SOMETHING ABOUT THE AUTHOR®

Something about
the Author *was named
an "**Outstanding
Reference Source,**"
the highest honor given
by the American
Library Association
Reference and Adult
Services Division.*

ISSN 0276-816X

SOMETHING ABOUT THE AUTHOR®

**Facts and Pictures about Authors
and Illustrators of Books for Young People**

volume 229

GALE
CENGAGE Learning™

Detroit • New York • San Francisco • New Haven, Conn • Waterville, Maine • London

Something about the Author, Volume 229

Project Editor: Lisa Kumar

Permissions: Leitha Etheridge-Sims

Imaging and Multimedia: Leitha
Etheridge-Sims, John Watkins

Composition and Electronic Capture:
Amy Darga

Manufacturing: Rhonda Dover

Product Manager: Mary Onorato

Gale, Cengage Learning
27500 Drake Rd.
Farmington Hills, MI, 48331-3535

LIBRARY OF CONGRESS CATALOG CARD NUMBER 62-52046

ISBN-13: 978-1-4144-6132-8
ISBN-10: 1-4144-6132-1

ISSN 0276-816X

This title is also available as an e-book.
ISBN-13: 978-1-4144-6461-9
ISBN-10: 1-4144-6461-4
Contact your Gale, Cengage Learning sales representative for ordering information.

Printed in Mexico
1 2 3 4 5 6 7 15 14 13 12 11

Contents

Authors in Forthcoming Volumes vii

Introduction ix

SATA Product Advisory Board xi

Illustrations Index 205

Author Index 241

A

Adams, S.J.
    See Selzer, Adam 176

Ahlberg, Jessica 1980- 1

Angaramo, Roberta 1974- 2

Aoyagi, Nora 3

B

Barrett, Jennifer
    See Plecas, Jennifer 151

Berman, Len 1947- 5

Birtha, Becky 1948- 7

Book, Rita
    See Holub, Joan 79

Breathed, Berke
    See Breathed, Berkeley 8

Breathed, Berkeley 1957- 8

Breathed, Guy Berkeley
    See Breathed, Berkeley 8

Brian, Dennis 1971- 14

Buckley, Michael 15

Bucks, Brad
    See Holub, Joan 79

Button, Lana 1968- 17

C

Calkhoven, Laurie 1959- 19

Campos, Maria de Fatima 20

Clement-Moore, Rosemary 21

Cody, Matthew 23

Collicutt, Paul 24

Cowles, Kathleen
    See Krull, Kathleen 95

Cuyler, Margery 1948- 26

Cuyler, Margery Stuyvesant
    See Cuyler, Margery 26

D

Davis, Nancy 34

Diaz, David 1959(?)- 35

Dickinson, Peter 1927- 41

Dickinson, Peter Malcolm de Brissac
    See Dickinson, Peter 41

Divine, L. 47

Dyer, Hadley 1973- 49

F

Fawcett, Katie Pickard 52

Fox, Karen C. 1969- 53

G

Garcia, Kami 1972- 54

Gardner, Sally 56

Graham, Ian 1953- 61

GrandPré, Mary 1954- 67

H

Hall, Teri 72

Hansen, Amy S. 73

Heldring, Thatcher 74

Helquist, Brett 75

Holub, Joan 79

Horley, Alex 1970- 86

Howells, Tania 86

J

Janni, Rebecca 89

Johnson, Stacie
  See Myers, Walter Dean 133
Johnson, Varian 1977- 90
Jones, Carrie 1971- 92

K
Kenny, Kathryn
  See Krull, Kathleen 95
Kenny, Kevin
  See Krull, Kathleen 95
Kinkade, Sheila 1962- 95
Krull, Kathleen 1952- 95

L
Larrañaga, Ana Martín 1969- 105
Leck, James 1973- 107
Logan, Alysia
  See Divine, L. 47
Loxton, Daniel 1975- 109
Lum, Kate 110

M
MacLachlan, Patricia 1938- 112
Malone, Marianne 121
Manivong, Laura 1967- 122
McKinley, Robin 1952- 123
Meschenmoser, Sebastian 1980- 129
Muldrow, Diane . . . .
Myers, Walter Dean 1937- 133
Myers, Walter M.
  See Myers, Walter Dean 133

N
Nelson, Jandy 145
Ngui, Marc 1972- 146

O
Orlandelli, Alessandro
  See Horley, Alex 86

P
Pearce, Carl 148
Peete, Holly Robinson 1964- 149

Plecas, Jennifer 1966- 151
Pon, Cynthia 155
Promitzer, Rebecca 155
Puybaret, Éric 1976- 157
Pyle, Charles S. 1954(?)- 158
Pyle, Chuck
  See Pyle, Charles S. 158

R
Rosen, Michael 160
Rostoker-Gruber, Karen 171

S
Sartell, Debra 173
Schröder, Monika 1965- 174
Selzer, Adam 1980- 176
Shinn, Sharon 1957- 178
Skovron, Jon 1976- 184
Snow, Sarah 185
Stower, Adam 186
Sumner, William 1971- 188

T
Tellegen, Toon 1941- 190
Tierney, Fiona 192
Triplett, Gina 193

V
Velásquez, Gloria 1949- 194

W
Wallace, Chad 197
Wallace, Daisy
  See Cuyler, Margery 26
Ward, Rachel 1964- 199
Wensell, Ulises 1945- 200

Y
Young, James
  See Graham, Ian 61

Authors in Forthcoming Volumes

Below are some of the authors and illustrators that will be featured in upcoming volumes of *SATA*. These include new entries on the swiftly rising stars of the field, as well as completely revised and updated entries (indicated with *) on some of the most notable and best-loved creators of books for children.

Rania al-Abdullah ▌ The wife of Jordan's King Abdullah II ibn Al Hussein, Queen Raina is beloved by many around the world, not only for the example she sets as a mother to her four children, but also for the grace she brings to her office. She is active in the education of future generations of Jordanians through her work promoting computer literacy, consistent teaching standards, and the increased involvement of families, businesses, and communities in the educational process. Her position as queen also allows her to work on the international level, advocating for the right of all children to a quality education and also serving as a spokesperson for UNICEF. On an individual basis, she also shares a lesson in tolerating differences in her picture book *The Sandwich Swap,* a story coauthored by Kelly DiPucchio and illustrated by Tricia Tusa.

Paul Brewer ▌ Only months out of college when he accepted his first illustration project, Brewer knew that he had found his niche: making readers laugh. This goal has inspired his own self-illustrated books *The Grossest Joke Book Ever, You Must Be Joking!: Lots of Cool Jokes,* and *You Must Be Joking, Two!: Even Cooler Jokes, Plus 11 1/2 Tips for Laughing Yourself into Your Own Stand-up Comedy Routine,* all geared for middle-grade readers. The husband of writer Kathleen Krull, he has also collaborated with his wife on several picture-book biographies, among them the quirky *Fartiste,* about a man who perfected a unique musical form.

*Steve Johnson ▌ Together with his wife, Lou Fancher, Johnson is a noted illustrator whose work has been paired with picture-book text by authors ranging from Kathleen Krull and Malachy Doyle to Jon Scieszka and Dr. Seuss. In addition to their work in book illustration, the couple has also created art for posters, business publications, commercial advertising, and periodicals and worked on the creative team that produced the animated films *Toy Story* and *A Bug's Life.*

*Lois Lowry ▌ Lowry, an award-winning author of young-adult novels, is perhaps best known for the Newbery Award-winning *Number the Stars* and her futuristic trilogy consisting of *The Giver, Gathering Blue,* and *Messenger.* Never one to shy from controversy, her books deal with topics ranging from the death of a sibling and the Nazi occupation of Denmark to the humorous antics of a rebellious teen named Anastasia Krupnik, to futuristic dystopian societies. Although Lowry's novels explore a variety of settings and characters, she distills from her work a single unifying theme: the importance of connections between people.

Charlotte Middleton ▌ Middleton's colorful picture-book illustrations meld engaging line drawings of dot-eyed characters with collage patterns to good effect. In addition to pairing her artwork with original stories in picture books such as *Tabitha's Terrifically Tough Tooth, Do You Still Love Me?,* and *Christopher Nibble,* the British-born author/illustrator also brings to life stories by a range of authors that include Betsy Franco, Titania Hardy, and Angela McAllister.

Phyllis Hornung Peacock ▌ Peacock illustrates books for young readers that range from fiction to nonfiction, although her ability to portray abstract concepts effectively has led her to specialize in mathematics-based texts. Beginning with Angeline Sparagna LoPresti's *A Place for Zero: A Math Adventure,* she has gone on to team up with author Julie Ellis on the award-winning picture book *What's Your Angle Pythagoras?: A Math Adventure,* Her art has also meshed well with the entertaining storylines in Karen Scalf Linamen's "Princess Madison" series, which include *Princess Madison and the Royal Darling Pageant, Princess Madison and the Whispering Woods,* and *Princess Madison and the Paisley Puppy.*

*Emily Rodda ▌ Rodda is considered one of Australia's favorite children's authors and has been honored with several of her country's top children's book awards. In addition to picture books, she has produced several novel series for older readers, most notably her "Rowan of Rin" and "Deltora Quest" books. Her fantasy novels introduce carefully drawn imaginary realms where quests are complicated by riddles, magic, and mixed motives. Rodda has also won fans for her middle-grade adventure/mystery series, "Teen Power Inc.," and also writes adult mysteries as well as cookbooks under her real name, Jennifer Rowe.

*Mark Alan Stamaty ▌ Beginning his career in the mid-1970s, Stamaty created several long-running cartoons in addition to his work as a children's book writer and illustrator. During the 1980s and 1990s his comic strip "MacDoodle Street" and "Washingtoon" entertained readers of the *Village Voice,* and his comics have also been syndicated. His 1973 picture book *Who Needs Donuts?,* which, with its complex and highly detailed illustrations was credited with inspiring the "Where Is Waldo?" phenomenon, is considered a cult classic and was re-released in 2003. Other books for children include *Alia's Mission: Saving the Books of Iraq* and *Shake, Rattle, and Turn That Noise Down!: How Elvis Shook up Music, Me, and Mom,* an entertaining memoir of Stamaty's memories as a preteen.

Anne Villeneuve ▌ A Canadian artist and illustrator who is based in Québec, Villeneuve has found success as a commercial illustrator as well as gaining fans through her work in picture books. Her illustrations have appeared in her own stories, as well as in works by writers such as Carmen Marois, Robert Souliéres, and sister Mireille Villeneuve that are geared for French-language readers. She was awarded both a Governor General's Literary Award for

children's illustration and a Canadian Children's Literature Award for her original story *L'écharpe rouge*, and she has gained English-language fans since this story was translated as *The Red Scarf.*

Mike Wohnoutka ▌ In addition to working in advertising and editorial illustration, where his work has achieved reknown, Wohnoutka has provided the artwork for numerous children's books, including *Cowboy Sam and Those Confounded Secrets* by coauthors Kitty Griffin and Kathy Combs as well as *When the Wizzy Foot Goes Walking* by Roni Schotter. He made his children's book debut in *Counting Sheep,* a story by Julie Glass, and his unique illustrations also appear in stories by Tim Kehoe, Stephen Krensky, Susanna Leonard Hill, and Marjorie Blain Parker.

Introduction

Something about the Author (*SATA*) is an ongoing reference series that examines the lives and works of authors and illustrators of books for children. *SATA* includes not only well-known writers and artists but also less prominent individuals whose works are just coming to be recognized. This series is often the only readily available information source on emerging authors and illustrators. You'll find *SATA* informative and entertaining, whether you are a student, a librarian, an English teacher, a parent, or simply an adult who enjoys children's literature.

What's Inside *SATA*

SATA provides detailed information about authors and illustrators who span the full time range of children's literature, from early figures like John Newbery and L. Frank Baum to contemporary figures like Judy Blume and Richard Peck. Authors in the series represent primarily English-speaking countries, particularly the United States, Canada, and the United Kingdom. Also included, however, are authors from around the world whose works are available in English translation. The writings represented in *SATA* include those created intentionally for children and young adults as well as those written for a general audience and known to interest younger readers. These writings cover the entire spectrum of children's literature, including picture books, humor, folk and fairy tales, animal stories, mystery and adventure, science fiction and fantasy, historical fiction, poetry and nonsense verse, drama, biography, and nonfiction. Obituaries are also included in *SATA* and are intended not only as death notices but also as concise overviews of people's lives and work. Additionally, each edition features newly revised and updated entries for a selection of *SATA* listees who remain of interest to today's readers and who have been active enough to require extensive revisions of their earlier biographies.

Autobiography Feature

Beginning with Volume 103, many volumes of *SATA* feature one or more specially commissioned autobiographical essays. These unique essays, averaging about ten thousand words in length and illustrated with an abundance of personal photos, present an entertaining and informative first-person perspective on the lives and careers of prominent authors and illustrators profiled in *SATA*.

Two Convenient Indexes

In response to suggestions from librarians, *SATA* indexes no longer appear in every volume but are included in alternate (odd-numbered) volumes of the series, beginning with Volume 57.

SATA continues to include two indexes that cumulate with each alternate volume: the Illustrations Index, arranged by the name of the illustrator, gives the number of the volume and page where the illustrator's work appears in the current volume as well as all preceding volumes in the series; the Author Index gives the number of the volume in which a person's biographical sketch, autobiographical essay, or obituary appears in the current volume as well as all preceding volumes in the series.

These indexes also include references to authors and illustrators who appear in *Gale's Yesterday's Authors of Books for Children, Children's Literature Review,* and *Something about the Author Autobiography Series.*

Easy-to-Use Entry Format

Whether you're already familiar with the *SATA* series or just getting acquainted, you will want to be aware of the kind of information that an entry provides. In every *SATA* entry the editors attempt to give as complete a picture of the person's life and work as possible. A typical entry in *SATA* includes the following clearly labeled information sections:

PERSONAL: date and place of birth and death, parents' names and occupations, name of spouse, date of marriage, names of children, educational institutions attended, degrees received, religious and political affiliations, hobbies and other interests.

ADDRESSES: complete home, office, electronic mail, and agent addresses, whenever available.

CAREER: name of employer, position, and dates for each career post; art exhibitions; military service; memberships and offices held in professional and civic organizations.

MEMBER: professional, civic, and other association memberships and any official posts held.

AWARDS, HONORS: literary and professional awards received.

WRITINGS: title-by-title chronological bibliography of books written and/or illustrated, listed by genre when known; lists of other notable publications, such as plays, screenplays, and periodical contributions.

ADAPTATIONS: a list of films, television programs, plays, CD-ROMs, recordings, and other media presentations that have been adapted from the author's work.

WORK IN PROGRESS: description of projects in progress.

SIDELIGHTS: a biographical portrait of the author or illustrator's development, either directly from the biographee—and often written specifically for the *SATA* entry—or gathered from diaries, letters, interviews, or other published sources.

BIOGRAPHICAL AND CRITICAL SOURCES: cites sources quoted in "Sidelights" along with references for further reading.

EXTENSIVE ILLUSTRATIONS: photographs, movie stills, book illustrations, and other interesting visual materials supplement the text.

How a *SATA* Entry Is Compiled

SATA editors examine a wide variety of published sources to gather information for an entry. Biographical and bibliographic sources are consulted, as are book reviews, feature articles, published interviews, and material sometimes obtained from the biographee's family, publishers, agent, or other associates. Whenever possible, the author or illustrator is sent a copy of the entry to check for accuracy and completeness.

Entries that have not been verified by the biographees or their representatives are marked with an asterisk (*).

Contact the Editor

We encourage our readers to examine the entire *SATA* series. Please write and tell us if we can make *SATA* even more helpful to you. Give your comments and suggestions to the editor:

Editor
Something about the Author
Gale, Cengage Learning
27500 Drake Rd.
Farmington Hills MI 48331-3535

Toll-free: 800-877-GALE
Fax: 248-699-8070

Something about the Author Product Advisory Board

The editors of *Something about the Author* are dedicated to maintaining a high standard of excellence by publishing comprehensive, accurate, and highly readable entries on a wide array of writers for children and young adults. In addition to the quality of the content, the editors take pride in the graphic design of the series, which is intended to be orderly yet inviting, allowing readers to utilize the pages of *SATA* easily and with efficiency. Despite the longevity of the *SATA* print series, and the success of its format, we are mindful that the vitality of a literary reference product is dependent on its ability to serve its users over time. As literature, and attitudes about literature, constantly evolve, so do the reference needs of students, teachers, scholars, journalists, researchers, and book club members. To be certain that we continue to keep pace with the expectations of our customers, the editors of *SATA* listen carefully to their comments regarding the value, utility, and quality of the series. Librarians, who have firsthand knowledge of the needs of library users, are a valuable resource for us. The *Something about the Author* Product Advisory Board, made up of school, public, and academic librarians, is a forum to promote focused feedback about *SATA* on a regular basis. The nine-member advisory board includes the following individuals, whom the editors wish to thank for sharing their expertise:

Eva M. Davis
Director,
Canton Public Library,
Canton, Michigan

Joan B. Eisenberg
Lower School Librarian,
Milton Academy,
Milton, Massachusetts

Francisca Goldsmith
Teen Services Librarian,
Berkeley Public Library,
Berkeley, California

Susan Dove Lempke
Children's Services Supervisor,
Niles Public Library District,
Niles, Illinois

Robyn Lupa
Head of Children's Services,
Jefferson County Public Library,
Lakewood, Colorado

Victor L. Schill
Assistant Branch Librarian/Children's Librarian,
Harris County Public Library/Fairbanks Branch,
Houston, Texas

Caryn Sipos
Community Librarian,
Three Creeks Community Library,
Vancouver, Washington

Steven Weiner
Director,
Maynard Public Library,
Maynard, Massachusetts

something about the author

ADAMS, S.J.
See SELZER, Adam

*   *   *

AHLBERG, Jessica 1980-

Personal

Born 1980; daughter of Allan (a writer) and Janet (an illustrator) Ahlberg. *Education:* Attended Winchester School of Art. *Hobbies and other interests:* Writing letters, looking at maps, reading books, baking cakes.

Addresses

Home—Brighton, England.

Career

Illustrator.

Illustrator

Allan Ahlberg, *Half a Pig,* Candlewick Press (Cambridge, MA), 2004.

Allan Ahlberg, *The Boy, the Wolf, the Sheep, and the Lettuce: A Little Search for Truth,* Puffin (London, England), 2004.

Mary Murphy, *Parrot Park,* Walker (London, England), 2006.

Mary Murphy, *Comings and Goings at Parrot Park,* Walker (London, England), 2008.

Toon Tellegen, *The Squirrel's Birthday and Other Parties* (translation of *De verjaardag van de eekhoorn*), Boxer Books (London, England), 2009.

Toon Tellegen, *Letters to Anyone and Everyone,* Boxer Books (London, England), 2009.

Vivian French, *Yucky Worms,* Candlewick Press (Somerville, MA), 2010.

Toon Tellegen, *Far Away across the Sea,* Boxer Books (London, England), 2011.

Sidelights

Jessica Ahlberg, the daughter of respected writer-illustrator team Allan and Janet Ahlberg, has followed in her parents' footsteps by providing the artwork for a number of critically acclaimed picture books. For her literary debut, *Half a Pig,* Ahlberg teamed up with her father, illustrating his humorous tale about a divorced couple's contentious battle over custody of their plump porker. When Mrs. Harbottle discovers that her ex-husband, who shares custody of Esmeralda the pig, wants his portion to be turned into sausage, the kind-hearted woman enlists her neighbors to kidnap and hide the creature. Daniel B. Schneider, reviewing *Half a Pig* in the *New York Times Book Review,* noted that Ahlberg "seems to share [her father's] puckish sensibility," and a *Publishers Weekly* critic remarked that her pencil-and-ink and watercolor "pictures call to mind the simple line and soft pastel shadings of her mother's artwork." In *Horn Book,* Roger Sutton commented that the "draw-

1

Jessica Ahlberg illustrates the English-language edition of several stories by Dutch author Toon Tellegen, among them **The Squirrel's Birthday and Other Parties.** (Illustration copyright © 2009 by Jessica Ahlberg. Reproduced by permission of Boxer Books Limited.)

ings aid readers in following the twists and turns of the pignapping and subsequent rescue-and-chase scenes," and *Booklist* contributor Diane Foote described the pictures in *Half a Pig* as "charmingly accessible."

A youngster learns to appreciate the slimy creatures inhabiting his grandmother's garden in *Yucky Worms*, featuring a text by Vivian French. This fictional tale includes a variety of facts about worms, such as a description of their diet and their contributions to the garden. Maryann H. Owen, writing in *School Library Journal*, complimented Ahlberg's "clear and appealing pencil and gouache illustrations" for *Yucky Worms*, while *Booklist* reviewer Hazel Rochman observed that the "artwork shows scenes both above and below the ground and weaves facts into each image," as well as in the worms' speech bubbles.

Ahlberg has enjoyed a successful collaboration with award-winning Dutch poet and author Toon Tellegen, illustrating the English-language translation of his story *The Squirrel's Birthday and Other Parties*, *Letters to Anyone and Everyone*, and *Far Away across the Sea*. In *The Squirrel's Birthday and Other Parties* Tellegen presents nine whimsical, surrealistic tales about friendship

and fun. In the words of *School Librarian* critic Anna Griffin, "Ahlberg's marvelous illustrations assist, giving a great insight into the stories," while *Books for Keeps* reviewer Annabel Gibb stated that "at her best she has a beautiful touch." In *Letters to Anyone and Everyone* Tellegen's animal protagonists share their thoughts and dreams through a series of messages. The "diminutive ink drawings look quite unstudied yet perfect in their scale and their innocent charm," Carolyn Phelan maintained in her *Booklist* appraisal of this work while Lynn K. Vanca wrote in *School Library Journal* that "Ahlberg's delicate illustrations" for the story collection *Far Away across the Sea.* "add visual appeal and bring out selected details."

Biographical and Critical Sources

PERIODICALS

Booklist, August, 2004, Diane Foote, review of *Half a Pig,* p. 1932; May 1, 2010, Hazel Rochman, review of *Yucky Worms,* p. 94; May 15, 2010, Carolyn Phelan, review of *Letters to Anyone and Everyone,* p. 44.
Books for Keeps, January, 2010, Annabel Gibb, reviews of *Letters to Anyone and Everyone* and *The Squirrel's Birthday and Other Parties.*
Guardian (London, England), June 12, 2004, Julia Eccleshare, review of *Half a Pig,* p. 33.
Horn Book, July-August, 2004, Roger Sutton, review of *Half a Pig,* p. 433.
Kirkus Reviews, April 15, 2004, review of *Half a Pig,* p. 389.
New York Times Book Review, September 19, 2004, Daniel B. Schneider, review of *Half a Pig,* p. 16.
Publishers Weekly, April 26, 2004, review of *Half a Pig,* p. 65.
School Librarian, spring, 2010, Anna Griffin, review of *The Squirrel's Birthday and Other Parties,* p. 32.
School Library Journal, August, 2004, Phyllis M. Simon, review of *Half a Pig,* p. 82; April, 2010, Shawn Brommer, review of *Letters to Anyone and Everyone,* p. 141; June, 2010, Maryann H. Owen, review of *Yucky Worms,* p. 70; November, 2010, Lynn K. Vanca, review of *Far Away across the Sea,* p. 85.
USA Today, April 8, 2010, review of *Yucky Worms,* p. D4.

ONLINE

Boxer Books Web site, http://www.boxerbooksltd.co.uk/ (May 1, 2011), "Jessica Ahlberg."*

*   *   *

ANGARAMO, Roberta 1974-

Personal

Born 1974, in Italy; married Daniele Cazzato (an artist). *Education:* European Institute of Design (Turin, Italy),

degree (painting and illustration). *Hobbies and other interests:* Mountain biking and sports, singing and dancing.

Addresses

Home—Bossolasco, Italy. *Agent*—BookStop Literary Agency, 67 Meadow View Rd., Orinda, CA 94563. *E-mail*—info@robertaangaramo.com.

Career

Illustrator and educator. Formerly worked as an advertising illustrator and trompe l'oeil artist; freelance illustrator of children's books, beginning 1999. Scuola d'Arte Novalia di Savigliano, children's teacher, beginning 2008. *Exhibitions:* Works exhibited throughout Italy and internationally.

Member

Associazione Culturale Sent'ed'art.

Awards, Honors

UNICEF Città di Chioggia contest first prize, 1997, for *Notte de Favola;* Hans Christian Andersen Award for Best Illustrated Series, 2005, for both *Le tre melarance* and *I musicanti di Brema.*

Illustrator

Tony Piuma, *Rosso Rosso dove vai?,* Happy Art, 1999.
Patrizia Nencini, *Che tempo fa?,* Giunti Kids (Florence, Italy), 2002.
Gianni Rodari, selector, *Favole della Fantasia,* Editori Riuniti (Italy), 2003.
Patrizia Nencini, *I colori dell'arcobaleno,* Giunti (Florence, Italy), 2003.
Anna Sarfatti, *Ri-trattini,* Giunti junior (Florence, Italy), 2003.
Chiara Carminati, *Il carnevale degli animali ispirato alla grande fantasia zoologica di Camille Saint-Saëns,* Fabbri (Milan, Italy), 2004.
Hans Christian Andersen, *The Ugly Duckling,* new edition, Purple Bear, 2006.
Julia Jarman, *Little Tiger and the Fire,* Franklin Watts (London, England), 2009.
David Conway, *Errol and His Extraordinary Nose,* Holiday House (New York, NY), 2010.
Dionigi Tettamanzi, *Santi subito: Lettera di natale al bambini,* Rizzoli (Milan, Italy), 2010.
Andrea Perry, *The Bicklebys' Birdbath,* Atheneum Books for Young Readers (New York, NY), 2010.
Greg Gormley, *Dog in Boots,* Holiday House (New York, NY), 2011.
David L. Harrison, *A Perfect Home for a Family,* Holiday House (New York, NY), 2012.
Nancy Walker Guye, *The Huge Splash,* Aracari Verlag (Berne Switzerland), 2012.

Author of books published in Hong Kong and Japan. Illustrator of other books published in Italy and Hong Kong, including *Notte da favola, Le tre melarance, I musicanti di Brema, L'arca di noè, Rime pitatesche,* and *L'enciclopedia della favola.*

Works featuring Angaramo's illustrations have been translated into Chinese, Finnish, French, German, Greek, Japanese, Korean, Spanish, Swiss, and Taiwanese.

Biographical and Critical Sources

PERIODICALS

Booklist, February 1, 2010, Patricia Austin, review of *The Bicklebys' Birdbath,* p. 48.
Kirkus Reviews, January 1, 2010, review of *The Bicklebys' Birdbath;* January 15, 2010, review of *Errol and His Extraordinary Nose;* February 1, 2011, review of *Dog in Boots.*
Publishers Weekly, April 24, 2006, review of *The Ugly Duckling,* p. 60; March 1, 2010, review of *Errol and His Extraordinary Nose,* p. 49.
School Library Journal, September, 2006, Margaret Bush, review of *The Ugly Duckling,* p. 158; March, 2010, Tanya Boudreau, review of *The Bicklebys' Birdbath,* p. 129; June, 2010, Catherine Callegari, review of *Errol and His Extraordinary Nose,* p. 66; March, 2011, Anne Beier, review of *Dog in Boots.*

ONLINE

Roberta Angaramo Home Page, http://www.robertaangaramo.com (April 24, 2011).

*   *   *

AOYAGI, Nora

Personal

Female.

Addresses

Home—Berkeley, CA. *E-mail*—noraspooked@yahoo.com.

Career

Illustrator and artist. *Exhibitions:* Work exhibited at galleries, including Incline Gallery, San Francisco, CA.

Illustrator

Mark Cassino, with Jon Nelson, *The Story of Snow: The Science of Winter's Wonder,* Chronicle Books (San Francisco, CA), 2009.

Biographical and Critical Sources

PERIODICALS

Booklist, December 1, 2009, John Peters, review of *The Story of Snow: The Science of Winter's Wonder,* p. 57.
Bulletin of the Center for Children's Books, December, 2009, Elizabeth Bush, review of *The Story of Snow,* p. 143.

Horn Book, January-February, 2010, Danielle J. Ford, review of *The Story of Snow,* p. 101.

Kirkus Reviews, October 15, 2009, review of *The Story of Snow.*

School Library Journal, November, 2009, Kathy Piehl, review of *The Story of Snow,* p. 93.

ONLINE

Nora Aoyagi Home Page, http://www.noraaoyagi.com (April 24, 2011).

Nora Aoyagi Web log, http://noraaoyagi.typepad.com (April 24, 2011).

B

BARRETT, Jennifer
See PLECAS, Jennifer

* * *

BERMAN, Len 1947-

Personal
Born June 14, 1947 in New York, NY; married; wife's name Jill (a real estate agent); children: three. *Education:* Syracuse University, B.S. (English and economics), M.A. (communications). *Religion:* Jewish.

Addresses
Home—Long Island, NY. *E-mail*—len@lenberman sports.com.

Career
Reporter, sports broadcaster, and author. WLWD-TV, Dayton, OH, reporter and news anchor, 1970-73; WBZ-TV, Boston, MA, sports director and play-by-play announcer, 1973-78; WCBS-TV, New York, NY, sports anchor, 1979-82; play-by-play announcer for Big East Basketball Conference, 1979-85; NBC Sports, New York, sports anchor, 1982-85; WNBC-TV, New York, sports anchor, 1985-2009, creator and host of "Sports Fantasy" segment for *Sportsworld,* 1985-90, creator of "Spanning the World" segment of *Today* show, 1989-2009. Also contributor to "One on One Sports" radio; cohost of "L.T.'s Place," 1991; host of TVKO Boxing, 1991-93.

Awards, Honors
Eight local Emmy awards; six-time New York Sportscaster of the Year, National Sportscasters and Sportswriters Association, including 1994, 1995, 1998, 2001; inducted into National Jewish Sports Hall of Fame, 2001.

Writings

And Nobody Got Hurt!: The World's Weirdest, Wackiest True Sports Stories, illustrated by Kent Gamble, Little, Brown (New York, NY), 2005.
Spanning the World: The Crazy Universe of Big-time Sports, All-star Egos, and Hall of Fame Bloopers, Morrow (New York, NY), 2005.
And Nobody Got Hurt Two!: The World's Weirdest, Wackiest, and Most Amazing True Sports Stories, illustrated by Kent Gamble, Little, Brown (New York, NY), 2007.
The Greatest Moments in Sports, Sourcebooks (Naperville, IL), 2009.
Twenty-five Greatest Baseball Players of All Time, Sourcebooks (Naperville, IL), 2010.

Sidelights
A popular, award-winning sportscaster, Len Berman has covered such major sporting events as the Super Bowl, the World Series, and the Olympic games during his long and distinguished career. For more than two decades Berman was a fixture on New York television, serving as the weekday sports anchor for WNBC and the creator of "Spanning the World," a monthly collection of bloopers that proved wildly popular with viewers. He garnered a host of honors for his work, including eight local Emmy awards and six New York Sportscaster of the Year citations. In addition to his career as a sports anchor, Berman has written several books for young readers, including *The Greatest Moments in Sports,* which landed him on the *New York Times* best-seller list.

Born in New York City in 1947, Berman began his career in broadcasting while attending Syracuse University, serving as sports director of the campus radio station for three years. After graduation, he started his television career as a reporter and news anchor in Dayton, Ohio, then moved to Massachusetts, where he served as sports director for WBZ and did play-by-play

for the Boston Celtics and New England Patriots. Berman eventually landed in New York City, joining WNBC in 1985 and leaving the station in 2009. Watching Berman, Michael Winerip commented in the *New York Times,* was "one of life's small pleasures. His voice is rich and strong without straining. He didn't have the tensed neck that seems to be the mark of the modern sportscaster. He wrote his own copy in simple, declarative sentences. Rarely did he use a superfluous word."

Employing his characteristic gentle wit, Berman presents audiences with a collection of anecdotes about bizarre and silly sports moments in both *And Nobody Got Hurt!: The World's Weirdest, Wackiest True Sports Stories* and its companion volume. In both volumes, Berman recounts tales from the world of sports—including a 1993 home run that bounced off the head of an outfielder—and also touches on such little-known oddities as a boxing match in England where the mum of one of the fighters jumped into the ring and began beating her son's opponent over his head with her shoe. According to Kim Dare, reviewing *And Nobody Got Hurt Two!: The World's Weirdest, Wackiest, and Most Amazing True Sports Stories* for *School Library Journal,* Berman "writes as he speaks, and his jovial style will engage reluctant readers." The author offers an equally unusual look at athletics in *Spanning the World: The Crazy Universe of Big-time Sports, All-star Egos, and Hall of Fame Bloopers.*

Berman draws on his experiences as a sportscaster in writing *The Greatest Moments in Sports,* "an eclectic roundup that's likely to have readers mulling their own

personal favorites," as a *Publishers Weekly* critic stated. Accompanied by a CD featuring broadcasts of relevant events, the work contains accounts of Babe Ruth's famous "called" home run, Roger Bannister's quest to break the four-minute mile, and Michael Phelps's gold-medal-winning performances at the Beijing Olympics. In the words of *School Library Journal* reviewer Kate Kohlbeck, Berman's "writing is lively, humorous, and informative—just right to sustain kids' (or adults') interest."

Berman still keeps in touch with fans through his Web site, *ThatsSports.com,* in which he offers his daily musings on the sporting world. He understands the perennial hold competitive sports has on the public's imagination, telling *New York Times* contributor Rahel Musleah: "There's a beginning to a game. There's an ending to a game. There's a result. There will be a champion at the end of this year. There will be another next year. That's all very understandable."

Biographical and Critical Sources

PERIODICALS

Booklist, June 1, 2005, Wes Lukowsky, review of *Spanning the World: The Crazy Universe of Big-time Sports, All-star Egos, and Hall of Fame Bloopers,* p. 1741; November 1, 2009, Todd Morning, review of *The Greatest Moments in Sports,* p. 31.

Kirkus Reviews, October 15, 2009, review of *The Greatest Moments in Sports.*

New York Daily News, March 31, 2009, Richard Huff, "Sports Anchor Len Berman Leaving WNBC after More than 20 Years at Station."

New York Times, July 11, 1993, Rahel Musleah, "Sportscaster Opts for Privacy"; April 7, 1996, Robert McG. Thomas, Jr., "A Love of Sports Inspired by the Yankees"; May 1, 2009, Michael Winerip, "My Sportscaster Is Gone, No Film at 11."

Publishers Weekly, October 3, 2005, review of *And Nobody Got Hurt!: The World's Weirdest, Wackiest True Sports Stories,* p. 73; November 30, 2009, review of *The Greatest Moments in Sports,* p. 46.

School Library Journal, November, 2007, Kim Dare, review of *And Nobody Got Hurt 2!: The World's Weirdest, Wackiest, Most Amazing True Sports Stories,* p. 142; January, 2010, Kate Kohlbeck, review of *The Greatest Moments in Sports,* p. 118.

ONLINE

Gothamist Web site, http://gothamist.com/ (March 20, 2007), Toby von Meistersinger, "Spanning Twenty Years with WNBC's Len Berman."

Len Berman Home Page, http://thatssports.com (April 15, 2011).

Championship batter Johnny Bench is among the top athletes profiled by Len Berman in his **The Twenty-five Greatest Baseball Players of All Time.** (Sourcebooks Jabberwocky, an imprint of Sourcebooks, Inc. Photograph reproduced by permission by AP Photo/Wide World Photos.)

BIRTHA, Becky 1948-

Personal

Born 1948; mother a librarian; partner's name Nancy; children: Tasha. *Education:* Earned college degree. *Religion:* Society of Friends (Quaker). *Hobbies and other interests:* Folk dancing, playing the hammered dulcimer.

Addresses

Home—Landsdowne, PA.

Career

Author. Worked variously as a camp counselor, daycare worker, preschool teacher, bookstore staffer, librarian aide, and writing teacher; member of staff of an adoption organization for many years. Presenter at conferences.

Awards, Honors

Golden Kite Honor Book designation, 2005, for *Grandmama's Pride.*

Writings

FOR CHILDREN

Grandmama's Pride, illustrated by Colin Bootman, Albert Whitman (Morton Grove, IL), 2005.
Lucky Beans, illustrated by Nicole Tadgell, Albert Whitman (Chicago, IL), 2010.

FOR ADULTS

(Compiler) *Literature by Black Women: A List of Books,* privately printed, 1983.
For Nights like This One: Stories of Loving Women, Frog in the Well (East Palo Alto, CA), 1983.
Lovers' Choice (short stories), Seal Press (Seattle, WA), 1987.
The Forbidden Poems, Seal Press (Seattle, WA), 1991.

Author's poems and short fiction have been included in anthologies.

Sidelights

Becky Birtha was named after her grandmother, a former slave who lived until age 103. Although Birtha was too young when her grandmother died to have any memory of the woman, she grew up with her grandmother's stories, and she learned to value her other relatives and their stories as well. Birtha shares several of these remembered tales in her picture books *Grandmama's Pride,* illustrated by Colin Bootman, and *Lucky Beans,* featuring artwork by Nicole Tadgell.

Birth grew up in Philadelphia, where her mother's job as a librarian meant that she was surrounded by books, and her favorite authors included Laura Ingalls Wilder, Frances Hodgeson Burnett, E. Nesbit, and Edward Eager. After completing college and exploring a bit of the world, Birtha worked at a variety of jobs while also writing poetry and short stories for adults. She even taught writing on the college level while building her reputation as an author. Her 1987 short-story collection *Lovers' Choice* focuses on black lesbians facing momentous change as well as on single mothers attempting to survive in a harsh urban environment. Her verse collection *The Forbidden Poems,* which features equally mature themes, prompted *Choice* contributor L.J. Parascandola to praise the "biting humor" and "stark, direct quality" of Birtha's writing.

Birtha's first picture book, *Grandmama's Pride,* takes place in the mid-1950s, as two African-American sisters and their mother make the bus trip south to visit the girls' grandmother. As the bus approaches Grandmama's home Mama schools the girls in the proper behavior of blacks under the Jim Crow laws of the pre-civil-rights-era south, such as sitting in the back of the bus and avoiding "whites only" public facilities that include preferred restaurant seating, lavatories, and drinking fountains. Praising Birtha's "strong, sensitive writing" in the book, Mary Hazleton also cited the "beautiful watercolor paintings" by Bootman in her *School Library Journal* review. The "slice of dramatic history" offered in *Grandmama's Pride* "will touch both heart and mind," predicted *Booklist* critic Julie Cummins, and a *Kirkus Reviews* writer commended Birtha's story as "a gentle introduction to an important and painful piece of our national past."

Lucky Beans draws on the memories of a relative of the author who grew up during the Great Depression of the 1930s. In Birtha's story, a boy named Marshall worries after his father becomes unemployed and various relatives arrive on the family's doorstep as a result of similar hardships. To feed everyone Marshall's mother cooks lots of beans, and the all-bean diet is becoming tiresome. When he learns about a local contest in which the person who correctly guesses the quantity of beans in a large glass jar will win a sewing machine, Marshall is determined to win. If his mom had the sewing machine, the boy reasons, she would not have to cook so many beans. Weaving mathematical problem-solving into her entertaining story, Birtha "also confronts the racism of the 1930s" and includes factual information in her author's note, according to *School Library Journal* contributor Mary Landrum. A *Kirkus Reviews* writer noted the upbeat elements of *Lucky Beans,* observing that Marshall and his "family work . . . together to survive and find . . . moments of love, appreciation and sheer happiness." "Math and wry comedy mix in this lively historical story," asserted Hazel Rochman in her *Booklist* review, while in *Horn Book* Susan Dove Lempke recommended Tadgell's "soft watercolor paint-

ings" and called *Lucky Beans* "a welcome addition to
. . . picture books about families getting through difficult times."

Biographical and Critical Sources

PERIODICALS

Booklist, November 1, 2005, Julie Cummins, review of
Grandmama's Pride, p. 51; February 1, 2010, Hazel
Rochman, review of *Lucky Beans,* p. 62.
Choice, October, 1991, L.J. Parascandola, review of *The
Forbidden Poems,* p. 276.
Horn Book, May-June, 2010, Susan Dove Lempke, review
of *Lucky Beans,* p. 62.
Kirkus Reviews, November 15, 2005, review of *Grandma-
ma's Pride,* p. 1230; February 15, 2010, review of
Lucky Beans.
New York Times, May 22, 1994, Hema N. Nair, "Learning
the Business at Writers' Conference."
Publishers Weekly, February 1, 1991, Penny Kaganoff, re-
view of *The Forbidden Poems,* p. 77.
School Library Journal, November, 2005, Mary Hazelton,
review of *Grandmama's Pride,* p. 83; February, 2010,
Mary Landrum, review of *Lucky Beans,* p. 75.
Village Voice, April 16, 1991, review of *The Forbidden
Poems,* p. 70.

ONLINE

Becky Birtha Home Page, http://www.beckybirtha.net
(April 24, 2011).*

* * *

BOOK, Rita
See HOLUB, Joan

* * *

BREATHED, Berke
See BREATHED, Berkeley

* * *

BREATHED, Berkeley 1957-
(Berke Breathed, Guy Berkeley Breathed)

Personal

Surname rhymes with "method"; born June 21, 1957, in
Encino, CA; son of John W. (an oil equipment execu-
tive) and Martha Jane Breathed; married Jody Boyman
(a photographer), May, 1986; children: two. *Education:*
University of Texas at Austin, B.A., 1979. *Politics:*
"Middle-winger."

Berkeley Breathed (Reproduced by permission.)

Addresses

Home—Southern CA. *Agent*—Esther Newberg, ICM, 40
W. 57th St., New York, NY 10019.

Career

Cartoonist and writer. Creator of comic strips "The
Academia Waltz," for *Daily Texan,* 1978-79, "Bloom
County," for syndication by Washington Post Writer's
Group, 1980-89, and "Opus Goes Home," for *Life,*
1987; creator of Sunday-only strips "Outland," 1989-
95, and "Opus," 2003-08.

Awards, Honors

Harry A. Schweikert, Jr., Disability Awareness Award,
Paralyzed Vets of America, 1982, and Pulitzer Prize for
editorial cartooning, 1987, both for "Bloom County";
Fund for Animal Genesis award, 1990, for "outstanding
cartoonist focusing on animal welfare issues."

Writings

SELF-ILLUSTRATED; FOR CHILDREN

A Wish for Wings That Work: An Opus Christmas Story,
Little, Brown (Boston, MA), 1991.
The Last Basselope: One Ferocious Story, Little, Brown
(Boston, MA), 1992.
Goodnight Opus, Little, Brown (Boston, MA), 1993.
*Red Ranger Came Calling: A Guaranteed True Christmas
Story,* Little, Brown (Boston, MA), 1994.

Edwurd Fudwupper Fibbed Big: Explained by Fannie Fud-wupper, Little, Brown (Boston, MA), 2000.

Flawed Dogs: The Year-end Leftovers at the Piddleton "Last Chance" Dog Pound, Little, Brown (Boston, MA), 2003.

Mars Needs Moms!, Philomel (New York, NY), 2007.

Pete and Pickles, Philomel (New York, NY), 2008.

Flawed Dogs: The Novel: The Shocking Raid on Westminster, Philomel (New York, NY), 2009.

CARTOON COLLECTIONS; UNDER NAME BERKE BREATHED

Bloom County: Loose Tails, Little, Brown (Boston, MA), 1983.

'Toons for Our Times: A Bloom County Book of Heavy Metal Rump 'n'Roll, Little, Brown (Boston, MA), 1984.

Penguin Dreams, and Stranger Things, Little, Brown (Boston, MA), 1985.

Bloom County Babylon: Five Years of Basic Naughtiness, Little, Brown (Boston, MA), 1986.

Billy and the Boingers Bootleg, Little, Brown (Boston, MA), 1987.

Tales Too Ticklish to Tell, Little, Brown (Boston, MA), 1988.

Night of the Mary Kay Commandos: Featuring Smell-O-Toons, Little, Brown (Boston, MA), 1989.

Classics of Western Literature: Bloom County, 1986-1989, Little, Brown (Boston, MA), 1990.

Happy Trails, Little, Brown (Boston, MA), 1990.

Politically, Fashionably, and Aerodynamically Incorrect: The First Outland Collection, Little, Brown (Boston, MA), 1992.

His Kisses Are Dreamy—But Those Hairballs down My Cleavage, Little, Brown (Boston, MA), 1994.

The Romantic Opus 'n' Bill, Little, Brown (Boston, MA), 1994.

One Last Little Peek, 1980-1995: The Final Strips, the Special Hits, the Inside Tips, Little, Brown (Boston, MA), 1995.

Opus: Twenty-five Years of His Sunday Best, Little, Brown (Boston, MA), 2004.

Bloom County: The Complete Library: Volume One, 1980-1982, IDW Publishing (San Diego, CA), 2009.

Bloom County: The Complete Library: Volume Two, 1982-1984, IDW Publishing (San Diego, CA), 2010.

Bloom County: The Complete Library: Volume Three, 1984-1986, IDW Publishing (San Diego, CA), 2010.

Contributor of illustrations to *The Emperor*, 1998.

Adaptations

A Wish for Wings That Work was adapted as a CBS-TV special and released on videocassette; *Edwurd Fudwupper Fibbed Big* was adapted as an animated short film for Nickelodeon Family Films; *Red Ranger Came Calling* was adapted as a musical; *Mars Needs Moms!* was adapted as a motion picture, Walt Disney Films, 2011.

Sidelights

Best known for his popular and satirical "Bloom County" comic strip, for which he earned the 1987 Pulitzer Prize for editorial cartooning, Berkeley Breathed

has also written and illustrated a host of well-received books for young readers, including *Red Ranger Came Calling: A Guaranteed True Christmas Story, Mars Needs Moms!*, and *Pete and Pickles*. Breathed, who further explored politics and pop culture in his "Outland" and "Opus" comic strips, told *Salon.com* interviewer Kerry Lauerman that his goal as a children's book author is to write "smart stories that leave people—OK, my children—feeling a bit better about the world at the end." "Stories for children are a refuge from the fire-fight going on above the foxhole," he added.

Breathed was born in Encino, California, in 1957, and after high school attended the University of Texas at Austin. In college he began a comic strip "because it was the most effective way to make a point and get people listening," Breathed told an interviewer in *Comics Journal*. While his overactive imagination may have gotten him into trouble as a child, as a cartoonist it became an asset, and he began working for the *Daily Texan*, his college school paper, in 1976 as a writer, photographer, and columnist. "I loved the idea of expressing myself in a mass medium . . . [and] when you drew a figure next to your words, it had an element of attraction for people that was unimaginable to me at the time."

During his senior year of college, Breathed approached several newspaper syndicates—companies that market articles, columns, and cartoons to a wide variety of newspapers at the same time—with samples of his work in the hope that he could find a new outlet for his cartoons. A year later he got a call from Al Leeds at the *Washington Post*, who commissioned the young cartoonist to create a new comic strip for the paper. Breathed's "Bloom County" debuted in newspapers in 1980.

Irreverent in tone, "Bloom County" boasts a quirky cast of characters that included scruffy Bill the Cat, who constantly "Ack!"s up hairballs; Opus the over-anxious penguin; and humans such as lowlife lawyer Steve Dallas, scientific whiz-kid Oliver Wendell Jones, disabled Vietnam veteran Cutter John, wimpy ten-year-old Michael Binkley, and ever-gloomy child-entrepreneur Milo Bloom. Touted by many critics as *the* comic strip of the 1980s, "Bloom County" gained a strong readership and Breathed received letters from loyal fans and offended detractors alike. According to *New York* contributor Brian Raftery, "Breathed's mix of political satire, pop-culture riffing, and interspecies existential crises—articulated through a band of small-town eccentrics, human and otherwise . . .—was anachronistic to the point of anarchy." By the end of the strip's almost-decade-long run, the Pulitzer Prize-winning "Bloom County" was carried in 1,300 newspapers nationwide and reached an estimated forty million readers. In addition, book collections of Breathed's strip sold in the millions of copies, while "Bloom County" critters appeared in numerous spin-off products, from T-shirts to stuffed animals.

Breathed collects the best of a quarter-century of the antics of Opus the penguin and friends in the definitive **Opus: Twenty-five Years of His Sunday Best.** (Illustration copyright © 2004 by Berkeley Breathed. Reproduced by permission of Little, Brown & Company, a division of Hachette Book Group.)

Bloom County Babylon: Five Years of Basic Naughtiness collects the first years of Breathed's popular strip, and a thumb through its pages reveals how each of the characters—as well as the strip's overall sarcastic slant—developed over time. Breathed "quickly hit his stride," noted Charles Solomon in the *Los Angeles Times Book Review,* "and turned his strip into something unique." Solomon also praised Breathed's strong characterizations, his improving artistic abilities, and the barbed wit that made "Bloom County" "one of the funniest and most relevant strips" in the newspaper.

Billy and the Boingers Bootleg collects the next batch of antics from the "Bloom County" gang. Poking fun at everything from movie stars and espionage rings to heavy metal music—Bill the Cat and his band the Boingers doing a feral rendition of "Deathtongue" are among those images brought to life by a pen heavily inked with satire—*Billy and the Boingers Bootleg* was sought out by the cartoonist's fans. In *Tales Too Ticklish to Tell* Bill the Cat trades in his amplified guitar for a microphone, a teleprompter, and a hat in order to start a new gig as the televangelist "Fundamentally Oral Bill." Conversion of all of "Bloom County" quickly follows; just as quick is its "deconversion" when the

entire list of comic characters decides to go on strike, demanding an end to crowded conditions in their small strip in the newspaper.

Other "Bloom County" collections include *The Night of the Mary Kay Commandos* and *Happy Trails* In the first volume the 1988 election sees Bill the Cat and Opus the penguin (not surprisingly) beaten at the polls, while steps are taken to break failed candidate Opus's mom out of the headquarters of Mary Kay Cosmetics, where she is in peril of being used for cosmetic testing. In *Happy Trails* Breathed's cast of characters indulges in one last round of sarcasm during a theatrical "wrap" party celebrating the end of their long-running performance. In the bittersweet final strip, Opus the Penguin abandons his regular haunts and, suitcases in hand, walks off the edge of the page. "A good comic strip is no more eternal than a ripe melon," Breathed stated on his home page, explaining his decision to end the strip in August of 1989. "The ugly truth is that in most cases, comics age even less gracefully than their creators. 'Bloom County' is retiring before the stretch marks show."

Fortunately for Breathed's fans, he quickly hit the presses with a new comic strip, the weekly "Outland," which appeared in the Sunday newspaper color supple-

ments. Although it contains a different cast of characters, the first anthology of "Outland" comics, *Politically, Fashionably, and Aerodynamically Incorrect: The First Outland Collection,* reveals, from its very title, that "Outland" covers the same territory—and steps on the same sets of toes—as "Bloom County" had.

While Breathed ended "Outland" in 1995, he returned to comics with his syndicated Sunday strip "Opus," featuring one of "Bloom County"'s favorite characters, and ran this strip from 2003 to 2008. As Breathed explained to *Los Angeles Times* contributor Geoff Boucher, "Cartooning was always unsatisfying for me because I couldn't explore storytelling in the fashion I wanted . . . and once you recognize you're in a declining art form, it's really hard to keep that energy up."

After ending "Opus," Breathed found a more-satisfactory outlet for his art: children's books. Opus the penguin makes a return appearance in several books Breathed has written and illustrated for children. *A Wish for Wings That Work: An Opus Christmas Story* Breathed tells of the penguin's desire to use his wings the same way other birds do: to fly. Opus gets his wish in a roundabout way after his swimming skills get Santa and his sleigh full of goodies out of a lake after a piece of the sleigh's harness snaps. Although some reviewers were disappointed that the book does not contain the sarcasm of "Bloom County," others wrote that *A Wish for Wings That Work* has a tone that is more appropriate for young readers. In *Publishers Weekly* a reviewer praised the book as one that "little ones will love for its own magic and logic."

Geared for slightly older readers, *The Last Basselope: One Ferocious Story* finds the sturdy penguin and his friends in a dark, creepy forest during a search for a ferocious and legendary beast. With vivid, full-color, full-page airbrushed illustrations, *The Last Basselope* lets readers follow Opus the "Great and Famous Discoverer" and his comrades—several characters from "Outland" along with the rangy Bill the Cat—as they hunt down and corner the terrible Basselope, only to discover . . . a quiet basset hound burdened with a set of tied-on, ten-times-too-large antlers and an allergy to dandelions. Ilene Cooper, writing in *Booklist,* praised Breathed's "dramatic, full-color" illustrations as "eye-popping," and Lisa Dennis predicted in *School Library Journal* that older children will appreciate the author's "delightfully sarcastic and sophisticated" humor while younger readers may enjoy the book's "sheer silliness."

In *Goodnight Opus*—a parody of Margaret Wise Brown's classic children's story *Goodnight Moon*—Opus listens to a favorite bedtime story read by his grandmother. When sleep and a vivid imagination carry the penguin away on a fantastic journey through the night, Opus joins such fantastic creatures as a pillow with a balloon for a head and a purple snorklewacker on a flying three-wheeler. On a voyage to see the cows of the Milky Way, the trio visits everyone from Abe

Lincoln to the tooth fairy during their dreamtime trip. While Dennis commented in *School Library Journal* that *Goodnight Opus* is "less sarcastic than that of his cartoon collections," other reviewers still detected the presence of Breathed's incorrigible sarcastic humor. Fellow cartoonist Gahan Wilson commented in the *New York Times Book Review* that *Goodnight Opus* "is so well disguised as a children's book that I suspect it will be purchased and actually read aloud to children by many people who would, if they understood it, burn the thing on sight . . . . I highly recommend this book."

A young disbeliever gives Santa one last chance in *Red Ranger Came Calling: A Guaranteed True Christmas Story,* published as a tribute to Breathed's father. The book takes place in 1939, when nine-year-old "Red" Breathed lives for the day when he will be the proud and rightful owner of an Official Buck Tweed Two-Speed Crime-Stopper Star-Hopper bicycle. When he is sent to spend Christmas with his aunt at her island home Red knows that all his pleas to his now-absent parents have been wasted. His only hope now lies with a mysterious toothless oldster who Red figures may or may not be Santa Claus. Surrounded by old gentlemen who look suspiciously elf-like and granting the boy a small wish make Red suspect that the old fellow is for real, and so he makes his demands. When Christmas morning dawns and there is no cycle in site, the boy chalks it up to another case of being let down by grown-ups. However, Breathed's surprise ending "reaffirm[s] a reader's belief in the spirit that is Santa," according to a *Publishers Weekly* reviewer. *Booklist* critic Carolyn Phelan hailed Breathed's "extraordinary full-color illus-

Cover of Breathed's humorous **Flawed Dogs,** *which introduces a collection of sad-sack pups.* (Illustration copyright © 2003 by Berkeley Breathed. Reproduced by permission of Little, Brown & Company, a division of Hachette Book Group.)

trations [that] seem three-dimensional," and concluded that *Red Ranger Came Calling* is "a most original Christmas book."

With *Edwurd Fudwupper Fibbed Big: Explained by Fannie Fudwupper* Breathed creates a new cast of characters to tell a cautionary tale about lying. The young, and very unpleasant, boy in question "gets out of many sticky situations by telling whoppers in this rhyming tale related by his neglected little sister," explained Ronald Jobe in a *School Library Journal* review. Although a critic for *Publishers Weekly* characterized the tone of the story, like its artwork, as "mean-spirited and unfunny," Jobe found more to like. "This is a highly moralistic tale, but a wildly zany one," the critic wrote, extending special praise to the author/illustrator's "wordplay, alliteration, and outrageously expressive" illustrations.

Flawed Dogs: The Year-End Leftovers at the Piddleton "Last Chance" Dog Pound is a poignant plea for better treatment of animals that is couched in a humorous story. "To the casual browser, the book is a rogue's gallery of unlovely pets," explained a reviewer for *Pub-*

lishers Weekly. Marge Loch-Wouters, writing in *School Library Journal,* noted that children "may enjoy the goofy humor and outrageousness of the poor unwanted pooches" in Breathed's catalogue of the current residents of a Vermont animal shelter, a "last chance" home for a wide assortment of misaligned, misbehaving, and mistreated pups. Along with Breathed's picture of each "too colorful, too gassy, too long, too hairy" dog, as Loch Wouters described them, the author includes a sad life history, told in rhyme. While the overall effect of the book is humorous, Breathed concludes with a plea for readers to adopt pets at their local animal shelters.

Aimed at middle-grade readers, *Flawed Dogs: The Novel: The Shocking Raid on Westminster* concerns the relationship between Heidy McCloud, an orphan forced to live with her unpleasant uncle, a former dog breeder, and her new pet. Sam the Lion, a prized dachshund, sports a rare genetic gift: the "Duuglitz tuft." When a jealous poodle frames Sam, he is cast from Heidy's home into the streets and endures a seemingly endless series of zany horrors, including the loss of a leg and a stint in an experimental lab. Winding up at the National Last-Ditch Dog Depository, Sam enlists a group of

Breathed's books for children include his humorous, self-illustrated animal story Pete and Pickles, *about two unlikely friends.* (Illustration copyright © 2008 by Berkeley Breathed. Reproduced by permission of Philomel Books, a division of Penguin Young Readers Group, a member of Penguin (USA) Inc., 345 Hudson St., NY 10014. All rights reserved.)

abandoned canines to help him crash the famed Westminster Dog Show, a plot that "combines the suspense of an over-the-top caper film with the slapstick of the Marx Brothers," remarked a critic in *Kirkus Reviews*. According to Ian Chipman in *Booklist*, "Breathed proves an able writer, laying on plenty of over-the-top ebullience," and Jessica Marie noted in *School Library Journal* that Breathed's black-and-white illustrations are found throughout the volume, "adding depth to an already engaging and well-paced tale."

A young boy must venture into space to rescue his kidnapped mother in *Mars Needs Moms!*, "a wacky treat," according to *School Library Journal* critic Lisa Gangemi Kropp. Although Milo is often critical of his mom's rules and regulations, he bravely stows away on a rocket ship when a trio of Martians abduct his parent. Arriving on the Red Planet, Milo quickly realizes why the aliens are so desperate for adult guidance, and he gains a greater appreciation for his own mother when she makes an incredible sacrifice to save Milo's life after his oxygen supply is cut off. "Breathed mockingly depicts children's love/hate relationships to disciplinarians," a reviewer observed in *Publishers Weekly*. Todd Morning, writing in *Booklist*, applauded Breathed's "colorful, almost three-dimensional computer-generated art," and Kropp noted that "the illustrations are lush, plush, and over-the-top with color, attitude, and craziness."

In *Pete and Pickles*, another self-illustrated picture book, a pig's routine life is interrupted by his encounter with a daredevil elephant. When Pete, a porker who loves order and predictability, discovers Pickles, a fugitive from the circus, hiding in his room, the two begin an unlikely friendship, with Pickles adding an element of excitement to Pete's staid existence. A reviewer in *Publishers Weekly* declared that Breathed creates "an emotional rollercoaster of a story, complete with a gripping life-or-death climax," and Beth Cuddy noted in *School Library Journal* that the "heartwarming tale is packed with adventure, imagination, and the all-important message of accepting differences." A contributor in *Kirkus Reviews* cited Breathed's digital artwork for *Pete and Pickles* as a highlight of this "comically silly, warmly affirmative package."

For Breathed, illustrating children's books requires a different approach than cartooning. He remarked to *Texas Monthly* interviewer Mike Shea: "The methodology in arriving at ideas for either is the same: staring at the ceiling and trimming my nails. Here the similarities stop. Writing a gag has little in common with writing a story whose emotional mission is to enter a vulnerable young brain."

Biographical and Critical Sources

PERIODICALS

Booklist, December 15, 1992, Ilene Cooper, review of *The Last Basselope: One Ferocious Story*, p. 735; January 1, 1994, Janice Del Negro, review of *Goodnight Opus*, p. 832; October 1, 1994, Carolyn Phelan, review of *Red Ranger Came Calling: A Guaranteed True Christmas Story*, p. 325; May 1, 2007, Todd Morning, review of *Mars Needs Moms!*, p. 96; October 15, 2009, Ian Chipman, review of *Flawed Dogs: The Novel: The Shocking Raid on Westminster*, p. 64.

Christian Science Monitor, February 8, 2001, May Wiltenburg, "Cartoonist Berke Breathed," p. 23.

Comics Journal, October, 1988, interview with Breathed.

Houston Chronicle,, October 6, 2009, Rene A. Guzman, review of *Bloom County: The Complete Library: Volume One, 1980-1982*, p. 1.

Kirkus Reviews, February 1, 2007, review of *Mars Needs Moms!*, p. 120; September 1, 2008, review of *Pete and Pickles*; August 15, 2009, review of *Flawed Dogs*.

Los Angeles Times Book Review, April 15, 1990, Charles Solomon, review of *Happy Trails*, p. 15.

Newsweek, September 22, 2003, Brad Stone, interview with Breathed, p. 103.

New York, October 19, 2009, Brian Raftery, "The Renegade Cartoonist; Enshrining Berkeley Breathed's *Bloom County*."

New York Times Book Review, December 5, 1993, Gahan Wilson, review of *Goodnight Opus*, p. 72; December 6, 2009, John Schwartz, review of *Flawed Dogs*, p. 51; March 14, 2010, Douglas Wolk, review of *Bloom County: The Complete Library: Volume One, 1980-1982*, p. 8.

People, August 6, 1984, Gail Buchalter, "Cartoonist Berke Breathed Feathers His Nest by Populating Bloom County with Rare Birds," p. 93.

Psychology Today, January-February, 2004, William Whitney, "Berkeley Breathed," p. 96.

Publishers Weekly, July 25, 1991, review of *A Wish for Wings That Work*, p. 52; November 2, 1992, review of *The Last Basselope*, p. 68; September 19, 1994, review of *Red Ranger Came Calling*, p. 28; August 28, 2000, review of *Edwurd Fudwupper Fibbed Big*, p. 82; November 24, 2003, review of *Flawed Dogs*, p. 62; March 26, 2007, review of *Mars Needs Moms!*, p. 93; August 4, 2008, review of *Pete and Pickles*, p. 60; July 20, 2009, review of *Flawed Dogs: The Novel*, p. 140.

School Library Journal, November, 2000, Ronald Jobe, review of *Edwurd Fudwupper Fibbed Big*, p. 110; January, 2004, Marge Loch-Wouters, review of *Flawed Dogs*, p. 88; May, 2007, Lisa Gangemi Kropp, review of *Mars Needs Moms!*, p. 85; January, 2009, Beth Cuddy, review of *Pete and Pickles*, p. 72; November, 2009, Jessica Marie, review of *Flawed Dogs: The Novel*, p. 101.

Texas Monthly, April, 2007, Mike Shea, "Berkeley Breathed," p. 64.

Time, December 25, 1989, Daniel S. Levy, "Berke Breathed: A Hooligan Who Wields a Pen," p. 10.

USA Today, October 25, 2004, Kathy Balog, "Cartoonist Delivers His Magnum 'Opus,'" p. 5D.

ONLINE

Berkeley Breathed Home Page, http://www.berkeley breathed.com (May 1, 2011).

Hero Complex Web log, http://herocomplex.latimes.com/ (November 4, 2008), Sherry Stern, "Berkeley Breathed: Opus Alive and Well, 'Dreaming of a More Hopeful Tomorrow'"; (October 3, 2009) Geoff Boucher, "Berkeley Breathed, Drawn Back to *Bloom County* but Looking Forward."

National Review Online, http://www.nationalreview.com/ (September 25, 2003), Radley Balko, "A Great Returns."

Onion A.V. Club Web site, http://www.theonionavclub.com/ (August 15, 2001), Tasha Robinson, "Berkeley Breathed."

Salon.com, http://www.salon.com/ (November 20, 2003), Jesse Jarnow, "The Penguin Is Mightier than the Sword"; (October 18, 2008) Kerry Lauerman, "The End of 'Opus.'"*

* * *

BREATHED, Guy Berkeley
See BREATHED, Berkeley

* * *

BRIAN, Dennis 1971-

Personal

Born 1971, in FL. *Hobbies and other interests:* Hiking, running.

Addresses

Home—San Diego, CA. *E-mail*—brian.dennis@usmc.mil.

Career

Marine and author. U.S. Marine Corps, enlisted, 1991, served in Special Forces in Iraq; currently F/A-18 fighter pilot; attained rank of major.

Writings

(With Mary Nethery and Kirby Larson) *Nubs: A Mutt, a Marine, and a Miracle,* Little, Brown Books for Young Readers (New York, NY), 2009.

Adaptations

Nubs was optioned for film by Warner Brothers, 2009.

Sidelights

Looking forward to adventure after graduating from his Florida high school, Dennis Brian achieved his goal during his career as a U.S. Marine. He also found something he did not expect during his tour of duty in war-torn Iraq, and he chronicles this special adventure in his book *Nubs: A Mutt, a Marine, and a Miracle.*

Dennis Brian (Photograph by Scott Linnett/San Diego Union-Tribune/ZUMA Press. Reproduced with permission by Little, Brown & Company, a division of Hachette Book Group.)

Although Brian now serves as an F/A-18 fighter pilot, he began his career in the Marines as a member of Special Forces. After his first deployment to Bosnia, he was sent to Iraq, where he and his unit were assigned to patrol a section of the Iraqi-Syrian border. Once a week they would camp at the site of some ruins where a pack of wild dogs made their home. The pack leader was a dog with ears that had been cut off, probably by a passing Iraqi soldier, and Brian gave this dog the name Nubs. He and his unit befriended the dogs, sharing their meals of exotic American food, and Brian and Nubs slowly built a strong friendship. On one visit, the Marines arrived at the ruins to find Nubs bleeding and sickly: he had been stabbed with a screwdriver by an Iraqi. During the night that followed, Brian and his team took care of the dog's wounds, and when they left the following morning Nubs was on the mend. Several days later, the dog appeared at Brian's base camp, having tracked the Marine's Humvee over seventy miles of desert terrain. Because Brian was not allowed to have a pet on base, he arranged to have Nubs transported to Jordan, where the dog received further care. Finally, in early 2008, the dog with the cut-off ears boarded a plane bound for the United States and his new home in California, his flight financed with donations. Nubs was introduced to the lifestyle of American dogs while staying at the home of Brian's friends until his beloved Marine returned stateside.

Working with authors Mary Nethery and Kirby Larson, Brian crafted his dog's saga into the picture book *Nubs,* which is illustrated by candid photographs by Brian's

friends and family. In *Kirkus Reviews* a contributor noted that the book "presents a view of the Iraq war that makes it accessible to very young" children, while in *School Library Journal* Kara Schaff Dean dubbed *Nubs* "a feel-good entry in the current trend of inspirational true animal stories." "Gritty, low-res" photographs showing Brian and his dog "against the bleak Iraqi horizon are married with text so gracefully that many of the compositions could be book jackets," asserted *Booklist* contributor Daniel Kraus, and a *Publishers Weekly* contributor recommended *Nubs* as a "moving" and "emotional . . . saga" that will appeal to fans of "stories of animals that triumph against the odds."

Biographical and Critical Sources

PERIODICALS

Booklist, October 1, 2009, Daniel Kraus, review of *Nubs: A Mutt, a Marine, and a Miracle*, p. 42.
Kirkus Reviews, October 15, 2009, review of *Nubs*.
People, November 15, 2009, Champ Clark, "Incredible Journey," p. 93.
Publishers Weekly, November 9, 2009, review of *Nubs*, p. 45.
St. Petersburg Times (St. Petersburg, FL), April 25, 2008, Stephanie Garry, "Nubs and His Friend Enjoy the Spotlight," p. B1.
School Library Journal, December, 2009, Kara Schaff Dean, review of *Nubs*, p. 97.*

* * *

BUCKLEY, Michael

Personal

Born in Akron, OH; married; wife's name Alison; children: Finn. *Education:* Ohio University, B.A. (with honors).

Addresses

Home—New York, NY.

Career

Children's book author. Worked variously as a stand-up comedian, lead singer of a punk-rock band, and pasta maker; children's programming developer at companies including Discovery Channel, Learning Channel, Music Television (MTV), MTV Animation, and Klasky Csupo, beginning 1996.

Awards, Honors

Borders Original Voices nomination; Oppenheim Toy Portfolio Platinum Award.

Writings

"SISTERS GRIMM" NOVEL SERIES; ILLUSTRATED BY PETER FERGUSON

The Fairy-tale Detectives, Amulet Books (New York, NY), 2005.
The Unusual Suspects, Amulet Books (New York, NY), 2005.
The Problem Child, Amulet Books (New York, NY), 2006.
Once upon a Crime, Amulet Books (New York, NY), 2007.
Magic and Other Misdemeanors, Amulet Books (New York, NY), 2007.
Tales from the Hood, Amulet Books (New York, NY), 2008.
The Everafter War, Amulet Books (New York, NY), 2009.
The Inside Story, Amulet Books (New York, NY), 2010.

"NERDS" NOVEL SERIES

NERDS: National Espionage, Rescue, and Defense Society, illustrated by Ethen Beavers, Amulet Books (New York, NY), 2009.
M Is for Mama's Boy, illustrated by Ethen Beavers, Amulet Books (New York, NY), 2010.

OTHER

Contributor to *Storyworks* magazine.

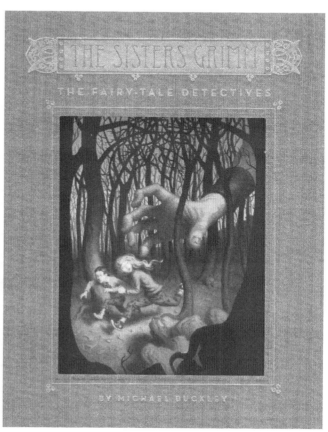

Cover of Michael Buckley's The Sisters Grimm: The Fairy-tale Detectives, *featuring an illustration by Peter Ferguson.* (Illustration © 2005 by Peter Ferguson. Reproduced by permission of Harry N. Abrams, Inc.)

Sidelights

A former television program developer, Michael Buckley is the creator of the popular "Sisters Grimm" and "NERDS" series for young readers, both of which have been praised for their adventure-filled plotlines, imaginative characters, and rich humor. On the *Sisters Grimm* Web site, Buckley explained that a childhood surrounded by books greatly influenced his success as a writer. "My parents were not wealthy people but they managed to find a way to get me books even when the checking account was empty," the author recalled. "I had more books than the library at my kindergarten school. To be a good writer you have to be a good reader and I had a great foundation to start from."

Buckley's "Sisters Grimm" novels for young readers, which include *The Fairy-tale Detectives* and *The Everafter War,* were inspired by his love of the stories collected by German scholars Jacob and Wilhelm Grimm during the eighteenth century. As he began researching other fairy tales to flesh out the world he was creating, Buckley realized how much these original folk stories differed from the Disney film versions he had been raised with.

The first "Sisters Grimm" novel, *The Fairy-tale Detectives* introduces eleven-year-old Sabrina and her seven-year-old sister Daphne. The sisters find themselves shuffling off to another in the series of foster families they have lived with since the disappearance of their parents. This foster home is different than others, however, and the sisters' new guardian, Granny Relda, actually claims to be the real-life grandmother they thought was dead. As if that was not strange enough, Granny's home town, Fairyport Landing, is actually the home of fairy-tale characters and creatures, called "Everafters," who live among the unknowing human population. When Granny and her companion, Mr. Canis (a.k.a. the Big Bad Wolf), are captured by a giant, Sabrina and Daphne have to decide who to trust in order to save the one person who may know the fate of their missing parents. "Fans of Lemony Snicket will adore this new series," wrote Annette Wells in a *Kliatt* review of *The Fairy-tale Detectives.* While citing some lags in the novel's plotline, along with Buckley's focus on world building, *Booklist* contributor Gillian Engberg praised the author's "gleefully fractured fairytales," and a *Kirkus Reviews* contributor dubbed *The Fairy-tale Detectives* a "tongue-in-cheek frolic" featuring "a pair of memorable young sleuths and a madcap plot."

In *The Unusual Suspects* Sabrina and Daphne begin school in Fairyport Landing when mystery once again surfaces. After one of their teachers is murdered, the girls learn that their whole school may be in danger. Sabrina would rather solve the mystery of her missing parents, however, and the girl's anger and frustration lead her to discover dangerous clues that may help her solve both mysteries, or may get her into even deeper trouble. A *Kirkus Reviews* contributor considered Buckley's second novel ti be "every bit as hilarious and scary" as *The Fairy-tale Detectives,* and Kathleen Meulen wrote in *School Library Journal* that "free-spirited Daphne is a perfect foil for her older, grumpier sister, Sabrina."

In *The Problem Child* Sabrina and Daphne face down one of their scariest opponents: Little Red Riding Hood. This familiar storybook character faced a terrible trauma after the traditional tale ended; Red was so traumatized by the Big Bad Wolf's brutal murder of her family that she actually went insane. Together with her "pet" Jabberwock, the orphaned girl now terrorizes the Grimm sisters. She even tries to kidnap Granny Relda so that she can complete her replacement family, a group that includes Sabrina and Daphne's unconscious parents. In *Kliatt,* Annette Wells described *The Problem Child* as "entertaining" and Tina Zubak recommended the third "Sisters Grimm" installment for readers who enjoy "a bit of dark humor rolled up with whimsy and adventure" in her *School Library Journal* review.

In *Once upon a Crime,* the fourth installment in Buckley's "Sisters Grimm" series, the sisters head to New York City after their friend Puck is injured. While searching for members of Puck's family, Sabrina and Daphne learn that Puck's father, Oberon, has been murdered. The two girls begin hunting for the killer, along the way discovering a surprising secret about their

Buckley's "Sisters Grimm" saga continues with **The Problem Child,** *featuring artwork by Peter Ferguson.* (Illustration © 2006 by Peter Ferguson. Reproduced by permission of Harry N. Abrams, Inc.)

mother's past. "A quick, fun read," Deidre Root stated in her *Kliatt* review of *Once upon a Crime*. Sabrina and Daphne travel to the future while investigating a series of thefts that confound the Everafters in *Magic and Other Misdemeanors*. "Fast-paced adventure" is one of the highlights of this "appealing choice for fairy-tale fans," wrote *Booklist* reviewer Kay Weisman in describing this adventure. The series continues with *Tales from the Hood*, in which the Grimms attempt to exonerate their friend, Mr. Canis, after he is placed on trial. In *The Everafter War*, conflict erupts between the notorious Scarlet Hand gang, led by the powerful Master, and a band of rebels led by Prince Charming. *The Inside Story* finds the girls transported to the Book of Everafter, where they chase the Master through several fairytales, altering their plotlines and raising the ire of the Editor.

Buckley shifts gears from his "Sisters Grimm" books to create his "NERDS" series of humorous adventure tales. Featuring a group of misfits turned superheroes, *NERDS: National Espionage, Rescue, and Defense Society* finds eleven-year-old Jackson Jones, a well-liked student at Nathan Hale Elementary School, relegated to social outcast after being fitted with highly magnetic braces and headgear. Jackson soon discovers that five of his fellow geeks are really part of an elite cadre of superspies whose foibles and weaknesses are turned into strengths through advanced technology. After joining NERDS, Jackson must rescue his new companions when they are taken hostage by Dr. Jigsaw, an evil genius who plans to destroy the planet by rearranging its plate tectonics. "Buckley has a flair for exaggerated humor," a critic noted in *Publishers Weekly*, and a *Kirkus Reviews* contributor maintained that "the inventive details, story and made-up futuristic technology will keep pages turning." According to *School Library Journal* reviewer Travis Jonker, "*NERDS* brings a worthy message to the fore—that uncool kids can grow up to be anything but."

In a sequel, *M Is for Mama's Boy*, the NERDS face off against a middle-aged computer whiz living in his mother's basement who hopes to strip the spies of their powers. Readers who enjoyed the first entry in the series "will find even more laughs here," Todd Morning predicted in his review of Buckley's humorous middle-grade novel for *Booklist*.

Biographical and Critical Sources

PERIODICALS

Booklist, November 15, 2005, Gillian Engberg, review of *The Fairy-tale Detectives*, p. 58; January 1, 2008, Kay Weisman, review of *Magic and Other Misdemeanors*, p. 76; October 15, 2009, Todd Morning, review of *NERDS: National Espionage, Rescue, and Defense Society*, p. 53; September 15, 2010, Todd Morning, review of *M Is for Mama's Boy*, p. 65.

Bulletin of the Center for Children's Books, December, 2005, review of *The Fairy-tale Detectives*, p. 172.
Children's Bookwatch, December, 2005, review of *The Fairy-tale Detectives*.
Kirkus Reviews, October 1, 2005, review of *The Fairy-tale Detectives*, p. 1077; November 1, 2005, review of *The Unusual Suspects*, p. 1182; March 15, 2006, review of *The Problem Child*, p. 286; August 15, 2009, review of *NERDS*.
Kliatt, September, 2005, Annette Wells, review of *The Fairy-tale Detectives*, p. 26; May, 2006, Annette Wells, review of *The Problem Child*, p. 6; January, 2008, Cara Chancellor, review of *The Problem Child*, p. 18; July, 2008, Deirdre Root, review of *Once upon a Crime*, p. 28.
Library Media Connection, February, 2006, Suzanne Libra, review of *The Fairy-tale Detectives*, p. 56.
Magazine of Fantasy and Science Fiction, September, 2006, Charles de Lint, reviews of *The Fairy-tale Detectives* and *The Unusual Suspects,* both p. 35.
Publishers Weekly, December 19, 2005, review of *The Fairy-tale Detectives*, p. 65; August 31, 2009, review of *NERDS,* p. 59.
School Library Journal, January, 2006, Sharon Grover, review of *The Fairy-tale Detectives,* and Kathleen Meulen, review of *The Unusual Suspects,* both p. 128; June, 2006, Tina Zubak, review of *The Problem Child,* p. 97; December, 2009, Travis Jonker, review of *NERDS,* p. 107.
Teacher Librarian, April, 2006, Betty Winslow, "Can You Keep a Secret?," p. 9; June, 2006, Betty Winslow, "More Fantastic Adventures," p. 44.

ONLINE

NERDS Web site, http://www.abramsbooks.com/nerds/ (May 1, 2011).
Sisters Grimm Web site, http://www.sistersgrimm.com/ (May 1, 2011).*

*   *   *

BUCKS, Brad
See HOLUB, Joan

*   *   *

BUTTON, Lana 1968-

Personal

Born 1968, in St. Stephen, New Brunswick, Canada; married 1992; children: three daughters. *Education:* Attended Concordia University for two years; studied early childhood education.

Addresses

Home—Burlington, Ontario, Canada. *E-mail*—button_4@sympatico.ca.

Lana Button (Photograph by Julie Johnson, courtesy of Vine Images. Reproduced by permission.)

Career

Early childhood educator and author. Childcare worker for over twenty years, including in Maryland. Presenter at schools.

Member

Writer's Union of Canada.

Awards, Honors

Outstanding Books for Young People with Disabilities selection, International Board on Books for Young People, 2010, Blue Spruce Award shortlist, Ontario Library Association, and Shining Willow Award shortlist, Saskatchewan Young Readers' Choice Award, both 2011, all for *Willow's Whispers*.

Writings

Willow's Whispers, illustrated by Tania Howells, Kids Can Press (Toronto, Ontario, Canada), 2010.

Contributor to periodicals, including *Child Care Exchange, Concordia University Magazine, Hamilton Spectator, Parents Canada,* and *Today's Parent.*

Sidelights

In her work as a child-care professional, Lana Button has had plenty of opportunities to hone her storytelling techniques and also draw on her college training in performance. A native of New Brunswick, Canada, Button enrolled in the theatre program at Concordia University, leaving after two years to work as an actress in both television and film. An interest in early childhood education gradually replaced her plans to pursue an acting career, and rapt audiences of children have now become her biggest fans. In addition to reading books by other writers, Button has also created the original picture book *Willow's Whispers,* which focuses on shyness, a childhood trait Button never experienced but often encounters in her work with young people.

Illustrated by Tania Howells, *Willow's Whispers* introduces a very shy young girl with a very quiet voice. Because her voice is virtually inaudible to others, Willow's friends cannot hear her welcome their invitation to join them at the lunch table, so she often sits alone. She also loses her favorite doll to a bully who cannot hear her quiet protests. Willow's patient and loving father offers her encouragement, however, and eventually the girl finds a way to express herself by using her creativity and her intelligence. "There is nothing cloying about the sweetness" of Button's story, noted Susan Perren in her *Globe & Mail* review of *Willow's Whispers,* while a *Kirkus Reviews* critic dubbed the picture book "cheerful inspiration even for readers who don't share [the girl's] . . . specific quandary." In *School Library Journal* Margaret R. Tassia also commended the story, noting that Button's mix of a basic "text and simple sentences" combines with "a strong character who solves her own problems" to produce a "successful" book. Praising Howells' use of "strong black outline and clear colors," Ellen Heaney added in her *Canadian Review of Materials* appraisal that *Willow's Whispers* "would be a success in a storytime about feelings or for a group discussion about problem solving."

Biographical and Critical Sources

PERIODICALS

Canadian Review of Materials, September 24, 2010, Ellen Heaney, review of *Willow's Whispers.*
Globe & Mail (Toronto, Ontario, Canada), May 8, 2010, Susan Perren, review of *Willow's Whispers,* p. F14.
Kirkus Reviews, January 15, 2010, review of *Willow's Whispers.*
Quill & Quire, April, 2010, Chelsea Donaldson, review of *Willow's Whispers.*
School Library Journal, May, 2010, Margaret R. Tassia, review of *Willow's Whispers,* p. 79.

ONLINE

Kids Can Press Web site, http://www.kidscanpress.com/ (April 20, 2011), "Lana Button."
Lana Button Home Page, http://www.lanabutton.com (April 24, 2011).

C

CALKHOVEN, Laurie 1959-

Personal

Born July 31, 1959, in Omaha, NE. *Education:* Syracuse University, B.A. (journalism and English literature). *Hobbies and other interests:* Travel.

Addresses

Home—New York, NY. *E-mail*—lcalkhoven@me.com.

Career

Author. Worked in publishing, New York, NY; currently freelance writer. Presenter at schools.

Writings

Flash, Boom, Blast!: Amazing Inventions from the War Front, Scholastic (New York, NY), 2004.

(Compiler with Ryan Herndon) *Guinness World Records Fearless Feats: Incredible Records of Human Achievement,* Scholastic (New York, NY), 2005.

(Compiler with Ryan Herndon) *Guinness World Records. Awesome Ocean Records,* Scholastic (New York, NY), 2005.

(Compiler with Ryan Herndon) *Guinness World Records: Top Ten Fantastic Flight Records,* Scholastic (New York, NY), 2005.

(Adaptor) *Just My Luck* (film novelization), Scholastic (New York, NY), 2006.

The Family Quiz Book, illustrated by Amanda Haley, American Girl (Middleton, WI), 2006.

Miles of Smiles, illustrated by Shannon Laskey, American Girl (Middleton, WI), 2007.

"STERLING BIOGRAPHIES" SERIES

George Washington: An American Life, Sterling Pub. Co. (New York, NY), 2007.

Laurie Calkhoven (Photograph by Elyse Fradkin. Reproduced by permission.)

Harriet Tubman: Leading the Way to Freedom, Sterling Publishing (New York, NY), 2008.

"BOYS OF WARTIME" SERIES

Daniel at the Siege of Boston, 1776, Dutton Children's Books (New York, NY), 2010.

Will at the Battle of Gettysburg, 1863, Dutton Children's Books (New York, NY), 2011.
Michael at the Invasion of France, 1943, Dial Books for Young Readers (New York, NY), 2012.

"INNERSTAR UNIVERSITY" SERIES

Fork in the Trail, Pleasant Company (Middleton, WI), 2010.
A Winning Goal, Pleasant Company (Middleton, WI), 2011.

Sidelights

"I've always loved reading, writing, and history," Laurie Calkhoven told *SATA.* "What I'm most interested in exploring in my fiction is how ordinary kids respond when they're confronted with extraordinary situations. That's how the 'Boys of Wartime' series was born. I hope I succeeded in making those extraordinary times real for today's readers while at the same time telling the truth about our American history."

Biographical and Critical Sources

PERIODICALS

Booklist, February 1, 2010, Carolyn Phelan, review of *Daniel at the Siege of Boston, 1776,* p. 42.
Kirkus Reviews, February 15, 2010, review of *Daniel at the Siege of Boston, 1776.*
School Library Journal, April, 2008, Kristen Oravec, review of *Harriet Tubman: Leading the Way to Freedom,* p. 158.

ONLINE

Laurie Calkhoven Home Page, http://www.lauriecalkhoven.com (April 24, 2011).

*   *   *

CAMPOS, Maria de Fatima

Personal

Born in Brazil; immigrated to England, 1989; married Richard Davis (a photographer), 1995; children: Victoria. *Education:* Studied industrial design (Curitiba, Brazil); degree (São Paolo, Brazil), c. 1980s; attended Westminister University.

Addresses

Home—London, England. *E-mail*—photos@campos-davis.com.

Career

Photographer and author. Instructor in photographic techniques. Film stills photographer, c. 1990s; photographer specializing in families, mothers to be, children, and all things Brazilian.

Member

Royal Photographic Society of Great Britain (associate member), British Professional Photographers Association (associate member).

Writings

AND PHOTOGRAPHER

Insight Guide to Rio de Janeiro, Insight Guides (London, England), 1999.
B Is for Brazil, Frances Lincoln (London, England), 1999, revised, 2009.
Cássio's Day: From Dawn to Dusk in a Brazilian Village, Frances Lincoln (London, England), 2001, revised, 2009.
In a Brazilian Village, Benchmark Books/Marshall Cavendish (New York, NY), 2002.
Victoria's Day, Frances Lincoln (London, England), 2007.
Hand Made Photos (photographs), Millennium Editions (London, England), 2008.
Victoria Goes to Brazil, Frances Lincoln (New York, NY), 2009.

Work included in anthologies, including *Literature brasileira em foco,* 2003; *Armadilhas ficcionais: modos de desarmar,* 2003; and *Linhas de fuga: transitos ficcionais,* edited by Ana Lúcia M. de Oliveira, 2007.

Sidelights

"I always thought that to be and feel really alive we had to create work in which, when we leave this life to another stage, there was something we have left to contribute to society," Maria de Fatima Campos told *SATA.* "Photography was the first thing I wanted to do.

"Before I left Brazil in 1989 I thought I should get to know my country as much as I could. I traveled all over Brazil and photographed what was there. Relocating to the U.K. was a very exciting thing to do, learning more about photography and Britain's culture. I was fascinated, but of course I missed my country very much. Fortunately, Frances Lincoln Publishers was looking for a photographer who wanted to write a book about Brazil, and I just happened to be there to say yes. I always wanted to write books, but honestly was too busy to think about it with so many others things I wanted to do. So I wrote *B Is for Brazil* and *Cássio's Day: From Dawn to Dusk in a Brazilian Village.*

"Then my daughter Victoria was born after four years of marriage, and life changed as she was born with Downs' syndrome.

"I tried to write books about Down's syndrome, but found it difficult. Then, when she was three and half, I wrote a book about her, *Victoria's Day.*

"Since my daughter was born, I have become very interested in inclusion and how it works in the U.K. [with regard to children with disabilities], and I wanted to

learn what I could. One thing I was completely sure of was that inclusion starts at home. But what are my child's right in society, and as a parent what I can do to support her? *Victoria's Day* is based on my belief regarding inclusion in mainstream education. Children with Downs' syndrome should be given as much opportunity as anyone else to be able to embrace their future.

"I wrote *Victoria Goes to Brazil* as part of a series of books in which children return to their roots and visit the countries where their parents were born. In this case Victoria traveled with me to Brazil to meet her family there, including her great grandmother of the indigenous Tupi-Guarani tribe."

Biographical and Critical Sources

PERIODICALS

Kirkus Reviews, October 15, 2009, review of *Victoria Goes to Brazil.*
School Librarian, autumn, 2007, Angela Redfern, review of *Victoria's Day;* autumn, 2009, Chris Brown, review of *Victoria Goes to Brazil,* p. 153.
Times Educational Supplement, September 17, 1999, review of *B Is for Brazil;* September, 2001, Tom Deveson, review of *Cássio's Day: From Dawn to Dusk in a Brazilian Village.*

ONLINE

Maria de Fatima Campos/Richard Davis Web site, http:// campos-davis.com (February 24, 2011).

* * *

CLEMENT-MOORE, Rosemary

Personal

Married. *Education:* Texas Christian University, M.A. *Hobbies and other interests:* Reading, sewing, sailing, music, vintage embroidery.

Addresses

Home—Arlington, TX. *E-mail*—rosemary@readrose mary.com.

Career

Writer. Former teacher, actress, and youth director for a community theater.

Writings

The Splendor Falls, Delacorte Press (New York, NY), 2009.

Also author of plays for community theater productions.

"MAGGIE QUINN: GIRL VS. EVIL" SERIES

Prom Dates from Hell, Delacorte Press (New York, NY), 2007.
Hell Week, Delacorte Press (New York, NY), 2008.
Highway to Hell, Delacorte Press (New York, NY), 2009.

Sidelights

A former actress and educator, Rosemary Clement-Moore is the author of *Prom Dates from Hell,* part of the "Maggie Quinn: Girl vs. Evil" series of supernatural thrillers that feature the exploits of a psychically gifted young woman who does battle with the forces of evil. Clement-Moore has also penned a well-received gothic romance *The Splendor Falls,* "an atmospheric tale with a complex heroine," according to *Booklist* reviewer Ilene Cooper. In a *Bildungsroman* online interview, Clement-Moore observed that "all my books in some ways . . . are about power. Do you get yours from in-

Cover of Rosemary Clement-Moore's teen novel **Prom Dates from Hell,** *featuring artwork by Angela Carlino and Andy Smith.* (Illustration copyright © www.asmithillustration.com. All rights reserved. Used by permission of Delacorte Press, an imprint of Random House Children's Books, a division of Random House, Inc.)

side yourself, from the person you are and the things you believe in? Or do you steal your power by putting down or bullying others?"

In her debut novel, *Prom Dates from Hell,* Clement-Moore mixes high-school life with the supernatural. Ace journalist and brainy senior Maggie Quinn has a passion, but it is not fellow student Stanley Dozer. When the über-geeky Stanley asks Maggie to be his date for Avalon High's senior prom, she balks and unknowingly causes the humiliated young man to unleash an evil that only Maggie can stop. Harnessing her latent ESP abilities, Maggie dons the hated prom dress, runs the gauntlet of condescension formed by Avalon's ruling clique, and appears at prom on the elbow of college friend Justin, hoping to avert a demon-led disaster.

In reviewing *Prom Dates from Hell,* critics praised Clement-Moore's ability to create a spunky and engaging heroine. Teen readers "will have fun with this one," predicted *Kliatt* contributor Claire Rosser, "especially if they like rather crazy, humorous stories" and sharp-witted teen heroines. Noting that the humorous plot of *Prom Dates from Hell* includes a touch of teen romance, Emily Rodriguez wrote in *School Library Journal* that "sharp writing and a satirical portrayal of the high school social scene make [the novel] . . . an enjoyable read." "There is a lot to like in this story that takes on magic, romance and even clique politics," concluded a *Publishers Weekly* contributor.

Maggie returns in *Hell Week* as an undercover stint draws her into the clutches of a sorority at her new college, where student mixers lead to secret meetings, bizarre pledging rituals, and a dark secret. Although noting that Clement-Moore's plot sometimes borders on the absurd, Stephanie L. Petruso added in *School Library Journal* that the author "makes it work by tempering the ridiculous with Maggie's dry humor and biting observations of Greek life in general." A contributor in *Kirkus Reviews* similarly cited "Maggie's snarky humor and quirky personality" as a highlight of the work, and in *Kliatt* Rosser dubbed *Hell Week* both "witty and entertaining."

A spring-break road trip takes a turn toward the bizarre in *Highway to Hell,* the third installment in the "Maggie Quinn" series. After the Jeep they are driving runs over the grisly remains of a dead cow, Maggie and her spell-casting companion, Lisa, are forced to stay in a small Texas town while their vehicle undergoes repairs. The duo quickly discovers from the townsfolk that El Chupacabra, a legendary blood-thirsty creature, roams the area, slaughtering the local livestock at will. As they look into the mystery, Maggie and Lisa encounter a strange evil that threatens both animals and humans. As with the previous two novels, *Highway to Hell* earned critical praise, *School Library Journal* contributor Jake Pettit noting that Clement-Moore's "story flows quickly with thrills, chills, and a first-rate mystery."

In a *Bildungsroman* online interview discussing her novel *The Splendor Falls,* Clement-Moore remarked that the book "is, at its heart, a Gothic novel in the vein of Mary Stewart, Phyllis A. Whitney, and Barbara Michaels. It's updated for modern sensibilities, but I think still timeless." *The Splendor Falls* focuses on Sylvie Davis, a professional ballerina who suffers a career-ending injury and then journeys to Alabama to visit her late father's family. While recovering from her physical and mental wounds, Sylvie moves into Bluestone Hill, an antebellum estate, where she draws the interest of both Shawn Maddox, a local teenager, and Rhys Griffith, a transplanted Welshman. The heroine begins to question her sanity, however, when she spies ghosts in the mansion, and her investigations lead to a number of startling discoveries about her family's past. A reviewer in *Publishers Weekly* offered praise for Clement-Moore's tale, noting that the author "anchors the story in actual locations and history, offering au courant speculations about the nature of ghosts and magic."

Cover of Clement-Moore's quirky teen novel Hell Week, *featuring cover art by Craig Phillips.* (Delacorte Press, 2008. Reproduced by permission of Random House, Inc.)

Biographical and Critical Sources

PERIODICALS

Booklist, March 15, 2009, Francisca Goldsmith, review of *Highway to Hell,* p. 55; September 15, 2009, Ilene Cooper, review of *The Splendor Falls,* p. 68.

Bulletin of the Center for Children's Books, July-August, 2007, Karen Coats, review of *Prom Dates from Hell,* p. 457.

Horn Book, May-June, 2007, Christine M. Heppermann, review of *Prom Dates from Hell,* p. 297.

Kirkus Reviews, February 15, 2007, review of *Prom Dates from Hell;* July 15, 2008, review of *Hell Week;* August 1, 2009, review of *The Splendor Falls.*

Kliatt, March, 2007, review of *Prom Dates from Hell,* p. 10; May, 2008, Claire Rosser, review of *Prom Dates from Hell,* p. 26; July, 2008, Claire Rosser, review of *Hell Week,* p. 10.

Publishers Weekly, March 26, 2007, review of *Prom Dates from Hell,* p. 95; September 28, 2009, review of *The Splendor Falls,* p. 66.

School Library Journal, March, 2007, Emily Rodriguez, review of *Prom Dates from Hell,* p. 206; February, 2008, Stephanie L. Petruso, review of *Hell Week,* p. 112; April, 2009, Jake Pettit, review of *Highway to Hell,* p. 130.

Voice of Youth Advocates, April, 2007, Jennifer Rummel, review of *Prom Dates from Hell,* p. 63; February, 2009, Stacey Hayman, review of *Highway to Hell,* p. 538.

ONLINE

Bildungsroman Web log, http://slayground.livejournal.com/ (May 20, 2009), interview with Clement-Moore.

Class of 2K7 Web site, http://classof2k7.com/ (March 15, 2008), "Rosemary Clement-Moore."

Cynsations Web log, http://cynthialeitichsmith.blogspot.com/ (February 11, 2008), Cynthia Leitich Smith, interview with Clement-Moore.

Random House Web site, http://www.randomhouse.com/ (April 15, 2011), interview with Clement-Moore.

Rosemary Clement-Moore Home Page, http://www.rosemaryclementmoore.com (April 15, 2011).

Rosemary Clement-Moore Web log, http://readrosemary.blogspot.com (April 15, 2011).*

*   *   *

CODY, Matthew

Personal

Born in St. Louis, MO; married; wife's name Alisha; children: Willem. *Education:* B.F.A. (theater and creative writing); M.F.A. (theatre).

Addresses

Home—New York, NY. *Agent*—Kate Schafer Testerman, KT Literary, contact@ktliterary.com. *E-mail*—matt@matthewcody.com.

Matthew Cody (Reproduced by permission.)

Career

Educator and author. Formerly worked at theaters in New York, NY; teacher of English, beginning 2004. Moderator, Symphony Space Thalia Book Club, New York, NY. Presenter at schools.

Writings

Powerless, Alfred A. Knopf (New York, NY), 2009.

Sidelights

A native of Missouri, Matthew Cody grew up reading adventure comics as well as classic tales that included Jules Verne's *20,000 Leagues under the Sea,* H.G. Wells' *The Time Machine, Tarzan* by Edgar Rice Burroughs, and Robert E. Howard's "Conan the Barbarian" novels. And after earning a master's degree in Shakespearean literature, he moved to New York City, intending to focus on writing for the theatre. Over time, Cody channeled his love of literature into a career as a teacher of English while continuing to keep his connection to the theatre through his writing. In addition to producing stage plays, he has also written short fiction and sequential stories intended as comic-book scripts. He began his first published novel, *Powerless,* the same year he began teaching; as Tim Wadham noted in *School Library Journal,* the book serves as "a loving tribute to [the] comic books and superhero stories" that Cody continues to enjoy.

Twelve-year-old Daniel Corrigan is the hero of *Powerless,* and his adventures begin after his family moves to the town of Noble's Green, Pennsylvania, to care for an elderly relative. When Daniel's new classmates reveal their many acts of heroism in saving people and averting catastrophes, they also explain that everyone in Noble's Green who is under the age of thirteen has amazing powers. The down side is that each of these children will lose both their powers and their memories of having them on the day they become a teenager: none of

the adults is aware that their children are special or that someone or something is stealing their special talents. As Daniel investigates the town's strange ability to breed young superheroes, he learns about a local legend involving a comic-book hero named Johnny Noble. Then his discoveries become more sinister, in a novel that ends with "a titanic climactic battle," according to a *Kirkus Reviews* writer. In *Booklist* Kathleen Isaacs remarked on Cody's skill in crafting "an intriguing premise, appealing characters, and a straightforward narrative arc with plenty of action," while a *Publishers Weekly* critic dubbed *Powerless* "a wholly satisfying debut" that encompasses "themes of heroism, sacrifice and coming-of-age." As the *Kirkus Reviews* writer observed, *Powerless* reads like "a Golden Age comic without the pictures."

"The only thing cooler than young readers are young writers," Cody noted in an interview for *Kidsreads.com*, discussing his time spent with groups of school children. "Kids are so honest in their opinions, and so perceptive, that it makes talking shop with them a real treat. Adults can get caught up in genres or literary labels, but kids just read what they like, and they write stories that they think will be entertaining. They try to write good stories, that's all. It's refreshing and humbling all at once."

Biographical and Critical Sources

PERIODICALS

Booklist, October 15, 2009, Kathleen Isaacs, review of *Powerless,* p. 65.
Kirkus Reviews, October 15, 2009, review of *Powerless.*
Publishers Weekly, November 2, 2009, review of *Powerless,* p. 52.
School Library Journal, January, 2010, Tim Wadham, review of *Powerless,* p. 98.

ONLINE

KidsReads.com, http://www.kidsreads.com/ (December, 2009), interview with Cody.
Matthew Cody Home Page, http://www.matthewcody.com (April 24, 2011).

* * *

COLLICUTT, Paul

Personal

Born in England. *Education:* Brighton Art College, B.F.A. (graphics illustration), 1984.

Addresses

Home—Hove, Sussex, England.

Career

Author and illustrator. Presenter at schools.

Awards, Honors

Parents' Choice Gold Award, c. 1999, for *This Train.*

Writings

SELF-ILLUSTRATED; FOR CHILDREN

This Train, Farrar Straus & Giroux (New York, NY), 1999.
This Plane, Farrar Straus & Giroux (New York, NY), 2000.
This Boat, Farrar, Straus & Giroux (New York, NY), 2001.
This Car, Farrar, Straus, & Giroux (New York, NY), 2002.
This Truck, Farrar Straus & Giroux (New York, NY), 2004.
This Rocket, Farrar, Straus & Giroux (New York, NY), 2005.

SELF-ILLUSTRATED; "ROBOT CITY ADVENTURES" GRAPHIC NOVEL SERIES

City in Peril!, Candlewick Press (Somerville, MA), 2009.
Rust Attack!, Candlewick Press (Somerville, MA), 2009.

Cover of Cody's teen novel Powerless, *featuring artwork by Geoffrey Lorenzen.* (Alfred A. Knopf, Inc., 2009. Reproduced with permission from Alfred A. Knopf, an imprint of Random House Children's Books, a division of Random House, Inc.)

Murder on the Robot City Express, Candlewick Press (Somerville, MA), 2010.

The Indestructible Metal Men, Candlewick Press (Somerville, MA), 2010.

ILLUSTRATOR

Carole Clements, *A Flavour of Normandy,* Headline (London, England), 1996.

Pepita Aris, *A Flavour of Tuscany,* Headline (London, England), 1996.

Pepita Aris, *A Flavour of Provence,* Headline (London, England), 1996.

Pepita Aris, *A Flavour of Andalusia,* Headline (London, England), 1996.

Brian Moses, selector, *Follow the Sea: Classic and Narrative Poems,* Longman (Harlow, England), 2000.

Karen Wallace, *Rockets,* Oxford University Press (Oxford, England), 2000.

ILLUSTRATOR; "CHINESE HOROSCOPES FOR LOVERS" SERIES BY LORI REID

The Rat, Element (Shaftesbury, England), 1996.
The Dog, Element (Shaftesbury, England), 1996.
The Snake, Element (Shaftesbury, England), 1996.
The Dragon, Element (Shaftesbury, England), 1996.
The Horse, Element (Shaftesbury, England), 1996.
The Monkey, Element (Shaftesbury, England), 1996.
The Pig, Element (Shaftesbury, England), 1996.
The Rabbit, Element (Shaftesbury, England), 1996.
The Ox, Element (Shaftesbury, England), 1996.
The Tiger, Element (Shaftesbury, England), 1996.
The Rooster, Element (Shaftesbury, England), 1996.
The Sheep, Element (Shaftesbury, England), 1996.

Sidelights

Based in the United Kingdom, Paul Collicutt is an illustrator who began his work in children's books in the mid-1990s. Collicutt's lighthearted art brings to life his original series of toddler-friendly books focusing on transportation, and he expands his work as a writer in his "Robot City Adventures" graphic-novel series.

Collicutt has loved to draw since childhood, when he discovered Marvel comics. On the back of rolls of old wallpaper supplied by his parents, he practiced drawing his favorite Marvel characters and then created several characters of his own while perfecting his cartoon style. He started his illustration career in 1984, after graduating from Brighton Art College where he had studied under children's author/illustrator Raymond Briggs. Although he originally intended to be a comic-book artist, Collicutt's art-school exposure to painting prompted him to refocus on commercial illustration. In the mid-1990s he earned his first book-illustration assignments, creating art for a trio of cookbooks by Pepita Aris and Carole Clements and also illustrating a series of horoscope guides. Collicutt turned to children's books a few years later beginning with the award-winning *This Train*.

In *This Train* Collicutt's brightly colored paintings of many different types of locomotives feature the kind of detail that young boys find intriguing. In addition to depicting different models of trains on the book's pages, *This Train* also features endpapers that contain even more drawings of trains. Collicutt employs a similar format in the related books *This Plane, This Boat,* and *This Car,* the last which Connie Fletcher noted in *Booklist* "uses eye-popping colors and varying perspectives to draw attention to a selection of vintage and a few modern vehicles." In *This Truck* young readers can scan what a *Kirkus Reviews* writer described as "captivating paintings [that are] laudable in their intricacy," while *This Rocket* will serve as a magnet for "kids who are space crazy," according to *Booklist* contributor Ilene Cooper.

While working on the illustrations for his transportation series, Collicutt realized how much fun drawing machinery could be. As he continued to draw, he created Curtis the Colossal Coast Guard, a robot that resembles a giant lighthouse. "I liked the fact that this figure was enormous and also that it was made out of lighthouse shapes and elements you might find on a ship," the author/artist recalled in an interview with John Hogan for *Graphic Novel Reporter* online. "I felt it had a retro feel to it, which I also liked, and I thought there must be some story behind it, and so I started to figure out what sort of a world it would live in. It seemed natural to me that it would live in Robot City and that city should be a big American city. I imagined New York with robots and people living together."

In *City in Peril!,* the first installment in Collicutt's "Robot City Adventures," the author/illustrator takes readers to Robot City, where robots can be found working side by side with their human creators. Along the hazardous coastline, Curtis the Colossal Coast Guard Robot is tall enough to perform the work of a lighthouse while also able to take hold of storm-tossed ships and guide them to safety. When a fire breaks out on an offshore oil-drilling platform, Curtis saves the day although a giant squid from the briny deep follows the robot back to land and causes some problems. Collicutt's illustrated series continues with *Rust Attack!, Murder on the Robot City Express,* and *The Indestructible Metal Men,* each which introduces helpful robots who win the admiration of their communities through their abilities to both serve and protect.

Reviewing both *City in Peril!* and *Rust Attack* for *Kirkus Reviews,* a critic cited the "retro-comic-book-style action and classic movie-serial banter" in a series that will draw upper-elementary-grade boys in with its "good, low-violence fun." "Retro not only in its look but also in its goofy earnestness," in the opinion of *Booklist* critic Ian Chipman, Collicutt's "Robot City Adventures" series "promises plenty of rock 'em sock 'em robot fun."

Biographical and Critical Sources

PERIODICALS

Booklist, March 15, 2001, Helen Rosenberg, review of *This Boat,* p. 1399; August, 2002, Connie Fletcher, review of *This Car,* p. 1967; March 15, 2004, Hazel Rochman, review of *This Truck,* p. 1307; December 1, 2005, Ilene Cooper, review of *This Rocket,* p. 66; November 1, 2009, Ian Chipman, review of *City in Peril!,* p. 46.

Kirkus Reviews, June 1, 2002, review of *This Car;* April 1, 2004, review of *This Truck;* August 15, 2005, review of *This Rocket,* p. 911; October 15, 2009, review of *City in Peril!*

Publishers Weekly, September 6, 1999, review of *This Train,* p. 101; August 21, 2000, review of *This Plane,* p. 75; September 10, 2001, review of *This Train,* p. 95; June 17, 2002, "True Champions," p. 67.

School Library Journal, July, 2001, Gay Lynn Van Vleck, review of *This Boat,* p. 92; August, 2002, Joy Fleishhacker, review of *This Car,* p. 174; July, 2004, Debbie Stewart Hoskins, review of *This Truck,* p. 92; September, 2005, Angela J. Reynolds, review of *This Rocket,* p. 191; January, 2010, Sadie Mattox, review of *City in Peril!,* p. 127.

ONLINE

Graphic Novel Reporter Online, http://www.graphicnovel reporter.com/ (April 20, 2011), John Hogan, interview with Collicutt.

Mindless Ones Web site, http://mindlessones.com/ (February 4, 2010), interview with Collicutt.*

* * *

COWLES, Kathleen
See KRULL, Kathleen

* * *

CUYLER, Margery 1948-
(Margery Stuyvesant Cuyler, Daisy Wallace)

Personal

Born December 31, 1948, in Princeton, NJ; daughter of Lewis Baker and Margery Cuyler; married John Perkins (a psychoanalyst), August 23, 1979; children Thomas, Timothy. *Education:* Sarah Lawrence College, B.A., 1970.

Addresses

Home—Princeton, NJ. *E-mail*—margery.cuyler@veri zon.net.

Margery Cuyler (Photograph by John Perkins. Reproduced by permission.)

Career

Publisher, editor, and author of children's books. Atlantic Monthly Press, Boston, MA, assistant to editor of children's books, 1970-71; Walker & Co., New York, NY, editor of children's books, 1972-74; Holiday House, New York, NY, vice president and editor-in-chief of children's books, 1974-95; Henry Holt & Co., New York, NY, vice president and associate publisher, Books for Young Readers, 1996-97; Golden Books Family Entertainment, vice president and director of trade publishing, 1997-99; Winslow Press, New York, NY, vice president and editor-in-chief, beginning 1999; Marshall Cavendish, Tarrytown, NY, currently director of trade publishing. Lecturer on children's book editing, Rutgers University, 1974, New School for Social Research, 1975, and Vassar College, 1984. Board member, Women's National Book Association and Children's Book Council, 1980-82. Library trustee and member of alumnae board, Sarah Lawrence College.

Awards, Honors

Children's Choice designation, International Reading Association (IRA)/Children's Book Council, 1976, for *Witch Poems,* 1982, for *The Trouble with Soap,* 1991, for *That's Good! That's Bad!;* New Jersey Institute of Technology Author's Award, 1988, for *Fat Santa;* Best Children's Book designation, Bank Street College of Education, Kentucky Bluegrass Award nomination, and Indiana Young Hoosier Award nomination, all 1998, all for *The Biggest, Best Snowman;* Best Children's Book

designation, Bank Street College of Education, Indiana Young Hoosier Award nomination, South Carolina Book Award nomination, and New Mexico Land of Enchantment nomination, all 1999, all for *The Battlefield Ghost;* Best Children's Book designation, Bank Street College of Education, and Teacher's Choice selection, IRA, both 2000, both for *One Hundredth Day Worries;* Best Children's Book designation, Bank Street College of Education, Tennessee Volunteer State Book Award, and Wisconsin Golden Archer Award, all 2002, all for *Skeleton Hiccups.*

Writings

PICTURE BOOKS

Jewish Holidays, illustrated by Lisa C. Wesson, Holt (New York, NY), 1978.

The All-around Pumpkin Book, illustrated by Corbett Jones, Holt (New York, NY), 1980.

The All-around Christmas Book, illustrated by Corbett Jones, Holt (New York, NY), 1982.

Sir William and the Pumpkin Monster, illustrated by Marcia Winborn, Holt (New York, NY), 1984.

Freckles and Willie, illustrated by Marcia Winborn, Holt (New York, NY), 1986.

Fat Santa, illustrated by Marcia Winborn, Holt (New York, NY), 1987.

Freckles and Jane, illustrated by Leslie Holt Morrill, Holt (New York, NY), 1989.

Shadow's Baby, illustrated by Ellen Weiss, Clarion (New York, NY), 1989.

Baby Dot, illustrated by Ellen Weiss, Clarion (New York, NY), 1990.

Daisy's Crazy Thanksgiving, illustrated by Robin Kramer, Holt (New York, NY), 1990.

That's Good! That's Bad!, illustrated by David Catrow, Holt (New York, NY), 1991.

The Christmas Snowman, illustrated by Johanna Westerman, Arcade, 1992.

Buddy Bear and the Bad Guys, illustrated by Janet Stevens, Clarion (New York, NY), 1993.

The Biggest, Best Snowman, illustrated by Will Hillenbrand, Scholastic (New York, NY), 1998.

From Here to There, illustrated by Yu Cha Pak, Henry Holt (New York, NY), 1999.

One Hundredth-Day Worries, illustrated by Arthur Howard, Simon & Schuster (New York, NY), 2000.

Road Signs: A Harey Race with a Tortoise: An Aesop Fable Adapted, illustrated by Steve Haskamp, Winslow Press, 2000.

Stop, Drop, and Roll: Fire Safety, illustrated by Arthur Howard, Simon & Schuster (New York, NY), 2001.

Skeleton Hiccups, illustrated by S.D. Schindler, Margaret K. McElderry Books (New York, NY), 2002.

That's Good! That's Bad! in the Grand Canyon, illustrated by David Catrow, Henry Holt (New York, NY), 2002.

Ah-choo!, illustrated by Bruce McNally, Scholastic (New York, NY), 2002.

Please Say Please!: Penguin's Guide to Manners, illustrated by Will Hillenbrand, Scholastic (New York, NY), 2004.

Big Friends, illustrated by Ezra Tucker, Walker & Co. (New York, NY), 2004.

The Bumpy Little Pumpkin, illustrated by Will Hillenbrand, Scholastic (New York, NY), 2005.

Groundhog Stays up Late, illustrated by Jean Cassels, Walker & Co. (New York, NY), 2005.

Please Play Safe!: Penguin's Guide to Playground Safety, illustrated by Will Hillenbrand, Scholastic (New York, NY), 2006.

That's Good! That's Bad! in Washington, DC, illustrated by Michael Garland, Henry Holt (New York, NY), 2007.

Kindness Is Cooler, Mrs. Ruler, illustrated by Sachiko Yohikawa, Simon & Schuster (New York, NY), 2007.

Hooray for Reading Day!, illustrated by Arthur Howard, Simon & Schuster (New York, NY), 2008.

Monster Mess!, illustrated by S.D. Schindler, Margaret K. McElderry Books (New York, NY), 2008.

(Adaptor) *We're Going on a Lion Hunt,* illustrated by Joe Mathieu, Marshall Cavendish (Tarrytown, NY), 2008.

Princess Bess Gets Dressed, illustrated by Heather Maione, Simon & Schuster (New York, NY), 2009.

Bullies Never Win, illustrated by Arthur Howard, Simon & Schuster (New York, NY), 2009.

That's Good! That's Bad! on Santa's Journey, illustrated by Michael Garland, Henry Holt (New York, NY), 2009.

The Little Dump Truck, illustrated by Bob Kolar, Henry Holt (New York, NY), 2009.

Guinea Pigs Add Up, illustrated by Tracey Campbell Pearson, Macmillan (New York, NY), 2010.

I Repeat, Don't Cheat!, illustrated by Arthur Howard, Simon & Schuster Books for Young Readers (New York, NY), 2010.

Tick Tock Clock, illustrated by Robert Neubecker, HarperCollins Children's Books (New York, NY), 2012.

NOVELS

The Trouble with Soap, Dutton (New York, NY), 1982.

Weird Wolf, illustrated by Dirk Zimmer, Holt (New York, NY), 1989.

Invisible in the Third Grade, illustrated by Mirko Gabler, Holt (New York, NY), 1995.

The Battlefield Ghost, illustrated by Arthur Howard, Scholastic (New York, NY), 1999.

FOR CHILDREN; EDITOR, UNDER PSEUDONYM DAISY WALLACE

Monster Poems, illustrated by Kay Chorao, Holiday House (New York, NY), 1976.

Witch Poems, illustrated by Trina Schart Hyman, Holiday House (New York, NY), 1976.

Giant Poems, illustrated by Margot Tomes, Holiday House (New York, NY), 1978.

Ghost Poems, illustrated by Tomie De Paola, Holiday House (New York, NY), 1979.

Fairy Poems, illustrated by Trina Schart Hyman, Holiday House (New York, NY), 1980.

Adaptations

Several of Cuyler's books have been adapted as audiobooks, including *That's Good! That's Bad!, The Biggest, Best Snowman, One Hundredth-Day Worries, I Repeat, Don't Cheat!,* and *Hooray for Reading Day!*

Sidelights

Margery Cuyler was already an experienced editor of children's books for New York City-based publisher Holiday House when she decided to try her hand at writing. While she once admitted to *SATA* that her passion has been for editing children's books, she has come to love writing as well, "since it exercises my imagination in a more personal and introspective fashion." In addition to authoring a wide range of both nonfiction and fiction picture books, including *Fat Santa, Skeleton Hiccups, Guinea Pigs Add Up,* and *I Repeat, Don't Cheat!,* Cuyler has also written chapter books for more talented readers.

Born in Princeton, New Jersey, Cuyler was raised in a large family that included four siblings and an equal number of cousins who had joined the household after their own mother died. She grew up in the oldest house in town, a colonial-style stone home where she still lives with her own family. After graduating from high school, Cuyler attended Sarah Lawrence College, earning her bachelor's degree in 1970. From there, it was a quick move to Boston to work for Atlantic Monthly Press before she returned to New York City and was offered a job with Holiday House. Cuyler found Holiday House to be the perfect fit with her own career aspirations; beginning there in 1974, she served as its editor-in-chief for children's fiction for many years before expanding her career to jobs at other publishers, among them Henry Holt, Golden Books, and Winslow Press.

For Cuyler's first self-penned work, *Jewish Holidays,* she relied on the generous assistance of Jewish friends to get her facts straight. Her second picture book, *The All-around Pumpkin Book,* was written in three days and was inspired by a dream. "I woke up . . . at two in the morning and I started writing," she told interviewer Jim Roginski in *Behind the Covers: Interviews with Authors and Illustrators of Books for Children and Young Adults.* Visualizing all the illustrations in her mind, Cuyler quickly made a dummy of the book, sketched out the pictures as she imagined them, and then added the text. Following the entire life span of the typical Halloween Jack-o'-lantern, from seed to garden to its ultimate destiny as a holiday decoration or pumpkin pie, the book was described by Ethel L. Heins in *Horn Book* as "a compendium of fascinating and practical facts," as well as a list of nontraditional uses for the fall squash. "Here's a way to stretch Halloween all around the year," commented Barbara Elleman in her *Booklist* appraisal of *The All-around Pumpkin Book.*

The All-around Christmas Book employs a format similar to *The All-around Pumpkin Book.* After presenting the story of the Nativity, Cuyler discusses folklore, crafts, recipes, games, and other information about the Christian holiday, both in its religious and secular manifestations. The wide variety of celebrations undertaken by many different Christian cultures around the world is explored, with answers to such questions as where the tradition of decorating trees came from and an explanation of the history of advent wreaths. Praising the information presented, a *Publishers Weekly* reviewer termed *The All-around Christmas Book* "a treasure of holiday lore."

Although her earliest books were nonfiction, Cuyler has more recently focused on creating entertaining picture books for preschoolers and children in the early grades. In *Shadow's Baby* a little dog is determined to take care of the new infant in his house, but when the child grows older and wants to play with other things, the attentive Shadow gets in the way. Fortunately, the dog's owner realizes that Shadow feels useless with nothing to care for; the introduction of a new puppy into the family provides a ready solution. Ann A. Flowers, reviewing the book for *Horn Book,* called *Shadow's Baby* "as warm and affectionate as a puppy," while a *Publishers Weekly* critic commended Cuyler's "sensitivity to the feelings of all involved" in this warmhearted story.

Although Cuyler admits to being a cat owner, dogs and their human companions figure prominently in several of her stories, including her tales about Freckles the dog and Willie, the teenage boy. In *Freckles and Willie* Freckles feels forlorn when Willie starts to spend most of his time with a girl named Jane; the girl, for her part, is obviously not a person of character—she dislikes dogs and makes Willie keep Freckles away from her when she is around. Ultimately, Willie recognizes where his true loyalty lies, and boy and dog are once again the best of friends—"a nice lesson in relationships and loyalty," according to a *Publishers Weekly* critic. However, despite her mistake in bringing a jar of flea powder to Freckles' birthday party, Jane redeems herself in *Freckles and Jane,* as Freckles gets the stuck-up teen out of a tight situation involving a German shepherd on the loose and finally wins her affection. A *Kirkus Reviews* commentator dubbed *Freckles and Jane* "a satisfying 'here and now' story."

With *Fat Santa* Cuyler returns to the subject of Christmas. Molly is determined to wait up for Santa's arrival; she settles into a comfortable chair and listens to Christmas carols on her headphones while she waits. Awakened out of a semi-sleep in the wee hours of the morning by a cloud of ash, the girl realizes that Santa has gotten stuck in the chimney! After his rescue, the jolly man exhibits some caution and convinces Molly to don his red jacket and complete his gift-giving rounds. Praising the book's energy, *Bulletin of the Center for Children's Books* contributor Betsy Hearne cited *Fat Santa* as "a holiday picture book that will be easy for children

Road Signs, *a picture book by Cuyler, features child-friendly illustrations by Steve Haskamp.* (Winslow Press Children, 2000. Illustration © 2000 by Steve Haskamp. All rights reserved. Reproduced by permission.)

to listen to, look at, and like." In *Booklist* Phillis Wilson pointed out that "the open end works in this well-constructed plot," while a *Publishers Weekly* critic praised Cuyler for "amiably captur[ing]" the spirit of Christmas Eve.

Cuyler focuses on another holiday in *Daisy's Crazy Thanksgiving*. Here Daisy begs to be excused from her parents' busy restaurant to join her grandparents for the holiday dinner, only to discover pandemonium in a house full of eccentric relatives, a menagerie of pet animals, and an absentminded Granny who has forgotten to turn on the oven to cook the turkey. "No getting around the success of the story's wacky humor," observed *Booklist* reviewer Denise Wilms, the critic going on to dub Cuyler's book "offbeat and, intermittently, very funny."

Skeleton Hiccups also contains a seasonal theme as it relates the efforts of a frustrated skeleton that cannot rid itself of the hiccups. Unfortunately, when you are a skeleton, the tried-and-true remedy of getting the hiccups scared out of you does not work; the most frightening "boo!" of Skeleton's best friend Ghost is nothing to be startled about, and drinking water while hanging

its head upside down causes puddles to run from Skeleton's empty eye sockets. Praising the quirky artwork contributed by S.D. Schindler, *Booklist* reviewer Jeanette Larson called *Skeleton Hiccups* "a treat for children who can laugh at the slightly macabre," and *Horn Book* critic Joanna Rudge Long predicted that Cuyler's simple text, with its "hic, hic, hic" refrain, is "sure to have kids giggling and joining in."

Groundhog Day is the holiday at the core of *Groundhog Stays up Late,* an updated Aesop's tale that features artwork by Jean Cassels. Here roly-poly Groundhog wants to play with his friends in the fall, and he puts off preparing his burrow for winter. When the snows come, Groundhog's playmates snuggle down for a long nap while he goes hungry, at least until he finds a way to trick them into thinking it is time for a spring feast. Although Groundhog ultimately snoozes through his appointed appearance when spring really does arrive, the playful creature does not learn his lesson, and the closing pages of the book find Groundhog once again playing rather than preparing for winter. In *School Library Journal* Linda L. Walkins praised Cassels' art, writing that "the colors and textures of the changing seasons are beautifully portrayed" in *Groundhog Stays*

up Late. Cuyler's accompanying text "bubbles with comic winks," wrote a *Publishers Weekly* reviewer, and its rhythm "will encourage even antsy youngsters to snuggle." "Children who like to test limits will identify with" Cuyler's impractical hero, concluded *Booklist* contributor Kay Weisman, the critic adding that the up-beat ending of *Groundhog Stays up Late* will entertain Groundhog Day story-hour audiences.

A more serious story is at the center of *From Here to There,* which helps young children gain perspective on their role as part of the larger world. In the book, Maria Mendoza introduces herself, at first within the context of her role in her family, then to her neighborhood, state, country, and beyond. Cuyler's concept-driven text is enhanced by "gorgeously rendered" watercolor and pastel illustrations by Yu Cha Pak, according to a *Publishers Weekly* critic. Praising *From Here to There* as a "heartfelt picture book," the *Publishers Weekly* reviewer added that Cuyler and Pak's work takes readers on an "enlightening journey" that serves as "both a meditation on humanity's small place in the universe and a cel-ebration of each person's immutable individuality."

That's Good! That's Bad!, Cuyler's story of a little boy traveling by balloon in a wild trip over a zoo, success-fully combines sound effects, a large format, and plenty of opportunity for audience participation where "kids will enjoy the push-me-pull-me tension," according to Roger Sutton in his review for the *Bulletin of the Center for Children's Books.* In the first of several sequels, *That's Good! That's Bad! in the Grand Canyon,* the boy joins his grandmother for a trip to the Grand Can-yon, where he again encounters good and bad in a se-ries of adventures. *That's Good! That's Bad! in Wash-ington, DC* finds him in the nation's capital while *That's Good! That's Bad! on Santa's Journey* adds levity to the boy's holiday-themed adventure. *School Library Jour-nal* contributor Marian Drabkin noted that, with its hu-morous plot and sing-songey text, *That's Good! That's Bad! in the Grand Canyon* "begs to be read aloud" and would be a "natural for storytime," and Wendy Luke-hart noted in the same periodical that "the sound effects and refrain" in Cuyler's text for *That's Good! That's Bad! in Washington, DC* "allow plenty of opportunities for audience participation." Reviewing *That's Good! That's Bad! on Santa's Journey* in *School Library Jour-nal,* Maureen Wade noted the story's "nonstop action" and "expressive, humorous illustrations" by Michael Garland, and a *Kirkus Reviews* writer observed that Cuyler's "bouncy text [is] full of sound-effect words that beg to be read with melodramatic expression."

Cuyler takes her readers to school along with a young girl named Jessica in *One Hundredth-Day Worries, Stop, Drop, and Roll: Fire Safety, Hooray for Reading Day!, Bullies Never Win,* and *I Repeat, Don't Cheat!,* all which feature illustrations by Arthur Howard. In *One Hundredth-Day Worries* readers worry right along with Jessica as she tackles the first weeks of school in Mr. Martin's class, while *Stop, Drop, and Roll* finds her ner-vous about messing up her role in a school-wide dem-onstration for Fire Prevention Week. *Bullies Never Win* finds Jessica tormented by tough-talking classmate Brenda, while in *Hooray for Reading Day!* an upcom-ing Reading Theatre day prompts the little worry-wart to get help with her read-aloud skills. In *Stop, Drop, and Roll* Cuyler "humorously driv[es] . . . home basic fire-safety tips for children to follow," according to *Booklist* critic Annie Ayres, while the "universal sce-nario" she presents in *Bullies Never Win* "will open up discussion and encourage kids to develop coping strate-gies," according to *Booklist* critic Hazel Rochman. Cuyler's "message of 'practice makes perfect'" and her depiction of an encouraging family in *Hooray for Read-ing Day!* "can serve to motivate children," asserted Lynne Mattern in *School Library Journal,* and Phelan concluded in *Booklist* that Cuyler's story about the young first grader "shows a practical solution while of-fering bits of humor along the way."

Another kindergarten classroom is the focus of *Kind-ness Is Cooler, Mrs. Ruler,* which emphasizes the re-ward to be found in good behavior via Cuyler's rhym-ing text and cartoon art by Sachiko Yoshikawa. The story features "the same enthusiasm, counting practice, and humor" that characterized *One Hundredth-Day Wor-ries,* concluded Weisman in *Booklist.*

Cuyler leads young readers to a reassuring ending in her book Bullies Never Win, *featuring cartoon artwork by Arthur Howard.* (Illustration copyright © 2009 by Arthur Howard. Reproduced with permission by Simon & Schuster, Inc.)

Teaming up with artist Will Hillenbrand, Cuyler presents a quirky slant on etiquette books with both *Please Say Please!: Penguin's Guide to Manners* and its companion volume, *Please Play Safe!: Penguin's Guide to Playground Safety.* In *Please Say Please!* Penguin plans a wonderful dinner for his friends and dresses the part, but is disappointed when guests Giraffe, Pig, and Elephant show that their table manners are not up to par with the fancy feast. Playtime manners and safety concerns are addressed in *Please Play Safe!*, in which Penguin and his friends survive some near misses on the playground. In *Publishers Weekly* a critic cited Cuyler for the "simple, crisp text" she creates for *Please Say Please!*, while *Horn Book* Christine M. Heppermann dubbed the same book "a natural read-aloud, with a generous helping of onomatopoeia." Writing that Cuyler "covers all the bases" in her focus on sharing, playing games, and the proper use of playground equipment, a *Kirkus Reviews* writer added that in *Please Play Safe!* Hillenbrand's ink-and-crayon cartoon art "masterfully portrays facial expressions." In *Booklist* Ilene Cooper described the playground guide as "activity-filled," noting that it "cleverly plays on young children's burgeoning sense of irony."

In *We're Going on a Lion Hunt* Cuyler teams up with illustrator Joe Mathieu to present an upbeat revision of a traditional song. Rather than a bear, as in "Going on a Bear Hunt," Cuyler's young characters ford streams, climb trees, and stomp along a muddy trail on their way to the mouth of a cave known to be the home of a lion. In *School Library Journal*, Lynn K. Vanca dubbed the book a "rollicking adaptation" of the well-known call-and-response song, and a *Kirkus Reviews* contributor recommended *We're Going on a Lion Hunt* for classrooms where students will view it as "a terrific invitation" to jumpstart "some happy dramatic play." Also praising the "entertaining" text, *Booklist* critic Shelle Rosenfeld recommended Mathieu's "bright, cartoonlike watercolor-and-pencil" artwork, which "highlight[s] the divers animals . . . in their native habitats."

Cuyler continues to entertain storytime audiences with her upbeat tales. In *Guinea Pigs Add Up,* which features artwork by Tracey Campbell Pearson, students worry about the loneliness of their new class pet until nature works its magic and the little guinea pig soon gives birth to a cage-full of tiny companions. Bob Kolar creates humorous digital art for *The Little Dump Truck,* in which Hard Hat Pete spends a busy day hauling all sorts of things in his trusty truck. While *The Little Dump Truck* has appeal to little boys, girls will be drawn to *Princess Bess Gets Dressed,* where Heather Maione's illustrations bring to life Cuyler's rhyming story about a princess whose duties require her to change into a steady series of fashionable outfits throughout her busy day, even though she longs to put on clothing that is far more ordinary. "Preschoolers will love this book," announced Sarah Polace in her *School Library Journal* review of *The Little Dump Truck,* while a *Kirkus Reviews* critic asserted that Cuyler's "repetitive" rhyming text

expands her story "with lots of details." Maione's "imaginative confections will satisfy even the most ardent of princess devotees," asserted a *Kirkus Reviews* writer in reviewing *Princess Bess Gets Dressed,* and a *Publishers Weekly* critic wrote of the same book that "Culyer's sprightly story brims over with little-girl appeal." Praised as a "rhythmic tale of ever-popular pets," *Guinea Pigs Add Up* "will work well as a read-aloud or with newly independent readers," according to *School Library Journal* contributor Kathleen Finn.

Cuyler's first book for older readers, *The Trouble with Soap,* was written after she attended a writer's conference in her capacity as editor. "I sat around for two weeks listening to people read their stuff," she told interviewer Roginski. "Then I started writing." *The Trouble with Soap* is based on its author's own experiences as a not-so-model child. In the novel, thirteen-year-old Lucinda Sokoloff—a.k.a Soap—is suspended from school due to her excessive zeal in playing practical jokes. After an incident involving a roll of plastic wrap and the toilets in the boys' lavatory cause her to be shipped off to Miss Pringle's Private School for Girls along with partner-in-crime and narrator Laurie Endersby, Soap rejects the snobbish students in favor of her own company. Laurie, on the other hand, desperately wants to be accepted by the in-crowd at her new school, and she ultimately tells a painful secret about Soap's father as a way of gaining that acceptance. A *Publishers Weekly* writer observed that *The Trouble with Soap* is completely unlike any of Cuyler's former works and "displays impressive versatility."

"I wanted to write about what it is that makes twelve- and thirteen-year-old kids so sensitive to peer pressure," Cuyler explained to Roginski of her decision to write books for older readers. "Why do they care so much about what other kids think of them? They're really imprisoned by collective values—how they think, how they dress, how they look at the world. It's a very conformist way of living. It's hard to be outside the collective spirit at that age and yet my character Soap is. That fascinates me because the whole key of life is to break through the walls that parents and society build around you, to be an individual, to express yourself."

Cuyler has followed *The Trouble with Soap* with several more novels for young people, including *Invisible in the Third Grade, Weird Wolf,* and *The Battlefield Ghost.* In *Weird Wolf* her protagonist again has trouble fitting in with his friends. It is not so much that nine-year-old Harry Walpole is unpopular, but he has a terribly embarrassing problem: he turns into a wolf when the moon is full. As inconvenient as this is—it gets increasingly difficult to come up with excuses for being caught running around naked outside at sunrise—Harry is fortunate that his blood lust only extends to hamburgers. A research trip to the library results in several possible cures for his problem, and one of them actually works, in a book critics praised as appropriately seductive for even the most reluctant of readers. Indeed, *Weird*

Wolf is "destined for greatness in the opinion of werewolf-crazy eight year olds," noted Kathryn Pierson in a review for the *Bulletin of the Center for Children's Books.*

The Battlefield Ghost marks a bit of a departure for Cuyler, because its story mixes historical fact with fiction. Actually, the book was inspired by the author's interest in her home town of Princeton, where she still lives in the same colonial-era house where she grew up. In the story, John and his sister move into what their new Princeton neighbors claim is a house inhabited by the spirits of the 1777 Battle of Princeton. After a series of uncanny but not terribly frightening hauntings, the children learn that their home is actually being haunted by a Hessian mercenary soldier who was killed while fighting for the British. When they discover that the soldier is wandering the area in search of his long-dead horse, John and his sister figure out how to put the spirit to rest in a novel that *Booklist* reviewer Jean Franklin praised as a "fast read" that "offers a nice blend of realism and the supernatural." A *Publishers Weekly* contributor also praised Cuyler for presenting the history of the battle in an entertaining fashion, noting that in addition to providing historical notes, *The Battlefield Ghost* ends with a "vivid, ghostly reenactment on the battlefield."

Biographical and Critical Sources

BOOKS

Roginski, Jim, *Behind the Covers: Interviews with Authors and Illustrators of Books for Children and Young Adults*, Libraries Unlimited (Littleton, CO), 1985, pp. 51-58.

PERIODICALS

Booklist, July 15, 1980, Barbara Elleman, review of *The All-around Pumpkin Book*, p. 1674; November 1, 1987, Phillis Wilson, review of *Fat Santa*, p. 474; October 1, 1990, Denise Wilms, review of *Daisy's Crazy Thanksgiving*, p. 338; December 1, 1991, Deborah Abbott, review of *That's Good! That's Bad! in the Grand Canyon*, pp. 702-703; December 15, 1998, Lauren Peterson, review of *The Biggest, Best Snowman*, p. 754; June 1, 1999, Susan Dove Lempke, review of *From Here to There*, p. 1838; November 1, 1999, GraceAnne A. DeCandido, review of *One Hundredth-Day Worries*, p. 537; November 15, 1999, Jean Franklin, review of *The Battlefield Ghost*, p. 626; December 1, 2000, Michael Cart, review of *Road Signs: A Harey Race with a Tortoise*, p. 717; September 15, 2001, Annie Ayres, review of *Stop, Drop, and Roll: Fire Safety*, p. 230; September 15, 2002, John Peters, review of *Skeleton Hiccups*, p. 245; February 1, 2004, Karin Snelson, review of *Please Say Please!: Penguin's Guide to Manners*, p. 980; April 15, 2004, Ha-

zel Rochman, review of *Big Friends*, p. 1445; September 1, 2005, Gillian Engberg, review of *The Bumpy Little Pumpkin*, p. 143; August 1, 2006, Ilene Cooper, review of *Please Play Safe!: Penguin's Guide to Playground Safety*, p. 84; May 15, 2007, Kay Weisman, review of *Kindness Is Cooler, Mrs. Ruler*, p. 52; June 1, 2008, Hazel Rochman, review of *Monster Mess!*, p. 91; August 1, 2008, Carolyn Phelan, review of *Hooray for Reading Day!*, p. 78; September 1, 2008, Shelle Rosenfeld, review of *We're Going on a Lion Hunt*, p. 109; February 15, 2009, Kristen McKulski, review of *Princess Bess Get Dressed*, p. 88; July 1, 2009, Hazel Rochman, review of *Bullies Never Win*, p. 65; September 15, 2009, Andrew Medlar, review of *The Little Dump Truck*, p. 65; May 1, 2010, Hazel Rochman, review of *Guinea Pigs Add Up*, p. 89; May 15, 2010, Hazel Rochman, review of *I Repeat, Don't Cheat!*, p. 43.

Bulletin of the Center for Children's Books, January, 1979, Zena Sutherland, review of *Jewish Holidays*, p. 77; November, 1987, Betsy Hearne, review of *Fat Santa*, p. 46; January, 1990, Kathryn Pierson, review of *Weird Wolf*, pp. 107-108; December, 1991, Roger Sutton, review of *That's Good! That's Bad! in the Grand Canyon*, p. 87; November, 2001, review of *Stop, Drop, and Roll*, p. 98; September, 2002, review of *Skeleton Hiccups*, p. 11; April 15, 2004, Hope Morrison, review of *Big Friends*, p. 1445; December 1, 2005, Kay Weisman, review of *Groundhog Stays up Late*, p. 53.

Horn Book, October, 1980, Ethel L. Heins, review of *The All-around Pumpkin Book*, p. 534; January, 1990, Ann A. Flowers, review of *Shadow's Baby*, p. 50; September-October, 2002, Joanna Rudge Long, review of *Skeleton Hiccups*, p. 549; May-June, 2004, Christine M. Hepperman, review of *Please Say Please!*, p. 310; July-August, 2006, Bridget T. McCaffrey, review of *Please Play Safe!*, p. 423.

Kirkus Reviews, November 1, 1989, review of *Freckles and Jane*, p. 602; March 15, 2002, review of *That's Good! That's Bad! in the Grand Canyon*, p. 408; April 1, 2004, reviews of *Skeleton Hiccups*, *Big Friends*, and *Please Say Please!*, p. 327; July 1, 2005, review of *The Bumpy Little Pumpkin*, p. 733; October 15, 2005, review of *Groundhog Stays up Late*, p. 1134; July 1, 2006, review of *Please Play Safe!*, p. 676; June 1, 2007, review of *Kindness Is Cooler, Mrs. Ruler*; July 1, 2007, review of *That's Good! That's Bad! in Washington, DC*; June 15, 2008, review of *Hooray for Reading Day!*; July 1, 2008, review of *Monster Mess!*; July 15, 2008, review of *We're Going on a Lion Hunt*; January 15, 2009, review of *Princess Bess Gets Dressed*; May 15, 2009, review of *Bullies Never Win*; September 15, 2009, review of *That's Good! That's Bad! on Santa's Journey*; September 15, 2009, review of *The Little Dump Truck*.

New York Times Book Review, September 16, 2007, Sara London, review of *Kindness Is Cooler, Mrs. Ruler*, p. 19.

Publishers Weekly, May 28, 1982, review of *The Trouble with Soap*, p. 72; September 17, 1982, review of *The All-around Christmas Book*, p. 115; April 25, 1986, review of *Freckles and Willie*, p. 78; October 30, 1987,

review of *Fat Santa,* p. 70; October 13, 1989, review of *Shadow's Baby,* p. 51; November 9, 1998, review of *The Biggest, Best Snowman,* p. 75; March 15, 1999, review of *From Here to There,* p. 56; September 27, 1999, review of *The Battlefield Ghost,* p. 106; December 13, 1999, review of *One Hundredth-Day Worries,* p. 81; July 10, 2000, review of *Road Signs,* p. 62; September 23, 2002, review of *Skeleton Hiccups,* p. 22; April 19, 2004, review of *Please Say Please!,* p. 59; August 1, 2005, review of *The Bumpy Little Pumpkin,* p. 64; November 14, 2005, review of *Groundhog Stays up Late,* p. 67; December 15, 2008, review of *Princess Bess Gets Dressed,* p. 52.

School Library Journal, January, 1979, Joan C. Feldman, review of *Jewish Holidays,* p. 41; September, 2000, Louise L. Sherman, review of *Road Signs,* p. 193; April, 2001, Teresa Bateman, review of *One Hundredth-Day Worries,* p. 74; October, 2001, Roxanne Burg, review of *Stop, Drop, and Roll,* p. 113; June, 2002, Marian Drabkin, review of *That's Good! That's Bad! in the Grand Canyon,* p. 92; October, 2002, Piper L. Nyman, review of *Skeleton Hiccups,* p. 100; April, 2004, Mary N. Oluonye, review of *Big Friends,* and Janet Blair, review of *Please Say Please!,* both p. 109; August, 2005, Kara Schaff Dean, review of *The Bumpy Little Pumpkin,* p. 87; December, 2005, Linda L. Walkins, review of *Groundhog Stays up Late,* p. 107; August, 2006, Maura Breshahan, review of *Please Play Safe!,* p. 78; June, 2007, Barbara Katz, review of *Kindness Is Cooler, Mrs. Ruler,* p. 96; September, 2007, Wendy Lukehart, review of *That's Good! That's Bad! in Washington, DC,* p. 161; July, 2008, Linda M. Kenton, review of *Monster Mess!,* p. 70; August, 2008, Lynne Mattern, review of *Hooray for Reading Day!,* p. 86; October, 2008, Lynn K. Vanca, review of *We're Going on a Lion Hunt,* p. 104; June, 2009, Maryann H. Owen, review of *Bullies Never Win,* p. 82; October, 2009, Maureen Wade, review of *That's Good! That's Bad! on Santa's Journey,* p. 79; November, 2009, Sarah Polace, review of *The Little Dump Truck,* p. 74; June, 2010, Mary Hazelton, review of *I Repeat, Don't Cheat!,* p. 66; July, 2010, Kathleen Finn, review of *Guinea Pigs Add Up,* p. 58; November, 2010, Lonna Pierce, review of *I Repeat, Don't Cheat,* p. 49.

ONLINE

Margery Cuyler Home Page, http://www.margerycuyler. com (April 15, 2011).*

*   *   *

CUYLER, Margery Stuyvesant
See CUYLER, Margery

D

DAVIS, Nancy

Personal
Female.

Addresses
Home—Las Vegas, NV. *Agent*—Libby Ford Artist Representative, 320 E. 57th St., Ste. 10B, New York, NY 10022. *E-mail*—nandavis@mac.com.

Career
Graphic designer and illustrator.

Writings

SELF-ILLUSTRATED

Who Uses a Drill?, Hearst Books (New York, NY), 2004.
Who Uses a Hammer?, Hearst Books (New York, NY), 2004.
Who Uses a Saw?, Hearst Books (New York, NY), 2004.
Who Uses a Wrench?, Hearst Books (New York, NY), 2004.
A Garden of Opposites, Schwartz & Wade Books (New York, NY), 2009.
Halloween Faces, Scholastic (New York, NY), 2010.
Who's at Home?, Little Simon (New York, NY), 2010.
Christmas Shapes, Little Simon (New York, NY), 2010.
The First Thanksgiving, Little Simon (New York, NY), 2010.
Wake Up! Wake Up!, Little Simon (New York, NY), 2011.

ILLUSTRATOR

Eency Weency Spider, Publications International (Lincolnwood, IL), 1998.
Joan Bransfield Graham, *Flicker Flash,* Houghton Mifflin (Boston, MA), 1999.

Jane E. Gerver, *What's for Dinner?,* Innovative Kids, 2002.
Lynne Roberts, *Daisy's Spring Surprise,* Publications International (Lincolnwood, IL), 2005.
Leo Mahon, *Fire under My Feet: A Memoir of God's Power in Panama,* Orbis Books (Maryknoll, NY), 2007.
Jill Ackerman, *My Body,* Scholastic (New York, NY), 2008.
Jill Ackerman, *Welcome Winter,* Little Simon (New York, NY), 2009.
Jill Ackerman, *Welcome Spring,* Little Simon (New York, NY), 2009.
Jill Ackerman, *Welcome Summer,* Little Simon (New York, NY), 2009.
Jill Ackerman, *Welcome Fall,* Little Simon (New York, NY), 2009.
Karen C. Fox, *Older than the Stars,* Charlesbridge (Watertown, MA), 2010.
Jane E. Gerver, *Who's at Home?: A Lift-the-flap Book,* Little Simon (New York, NY), 2010.

Contributor to periodicals, including *3x3 Illustration Annual* and *3x3 Showcase.*

Sidelights
A graphic designer and illustrator based in Las Vegas, Nevada, Nancy Davis began her work in picture books in 1998, by capturing her unique vision of a childhood rhyme in *Eency Weency Spider.* Her brightly colored digital illustrations, with their simple shapes and touches of humor, have proved to be a perfect fit for the toddler-friendly texts in board books that include *Daisy's Spring Surprise* by Lynne Roberts and Jill Ackerman's *Welcome Winter* and its three season-spanning companions. Beginning in 2004, Davis has also paired her artwork with original texts in interactive board books such as *Halloween Faces,* which is composed of a series of masks, and energetic stories such as *Wake Up! Wake Up!* and *A Garden of Opposites,* the latter which was recommended by *School Library Journal* contributor Sally R. Dow for its "bright, crisp, childlike illustrations" and "clean, uncluttered design." In addition to

children's books, Davis also creates artwork for greeting cards and other educational materials.

A collaboration between Davis and author Joan Bransfield Graham, *Flicker Flash* features concrete poems about the many different ways that light is generated in a child's world. "Graphic design is the outstanding feature here," asserted a *Horn Book* contributor, recommending *Flicker Flash* as a book with "particular appeal to visual learners," and in *Booklist* GraceAnne DeCandido predicted that the "extraordinarily clever" designs created by the artist using "flat geometric forms" "will bewitch readers." Reviewing Davis's work for Karen C. Fox's *Older than the Stars,* Kathleen Kelly MacMillan asserted in *School Library Journal* that author and illustrator successfully "tackle the challenge of creating an engaging read-aloud about the Big Bang theory with energy and style."

Biographical and Critical Sources

PERIODICALS

Booklist, January 1, 2000, GraceAnne DeCandido, review of *Flicker Flash,* p. 909.
Horn Book, January, 2000, review of *Flicker Flash,* p. 90.
Kirkus Reviews, February 15, 2009, review of *A Garden of Opposites.*
Publishers Weekly, November 22, 1999, review of *Flicker Flash,* p. 55; May 20, 2002, review of *What's for Dinner?,* p. 69.
School Library Journal, December, 1999, Patricia Manning, review of *Flicker Flash,* p. 119; April, 2009, Sally R. Dow, review of *A Garden of Opposites,* p. 102; February, 2010, Kathleen Kelly MacMillan, review of *Older than the Stars,* p. 100.

ONLINE

Libby Ford Artist Representative Web site, http://www.libbyford.com/ (April 15, 2011), "Nancy Davis."
Nancy Davis Home Page, http://www.nancydavis.org (April 24, 2011).*

*　　*　　*

DIAZ, David 1959(?)-

Personal

Born c. 1959, in New York, NY; married; wife's name Cecelia (an artist); children: Jericho, Ariel, Gabrielle. *Education:* Fort Lauderdale Art Institute, diploma. *Hobbies and other interests:* Music.

Addresses

Home—Carlesbad, CA.

Career

Graphic artist, illustrator, and ceramic artist. Worked variously as a newspaper illustrator, graphic designer, and graphic artist, beginning 1980.

Awards, Honors

Caldecott Medal, American Library Association, 1995, for *Smoky Night* by Eve Bunting; Newbery Award Honor citation, 2000, for *The Wanderer* by Sharon Creech; Best Children's Book designation, Bank Street College of Education, 2002, and Pura Belpré Honor Book for Illustration citation, 2004, both for *The Pot That Juan Built* by Nancy Andrews-Goebel; Pura Belpré Honor citation, 2009, for *Diego: Bigger than Life* by Carmen T. Bernier-Grand; awards from *Communications Arts, American Illustration,* American Institute of Graphic Arts, and New York Art Directors Club.

Illustrator

Gary Soto, *Neighborhood Odes,* Harcourt, Brace (New York, NY), 1992

Len Cabral, *Anansi's Narrow Waist,* Addison-Wesley (New York, NY), 1994.

Eve Bunting, *Smoky Night,* Harcourt, Brace (New York, NY), 1994.

Eve Bunting, *Going Home,* HarperCollins (New York, NY), 1996.

Marybeth Lorbiecki, *Just One Flick of a Finger,* Dial Books (New York, NY), 1996.

Eve Merriam, *The Inner City Mother Goose,* 3rd edition, Simon & Schuster (New York, NY), 1996.

Joseph A. Citro, *Passing Strange: True Tales of New England Hauntings and Horrors,* Chapters, 1996.

Kathleen Krull, *Wilma Unlimited: How Wilma Rudolph Became the World's Fastest Woman,* Harcourt, Brace (New York, NY), 1996.

Pauline Cartwright, *Table for Two: An African Folktale,* Celebration Press (Glenview, IL), 1996.

Eve Bunting, *The Christmas House,* Harcourt, Brace (New York, NY), 1997.

Eve Bunting, *December,* Harcourt, Brace (New York, NY), 1997.

Richard Wilbur, *The Disappearing Alphabet,* Harcourt, Brace (San Diego, CA), 1998.

Margaret Wise Brown, *The Little Scarecrow Boy,* HarperCollins (New York, NY), 1998.

Eric A. Kimmel, *Be Not Far from Me: The Oldest Love Story: Legends from the Bible,* Simon & Schuster (New York, NY), 1998.

Nancy Willard, *Shadow Story,* Harcourt, Brace (San Diego, CA), 1999.

Afi Scruggs, *Jump Rope Magic,* Blue Sky Press (New York, NY), 1999.

Joyce Carol Thomas, *The Gospel Cinderella,* HarperCollins (New York NY), 2000.

Rudolfo A. Anaya, *Roadrunner's Dance,* Hyperion Books for Children (New York, NY), 2000.

Sharon Creech, *The Wanderer,* HarperCollins (New York, NY), 2000.

Sarah Weeks, *Angel Face,* Atheneum (New York, NY), 2002.

Nancy Andrews-Goebel, *The Pot That Juan Built,* Lee & Low Books (New York, NY), 2002.

José Feliciano, *Feliz Navidad!: Two Stories Celebrating Christmas,* Scholastic (New York, NY), 2003.

Sharon Creech, *Who's That Baby?: New-Baby Songs,* Joanna Cotler Books (New York, NY), 2005.

José-Luis Orozco, *Rin, Rin, Rin/Do, Re, Mi,* Scholastic (New York, NY), 2005.

Sarah Weeks, *Counting Ovejas,* Atheneum (New York, NY), 2006.

Carmen T. Bernier-Grand, *Cèsar: Sí se puede!/Yes We Can!,* Marshall Cavendish (New York, NY), 2006.

Sharon Creech, *The Castle Corona,* Joanna Cotler Books (New York, NY), 2007.

Kathleen Krull, *Pocahontas: Princess of the New World,* Walker & Co. (New York, NY), 2007.

De colores: Bright with Colors, Marshall Cavendish (New York, NY), 2008.

Christine Ford, *Ocean's Child,* Random House (New York, NY), 2009.

Carmen T. Bernier-Grand, *Diego: Bigger than Life,* Marshall Cavendish (New York, NY), 2009.

Debbi Chocolate, *El Barrio,* Henry Holt (New York, NY), 2009.

Jill Jackson and Sy Miller, *Let There Be Peace on Earth: And Let It Begin with Me* (includes audio CD), Tricycle Press (Berkeley, CA), 2009.

Amy Novesky, *Me, Frida: Frida Kahlo in San Francisco,* Abrams Books for Young Readers (New York, NY), 2010.

Lee Bennett Hopkins, selector, *Sharing the Seasons: A Book of Poems,* Margaret K. McElderry Books (New York, NY), 2010.

Patricia MacLachlan and Emily MacLachlan Charest, *Before You Came,* Katherine Tegen Books (New York, NY), 2011.

Contributor of illustrations to periodicals, including *Atlantic Monthly* and *Washington Post.*

Books featuring Diaz's art have been translated into Spanish.

Sidelights

After establishing a successful career as a graphic and commercial artist, David Diaz decided to illustrate picture books as a creative outlet. Choosing his projects carefully, he quickly established himself as an illustrator of high reputation, winning a Caldecott medal in 1995 for his work on *Smoky Night* by Eve Bunting and joining author Sharon Creech in receiving a Newbery Honor citation for *The Wanderer.* In the many books he has illustrated since, Diaz has avoided repetition, using a variety of media to enliven an array of titles ranging from folk tales to biography and other nonfiction. In the *New York Times Book Review,* Bill Ott observed that Diaz's images "reveal the way finished art integrates multiple levels of detail into a coordinated whole."

Born in New York City, Diaz grew up in Florida, where he decided to be a "drawer" from an early age. After graduating from high school, he attended the Fort Lauderdale Art Institute, and then moved to southern California, where he established himself as a commercial designer and illustrator. Diaz shifted his focus to illustration in the early 1990s because he did not want the regret of having missed creative opportunities later in his life. In 1994 he accepted his first illustration project: Eve Bunting's picture-book text about the Los Angeles riots titled *Smoky Night.*

Diaz was given the job of illustrating *Smoky Night* on the strength of a book he had designed that interspersed found objects and drawings to reflect a summer spent in Brazil. The book depicts a young boy's reaction to rioting on the streets below his family's apartment in an ethnically diverse urban neighborhood. In his illustrations for Bunting's story Diaz mixes heavily outlined acrylic paintings incorporating soothing blue, purple, and green tones with collages of photographs capturing elements of Bunting's tale. In the illustrations depicting the looting of a grocery store, for instance, his artwork is layered over a photographed backdrop of spilled cereal. As Diaz recalled in his Caldecott Medal acceptance speech as printed in *Horn Book:* "Bunting had taken a timely subject and had handled it in a truly sensitive and thoughtful way. I felt the book could have a positive effect and help erode barriers of prejudice and intolerance. And above all, it was a book that could be part of the post-riot healing process."

Commenting on Diaz's efforts to make characters of diverse ethnic backgrounds appear physically similar in *Smoky Night,* a *Publishers Weekly* critic asserted that his artwork "cautions the reader against assumptions about race." Likewise, Ellen Fader observed in *Horn Book* that "Diaz's bold artwork is a perfect match for the story. . . . Because each double-page spread is so carefully designed, because the pictorial elements work together harmoniously, the overall effect is that of urban energy, rather than cacophony. Both author and illustrator insist on an headlong confrontation with the issue of rapport between different races, and the result is a memorable, thought-provoking book."

With *Smoky Night* Diaz won one of the most prestigious illustration honors in the United States: the American Library Association's 1995 Caldecott Medal. Commenting on his illustrations, Caldecott Award selection committee chair Grace W. Ruth was quoted in *School Library Journal* as calling the book "dramatic and groundbreaking," adding that the artist effectively "uses thickly textured, expressionistic acrylic paintings to portray a night of urban rioting from a child's perspective." In *Booklist* Hazel Rochman characterized Diaz's art for *Smoky Night* as "powerful—pulsating and crowded; part street mural, part urban collage."

Expanding his work in children's literature, Diaz has illustrated several other picture books that feature urban settings and social problems. A new edition of *The In-*

David Diaz's many picture-book projects include creating the artwork for Jose-Luis Orozco's upbeat story in **Rin, Rin, Rin, Do, Re, Mi.** (Orchard Books, 2005. Illustration copyright © 2005 by David Diaz. Reproduced by permission of Scholastic, Inc.)

ner City Mother Goose, Eve Merriam's poetic reflection on the problems of the inner city, hones in on a teen audience with the help of Diaz's bold use of color and line. In *Booklist,* Carolyn Phelan praised the book by noting that the artist's "small, intense paintings create portraits rich in composition, color, and gesture." "The images, almost mythic in their sense of representing more than individual people, seem to move with the rhythm of the verse," added the critic.

In Marybeth Lorbiecki's *Just One Flick of a Finger,* urban teen violence is explored. A young man's act of taking a gun to school to ward off a local bully is portrayed in Diaz's characteristic heavy style against a "background [that] evokes a kind of feverish excitement with neon-lit graffiti, peeling walls, flashing color," according to *Booklist* reviewer Hazel Rochman. *December,* also by Bunting, explores the fate of a homeless child who takes solace in the picture of an angel that he has pinned to the side of the cardboard box in which he lives. When Christmas Day comes, an act of kindness performed by the boy and his mother results in a visit from an angel and an improvement in their circumstances. Grace Oliff, writing in *School Library Journal,* concluded that Diaz's woodcuts for *December* "amplify the theme" in the holiday tale.

Diaz and Bunting collaborate again on *Going Home,* a picture book in which a migrant family returns to the Mexican town of their birth. Calling the work a "veritable treat for the eyes," a *Publishers Weekly* reviewer added that Diaz "sets his artwork within photographic backdrops that show gaily painted pottery, folk art figurines, Mexican Christmas decorations, festive flowers and other shiny holiday trinkets." "Bunting conveys her message softly, leaving the major role to Diaz," maintained Barbara Kiefer in her *School Library Journal* review of *Going Home.* "His distinctive style is well suited to the setting and the mood of the book."

Diaz imbues each book project he takes with an individual flair and a unique theme. A new edition of poet Gary Soto's *Neighborhood Odes* features woodcut silhouettes that complement Soto's twenty-one verses in what *Booklist* contributor Phelan called "an unobtrusive, playful way." Whimsical letters of both upper and lower case sneak across whole-page spreads in Richard Wilbur's *The Disappearing Alphabet,* a book that muses on what would happen to words if certain letters decided not to cooperate. In *Horn Book* Jennifer M. Brabander commended Diaz's pictures for the latter work as "bold and appropriately playful." The acrylic paintings the artist creates for Joyce Carol Thomas's *The Gospel Cinderella* consist of "humorous, bold, and colorful images" that help make the fairy-tale adaptation "delightful," according to *School Library Journal* critic Mary N. Oluonye. In the pages of Debbi Chocolate's *El*

Barrio Diaz "returns to his classic thick-outlined wood-cuts, but [uses] . . . a rainbow of hues" and positions his "framed spreads . . . over photographic collages that evoke" Chocolate's urban setting, according to *School Library Journal* contributor Nina Lindsay.

In Carmen T. Bernier-Grand's poetry collection about the live of activist Cèsar Chavez, Diaz contributes what *School Library Journal* critic Scott La Counte described as "stylized, computer-drawn, folk-art" images that bring to life a man dedicated to improving the lot of migrant farm workers in the United States.

Another collaboration between author and artist, *Diego: Bigger than Life,* captures the life of Diego Rivera, one of the best-known Mexican muralists of the twentieth century, in multimedia art by Diaz. Praising these illustrations as "luminous scenes drenched in color," Wendy Lukehart added in her *School Library Journal* review that *Diego* shows Diaz to be "in top form." Calling the same volume "a lively verse portrait illuminated with incandescent illustrations," Phelan wrote that the book's "iconic images glow with warmth, light, and color," while *Horn Book* critic Jonathan Hunt recommended

Diego for its effectiveness in highlighting "the symbiotic relationship between art and politics in Latino culture." Working with author Amy Novesky, Diaz also crafts a visual portrait of Rivera's wife, fellow artist Frida Kahlo, in *Me, Frida: Frida Kahlo in San Francisco,* which reflects Kahlo's own aesthetic through his use of what a *Publishers Weekly* contributor described as "intense hues and [a] folk/naive style."

Another picture-book biography, *The Pot That Juan Built,* introduces youngsters to artist Juan Quezada, a Mexican potter famous for reviving Native-American techniques. The story by Nancy Andrews-Goebel uses built rhymes to explain the process of creating a new pot, a process that is understood by Diaz through his work as a potter as well as painter. According to a *Publishers Weekly* reviewer, the artwork's "glowing tones . . . capture the sweep and heat of the sun-bleached landscape" in a story that is both "inventive and engrossing." In Diaz's stylized images, noted *Booklist* critic Todd Morning, the illustrator captures "the shimmering light and heat of the desert," as well as including Quezada's unique pattern styles.

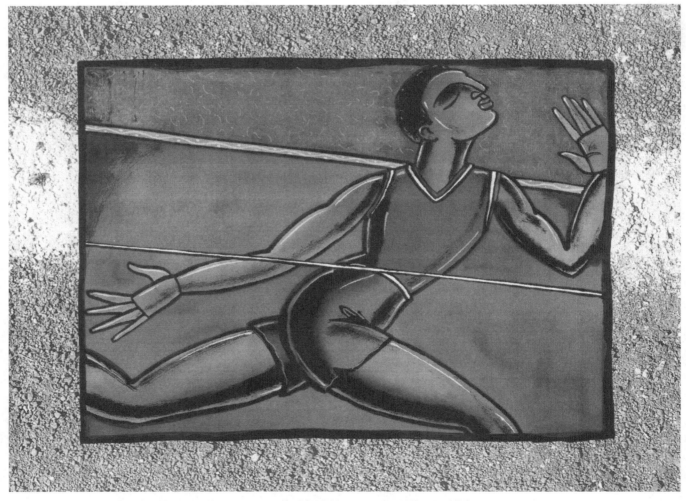

Diaz's artwork for Katherine Krull's* Wilma United *portrays the life of Olympic runner Wilma Rudolph. (Illustration copyright © 1996 by David Diaz. All rights reserved. Reproduced by permission of Harcourt, Inc. in the UK by permission of Writer's House Ltd., on behalf of author.)

One of Diaz's most popular illustration projects, *Wilma Unlimited: How Wilma Rudolph Became the World's Fastest Woman,* is a picture book that explores the inspiring life of Olympic gold medalist Wilma Rudolph, who overcame childhood illnesses and racism to become a champion on the track. Kathleen Krull's text is graced by "richly colored, stylized illustrations that—though painted—have the look and permanence of wood carvings" and are paired with a font of Diaz's own design, according to *Booklist* reviewer Michael Cart. In illustrating the story, Diaz uses sepia tones of watercolor, gouache, and acrylic in his characteristic stylized manner to "artfully capture [Rudolph's] physical and emotional determination, as well as the beauty of her body in motion," in the words of *Horn Book* critic Ellen Fader.

Krull and Diaz also team up in *Pocahontas,* a sophisticate picture-book treatment of the Native-American woman whose work on behalf of the Jamestown colonists and "rescue of Captain John Smith from an apparent execution" are presented "as one aspect of a broader life story," according to *Booklist* contributor Jennifer Mattson. Diaz's "striking artwork" is "bold, unexpected and inventive" in its interpretation, Mattson added while also expressing concern that the images imbue the story with a fanciful rather than realistic air. In *Publishers Weekly* a critic cited the book's "radiant illustrations and attention-grabbing narrative," while in *School Library Journal* Lucinda Snyder Whitehurst maintained that the characters in *Pocahontas* "burst from the page with exuberance and energy."

In Creech's award-winning *The Wanderer* a thirteen year-old joins her adopted family on an event-filled and sometimes frightening sailing trip from Connecticut to England. Diaz's "small ink drawings . . . add pleasure to this memorable voyage of discovery," according to Phelan. His "warm, melon-colored, pattern-filled paintings" for Creech's *Who's That Baby?: New-Baby Songs* "exalt babyhood and its rounded, soft-skinned perfection," according to *Booklist* critic Karin Snelson. Also reviewing Creech's book, a *Kirkus Reviews* writer deemed Diaz's contribution "gorgeous," due to his "extraordinary mastery of pattern" and his use of radiant colors and "sinuous line." *The Castel Corona,* Creech's original fairy story about a rich king and the two young orphans who teach him how to value life, also benefits from Diaz's illustrations, which "capture the feeling of medieval illuminations" and feature a "formal stiffness [that] is a perfect counterpoint to Creech's satisfying tale," according to *School Library Journal* critic Barbara Scotto.

Diaz employs a palette of autumn hues to illustrate *The Little Scarecrow Boy,* a story by legendary children's author Margaret Wise Brown. The little scarecrow wants to follow his father into the field to scare crows but is told that he is "not fierce enough." One day, determined to do his part, he ventures into the field and attempts an array of scary faces, finally finding one that sends the

Diaz lends an exotic air to a familiar story from history in his illustrations for Kathleen Krull's **Pocahontas, Princess of the New World.** (Illustration copyright © 2007 by David Diaz. Reprinted by permission of Walker & Co.)

crows packing. A *Publishers Weekly* reviewer liked the way Diaz created scarecrow faces, calling his renditions "a droll caricature of the kind of grimaces children concoct." A song by author José-Luis Orozco comes to life in Diaz's "powerful, arresting art," according to Maria Otero-Boisvert in her *School Library Journal* review of *Rin, Rin, Rin/Do, Re, Mi.* "Most readers will bypass the text in [favor of] . . . the illustrations," the critic added.

Diaz captures the subtleties of a challenging setting in his artwork for Christine Ford's *Ocean's Child,* depicting a range of Arctic animals preparing for sleep against the icy cool dusk of the northern regions. "Finely crafted" in tones of blue, violet, gold, and green, according to *School Library Journal* contributor Susan Scheps, his images here feature "swirly reflectionlike patterns in the water . . . along with representations of plant life and bubbles," all woven into what a *Kirkus Reviews* critic dubbed "stylized compositions whose motifs include watery batik and the totemic iconography of First Nation Alaskans." "The soothing flow of rhythmic language and elegant images creates a serenity just right for bedtimes," concluded Linda Perkins in her *Booklist* review of Ford's story, and a *Publishers Weekly* critic hailed Diaz's illustrations for *Ocean's Child* as "transcendent."

Diaz enjoys teaching children how to draw at workshops, and he is also an avid reader. As for his own

work for picture books, he once noted in a *BookPage.com* interview: "I never try to second-guess what's going to make kids laugh or hold their attention. I just try to make the images as appropriate to the text as possible. . . . I never try to make something cute just because it's for kids."

Biographical and Critical Sources

PERIODICALS

Booklist, June 15, 1992, Carolyn Phelan, review of *Neighborhood Odes,* p. 1838; March 1, 1994, Hazel Rochman, review of *Smoky Night,* pp. 1266-1267; April 15, 1996, Carolyn Phelan, review of *The Inner City Mother Goose,* p. 1432; May 1, 1996, Michael Cart, review of *Wilma Unlimited: How Wilma Rudolph Became the World's Fastest Woman,* p. 1503; June 1, 1996, Hazel Rochman, review of *Just One Flick of the Finger,* p. 1718; September 1, 1998, Carolyn Phelan, review of *The Little Scarecrow Boy,* p. 124; April 1, 2000, Carolyn Phelan, review of *The Wanderer,* p. 1456; September 15, 2002, Todd Morning, review of *The Pot That Juan Built,* p. 229; October 15, 2004, Jennifer Mattson, review of *Cèsar: Sí se puede!/Yes We Can,* p. 400; August, 2005, Karin Snelson, review of *Who's That Baby?: New-Baby Songs,* p. 2032; June 1, 2007, Jennifer Mattson, review of *Pocahontas: Princess of the New World,* p. 96; September 1, 2007, Jennifer Mattson, review of *The Castle Corona,* p. 113; March 1, 2008, Carolyn Phelan, review of *De Colores: Bright with Colors,* p.

Diaz's stylized and colorful art is a highlight of **Let There Be Peace on Earth and Let It Begin with Me,** *which features song lyrics by Jill Jackson and Sy Miller.* (Illustration copyright © 2009 by David Diaz. Reproduced with permission of Tricycle Press, an imprint of Random House Children's Books, a division of Random House, Inc.)

71; February 15, 2009, Carolyn Phelan, review of *Diego: Bigger than Life,* p. 80; April 1, 2009, Linda Perkins, review of *Ocean's Child,* p. 44; March 1, 2010, Gillian Engberg, review of *Sharing the Seasons: A Book of Poems,* p. 73; November 1, 2010, Carolyn Phelan, review of *Me, Frida: Frida Kahlo in San Francisco,* p. 60.

Horn Book, May-June, 1994, Ellen Fader, review of *Smoky Night,* p. 309; July-August, 1995, David Diaz, transcript of Caldecott Medal speech, pp. 430-433; September-October, 1996, Ellen Fader, review of *Wilma Unlimited;* September-October, 1998, Jennifer M. Brabander, review of *The Disappearing Alphabet,* p. 618; November-December, 2007, Susan Dove Lempke, review of *The Castle Corona,* p. 675; May-June, 2009, Jonathan Hunt, review of *Diego,* p. 320.

Kirkus Reviews, August 15, 2005, review of *Who's That Baby?,* p. 911; July 1, 2006, review of *Counting Ovejas,* p. 683; April 1, 2007, review of *Pocahontas;* September 1, 2007, review of *The Castle Corona;* May 1, 2009, review of *Ocean's Child;* January 15, 2010, review of *Sharing the Seasons.*

Kliatt, September, 2007, Paula Rohrlick, review of *The Castle Corona,* p. 9.

New York Times Book Review, May 21, 1995, Selma G. Lanes, "Violence from a Distance," p. 25; February 9, 2003, Bill Ott, review of *The Pot That Juan Built,* p. 21.

Publishers Weekly, January 31, 1994, review of *Smoky Night,* p. 89; September 23, 1996, review of *Going Home,* p. 76; August 17, 1998, review of *The Disappearing Alphabet,* p. 70; August 26, 2002, review of *The Pot That Juan Built,* p. 68; September 22, 2003, review of *Feliz Navidad,* p. 70; April 15, 2007, review of *Pocahontas,* p. 51; September 17, 2007, review of *The Castle Corona,* p. 54; May 4, 2009, review of *Ocean's Child,* p. 47; February 8, 2010, review of *Poems to Grow On,* p. 48; October 4, 2010, review of *Me, Frida,* p. 46.

School Library Journal, March, 1995, "Newbery, Caldecott Medals Go to New Creators," p. 108; September, 1996, Barbara Kiefer, review of *Going Home,* p. 171; July 20, 1998, review of *The Little Scarecrow Boy,* p. 218; September, 2002, Ann Welton, review of *The Pot That Juan Built,* p. 209; September, 2003, Grace Oliff, review of *December,* p. 84; March, 2004, Andrew Medlar, review of *Wilma Unlimited,* p. 69; May, 2004, Mary N. Oluonye, review of *The Gospel Cinderella,* p. 136; October, 2004, Scott La Counte, review of *Cèsar,* p. 138; March, 2005, Kathleen T. Isaacs, review of *The Pot That Juan Built,* p. 68; October, 2005, Bina Williams, review of *Who's That Baby?,* p. 136; February, 2006, Maria Otero-Boisvert, review of *Rin, Rin, Rin/Do, Re, Mi,* p. 127; June, 2006, Maria Otero-Boisvert, review of *Counting Ovejas,* p. 145; April, 2007, Lucinda Snyder Whitehurst, review of *Pocahontas,* p. 123; October, 2007, Barbara Scotto, review of *The Castle Corona,* p. 146; May, 2008, Barbara Katz, review of *De Colores,* p. 114; March, 2009, Nina Lindsay, review of *El Barrio,* p. 107; April, 2009, Wendy Lukehart, review of *Diego,* p. 146; July, 2009, Susan Scheps, review of *Ocean's Child,* p. 62; June,

2010, Lauralyn Persson, review of *Sharing the Seasons,* p. 88; December, 2010, Jody Kopple, review of *Me, Frida,* p. 96; April, 2011, Wendy Lukehart, review of *Before You Came,* p. 148.

Teaching and Learning Literature, September-October, 1995, Michael Patrick Hearne, "After the Smoke Has Cleared," pp. 54-56.

ONLINE

BookPage.com, http://www.bookpage.com/ (December 6, 2003), Alice Cary, "Fast Book to Honor World's Fastest Woman."

Lee & Low Books Web site, http://www.leeandlow.com/ booktalk/ (April 15, 2011), "David Diaz."*

*   *   *

DICKINSON, Peter 1927-
(Peter Malcolm de Brissac Dickinson)

Personal

Born December 16, 1927, in Livingstone, Northern Rhodesia (now Zambia); son of Richard Sebastian Willoughby (a colonial civil servant) and May Southey (a tomb restorer) Dickinson; married Mary Rose Barnard (an artist), April 20, 1953 (died, 1988); married Robin McKinley (an author), January, 1992; children: (first marriage) Philippa Lucy Anne, Dorothy Louise, John Geoffrey Hyett, James Christopher Meade. *Education:* Attended Eton College; King's College, Cambridge, B.A., 1951. *Politics:* "Leftish." *Religion:* "Lapsed Anglican."

Addresses

Home—Hampshire, England. *Agent*—A.P. Watt, Ltd., 20 John St., London WC1N 2DL, England. *E-mail*—hahoro@peterdickinson.com.

Career

Author of mystery novels and juvenile books. *Punch,* London, England, assistant editor, 1952-69. *Military service:* British Army, conscripted, 1946-48.

Member

Crime Writers Association, Society of Authors, Royal Society of Literature.

Awards, Honors

Gold Dagger award for best mystery of the year, Crime Writers Association, 1968, for *The Glass-sided Ants' Nest,* and 1969, for *The Old English Peep Show;* American Library Association (ALA) Notable Book Award, 1971, for *Emma Tupper's Diary; Horn Book* nonfiction award, c. 1976, for *Chance, Luck, and Destiny;* London *Guardian* Award, 1977, for *The Blue Hawk; Boston Globe/Horn Book* Award for nonfiction, 1977; Whitbread Award, and Carnegie Medal, both 1979, both for *Tulku;* ALA Best Books for Young Adults designation, 1979, for both *The Flight of Dragons* and *Tulku;* Carnegie Medal, 1982, for *City of Gold, and Other Stories from the Old Testament;* Whitbread Award, 1990, for *AK;* Blue Ribbon citation, *Bulletin of the Center for Children's Books,* 1996, for *Chuck and Danielle;* Phoenix Award, Children's Literature Association, 2001, for *The Seventh Raven,* 2008, for *Eva;* Mythopoeic Fantasy Award for children's literature, 2002, for *The Ropemaker;* named to Order of the British Empire, 2009, for services to literature.

Writings

JUVENILE FICTION

Emma Tupper's Diary, Little, Brown (Boston, MA), 1971.
The Dancing Bear, illustrated by David Smee, Gollancz (London, England), 1972, Little, Brown (Boston, MA), 1973.
The Iron Lion, illustrated by Marc Brown, Little, Brown (Boston, MA), 1972.
The Gift, illustrated by Gareth Floyd, Gollancz (London, England), 1973, Little, Brown (Boston, MA), 1974.
(Editor) *Presto! Humorous Bits and Pieces,* Hutchinson (London, England), 1975.
Chance, Luck, and Destiny (miscellany), illustrated by David Smee and Victor Ambrus, Gollancz (London, England), 1975, Little, Brown (Boston, MA), 1976.
The Blue Hawk, illustrated by David Smee, Little, Brown (Boston, MA), 1976, reprinted, Macmillan (London, England), 2002.
Annerton Pit, Gollancz (London, England), 1976, Little, Brown (Boston, MA), 1977.
Hepzibah, illustrated by Sue Porter, Eel Pie (Twickenham, England), 1978, David R. Godine (New York, NY), 1980.
Tulku, Dutton (New York, NY), 1979.
The Flight of Dragons, illustrated by Wayne Anderson, Harper & Row (New York, NY), 1979.
City of Gold, and Other Stories from the Old Testament, illustrated by Michael Foreman, Gollancz (London, England), 1979, Pantheon (New York, NY), 1980, published as *City of Gold,* Houghton Mifflin (New York, NY), 1992.
The Seventh Raven, Dutton (New York, NY), 1981.
Giant Cold, illustrated by Alan E. Cober, Dutton (New York, NY), 1981.
Healer, Gollancz (London, England), 1983, Delacorte (New York, NY), 1985.
(Editor) *Hundreds and Hundreds,* Penguin (London, England), 1984.
Mole Hole, Peter Bedrick (London, England), 1987.
Merlin Dreams, illustrated by Alan Lee, Chivers Press (London, England), 1987, Delacorte (New York, NY), 1988.

A Box of Nothing, illustrated by Ian Newsham, Delacorte (New York, NY), 1988.

Eva, Delacorte (New York, NY), 1989.

AK, Gollancz (London, England), 1990, Doubleday (New York, NY), 1992.

A Bone from a Dry Sea, Delacorte (New York, NY), 1993.

Time and the Clock Mice, Etcetera, illustrated by Emma Chichester-Clark, Doubleday (London, England), 1993, Delacorte (New York, NY), 1994.

Shadow of a Hero, Delacorte (New York, NY), 1994.

Chuck and Danielle, illustrated by Robin Lawrie, Doubleday (London, England), 1994, illustrated by Kees de Kiefte, Bantam (New York, NY), 1996.

The Lion Tamer's Daughter and Other Stories, Delacorte (New York, NY), 1997.

Touch and Go, and Other Stories, Macmillan (London, England), 1997.

The Ropemaker, Delacorte (New York, NY), 2001.

(With wife Robin McKinley) *Water: Tales of Elemental Spirits* (stories) Putnam (New York, NY), 2002, published as *Elementals: Water,* David Fickling Books (London, England), 2002.

The Tears of the Salamander, Random House (New York, NY), 2003.

Inside Grandad, Random House (New York, NY), 2004, published as *The Gift Boat,* Macmillan (London, England), 2004.

Angel Isle (sequel to *The Ropemaker*), Macmillan (London, England), 2006, Wendy Lamb Books (New York, NY), 2007.

(With Robin McKinley) *Fire: Tales of Elemental Spirits* (stories) Putnam (New York, NY), 2009.

"CHANGES" SERIES; YOUNG-ADULT NOVELS

The Weathermonger, Gollancz (London, England), 1968, Little, Brown (Boston, MA), 1969, reprinted, Collins Voyager (London, England), 2003.

Heartsease, illustrated by Robert Hales, Little, Brown (Boston, MA), 1969.

The Devil's Children, illustrated by Robert Hales, Little, Brown (Boston, MA), 1970.

The Changes: A Trilogy (contains *The Weathermonger, Heartsease,* and *The Devil's Children*), Gollancz (London, England), 1975.

"KIN" SERIES; YOUNG-ADULT NOVELS

Noli's Story (also see below), Grosset & Dunlap (New York, NY), 1998.

Po's Story (also see below), Grosset & Dunlap (New York, NY), 1998.

Suth's Story (also see below), Grosset & Dunlap (New York, NY), 1998.

The Kin (omnibus), Macmillan (London, England), 1998, Penguin (New York, NY), 2003.

Mana's Story (also see below), Grosset & Dunlap (New York, NY), 1999.

ADULT MYSTERY NOVELS

The Glass-sided Ants' Nest, Harper & Row (New York, NY), 1968, published as *Skin Deep,* Hodder & Stoughton (London, England), 1968.

The Old English Peep Show, Harper & Row (New York, NY), 1969, published as *A Pride of Heroes,* Hodder & Stoughton (London, England), 1969.

The Sinful Stones, Harper & Row (New York, NY), 1970, published as *The Seals,* Hodder & Stoughton (London, England), 1970.

Sleep and His Brother, Harper & Row (New York, NY), 1971, reprinted, Felony & Mayhem Press (New York, NY), 2009.

The Lizard in the Cup, Hodder & Stoughton (London, England), 1971, Harper & Row (New York, NY), 1972.

The Green Gene, Pantheon (New York, NY), 1973.

The Poison Oracle, Pantheon (New York, NY), 1974.

The Lively Dead, Pantheon (New York, NY), 1975.

King and Joker, Pantheon (New York, NY), 1976.

Walking Dead, Hodder & Stoughton (London, England), 1977, Pantheon (New York, NY), 1978.

One Foot in the Grave, Hodder & Stoughton (London, England), 1979, Pantheon (New York, NY), 1980.

The Last House-Party, Pantheon (New York, NY), 1982.

Hindsight, Pantheon (New York, NY), 1983.

Death of a Unicorn, Pantheon (New York, NY), 1984.

Skeleton-in-Waiting, Pantheon (New York, NY), 1989.

Play Dead, Bodley Head (London, England), 1991, Mysterious Press (New York, NY), 1992.

The Yellow Room Conspiracy, Mysterious Press (New York, NY), 1994.

Some Deaths before Dying, Mysterious Press (New York, NY), 1999.

ADULT NOVELS

A Summer in the Twenties (novel), Pantheon (New York, NY), 1981.

Tefuga, Bodley Head (London, England), 1985, Pantheon (New York, NY), 1986.

Perfect Gallows, Pantheon (New York, NY), 1987.

OTHER

Mandog (television series), British Broadcasting Corporation (BBC-TV), 1972.

The Weir (poetry), Peter Dickinson Books (Alresford, England), 2007.

Contributor to anthologies, including: Otto Penzler, editor, *The Great Detectives,* Little, Brown (Boston, MA), 1978; and Julian Symons, editor, *Verdict of Thirteen,* Harper & Row (New York, NY), 1979.

Adaptations

The British Broadcasting Corporation produced a television serial based on Dickinson's *Changes* trilogy, 1975. *The Flight of Dragons* was adapted as an ani-

mated television film by the American Broadcasting Co. (ABC), 1982. *A Box of Nothing* was adapted for audiobook by G.K. Hall, 1988. *Hindsight* was adapted for audiobook by Oasis (Oxford, England), 1989. Audiobook adaptations by Isis (Oxford, England) include *Perfect Gallows,* 1988, *Play Dead,* 1991, and *The Yellow Room Conspiracy.*

Sidelights

The recipient of a prestigious Carnegie medal, Whitbread award, and Phoenix award, Peter Dickinson is one of the United Kingdom's most popular and distinguished storytellers. Dickinson's fertile imagination distinguishes his children's books, such as *Tulku, Eva,* and *Angel Isle,* resulting in stories that contain oddities ranging from youngsters with remarkable healing powers to an aged magician doped up on morphine. "The versatility, the narrative power, and the dry authorial humour that is found throughout Dickinson's work is astonishing and forbids any summary beyond the crudest kind of categorization," Brian Alderson asserted in *Books for Keeps.* "For all their variety," John Rowe Townsend wrote in his *A Sounding of Storytellers: New*

Cover of Peter Dickinson's short-story collection **The Lion-Tamer's Daughter,** *featuring artwork by Kamil Vojnar.* (Illustration copyright © 1997 by Delacorte Press. Reproduced by permission of Delacorte Press, an imprint of Random House Children's Books, a division of Random House, Inc.)

and Revised Essays on Contemporary Writers for Children, "the books have much in common: strong professional storytelling, rapid action and adventure, continual invention, a proliferating interest in ideas, and an understanding of how things are done. Behind all this one glimpses an energetic, speculative mind with a leaning towards the exotic."

Like his writing, Dickinson's personal background is exotic. His father, a British civil servant, worked in Zambia, then the colony of Northern Rhodesia. It was there that Dickinson was born and lived the first seven years of his life. Shortly after their return to England in 1935, his father died, but Dickinson's fortune took a turn for the better a few years later when he won a scholarship to attend Eton College. After leaving Eton and serving his country in the aftermath of World War II as a district signals officer, he enrolled at King's College Cambridge. Although he began studying Latin, Dickinson later switched to English literature, and it was one of his English tutors who convinced him to apply for a position as assistant editor at *Punch,* a well-known London humor magazine.

Getting an appointment for an interview did not turn out to be as difficult as actually arriving at the *Punch* offices, for on his way there Dickinson was hit by a tram. Despite the accident, the aspiring editor made it to the interview, his clothing stained with blood, and was accepted for the job. For the next seventeen years Dickinson worked for *Punch,* including a five-year stint reviewing crime novels. After reading and analyzing literally thousands of these books, Dickinson began to think about writing one of his own, although he hoped to write more than just another story about a murder. He drew on his knowledge of a wide variety of topics—including anthropology, trains, languages, antiques, and history—and produced *Skin Deep* (published in the United States as *The Glass-sided Ants' Nest*). The story employs certain facts about anthropology to weave a bizarre mystery concerning a tribe of aborigines from New Guinea who have settled in London only to have their chief murdered.

Of his adult mysteries, Dickinson's books featuring detective James Pibble are best known, but he has also written several quirky whodunnits featuring out-of-the-ordinary detectives faced with unusual challenges. Dickinson's stories are often set in familiar places made slightly off-balance by science-fiction-like elements, and this sort of invention is also key to his children's novels. A vivid dreamer, Dickinson sometimes envisions elements of his plots in his dreams, then wakes and builds a story around them. "I believe the crucial thing for a writer is the ability to make up coherent worlds," he explained to *New York Times Book Review* contributor Eden Ross Lipson. "I'm like a beachcomber walking along the shores of invention, picking up things and wondering what kinds of structures they could make. . . . The imagination is like the sea, full of things you can't see but can possibly harvest and use."

Dickinson published his first book for children, *The Weathermonger,* the same year as his first adult mystery, and it became the first book in his "Changes" trilogy, which includes *Heartsease* and *The Devil's Children.* In the series Geoffrey is growing up in a near-future England where society has developed a mysterious aversion to all types of technology—as well as a general xenophobia—with the result that the entire country is thrown into another Dark Age. Another side effect of the Changes is that it gives some people the power to manipulate the weather. In *The Weathermonger* Geoffrey, along with his sister, Sally, is sent on a mission to find out what has been causing the Changes. The source turns out to be of a magical nature: a chemist named Furbelow has revived King Arthur's wizard, Merlin, from a centuries-old sleep and now manipulates him after getting the magician addicted to morphine. In *Heartsease* Margaret and Jonathan discover the hiding place of an American investigator who has been stoned by the British because they thought he was a witch. The two children, along with their house servant, Lucy, help the man escape to Gloucester and the boat that will return him to the United States. Set at the beginning of the Changes, *The Devil's Children* finds a group of Sikhs—who have not developed the fear of technology like the British—escaping persecution with the help of a twelve-year-old English girl named Nicola. S.F. Said noted in the London *Daily Telegraph* that Dickinson's "Changes" novels "were landmarks of the Sixties, read in schools and broadcast on TV." The trilogy is still in print and is sometimes recommended to students who enjoy challenging and morally ambiguous stories.

Dickinson's novels *The Gift, Annerton Pit,* and *Healer* have contemporary, realistic settings upon which the author imposes extraordinary elements. In each of these novels, a child possesses—or seems to possess—amazing powers: Davy Price in *The Gift* has inherited the ability to see the images that other people form in their minds, while in *Annerton Pit* a blind boy named Jake is kidnapped by a group of environmental terrorists and imprisoned in an abandoned mine and discovers his telepathic abilities while attempting to escape. With *Healer* Dickinson explores the emotions and thoughts of both Barry, a sixteen year old, and his inner personality, "Bear," a being with animalistic impulses.

Ostensibly a tale of adventure, *Healer* is also one "from which [the reader] . . . peels different levels of meaning layer by layer," according to a *Junior Bookshelf* reviewer. While *The Gift, Annerton Pit,* and *Healer* reveal Dickinson's interest in the psychology of his characters, *Healer* also explores his preoccupation with religion and religious faith. This fascination is also manifested in some of the author's other novels, such as the distant-future science-fiction work *The Blue Hawk* and the historical novel *Tulku.*

Merlin Dreams effectively displays Dickinson's talent for language and storytelling. A series of nine stories, all dealing with powers of one sort or another, are pre-sented as the dreams of a sleeping Merlin as the wizard nears the end of his life. All of the stories contain medieval elements such as knights and damsels, and Merlin himself appears in some of them. *Horn Book* contributor Ann A. Flowers, while asserting that the interludes of the dreaming Merlin may be "puzzling to the young reader," noted that "all the stories are splendid and a pleasure to read." Christina L. Olson stated in *School Library Journal* that while Dickinson's collection "works on the level of pure story," his "language works *on* readers as well." "It's the language of a spellbinder," Barbara Sherrard-Smith explained in *School Librarian,* concluding that *Merlin Dreams* "is one of those rare joys, a book to be read quickly to find out what happens next, then to be savoured again and again."

One of Dickinson's most controversial works for children, *Eva,* addresses the author's concerns about human society and the impact it has had on the ecology of the earth. Severely injured and paralyzed in a car accident, Eva is "saved" by having her memory transplanted into the body of a chimpanzee. After regaining consciousness, Eva must adjust not only to her new body, with its chimp impulses, but to the corporate sponsorship that makes her the focus of media attention. She eventually decides to leave human society, taking a group of captive chimps with her to a remote island. Calling *Eva* "an astonishing work of biological science fiction," *Horn Book* writer Ethel L. Heins remarked that Dickinson's adventure story "is also a work of passion and eloquence, and its sobering significance increases in proportion to the reader's maturity." *Times Literary Supplement* reviewer Neil Philip dubbed *Eva* "highly provocative" and a story that "involves the reader from the very first page and will not quickly leave the mind." In *Horn Book* Betty Carter wrote that "Dickinson shows tremendous respect for his readers and their ability to grapple with hard issues that range from euthanasia to the influence of the media. . . . He gives readers no logical wiggle room in which to build a softer interpretation of this deteriorating society. They can question, challenge, regret, confront, dismiss, or accept it, but they cannot change it. . . . Here readers are on their own, as they should be, full of questions with no certain answers. And that is the power of literature—to provide an arena where young people can encounter unimaginable situations."

A similarly provocative work, *AK,* focuses on a fictional African nation that has been torn by civil war. Paul Kagomi has known nothing but conflict during his twelve years, having grown up as part of the Nagala Liberation Army. He defines himself by his weapon—the AK-47 of the title—and is left confused when the war ends and he is sent to school by his foster father, who is now a member of the government. When a coup erupts, Paul escapes from his father's enemies, retrieves his gun, and mounts a rescue attempt. Dickinson shows, however, that victories achieved through violence are fragile, and he "carefully structures his conclusion so the lesson of ambiguity is the one we carry away," as

Michele Slung summarized in the *New York Times Book Review*. Although the story's locale is imaginary, the events are truthful, Margaret A. Bush observed in *Horn Book: AK* is "disturbing in its plausibility and creates a thoughtful exploration of the dynamics of war."

In contrast to his more serious novels, Dickinson has also created stories featuring animals as central characters. *Chuck and Danielle* is a story about a young girl and her high-strung dog—a whippet nicknamed Chuck. Danielle has made a bet with her mother that someday her energetic pooch, which a *Kirkus Reviews* critic described as an "antihero," will save the universe. In his *Time and the Clock Mice, Etcetera* the main attraction of Branton, a ninety-nine-year-old town hall clock, stops. The clockmaker's grandson, who is now elderly, comes to repair the clock and discovers a group of super-intelligent mice who can communicate via ESP, and whose safety and existence are threatened by cats and human research scientists. As the man befriends the mice and describes both how to fix the clock and how it works, Dickinson's book becomes a series of "essays" on such topics as bells, people, clocks, science, and cats, among others. *Time and the Clock Mice, Etcetera* is enhanced by the illustrations of Emma Chichester-Clark, and the result, noted *School Librarian* contributor Alisdair Campbell, "becomes a visual treat as well as a literary hotch-potch."

The Kin was first published in the United States as four separate volumes: *Noli's Story,, Po's Story, Suth's Story,* and *Mana's Story.* Set in Africa approximately 200,000 years ago, Dickinson's saga follows four children as they venture into adulthood together, struggling to survive after they are separated from their extended family group and threatened by a series of natural disasters and animal predators. What separates *The Kin* from pure adventure yarn is its author's preoccupation with deeper questions of humanity, as represented by these proto-*homo sapiens* youngsters. They communicate by language but befriend a wounded man who does not speak. They must use their wits to find food and shelter and to thwart danger, but they also have time to think about what they mean to each other and how the world has come to be. In the London *Daily Telegraph*, Mary Hoffman called *The Kin* "a remarkable work" in which "Dickinson has created a completely believable and compelling culture and history from a period which has left virtually no trace." A reviewer for *Books for Keeps* cited the saga for featuring "writing of the finest quality," and a *Publishers Weekly* reviewer praised *Noli's Story* for "the exhilarating mix of ideas the novel so nimbly sets forth."

With *The Ropemaker, Angel Isle,* and *The Tears of the Salamander* Dickinson returns to fantasy and science-fiction themes. In *The Ropemaker* Tilja and Tahl must undertake a pilgrimage to find the powerful magician who has traditionally protected their homeland from its war-mongering neighbors. Part adventure tale, part character study, *The Ropemaker* explores how young people

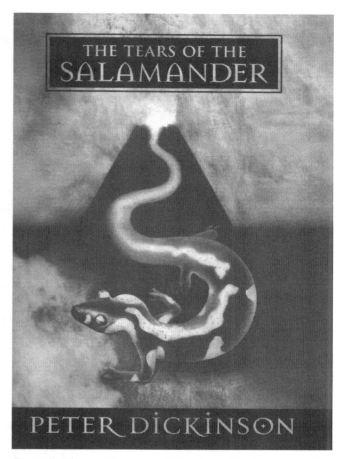

Cover of Dickinson's fantasy novel **The Tears of the Salamander,** *featuring cover art by Dave McKean.* (Illustration copyright © 2003 by Dave McKean. Used by permission of Random House Children's Books, a division of Random House, Inc.)

come to terms with their special skills. "While on one level this tale is a fantasy, it is also a wonderful coming-of-age story," noted Bruce Anne Shook in her *School Library Journal* review. A *Publishers Weekly* critic declared Dickinson's mythic world in *The Ropemaker* to be "as breathtakingly fresh as it is archetypal."

Angel Isle, a sequel to *The Ropemaker,* "is a complex, thrilling fantasy that should challenge readers' imaginations and intellects," observed Rosser. Twenty generations removed from the heroics of Tilja and Tahl, the people of the Valley now find themselves under the control of the Watchers, prompting an adventurous band of characters to venture through a dangerous realm in search of the life-giving Ropemaker. "The complex and intricate plot illustrates just how artful a writer Dickinson is," a *Kirkus Reviews* critic stated, and Anita L. Burkam wrote in *Horn Book* that Dickinson's "bravura performance of created worlds and rock-solid plotting [is] sure to please fantasy lovers."

Thirteen-year-old Alfredo is thrust into a fantastic world in *The Tears of the Salamander.* When his beloved father's bakery burns down, Alfredo is orphaned with no prospects, save the unsavory fate of submitting to castration so that he can always sing soprano for the

Church. Arriving in the nick of time, Uncle Giorgio offers another option: Alfredo can come and live on the slopes of Mount Etna in the family's ancestral home. Alfredo soon discovers that much is amiss in the shadow of the mighty volcano, and as his beautiful singing wrings tears from a magic salamander, he realizes that his uncle has sinister ambitions for immortality and world domination. As a *Publishers Weekly* critic noted, "burning questions" animate what the critic praised as an "engrossing, almost operatic novel," and in *Horn Book* Joanna Rudge Long concluded that *The Tears of the Salamander* "makes a unique and satisfying addition to Dickinson's remarkable oeuvre." Noting that the story offers readers a challenging narrative, Rosser stated that, "for those . . . who are fascinated by metaphysics, by music, by intricate fantasy, this is a special treat."

Inside Grandad is a gentler tale of fantasy in which Dickinson's focus in on reconciling oneself to the changes wrought by the passage of time. Gavin and his grandfather enjoy a deep bond in their Scottish seacoast town. As Gavin's grandfather completes a model boat,

Cover of Dickinson's novel Angel Isle, *featuring cover art by Steve Rawlings.* (Lamb Books, 2009. Reproduced by permission of Wendy Lamb Books, an imprint of Random House Children's Books, a division of Random House, Inc.)

he recounts legends of the selkies—a mystical race of seal-people who can work good or ill in humans' lives. Shortly after completing the boat, the elderly man suffers a crippling stroke, leaving Gavin to bargain with the selkies for restoration of his grandfather's health. "The road to the hopeful but honest conclusion is thoughtful but never maudlin," a contributor maintained in *Publishers Weekly*. A *Kirkus Reviews* critic deemed *Inside Grandad* "a touching story of love and determination," and Hazel Rochman commented in *Booklist* that Dickinson's "simple, beautiful words . . . root the fantasy in real places and daily routine."

In addition to his own works, Dickinson has also collaborated with his wife, celebrated fantasy writer Robin McKinley, on two collections of short stories. In *Water: Tales of Elemental Spirits* each writer presents three stories united by an aquatic theme. While Dickinson's contributions "lean toward the dark, the violent, the malevolent," according to a *Kirkus Reviews* critic, John Peters remarked in *School Library Journal* that *Water* as a whole "focus[es] as strongly on action as on character." In the companion volume, *Fire: Tales of Elemental Spirits*, Dickinson's "Phoenix" concerns a British girl's unlikely relationship with the guardian of an ancient creature, while "Fireworm" finds a prehistoric cave dweller embarking on a spirit-walk to defeat his clan's mortal enemies. "Dickinson's offerings are notable for their sophisticated magical thinking and subtlety of expression," Burkam declared of *Fire,* while Shelly Shaffer reported in the *Journal of Adolescent & Adult Literacy* that the story collection treats readers to "an engaging read, packed with fantasy and excitement."

Creating finely realized fictional worlds has always been of the utmost concern for Dickinson. "The primary function of my books, indeed of all fiction, is to provide exercise for the reader's imagination, in the case of children to help to strengthen and develop it, and thereafter to keep it fit and active, because our imaginative life is an essential aspect of our humanity," he stated in his Phoenix Award acceptance speech, reprinted on his home page. "What story-tellers do is controlled dreaming. Dreams for others to share. It is no surprise that a book should arise from a dream." In a media-saturated world, Dickinson maintains, literature remains an essential part of human life. As he stated in an article for *Children's Literature in Education,* the act of reading "invites the exercise of the imagination, the enlargement of the imaginative sympathies, the increase of our potential as human beings."

Biographical and Critical Sources

BOOKS

Children's Literature Review, Volume 29, Gale (Detroit, MI), 1993.

Contemporary Literary Criticism, Volume 35, Gale (Detroit, MI), 1985.

Dictionary of Literary Biography, Volume 161: *British Children's Writers since 1960, First Series,* Gale (Detroit, MI), 1996.

St. James Guide to Young Adult Writers, 2nd edition, St. James (Detroit, MI), 1999.

Townsend, John Rowe, *A Sounding of Storytellers: New and Revised Essays on Contemporary Writers for Children,* Lippincott (Philadelphia, PA), 1979, pp. 41-54.

Townsend, John Rowe, *Writing for Children: An Outline of English-Language Children's Literature,* revised edition, Lippincott (Philadelphia, PA), 1974.

PERIODICALS

Booklist, May 15, 2003, Ilene Cooper, review of *The Tears of the Salamander,* p. 1659; January 1, 2004, Hazel Rochman, review of *Inside Grandad,* p. 854; October 15, 2007, Sally Estes, review of *Angel Isle,* p. 46; September 1, 2009, Krista Hutley, review of *Fire: Tales of Elemental Spirits,* p. 81.

Books for Keeps, July, 1999, review of *The Kin,* p. 25; September, 2008, Brian Alderson, "Peter Dickinson and the Hazards of Storytelling."

Bulletin of the Center for Children's Books, January, 1995, Roger Sutton, review of *Shadow of a Hero,* pp. 163-164.

Children's Literature in Education, spring, 1986, Peter Dickinson, "Fantasy: The Need for Realism," pp. 39-51.

Daily Telegraph (London, England), October 15, 1998, Mary Hoffman, "What It Is to Be Human"; September 15, 2001, S.F. Said, "Power of a Word Wizard: Peter Dickinson Is the Children's Author That All the Rest Admire."

Guardian (London, England), November 9, 2002, "In Their Element," p. 33; July 12, 2003, Jan Mark, "Burning Desire," p. 33.

Horn Book, March-April, 1989, Ann A. Flowers, review of *Merlin Dreams,* p. 210; July-August, 1989, Ethel L. Heins, review of *Eva,* pp. 487-488; September-October, 1992, Margaret A. Bush, review of *AK,* p. 588; March-April, 1995, Ann A. Flowers, review of *Shadow of a Hero,* pp. 199-200; March-April, 1997, Nancy Vasilakis, review of *The Lion Tamer's Daughter and Other Stories,* pp. 195-196; September, 2001, Betty Carter, review of *Eva,* p. 541; November-December, 2001, Anita L. Burkam, review of *The Ropemaker,* p. 745; July-August, 2003, Joanna Rudge Long, review of *The Tears of the Salamander,* p. 453; January-February, 2004, Joanna Rudge Long, review of *Inside Grandad,* p. 80; November-December, 2007, Anita L. Burkam, review of *Angel Isle,* p. 678; November-December, 2009, Anita L. Burkam, review of *Fire,* p. 681.

Independent, October 24, 1998, Nicholas Tucker, "Visionary Angels on a Bloody Earth."

Journal of Adolescent & Adult Literacy, September, 2010, Shelly Shaffer, review of *Fire,* p. 72.

Junior Bookshelf, October, 1983, review of *Healer,* p. 212.

Kirkus Reviews, December 1, 1995, review of *Chuck and Danielle,* p. 1701; June 1, 2002, review of *Water: Tales of Elemental Spirits,* p. 808; July 15, 2003, review of *The Tears of the Salamander,* p. 962; December 15, 2003, review of *Inside Grandad,* p. 1449.

Kliatt, July, 2003, Claire Rosser, review of *The Tears of the Salamander,* p. 10, and Lesley S.J. Farmer, review of *Water,* p. 33; May, 2004, Karen Reeds, review of *The Ropemaker,* p. 28; September, 2007, Claire Rosser, review of *Angel Isle,* p. 10.

New York Times Book Review, April 20, 1986, Eden Ross Lipson, "Write, Then Research, Then Rewrite"; September 27, 1992, Michele Slung, review of *AK,* p. 33.

Publishers Weekly, June 29, 1998, review of *Noli's Story;* November 5, 2001, review of *The Ropemaker,* p. 70; August 11, 2003, review of *The Tears of the Salamander,* p. 281; February 2, 2004, review of *Inside Grandad,* p. 78; October 29, 2007, review of *Angel Isle,* p. 58.

School Librarian, February, 1989, Barbara Sherrard-Smith, review of *Merlin Dreams,* p. 21; May, 1994, Alasdair Campbell, review of *Time and the Clock Mice, Etcetera,* p. 60.

School Library Journal, December, 1988, Christina L. Olson, review of *Merlin Dreams,* p. 120; April, 1989, Kathryn Harris, review of *Eva,* p. 118; November, 2001, Bruce Anne Shook, review of *The Ropemaker,* p. 154; June, 2002, John Peters, review of *Water,* p. 142; August, 2003, Renee Steinberg, review of *The Tears of the Salamander,* p. 158; January, 2004, Lauralyn Persson, review of *Inside Grandad,* p. 129; November, 2007, Kristin Anderson, review of *Angel Isle,* p. 120; September, 2009, Misti Tidman, review of *Fire,* p. 166.

Times Educational Supplement, October 23, 1998, Michael Thorn, "Back to Africa," p. 10.

Times Literary Supplement, March 3-9, 1988, Neil Philip, "Working with Nature," p. 232.

Washington Post Book World, August 9, 1992, Michael Dirda, review of *AK,* p. 11.

ONLINE

Peter Dickinson Home Page, http://www.peterdickinson. com (April 15, 2011).

Random House Web site, http://www.randomhouse.com/ (April 15, 2011), profile of Dickinson.

* * *

DICKINSON, Peter Malcolm de Brissac See DICKINSON, Peter

* * *

DIVINE, L.
(Alysia Logan)

Personal

Born in CA; children: one daughter, one son. *Education:* University of California—Los Angeles, B.A.

(African-American studies), 1999, M.A. (African-American studies/educational psychology), 2000.

Addresses

Home—Atlanta, GA.

Career

Author and educator. Teacher of high-school English in Los Angeles, CA, and Atlanta, GA. University of California—Los Angeles, visiting research scholar at Center for the Study of Women, 2006, and guest lecturer of women's studies and African-American studies. Speaker and presenter at schools.

Awards, Honors

A Room of Her Own retreat scholarship, 2007.

Writings

"DRAMA HIGH" YOUNG-ADULT NOVEL SERIES

The Fight, Dafina Books for Young Readers (New York, NY), 2006.
Second Chance, Dafina Books for Young Readers (New York, NY), 2006.
Jayd's Legacy, Dafina Books for Young Readers (New York, NY), 2007.
Frenemies, Dafina Books for Young Readers (New York, NY), 2008.
Lady J, Dafina Books for Young Readers (New York, NY), 2008.
Courtin' Jayd, Dafina Books for Young Readers (New York, NY), 2008.
Hustlin', Dafina Books for Young Readers (New York, NY), 2009.
Keep It Movin', Dafina Books for Young Readers (New York, NY), 2009.
Holidaze, Dafina Books for Young Readers (New York, NY), 2009.
Culture Clash, Dafina Books for Young Readers (New York, NY), 2010.
Pushin', Dafina Books for Young Readers (New York, NY), 2010.
Cold as Ice, Dafina Books for Young Readers (New York, NY), 2011.
The Meltdown, Dafina Books for Young Readers (New York, NY), 2011.
So, So Hood, Dafina Books for Young Readers (New York, NY), 2011.

Sidelights

Raised in California and now living in Atlanta, Georgia, L. Divine sets her stories in Los Angeles, where she earned her master's degree and once taught high-school English. Her experiences as an African American, a mother, and an educator with a front-row seat to con-

temporary teen culture inspired Divine (the pen name of Alysia Logan) to begin her "Drama High" novels, which feature a bright and likeable young black woman who, with wise guidance from her grandmother, models self-respect as she embraces challenges, gravitates toward healthy relationships, and exhibits a super fashion sense.

In her first "Drama High" series installment, *The Fight,* Divine introduces sixteen-year-old Jayd Jackson. Growing up south of Los Angeles, in Compton, where gang activity and drug use are commonplace, the intelligent and perceptive Jayd has also gained a healthy dose of street smarts. The teen's common-sense approach to life becomes clear when she becomes part of a group of high-achieving students being bussed to South Bay High, a wealthier suburb of Los Angeles. When basketball star KJ makes his moves on the pretty new student, Jayd enjoys his attentions until KJ's jealous girlfriend makes her claims on the sports star known. With the counsel of her grandmother, Jayd knows what to do when KJ turns out to be just another player.

Jayd's junior-year challenges continue in *Second Chance,* as she begins a new relationship with wealthy

Cover of L. Divine's Keep It Movin,' *a "Drama High" novel featuring cover art by George Kerrigan.* (Kensington Publishing Group, 2009. Cover photography by George Kerrigan. Reproduced by permission of George Kerrigan.)

and with-it Jewish classmate Jeremy Weiner. Jeremy's noncommittal rich-boy attitude is beginning to become tiresome in *Frenemies,* but Jayd is more concerned over her fragmenting friendship with former best friend Nellie, especially since Nellie was named homecoming princess. The teen decides to buck some students' objections and form the school's first African Student Union in *Culture Clash,* and Jayd decides that exams take precedence over time with her friends in *Cold as Ice.* Reviewing *Holidaze,* which finds Jayd courted by three handsome guys as Valentine's Day approaches, a *Kirkus Reviews* critic recommended the story's "abundant, juicy drama," adding that "Divine juggles the numerous subplots and characters skillfully."

Biographical and Critical Sources

PERIODICALS

Kirkus Reviews, December 15, 2009, review of *Holidaze.*
Library Journal, June 15, 2010, review of *Cold as Ice,* p. 5.
Tribune Books (Chicago, IL), August 11, 2007, Mia Sartin, review of *The Fight,* p. 7.

ONLINE

L. Divine Home Page, http://www.dramahigh.com (April 24, 2011).
Mastermedia Speakers Web site, http://www.mastermedia speakers.com/ (April 30, 2011), "L. Divine."*

*   *   *

DYER, Hadley 1973-

Personal

Born September 12, 1973, in Halifax, Nova Scotia, Canada; daughter of a lawyer and a homemaker. *Education:* University of King's College, B.A. (English).

Addresses

Home—Toronto, Ontario, Canada.

Career

Writer and editor. Woozles (bookstore), Halifax, Nova Scotia, Canada, bookseller and assistant manager; Chapter's (bookstore), London, Ontario, Canada, bookseller; Canadian Children's Book Centre, Toronto, Ontario, library coordinator, 1999-2001; Groundwood Books, Toronto, editor marketing manager, 2001-02; James Lorimer & Company, Halifax, editor, until 2007; HarperCollins Canada, Toronto, executive editor of children's books, 2011—. Teacher in publishing program at Ryerson University.

Member

International Board on Books for Young People Canada (former president), Canadian Society of Children's Authors, Illustrators, and Performers.

Awards, Honors

Book of the Year for Children selection, and Young-Adult Book Award Honour Book selection, both Canadian Library Association, TD Canadian Children's Literature Award Honour Book selection, Hackmatack Award finalist, Rocky Mountain Book Award finalist, Red Cedar Award finalist, and Red Maple Award finalist, Ontario Library Association, all c. 2006, all for *Johnny Kellock Died Today;* Red Maple Award shortlist inclusion, and Notable Social Studies Trade Books for Young People selection, National Council for the Social Studies/Children's Book Council, both 2011, both for *Watch This Space.*

Writings

(With Bobbie Kalman) *The Life Cycle of a Mosquito,* Crabtree Publishing (New York, NY), 2004.
(With Bobbie Kalman) *The Life Cycle of an Earthworm,* Crabtree Publishing (New York, NY), 2004.
(With Bobbie Kalman) *Field Events in Action,* Crabtree Publishing (New York, NY), 2005.
(With Bobbie Kalman) *Endangered Chimpanzees,* Crabtree Publishing (New York, NY), 2005.
(With Bobbie Kalman) *Endangered Leopards,* Crabtree Publishing (New York, NY), 2005.
(With Bobbie Kalman) *Endangered Manatees,* Crabtree Publishing (New York, NY), 2006.
(With Bobbie Kalman) *Fishing in Action,* Crabtree Publishing (New York, NY), 2006.
(With Bobbie Kalman) *The Life Cycle of an Ant,* Crabtree Publishing (New York, NY), 2006.
(With Bobbie Kalman) *Wonderful Whales,* Crabtree Publishing (New York, NY), 2006.
Johnny Kellock Died Today (novel), HarperCollins (Toronto, Ontario, Canada), 2006.
(With Bobbie Kalman) *Australian Outback Food Chains,* Crabtree Publishing (New York, NY), 2007.
(With Bobbie Kalman) *Batter up Baseball,* Crabtree Publishing (New York, NY), 2007.
(With Bobbie Kalman) *Savanna Food Chains,* Crabtree Publishing (New York, NY), 2007.
Watch This Space: Designing, Defending, and Sharing Public Spaces, illustrated by Marc Ngui, Kids Can Press (Toronto, Ontario, Canada), 2010.

Author of "Live Better" column, *Globe & Mail;* columnist for *Canadian Family* magazine for eight years. Contributor to periodicals, including *Children's Book News, Quill & Quire, Owl, Chickadee,* and *Toronto Life.*

Sidelights

Hadley Dyer, a publishing industry veteran who has worked as a bookseller, publicist, and library coordinator, is the author of the young-adult novel *Johnny*

Hadley Dyer encourages young readers to view common spaces such as parks and playgrounds differently in her book Watch This Space!, *featuring artwork by Marc Ngui.* (Illustration copyright © 2010 by Marc Ngui. Reproduced by permission of Kids Can Press Ltd., Toronto.)

Kellock Died Today as well as *Watch This Space: Designing, Defending, and Sharing Public Spaces,* a critically acclaimed work of nonfiction. Now an executive editor at HarperCollins Canada, Dyer is also a regular contributor to such publications as *Owl* and *Toronto Life,* and she teaches in the publishing program at Ryerson University.

Born in 1973 in Halifax, Nova Scotia, Dyer was raised in nearby Kingston, where she developed an early interest in writing and storytelling. As she recalled to *Canadian Review of Materials* interviewer Dave Jenkinson, "I think from the time I was about eight or nine years old, I knew writing was something I would like to do. . . . My mom was very encouraging of my writing from the time I was pretty young. I didn't know if I was going to be able to be a full-time writer of books someday, but I thought I would want to do something

with writing or words." After graduating from high school, Dyer returned to Halifax to attend the University of King's College and there she began working at Woozles, a children's book store, while also writing book reviews. "I really cut my teeth on children's literature at Woozles, which was my first big job," she told Jenkinson; "I learned so much . . . about not just what makes a good book but about how kids respond to books, why they like the books they do, and why people choose books."

Dyer later served as a library coordinator for the Canadian Children's Book Centre, a marketing manager for Groundwood Books, and an editor for James Lorimer & Company. "I'm part of that last gasp of people who work in publishing or in journalism who didn't need a certificate to get in and where the sum of my experience had value," she admitted in her *Canadian Review*

of Materials interview. During this time, she coauthored a variety of nonfiction books with Bobbie Kalman for Crabtree Publishing. The experience proved valuable, she told Jenkinson. "When you're a writer and you work with a variety of editors, you learn all of these different practices and what works and what doesn't and what's important and how you like to communicate."

Johnny Kellock Died Today won the Canadian Library Association's Book of the Year for Children Award as well as several other honors. Set in 1959, it focuses on Rosalie Norman, a sensitive and curious twelve year old from Halifax. When Rosalie learns that her older cousin, Johnny, has gone missing, she enlists the help of David, a neighbor, to help her investigate Johnny's disappearance, in the process uncovering a host of family secrets. "In the end," Caitlin J. Berry stated in the *Canadian Review of Materials,* "Rosalie discovers that, in order to truly understand life's complexities—those both beautiful and terrible—one must be willing to let old perspectives die away." In *Resource Links* Joanne de Groot offered praise for the work, stating that "Rosalie Norman is a memorable narrator, full of charm and curiosity and a keen sense of observation." Jennifer Waters, writing in *Quill & Quire,* similarly noted of *Johnny Kellock Died Today* that "Rosalie's voice is charmingly original."

In *Watch This Space* Dyer highlights the importance of public spaces, particularly for young adults, and explores ways to create and preserve such areas while touching on such topics as urban design and social justice. Discussing the origins of the book with an interviewer in *Curriculum Review,* she stated: "A lot of my nonfiction for youth has suggested ways for kids to take action on global issues, and I loved the idea of encouraging them to take ownership of their towns and cities." Caroline Higgins, writing in the *Canadian Review of Materials,* maintained that "the true value of *Watch This Space* . . . is providing an entrance for youth into public policy discussions surrounding public space." "Dyer arms her young readers with good information, practical solutions and the responsibility to act now," the critic added.

Biographical and Critical Sources

PERIODICALS

Canadian Review of Materials, March 17, 2006, Caitlin J. Berry, review of *Johnny Kellock Died Today;* May 21, 2010, Caroline Higgins, review of *Watch This Space: Designing, Defending, and Sharing Public Spaces.*

Curriculum Review, April, 2010, review of *Watch This Space,* p. 7.

Globe & Mail (Toronto, Ontario, Canada), April 8, 2006, Susan Perren, review of *Johnny Kellock Died Today,* p. D20.

Kirkus Reviews, February 15, 2010, review of *Watch This Space.*

Publishers Weekly, March 8, 2010, review of *Watch This Space,* p. 58.

Quill & Quire, April, 2006, Jennifer Waters, review of *Johnny Kellock Died Today.*

Resource Links, October, 2005, Rosemary Anderson, review of *Endangered Chimpanzees,* p. 25; April, 2006, Heather Empey, review of *The Life Cycle of an Ant,* p. 33; October, 2006, Joanne de Groot, review of *Johnny Kellock Died Today,* p. 34; April, 2007, Maria Forte, reviews of *Australian Outback Food Chains* and *Savanna Food Chains,* both p. 25.

School Library Journal, December, 2005, Kathy Piehl, review of *Endangered Chimpanzees,* p. 125; June, 2007, Judith V. Lechner, reviews of *Australian Outback Food Chains* and *Savanna Food Chains,* both p. 134; May, 2010, Jody Kopple, review of *Watch This Space,* p. 130.

ONLINE

Canadian Review of Materials Online, http://umanitoba.ca/outreach/cm/profiles/ (December, 2007), Dave Jenkinson, profile of Dyer."

Hadley Dyer Web log, http://hadleydyer.blogspot.com (April 15, 2011).

Kids Can Press Web site, http://www.kidscanpress.com/ (April 15, 2011), "Hadley Dyer."*

F-G

FAWCETT, Katie Pickard

Personal

Born in Barbourville, KY; married; children: one son. *Education:* Union College, B.S. *Hobbies and other interests:* Travel, birdwatching, gardening, reading, cooking.

Addresses

Home—McLean, VA. *E-mail*—Klzfawcett@gmail.com.

Career

Social worker and writer. Social worker in Knox County, KY, c. early 1970s; counselor and tutor in McLean, VA; freelance copywriter for international nonprofits and other agencies. Volunteer in Fairfax County, VA, public schools; cofounder of an orphanage library in San Miguel de Allende, Mexico.

Member

Nature Conservancy, Audubon Society, National Geographic Society.

Awards, Honors

Best Children's Book designation, Bank Street College of Education, 2010, for *To Come and Go like Magic.*

Writings

To Come and Go like Magic, Alfred A. Knopf (New York, NY), 2010.

Contributor of articles to periodicals.

Sidelights

Katie Pickard Fawcett was raised in eastern Kentucky, and she uses this region as the setting for her first novel, *To Come and Go like Magic.* A freelance writer who has worked for organizations ranging from the World Bank to the Peace Corps, Fawcett also worked as a counselor to families living in the coal-mining regions of Appalachia, where poverty and isolation have combined to create a uniquely clannish rural American culture.

Set in 1975, *To Come and Go like Magic* introduces Chili Sue Mahoney, a twelve year old who has never left her Kentucky home town. Things are crowded in the Mahoney's house now that several relatives have taken refuge there, and now her older sister has returned, pregnant and fleeing from a brief and unhappy marriage. When a former town resident, Miss Matlock, returns years after leaving town, earning her college education, and living well-traveled life, Chili is excited to find that the elderly woman will be teaching her seventh-grade class. As the girl listens to the new teacher's stories of the wider world, however, she begins to realize that Miss Matlock's view of their shared home town is very different from her own, and that the close-knit community of Mercy Hill, Kentucky, may be less a prison and more an oasis in the wider world.

Reviewing Fawcett's middle-grade novel in *School Library Journal,* Kim Dare noted that "Chili is a likable protagonist"whose "descriptions of family and friends make them fully realized characters in their own right." Praising the author's "engaging, lyrical" tale, Courtney Jones added in *Booklist* that *To Come and Go like Magic* "is laced with wistful longing even while exploring heady themes like gender, class, love, and loyalty," while a *Publishers Weekly* critic wrote that Chili's "insights are absorbing and her setbacks heartbreaking."

Cover of Katie Picard Fawcett's novel To Come and Go like Magic, *featuring artwork by Jen Lobo.* (Cover copyright © 2010 by Knopf Children. Reproduced by permission of Alfred A. Knopf, an imprint of Random House Children's Books, a division of Random House, Inc.)

Biographical and Critical Sources

PERIODICALS

Booklist, March 1, 2010, Courtney Jones, review of *To Come and Go like Magic,* p. 74.

Bulletin of the Center for Children's Books, March, 2010, Hope Morrison, review of *To Come and Go like Magic,* p. 285.

Journal of Adolescent & Adult Literacy, September, 2010, Hannah Peevey, review of *To Come and Go like Magic,* p. 71.

Kirkus Reviews, February 15, 2010, review of *To Come and Go like Magic.*

Publishers Weekly, February 1, 2010, review of *To Come and Go like Magic,* p. 49.

School Library Journal, February, 2010, Kim Dare, review of *To Come and Go like Magic,* p. 108.

Voice of Youth Advocates, April, 2010, Karen Jensen, review of *To Come and Go like Magic,* p. 56.

ONLINE

Katie Pickard Fawcett Web log, http://katiepickardfawcett.wordpress.com (April 15, 2011).*

FOX, Karen C. 1969-

Personal

Born December 11, 1969, in Washington, DC; daughter of Patricia Smith (founder of nonprofit agencies); married, 2007; husband's name Steve. *Education:* Amherst College, B.S. (physics and English), 1991; University of California, Santa Cruz, M.A. (science writing), 1993.

Addresses

Home—Washington, DC. *E-mail*—kfox@nasw.org.

Career

Author, journalist, and speaker. *Science Report Radio* (radio program), writer and producer, 1994-98; Goddard Space Flight Center, NASA, science writer covering heliophysics and solar science; lecturer on scientific topics.

Member

National Association of Science Writers.

Writings

The Chain Reaction: Profiles in Nuclear Science, Grolier, 1998.

The Big Bang Theory: What It Is, Where It Came From, and Why It Works, Wiley (New York, NY), 2002.

(With Aries Keck) *Einstein: A to Z,* J. Wiley (Hoboken, NJ), 2004.

Older than the Stars, illustrated by Nancy Davis, Charlesbridge (Watertown, MA), 2010.

Contributor of articles to periodicals, including *Amherst Magazine, Discover, MIT Technology Review, Nature, Popular Mechanics, Science & Spirit,* and *USA Weekend.* Online relationship columnist, under name "The Dating Diva," 1997-2001.

Sidelights

A journalist and columnist, Karen C. Fox has a special expertise in solar physics, astronomy, and the history of science, and she works to inspire interest in these subjects in her writing for both adults and children. In her books *The Chain Reaction: Profiles in Nuclear Science* and *The Big Bang Theory: What It Is, Where It Came From, and Why It Works,* as well as in her magazine articles and her work for agencies such as the National Institute of Standards and Technology, Fox translates the work of scientists into a format that lay audiences can both understand and find interesting.

Although her childhood dream was to be a physicist, Fox double-majored in physics and English while earning her B.S. at Amherst College in western Massachu-

setts. She ultimately decided against further science study and instead pursued a career in science writing. After earning an advanced degree in science communication, Fox wrote and produced a science radio program. During that time, she also wrote *The Chain Reaction,* her first book, and shared relationship advice under the moniker "The Dating Diva" for AOL and for Dating911.com. In 1999 Fox began a full-time freelance-writing career focusing on scientific topcis and she published *The Big Bang Theory* in 2002. Praising *The Big Bang Theory* in *Science News,* a contributor maintained that Fox's "accessible and engaging introduction" to the theory by which many scientists explain the formation of the universe incorporates both the factual basis for the hypothesis and the "emerging theories" that now compete with it.

In *Older than the Stars* Fox teams up with illustrator Nancy Davis to translate the Big Bang theory into terms that early-elementary-grade children can understand. Using the cumulative format of the nursery rhyme "The House That Jack Built," she takes readers from the Big Bang that created the universe to the gradual ordering of matter into planets, oceans and mountains, and diverse forms of life. "Fox and Davis tackle the challenge of creating an engaging read-aloud about the Big Bang theory with energy and style," asserted *School Library Journal* contributor Kathleen Kelly MacMillan, the critic adding that the book's use of repetition makes it "an intriguing introduction to a difficult-to-understand concept" that is "perfect for the classroom." In *Kirkus Reviews* a contributor also praised the book, recommending its timeline and glossary as well as Fox's inclusion of "breezy paragraph[s] of more comprehensive" information. Other books by Fox include *Einstein: A to Z,* a collaboration with fellow journalist Aries Keck that features over a hundred facets of the life of German-born physicist Albert Einstein, from "absentmindedness" to "Zionism." Writing in *Science News,* a contributor praised *Einstein: A to Z* as "an accessible and lively overview of this iconic figure."

Biographical and Critical Sources

PERIODICALS

Kirkus Reviews, January 1, 2010, review of *Older than the Stars.*
School Library Journal, February, 2010, Kathleen Kelly MacMillan, review of *Older than the Stars,* p. 100.
Science News, April 20, 2002, review of *The Big Bang Theory: What It Is, Where It Came From, and Why It Works,* p. 255; August 14, 2004, review of *Einstein: A to Z.*

ONLINE

Charlesbridge Web site, http://www.charlesbridge.com/ (April 15, 2011), interview with Fox.

Karen C. Fox Home Page, http://www.karenceliafox.com (April 24, 2011).

*   *   *

GARCIA, Kami 1972-

Personal

Born 1972; married; children: one son, one daughter. *Education:* Earned M.A. (education). *Hobbies and other interests:* Reading, painting, watching disaster movies.

Addresses

Home—Los Angeles, CA. *E-mail*—kamigarcia@aol. com.

Career

Educator, writer, and artist. Taught in Washington, DC; reading specialist based in CA. *Exhibitions:* Garcia's paintings have been shown in Santa Monica, CA.

Awards, Honors

(With Margaret Stohl) Morris Award finalist, American Library Association, 2010, for *Beautiful Creatures.*

Writings

"BEAUTIFUL CREATURES" NOVEL SERIES; WITH MARGARET STOHL

Beautiful Creatures, Little, Brown (New York, NY), 2009.
Beautiful Darkness, Little, Brown (New York, NY), 2010.
Beautiful Chaos, Little, Brown (New York, NY), 2011.

Sidelights

A reading specialist based in California, Kami Garcia is the coauthor, along with Margaret Stohl, of the Southern Gothic romance *Beautiful Creatures,* the first work in their "Beautiful Creatures" series. The novel follows the adventures of Ethan Wate, a smart, sensitive adolescent who feels stifled both at home and at school. Ethan's life changes when Lena Duchannes, a mysterious girl from Ethan's dreams, arrives in town under a dreaded curse. "I write for teens because, as a teacher, those are the people I spend time with," Garcia remarked to Lyn Burns during a *Young Adult Library Services Association Web log* interview. "Those are the people I know. I also believe that YA is the most important genre in literature because finding the right book as a teen—when everything is so lonely and frightening and out of control—can change your life. More importantly, it can remind you that you aren't alone."

Garcia and Stohl began writing *Beautiful Creatures* in response to a challenge from Stohl's daughters: to create a story with a strong female character who does not

Kami Garcia (Photograph by Vania Stoyanova. Reproduced by permission.)

simply serve as the love interest for a male protagonist. Originally titled "Sixteen Moons," the work quickly took form as the pair dashed off a new chapter every few days, at the constant urging of Stohl's children and their classmates. "We were writing as fast as we could," Garcia told Jessica Harrison in the *Deseret News.* "And when we finished, it was virally going through two or three high schools." After one of Stohl's friends, author Pseudonymous Bosch, caught wind of the project, he sent the manuscript to his agent, who eventually sold it to Little, Brown & Company.

Beautiful Creatures takes place in the fictional town of Gatlin, South Carolina, a setting based in part on Garcia's childhood memories of visiting relatives in rural North Carolina and in part on Stohl's family roots in a small town in the west. Ethan, a high-school sophomore, wants nothing more than to leave his hometown, which is cloaked in a suffocating history. When Lena, the niece of Gatlin's reclusive Macon Ravenwood, enrolls at his school, Ethan recognizes her as the girl who haunts his dreams. As the two learn that they can communicate telepathically, Ethan discovers that Lena comes from a family of magical Casters and will be claimed by light or dark (essentially good or evil) forces on her sixteenth birthday. "The intensity of Ethan and Lena's need to be together is palpable, [and] the detailed descriptions create a vivid, authentic world," observed *School Library Journal* critic Amy J. Chow. A reviewer in *Publishers Weekly* also praised *Beautiful Creatures,* declaring that "readers who like angst-filled teenage romance will be swept up by the haunting and detailed atmosphere." Lidia Perez, writing in the *Jour-*

nal of Adolescent & Adult Literacy, noted that "Garcia and Stohl write clearly and lyrically, appealing to the dreamer in all young adults and keeping them captivated."

Garcia and Stohl have also completed *Beautiful Darkness* and *Beautiful Chaos,* which continue the series. "Our books really deal with the idea of being yourself and being brave enough to be yourself in a community or world where you might be different," Garcia told Harrison. "With kids, teens are going through that all the time right now. . . . They're trying to be themselves and be their own person but at the same time, everybody wants to be part of a community and fit in also. It's a really difficult thing to do."

Biographical and Critical Sources

PERIODICALS

Booklist, November 1, 2009, Ilene Cooper, review of *Beautiful Creatures,* p. 31; October 1, 2010, Ilene Cooper, review of *Beautiful Darkness,* p. 83.

Cover of Garcia and Margaret Stohl's first collaborative Southern gothic novel, **Beautiful Creatures.** (Little, Brown & Company, 2010. Reproduced by permission of Little, Brown & Company, a division of Hachette Book Group, Inc.)

Deseret News (Salt Lake City, UT), October 16, 2010, Jessica Harrison, "*Beautiful Darkness* Authors Garcia, Stohl in Tune with Complexities of Teenage Life."

Journal of Adolescent & Adult Literacy, October, 2010, Lidia Perez, review of *Beautiful Creatures,* p. 154.

Kirkus Reviews, December 1, 2009, review of *Beautiful Creatures.*

Publishers Weekly, November 16, 2009, review of *Beautiful Creatures,* p. 55.

School Librarian, spring, 2010, Sandra Bennett, review of *Beautiful Creatures,* p. 47.

School Library Journal, December, 2009, Amy J. Chow, review of *Beautiful Creatures,* p. 118.

ONLINE

Amazon.com, http://www.amazon.com/ (April 15, 2011), interview with Garcia and Margaret Stohl.

Beautiful Creatures Web site, http://beautifulcreaturesthebook.com (April 15, 2011).

Kami Garcia Web log, http://kamimgarcia.typepad.com (April 15, 2011).

Salt Lake Tribune Online, http://www.sltrib.com/ (February 17, 2011), Sheena McFarland, "*Beautiful Darkness* Gives Girls the Power."

Young Adult Library Services Association Web log, http://yalsa.ala.org/blog/ (December 21, 2009), Liz Burns, interview with Garcia and Margaret Stohl.

*   *   *

GARDNER, Sally

Personal

Born in England; children: twin daughters, one son. *Education:* Degree from London art college (with highest honors); attended theatre school.

Addresses

Home—North London, England.

Career

Children's book author and illustrator. Theatre designer in London, England, for fifteen years, specializing in costume design.

Awards, Honors

Smarties' Book Prize Bronze Award, 2003, for *The Countess's Calamity;* Carnegie Medal longlist inclusion, and Nestlé Children's Book Prize Gold Award, both 2005, and British Children's Book of the Year shortlist inclusion, 2006, all for *I, Coriander;* London *Guardian* Award longlist selection, 2009, for *The Silver Blade;* various awards for costume design.

Writings

FOR CHILDREN; SELF-ILLUSTRATED

The Little Nut Tree, Tambourine Books (New York, NY), 1993.

My Little Princess, Orion (London, England), 1994.

A Book of Princesses, Orion (London, England), 1997.

The Fairy Catalogue: All You Need to Make a Fairy Tale, Orion (London, England), 2000, published as *The Fairy Tale Catalog: Everything You Need to Make a Fairy Tale,* Chronicle Books (San Francisco, CA), 2001.

(Adaptor) *The Glass Heart: A Tale of Three Princesses* (based on "Die drie Schwestern mit den gläsernen Herzen" by Richard Volkmann-Leander), Orion (London, England), 2001.

(And illustrator) *Mama, Don't Go out Tonight,* Bloomsbury Children's Books (New York, NY), 2002, published as *Mummy, Don't Go out Tonight,* Bloomsbury (London, England), 2002.

Fairy Shopping, Orion (London, England), 2003.

Lucy Willow, illustrated by Peter Bailey, Orion (London, England), 2006.

The Red Necklace: A Story of the French Revolution, Orion (London, England), 2007, Dial Books (New York, NY), 2008.

The Silver Blade (sequel to *The Red Necklace*), Dial Books (New York, NY), 2009.

"MAGICAL CHILDREN" SERIES; SELF-ILLUSTRATED

The Strongest Girl in the World (also see below), Dolphin (London, England), 1999.

The Smallest Girl Ever (also see below), Dolphin (London, England), 2000.

The Boy Who Could Fly (also see below), Dolphin (London, England), 2001.

The Invisible Boy (also see below), Dolphin (London, England), 2002.

The Boy with the Magic Numbers, Dolphin (London, England), 2003.

Magical Children (includes *The Strongest Girl in the World, The Invisible Boy,* and *The Boy Who Could Fly*), Dolphin (London, England), 2004.

The Boy with Lightning Feet, illustrated by Lydia Corry, Dolphin (London, England), 2006.

Magical Kids: The Strongest Girl in the World/The Invisible Boy, Dial (New York, NY), 2007.

Magical Kids: The Boy Who Could Fly/The Smallest Girl Ever, Dial (New York, NY), 2009.

"TALES FROM THE BOX" SERIES; SELF-ILLUSTRATED

The Countess's Calamity, Bloomsbury Children's Books (New York, NY), 2003.

Boolar's Big Day Out, Bloomsbury Children's Books (New York, NY), 2003.

ILLUSTRATOR

Marjorie Newman, *Robert and the Giant,* Hamish Hamilton (London, England), 1990.

Beverley Birch, *Suzi, Sam, George, and Alice,* Bodley Head (London, England), 1993.

Playtime Rhymes, Orion (London, England), 1995.

Adrian Mitchell, *Gynormous: The Ultimate Book of Giants,* Orion (London England), 1996.

Jostein Gaarder, *Hello? Is Anybody There?,* translated by James Anderson, Farrar, Straus & Giroux (New York, NY), 1998.

Georgie Adams, *The Real Fairy Storybook,* Orion (London, England), 1998.

Frances Thomas, *Polly's Running Away Book,* Bloomsbury (London, England), 2000, published as *Polly's Really Secret Diary,* Delacorte Press (New York, NY), 2002.

Frances Thomas, *Polly's Absolutely Worst Birthday Ever,* Bloomsbury (London, England), 2001, Delacorte Press (New York, NY), 2003.

OTHER

I, Coriander (young-adult novel), Dial (New York, NY), 2005.

Adaptations

The Boys with the Magic Numbers was adapted for audiobook, read by Stephen Greif, Chivers Children's Audio, 2005. *I, Coriander* was adapted for audiobook, read by Juliet Stevenson, Listening Library, 2006. *The Red Necklace* was adapted for audiobook, read by Carrington Macduffie, Listening Library, 2008. Orion adapted several other books by Gardner as book-and-CD packages.

Sidelights

During Sally Gardner's school-aged years, poor reading skills found the British schoolgirl struggling to pass class after class. No one—least of all Gardner herself—would have guessed that she would eventually grow up to become a successful children's book author. Fortunately, her difficulty with reading was combatted once she was diagnosed with dyslexia, and Gardner's whimsical imagination and unique perspective now finds an outlet in self-illustrated picture books such as *The Little Nut Tree* and *Mama, Don't Go out Tonight* as well as chapter books such as *The Countess's Calamity* and the multi-volume "Magical Children" series: *The Invisible Boy, The Boy Who Could Fly, The Smallest Girl Ever,* and *The Strongest Girl in the World.* Written for older readers, Gardner's young-adult novels include *The Red Necklace: A Story of the French Revolution, The Silver Blade,* and *I, Coriander,* the last which earned its author the coveted 2006 Nestlé Children's Book Prize in her native England.

Born and raised in London, Gardner found her success in school hampered by the fact that, due to dyslexia, she could neither read nor write until her early teens. In fact, she even changed her first name from Sarah to Sally so she would be able to spell it correctly. Dismissed from several schools after being deemed uneducable, Gardner was eventually enrolled in a program for maladjusted children. Fortunately, by the time she reached age fourteen, advances in learning allowed her to deal with her condition, and the first book she read was Charlotte Brontë's *Wuthering Heights.* Writers that soon became favorites included Charles Dickens, E. Nesbit, Rachel Compton, and Jane Austen; in fact, Gardner still ranks Dickens' *Great Expectations* as her favorite book of all time.

While reading was not Gardner's strong suit, her talent for dealing with three-dimensional form combined with her strong artistic sense to fuel her success at art college and eventually earn a scholarship to study theatre design. For the next fifteen years Gardner worked on the London stage as a designer, and her costume designs won her several awards. She moved to book illustration following the births of twin daughters and a son, and from there to writing. Her first self-illustrated picture book, *The Little Nut Tree,* was published in 1994 and has also been translated into Spanish.

Gardner's picture books and chapter books often feature fairytale themes and magical elements. *Mama, Don't Go out Tonight,* a picture book praised for its "gentle humor" by *Booklist* contributor Ellen Mandel, finds a young girl conjuring up a series of fantastical catastrophes that might potentially befall her mother on a night out: from being captured by pirates to becoming a monster's evening appetizer. Her "Tales from the Box" chapter-book series brings to life the story of five abandoned dolls as they struggle to survive in a hostile world. Helped by a nearby mouse family in *The Countess's Calamity,* Boolar, Stitch, the Chinese doll Ting Tang, the sailor doll Quilt, and the Countess are appreciative of their new home, although the fashionably dressed Countess demands a more luxurious abode. Ultimately, when her life is threatened by the sinister Mr. Cuddles, a local cat, the now-tattered doll learns to appreciate the charity of others with the help of a new heart. In *School Library Journal* Susan Helper praised *The Countess's Calamity* for its "fresh and lively" plot, while a *Publishers Weekly* writer deemed it a "diverting and clever fantasy."

Gardner's diminutive doll saga continues in *Boolar's Big Day Out,* as the resourceful Boolar leaves the group to join a puppet troupe as the lead in a production of *The Adventures of Tom Thumb.* While his time away is supposed to be brief, Boolar quickly falls in love with the performing life as well as with his captivating marionette costar. With cold weather coming, the dolls left behind are forced to seek much-needed supplies for themselves, forgotten by their stage-struck friend. Ultimately, however, Boolar learns about the theatre's fickle side and when his leading role is given to another he returns to the toy box, where all is forgiven. Reviewing *Boolar's Big Day Out,* a *Kirkus Reviews* writer praised

Part of Sally Gardner's "Tales from the Box" series, **The Countess's Calamity** *finds a mouse family befriending a group of lost dolls.* (Bloomsbury Publishing, PLC, 2003. Illustration copyright © 2003. Reproduced by permission.)

Gardner's "charming pencil drawings," while JoAnn Jonas deemed the tale a "satisfying read" in her review for *School Library Journal.* Jonas further praised *Boolar's Big Day Out,* noting that it boasts "engaging writing, an entertaining story line, plus a lesson in friendship and loyalty."

Set in London during the 1600s, *I, Coriander* weaves together fantasy and history in its story of the unhappy daughter of a silk merchant. Following the death of England's King Charles I and the rise to power of Oliver Cromwell, Coriander Hobie's widowed father is forced to flee due to his loyalty to the English crown. Left in the care of an unloving stepmother, the imaginative nine year old is now an obstacle for the grasping woman and her friend, a coldhearted Puritan minister. Locked in a trunk and left to die, the girl instead finds herself in a dream world where she learns that her real mother, a fairy princess, has left her with a quest: to locate a secret object and save fairyland from the control of a destructive queen. The story's use of time shifts— Coriander ages six years during the retrospective tale— and Gardner's juxtaposition of "turbulent seventeenth-century London and the shimmering mysteries of fairyland" reflect the history of England's tumultuous Restoration period, as Jennifer Mattson noted in *Booklist,* the critic adding that *I, Coriander* presents readers with a rewarding challenge. In *Kliatt* Janis Flint-Ferguson characterized the novel as "one of good triumphing over evil and of true love saving the lives of honest people," while Beth Wright deemed *I, Coriander* an "absorbing, picturesque tale." Also commenting on Gardner's use of time travel and dual worlds, Wright predicted that the novel will appeal to both fantasy fans and those who enjoy historical fiction, while "readers who love romantic fairy tales will delight" in Coriander's discovery of true love and "the way her dual heritage allows her to honor her human father and still have her fairy prince." "Deft and dulcet language . . . and the tie to a grim historical season will hold readers fast," predicted a *Kirkus Reviews* writer of Gardner's award-winning novel.

In *The Red Necklace* Gardner takes readers back to late-eighteenth-century France, as fourteen-year-old gypsy ventriloquist and magician's assistant Yann Margoza is drawn into the world of Sidonie, the twelve-year-old daughter of a corrupt aristocrat. As the people around him begin to revolt against the French noble families, Yann also hopes to avenge the death of his former employer at the hand of a villainous and murderous count. In *Kliatt* Claire Rosser noted the "challenging vocabulary and historical reverences" that enrich Gardner's historical novel, while a *Kirkus Reviews* writer wrote of the melodramatic story that "Gardner keeps tight control over [her] . . . lush tale of magic, betrayal and Revolution. "Enthrallingly told . . . ," according to London *Sunday Times* critic Nicolette Jones, *The Red Necklace* "offers action, surprises and protagonists to care about."

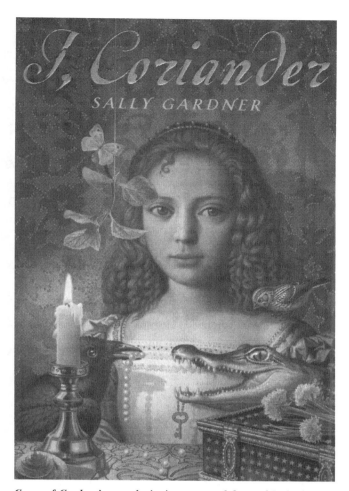

Cover of Gardner's award-winning young-adult novel **I, Coriander,** *featuring cover art by Dan Craig.* (Illustration © 2005 by Dan Craig. Reproduced by permission of Dial Books, a division of Penguin Putnam Books for Young Readers, a member of Penguin (USA) Inc., 345 Hudson St., NY 10014. All rights reserved.)

Continuing Gardner's story of the French Revolution, *The Silver Blade* draws on the legend of the Scarlet Pimpernel in describing Yann's efforts to save French aristocrats from a date with Madame Guillotine as Robespierre's policies usher in the notorious Reign of Terror. Although he believes Sidonie to be safe in England, the news of her kidnapping forces the gypsy to turn his attention to her abductor, the evil Count Kalliovski. In a story that Sue Giffard described in *School Library Journal* as "skillfully plotted and with an unflagging pace," Gardner captures "the fears and anxieties of ordinary people" in her "gorgeous writing and evocative descriptions." Reviewing *The Silver Blade* in the London *Times,* Amanda Craig drew comparisons between Gardner's novel and the works of authors such as Angela Carter and Charles Dickens, writing that "the resonance of traditional fantasy is woven into a first-rate suspense novel" in which "the tension between the cruel steel and frail flesh is heightened by ardent love." "With its reversals, surprises, scholarship and dramatic details of an era so soaked in blood that the Seine ran red," added Craig, "*The Silver Blade* is historical fiction at its height." "A luscious melodrama," according to a *Kirkus Reviews* writer, *The Silver Blade* is also "rich in

sensuous detail from horrific to sublime, with an iridescent overlay of magic" that will tantalize teen readers.

As an illustrator, Gardner has created art for Frances Thomas's amusing diaries of a nine year old named Polly, whose antic life is recounted in *Polly's Running Away Book*—published as *Polly's Really Secret Diary* in the United States—and *Polly's Absolutely Worst Birthday Ever*. She has also served as illustrator for Jostein Gaarder's novel *Hello? Is Anybody There?*, a story about a boy's encounter with a young space traveler. Through what a *Kirkus Reviews* writer characterized as a "combination of childlike pencil illustrations, magazine cut-outs, clip-art, and family photos," Gardner effectively brings to life the "frenetic, yet completely believable" account of Thomas's spunky and single-minded narrator in *Polly's Absolutely Worst Birthday Ever*.

"Fairy tales are the soul of the world," Gardner explained to Orion Web site contributor Danuta Kean while discussing her motivation for writing for children. "They talk of great universal truths in a way that is ac-

cessible. When you write about a child living in a tower block with a crackhead mother, it is too close to her reality for her to see what else is in the story." However, "place her in a fairy tower with a horrible witch whom she is trying to escape," the author added, "and she can take inspiration from the message that good can triumph over evil."

Biographical and Critical Sources

PERIODICALS

Booklist, June 1, 2002, Kelly Milner Halls, review of *Polly's Really Secret Diary,* p. 1726; January 1, 2003, Ellen Mandel, review of *Mama, Don't Go out Tonight,* p. 906; July, 2003, Kay Weisman, review of *Polly's Absolutely Worst Birthday Ever,* p. 1892; August, 2005, Jennifer Mattson, review of *I, Coriander,* p. 2015; April 15, 2008, Ilene Cooper, review of *The Red Necklace: A Story of the French Revolution,* p. 54; December 15, 2008, Hazel Rochman, review of *Magical Kids: The Smallest Girl Ever/The Boy Who Could Fly,* p. 44; August 1, 2009, Ilene Cooper, review of *The Silver Blade,* p. 61.

Guardian (London, England), February 23, 2008, Adéle Géras, review of *The Red Necklace,* p. 20.

Horn Book, November-December, 2005, Jennifer M. Brabander, review of *I, Coriander,* p. 719; July-August, 2008, Megan Lynn Isaac, review of *The Red Necklace,* p. 444; September-October, 2009, Megan Lynn Isaac, review of *The Silver Blade,* p. 559.

Kirkus Reviews, June 1, 2003, review of *Polly's Absolutely Worst Birthday Ever,* p. 812; November 1, 2003, review of *Boolar's Big Day Out,* p. 1310; July 15, 2005, review of *I, Coriander,* p. 789; February 15, 2007, review of *Magical Kids: The Smallest Girl Ever/The Boy Who Could Fly*; April 1, 2008, review of *The Red Necklace*; August 1, 2009, review of *The Silver Blade.*

Kliatt, September, 2005, Janis Flint-Ferguson, review of *I, Coriander,* p. 8; May, 2008, Claire Rosser, review of *The Red Necklace,* p. 8.

Publishers Weekly, May, 23, 1994, review of *The Little Nut Tree,* p. 87; August 10, 1998, review of *Hello? Is Anybody There?,* p. 388; June 3, 2002, review of *Polly's Really Secret Diary,* p. 88; October 28, 2002, review of *Mama, Don't Go out Tonight,* p. 71; March 24, 2003, review of *The Countess's Calamity,* p. 76; July 18, 2005, review of *I, Coriander,* p. 206; March 12, 2007, review of *Magical Kids: The Strongest Girl in the World/The Invisible Boy,* p. 58; May 26, 2008, review of *The Red Necklace,* p. 66.

School Librarian, spring, 1998, reviews of *Hello? Is Anybody out There?* and *A Book of Princesses,* both p. 24; spring, 2001, review of *The Fairy Catalogue: All You Need to Make a Fairy Tale,* p. 33; spring, 2002, reviews of *The Glass Heart* and *The Boy Who Could Fly,* both p. 24; winter, 2002, review of *The Invisible Boy,* p. 186; autumn, 2003, review of *The Countess's Calamity,* p. 136; autumn, 2005, Barbara Sherrard-

Cover of Gardner's young-adult novel The Silver Blade, *a sequel to* **The Red Necklace** *that is also set during the French Revolution.* (Cover photography by Michael Frost. Reproduced by permission of Dial Books for Young Readers, a division of Penguin Young Readers Group, a member of Penguin (USA) Inc., 345 Hudson St., NY 10014. All rights reserved.)

Smith, review of *I, Coriander,* p. 155; autumn, 2006, Rosemary Woodman, review of *The Boy with the Lightning Feet,* p. 141.

School Library Journal, July, 1994, Cyrisse Jaffee, review of *The Little Nut Tree,* p. 76; August, 2002, Marietta Barral Zacker, review of *The Fairy Catalog,* p. 55, and Amy Stultz, review of *Polly's Really Secret Diary,* p. 171; December, 2002, Steven Engelfried, review of *Mama, Don't Go out Tonight,* p. 96; August, 2003, Susan Hepler, review of *The Countess's Calamity,* p. 128; November, 2003, Carolyn Janssen, review of *Polly's Absolutely Worst Birthday Ever,* p. 116; January, 2004, JoAnn Jonas, review of *Boolar's Big Day Out,* p. 98; September, 2005, Beth Wright, review of *I, Coriander,* p. 203; August, 2006, Veronica Schwartz, review of *The Boy with the Magic Numbers,* p. 53; July, 2007, Kathleen Meulen, review of *Magical Kids: The Strongest Girl in the World/The Invisible Boy,* p. 76; May, 2008, Jill Heritage Maza, review of *The Red Necklace,* p. 124; February, 2009, Elaine Lesh Morgan, review of *Magical Kids: The Boy Who Could Fly/The Smallest Girl Ever,* p. 74; November, 2009, Sue Giffard, review of *The Silver Blade,* p. 106.

Sunday Times (London, England), November 4, 2007, Nicolette Jones, review of *The Red Necklace,* p. 56.

Times Educational Supplement, November 16, 2001, review of *The Boy Who Could Fly,* p. 20; September 5, 2003, review of *The Countess's Calamity,* p. 14; July 29, 2005, Linda Newbery, review of *I, Coriander,* p. 26.

ONLINE

BookBrowse, http://www.bookbrowse.com/ (August 15, 2005), interview with Gardner.

Guardian Unlimited, http://books.guardian.co.uk/ (December 14, 2005), Michelle Pauli, "Dyslexic Writer Savours Nestlé Victory."

Orion Web site, http://www.orionbooks.co.uk/ (March 7, 2007), Danuta Kean, interview with Gardner.

Sally Gardner Home Page, http://www.sallygardner.net (April 20, 2011).*

* * *

GRAHAM, Ian 1953-
(James Young)

Personal

Born September 9, 1953, in Belfast, Northern Ireland. *Education:* City University, London, B.S. (applied physics), 1975, graduate diploma (journalism), 1978. *Hobbies and other interests:* Keeping fish, growing bonsai trees, crosswords, photography, lateral thinking, coin collecting, banknote collecting, special-issue stamp collecting, watching too much television.

Addresses

Home—Ash Vale, England.

Career

Freelance writer and editor, 1982—. Argus Specialist Publications, member of editorial staff, serving as assistant editor of *Electronics Today International,* and deputy editor of *Which Video,* 1978-82. Consultant editor to magazines *Space Voyager,* 1983-84, and *Micro Challenge,* 1985.

Member

American Institute of Aeronautics & Astronautics, Authors' Lending & Copyright Society, British Association for the Advancement of Science, British Interplanetary Society, Institute of Journalist, Society of Authors, Farnborough Air Sciences Association, Mensa.

Writings

NONFICTION

Computer and Video Games, Usborne (London, England), 1982.

(With Lynn Myring) *Information Revolution,* Usborne (London, England), 1983.

The Inside Story: Computer, illustrated by Denis Bishop and others, Gloucester Press (New York, NY), 1983.

(With Helen Varley) *The Personal Computer Yearbook,* Pan (London, England), 1983, published as *The Home Computer Handbook: The Foremost Guide to the New Home Technology,* Simon & Schuster (New York, NY), 1984.

(Editor) *Choose Your Own Video: A Guide to Buying the Best Video System for Your Money,* Barron's Educational (Hauppauge, NY), 1983.

Step-by-Step Programming for the Sinclair Spectrum, two volumes, Dorling Kindersley (London, England), 1984.

Step-by-Step Programming for the Sinclair Spectrum Plus, two volumes, Dorling Kindersley (London, England), 1984.

Step-by-Step Programming for the BBC Micro, two volumes, Dorling Kindersley (London, England), 1984.

Step-by-Step Programming for the Acorn Electron, two volumes, Dorling Kindersley (London, England), 1984.

Inventions, Wayland (Hove, England), 1986, published as *Topics: Inventions,* Bookwright Press (New York, NY), 1987.

How to Look after Your Home Computer, Editorial Gustavo Gili (Barcelona, Spain), 1986.

(With Douglas Garr) *The Video Maker's Handbook,* Octopus (London, England), 1986, published as *The Home Video Makers' Handbook,* St. Martin's Press (New York, NY), 1986.

Science Frontiers: Communications, Macdonald (London, England), 1988, Hampstead (New York, NY), 1989.

Science Frontiers: Transportation, Macdonald (London, England), 1988, Hampstead (New York, NY), 1989.

Engineers at Work: Attack Submarine, Gloucester Press (New York, NY), 1989.

Engineers at Work: Salvage at Sea, Gloucester Press (New York, NY), 1990.

Our Solar System, Two-Can Publishing (London, England), 1990, Scholastic (New York, NY), 1991.

The Universe, Two-Can Publishing (London, England), 1990.

Space Travel, Two-Can Publishing (London, England), 1990.

Stars and Galaxies, Two-Can Publishing (London, England), 1990.

Facing the Future: Communications, Raintree Steck-Vaughn (Austin, TX), 1991.

Concorde, Pan (London, England), 1991.

Be an Expert: Astronomer, Gloucester Press (New York, NY), 1991.

Facing the Future: Space Science, Evans Brothers (London, England), 1992, Raintree Steck-Vaughn (Austin, TX), 1993.

Skyscrapers, Pan (London, England), 1992.

Channel Tunnel, Pan (London, England), 1992.

Facing the Future: Transport, Evans Brothers (London, England), 1992, published as *Facing the Future: Transportation,* Raintree Steck-Vaughn (Austin, TX), 1993.

The Big Book of Flight, Hamlyn (London, England), 1993.

How Things Work: Cars, Bikes, Trains, and Other Land Machines, Kingfisher (New York, NY), 1993.

How Things Work: Boats, Ships, Submarines, and Other Floating Machines, Kingfisher (London, England), 1993.

101 Questions and Answers: How Things Work, Hamlyn (London, England), 1993, Facts on File (New York, NY), 1995.

Pointers: Cars, illustrated by Mick Gillah, Simon & Schuster (Hemel Hempstead, England), 1993, Raintree Steck-Vaughn (Austin, TX), 1994.

Pointers: Spacecraft, illustrated by Roger Stewart, Simon & Schuster (Hemel Hempstead, England), 1994, Raintree Steck-Vaughn (Austin, TX), 1995.

101 Questions and Answers: Transport, Hamlyn (London, England), 1994.

Transport by Design, Simon & Schuster (Hemel Hempstead, England), 1995, published as *Transport: How It Works,* Sterling (New York, NY), 1995.

How It Goes: Racing Cars, Barron's Educational (Hauppauge, NY), 1995.

How It Goes: Boats, Barron's Educational (Hauppauge, NY), 1995.

Supercutaways: Aircraft and Spacecraft, Colour Library Books (Godalming, England), 1995.

Visual Reality: Aircraft, Vineyard Books (Abingdon, England), 1995.

Discoveries: How Things Work, Time-Life Books (Alexandria, VA), 1996.

(With Paul Sterry) *Questions and Answers Book of Facts,* Vineyard Books (Abingdon, England), 1996, published as *Questions and Answers Book of Science Facts,* Facts on File (New York, NY), 1997.

Worldwise: Photography and Film, illustrated by Nicholas Hewetson, Franklin Watts (New York, NY), 1997.

Collect-a-Classic: Ford Mustang, Templar Communications, 1997.

Collect-a-Classic: Chevrolet Corvette, Templar Communications, 1997.

Spaceflight, Disney (New York, NY), 1997.

Worldwise: Motorcycles, Franklin Watts (New York, NY), 1998.

My Best Book of Spaceships, Kingfisher (London, England), 1998, published as published as *The Best Book of Spaceships,* Kingfisher (New York, NY), 1999.

The World of Computers and Communications, Horus Editions (London, England), 1998, Gareth Stevens (Milwaukee, WI), 2000.

Energy, Motion, and Machines, Miles Kelly Publishing (Great Bardfield, England), 1998.

(With Andrew Langley) *What Do You Know about Science and Technology?: Over 101 Questions and Answers,* Vineyard (Abingdon, England), 1998.

(With Andrew Langley and Paul Sterry) *What Do You Know about Earth and Space?: Over 101 Questions and Answers,* Andromeda Oxford (Abingdon, England), 1998.

My Best Book of the Moon, Kingfisher (London, England), 1999, published as *The Best Book of the Moon,* Kingfisher (New York, NY), 1999.

Investigations: Space, Anness Publishing, 1999.

Future Tech: Space, Belitha Press (London, England), 1999.

Future Tech: Transport, Belitha Press (London, England), 1999.

Space: Now and into the Future, Belitha Press (London, England), 1999.

(With Andrew Langely and Paul Sterry) *The Best Ever Book of Questions and Answers,* Vineyard (Abingdon, England), 1999.

Transport Now and into the Future, illustrated by Alex Pang, Belitha Press (London, England), 1999.

Space, Lorenz (London, England), 1999, published as *All about Space: Amazing Cosmic Facts,* Southwater (London, England), 2000.

How to Fly a 747, Candlewick Press (Cambridge, MA), 2000.

Computers, Hodder Wayland (London, England), 2000, Raintree Steck-Vaughn (Austin, TX), 2001.

The Internet: The Impact on Our Lives, Hodder Wayland (London, England), 2000, Raintree Steck-Vaughn (Austin, TX), 2001.

Music and Sound, Barron's Educational (Hauppauge, NY), 2000.

Satellites and Communications, Hodder Wayland (London, England), 2000, Raintree Steck-Vaughn (Austin, TX), 2001.

Planes, Rockets, and Other Flying Machines, illustrated by Nick Hewetson, Franklin Watts (New York, NY), 2000, revised edition, Book House (Brighton, England), 2009.

Ships and Submarines, illustrated by Dave Antram, Franklin Watts (New York, NY), 2000.

Cars, illustrated by Mark Bergin, Franklin Watts (New York, NY), 2000, revised edition, Book House (Brighton, England), 2009.

Genetics: The Study of Heredity, Ticktock Media (Tunbridge Wells, England), 2001, Gareth Stevens (Milwaukee, WI), 2002.

Super Trucks, illustrated by Nick Hewetson, Franklin Watts (New York, NY), 2001, revised edition, Book House (Brighton, England), 2009.

My Book of Space, Kingfisher (London, England), 2001.

Flight, Kingfisher (London, England), 2001.

Super Bikes, illustrated by Nick Hewetson, Franklin Watts (New York, NY), 2001, revised edition, Book House (Brighton, England), 2009.

Communications, illustrated by Alex Pang, Raintree Steck-Vaughn (Austin, TX), 2001.

Going Digital, Raintree Steck-Vaughn (Austin, TX), 2001.

Wonders of Our World, Time Life Books (Alexandria, VA), 2001.

The Internet Revolution, Heinemann Library (Oxford, England), 2002, Heinemann Library (Chicago, IL), 2003.

My Best Book of Speed Machines, Kingfisher (London, England), 2002, published as *The Best Book of Speed Machines,* Kingfisher (New York, NY), 2002.

Artificial Intelligence, Heinemann Library (Oxford, England), 2002, Heinemann Library (Chicago, IL), 2003.

E.T. the Extra-Terrestrial Discovers the Solar System, Kingfisher (New York, NY), 2002.

E.T. the Extra-terrestrial Discovers Communication, Kingfisher (New York, NY), 2002.

The Caribbean, Franklin Watts (London, England), 2002, Smart Apple Media (Mankato, MN), 2003, revised edition, Franklin Watts (London, England), 2005, Sea-to-Sea Publications (Mankato, MN), 2009.

Judaism, Chrysalis Education (Mankato, MN), 2003.

The Wright Brothers and the Science of Flight, illustrated by David Antram, Book House (Brighton, England), 2003, published as *The Wright Brothers: Pioneers of Flight,* Barron's Educational (Hauppauge, NY), 2003.

Superbikes, Heinemann Library (Chicago, IL), 2003, revised edition, 2008.

Sports Cars, Heinemann Library (Chicago, IL), 2003, revised edition, 2008.

Racing Cars, Heinemann Library (Oxford, England), 2003, published as *Race Cars,* Heinemann Library (Chicago, IL), 2003, revised edition, 2008.

Spain, Franklin Watts (London, England), 2003, revised edition, 2005, Sea-to-Sea Publications (Mankato, MN), 2009.

Pakistan, Franklin Watts (London, England), 2003, revised edition, 2005, Sea-to-Sea Publications (Mankato, MN), 2009.

Off-road Vehicles, Heinemann Library (Chicago, IL), 2003, revised edition, 2008.

Military Vehicles, Heinemann Library (Chicago, IL), 2003, revised edition, 2008.

Kenya, Franklin Watts (London, England), 2003.

Superboats, Heinemann Library (Chicago, IL), 2003, revised edition, 2008.

(With John Farndon) *Discovering Science,* Miles Kelly Publishing (Great Bardfield, England), 2003, MC Publishers, (Broomall, PA), 2004.

Attack Fighters, Heinemann Library (Chicago, IL), 2003, revised edition, 2008.

Nigeria, Smart Apple Media (Mankato, MN), 2004, revised edition, Franklin Watts (London, England), 2006.

Curie and the Science of Radioactivity, illustrated by David Antram, Book House (Brighton, England), 2004, Barron's Educational (Hauppauge, NY), 2006.

Space Travel, Dorling Kindersley (New York, NY), 2004, revised edition, 2006.

Build Your Own Cool Cars, Tangerine Press (New York, NY), 2004.

South Africa, Franklin Watts (London, England), 2004, Smart Apple Media (Mankato, MN), 2005 revised edition, Franklin Watts (London, England), 2006.

The Search for the Ultimate Race Car, Gareth Stevens (Milwaukee, WI), 2005.

Tanks, Raintree (Oxford, England), 2005, Raintree (Chicago, IL), 2006.

Italy, revised edition, Franklin Watts (London, England), 2006.

Trucks and Earthmovers, Raintree (Chicago, IL), 2006.

Motorbikes, Raintree (Chicago, IL), 2006.

Space Vehicles, Raintree (Chicago, IL), 2006.

Race Cars, Raintree (Chicago, IL), 2006.

Mighty Aircraft, Franklin Watts (London, England), 2006, published as *Aircraft,* Smart Apple Media (Mankato, MN), 2007.

Mighty Cars, Franklin Watts (London, England), 2006.

Mighty Ships, Franklin Watts (London, England), 2006.

Warplanes, Raintree (Chicago, IL), 2006.

On the Building Site, QED Publishing (London, England), 2006, published as *At a Construction Site,* QEB Publishing (Laguna Hills, CA), 2006.

On the Farm, QEB Publishing (Laguna Hills, CA), 2006.

On the Water, QEB Publishing (Laguna Hills, CA), 2006.

On the Rails, QED Publishing (London, England), 2006, QEB Publishing (Laguna Hills, CA), 2007.

Emergency!, QEB Publishing (Laguna Hills, CA), 2006.

Cars and Bikes, QED Publishing (London, England), 2006, QEB Publishing (Laguna Hills, CA), 2007.

In the Air, QED Publishing (London, England), 2006, QEB Publishing (Laguna Hills, CA), 2007.

In Space, QED Publishing (London, England), 2006, QEB Publishing (Laguna Hills, CA), 2007.

Trucks, Franklin Watts (London, England), 2006, Smart Apple Media (Mankato, MN), 2008.

The World of Flight, Kingfisher (Boston, MA), 2006.

Voyage through Space, illustrated by Sebastian Quigley and Gary Slater, Barron's Educational (Hauppage, NY), 2007.

Ships, Smart Apple Media (Mankato, MN), 2007.

Machines and Inventions, Children's Press (New York, NY), 2008.

Transport, QED Publishing (London, England), 2008, published as *Transportation,* QED Publishing (Laguna Hills, CA), 2008.

Communication, QEB Publishing (Laguna Hills, CA), 2008.

Dump Trucks and Other Big Machines, QEB Publishing (Irvine, CA), 2008.

Science and Technology, QEB Publishing (Laguna Hills, CA), 2008.

Cars, QEB Publishing (Laguna Hills, CA), 2008.

The Science in a Bicycle: The Science of Forces and More, Franklin Watts (London, England), 2008, published as *The Science of a Bicycle: The Science of Forces,* Gareth Stevens (Pleasantville, NY), 2009.

Earth and the Universe, Book House (Brighton, England), 2008.

Emergency Vehicles, Franklin Watts (London, England), 2008, Smart Apple Media (Mankato, MN), 2009.

Fast Cars, Franklin Watts (London, England), 2008, Smart Apple Media (Mankato, MN), 2009.

Inventions in the Home, QED Publishing (London, England), 2008, QED Publishing (Mankato, MN), 2009.

Bikes, QED Publishing (London, England), 2008.

Monster Trucks, QEB Publishing (Laguna Hills, CA), 2008.

Comets and Asteroids, Smart Apple Media (Mankato, MN), 2008.

Military Technology, Smart Apple Media (Mankato, MN), 2008.

Motorcycles, QEB Publishing (Irvine, CA), 2008.

Stars and Galaxies, Smart Apple Media (Mankato, MN), 2008.

The Far Planets, Smart Apple Media (Mankato, MN), 2008.

The Moon, Smart Apple Media (Mankato, MN), 2008.

The Near Planets, Smart Apple Media (Mankato, MN), 2008.

The Sun, Smart Apple Media (Mankato, MN), 2008.

Farming in the Future, Wayland (London, England), 2009.

Fighting Crime, Heinemann Library (Chicago, IL), 2009.

Food Technology, Smart Apple Media (Mankato, MN), 2009.

(With Jean Coppendale) *The Great Big Book of Mighty Machines,* Firefly (Tonawanda, NY), 2009.

Ripley's Mighty Machines, Ripley Publishing (Orlando, FL), 2009.

Tremendous Tunnels, Franklin Watts (London, England), 2009, Amicus (Mankato, MN), 2011.

Farming and the Future, PowerKids Press (New York, NY), 2010.

Microscopic Scary Creatures, Franklin Watts (New York, NY), 2010.

Technology Careers, Amicus (Mankato, MN), 2010.

Amazing Stadiums, Amicus (Mankato, MN), 2011.

Bullet Trains, QEB Publishing (Mankato, MN), 2011.

Fabulous Bridges, Amicus (Mankato, MN), 2011.

Jet Planes, QEB Publishing (Mankato, MN), 2011.

Military and Government Technology, Raintree (Chicago, IL), 2011.

Speedboats, QEB Publishing (Mankato, MN), 2011.

Supercars, QEB Publishing (Mankato, MN), 2011.

Forensic Technology, Smart Apple Media (Mankato, MN), 2012.

Robot Technology, Smart Apple Media (Mankato, MN), 2012.

What Do We Know about the Solar System?, Raintree (Chicago, IL), 2012.

Contributor to periodicals, including *Air World International, Autocar, Choice, Complete Traveller, Computing Today, Everyday Electronics, Electronics Australia, Fishkeeping Answers, Gold, High Fidelity, Hobby Electronics, Movies, Practical Fishkeeping, Space Voyager, Video Today, Wallace and Grommit's Techno Quest, What Hi-Fi,* and *What Video.* Contributor to reference books, including *Kingfisher Children's Science Encyclopedia,* Kingfisher, 1991, and *Kingfisher Children's Encyclopedia,* 1998.

Also author of books under pseudonym James Young.

"HOW IT WORKS" SERIES

Submarines, Gloucester Press (New York, NY), 1989.

Helicopters, illustrated by Aziz Khan, Gloucester Press (New York, NY), 1989.

Space Shuttles, Gloucester Press (New York, NY), 1989.

Combat Aircraft, Gloucester Press (New York, NY), 1989.

Racing Cars, Gloucester Press (New York, NY), 1990.

Battle Tanks, illustrated by Aziz Khan, Gloucester Press (New York, NY), 1990.

Trucks, illustrated by Aziz Khan, Gloucester Press (New York, NY), 1990.

Television and Video, illustrated by Alex Pang and Ian Moores, Gloucester Press (New York, NY), 1991.

Cameras, Gloucester Press (New York, NY), 1991.

Lasers and Holograms, Gloucester Press (New York, NY), 1991.

Telescopes, Gloucester Press (New York, NY), 1991.

Computers, Gloucester Press (New York, NY), 1992.

"SCIENCE SPOTLIGHT" SERIES

Crime-Fighting, Evans Brothers (London, England), 1993, Raintree Steck-Vaughn (Austin, TX), 1995.

Fighting Disease, Evans Brothers (London, England), 1994, Raintree Steck-Vaughn (Austin, TX), 1995.

Fakes and Forgeries, Evans Brothers (London, England), 1994, Raintree Steck-Vaughn (Austin, TX), 1995.

Astronomy, Evans Brothers (London, England), 1994, Raintree Steck-Vaughn (Austin, TX), 1995.

Sport, Evans Brothers (London, England), 1994, published as *Sports,* Raintree Steck-Vaughn (Austin, TX), 1995.

Stage and Screen, Raintree Steck-Vaughn (Austin, TX), 1995.

"BUILT FOR SPEED" SERIES

Aircraft, illustrated by Tom Connell, Belitha Press (London, England), 1997, Raintree Steck-Vaughn (Austin, TX), 1999.

Boats, illustrated by Tom Connell, Belitha Press (London, England), 1997, Raintree Steck-Vaughn (Austin, TX), 1999.

Cars, illustrated by Tom Connell, Belitha Press (London, England), 1997, Raintree Steck-Vaughn (Austin, TX), 1999.

Motorcycles, illustrated by Tom Connell, Belitha Press (London, England), 1997, Raintree Steck-Vaughn (Austin, TX), 1999.

Motorbikes, illustrated by Tom Connell, Belitha (London, England), 1998, Raintree Steck-Vaughn (Austin, TX), 1999.

"SKY FLIES" SERIES

Modern Passenger Aircraft, Hawkswell Associates (Axminster, England), 1997.
History of Flying Machines, Hawkswell Associates (Axminster, England), 1997.
Record Breakers, Hawkswell Associates (Axminster, England), 1997.
At the Controls, Hawkswell Associates (Axminster, England), 1997.
At the Airport, Hawkswell Associates (Axminster, England), 1997.
Fighters and Bombers, Hawkswell Associates (Axminster, England), 1997.

"ENERGY FOREVER?" SERIES

Water Power, Wayland (Hove, England), 1997, Raintree Steck-Vaughn (Austin, TX), 1999.
Solar Power, Wayland (Hove, England), 1998, Raintree Steck-Vaughn (Austin, TX), 1999.
Wind Power, Wayland (Hove, England), 1998, Raintree Steck-Vaughn (Austin, TX), 1999.
Fossil Fuels, Wayland (Hove, England), 1998, Raintree Steck-Vaughn (Austin, TX), 1999.
Nuclear Power, Raintree Steck-Vaughn (Austin, TX), 1999.
Geothermal and Bio Power, Wayland (Hove, England), 1999, published as *Geothermal and Bio-Energy,* Raintree Steck-Vaughn (Austin, TX), 1999.

"COMMUNICATIONS" SERIES

Books and Newspapers, Evans Brothers (London, England), 1999, Raintree Steck-Vaughn (Austin, TX), 2001.
Photography and Film, Evans Brothers (London, England), 2000, published as *Film and Photography,* Raintree Steck-Vaughn (Austin, TX), 2001.
Radio and TV, Evans Brothers (London, England), 2000, published as *Radio and Television,* Raintree Steck-Vaughn (Austin, TX), 2001.
Global Networks, Evans Brothers (London, England), 2000, Raintree Steck-Vaughn (Austin, TX), 2001.

"RESOURCE OUR WORLD DEPENDS ON" SERIES

Soil, Heinemann Library (Oxford, England), 2004, Heinemann Library (Chicago, IL), 2005.
Rocks, Heinemann Library (Oxford, England), 2004, Heinemann Library (Chicago, IL), 2005.
Minerals, Heinemann Library (Oxford, England), 2004, Heinemann Library (Chicago, IL), 2005.
Water, Heinemann Library (Oxford, England), 2004, Heinemann Library (Chicago, IL), 2005.
Plants, Heinemann Library (Oxford, England), 2004, Heinemann Library (Chicago, IL), 2005.

Fossil Fuels, Heinemann Library (Oxford, England), 2004, Heinemann Library (Chicago, IL), 2005.
Air, Heinemann Library (Oxford, England), 2004, Heinemann Library (Chicago, IL), 2005.

"DANGER ZONE" SERIES

You Wouldn't Want to Work on the Railroad!: A Track You'd Rather Not Go Down, illustrated by David Antram, Franklin Watts (New York, NY), 2001.
Avoid Being on Apollo 13!, illustrated by David Antram, Book House (Brighton, England), 2003.
Avoid Being in the First Submarine!, illustrated by David Antram, Book House (Brighton, England), 2008, published as *You Wouldn't Want to Be in the First Submarine!: An Undersea Expedition You'd Rather Avoid,* Franklin Watts (New York, NY), 2009.
Avoid Flying on the Hindenburg!, illustrated by David Antram, Book House (Brighton, England), 2008, published as *You Wouldn't Want to Be on the Hindenburg!: A Transatlantic Trip You'd Rather Skip,* Franklin Watts (New York, NY), 2009.
Avoid Being a World War II Pilot!, illustrated by David Antram, Book House (Brighton, England), 2009, published as *You Wouldn't Want to Be a World War II Pilot!: Air Battles You Might Not Survive,* Franklin Watts (New York, NY), 2010.

Sidelights

Ian Graham, a prolific nonfiction writer with hundreds of books to his credit, shares his expertise and enthusiasm on a number of topics, in particular the ever-changing areas of science and technology. Among his titles are *How Things Work: Boats, Ships, Submarines, and Other Floating Machines, Bullet Trains,* and the "Danger Zone" series of history books, which includes *You Wouldn't Want to Be on the Hindenburg!: A Transatlantic Trip You'd Rather Skip.* "In general, I find it impossible NOT to write," the Irish-born Graham once admitted to *SATA.* "I am always either writing commissioned books, or writing articles for a major international CAD software company, or penning poetry (usually nonsense rhymes for children)."

Born in 1953, Graham pursued a bachelor of science degree before indulging in his other interest—writing—and earning an advanced degree in journalism. He worked on the editorial staff of Argus Specialist Publications, a trade-magazine publisher, before breaking out into a career as a freelance writer and editor in 1982. Since then, Graham has produced, on average, four or more books a year. While most books are written under his own name, he has published books using the pseudonym James Young on a few occasions.

Graham enjoys informing elementary-aged young people about their ever-changing world, and to this end he has written books on computers and peripheral technology that keep pace with constantly evolving technology. In *The Inside Story: Computer* he discusses every-

thing from microchips to mainframes, showing both how computers are manufactured and how they impact society. Regarded as "accessible and authoritative" by *School Library Journal* reviewer Linda Wadleigh, *The Internet: The Impact on Our Lives* discusses censorship and privacy issues, the World Wide Web's effect on commerce, and other topics. In *Military Technology,* Graham examines developments in land, sea, and air vehicles and weaponry, as well as advancements in satellites and robotics. The combination of his clearly written narrative and the book's photos and graphics "will make [*Military Technology*] especially appealing to reluctant readers," Ed Sullivan noted in his review for *Booklist.*

In *Transportation,* which is part of the "Science Frontiers" series, Graham reviews the various ways in which people and things move over long distances. Against a backdrop of photographs and other illustrations, he explains improvements in transportation that we now benefit from, as well as those, such as solar power, which are still developing. He also looks at trends in technology within the transportation industry, efforts to improve the design of aircraft wings. Praising *Transportation,* as well *Communications* and several other books in the "Science Frontiers" series, *Booklist* contributor Beth Herbert noted that the author's "international approach will be especially welcome to technologically curious youngsters, who will appreciate the well-researched texts."

Graham's *The Great Big Book of Mighty Machines,* co-authored with Jean Coppendale, "offers a visual feast for young gearheads," as Gillian Engberg declared in *Booklist.* This work presents descriptions of transportation and construction vehicles ranging from a simple bicycle to a tractor to a high-speed train. A contributor in *Kirkus Reviews* also applauded the work, observing of *The Great Big Book of Mighty Machines* that even "the youngest grease monkeys will feel completely fulfilled by the heft and breadth of this tome."

Graham has contributed volumes on a wide range of interesting subjects to the "Science Spotlight" series. Not only science but entertainment and social life also come under scrutiny in books such as *Sports, Fighting Disease, Stage and Screen,* and *Fakes and Forgeries.* In *Fighting Disease* Graham focuses on ailments such as coronary disease and other problems that plague modern man and discusses the advances that make these illnesses less of a threat than they were for previous generations. *Fakes and Forgeries* looks at the process whereby works of art are dated and authenticated prior to changing hands, to ensure that private collectors and museums are getting what they are paying for. It also strays beyond the museum walls; other topics Graham includes are the Shroud of Turin, UFO sightings, the Loch Ness monster, and crop circles. In *Sports* training techniques used by modern athletes are explained, and the scientific principles involved in different sporting events are also discussed. While *School Journal* reviewer Ann M. Burlingame remarked of *Sports* that students seeking detailed information about organized athletics will require "additional sources," other reviewers found Graham's coverage to be adequate. Praising the "Science Spotlight" series as a whole, an *Appraisal* contributor concluded that these books "[discuss] in an eminently readable fashion, a large number of sophisticated scientific techniques and concepts," and judged the series to be "well worth the time and effort for readers."

Graham explores the mysteries of the universe in works such as *Voyage through Space,* an interactive title complete with pop-ups and sliding panels. In *The Best Book of Spaceships* the author "does a creditable job" describing various types of rockets and explaining liftoff and reentry procedures, according to *Booklist* contributor Hazel Rochman. Passenger planes, military planes, and cargo planes are the focus of Graham's *Aircraft,* which features cutaway drawings of the machines and their components. In *Booklist* Daniel Kraus described the last-named volume as "good stuff for budding pilots." The author takes a broader view of humankind's attempts to soar through the sky in *Flight,* a book described as being both "systematic" and "visually appealing" by *School Library Journal* critic John Peters.

You Wouldn't Want to Work on the Railroad!: A Track You'd Rather Not Go Down and *You Wouldn't Want to Be in the First Submarine!: An Undersea Expedition You'd Rather Avoid* are part of Graham's "Danger Zone" series, which gives readers an unorthodox look at historical events. In *You Wouldn't Want to Work on the Railroad!* Graham asks readers to put themselves in the place of the immigrant laborers—many of them Chinese—who helped build the transcontinental railroad, describing the often-harsh conditions facing these workers. In *You Wouldn't Want to Be in the First Submarine!* Graham recounts the dangers facing the ill-fated crew of the *H.L. Hunley,* an experimental submersible Confederate ship that saw only brief combat duty before sinking to the bottom of Charleston, South Carolina's outer harbor during the U.S. Civil War. The "lively text" in the latter work garnered praise from *Booklist* reviewer Carolyn Phelan.

Biographical and Critical Sources

PERIODICALS

Appraisal, autumn, 1995, review of "Science Spotlight" series, pp. 88-89.

Booklist, December 15, 1998, Kay Weisman, review of *The Best Book of Spaceships,* p. 753; June 1, 1989, Beth Herbert, review of *Science Frontiers: Transportation,* p. 1720; October 15, 2008, Ed Sullivan, review of *Military Technology,* p. 58; December, 2008, Daniel Kraus, review of *Aircraft,* p. 64; December 1, 2008, Carolyn Phelan, review of *You Wouldn't Want to Be in*

the First Submarine!: An Undersea Expedition You'd Rather Avoid, p. 64; December 15, 2009, Gillian Engberg, review of *The Great Big Book of Mighty Machines*, p. 41.

Kirkus Reviews, November 15, 2009, review of *The Great Big Book of Mighty Machines*.

Publishers Weekly, July 23, 2001, review of *Space*, p. 79; December 3, 2007, review of *Voyage through Space*, p. 73.

School Library Journal, September, 1989, Sylvia S. Marantz, reviews of *Science Frontiers: Communications* and *Science Frontiers: Transportation*, both p. 259; July, 1995, Ann M. Burlingame, review of *Fakes and Forgeries*, p. 86; March, 2001, Kathleen Isaacs, review of *The World of Computers and Communications*, p. 265; November, 2001, Linda Wadleigh, review of *The Internet: The Impact on Our Lives*, p. 176; December, 2001, John Peters, review of *Flight*, p. 161; March, 2002, Ann Chapman, review of *You Wouldn't Want to Work on the Railroad!: A Track You'd Rather Not Go Down*, p. 250; May, 2003, Elizabeth Stumpf, review of *Genetics: The Study of Heredity*, p. 166; November, 2006, Anne Chapman Callaghan, review of *Curie and the Science of Radioactivity*, p. 160; January, 2008, John Peters, review of *Voyage through Space*, p. 139; March, 2009, Christine Markley, review of *Machines and Inventions*, p. 132; December, 2009, Lori A. Guenthner, review of *Microscopic Scary Creatures*, p. 96; March, 2010, Eldon Younce, review of *The Great Big Book of Mighty Machines*, p. 138; April, 2010, S. McClendon, review of *Discovering Science*, p. 175.*

*   *   *

GRANDPRÉ, Mary 1954-

Personal

Born 1954, in SD; father a carpenter, mother a cashier; married Kevin Whaley (a designer; divorced); married Tom Casmer (an illustrator and educator), c. 2001; children: Julia Wren (adopted), three other children. *Education:* Pomona College, B.A. (fine arts); Minneapolis College of Art and Design, degree.

Addresses

Home—Sarasota, FL.

Career

Commercial illustrator, graphic designer, and fine artist. Worked for Hallmark Cards, c. 1970s; freelance illustrator. Film work includes environment/scenery development for DreamWorks' animated film *Antz* and character development for Disney's *Ice Age. Exhibitions:* Work exhibited at Cedar Rapids Museum of Art, Cedar Rapids, IA, 2008.

Awards, Honors

Middle East Book Award, Middle East Outreach Council, 2001, for *The House of Wisdom*; awards from Society of Illustrators, *Communication Arts, Graphis, Print,* and *Art Direction.*

Writings

(And illustrator, with husband, Tom Casmer) *Henry and Pawl and the Round Yellow Ball,* Dial (New York, NY), 2005.

ILLUSTRATOR

Aleksandr Sergeevich Pushkin, *The Snow Storm,* Creative Education (Mankato, MN), 1983.

Jennifer Armstrong, *Chin Yu Min and the Ginger Cat,* Crown (New York, NY), 1993.

Christopher King, *The Vegetables Go to Bed,* Crown (New York, NY), 1994.

Domenico Vittorini, *The Thread of Life: Twelve Old Italian Tales,* new edition, Crown (New York, NY), 1995.

Marguerite W. Davol, *Batwings and the Curtain of Night,* Orchard (New York, NY), 1997.

Jennifer Armstrong, *Pockets,* Crown (New York, NY), 1998.

Florence Parry Heide and Judith Heide Gilliland, *The House of Wisdom,* Dorling Kindersley (New York, NY), 1999.

Rozanne Lanczak Williams, *The Purple Snerd,* Harcourt (San Diego, CA), 2000.

Deborah Blumenthal, *Aunt Claire's Yellow Beehive Hair,* Dial (New York, NY), 2001.

Toni Buzzeo, *The Sea Chest,* Dial (New York, NY), 2002.

Tony Mitton, *Plum: Poems,* Arthur A. Levine (New York, NY), 2003.

Nancy Willard, *Sweep Dreams,* Little, Brown (New York, NY), 2005.

Phyllis Root, *Lucia and the Light,* Candlewick (Cambridge, MA), 2006.

Jason Robert Brown, *Tickety Tock,* Laura Geringer Books (New York, NY), 2008.

Roderick Townley, *The Blue Shoe: A Tale of Thievery, Villainy, Sorcery, and Shoes,* Alfred A. Knopf (New York, NY), 2009.

Jack Prelutsky, *The Carnival of the Animals by Camille Saint-Saëns: New Verses,* Alfred A. Knopf (New York, NY), 2010.

Chinua Achebe and John Iroaganachi, *How the Leopard Got His Claws,* Candlewick Press (Somerville, MA), 2011.

Betty MacDonald, *Nancy and Plum,* Alfred A. Knopf (New York, NY), 2011.

Contributor of illustrations to periodicals, including *Atlantic Monthly, Business Week, New Yorker, Wall Street Journal,* and *Time.*

ILLUSTRATOR; "HARRY POTTER" NOVEL SERIES BY J.K. ROWLING

Harry Potter and the Sorcerer's Stone, Arthur A. Levine (New York, NY), 1998.

Harry Potter and the Chamber of Secrets, Arthur A. Levine (New York, NY), 1999.

Harry Potter and the Prisoner of Azkaban, Arthur A. Levine (New York, NY), 1999.

Harry Potter and the Goblet of Fire, Arthur A. Levine (New York, NY), 2000.

Harry Potter and the Order of the Phoenix, Arthur A. Levine (New York, NY), 2003.

Harry Potter and the Half Blood Prince, Arthur A. Levine (New York, NY), 2005.

Harry Potter and the Deathly Hallows, Arthur A. Levine (New York, NY), 2007.

GrandPré's illustrations also appear in the Hebrew translations of the "Harry Potter" series.

Sidelights

Illustrator Mary GrandPré is best known to fantasy fans for her work creating cover art for the U.S. edition of J.K. Rowling's phenomenally popular "Harry Potter" novels, and her first illustration of Harry was actually created using herself as a model. Each of the seven novels in the series were illustrated—cover art plus several dozen interior line illustrations—in only two months, and as the first recipient of a manuscript that Rowling's fans awaited with bated breath, GrandPré had to keep the book's galley pages hidden from even her own family. "I've learned to accept it and be grateful for what it brings to my life," she noted in discussing her "Harry Potter" experience with *Sarasota Herald Tribune* interviewer Ruth Lando. "It open[ed] . . .

Mary GrandPré's artwork for Toni Buzzeo's **The Sea Chest** ***reflects the story's sense of mystery and adventure.*** (Illustration © 2002 by Mary GrandPré. Reproduced by permission of Dial Books for Young Readers, a division of Penguin Putnam Books for Young Readers, a member of Penguin (USA) Inc., 345 Hudson St., NY 10014. All rights reserved.)

A child's mystical journey comes to life in GrandPré's paintings for Phyllis Root's picture book Lucia and the Light. (Illustration copyright © 2006 by Mary GrandPré. Reproduced by permission of Candlewick Press, Somerville, MA.)

doors to expose the rest of who I am as an artist," she added, referencing the "wonderful messages, fun and freedom" she has found as a children's-book illustrator.

Born in South Dakota as the youngest of four siblings and raised in Minnesota, GrandPré started drawing illustrations of Mickey Mouse when she was five. Her parents modeled a life of industry and creativity, and by age ten she was mimicking the art of Spanish surrealist painter Salavador Dali. GrandPré developed her own unique style while attending the Minneapolis College of Art and Design in her late twenties. After gaining the skills and focus she needed, she left college before completing her degree, determined to make illustration her career. "I'd always thought of illustration as kind of a boring, commercial thing. I was a fine arts major, so I approached illustration with that attitude. And it came to a point where it really worked for me because I started solving illustration ideas with the natural way that I draw," she explained to John Jarvis in *Communication Arts.*

GrandPré has collaborated with a number of authors in the course of her career as an illustrator. Reviewing the artist's work for Jennifer Armstrong's *Chin Yu Min and the Ginger Cat, Horn Book* contributor Nancy Vasilakis wrote that the "strong, almost exaggerated, characterizations" reveal both "humor and fine style." Writing about the same title, a *Publishers Weekly* contributor maintained that GrandPré's "sumptuous palette of golds, gingers, browns and maroons suffuses the illustrations

with warmth, and . . . create an aura of mystery befitting the [book's] exotic locale." Another *Publishers Weekly* critic commented on the art in Christopher King's *The Vegetables Go to Bed,* writing that it "displays her flair for unusual perspectives and lighting." Kathy Broderick, writing in *Booklist,* commented on the "beautiful new illustrations" GrandPré crafted a new edition of Domenico Vittorini's *The Thread of Life: Twelve Old Italian Tales,* while a *Publishers Weekly* critic commented that the "lush, dramatic pastel drawings" the artist pairs with Marguerite W. Davol's text in the picture book *Batwings and the Curtain of Night* "evoke motion so adroitly."

The House of Wisdom, set in ancient Baghdad and featuring a text by Florence Parry Heide and Judith Heide Gilliland, received a Middle East Book Award for its contribution to promoting young readers' understanding of the Middle East. As Alicia Eames wrote in *School Library Journal,* GrandPré's "brilliantly hued, detailed pastels capture the grandeur and beauty" of the story's exotic setting. In Rozanne Lanczak Williams' *The Purple Snerd,* GrandPré creates a strange creature with a curling purple tail; "The book has great visual appeal," wrote Melanie S. Wible in *School Library Journal.* Barbara Buckley, reviewing Toni Buzzeo's *The Sea Chest* for the same publication, wrote that "GrandPré's oil paintings create the dramatic effects of the story," while John Peters noted in *Booklist* that her art "creates luminous New England scenes in rich, warm colors." In *School Library Journal* Jane Barrer commented of

Nancy Willard's *Sweep Dreams* that the artist's "oil-wash and colored-pencil artwork is as tender and expressive as the story." GrandPré's "evocative, dimly lit acrylics" for *Lucia and the Light* "capture the eerie mystery and shivery suspense" of Phyllis Root's story, according to *Booklist* contributor Gillian Engberg.

Benefitting from GrandPré's talent for capturing the fanciful, Jason Robert Brown's folktale-like story in *Tickety Tock* follows a young tailor whose life is consumed by work until he is transformed by the chime of a magic clock. *The Blue Shoe: A Tale of Thievery, Villainy, Sorcery, and Shoes,* a story by Roderick Townley, falls even further into the fanciful in its saga of a young teen whose unjust imprisonment leads to a newfound appreciation for his mild-mannered shoemaker father. Reviewing *Tickety Tock* for *School Library Journal,* Martha Simpson noted that "GrandPré's swirling style captures scenes of light and dark, . . . reinforcing a sense of fantasy," while a *Kirkus Reviews* writer asserted that the book's "collage" images "artfully depict a boy's progression from child to man." The blue-and-white charcoal drawings art GrandPré creates for Town-

GrandPré's many illustration projects include Roderick Townley's **The Blue Shoe: A Tale of Thievery, Villainy, Sorcery, and Shoes.** (Illustration copyright © 2009 by Mary GrandPré. Reproduced by permission of Alfred A. Knopf, an imprint of Random House Children's Books, a division of Random House, Inc.)

ley's story "partner well with the tongue-in-cheek narrative voice," according to a *Publishers Weekly* critic, while a *Kirkus Reviews* writer deemed them an "arresting" element in the author's "sometimes dark but ultimately cheerful adventure." Another imaginative picture-book project, illustrating Jack Prelutsky's poetic adaptation of Camille Saint-Saëns' musical suite "Carnival of the Animals," feature "vibrant acrylic and paper collage" images that "exude the same imaginative insights" as Saint-Saëns' music, according to another *Publishers Weekly* writer.

GrandPré and her husband, Tom Casmer, are the joint author-illustrators of *Henry and Pawl and the Round Yellow Ball.* Henry is a young artist who is frustrated because he cannot create "something important." When his dog Pawl loses a beloved yellow ball, Henry creates posters to help them locate it; when a man returns the ball and compliments Henry's posters, the boy realizes that his art has accomplished something. "Smoothly sculpted 3D figures and flat, childlike drawings co-exist harmoniously," wrote a *Kirkus Reviews* contributor in reviewing the work, and Joy Fleishhacker noted in *School Library Journal* that "Henry's frustrations over his abilities are realistically portrayed, as is the antidote to his problem." GrandPré discussed the husband-and-wife collaboration in an article for the *Sarasota Herald Tribune.* "Our challenge was for the two of us to blend our styles together," she explained. "Tom's style is based in line, a strong sense of line work and structure. But it also has kind of a quirkiness and a funky edge to it, and really vibrant color. It's everything that I love in artwork, and it's not like mine; we're kind of opposites in our work, and that's where we had to find how to make those things blend. And we really did."

Biographical and Critical Sources

PERIODICALS

Booklist, November 1, 1995, Kathy Broderick, review of *The Thread of Life: Twelve Old Italian Tales,* p. 469; August, 1998, John Peters, review of *Pockets,* p. 2012; September 15, 2002, John Peters, review of *The Sea Chest,* p. 238; July, 2005, Hazel Rochman, review of *Sweep Dreams,* p. 1931; December 1, 2006, Gillian Engberg, review of *Lucia and the Light,* p. 45; January 1, 2009, Ilene Cooper, review of *Tickety Tock,* p. 96; September 1, 2009, Kimberly Garnick, review of *The Blue Shoe: A Tale of Thievery, Villainy, and Sorcery, and Shoes,* p. 88.
Communication Arts, January-February, 2000, John Jarvis, interview with GrandPré, p. 108.
Detroit Free Press, June 21, 2007, "Potter Artist Mary GrandPré Makes Magic."
Horn Book, May-June, 1993, Nancy Vasilakis, review of *Chin Yu Min and the Ginger Cat,* p. 326.
Interview, November, 2000, Steven Heller, "Talk Back," p. 40A.

Kirkus Reviews, January 15, 2005, review of *Henry and Pawl and the Round Yellow Ball,* p. 118; October 15, 2006, review of *Lucia and the Light,* p. 1079; November 15, 2008, review of *Tickety Tock*; September 15, 2009, review of *The Blue Shoe.*

Publishers Weekly, March 15, 1993, review of *Chin Yu Min and the Ginger Cat,* p. 86; July 12, 1993, "Flying Starts," p. 24; April 11, 1994, review of *The Vegetables Go to Bed,* p. 63; March 3, 1997, review of *Batwings and the Curtain of Night,* p. 75; August 23, 1999, review of *The House of Wisdom,* p. 58; February 17, 2003, review of *Plum: Poems,* p. 75; November 27, 2006, review of *Lucia and the Light,* p. 50; November 24, 2008, review of *Tickety Tock,* p. 57; October 26, 2009, review of *The Blue Shoe,* p. 58; August 2, 2010, review of *The Carnival of the Animals,* p. 45.

Sarasota, November, 2003, Kay Kipling, "Mary's Magic," p. 72.

Sarasota Herald Tribune, April 2, 2006, Ruth Lando, "Illustrating Harry," p. L96.

School Library Journal, January, 2001, Melaine S. Wible, review of *The Purple Snerd,* p. 112; July, 2001, Jeanne Clancy Watkins, review of *Aunt Claire's Yellow Beehive Hair,* p. 72; August, 2002, Barbara Buckley, review of *The Sea Chest,* p. 147; January, 2003, Alicia Eames, review of *The House of Wisdom,* p. 83; May, 2003, Grace Oliff, review of *Plum,* p. 140; May, 2005, Joy Fleishhacker, review of *Henry and Pawl and the Round Yellow Ball,* p. 78; July, 2005, Jane Barrer, review of *Sweep Dreams,* p. 84; December, 2006, Tamara E. Richman, review of *Lucia and the Light,* p. 114; January, 2009, Martha Simpson, review of *Tickety Tock,* p. 72; December, 2009, Nancy D. Tolson, review of *The Blue Shoe,* p. 135.

ONLINE

Mary GrandPré Home Page, http://www.marygrandpre. com (April 15, 2011).

Scholastic Web site, http://www.scholastic.com/ (April 15, 2011), "Mary GrandPré."*

H

HALL, Teri

Personal
Female.

Addresses
Home—WA. *Agent*—Kirby Kim, William Morris Endeavor; kkim@wmeentertainment.com.

Career
Writer.

Awards, Honors
Children's Choices listee, International Reading Association/Children's Book Council, 2011, for *The Line.*

Writings

The Line, Dial Books (New York, NY), 2010.
Away, Dial Books (New York, NY), 2011.

Sidelights
In her debut novel *The Line,* as well as its sequel, both of which are set in a dystopian, near-future North America, Teri Hall addresses themes of courage, authoritarianism, and rebellion. Inspired by a dream the author once had of a girl sitting in a glass-walled room during a rainstorm, *The Line* centers on Rachel, a curious and sensitive teen who lives a quiet life with her widowed mother on The Property, an estate near the Line, a protective, invisible barrier that runs along the border of the United States. Homeschooled because her mother distrusts the government's repressive policies, Rachel wonders about the fate of the Others, a group of displaced citizens that inhabits the Away, a region beyond the Line that suffered a devastating nuclear attack.

Cover of Teri Hall's futuristic YA novel **The Line,** *which finds a teen searching for escape from a repressive and controlling U.S. government.* (Cover photograph by Jan Rietz © Getty Images. Reproduced by permission of Dial Books for Young Readers, a division of Penguin Young Readers Group, a member of Penguin (USA) Inc., 345 Hudson St., NY 10014. All rights reserved.)

When Rachel discovers a mysterious message from someone beyond the border, she journeys to the Line to offer her help, a decision fraught with peril.

"Hall's clear, controlled prose builds burgeoning tension," a critic in *Publishers Weekly* observed, and Lynn Rutan, writing in *Booklist,* applauded the "tense narrative that will leave readers intrigued with the mysterious Away." According to a contributor in *Kirkus Reviews,* Hall's narrative stirs audiences to consider "the tension between freedom and security while keeping them engrossed in a suspenseful story."

Biographical and Critical Sources

PERIODICALS

Booklist, February 1, 2010, Lynn Rutan, review of *The Line,* p. 42.
Kirkus Reviews, January 15, 2010, review of *The Line.*
Publishers Weekly, March 1, 2010, review of *The Line,* p. 51.
School Library Journal, April, 2010, Jane Henriksen Baird, review of *The Line,* p. 158.

ONLINE

Teri Hall Home Page, http://www.terihall.com (April 15, 2011).*

*   *   *

HANSEN, Amy S.

Personal

Female. *Education:* Oberlin College, B.A. (English and economics), 1987; University of Michigan, M.A/M.S. (journalism/natural resources), 1991.

Addresses

Home—Greenbelt, MD.

Career

Author of books for children. Journalist, including staff reporter for *Milwaukee Journal, Elyria Chronicle-Telegram,* and *Amherst News-Times;* 1987-98; Low & Associates, senior writer and editor, 1994-98; freelance author beginning 1998. Presenter at schools.

Member

Society of Children's Book Writers and Illustrators, National Association of Science Writers, Children's Book Guild.

Awards, Honors

Parents' Choice selection, 1996; Blue Pencil award, *Frontiers,* 1997; Apex Award for Excellence in Feature Writing, 1997; Society of Children's Book Writers and Illustrators Work-in-Progress Letter of Merit, 2008; John Burroughs List for Excellence in Nature Writing for Young Readers inclusion, American Museum of Natural History/John Burroughs Society, and Best Children's Book selection, Bank Street College, both 2011, both for *Bugs and Bugsicles.*

Writings

Kidsource: Science Experiments, illustrated by Mike Moran, Lowell House Juvenile (Los Angeles, CA), 2000.
Eastern Himalayas, World Wildlife Fund, 2001.
How Things Work, Publications International (Lincolnwood, IL), 2006.
Wild Animals, illustrated by William Fraccaro, Publications International (Lincolnwood, IL), 2007.
Touch the Earth, National Aeronautic and Space Administration/NFB, 2009.
Hubble, an Out-of-This-World Telescope, Reading A-Z, 2010.
Bugs and Bugsicles: Insects in the Winter, illustrated by Robert C. Kray, Boyds Mills Press (Honesdale, PA), 2010.
Where Does the Sun Go at Night? (graphic novel), Capstone Press (Mankato, MN), 2011.
How Do I Stay on Earth? (graphic novel), Capstone Press (Mankato, MN), 2011.

Contributor to numerous periodicals, including *Children's Writer, Cricket, CLICK, Highlights for Children,* and the *Washington Post.* Author of plays and short stories. Contributor of book reviews to Children's Literature Comprehensive Database, beginning 2002; editor of reference material.

"POWERING OUR WORLD" SERIES

Fossil Fuels: Buried in the Earth, PowerKids Press (New York, NY), 2010.
Geothermal Energy: Hot Stuff!, PowerKids Press (New York, NY), 2010.
Hydropower: Making a Splash!, PowerKids Press (New York, NY), 2010.
Nuclear Energy: Amazing Atoms, PowerKids Press (New York, NY), 2010.
Solar Energy: Running on Sunshine, PowerKids Press (New York, NY), 2010.
Wind Energy: Blown Away!, PowerKids Press (New York, NY), 2010.

Biographical and Critical Sources

PERIODICALS

Booklist, March 1, 2010, Carolyn Phelan, review of *Bugs and Bugsicles: Insects in the Winter,* p. 66.
Kirkus Reviews, February 15, 2010, review of *Bugs and Bugsicles.*

School Library Journal, April, 2010, Karey Wehner, review of *Bugs and Bugsicles,* p. 145.

ONLINE

Amy S. Hansen Home Page, http://www.amyshansen.com (April 15, 2011).
Children's Literature Database, http://www.childrenslit. com/ (April 15, 2011), "Amy S. Hansen."*

* * *

HELDRING, Thatcher

Personal

Born in WA; married; wife's name Staci. *Education:* Degree (history). *Hobbies and other interests:* Playing indoor sports.

Addresses

Home—Seattle, WA.

Career

Author. Worked in publishing industry, New York, NY.

Writings

MIDDLE-GRADE FICTION

Toby Wheeler, Eighth-grade Benchwarmer, Delacorte Press (New York, NY), 2007.
Roy Morelli Steps up to the Plate, Delacorte Press (New York, NY), 2010.

Work included in anthology *Not like I'm Jealous or Anything.*

Sidelights

Thatcher Heldring was raised in the Pacific Northwest and still lives there, although he spent several years after college working for a New York City publisher. His middle-grade novels *Toby Wheeler, Eighth-grade Benchwarmer* and *Roy Morelli Steps up to the Plate* tap into Heldring's love of team sports and of his own boyhood memories. "As a history major in college I learned to go an awfully long way on very little fact," he explained on his home page in discussing his background as a writer. "This skill is very important if you want to be a novelist. I also rely heavily on other books . . . [because] reading stacks and stacks of other middle-grade and young-adult books has given me a sense of what I like, what I don't like, and where I think I fit in." "But the most important training is [real-world] experience," Heldring asserted. "In order for fiction to come out, something has to go in. That some something is experience."

Heldring's experience as a benched player on his high-school varsity basketball team comes into play in his debut novel, *Toby Wheeler, Eighth-grade Benchwarmer.* In the story, Toby joins best friend JJ in signing up to play basketball on his junior-high-school team. Although he tries his hardest, the preteen does not share JJ's athletic talents, leaving a disappointed Toby warming the bench while JJ is out on the court. Taking his last-place position in stride, the boy's enthusiasm continues unabated, and he also continues to work on his shooting, passing, and free-throw skills in a story that leads to a traditional but nonetheless inspiring conclusion. Calling *Toby Wheeler, Eighth-grade Benchwarmer* "engaging," Diana Pierce added in *School Library Journal* that Heldring's story will attract fans of author Matt Christopher. In *Booklist* Ilene Cooper recognized another positive aspect of the middle-grade novel, writing that, "with so much written about the friction between girl friends, it's good to have a book that acknowledges that left-out feeling happens to boys, too."

Roy Morelli Steps up to the Plate finds eight-grader Roy Morelli looking forward to another year playing

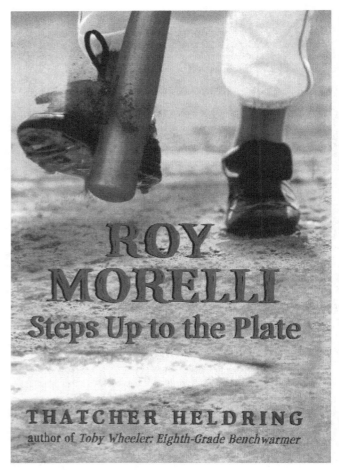

Cover of Thatcher Heldring's **Roy Morelli Steps up to the Plate,** *which finds a cocky eighth grader learning a few lessons after his parents decide to prohibit his sports involvement to playing for the local rec. league.* (Jacket photography by Jim Cummins/Corbis. Delacorte Press, 2010. Reproduced by permission of Delacorte Press, an imprint of Random House Children's Books, a division of Random House, Inc.)

shortstop on his local all-star baseball team. From there, he figures, it should be a quick step to the varsity team when he reaches high school. Then Roy's lackluster report card arrives in the mail, prompting his divorced parents to finally agree on one thing: from now on less time will be spent on sports and more time will be spent on schoolwork. In between his school classes and meetings with his history tutor, Roy now only has time to play on the worst team in his town's recreation league. He brings his negative attitude onto the baseball field until his perceptive coach and the reaction of his teammates inspire Roy to make an attitude adjustment that reaps positive results. Noting the "fast paced and exciting" baseball references in *Roy Morelli Steps up to the Plate*, Richard Luzer added in *School Library Journal* that Heldring's "depiction of middle school dynamics rings true," while a *Kirkus Reviews* critic cited the novel for its "well-described baseball action and a protagonist to care about."

Biographical and Critical Sources

PERIODICALS

Booklist, September 1, 2007, Ilene Cooper, review of *Toby Wheeler: Eighth-grade Benchwarmer*, p. 136; February 15, 2010, John Peters, review of *Roy Morelli Steps up to the Plate*, p. 78.
Kirkus Reviews, February 15, 2010, review of *Roy Morelli Steps up to the Plate*.
School Library Journal, September, 2007, Diana Pierce, review of *Toby Wheeler: Eighth-grade Benchwarmer*, p. 198; February, 2010, Richard Luzer, review of *Roy Morelli Steps up to the Plate*, p. 112.

ONLINE

Class of 2k7 Web site, http://classof2k7.com/ (April 15, 2011), "Thacher Heldring."
Random House Web site, http://www.randomhouse.com/ (April 15, 2011), "Thatcher Heldring."
Thatcher Heldring Home page, http://www.thatchertheauthor.typepad.com (April 15, 2010).*

*   *   *

HELQUIST, Brett

Personal

Born in Gonado, AZ; married Mary Jane Callister. *Education:* Brigham Young University, B.F.A., 1993. *Hobbies and other interests:* Playing old-time fiddle music.

Addresses

Home—Brooklyn, NY. *Agent*—Steven Malk, Writers House, 3368 Governor Dr., Ste. 224F, San Diego, CA 92122.

Career

Illustrator and author.

Writings

SELF-ILLUSTRATED

Roger, the Jolly Pirate, HarperCollins (New York, NY), 2004.
Bedtime for Bear, HarperCollins (New York, NY), 2010.

ILLUSTRATOR

Tor Seidler, *The Revenge of Randal Reese-Rat*, Farrar, Straus & Giroux (New York, NY), 2001.
Shana Corey, *Milly and the Macy's Parade*, Scholastic (New York, NY), 2002.
Peter W. Hassinger, *The Book of Alfar: A Tale of the Hudson Highlands*, Laura Geringer (New York, NY), 2002.
Blue Balliett, *Chasing Vermeer*, Scholastic (New York, NY), 2003.
James V. Hart, *Captain Hook: The Adventures of a Notorious Youth*, Laura Geringer Books (New York, NY), 2005.
Elizabeth Haydon, *The Floating Island* ("Lost Journals of Ven Polypheme" series), Tor (New York, NY), 2006.
Blue Balliett, *The Wright Three*, Scholastic (New York, NY), 2006.
Blue Balliett, *The Calder Game*, Scholastic (New York, NY), 2008.
Lemony Snicket, *The Lump of Coal*, HarperCollins (New York, NY), 2008.
Charles Dickens, *A Christmas Carol*, abridged by Josh Greenhut, HarperCollins Children's Books (New York, NY), 2009.
Neil Gaiman, *Odd and the Frost Giants*, Harper (New York, NY), 2009.
Jennifer Trafton, *The Rise and Fall of Mount Majestic*, Dial Books for Young Readers (New York, NY), 2010.

Contributor of illustrations to publications such as *New York Times*, *Time for Kids*, and *Cricket*.

ILLUSTRATOR; "A SERIES OF UNFORTUNATE EVENTS" SERIES BY LEMONY SNICKET

The Bad Beginning, HarperCollins (New York, NY), 1999.
The Reptile Room, HarperCollins (New York, NY), 1999.
The Wide Window, HarperCollins (New York, NY), 2000.
The Miserable Mill, HarperCollins (New York, NY), 2000.
The Austere Academy, HarperCollins (New York, NY), 2000.
The Ersatz Elevator, HarperCollins (New York, NY), 2001.
The Vile Village, HarperCollins (New York, NY), 2001.
The Hostile Hospital, HarperCollins (New York, NY), 2001.

The Carnivorous Carnival, HarperCollins (New York, NY), 2002.

The Slippery Slope, HarperCollins (New York, NY), 2003.

The Grim Grotto, HarperCollins (New York, NY), 2004.

The Ominous Omnibus (includes *The Bad Beginning, The Reptile Room,* and *The Wide Window*), HarperCollins (New York, NY), 2005.

The Penultimate Peril, HarperCollins (New York, NY), 2005.

The End, HarperCollins (New York, NY), 2006.

The Beatrice Letters, HarperCollins (New York, NY), 2006.

ILLUSTRATOR; "TALES FROM THE HOUSE OF BUNNICULA" SERIES BY JAMES HOWE

It Came from beneath the Bed!, Atheneum Books for Young Readers (New York, NY), 2002.

Howie Monroe and the Doghouse of Doom, Atheneum Books for Young Readers (New York, NY), 2002.

Invasion of the Mind Swappers from Asteroid Six!, Atheneum Books for Young Readers (New York, NY), 2002.

Screaming Mummies of the Pharaoh's Tomb II, Atheneum Books for Young Readers (New York, NY), 2003.

Brett Helquist's long-running collaboration with author Lemony Snicket began with his illustrations for The Bad Beginning, *the first in* "A Series of Unfortunate Events." (Illustration copyright © 1999 by Brett Helquist. Used by permission HarperCollins Children's Books, a division of HarperCollins Publishers.)

Budd Barkin, Private Eye, Atheneum Books for Young Readers (New York, NY), 2003.

The Amazing Odorous Adventures of Stinky Dog, Atheneum Books for Young Readers (New York, NY), 2003.

Sidelights

Artist and author Brett Helquist is known to most readers as the illustrator of Lemony Snicket's highly popular "A Series of Unfortunate Events" novels. Published in thirteen volumes between 1999 and 2006, the arch melodrama in Snicket's series was given an extra dimension in Helquist's line drawings. A 1993 graduate of Brigham Young University, Helquist has produced a large body of published work in addition to his "Unfortunate" books, creating illustrations for texts by such well-known writers as Tor Seidler, James Howe, Neil Gaiman, and Blue Balliett. Reviewing Balliett's *The Calder Game,* part of a series of middle-grade novels about three seventh-grade sleuths who track down missing works of art, Connie Tyrell Burns noted in *School Library Journal* that "Helquist's detailed illustrations enhance this multilayered story" and add a layer of intrigue by featuring clues to the ongoing mystery.

In his collaboration with Snicket, Helquist chronicles the downbeat, sometimes entirely grim adventures of the Baudelaire orphans: fourteen-year-old Violet, twelve-year-old Klaus, and baby Sonny. The children become orphans when a fire destroys their home and kills their parents in *The Bad Beginning,* but the executor of their parents' estate completely ignores any of the siblings' wishes. As the series unfolds, their villainous guardian, Count Olaf, relentlessly makes the Baudelaire family fortune his own, no matter the cost to its rightful heirs. Peril follows misfortune for the Baudelaire children, and narrator Snicket takes pains to warn readers throughout the series that a happy ending will not be forthcoming. In a review of *The Bad Beginning,* a *Publishers Weekly* reviewer remarked on Helquist's illustrations, noting that "exquisitely detailed drawings of Gothic gargoyles and mischievous eyes echo the contents of this elegantly designed hardcover."

Woe and danger continue to plague Violet, Klaus, and Sonny for the duration of Snicket's "A Series of Unfortunate Events" novels. In *The Vile Village* the siblings are adopted by the entire village of V.F.D. because of the old saying that "it takes a village to raise a child." They elude Count Olaf by relying on their skills and resourcefulness as the idea of being adopted by a village proves to have been ill-conceived. Threats become more personal in *The Hostile Hospital,* as Count Olaf and his henchmen threaten to behead anesthetized Violet, try to crush the children with filing cabinets, and trap the Baudelaire siblings in a burning building. "Perfectly capturing the atmosphere of the stories, Helquist's stylized pencil sketches are among his best yet," commented Carolyn Phelan in *Booklist.* The children don disguises in order to investigate a fortune teller in *The Carnivorous Carnival,* but carnival life is not the con-

Helquist's illustrations for Blue Balliett's Chasing Vermeer *prove as engaging to readers as the novel's unique storyline.* (Illustration copyright © 2004 by Brett Helquist. Reprinted by permssion of Scholastic, Inc.)

Howie Monroe, the Monroe family's resident wirehaired dachshund. An aspiring literary light, Howie seeks glory via his imaginative tales and undertakes a number of creative-writing projects. In *Howie Monroe and the Doghouse of Doom* the pup writes himself into a parody of the "Harry Potter" novels, while his friend Delilah finds herself transformed into a squirrel by aliens in another of Howie's stories, *Invasion of the Mind Swappers from Asteroid Six!* Howie acquires Harold, an unwanted editor, in *It Came from beneath the Bed!*, wherein Howie writes and Harold criticizes a story about a crazed, stuffed koala bear that comes to life. Wendy S. Carroll, writing in *School Library Journal*, called *Invasion of the Mind Swappers from Asteroid Six!* "lighthearted fun" that benefits from Helquist's "humorous black-and-white drawings."

Another of Helquist's illustrations projects is Tor Siedler's *The Revenge of Randal Reese-Rat*, which recounts a romance between two young rodents that is fraught by scandal, arson, revenge, and jealously. Helquist's detailed black-and-white illustrations for the story "make it clear that these lithe, sociable New York

stant fun it might seem—especially when one of the performers is about to be thrown to the lions. The fittingly titled *The End* finds the Baudelaire's saga at a dangerous close, as Violet, Klaus, and Sonny are tempest-tossed in an ocean where Count Olaf floats menacingly nearby.

For his contribution to Snicket's series, Helquist earned high remarks from critics. "Some brilliant publishing person or cabal saw the pleasure in these tales—anarchy masked as propriety—and decided, brilliantly, to engage Brett Helquist to do the spiky and droll line drawings," observed Gregory Maguire in a review of *The Austere Academy* for the *New York Times Book Review*. In their look, weight, and feel, the "A Series of Unfortunate Events" novels are "evocative of gift books of an earlier day," Maguire added, and "the presentation is inspired."

Helquist's illustrations are equally effective in more whimsical, lighthearted volumes. James Howe's "Tales from the House of Bunnicula" books feature puppy

Helquist and Balliett team up again on The Calder Game, *which continues the art-related adventures of three young sleuths.* (Illustration copyright © 2008 by Brett Helquist. Reproduced by permission of Scholastic Press, an imprint of Scholastic, Inc.)

A mastery of the quirkily macabre makes Helquist's art an effective match for Alvin Schwartz's story collection **Scary Stories to Share in the Dark.** (Illustration copyright © 2007 by Brett Helquist. Reproduced by permission of HarperCollins Children's Books, a division of HarperCollins Publishers.)

rodents have busy lives and unique personalities," wrote Eva Mitnick in a review of Siedler's book for *School Library Journal,* and a *Kirkus Reviews* writer deemed *The Revenge of Randal Reese-Rat* "loyally and lovably ratty."

Another imaginative pairing between author and illustrator finds Helquist and writer Balliett collaborating on a series of imaginative middle-grade novels that mix puzzles with a mystery. *Chasing Vermeer* finds two children on the trail of a missing painting. Helquist "outdoes himself," according to *Booklist* critic Ilene Cooper, the reviewer adding in her appraisal of the book that the illustrator enhances Balliett's imaginative text by "providing an interactive mystery in his pictures."

Helquist's holiday-themed art for *Milly and the Macy's Parade* bring to life a story by Shana Corey that is based on New York City-based retailer Macy's historical archives. Dubbed "charming" by Deborah Hopkinson in a *BookPage* online review, the unusual book follows Milly, a Polish immigrant who visits her father every day at his job at New York City's famed depart-

ment store. While in Macy's Milly luxuriates in the atmosphere, riding the escalators and inspecting the cheerful holiday items on sale. However, during the 1924 holiday season Milly finds her father and his friends depressed and wistful for the music, caroling, and parades they remember from their childhood in Poland. When the girl bravely suggests to Mr. Macy himself that a parade would cheer up his workers and inspire a holiday spirit, he agrees and a holiday tradition is born. "Lusciously illustrated," *Milly and the Macy's Parade* features richly colored, stylized illustrations that "convey a sense of luxury associated with Macy's," observed a *Kirkus Reviews* critic. Susan Pine, writing in *School Library Journal,* called the book "an entertaining and lively" addition to holiday-book collections.

Gaiman's *Odd and the Frost Giants* and Jennifer Trafton's *The Rise and Fall of Mount Majestic* are two more stories that have benefited from Helquist's artwork. In Gaiman's novel, a Nordic winter provides the setting as a lonely young orphaned boy befriends three animals that turn out to be the powerful gods Thor, Odin, and Loki. The full-page drawings that Helquist contributes are "distinguished by their sturdy characterizations and angular drafting," observed Joanna Rudge Long, the *Horn Book* contributor adding that they "deftly evoke Gaiman's wintry Norse world" in a story that features both an "impeccable" narrative and "humor in many a turn of phrase." In a similar fashion, the artist's "black-and-white [pencil] illustrations add to the humor and nonstop action" of *The Rise and Fall of Mount Majestic,* an entertaining preteen mystery that features "an unique setting with unusual and detailed characters," according to *School Library Journal* critic Beth L. Meister.

While most of his work has consisted of illustrating stories by other writers, Helquist has also created the original self-illustrated stories *Roger, the Jolly Pirate* and *Bedtime for Bear.* Featuring full-color, large-format illustrations, *Roger, the Jolly Pirate* is a porquois-tale of sorts in which Helquist's story and art transport young readers out onto the high seas and introduce them to a good-tempered pirate who remains on an even keel despite the malevolent mood of his crewmates. Although the upbeat Roger is viewed as less-than-useless in battle, when the pirate ship encounters a British Man-o-War, it is Roger the pirate who ultimately wins the day—and creates the skull-and-crossbones flag that has since become the sign of all-things piratical. In a review of *Roger, the Jolly Pirate* for *Publishers Weekly,* a critic praised Helquist's debut for its "exceptionally dynamic" watercolor-and-pencil artwork, and in *School Library Journal* Marge Loch-Wouters wrote that the story is "told with a rhythm and bounce that begs to be read aloud." Loch-Wouters dubbed *Roger, the Jolly Pirate* "a rousing and humorous tale," while in *Booklist* Hazel Rochman predicted that Helquist's "lively picture book" will appeal to young buccaneers.

In *Bedtime for Bear* young Bear has curled up for the winter when the sound of some playful friends disturbs his slumber and ultimately prompts him to postpone the

inevitable hibernation. Crafted in a sequential "comic-book" format, the book pairs Helquist's simple story with detailed images that feature "just the right quirky details to catch viewers' attention," according to *School Library Journal* contributor Jayne Damron. In *Booklist* Andrew Medlar commented on the story's "action-filled" illustrations, predicting in *Booklist* that *Bedtime for Bear* serves up a "wintry romp [that] will make an enjoyable choice for sharing."

Biographical and Critical Sources

PERIODICALS

Booklist, October 15, 2001, Carolyn Phelan, review of *The Hostile Hospital,* p. 392; October 1, 2002, Kathleen Odean, review of *Howie Monroe and the Doghouse of Doom,* p. 326; December 15, 2002, Susan Dove Lempke, review of *The Carnivorous Carnival,* p. 761; April 1, 2004, Ilene Cooper, review of *Chasing Vermeer,* p. 1365; July, 2004, Hazel Rochman, review of *Roger, the Jolly Pirate,* p. 184; July, 2005, Gillian Engberg, review of *Captain Hook: The Adventures of a Notorious Youth,* p. 1916; February 1, 2006, Jennifer Mattson, review of *The Wright Three,* p. 47; September 1, 2006, Diana Tixier Herald, review of *The Floating Island,* p. 126; May 1, 2008, Ilene Cooper, review of *The Calder Game,* p. 51; September 15, 2008, Thom Barthelmess, review of *The Lump of Coal,* p. 57; July 1, 2009, Ian Chipman, review of *Odd and the Frost Giants,* p. 61; October 15, 2009, John Peters, review of *A Christmas Carol,* p. 52; October 15, 2010, Andrew Medlar, review of *Bedtime for Bear,* p. 54; January 1, 2011, Ilene Cooper, review of *The Rise and Fall of Mount Majestic,* p. 108.
Bulletin of the Center for Children's Books, February, 2010, April Spisak, review of *Odd and the Frost Giants,* p. 246; December, 2010, Kate Quealy-Gainer, review of *The Rise and Fall of Mount Majestic,* p. 208.
Childhood Education, winter, 2001, Elizabeth K. Liddicoat, review of *The Ersatz Elevator,* p. 112.
Family Life, November 1, 2001, Sara Nelson, review of *The Hostile Hospital,* p. 95.
Globe & Mail (Toronto, Ontario, Canada), October 24, 2009, Susan Perren, review of *Odd and the Frost Giants,* p. F17.
Horn Book, March-August, 2006, Roger Sutton, review of *The Wright Three,* p. 176; July-August, 2008, Roger Sutton, review of *The Calder Game,* p. 437; November-December, 2009, Joanna Rudge Long, review of *Odd and the Frost Giants,* p. 672.
Kirkus Reviews, August 15, 2001, review of *The Revenge of Randal Reese-Rat,* p. 1221; October 1, 2002, review of *Milly and the Macy's Parade,* p. 1464; November 15, 2002, review of *Screaming Mummies of the Pharaoh's Tomb II,* p. 1695; March 1, 2004, review of *Roger, the Jolly Pirate,* p. 223; August 1, 2005, review of *Captain Hook,* p. 848; March 15, 2006, review of *The Wright Three;* May 1, 2008, review of *The Calder Game;* November 1, 2008, review of *The Lump of Coal;* September 15, 2009, reviews of *A Christmas Carol* and *Odd and the Frost Giants.*

New York Times Book Review, October 15, 2000, Gregory Maguire, review of *The Austere Academy,* p. 30; June 17, 2001, review of *The Vile Village,* p. 24; November 18, 2001, Nora Krug, review of *The Revenge of Randal Reese-Rat,* p. 52.
Publishers Weekly, September 6, 1999, review of *The Bad Beginning,* p. 104; July 30, 2001, review of *The Revenge of Randal Reese-Rat,* p. 85; May 3, 2004, review of *Roger, the Jolly Pirate,* p. 191; August 29, 2005, review of *Captain Hook,* p. 56; February 27, 2006, review of *The Wright Three,* p. 61; September 18, 2006, review of *The Floating Island,* p. 54; May 19, 2008, review of *The Calder Game,* p. 54; August 17, 2009, review of *Odd and the Frost Giants,* p. 62; October 26, 2009, review of *A Christmas Carol,* p. 57.
School Library Journal, January, 2000, Marlene Gawron, review of *The Wide Window,* p. 136; October, 2000, Ann Cook, review of *The Austere Academy,* p. 171; August, 2001, Farida S. Dowler, review of *The Vile Village,* p. 188; October, 2001, Eva Mitnick, review of *The Revenge of Randal Reese-Rat,* p. 170; November, 2001, Jean Gaffney, review of *The Hostile Hospital,* p. 164; October, 2002, Susan Pine, review of *Milly and the Macy's Parade,* pp. 99-100; November, 2002, JoAnn Jonas, review of *Howie Monroe and the Doghouse of Doom,* Wendy S. Carroll, review of *Invasion of the Mind Swappers from Asteroid Six,* and John Sigwald, review of *It Came from beneath the Bed!,* all p. 169; August, 2003, Elaine E. Knight, review of *Bud Barkin, Private Eye,* p. 129; April, 2004, Marge Loch-Wouters, review of *Roger, the Jolly Pirate,* p. 112; October, 2005, Beth L. Meister, review of *Captain Hook,* p. 161; April, 2006, Caitlin Augusta, review of *The Wright Three,* p. 133; December, 2006, Mara Alpert, review of *The Floating Island,* p. 144; June, 2008, Connie Tyrrell Burns, review of *The Calder Game,* p. 134; October, 2008, Linda Israelson, review of *The Lump of Coal,* p. 98; October, 2009, Mara Alpert, review of *A Christmas Carol,* p. 79, and Lauralyn Persson, review of *Odd and the Frost Giant,* p. 126; February, 2011, Jayne Damron, review of *Bedtime for Bear,* p. 81; March, 2011, Beth L. Meister, review of *The Rise and Fall of Mount Majestic,* p. 172.

ONLINE

BookPage, http://www.bookpage.com/ (May 21, 2003), Deborah Hopkinson, review of *Milly and the Macy's Parade.*
Brett Helquist Home Page, http://www.bretthelquist.com (March 15, 2008).*

* * *

HOLUB, Joan (Rita Book, Brad Bucks)

Personal

Female. *Education:* B.F.A. *Hobbies and other interests:* Aerobics, pet care, hiking, reading, traveling, eating chocolate.

Joan Holub (Reproduced by permission.)

Addresses

E-mail—joanholub@aol.com.

Career

Writer and illustrator. Art director in an advertising firm, 1980-89; Scholastic, New York, NY, associate art director, children's trade books, 1989-91; author and illustrator, 1991—. *Exhibitions:* Work included in juried exhibit at Frye Art Museum, Seattle, WA, 2002.

Member

Society of Children's Book Writers and Illustrators.

Awards, Honors

Society of Children's Book Writers and Illustrators Magazine Illustration Merit Honor designation, 1993; Honor Book designation, Society of School Librarians International, 2000, for *I Have a Weird Brother Who Digested a Fly;* Pick of the List selections, American Booksellers Association, 2001, for *Why Do Cats Meow?* and *Why Do Dogs Bark?;* Western Writers of America Honor Book selection, 2002; Children's Literature Choice listee, 2002; Best Books for Children selection, Association of Booksellers for Children, 2003, for *Riddle-iculous Math;* Best Children's Books of the Year selection, Bank Street College of Education, 2003, for *Why Do Horses Neigh?;* Lasting Connections selection, American Library Association, 2006, for *The Man Who Named the Clouds;* Best Children's Books of the Year selection, Bank Street College of Education, 2009, for *Shampoodle.*

Writings

Pajama Party, illustrated by Julie Durrell, Grosset & Dunlap (New York, NY), 1998.

Space Dogs on Planet K-9, illustrated by Mike Reed, Troll Associates (Mahwah, NJ), 1998.

I Have a Weird Brother Who Digested a Fly, illustrated by Patrick Girouard, Albert Whitman (Morton Grove, IL), 1999.

The Spooky Sleepover, illustrated by Cynthia Fisher, Grosset & Dunlap (New York, NY), 1999.

Backwards Day, illustrated by Jean Kurisu, Scholastic (New York, NY), 2000.

Light the Candles: A Hanukkah Lift-the-Flap Book, illustrated by Lynne Cravath, Puffin (New York, NY), 2000.

(As Rita Book) *My Soccer Mom from Mars,* illustrated by Amy Wummer, Grosset & Dunlap (New York, NY), 2001.

Scat, Cats!, illustrated by Rich Davis, Viking (New York, NY), 2001.

Silly Bears, illustrated by Priscilla Burris, Scholastic (New York, NY), 2001.

Why Do Cats Meow?, illustrated by Anna DiVito, Dial Books for Young Readers (New York, NY), 2001.

Why Do Dogs Bark?, illustrated by Anna DiVito, Dial Books for Young Readers (New York, NY), 2001.

The Garden That We Grew, illustrated by Hiroe Nakata, Viking (New York, NY), 2001.

The Pizza That We Made, illustrated by Lynne Cravath, Puffin (New York, NY), 2001.

The Gingerbread Kid Goes to School, illustrated by Debbie Palen, Grosset & Dunlap (New York, NY), 2002.

Company's Coming: A Passover Lift-the-Flap Book, illustrated by Renée Andriani, Puffin (New York, NY), 2002.

Hooray for St. Patrick's Day!, illustrated by Paul Meisel, Puffin (New York, NY), 2002.

Jack and the Jellybeanstalk, illustrated by Benton Mahan, Grosset & Dunlap (New York, NY), 2002.

Turkeys Never Gobble, illustrated by Jennifer Beck Harris, HarperFestival (New York, NY), 2002.

Kwanzaa Kids, illustrated by Ken Wilson-Max, Puffin (New York, NY), 2002.

Why Do Horses Neigh?, illustrated by Anna DiVito, Dial Books for Young Readers (New York, NY), 2003.

Why Do Rabbits Hop?, and Other Questions about Rabbits, Guinea Pigs, Hamsters, and Gerbils, illustrated by Anna DiVito, Dial Books for Young Readers (New York, NY), 2003.

Yankee Doodle Riddles: American History Fun, illustrated by Elizabeth Butler, Albert Whitman (Morton Grove, IL), 2003.

Apples and Honey: A Rosh Hashanah Lift-the-Flap Book, illustrated by Cary Pillo, Puffin (New York, NY), 2003.

Dragon Dance: A Chinese New Year Lift-the-Flap Book, illustrated by Cary Pillo, Puffin (New York, NY), 2003.

Fourth of July, Sparkly Sky, illustrated by Amanda Haley, Simon & Schuster (New York, NY), 2003.

Riddle-iculous Math, illustrated by Regan Dunnick, Albert Whitman (Morton Grove, IL), 2003.

Why Do Birds Sing?, illustrated by Anna DiVito, Dial Books for Young Readers (New York, NY), 2004.

Why Do Snakes Hiss?, and Other Questions about Snakes, Lizards, and Turtles, illustrated by Anna DiVito, Dial Books for Young Readers (New York, NY), 2004.

The Halloween Queen, illustrated by Theresa Smythe, Albert Whitman (Morton Grove, IL), 2004.

Geogra-fleas!: Riddles All over the Map, illustrated by Regan Dunnick, Albert Whitman (Morton Grove, IL), 2004.

Who Was Johnny Appleseed?, illustrated by Anna DiVito, Grosset & Dunlap (New York, NY), 2005.

(With Julie Hannah) *The Man Who Named the Clouds,* illustrated by Paige Billin-Frye, Albert Whitman (Morton Grove, IL), 2006.

More Snacks!: A Thanksgiving Play, illustrated by Will Terry, Aladdin (New York, NY), 2006.

Big Heart!: A Valentine's Day Story, illustrated by Will Terry, Aladdin (New York, NY), 2007.

Cleopatra and the King's Enemies: Based on a True Story of Cleopatra in Egypt, illustrated by Nonna Aleshina, Aladdin (New York, NY), 2007.

Elizabeth and the Royal Pony: Based on a True Story of Elizabeth I of England, illustrated by Nonna Aleshina, Aladdin (New York, NY), 2007.

Good Luck!: A St. Patrick's Day Story, illustrated by Will Terry, Aladdin (New York, NY), 2007.

Isabel Saves the Prince: Based on a True Story of Isabel I of Spain, illustrated by Nonna Aleshina, Aladdin (New York, NY), 2007.

Lydia and the Island Kingdom: A Story Based on the Real Life of Princess Liliuokalani of Hawaii, illustrated by Nonna Aleshina, Aladdin (New York, NY), 2007.

Scaredy Pants!: A Halloween Story, illustrated by Will Terry, Aladdin (New York, NY), 2007.

Who Was Marco Polo?, illustrated by John O'Brien, Grosset & Dunlap (New York, NY), 2007.

Bed, Bats, and Beyond, illustrated by Mernie Gallagher-Cole, Darby Creek Publshing (Plain City, OH), 2008.

Five Spring Fairies: A Counting Book with Flaps and Pop-ups!, illustrated by Kathy Couri, Simon & Schuster (New York, NY), 2008.

Knuckleheads, illustrated by Michael Slack, Chronicle Books (San Francisco, CA), 2008.

Snow Day!, illustrated by Will Terry, Aladdin (New York, NY), 2008.

Spring Is Here!: A Story about Seeds, illustrated by Will Terry, Aladdin (New York, NY), 2008.

Apple Countdown, illustrated by Jan Smith, Albert Whitman (Morton Grove, IL), 2009.

Groundhog Weather School, illustrated by Kristin Sorra, Putnam (New York, NY), 2009.

Shampoodle, illustrated by Tim Bowers, Random House (New York, NY), 2009.

Twinkle, Star of the Week, illustrated by Paul Nicholls, Albert Whitman (Chicago, IL), 2010.

Who Was Jim Henson?, illustrated by Nancy Harrison, Grosset & Dunlap (New York, NY), 2010.

What Does Cow Say?, illustrated by Jannie Ho, Scholastic (New York, NY), 2011.

(With George Hallowell) *Wagons Ho!,* illustrated by Lynne Avril, Albert Whitman (Chicago, IL), 2011.

Who Was Babe Ruth?, illustrated by Ted Hammond, Grosset & Dunlap (New York, NY), 2012.

Countdown, illustrated by Jan Smith, Albert Whitman (Morton Grove, IL), 2012.

A Little Had Can Blow a Kiss, illustrated by Caroline Jayne Church, Scholastic (New York, NY), 2012.

Zero the Hero, illustrated by Tom Lichtenheld, Holt (New York, NY), 2012.

"DOLL HOSPITAL" SERIES

Tatiana Comes to America: An Ellis Island Story, illustrated by Cheryl Noll Kirk, Scholastic (New York, NY), 2002.

Goldie's Fortune: A Story of the Great Depression, illustrated by Cheryl Noll Kirk, Scholastic (New York, NY), 2002.

Glory's Freedom: A Story of the Underground Railroad, illustrated by Cheryl Noll Kirk, Scholastic (New York, NY), 2003.

Saving Marissa, illustrated by Anne Iosa, Scholastic (New York, NY), 2003.

Danielle's Dollhouse Wish, illustrated by Anne Iosa, Scholastic (New York, NY), 2003.

Charlotte's Choice, illustrated by Anne Iosa, Scholastic (New York, NY), 2004.

"GODDESS GIRLS" SERIES; WITH SUZANNE WILLIAMS

Athena the Brain, Aladdin (New York, NY), 2010.

Persephone the Phony, Aladdin (New York, NY), 2010.

Aphrodite the Beauty, Aladdin (New York, NY), 2010.

Artemis the Brave, Aladdin (New York, NY), 2010.

Athena the Wise, Aladdin (New York, NY), 2011.

Aphrodite the Diva, Aladdin (New York, NY), 2011.

Artemis the Loyal, Aladdin (New York, NY), 2011.

Medusa the Mean, Aladdin (New York, NY), 2012.

SELF-ILLUSTRATED

Pen Pals, Grosset & Dunlap (New York, NY), 1997.

Boo Who? A Spooky Lift-the-Flap Book, Scholastic (New York, NY), 1997.

Red, Yellow, Green: What Do Signs Mean?, Scholastic (New York, NY), 1998.

Happy Monster Day!, Scholastic (New York, NY), 1999.

Eek-a-Boo! A Spooky Lift-the-Flap Book, Scholastic (New York, NY), 2000.

Abby Candabra, Super Speller, Grosset & Dunlap (New York, NY), 2000.

How to Find Lost Treasure in All Fifty States . . . and Canada, Too!, Aladdin (New York, NY), 2000.

Cinderdog and the Wicked Stepcat, Albert Whitman (Morton Grove, IL), 2001.

(As Brad Bucks) *Vincent van Gogh: Sunflowers and Swirly Stars,* Grosset & Dunlap (New York, NY), 2001.

The Haunted States of America: Haunted Houses and Spooky Places in All Fifty States . . . and Canada, Too!, Aladdin (New York, NY), 2001.

The Valley of the Golden Mummies, Grosset & Dunlap (New York, NY), 2002.

(Illustrated with Dana Regan) *Animals,* Price Stern Sloan (New York, NY), 2002.

(Illustrated with Dana Regan) *Cars and Trucks,* Price Stern Sloan (New York, NY), 2002.

(Illustrated with Dana Regan) *Dinosaurs,* Price Stern Sloan (New York, NY), 2003.

(Illustrated with Dana Regan) *Magical Creatures,* Price Stern Sloan (New York, NY), 2003.

Somebunny Loves Me, Simon & Schuster (New York, NY), 2003.

What Can Our New Baby Do?, Simon & Schuster (New York, NY), 2004.

Ivy Queen, Cootie Queen, Scholastic (New York, NY), 2004.

Happy Easter Eggs, Aladdin (New York, NY), 2005.

Glorious Grandmas, Aladdin (New York, NY), 2006.

Marvelous Moms, Aladdin (New York, NY), 2006.

ILLUSTRATOR

Elizabeth Levy, *If You Were There When They Signed the Constitution,* Scholastic (New York, NY), 1992.

Judy Gire, *A Boy and His Baseball: The Dave Dravecky Story,* Zondervan (Grand Rapids, MI), 1993.

Mary Winston, editor, *The American Heart Association Kids' Cookbook,* Times Books (New York, NY), 1994.

Rick Bunsen, *Nursery School ABC,* Western Publishing (Racine, WI), 1994.

Kirsten Hall, *My Brother, the Brat,* Scholastic (New York, NY), 1995.

My First Book of Sign Language, Troll Associates (Mahwah, NJ), 1996.

Wendy Lewison, *Ten Little Ballerinas,* Grosset & Dunlap (New York, NY), 1996.

Angela Shelf Medearis, *The 100th Day of School,* Scholastic (New York, NY), 1996.

Caren Holtzman, *No Fair!,* Scholastic (New York, NY), 1997.

Iris Hiskey Arno, *I Love You, Mom,* Troll Associates (Mahwah, NJ), 1997.

Iris Hiskey Arno, *I Love You, Dad,* Troll Associates (Mahwah, NJ), 1998.

Josephine Nobisso, *Hot Cha-Cha!,* Winslow Press (Delray Beach, FL), 1998.

Gina Shaw, *Shadows Everywhere,* Scholastic (New York, NY), 1999.

Lee Wardlaw, *Hector's Hiccups,* Random House (New York, NY), 1999.

Ruth Horowitz, *Breakout at the Bug Lab,* Dial Books for Young Readers (New York, NY), 2001.

Patty Rutland Mullins, *All about You with Inspector McQ,* World Book (Chicago, IL), 2004.

Ruth Horowitz, *Big Surprise in the Bug Tank,* Dial Books for Young Readers (New York, NY), 2005.

Contributor to periodicals, including *Instructor, Lady-Bug, Let's Find Out, Pre-K Today, Spider,* and *Children's Book Insider.*

Sidelights

A versatile and talented author and illustrator, Joan Holub has over 130 books to her credit, including such award-winning tales as *Groundhog Weather School,*

Leo and his brother have to think like a bug to find Max, a giant cockroach, before party guests arrive in Ruth Horowitz's Breakout at the Bug Lab, *illustrated in watercolor, gouache, and acrylic paints by Joan Holub.* (Illustration copyright © 2001 by Joan Holub. Used by permission of Dial Books for Young Readers, a division of Penguin Young Readers Group, a member of Penguin (USA) Inc., 345 Hudson St., NY 10014. All rights reserved.)

Why Do Dogs Bark?, and *Shampoodle.* Writing and illustrating children's books "is a great job," Holub commented in an essay on the Penguin Group Web site. "When I think of an idea, I write it down so that whenever I finish one story I'll have a bunch of ideas waiting that I can begin working on next."

Holub developed an interest in literature and art as a child, once telling *SATA:* "I loved elementary school and made good grades. English and math were my favorite subjects. My family moved every few years because of my father's job with an oil company. Sometimes it took a while to make new friends because I was shy. (I grew out of it.) My family didn't own many books, but my mom took my brother, sister, and me to the public library regularly. She enjoyed and valued books and reading, and through her, I learned to love books."

After graduating from college with a bachelor of fine arts degree, Holub spent several years working as an art director for a graphics design firm. As she once recalled to *SATA:* "In 1989, I left a lucrative job in Texas and moved to New York because I wanted to work in the children's book field. New York City was exciting and my new job in the book design department at Scholastic was a great learning experience.

"When I left Scholastic, I began freelancing as an illustrator full time. Because of my art background, I'd always primarily focused on art rather than the stories in children's books. But once I began reading children's books, I wanted to write them. It took a lot of reading and about five years before I sold my first book manuscript. Then I sold three manuscripts in three months. In the years since then, I've written and/or illustrated board books, novelty books, easy-to-reads, chapter books, 'tween books, and middle-grade nonfiction. Some people ask why I write so many different kinds of books. My answer is that I write the ideas that come to me. Ideas are easy to come by. The real work is turning an idea into a satisfying book that works from beginning to end."

Among Holub's nonfiction works are *Vincent van Gogh: Sunflowers and Swirly Stars* as well as her "Who Was. . .?" and "Why Do . . .?" books, which includes *Why Do Cats Meow?, Why Do Dogs Bark?, Why Do Horses Neigh?,* and several other titles. These books give children useful information about familiar animals in a simple, easy-to-read format and pair "a winning combination of tightly written narrative [with] age-appropriate vocabulary," as Pamela K. Bomboy wrote in a *School Library Journal* review of *Why Do Horses Neigh?* and *Why Do Rabbits Hop?, and Other Questions about Rabbits, Guinea Pigs, Hamsters, and Gerbils.* Holub works into the text of all her nonfiction "some surprising facts that children will enjoy, such as the fact that horses sleep only three hours per day," noted a *Kirkus Reviews* contributor in a review of *Why Do Horses Neigh?* Another *Kirkus Reviews* critic pre-

Holub teams up with artist Regan Dunnick to mix word games with number puzzles in the humorous **Riddle-iculous Math.** (Albert Whitman & Company, 2003. Illustration copyright © 2003 by Regan Dunnick. Reproduced by permission.)

dicted that children "with an affinity for all creatures green and scaly" will appreciate Holub's "easy but specific text" in *Why Do Snakes Hiss?, and Other Questions about Snakes, Lizards, and Turtles.*

Holub has contributed a number of books to Viking's "Easy-to-Read" series, including *The Garden That We Grew, The Pizza That We Made,* and *Scat, Cats!,* the last which tells a story about a boy and a girl who rid their house of several mischievous felines but then invite them back in. "With its easy vocabulary and rhyming verse," *Scat, Cats!* "is well suited for beginning readers," as Louie Lahana wrote in *School Library Journal.* A *Kirkus Reviews* contributor dubbed the same book "a model for the genre: a funny, satisfying story with solid educational underpinnings." *The Garden That We Grew* was praised by a *Horn Book* critic who commented that Holub's story about children raising pumpkins has "the necessary qualities of a beginning reader—simplicity, repetition, predictability, and pictorial cues."

A humorous tale about insomnia, *Bed, Bats, and Beyond* centers on Fink, a young bat that has trouble falling to sleep. Hoping to soothe their brother, siblings Fang, Batrick, and Batsy each tell a story that only serves to frighten and excite Fink. Finally, Mom Bat arrives with the perfect tale to quiet her child. "Charming and full of humor, this is sure to be a favorite," Jackie

Partch predicted in *School Library Journal,* and a *Kirkus Reviews* contributor believed that young readers would appreciate the work, "filled as it is with silly wordplay, funny stories and frequent spot drawings." In *Knuckle-heads,* Holub presents her offbeat take on a quartet of familiar fairy tales, featuring such characters as Nose White and Handsel and Gretel. "Jokes, both visual and verbal, abound, as do puns and other forms of word-play," a contributor remarked in a *Kirkus Reviews* appraisal of the book.

A forecast gone awry is at the heart of Holub's *Ground-hog Weather School,* which "combines elements of comic books, science lessons, a holiday tale, and history class," according to *School Library Journal* critic Lisa Egly Lehmuller. Frustrated by an optimistic but wildly inaccurate report of spring's arrival, a group of animals express disappointment with Groundhog, prompting him to offer lessons in weather prognostication. Although Holub's story introduces readers to a plethora of topics, including seasonal changes and burrowing, her "approach is so varied and so often witty that children will absorb the facts effortlessly," Carolyn Phelan noted in *Booklist.* In *Shampoodle* Holub de-

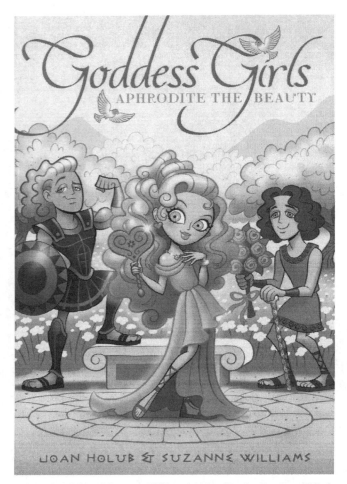

Cover of Holub and Suzanne Williams' **Aphrodite the Beauty,** *a "Goddess Girls" novel featuring artwork by Glen Hanson.* (Illustration by Glen Hanson. Aladdin Paperbacks, 2010. Reproduced by permission of Aladdin, an imprint of Simon & Schuster Children's Publishing Division.)

scribes the frantic efforts of several hairdressers to beautify an energetic group of canines. "Snappy rhyming verses lead children through the fiasco," remarked a *Kirkus Reviews* critic, and Shelle Rosenfeld, writing in *Booklist,* described *Shampoodle* as a "sympathetic portrayal of overcoming disappointment and discovering personal talents."

Coauthored with Suzanne Williams, the "Goddess Girls" books—including *Athena the Brain, Persephone the Phony,* and *Artemis the Brave*—offer a contemporary and humorous spin on characters from Greek mythology. "The myths themselves suggested the personalities of our characters and helped us plot our stories," Holub remarked in an essay on the *Cynsations Web log.* "Athena is the goddess of wisdom, among other things, so she's the brainy goddess girl. An over-achiever in fact, who tries to juggle too much (cheer, extra-credit projects, a big course-load) in order to keep up with the other amazing goddess girls and godboys she meets at MOA (Mount Olympus Academy)." *School Library Journal* contributor Adrienne L. Strock applauded the 'tween-centered tales, stating that Holub and Williams "intertwine an enchanting mythological world with middle-school woes compounded by life as a deity or blessed mortal."

As an author/illustrator, Holub has also created many board books and novelty books, including *What Does Cow Say?* and *Eek-a-Boo! A Spooky Lift-the-Flap Book.* Another of these works, *Boo Who? A Spooky Lift-the-Flap Book,* was considered "an engaging book for youngsters" by *School Library Journal* critic Debra Gold, the critic going on to call *Boo Who?* "a wonderful one-on-one choice."

As an illustrator, Holub's projects include providing the artwork for *Breakout at the Bug Lab* by Ruth Horowitz, as well as its sequel, *Big Surprise in the Bug Tank.* In the first book, two brothers accidentally let loose a Madagascar cockroach, a giant hissing bug, in their mother's environmental entomology lab and must recapture the insect before anything too bad happens; the second finds them convincing their mom to let them bring two of the cockroaches home, with unexpected consequences. Leslie S. Hilverding, writing in *School Library Journal,* deemed *Breakout at the Bug Lab* "a book in which everything is just right," while a *Kirkus Reviews* critic offered praise for *Big Surprise in the Bug Tank,* citing Holub's "small cartoon scenes featuring smiling, thumb-sized insects with appealingly googly eyes." In *School Library Journal* Heather Ver Voort commented of the same book that "the cartoon illustrations are colorful and clear."

Working in the field of children's literature is a dream come true for Holub. In her essay on the Penguin Group Web site, she noted: "The reason I'm a children's book author/illustrator today is that I have a lot of determination. I practiced drawing and revised my stories over

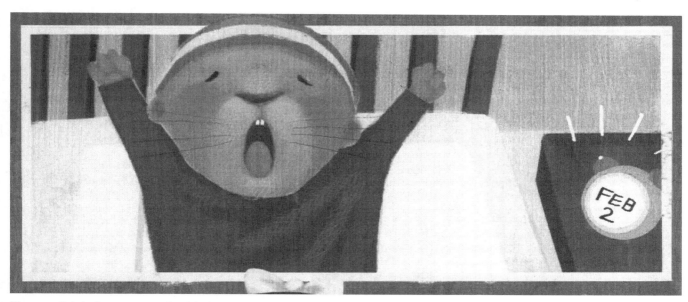

Illustrator Kristin Sorra captures the child-friendly elements of Holub's picture-book story **Groundhog Weather School.** (Illustration copyright © 2009 by Kristin Sorra. Reproduced by permission of G.P. Putnam's Sons, a division of Penguin Young Readers Group, a member of Penguin (USA) Inc., 345 Hudson St., NY 10014. All rights reserved.)

and over because I wanted nothing more than to do what I'm doing now—writing and illustrating children's books."

Biographical and Critical Sources

PERIODICALS

ARTnews, December, 2001, review of *Vincent van Gogh: Sunflowers and Swirly Stars,* pp. 102-104.

Booklist, February 15, 2001, Ilene Cooper, reviews of *Why Do Cats Meow?* and *Why Do Dogs Bark?,* both p. 1143; April 15, 2001, Stephanie Zvirin, review of *Scat, Cats!,* p. 1568; July, 2001, Hazel Rochman, review of *The Garden That We Grew,* p. 2023; November, 2001, Gillian Engberg, review of *The Pizza That We Made,* p. 486; November 15, 2002, Ilene Cooper, review of *Why Do Horses Neigh?,* p. 605; October 15, 2003, Hazel Rochman, review of *Riddle-iculous Math,* p. 406; November 1, 2004, Carolyn Phelan, review of *Why Do Birds Sing?,* p. 487; August 1, 2006, Carolyn Phelan, review of *The Man Who Named the Clouds,* p. 70; November 15, 2009, Carolyn Phelan, review of *Groundhog Weather School,* p. 42; March 1, 2010, Shelle Rosenfeld, review of *Twinkle, Star of the Week,* p. 80.

Horn Book, July, 2001, reviews of *The Garden That We Grew* and *Breakout at the Bug Lab,* both p. 452; May-June, 2005, Betty Carter, review of *Big Surprise in the Bug Tank,* p. 326.

Kirkus Reviews, June 1, 2001, review of *Scat, Cats!;* November 15, 2002, reviews of *Why Do Horses Neigh?* and *Why Do Rabbits Hop?, and Other Questions about Rabbits, Guinea Pigs, Hamsters, and Gerbils,* both p. 1695; September 1, 2004, review of *Why Do*

Snakes Hiss?, and Other Questions about Snakes, Lizards, and Turtles, p. 867; January 1, 2005, review of *Big Surprise in the Bug Tank,* p. 52; September 1, 2008, review of *Bed, Bats, and Beyond;* October 15, 2008, review of *Knuckleheads;* September 15, 2009, review of *Groundhog Weather School;* October 1, 2009, review of *Shampoodle;* February, 2010, review of *Twinkle, Star of the Week.*

Publishers Weekly, May 29, 2000, review of *How to Find Lost Treasure in All Fifty States . . . and Canada, Too!,* p. 84; September 25, 2000, reviews of *Eek-a-Boo! A Spooky Lift-the-Flap Book,* p. 64, and *Light the Candles: A Hanukkah Lift-the-Flap Book,* p. 66; February 19, 2001, review of *Cinderdog and the Wicked Stepcat,* p. 90; November 19, 2001, review of *Vincent van Gogh,* p. 70; December 17, 2001, review of *The Haunted States of America,* p. 94.

School Library Journal, June, 1993, Todd Morning, review of *A Boy and His Baseball: The Dave Dravecky Story,* pp. 117-118; October, 1997, Debra Gold, review of *Boo Who?: A Spooky Lift-the-Flap Book,* p. 98; February, 1998, Amelia Kalin, review of *Pen Pals,* p. 85; December, 1998, Carolyn Jenks, review of *Hot-Cha-Cha!,* p. 88; December, 1999, Anne Knickerbocker, review of *Hector's Hiccups,* p. 114, and Gay Lynn Van Vleck, review of *I Have a Weird Brother Who Digested a Fly,* p. 120; August, 2000, Donna L. Scanlon, review of *How to Find Lost Treasure in All Fifty States . . . and Canada, Too!,* p. 200; April, 2001, Leslie S. Hilverding, review of *Breakout at the Bug Lab,* p. 112; May, 2001, Karen Scott, review of *Cinderdog and the Wicked Stepcat,* p. 123, and Wanda Meyers-Hines, reviews of *Why Do Cats Meow?* and *Why Do Dogs Bark?,* both p. 143; August, 2001, Carolyn Jenks, review of *The Garden That We Grew,* and Louie Lahana, review of *Scat, Cats!,* both p. 153; September, 2001, Anne Chapman Callaghan, review of *The Haunted States of America,* p. 246; November,

2001, Lisa Smith, review of *The Pizza That We Made,* p. 124; December, 2002, Cynthia M. Sturgis, review of *Valley of the Golden Mummies,* p. 122; February, 2003, Pamela K. Bomboy, reviews of *Why Do Horses Neigh?* and *Why Do Rabbits Hop?,* both p. 132; January, 2004, Mary Elam, review of *Yankee Doodle Riddles: American History Fun,* p. 118; March, 2004, Nancy A. Gifford, review of *Riddle-iculous Math,* p. 196; October, 2004, Mary Hazelton, review of *The Halloween Queen,* p. 118; November, 2004, Bethany L.W. Hankinson, review of *Geogra-fleas!: Riddles All over the Map,* p. 124, and Heather Ver Voort, review of *Why Do Birds Sing?,* p. 126; February, 2005, Heather Ver Voort, review of *Big Surprise in the Bug Tank,* p. 103; December, 2006, Sandra Welzenbach, review of *More Snacks!: A Thanksgiving Play,* p. 100; July, 2007, Jayne Damron, review of *Cleopatra and the King's Enemies: A True Story of Cleopatra in Egypt,* p. 92; December, 2008, Jackie Partch, review of *Bed, Bats, and Beyond,* p. 92; June, 2009, Kristine M. Casper, review of *Apple Countdown,* p. 90; November, 2009, Lisa Egly Lehmuller, review of *Groundhog Weather School,* p. 82; February, 2010, Heidi Estrin, review of *Twinkle, Star of the Week,* p. 86; April, 2010, Adrienne L. Strock, reviews of *Athena the Brain* and *Persephone the Phony,* both p. 160.

Virginian Pilot, June 28, 2001, review of *Breakout at the Bug Lab,* p. E13.

Writer, March, 2000, "Quotes for Writers: They Say . . . ," p. 3.

ONLINE

Bildungsroman Web log, http://slayground.livejournal.com/ (November 20, 2009), interview with Holub; (April 7, 2010) interview with Holub and Suzanne Williams.

Cynsations Web log, http://cynthialeitichsmith.blogspot.com/ (April 6, 2010), "Guest Post: Joan Holub and Suzanne Williams on the 'Goddess Girls' series."

Joan Holub Home Page, http://www.joanholub.com (April 15, 2011).

Joan Holub Web log, http://joanholub.blogspot.com (April 15, 2011).

Penguin Group Web site, http://us.penguingroup.com/ (April 15, 2011), "Joan Holub."

*　　*　　*

HORLEY, Alex 1970-
(Alessandro Orlandelli)

Personal

Born Alessandro Orlandelli, 1970, in Opera, Italy. *Education:* Academy of Fine Arts of Milan, degree.

Addresses

Home—Italy; United States.

Career

Sequential and layout artist and illustrator. Creator of character art for video and role-playing games, comic books, CD covers, and promotion and advertising. Creator of licensed characters for Wizards of the Coast, Upper Deck Entertainment, and other gaming publishers. *Exhibitions:* Work included in exhibition at Museum of Contemporary Art Taiwan, 2010.

Illustrator

(With Dean Robinson) Greg Hildebrandt, *Blood Brother* ("Realm of the Rodent" series), Sourcebooks (Napierville, OH), 2009.

Alex Horley Sketchbook, Vanguard Productions, 2010.

Contributor to comic books and to periodicals, including *Draw!, Heavy Metal, Imagine FX, Online Gamer,* and *Rough Stuff.*

Biographical and Critical Sources

PERIODICALS

School Library Journal, February, 2010, Eric Norton, review of *Blood Brother,* p. 112.

ONLINE

Alex Horley Home Page, http://www.alexhorleyart.com (February 24, 2011).*

*　　*　　*

HOWELLS, Tania

Personal

Married; children: Finch. *Education:* Ontario College of Art and Design, degree, 1997. *Hobbies and other interests:* Reading, gardening, baking, knitting.

Addresses

Home—Toronto, Ontario, Canada. *E-mail*—taniahowells @yahoo.ca.

Career

Illustrator. Worked variously as a clay elephant maker, jewelry maker's assistant, hat maker's assistant, production assistant on the *Hour* with George Stromboulopoulos, and library aide.

Awards, Honors

Outstanding Books for Young People with Disabilities selection, International Board on Books for Young People, 2010, Blue Spruce Award shortlist, Ontario Li-

brary Association, and Shining Willow Award shortlist, Saskatchewan Young Readers' Choice Award, both 2011, all for *Willow's Whispers* by Lana Button.

Illustrator

Tera Johnson, *Berkeley's Barn Owl Dance,* Kids Can Press (Toronto, Ontario, Canada), 2008.

Lana Button, *Willow's Whispers,* Kids Can Press (Toronto, Ontario, Canada), 2010.

Contributor to books, including *The Crafter's Companion* and *No Sheep for You.* Contributor to periodicals, including *Today's Parent, Cottage Life, Chirp,* and Canada's *National Post.*

Sidelights

A freelance illustrator based in Toronto, Ontario, Canada, Tania Howells has provided the artwork for *Berkeley's Barn Owl Dance,* a whimsical picture book by Tera Johnson, and *Willow's Whispers,* an award-winning title by Lana Button. In the former, a young owl with a love of rhythm and dance struts her stuff at the Leave the Nest Fall Fest, an event signaling that the time has come for fledglings to find their own homes.

Tania Howells' illustration projects include creating the naïf line-and-wash art for Tera Johnson's picture book **Berkeley's Barn Owl Dance.** (Illustration copyright © 2008 by Tania Howells. Reproduced by permission of Kids Can Press Ltd., Toronto.)

Content to live with parents, however, Berkeley needs a reassuring pep talk before she reluctantly flies off with her brother and sister, exploring a number of barns before settling on one whose inhabitants appreciate her unique talents. Devon Greyson offered praise for Howell's artwork in her *Canadian Review of Materials* review, observing that the "illustrations are digitally rendered art with a soft, retro, watercolour feel." Gwyneth Evans, writing in *Quill & Quire,* stated that "Howells' gently coloured drawings, with their very expressive barn owl faces, are both humorous and reassuring."

An incredibly soft-spoken youngster discovers a way to make herself heard in *Willow's Whispers.* Because her voice is virtually inaudible to others, shy and sensitive Willow sits alone at lunch because her friends do not hear her invitation to join them and loses her favorite toy to a bully who cannot hear her protests. Willow's patient and loving father offers encouragement, however, and helping the girl devise a clever solution to her problem by employing creativity and intelligence. In *Quill & Quire* Chelsea Donaldson applauded Howell's use of "bold colours, spare lines, and plain white backgrounds" in her illustrations for Button's story, and a *Kirkus Reviews* critic believed that the minimalist drawings" in *Willow's Whispers* "have enough facial energy to carry the plot's emotions."

Biographical and Critical Sources

PERIODICALS

Canadian Review of Materials, November 7, 2008, Devon Greyson, review of *Berkeley's Barn Owl Dance*; September 24, 2010, Ellen Heaney, review of *Willow's Whispers.*

Globe & Mail (Toronto, Ontario, Canada), May 8, 2010, Susan Perren, review of *Willow's Whispers,* p. F14.

Kirkus Reviews, September 1, 2008, review of *Berkeley's Barn Owl Dance.*

Publishers Weekly, January 25, 2010, review of *Willow's Whispers,* p. 116.

Quill & Quire, October, 2008, Gwyneth Evans, review of *Berkeley's Barn Owl Dance*; April, 2010, Chelsea Donaldson, review of *Willow's Whispers.*

School Library Journal, December, 2008, Susan Scheps, review of *Berkeley's Barn Owl Dance,* p. 94; May, 2010, Margaret R. Tassia, review of *Willow's Whispers,* p. 79.

ONLINE

Tania Howells Home Page, http://www.taniahowells.com (April 15, 2011).

J

JANNI, Rebecca

Personal

Married; husband's name James; children: three sons, one daughter. *Education:* M.Ed. (English education). *Hobbies and other interests:* Reading, biking.

Addresses

Home—IA. *Agent*—Jamie Weiss Chilton, Andrea Brown Literary Agency; jamie@andreabrownlit.com. *E-mail*—rebecca@rebeccajanni.com.

Career

Educator and author. Teacher of high-school and college English and creative writing.

Member

Society of Children's Book Writers and Illustrators, PAL of Central Iowa, Des Moines Area Writers Group.

Writings

Every Cowgirl Needs a Horse, illustrated by Lynne Avril, Dutton Children's Books (New York, NY), 2010.
Every Cowgirl Needs Dancing Boots, illustrated by Lynne Avril, Dutton Children's Books (New York, NY), 2011.

Sidelights

Rebecca Janni celebrates the power of a child's imagination in her debut picture book, *Every Cowgirl Needs a Horse.* The work focuses on Nellie Sue, an expressive and energetic youngster who is eagerly anticipating her upcoming birthday. A country girl at heart, Nellie Sue becomes convinced that she will receive a horse for a present, and the imaginative child practices for the added responsibilities while performing her chores, which include filling her dog's water trough (his water bowl) and gathering hay (lawn clippings). With the party in full swing, the youngster's hopes are dashed when her mother and father wheel out a new bicycle, but she ultimately finds a way to make the best of the situation. "This entertaining picture book features a spunky protagonist," remarked *Booklist* critic Shelle

Rebecca Janni's story about a resourceful young heroine in Every Cowgirl Needs a Horse *features humorous artwork by Lynne Avril Cravath.* (Illustration copyright © 2010 by Lynne Avril Cravath. Reproduced by permission of Dutton Children's Books, a division of Penguin Young Readers Group, a member of Penguin (USA) Inc., 345 Hudson St., NY 10014. All rights reserved.)

Rosenfeld, who also praised Janni's "folky narrative." Marge Loch-Wouters, writing in *School Library Journal*, maintained that Janni's "lesson on dealing positively with disappointment is gently delivered." A *Kirkus Reviews* contributor asserted that Nellie Sue's "hopeful, unbroken spirit" is appealing to younger children and a *Publishers Weekly* critic predicted that story-hour audiences "should identify with her longing, as well as her powerful sense of imagination." The upbeat Nellie Sue makes a return appearance in *Every Cowgirl Needs Dancing Boots.*

Biographical and Critical Sources

PERIODICALS

Booklist, February 1, 2010, Shelle Rosenfeld, review of *Every Cowgirl Needs a Horse,* p. 49.
Kirkus Reviews, January 1, 2010, review of *Every Cowgirl Needs a Horse.*
Publishers Weekly, January 4, 2010, review of *Every Cowgirls Needs a Horse,* p. 44.
School Library Journal, February, 2010, Marge Loch-Wouters, review of *Every Cowgirl Needs a Horse,* p. 88.

ONLINE

Cynsations Blog, http://cynthialeitichsmith.blogspot.com/ (February 19, 2011), Cynthia Leitich Smith, interview with Janni.
Rebecca Janni Home Page, http://www.rebeccajanni.com (April 15, 2011).*

*　　*　　*

JOHNSON, Stacie
See MYERS, Walter Dean

*　　*　　*

JOHNSON, Varian 1977-

Personal

Born 1977, in Florence, SC; married November, 2003; wife's name Crystal. *Education:* University of Oklahoma, B.S. (civil engineering); Vermont College of Fine Arts, M.F.A. (writing for children and young adults).

Addresses

Home—Austin, TX. *Agent*—Sara Crowe, Harvey Klinger, Inc., 300 W. 55th St., Ste. 11V, New York, NY 10019. *E-mail*—vcj@varianjohnson.com.

Career

Civil engineer and author. Bridge designer for civil engineering firm in Austin, TX, beginning 2004. Cofounder, Brown Bookshelf (online community). Presenter at schools.

Member

Society of Children's Book Writers and Illustrators, Assembly on Literature for Adolescents, Writers' League of Texas.

Awards, Honors

Tayshas High-school Reading List inclusion, Texas Library Association, and Stuff for the Teen Age selection, New York Public Library, both 2009, both for *My Life as a Rhombus.*

Writings

A Red Polka Dot in a World Full of Plaid, Genesis Press (Columbus, MS), 2005.
My Life as a Rhombus, Flux (Woodbury, MN), 2007.
Saving Maddie, Delacorte Press (New York, NY), 2010.

Adaptations

A Red Polka Dot in a World Full of Plaid was adapted for audiobook, Recorded Books, 2006.

Sidelights

A South Carolina native who now makes his home in Austin, Texas, Varian Johnson has an unusual dual career: in addition to working as a civil engineer designing bridges, he also has several young-adult novels to his credit. His first novel, *A Red Polka Dot in a World Full of Plaid,* was written for adults but anticipates Johnson's interest in teens through its coming-of-age story about a girl who travels across several states in search of the father she never knew. Johnson's more-recent novels, *My Life as a Rhombus* and *Saving Maddie,* directly address adolescent readers through their focus on adolescent issues from a teen point of view. "Everything seems so immediate and fresh and awe-inspiring when you're a teenager," the author explained in an online interview with Cynthia Leitich Smith for *Cynsations.* "The teen years are when most people are figuring out who and what they're destined to be. It's an age where the simplest things can cause the most spectacular results." "Looking back at my own teen years, I clearly remember certain people and events that had profound effects on who I am today," Johnson added. "The teen years really are a time of wonder and enlightenment."

Although Johnson was a well-rounded student during high school—he performed in the school marching band and excelled at his studies—his aptitude for and interest

in math and science signaled a promising career in engineering. After he and his twin brother graduated from high school as co-valedictorians, Johnson attended the University of Oklahoma, graduating with a degree in civil engineering. In addition to completing his degree, he also found the time to write the first draft of what would become *A Red Polka Dot in a World Full of Plaid*. Marriage, a job, and a move to Austin, Texas, followed, and while building his engineering career Johnson has also continued to develop as a writer, honing his skills and tapping the many creative resources within that city's active writers' community.

Inspired by a personal experience, *My Life as a Rhombus* also taps Johnson's knowledge of mathematics through its focus on high-school senior Rhonda Lee. A math wiz, Rhonda is assigned to tutor popular junior student Sarah Gamble, but she evolves into a needed confidante when Sarah discovers that she is pregnant. While learning to listen and not to judge, Rhonda also revisits her decision to abide by her father's wishes and terminate her own unplanned pregnancy three years be-

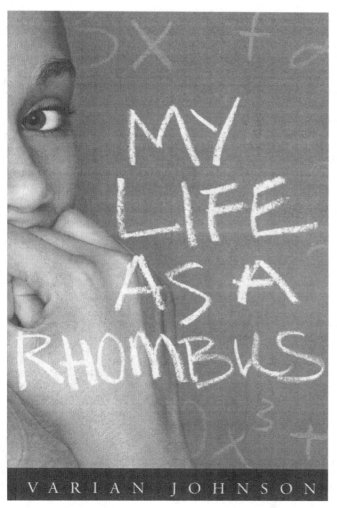

Cover of Varian Johnson's young-adult novel **My Life as a Rhombus**, *which finds a young math prodigy using logic to solve the problems of the heart.* (Cover photograph by Image Source/Shutterstock. Flux, 2010. Reproduced by permission of Flux, an imprint of Llewellyn Publications.)

fore. Noting that Johnson deals with a "loaded topic [that] will naturally lend itself to intense discussions," *Kliatt* reviewer Amanda MacGregor added of *My Life as a Rhombus* that the "variety of reactions, choices, and feelings" experienced by its teen characters "are realistic and nuanced." According to *Booklist* critic Stephanie Zvirin, Johnson creates interest by describing Rhoda's efforts to "channel . . . her anger and pain into numbers and theorems," and *My Life as a Rhombus* benefits from a "wry humor" and the teen characters' realistic dialogue.

Set in Johnson's native South Carolina, *Saving Maddie* finds seventeen-year-old Joshua Wynn conflicted when a childhood friend returns to their small town after a five-year absence. The son of a preacher who recognizes that his behavior should be beyond reproach, Joshua is both shocked and attracted to Maddie Smith in her new incarnation as an attractive, sexually provocative, and worldly-wise college student. Throwing off the hurt of a recent romantic break-up, he now funnels all his energy into rescuing Maddie, even though his sheltered life makes him incapable of understanding the experiences that have changed her. While noting that Johnson's characters "sometimes feel as if they've been set up to illustrate certain points," *School Library Journal* contributor Eliza Langhans dubbed *Saving Maddie* both "lively and endearing." According to a *Kirkus Reviews* writer, the author "avoids heavy-handed messages" and enriches his coming-of-age story "with nuanced characters and a realistic treatment of Joshua and Maddie's complex relationship." "Joshua's confusion about how narrow his path must be . . . keeps readers turning pages," asserted *Booklist* critic Ilene Cooper, while a *Publishers Weekly* writer wrote of *Saving Maddie* that "both the portrayal of awkward teen moments . . . and the questions Josh weighs about morality, God, and desire feel wholly genuine."

Biographical and Critical Sources

PERIODICALS

Austin American-Statesman, June 20, 2010, Joe Gross, "Austin Festival Turns Focus to Black Male Writers," p. H5.
Booklist, December 1, 2007, Stephanie Zvirin, review of *My Life as a Rhombus,* p. 36; April 15, 2010, Ilene Cooper, review of *Saving Maddie,* p. 42.
Bulletin of the Center for Children's Books, February, 2008, Karen Coats, review of *My Life as a Rhombus,* p. 252; March, 2010, Deborah Stevenson, review of *Saving Maddie,* p. 291.
Kirkus Reviews, February 15, 2010, review of *Saving Maddie.*
Kliatt, March, 2008, Amanda MacGregor, review of *My Life as a Rhombus,* p. 25.
Publishers Weekly, February 8, 2010, review of *Saving Maddie,* p. 52.

School Library Journal, February, 2010, Eliza Langhans, review of *Saving Maddie,* p. 114.

State (Columbia, SC), February 17, 2008, Rebekah Buffington, "No Right or Wrong Answers in Johnson's Young-Adult Novels."

Voice of Youth Advocates, June, 2010, Karen Sykeny, review of *Saving Maddie,* p. 155.

ONLINE

Cynsations Web log, http://cynthialeitichsmith.blogspot.com/ (July 31, 2008), Cynthia Leitich Smith, interview with Johnson.

Varian Johnson Home Page, http://www.varianjohnson.com (April 24, 2011).*

*   *   *

JONES, Carrie 1971-

Personal

Born March 1, 1971, in Manchester, NH; daughter of Lew (a truck driver) and Betty (an office manager) Bernard; married; husband's name Doug (a hospital president); children: Emily. *Education:* Bates College, B.A., 1993; Vermont College, M.F.A., 2007. *Politics:* Democrat. *Hobbies and other interests:* Kayaking, sailing, running.

Addresses

Home and office—Ellsworth, ME. *Agent*—Edward Necarsulmer IV, McIntosh & Otis, Inc., 353 Lexington Ave., New York, NY 10016.

Career

Author, journalist, and editor. Former reporter and editor for *Ellsworth Weekly,* Ellsworth, ME, and reporter for *Ellsworth American,* Ellsworth, and *Bar Harbor Times,* Bar Harbor, ME. Member of Ellsworth City Council, 2001-03.

Member

Society of Children's Book Writers and Illustrators.

Awards, Honors

Martin Dibner Award for Most-Promising Maine writer; Maine Literary Award for adult nonfiction; Maine Press Association awards for column, editorial, and sports writing; Independent Publishers Book Award for Best Young Adult/Juvenile Novel, Maine Literary Award for Children's Fiction, and Quick Pick for Reluctant Readers designation, American Library Association, all 2007 all for *Tips on Having a Gay (ex) Boyfriend.*

Writings

YOUNG-ADULT NOVELS

Tips on Having a Gay (ex) Boyfriend, Flux (Woodbury, MN), 2007.

Love (and Other Uses for Duct Tape), Flux (Woodbury, MN), 2008.

Girl, Hero, Flux (Woodbury, MN), 2008.

Sarah Emma Edmonds Was a Great Pretender: The True Story of a Civil War Spy, illustrated by Mark Oldroyd, Carolrhoda Books (Minneapolis, MN), 2011.

"NEED" YOUNG-ADULT NOVEL SERIES

Need, Bloomsbury (New York, NY), 2009.
Captivate, Bloomsbury (New York, NY), 2010.
Entice, Bloomsbury Children's Books (New York, NY), 2010.

OTHER

Also editor of poetry journals.

Adaptations

Jones' "Need" novels were adapted for audiobook by Briliance Audio, beginning 2009.

Sidelights

Carrie Jones, a former editor and journalist who makes her home in Maine, is the author of the young-adult

Cover of Carrie Jones' compellingly titled teen novel **Tips on Having a Gay (ex) Boyfriend.** (Cover image copyright © 2006 Brand X Illustration. All rights reserved. Reproduced by permission.)

novels *Tips on Having a Gay (ex) Boyfriend* and its sequel, *Love (and Other Uses for Duct Tape),* as well as *Girl, Hero* and a trilogy of supernatural stories that include *Entice, Need,* and *Captivate.* In an online interview with Cynthia Leitich Smith for *Cynsations,* Jones noted that "young adult books are about more than an age. They are about an openness to change, about the questioning of personal and political identity as well as the evaluation of cultural mores and practices. There's an amazing freedom in writing for people who are into that."

Jones began *Tips on Having a Gay (ex) Boyfriend* upon hearing about a local high-school student who suffered at the hands of her classmates after they learned that her former boyfriend was homosexual. Set in small-town Maine, the novel concerns Belle Philbrick, a senior who is devastated when her longtime boyfriend, Dylan, reveals that he is gay. Belle soon finds herself targeted by a homophobic thug, and she turns to Dylan and another classmate, Tom, for support. *Tips on Having a Gay (ex) Boyfriend* garnered strong reviews. A critic in *Publishers Weekly* stated that Jones' "poetic prose ably captures her heroine's emotional upheavals," and *School Library Journal* contributor Amy S. Pattee remarked that *Tips on Having a Gay (ex) Boyfriend* "offers an atypical perspective of the coming-out story by legitimizing the love that is not lost, but changed, when young people grow up and apart."

In *Love (and Other Uses for Duct Tape)* a jealous classmate begins to spread rumors after spotting Belle in a drug store purchasing a pregnancy test for her best friend, Emily. The brouhaha prompts the high-school senior to question several things, including the health of her relationship with her demanding jock boyfriend, Tom. Meanwhile, she must watch as her divorce mom begins dating, and the free time to process all the changes in her life is hard to come by given the demands of school, friends, and her job teaching gymnastics. Jones' "story is honest, earthy, and appealing," Claire Rosser observed in *Kliatt,* while in *School Library Journal* critic Kathleen E. Graver called Jones' heroine "a likable, believable character whose emotional crises will resonate with teens."

Musically gifted high-school freshman Liliana Faltin copes with the loss of her stepfather, an abusive brother-in-law, and an untrustworthy best friend by penning letters to heroic (but deceased) actor John Wayne in *Carrie, Girl Hero,* Jones' third novel. According to a contributor in *Kirkus Reviews,* teens "will respond to the self-aware but vulnerable Lily as she grows over time into her own unique hero," and in *School Library Journal* Leah Krippner dubbed *Carrie, Girl Hero* "a compelling read" in which Lili's "Western-style banter à la John Wayne is charming."

In *Need* Jones begins her four-volume series about a Bedford, Maine, high-schooler who is pulled into a supernatural world when she attracts the unwanted atten-

Cover of Jones' young-adult novel **Need,** *which finds a teen encountering supernatural creatures as well as romance while living with her grandparents in Maine.* (Bloomsbury, 2009. Cover photograph copyright © by Moodboard/Corbis. Reproduced by permission of Corbis.)

tion of a pixie. The creature lurks in the shadows and haunts Zara while attempting to increase his power for evil. Fortunately, the young woman finds an ally in Nick, a handsome classmate who also takes on the role of romantic liaison while gradually revealing his true nature as a shape-shifting pixie hunter. Zara's complicated family history has been revealed by the time readers reunite with her in *Captivate,* and now she must defend the pixie king from Nick while also keeping a secret that may doom the duo's growing romance. A *Publishers Weekly* critic noted the influence of Stephenie Meyer's "Twilight" books while also predicting that fans of supernatural romance will "enjoy the sizzle" in the romance between Nick and the "funny, globally conscious" Zara. While remarking on Jones' "trademark idiosyncratic figurative prose," a *Kirkus Reviews* critic wrote that the "fusion of self-sacrifice and burning love" in *Captivate* "will fully slake the thirst of eager *Need* fans."

Jones' "Need" series continues with *Entice,* in which Zara mourns Nick's death but holds out hope that he can be reconstituted by supernatural means. For now,

however, her efforts must focus on the pixie band that has been feeding off the teenaged population of Bedford, as well as on the possibility that the kiss she received from the pixie king may signal her doom. Praising *Entice* as "a strong successor" to Jones' first two series installments, Misti Tidman added in her *School Library Journal* review that "Zara is a strong and believable heroine" in a story that will attract "fans of urban fantasy and paranormal romance."

"I write for teens because I want to empower them," Jones noted in a *Class of 2k7* online interview. "I want to create a world they recognize and legitimize their world by presenting it as truth, but I also want teens to question that world a little bit, shake up that world view, question it. It's only by searching and exploring that we can figure our way back to the truth that is our own."

Biographical and Critical Sources

PERIODICALS

Bangor Daily News (Bangor, ME), June 30, 2008, "Maine People Inspire Novelist Carrie Jones."

Booklist, April 1, 2010, Lolly Gepson, review of *Captivate*, p. 80.

Bulletin of the Center for Children's Books, February, 2009, Karen Coats, review of *Need*, p. 244.

Kirkus Reviews, July 1, 2008, review of *Girl, Hero*; December 1, 2008, review of *Need*; December 1, 2009, review of *Captivate*.

Kliatt, May, 2007, Claire Rosser, review of *Tips on Having a Gay (ex) Boyfriend*, p. 14; March, 2008, Claire Rosser, review of *Love (and Other Uses for Duct Tape)*, p. 16.

Publishers Weekly, June 4, 2007, review of *Tips on Having a Gay (ex) Boyfriend*, p. 51; November 24, 2008, review of *Need*, p. 58.

School Library Journal, May, 2007, Amy S. Pattee, review of *Tips on Having a Gay (ex) Boyfriend*, p. 134; August, 2008, Kathleen E. Gruver, review of *Love (and Other Uses for Duct Tape)*, p. 124; January, 2009, Leah Krippner, review of *Girl, Hero*, p. 106; June, 2010, Genevieve Gallagher, review of *Captivate*, p. 50; March, 2011, Misti Tidman, review of *Entice*, p. 164; April, 2011, Lucinda Snyder Whitehurst, review of *Sarah Emma Edmonds Was a Great Pretender: The True Story of a Civil-War Spy*, p. 161.

Voice of Youth Advocates, June, 2007, Jenny Ingram and Kristen Moreland, review of *Tips on Having a Gay (ex) Boyfriend*, p. 143; June, 2008, Caitlin Augusta, review of *Love (and Other Uses for Duct Tape)*, p. 144; December, 2008, review of *Need*, p. 452; April, 2010, Alissa Lauzon and Mary Boutet, review of *Captivate*, p. 70; February, 2011, Susan Hampe and Linda Infantino, review of *Entice*, p. 570.

ONLINE

Carrie Jones Home Page, http://www.carriesjonesbooks.com (May 15, 2011).

Carrie Jones Web log, http://carriejones.livejournal.com (May 15, 2011).

Class of 2k7 Web site, http://www.classof2k7.com/ (August 1, 2008), "Carrie Jones."

Cynsations Web site, http://cynthialeitichsmith.blogspot.com/ (September 24, 2007), Cynthia Leitich Smith, interview with Jones.

Writing Life Web log, http://ellsworthmaine.com/ (August 1, 2008), "Carrie Jones."*

K-L

KENNY, Kathryn
See KRULL, Kathleen

*   *   *

KENNY, Kevin
See KRULL, Kathleen

*   *   *

KINKADE, Sheila 1962-

Personal
Born 1962. *Education:* Duke University, B.A. (English and political science), 1984; Columbia University, M.S. (journalism), 1987. *Hobbies and other interests:* Travel.

Addresses
Home—Baltimore, MD.

Career
Communications consultant and author. Artemis Communications, founder and principal, 2008—; consultant to organizations, including African Development Foundation, Baklans YouthLink-Albania, Inter-American Development Bank, International Youth Foundation, and World Bank. Corfu Foundation, member of board; Humanity International, member of advisor board.

Writings

Children of the Philippines, photographs by Elaine Little, Carolrhoda Books (Minneapolis, MN), 1996.
Travel Smart: Maryland/Delaware, John Muir Publications, 1999.
Children of Slovakia, photographs by Elaine Little, Carolrhoda Books (Minneapolis, MN), 2001.

(With Christina Macy) *Our Time Is Now: Young People Changing the World,* foreword by Archbishop Desmond Tutu, Pearson Foundation (New York, NY), 2005.
My Family, photographs by Elaine Little, Charlesbridge (Watertown, MA), 2006.
(With Maya Ajmera and Cynthia Pon) *Our Grandparents: A Global Album,* Charlesbridge (Watertown, MA), 2010.

Biographical and Critical Sources

PERIODICALS

Booklist, December 1, 1996, Susan Dove Lempke, review of *Children of the Philippines,* p. 650; January 1, 2006, Hazel Rochman, review of *My Family,* p. 105.
Children's Bookwatch, January, 2007, review of *My Family.*
School Library Journal, June, 2001, Tammy K. Baggett, review of *Children of Slovakia,* p. 136; February, 2006, Genevieve Gallagher, review of *My Family,* p. 120.

ONLINE

Charlesbridge Web site, http://www.charlesbridge.com/ (April 15, 2011), "Sheila Kinkade."*

*   *   *

KRULL, Kathleen 1952-
(Kathleen Cowles, Kathryn Kenny, Kevin Kenny)

Personal
Born July 29, 1952, in Fort Leonard Wood, MO; daughter of Kenneth (an artists' representative) and Helen (a counselor) Krull; married Paul W. Brewer (an artist and

Kathleen Krull (Photograph by Paul Brewer. Reproduced by permission.)

writer), October 31, 1989; stepchildren: Jacqui, Melanie. *Education:* Lawrence University, B.A. (magna cum laude), 1974. *Hobbies and other interests:* Music, gardening, quilting, travel.

Addresses

Home—San Diego, CA. *E-mail*—kkrull1@san.rr.com.

Career

Author. Harper & Row Publishers, Evanston, IL, editorial assistant, 1973-74; Western Publishing, Racine, WI, associate editor, 1974-79; Raintree Publishers, Milwaukee, WI, managing editor, 1979-82; Harcourt Brace Jovanovich, San Diego, CA, senior editor, 1982-84; freelance writer, 1984—.

Member

Society of Children's Book Writers and Illustrators.

Awards, Honors

Notable Children's Trade Book in the Field of Social Studies designation, National Council for the Social Studies (NCSS)/Children's Book Council (CBC), 1980, for *Sometimes My Mom Drinks Too Much;* Chicago Book Clinic Award, 1980, for *Beginning to Learn about Colors;* New York Art Directors Club Award, 1980, for *Beginning to Learn about Shapes;* Notable Book designation, American Library Association (ALA), 1992, for *I Hear America Singing;* Golden Kite Honor Award, Society of Children's Book Writers and Illustrators, ALA Notable Book designation, PEN West Children's Literature Award, and *Boston Globe/Horn Book* Honor Award, all c. 1993, all for *Lives of the Musicians;* ALA Best Books for Young Adults selection, Notable Children's Trade Books in the Language Arts designation, and International Reading Association (IRA) Teacher's Choice citation, all c. 1994, all for *Lives of the Writers;* IRA Teacher's Choice citation, and One Hundred Titles for Reading and Sharing selection, New York Public Library, both 1995, both for *Lives of the Artists;* Books for the Teen Age selection, New York Public Library, 1995, for *V Is for Victory;* Jane Addams Picture Book Award, Jane Addams Peace Association, ALA Notable Book designation, One Hundred Titles for Reading and Sharing selection, and Parents' Choice Award, all c. 1996, all for *Wilma Unlimited;* IRA Teacher's Choice citation, One Hundred Titles for Reading and Sharing selection, and Notable Children's Trade Book in the Field of Social Studies designation, NCSS/CBC, all c. 1997, all for *Lives of the Athletes;* Books for the Teen Age selection, 1998, for *Lives of the Presidents;* ALA Best Books for Young Adults selection, 2003, for *The Book of Rock Stars;* Jane Addams Picture Book Award, ALA Notable Book designation, Carter G. Woodson Honor Book Award, and Americas Award Honor designation, all 2003, and Christopher Award, 2004, all for *Harvesting Hope;* NCSS/CBC Notable Children's Trade Book in the Field of Social Studies designation, and One Hundred Titles for Reading and Sharing selection, both c. 2004, both for *A Woman for President;* Notable Children's Trade Book in the Field of Social Studies designation, 2005, for *Houdini;* ALA Notable Book designation, and NCSS/CBC Outstanding Science Book of the Year selection, both 2006, both for *Leonardo da Vinci;* ALA Notable Book designation, 2006, for *Isaac Newton;* ALA Notable Book designation, NCSS/CBC Outstanding Science Book of the Year designation, and Books for the Teen Age selection, all 2006, all for *Sigmund Freud;* One Hundred Titles for Reading and Sharing selection, 2008, for *Fartiste;* Parents' Choice Silver Honor selection, and Orbis Pictus Award finalist, National Council of Teachers of English, both 2009, both for *The Boy Who Invented TV;* One Hundred Titles for Reading and Sharing selection, 2010, for *Kubla Khan;* Children's Book Guild Nonfiction Award for body of work, 2011.

Writings

FICTION; FOR CHILDREN

(Under house pseudonym Kathryn Kenny) *Trixie Belden and the Hudson River Mystery,* Western Publishing (Racine, WI), 1979.

(Under pseudonym Kevin Kenny; with mother, Helen Krull) *Sometimes My Mom Drinks Too Much,* illustrated by Helen Cogancherry, Raintree (Milwaukee, WI), 1980.

Alex Fitzgerald's Cure for Nightmares, illustrated by Irene Trivas, Little, Brown (Boston, MA), 1990, revised edition, illustrated by Wendy Edelson, Troll Associates (Mahwah, NJ), 1998.

Alex Fitzgerald, TV Star, illustrated by Irene Trivas, Little, Brown (Boston, MA), 1991, revised edition, illustrated by Wendy Edelson, Troll Associates (Mahwah, NJ), 1998.

Maria Molina and the Days of the Dead, illustrated by Enrique Sanchez, Macmillan (New York, NY), 1994.

Clip, Clip, Clip: Three Stories about Hair, illustrated by husband Paul Brewer, Holiday House (New York, NY), 2002.

(Compiler and adapter) *A Pot o' Gold: A Treasury of Irish Stories, Poetry, Folklore, and (of Course) Blarney,* illustrated by David McPhail, Hyperion Books (New York, NY), 2004.

How to Trick or Treat in Outer Space, illustrated by Paul Brewer, Holiday House (New York, NY), 2004.

"BEGINNING TO LEARN ABOUT" SERIES; WITH RICHARD L. ALLINGTON

Colors, illustrated by Noel Spangler, Raintree (Milwaukee, WI), 1979.

Shapes, illustrated by Lois Ehlert, Raintree (Milwaukee, WI), 1979.

Numbers, illustrated by Tom Garcia, Raintree (Milwaukee, WI), 1979.

Opposites, illustrated by Eulala Conner, Raintree (Milwaukee, WI), 1979.

Hearing, illustrated by Wayne Dober, Raintree (Milwaukee, WI), 1980.

Looking, illustrated by Bill Bober, Raintree (Milwaukee, WI), 1980.

Tasting, illustrated by Noel Spangler, Raintree (Milwaukee, WI), 1980.

Smelling, illustrated by Lee Gatzke, Raintree (Milwaukee, WI), 1980.

Feelings, illustrated by Brian Cody, Raintree (Milwaukee, WI), 1980.

Touching, illustrated by Yoshi Miyake, Raintree (Milwaukee, WI), 1980.

Thinking, illustrated by Tom Garcia, Raintree (Milwaukee, WI), 1980.

Writing, illustrated by Yoshi Miyake, Raintree (Milwaukee, WI), 1980.

Reading, illustrated by Joel Naprstek, Raintree (Milwaukee, WI), 1980.

Talking, illustrated by Rick Thrun, Raintree (Milwaukee, WI), 1980.

Spring, illustrated by Lynn Uhde, Raintree (Milwaukee, WI), 1981.

Summer, illustrated by Dennis Hockerman, Raintree (Milwaukee, WI), 1981.

Winter, illustrated by John Wallner, Raintree (Milwaukee, WI), 1981.

Autumn, illustrated by Bruce Bond, Raintree (Milwaukee, WI), 1981.

Letters, illustrated by Tom Garcia, Raintree (Milwaukee, WI), 1983.

Words, illustrated by Ray Cruz, Raintree (Milwaukee, WI), 1983.

Stories, illustrated by Helen Cogancherry, Raintree (Milwaukee, WI), 1983.

Science, illustrated by James Teason, Raintree (Milwaukee, WI), 1983.

Time, illustrated by Yoshi Miyake, Raintree (Milwaukee, WI), 1983.

Measuring, illustrated by Noel Spangler, Raintree (Milwaukee, WI), 1983.

NONFICTION; FOR CHILDREN

(Piano arranger) *The Christmas Carol Sampler,* illustrated by Margaret Cusack, Harcourt (San Diego, CA), 1983.

(Piano arranger and editor) *Songs of Praise,* illustrated by Kathryn Hewitt, Harcourt (San Diego, CA), 1989.

Gonna Sing My Head Off! American Folk Songs for Children, illustrated by Allen Garns, Knopf (New York, NY), 1992, published with CD as *I Hear America Singing: Folk Songs for American Families,* 2003.

It's My Earth, Too: How I Can Help the Earth Stay Alive, illustrated by Melanie Hope Greenberg, Doubleday (New York, NY), 1992.

V Is for Victory: America Remembers World War II, Knopf (New York, NY), 1995.

Wilma Unlimited: How Wilma Rudolph Became the World's Fastest Woman, illustrated by David Diaz, Harcourt (San Diego, CA), 1996.

Wish You Were Here: Emily's Guide to the Fifty States, illustrated by Amy Schwartz, Doubleday (New York, NY), 1997.

They Saw the Future: Psychics, Oracles, Scientists, Inventors, and Pretty Good Guessers, illustrated by Kyrsten Brooker, Atheneum (New York, NY), 1999.

A Kid's Guide to America's Bill of Rights: Curfews, Censorship, and the 100-Pound Giant, illustrated by Anna DiVito, Avon Books (New York, NY), 1999.

Supermarket, illustrated by Melanie Hope Greenberg, Holiday House (New York, NY), 2001.

M Is for Music, illustrated by Stacy Innerst, Harcourt (Orlando, FL), 2003.

What Really Happened in Roswell?: Just the Facts (Plus the Rumors) about UFOs and Aliens, illustrated by Chris Santoro, HarperCollins (New York, NY), 2003.

Harvesting Hope: The Story of Cesar Chavez, illustrated by Yuyi Morales, Harcourt (San Diego, CA), 2003.

The Book of Rock Stars: Twenty-four Musical Icons That Shine through History, illustrated by Stephen Alcorn, Hyperion Books for Children (New York, NY), 2003.

The Night the Martians Landed: Just the Facts (Plus the Rumors) about Invaders from Mars, illustrated by Christopher Santoro, HarperCollins (New York, NY), 2003.

The Boy on Fairfield Street: How Ted Geisel Grew Up to Become Dr. Seuss, illustrated by Steve Johnson and Lou Fancher, Random House (New York, NY), 2004.

A Woman for President: The Story of Victoria Woodhull, illustrated by Jane Dyer, Walker (New York, NY), 2004.

(With Anne Elizabeth Rector) *Anne Elizabeth's Diary: A Young Artist's True Story,* illustrated by Anne Elizabeth Rector, Little, Brown (New York, NY), 2004.

Houdini: World's Greatest Mystery Man and Escape King, illustrated by Eric Velasquez, Walker (New York, NY), 2005.

Pocahontas: Princess of the New World, illustrated by David Diaz, Walker (New York, NY), 2007.

(With husband Paul Brewer) *Fartiste: An Explosively Funny, Mostly True Story,* illustrated by Boris Kulikov, Simon & Schuster (New York, NY), 2008.

Hillary Rodham Clinton: Dreams Taking Flight, illustrated by Amy June Bates, Simon & Schuster (New York, NY), 2008.

The Road to Oz: Twists, Turns, Bumps, and Triumphs in the Life of L. Frank Baum, illustrated by Kevin Hawkes, Knopf (New York, NY), 2008.

The Boy Who Invented TV: The Story of Philo Farnsworth, illustrated by Greg Couch, Knopf (New York, NY), 2009.

Kubla Khan: Emperor of Everything, illustrated by Robert Byrd, Viking (New York, NY), 2010.

(With Paul Brewer) *Lincoln Tells a Joke: How Laughter Saved the President (and the Country),* illustrated by Stacy Innerst, Houghton Mifflin Harcourt (Boston, MA), 2010.

The Brothers Kennedy: John, Robert, Edward, illustrated by Amy June Bates, Simon & Schuster (New York, NY), 2010.

A Boy Named FDR: How Franklin D. Roosevelt Grew up to Change America, illustrated by Steve Johnson and Lou Fancher, Knopf (New York, NY), 2011.

Big Wig: A Little History of Hair, illustrated by Peter Malone, Arthur A. Levine Books (New York, NY), 2011.

Jim Henson: The Guy Who Played with Puppets, illustrated by Steve Johnson and Lou Fancher, Random House (New York, NY), 2011.

Contributor to *Open Your Eyes: Extraordinary Experiences in Far Away Places,* Viking (New York, NY), 2003.

"WORLD OF MY OWN" NONFICTION SERIES; PHOTOGRAPHS BY DAVID HAUTZIG

City within a City: How Kids Live in New York's Chinatown, Lodestar (New York, NY), 1994.

The Other Side: How Kids Live in a California Latino Neighborhood, Lodestar (New York, NY), 1994.

Bridges to Change: How Kids Live on a South Carolina Sea Island, Lodestar (New York, NY), 1995.

One Nation, Many Tribes: How Kids Live in Milwaukee's Indian Community, Lodestar (New York, NY), 1995.

"LIVES OF . . ." NONFICTION SERIES; FOR CHILDREN; ILLUSTRATED BY KATHRYN HEWITT

Lives of the Musicians: Good Times, Bad Times (and What the Neighbors Thought), Harcourt (San Diego, CA), 1993.

Lives of the Writers: Comedies, Tragedies (and What the Neighbors Thought), Harcourt (San Diego, CA), 1994.

Lives of the Artists: Masterpieces, Messes (and What the Neighbors Thought), Harcourt (San Diego, CA), 1995.

Lives of the Athletes: Thrills, Spills (and What the Neighbors Thought), Harcourt (San Diego, CA), 1997.

Lives of the Presidents: Fame, Shame (and What the Neighbors Thought), Harcourt (San Diego, CA), 1998, updated edition, 2011.

Lives of Extraordinary Women: Rulers, Rebels (and What the Neighbors Thought), Harcourt (San Diego, CA), 2000.

Lives of the Pirates: Swashbucklers, Scoundrels (Neighbors Beware!), Houghton Mifflin Harcourt (Boston, MA), 2010.

"GIANTS OF SCIENCE" SERIES; ILLUSTRATED BY BORIS KULIKOV

Leonardo da Vinci, Viking (New York, NY), 2005.

Isaac Newton, Viking (New York, NY), 2006.

Sigmund Freud, Viking (New York, NY), 2006.

Marie Curie, Viking (New York, NY), 2008.

Albert Einstein, Viking (New York, NY), 2009.

Charles Darwin, Penguin (New York, NY), 2010.

FOR CHILDREN; UNDER PSEUDONYM KATHLEEN COWLES

The Bugs Bunny Book, Western Publishing (Racine, WI), 1975.

The Seven Wishes, Western Publishing (Racine, WI), 1976.

Golden Everything Workbook Series, Western Publishing (Racine, WI), 1979.

What Will I Be? A Wish Book, Western Publishing (Racine, WI), 1979.

OTHER

Twelve Keys to Writing Books That Sell (for adults), Writer's Digest (Cincinnati, OH), 1989.

Presenting Paula Danziger, Twayne (New York, NY), 1995.

Coauthor of middle-school textbook for Pearson social studies program, 2011.

Author's papers are housed at the Kerlan Collection, University of Minnesota.

Sidelights

The recipient of the 2011 Children's Book Guild Nonfiction Award for her body of work, Kathleen Krull has made a career of educating and entertaining both children and young adults. The author of critically acclaimed works of fiction and nonfiction, including the *Boston Globe/Horn Book* Honor title *Lives of the Musicians: Good Times, Bad Times (and What the Neighbors Thought),* Krull has established herself as "a fixture in the children's literature world," noted Deborah Stevenson in the *Bulletin of the Center for Children's Books Online.* Among her many books, Krull is perhaps

best known for *Harvesting Hope: The Story of Cesar Chavez, The Boy Who Invented TV: The Story of Philo Farnsworth, Lincoln Tells a Joke: How Laughter Saved the President (and the Country),* and other biographies, all which employ "a conversational tone, well-integrated facts, vivid anecdotes, and sly asides," according to *Booklist* critic Gillian Engberg.

Krull was a self-proclaimed "book addict" from the time she could read; as she once told *SATA,* "Reading a lot is the main job requirement for being a writer." Encouraged by several of the nuns who taught her in Catholic school, she quickly began writing. Her earliest works, as Krull recalled, included "*A Garden Book* (second grade) and *Hair-Dos and People I Know* (fifth)." By the time she graduated from college, she was certain she wanted to be a writer, but to make a living while she developed her craft, she entered the publishing business. "It was a way to work with real writers, learn from them, participate in a highly creative world, and get a paycheck all at the same time," Krull explained to *SATA.* Over the next decade, through a series of jobs with various publishers, she rose from editorial assistant to senior editor and moved from the Midwest to San Diego, California. Editing hundreds of books, she worked with such authors as Tomie dePaola, Eve Bunting, Patricia Hermes, Anne Lindbergh, Jane Yolen, Charles Mikolaycak, Arnold Adoff, Amy Schwartz, Judy Delton, and Lael Littke.

Krull's first published works were issued by companies that employed her. Then, in 1984, with her solid credentials in writing and publishing, she made the break to full-time writer. Since then she has produced books covering a wide range of interests and age groups, and she is especially well regarded by critics for her contributions to children's music appreciation. Krull's extensive background in music—she played several instruments as a child and minored in music during college—has made her "passionate about helping to ensure that music remains important in the lives of children."

Inspired by Krull's eight years serving as a church organist (which began at age twelve), *Songs of Praise* collects fifteen hymns accompanied by historical notes, alternative verses, piano scores, and guitar chords. Praised as a "stylish collection" by a *Publishers Weekly* contributor, *Songs of Praise* features hymns from England, Germany, Holland, and North America, among them "Amazing Grace," "Jesus Loves Me," and the Doxology. Phillis Wilson concluded in *Booklist* that Krull's work, which is paired with illustrations by Kathryn Hewitt, creates a "veritable feast for the ears, the eyes, and the heart."

Gonna Sing My Head Off! American Folk Songs for Children, a comprehensive collection of sixty-two American songs, grew out of a love for the folk music Krull learned from her parents, from her guitar study, and from her "fear that traditional music was losing its place in the lives of children." From "I've Been Work-

ing on the Railroad," "Take Me out to the Ball Game," and "Oh, Susanna" to "What Have They Done to the Rain?," this "superbly edited" collection, according to a *Publishers Weekly* contributor, provides readers with "an invigorating musical tour of American history and American regions." As Oscar Brand wrote in the *New York Times Book Review,* the keys of the arrangements "are eminently singable, the chords easily playable," making the collection "totally enjoyable." A *Kirkus Reviews* critic praised the "scrupulous" care Krull takes in relating the origins of the songs, and Hazel Rochman stated in *Booklist* that the headnotes "express the sense of connection with ordinary people's lives that is at the heart of this collection." *School Library Journal* reviewer Ann Stell concluded that *Gonna Sing My Head Off!* contains "so many outstanding selections that no one will be disappointed." Krull's book made a reappearance in 2003 under the title *I Hear America Singing: Folk Songs for American Families,* complete with a compact disc containing twenty-three of the sixty-two songs featured in the book.

In *M Is for Music* Krull creates an eclectic, largely pictorial introduction to the world of song. "The range of

Krull takes a unique view of the life of classical musicians such as J.S. Bach in **Lives of the Musicians,** *featuring illustrations by Kathryn Hewitt.* (Sandpiper, 2002. Illustration copyright © 2002 by Kathryn Hewitt. Reproduced by permission of Houghton Mifflin Harcourt.)

words explored [in *M Is for Music*] is almost as vast as the world of music itself," commented *School Library Journal* contributor Jane Marino. For example, on the "B is for Beatles" page, three "bees" labeled with the names of classical composers—Bach, Beethoven, and Brahms—fly around the modern British rock band. Performers from jazz trumpeter Louis Armstrong to rock musician Frank Zappa, instruments from accordion to zither, and musical styles from *a cappella* to zydeco are also included. "I wanted to do *M Is for Music* as a unique, all-encompassing, eclectic tribute to the power of music in our lives," Krull told an interviewer on the Harcourt Books Web site. "It's meant as a springboard to musical activities and discussion of all kinds." Featuring complex, collage-like illustrations by Stacy Innerst, *M Is for Music* is a good choice "for those ready to explore an interest in music" and "will also appeal to those just learning the alphabet," according to a *Kirkus Reviews* critic.

Lives of the Musicians reveals Krull's passion for music and her use of research to unearth quirky facts. This work, which grew out of a lunchtime conversation, profiles the lives of twenty composers in a work that, as Malcolm Jones wrote in *Newsweek,* "unstuffs a host of shirts and delivers wonderful musical trivia." Classical composers Bach, Beethoven, Brahms, Mozart, and Vivaldi, operetta composers Gilbert and Sullivan, ragtime composer Scott Joplin, and even folk singer Woody Guthrie are all featured here in humorous detail. A *Publishers Weekly* critic praised Krull's editorial work, writing that the author "masterfully distills the essentials of each musician's life into snappy prose." "Even those only remotely interested in music will be hooked," concluded the critic in a reaffirmation of Krull's intent.

In addition to *Lives of the Musicians,* Krull has also produced *Lives of the Writers: Comedies, Tragedies (and What the Neighbors Thought), Lives of the Presidents: Fame, Shame (and What the Neighbors Thought), Lives of the Athletes: Thrills, Spills (and What the Neighbors Thought), Lives of Extraordinary Women: Rulers, Rebels (and What the Neighbors Thought),* and *Lives of the Pirates: Swashbucklers, Scoundrels (Neighbors Beware!).* Describing *Lives of the Writers,* a *Kirkus Reviews* critic called Krull's work "another colorful, enthralling excursion into our cultural heritage." With entertaining details about authors from Hans Christian Andersen to Jack London, the author "knows exactly how to captivate her audience," combining historical particulars with "amusing anecdotes that put flesh and blood on dry literary bones," according to a *Publishers Weekly* critic. Nevertheless, "the glimpses she provides are respectful of their times and influences without being dull," *School Library Journal* contributor Sally Margolis noted, the critic going on to predict that her approach will "whet readers' appetites for more biography and for the writers' actual works," as Mary Harris Veeder concluded in *Booklist.*

Krull ventures into the world of painting, sculpture, and other fine arts in her intriguing companion volume,

Lives of the Artists, while *Lives of the Presidents* features both political and personal details about each U.S. chief executive, including hints of scandals such as President Bill Clinton's extramarital affairs. *Lives of the Presidents,* like the other books in the series, displays Krull's "proven knack for delivering generous dollops of covert asides along with fun facts and pertinent information," commented a *Publishers Weekly* reviewer. Discussing her approach to writing biographies, Krull noted on her home page: "I use a 'warts and all' approach because I want to write biographies for kids living in the real world. I know readers have to survive all kinds of hurts and traumas; my way of helping is to dramatize how people in the past have done it."

Outside the "Lives of" series but in a similar vein, *They Saw the Future: Psychics, Oracles, Scientists, Inventors, and Pretty Good Guessers* profiles a dozen people—including Nostradamus, Marshall McLuhan, and Jeane Dixon—who made detailed predictions about the world with varying degrees of success. This volume has a "healthily skeptical" tone, encouraging readers to scrutinize even apparently accurate projections, while also providing extensive information about the times and cultures in which each subject lived, reported a *Publishers Weekly* contributor.

In her writing, Krull likes to show how famous people overcame adversity. Many of the men and women she profiles have had to surmount major obstacles, and reading about their efforts can inspire children. One inspiring life is presented in *Wilma Unlimited: How Wilma Rudolph Became the World's Fastest Woman.* After contracting polio as a child, Rudolph was told she was unlikely to regain the ability to walk. However, she managed not only to walk but to run, and she eventually became an Olympic champion. Krull originally set out to write about Rudolph in *Lives of the Athletes,* but quickly realized that the runner's story was so fascinating that it merited an entire book. "My interest in biography as a literary form comes from curiosity about the details of others' lives," Krull stated on her home page. "To put it in a simple way, I'm nosy." The author continued, "More intellectually, I'm intrigued by the shape and structure of a person's life—the arc, the story of it. As stories, biographies are some of the very best—people have definite beginnings, middles, and demises. I'm motivated by the challenge of trying to write about a life in a pithy, meaningful way—sculpting with words a portrait that conveys the essence of a person—accurately yet dramatically."

Labor activist Cesar Chavez is profiled in *Harvesting Hope.* Although this biography, aimed at elementary school children, gives the details of the activist's childhood and discusses Chavez's early efforts to organize migrant farm workers in California, the majority of *Harvesting Hope* deals with the National Farm Workers Association's 1965 strike. "Focusing on one event makes the story appealing to younger readers," maintained *School Library Journal* contributor Sue Morgan.

Because of that limited focus, Krull was able to provide gripping details of the strike and the accompanying three-hundred-mile protest march. For readers who are interested in what happened to Chavez after 1965, Krull provides an author's note outlining the activists' later life. Overall, as Susan Dove Lempke concluded in *Horn Book, Harvesting Hope* "is a powerfully moving tribute to an important person in U.S. history."

In *A Woman for President: The Story of Victoria Woodhull* Krull shares the little-known story of the first woman to run for the presidency of the United States. Woodhull, a fortune teller, financial whiz, and suffragist, was the candidate of the Equal Rights Party in 1872. "Krull's writing style is lively and engaging," observed *School Library Journal* contributor Ann Welton in a review of *A Woman for President*. A "perceptive and dramatic tribute," according to a critic in *Kirkus Reviews, Houdini* examines the life of famed escape artist Harry Houdini, who mesmerized audiences with his feats of derring-do in the early twentieth century. "The author's crisp narrative style and careful choice of detail are evident here," wrote Heide Piehler in a review of Krull's biography for *School Library Journal*. The author also looks at an important figure in America's colonial history in *Pocahontas: Princess of the New World*, "an accessible portrait of the Native American girl who helped maintain a fragile peace between her tribe and English colonists," according to a *Publishers Weekly* reviewer. A critic in *Kirkus Reviews* noted that Krull's "narrative economically continues the intertwined stories of Pocahontas's maturation and the travails of the white settlers," men who include John Smith, the English captain who owed his life to the Powhatan girl, and John Rolfe, the tobacco farmer who married her.

The story of nineteenth-century performance artist Joseph Pujol—better known by his stage name Le Pétomane—is the subject of *Fartiste: An Explosively Funny, Mostly True Story*, a book coauthored with Krull's husband, Paul Brewer. Pujol mesmerized audiences with his ability to break wind at will, demonstrating this strange skill at such famous venues as the Moulin Rouge in Paris. "Written in well-rhymed couplets," remarked *School Library Journal* reviewer Catherine Threadgill, "this gleefully tasteless tale reads easily." *Booklist* critic Ilene Cooper observed that "Krull and Brewer easily find humor in gassiness," and a *Kirkus Reviews* contributor described the biography as "a total blast." Krull and Brewer also collaborated on *Lincoln Tells a Joke*, a portrait of U.S. President Abraham Lincoln that focuses on his ability to use humor to cope with both personal difficulties and national crises. The sixteenth president "is portrayed as an accessible, endearing, and sympathetic figure," Jody Kopple declared in *School Library Journal*, and in *Horn Book* Betty Carter applauded the authors' "inclusion of less amusing, but perhaps more instructive, information on his love of language, grammar, and elocution."

Krull profiles other political figures in *Hillary Rodham Clinton: Dreams Taking Flight* and *The Brothers Kennedy: John, Robert, Edward*. In the former, she follows Clinton from her childhood, when she hoped to become an astronaut, through the 2008 presidential campaign. According to Cooper, the work "offers an appealing portrait of a person who pursued her goals with a single-mindedness others lack." *The Brothers Kennedy*, which describes a pivotal event from each individual's life, "serves as a good introduction to this important American political dynasty," Grace Oliff wrote in *School Library Journal*. Krull explores another leader, a thirteenth-century Mongolian statesman and general, in *Kubla Khan: Emperor of Everything*. Noting that reliable biographical information about Khan is not readily available, *Booklist* critic Ian Chipman still concluded that Krull "assembles a convincingly grand impression" of the founder of the Yuan dynasty.

In *The Road to Oz: Twists, Turns, Bumps, and Triumphs in the Life of L. Frank Baum* Krull casts her eye on the writer behind an American classic. She describes nineteenth-century author Baum's unlikely road to literary success, a road that included such failed business ventures as stints as a chicken breeder and window dresser. Finally, in 1900, his book *The Wonderful Wizard of Oz* became a bestseller at the turn of the twentieth century. Writing in *Horn Book*, J.L. Bell described *The Road to Oz* as "an entertaining look at how a peripatetic man in a rapidly changing society produced a lasting fantasy tale." *The Boy Who Invented TV* describes the moment of inspiration that led fourteen-year-old farm boy Philo Farnsworth to make an incredible breakthrough in technology. "It is the inventor's passion and genius that come through in this picture-book biography," commented Janet S. Thompson in *School Library Journal*. "Beautiful and beautifully told," observed Rich Cohen in the *New York Times Book Review, The Boy Who Invented TV* "tracks like the sort of graphic novel that breaks your heart, with its implied passage of time and slipping away of early dreams."

In 2005 Krull introduced her "Giants of Science" biography series, illustrated by Boris Kulikov. The works "show how scientific discovery is never a revelation arriving in a single, mind-blowing flash," as the author wrote in a *Book Links* essay. In *Leonardo da Vinci* she focuses on the great artist's scientific achievements and describes life in the Middle Ages. "Readers will come away from this accessible volume with an understanding of who Leonardo was," remarked *School Library Journal* reviewer Laura Younkin, and *Booklist* critic Carolyn Phelan described the work as a "very readable, vivid portrait set against the backdrop of remarkable times."

Albert Einstein highlights the Nobel-winning physicist whose insights into the nature of the physical world revolutionized scientific thought. Despite the complexity of Einstein's theories, the author "explains them in a fashion appropriate for her middle-school audience," Kathleen Isaacs remarked in *Booklist*. Thompson simi-

Krull captures the life of one of history's most fascinating leaders in* Kubla Khan, the Emperor of Everything, *featuring detailed artwork by Robert Byrd. (Illustration copyright © 2010 by Robert Byrd. Reproduced by permission of Viking Children's Books, a division of Penguin Young Readers Group, a member of Penguin (USA) Inc., 345 Hudson St., NY 10014. All rights reserved.)

larly noted in *School Library Journal* that Krull "employs colloquial terms and concrete examples to make her work both engaging and accessible to young audiences."

In *Isaac Newton* Krull profiles the seventeenth-century British scientist who invented calculus and discerned the basic principles of physics. The author's "conversational tone . . . lends a lively voice to a biography chock-full of information," Betty Carter wrote in *Horn Book.*

Krull looks at the father of psychoanalysis in *Sigmund Freud,* a "lucid and thoughtful examination of Freud's life, work and legacy," a contributor in *Kirkus Reviews* stated. Appraising the same work, *Booklist* reviewer GraceAnne A. DeCandido praised the author for her "breezy, forthright, and intelligent approach" to her subject. *Marie Curie* centers on the life of the acclaimed physicist who became the first woman to receive the Nobel Prize. According to *Booklist* critic John Peters, "Krull presents her as a reserved, focused brainiac, whose cold exterior concealed a sense of compassion," and Kristen Oravec, writing in *School Library Journal,* applauded the author's honest presentation of Curie's failures as well as her triumphs, describing the work as "a realistic portrait of a flesh-and-blood woman, not just a famous name."

It's My Earth, Too: How I Can Help the Earth Stay Alive provides a good example of Krull's contribution of other nonfiction subjects to children's literature. The volume received attention as the first children's book to be printed on recycled paper using environmentally friendly soybean inks and water-soluble glue, thus reinforcing the book's message. Throughout the book, the author reminds readers that judicious use of technology is best, and she provides twelve suggestions for children that generally emphasize changing habits, thinking about one's actions, and trying to avoid greediness. With its list of suggestions, *It's My Earth, Too* "could be very useful as an idea starter or discussion book in classrooms," Tina Smith Entwistle remarked in a *School Library Journal* review, while Kay Weisman wrote in *Booklist* that the "simple, rhythmic text" is "particularly appropriate for this age level."

Krull also investigates America's ethnic communities, such as New York City's Chinatown and California's Latino neighborhoods, in her "World of My Own" series. Reviewing the first two books, *City within a City: How Kids Live in New York's Chinatown* and *The Other Side: How Kids Live in a California Latino Neighborhood,* Rochman noted in *Booklist* that Krull's "lively photo-essays" are written in "an informal, chatty style, weaving together information about family, friends, school, [and] religion," among other things. Krull uses quotations to allow her subjects to speak for themselves; as a result, as Roger Sutton remarked in the *Bulletin of the Center for Children's Books,* "in many ways, these books are a model for the genre." Reviewing all of the books in the series, Leigh Fenly similarly concluded in the *San Diego Union-Tribune* that while multicultural books have become a "hot market," Krull "refreshingly takes the genre into the reality zone."

In addition to her nonfiction, Krull has also written fictional tales for children, some of which feature the character Alexandra Fitzgerald. In *Alex Fitzgerald's Cure for Nightmares,* the nine year old attempts to cope with the scary dreams she has been having since she began to live with her father in California. Alexandra is worried that the other children in school will find out about her nightmares, but when she finally tells a friend about her problem, she is given some worry dolls and the night frights finally stop. Krull once commented, "The inspiration for this book combined my stepdaughter's insomnia (and her resulting obsession with worry dolls) with my own experiences as a California transplant." *Booklist* critic Wilson found the story to be "a sensitive and upbeat handling of a problem" that is "presented within an engaging school-activities plot."

Alexandra returns in *Alex Fitzgerald, TV Star,* which was inspired by an article about a girl "chosen to play the part of the young Madonna in a Pepsi commercial," as Krull once noted. "I got to wondering how sudden fame would affect an ordinary kid. Also, with hours of

Krull's talent for bringing her characters to vivid life is revealed in **The Boy Who Invented TV,** *a biography of Philo Farnsworth that features artwork by Greg Couch.* (Illustration copyright © 2009 by Greg Couch. Reproduced by permission of Alfred A. Knopf, an imprint of Random House Children's Books, a division of Random House, Inc.)

my childhood spent at the piano, I've had my own visions of fame and stardom." In this story, fourth grader Alex is invited to audition for a music video. Excited about the celebrity status she imagines, she forgets to buy her father a Christmas present, asks him to spend more money than he has, and annoys her friends. Krull's "pleasant, entertaining story," according to *Booklist* reviewer Stephanie Zvirin, is "wrapped around an important lesson," while a *Kirkus Reviews* writer praised the author's "good ear for dialogue." *Bulletin of the Center for Children's Books* critic Ruth Ann Smith concluded of *Alex Fitzgerald, TV Star* that readers will "sympathize with Alex's dreams of stardom, especially since they don't materialize."

With more dozens of titles to her credit, Krull remains dedicated to providing children with meaningful reading experiences. "As a child I thought books were the most important thing in the world, and that perception is actually more intense now," she commented on her home page. "I'm grateful, for so many reasons, to be able to work in a vital and exhilarating field: preserving literacy."

Biographical and Critical Sources

BOOKS

Graham, Paula, editor, *Speaking of Journals: Children's Book Writers Talk about Their Diaries,* Boyds Mills Press (Honesdale, PA), 1999.

Robb, Laura, *Nonfiction Writing from the Inside Out,* Scholastic (New York, NY), 2004.

PERIODICALS

Book Links, November, 2005, Kathleen Krull, "The 'Anti-Eureka' Series," p. 46.

Booklist, November 15, 1988, Phillis Wilson, review of *Songs of Praise,* p. 586; June 15, 1990, Phillis Wilson, review of *Alex Fitzgerald's Cure for Nightmares,* p. 1986; March 1, 1991, Stephanie Zvirin, review of *Alex Fitzgerald, TV Star,* p. 1388; July, 1992, Kay Weisman, review of *It's My Earth, Too: How I Can Help the Earth Stay Alive,* p. 1941; October 15, 1992, Hazel Rochman, review of *Gonna Sing My Head Off! American Folk Songs for Children,* p. 424; April 15, 1994, Hazel Rochman, reviews of *City within a City: How Kids Live in New York's Chinatown* and *The Other Side: How Kids Live in a California Latino Neighborhood;* September 15, 1994, Mary Harris Veeder, review of *Lives of the Writers: Comedies, Tragedies (and What the Neighbors Thought);* March 1, 2002, Ilene Cooper, review of *Lives of Extraordinary Women: Rulers, Rebels (and What the Neighbors Thought),* p. 1147; June 1, 2003, Traci Todd, review of *Harvesting Hope: The Story of Cesar Chavez,* pp. 1795-1796; August 1, 2003, review of *M Is for Music,* p. 1019; March 1, 2005, Jennifer Mattson, review of

Houdini: World's Greatest Mystery Man and Escape King, p. 1200; September 1, 2005, Carolyn Phelan, review of *Houdini,* p. 126; April 1, 2006, Kay Weisman, review of *Isaac Newton,* p. 38; December 1, 2006, GraceAnne A. DeCandido, review of *Sigmund Freud,* p. 36; December 15, 2007, John Peters, review of *Marie Curie,* p. 45; June 1, 2008, Gillian Engberg, review of *The Road to Oz: Twists, Turns, Bumps, and Triumphs in the Life of L. Frank Baum,* p. 100; August 1, 2008, Ilene Cooper, review of *Fartiste: An Explosively Funny, Mostly True Story,* p. 75; November 1, 2008, Ilene Cooper, review of *Hillary Rodham Clinton: Dreams Taking Flight,* p. 44; June 1, 2009, Ilene Cooper, review of *The Boy Who Invented TV: The Story of Philo Farnsworth,* p. 84; September 1, 2009, Kathleen Isaacs, review of *Albert Einstein,* p. 79; February 15, 2010, Andrew Medlar, review of *Lincoln Tells a Joke: How Laughter Saved the President (and the Country),* p. 73; March 15, 2010, Andrew Medlar, review of *The Brothers Kennedy: John, Robert, Edward,* p. 40; July 1, 2010, Ian Chipman, review of *Kubla Khan: The Emperor of Everything,* p. 54.

Bulletin of the Center for Children's Books, May, 1991, Ruth Ann Smith, review of *Alex Fitzgerald, TV Star,* pp. 221-222; May, 1994, Roger Sutton, reviews of *City within a City* and *The Other Side.*

Children's Digest, September-October, 2003, review of *I Hear America Singing!: Folk Songs for American Families,* p. 28.

Christian Science Monitor, August 23, 2001, review of *Lives of Extraordinary Women,* p. 21.

Constitutional Commentary, summer, 2002, Luke Paulsen, review of *A Kid's Guide to America's Bill of Rights,* pp. 291-295.

Horn Book, July-August, 2003, Susan Dove Lempke, review of *Harvesting Hope,* pp. 480-481; January-February, 2004, Joanna Rudge Long, review of *The Boy on Fairfield Street: How Ted Geisel Grew up to Become Dr. Seuss,* p. 103; September-October, 2005, Betty Carter, review of *Leonardo da Vinci,* p. 345; May-June, 2006, Betty Carter, review of *Isaac Newton,* p. 345; September-October, 2006, Betty Carter, review of *Sigmund Freud,* p. 607; September-October, 2008, Christine M. Heppermann, review of *Fartiste,* and J.L. Bell, review of *The Road to Oz,* p. 610; November-December, 2009, Tanya D. Auger, review of *The Boy Who Invented TV,* p. 694, and *Albert Einstein,* p. 695; May-June, 2010, Betty Carter, review of *Lincoln Tells a Joke,* p. 109; November-December, 2010, Christine M. Heppermann, review of *Kubla Khan,* p. 115.

Instructor, October, 1997, Judy Freeman, review of *Lives of the Athletes: Thrills, Spills (and What the Neighbors Thought),* p. 24.

Kirkus Reviews, June 1, 1991, review of *Alex Fitzgerald, TV Star,* p. 730; October 1, 1992, review of *Gonna Sing My Head Off!,* p. 1257; September 15, 1994, review of *Lives of the Writers;* January 15, 2002, review of *Clip Clip Clip: Three Stories about Hair,* p. 106; May 15, 2003, review of *What Really Happened in Roswell?: Just the Facts (Plus the Rumors) about UFOs and Aliens,* p. 753; July 1, 2003, review of

Harvesting Hope, p. 911; August 1, 2003, review of *M Is for Music*, p. 1019; September 15, 2003, review of *The Book of Rock Stars: Twenty-four Musical Icons That Shine through History*, p. 1177; March 1, 2005, review of *Houdini*, p. 289; June 15, 2005, review of *Leonardo da Vinci*, p. 685; March 1, 2006, review of *Isaac Newton*, p. 233; September 1, 2006, review of *Sigmund Freud*, p. 906; April 1, 2007, review of *Pocahontas: Princess of the New World*; September 1, 2007, review of *Marie Curie*; May 15, 2008, review of *Fartiste*; August 1, 2008, review of *The Road to Oz*; August 15, 2008, review of *Hilary Rodham Clinton*; August 15, 2009, review of *The Boy Who Invented TV.*

Newsweek, November 22, 1993, Malcolm Jones, review of *Lives of the Musicians: Good Times, Bad Times (and What the Neighbors Thought).*

New York Times Book Review, November 8, 1992, Oscar Brand, review of *Gonna Sing My Head Off!*, p. 44; November 16, 2003, Paul O. Zelinsky, review of *M Is for Music*, p. 37; October 17, 2004, Cokie Roberts, review of *A Woman for President: The Story of Victoria Woodhull*, p. 20; December 20, 2009, Rich Cohen, review of *The Boy Who Invented TV*, p. 12.

Publishers Weekly, October 5, 1992, review of *Gonna Sing My Head Off!*, p. 72; January 25, 1993, review of *Songs of Praise*, p. 88; February 22, 1993, review of *Lives of the Musicians*, pp. 96-97; August 1, 1994, review of *Lives of the Writers*, p. 79; May 15, 1995, review of *V Is for Victory: America Remembers World War II*, p. 75; April 29, 1996, review of *Wilma Unlimited: How Wilma Rudolph Became the World's Fastest Woman*, p. 73; June 8, 1998, review of *Lives of the Presidents: Fame, Shame (and What the Neighbors Thought)*, p. 60; June 7, 1999, review of *They Saw the Future: Psychics, Oracles, Scientists, Inventors, and Pretty Good Guessers*, p. 84; February 25, 2002, review of *Clip Clip Clip*, p. 66; June 3, 2002, review of *V Is for Victory*, p. 91; May 5, 2003, review of *Harvesting Hope*, p. 221; July 7, 2003, review of *What Really Happened in Roswell?*, p. 73; September 8, 2003, review of *M Is for Music*, p. 74; December 22, 2003, *The Book of Rock Stars*, p. 62; January 12, 2004, review of *The Boy on Fairfield Street*, p. 54; April 4, 2005, review of *Houdini*, p. 59; June 2, 2008, review of *Fartiste*, p. 46; August 11, 2008, review of *Hillary Rodham Clinton*, p. 46; August 25, 2008, review of *The Road to Oz*, p. 74; March 22, 2010, review of *Lincoln Tells a Joke*, p. 69.

San Diego Union-Tribune, August 7, 1994, Leigh Fenly, review of "World of My Own" series.

School Library Journal, July, 1992, Tina Smith Entwistle, review of *It's My Earth, Too*, p. 70; October, 1992, Ann Stell, review of *Gonna Sing My Head Off!*, p. 105; October, 1994, Sally Margolis, review of *Lives of the Writers*, pp. 134-135; March, 2002, Jody McCoy, review of *Clip Clip Clip*, p. 192; February, 2003, Lee Bock, review of *Wilma Unlimited*, p. 97; June, 2003, Sue Morgan, review of *Harvesting Hope*, pp. 129-130; September, 2003, Jane Marino, review of *M Is for Music*, pp. 200-201; October, 2003, Ann G. Brouse, review of *What Really Happened in Roswell?*,

p. 194; January, 2004, Anne Chapman Callaghan, review of *The Boy on Fairfield Street*, p. 119; November, 2004, Catherine Threadgill, review of *How to Trick or Treat in Outer Space*, p. 110; September, 2004, Ann Welton, review of *A Woman for President*, p. 189; December, 2004, Ginny Gustin, review of *Lives of the Musicians*, p. 60; April, 2005, Heide Piehler, review of *Houdini*, p. 124; October, 2005, Laura Younkin, review of *Leonardo da Vinci*, p. 190; March, 2006, John Peters, reviews of *A Woman for President*, p. 90, and *Isaac Newton*, p. 243; December, 2006, Nancy Silverrod, review of *Sigmund Freud*, p. 164; April, 2007, Lucinda Snyder Whitehurst, review of *Pocahontas*, p. 123; December, 2007, Kristen Oravec, review of *Marie Curie*, p. 154; April, 2007, Lucinda Snyder Whitehurst, review of *Pocahontas*, p. 123; July, 2008, Catherine Threadgill, review of *Fartiste*, p. 89; September, 2008, Jayne Damron, review of *The Road to Oz*, p. 165; September, 2009, Janet S. Thompson, review of *The Boy Who Invented TV*, p. 144; October, 2009, Janet S. Thompson, review of *Albert Einstein*, p. 147; March, 2010, Grace Oliff, review of *The Brothers Kennedy*, p. 141, and Jody Kopple, review of *Lincoln Tells a Joke*, p. 142; October, 2010, Barbara Scotto, review of *Kubla Khan*, p. 100.

Teacher Librarian, September-October, 1998, Teri Lesesne, "The Many Lives of Kathleen Krull."

ONLINE

Bulletin of the Center for Children's Books Online, http://bccb.lis.uiuc.edu/ (April 1, 2007), Deborah Stevenson, "True Blue: Kathleen Krull."

Children's Book Guild Web site, http://www.childrensbookguild.org/ (October 1, 2010), "Kathleen Krull 2011 Nonfiction Award Winner."

Harcourt Books Web site, http://www.harcourtbooks.com/ (April 15, 2011), interview with Krull.

Kathleen Krull Home page, http://www.kathleenkrull.com (April 15, 2011).

Random House Web site, http://www.randomhouse.com/ (April 15, 2011), "Kathleen Krull."

* * *

LARRAÑAGA, Ana Martín 1969-

Personal

Born 1969, in San Sebastian, Spain; immigrated to Germany; married; children. *Education:* University of Salamanca, B.F.A. (graphic design).

Addresses

Home—Germany. *Agent*—Herman Agency, 350 Central Park W., New York, NY 10025. *E-mail*—ana@conclu.de.

Career

Author and illustrator of children's books.

Writings

SELF-ILLUSTRATED

The Big Wide-mouthed Frog: A Traditional Tale, Candlewick Press (Cambridge, MA), 1999.

Woo!: The Not-so-scary Ghost, Arthur A. Levine Books (New York, NY), 2000.

Whose Toes Are Those?, Little Simon (New York, NY), 2001.

Is That My Chick?, Little Simon (New York, NY), 2001.

Pepo and Lolo Are Friends, Candlewick Press (Cambridge, MA.), 2004.

Pepo and Lolo and the Red Apple, Candlewick Press (Cambridge, MA), 2004.

Farm Faces: A Book of Masks, Innovative Kids, 2006.

Goodnight, Baby, Innovative Kids, 2006.

Quacky and Hoppy: Hide-and-seek Pond Bath Book, Barrons Educational (Hauppauge, NY), 2007.

Snuggle in the Snow, Little Tiger Press (New York, NY), 2007.

Squishy and Squirty: Hide-and-seek Ocean Pool Bath Book, Barrons Educational (Hauppauge, NY), 2007.

ILLUSTRATOR

B.G. Hennessy, *Meet Dinah Dinosaur,* Candlewick Press (Cambridge, MA), 2000.

B.G. Hennessy, *Busy Dinah Dinosaur,* Candlewick Press (Cambridge, MA), 2000.

B.G. Hennessy, *Little and Big,* Candlewick Press (Cambridge, MA), 2000.

B.G. Hennessy, *Dinah's Dream,* Candlewick Press (Cambridge, MA), 2000.

B.G. Hennessy, *Dinah Likes to Eat,* Candlewick Press (Cambridge, MA), 2000.

Richard Powell, *Jolly Jungle,* Treehouse Children's Books, 2000.

Richard Powell, *Guess What I Have!,* Barron's (Hauppauge, NY), 2001.

Richard Powell, *Guess Who's Hiding!,* Barron's (Hauppauge, NY), 2001.

Richard Powell, *Hoot! Hoot!,* Candlewick Press (Cambridge, MA), 2003.

Richard Powell, *Flap My Wings,* Tiger Tales (London, England), 2003.

Richard Powell, *Wag My Tail,* Tiger Tales (London, England), 2003.

Richard Powell, *Wiggle My Ears,* Tiger Tales (London, England), 2003.

Richard Powell, *The Black Cat,* Candlewick Press (Cambridge, MA), 2003.

Kathleen Long Bostrom, *Easter, Easter, Almost Here!,* Zonderkidz (Grand Rapids, MI), 2005.

Phyllis Root, *Who Said Boo?,* Little Simon (New York, NY), 2005.

Ana Martín Larrañaga's illustration projects include creating the interactive artwork for Susan Leonard Hill's **Freight Train Trip!** (Illustration copyright © 2009 by Ana Martin Larranaga. Reproduced by permission of Simon & Schuster Children's Publishing.)

Jan Jugran, *Hello, Baby,* Innovative Kids (Norwalk, CT), 2005.

Tish Rabe, *I'm a Baby,* Innovative Kids (Norwalk, CT), 2006.

Susanna Leonard Hill, *Airplane Flight!: A Lift-the-flap Adventure,* Little Simon (New York, NY), 2009.

Also illustrator of "Ana's Mini Movers" board books by Richard Powell.

Sidelights

Ana Martín Larrañaga was born in San Sebastian, Spain, and spent much of her childhood playing outside with her cousins. Her interest in art led Larrañaga to earn her B.F.A. at the University of Salamanca, where she focused on graphic design. Moves to Scotland and then to New York City exposed her to new ideas as well as a new language, but she has finally found a home in Germany, where raising her own children has helped to inspire her work as an illustrator and author of children's stories.

Larrañaga's first self-illustrated picture book, *The Big Wide-mouthed Frog: A Traditional Tale,* premiered her work for young readers. In the story, a talkative and boastful frog introduces itself to a succession of animals—including a koala and a kangaroo—before meeting up with a hungry crocodile and realizing that its bravado may inspire the toothy crocodile to put frog on the dinner menu. Other original stories that pair Larrañaga's text and art include *Pepo and Lolo Are Friends* and *Pepo and Lolo and the Red Apple,* two tales staring a young piglet and a fluffy chick who discover ways to work together despite their many differences. Designed for toddlers, *Woo! The Not-So-Scary Ghost* focuses on a young apparition that rebels against ghostly tradition by emerging during the daytime, only to discover much to be fearful of. Noting that Larrañaga's "crisp text is easy to read," Lisa Dennis added in her *School Library Journal* review that *Woo!* also benefits from "simple, stylized pictures" featuring bright colors and heavy black outlines that contribute "added energy and definition."

In addition to crafting original illustrated stories for very young children, Larrañaga has contributed artwork to beginning readers by B.G. Kennedy, Richard Powell, Phyllis Root, and Susanna Leonard Hill, among others. Dinah Dinosaur, the star of several stories by B.G. Kennedy, appears in *Meet Dinah Dinosaur, Little and Big, Dinah's Dream, Dinah Likes to Eat,* and *Busy Dinah Dinosaur.* Each book contains four short stories that feature what *Booklist* contributor Hazel Rochman described as Larrañaga's "big, bright . . . watercolor, pastel, and ink" images. Reviewing *Busy Dinah Dinosaur* in *School Library Journal,* Christina F. Renaud predicted that the inclusion of "endearing protagonists" make the series "appealing to the earliest readers," while Adele Greenlee noted in the same periodical that *Meet Dinah Dinosaur* combines a simple text with "illustrations [that] are done in a simple, colorful, childlike style."

Biographical and Critical Sources

PERIODICALS

Booklist, October 1, 2000, Hazel Rochman, reviews of *Meet Dinah Dinosaur* and *Busy Dinah Dinosaur,* both p. 351; December 1, 2000, Hazel Rochman, review of *Busy Dinah Dinosaur,* p. 725.

Publishers Weekly, August 1, 2005, review of *Who Said Boo? A Lift-the-Flap Book,* p. 66; May 7, 2007, review of *Hello, Baby,* p. 62.

School Library Journal, September, 2000, Lisa Dennis, review of *Woo! The Not-So-Scary Ghost,* p. 203; February, 2001, Adele Greenlee, review of *Meet Dinah Dinosaur,* p. 100; March, 2001, Christina F. Renaud, review of *Busy Dinah Dinosaur,* p. 194.

ONLINE

Ana Martín Larrañaga Home Page, http://www.conclu.de/ana (April 24, 2011).

Herman Agency Web site, http://www.hermanagencyinc.com/ (April 15, 2011), "Ana Martín Larrañaga."*

*   *   *

LECK, James 1973-

Personal

Born 1973, in Dartmouth, Halifax, Nova Scotia, Canada; married; wife's name Heather; children: Zoe, Isaac. *Education:* Mount Saint Vincent University, B.Ed. (English), 2005. *Hobbies and other interests:* Travel.

Addresses

Home—Kuwait City, Kuwait.

Career

Educator and author. Teacher of high school in Canada, Japan, and Kuwait.

Member

Top Ten First Novels for Youth selection, 2010, for *Booklist,* for *The Adventures of Jack Lime.*

Writings

The Adventures of Jack Lime, Kids Can Press (Toronto, Ontario, Canada), 2010.

Sidelights

James Leck loved to read mysteries while growing up in Canada, and in his first published book, *The Adventures of Jack Lime,* he draws on everything from Sir

Arthur Conan Doyle's legendary sleuth Sherlock Holmes and the hard-boiled detectives of the 1940s to 1970s television series *Colombo* and popular Saturday-morning cartoon series *Scooby Do*. A native of Nova Scotia, Leck gained a strong sense of what young readers look for in a book while working as an English teacher; in addition to teaching in North America, Leck has taught in Asia and now works as an English instructor in Kuwait City, Kuwait. "Detective novels tend to be fairly structured, which suits my writing style," Leck explained of his genre choice to *Halifax Newsnet.com* interviewer Kate Watson. "but at the same time you can have fun creating sinister villains and slipping in plot twists and red herrings." "In the tradition of all heroes," he revealed to Watson, his hero Jack Lime has a special challenge: "For Jack, it's his narcolepsy that kicks in at the worst possible times."

In the three interconnected stories in *The Adventures of Jack Lime* the fifteen-year-old sleuth lives with his grandmother in a modest older house is now surrounded by million-dollar homes as part of an exclusive gated community. Hoping to be accepted by his well-heeled classmates, Jack uses his tenacity and his powers of observation to raise his social status at Iona High School, trading his help for favors to be called upon when needed. In his first case as class problem-solver, Jack goes on the trail of a missing bicycle, while the next tale finds him tracking down the kidnapper of a classroom hamster. A clever student who is guaranteed to help Iona High win a local trivia tournament goes missing in Leck's third tale, again challenging his sleuthing skill and his ability to stay awake at important moments. Calling Jack "totally serious and tightly focused," a *Kirkus Reviews* writer recommended the novel's "tongue-in-cheek Raymond Chandler-esque first-person narration," which is "laced with gleefully clichéd slag." "The essence of 'cool' is hard to define," wrote Mary Thomas in her positive review of *The Adventures of Jack Lime* in the *Canadian Review of Materials;* "Jack doesn't have it, but he appreciates it, acknowledges it, and is not overly impressed by it. . . . Instead, he has smarts, a certain power of observation, and a logical mind that can reason from A to B and deduce C." "You don't need to reinvent the wheel for a great detective story," wrote *Booklist* critic Ian Chipman in discussing the strands of other mysteries that Leck weaves into *The Adventures of Jack Lime*. "But you do need a terrific sense of style. Jack Lime's got it in spades."

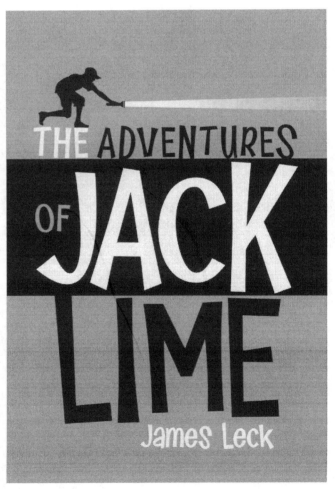

Cover of James Leck's young-adult novel The Adventures of Jack Lime, *which focuses on a teen sleuth who fancies himself a modern-day Sam Spade.* (Cover illustration adapted from images at iStockPhoto/A-Digit/marlanu/johnwoodcock. Kids Can Press, 2010. Reproduced by permission of Kids Can Press Ltd., Toronto.)

Biographical and Critical Sources

PERIODICALS

Booklist, February 15, 2010, Ian Chipman, review of *The Adventures of Jack Lime,* p. 76.
Canadian Review of Materials, June 25, 2010, Mary Thomas, review of *The Adventures of Jack Lime.*
Kirkus Reviews, December 15, 2009, review of *The Adventures of Jack Lime.*
School Library Journal, March, 2010, Natasha Forrester, review of *The Adventures of Jack Lime,* p. 162.
Voice of Youth Advocates, April, 2010, Debbie Wenk, review of *The Adventures of Jack Lime,* p. 59.

ONLINE

Halifax Weekly News Online, http://www.halifaxnewsnet.ca/ (February 26, 2010), Kate Watson, profile of Leck.
Kids Can Press Web site, http://www.kidscanpress.com/ (April 30, 2011), "James Leck."*

*   *   *

LOGAN, Alysia
See DIVINE, L.

LOXTON, Daniel 1975-

Personal

Born 1975, in British Columbia, Canada; son of tree-planting contractors. *Education:* Attended university.

Addresses

Home—Victoria, British Columbia, Canada. *E-mail*—juniorskeptic@skeptic.com.

Career

Writer, editor, and artist. Loxton Sheep Company, Prince George, British Columbia, Canada, professional shepherd for ten years; *Skeptic* magazine, editor and illustrator of "Junior Skeptic" section. Guest appearances on podcasts *Skepticality* and *The Skeptics Guide to the Universe.*

Member

Skeptics Society.

Awards, Honors

Silver Birch Award nomination, Ontario Library Association, 2011, for *Evolution.*

Writings

Evolução, Calouste Gulbenkian Foundation (Lisbon, Portugal), 2009.

(And illustrator, with Jim W.W. Smith) *Evolution: How We and All Living Things Came to Be,* Kids Can Press (Toronto, Ontario, Canada), 2010.

Contributor to periodicals, including *Skeptical Briefs* and *Skeptical Inquirer.*

ILLUSTRATOR

Contributor to *Dino's en Draken,* Teylers Museum (Haalems, Netherlands). Contributor to periodicals, including *Geotimes, Skeptic, Yes,* and *Free Inquiry.*

Sidelights

Daniel Loxton, a Canadian writer and artist who specializes in the subjects of science and critical thinking, serves as the "Junior Skeptic" editor of *Skeptic* magazine. In this capacity, Loxton uses a mix of writing and art to explore a wide range of subjects of interest to young readers, including extraterrestrial life, the Bermuda Triangle, fortune telling, the moon-landing hoax, and the search for Atlantis. Loxton is also the author and illustrator of *Evolution: How We and All Living Things Came to Be,* a nonfiction work described by

Quill & Quire reviewer Nathan Whitlock as "a good primer on a topic that, for reason[s] both good and bad, never seems to be out of the public eye."

Born in 1975 as the son of tree-planting contractors, Loxton was raised in Victoria, British Columbia, and lived in the Canadian outback during the summer months. A voracious reader as a child, he was fascinated by the paranormal, especially cryptozoology, the study of mysterious creatures such as Bigfoot. While attending a science-fiction convention as a high-school student, Loxton attended a panel led by Barry Beyerstein, a psychology professor and scientific skeptic, who fueled Loxton's interest in critical thinking. After his parents began a vegetation management company, using thousands of sheep to control plants that would overwhelm deforested regions, Loxton became a professional shepherd, spending a decade doing seasonal work along the British Columbia side of the Alaskan Panhandle. He attended school during the winter, and after graduation he performed freelance illustration work for *Free Inquiry* and *Skeptic* magazines, which eventually led to his appointment as the editor of "Junior Skeptic."

Loxton's *Evolution,* which he co-illustrated with Jim W.W. Smith, examines the studies of celebrated

In his text as well as his original art, Daniel Loxton provides a detailed look at the development of life as we know it in Evolution: How We and All Living Things Came to Be. *(Illustration copyright © 2010 by Daniel Loxton. Reproduced by permission of Kids Can Press Ltd., Toronto.)*

nineteenth-century British scientist Charles Darwin and explains the concepts of natural selection and survival of the fittest. A second section of the work offers a series of commonly asked questions and answers about evolutionary theory, including queries about transitional fossils and the issue of religion. "Loxton has a wonderful knack for simplifying without condescending and for challenging young readers to grapple with complicated concepts," observed Harriet Hall in her *Skeptical Inquirer* review, the critic adding that the author/artist's "illustrations are colorful, informative, and whimsical." According to *Wired* online reviewer Jason B. Jones, *Evolution* "is easy to read without being childish," and Katarin MacLeod noted in the *Canadian Review of Materials* that the volume "has a descriptive text, uses common analogies to aid in understanding possibly difficult aspects of the theory, and the graphics are frequently related to the accompanying text."

Biographical and Critical Sources

PERIODICALS

Canadian Review of Materials, May 7, 2010, Katarin MacLeod, review of *Evolution: How We and All Living Things Came to Be.*
Kirkus Reviews, January 15, 2010, review of *Evolution.*
Quill & Quire, January, 2010, Nathan Whitlock, review of *Evolution.*
Resource Links, June, 2010, review of *Evolution,* p. 10.
School Library Journal, May, 2010, Patricia Manning, review of *Evolution,* p. 133.
Skeptical Inquirer, September-October, 2010, Harriet Hall, review of *Evolution,* p. 57.

ONLINE

Daniel Loxton Web log, http://skepticblog.org/author/loxton (April 15, 2011).
Kids Can Press Web site, http://www.kidscanpress.com/ (April 15, 2011), "Daniel Loxton."
Skeptic Online, http://www.skeptic.com/ (April 15, 2011), "Daniel Loxton."
Wired Online, http://www.wired.com/ (March 16, 2010), Jason B. Jones, "The Junior Skeptic Explains Evolution: Daniel Loxton on Natural Selection."

*   *   *

LUM, Kate

Personal

Immigrated to Canada; married; children: one son, one daughter. *Education:* College degree.

Addresses

Home—Niagara-on-the-Lake, Ontario, Canada.

Career

Author.

Writings

(With Adrian Johnson) *What!,* illustrated by Adrian Johnson, Bloomsbury Children's Books (London, England), 1998, published as *What! Cried Granny: An Almost Bedtime Story,* Dial Books for Young Readers (New York, NY), 1999.
Stanley's No-Hic! Machine, illustrated by Bernice Lum, Bloomsbury (New York, NY), 1999.
Princesses Are Not Quitters!, illustrated by Sue Hellard, Bloomsbury Children's Books (New York, NY), 2003.
Princesses Are Not Perfect, illustrated by Sue Hellard, Bloomsbury (New York, NY), 2010.

Sidelights

A New England native, Kate Lum now makes her home in Ontario, Canada, where she attended college, met and married, and now raises her family. Her first published book, *What! Cried Granny: An Almost Bedtime Story,* was written for her son when he was a toddler, and she balanced this not to one child by writing *Princesses Are Not Quitters!* for her daughter. Another of Lum's stories for younger children, *Stanley's No-Hic Machine,* allowed the author to collaborate with her sister in law, prolific artist and illustrator Bernice Lum.

Reviewing *What! Cried Granny,* which is illustrated by Adrian Johnson, *Horn Book* critic Joanna Rudge Long wrote that the author's cumulative story "is paced with panache" and results in "a refreshing new take on a familiar scenario." Lum's chronicle of a battle between a wise grandmother and a toddler who is determined not to go to bed produces a "chuckler of a bedtime romp," according to a *Publishers Weekly* critic, while "Johnson's elastic artwork . . . stretches the story's humorous elements with a kind of manic glee."

Illustrated by Sue Hellard, *Princesses Are Not Quitters!* introduces a trio of energetic but bored young ladies who are determined to make life in the family castle more exciting. Princesses Allie, Libby, and Mellie trade places with three palace servants, and diligently complete every task that housekeeper Mrs. Blue sets before them. The next morning the three girls have far more appreciation for the many people who service their castle, and they take over several chores themselves in order to allow the castle staff some well-deserved time off. *Princesses Are Not Perfect,* the girls decide to trade off their favorite task; for Princess Allie, baking breads and cakes is her special talent, while Princess Libby shows a knack for building things from wood and Princess Mellie enjoys time spent working in the castle gar-

den. Although the girls assumed that, as princesses, they are interchangeable, they quickly learn to appreciate that each of their abilities is unique.

Reviewing *Princesses Are Not Quitters* for *Booklist*, Gillian Engberg predicted that Lum's "whimsical text will lend itself well to reading aloud," while "scribbly watercolors" by Hellard "enhance the cheeky fun." "Children will enjoy the role reversal in this lighthearted tale," concluded Linda Ludke in her *School Library Journal* appraisal of the same book, while a *Kirkus Reviews* contributor cited the mix of a "light, humorous approach and fairytale language" Lum employs her "gentle social commentary." "Frilly dresses, pink puppies, golden table settings, and sumptuous, far-fetched desserts abound" in Hellard's illustrations for *Princesses Are Not Perfect*, according to *School Library Journal* contributor Sara Lissa Paulson, while a *Kirkus Reviews* writer dubbed the same book a "rollicking sequel" in which Lum's "sprightly tale will enchant aspiring princesses." "The well-structured, gracefully written text" in *Princesses Are Not Perfect* "tells the story with a light touch," asserted *Booklist* contributor Carolyn Phelan, and Nicolette Jones predicted in her London *Sunday Times* review that Lum's "Princess" stories may be "an antidote to wishy-washy girly aspirations to swan about in pretty clothes."

Biographical and Critical Sources

PERIODICALS

Booklist, May 1, 1999, Hazel Rochman, review of *What! Cried Granny: An Almost Bedtime Story,* p. 1600; June 1, 2003, Gillian Engberg, review of *Princesses Are Not Quitters!,* p. 1787; December 1, 2009, Carolyn Phelan, review of *Princesses Are Not Perfect,* p. 48.

Horn Book, March, 1999, Joanna Rudge Long, review of *What! Cried Granny,* p. 197.

Kirkus Reviews, April 1, 2003, review of *Princesses Are Not Quitters!,* p. 536; February 15, 2010, review of *Princesses Are Not Perfect.*

Publishers Weekly, April 19, 1999, review of *What! Cried Granny,* p. 72; March 31, 2003, review of *Princesses Are Not Quitters!,* p. 66; February 22, 2010, review of *Princesses Are Not Perfect,* p. 66.

Quill & Quire, May, 2002, Joanne Findon, review of *Princesses Are Not Quitters!*

School Library Journal, May, 2003, Linda Ludke, review of *Princesses Are Not Quitters!,* p. 124; March, 2010, Sara Lissa Paulson, review of *Princesses Are Not Perfect,* p. 124.

Sunday Times (London, England), May 5, 2002, Nicolette Jones, review of *Princesses Are Not Quitters!,* p. 46.*

M

MacLACHLAN, Patricia 1938-

Personal

Born March 3, 1938, in Cheyenne, WY; daughter of Philo (a teacher) and Madonna (a teacher) Pritzkau; married Robert MacLachlan (a clinical psychologist), April 14, 1962; children: John, Jamie, Emily. *Education:* University of Connecticut, B.A., 1962.

Addresses

Home—Williamsburg, MA. *Office*—Department of Education, Smith College, Northampton, MA 01063.

Career

Writer and educator. Bennett Junior High School, Manchester, CT, English teacher, 1963-79; Smith College, Northampton, MA, visiting lecturer, 1986—; writer. Lecturer; social worker; teacher of creative writing workshops for adults and children. Member of board, Children's Aid Family Service Agency, 1970-80, and National Children's Book and Literacy Alliance.

Awards, Honors

Golden Kite Award, Society of Children's Book Writers, 1980, for *Arthur, for the Very First Time;* Notable Book citation, American Library Association (ALA), 1980, for *Arthur, for the Very First Time,* 1984, for both *Unclaimed Treasures* and *Sarah, Plain and Tall,* and 1988, for *The Facts and Fictions of Minna Pratt;* Notable Children's Trade Book designation, National Council for Social Studies/Children's Book Council, 1980, for *Through Grandpa's Eyes,* 1982, for *Mama One, Mama Two,* 1985, for *Sarah, Plain and Tall;* Boston Globe/Horn Book Award, 1984, for *Unclaimed Treasures; Horn Book* Honor List inclusion, 1984, for *Unclaimed Treasures,* 1985, for *Sarah, Plain and Tall;* Golden Kite Award, Scott O'Dell Historical Fiction Award, and *New York Times* Notable Children's Books

Patricia MacLachlan (Photo AP/Wide World Photos.)

of the Year designation, both 1985, Newbery Medal, ALA, Jefferson Cup Award, Virginia Library Association, Christopher Award, and Child Study Association of America Children's Books of the Year selection, all 1986, Garden State Children's Book Award, New Jersey Library Association, Charlie May Simon Book Award, Elementary Council of the Arkansas Department of Education, and International Board on Books for Young People Honor List selection, both 1988, all for *Sarah, Plain and Tall;* Parents' Choice Award, Parents' Choice Foundation, 1988, and *Horn Book* Fanfare citation, 1989, both for *The Facts and Fictions of Minna*

Pratt; University of Southern Mississippi Medallion, for body of work; National Humanities Medal, 2003, for body of work.

Writings

FOR CHILDREN

The Sick Day (picture book), illustrated by William Pene Du Bois, Pantheon (New York, NY), 1979.

Arthur, for the Very First Time (novel), illustrated by Lloyd Bloom, Harper (New York, NY), 1980.

Moon, Stars, Frogs, and Friends, illustrated by Tomie de Paola, Pantheon (New York, NY), 1980.

Through Grandpa's Eyes (picture book), illustrated by Deborah Ray, Harper (New York, NY), 1980.

Cassie Binegar (novel), Harper (New York, NY), 1982.

Mama One, Mama Two (picture book), illustrated by Ruth Lercher Bornstein, Harper (New York, NY), 1982.

Tomorrow's Wizard, illustrated by Kathy Jacobi, Harper (New York, NY), 1982.

Seven Kisses in a Row (picture book), illustrated by Maria Pia Marrella, Harper (New York, NY), 1983.

Unclaimed Treasures (novel), Harper (New York, NY), 1984.

Sarah, Plain and Tall (novel), Harper (New York, NY), 1985.

The Facts and Fictions of Minna Pratt (novel), Harper (New York, NY), 1988.

Journey, Delacorte Press (New York, NY), 1991, published with *Baby,* 2007.

Three Names, illustrated by Alexander Pertzoff, HarperCollins (New York, NY), 1991.

Baby, Delacorte Press (New York, NY), 1993, published with *Journey,* 2007.

All the Places to Love, paintings by Mike Wimmer, HarperCollins (New York, NY), 1994.

Skylark (sequel to *Sarah, Plain and Tall*), HarperCollins (New York, NY), 1994.

What You Know First, engravings by Barry Moser, HarperCollins (New York, NY), 1995.

Caleb's Story (sequel to *Skylark*), Joanna Cotler Books (New York, NY), 2001.

(With daughter, Emily MacLachlan) *Painting the Wind,* illustrated by Katy Schneider, Joanna Cotler Books (New York, NY), 2003.

(With Emily MacLachlan) *Bittle,* illustrated by Dan Yaccarino, Joanna Cotler Books (New York, NY), 2004.

More Perfect than the Moon (sequel to *Caleb's Story*), Joanna Cotler Books (New York, NY), 2004.

Who Loves Me?, illustrated by Amanda Shepherd, Joanna Cotler Books (New York, NY), 2005.

Grandfather's Dance (sequel to *Skylark*), HarperCollins (New York, NY), 2006.

(With Emily MacLachlan) *Once I Ate a Pie,* illustrated by Katy Schneider, Joanna Cotler Books (New York, NY), 2006.

Edward's Eyes, Atheneum Books for Young Readers (New York, NY), 2007.

(With Emily MacLachlan Charest) *Fiona Loves the Night,* illustrated by Amanda Shepherd, Joanna Cotler Books (New York, NY), 2007.

The True Gift: A Christmas Story, illustrated by Brian Floca, Atheneum Books for Young Readers (New York, NY), 2009.

(With Emily MacLachlan Charest) *I Didn't Do It,* illustrated by Katy Schneider, Katherine Tegen Books (New York, NY), 2010.

Word after Word after Word, Katherine Tegen Books (New York, NY), 2010.

Your Moon, My Moon: A Grandmother's Words to a Faraway Child, illustrated by Bryan Collier, Simon & Schuster Books for Young Readers (New York, NY), 2010.

(With Emily MacLachlan Charest) *Before You Came,* illustrated by David Diaz, Katherine Tegen Books (New York, NY), 2011.

Lala Salama: A Tanzanian Lullaby, illustrated by Liz Zunon, Candlewick Press (Somerville, MA), 2011.

Waiting for the Magic, Atheneum Books for Young Readers (New York, NY), 2011.

Author of *Skylark* (teleplay), CBS-TV, 1993; author of teleplay for *Sarah, Plain and Tall,* broadcast as a *Hallmark Hall of Fame* presentation, 1991. Work included in anthologies such as *Newbery Award Library II,* edited by Joseph Krumgold, Harper (New York, NY), 1988; and *Acting Out: Six One-act Plays! Six Newbery Stars!,* edited by Justin Chanda, Atheneum (New York, NY), 2008.

Adaptations

Arthur, for the Very First Time was adapted as a filmstrip with cassette, Pied Piper, 1984. *Sarah, Plain and Tall* was adapted as a filmstrip with cassette, Random House, 1986, as a television film starring Glenn Close, 1991, and as a musical by Julia Jordan, Nell Benjamin, and Laurence O'Keefe, produced in New York, NY, 2002. *Mama One, Mama Two, Through Grandpa's Eyes,* and *The Sick Day* were adapted for audiocassette, Caedmon, 1987. *Baby* was adapted for film.

Sidelights

Patricia MacLachlan is known for her award-winning picture books and novels for children, among them *The Sick Day; Arthur, for the Very First Time; Sarah, Plain and Tall;* and *The Facts and Fictions of Minna Pratt.* Populated by eccentric, endearing characters and often focusing on family relationships, MacLachlan's works are considered to be tender, humorous, and perceptive. Although she usually concentrates on the realities of everyday life in her books, MacLachlan has also penned fanciful tales such as *Tomorrow's Wizard* and *Moon, Stars, Frogs, and Friends.* Reviewers generally praise her work, indicating that her graceful, easy-to-read prose is particularly suitable for reading aloud and that her warm, optimistic stories both enlighten and entertain young readers. "MacLachlan is the critically acclaimed author of the kind of children's stories so compelling

MacLachlan's elementary-grade novel* Arthur, for the Very First Time *features engaging artwork by Lloyd Bloom. (Illustration copyright © 1980 by Lloyd Bloom. Reproduced by permission of HarperCollins Publishers.)

that readers clasp the book to their chest and sigh when the last page is turned," wrote Catherine Keefe in the *Orange County Register.*

Born in Wyoming and reared in Minnesota, MacLachlan was shaped by her prairie upbringing, and as an adult she continues to keep with her a sack containing soil from her homeplace as a symbol of the austere prairie environment. An only child, she developed strong family relationships and an active imagination. MacLachlan's parents were teachers and they encouraged her to read; as her mother often said, "read a book and find out who you are," the author related in *Horn Book.* She did read voraciously, sometimes discussing and acting out scenes in books with her parents. As she recalled in *Horn Book,* "I can still feel the goose bumps as I, in the fur of Peter Rabbit, fled from the garden and Mr. McGregor—played with great ferocity by my father—to the coat closet. . . . Some days I would talk my father into acting out the book a dozen times in a row, with minor changes here and there or major differences that reversed the plot."

MacLachlan was also kept company by her imaginary friend, Mary, "who was real enough for me to insist that my parents set a place for her at the table," the author recalled in *Horn Book.* "Mary was a free spirit. She talked me into drawing a snail on the living room wall, larger and larger, so that the room had to be repainted. . . . My parents tolerated Mary with good humor, though I'm sure it was trying. Mary was ever present. 'Don't sit there,' I'd cry with alarm. 'Mary's there!' One of my early memories is of my father, negotiating with Mary for the couch after dinner."

Though she was creative enough to invent a friend and concoct elaborate fantasies, MacLachlan did not write stories as a child. The author remembers being intimidated by the intensely personal nature of writing. In an autobiographical essay in *Authors and Adults for Young Adults,* she confessed: "I was afraid of putting my own feelings and thoughts on a page for everyone to read. This is still a scary part of writing." She also admitted in *Horn Book* that she believed "writers had all the answers." For one memorable school assignment "I wrote a story on a three by five card," she recalled. "I still have it: 'My cats have names and seem happy. Often they play. The end.' My teacher was not impressed. I was discouraged, and I wrote in my diary: 'I shall try not to be a writer.'"

MacLachlan was successful at not being a writer until age thirty-five. Married and with children of her own, she kept busy by working with foster mothers at a family services agency and spending time with her family. As her children grew older, though, she "felt a need to do something else—go to graduate school or go back to teaching, perhaps," she once noted. "It dawned on me that what I really wanted to do was to write. How would I ever have the courage, I wondered. It was very scary to find myself in the role of student again, trying to learn something entirely new."

MacLachlan started her successful writing career by creating picture books. Her first, *The Sick Day,* details how a little girl with a cold is cared for by her father. Another work, *Through Grandpa's Eyes,* explores how a young boy is taught by his blind grandfather to "see" the world through his other senses. *Mama One, Mama Two,* a somewhat later book, takes a frank yet comforting look at mental illness and foster parenting. In it a girl is taken in by "Mama Two" while waiting for her natural mother, "Mama One," to recover from psychological problems. MacLachlan, praised for the simplicity and sensitivity she brings to these stories, is especially noted for her deft handling of unconventional subject matter.

Encouraged by her editor, MacLachlan also started to write novels intended for a slightly older audience. Her first, *Arthur, for the Very First Time,* describes a young boy's emotional growth during a summer spent with his great-uncle and great-aunt. "Fine characterization, an intriguing mix of people and problems, and the author's remarkable knack for leaving between the lines things best unsaid are some of the strengths of the novel," maintained *Booklist* reviewer Judith Goldberger. Zena Sutherland, reviewing *Arthur, for the Very First Time* in the *Bulletin of the Center for Children's Books,* commented that MacLachlan's debut novel "has a deep tenderness, a gentle humor, and a beautifully honed writing style."

A character in *Arthur, for the Very First Time* provided the seed for what has become the author's best-known work: *Sarah, Plain and Tall.* The character of Aunt Mag, a mail-order bride (a woman who, in past times, attained a husband by answering a newspaper advertisement), was actually a distant relative of MacLachlan's. In *Sarah, Plain and Tall* the title character answers a newspaper advertisement and then travels to meet Jaco Witting, a lonely widower, and his children on the Midwestern prairie. When Sarah arrives, the children take to her immediately and hope she will stay and marry their father. Considered a poignant and finely wrought tale, *Sarah, Plain and Tall* garnered widespread critical acclaim and earned MacLachlan a Newbery medal in 1986. Margery Fisher, writing in *Growing Point,* hailed the novel as a "small masterpiece."

"My mother told me early on about the real Sarah, who came from the coast of Maine to the prairie to become a wife and mother to a close family member . . . .," MacLachlan explained in her Newbery Medal acceptance speech. "So the fact of Sarah was there for years, though the book began as books often do, when the past stepped on the heels of the present; or backward, when something *now* tapped something *then.*" Shortly before two of her children were to leave for college, MacLachlan and her family visited the prairie where MacLachlan and her parents were all born. This trip made the connection between the past and the present more evident to both MacLachlan and her mother, who was beginning to lose her memory because of Alzheimer's disease.

"When I began *Sarah,*" continued MacLachlan in her speech, "I wished for several things and was granted something unexpected. Most of all I wished to write my mother's story with spaces, like the prairie, with silences that could say what words could not. . . . But books, like children, grow and change, borrowing bits and pieces of the lives of others to help make them who and what they are. And in the end we are all there, my mother, my father, my husband, my children, and me. We gave my mother better than a piece of her past. We gave her the same that Anna and Caleb and Jacob received—a family."

A sequel to *Sarah, Plain and Tall, Skylark* "does not suffer in such a pairing [with the original], for it has its own center and momentum," according to Mary M. Burns in *Horn Book.* A terrible drought has overwhelmed Sarah and Jacob Witting's farm. The crops wither and die, drinking water is scarce, neighbors leave for better conditions elsewhere, and the barn burns down after a freak rainless lightning strike. "Sarah is increasingly on edge, not so firmly rooted as her husband, Jacob," wrote a *Publishers Weekly* critic. To alleviate their problems, Sarah takes the children Anna and Caleb, and goes to visit her aunts in coastal Maine, where water is plentiful and life is easier than on a hardscrabble farm in the plains. The only connection she and the children have with the farm is letters from Jacob, until one day he appears in Maine to collect his family. Rain has come to the farm, and Sarah is by now expecting a new baby. With renewed hope, the family returns to the farm, where Sarah symbolically writes her own name in the land. "*Skylark* is one sequel that is as successful as the original," Burns wrote. "This stirring novel's flawlessly crafted dialogue and imagery linger long after the final, hopeful message is delivered" by young Caleb, "who looks forward to arrival of spring and of his new sibling," wrote the *Publishers Weekly* reviewer.

Caleb narrates the continuing history of the Witting family in the aptly titled *Caleb's Story.* Anna has moved to town to attend school and work for the local doctor while the newest arrival to the family, Cassie, grows up on the farm. Then Jacob's father, who had abandoned his farm and his family and who Jacob thought was dead, returns and a conflict sparks between father and son. Finally it emerges that Jacob's father is illiterate, which may have contributed to his past actions. Now Caleb takes on the task of teaching his grandfather to read and Sarah urges Jacob to find the courage to forgive. In *Caleb's Story* "the relationships are believable, the emotions ring true, and MacLachlan has an unabated gift for clean, well-honed dialogue that carries its resonant meanings with unusual grace," wrote a *Horn Book* reviewer. A *Kirkus Reviews* critic predicted of the novel that "MacLachlan's appreciative readers will savor this new addition to the chronicle of a delightful family" while hoping for more volumes in the ever-growing series.

The Witting family's saga continues in *More Perfect than the Moon,* in which narrator Cassie is now eight years old and a budding writer. In her journal she records the things that happen to her family and her feelings about them, as well as including stories she makes up for herself. Many of Cassie's entries anticipate the arrival of a new younger brother or sister, an event Cassie is not looking forward to. She is convinced that the baby will be "ugly and mean," and wishes instead for a pet lamb. By the time the baby is born, however, the girl agrees with Sarah that the new child is a gift "more perfect than the moon." "The tale is charming," wrote a *Kirkus Reviews* contributor, "and Cassie is a delightful narrator." As Kay Weisman commented in her *Booklist* review of *More Perfect than the Moon,* the story's "solid, believable characters face classic dilemmas, yet the ending feels neither pat nor predictable," and *Horn Book* contributor Christine M. Heppermann wrote that, "as usual, MacLachlan infuses her story with graceful, affectionate images of life on the prairie."

Grandfather's Dance completes the saga MacLachlan began with *Sarah, Plain and Tall* as Anna is aided by Sarah in planning her wedding day. Far-away family members come home for the celebration, Caleb from school and William from Maine. Cassie, the narrator, is now in fourth grade and joins little brother Jack in anticipating the event-filled occasion. Characterizing the girl's descriptions as poetic, a *Publishers Weekly* contributor observed that "the real story" in the book is the "relationship between Jack and 'Boppa', the boy's special name for his elderly grandfather." As the characters' activities reflect "the changing times," MacLachlan's final plot twist also reflects the inevitable transition from generation to generation, her "beautifully straightforward language" capturing the honorable foundation of her midwestern characters, according to *School Library Journal* critic Pat Leach. Dubbing *Grandfather's Dance* "heartwarming," Hazel Rochman observed in *Booklist* that the author's narrative voice "is always true to a child's viewpoint, whether dealing with the joyous celebration of a marriage or the sad loss of a beloved family member."

Echoing themes explored by MacLachlan in *Skylark,* *What You Know First* tells the story of a girl whose parents have been forced to sell their farm and move elsewhere. Heartbroken, she begins to catalogue the things about the farm and the country that she will miss, and even tries to come up with reasons for not moving. In the end, she cannot avoid the inevitable, but she takes some tangible reminders with her: a bag of prairie dirt and cuttings from a beloved cottonwood tree. The book "touches the heart," wrote a *Publishers Weekly* reviewer. MacLachlan is a real-life example of the character in the story: she also carries a bag of prairie dirt with her wherever she goes, to remind her of where she came from. "It is the prairie dirt—clutched in a plastic sandwich bag, dusty and twiggy and brown, toted every-

where that MacLachlan goes—that speaks volumes about the connection between her own life and her work," Keefe observed.

The Facts and Fictions of Minna Pratt finds eleven-year-old Minna teetering on the edge of adolescence, confronting many changes while also striving to develop a vibrato. While she practices her cello to attain this dream, Minna also longs for her eccentric mother, a writer, to be more like a typical "mother." In the midst of all this appears Lucas Ellerby, a violinist who has the quiet and peaceful home Minna desires. Raised in a traditional home, Lucas is fascinated with the unusual ways of Minna's family, and the two ultimately experience their first romance. In *The Fact and Fictions of Minna Pratt* "MacLachlan has created a wonderfully wise and funny story with such satisfying depths and unforgettable characters that one is reluctant to let it go," according to a *Horn Book* reviewer. Heather Vogel Frederick, writing in the *New York Times Book Review,* was prompted to declare that "if writers of children's fiction were organized into a guild, the title of master craftsman would be bestowed upon Patricia MacLachlan. Her crisp, elegant prose and superb storytelling ability . . . grace . . . *The Facts and Fictions of Minna Pratt.*"

MacLachlan continued to hone her realistic storytelling skills with two tales of loss: *Journey* and *Baby.* In its focus on abandonment, *Journey* finds Journey and his sister Cat living with their grandparents now that their mother has abandoned them. Each member of the re-shuffled family copes with the woman's absence differently, and piecing together some old photographs of his mother enables Journey to attain the love that he seeks. In contrast, *Baby* finds a family dealing with an anticipated loss. Shortly after twelve-year-old Larkin's infant brother dies, his family finds a baby girl, Sophie, abandoned on their driveway. Although they realize that her mother will be coming back for her, the members of the family break down and let Sophie into their hearts, an act that allows them to mourn their recent loss. Nancy Bray Cardozo wrote in her *New York Times Book Review* appraisal of *Journey* that MacLachlan's "language . . . is beautiful, emotionally articulate," "as though an eloquent adult is reminiscing about a childhood tragedy, the sadness still keenly remembered." The author's "style remains masterly" in *Baby,* concluded a *Publishers Weekly* commentator, the critic adding that "it is difficult to read her sentences only once, and even more difficult to part from her novel."

In the middle-grade novel *Edward's Eyes* love is again the focus, as Jake explains how much he enjoys spending time with his new baby brother, even as he learns that deep affection can sometimes translate into deep sadness. "Both unbearably sad and uplifting," according to a *Publishers Weekly* critic, MacLachlan's story in *Edward's Eyes* is "delivered . . . in perfect pitch," while Marie Orlando wrote in *School Library Journal* that the poignant story "includes light touches of humor and weaves a spell that draws readers into an intimate family circle in which hope prevails."

In *Word after Word after Word* MacLachlan draws from her life as a writer, presenting a fictional story that acknowledges the many teachers and other mentors that have supported her along the way. When Ms. Mirabel comes to spend a month with the students in her fourth-grade class, Lucy is excited, especially when the teacher helps Lucy to use stories to discover the things in her everyday life that make her world unique. Evie, Henry, and Russell also find Ms. Mirabel's enthusiasm for writing contagious, and soon they are meeting after school to write and make sense of the many changes in other's lives. "MacLachlan creates marvelous characters, children who can empathize with and support one another," asserted *School Library Journal* contributor Carole Phillips, and in *Booklist* Carolyn Phelan praised *Word after Word after Word* as "a memorable chapter book" that brings to light "the swift, subtle depiction of characters' realizations, revelations, and connections." MacLachlan's "strong, spare novel" also holds inspiration for budding writers, asserted a *Publishers Weekly* critic, through its "message that everyone has a story in them."

Cover of MacLachlan's middle-grade novel **Word after Word after Word,** *which features artwork by Erwin Madrid.* (Katherine Tegen Books, 2010. Illustration by Erwin Madrid. Reproduced by permission of HarperCollins Publishers.)

Cover of MacLachlan's middle-grade novel Edward's Eyes, *in which an older brother recalls the many talents of a little brother who died too young.* (Atheneum Books for Young Readers, 2007. Jacket photograph by Marc Yankus. Reproduced by permission of Marc Yankus.)

While finding success in longer fiction, MacLachlan has continued to produce picture books, among them *Who Loves Me?* and *The True Gift: A Christmas Story,* and *Your Moon, My Moon: A Grandmother's Words to a Faraway Child,* the last illustrated by Bryan Collier. In *Who Loves Me?* a little girl gets ready to go to bed and repeatedly asks her cat the titular question. Each time, the cat replies with the name of someone who loves her and then describes how this person uniquely shows his or her affection. Featuring artwork by Brian Floca, *The True Gift* echoes O. Henry's classic "The Gift of the Magi" in its story about a boy who sells his most valued possessions in order to bring happiness to a lonely creature, producing what Virginia Walter described in *School Library Journal* as a "warm family story with a classic holiday theme." "The lyrical text" in *Who Loves Me?* "rises and falls in waves and curves, echoing the cat's tail," remarked a *Kirkus Reviews* contributor. Catherine Threadgill, writing in *School Library Journal,* also praised the story's text, noting that "MacLachlan's cozy, comforting dialogue meanders like a song."

MacLachlan's picture books also include several collaborations with her daughter, Emily MacLachlan Charest. In *Painting the Wind* a young artist finds inspiration from the dozens of other painters who migrate to his island and work at their easels every summer. At summer's end, an exhibition staged by all these artists lets the narrator find new ways to view his work and also appreciate the work of others. *Painting the Wind* "bears insights into how artists look at their world, and their work, and will broaden children's understanding of how and why art is made," a *Kirkus Reviews* critic remarked. *Booklist* reviewer Julie Cummins noted that the coauthors' text "gets to the heart of creativity in a way children will understand," and a *Publishers Weekly* contributor described *Painting the Wind* as a "thoughtful volume [that] conveys a respect for and understanding of the many ways the creative process manifests itself."

Mother and daughter have also teamed up for *Bittle,* as older siblings cope with the arrival of a new baby. Rather that focusing on children, the story focuses on a cat named Nigel and a pessimistic hound dog named Julia. Reigning household pets, Nigel and Julia are initially disdainful of "Bittle," as they dub the sleepy-eyed infant their owners now bring home, but they eventually come to enjoy the child's presence. *Bittle* is full of "vim and humor," declared a *Kirkus Reviews* critic, while *School Library Journal* reviewer Kelley Rae Unger noted that "the authors cleverly highlight the changes a new baby brings to a home."

Illustrated by Amanda Shepherd, *Fiona Loves the Night,* also features a text coauthored by MacLachlan and Charest. Here a little girl leaves her room and goes outside in the middle of the night, where she experiences a different world than the sunlight one she inhabits during the day. The companion picture books *Once I Ate a Pie* and *I Didn't Do It* pair artwork by Katy Schneider with free-verse poems that reflect the world view of a succession of disobedient dogs, while in *Before You Came* taps a picture-book tradition in its evocation of the love between mother and child. A *Publishers Weekly* contributor praised *Fiona Loves the Night* for its "simple, lyrical prose" and illustrations that capture the nighttime world in "lush, comforting tones," while Jessica Bruder noted in her *New York Times Book Review* appraisal that the mother-daughter collaboration evokes a "serene, lulling rhythm [that] creates a sense of safety, a balm for young readers." In *School Library Journal* Linda Ludke dubbed *I Didn't Do It* "an irresistible treat for animal lovers," while *Once I Ate a Pie* could serve young readers "as inspiration . . . for young poets trying to describe their own pets," according to Judith Constantinides in the same periodical.

MacLachlan is heartened by children's reactions to her work. "It's hugely gratifying to know that kids all over read what I write," she once noted. Affirming the importance of encouraging young writers, she visits schools to speak with students and give writing workshops. "In my experience, children believe that writers are like movie stars. I am often asked if I arrived in a limousine," MacLachlan remarked. "I admit that sometimes I'm a little flattered at the exalted idea kids have about writers. But more importantly, I feel it's crucial

that kids who aspire to write understand that I have to rewrite and revise as they do. Ours is such a perfectionist society—I see too many kids who believe that if they don't get it right the first time, they aren't writers."

Reflecting on her long career as an author, MacLachlan noted to *Publishers Weekly Online* interviewer Ingrid Roper: "There is so much more I want to write. Sometimes I look back at my books and even read them and I think that I'm getting better. And sometimes I read something I wrote and I don't even recognize it. I once read a newspaper article that quoted something I thought was rather insightful about the prairie, and when I looked more closely at it, I saw my name and realized that someone had interviewed me and it had been quoted. That was the funniest experience. So really I think about what's to come more than looking back."

MacLachlan shared some advice for beginning writers in an interview with Ann Courtney in *Language Arts.* "Only write books for children if you really love children's books and want to do it," she counseled. "Writing for children is special because I think children read with a great true belief in what they're reading. The other thing is to read. One must understand the far reaches of children's books because they're really about many of the same subjects as adults are concerned with. Don't be condescending. I hate the didacticism that sometimes comes through in children's books. I would read and read and read. There is no better model than a good book."

Biographical and Critical Sources

BOOKS

Children's Literature Review, Volume 14, Gale (Detroit, MI), 1988.

MacLachlan, Patricia, *More Perfect than the Moon,* Joanna Cotler Books (New York, NY), 2004.

MacLachlan, Patricia, and Emily MacLachlan, *Bittle,* illustrated by Dan Yaccarino, Joanna Cotler Books (New York, NY), 2004.

Russell, David L., *Patricia MacLachlan,* Twayne (New York, NY), 1997.

PERIODICALS

Booklist, October 15, 1980, Judith Goldberger, review of *Arthur, for the Very First Time,* pp. 328-329; April 1, 1982, Denise M. Wilms, review of *Mama One, Mama Two,* pp. 1019-1020; May 1, 1985, Betsy Hearne, review of *Sarah, Plain and Tall,* pp. 1254, 1256; March 15, 1992, review of *Journey,* p. 1364; May 1, 1992, review of *Sarah, Plain and Tall,* p. 1612; September 1, 1993, review of *Baby,* p. 51; January 1, 1994, review of *Skylark,* p. 827; March 15, 1994, review of *Baby,* p. 1355; May 15, 1994, Nancy McCray, review

of *Baby,* p. 1701; June 1, 1994, Stephanie Zvirin, review of *All the Places to Love,* p. 1810; June 1, 1997, review of *Sarah, Plain and Tall,* p. 1701; March 1, 1999, review of *Sarah, Plain and Tall,* p. 1212; February 15, 2001, review of *The Sick Day,* p. 1141; September 1, 2001, review of *Caleb's Story,* p. 107; December 15, 2001, review of *The Sick Day,* p. 728; August, 2003, Julie Cummins, review of *Painting the Wind,* p. 1980; June 1, 2004, Kay Weisman, review of *More Perfect than the Moon,* p. 1726, Jennifer Mattson, review of *Bittle,* p. 1743; June 1, 2005, Jennifer Mattson, review of *Who Loves Me?,* p. 1822; May 1, 2006, Abby Nolan, review of *Once I Ate Pie,* p. 87; July 1, 2006, Hazel Rochman, review of *Grandfather's Dance,* p. 55; March 15, 2010, Carolyn Phelan, review of *Word after Word after Word,* p. 43.

Books for Keeps, May, 1993, review of *Journey,* p. 15; July, 1994, review of *Skylark,* p. 11; September, 1998, review of *Sarah, Plain and Tall,* p. 22.

Books for Your Children, autumn, 1994, review of *Baby,* p. 21.

Bulletin of the Center for Children's Books, September, 1979, Zena Sutherland, review of *The Sick Day,* pp. 11-12; September, 1980, Zena Sutherland, review of *Arthur, for the Very First Time,* pp. 15-16; April, 1982, Zena Sutherland, review of *Mama One, Mama Two,* pp. 153-154; January, 1992, review of *Three Names,* p. 132; September, 1993, review of *Baby,* p. 16; February, 1994, review of *Skylark,* p. 194; July, 1994, review of *All the Places to Love,* p. 367; December, 1995, review of *What You Know First,* p. 132; October, 2001, review of *Caleb's Story,* p. 68; November, 2004, Karen Coates, review of *More Perfect than the Moon,* p. 134; November, 2010, Deborah Stevenson, review of *I Didn't Do It,* p. 139.

Changing Men, winter, 1994, review of *Through Grandpa's Eyes,* p. 40.

Childhood Education, summer, 1992, review of *Three Names,* p. 245.

Children's Book Review Service, April, 1980, Ruth W. Bauer, review of *Through Grandpa's Eyes,* p. 84; June, 1994, review of *All the Places to Love,* p. 126; September, 1995, review of *What You Know First,* p.7.

Children's Book Watch, January, 1992, review of *Three Names,* p. 2; March, 1994, review of *Baby,* p. 3; November, 1995, review of *What You Know First,* p. 8; May, 2001, review of *The Sick Day,* p. 7.

Children's Literature, March, 1995, review of *Unclaimed Treasures,* p. 202.

Christian Science Monitor, November 5, 1993, review of *Baby,* p. 10; May 6, 1994, review of *Skylark,* p. 12.

Day Care & Early Education, summer, 1995, review of *All the Places to Love,* p. 42.

Emergency Librarian, January, 1992, review of *Journey,* p. 50; January, 1992, review of *Three Names,* p. 50; November, 1993, review of *Baby,* p. 46; May, 1994, review of *Skylark,* p. 45.

Entertainment Weekly, April 8, 1994, review of *Skylark,* p. 69.

Five Owls, November, 1993, review of *Sarah, Plan and Tall,* pp. 29-30; November, 1994, review of *All the Places to Love,* p. 25, 28; May, 1995, review of *Skylark,* p. 95, 100.

Growing Point, March, 1987, Margery Fisher, review of *Sarah, Plain and Tall,* p. 4750.

Horn Book, February, 1983, Ann A. Flowers, review of *Cassie Binegar,* pp. 45-46; July-August, 1986, Patricia MacLachlan, transcript of Newbery Medal acceptance speech, pp. 407-413; July-August, 1986, Robert MacLachlan, "A Hypothetical Dilemma," pp. 416-419; July-August, 1988, review of *The Facts and Fictions of Minna Pratt,* pp. 495-496; November-December, 1989, Charlotte Zolotow, interview with MacLachlan, pp. 736-745; November-December, 1993, Mary M. Burns, review of *Baby,* pp. 746-747; July-August, 1994, Mary M. Burns, review of *Skylark,* pp. 453-454; January-February, 1996, Nancy Vasilakis, review of *What You Know First,* pp. 66-67; January, 1998, review of *Sarah, Plain and Tall,* p. 26; September, 2001, review of *Caleb's Story,* p. 590; September-October, 2004, Christine M. Heppermann, review of *More Perfect than the Moon,* p. 590; November-December, 2006, Christine M. Heppermann, review of *Grandfather's Dance,* p. 719; November-December, 2009, Jennifer M. Brabander, review of *The True Gift: A Christmas Story,* p. 644.

Hungry Mind Review, summer, 1994, review of *Skylark,* p. 55.

Instructor, January, 1993, review of *Through Grandpa's Eyes,* p. 51; October, 1993, review of *Journey,* p. 68.

Journal of Adult Reading, March, 1994, review of *Baby,* p. 519.

Journal of Reading, March, 1992, review of *Journey,* p. 501; November, 1992, review of *Sarah, Plain and Tall,* p. 174.

Junior Bookshelf, April, 1992, review of *Journey,* p. 75.

Kirkus Reviews, January 1, 1994, review of *Skylark,* p. 71; June 15, 1994, review of *All the Places to Love,* p. 848; August, 15, 1995, review of *What You Know First,* p. 1190; October 1, 2001, review of *Caleb's Story,* p. 1428; April 15, 2003, review of *Painting the Wind,* p. 609; May 15, 2004, review of *Bittle,* p. 494; July 15, 2004, review of *More Perfect than the Moon,* p. 690; May 1, 2005, review of *Who Loves Me?,* p. 542; August 1, 2006, review of *Grandfather's Dance,* p. 791; July 15, 2007, review of *Edward's Eyes*; September 15, 2009, review of *The True Gift.*

Kliatt, March, 1994, reviews of *Journey* and *Baby,* both p. 54.

Language Arts, November, 1985, Ann Courtney, interview with MacLachlan, pp. 783-787; March, 1992, review of *Three Names,* p. 218; November, 1992, review of *Journey,* p. 516; October, 1994, review of *Baby,* p. 460; February, 1995, review of *Skylark,* p. 142; October, 1995, review of *All the Places to Love,* p. 435; April, 1996, review of *What You Know First,* p. 263.

Learning, October, 1995, review of *Journey,* p. 83.

Library Talk, January, 1992, review of *Journey,* p. 33; September, 1992, review of *Three Names,* p. 46; May, 1994, review of *Baby,* p. 44; September, 1994, review of *Skylark,* p. 42; September, 1994, review of *All the Places to Love,* p. 11.

Los Angeles Times Book Review, December 17, 1995, review of *What You Know First,* p. 15.

Magpies, July, 1993, review of *Journey,* p. 39.

Newsweek, December 28, 1992, review of *Through Grandpa's Eyes,* p. 54.

New York Times Book Review, September 28, 1980, Natalie Babbitt, review of *Through Grandpa's Eyes,* p. 36; May 19, 1985, Martha Saxton, review of *Sarah, Plain and Tall,* p. 20; January 8, 1989, Heather Vogel Frederick, review of *The Facts and Fictions of Minna Pratt,* p. 36; March 22, 1992, Nancy Bray Cardozo, review of *Journey,* p. 25; November 14, 1993, review of *Baby,* p. 34; June 5, 1994, review of *All the Places to Love,* p. 30; November 16, 1996, review of *Sarah, Plain and Tall,* p. 26; January 20, 2002, review of *Caleb's Story,* p. 15; February 17, 2008, Jessica Bruder, review of *Fiona Loves the Night,* p. 23; December 20, 2009, Julie Just, review of *The True Gift,* p. 13.

Orange County Register, September 21, 1994, Catherine Keefe, interview with MacLachlan.

Parents, December, 1994, review of *Skylark,* p. 24.

Plays, March, 1997, review of *Tomorrow's Wizard,* p. 64.

Publishers Weekly, May 9, 1980, review of *Through Grandpa's Eyes,* p. 57; December 26, 1980, review of *Arthur, for the Very First Time,* p. 59; April 16, 1993, review of *Baby,* p. 104; November 29, 1993, review of *Skylark,* p. 65; March 21, 1994, review of *All the Places to Love,* p. 70; April 25, 1994, review of *Three Names,* p. 81; July 31, 1995, review of *What You Know First,* p. 79; September 11, 1995, review of *Baby,* p. 87; February 3, 1997, review of *Skylark,* p. 108; March 23, 1998, review of *What You Know First,* p. 102; May 28, 2001, review of *The Sick Day,* p. 990; September 24, 2001, review of *Caleb's Story,* p. 94; October 22, 2001, Jason Britton, review of *Caleb's Story,* p. 26; February 10, 2003, review of *Painting the Wind,* p. 185; July 5, 2004, review of *Bittle,* p. 55; March 28, 2005, review of *Who Loves Me?,* p. 79; August 7, 2006, review of *Grandfather's Dance,* p. 59, and Jennifer M. Brown, interview with MacLachlan, p. 60; July 16, 2007, review of *Edward's Eyes,* p. 165; August 20, 2007, review of *Fiona Loves the Night,* p. 67; May 17, 2010, review of *Word after Word after Word,* p. 49; August 9, 2010, review of *I Didn't Do It,* p. 50.

Quill & Quire, November, 1993, review of *Baby,* p. 40; February, 1996, review of *What You Know First,* p. 43.

Reading Teacher, December, 1992, review of *Three Names,* p. 333; May, 1993, review of *Journey,* p. 692; September, 1994, review of *Skylark,* p. 71; November, 1994, review of *Baby,* p. 241; March, 1995, review of *All the Places to Love,* p. 510; November, 1995, review of *All the Places to Love,* p. 238; October, 1996, review of *What You Know First,* p. 153; April, 2002, review of *Caleb's Story,* p. 697.

San Francisco Review of Books, September, 1995, review of *Baby,* p. 46.

School Librarian, May, 1992, review of *Journey,* p. 71.

School Library Journal, September, 1982, Wendy Dellett, review of *Cassie Binegar,* p. 124; May, 1985, Trev Jones, review of *Sarah, Plain and Tall,* p. 93; April, 1992, review of *Journey,* p. 44; November, 1993, review of *Baby,* p. 109; March, 1994, review of *Skylark,*

p. 222; June, 1994, review of *All the Places to Love,* p. 110; June, 1996, review of *Arthur, for the Very First Time,* p. 55; January, 1998, review of *Journey,* p. 43; August, 1998, review of *Baby,* p. 27; September, 2001, review of *Caleb's Story,* p. 230; May, 2003, Lee Bock, review of *Painting the Wind,* p. 125; June, 2004, Kelley Rae Unger, review of *Bittle,* p. 114; August, 2004, Caroline Ward, review of *More Perfect than the Moon,* p. 90; December, 2004, Ginny Gustin, review of *The Facts and Fictions of Minna Pratt,* p. 60; May, 2005, Catherine Threadgill, review of *Who Loves Me?,* p. 90; May, 2006, Judith Constantinides, review of *Once I Ate a Pie,* p. 114; November, 2006, Pat Leach, review of *Grandfather's Dance,* p. 105; September, 2007, Mary Jean Smith, review of *Fiona Loves the Night,* p. 171; October, 2007, Marie Orlando, review of *Edward's Eyes,* p. 160; October, 2009, Virgina Walter, review of *The True Gift,* p. 82; July, 2010, Carole Phillips, review of *Word after Word after Word,* p. 65; October, 2010, Linda Ludke, review of *I Didn't Do It,* p. 90.

Smithsonian, November, 1994, review of *All the Places to Love,* p. 34.

Social Education, April, 1992, review of *Journey,* p. 262; April, 1995, review of *All the Places to Love,* p. 217.

Social Studies, March, 1995, review of *Through Grandpa's Eyes,* p. 92.

Times Educational Supplement, February 14, 1992, review of *Journey,* p. 30; September 16, 1994, review of *Baby,* p. 20; June 26, 1998, review of *Sarah, Plain and Tall,* p. 10.

Tribune Books (Chicago, IL), November 14, 1993, review of *Baby,* p. 7; March 13, 1994, review of *Skylark,* p. 7; April 10, 1994, review of *All the Places to Love,* p. 8; January 14, 1996, review of *What You Know First,* p. 7; October 21, 2001, review of *Caleb's Story,* p. 4.

Wilson Library Bulletin, May, 1992, review of *Journey,* p. S5; January, 1994, review of *Baby,* p. 119.

ONLINE

Eduplace.com, http://www.eduplace.com/ (May 28, 2003), Katy Smith, review of *All the Places to Love.*

HarperCollins Children's Web site, http://www.harpercollinschildrens.com/ (April 20, 2011), "Patricia MacLachlan."

Publishers Weekly Online, http://www.publishersweekly.com/ (June 24, 2010), Ingrid Roper, interview with MacLachlan.*

*　　*　　*

MALONE, Marianne

Personal

Born in IL; married Jonathan Fineberg; children: Maya, Noni, Henry. *Education:* University of Illinois, B.A. (art history). *Hobbies and other interests:* Painting.

Addresses

Home—Urbana, IL. *E-mail*—mariannemalonebooks@gmail.com.

Career

Author and artist. Former jewelry designer; Campus Middle School for Girls, IL, art teacher for ten years.

Writings

The Sixty-eight Rooms, illustrated by Greg Call, Random House (New York, NY), 2010.

Sidelights

Illinois native Marianne Malone traces her fascination with dollhouses to her visit to the Thorne Rooms, an exhibit housed in the basement of the Art Institute of Chicago. Sixty-eight miniature rooms installed in the museum in 1942, the Thorne Rooms feature intriguing levels of detail in their Asian, European, and early American furnishings and decor. As a child, Malone was inspired by her visit to the Thorne Rooms to create her own doll house. As an adult, memories of the visit inspired her to write her first children's novel, *The Sixty-eight Rooms.*

The youngest of four children, Malone grew up watching her mother paint landscapes, and she shares the same talent: her painting has grwon into a business painting portraits of client's pets. Although she enrolled at the University of Illinois intending to study art, she ended up majoring in art history, then worked for several years as a jewelry designer. While raising her children, Malone helped several friends co-found a private middle school, the Campus Middle School for Girls, and she worked there as an art teacher for over a decade. She began writing *The Sixty-eight Rooms* after her children left home for college and she ended her work as a teacher.

Featuring illustrations by Greg Call, *The Sixty-eight Rooms* finds sixth graders Jack Tucker and Ruthie Stewart visiting the Thorne Rooms on a school field trip. As Ruthie explains in the novel's first-person narrative, while studying the rooms she feels pulled into this miniature reality. Then Jack discovers an old key and places it in her hand, whereupon both children shrink down to Thorne-Room size. Now five inches tall, the eleven year olds explore the many rooms, only to discover that someone has been there before them. Soon, their visit turns into a quest as Jack and Ruthie attempt to locate a book of photographs belonging to the daughter of one of the museum guards, even as the Thorne Rooms reveal their own dangers. Reviewing *The Sixty-eight Rooms* for *Kirkus Reviews,* a contributor noted the research that went into the story, adding that Malone's "premise is engaging and the plotting [is] easy to follow." "Malone carefully crafts a fantastical story with plenty of real-world elements," added *Booklist* contributor Ilene Cooper, and in *School Library Journal* Misti Tidman characterized *The Sixty-eight Rooms* as a book that will appeal to readers who enjoy "stories that

Marianne Malone tells a fanciful story about two preteens who shrink to doll-house size in order to solve a life-size mystery in **The Sixty-eight Rooms,** *a novel featuring artwork by Greg Call.* (Illustration copyright © 2010 by Greg Call. Reproduced by permission of Random House, Inc.)

incorporate a touch of fantasy into a cozy mystery." Dubbing Malone's novel "a fantasy that is both very Chicago and completely universal," a Chicago *Tribune Books* critic also noted the subtle cultural history lessons that can be gleaned by readers. In addition to including "excellent, accurate details regarding the rooms' inception [and] . . . the many true-to-life items extracted from the interiors themselves," the critic noted, the children's "pint-sized adventures take them to Salem Witch Trial-era Massachusetts and pre-Revolutionary France as the magic extends beyond the rooms themselves and into those painted vistas and hidden hallways, the kids becoming avid history buffs in the process."

"As a teacher, a parent, and now a writer, I enjoy the responsibility we have to children, to offer stories that engage their imaginations, to offer characters they can relate to," Malone noted in an online interview with Cynthia Leitich Smith for *Cynsations.* "It's that generative process of passing something good on to our children. So even as the world changes so fast we could lose our balance, we don't let them fall."

Biographical and Critical Sources

PERIODICALS

Booklist, January 1, 2010, Ilene Cooper, review of *The Sixty-eight Rooms,* p. 84.
Bulletin of the Center for Children's Books, March, 2010, Jeannette Hulick, review of *The Sixty-eight Rooms,* p. 294.
Kirkus Reviews, February 15, 2010, review of *The Sixty-eight Rooms.*
Publishers Weekly, January 18, 2010, review of *The Sixty-eight Rooms,* p. 48.
School Library Journal, February, 2010, Misti Tidman, review of *The Sixty-eight Rooms,* p. 118.
Tribune Books (Chicago, IL), May 22, 2010, review of *The Sixty-eight Rooms,* p. 13.

ONLINE

Cynsations Web log, http://cynthialeitichsmith.blogspot. com/ (July 21, 2010), Cynthia Leitich Smith, interview with Malone.
Marianne Malone Home Page, http://www.mariannema lone.com (April 24, 2011).

*   *   *

MANIVONG, Laura 1967-

Personal

Born 1967, in Kansas City, MO; married Troy Manivong; children: Clara, Aidan. *Education:* Missouri State University, degree (television production).

Addresses

Home—Kansas City, KS. *E-mail*—laura@lauramani vong.com.

Career

Television producer and writer. Formerly worked as a camp counselor.

Awards, Honors

Emmy Award for television production.

Writings

One Smart Fish, illustrated by Suzanne Beaky, Children's Press (New York, NY), 2006.
Escaping the Tiger, Harper (New York, NY), 2010.

Contributor to periodicals, including *Skipping Stones.*

Sidelights

A television producer and author who is based in Kansas City, Missouri, Laura Manivong was inspired to write her first children's novel after hearing her husband recount his experiences as a Laotian refugee during the early 1980s. In addition to *Escaping the Tiger,* which finds a boy and his family fleeing from their communist country and encountering obstacles on their way to a better life, Manivong has also written the beginning reader *One Smart Fish,* a humorous rhyming story about a little girl's efforts to catch a fish using several of her favorite foods as bait.

Manivong was born and raised in Kansas City, Missouri, and with a mother and grandfather who were writers she accepted writing as a realistic career possibility. While attending Missouri State University she opted to study television production and during the course of her career managed to meld her production skills and her interest in writing into work creating television scripts. While raising her own two children, Manivong retooled as a writer and produced her first children's book, *One Smart Fish; Escaping the Tiger* was completed several years later.

In *Escaping the Tiger* twelve-year-old Vonlai Sirivong and his older sister Dalah have grown up under the repressive communist government in Laos, near the Mekong River. Vonlai's parents know that a better life is possible so they brave the dangerous trip across the Mekong to Na Pho, Thailand. Unfortunately, the family must spend the next four years in a U.N.-sponsored refugee camp, where living conditions are primitive, sanitation is lacking, and food is rationed. School and soccer become an escape for Vonlai, who is haunted by hunger and thirst. He is also inspired by the hope of a new friend: an elderly Laotian colonel who shares his dreams of what life will be like in the United States. As time passes, camp life becomes more menacing, and when sixteen-year-old Dalah is threatened by a camp guard Vonlai's hope for the future strengthens his determination to defend her.

As a *Kirkus Reviews* writer noted, Manivong's story in *Escaping the Tiger* has a strong basis in fact; her afterword describing the experiences of her husband contributes "further depth to an already moving tale." Praising *Escaping the Tiger* as "compelling," Alison Follos added in *School Library Journal* that Manivong's story will "certainly . . . prompt purposeful discussion to increase historical and multicultural awareness." Hazel Rochman cited another appreciative audience for the novel, writing in *Booklist* that "refugee families. . . . will recognize the cruel dislocation, the interminable wait, and the search for home."

Biographical and Critical Sources

PERIODICALS

Booklist, January 1, 2010, Hazel Rochman, review of *Escaping the Tiger,* p. 60.

Bulletin of the Center for Children's Books, April, 2010, Maggie Hommel, review of *Escaping the Tiger,* p. 345.

Kirkus Reviews, January 1, 2010, review of *Escaping the Tiger.*

School Library Journal, March, 2010, Alison Follos, review of *Escaping the Tiger,* p. 163.

ONLINE

Laura Manivong Home Page, http://www.lauramanivong. com (April 24, 2011).

Laura Manivong Web log, http://lauramanivong.wordpress. com (April 24, 2011).*

*   *   *

McKINLEY, Robin 1952-

Personal

Born November 16, 1952, in Warren, OH; daughter of William (in the U.S. Navy and Merchant Marines) and Jeanne Carolyn (a teacher) McKinley; married Peter Dickinson (an author), January 3, 1992. *Education:* Attended Dickinson College, 1970-72; Bowdoin College, B.A. (summa cum laude), 1975. *Hobbies and other interests:* Gardening, horses, walking, travel, many kinds of music, "life as an expatriate and the English-American culture chasm."

Addresses

Home—Hampshire, England. *E-mail*—nuraddin@robin mckinley.com.

Career

Writer, 1975—. Ward & Paul (stenographic reporting firm), Washington, DC, editor and transcriber, 1972-73; Research Associates, Brunswick, ME, research assistant, 1976-77; bookstore clerk in Maine, 1978; teacher and counselor at private secondary school in Natick, MA, 1978-79; Little, Brown, Inc., Boston, MA, editorial assistant, 1979-81; barn manager on a horse farm in Holliston, MA, 1981-82; Books of Wonder, New York, NY, clerk, 1983; freelance reader, copy-and line-editor, general all-purpose publishing dogsbody, 1983-91.

Awards, Honors

Horn Book Honor Book designation, 1978, for *Beauty,* 1985, for *The Hero and the Crown,* 1988, for *The Outlaws of Sherwood,* and 1995, for *Knot in the Grain;* Best Books for the Teen Age citation, New York Public Library, 1980, 1981, 1982, all for *Beauty;* Best Young-Adult Books citation, American Library Association (ALA), 1982, and Newbery Honor Book designation, ALA, 1983, both for *The Blue Sword;* Newbery Medal, and ALA Notable Book designation, both 1985, both

for *The Hero and the Crown;* D.H.L., Bowdoin College, 1986; World Fantasy Award for best anthology, 1986, for *Imaginary Lands;* Best Books for the Teen Age citation, and ALA Best Adult Book for the Teen Age designation, both 1994, both for *Deerskin;* D.H.L., Wilson College, 1996; Mythopoeic Award for Adult Literature, 2004, for *Sunshine.*

Writings

FICTION

Beauty: A Retelling of the Story of Beauty and the Beast, Harper (New York, NY), 1978.

The Door in the Hedge (short stories), Greenwillow (New York, NY), 1981.

The Blue Sword, Greenwillow (New York, NY), 1982, reprinted, Ace Books (New York, NY), 2007.

The Hero and the Crown, Greenwillow (New York, NY), 1984, reprinted, Ace Books (New York, NY), 2007.

(Editor and contributor) *Imaginary Lands* (short stories; includes "The Stone Fey"), Greenwillow (New York, NY), 1985.

The Outlaws of Sherwood, Greenwillow (New York, NY), 1988, reprinted, Firebird (New York, NY), 2002.

My Father Is in the Navy (picture book), illustrated by Martine Gourbault, Greenwillow (New York, NY), 1992.

Rowan (picture book), illustrated by Donna Ruff, Greenwillow (New York, NY), 1992.

Deerskin (adult fantasy), Putnam (New York, NY), 1993.

A Knot in the Grain and Other Stories, Greenwillow (New York, NY), 1994.

Rose Daughter, Greenwillow (New York, NY), 1997.

Stone Fey, illustrated by John Clapp, Harcourt (San Diego, CA), 1998.

Spindle's End, Putnam (New York, NY), 2000.

(With husband, Peter Dickinson) *Water: Tales of Elemental Spirits,* Putnam (New York, NY), 2002.

Sunshine (adult novel), Berkeley Books (New York, NY), 2003.

Dragonhaven, Putnam (New York, NY), 2007.

Chalice, Putnam (New York, NY), 2008.

(With Peter Dickinson) *Fire: Tales of Elemental Spirits,* Putnam (New York, NY), 2009.

Pegasus, G.P. Putnam's Sons (New York, NY), 2010.

Contributor to anthologies, including *Elsewhere II,* edited by Terri Windling and Mark Arnold, Ace Books, 1982; *Elsewhere III,* edited by Windling and Arnold, Ace Books, 1984; and *Faery,* edited by Windling, Ace Books, 1985. Also contributor of book reviews to numerous periodicals. Author of column, "In the Country," for *New England Monthly,* 1987-88.

ADAPTER

Rudyard Kipling, *Tales from the Jungle Book,* Random House (New York, NY), 1985.

Anna Sewell, *Black Beauty,* illustrated by Susan Jeffers, Random House (New York, NY), 1986.

George MacDonald, *The Light Princess,* illustrated by Katie Thamer Treherne, Harcourt (San Diego, CA), 1988.

Adaptations

Random House produced audio versions of *The Hero and the Crown,* 1986, and *The Blue Sword,* 1994.

Sidelights

Robin McKinley is the award-winning author of novels, short stories, and picture books that mine the world of fantasy and fairy tales. Her renditions of classic fairy tales have a feminist twist; no weak-kneed damsels in distress, McKinley's protagonists are young women who do things rather than "waiting limply to be rescued by the hero," as the author explained on her home page. In novels such as *Beauty: A Retelling of the Story of Beauty and the Beast, The Hero and the Crown, Rose Daughter, Spindle's End,* and *Chalice,* McKinley fills

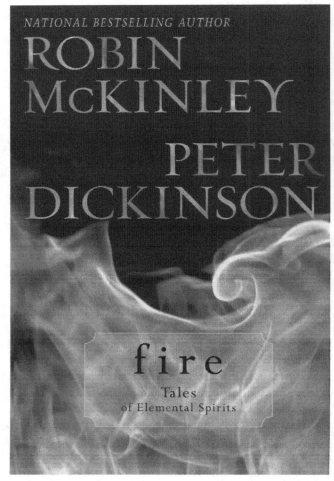

Robin McKinley teams up with her husband, author Peter Dickinson, on several short-story collections, among them Fire: Tale of Elemental Spirits. (Cover photograph by 2Happy used under license from Shutterstock.com. Reproduced by permission of G.P. Putnam's Sons, a division of Penguin Young Readers Group, a member of Penguin (USA) Inc., 345 Hudson St., NY 10014. All rights reserved.)

her fantasy realms with realistic detail and powerful characters, attracting readers both young and old. She has also collaborated with writer husband Peter Dickinson on the story collections *Water: Tales of Elemental Spirits* and *Fire: Tales of Elemental Spirits*, the first of which John Peters praised in *School Library Journal* as "masterfully written stories" that, with their "distinct, richly detailed casts and settings," will "excite, enthrall, and move even the pickiest readers."

Although she now makes her home in the United Kingdom, McKinley was born in the United States and "grew up a military brat and an only child [who] decided early on that books were much more reliable friends than people," as she wrote on her home page. Moving every two years, from California to Japan to New York, she found comfort in fictional worlds. "Writing has always been the other side of reading for me," McKinley further commented. "It never occurred to me not to make up stories." However, as a young girl, she also had identity issues. "I despised myself for being a girl," she once told *SATA*, "and ipso facto being someone who stayed at home and was boring, and started trying to tell myself stories about girls who did things and had adventures."

"Once I got old enough to realize that authorship existed as a thing one might aspire to, I knew it was for me," McKinley recalled on her home page. "I even majored in English literature in college, a good indication of my fine bold disdain for anything so trivial as earning a living." She saw herself as a writer in the J.R.R. Tolkien or H. Rider Haggard vein, but unlike those authors, she was "going to tell breathtaking stories about *girls* who had adventures." McKinley's first publication, written only a few years after her graduation from Bowdoin, was inspired by viewing a television adaptation of "Beauty and the Beast." She was so disappointed with what she saw that she began to write a version of the classic fairy tale herself.

Beauty won praise from readers and critics alike. According to Michael Malone in the *New York Times Book Review,* the novel is "much admired not only for its feminism but for the density of detail in the retelling." "It's simply a filling out of the story, with a few alterations," wrote a *Kirkus Reviews* critic. Beauty—or Honour, as the heroine in McKinley's version is named—is an awkward child, not a beauty, and her "evil sisters" are caring and kind. Reviewers also praised McKinley's handling of fantasy in the medieval setting. "The aura of magic around the Beast and his household comes surprisingly to life," commented a *Choice* critic. The winner of several literary awards, *Beauty* instantly established McKinley as a powerful new voice in young-adult literature and it has remained one of her most-popular novels.

Years after publishing *Beauty,* McKinley returns to the fairy tale that novel was based on in *Rose Daughter.* Over 300 pages in length, *Rose Daughter* has "a more

mystical, darker edge," according to Estes. In the novel, readers learn about the early family life and personalities of the three sisters: the acerbic Jeweltongue; Lionheart, a physically daring girl; and the title character, Beauty. Unlike the original "Beauty and the Beast," the relationship between the three sisters in McKinley's novel is a loving rather than hostile one. Although the girls have been raised in the city by their wealthy and widowed father, when he loses his business they relocate to a rural cottage where new hardships bring the family closer together.

One central element of *Rose Daughter* is the flower of the title: at the sisters' new country home roses are extremely difficult to cultivate. Beauty discovers, while working in her garden, that she possesses a skill for raising the beautiful flower. She also finds herself plagued by disturbing dreams of a dark corridor, a memory of her mother, and the heavy scent of roses. The Beast in this novel is a legendary local figure, a tragic hero who is half man. When Beauty journeys to his castle and begins tending the magic roses in his gar-

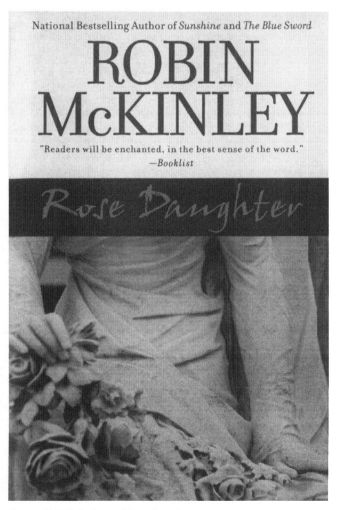

Cover of McKinley's novel Rose Daughter. (Cover art by B. Schmid/Photonica/ Getty Images. The Berkley Publishing Group copyright © 1977. Reproduced by permission of The Berkley Publishing Group, a division of Penguin Putnam Books for Young Readers and Getty Images.)

den, other flora and fauna return to the Beast's former wasteland. A romance develops between the two and Beauty's tenderness toward the Beast eventually unlocks the curse that has beset him. "As before, McKinley takes the essentials of the traditional tale and embellishes them with vivid and quirky particulars," declared a contributor for *Publishers Weekly*. Jennifer Fakolt, reviewing *Rose Daughter* for *Voice of Youth Advocates*, asserted that the author "has captured the timelessness of the traditional tale and breathed into it passion and new life appropriate to the story's own 'universal themes' of love and regeneration," while a *Publishers Weekly* reviewer concluded that McKinley's "heady mix of fairy tale, magic and romance has the power to exhilarate."

Prior to writing *Beauty*, McKinley had begun work on several stories set in a fictional world she has named Damar. As she once explained to *SATA*, "I had begun . . . to realize that there was more than one story to tell about Damar, that in fact it seemed to be a whole history, volumes and volumes of the stuff, and this terrified me. I had plots and characters multiplying like mice and running in all directions." The first "Damar" book to appear was the story collection *The Door in the Hedge*, which was published in the late 1970s. In the second, the novel *The Blue Sword*. The hero is Harry Crewe, a young woman who must forge her identity and battle an evil force at the same time. After Harry is abducted she learns from her kidnappers how to ride a horse and battle as a true warrior. While she struggles in the tradition of the legendary female hero of Damar, Aerin, the teen becomes a hero in her own right.

Although *The Blue Door* is set in a fantasy world—Damar was characterized as "pseudo-Victorian" by Darrell Schweitzer in *Science Fiction Review*—critics have found Harry to be a heroine that contemporary readers may well understand. Like *Beauty*, *The Blue Sword* earned McKinley both recognition and praise. It also earned a Newbery Honor Book designation. In *Booklist* Sally Estes described the novel as "a zesty, romantic heroic fantasy with . . . a grounding in reality that enhances the tale's verve as a fantasy."

In *The Hero and the Crown*, the next "Damar" novel, readers are taken back in time to learn the story of Aerin, the legendary warrior woman Harry so reveres. As McKinley once explained to *SATA*, "I recognized that there were specific connections between Harry and Aerin, and I deliberately wrote their stories in reverse chronological order because one of the things I'm fooling around with is the idea of heroes: real heroes as opposed to the legends that are told of them afterwards. Aerin is one of her country's greatest heroes, and by the time Harry comes along, Harry is expected—or Harry thinks she is—to live up to her. When you go back and find out about Aerin in *The Hero and the Crown*, you discover that she wasn't this mighty invincible figure. . . . She had a very hard and solitary time [because] of her early fate."

When readers first meet Aerin in *The Hero and the Crown*, she is graceless and clumsy; it takes her a long time to turn herself into a true warrior and she suffers many traumas in the process. Yet she is also clever and courageous, bravely battling and killing the dragons that are threatening Damar. Merri Rosenberg asserted in the *New York Times Book Review* that in *The Hero and the Crown* McKinley has "created an utterly engrossing fantasy, replete with a fairly mature romantic subplot as well as adventure." According to *Horn Book* contributor Mary M. Burns, *The Hero and the Crown* is "as richly detailed and elegant as a medieval tapestry. . . . Vibrant, witty, compelling, the story is the stuff of which true dreams are made." Writing in the *New Statesman*, Gillian Wilce cited the novel's "completeness, [and] its engaging imagination," while *Wilson Library Bulletin* contributor Frances Bradburn called McKinley's novel a "marvelous tale of excitement and female ingenuity."

Upon winning the coveted Newbery Medal in 1985 for *The Hero and the Crown*, McKinley shared her feelings with *SATA*: "The Newbery award is supposed to be the peak of your career as a writer for children or young adults. I was rather young to receive it; and it is a little disconcerting to feel—okay, you've done it; that's it, you should retire now."

Far from retiring, however, McKinley has continued to write retellings of traditional favorites as well as original novels and stories. She has also returned, on occasion to Damar, as she does in *A Knot in the Grain and Other Stories*. The tales in this collection, according to *Bulletin of the Center for Children's Books* critic Betsy Hearne, bear "McKinley's signature blend of the magical and the mundane in the shape of heroines" who triumph and find love despite the obstacles they face. They also demonstrate the author's "remarkable ability to evoke wonder and belief," asserted *Horn Book* contributor Ann A. Flowers. A reviewer for *Publishers Weekly* called *A Knot in the Grain* a "thrilling, satisfying and thought-provoking collection."

Also set in the world of Damar, McKinley's short story "The Stone Fey" first appeared in *Imaginary Lands* and was republished as an illustrated book with artwork by John Clapp. In the story Maddy, a shepherdess, falls in love with a stone fey, a fairy with skin the color of stone. Entranced by her new love, Maddy drifts away from the people and things she has always cared about until she realizes that the fey can not return her love. A contributor for *Publishers Weekly* noted that, "while staying true to her penchant for presenting strong female protagonists, . . . McKinley strikes a softer note with this deeply romantic yet ultimately clear-eyed love story." In *Booklist* Carolyn Phelan deemed *The Stone Fey* a "haunting story," and Virginia Golodetz described McKinley's writing in *School Library Journal* as "passionate."

Like *Beauty*, *The Outlaws of Sherwood* showcases McKinley's talent for revising and reviving traditional tales. Instead of concentrating on Robin Hood—or glo-

rifying him—this novel focuses on other members in Robin's band of outlaws and provides carefully wrought details about their daily lives: how they get dirty, and sick, and how they manage their outlaw affairs. Robin is not portrayed as the bold, handsome marksman and sword handler readers find in traditional versions of the "Robin Hood" story. Instead, he is nervous, a poor shot, and even reluctant to form his band of merry men. Not surprisingly, McKinley's merry men include merry *women* among their number. "The young women are allowed to be angry, frankly sexual, self willed—and even to outshoot the men, who don't seem to mind," observed *Washington Post Book World* reviewer Michele Landsberg in discussing the author's alteration of the well-known story. In another characteristic revisioning by McKinley, Maid Marian stands out as a brilliant, beautiful leader and an amazingly talented archer. *The Outlaws of Sherwood* is "romantic and absorbing . . . [and] the perfect adolescent daydream where happiness is found in being young and among friends," concluded Shirley Wilton in her review of the book for *Voice of Youth Advocates.*

The adult novel *Deerskin* also demonstrates McKinley's talent for creating new tales out of the foundations of old ones. As Hearne noted, *Deerskin* presents a "darker side of fairy tales." Based on Perrault's "Donkeyskin," a story in which a king assaults his own daughter after his queen dies, the novel relates how a beautiful princess is raped by her father after the death of her mother. This "is also a dog story," Hearne reminded readers: Princess Lissar survives the brutal attack and heals emotionally because of her relationship with her dog, Ash. "Written with deep passion and power, *Deerskin* is an almost unbearably intense portrait of a severely damaged young woman. . . . There is also romance, humor, and sheer delight," commented Christy Tyson in *Voice of Youth Advocates.* In *School Library Journal,* Cathy Chauvette deemed the book "a riveting and relentless fairy tale, told in ravishing prose." Another novel with adult themes, McKinley's vampire novel *Sunshine,* was awarded the Mythopoeic Fantasy Award for Adult Literature in 2003.

With *Spindle's End* McKinley once again revamps a fairy tale for modern readers. Using "Sleeping Beauty" as a template, she creates a "novel of complex imagery and characters," according to a critic for *Family Life.* In this tale the infant princess Briar Rose is cursed on her name day by the evil fairy, Pernicia. Then—as in the original—she is taken away to a remote and magical land to be raised—her real identity concealed—in an attempt to escape Pernicia's wrath. In McKinley's take, good fairy Katriona takes the young princess away to her village of Foggy Bottom, renames her Rosie, and raises the girl while awaiting the ill-fated twenty-first birthday, when Briar Rose will supposedly prick her finger on a spinning-wheel spindle and fall into an eternal sleep. In order to confound Pernicia, Rosie and her friend Peony trade places at on the prophecied birthday.

Rosie's kiss awakens the sleeping Peony, setting into motion a chain of events that lead to true love for all concerned.

Writing in *School Library Journal,* Connie Tyrrell Burns observed that in *Spindle's End* "McKinley once again lends a fresh perspective to a classic fairy tale, developing the story of 'Sleeping Beauty' into a richly imagined, vividly depicted novel." In *Booklist* Estes similarly noted that the author's reinterpretation of the beloved fairy tale "takes readers into a credibly developed world." "Full of humor and romance as well as magic and adventure, and with an ending that has a decided twist," Estes concluded, the "spellbinding novel is bound to attract McKinley's fans and those who relish the genre." A critic for *Publishers Weekly* called *Spindle's End* a "luscious, lengthy novel" that is "dense with magical detail and all-too-human feeling."

"Elegant prose and lyrical descriptions capture reader interest while an increasingly tense plot maintains it," wrote a *Kirkus Reviews* contributor in a review of *Chalice.* In this original fantasy, McKinley spins a story that focuses on a young woman named Mirasol. Serving the Master of Willowlands as a chalice, or servant, Mirasol is also a beekeeper. However, her task now is a pressing one: to mend her damaged world by finding a way to bind her master—a Prince of Fire who causes everything he touches to burn—to the fragile land that is now wracked by earthquakes and other destruction. Noting that Mirasol is a characteristic McKinley heroine "who discovers her impressive powers as she finds her way," *Booklist* critic Lynn Rutan praised the novel's evocative narration as "a sensory delight." In *Publishers Weekly* an equally impressed reviewer characterized *Chalice* as a "high fantasy as perfectly shaped and eloquently told" as McKinley's best-known novels, the critic concluding that this romantic tale will be greeted as "a lavish and lasting treat" by the author's many fans. "Teens who long for beautiful phrases and descriptive writing will find themselves drinking in this rich fairy tale as if it were honey," predicted Heather M. Campbell in her review of *Chalice* for *School Library Journal.*

According to *Booklist* contributor Jennifer Mattson, *Dragonhaven* may be something of "a curveball" for McKinley's fans due to its modern-day setting. However, readers soon discover what Mattson dubbed "a distinctly fantastical aspect" to the Wyoming nature preserve where fifteen-year-old protagonist Jake lives with his naturalist father. Jake is studying Draca Australiensis, the last remaining species of dragon on Earth. When he secretly raises a young dragon whose mother has been killed by poachers, the teen challenges prevailing theories about how humans and dragons have coevolved and also gains an intimate knowledge of the gigantic fire-breathing creatures. In *Dragonhaven* "McKinley renders her imagined universe . . . potently," wrote a *Publishers Weekly* reviewer, the critic adding that the "tightly wound and solitary Jake" is a

including the powerful Fthoom, who determines to end the girl's relationship with pegasus by any means necessary. Noting that *Pegasus* is a novel that McKinley's fans will treasure, a *Publishers Weekly* critic commended the story as "leisurely in its pacing, but rich in language and character development." "McKinley's storytelling is to be savored," asserted Daniel Kraus in *Booklist,* the critic noting the author's ability to craft an "intricately constructed world" and communicate a "masterful sense of pegasi physicality and mannerisms."

In addition to novel-length fiction, McKinley has also written original picture books for children. *Rowan* is a story about a girl selecting and loving a pet dog, while *My Father Is in the Navy* portrays a young girl whose father has been away for some time: as he is about to return, she tries to remember what the man looks like. Reviewing *Rowan,* a contributor for *Publishers Weekly* deemed it an "affable tale of a girl and her pet," while in *School Library Journal* JoAnn Rees called *My Father Is in the Navy* a "warm, loving look at a family group." Other books by McKinley that are geared for younger readers include short retellings of childhood classics like Anna Sewell's *Black Beauty,* George MacDonald's *The Light Princess,* and Rudyard Kipling's *The Jungle Book.*

"As a compulsive reader myself, I believe that you are what you read . . . ," McKinley once told *SATA.* "My books are also about hope—I hope. Much of modern literature has given up hope and deals with anti-heroes and despair. It seems to me that human beings by their very natures need heroes, real heroes, and are happier with them. I see no point in talking about how life is over and it never mattered anyway. I don't believe it."

Cover of McKinley's novel Chalice, **featuring cover art by Cory and Catska Ench.** (Ace Books, 2009. Illustration by Cory Ench and Catska Ench. Reproduced by permission of Berkley Publishing Group, a division of Penguin Group (U.S.A.) Inc.)

"classic McKinley" protagonist. According to a *Kirkus Reviews* writer, *Dragonhaven* treats readers to a "sharply incisive, wildly intelligent dragon fantasy involving profound layers of science and society, love and loss and nature and nurture." In *Kliatt* Paula Rohrlick wrote that McKinley's "engrossing fantasy is suspenseful and highly detailed," and Jake's "self-deprecating sense of humor helps make [*Dragonhaven*] . . . a truly wonderful read."

In *Pegasus* readers are drawn into the story of Sylvie, a twelve-year-old princess of a land where magicians and fantasy creatures dwell. For over 1,000 years humans have dwelled peacefully alongside the herds of wingéd horses that share the region. Language difficulties prevented a true partnership until now as Sylvi and the black pegasus Ebon realize that they can communicate telepathically. As the girl begins to bond with Ebon and is allowed entrance into the pegasi's secret caves, her knowledge becomes a threat to several local magicians,

Biographical and Critical Sources

BOOKS

Children's Literature Review, Volume 10, Gale (Detroit, MI), 1986.
Dictionary of Literary Biography, Volume 52: *American Writers for Children since 1960: Fiction,* Gale (Detroit, MI), 1986, pp. 262-266.
St. James Guide to Fantasy Writers, St. James Press (Detroit, MI), 1996.
St. James Guide to Young-Adult Writers, 2nd edition, St. James Press (Detroit, MI), 1999.

PERIODICALS

Booklist, October 1, 1982, Sally Estes, review of *The Blue Sword,* p. 198; August, 1994, Frances Bradburn, review of *A Knot in the Grain and Other Stories,* p. 2039; August, 1997, Sally Estes, review of *Rose Daughter,* p. 1898; November 1, 1998, Carolyn Phelan, review of *The Stone Fey,* p. 484; April, 15,

2000, Sally Estes, review of *Spindle's End,* p. 1543; April 15, 2002, Sally Estes, review of *Water: Tales of Elemental Spirits,* p. 1416; October 15, 2003, Kristine Huntley, review of *Sunshine,* p. 399; October 1, 2007, Jennifer Mattson, review of *Dragonhaven,* p. 44; September 1, 2008, Lynn Rutan, review of *Chalice,* p. 89; September 1, 2009, Krista Hutley, review of *Fire: Tales of Elemental Spirits,* p. 81; October 1, 2010, Daniel Kraus, review of *Pegasus,* p. 88.

Bulletin of the Center for Children's Books, September, 1993, Betsy Hearne, review of *Deerskin,* p. 16; June, 1994, Betsy Hearne, review of *A Knot in the Grain and Other Stories,* p. 327.

Choice, July-August, 1979, review of *Beauty: A Retelling of the Story of Beauty and the Beast,* p. 668.

Christian Science Monitor, November 26, 2008, Yvonne Zipp, review of *Chalice,* p. 25.

Family Life, December 1, 2000, review of *Spindle's End,* p. 127.

Horn Book, January-February, 1985, Mary M. Burns, review of *The Hero and the Crown,* pp. 59-60; July-August, 1985, Robin McKinley, transcript of Newbery Medal acceptance speech, pp. 395-405, and Terri Windling and Mark Alan Arnold, "Robin McKinley," pp. 406-409; July-August, 1994, Ann A. Flowers, review of *A Knot in the Grain and Other Stories,* pp. 458-459; September-October, 1997, Lauren Adams, review of *Rose Daughter,* pp. 574-575; May-June, 2000, Anita L. Burkam, review of *Spindle's End,* p. 317; July-August, 2002, Anita L. Burkham, review of *Water,* p. 466; September-October, 2007, Deirdre F. Baker, review of *Dragonhaven,* p. 581; November-December, 2009, Anita L. Burkam, review of *Fire,* p. 681.

Kirkus Reviews, December 1, 1978, review of *Beauty,* p. 1307; June 1, 2002, review of *Water,* p. 808; August 15, 2003, review of *Sunshine,* p. 1039; August 1, 2007, review of *Dragonhaven;* August 15, 2008, review of *Chalice;* October 1, 2009, review of *Fire.*

Kliatt, May, 2005, Donna Scanlon, review of *Sunshine,* p. 34; September, 2007, Paula Rohrlick, review of *Dragonhaven,* p. 15.

New Statesman, November 8, 1985, Gillian Wilce, review of *The Hero and the Crown,* p. 28.

New York Times Book Review, January 27, 1985, Merri Rosenberg, review of *The Hero and the Crown,* p. 29; November 13, 1988, Michael Malone, review of *The Outlaws of Sherwood,* p. 54; January 18, 1998, Kathryn Harrison, review of *Rose Daughter,* p. 18; May 14, 2000, Elizabeth Devereaux, review of *Spindle's End,* p. 27.

Publishers Weekly, April 25, 1994, review of *A Knot in the Grain and Other Stories,* p. 80; June 16, 1997, review of *Rose Daughter,* p. 60; August 31, 1998, review of *The Stone Fey,* p. 77; March 27, 2000, review of *Spindle's End,* p. 82; September 2, 2002, review of *Water,* p. 77; September 29, 2003, review of *Sunshine,* p. 47, and Mitzi Brunsdale, interview with McKinley, p. 48; August 20, 2007, review of *Dragonhaven,* p. 69; July 21, 2008, review of *Chalice,* p. 159; October 11, 2010, review of *Pegasus,* p. 45.

School Library Journal, January, 1983, Karen Stang Hanley, review of *The Blue Sword,* p. 86; May, 1992,

JoAnn Rees, review of *My Father Is in the Navy,* p. 91; September, 1993, Cathy Chauvette, review of *Deerskin,* p. 261; September, 1997, Julie Cummins, review of *Rose Daughter,* pp. 219-220; January, 1999, Virginia Golodetz, review of *The Stone Fey,* p. 130; June, 2000, Connie Tyrrell Burns, review of *Spindle's End,* p. 150; June, 2002, John Peters, review of *Water,* p. 142; December, 2004, Beth Wright, "Once upon a Time: A Librarian Looks at Recent Young-Adult Novels Based on Fairy Tales," p. 40; September, 2007, Beth Wright, review of *Dragonhaven,* p. 203; October, 2008, Heather M. Campbell, review of *Chalice,* p. 154; September, 2009, Misti Tidman, review of *Fire,* p. 166.

Science Fiction Review, August, 1983, Darrell Schweitzer, review of *The Blue Sword,* p. 46.

Voice of Youth Advocates, April, 1989, Shirley Wilton, review of *The Outlaws of Sherwood,* p. 44; August, 1993, Christy Tyson, review of *Deerskin,* p. 168.

Washington Post Book World, November 6, 1988, Michele Landsberg, review of *The Outlaws of Sherwood,* p. 15.

Wilson Library Bulletin, January, 1987, Frances Bradburn, review of *The Hero and the Crown,* p. 60.

ONLINE

Robin McKinley Home Page, http://www.robinmckinley. com (April 15, 2011).

Robin McKinley Web log, http://robinmckinleyblog.com (April 15, 2011).*

*   *   *

MESCHENMOSER, Sebastian 1980-

Personal

Born 1980, in Frankfurt am Main, Germany. *Education:* Attended Freien Bildenden Kunst and École National Supériure d'Art; Akademie für Bildende Künste Mainz, diploma, 2007.

Addresses

Home—Frankfurt, Germany. *E-mail*—semesch@gmx. de.

Career

Artist and author/illustrator of children's books. Resident artist, VG.& S. Art Development, Frankfurt, Germany, 2011. *Exhibitions:* Works exhibited at Galerie Greulich, Frankfurt am Main, Germany; Kunsthaus Dresden, Dresden, Germany; Institute of Contemporary Art, Danzig, Germany; Galeri Krethlow, Bern, Switzerland; and Kunstverein Familie Montez.

Awards, Honors

Best Children's Book of the Year selection, Bank Street College of Education, and Comstock Award Honor Book designation, both 2006, both for *Learning to Fly;*

Deutschen Jugendliteraturpreis nomination, 2007; Kulturförderpreis Wtttlich, and Silver Pencil award, Rijksmuseum (Amsterdam, Netherlands), both 2008; Notable Children's Book designation, American Library Association, 2009, for *Waiting for Winter;* Balmoral-Schloss Wipersdorf award, 2010.

Writings

SELF-ILLUSTRATED

Fliegen Lernen, Esslinger (Esslingen, Germany), 2005, translation published as *Learning to Fly,* Kane/Miller (La Jolla, CA), 2006.

Herr Eichhorn und der Mond, Esslinger (Esslingen, Germany), 2006.

Herr Eichhorn und der erste Schnee, Esslinger (Esslingen, Germany), 2007.

Wünsche für Mopsmann, Esslinger (Esslingen, Germany), 2008.

Der Selenit etc., Galerie Greulich (Frankfurt am Main, Germany), 2008.

Wo auch immer, Galerie Greulich (Frankfurt am Main, Germany), 2009, translation published as *Waiting for Winter,* Kane Miller (Tulsa, OK), 2009.

Herr Eichhorn weiß den Weg zum Glück, Esslinger (Esslingen, Germany), 2009.

Author's work has been translated into Dutch.

Sidelights

Sebastian Meschenmoser is an artist and author whose work in the realm of children's literature has gained him many young fans in his native Germany. The picture books *Fliegen Lernen* and *Wo auch immer* have been the first books to introduce Meschenmoser's work to English-language readers; they have been translated, respectively, as *Learning to Fly* and *Waiting for Winter.*

Featuring charcoal drawings by the author, *Learning to Fly* begins its inspiring story with a quirky premise. According to Meschenmoser's spare, droll narrative, the man meets a penguin that claims that it knew how to fly until it was told by other birds that penguins cannot fly. As readers follow the story and art, the bearded narrator (who looks surprisingly like Meschenmoser himself) brings this penguin home and tries to help the Arctic creature reclaim its flying abilities. In addition to building up wing muscles with exercise, man and bird experiment with various flight aids, among them a kite attachment and wing enhancements crafted from strong-quilled chicken feathers. Ultimately, the penguin regains its inspiration and is able to soar in Meschenmoser's mock-serious epic.

Praised by a *Publishers Weekly* contributor as "a quiet, atmospheric and offbeat treasure," *Waiting for Winter* also pairs Meschenmoser's detailed art with a quirky tale. When Deer remarks that winter is coming and snow will be falling soon, three young animals look forward to experiencing their first cold-weather season. With their excitement over seeing this substance called snow, Squirrel, Bear, and Hedgehog decide to postpone snuggling down in their cozy burrows and caves for the winter and await snow's forecasted coming. But what does snow look like? They know that snow is white, cold, wet, and soft to the touch, but so are other things, leading to a great deal of slapstick humor. Praising *Waiting for Winter* as "a beautiful title to share with children," Lisa Gangemi Kropp added that Meschenmoser's "deftly drawn" and subtly tinted colored-pencil illustrations are enhanced by "broadly stroked hues of azure paint" that "make the white space of the page really come to life." The author/illustrator "sketches freely . . . in dark gray and sepia, drawing with casual grace and unerring comic instinct," wrote the *Publishers Weekly* critic, while a *Kirkus Reviews* writer dubbed *Waiting for Winter* "a perfect marriage of words and pictures."

In the *New York Times* David Barringer commented on the unique manner in which Meschenmoser captures the animal qualities of his anthropomorphized cast of picture-book characters. These childlike animal "creatures are not slickly cute but refreshingly sympathetic," the critic noted. "They do not ask to be admired. They look as if they need a hairbrush—and a cup of hot chocolate."

Biographical and Critical Sources

PERIODICALS

Booklist, November 1, 2009, Kay Weisman, review of *Waiting for Winter,* p. 55.

Children's Bookwatch, October, 2009, review of *Waiting for Winter.*

Kirkus Reviews, October 15, 2009, review of *Waiting for Winter.*

New York Times Book Review, November 8, 2009, David Barringer, review of *Waiting for Winter,* p. 22.

Publishers Weekly, January 30, 2006, review of *Learning to Fly,* p. 68; September 21, 2009, review of *Waiting for Winter,* p. 58.

School Library Journal, September, 2009, Lisa Gangemi Kropp, review of *Waiting for Winter,* p. 129.

ONLINE

Kane/Miller Book Publishers Web site, http://www.kanemiller.com/ (April 15, 2011), "Sebastian Meschenmoser."

Sebastian Meschenmoser Home Page, http://www.sebastian-meschenmoser.de (April 24, 2011).*

MULDROW, Diane

Personal

Female. *Education:* Ohio University, degree (magazine journalism, dance), 1987.

Addresses

Home—Brooklyn, NY.

Career

Author and editor of books for children. Worked as a dancer and actor in New York, NY; Golden Books (now Golden Books/Random House), New York, NY, junior editor, 1987, then editor until 1994, editorial director, beginning 1999; Scholastic, Inc., New York, NY, editor of Cartwheel Books imprint, 1994-98; freelance writer, beginning 2001. Speaker at conferences.

Writings

FOR CHILDREN

(Selector) *Mother Goose on the Farm,* illustrated by Amy Aitken, Western Pub. Co. (Racine, WI), 1989.

(Selector) *My Little Book of Mother Goose Rhymes,* illustrated by Leonard Lubin, Western Pub. Co. (Racine, WI), 1989.

Walt Disney's Bambi: Count to Five, Western Pub. Co. (Racine, WI), 1991.

(Adaptor) *Walt Disney's Pinocchio,* illustrated by Fred Marvin, Western Pub. Co. (Racine, WI), (New York, NY), 1992.

(With Margo Lundell) *Dearest Baby,* illustrated by Barbara Lanza, Western Pub. Co. (Racine, WI), 1993.

Walt Disney's Dumbo: The Circus Baby, illustrated by Peter Emslie, Western Pub. Co. (Racine, WI), 1993.

Disney's Aladdin Action Words, illustrated by Kenny Thompkins, Western Pub. Co. (Racine, WI), 1994.

(Reteller) The Brothers Grimm, *The Twelve Dancing Princesses,* illustrated by Fred Marvin, Western Pub. Co. (Racine, WI), 1995.

The Picnic Surprise, illustrated by Darrell Baker, Western Pub. Co. (Racine, WI), 1996.

(Adaptor) *Disney's Beauty and the Beast: The Enchanted Christmas,* illustrated by Alan Nowell, Golden Books (New York, NY), 1997.

(Adaptor) *Margaret Wise Brown's Pussy Willow,* illustrated by Jo-Ellen C. Bosson, Golden Books (New York, NY), 1997.

Jingle Bells, illustrated by Joe Ewers, Golden Books (New York, NY), 1998.

Lassie: The Great Escape, Golden Books (New York, NY), 1998.

Shapes at the Ballet, Golden Books (New York, NY), 1998.

Walt Disney's Mickey and Friends: Haunted Halloween, illustrated by Scott Tilley and Brent Ford, Golden Books (New York, NY), 1998.

(Adaptor) *Toy Story 2* (based on the animated film), Golden Books (New York, NY), 1999.

(Adaptor) *Buzz Lightyear: Space Ranger,* (based on the animated film *Toy Story 2*), Golden Books (New York, NY), 1999.

Counting Book, Golden Books (New York, NY), 1999.

Counting Fun on the Farm!, Golden Books (New York, NY), 1999.

Jacky and the Giant, illustrated by Vince Andriani, Scholastic (New York, NY), 1999.

Kindness, illustrated by Mary O'Keefe Young, Rourke Book Co. (Vero Beach, FL), 1999.

Mewtwo Strikes Back, Golden Books (New York, NY), 1999.

The Happy Book, illustrated by Patti Ann Harris, Scholastic (New York, NY), 1999.

A Shipful of Shivers, illustrated by Chris Nowell, Golden Books (New York, NY), 2000.

Barbie and Kelly's Super Saturday: A Big Lift and Learn Flap Book, Reader's Digest (Pleasantville, NY), 2000.

Electric Shock Showdown, Golden Books (New York, NY), 2000.

The Pokemon Book of Colors, Golden Books (New York, NY), 2000.

Frosty the Snowman, Golden Books (New York, NY), 2001.

Jingle Bells, Golden Books (New York, NY), 2001.

Rapunzel, Golden Books (New York, NY), 2001.

Little Golden Picture Dictionary, Golden Books (New York, NY), 2002.

The Sleepy Book, Scholastic, Inc. (New York, NY), 2002.

(With Barbara Shook Hazen) *Noah's Ark,* illustrated by Mircea Catusanu, Random House (New York, NY), 2003.

How Do Lions Say I Love You?, Random House (New York, NY), 2009.

(Reteller with Pamela Broughton) *Miracles of Jesus,* illustrated by Jerry Smath, Golden Books (New York, NY), 2009.

Somewhere So Sleepy, illustrated by Jui Ishida, Random House (New York, NY), 2010.

We Planted a Tree, illustrated by Bob Staake, Golden Books (New York, NY), 2010.

Who's Your Daddy?, illustrated by Rick Peterson, Random House (New York, NY), 2010.

Where Do Giggles Come From?, Random House (New York, NY), 2011.

"BARBIE" SERIES

I Am Barbie, Golden Books (Racine WI), 1997.

Busy Careers, Golden Books (New York, NY), 1997.

Holiday Helpers, Golden Books (New York, NY), 1998.

A Colorful Beach Day, Golden Books (New York, NY), 1998.

My Favorite Teacher, Golden Books (New York, NY), 1998.

The New Counselor, Golden Books (New York, NY), 1998.

Ice Skating Dreams, Golden Books (New York, NY), 1999.

Gymnastics Fun, Golden Books (New York, NY), 2000.

A Happy Holiday, Golden Books (New York, NY), 2001.

"DISH" NOVEL SERIES

Boiling Point, illustrated by Barbara Pollak, Grosset & Dunlap (New York, NY), 2002.

Into the Mix, illustrated by Barbara Pollak, Grosset & Dunlap (New York, NY), 2002.

Stirring It Up, illustrated by Barbara Pollak, Grosset & Dunlap (New York, NY), 2002.

Truth without the Trimmings, illustrated by Barbara Pollak, Grosset & Dunlap (New York, NY), 2002.

Turning up the Heat, illustrated by Barbara Pollak, Grosset & Dunlap (New York, NY), 2002.

A Measure of Thanks, illustrated by Barbara Pollak, Grosset & Dunlap (New York, NY), 2003.

Lights! Camera! Cook!, illustrated by Barbara Pollak, Grosset & Dunlap (New York, NY), 2003.

On the Back Burner, illustrated by Barbara Pollak, Grosset & Dunlap (New York, NY), 2003.

Recipe for Trouble, illustrated by Barbara Pollak, Grosset & Dunlap (New York, NY), 2003.

Diane Muldrow's upbeat nature story in **We Planted a Tree** *comes to life in Bob Staake's stylized and retro-inspired illustrations.* (Golden Books, 2010. Illustration copyright © 2010 by Bob Staake. Reproduced by permission of Random House Children's Books, a division of Random House, Inc.)

Sweet-and-sour Summer, illustrated by Barbara Pollak, Grosset & Dunlap (New York, NY), 2003.

Winner Takes the Cake, illustrated by Barbara Pollak, Grosset & Dunlap (New York, NY), 2003.

Deep Freeze, illustrated by Barbara Pollak, Grosset & Dunlap (New York, NY), 2007.

Sidelights

Diane Muldrow is a prolific writer whose books for children range from stories based on feature films to toddler-friendly picture books to her "Dish" series of middle-grade novels featuring artwork by Barbara Pollak. As editorial director of Golden Books, Muldrow is also involved in publishing stories by other writers as well as reprinting classic Golden Books, sometimes selecting new illustrations that will attract contemporary picture-book audiences. "Don't write to be published," the author/editor advised an audience of writers, as quoted on the Web site of the Metropolitan New York chapter of the Society of Children's Book Writers and Illustrators. "This should be what you're doing because it's what you love to do."

Featuring stylized illustrations by Bob Staake, *We Planted a Tree* is Muldrow's first large-format picture book. The story was inspired by the work of Wangari Maathai, the Kenyan woman who marshaled her nation's farmwomen to plant over thirty million new trees in what has been called the Greenbelt Movement. In Muldrow's rhyming text, families from diverse regions of the earth plant young trees near their homes and then tend them. As these trees grow—whether in a Brooklyn backyard, on the Kenyan savannah, in Continental Europe, or in Asia—so do the families' children. The trees leaf out, help freshen the air, and become an important part of their environment while the children grow into adults and contribute too, each in their own way. "Illustrating the simple poetry are clean-lined digital illustrations" by Staake that included scientific detail and also "celebrate the connections between plants and people," noted *Booklist* contributor Hazel Rochman, while in *School Library Journal* Kathleen Kelly MacMillan recommended *We Planted a Tree* as an "enjoyable and informative" choice for Earth Day or Arbor Day storyhours.

In *Stirring It Up,* the first volume in Muldrow's "Dish" series, readers meet Amanda and Molly Moore, preteen twins who live in Brooklyn, New York. To keep themselves busy during their summer holiday, the girls decide to learn to cook and help out the family. Muldrow follows the girls as they select a recipe online and then go to the grocery store to seek out the proper ingredients and prepare an evening meal. Encouraged by their first effort, Amanda and Molly decide to take a cooking class, where they are joined by friends Peichi and Shawn. Other events play out over the girl's busy summer, including a visit with Grandfather, baby-sitting assignments, and dealing with a difficult classmate. The "Dish" series continues in *Turning up the Heat,* in

which the sisters decide to start a cooking service for busy neighbors, as well as *Into the Mix, Truth without the Trimmings, Recipe for Trouble,* and several other stories. In addition to recommending *Stirring It Up* for reluctant readers, Shelle Rosenfeld added in *Booklist* that Muldrow's book "may also inspire some kids to try their hand in the kitchen." Although Wendy S. Carroll concluded that the novel's "plot play[s] . . . second fiddle to talk of food and cooking," the critic added that the inclusion of three kid-tested recipes as well as "cooking tips" will make the "Dish" books attractive to creative middle-graders in families where healthy eating is a way of life.

Biographical and Critical Sources

PERIODICALS

Booklist, July, 2002, Shelle Rosenfeld, review of *Stirring It Up,* p. 1848; February 15, 2010, Hazel Rochman, review of *We Planted a Tree,* p. 89.

California Kids, October, 2009, Patricia Newman, profile of Muldrow.

Kirkus Reviews, February 15, 2010, review of *We Planted a Tree.*

School Library Journal, August, 2002, Wendy S. Carroll, review of *Stirring It Up,* p. 195; March, 2010, Kathleen Kelly MacMillian, review of *We Planted a Tree,* p. 128.

ONLINE

Society of Children's Book Writers and Illustrators Metro New York Chapter Web site, http://metro.nyscbwi.org/ (April 15, 2011), "Diane Muldrow on Golden Books, Storytelling, and Craft."*

*   *   *

MYERS, Walter Dean 1937-
(Stacie Johnson, Walter M. Myers)

Personal

Born Walter Milton Myers, August 12, 1937, in Martinsburg, WV; son of George Ambrose and Mary Myers; raised from age three by Herbert Julius (a shipping clerk) and Florence (a factory worker) Dean; married (marriage dissolved); married Constance Brendel, June 19, 1973; children: (first marriage) Karen, Michael Dean; (second marriage) Christopher. *Education:* Attended City College of the City University of New York; Empire State College, B.A., 1984.

Addresses

Home—Jersey City, NJ. *Agent*—Miriam Altshuler Literary Agency, 53 Old Post Rd. N., Red Hook, NY 12571.

Walter Dean Myers (Photograph by David Godlis. Reproduced by permission of Walter Dean Myers.)

Career

Author of books for children. New York State Department of Labor, New York, NY, employment supervisor, 1966-70; Bobbs-Merrill Co., Inc. (publisher), New York, NY, senior trade books editor, 1970-77; full-time writer, beginning 1977. Teacher of creative writing and black history on a part-time basis in New York, NY, 1974-75; worked variously as a post-office clerk, inter-office messenger, and an interviewer at a factory. *Military service:* U.S. Army, 1954-57.

Member

PEN, Harlem Writers Guild.

Awards, Honors

Council on Interracial Books for Children Award, 1968, for *Where Does the Day Go?;* Children's Book of the Year, Child Study Association of America (CSAA), 1972, for *The Dancers;* Notable Book designation, American Library Association (ALA), 1975, and Woodward Park School Annual Book Award, 1976, both for *Fast Sam, Cool Clyde, and Stuff;* Best Books for Young Adults designation, ALA, 1978, for *It Ain't All for Nothin',* and 1979, for *The Young Landlords;* Coretta Scott King Award, ALA, 1980, for *The Young Landlords,* and 1985, for *Motown and Didi;* ALA Best Books for Young Adults designation, 1981, and Notable Children's Trade Book in the Field of Social Studies designation, National Council for Social Studies/Children's Book Council, 1982, both for *The Legend of Tarik;*

Edgar Allan Poe Award runner up, Mystery Writers of America, and ALA Best Books for Young Adults designation, both 1982, both for *Hoops;* Parents' Choice Award, Parents' Choice Foundation, 1982, for *Won't Know till I Get There,* 1984, for *The Outside Shot,* 1987, for *Crystal,* 1988, for *Fallen Angels,* 1990, for *The Mouse Rap,* and 1992, for *The Righeous Revenge of Artemis Bonner;* New Jersey Institute of Technology Authors Award, 1983, for *Tales of a Dead King;* Children's Book of the Year selection, CSAA, 1987, for *Adventure in Granada;* New Jersey Institute of Technology Authors Award, and ALA Best Books for Young Adults designation, 1988, Coretta Scott King Award, 1989, and Children's Book Award, South Carolina Association of School Librarians, 1991, all for *Fallen Angels;* ALA Notable Book designation and Best Books for Young Adults designation, both 1988, both for *Me, Mop, and the Moondance Kid;* ALA Notable Book designation, 1988, and Newbery Medal Honor Book designation, 1989, both for *Scorpions;* Golden Kite Award Honor Book selection, and Jane Addams Award Honor Book designation, both 1991, and Coretta Scott King Award, and Orbis Pictus Award Honor Book designation, both 1992, all for *Now Is Your Time!; Boston Globe/Horn Book* Award Honor Book selection, 1992, and Coretta Scott King Award Honor Book selection, and Newbery Medal Honor Book designation, both 1993, all for *Somewhere in the Darkness;* Jeremiah Ludington Award, Educational Paperback Association, 1993, for "18 Pine St." series; CRABberry Award, 1993, for *Malcolm X;* Margaret A. Edwards Award, ALA/ *School Library Journal,* 1994, for contributions to young-adult literature; Coretta Scott King Award, 1997, for *Slam!; Boston Globe/Horn Book* Award Honor Book designation, 1997, for *Harlem: A Poem;* Michael L. Printz Award, ALA, and Coretta Scott King Award Honor Book designation, both 2000, both for *Monster;* Books for the Teen Age citation, New York Public Library, and ALA Quick Pick for Reluctant Young-Adult Readers citation, both 2004, both for *Shooter;* Lee Bennett Hopkins Poetry Award, International Reading Association, 2005, for *Here in Harlem;* Books for the Teen Age citation, ALA Best Books for Young Adults designation, and National Book Award finalist for Young People's Literature, all 2005, all for *Autobiography of My Dead Brother;* Cooperative Children's Book Center Choice selection, 2008, for *Game;* NSK Neustadt Prize in Children's Literature nomination, 2006; May Hill Arbuthnot Honor Lecture Award, ALA, 2009; ALA Top-Ten Quick Pick for Reluctant Young-Adult Readers inclusion, 2010, for *Dope Sick;* National Book Award finalist for Young People's Literature, 2010, for *Lockdown;* Coretta Scott King/Virginia Hamilton Award for Lifetime Achievement, 2010; several child-selected awards.

Writings

FICTION; FOR CHILDREN AND YOUNG ADULTS

Fast Sam, Cool Clyde, and Stuff, Viking (New York, NY), 1975.

Brainstorm, photographs by Chuck Freedman, F. Watts (New York, NY), 1977.

Mojo and the Russians, Viking (New York, NY), 1977.

Victory for Jamie, Scholastic (New York, NY), 1977.

It Ain't All for Nothin', Viking (New York, NY), 1978.

The Young Landlords, Viking (New York, NY), 1979.

The Golden Serpent, illustrated by Alice and Martin Provensen, Viking (New York, NY), 1980.

Hoops, Delacorte (New York, NY), 1981.

The Legend of Tarik, Viking (New York, NY), 1981.

Won't Know till I Get There, Viking (New York, NY), 1982.

The Nicholas Factor, Viking (New York, NY), 1983.

Tales of a Dead King, Morrow (New York, NY), 1983.

Motown and Didi: A Love Story, Viking (New York, NY), 1984.

The Outside Shot, Delacorte (New York, NY), 1984.

Sweet Illusions, Teachers & Writers Collaborative, 1986.

Crystal, Viking (New York, NY), 1987, reprinted, Harper-Trophy (New York, NY), 2001.

Scorpions, Harper (New York, NY), 1988.

Me, Mop, and the Moondance Kid, illustrated by Rodney Pate, Delacorte (New York, NY), 1988.

Fallen Angels, Scholastic (New York, NY), 1988.

The Mouse Rap, HarperCollins (New York, NY), 1990.

Somewhere in the Darkness, Scholastic (New York, NY), 1992.

Mop, Moondance, and the Nagasaki Knights, Delacorte (New York, NY), 1992.

The Righteous Revenge of Artemis Bonner, HarperCollins (New York, NY), 1992.

The Glory Field, Scholastic (New York, NY), 1994.

Darnell Rock Reporting, Delacorte (New York, NY), 1994.

Shadow of the Red Moon, illustrated by son Christopher Myers, Scholastic (New York, NY), 1995.

Sniffy Blue, Ace Crime Detective: The Case of the Missing Ruby and Other Stories, illustrated by David J.A. Sims, Scholastic (New York, NY), 1996.

Slam!, Scholastic (New York, NY), 1996.

The Journal of Joshua Loper: A Black Cowboy, Atheneum (New York, NY), 1999.

The Journal of Scott Pendleton Collins: A World War II Soldier, Normandy, France, 1944, Scholastic (New York, NY), 1999.

Monster, illustrated by Christopher Myers, HarperCollins (New York, NY), 1999.

The Blues of Flats Brown, illustrated by Nina Laden, Holiday House (New York, NY), 2000.

145th Street: Short Stories, Delacorte Press (New York, NY), 2000.

Patrol: An American Soldier in Vietnam, illustrated by Ann Grifalconi, HarperCollins (New York, NY), 2001.

The Journal of Biddy Owens and the Negro Leagues, Scholastic (New York, NY), 2001.

Three Swords for Granada, illustrated by John Speirs, Holiday House (New York, NY), 2002.

Handbook for Boys, illustrated by Matthew Bandsuch, HarperCollins (New York, NY), 2002.

A Time to Love: Stories from the Old Testament, illustrated by Christopher Myers, Scholastic (New York, NY), 2003.

The Beast, Scholastic (New York, NY), 2003.

The Dream Bearer, HarperCollins (New York, NY), 2003.

Shooter, HarperTempest (New York, NY), 2004.

Southern Fried, St. Martin's Minotaur (New York, NY), 2004.

Autobiography of My Dead Brother, HarperTempest/Amistad (New York, NY), 2005.

Street Love, HarperTempest/Amistad (New York, NY), 2006.

Harlem Summer, Scholastic (New York, NY), 2007.

What They Found: Love on 145th St. (short stories), Wendy Lamb Books (New York, NY), 2007.

Game, HarperTeen (New York, NY), 2008.

Sunrise over Fallujah (sequel to *Fallen Angels*), Scholastic (New York, NY), 2008.

Dope Sick, HarperTeen/Amistad (New York, NY), 2009.

Riot, Egmont (New York, NY), 2009.

Lockdown, HarperTeen/Amistad (New York, NY), 2010.

The Cruisers, Scholastic (New York, NY), 2010.

(With Ross Workman) *Kick,* HarperTeen (New York, NY), 2011.

Creator and editor of "18 Pine Street" series of young-adult novels, Bantam, beginning 1992. Work represented in anthologies, including *What We Must SEE: Young Black Storytellers,* Dodd, 1971, and *We Be Word Sorcerers: Twenty-five Stories by Black Americans.*

"ARROW" SERIES

Adventure in Granada, Viking (New York, NY), 1985.

The Hidden Shrine, Viking (New York, NY), 1985.

Duel in the Desert, Viking (New York, NY), 1986.

Ambush in the Amazon, Viking (New York, NY), 1986.

JUVENILE NONFICTION

The World of Work: A Guide to Choosing a Career, Bobbs-Merrill (New York, NY), 1975.

Social Welfare, F. Watts (New York, NY), 1976.

Now Is Your Time! The African-American Struggle for Freedom, HarperCollins (New York, NY), 1992.

A Place Called Heartbreak: A Story of Vietnam, illustrated by Frederick Porter, Raintree (Austin, TX), 1992.

Young Martin's Promise (picture book), illustrated by Barbara Higgins Bond, Raintree (Austin, TX), 1992.

Malcolm X: By Any Means Necessary, Scholastic (New York, NY), 1993.

One More River to Cross: An African-American Photograph Album, Harcourt (New York, NY), 1995.

Turning Points: When Everything Changes, Troll Communications (Matwah, NJ), 1996.

Toussaint L'Ouverture: The Fight for Haiti's Freedom, illustrated by Jacob Lawrence, Simon & Schuster (New York, NY), 1996.

Amistad: A Long Road to Freedom, Dutton (New York, NY), 1998.

At Her Majesty's Request: An African Princess in Victorian England, Scholastic (New York, NY), 1999.

Malcolm X: A Fire Burning Brightly, illustrated by Leonard Jenkins, HarperCollins (New York, NY), 2000.

The Greatest: Muhammad Ali, Scholastic (New York, NY), 2001.

Bad Boy: A Memoir, HarperCollins (New York, NY), 2001.

USS Constellation: Pride of the American Navy, Holiday House (New York, NY), 2004.

I've Seen the Promised Land: The Life of Dr. Martin Luther King, Jr., illustrated by Leonard Jenkins, HarperCollins (New York, NY), 2004.

Antarctica: Journeys to the South Pole, Scholastic (New York, NY), 2004.

(With William Miles) *The Harlem Hellfighters: When Pride Met Courage,* HarperCollins (New York, NY), 2006.

Ida B. Wells: Let the Truth Be Told, HarperCollins (New York, NY), 2008.

PICTURE BOOKS

(Under name Walter M. Myers) *Where Does the Day Go?,* illustrated by Leo Carty, Parents Magazine Press, 1969.

The Dragon Takes a Wife, illustrated by Ann Grifalconi, Bobbs-Merrill (New York, NY), 1972.

The Dancers, illustrated by Anne Rockwell, Parents Magazine Press, 1972.

Fly, Jimmy, Fly!, illustrated by Moneta Barnett, Putnam (New York, NY), 1974.

The Black Pearl and the Ghost; or, One Mystery after Another, illustrated by Robert Quackenbush, Viking (New York, NY), 1980.

Mr. Monkey and the Gotcha Bird, illustrated by Leslie Morrill, Delacorte (New York, NY), 1984.

The Story of the Three Kingdoms, illustrated by Ashley Bryan, HarperCollins (New York, NY), 1995.

How Mr. Monkey Saw the Whole World, illustrated by Synthia Saint James, Bantam (New York, NY), 1996.

Harlem: A Poem, illustrated by Christopher Myers, Scholastic (New York, NY), 1997.

Jazz, illustrated by Christopher Myers, Holiday House (New York, NY), 2006.

Amiri and Odette: A Love Story, illustrated by Javaka Steptoe, Scholastic (New York, NY), 2009.

Muhammad Ali: The People's Champion, illustrated by Alix Delinois, Collins Amistad (New York, NY), 2010.

Looking for the Easy Life, illustrated by Lee Harper, HarperCollins (New York, NY), 2010.

We Are America: A Tribute from the Heart, illustrated by Christopher Myers, HarperCollins (New York, NY), 2011.

POETRY

Brown Angels: An Album of Pictures and Verse, HarperCollins (New York, NY), 1993.

Remember Us Well: An Album of Pictures and Verse, HarperCollins (New York, NY), 1993.

Glorious Angels: A Celebration of Children, HarperCollins (New York, NY), 1995.

Angel to Angel: A Mother's Gift of Love, HarperCollins (New York, NY), 1998.

Blues Journey, illustrated by Christopher Myers, Holiday House (New York, NY), 2003.

Here in Harlem: Poems in Many Voices, Holiday House (New York, NY), 2004.

Looking like Me, illustrated by Christopher Myers, Egmont (New York, NY), 2009.

UNDER NAME STACIE JOHNSON

Sort of Sisters, Delacorte (New York, NY), 1993.

The Party, Delacorte (New York, NY), 1993.

The Prince, Delacorte (New York, NY), 1993.

Contributor of articles and fiction to books and to periodicals, including *Alfred Hitchcock Mystery Magazine, Argosy, Black Creation, Black World, Boy's Life, Ebony, Jr.!, Espionage, Essence, McCall's, National Enquirer, Negro Digest,* and *Scholastic;* also contributor of poetry to university reviews and quarterlies.

Adaptations

The Young Landlords was adapted for film by Topol Productions. *Mojo and the Russians* was adapted for film by Children's Television International, Great Plains National Instructional Television Library, 1980. Demco Media released videos of *Fallen Angels* and *Me, Mop, and the Moondance Kid,* both 1988, *Scorpions,* 1990, and *The Righteous Revenge of Artemis Bonner,* 1996. *Darnell Rock Reporting* was adapted for video, 1996. *Harlem: A Poem* was released as a combination book-and-CD, 1997. *Scorpions* was adapted as a sound recording, 1998.

Sidelights

Deemed "a giant among children's and young adult authors" by Frances Bradburn in the *Wilson Library Bulletin,* Walter Dean Myers ranks among the best-known contemporary American writers for children and teens. An author of African-American descent, Myers is credited with helping to redefine the image of blacks in juvenile literature through books such as *Scorpions,* a Newbery Medal Honor Book, *Monster,* winner of the Michael L. Printz Award, and *Lockdown,* a National Book Award finalist. "As a Black writer I want to talk about my people," he observed in the *Something about the Author Autobiography Series (SAAS).* "I want to tell Black children about their humanity and about their history and how to grease their legs so the ash won't show and how to braid their hair so it's easy to comb on frosty winter mornings. The books come. They pour from me at a great rate."

During the 1960s and 1970s African-American writers such as Alice Childress, Lucille Clifton, Eloise Greenfield, Virginia Hamilton, and Sharon Bell Mathis sought to provide books for young readers that featured realistic storylines and well-rounded portrayals of black characters. As a member of this group, Myers distinguished himself by bringing both humor and poignancy to his

work as well by creating books with special appeal to boys; in addition, he is considered the only prominent male writer of the group to have consistently published books of high quality that range from realistic and historical fiction to mysteries, adventure stories, and fantasies as well as nonfiction, poetry, and picture books. A versatile and prolific author, Myers is perhaps best known for his books geared for readers in middle school and high school, stories that range from farcical, light-hearted tales for preteens to powerful, moving novels for older adolescents. Myers stresses the more positive aspects of black urban life in his works; often setting his stories in his boyhood home of Harlem, he depicts the strength and dignity of his characters without downplaying the harsh realities of their lives.

Although he features both young men and women as protagonists, Myers is noted for his focus on young black males. His themes often include the relationship between fathers and sons as well as the search for identity and self-worth in an environment of poverty, drugs, gang violence, and racism. Although his characters confront difficult issues, Myers stresses survival, pride, and hope in his works, which are filled with love and laughter and a belief in the possibility of a better future.

Calling Myers "a unique voice," Rudine Sims Bishop wrote in *Presenting Walter Dean Myers* that the author is significant "because he creates books that appeal to young adults from many cultural groups. They appeal because Myers knows and cares about the things that concern his readers and because he creates characters . . . readers are happy to spend time with." R.D. Lane noted in the *African American Review* that the author "celebrates children by weaving narratives of the black juvenile experience in ways that reverse the effects of mediated messages of the black experience in public culture. . . . Myers's stratagem is revolutionary: the intrinsic value to black youth of his lessons stands priceless, timeless, and class-transcendent." In her entry in the *Dictionary of Literary Biography,* Carmen Subryan concluded that "Myers's books demonstrate that writers can not only challenge the minds of black youths but also emphasize the black experience in a nondidactic way that benefits all readers."

Born in Martinsburg, West Virginia, Myers lost his mother at age two, during the birth of his younger sister Imogene. Since his father, George Ambrose Myers, was struggling economically, Walter and two of his sisters were informally adopted by family friends Florence and Herbert Dean; Myers has written about surrogate parenting in several of his stories, including *Won't Know Till I Get There* and *Me, Mop, and the Moondance Kid.*

The Dean family moved to Harlem when Myers was about three years old. He recalled in *SAAS,* "I loved Harlem. I lived in an exciting corner of the renowned Black capital and in an exciting era. The people I met there, the things I did, have left a permanent impression on me." When he was four years old Myers was taught

to read by his foster mother while his foster father sat the boy on his knee and told him "endless stories." As the author later wrote in *Children's Books and Their Creators,* "Somewhere along the line I discovered that books could be part of a child's world, and by the time I was nine I found myself spending long hours reading in my room. The books began to shape new bouts of imagination."

When not reading, Myers enjoyed playing sports, especially stickball, baseball, and basketball, and sports provide the background for young-adult novels such as *Hoops, The Outside Shot,* and *Slam!* At school, he enjoyed classwork although a speech impediment caused him some difficulty. When his fellow classmates laughed at him he would fight back; consequently, he was often suspended from school. When Myers reached the fifth grade, as he recalled in *SAAS,* "a marvelous thing happened." Made to sit at the back of the class as punishment for fighting, he was reading a comic book during a math lesson when the teacher, Mrs. Conway, caught him. Mrs. Conway, who was known for her strictness, surprised Walter by saying that if he was going to read, he might as well read something decent and brought him a selection of children's books. Mrs. Conway also required her students to read aloud in class. In order to avoid some of the words that he had trouble speaking, she suggested that Walter write something original to read before the class.

After junior high, Myers attended all-male Stuyvesant High School. Although he struggled somewhat due to the school's focus on science and academic achievement, he met another influential teacher, Bonnie Liebow, who interviewed each of her students and made up individualized reading lists for them. Myers's list included works by such European authors as Emile Zola and Thomas Mann. Liebow also told Myers that he was a gifted writer, inspiring the teen to consider writing as a career.

Despite this encouragement, Myers realized that writing "had no practical value for a Black child," as he recalled. "These minor victories did not bolster my ego. Instead, they convinced me that even though I was bright, even though I might have some talent, I was still defined by factors other than my ability." In addition, Myers was depressed by the fact that he would not be able to attend college due to his family's financial status. Consequently, he wrote in *SAAS,* he began "writing poems about death, despair, and doom" and began "having doubts about everything in my life."

When not writing or working odd jobs, Myers hung out in the streets: "I was steeped in the mystique of the semi-hoodlum," he recalled in *SAAS.* He acquired a stiletto and acted as a drug courier; he also became a target for one of the local gangs after intervening in a fight between three gang members and a new boy in the neighborhood.

In *Bad Boy: A Memoir* Myers recounts his childhood and adolescence, during which he often skipped school and sometimes made deliveries for drug dealers. He also describes his beginnings as a writer. Rochman said of this work that "the most beautiful writing is about Mama: how she taught him to read, sharing *True Romance* magazines." "The author's growing awareness of racism and of his own identity as a black man make up one of the most interesting threads" of *Bad Boy,* wrote Miranda Doyle in *School Library Journal.* Myers' "voice and heart are consistently heard and felt throughout," concluded a *Horn Book* contributor.

Finally, influenced by the war poems of British writer Rupert Brooke, Myers joined the army at age seventeen in order to, as he wrote in *SAAS,* "hie myself off to some far-off battlefield and get killed. There, where I fell, would be a little piece of Harlem."

Myers' army experience was not the glorious adventure promised by the poetry he had read; he went to radio-repair school and spent most of his time playing basketball. "I also learned several efficient ways of killing human beings," he later recalled. In addition, as he told Bishop in *Presenting Walter Dean Myers,* "I learned something about dying. I learned a lot about facilitating the process, of making it abstract." During his military service, Myers also developed the strong antiwar attitude that would later become part of his young-adult novel *Fallen Angels,* the story of a young black soldier in Vietnam.

After three years in the U.S. Army, Myers returned home to live with his parents, who had by now moved to Morristown, New Jersey. Then he moved back to Harlem, where he took an apartment and began to work at becoming a professional writer. In what he recalled as his "starving artist period," Myers wrote poetry and read books about the Bohemian life by such authors as George Orwell and André Gide; he also lived on two dollars a week from unemployment compensation and lost fifty pounds. While working briefly for the U.S. Post Office, he married Joyce, a woman he later called "wonderful, warm, beautiful, religious, caring."

Even after becoming a father—two of his three children, Karen and Michael, are from his first marriage—Myers continued to try to live a romantic lifestyle. While working odd jobs in a factory and an office, he played bongos with a group of jazz musicians, some of whom were into heroin and cocaine. His jazz-based poetry was published in Canada. He also began to be published in African-American magazines such as the *Negro Digest* and the *Liberator* as well as in men's magazines such as *Argosy* and *Cavalier.* During this time, his first marriage collapsed.

In 1961, Myers enrolled in a writing class with author Lajos Egri, who told him that he had a special talent. A few years later, he attended City College of the City University of New York as a night student, but dropped out. At a writer's workshop at Columbia University led by novelist John Oliver Killens, Myers was recommended for a new position at the publishing house Bobbs-Merrill and became their acquisitions editor. In 1968, he won first prize in a contest for black writers sponsored by the Council on Interracial Books for Children and a year later his picture-book text was published by Parents' Magazine Press as *Where Does the Day Go?*

Where Does the Day Go? features Steven, a small black boy whose father takes him and a group of children of various races for an evening walk in the park. When Steven wonders where the day goes, his friends each provide imaginative opinions of their own. Finally, Steven's dad explains that day and night are different, just like people, and that the times of day are caused by the rotation of the Earth. "Integration, involvement, and togetherness are all deftly handled," noted Mary Eble in *School Library Journal,* while Zena Sutherland, Dianne L. Monson, and May Hill Arbuthnot claimed in *Children and Books* that the story has "other strong values in addition to its exploration of the mystery of night and day." The critics noted that *Where Does the Day Go?* "explains natural phenomena accurately, and it presents an exemplary father."

After the publication of his first book, Myers changed his name from Walter Milton Myers to "one that would honor my foster parents, Walter Dean Myers." He also remarried, and he and new wife Connie had a son, Christopher, whi is now an artist and the illustrator of several of his father's works. In 1972, Myers published *The Dragon Takes a Wife,* a picture book about Harry, a lonely dragon who cannot fight, and Mabel May, the African-American fairy who helps him. In order to acquire a wife, Harry must defeat a knight in battle. When Mabel May turns into a dragon to show Harry how to fight, Harry falls in love with her, defeats the knight, and wins her hand, not to mention a good job at the post office.

One of several picture-book collaborations between Myers and son Christopher, *Jazz* serves as "a scintillating paean to jazz," according to a *Publishers Weekly* critic. Noting the efforts by other authors who struggle to capture the spirit of the music form in text, *Booklist* reviewer Bill Ott deemed *Jazz* "an absolutely airtight melding of words and pictures that is perfectly accessible to a younger audience." Through a series of poems accompanied by brightly colored illustrations, father and son chronicle the evolution of the uniquely American music form, from fast-paced New Orleans jazz to be-bop, so effectively that "readers will find music coming irresistibly into their heads," suggested Roger Sutton in *Horn Book.* In *Looking like Me* the Myers' offer a lyrical and uplifting portrait of a Harlem youth, focusing on the boy's relationships with his family and his community. "The rhyme and repetition flow naturally, capturing the rhythms of everyday conversation and the hip-hop beats many children hear daily,"

Mary Landrum observed in *School Library Journal.* Praising the vibrant text and colorful photo collages, *Booklist* critic Andrew Medlar described *Looking like Me* as "encouraging, energetic, and inspired."

In 1975, Myers published his first novel for young adults, *Fast Sam, Cool Clyde, and Stuff.* Set in a Harlem neighborhood much like the one in which its author grew up, the story describes a group of young teens who take a positive approach to living in a difficult environment. The story is narrated by eighteen-year-old Stuff, who recalls the year he was thirteen and formed a sort of anti-gang, the Good People, with his best friends Fast Sam and Cool Clyde plus five other boys and girls from the neighborhood. The Good People have several hilarious adventures, including one where Sam and Clyde—who is dressed as a girl—win a dance contest. However, they also deal with such problems as mistaken arrest and the deaths of one of their fathers and a friend who has turned to drugs. The children survive, both through their inner strength and the fellowship of dependable friends who are respectful of one another. Writing in *English Journal,* Alleen Pace Nilsen called *Fast Sam, Cool Clyde, and Stuff* "a rich, warm story about black kids in which Myers makes the reader feel so close to the characters that ethnic group identification is secondary." In *Horn Book,* Paul Heins noted that "the humorous and ironic elements of the plot give the book the flavor of a Harlem *Tom Sawyer* or *Penrod.*"

In 1977, after leaving Bobbs-Merrill, Myers became a full-time writer. *It Ain't All for Nothin',* a young-adult novel published the next year, is considered the first of his more serious, thought-provoking works. The novel features twelve-year-old Tippy, a motherless Harlem boy who has been living with his loving, principled grandmother since he was a baby. When she goes into a nursing home, Tippy moves in with his father Lonnie, an ex-con who makes his living by stealing and who beats his son viciously. Lonely and afraid, Tippy begins drinking whiskey. When Lonnie and his pals rob a store, he coerces Tippy into participating. *It Ain't All for Nothin'* was praised by Steven Matthews in *School Library Journal* as "a first-rate read," and by a *Kirkus Reviews* critic as "like Tippy—a winner." Although questioning "how many children are really going to 'drop a dime' on their father?," Ashley Jane Pennington concluded in her review for *Interracial Books for Children Bulletin* that *It Ain't All for Nothin'* "is a devastating book which needed to be written." *Motown and Didi: A Love Story,* a highly praised sequel, features two of the peripheral characters from *It Ain't All for Nothin'* and includes a strong anti-drug message as well as the theme that love can conquer all.

In *Monster* Myers explored another complicated topic in its story recounting a young man's experience in prison awaiting trial after he takes part in a fatal robbery. In 2000 the novel was awarded the first Michael L. Printz Award by the American Valcan Library Association

for excellence in young-adult literature. "Myers combines an innovative format, complex moral issues, and an intriguingly sympathetic but flawed protagonist in this cautionary tale," *Booklist* critic Debbie Carton remarked. *Shooter* focuses on the events leading up to and following a school shooting. Many reviewers compared the book to the real-life and well-publicized Columbine school tragedy, which occurred months prior to *Shooter*'s 2004 publication. The novel is told through a unique narrative approach: it consists of police reports, news articles, a journal, and other "real-life" documentation of the event. Of *Shooter,* Lauren Adams wrote in *Horn Book* that Myers's "exacting look at the many possible players and causes in the events makes for a compelling story." A *Publishers Weekly* reviewer praised the author for his handling of a controversial subject in which "no one is completely innocent and no one is entirely to blame." The reviewer concluded, "Readers will find themselves racing through the pages, then turning back to pore over the details once more."

Although Myers turns to a lighter subject in *Game,* he still explores serious themes through the first-person perspective of Drew, a seventeen year old from Harlem who hopes to earn a college basketball scholarship and play at the professional level. Like several of the author's earlier novels, *Game* features an African-American male from the inner city who reflects on the urban environment around him and questions his place within it. In addition to narrating Drew's struggle to chart his future, Myers includes "tautly choreographed game sequences that . . . bristle with the electricity of the sport," noted a *New York Times Book Review* critic. Predicting that the book will appeal to fans of *Monster* and *Slam,* a *Kirkus Reviews* contributor wrote that *Game* offers readers "a sensitive portrait of a likable young man, his family, city and dreams."

The middle-grade novels *Scorpions* and *Fallen Angels* are considered among Myers' best. In *Scorpions* twelve-year-old Jamal lives in Harlem with his mother and younger sister. He is approached to take the place of his older brother Randy—who has been jailed for killing a man—as the leader of his gang, the Scorpions. At first, Jamal refuses; however, he is fascinated with the gun that Randy's friend Mack gives him. Vieing the move as a way to help his family raise the money for Randy's appeal, Jamal joins the Scorpions, who are dealing cocaine. During a confrontation, Jamal is defended by best friend Tito, a sensitive Puerto Rican teen who uses the gun Mack had given Jamal to kill to protect his friend. Marcus Crouch wrote in *Junior Bookshelf* that Myers "writes with great power, capturing the cadences of black New York, and keeps a firm hold on his narrative and his emotions. He is a fine story-teller as well as a social critic and, I suspect, a moralist."

Myers wrote *Fallen Angels* as a tribute to his older brother Sonny, who was killed on his first day as a soldier in Vietnam; he also based much of the book on his own experience in the U.S. Army. *Fallen Angels* de-

scribes the horrors of the Vietnam War from the perspective of Richie Perry, a seventeen-year-old African American who has joined the U.S. Army as a way to make life easier for his mother and younger brother at home in Harlem. During the course of a year, Richie experiences fear and terror as he fights in the war; he burns the bodies of American soldiers because they cannot be carried and—with a rifle at his head—shoots a North Vietnamese soldier in the face; finally, after being wounded twice, he is sent home. Underscoring the novel, which includes rough language and gallows humor, is a strong antiwar message; Myers also addresses such issues as racial discrimination within the service and the conditions faced by the Vietnamese people. Calling Myers "a writer of skill, maturity, and judgment," Ethel L. Heins maintained in *Horn Book* that, "with its intensity and vividness in depicting a young soldier amid the chaos and the carnage of war, the novel recalls Stephen Crane's *The Red Badge of Courage*." W. Keith McCoy, writing in *Voice of Youth Advocates*, commented that "everything about this book rings true," while Mary Veeder noted in Chicago's *Tribune Books* that *Fallen Angels* "may be the best novel for young adults I've read this year."

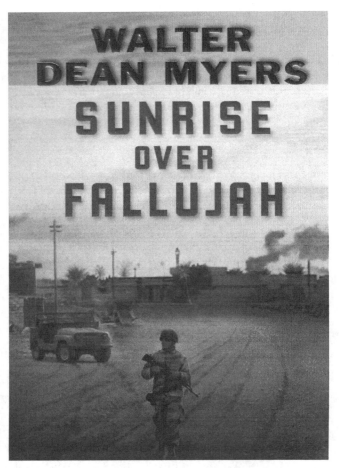

Cover of Sunrise over Fallujah, *Myers' novel about the American servicemen and women serving in Operation Iraqi Freedom.* (Illustration copyright © 2008 by Tim O'Brien. Reproduced by permission of Scholastic, Inc.)

In *Sunrise over Fallujah* Myers returns to the family depicted in his award-winning *Fallen Angels* and focuses on the Second Gulf War in Iraq. Enlisting in the army after the terrorist attacks of September 11, 2001, Richie's nephew Robin narrates his experiences in the letters he sends home during his time overseas. Initially assigned to a Civil Affairs unit working to gain the cooperation of Iraqi citizens, Robin struggles to comprehend the collateral bloodshed occurring as the conflict progresses as well as deal with the constant threat to his life from Iraqis fighting against the presence of American troops in their country. By experiencing firsthand the horrors of war similar to those his uncle endured, the young soldier finally understands why Uncle Richie kept silent about his experiences in the jungles of Southeast Asia a generation earlier. Writing in *School Library Journal,* Diane P. Tuccillo wrote that Myers avoids editorializing about the war and instead offers an "expert portrayal of a soldier's feelings and perspectives . . . allow[ing] the circumstances to speak for themselves." Noting the lack of Y.A. material about the Gulf War, a *Kirkus Reviews* writer deemed *Sunrise over Fallujah* "an important volume, covering much ground and offering much insight," while a *Publishers Weekly* critic suggested that Myers has written "the novel that will allow American teens to grapple intelligently and thoughtfully with the war in Iraq."

Returning to the past and the U.S. Civil War, *Riot* employs a screenplay format to tell the story of the New York Draft Riots of 1863. Myers' work focuses on Claire Johnson, a biracial teen who finds herself caught in a heated conflict that pits Irish immigrants against the city's African-American inhabitants. The inventive narrative "gives a sense of the proportion and chaos of the times," Jill Heritage Maza commented in *School Library Journal,* and Hazel Rochman, writing in *Booklist,* maintained that the "diverse voices, from all sides . . . will draw readers into the fiery debates." "Another innovative work by an author constantly stretching the boundaries of what fiction can be," noted a critic in a *Kirkus Reviews* appraisal of *Riot.*

In *Dope Sick* Myers offers a "gritty depiction of one young man's struggle to overcome the lure of the streets," in the words of *School Library Journal* reviewer Meredith Robbins. Seventeen-year-old Jeremy Dance, also known as Lil J, must hide in an abandoned building after he is wounded during a botched drug deal involving the shooting of a police officer. There he encounters Kelly, a mystical vagrant whose television displays scenes from Lil J's life, allowing the young man to reflect on the choices he has made that have led to this dire situation. In *Horn Book* Jonathan Hunt remarked that "Myers communicates powerfully the pitfalls of the urban neighborhood," and Michael Cart wrote in *Booklist* that the author's dramatic plotline "captures his readers' attentions and imaginations, inviting not only empathy but also thoughtful discussion."

Another troubled youth is the focus of *Lockdown,* a work that explores the nation's troubled juvenile deten-

Cover of Myers' novel Riot, *which takes readers back to the U.S. Civil War era and the racial tensions that engulfed northern blacks in response to Lincoln's call for immigrants to join the Union army.* (Jacket photographs courtesy of Walter Dean Myers; jacket design by Michael Nagin. Egmont, 2009. Reproduced by permission of Egmont USA.)

tion system. Reese Anderson, a fourteen year old serving time for stealing prescription forms, faces a number of personal obstacles as he prepares for his upcoming parole hearing, including his penchant for brawling and his contentious relationship with a fellow inmate who accuses Reese of a crime he did not commit. According to Hunt, Myers uses the prison setting to "riff on favorite themes: hard luck, second chances, overcoming adversity, living with purpose and determination." *New York Times Book Review* critic Jessica Bruder stated that "*Lockdown* isn't a straightforward morality tale. It's a keenly observed portrait of what it means to serve time, full of hard choices and shaky shots at redemption." Discussing his motivation for writing the novel, Myers told an interviewer on the National Book Foundation Web site: "Over the years I've spent a lot of time in Juvenile Detention facilities and corresponding with young men and women who are locked up." "Incarcerated children need to somehow find the strength within their own psyches to break from negative influences," he continued. "I hope that giving voice to their problems will help."

The Cruisers centers on a a group of smart but underachieving students at a Harlem school for the gifted and talented. After the four—Zander, LaShonda, Kambui, and Bobbi—publish a controversial article in their underground newspaper, the administration challenges the quartet to negotiate a peace between factions that have arisen during a classroom project on the U.S. Civil War, threatening them with expulsion if they fail. "Once again, Myers integrates difficult and significant conversations into his work," Jennifer Miskec reported in her *School Library Journal* review of *The Cruisers*, and *Booklist* critic Ian Chipman praised the "unusual story that can maneuver whip-quick from light to heavy and right back again."

In his highly praised informational books for children and young people, Myers characteristically outlines the fight for freedom by people of color; he has also written biographies of such figures as Toussaint L'Ouverture, the Reverend Martin Luther King, Jr., and Malcolm X. In *Now Is Your Time! The African-American Struggle for Freedom* Myers recounts the history of black Americans through both overviews and profiles of individuals. "What happens," wrote a *Kirkus Reviews* critic, "when a gifted novelist chooses to write the story of his people? In this case, the result is engrossing history with a strong unifying theme, the narrative enriched with accounts of outstanding lives." Michael Dirda, writing in the *Washington Post Book World,* added that Myers "writes with the vividness of a novelist, the balance of a historian, and the passion of an advocate. He tells a familiar story and shocks us with it all over again." In the *Voice of Youth Advocates,* Kellie Flynn called *Now Is Your Time!* "alive and vital—with breathing biographical sketches and historic interpretations like rabbit punches."

Amistad: A Long Road to Freedom recounts the dramatic story of the captive Africans who mutinied against their captors on the slave ship *Amistad* in the late 1830s. The book recounts the hellish voyage and forced landing in Connecticut as well as the landmark trial and the struggle of the West Africans to return home. Writing in *Booklist,* Hazel Rochman stated that Myers' "narrative is exciting, not only the account of the uprising but also the tension of the court arguments about whether the captives were property and what their rights were in a country that banned the slave trade but allowed slavery." Gerry Larson added in a review of *Amistad* for *School Library Journal* that, "with characteristic scholarship, clarity, insight, and compassion, Myers presents readers with the facts and the moral and historical significance of the *Amistad* episode."

A longtime collector of historical photographs and documents depicting the lives and culture of African Americans, Myers has used his personal archive to illustrate several of his informational books. The photos and letters from the author's collection have also inspired several of his works, including the biography *At Her Majesty's Request: An African Princess in Victorian*

England. The book focuses on a child of royal African descent who became a goddaughter of Queen Victoria as well as a British celebrity. Saved from a sacrificial rite in Dahomey by English sea captain Frederick E. Forbes, orphaned African Sarah Forbes Bonetta—named after her rescuer and his ship—was brought to England as a gift for Queen Victoria from the Dahomian king who slaughtered her family. Working from a packet of letters he discovered in a London bookstore, Myers tells Sally's story, which he embellishes with quotes from Queen Victoria's diary as well as from newspapers and other chronicles of the time. As a critic in *Kirkus Reviews* commented, "This vividly researched biography will enthrall readers, and ranks among Myers's best writing." Calling *At Her Majesty's Request* a "fascinating biography" and a "moving and very humane portrait of a princess," a reviewer in *Publishers Weekly* concluded that Myers "portrays a young woman who never truly belongs."

Myers' *Malcolm X: A Fire Burning Brightly,* focuses on the stages of Malcolm's life and is illustrated by Leonard Jenkins' "full-color montage illustrations, in acrylic, pastel, and spray paint" that feature "larger-than-life individual portraits set against the crowded streets and the swirl of politics," according to *Booklist* contributor Rochman. Along with numerous quotes from Malcolm's speeches or writings, Myers chronicles the activist's childhood, his time in Charlestown State Prison, his conversion to Islam and leadership of the Black Muslims until his break with Black Muslim leader Elijah Muhammad, and his pilgrimage to Mecca prior to his assassination in 1965. Myers revisits the life of the civil-rights leader in the biography *Malcolm X—By Any Means Necessary.*

In *Ida B. Wells: Let the Truth Be Told,* another picture-book biography, Myers chronicles the life of a nineteenth-century African-American suffragist, journalist, and civil rights activist. Writing in *Horn Book,* Susan Dove Lempke called the work "an understandable and compelling picture of a remarkable woman."

In his biography *The Greatest: Muhammad Ali* Myers documents the life of the boxer born Cassius Clay, moving from Ali's childhood in segregated St. Louis to his Olympic win in 1960 and his success as a world-class athlete. In addition to describing major fights against Sonny Liston, Joe Frazier, and Goerge Foreman, Myers also relates the athlete's commitment as a Black Muslim and his political activism as a conscientious objector during the Vietnam War. In *Horn Book* Jack Forman described the book as "more a portrait of Ali's character and cultural impact than a narrative of his life," while Ott cited the biography as "a story about a black man of tremendous courage, the kind of universal story that needs a writer as talented as Myers to retell it for every generation." Khafre K. Abif noted in *Black Issues Book Review* that in *The Greatest* Myers "inspires a new generation of fans by exposing the hazards Ali faced in boxing, the rise of a champion, and now his

battle against Parkinson's disease." In *Muhammad Ali: The People's Champion,* Myers teams up with illustrator Alix Delenois to offer a biography of the famed athlete and activist aimed at young readers. "Unexpectedly far reaching," Daniel Kraus noted in *Booklist,* "this is a Muhammad All for the thinking child."

Myers' nonfiction title *USS Constellation* relates the entire story of the famous warship, from her construction in 1854 to her war victories, encounters with slave ships, and crew training. The book is complemented by first-person accounts, along with illustrations and charts. Phelan, writing in *Booklist,* praised *USS Constellation* as a "well-researched" and "unique addition to American history collections." In *Publishers Weekly* a reviewer deemed it a "meticulously researched, fast-flowing chronicle" and applauded it for offering "a larger view of the shaping of America." Betty Carter, writing in *Horn Book,* noted that the author's inclusion of first-person accounts "lend[s] authenticity while personalizing events."

In *Here in Harlem: Poems in Many Voices* Myers presents over fifty poems that explore the streets of Harlem through the experiences of dozens of characters. Varying in his style from free verses to conversation, he "treats readers to a tour of Harlem's past and present," remarked a *Publishers Weekly* contributor, covering a wide variety of city settings that include a church, hair salons, and several restaurants. Accompanying the poems are period photographs of Harlem that offer readers a visual context for the poems. In *Booklist* Phelan dubbed *Here in Harlem* "a colorful and warmly personal portrayal of Harlem," before going on to predict, "this unusual book will be long remembered."

Myers presents a contemporary retelling of Pyotr Tchaikovsky's classic nineteenth-century ballet *Swan Lake* in *Amiri and Odette: A Love Story.* "I had seen the ballet of *Swan Lake* as a child but it was as an adult . . . that I first noticed how significant a part the ever-present threat of violence played," the author commented in an essay on the Scholastic Web site. "This juxtaposition of great beauty and grace with a backdrop of pure evil stayed with me for years." Told in a rhyming narrative, *Amiri and Odette* centers on the ill-fated romance between Amiri, a young man living in an urban housing project, and Odette, an addict who is promised to Big Red, a notorious drug dealer. "Myers's words carry the force of blows," observed a contributor in *Publishers Weekly,* and Nina Lindsay commented in *School Library Journal* that the "verse is almost overwrought—as it should be to suit the story, and the intensity of teenage love."

"Children and adults must have role models with which they can identify," wrote Myers in *SAAS;* in his writing he has attempted to "deliver images upon which [they] could build and expand their own worlds." Reflecting on his long and distinguished literary career, Myers remarked in a *Teenreads.com* essay: "I so love writing. It

is not something that I am doing just for a living, this is something that I love to do." He concluded, "Ultimately, what I want to do with my writing is to make connections—to touch the lives of my characters and, through them, those of my readers."

Biographical and Critical Sources

BOOKS

Bishop, Rudine Sims, *Presenting Walter Dean Myers,* Twayne (Boston, MA), 1991.

Dictionary of Literary Biography, Volume 33: *Afro-American Fiction Writers after 1955,* Gale (Detroit, MI), 1984.

Myers, Walter Dean, *Bad Boy: A Memoir,* HarperCollins (New York, NY), 2001.

Novels for Students, Gale (Detroit, MI), Volume 30, 2010, Volume 33, 2010.

Short Stories for Students, Volume 31, Gale (Detroit, MI), 2010.

Something about the Author Autobiography Series, Gale (Detroit, MI), 1986.

Sutherland, Zena, *Children and Books,* Longman (New York, NY), 1997.

PERIODICALS

African American Review, spring, 1988, R.D. Lane, "Keepin It Real: Walter Dean Myers and the Promise of African-American Children's Literature," p. 125.

Black Issues Book Review, May, 2001, Khafre K. Abif, review of *The Greatest: Muhammad Ali,* p. 80.

Booklist, February 15, 1998, Hazel Rochman, "Some Versions of *Amistad,*" p. 1003; May 1, 1999, Debbie Carton, review of *Monster,* p. 1587; February 15, 2000, Hazel Rochman, review of *Malcolm X: A Fire Burning Brightly,* p. 1103; March 1, 2000, Shelle Rosenfeld, review of *The Blues of Flats Brown,* p. 1242; January 1, 2001, Bill Ott, review of *The Greatest,* p. 952; May 1, 2001, Hazel Rochman, review of *Bad Boy,* p. 1673; July, 2004, Carolyn Phelan, review of *USS Constellation,* p. 1841; November 1, 2004, Carolyn Phelan, review of *Here in Harlem: Poems in Many Voices,* p. 480; February 1, 2006, Jennifer Hubert, review of *The Harlem Hellfighters: When Pride Met Courage,* p. 62; September 1, 2006, Bill Ott, review of *Jazz,* p. 127; October 1, 2006, Hazel Rochman, review of *Street Love,* p. 52; February 1, 2007, Michael Cart, review of *Harlem Summer,* p. 56; July 1, 2007, Hazel Rochman, review of *What They Found: Love on 145th Street,* p. 61; February 1, 2008, Gillian Engberg, review of *Game,* p. 51; February 15, 2008, Jennifer Mattson, review of *Sunrise over Fallujah,* p. 76; November 15, 2008, Michael Cart, review of *Dope Sick,* p. 37; December 1, 2008, Hazel Rochman, review of *Amiri and Odette: A Love Story,* p. 47; August 1, 2009, Hazel Rochman, review of *Riot,* p. 67; October 15, 2009, Andrew Medlar, review of *Looking like Me,* p. 50; November 1, 2009, Daniel Kraus, review of *Muhammad Ali: The People's Champion,* p. 50; September 1, 2010, Ian Chipman, review of *The Cruisers,* p. 96.

Bulletin of the Center for Children's Books, July-August, 1988, review of *Scorpions,* p. 235.

English Journal, March, 1976, Alleen Pace Nilsen, "Love and the Teenage Reader," pp. 90-92.

Horn Book, August, 1975, Ethel L. Heins, review of *Fallen Angels,* pp. 503-504; July-August, 1988, Paul Heins, review of *Fast Sam, Cool Clyde, and Stuff,* pp. 388-389; May, 2000, review of *Malcolm X: A Fire Burning Brightly,* p. 336; January, 2000, Jack Forman, review of *The Greatest,* p. 115; July, 2001, review of *Bad Boy,* p. 473; May-June, 2004, Lauren Adams, review of *Shooter,* p. 335; July-August, 2004, Betty Carter, review of *USS Constellation,* p. 469; November-December, 2006, Claire E. Gross, review of *Street Love,* p. 722, and Roger Sutton, review of *Jazz,* p. 735; May-June, 2007, Roger Sutton, review of *Harlem Summer,* p. 286; May-June, 2008, Betty Carter, review of *Sunrise over Fallujah,* p. 324; January-February, 2009, Susan Dove Lempke, review of *Ida B. Wells: Let the Truth Be Told,* p. 119; March-April, 2009, Jonathan Hunt, review of *Dope Sick,* p. 201; November-December, 2009, Roger Sutton, review of *Looking like Me,* p. 656; March-April, 2010, Jonathan Hunt, review of *Lockdown,* p. 65.

Interracial Books for Children Bulletin, Volume 10, number 4, 1979, Ashley Jane Pennington, review of *It Ain't All for Nothin',* p. 18.

Journal of Adolescent & Adult Literacy, May, 2007, Keith Miller and Allison Parker, interview with Myers, p. 688.

Junior Bookshelf, August, 1990, Marcus Crouch, review of *Scorpions,* pp. 190-191.

Kirkus Reviews, March 1, 1972, review of *The Dragon Takes a Wife,* p. 256; October 15, 1978, review of *It Ain't All for Nothin',* p. 1143; October 1, 1991, review of *Now Is Your Time!,* p. 1537; December 15, 1998, review of *At Her Majesty's Request: An African Princess in Victorian England,* p. 1802; November 15, 2005, review of *The Harlem Hellfighters,* p. 1235; December 15, 2007, review of *Game;* April 1, 2008, review of *Sunrise over Fallujah;* October 1, 2008, review of *Ida B. Wells;* December 15, 2008, review of *Amiri and Odette;* January 1, 2009, review of *Dope Sick;* August 1, 2009, review of *Riot;* September 15, 2009, review of *Looking like Me;* December 15, 2009, review of *Muhammad Ali;* January 1, 2010, review of *Lockdown.*

Kliatt, July, 2005, KaaVonia Hinton, review of *Autobiography of My Dead Brother,* p. 14; March, 2007, Paula Rohrlick, review of *Harlem Summer,* p. 17; January, 2008, Paula Rohrlick, review of *Game,* p. 11; May, 2008, Paula Rohrlick, review of *Sunrise over Fallujah,* p. 15.

New York Times Book Review, April 19, 1972, Nancy Griffin, review of *The Dragon Takes a Wife,* p. 8; October 21, 2001, Kermit Frazier, review of *Bad Boy,* p. 31; May 11, 2008, review of *Game* and *Sunrise over Fallujah,* p. 26; May 16, 2010, Jessica Bruder, review of *Lockdown,* p. 22.

Publishers Weekly, February 26, 1988, "Walter Dean Myers," p. 117; February 8, 1999, review of *At Her Majesty's Request,* p. 215; January 24, 2000, review of *The Blues of Flats Brown,* p. 311; March 22, 2004, review of *Shooter,* p. 87; June 28, 2004, review of *USS Constellation,* p. 52; November 15, 2004, review of *Here in Harlem,* p. 61; September 19, 2005, review of *Autobiography of My Dead Brother,* p. 68; August 7, 2006, review of *Jazz,* p. 57; March 26, 2007, review of *Harlem Summer,* p. 94; April 21, 2008, review of *Sunrise over Fallujah,* p. 59; November 17, 2008, review of *Amiri and Odette,* p. 57; January 19, 2009, review of *Dope Sick,* p. 61; January 11, 2010, review of *Lockdown,* p. 49; July 26, 2010, review of *The Cruisers,* p. 76.

School Librarian, August, 1990, Allison Hurst, review of *Fallen Angels,* pp. 118-119.

School Library Journal, April 15, 1970, Mary Eble, review of *Where Does the Day Go?,* p. 111; October, 1978, Steven Matthews, review of *It Aint' All for Nothin',* p. 158; May, 1998, Gerry Larson, review of *Amistad: A Long Road to Freedom,* p. 158; March, 2000, Karen James, review of *The Blues of Flats Brown,* p. 210; May, 2001, Miranda Doyle, review of *Bad Boy,* p. 169; December, 2001, Kathleen Baxter, review of *The Greatest,* p. 39; April, 2005, Nina Lindsay, review of *Here in Harlem,* p. 57; August, 2005, Francisca Goldsmith, review of *Autobiography of My Dead Brother,* p. 132; March, 2007, Hillias J. Martin, review of *Harlem Summer,* p. 216; August, 2007, Chris Shoemaker, review of *What They Found,* p. 122; April, 2008, Diane P. Tuccillo, review of *Sunrise over Fallujah,* p. 146; February, 2008, Richard Luzer, review of *Game,* p. 122; November, 2008, Lee Bock, review of *Ida B. Wells,* p. 146; January, 2009, Nina Lindsay, review of *Amiri and Odette,* p. 114; April, 2009, Meredith Robbins, review of *Dope Sick,* p. 140; September, 2009, Jill Heritage Maza, review of *Riot,* p. 168; November, 2009, Mary Landrum, review of *Looking like Me,* p. 96; February, 2010, Blair Christolon, review of *Muhammad Ali,* p. 101, and Chris Shoemaker, review of *Lockdown,* p. 118; October, 2010, Jennifer Miskec, review of *The Cruisers,* p. 124.

Teaching and Learning Literature, September-October, 1998, Ellen A. Greever, "Making Connections in the Life and Works of Walter Dean Myers," pp. 42-54.

Tribune Books (Chicago, IL), November 13, 1988, Mary Veeder, "Some Versions of *Fallen Angels,*" p. 6.

USA Today, April 24, 2008, Bob Minzesheimer, interview with Myers, p. D7.

Voice of Youth Advocates, August, 1988, W. Keith McCoy, review of *Fallen Angels,* p. 133; February, 1992, Kellie Flynn, review of *Now Is Your Time!,* p. 398.

Washington Post Book World, March 8, 1992, Michael Dirda, review of *Now Is Your Time!,* p. 11.

Wilson Library Bulletin, January, 1993, Frances Bradburn, review of *The Righteous Revenge of Artemis Bonner,* p. 88.

World Literature Today, May-June, 2007, Olubunmi Ishola, interview with Myers, p. 63.

ONLINE

National Book Foundation Web site, http://www.nationalbook.org/ (May 1, 2011), Eisa Ulen, interview with Myers.

National Public Radio Web site, http://www.npr.org/ (August 19, 2008), Juan Williams, "Walter Dean Myers: A 'Bad Boy' Makes Good."

Scholastic Web site, http://www2.scholastic.com/ (May 1, 2011), "Walter Dean Myers."

Teenreads.com, http://www.teenreads.com/ (September, 2010), interview with Myers.

Walter Dean Myers Home Page, http://www.walterdeanmyers.net (April 15, 2011).*

*   *   *

MYERS, Walter M.
See MYERS, Walter Dean

N-P

NELSON, Jandy

Personal
Female. *Education:* Cornell University, B.A. (with honors); Brown University, M.F.A. (poetry); Vermont College of Fine Arts, M.F.A. (writing for children and young adults).

Addresses
Home—San Francisco, CA. *Agent*—Holly McGhee, Pippin Properties, Inc., 155 E. 38th St., Ste. 2H, New York, NY 10016. *E-mail*—Jandy@JandyNelson.com.

Career
Author, poet, and literary agent. Worked variously as a film producer and dramaturge; Manus & Associates Literary Agency, Palo Alto, CA, former literary agent. Brown University, former teacher of creative writing. Word for Word Performing Arts Council, member of leadership council. Presenter and panelist at conferences and writers' workshops.

Awards, Honors
Several awards for poetry; Outstanding Book designation, Bank Street College of Education, New Voices selection, Association of Booksellers for Children, and Chicago Public Library Best of the Best selection, Carnegie Medal long list inclusion, Leserpreis short list (Germany), and Prix des Sorciéres short list inclusion (France), all 2010, and Best Fiction for Young Adults selection, YALSA/American Library Association, 2011, all for *The Sky Is Everywhere.*

Writings
The Sky Is Everywhere, Dial Books (New York, NY), 2010.

Author's work has been translated into Chinese, Danish, Dutch, French, German, Italian, Norwegian, Polish, Portuguese, Spanish, Swedish, and Turkish.

Adaptations
The Sky Is Everywhere was adapted for audiobook, ready by Julia Whelan, Brilliance Audio, 2010.

Sidelights
A senior agent at a West Coast literary agency, Jandy Nelson specialized in a range of fiction and nonfiction and was successful in marketing film and television rights for her clients. Prior to becoming a literary agent, she produced films, wrote poetry, worked as a dramaturg for theatres in the San Francisco area, and taught creative writing. In the late 2000s Nelson found herself on the other side of the agent's desk while she was seeking a publisher for what became her first young-adult novel, *The Sky Is Everywhere.*

Nelson considered herself to be a poet before she was a novelist, and *The Sky Is Everywhere* inspired that transition. "*The Sky Is Everywhere* actually started as a novel in verse," she explained in an interview posted on the *The Sky Is Everywhere Web site.* "I had this image in my mind of a grief-stricken girl scattering her poems all over a town—that was really the inciting image for the whole book and key right from the start to Lennie's character. I kept thinking of her, this bereft girl, who wanted so badly to communicate with someone who was no longer there that she just began writing her words on everything and anything she could, scattering her poems and thoughts and memories to the winds. In my mind, it was a way for Lennie to write her grief on the world, to mark it, to reach out to her sister and at the same time to make sure, in this strange way, that their story was part of everything. So it all began with Lennie's poems, but very early on, like after a couple weeks of writing, it became clear that Lennie's story needed to be told primarily in prose so I dove in and

Cover of Jandy Nelson's debut novel **The Sky Is Everywhere,** *which focuses on a teen's complex rush of emotions following her sister's tragic death.* (Cover photograph © Johner Images/Veer. Reproduced by permission of Dial Books for Young Readers, a division of Penguin Young Readers Group, a member of Penguin (USA) Inc., 345 Hudson St., NY 10014. All rights reserved.)

found myself falling in love with writing fiction—it was a total revelation! After that, I wrote both the prose and poems simultaneously, weaving the poems in as I went along."

Seventeen-year-old Lennie Walker is the main character in *The Sky Is Everywhere.* A bookish student who writes poetry and plays clarinet in her high-school band, Lennie is comfortable being overshadowed by her older sister, Bailey, but when Bailey dies unexpectedly from a heart ailment Lennie suddenly has no place to hide. As she begins to assert her own personality, she also opens herself up to romance. Toby, Bailey's boyfriend, is mourning his lost love just as Lennie is mourning her sister, and now the two teens find themselves bonding through their shared feelings. Then Joe Fontaine arrives in town, a Parisian transplant, his talent for music is matched by his upbeat outlook. As the young woman's grief begins to change over time, so do her separate feelings for both Joe and Toby, in a novel that *School Library Journal* contributor Jennifer Schultz praised as a "realistic, sometimes funny, and heartbreaking story." An intimate story about coping with loss, Nelson's first

novel is tender, romantic, and loaded with passion," wrote *Horn Book* critic Lauren Adams, while a *Publishers Weekly* reviewer noted of *The Sky Is Everywhere* that Nelson's "honest, complex debut is distinguished by a dreamy California setting and poetic images that will draw readers into Lennie's world." "Lennie is sympathetic, believable, and complex," asserted Shauna Yusko in *Booklist,* and her story "will resonate with readers."

Biographical and Critical Sources

PERIODICALS

Booklist, January 1, 2010, Shauna Yusko, review of *The Sky Is Everywhere,* p. 70.
Bulletin of the Center for Children's Books, April, 2010, Deborah Stevenson, review of *The Sky Is Everywhere,* p. 347.
Horn Book, March-April, 2010, Lauren Adams, review of *The Sky Is Everywhere,* p. 65.
Kirkus Reviews, February 15, 2010, review of *The Sky Is Everywhere.*
Publishers Weekly, February 22, 2010, review of *The Sky Is Everywhere,* p. 69.
San Francisco Chronicle, March 11, 2010, Louis Peitzman, "Out Loud: Jandy Nelson," p. G28.
School Library Journal, March, 2010, Jennifer Schultz, review of *The Sky Is Everywhere,* p. 165.

ONLINE

Jandy Nelson Home Page, http://www.jandynelson.com (April 24, 2011).
The Sky Is Everywhere Web site, http://www.theskyisevery where.com/ (April 24, 2011).*

*   *   *

NGUI, Marc 1972-

Personal

Born 1972, in Georgetown, Guyana; partner of Magda Wojtyra (an artist and designer). *Education:* University of Waterloo, B.E.S., 1994. *Hobbies and other interests:* Science, poetry, drawing, diagrams, philosophy, design.

Addresses

Home—Cambridge, Ontario, Canada. *E-mail*—marc@happysleepy.com.

Career

Cartoonist, animator, and illustrator. Graphic novelist, 1989—; Bumblenut Pictures, Toronto, Ontario, Canada, illustrator, cartoonist, and animator, 1994—; *This* maga-

zine, Toronto, illustrator, 2000-05; ZeD television, video journalist, 2003-04. *Exhibitions:* Work exhibited at museums and galleries, including Doris McCarthy Gallery, Toronto, Ontario, Canada, 2006; McMaster Museum of Art, Hamilton, Ontario, Canada, 2007; Open Space Gallery, Victoria, British Columbia, Canada, 2008; Art Gallery of Algoma, Sault Ste. Marie, Ontario, 2009; Gallery Lambton, Sarnia, Ontario, 2009; and Doris McCarthy Gallery, University of Toronto Scarborough, 2010.

Awards, Honors

Creative writing grants, Canada Council for the Arts, 2005, 2007; Best Emerging Artist nomination, Doug Wright Awards, 2005; Notable Social Studies Trade Books for Young People, National Council for the Social Studies/Children's Book Council, 2011, for *Watch This Space.*

Writings

SELF-ILLUSTRATED

Senser non ules: The Complete Baby, Thompson Block Press (Windsor, Ontario, Canada), 1997.
Tract Atlas (chapbook), Bumblenut Pictures, 1999.
Enter Avariz (graphic novel), Conundrum Press (Montreal, Quebec, Canada), 2003.
The Unexpurgated Tale of Lordie Jones: A Modern Retelling of an Obscure Caribbean Folktale (graphic novel), Conundrum Press (Montreal, Quebec, Canada), 2005.

Author and illustrator of self-published comics series, including "Hysterium Motel," 1991-92; "Ferdinand a Fish's Tale," 1992-93; "The Boy with a Pig . . .," 1996; "Instant Comic after the Night before Thinking," 1998; "Six Tail Sushi," 1998; "Untitanic Tales," 1998; "A Puddle to Call My Own," 1999; "Almost All Weather," 2000; and "Zak Meadow Minis," 2000. Contributor of comics to anthologies, including *GreenTopia,* Coachhouse Press, and *Girls Who Bite Back,* edited by Emily Pohl Weary, Sumac Press, 2004. Also contributor to periodicals, including *Arcane* and *Headtrip,* 1987-90.

ILLUSTRATOR

(With Hoge Day) Hal Niedzviecki, *Lurvy: A Farmer's Almanac,* Coach House Press (Toronto, Ontario, Canada), 1999.
Derrick de Kerckhove, *The Architecture of Intelligence,* Birkhäuser (Basel, Switzerland), 2002.
Hal Niedzviecki and Darren Wershler-Henry, *The Original Canadian City Dweller's Almanac: Facts, Rants, Anecdotes, and Unsupported Assertions for Urban Residents,* Viking Canada (Toronto, Ontario, Canada), 2002.
Hal Niedzviecki, *The Big Book of Pop Culture: A How-to Guide for Young Artists,* Annick Press (Toronto, Ontario, Canada), 2007.

Jim Munroe, *Time Management for Anarchists,* IDW Publishing (San Diego, CA), 2008.
Hadley Dyer, *Watch This Space: Designing, Defending, and Sharing Public Spaces,* Kids Can Press (Toronto, Ontario, Canada), 2010.

Sidelights

A Canadian artist and designer, Marc Ngui has written and illustrated numerous comic books and graphic novels, among them the book-length works *Enter Avariz* and *The Unexpurgated Tale of Lordie Jones: A Modern Retelling of an Obscure Caribbean Folktale.* In addition, Ngui, a native of Guyana, has provided the artwork for *Watch This Space: Designing, Defending, and Sharing Public Spaces,* an award-winning nonfiction work by Hadley Dyer that is aimed at teen readers. In the work, Dyer explores the history, characteristics, and significance of public spaces, particularly for young adults, and suggests ways to create and preserve such areas while touching on such topics as age discrimination, graffiti, and social activism. "Supported by the bold illustrations and graphics of Marc Ngui, every page arrests the reader with historical and contemporary developments, case studies, and projects from cities around the world," Caroline Huggins asserted in the *Canadian Review of Materials.* "The book benefits greatly from . . . Ngui's vibrant illustrations," Emily Donaldson remarked in her *Quill & Quire* review of *Watch This Space.* "Using a colourful but restrained palette, his expressive visuals are a wonderful complement to the refreshingly clean text," Donaldson added, while a *Publishers Weekly* critic stated that the artist's "sketch-like ink drawings suggest the energy and diversity of city life." Jody Kopple, writing in *School Library Journal,* commented that the "engaging and informative" illustrations in *Watch This Space* "complement[Dyer's] . . . text without overwhelming it."

Biographical and Critical Sources

PERIODICALS

Canadian Review of Materials, May 21, 2010, Caroline Higgins, review of *Watch This Space: Designing, Defending, and Sharing Public Spaces.*
Kirkus Reviews, February 15, 2010, review of *Watch This Space.*
Publishers Weekly, March 8, 2010, review of *Watch This Space,* p. 58.
Quill & Quire, April, 2010, Emily Donaldson, review of *Watch This Space.*
Resource Links, June, 2007, Leslie L. Kennedy, review of *The Big Book of Pop Culture: A How-to Guide for Young Artists,* p. 38.
School Library Journal, May, 2010, Jody Kopple, review of *Watch This Space,* p. 130.
This, May, 2010, Jody Kopple, review of *Watch This Space,* p. 130.

ONLINE

Happy Sleepy Web site, http://www.happysleepy.com/ (May 1, 2011), "About Marc Ngui."
Marc Ngui Home Page, http://www.bumblenut.com (May 1, 2011).*

*   *   *

ORLANDELLI, Alessandro
See HORLEY, Alex

*   *   *

PEARCE, Carl

Personal

Born in Wales. *Education:* North Wales School of Art and Design, degree, 2004. *Hobbies and other interests:* Reading, watching films, walking, photography.

Addresses

Home—North Wales, United Kingdom. *E-mail*—jimoakley666@hotmail.com; carlpearceartist@yahoo. co.uk.

Career

Illustrator. *Exhibitions:* Work exhibited in Advocate Gallery, Ashtead, Surrey, England.

Awards, Honors

Dundee City of Discovery Picture Book Award shortlist, 2006, for *The Night the Lights Went Out* by Anna Perera; First Prize for Illustrated Text (Large Nonprofit Publishers), Washington Book Publishers' Book Design and Effectiveness Awards, 2010, for *Attention, Girls!* by Patricia O. Quinn.

Illustrator

Annie Dalton, *Ferris Fleet the Wheelchair Wizard,* Tamarind (Camberley, England), 2005.

Carl Pearce's illustration projects include creating the artwork for Ben Morley's **The Silence Seeker.** (Tamarind Books, 2009. Illustration copyright © 2009 by Carl Pearce. Reproduced by permission of Random House (UK).)

Anna Perera, *The Night the Lights Went Out,* Tamarind (Northwood, England), 2006.

Edel Wignell, *Big Eyes, Scary Voice,* Tamarind (Northwood, England), 2008.

Ben Morley, *The Silence Seeker,* Tamarind (London, England), 2009.

Patricia O. Quinn, *Attention, Girls!: A Guide to Learn All about Your AD/HD,* Magination Press (Washington, DC), 2009.

Sidelights

Based in northern Wales, where he studied at the North Wales School of Art and Design, Carl Pearce is an illustrator whose comics-style images are characterized by their graphic details and his use of clear tints of color. Bucking the trend of his genre, Pearce does pencil drawings and then inks his lines with a pen rather than creating his line art on computer; the color is the only element that is done digitally. His artwork has appeared in several books for children, including stories by Annie Dalton, Anna Perera, Edel Winnell, and Ben Morley. Appraising another illustration project, physician Patricia O. Quinn's *Attention, Girls!: A Guide to Learn All about Your AD/HD,* Elaine Lesh Morgan noted in *School Library Journal* that the "attractive and inviting" book gains visual appeal from Pearce's "colorful cartoon illustrations."

"Pearce's sharp-edged, bright, almost graphic-novel-style artwork brings out the cacophonous, tense urban atmosphere" in Morley's *The Silence Seeker,* according to a *Kirkus Reviews* writer. An evocative story about a young boy's misunderstanding regarding an immigrant family's search for political asylum, *The Silence Seeker* begins as Joe offers the family's teenaged son a sandwich. Understanding "asylum" as the search for silence, Joe takes boy on a tour of all the quiet places in the city, realizing in the process that layers of noise exist everywhere. Despite the fact that his new friend does not speak English, Joe enjoys the day with his new friend; the next day, however, the immigrant family has gone. While noting that Morley's story will inspire discussion, Jane Doonan had particular praise for Pearce's "robust" illustrations in her *School Librarian* review of *The Silence Seeker.* Citing the artist's detailed use of background elements, she asserted that "strong clean outlines" and a controlled use of perspective "bring solidity and presence to the pictured world," while Pearce's use of sunlit tones of color "does much to mitigate the raw unglamorous [urban] setting" of Morley's tale.

Biographical and Critical Sources

PERIODICALS

Kirkus Reviews, February 15, 2010, review of *The Silence Seeker.*

School Librarian, spring, 2010, Jane Doonan, review of *The Silence Seeker,* p. 36.

School Library Journal, October, 2009, Elaine Lesh Morgan, review of *Attention, Girls!: A Guide to Learn All about Your AD/HD,* p. 150; April, 2010, Joan Kindig, review of *The Silence Seeker,* p. 136.

ONLINE

Carl Pearce Home Page, http://carlpearce.daportfolio.com (April 24, 2011).

Carl Pearce Web log, http://carlpearce.blogspot.com (April 15, 2011).*

*   *   *

PEETE, Holly Robinson 1964-

Personal

Born September 18, 1964, in Philadelphia, PA; daughter of Matt (a television producer and an actor on *Sesame Street*) and Dolores (a teacher) Robinson; married Rodney Peete (a football player), June 10, 1995; children: Rodney Jackson, Jr., and Ryan Elizabeth (twins), Robinson, Roman. *Education:* Sarah Lawrence College, B.S. (psychology and French); attended University of Paris, Sorbonne.

Addresses

Home—Los Angeles, CA.

Career

Actor, author, and philanthropist. Worked as a singer in Paris, France. Television work includes: (as Sally) *Sesame Street,* 1969; (as Genettia Lang) *Dummy,* 1979; (as Officer Judy Hoffs) *21 Jump Street,* 1987-91; (as Detective Judy Hoffs) *Booker,* 1989; (as Jackie Tate) *Gabriel's Fire,* 1991; (as Diana Ross) *The Jacksons: An American Dream* (movie), 1992; (as Venessa Russell) *Hangin' with Mr. Cooper,* 1992-98; (as Vanessa Hamilton) *Touched by an Angel,* 1997; (as Jennie Sawyer) *Killers in the House* (movie), 1998; (as Michelle Troussaint) *After All* (movie), 1999; (as Stacy) *One on One,* 2001-02; (as Halle Ellis) *Strong Medicine,* 2001; (as Samika) *My Wonderful Life* (movie), 2002; (as Malena Ellis) *For Your Love,* 2002; (as Tanya Ward) *Like Family,* 2003; (as Jackie Jameson) *Football Wives* (movie), 2007; (as Macy) *The Bridget Show* (series pilot), 2009; and (as Gayle) *Speed Dating,* 2010. Film work includes: (as K.C.) *Howard the Duck.* Recording artist, appearing on film and television soundtracks. Co-host, with husband Rodney Peete, of radio talk show *Meet the Peetes,* 2008; co-host of television talk show *The Talk,* beginning 2010. Guest appearance on *Celebrity Apprentice,* 2010. Founder, with Rodney Peete, of HollyRod Foundation, 1997. Member of board, Autism Speaks, Los Angeles Zoo Association, and Keck School of Medicine.

Holly Robinson Peete (Fred Prouser/Reuters/Landov. © 2003 Landov LLC. All rights reserved. Reproduced by permission.)

Awards, Honors

Quills Award (with Danile Paisner), 2006, for *Get Your Own Damn Beer, I'm Watching the Game!;* American Mentor Award, Ford's Freedom Sisters; Buddy Award, National Organization for Women Legal Defense and Education Fund; Community Service Award, Southern California Broadcasters' Association; People Helping People award, Gerald R. Ford Foundation; Healthy Babies, Healthy Futures Award, March of Dimes; named University of Southern California Woman of Distinction; John E. Jacob Community Service Award, Anheuser-Busch; distinguished achievement award, Huntington Disease Society; Mentor Award, Girls Inc.; A Place Called Home Humanitarian Award; McDonald's 365 Black Award.

Writings

(With Daniel Paisner) *Get Your Own Damn Beer, I'm Watching the Game!: A Woman's Guide to Loving Pro Football,* foreword by Ronnie Lott, Rodale (Emmaus, PA), 2005.

(With daughter Ryan Elizabeth Peete) *My Brother Charlie: A Sister's Story of Autism,* illustrated by Shane Evans, Scholastic Press (New York, NY), 2010.

Sidelights

An actress and vocalist working in both television and radio, as well as coauthor of the humorous *Get Your Own Damn Beer, I'm Watching the Game!: A Woman's Guide to Loving Pro Football,* Holly Robinson Peete also has a busy life outside the celebrity limelight: she is the mother of four children as well as a dedicated philanthropist who advocates on behalf of several charities. In 2010 she teamed up with her oldest daughter, Ryan Elizabeth Peete, to express Ryan's affection for her twin brother Rodney Peete, Junior, who is autistic.

Peete's career as a performer had an unusual start: her mother, Dolores Robinson, was a teacher who inspired Peete with a love of learning. Matt Robinson, Peete's father, was involved in educational television, and in 1969, a five-year-old Peete made her television debut on the first episode of *Sesame Street,* where her dad performed the part of the popular character Gordon. In 1974 her family moved west to California, but Peete later returned to the east coast to study at Sarah Lawrence College. After a year spent abroad studying at the Sorbonne in Paris, she graduated with a degree in psychology and French.

Peete began her adult career as a performer during that year in France, singing in Paris nightclubs. Her acting career started in 1979, and she has had feature roles in television series that include *21 Jump Street* and *Hangin' with Mr. Cooper.* She has found more-recent suc-

Peete teams up with her daughter Ryan to introduce readers to a young autistic boy (Ryan's brother) in **My Brother Charlie,** *featuring artwork by Shane W. Evans.* (Scholastic Press, 2010. Illustration copyright © 2010 by Shane W. Evans. Reproduced by permission of Scholastic, Inc.)

cess by letting her energetic personality shine through in stints on television programs such as *Celebrity Apprentice* and her co-hosting role on *The Talk*. In 1995 she married N.F.L. quarterback Rodney Peete. Her father's battle with Parkinson's disease, as well as her oldest son's diagnosis of autism, inspired Peete and her husband to establish the HollyRod Foundation to support families living with autism and Parkinson's disease.

Illustrated by Shane Evans in colorful mixed-media art, *My Brother Charlie* features what *Booklist* contributor Hazel Rochman characterized as "an honest, simple narrative" in which a girl named Callie describes her experiences living with her autistic brother Charlie. In addition to describing what autism is, Callie also explains how her family deals with Charlie's unpredictable, sometime humorous, and sometimes volatile behavior. Although the girl's admiration for her brother is clear as she praises his musical talent and his many accomplishments, the text in *My Brother Charlie* remains "warm but never sentimental," according to Rochman. In *Publishers Weekly* a critic praised *My Brother Charlie* as a "thoughtful and moving story" from a "mother-daughter author team" that is supplemented by "background and advice for families dealing with someone with autism." The Peetes' "theme is of love, patience, and acceptance," observed Laura Butler in her laudatory review for *School Library Journal*, and a *Kirkus Reviews* writer hailed the book for featuring "a seldom-seen perspective on autism [that is] delivered concisely and with empathy."

Biographical and Critical Sources

PERIODICALS

Booklist, September 15, 2005, Mary Frances Wilkens, review of *Get Your Own Damn Beer, I'm Watching the Game!: A Woman's Guide to Loving Pro Football*, p. 19; March 1, 2010, Hazel Rochman, review of *My Brother Charlie*, p. 78.

Kirkus Reviews, January 15, 2010, review of *My Brother Charlie*.

People, June 4, 2007, Amy Elisa Keith, interview with Peete, p. 69.

Publishers Weekly, January 25, 2010, review of *My Brother Charlie*, p. 119.

Redbook, May, 2010, Kate Meyers, "'Our Son's Autism Almost Tore Us Apart'" (interview), p. 118.

School Library Journal, March, 2010, review of *My Brother Charlie*, p. 129.

ONLINE

HollyRod Foundation Web site, http://www.hollyrod.org/ (April 20, 2011), "Holly Robinson Peete."*

PLECAS, Jennifer 1966-
(Jennifer Barrett)

Personal

Born March 3, 1966, in Washington, DC; daughter of James Edward (a behavioral pharmacologist) and Maura Barrett; married Tomislav Plecas, November 24, 1991; children: two. *Education:* Attended Hamilton College, 1985-87, and University of the Arts, 1987-88; Moore College of Art and Design, B.F.A., 1991.

Addresses

Home—Blue Springs, MO. *E-mail*—Jennifer@jennifer plecas.com.

Career

Artist and illustrator. AR & T Animation Studio, Philadelphia, PA, animation assistant intern, 1988; Hallmark Cards, Kansas City, MO, artist, 1991-93; freelance artist and writer, 1993—.

Awards, Honors

Notable Children's Book citation, American Library Association (ALA), 1994, and One Hundred Titles for Reading and Sharing selection, New York Public Library, both for *The Outside Dog* by Charlotte Pomerantz; Notable Children's Book citation, ALA, 2000, for both *Good Night, Good Knight* by Shelley Moore Thomas and *Emma's Yucky Brother* by Jean Little, and 2004, for *Baby Danced the Polka* by Karen Beaumont.

Writings

SELF-ILLUSTRATED

(As Jennifer Barrett) *Kiki's New Sister*, Bantam (New York, NY), 1992.
Pretend!, Philomel Books (New York, NY), 2011.

ILLUSTRATOR

Betsy Byars, *The Seven Treasure Hunts*, HarperCollins (New York, NY), 1991.
Pamela Greenwood, *What about My Goldfish?*, Clarion (New York, NY), 1993.
Charlotte Pomerantz, *The Outside Dog*, HarperCollins (New York, NY), 1993.
Fran Manushkin, *Peeping and Sleeping*, Clarion (New York, NY), 1994.
Pamela Greenwood, *I Found Mouse*, Clarion (New York, NY), 1994.
Sylvia Andrews, *Rattlebone Rock*, HarperCollins (New York, NY), 1995.
Barbara M. Joosse, *Snow Day!*, Clarion (New York, NY), 1995.

Barthe DeClements, *Spoiled Rotten,* Hyperion (New York, NY), 1996.

Susan Beth Pfeffer, *The Trouble with Wishes,* Holt (New York, NY), 1996.

Patricia Hubbell, *Wrapping Paper Romp,* HarperFestival (New York, NY), 1998.

Jean Little, *Emma's Magic Winter,* HarperCollins (New York, NY), 1998.

Joy Cowley, *Agapanthus Hum and the Eyeglasses,* Philomel Books (New York, NY), 1999.

Shirley Mozelle, *The Pig Is in the Pantry, the Cat Is on the Shelf,* Clarion (New York, NY), 2000.

Shelley Moore Thomas, *Good Night, Good Knight,* Dutton (New York, NY), 2000.

Jean Little, *Emma's Yucky Brother,* HarperCollins (New York, NY), 2000.

Harriet Ziefert, *Grandmas Are for Giving Tickles,* Puffin Books (New York, NY), 2000.

Harriet Ziefert, *Grandpas Are for Finding Worms,* Puffin Books (New York, NY), 2000.

Joy Cowley, *Agapanthus Hum and Major Bark,* Philomel Books (New York, NY), 2001.

Shelley Moore Thomas, *Get Well, Good Knight,* Dutton (New York, NY), 2002.

Joy Cowley, *Agapanthus Hum and the Angel Hoot,* Philomel Books (New York, NY), 2003.

Jean Little, *Emma's Strange Pet,* HarperCollins (New York, NY), 2003.

Kathryn Lasky, *Love That Baby!: A Book about Babies for New Big Brothers, Sisters, Cousins, and Friends,* Candlewick Press (Cambridge, MA), 2004.

Barbara M. Joosse, *Bad Dog School,* Clarion (New York, NY), 2004.

Karen Beaumont, *Baby Danced the Polka,* Dial (New York, NY), 2004.

Shelley Moore Thomas, *Happy Birthday, Good Knight,* Dutton (New York, NY), 2006.

Barbara M. Joosse, *Please Is a Good Word to Say,* Philomel Books (New York, NY), 2007.

Barbara M. Joosse, *Love Is a Good Thing to Feel,* Philomel Books (New York, NY), 2008.

Shelley Moore Thomas, *A Cold Winter's Good Knight,* Dutton (New York, NY), 2008.

Lee Fox, *Ella Kazoo Will Not Brush Her Hair,* Walker (New York, NY), 2010.

Shelley Moore Thomas, *A Good Knight's Rest,* Dutton (New York, NY), 2011.

Esme Raji Codell, *The Basket Ball,* Abrams (New York, NY), 2011.

Contributor of illustrations to periodicals, including *Ladybug, Spider,* and *Cricket.*

Sidelights

Illustrator Jennifer Plecas has provided the images for dozens of children's books, including Shelley Moore Thomas's *Good Night, Good Knight* and its sequel as well as Barbara M. Joosse's *Love Is a Good Thing to Feel* and Lee Fox's *Ella Kazoo Will Not Brush Her Hair.* While she has illustrated a wide variety of picture books, Plecas earns particular notice from critics for her efforts at decorating books for children just learning to read independently. "There are plenty of illustrators making a splash with big, gorgeous picture books," wrote Deborah Stevenson for the *Bulletin of the Center for Children's Books* online, "but Jennifer Plecas has made a career in an unusual artistic excellence—illustration of easy readers." While noting that the artist "can turn out perfectly dandy larger illustrations," Stevenson claimed, "It's in those small, underserved pages that she really outshines the competition."

One of Plecas's first books as an illustrator, Fran Manushkin's *Peeping and Sleeping,* is an affectionate tale about a young boy named Barry who goes on a nighttime walk with his father to see the frogs whose peeps he can hear from his bedroom. Reviewers praised Plecas's illustrations of the pair, who, as Ellen Fader noted in *Horn Book,* are pictured against "a densely starred, deep blue sky [and] an abundance of beautiful deep green grass." A *Publishers Weekly* reviewer commented that Plecas's "velvety, smudged pastels" in *Peeping and Sleeping* do a good job of reflecting the "warmth and ease" of the father-son relationship.

A knight heroically fetches a drink of water, reads a story, and gives goodnight kisses to three sleepy little dragons in Shelley Moore Thomas's Good Night, Good Knight, *a story illustrated by Plecas.* (Illustration copyright © 2000 by Jennifer Plecas. Used by permission of Dutton Children's Books, a division of Penguin Young Readers Group, a member of Penguin Group (USA) Inc., 345 Hudson St., New York, NY 10014. All rights reserved.)

Plecas's illustrations are paired with a humorous, family-centered story by prolific writer Harriet Ziefert titled **Grandma's Are for Giving Tickles.** (Illustration copyright © 2000 by Jennifer Plecas. Reproduced by permission of Puffin Books, a division of Penguin Young Readers Group, a member of Penguin (USA) Inc., 345 Hudson St., NY 10014. All rights reserved.)

Agapanthus Hum, an exuberant, accident-prone little girl, is the heroine of a series of books written by Joy Cowley and illustrated by Plecas. In various volumes, the girl breaks her glasses while doing gymnastics, adopts a dog who also has a penchant for mishaps, and loses a tooth. The illustrator "plays up the text's sweet-natured humor with her springy-limbed heroine, who indeed looks as if she can barely contain her energy," a *Publishers Weekly* contributor commented in a critique of *Agapanthus Hum and the Eyeglasses.* Reviewing *Agapanthus Hum and Major Bark* in *School Library Journal,* Laura Scott wrote that "Plecas's bright, watercolor cartoons . . . capture and extend this story, and will keep beginning readers enthralled." In *Booklist* Gillian Engberg remarked of *Agapanthus Hum and the Angel Hoot* that "Plecas once again contributes charming paint-and-ink sketches" of the "ever-exuberant" youngster.

Good Night, Good Knight and its sequel, *Get Well, Good Knight,* are tales which turn the usual narrative of armor-clad knights and fire-breathing dragons on its head. This Good Knight is on watch in his tower one night when he hears a roar and investigates, only to find three little pajama-clad dragons that do not want to go to bed. The Good Knight gives the first dragon a drink of water and rides home, only to be called back by the second, who wants to be read a bedtime story. After complying, the knight rides home again, only to be called back a third time to sing a lullaby to the last little dragon. Thinking his work done, the frustrated knight returns to his guard duty, until the dragons refuse to fall asleep until their most important request is met. "Plecas's illustrations show that with each innocent demand the knight grows increasingly impatient, thus extending the text rather than just duplicating it," a *Horn Book* reviewer commented of *Good Night, Good Knight.* Plecas's "charming, hilarious" images "make the book

. . . irresistible," Engberg wrote in *Booklist,* while *School Library Journal* contributor Maura Bresnahan noted that "observant viewers will enjoy the expressions of the horse as he awaits his master upon each visit to the cave."

The dragons from *Good Night, Good Knight* return in *Get Well, Good Knight,* and this time they have terrible colds. Trying to help his suffering friends, the Good Knight administers icky-tasting potions from the wizard, with little effect. The knight's own concoction also does nothing, so he looks to his secret weapon: his own mother's chicken soup. *Book* contributor Kathleen Odean deemed *Get Well, Good Knight* "outstanding" and commended Plecas's "sprightly illustrations," while *School Library Journal* critic Laura Scott described the story as "a royal treat to soothe any beginning reader's blues."

In *Happy Birthday, Good Knight,* the third installment in Thomas's series, the dragon trio wants to make a personalized birthday gift for a special someone and the Good Knight is eager to offer suggestions. After they fail in their efforts to bake a cake, design a card, and put on a magic show, however, the dragons confess that the gifts were really meant for the knight, and his surprising reaction lifts their spirits. "The warm friendship story is beautifully captured in Plecas' ink-and-watercolor pictures," Hazel Rochman stated in *Booklist,* and Bobbee Pennington noted in *School Library Journal* that the pictures "enhance the setting and mood of this sweet, well-told story."

The young dragons wreak havoc at a fancy ball in *A Cold Winter's Good Knight.* Rescued from their chilly cave by the Good Knight, they find themselves in the midst of a formal dance at the castle, where they are warned to avoid mischief. Unfortunately, the creatures have had no training in etiquette, and their behavior soon creates a series of disruptions. Engberg praised this series installment as an "entertaining, charmingly illustrated story," while *School Library Journal* critic Angela J. Reynolds noted that the author's switch to a picture-book format "allows Plecas to pack the pages with more detail, action, and humor."

Plecas's collaboration with Joosse on *Bad Dog School* brings to life the story of an all-too-energetic pooch. Although Harris does not mind the rascally antics of his pet, Zippy, the youngster's family forces the boy to enroll the mutt in obedience school. The training works too well for Harris's taste, robbing Zippy of his enthusiasm, and he proposes sending the canine to "Bad Dog School" to rekindle the spark. Plecas's illustrations "bring little Zippy to life, with particularly expressive eyes and ears and a variety of appealing poses," a contributor in *Kirkus Reviews* observed.

In *Please Is a Good Word to Say* Joosse introduces young Harriet, a spunky redhead who offers cheery and helpful advice on manners and etiquette, such as the

proper time to offer a hug. According to *School Library Journal* reviewer Catherine Callegari, "Plecas's ink-and-watercolor cartoons imbue the already spirited commentary with personality, dimension, and even more energy." In a companion volume, *Love Is a Good Thing to Feel*, Harriet counsels young readers on the myriad way to express love with the help of her faithful companion, a stuffed rabbit named Squeezie. Here Plecas's "adorable pictures . . . capture the effervescence love can engender," as Ilene Cooper maintained in *Booklist*.

A toddler refuses to settle down for a nap, preferring to boogie down with his stuffed animals in *Baby Danced the Polka*, a lift-the-flap book by Karen Beaumont that features artwork by Plecas. The illustrator "captures hilarious facial expressions and jubilant dance poses," reported a critic in *Publishers Weekly*. Cooper compared Plecas's illustrations to those of Helen Oxenbury, noting that "their warm, cozy feeling has the same appeal." In *Love That Baby!: A Book about Babies for New Big Brothers, Sisters, Cousins, and Friends* Kathryn Lasky helps youngsters prepare for life with an infant sibling. "Plecas' plentiful watercolor-and-ink illustrations have the bright, airy tone of kid-friendly greeting cards," as Abby Nolan wrote in her *Booklist* review.

Plecas joins forces with Lee Fox on *Ella Kazoo Will Not Brush Her Hair*, a humorous picture book about a stubborn gal whose free-flowing locks threaten to overrun her household. Plecas "gets good comic mileage out of turning Ella's hair into a force of nature," a contributor declared in *Publishers Weekly*. A critic in *Kirkus Reviews* remarked that the "colorful and detailed watercolor illustrations deftly capture the feelings of all the

characters" in *Ella Kazoo Will Not Brush Her Hair*, and Susan Weitz similarly remarked that Plecas "makes great use of the space on each page to highlight the child's mood" in her *School Library Journal* critique.

In addition to her work as an illustrator, Plecas has created several original stories for children. The first, *Kiki's New Sister*, was published in the early 1990s, at the start of her career. With *Pretend!* Plecas returned to writing after almost twenty years, creating a self-illustrated father-and-son story about an imaginative adventure that transforms an uneventful afternoon into something magical.

Biographical and Critical Sources

PERIODICALS

Book, March-April, 2003, Kathleen Odean, review of *Get Well, Good Knight*, pp. 36-37.

Booklist, September 15, 1993, Ilene Cooper, review of *The Outside Dog*, p. 151; November 1, 1993, Hazel Rochman, review of *What about My Goldfish?*, pp. 528-529; June 1, 1994, Hazel Rochman, review of *Peeping and Sleeping*, p. 1841; September 15, 1995, Ilene Cooper, review of *Rattlebone Rock*, p. 168; November 1, 1998, Carolyn Phelan, review of *Emma's Magic Winter*, p. 507; December 1, 1998, Carolyn Phelan, review of *Wrapping Paper Romp*, p. 670; February 15, 2000, Gillian Engberg, review of *Good Night, Good Knight*, p. 1124; February 15, 2001, review of *Agapanthus Hum and Major Bark*, p. 1143; February 15, 2003, Gillian Engberg, review of *Agapanthus Hum and the Angel Hoot*, p. 1072; July, 2003, Stephanie Zvirin, review of *Emma's Strange Pet*, p. 1899; November 1, 2003, Abby Nolan, review of *Love That Baby!: A Book about Babies for New Big Brothers, Sisters, Cousins, and Friends*, p. 501; February 15, 2004, Ilene Cooper, review of *Baby Danced the Polka*, p. 1061; January 1, 2006, Hazel Rochman, review of *Happy Birthday, Good Knight*, p. 119; June 1, 2007, Connie Fletcher, review of *Please Is a Good Word to Say*, p. 84; January 1, 2009, Ilene Cooper, review of *Love Is a Good Thing to Feel*, p. 92; February 1, 2009, Gillian Engberg, review of *A Cold Winter's Good Knight*, p. 47.

Horn Book, January-February, 1994, Maeve Visser Knoth, review of *The Outside Dog*, p. 68; May-June, 1994, Ellen Fader, review of *Peeping and Sleeping*, p. 317; September-October, 1998, Martha V. Parravano, review of *Emma's Magic Winter*, pp. 610-611; January, 2000, review of *Good Night, Good Knight*, p. 84; May-June, 2004, Jennifer M. Brabander, review of *Baby Danced the Polka*, p. 307; January-February, 2009, Susan Dove Lempke, review of *A Cold Winter's Good Knight*, p. 85.

Instructor, January-February, 2003, Judy Freeman, review of *Get Well, Good Knight*, p. 78.

Kirkus Reviews, September 15, 2002, review of *Get Well, Good Knight*, p. 1402; December 15, 2003, review of *Love That Baby!*, p. 1452; January 1, 2004, review of

Plecas's illustration assignments included creating the line-and-wash art for Karen Beaumont's upbeat story in **Baby Danced the Polka.** *(Illustration copyright © 2004 by Jennifer Plecas. Reproduced by permission of Dial Books for Young Readers, a division of Penguin Young Readers Group, a member of Penguin (USA) Inc., 345 Hudson St., NY 10014. All rights reserved.)*

Baby Danced the Polka, p. 33; July 15, 2004, review of *Bad Dog School,* p. 688; April 15, 2007, review of *Please Is a Good Word to Say*; November 15, 2008, review of *Love Is a Good Thing to Feel*; December 15, 2009, review of *Ella Kazoo Will Not Brush Her Hair.*

New York Times Book Review, November 12, 1995, Roni Schotter, review of *Snow Day!,* p. 42.

Publishers Weekly, September 20, 1993, review of *What about My Goldfish?,* p. 72; April 25, 1994, review of *Peeping and Sleeping,* p. 77; September 18, 1995, review of *Rattlebone Rock,* p. 89; December 21, 1998, review of *Agapanthus Hum and the Eyeglasses,* p. 68; November 1, 1999, review of *Agapanthus Hum and Major Bark,* p. 56; December 13, 1999, review of *Good Night, Good Knight,* p. 81; March 27, 2000, review of *The Pig Is in the Pantry, the Cat Is on the Shelf,* p. 79; March 15, 2004, review of *Baby Danced the Polka,* p. 73; June 25, 2007, review of *Please Is a Good Word to Say,* p. 62; December 22, 2008, review of *Love Is a Good Thing to Feel,* p. 50; December 21, 2009, review of *Ella Kazoo Will Not Brush Her Hair,* p. 59.

School Library Journal, November, 1993, Gale W. Sherman, review of *The Outside Dog,* p. 88; January, 1994, Elizabeth Hanson, review of *What about My Goldfish?,* p. 88; June, 1994, Lisa Wu Stowe, review of *Peeping and Sleeping,* p. 110; October, 1994, Gale W. Sherman, review of *I Found Mouse,* p. 90; September, 1995, Eunice Weech, review of *Snow Day!,* pp. 179-180; November, 1995, Nancy Seiner, review of *Rattlebone Rock,* p. 64; June, 1996, Christina Dorr, review of *The Trouble with Wishes,* p. 107; July, 1996, William C. Heckman, review of *Spoiled Rotten,* p. 58; February, 1999, Blair Christolon, review of *Wrapping Paper Romp,* pp. 83-84; April, 1999, Gale W. Sherman, review of *Agapanthus Hum and the Eyeglasses,* p. 91; March, 2000, Maura Bresnahan, review of *Good Night, Good Knight,* p. 218; May, 2000, Christine Lindsey, review of *The Pig Is in the Pantry, the Cat Is on the Shelf,* p. 150; December, 2000, review of *Good Night, Good Knight,* p. 55; January, 2001, Maura Bresnahan, review of *Emma's Yucky Brother,* p. 103; February, 2001, Laura Scott, review of *Agapanthus Hum and Major Bark,* p. 93; November, 2002, Laura Scott, review of *Get Well, Good Knight,* p. 139; February, 2003, Mary Elam, review of *Agapanthus Hum and the Angel Hoot,* p. 103; October, 2003, Anne Knickerbocker, review of *Emma's Strange Pet,* p. 129; September, 2004, Gloria Koster, review of *Bad Dog School,* p. 169; March, 2006, Bobbee Pennington, review of *Happy Birthday, Good Knight,* p. 203; July, 2007, Catherine Callegari, review of *Please Is a Good Word to Say,* p. 78; December, 2008, Heidi Estrin, review of *Love Is a Good Thing to Feel,* p. 94, and Angela J. Reynolds, review of *A Cold Winter's Good Knight,* p. 104; February, 2010, Susan Weitz, review of *Ella Kazoo Will Not Brush Her Hair,* p. 84.

ONLINE

Bulletin of the Center for Children's Books Web site, http://bccb.lis.illinois.edu/ (April, 2001), Deborah Stevenson, "True Blue: Jennifer Plecas."

Jennifer Plecas Home Page, http://www.jenniferplecas. com (April 15, 2011).

* * *

PON, Cynthia

Personal

Born in Hong Kong. *Education:* University of Hong Kong, B.A.; University of Michigan, M.A. (comparative literature), Ph.D. (comparative literature).

Addresses

Home—Washington, DC.

Career

Administrator and writer. Southern Poverty Law Center, member of editorial staff of Teaching Tolerance project; Global Fund for Children's Books, director.

Awards, Honors

Rodda Award, Church and Synagogue Library Association, 2011, for *Faith.*

Writings

(With Maya Ajmera and Magda Nakassis) *Faith,* Charlesbridge (Watertown, MA), 2009.
(With Maya Ajmera and Sheila Kinkade) *Our Grandparents: A Global Album,* Charlesbridge (Watertown, MA), 2010.

Biographical and Critical Sources

PERIODICALS

Booklist, March 1, 2009, Ilene Cooper, review of *Faith,* p. 49.
School Library Journal, April, 2009, review of *Faith,* p. S16; February, 2010, Margaret R. Tassia, review of *Our Grandparents: A Global Album,* p. 98.

ONLINE

Global Fund for Children Web site, http://www.globalfund orchildren.org/ (April 15, 2011).*

* * *

PROMITZER, Rebecca

Personal

Born in Austria; immigrated to England. *Education:* Goldsmiths College London, M.A., 1999.

Addresses

Home—London, England. *Agent*—Meg Davis and Sophie Gorell-Barnes, MBA Literary Agents, 62 Grafton Way, London W1T 5DW, England.

Career

Screenwriter, playwright, novelist, singer, and songwriter. University of York, York, England, teacher of English. Director and producer of play *Mouth to Mouth.*

Awards, Honors

Performance Award, Film Stock Film Festival, and highly commended citation, Turner Classic Movies Classic Shorts competition, both for *Keepers.*

Writings

The Pickle King (middle-grade novel), Chicken House (Frome, England), 2009, Scholastic, Inc. (New York, NY), 2010.

Writer and director of *Keeper* (short film); author of screenplays, including *Out to Lunch, Chasing a Kiss,* and *Retro.* Contributor of screenplays for episodes of *The Secret of Eel Island* (children's television series). Writer, director, and producer of *Mouth to Mouth* (play), University of York; adaptor of Edgar Allan Poe's *The Fall of the House of Usher* for the stage.

Sidelights

A native of Austria who lives in London, England, Rebecca Promitzer is the author of *The Pickle King,* a novel for middle graders. Inspired in part by a rainy, dreary vacation in San Francisco, California, Promtizer's novel centers on Beatrice Klednik, an eleven year old living in the dead-end town of Elbow, where the summers are marked by seemingly endless downpours. When friend Sam discovers a one-eyed corpse in the waterlogged basement of a dilapidated old house and asks Bea, a camera bug, to photograph the scene, it sparks a bizarre and frightening series of events revolving around the owner of the town's leading employer, a pickle company. With the help of some misfit classmates, Bea and Sam uncover a conspiracy that involves a murderous surgeon, a bag of human intestines, a community of outcasts living in a dump, a crooked police force, and a shadowy group known as the Brotherhood.

"There is plenty of truly gross action" in the story, observed *School Library Journal* critic Elaine E. Knight in her review of *The Pickle King,* and *Booklist* reviewer Andrew Medlar predicted that readers with "a taste for quirky and circuitous adventures may want to take a bite." Similarly, a contributor in *Publishers Weekly* wrote that *The Pickle King* contains "enough adventure elements—especially for readers with an appetite for grisly details—to make for an entertaining read."

Cover of Rebecca Promitzer's middle-grade novel The Pickle King, *featuring artwork by Oliver Purston.* (Chicken House, 2010. Illustration by Oliver Purston. Reproduced by permission of Scholastic, Inc.)

Biographical and Critical Sources

PERIODICALS

Booklist, February 1, 2010, Andrew Medlar, review of *The Pickle King,* p. 46.

Bulletin of the Center for Children's Books, April, 2010, Karen Coats, review of *The Pickle King,* p. 351.

Journal of Adolescent & Adult Literacy, October, 2010, Donna L. Miller, review of *The Pickle King,* p. 155.

Kirkus Reviews, January 1, 2010, review of *The Pickle King.*

Observer (London, England), July 26, 2009, Lisa O'Kelly, review of *The Pickle King.*

Publishers Weekly, February 22, 2010, review of *The Pickle King,* p. 65.

School Library Journal, June, 2010, Elaine E. Knight, review of *The Pickle King,* p. 117.

ONLINE

MBA Literary Agents Web site, http://www.mbalit.co.uk/ (April 15, 2011), "Rebecca Promitzer."

Rebecca Promitzer Home Page, http://www.rebecca
promitzer.com (April 15, 2011).

*   *   *

PUYBARET, Éric 1976-

Personal

Born 1976, in France. *Education:* Attended École National Supérieure des Arts Décoratifs.

Addresses

Home—France.

Career

Illustrator. *Exhibitions:* Work exhibited at Bologna Children's Book Fair, 1999.

Writings

SELF-ILLUSTRATED

Les échasses rouges, Gautier-Languereau (Paris, France), 2006.
Cache-lune, Gautier-Languereau (Paris, France), 2007.
Les îlots de Piédestal ("Voyage au pays des mages" series), Gautier-Languereau (Paris, France), 2008.
Le grand mage d'Uzinagaz ("Voyage au pays des mages" series), Gautier-Languereau (Paris, France), 2009.
Mes masques de contes de fées, Gautier-Languereau (Paris, France), 2009.
Les échasses rouges, Gautier-Languereau (Paris, France), 2009.

ILLUSTRATOR

Laurence Tichit, *Gaspard le renard et gaston le héron,* Gautier-Languereau (Paris, France), 2000.
Florence Grazia, *Barnabé le chat beauté,* Gautier-Languereau (Paris, France), 2000.
Christine Frasseto, *Moitié de poulet,* Flammarion (Paris, France), 2001.
Christine Frasseto, *Un cadeau en hiver,* Flammarion (Paris, France), 2002.
Claire Mazard, *L'été de mes dix ans,* Flammarion (Paris, France), 2002.
Christian Jolibois, *Le grand voyage de mimolette,* Flammarion (Paris, France), 2002.
Philippe Barbeau, *Gare au Dragon!,* Flammarion (Paris, France), 2002.
Anne-Sophie Baumann, *Au Zoo!,* Mondo Mino (Paris, France), 2003.
Catherine Lamon-Mignot, *Une sorcière dans le coffre à jouets,* Hachette (Paris, France), 2004.
Mathilde Barat, *Le grand orchestre von Bémol,* Gautier-Languereau (Paris, France), 2005.

Philippe Lechermeier, *Graines de cabanes,* Gautier-Languereau (Paris, France), 2005.
Didier Sustrac, *Chut, le roi pourrait t'entendre!,* Gautier-Languereau (Paris, France), 2007.
Pol-Serge Kakon, *L'opéra plouf* (with CD), Père Castor Flammarion (Paris, France), 2007.
Peter Yarrow and Lenny Lipton, *Puff, the Magic Dragon* (with CD), Sterling Publishing (New York, NY), 2007.
Marie-Claire Baillaud, adapter, *Qamar az-Zaman et la princesse de la Chine,* Éditions du Jasmin (Clichy, France), 2007.
Corinne Albaut, *Le château de Vincennes,* Monum/Patrimoine (Paris, France), 2007.
Emmanuelle et Benoît de Saint Chamas, *Contes des six trésors,* Éditions du Jasmin (Clichy, France), 2007.
Marie-Astrid Bailly-Maître, *Angèle au bout de la nuit,* Gautier-Languereau (Paris, France), 2007.
(With Florence Vandermarlière) Charles Delhez, *Jésus, qui est-il?,* Mame (Paris, France), 2007.
Nathaniel Hawthorne, *Le premier livre des merveilles,* Le Livre de Poche Jeunesse (Paris, France), 2007.
Jennifer Berne, *Manfish: The Story of Jacques Cousteau,* Chronicle Books (New York, NY), 2008.
Universal Declaration of Human Rights, United Nations (New York, NY)/Gautier-Languereau (Paris, France), 2008.
(With Chantal Cazin and Stéphane Girel) Charles Delhez, *La prière, c'est facile!,* Mame (Paris, France), 2008.
Philippe Lechermeier, *Graines de cabanes,* Gautier-Languereau (Paris, France), 2008.
Agnès Bertron-Martin, *La flûte prodigieuse,* Père Castor-Flammarion (Paris, France), 2008.
Virginie Aladjidi and Caroline Pellissier, editors, *Poésies du monde entier,* Fleurus (Paris, France), 2008.
Juliette Saumande, *In Search of Happiness,* Hammond (Long Island City, NY), 2009.
John Cech, reteller, *The Nutcracker* (based on the story by E.T.A. Hoffmann), Sterling Publishing (New York, NY), 2009.
Virginie Aladjidi and Caroline Pellissier, editors, *Poésies du petits bonheurs,* Fleurus (Paris, France), 2009.
Karine-Marie Amiot and Sophie de Mullenheim, *Mon baptême,* Mame (Paris, France), 2009.
Le livre magique des contes infinis, Gautier-Languereau (Paris, France), 2010.
Joseph Jacobs, *Les trois petits cochons,* Magnard Jeunesse (Paris, France), 2010.
Mayumi Watanabe, *Contes du Japon,* Éditions du Jasmin (Clichy, France), 2010.
Harold Arlen and E.Y. Harburg, *Over the Rainbow,* Imagine Publishing (Morganville, NJ), 2010.
Clement C. Moore, *The Night before Christmas* (with CD), Imagine Publishing (Morganville, NJ), 2010.

Sidelights

An accomplished French illustrator, Éric Puybaret has provided the artwork for numerous children's books, including several that have been published in English. *Puff, the Magic Dragon,* a work based on the popular 1963 song recorded by the folk trio Peter, Paul & Mary, follows the relationship between the title character—a

sensitive, warmhearted creature—and his loyal human companion, Jackie Paper, who together roam the magical island of Honalee. Originally a poem by Paul Yarrow and Lenny Lipton concerning a child's loss of innocence, *Puff, the Magic Dragon* features "Puybaret's atmospheric paintings, all gently curving lines and scrupulous precision," as Nicolette Jones remarked in the London *Sunday Times*. A reviewer in *Publishers Weekly* also complimented the illustrations, stating that "Puybaret's graceful acrylic on linen paintings are intermittently misty and sunny." A number of critics observed that, in his final spread, Puybaret tempers the song's wistful conclusion, although Jackie grows up and leaves Honalee, "his young daughter takes his place as Puff's best buddy," according to Janice Del Negro in *Booklist*.

Puybaret helps bring another favorite tune to life in *Over the Rainbow,* a work inspired by the Academy Award-winning song from *The Wizard of Oz.* Depicting a young girl's magical journey from her farmhouse to a celestial world of castles and bluebirds, *Over the Rainbow* garnered praise for its colorful, dreamlike pictures. "The art is unique, delicate, and detailed," Mary Elam reported in *School Library Journal.* "Creatively meshing folk-art flourishes with an ethereal sensibility," as a *Publishers Weekly* reviewer noted, Puybaret's "illustrations well match the fantasy of the lyrics."

John Cech's retelling of *The Nutcracker,* a picture book based on the 1816 story by E.T.A. Hoffmann, describes the adventures of a Christmas toy that comes to life. Here "Puybaret's acrylic paintings show an art deco influence," a critic in *Kirkus Reviews* stated, and a *Publishers Weekly* contributor observed that the "stylized illustrations . . . suggest a dizzying fever-dream." Puybaret's art was cited as a highlight of *The Night before Christmas,* a version of the classic poem by Clement C. Moore. In the words of *School Library Journal* reviewer Eva Mitnick, Puybaret's illustrations "create a magical, yet cozy, setting for Santa's visit."

Jennifer Berne offers a picture-book biography of a celebrated French explorer, oceanographer, conservationist, and filmmaker in *Manfish: The Story of Jacques Cousteau.* "Almost poetic in its rich descriptions, the text is superimposed on ethereal acrylic paintings," wrote Nicki Clausen-Grace in her review of the book for *School Library Journal.* Gillian Engberg similarly noted in her *Booklist* review that Puybaret's illustrations "extend the words' elegant simplicity and beautifully convey the sense of infinite, underwater space," and *New York Times Book Review* contributor Lawrence Downes applauded the inclusion of an inventive "pull-out page that, turned vertically, gives a suggestion of the teeming depths of the kingdoms that so captivated Cousteau." Pubyaret's illustrations are also a feature of Juliette Saumande's *In Search of Happiness,* a whimsical tale of a boy's journey through a series of strange lands. Here his "stunning use of line and color . . . pulls readers' eyes through the pages," Patricia Austin declared in her *Booklist* review of the work.

Biographical and Critical Sources

PERIODICALS

Booklist, September 15, 2007, Janice Del Negro, review of *Puff, the Magic Dragon,* p. 70; June 1, 2008, Gillian Engberg, review of *Manfish: The Story of Jacques Cousteau,* p. 104; September 1, 2009, Diane Foote, review of *The Nutcracker,* p. 91; February 15, 2010, Patricia Austin, review of *In Search of Happiness,* p. 80.

Kirkus Reviews, July 15, 2007, review of *Puff, the Magic Dragon;* May 15, 2008, review of *Manfish;* September 15, 2009, review of *The Nutcracker.*

New York Times Book Review, November 11, 2007, Steven Heller, review of *Puff, the Magic Dragon,* p. 36; May 10, 2009, Lawrence Downes, review of *Manfish,* p. 16.

Publishers Weekly, June 11, 2007, review of *Puff, the Magic Dragon,* p. 58; October 26, 2009, review of *The Nutcracker,* p. 57; December 21, 2009, review of *In Search of Happiness,* p. 60; February 8, 2010, review of *Over the Rainbow,* p. 48.

School Library Journal, August, 2007, Marge Loch-Wouters, review of *Puff, the Magic Dragon,* p. 108; November, 2008, Nicki Clausen-Grace, review of *Manfish,* p. 105; October, 2009, Virginia Walter, review of *The Nutcracker,* p. 78; June, 2010, Mary Elam, review of *Over the Rainbow,* p. 88; October, 2010, Eva Mitnick, review of *The Night before Christmas,* p. 75.

Sunday Times (London, England), August 19, 2007, Nicolette Jones, review of *Puff, the Magic Dragon,* p. 49.

Times (London, England), September 1, 2007, Tom Gatti, review of *Puff, the Magic Dragon,* p. 15.

ONLINE

Ricochet-Jeunes Web site, http://www.ricochet-jeunes.org/ (December 15, 2008), "Éric Puybaret."*

*   *   *

PYLE, Charles S. 1954(?)- (Chuck Pyle)

Personal

Born c. 1954, in CA. *Education:* Academy of Art University, B.F.A., 1976.

Addresses

Home—San Francisco, CA. *E-mail*—charles@charles pylestudio.com.

Career

Illustrator, fine artist, and educator. Freelance artist, beginning 1977; Academy of Arts University, San Francisco, CA, director of school of illustration, 2004—. *Exhibitions:* Work exhibited in numerous galleries and included in private collections.

Awards, Honors

President's Award, Academy of Art University, 2010.

Illustrator

Lin Oliver, *The Daylight Limited,* Learning Curve (Chicago, IL), 1998.

John Boswell and Lenore Skenazy, *Dysfunctional Family Christmas Songbook,* Broadway Books (New York, NY), 2004.

Fred Bowen, *No Easy Way: The Story of Ted Williams and the Last .400 Season,* Dutton (New York, NY), 2010.

UNDER NAME CHUCK PYLE

Laura Lee Hope, *Freddie and Flossie,* Aladdin (New York, NY), 2005.

Laura Lee Hope, *Freddie and Flossie and the Train Ride,* Aladdin (New York, NY), 2005.

Laura Lee Hope, *Freddie and Flossie and Snap,* Aladdin (New York, NY), 2005.

Laura Lee Hope, *Freddie and Flossie at the Beach,* Aladdin (New York, NY), 2005.

Biographical and Critical Sources

PERIODICALS

Booklist, December 15, 2009, Bill Ott, review of *No Easy Way: The Story of Ted Williams and the Last .400 Season,* p. 41.

Kirkus Reviews, February 15, 2010, review of *No Easy Way.*

School Library Journal, January, 2010, Marilyn Taniguchi, review of *No Easy Way,* p. 85.

ONLINE

Charles Pyle Home Page, http://www.charlespylestudio.com (April 24, 2011).

Charles Pyle Web log, http://chuckplyeart.blogspot.com (April 24, 2011).*

*   *   *

PYLE, Chuck
See PYLE, Charles S.

R-S

ROSEN, Michael

Personal

Born in Harrow, Middlesex, England; son of Harold (a professor) and Connie Ruby (a college lecturer) Rosen; married Elizabeth Susanna Steele, 1976 (divorced, 1987); married Geraldine Clark, 1987 (divorced, 1997); married Emma-Louise Williams; children: (first marriage) Joseph Steele, Eddie Steele (deceased); (second marriage) Isaac Louis; (step-daughters) Naomi Imogen Hill, Laura Clark; (third marriage) Elsie Lavender Ruby. *Education:* Attended Middlesex Hospital Medical School, 1964-65, and National Film School, 1973-76; Wadham College, Oxford, B.A. (English language and literature), 1969; University of Reading, M.A. (children's literature; with distinction), 1993; University of North London, Ph.D., 1997. *Politics:* "Socialist.' *Religion:* 'Atheist.' *Hobbies and other interests:* Watching the Arsenal Football Club.

Addresses

Home—Hackney, London, England. *Agent*—Katy Jones, United Agents, kjones@unitedagents.co.uk. *E-mail*—michael@michaelrosen.co.uk.

Career

Writer, poet, educator, playwright, performer, and broadcaster. Host and guest on British Broadcasting Corporation (BBC) television and radio shows, including *Meridian Books, Treasure Islands,* 1988-89, *Best Worlds,* and *Word of Mouth,* beginning 1998. Writer-in-residence at schools in London, England; lecturer at universities and colleges in the United Kingdom and Canada, including at Birbeck College, London Metropolitan University, and Middlesex University. Presenter at conferences in the United Kingdom, Australia, United States, Canada, Singapore, and Italy; performer at venues in the United Kingdom, including the Shaw Theatre, National Theatre, Edinburgh Book Festival, and BBC Children's Poetry Festival. Political candidate representing the Respect Coalition, c. 2006.

Michael Rosen (Reproduced by permission of Peters, Fraser & Dunlop Group Ltd.)

Member

National Union of Journalists.

Awards, Honors

Best Original Full-Length Play Award, London *Sunday Times* National Union of Students Drama Festival, 1968, for *Backbone; Signal* magazine Poetry Award, 1982, for *You Can't Catch Me!;* Other Award, *Children's Book Bulletin,* 1983, for *Everybody Here;* British Book Award runner-up, 1989; Nestlé Smarties Best Children's Book

of the Year Award, and *Boston Globe/Horn Book* Award, both 1990, and Japanese Picture Book Award, 1991, all for *We're Going on a Bear Hunt;* Cuffies Award for best anthology, *Publishers Weekly,* 1992, and Best Book Award, National Association of Parenting Publications, 1993, both for *Poems for the Very Young;* Glennfiddich Award for best radio program on the subject of food, 1996, for "*Treasure Islands* Special: Lashings of Ginger Beer"; Eleanor Farjeon Award for distinguished services to children's literature, 1997; Play and Learn Award, *Parent* magazine, 1998, for *Snore;* Talkies Award for best poetry audiotape of the year, 1998, for *You Wait till I'm Older than You;* International Reading Association Teachers' Choice selection, 1999, for *Classic Poetry;* Sony Radio Academy Silver Award, 2000, for radio feature "Dr. Seuss: Who Put the Cat in the Hat?," and Gold Award, 2003, for "On Saying Goodbye"; English Association Exceptional Award, 2004, and *Boston Globe/Horn Book* Nonfiction Honor Book designation, 2006, both for *Michael Rosen's Sad Book;* honorary doctorate, Open University, 2005; National Literacy WOW Award, 2005, for *Alphabet Poem;* appointed Children's Laureate of Great Britain, 2007-09; named chevalier, Ordre des Arts et des Letters (France), 2008; Oxfordshire Book Award, 2009, for *Dear Mother Goose;* Fred and Anne Jarvis Award, National Union of Teachers, 2010; honorary D.Ed., Nottingham Trent University, 2010.

Writings

FOR CHILDREN

Once There Was a King Who Promised He Would Never Chop Anyone's Head Off, illustrated by Kathy Henderson, Deutsch (London, England), 1976.

She Even Called Me Garabaldi, BBC Books (London, England), 1977.

The Bakerloo Flea, illustrated by Quentin Blake, Longman (London, England), 1979.

Nasty!, illustrated by Amanda Macphail, Longman (London, England), 1982, revised edition, Puffin (Harmondsworth, England), 1984.

How to Get out of the Bath, and Other Problems, illustrated by Graham Round, Scholastic (New York, NY), 1984.

Hairy Tales and Nursery Crimes, illustrated by Alan Baker, Deutsch (London, England), 1985.

You're Thinking about Doughnuts, illustrated by Tony Pinchuck, Deutsch (London, England), 1987.

Beep Beep! Here Come—The Horribles!, illustrated by John Watson, Walker (London, England), 1988.

Jokes and Verses, illustrated by Quentin Blake, BBC Books (London, England), 1988.

Norma and the Washing Machine, illustrated by David Hingham, Deutsch (London, England), 1988.

Silly Stories (jokes), illustrated by Mik Brown, Kingfisher (London, England), 1988 revised as *Michael Rosen's Horribly Silly Stories,* 1994, revised as *Off the Wall: A Very Silly Joke Book,* Kingfisher (New York, NY), 1994.

(Editor) *Ribticklers: Funny Stories,* Kingfisher (London, England), 1988, Kingfisher (Boston, MA), 2007.

The Class Two Monster, illustrated by Maggie King, Heinemann (London, England), 1989.

The Deadman Tapes, Deutsch (London, England), 1989.

The Royal Huddle [and] *The Royal Muddle,* illustrated by Colin West, Macmillan (London, England), 1990.

Clever Cakes, illustrated by Caroline Holden, Walker (London, England), 1991.

Burping Bertha, illustrated by Tony Ross, Andersen (London, England), 1993.

Moving, illustrated by Sophy Williams, Viking (New York, NY), 1993.

Songbird Story, illustrated by Jill Down, Frances Lincoln (London, England), 1993.

The Arabian Frights and Other Gories, illustrated by Chris Fisher, Scholastic (London, England), 1994.

Dad, illustrated by Tony Ross, Longman (Harlow, England), 1994, Sundance (Littleton, MA), 1997.

Figgy Roll, illustrated by Tony Ross, Longman (Harlow, England), 1994, published as *Dad's Fig Bar,* Sundance (Littleton, MA), 1997.

Lisa's Letter, illustrated by Tony Ross, Longman (Harlow, England), 1994, Sundance (Littleton, MA), 1997.

Fantastically Funny Stories, illustrated by Mik Brown, Kingfisher (London, England), 1994, Kingfisher (Boston, MA), 2005.

Even Stevens, F.C., illustrated by John Rogan, Collins (London, England), 1995.

This Is Our House, illustrated by Bob Graham, Candlewick Press (Cambridge, MA), 1996.

Norma's Notebook, illustrated by Tony Ross, Sundance (Littleton, MA), 1997.

(Author of text) *I Want to Be a Superhero,* score by Robert Kapilow, G. Schirmer (New York, NY), 1998.

Snore!, illustrated by Jonathan Langley, HarperCollins (London, England), 1998.

Mission Ziffoid, illustrated by Arthur Robins, Walker (London, England), Candlewick Press (Cambridge, MA), 1999.

Rover, illustrated by Neal Layton, Bloomsbury (London, England), Random House (New York, NY), 1999.

Lunch Boxes Don't Fly, illustrated by Korky Paul, Puffin (London, England), 1999.

A Thanksgiving Wish, illustrated by John Thompson, Blue Sky Press (New York, NY), 1999.

Lovely Old Roly, illustrated by Pricilla Lamont, Frances Lincoln (London, England), 2002.

One Push, illustrated by Martin Olsson, Storycircus.com, 2002.

Oww!: A Wriggly Piglet with a Prickly Problem, illustrated by Jonathan Langley, HarperCollins (London, England), 2003, Trafalgar, 2005.

Howler, illustrated by Neal Layton, Bloomsbury (London, England), 2003, Bloomsbury (New York, NY), 2004.

Michael Rosen's Sad Book, illustrated by Quentin Blake, Candlewick Press (Cambridge, MA), 2005.

Totally Wonderful Miss Plumberry, illustrated by Chinlun Lee, Candlewick Press (Cambridge, MA), 2006.

Bear's Day Out, illustrated by Adrian Reynolds, Bloomsbury Children's Books (New York, NY), 2007.

Something's Drastic, illustrated by Tim Archbold, Collins (London, England), 2007.

Shoo!, illustrated by Jonathan Langley, HarperCollins Children's (London, England), 2007.

Bear Flies High, illustrated by Adrian Reynolds, Bloomsbury (New York, NY), 2009.

I'm Number One, illustrated by Bob Graham, Candlewick Press (Somerville, MA), 2009.

Red Ted and the Lost Things, illustrated by Joel Stewart, Candlewick Press (Somerville, MA), 2009.

Tiny Little Fly, illustrated by Kevin Waldron, Candlewick Press (Somerville, MA), 2010.

Contributor of short fiction to *Round about Six,* edited by Kaye Webb, Frances Lincoln (London, England, 1993.

Author's works have been translated into numerous languages, including Albanian, Bengali, Gujarati, Somali, and Welsh.

POETRY; FOR CHILDREN

Mind Your Own Business, illustrated by Quentin Blake, Deutsch (London, England), 1974.

Wouldn't You Like to Know, illustrated by Quentin Blake, Deutsch (London, England), 1977, revised edition, Penguin (Harmondsworth, England), 1981.

Bathtime, BBC Books (London, England), 1979.

(With Roger McGough) *You Tell Me,* illustrated by Sara Midda, Kestrel (London, England), 1979.

You Can't Catch Me! (also see below), illustrated by Quentin Blake, Deutsch (London, England), 1981, reprinted, 1996.

Quick, Let's Get out of Here, illustrated by Quentin Blake, Deutsch (London, England), 1983.

Smacking My Lips, illustrated by Quentin Blake, Puffin (London, England), 1983.

Don't Put Mustard in the Custard (also see below), illustrated by Quentin Blake, Deutsch (London, England), 1985.

Chocolate Cake, illustrated by Amelia Rosato, BBC Books (London, England), 1986.

When Did You Last Wash Your Feet?, illustrated by Tony Pinchuck, Deutsch (London, England), 1986.

The Hypnotiser, illustrated by Andrew Tiffen, Deutsch (London, England), 1988.

We're Going on a Bear Hunt, illustrated by Helen Oxenbury, Walker (London, England), 1989, Aladdin (New York, NY), 1992, published with audio CD, Little Simon (New York, NY), 2007, twentieth-anniversary edition, Walker (London, England), 2009.

Freckly Feet and Itchy Knees, illustrated by Sami Sweeten, Doubleday (New York, NY), 1990.

Never Mind!, BBC Books (London, England), 1990.

Little Rabbit Foo Foo, illustrated by Arthur Robins, Simon & Schuster (New York, NY), 1990, published with audio CD, Walker (London, England), 2007.

Who Drew on the Baby's Head?, Deutsch (London, England), 1991.

Mind the Gap, Scholastic (London, England), 1992.

Nuts about Nuts, illustrated by Sami Sweeten, Collins (London, England), 1993.

The Best of Michael Rosen, illustrated by Quentin Blake, RDR Books (Oakland, CA), 1995.

Michael Rosen's ABC, illustrated by Bee Wiley, Macdonald (London, England), 1996.

You Wait till I'm Older than You, illustrated by Shoo Rainer, Viking (London, England), 1997.

The Michael Rosen Book of Nonsense, illustrated by Clare Mackie, Wayland Macdonald (Brighton, England), 1997.

Tea in the Sugar Bowl, Potato in My Shoe, illustrated by Quentin Blake, Walker (London, England), 1998.

Centrally Heated Knickers, illustrated by Harry Horse, Puffin (London, England), 1999.

Even More Nonsense from Michael Rosen, illustrated by Clare Mackie, Hodder (London, England), 2000.

Views of Notley Green, photographs by Ed Clark, Design Council (London, England), 2000.

Uncle Billy Being Silly, illustrated by Korky Paul, Puffin (London, England), 2001.

No Breathing in Class, illustrated by Korky Paul, Puffin (London, England), 2003.

Alphabet Poem, illustrated by Herve Tullet, Milet (London, England), 2004.

Something's Drastic (collection), illustrated by Tim Archbold, Collins (London, England), 2007.

Mustard, Custard, Grumble Belly, and Gravy (with audio CD; includes *Don't Put Mustard in the Custard* and *You Can't Catch Me*), illustrated by Quentin Blake, Bloomsbury (London, England), 2007.

Fighters for Life: Selected Poems, Bookmarks Publications (London, England), 2007.

The Bear in the Cave (with CD), illustrated by Adrien Reynolds, Bloomsbury (London, England), 2007.

Selected Poems, Penguin (London, England), 2007.

Michael Rosen's Big Book of Bad Things, Puffin (London, England), 2010.

Also author of *Zoo at Night,* illustrated by Bee Willey, Tradewind Books (Vancouver, British Columbia, Canada). Contributor of poetry to educational materials.

RETELLINGS; FOR CHILDREN

A Cat and Mouse Story, illustrated by William Rushton, Deutsch (London, England), 1982.

The Wicked Tricks of Till Owlyglass, illustrated by Fritz Wegner, Walker (London, England), 1989.

Peter Pan, illustrated by Francesca Rovira, Firefly (Hove, England), 1989.

Aladdin, illustrated by Jose M. Lavarello, Firefly (Hove, England), 1989.

Alice in Wonderland, illustrated by Francesca Rovira, Firefly (Hove, England), 1989.

Cinderella, illustrated by Agusti Ascensio, Firefly (Hove, England), 1989.

The Three Little Pigs, illustrated by Agusti Ascensio, Firefly (Hove, England), 1989.

Goldilocks and the Three Bears, illustrated by Jose M. Lavarello, Firefly (Hove, England), 1989.

Hansel and Gretel, illustrated by Francesca Rovira, Firefly (Hove, England), 1989.

Little Red Riding Hood, illustrated by Jose M. Lavarello, Firefly (Hove, England), 1989.

Snow White, illustrated by Agusti Ascensio, Firefly (Hove, England), 1989.

The Little Tin Soldier, illustrated by Agusti Ascensio, Firefly (Hove, England), 1990.

The Princess and the Pea, illustrated by Francesca Rovira, Firefly (Hove, England), 1990.

Sinbad the Sailor, illustrated by Francesca Rovira, Firefly (Hove, England), 1990.

The Golem of Old Prague, illustrated by Val Biro, Deutsch (London, England), 1990, illustrated by Brian Simons, Five Leaves (Nottingham, England), 1997.

How the Animals Got Their Colours: Animal Myths from around the World, illustrated by John Clementson, Harcourt (New York, NY), 1992.

The First Giraffe, illustrated by John Clementson, Studio Editions (London, England), 1992, published as *How Giraffe Got Such a Long Neck . . . and Why Rhino Is So Grumpy,* Dial (New York, NY), 1993.

The Old Woman and the Pumpkin, illustrated by Bob Hewis, Learning by Design (London, England), 1994.

The Man with No Shadow (based on a story by Adelbert von Chamisso), illustrated by Reg Cartwright, Longmans (London, England), 1994, published as *The Man Who Sold His Shadow,* 1998.

Crow and Hawk: A Traditional Pueblo Indian Story, illustrated by John Clementson, Harcourt (New York, NY), 1995.

Two European Tales, illustrated by Barry Wilkinson and Gwen Touret, Pearson Education (Harlow, England), 2001.

A Jewish Tale, Longman (Harlow, England), 2002.

Shakespeare's Romeo and Juliet, illustrated by Jane Ray, Candlewick Press (Cambridge, MA), 2004.

"SCRAPBOOK" SERIES; POETRY AND PROSE COLLECTIONS; FOR CHILDREN; ILLUSTRATED BY QUENTIN BLAKE

Smelly Jelly Smelly Fish, Prentice-Hall (New York, NY), 1986.

Under the Bed, Prentice-Hall (New York, NY), 1986.

Hard-boiled Legs, Prentice-Hall (New York, NY), 1987.

Spollyollydiddilytiddlyitis, Walker (London, England), 1987, published as *Down at the Doctor's: The Sick Book,* Simon & Schuster (New York, NY), 1987.

NONFICTION; ADAPTED FROM SPANISH; FOR CHILDREN

Fear, the Attic, illustrated by Agusti Ascensio, Firefly (Hove, England), 1989.

Friendship, the Oar, illustrated by H. Elena, Firefly (Hove, England), 1989.

Imagination, the Tree, illustrated by Conxita Rodriguez, Firefly (Hove, England), 1989.

Intelligence, the Formula, illustrated by Carme Peris, Firefly (Hove, England), 1989.

Shyness, Isabel, illustrated by F. Infante, Firefly (Hove, England), 1989.

Lying, the Nose, illustrated by Carme Peris, Firefly (Hove, England), 1989.

"ZOOMABABY" SERIES; FOR CHILDREN; ILLUSTRATED BY CAROLINE HOLDEN

Zoomababy and the Great Dog Chase, Longman (Harlow, England), 2002.

Zoomababy and the Locked Cage, Longman (Harlow, England), 2002.

Zoomababy and the Mission to Mars, Longman (Harlow, England), 2002.

Zoomababy and the Rescue, Longman (Harlow, England), 2002.

Zoomababy and the Search for the Lost Mummy, Longman (Harlow, England), 2002.

Zoomababy at the World Cup, Longman (Harlow, England), 2002.

EDITOR; FOR CHILDREN

Everybody Here (miscellany), Bodley Head (London, England), 1982.

(With Susanna Steele) *Inky Pinky Ponky: Children's Playground Rhymes,* illustrated by Dan Jones, Granada (London, England), 1982.

(With David Jackson) *Speaking to You,* Macmillan (London, England), 1984.

(With Joan Griffiths) *That'd Be Telling,* Cambridge University Press (Cambridge, England), 1985.

The Kingfisher Book of Children's Poetry, illustrated by Alice Englander, Kingfisher (London, England), 1985, reprinted, 2008.

A Spider Bought a Bicycle, and Other Poems for Young Children, illustrated by Inga Moore, Kingfisher (Boston, MA), 1986.

The Kingfisher Book of Funny Stories, illustrated by Tony Blundell, Kingfisher (London, England), 1988.

Ribticklers: Funny Stories, Kingfisher (London, England), 1988, Kingfisher (Boston, MA), 2007.

Culture Shock, Viking (London, England), 1990.

Stories from Overseas/Histoires d'outre-mer, Ges-editions (Paris, France), 1990.

Give Me Shelter, Bodley Head (London, England), 1991.

A World of Poetry, Kingfisher (London, England), 1991.

Minibeasties, illustrated by Alan Baker, Firefly (Hove, England), 1991, published as *Itsy-Bitsy Beasties: Poems from around the World,* Carolrhoda (Minneapolis, MN), 1992.

Sonsense Nongs, illustrated by Shoo Rayner, A. & C. Black (London, England), 1992.

South and North, East and West: The Oxfam Anthology of Children's Stories, Candlewick (Cambridge, MA), 1992.

Action Replay, Anecdotal Poems, illustrated by Andrzej Krauze, Viking (London, England), 1993.

Poems for the Very Young, illustrated by Bob Graham, Kingfisher (London, England), 1993, Kingfisher (Boston, MA), 1994.

Pilly Soems, illustrated by Shoo Rayner, A. & C. Black (London, England), 1994.

A Different Story: Poems from the Past, English & Media Centre (London, England), 1994.

Rap with Rosen, Longmans (London, England), 1995.

Walking the Bridge of Your Nose, illustrated by Chloe Cheese, Kingfisher (London, England), 1996.

The Secret Life of Schools, Channel 4 Learning (London, England), 1997.

Classic Poetry: An Illustrated Collection, illustrated by Paul Howard, Candlewick Press (Cambridge, MA), 1998.

Night-Night, Knight, and Other Poems, illustrated by Sue Heap, Walker (London, England), 1998.

Poems Are Crazy, Longman (Harlow, England), 2002.

Poems Are Noisy, Longman (Harlow, England), 2002.

Poems Are Pictures, Longman (Harlow, England), 2002.

Poems Are Private, Longman (Harlow, England), 2002.

Poems Are Public, Longman (Harlow, England), 2002.

Poems Are Quiet, Longman (Harlow, England), 2002.

Michael Rosen's A to Z: The Best Children's Poetry from Agard to Zephaniah, illustrated by Joe Berger, Puffin (London, England), 2009.

NONFICTION; FOR ADULTS

Did I Hear You Write?, illustrated by Alan Pinchuck, Deutsch (London, England), 1989.

Goodies and Daddies: An A-Z Guide to Fatherhood, Murray (London, England), 1991.

(Coauthor) *Holocaust Denial: The New Nazi Lie,* Anti-Nazi League (London, England), 1992.

(With Jill Burridge) *Treasure Islands II: An Adult Guide to Children's Writers,* BBC Books (London, England), 1992.

Just Kids: How to Survive the Twos to Tens, illustrated by Caroline Holden, John Murray (London, England), 1995.

(And editor, with Myra Barrs) *A Year with Poetry: Teachers Write about Teaching Poetry,* Centre for Language in Primary Education (London, England), 1997.

(With Simon Elmes) *Word of Mouth,* Oxford University Press (Oxford, England), 2002.

ANTHOLOGIES; FOR ADULTS

Rude Rhymes, illustrated by Riana Duncan, Deutsch (London, England), 1989, revised edition published with *Dirty Ditties* and *Vulgar Verses,* Signet (London, England), 1992.

Dirty Ditties, illustrated by Riana Duncan, Deutsch (London, England), 1990 published with *Rude Rhymes* and *Vulgar Verses,* Signet (London, England), 1992.

Vulgar Verses, illustrated by Riana Duncan, Deutsch (London, England), 1991, published with *Dirty Ditties* and *Rude Rhymes,* Signet (London, England), 1992.

(With David Widgery) *The Chatto Book of Dissent,* Chatto & Windus (London, England), 1991.

Penguin Book of Childhood, Penguin (New York, NY), 1994.

Rude Rhymes Two, Signet (London, England), 1994.

POETRY; FOR ADULTS

Bloody L.I.A.R.S., illustrated by Alan Gilbey, privately printed, 1984.

You Are, Aren't You?, Jewish Socialist Group & Mushroom Bookshop (Nottingham, England), 1993.

The Skin of Your Back, Five Leaves Press (Nottingham, England), 1996.

Selected Poems, Penguin (Harmondsworth, England), 2007.

OTHER

Stewed Figs (play), produced at Oxford University, 1966.

Backbone (play; produced at Oxford University, 1967; produced on the West End, 1968), Faber (London, England), 1968.

Regis Debray (radio play), BBC-Radio 4, 1971.

I See a Voice (on poetry), Thames Television-Hutchinson (London, England), 1981.

Mordecai Vanunu: A Reconstruction (play), produced in London, England, 1993.

Pinocchio in the Park (play), produced in London, England, 2001.

Shakespeare: His Work and His World (nonfiction), illustrated by Robert Ingpen, Candlewick Press (Cambridge, MA), 2001, revised and abridged as *What's So Special about Shakespeare?,* Walker (London, England), 2007.

Carrying the Elephant: A Memoir of Love and Loss, Penguin (London, England), 2002.

This Is Not My Nose: A Memoir of Illness and Recovery, Penguin (London, England), 2004.

Dickens: His Work and His World (nonfiction), illustrated by Robert Ingpen, Candlewick Press (Cambridge, MA), 2005, revised and abridged as *What's So Special about Dickens?,* Walker (London, England), 2007.

Contributor to books, including *There's a Poet behind You!,* edited by Morag Styles and Helen Cook, A. & C. Black (London, England), 1988; *After Alice: Exploring Children's Literature,* edited by Styles, Victor Watson, and Eve Bearne, Cassell (London, England), 1992; and *Tales, Tellers, and Texts,* edited by Gabrielle Cliff Hodges, Mary Jane Drummind, and Styles, Cassell, 2000. Contributor to periodicals, including London *Guardian, Books for Keeps,* London *Daily Telegraph, Signal, Times Educational Supplement,* and *Children's Literature in Education.*

Author and presenter of radio programs for BBC Radio 4, BBC Radio 3, BBC World Service, and BBC Schools Radio, 1970—, including "*Treasure Islands* Special: Lashings of Ginger Beer" and "Dr. Seuss: Who Put the Cat in the Hat?" Author of scripts for television series, including *The Juice Job,* Thames TV, 1981, 1984; *You Tell Me,* Thames TV, 1982; *Everybody Here,* BBC Channel 4, 1982; *Black and White and Read All Over,* BBC Channel 4, 1984; and *Talk Write Read,* Central TV, 1986. Editor of video scripts, including *Why Poetry, Mike Rosen, Count to Five and Say I'm Alive,* Po-

etry Workshop, and *A Poet's Life.* Author of five plays about grandparenting for British Social Action Unit, BBC Radio, 2000.

Adaptations

Many of Rosen's books have been adapted for audio-cassette, read by the author, including *The Bakerloo Flea, You Can't Catch Me, Quick, Let's Get out of Here, Hairy Tales and Nursery Crimes, Don't Put Mustard in the Custard, Sonsense Nongs, The Wicked Tricks of Till Owlyglass, You Wait till I'm Older than You,* and *Centrally Heated Knickers.*

Sidelights

As *School Librarian* critic Margaret Meek proclaimed, anyone "who has seen Michael Rosen on TV, at work with children in school," or reading to children "testifies to his Pied Piper magic with words." Rosen's love of words, his talent for combining them in fresh and exciting ways, and his delightful ability to speak words the way a child would speak them has made him one of the United Kingdom's most popular children's storytellers and poets. It also contributed to his two-year appointment as U.K. child's laureate in 2007. Describing *The Best of Michael Rosen,* a collection of over sixty of the author's best-loved poems, *Booklist* contributor Carolyn Phelan praised Rosen's "excellent descriptions of childhood experiences, sharp insights into people, and . . . humor."

Rosen's love of words is reflected in his enthusiasm for compiling or creating anecdotes, jokes, songs, folk tales, fairytales, vignettes, and nonsense verse, and he shares these collections in books such as *Action Replay, Anecdotal Poems, That'd Be Telling, You're Thinking about Doughnuts,* and *The Deadman Tapes.* His many popular picture-book texts for pre-and beginning readers include *This Is Our House, We're Going on a Bear Hunt, Totally Wonderful Miss Plumberry, Mission Ziffoid,* and *Red Ted and the Lost Things.*

Rosen realized the importance of following his own muse after reading twentieth-century Irish author James Joyce's unconventional novel *Portrait of the Artist as a Young Man* as a teenager. "That book really came home to me," he told an interviewer for *Language Matters.* "It was really quite extraordinary, because for the first time I realized that you could actually play around with different ways of saying something. So, for example, you could do a stream of consciousness or you could write about things that happened to you when you were six, and you could do it in the voice of a child of six. So I became absolutely fascinated by this idea and I started to write a few things of that sort."

In college, Rosen developed an interest in drama, and one of his plays was performed at London's Royal Court theatre. A study of the poems his mother selected for a British Broadcasting Corporation (BBC) program she helped produce inspired him to combine his interests in drama and verse and write his own poems for radio and television programming. Although his poems quickly made the air waves, it took longer for them to find a home on the printed page. As Rosen recalled in *Language Matters,* publishers first rejected his submissions, "saying that 'Children don't like poems written from the child's point of view.'" That dictum would be proved wrong in 1974 when an editor at Deutsch paired Rosen's verse with quirky drawing by illustrator Quentin Blake to create his first children's book, *Mind Your Own Business.*

According to *Times Educational Supplement* critic Edward Blishen, reviewing two other early works by Rosen and Blake, *You Can't Catch Me!* and *Wouldn't You Like to Know,* the author quickly revealed his ability to show "how far from being ordinary are the most ordinary of events." In *You Can't Catch Me!,* for example, one poem finds a father and child teasing one another, another ponders the joy of sailing, and still another focuses on the fear of the dark. *Wouldn't You Like to Know* also focus on relationships, fears, and simple joys. A reviewer for *Junior Bookshelf* deemed *You Can't Catch Me!* a "gorgeous book," while a *Junior Bookshelf* contributor asserted of *Wouldn't You Like to Know* that Rosen's verse gives young teens "comforting insights into the problems that can make adults so troublesome."

The free-verse poems in *Quick, Let's Get out of Here* recall the events, episodes, and special moments of childhood: fights, birthday parties, tricks and schemes, and the like. As Helen Gregory related in *School Library Journal,* here Rosen evokes emotions ranging from the "hysteria of silly joking" to "the agony of breaking a friend's toy." In *You Wait till I'm Older than You* he continues his poetic take on childhood with his characteristic "originality, authenticity, wit and affection," in the opinion of a *Books for Keeps* contributor. Noting that the collection "fully lives up to expectations," *School Librarian* reviewer Diane Broughton also had praise for the "moments of poignancy" provided by a series of verses evoking the poet's own childhood, as well as for Shoo Rayner's "appealing" pen-and-ink illustrations. Another verse collection by Rosen, the twenty-two-page *Tea in the Sugar Bowl, Potato in My Shoe,* prompted *New Statesman* reviewer Michael Glover to dub it "a beautiful piece of work and an exemplary piece of publishing."

Rosen's ability to bring smiles to the faces of his young readers through rhyme also manifests itself in several collections of silly verses and songs. *Freckly Feet and Itchy Knees* lists a human's body parts, describes their owners, and explains their functions, all in rhythmic verse. Before the end of the book, children are encouraged to wiggle and jiggle their own body parts. *Nuts about Nuts* contains another list set to rhyme, but this time the focus is on food: sweets like ice cream, cake, and honey as well as staples like bread, eggs, nuts, and

rice. In the opinion of a *Publishers Weekly* reviewer, *Freckly Feet and Itchy Knees* is "always lighthearted" and "ideal for reading aloud."

The English alphabet is humorously reworked in *Michael Rosen's ABC,* as easily recognizable characters like Goldilocks, Rudolph the Red-nosed Reindeer, Humpty Dumpty, King Kong, and actor Charlie Chaplin team with well-known objects beginning with various letters of the alphabet to parade before readers in what *School Library Journal* contributor Tania Elias characterized as "tongue-twisting" fashion. Describing the text as a "glorious glut of alliterative nonsense," Jill Bennett noted in her *Books for Keeps* review of *Michael Rosen's ABC* that the collection is "peppered with wondrous words."

The works in *Sonsense Nongs*—eight ballads, parodies, and silly songs written by Rosen with contributions from children—are meant to be sung out loud. According to a *Junior Bookshelf* reviewer, this whimsical work will likely help children gain a "deeper understanding of language as well as much fun and laughter." Children can also sing the words to *Little Rabbit Foo Foo,* Rosen's rhyming adaptation of a children's finger-play song in which a little rabbit bops his helpless victims on the head. Judith Sharman testified in *Books for Keeps* that her son found *Little Rabbit Foo Foo* so charming that she had to "sneak" the book away from him while he slept in order to write her review of it.

Many children will recognize the story in Rosen's multi-award-winning picture book *We're Going on a Bear Hunt,* which is based on a traditional British children's song and also inspired the sequel *The Bear in the Cave.* Eager to find a bear, a young family wades through mud, water, grass, and snow, braving the dangers of a forest, a river, and a cave. As they meet each obstacle, they make their way through it all with joyful chants. When the family finally finds the bear, the creature scares them so much that they turn around and hurry back through each obstacle. The tables turn in *The Bear in the Cave* as the brown bear decides to leave its forest habitat and explore the city, but the noises, strange "creatures", and tall buildings ultimately make it hurry back home. As Elizabeth S. Watson commented in her *Horn Book* review of *We're Going on a Bear Hunt,* Rosen's text has "a driving rhythm" and "new sounds" that give the familiar tale added "sparkle." Reviewing the sequel, London *Guardian* critic Diane Samuels concluded that Adrian Reynolds' watercolor illustrations for *The Bear in the Cave* feature a "robust vigour that matches the rhythmic text perfectly."

Reynolds and Rosen have paired up on several other stories featuring a bear and his friends, among them *Bear's Day Out* and *Bear Flies High.* A bear also stars in *Red Ted and the Lost Things,* a picture book featuring comic-strip speech balloons and artwork by Joel Stewart. In this story, poor Red Ted, the favored toy bear of a girl named Stevie, is left on the commuter train and winds up in the station's lost-property room, where it meets and befriends the curmudgeonly Crocodile. Together with a white cat that can track down Stevie due to her love of cheese, the two toys search the grey, rainy city, where a happy reunion is their ultimate reward. "Readers will ponder the tangents and possibilities of this funny-sad story long after they put it down," maintained a *Publishers Weekly* contributor, while *School Librarian* critic Peter Andrews concluded that *Red Ted and the Lost Things* treats readers to "a thoughtfully presented story making its points very subtly." According to Barbara Elleman in *School Library Journal,* "Rosen's quirky combination of characters is matched by Stewart's muted colors and [the] deliberately hazy backgrounds" in his sequential cartoon panels, "which nicely spotlight" Red Ted and his unique companions.

Rosen shows his mastery of prose in *This Is Our House,* in which a cardboard box takes on a new life and a group of playground friends learns an important lesson about acceptance. Other prose stories include *Rover* and its sequel, *Howler.* Featuring entertaining art by Neal Layton, these two stories overturn the usual perspective on children and their pets as the family dog narrates its account of life with his pet humans. In *Rover* we see the customs of dog owners Rex and Cindy through doggy eyes: at the seashore they run around and then lie down and play dead, while at home they stare for hours at a loud box rather than playing with toys. Rover is concerned when Cindy's tummy grows visibly larger in *Howler,* but when she leaves and then returns home several days later with a small, loud, prunelike creature the dog quickly names Howler, the pup goes from concerned to dismayed. "Rosen has an instinctive feel for the way children confront one another, ponder, negotiate and form alliances," concluded a *Publishers Weekly* contributor in reviewing *This Is Our House,* the critic adding that "every word" of Rosen's text "rings true." *Magpies* critic Barbara James praised *Rover* as a "bright and breezy" tale enlivened by "the leap of imagination of seeing humans from a dog's point of view," and a *Kirkus Reviews* writer dubbed *Howler* a "lively, equally droll follow-up."

Rosen spins an offbeat story in *Mission Ziffoid,* as a boy builds a faulty spaceship and winds up in the center of a football game played by small, greenish alien beings . . . at least, according to the ship-builder's little brother. Praising the text as "laconic and hilarious," a *Magpies* reviewer noted that the tale's "imaginative flights of fancy" result from Rosen's care in listening "to young children telling cumulative yarns." Calling *Mission Ziffoid* "a natural readaloud with a generous dose of kid-pleasing hilarity," Janice M. Del Negro added in her review for the *Bulletin of the Center for Children's Books* that "the text zips right along," fueled by Arthur Robins' over-the-top, neon-colored illustrations.

Whimsy is also at the core of *I'm Number One,* a picture book illustrated by Bob Graham. When a child leaves his room for the day, his toy soldier, A-One, de-

clares himself commander of several other toys after he ask for their help in turning his windup key. A-One then plays the role of drill sergeant to a doll and two stuffed animals. When his brash bossiness is answered with a wink, nod, and smile from the other toys, A-One learns that he should treat his fellow toys with the same tolerance that they now extend to him. Praising *I'm Number One* as a "simple, affecting story," Andrew Medlar added in *Booklist* that Graham's ink-and-watercolor illustrations "are filled with expressive characters and . . . whimsical details." A "light tale about dealing with bullies," *I'm Number One* will encourage young readers to "easily find real-life parallels," according to a *Publishers Weekly* critic.

While the majority of Rosen's stories are optimistic and upbeat, *Michael Rosen's Sad Book* and *Michael Rosen's Big Book of Bad Things* explore a different part of the emotional spectrum. Featuring a spare text and scribbly pen-and-wash illustrations by Blake, *Michael Rosen's Sad Book* was inspired by the author's depression following the death of his teenaged son, Eddie. In the free verse poems in *Michael Rosen's Big Book of Bad Things* the author also touches on Eddie's loss as well as his memories of the many youthful missteps and indiscre-

Rosen's ability to capture, in few words, a range of emotions pairs with Quentin Blake's line art in the highly acclaimed **Michael Rosen's Sad Book.** (Illustration © 2004 by Quentin Blake. All rights reserved. Reproduced by permission of the publisher Candlewick Press, Inc., Cambridge, MA on behalf of Walker Books Ltd., London.)

tions that seemed dire at the time but proved less consequential through the eyes of loving parents. Discussing the mature focus of *Michael Rosen's Sad Book, Booklist* critic Ilene Cooper noted: "Sadness is part of the human condition. Children know this as well as adults and perhaps feel it even more keenly since they haven't had as much time to develop defenses." "Rosen's poetic revelation of his conflicting emotions and coping strategies will resonate with—and help—anyone mourning a loss or dealing with an indefinable sadness," asserted a *Publishers Weekly* of the work, while *Horn Book* reviewer Joanna Rudge Long described Rosen and Blake's collaboration as "a beautiful, solacing book." In a London *Sunday Times* review of *Michael Rosen's Big Book of Bad Things,* Nicolette Jones concluded that the work "proves its author's talent for saying much in the simplest way" and "gives permission for imagination, silliness and experimentation."

Rosen's treatment of folktales is tempered by his respect for their origins. Described by *School Library Journal* contributor Lee Bock as "lively" and "bright," *How Giraffe Got Such a Long Neck . . . and Why Rhino Is So Grumpy* is his version of an Eastern and Southern African *porquoi* tale that tells how Giraffe—originally a small beast—and the much larger Rhino implore Man to help them survive the drought. Although Man instructs Giraffe and Rhino to visit him the next day for help reaching the leaves high in the trees, Rhino does not arrive on time, and Giraffe eats his portion of Man's remedy as well as her own. As a result, Giraffe's neck grows long. Rhino, who feels cheated, only grows grumpy.

The Golem of Old Prague collects stories concerning the legendary Rabbi Loeb of Prague, including how the rabbi creates a golem—a huge, strong, but mindless creature—out of clay and gives him life. With the help of the powerful and loyal golem, Rabbi Loeb ensures the Jewish community's survival when they are persecuted by the monk Thaddeus. Writing in *Books for Your Children,* S. Williams concluded that *The Golem of Old Prague* "gives insight to Jewish thinking, customs, and way of life" in sixteenth-century Prague.

South and North, East and West: The Oxfam Anthology of Children's Stories, which Rosen edited, is a collection of twenty-five stories that includes tales from Cyprus, Korea, the Dominican Republic, Bangladesh, China, Jamaica, Malta, Vietnam, and England. Betsy Hearne, writing in the *Bulletin of the Center for Children's Books,* found these retellings to be "fresh and colloquial." The royalties from *South and North, East and West* benefit Oxfam, the international organization that establishes self-help development programs in countries disrupted by natural or man-made disasters.

Unlike his picture books, Rosen's books for older children and teenagers frequently address serious issues. His original poetry collection *When Did You Last Wash Your Feet?,* for example, deals with topics from racism to terminal illness. *Mind the Gap,* a collection of poems

Rosen teams up with artist Joel Stewart to follow the adventures of a lost teddy bear as it searches for its owner in **Red Ted and the Lost Things.** (Illustration copyright © 2010 by Joel Stewart. Reproduced by permission of Candlewick Press, Somerville, NA on behalf of Walker Books, London.)

Sue Rogers described in *School Librarian* as "brilliant," touches on "comic, sad," and "controversial" themes all at once and includes one poem that recalls the past as the narrator's mother is dying. *Books for Keeps* critic Adrian Jackson advised librarians to buy many copies in *Mind the Gap,* predicting that "teenagers will love it." In *Culture Shock,* a collection of poems Rosen selected from around the world, racism, sexism, love, and hate are also addressed.

Like Rosen's more serious poetry, several of his novels contain serious undertones. *The Deadman Tapes* presents a series of stories within a larger plot. When Paul Deadman plays some tapes he has found in the attic of his new house, he is introduced to the voices and stories of eight troubled teens. With occasional interruptions from Paul, these stories make up the novel's text. The short novel *You're Thinking about Doughnuts* also contains several stories, in this case told from strange perspectives. Frank, who is just eight years old, must wait in the dark halls of the museum where his mother works every Friday night. One night, the exhibits—including a skeleton, a space suit, several Greek statues, and a stuffed tiger—come alive. As these exhibits tell Frank about their lives before they were taken to the

quiet museum, Rosen also injects questions about the "honesty and integrity of an institutional building like a museum," according to *School Librarian* contributor Tom Lewis.

As with his poetry, Rosen's prose for older children often develops around episodes and anecdotes, calls upon his performer's love of dialogue, and insightfully expresses the perspectives of his protagonist. In one example, the story collection *Nasty!* is narrated by a talkative Cockney cleaning woman known as the Bakerloo Flea Woman. She tells the story of the giant Bakerloo flea, recalls how wasps plagued the residents of London's East End one winter, and remembers how they dealt with the mice that invaded their homes. Rosen's love of drama, as well as his appreciation for literature, are also apparent in his biographies of two literary giants. Featuring highly detailed paintings by Robert Ingpen, both *Shakespeare: His Work and His World* and *Dickens: His Work and His World* put highly influential English writers into a cultural context that makes each man come alive for readers while also retelling several of his major works. Reviewing *Dickens* in *Booklist,* Cooper called Rosen's retelling of the nineteenth-century novelist's life "a tale as gripping as any of his [Charles Dickens'] stories," and a *Kirkus Reviews* writer dubbed *Shakespeare* "beautiful and engaging."

In addition to his original work, Rosen has also edited several volumes of poetry for young listeners. *Walking the Bridge of Your Nose* includes traditional and composed poems that "play with words, their sounds and their spellings, [and] their punctuations," according to *Junior Bookshelf* contributor Marcus Crouch. Readers will relish the puns, tongue twisters, chants, and quips Rosen serves up while "demonstrating the peculiarities and foolishness of the English language," Judith Constantinides protected her *School Library Journal* review of the work. Other edited anthologies include the 250-verse *The Kingfisher Book of Children's Poetry,* the multi-volume "Poems Are" books, and *Classic Poetry: An Illustrated Collection,* the last in which Rosen couples brief biographies of noted English-language poets from Shakespeare to Langston Hughes with selections from their works. Containing over eighty poems, *Classic Poetry* "reaffirms the English poetry canon familiar to students throughout the English-speaking world since the 1940s," explained a *Magpies* contributor of the historic overview.

Rosen enjoys sharing the techniques that have made him a successful children's writer. He has published books on writing such as *Did I Hear You Write?,* and also visits schools and libraries. He revealed one of the secrets of his unique style to *Language Matters:* "What I try to do in my mind is to go back and write about my feelings when I was ten. . . . I write about my experience using the voice of a ten year old. I write in that voice, using what I know as a performer will work, knowing, that is, what children can take off a page." Discussing his work as children's laureate, Rosen told *Bookseller* interviewer Caroline Horn: "I have been do-

***Robert Igpen contributes his artistic talents to Rosen's detailed profile of one of the most popular English writers of all time in* Shakespeare: His Work and His World.** (Illustration © 2001 by Robert Ingpen. All rights reserved. Reproduced by permission of the publisher Candlewick Press, Inc., Cambridge, MA on behalf of Walker Books Ltd., London.)

ing performance poetry for 30 years and I know how children respond to it. You look at their faces when you start and it's like an infection—it spreads across their face, through their bodies, around them. They move, they light up. Wouldn't it be lovely to see more and more of that?"

Biographical and Critical Sources

BOOKS

Children's Literature Review, Volume 45, Gale (Detroit, MI), 1997, pp. 127-152.

Language Matters, Centre for Language in Primary Education (London, England), 1983.

Nettell, Stephanie, editor, *Meet the Authors,* Scholastic (New York, NY), 1994.

Powling, Chris, *What It's Like to Be Michael Rosen,* Ginn (Oxford, England), 1990.

St. James Guide to Children's Writers, 5th edition, St. James Press (Detroit, MI), 1999.

Styles, Morag, and Helen Cook, editors, *There's a Poet behind You,* A. & C. Black (London, England), 1988.

PERIODICALS

Booklist, December 1, 1993, Elizabeth Bush, review of *How Giraffe Got Such a Long Neck . . . and Why Rhino Is So Grumpy,* p. 695; December 15, 1993, Julie Corsaro, review of *Moving,* p. 766; January 1, 1994, Carolyn Phelan, review of *Poems for the Very Young,* p. 821; April 15, 1995, Karen Hutt, review of *Crow and Hawk: A Traditional Pueblo Indian Story,* p. 1503; February 1, 1996, Carolyn Phelan, review of *The Best of Michael Rosen,* p. 929; November 1, 1996, Carolyn Phelan, review of *This Is Our House,* p. 510; June 1, 1997, Kathleen Squires, review of *Michael Rosen's ABC,* p. 1712; January 1, 1999, Carolyn Phelan, review of *Classic Poetry: An Illustrated Collection,* p. 862; July, 1999, Stephanie Zvirin, review of *Rover,* p. 1953; November 1, 2001, John Peters, review of *Shakespeare: His Work and His World,* p. 477; December 1, 2003, Hazel Rochman, review of *Shakespeare's Romeo and Juliet,* p. 659; May 15, 2005, Ilene Cooper, review of *Michael Rosen's Sad Book,* p. 1658; September 15, 2005, Ilene Cooper, review of *Dickens: His Work and His World,* p. 62; August 1, 2006, Ilene Cooper, review of *Totally Wonderful Miss Plumberry,* p. 96; December 15, 2009, Ilene Cooper, review of *Bear Flies High,* p. 43, and Andrew Medlar, review of *I'm Number One,* p. 46.

Bookseller, June 15, 2007, Caroline Horn, interview with Rosen.

Books for Keeps, May, 1992, Judith Sharman, review of *Little Rabbit Foo Foo,* p. 11; September, 1992, Adrian Jackson, review of *Mind the Gap,* p. 13; March, 1996, Jill Bennett, review of *Michael Rosen's ABC,* p. 28; January, 1997, review of *You Wait till I'm Older than You,* p. 25; September, 1999, review of *Rover,* p. 21.

Books for Your Children, spring, 1991, S. Williams, review of *The Golem of Old Prague,* p. 24.

Bulletin of the Center for Children's Books, December, 1992, Betsy Hearne, review of *South and North, East and West,* pp. 121-122; June, 1999, Deborah Stevenson, review of *Rover,* p. 363; November, 1999, Janice M. Del Negro, review of *Mission Ziffoid,* pp. 104-105; April, 2005, Deborah Stevenson, review of *Michael Rosen's Sad Book,* p. 355; March, 2006, April Spisak, review of *Dickens,* p. 325.

Horn Book, June, 1984, Anne A. Flowers, review of *Quick, Let's Get out of Here,* p. 345; December, 1989, Elizabeth S. Watson, review of *We're Going on a Bear Hunt,* p. 765; September-October, 1993, Maeve Visser Knoth, review of *How Giraffe Got Such a Long Neck . . . and Why Rhino Is So Grumpy,* p. 611; July-August, 1996, Margaret A. Bush, review of *This Is Our House,* p. 454; May-June, 2005, Joanna Rudge Long, review of *Michael Rosen's Sad Book,* p. 313.

Guardian (London, England), October 20, 2007, Diane Samuels, review of *The Bear in the Cave,* p. 20; July 21, 2009, Laura Barnett, interview with Rosen, p. 23.

Junior Bookshelf, February, 1982, review of *You Can't Catch Me!,* p. 22; October, 1992, review of *Sonsense Nongs,* p. 201; June, 1993, review of *Nuts about Nuts,* p. 100; June, 1995, pp. 93-94; April, 1996, Marcus Crouch, review of *Walking the Bridge of Your Nose,* p. 71; October, 1996, review of *You Can't Catch Me,* p. 194; December, 1996, review of *Wouldn't You Like to Know,* pp. 259-260.

Kirkus Reviews, June 1, 1996, review of *This Is Our House,* p. 829; October 15, 2001, review of *Shakespeare,* p. 149; November 15, 2003, review of *Shakespeare's Romeo and Juliet,* p. 1363; April 15, 2004, review of *Howler,* p. 400; January 15, 2005, review of *Michael Rosen's Sad Book,* p. 125; April 1, 2005, review of *Oww!: A Wriggly Piglet with a Prickly Problem,* p. 423; September 15, 2005, review of *Dickens,* p. 1033; August 15, 2006, review of *Totally Wonderful Miss Plumberry,* p. 850; October 15, 2009, review of *Red Ted and the Lost Things*; November 1, 2009, review of *I'm Number One.*

Kliatt, January, 2007, Peter Neissa, review of *Shakespeare,* p. 35.

Magpies, March, 1996, review of *Crow and Hawk,* p. 29; November, 1998, review of *Classic Poetry,* pp. 18-19; July, 1999, review of *Mission Ziffoid,* pp. 26-27; November, 1999, review of *Rover,* p. 28.

New Statesman, December 5, 1997, review of *Tea in the Sugar Bowl, Potato in My Shoe,* p. 63.

Observer (London, England), May 30, 1999, review of *The Kingfisher Book of Children's Poetry,* p. 13.

Publishers Weekly, June 30, 1989, review of *We're Going on a Bear Hunt,* p. 104; June 8, 1990, review of *Freckly Feet and Itchy Knees,* p. 54; September 21, 1992, review of *South and North, East and West,* p. 94; July 26, 1993, review of *How Giraffe Got Such a Long Neck . . . and Why Rhino Is So Grumpy,* p. 71; February 27, 1995, review of *Crow and Hawk,* p. 102; October 16, 1995, review of *Walking the Bridge of Your Nose,* p. 61; December 18, 1995, review of *The Best of Michael Rosen,* p. 54; June 24, 1996, review of *This Is Our House,* p. 58; March 3, 1997, review of *Michael Rosen's ABC,* p. 77; December 14, 1998, review of *Classic Poetry,* p. 77; April 26, 1999, review of *Walking the Bridge of Your Nose,* p. 85; June 7,

1999, review of *Rover,* p. 83; December 3, 2001, review of *Shakespeare,* p. 61; April 4, 2005, review of *Michael Rosen's Sad Book,* p. 58; October 1, 2007, review of *Bear's Day Out,* p. 56; November 16, 2009, review of *Red Ted and the Lost Things,* p. 53; November 30, 2009, review of *I'm Number One,* p. 47.

School Librarian, March, 1985, Colin Walter, review of *Hairy Tales and Nursery Crimes,* p. 40; May, 1988, Tom Lewis, review of *You're Thinking about Doughnuts,* p. 59; August, 1989, Margaret Meek, review of *Did I Hear You Write?,* p. 128; November, 1992, Sue Rogers, review of *Mind the Gap,* p. 156; February, 1997, Diane Broughton, review of *You Wait till I'm Older than You!,* p. 43; winter, 1999, Anne Rowe, review of *Lunch Boxes Don't Fly,* p. 208; spring, 2010, Peter Andrews, review of *Red Ted and the Lost Things,* p. 32.

School Library Journal, May, 1982, review of *You Can't Catch Me,* p. 56; November, 1983, Margaret L. Chatham, review of *A Cat and Mouse Story,* p. 69; October, 1984, Helen Gregory, review of *Quick, Let's Get out of Here,* p. 161; January, 1987, Barbara McGinn, review of *Don't Put Mustard in the Custard,* p. 78; May, 1989, Lucy Young Clem, review of *Down at the Doctor's,* p. 101; February, 1991, JoAnn Rees, review of *Little Rabbit Foo Foo,* p. 74; December, 1992, Karen Wehner, review of *Itsy-Bitsy Beasties,* p. 127; October, 1993, Lee Bock, review of *How Giraffe Got Such a Long Neck . . . and Why Rhino Is So Grumpy,* pp. 121-22; March, 1994, Carolyn Noah, review of *Moving,* p. 208; July, 1995, Lisa Dennis, review of *Crow and Hawk,* p. 74; January, 1996, Judith Constantinides, review of *Walking the Bridge of Your Nose,* p. 105; July, 1996, Steven Engelfried, review of *This Is Our House,* p. 71; March, 1997, Tana Elias, review of *Michael Rosen's ABC,* p. 165; June, 1999, Carol Ann Wilson, review of *Rover,* p. 106; December, 1999, Sally R. Dow, review of *Mission Ziffoid,* p. 112; November, 2001, Patricia Lothrop-Green, review of *Shakespeare,* p. 184; February, 2004, Nancy Menaldi-Scanlan, review of *Shakespeare's Romeo and Juliet,* p. 168; August, 2004, Wendy Woodfill, review of *Howler,* p. 93; March, 2005, Maryann H. Owen, review of *Michael Rosen's Sad Book,* p. 218; November, 2005, Nancy Menaldi-Scanlan, review of *Dickens,* p. 170; September, 2006, Piper L. Nyman, review of *Totally Wonderful Miss Plumberry,* p. 183; October, 2007, Susan Moorhead, review of *Bear's Day Out,* p. 127; November, 2009, Barbara Elleman, review of *Red Ted and the Lost Things,* p. 86; February, 2010, James K. Irwin, review of *Bear Flies High,* p. 93.

Sunday Times (London, England), August 29, 2010, Nicolette Jones, review of *Michael Rosen's Big Book of Bad Things,* p. 50.

Times Educational Supplement, November 20, 1981, Edward Blishen, "Nonsense Not Nauseous," p. 34; October 31, 1997, review of *Tea in the Sugarbowl, Potato in My Shoe,* p. 244; October 19, 2001, John Mole, review of *Shakespeare,* p. B22.

Times Higher Education Supplement, May 6, 1994, Colwyn Williamson, review of *The Chatto Book of Dissent,* p. 28.

Times Literary Supplement, March 8, 1985, George Szirtes, review of *Hairy Tales and Nursery Crimes,* p. 270;

April 7, 1989, Carol Ann Duffy, review of *Didn't I Hear You Write?,* p. 381; November 24, 1989, D.J. Enright, review of *Rude Rhymes,* p. 1310.

Voice of Youth Advocates, August, 2004, review of *Shakespeare's Romeo and Juliet,* p. 241; February, 2007, Jonatha Masters, review of *Shakespeare,* p. 556.

ONLINE

Michel Rosen Home Page, http://www.michaelrosen.co.uk (April 15, 2011).

WriteWords Writers' Community Web site, http://www.writewords.org/ (February, 2006), interview with Rosen.*

*   *   *

ROSTOKER-GRUBER, Karen

Personal

Born in Brooklyn, NY.

Addresses

Home—Branchburg, NJ. *E-mail*—Karen@karenrostoker-gruber.com.

Career

Author and puppeteer. Member, Rutgers University Council on Children's Literature. Presenter at schools.

Karen Rostoker-Gruber (Reproduced by permission.)

Member

Authors Guild, Society of Children's Book Writers and Illustrators.

Awards, Honors

Works included in New Jersey Bureau of Education and Research's "Best of the Year" list; work included on state reading lists.

Writings

FOR CHILDREN

Food Fright!: A Mouthwatering Novelty Book, illustrated by Sheila Aldridge, Price Stern Sloan (New York, NY), 2003.

Rooster Can't Cock-a-doodle-doo, illustrated by Paul Rátz de Tagyos, Dial Books for Young Readers (New York, NY), 2004.

Bandit, illustrated by Vincent Nguyen, Marshall Cavendish (New York, NY), 2008.

Bandit's Surprise, illustrated by Vincent Nguyen, Marshall Cavendish Children (Tarrytown, NY), 2010.

Tea Time (board book), illustrated by Viviana Garofoli, Marshall Cavendish (New York, NY), 2010.

Ferret Fun, illustrated by Paul Rátz de Tagyos, Marshall Cavendish Children's (New York, NY), 2011.

OTHER

the Unofficial College Survival Guide, Great Quotations, 1992.

Remote Controls Are Better than Women Because . . . ; or, What Men Would Say If They Dared, Longstreet Press (Atlanta, GA), 1993.

Telephones Are Better than Men Because . . . ; or, What Women Would Say If They Dared, illustrated by Don Smith, Longstreet Press (Atlanta, GA), 1996.

If Men Had Babies . . . , C.C.C. Publications, 2001.

Sidelights

New Jersey-based author Karen Rostoker-Gruber began her writing career as a humorist who also wrote children's books. She began to focus increasingly on the children's market at the suggestion of publishers, who found her upbeat stories and use of puns and other wordplay to be a perfect fit for the story-hour crowd. In addition to picture books such as *Rooster Can't Cock-a-doodle-doo,* which *School Library Journal* critic Carolyn Janssen described as "packed with amusing puns," Rostoker-Gruber has created the stories *Bandit* and *Fer-*

Karen Rostoker-Gruber's story **Bandit's Surprise** *features artwork by Vincent Nguyen that captures the competition between a family cat and a competitive new kitten.* (Illustration copyright © 2010 by Vincent Nguyen. Reproduced by permission of Marshall Cavendish Children.)

ret Fun. She also entertains children as a ventriloquist, appearing before young audiences together with her puppet, Maria.

Rostoker-Gruber was born in Brooklyn, New York, but moved to New Jersey at age eight. She published her first book, *The Unofficial College Survival Guide,* in 1992, and followed that with *Remote Controls Are Better than Women Because . . . ; or, What Men Would Say If They Dared.* She has continued her focus on male-female relationships in *Telephones Are Better than Men Because . . . ; or, What Women Would Say If They Dared,* and the provocatively-titled *If Men Had Babies . . . ,* in addition to shifting her central focus to children. A hard-working writer, Rostoker-Gruber has dozens of manuscripts in play at any one time, most of which are geared for children. "I write on two levels," the author explained to *My Central Jersey Online* contributor Dominic Serrao. "The first is for the children, but the books that I write need to make the parents laugh as well. If you're going to read the same story over and over again to your child, that book better be laugh-out-loud funny."

Illustrated by Vincent Nguyen, both *Bandit* and *Bandit's Surprise* focus on a spunky orange tiger kitten that lives with a little girl named Michelle. In *Bandit* the kitty finds its home in an uproar as the family prepares to move to a new home, and even when its toys are scattered all around the new house Bandit views its old house as home. *Bandit's Surprise* finds the kitten forced to share Michelle's affections with a new kitten, the insufferable Mitzy, whose cuteness and constant antics prompt the jealous Bandit to escape through an open window and run away from home. In *Booklist* Ilene Cooper praised the "witty" story in *Bandit,* while in *School Library Journal* Kara Schaff Dean asserted that Rostoker-Gruber's "fresh" approach to a familiar childhood trauma—a family move—"will resonate with children who have moved themselves." Praising the "well-paced story" in *Bandit's Surprise,* Gillian Engberg added of Bandit's second outing that Nguyen's "polished, simply shaded drawings" "add to the book's read-aloud appeal." In her *School Library Journal* of *Bandit's Surprise,* Carrie Rogers-Whitehead commended Rostoker-Gruber's ability to craft "laugh-out-loud dialogue," adding that the artist's "clever" illustrations feature cat characters with "humanlike expressions [that] give feeling to the text."

Biographical and Critical Sources

PERIODICALS

Booklist, May 15, 2008, Ilene Cooper, review of *Bandit,* p. 46; April 1, 2010, Gillian Engberg, review of *Bandit's Surprise,* p. 45.

Horn Book, July-August, 2004, Kitty Flynn, review of *Rooster Can't Cock-a-doodle-doo,* p. 441.

Kirkus Reviews, May 1, 2004, review of *Rooster Can't Cock-a-doodle-doo,* p. 447; February 15, 2010, review of *Bandit's Surprise.*

Record (Bergen County, NJ), May 9, 2010, Mike Kerwick, "Kids Author Finds Hard-Won Success," p. F7.

School Library Journal, July, 2004, Carolyn Janssen, review of *Rooster Can't Cock-a-doodle-doo,* p. 88; May, 2008, review of *Bandit,* p. 107; March, 2010, Carrie Rogers-Whitehead, review of *Bandit's Surprise,* p. 130.

ONLINE

Karen Rostoker-Gruber Home Page, http://www.karen rostoker-gruber.com (April 24, 2011).

MyCentralJersey.com, http://www.mycentraljersey.com/ (August 21, 2008), Dominic Serrao, profile of Rostoker-Gruber.*

*   *   *

SARTELL, Debra

Personal

Born in Clarkston, MI; father a firefighter; married; husband's name Darrell; children: Cole, Stella. *Education:* Attended college. *Hobbies and other interests:* Photography.

Addresses

Home—Corte Madera, CA. *E-mail*—author@debrasartell.com.

Career

Writer and talent coordinator. Booked shows for stand-up comedians for sixteen years in CA; actor with Haight Ashbury Theatre Company.

Member

Society of Children's Book Writers and Illustrators.

Writings

Time for Bed, Baby Ted, illustrated by Kay Chorao, Holiday House (New York, NY), 2010.

Sidelights

A former talent coordinator who spent more than a decade booking shows for stand-up comedians, Debra Sartell has also created *Time for Bed, Baby Ted,* a picture book inspired by a humorous incident involving her husband, Darrell, and her son, Cole. In her story Sartell uses a rhyming narrative to describe the efforts of her young protagonist to delay his bedtime. After Fa-

ther finishes reading a bedtime story, Ted refuses to crawl under the covers, instead devising a clever guessing game meant to divert his dad's attention. As Ted nibbles on a snack, brushes his teeth, and uses the potty, he pretends to be one of the animals from the book they just finished, challenging his ever-so-patient dad to identify the various creatures. "The interactive concept is a fun idea," wrote *School Library Journal* critic Martha Simpson, and a contributor to *Kirkus Reviews* observed that "Sartell keeps the structured, rhyming text predictable and satisfying for young ears." In *Booklist*, Randall Enos offered parents a tongue-in-cheek warning, commenting that "reading this at bedtime could lengthen your nightly routine."

Discussing the origins of *Time for Bed, Baby Ted*, on her home page, Sartell explained that she received a camera after the birth of Cole, her first child, and quickly developed an interest in photography, often documenting her son's exploits on film. "*Time for Bed, Baby Ted* sprang from one of those frozen snapshot moments in parenting when one can only laugh while looking back on it," as she recalled. "The photograph captures my husband trying to put our son Cole to bed. In the end, it was Cole tucking his dad into bed."

Biographical and Critical Sources

PERIODICALS

Booklist, January 1, 2010, Randall Enos, review of *Time for Bed, Baby Ted*, p. 100.
Bulletin of the Center for Children's Books, March, 2010, Hope Morrison, review of *Time for Bed, Baby Ted*, p. 303.

Debra Sartell's family-centered nighttime story* Time for Bed, Baby Ted *is enriched by Kay Chorao's evocative ink-and-watercolor art. (Illustration copyright © 2010 by Kay Chorao. Reproduced by permission of Holiday House.)

Kirkus Reviews, February 15, 2010, review of *Time for Bed, Baby Ted*.
School Library Journal, March, 2010, Martha Simpson, review of *Time for Bed, Baby Ted*, p. 130.

ONLINE

Debra Sartell Home Page, http://www.debrasartell.com (April 15, 2011).
Debra Sartell Web log, http://debrasartell.blogspot.com (April 15, 2011).*

*　　　*　　　*

SCHRÖDER, Monika 1965-

Personal

Born 1965, in Germany; married; husband a teacher. *Education:* Ruhr University, M.A. (history and social studies). *Hobbies and other interests:* Travel, reading, baking, watching films.

Addresses

Home—New Delhi, India. *E-mail*—monika.schroeder. author@gmail.com.

Career

Librarian, educator, and author. German Parliament, former research assistant; teacher of elementary-grade students in Germany, Egypt, Chile, and Oman; American Embassy School, New Delhi, India, elementary-school librarian, beginning 2002.

Awards, Honors

Notable Social Studies Trade Book for Young People selection, National Council on the Social Studies, and Best Children's Book designation, Bank Street College, both 2010, both for *Saraswati's Way*.

Writings

MIDDLE-GRADE NOVELS

The Dog in the Wood, Front Street (Honesdale, PA), 2009.
Saraswati's Way, Farrar, Straus & Giroux (New York, NY), 2010.
My Brother's Shadow, Farrar, Straus & Giroux (New York, NY), 2011.

Contributor of book reviews and interviews to *Booklist* and *School Library Journal*; contributor of articles to *BookLinks*.

Sidelights

German-born teacher and writer Monika Schröder based her first novel, *The Dog in the Wood*, on her father's experiences as a boy growing up in post-World War II

Monika Schröder (Photograph by Tim Steadman. Reproduced by permission.)

Germany. A student of history, Schröder worked in government for several years, then became a teacher. After marrying a fellow educator, she and her husband taught in several countries, including Egypt, Chile, and Oman. She began writing in 2005, while working as the elementary-school librarian at the American Embassy School in New Delhi, India. Schröder's other novels include *Saraswati's Way,* which is set in India, and *My Brother's Shadow,* which takes readers back in time to war-torn Berlin in the fall of 1918.

Eleven-year-old Fritz, who readers meet in *The Dog in the Wood,* lives on a family farm in eastern Germany, together with his fraternal grandparents, mother, and older sister. It is 1945 and news of German Chancellor Adolf Hitler's death means that World War II has ended. Fritz's grandparents, loyal Nazis, commit suicide when they hear that their region has fallen under the control of Soviet-run Russia. Soon Soviet officers oust the remaining family members from their home and locals are threatened by the brutality of armed soldiers hardened by war. Ultimately the land reform commission divides up the family's farm among local communist supporters, leaving Fritz homeless and on his own. As the boy attempts to make sense of the seismic changes in not only his own life but also the life of his country,

he finds guidance from surprising places, making *The Dog in the Wood* "a powerful, inspiring read," according to *School Library Journal* contributor Bethany Isaacson. A "poignant look at the effects of war and propaganda," Schröder's first novel "resonates with candor and eloquence," according to a *Kirkus Reviews* writer, while in *Booklist* Hazel Rochman asserted that *The Dog in the Wood* presents "an excellent, authentic portrait of children in war" in a story that "will grab readers."

Reflecting Schröder's familiarity with the lives of East Indian culture, *Saraswati's Way* also focuses on a pre-teen boy confronted by challenges. Akash is twelve years old and lives in a rural town in India, where he dreams of pursuing his fascination for mathematics in college. When his father, a farmer, dies, the boy is sent to work at a quarry. Akash quickly realizes that his wages will never be enough to release his family from their debt to local moneylenders. Going against the fatalism that he has been taught as a Hindu, he leaves home and travels to New Delhi, hoping to make his dream come through. He is forced to live on the street, learning to survive from other homeless children. Fortunately, Akash has a dream, and this enables him to spot opportunities while others do not. In her story, Schröder features "details about life on the streets of Delhi," wrote a *Publishers Weekly* critic, and Marilyn Taniguchi noted in *School Library Journal* that the author "adds interest with references to Vedic math and Hindu gods." For *Booklist* critic Gillian Engberg, *Saraswati's Way* presents middle-grade readers with "a view, sobering and inspiring, of remarkably resilient young people surviving poverty without losing themselves."

Biographical and Critical Sources

PERIODICALS

Booklist, October 15, 2009, Hazel Rochman, review of *The Dog in the Wood,* p. 59; January 1, 2010, Monika Schröder, "After the Russians Came," p. S14; December 1, 2010, Gillian Engberg, review of *Saraswati's Way,* p. 61.

Bulletin of the Center for Children's Books, January, 2010, Elizabeth Bush, review of *The Dog in the Wood,* p. 216; December, 2010, Hope Morrison, review of *Saraswati's Way,* p. 205.

Kirkus Reviews, October 15, 2009, review of *The Dog in the Wood.*

Publishers Weekly, November 16, 2009, review of *The Dog in the Wood,* p. 54; October 18, 2010, review of *Saraswati's Way,* p. 49.

School Library Journal, January, 2010, Bethany Isaacson, review of *The Dog in the Wood,* p. 113; December, 2010, Marilyn Taniguchi, review of *Saraswati's Way,* p. 126.

ONLINE

Macmillan Web site, http://us.macmillan.com/ (April 20, 2011), "Monika Schröder."

Monika Schröder Home Page, http://www.monika
schroeder.com (February 24, 2011).

*   *   *

SELZER, Adam 1980-
(S.J. Adams)

Personal

Born 1980, in Des Moines, IA.

Addresses

Home—Chicago, IL. *E-mail*—adam.selzer@gmail.com.

Career

Writer, musician, historian, and tour guide. Chicago
Unbelievable (tour company), Chicago, IL, founder,
tour guide, and ghost investigator. Performer with Adam
Selzer and His Revolving-Door All-Stars. Presenter at
schools.

Writings

How to Get Suspended and Influence People, Delacorte
   Press (New York, NY), 2007.
Pirates of the Retail Wasteland, Delacorte Press (New
   York, NY), 2008.
*I Put a Spell on You: From the Files of Chrissie Wood-
   ward, Spelling Bee Detective,* Delacorte Press (New
   York, NY), 2008.
Lost and Found, Delacorte Press (New York, NY), 2009.
Andrew North Blows up the World, Delacorte Press (New
   York, NY), 2009.
The Smart Aleck's Guide to American History, Delacorte
   Press (New York, NY), 2009.
*Your Neighborhood Gives Me the Creeps: True Tales of an
   Accidental Ghost Hunter,* Llewellyn Publications
   (Woodbury, MN), 2009.
I Kissed a Zombie, and I Liked It, Delacorte Press (New
   York, NY), 2010.
*Extraordinary: The True Story of My Fairy Godparent,
   Who Almost Killed Me, and Certainly Never Made Me
   a Princess,* Random House (New York, NY), 2011.
(Under pseudonym S.J. Adams) *Sparks,* Flux Press, 2011.

Contributor to books, including *Weird Chicago: Forgotten History, Strange Legend, and Mysterious Hauntings
of the Windy City,* two volumes. Author of numerous
Web logs, including *Chicagounbelievable.com.*

Sidelights

Chicago-based writer, historian, and musician Adam
Selzer is the author of several off-beat books for middle-
grade readers, including *How to Get Suspended and Influence People, I Put a Spell on You: From the Files of
Chrissie Woodward, Spelling Bee Detective, Pirates of
the Retail Wasteland,* and *I Kissed a Zombie and I Liked
It.*

Described as a "farcical mystery" by a *Kirkus Reviews*
writer, Selzer's novel *I Put a Spell on You* mixes a list
of new vocabulary words with an antic story about
sixth-grader Chrissie and a middle-school spelling bee
that turns vicious. "Framed as Chrissie's case notes, interview transcripts, and emails," *I Put a Spell on You*
serves up a "funny light mystery" that features "a casual, conversational tone." "Suspension of disbelief is
definitely in order here," asserted the *Kirkus Reviews*
writer, although Selzer's ability to portray his cast of
adult characters as "overachievement-obsessed lunatics"
will provide a tantalizing hook for reluctant readers.

In *How to Get Suspended and Influence People* readers
meet Leon Noside Harris, an eighth-grade geek who
suffers from the stigma of being a gifted student of very
eccentric but brainy parents. When Mrs. Smollet, the
teacher of the Gifted Pool students, agrees to allow
Leon to embark on a filmmaking project, his finished
project—an open-minded, Fellini-esque sex documen-

Cover of Adam Selzer's **How to Get Suspended and Influence People,**
featuring artwork by Matt Straub. (Reproduced by permission of Random House
Children's Books, a division of Random House, Inc.)

tary for preteens—gets him both suspended from school and transformed into a classroom hero. In his humorous text, "Selzer manages to capture the voice of a smarter-than-average young teen," according to a *Kirkus Reviews* writer, and Leon's narrative is rich with what a *Publishers Weekly* critic described as "heavy doses of sarcasm, smart aleck wit and adolescent frustration." In *School Library Journal* Pat Scales remarked on Selzer's inclusion of "a lesson or two about free speech" in his "funny, fast-paced novel," and Jennifer Mattson maintained in her *Booklist* review of *How to Get Suspended and Influence People* that "creative" readers "will appreciate the plot's outrageousness and applaud Leon's commitment to his quirky vision."

Leon returns in *Pirates of the Retail Wasteland,* as the students of Mrs. Smollet's Gifted Pool turn their attention to the local branch of mega-coffee-shop Wackfords. Film again becomes the tool of choice as the gifted group stages a takeover of Wackfords that they capture on video in order to raise awareness regarding the commercial sprawl overtaking their community. As if it is not bad enough to be continually mortified by the antics of his braniac, off-the-chart parents, life becomes even more complicated for Leon when the geeky teen attracts the romantic attention of a persistent female classmate. Selzer's "lighter-than-air comedy" will have a special attraction for "tweener sitcom fans," according to a *Kirkus Reviews* writer, while Paula Rohrlick wrote in *Kliatt* that "the clever repartee and humor" in *Pirates of the Retail Wasteland* "will amuse junior high students."

Andrew "Danger" North is the third-grade hero of *Andrew North Blows up the World,* a story geared for younger readers. Here Selzer's hero is part of a family of spies: at least teenaged brother Jack has convinced Andrew that both he and the boys' dad are secret agents. The fact that Dad watches lots of movies about spies serves as confirmation of Jack's assertion, and the unusually complex calculator that Jack keeps in his desk, with all its strange symbols, proves that Jack must keep busy typing out secret codes. When Andrew nabs Jack's communication device (in reality a graphing calculator) and fiddles with it during class, his math teacher confiscates the instrument and locks it away. Now the imaginative Andrew has a true spy mission of his own: to outsmart criminal mastermind Dr. Cringe (in reality the school janitor) and retrieve the device, which may have been set to blow up the world. "It will be obvious to readers that Andrew's dad is actually an insurance salesman and that the boy attends a normal school," asserted *School Library Journal* Clare A. Dombrowski, the critic adding that the titular young hero of *Andrew North Blows up the World* "has a great imagination."

Geared for older teens, *I Kissed a Zombie, and I Liked It* parodies supernatural teen romance novels (think Stephenie Meyer's *Twilight* and its ilk) in its story of eighteen-year-old Algonquin "Alley" Rhodes. Alley lives a few years in the future, and by now it has be-

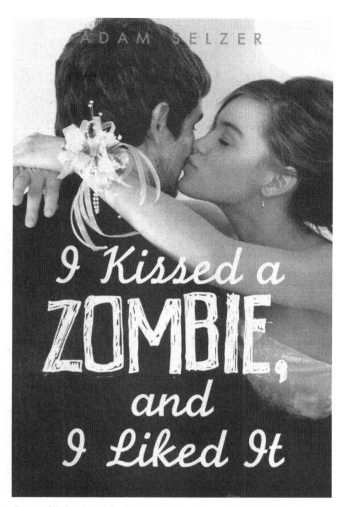

Cover of Selzer's quirky **I Kissed a Zombie, and I Liked It,** *a humorous parody of the supernatural romance genre spawned by Stephenie Meyer's* **Twilight.** (Delacorte Press, 2010. Photograph by Veer. Reproduced by Random House Children's Books, a division of Random House, Inc.)

come cool to be post-human. While all the other girls in her school have gone gaga for vampires and werewolves, Alley refuses to follow the pack and date a member of the undead. Then she meets Doug, a talented musician who seems different even though he sports the same Goth look: pale skin, tatty black suit, and a just-rolled-out-of-bed hairstyle. As Alley soon discovers, Doug may be the real thing—a zombie—and she has to rethink her declaration of love now that she knows that the object of her affection is a car-crash victim who is wearing the suit he was buried in four years ago. "This is one smart goth caper, with plenty of appeal to those who normally wouldn't . . . be caught reading a romance," asserted Francisca Goldsmith in her *Booklist* review of *I Kissed a Zombie, and I Liked It.* Selzer "takes a delightfully wicked but thoughtful poke at teenage infatuations, vampire groupies, and pretentious goths," noted a *Publishers Weekly* critic, and in *School Library Journal* Donna Rosenblum dubbed the novel "original, funny, unpredictable, romantic, and tragic." "A scathing parody of the paranormal-romance genre," according to a *Kirkus Reviews* writer, *I Kissed a*

Zombie, and I Liked It also stands as "a sweetly romantic paranormal love story in its own right."

In addition to fiction, Selzer also deals with real life (and death) in his book *Your Neighborhood Gives Me the Creeps: True Tales of an Accidental Ghost Hunter,* which was inspired by his interest in ferreting out odd aspects of local history as well as his work as founder, chief guide, and head ghost investigator for the off-beat tour company Chicago Unbelievable. Another work of nonfiction, *The Smart Aleck's Guide to American History* presents a humorous and enlightened antidote to politically correct history books that skewers the cultural oddities of several centuries of U.S. history while illuminating the idealism and rationality that inspired the country's founding. "I spent seven years learning Kung Fu at Daniel Pinkwater's Tibetan compound," Selzer confided to *SATA,* exhibiting his exacting respect for the truth, "and I now work part time as an assassin for hire."

Biographical and Critical Sources

PERIODICALS

Booklist, January 1, 2007, Jennifer Mattson, review of *How to Get Suspended and Influence People,* p. 83; April 15, 2010, Francisca Goldsmith, review of *I Kissed a Zombie, and I Liked It,* p. 42.

Bulletin of the Center for Children's Books, May, 2007, Karen Coats, review of *How to Get Suspended and Influence People,* p. 385; May, 2008, Karen Coats, review of *Pirates of the Retail Wasteland,* p. 400; September, 2008, Deborah Stevenson, review of *I Put a Spell on You: From the Files of Chrissie Woodward, Spelling Bee Detective,* p. 45; March, 2010, Karen Coats, review of *I Kissed a Zombie, and I Liked It,* p. 304, and Elizabeth Bush, review of *The Smart Aleck's Guide to American History,* p. 305.

Horn Book, September-October, 2008, Susan Dove Lempke, review of *I Put a Spell on You,* p. 596.

Kirkus Reviews, February 1, 2007, review of *How to Get Suspended and Influence People,* p. 128; March 15, 2008, review of *Pirates of the Retail Wasteland;* July 15, 2008, review of *I Put a Spell on You;* July 15, 2009, review of *Andrew North Blows up the World;* November 1, 2009, review of *The Smart Aleck's Guide to American History;* December 1, 2009, review of *I Kissed a Zombie, and I Liked It.*

Kliatt, January, 2007, Paula Rohrlick, review of *How to Get Suspended and Influence People,* p. 18; March, 2008, Paula Rohrlick, review of *Pirates of the Retail Wasteland,* p. 19.

Publishers Weekly, February 26, 2007, review of *How to Get Suspended and Influence People,* p. 91; March, 2007, Pat Scales, review of *How to Get Suspended and Influence People,* p. 218; December 21, 2009, review of *I Kissed a Zombie, and I Liked It,* p. 63.

School Library Journal, March, 2007, Pat Scales, review of *How to Get Suspended and Influence People,* p. 281; July, 2008, Chris Shoemaker, review of *Pirates of the Retail Wasteland,* p. 107; November, 2008, Geri Diorio, review of *I Put a Spell on You,* p. 136; September, 2009, Clare A. Dombrowski, review of *Andrew North Blows up the World,* p. 173; January, 2010, Donna Rosenblum, review of *I Kissed a Zombie, and I Liked It,* p. 113, and Brian Odom, review of *The Smart Aleck's Guide to American History,* p. 125.

Voice of Youth Advocates, April, 2007, Dave Goodale, review of *How to Get Suspended and Influence People,* p. 56; April, 2010, Debbie Wenk, review of *The Smart Aleck's Guide to American History,* p. 83.

ONLINE

Adam Selzer Home Page, http://www.adamselzer.com (April 24, 2011).

*   *   *

SHINN, Sharon 1957-

Personal

Born April 28, 1957, in Wichita, KS; daughter of Raymond, Jr. (a college professor) and Carol (a secretary) James. *Education:* Northwestern University, B.S., 1979.

Addresses

Home—Brentwood, MO. *Agent*—Ethan Ellenberg, 548 Broadway, No. 5E, New York, NY 11012; agent@ethanellenberg.com. *E-mail*—sharon@sharonshinn.net.

Career

Author and editor. *Professional Photographer* magazine, Chicago, IL, assistant editor, 1979-83; *Decor* magazine, St. Louis, MO, managing editor, 1983-2001; *Biz Ed* magazine, co-editor, beginning 2001.

Member

Alternate Historians.

Awards, Honors

William Crawford Award for best first novel, International Association for the Fantastic in the Arts, 1996, for *The Shape-changer's Wife;* Best Books for Young Adults citation, American Library Association (ALA), 2000, for *Summers at Castle Auburn;* Reviewer's Choice award, *Romantic Times,* 2004, for *Angel-Seeker;* twice nominated for William Campbell Award for best new writer; Best Books for Young Adults citation, ALA, 2004, for *The Safe-keeper's Secret;* Books for the Teen Age selection, New York Public Library, and Best Children's Books of the Year designation, Bank Street College of Education, both 2006, both for *The Truth-teller's Tale;* Career Achievement award in Science Fiction and Fantasy, *Romantic Times,* 2010.

Writings

FANTASY AND SCIENCE-FICTION NOVELS

The Shape-changer's Wife, Ace (New York, NY), 1995.
Wrapt in Crystal, Ace (New York, NY), 1999.
Heart of Gold, Ace (New York, NY), 2000.
Summers at Castle Auburn, Ace (New York, NY), 2000.
Jenna Starborn, Ace (New York, NY), 2002.
The Safe-keeper's Secret, Viking (New York, NY), 2004.
The Truth-teller's Tale (sequel to *The Safe-keeper's Secret*), Viking (New York, NY) 2005.
The Dream-maker's Magic (sequel to *The Truth-teller's Tale*), Viking (New York, NY), 2006.
General Winston's Daughter, Viking (New York, NY), 2007.
Gateway, Viking (New York, NY), 2009.
Quatrain (novellas), Ace Books (New York, NY), 2009.
Troubled Waters, Ace Books (New York, NY), 2010.

"SAMARIA" NOVEL SERIES

Archangel, Ace (New York, NY), 1996.
Jovah's Angel, Ace (New York, NY), 1997.
The Alleluia Files, Ace (New York, NY), 1998.
Angelica, Ace (New York, NY), 2003.
Angel-Seeker, Ace (New York, NY), 2004.

Also author of novella *Fallen Angels,* published in *To Weave a Web of Magic,* Berkley Books (New York, NY), 2004.

"TWELVE HOUSES" NOVEL SERIES

Mystic and Rider, Berkley Books (New York, NY), 2005.
The Thirteenth House, Ace (New York, NY), 2006.
Dark Moon Defender, Ace Books (New York, NY), 2006.
Reader and Raelynx, Ace Books (New York, NY), 2007.
Fortune and Fate, Ace Books (New York, NY), 2008.

Also author of story "When Winter Comes," published in *The Queen in Winter,* Berkley Books (New York, NY), 2006.

OTHER

Contributor to books, including *Powers of Detection,* edited by Dana Stabenow, Ace Books (New York, NY), 2004; *Elemental Magic,* Berkley Books (New York, NY), 2007; and *Never After,* Jove Books (New York, NY), 2009.

Sidelights

Sharon Shinn writes novels that critics have described as innovative and compelling in their blend of fantasy, science fiction, mystery, and romance. In works such as *Archangel, General Winston's Daughter,* and her "Twelve Houses" series, Shinn offers thought-provoking narratives, fully realized characters, and complex fantasy worlds. "I think that's just the way my mind works," the author remarked to *BSC Review* online contributor Elena Nola. "When a story presents itself to me, it's almost always in a fantasy or speculative world. Although I do like the fantasy conventions: the quest, the self-discovery, the magic, the chance to battle great evil and save the world. These story elements never cease to be satisfying to me."

Shinn's award-winning debut, *The Shape-changer's Wife,* centers on Aubrey, whose training to become a wizard entails an apprenticeship with Glyrenden, a master wizard who teaches the boy about shape-changing. As Aubrey learns the magical art he encounters Lilith, Glyrenden's remote wife; Arachne, the wizard's housekeeper; and two others: a large man named Orion and a shy young woman named Eve. When Aubrey comes to suspect Glyrenden of Shape-changing these people—Arachne is really a spider, Orion a bear, Lilith a willow, and Eve a fawn—he must decide whether to take his master's life and end the magical entrapment. "Fantasy fans will love this book," averred Gail E. Roberts in *Kliatt,* calling *The Shape-changer's Wife* "a very good . . . first novel."

Cover of Sharon Shinn's fantasy novel The Safe-Keeper's Secret, *featuring cover art by Matt Mahurin.* (Jacket art © 2004 by Matt Mahurin. Reproduced by permission of Viking Children's Books, a division of Penguin Young Readers Group, a member of Penguin (USA) Inc., 345 Hudson St., NY 10014. All rights reserved.)

In *Archangel* Shinn creates a world centering on Samaria, which is either an alternate ancient Israel or a vision of that country's distant future. The angel Gabriel, due to inherit the role of archangel from Raphael, seeks a wife to help him lead the next festival of song to the glory of Jovah, the god of Samaria. The oracle Josiah directs Gabriel to Rachel, a slave girl living in a remote village, but no sooner are the two married than the relationship becomes strained as Rachel attempts to use her newfound position to aid her fellow slaves in Samaria. A critic for *Kirkus Reviews* described *Archangel* as "taut, inventive, often mesmerizing, with a splendid pair of disaffected, predestined lovers," while *Booklist* reviewer Carl Hays praised Shinn's "sure command of characterization and vividly imagined settings." References to the technology that allows Samarians to contact their gods infuses the ethereal realm of angels with a science-fiction air "that should please fans of both genres," Hays added.

Angels are also central to *Jovah's Angel,* a sequel to *Archangel.* Here, the god Jovah must be appeased by the singing of the angels in order for the planet Samaria to avoid the violent storms that otherwise make life there untenable. When the archangel Delilah is wounded in one of these storms, the oracles gather to petition Jovah to send them a replacement. Jovah chooses shy Alleya, whose prayerful singing is the only voice Jovah has lately heeded. In partnership with the mechanic Caleb, Alleya now questions the god's recent neglect and discovers that both she and Caleb are actually descended from earlier colonists from another planet. These colonists created the genetically engineered race of angels in order to continue to control the planet's weather with their technology in perpetuity. The resulting crisis of belief is "thoughtfully discussed and resolved," according to Liz LaValley in *Kliatt,* the critic calling *Jovah's Angel* "a lovely, lyrical read with sympathetic characters." LaValley noted the many topics addressed in the book, including the nature of religious faith and the benefits and costs of technology. "Fans of *Archangel* will be gratified" by the appearance of *Jovah's Angel,* concluded a contributor to *Kirkus Reviews.*

The "Samaria" series continues with *The Alleluia Files,* in which the archangel Bael continues his persecution of a heretic sect of Jacobites and a rebellious angel hooks up with a runaway mortal to search for the Alleluia Files. Here, Shinn showcases her signature blend of high-tech sci-fi, mystery, romance, and fantasy, creating "a fresh and innovative tale full of surprising turns of plot," according to Jackie Cassada in *Library Journal.*

Other "Samaria" novels include *Angelica*, the story of a woman who is called to be the wife of an angel, and *Angel-Seeker.* In *Angelica* Susannah is heartbroken and homesick among the angels, and her new husband, Gaaron, is uncommunicative and distant until the couple join to face an alien threat. A *Publishers Weekly* critic noted that *Angelica* "will win new readers and delight

existing fans," while Roberta Johnson wrote in *Booklist,* that "Shinn blends romance and sf gracefully enough to satisfy fantasy fans." In *Angel-Seeker* Rebekah hails from a tribe that hates angels. When the angel Obadiah is attacked and wounded, Rebekah finds herself nursing him back to health, in the process questioning her family's assumptions about the world. "Shinn smoothly blends the romantic sensibility of yesteryear with the feminism of today," complimented a critic for *Publishers Weekly. Booklist* reviewer Regina Schroeder considered *Angel-Seeker* "a solid read," and Cassada noted in *Library Journal* that the novel "fills a gap in the history" of Samaria.

Shinn introduced a series specifically written for young-adult readers with *The Safe-keeper's Secret.* Damiana is a "Safe-keeper," one who listens to the secrets of others but pledges not to repeat them. Her daughter, Fiona, and her ward, the boy Reed, whose parents are a mystery, are planning to apprentice in their chosen professions; Fiona wants to become a Safe-keeper like her mother, but is trained in the study of herbs, while Reed goes from one apprenticeship to the next, good at all but happy with none. When Damiana reaches the end of her life, Fiona takes on her mother's secrets, only to realize that perhaps this is not the path she is best suited for, because the secret of Reed's true parents is a difficult one to keep. "Teens will connect with Shinn's vividly drawn world," commented Gillian Engberg in a *Booklist* review, while Michele Winship noted in *Kliatt* that in *The Safe-keeper's Secret,* "Shinn skillfully weaves a tale of fantasy to rival the classics." A *Kirkus Reviews* contributor praised the novel's ending, which, "with its revelations of true identity and hints of romance, is quite satisfying."

In *The Truth-teller's Tale* Eleda is a Truth-teller, and her mirror-twin, Adele, is a Safe-keeper. Both are friends with Roelynn, whose father is grooming her to marry the prince despite her own ideas about romance. When Roelynn falls in love with a dancing-master's apprentice and the twins are mistaken for each other, a comedy of "romantic mayhem" ensues, according to a *Kirkus Reviews* critic, who concluded, "Romance reigns for all in this engaging page-turner of mistaken identity." In *Kliatt* Winship noted that the events of *The Safe-keeper's Secret* "lead readers into an intrigue with more than a few twists." Cheri Dobbs, writing in *School Library Journal,* commented that "Teen readers will be captivated by this medieval tale," adding: "Shinn has a beautiful turn of phrase and a knack for writing a sentence that will stop readers in their tracks."

The Dream-maker's Magic, "a warm-hearted conclusion to a trilogy of novels set in the same rustic kingdom," in the words of *Booklist* critic Jennifer Mattson, centers on the relationship between Kellen, whose mother confusingly raises her as a boy, and Gryffin, a disabled youth who has the ability to affect people's dreams. "Shinn has once again deftly mixed magic with

human struggles and adolescent foibles," a contributor in *Kirkus Reviews* stated, and Beth L. Meister noted in *School Library Journal* he author "has created a fully realized world full of unusual characters."

Mystic and Rider is the first book in Shinn's "Twelve Houses" series. The novel is set on the fantasy world of Gillengaria, where those who have magic abilities, called Mystics, are treated with suspicion. The king recognizes the usefulness of the mystics, however, and when trouble stirs the team he sends to investigate includes Senneth, a fire mystic; Kirra and her servant Donnal, both who can change shape; and Tayse and Justin, Riders, or elite soldiers of the crown. The Riders have an instant distrust for the Mystics, but they overcome their differences for the sake of the kingdom. The "promise of her characters' lives 'changed by love' in future" books in the ongoing series "make for a rich beginning," according to a *Publishers Weekly* reviewer. Paula Luedtke, writing for *Booklist,* applauded the novel's "entirely likeable major characters and an interesting group-development narrative."

The kingdom of Gillengaria is the setting of Shinn's **Mystic and Rider,** *which finds several powerful families suspect that those possessing magic abilities are a threat to their survival.* (Ace Books, 2005. Jacket illustration © by Donato Giancola. All rights reserved. Used by permission of the designer, Annette Fiore.)

In *The Thirteenth House,* the second installment in the series, Casserah, Kirra's younger sister and the newly declared heir to House Danalustrous, refuses to attend any social affairs held by the Twelve Houses. Assuming her sibling's form, Kirra goes in her stead, encountering the beautiful Princess Amalie and entering an affair with Lord Romar, both of whom are in peril. Shinn's novel "abounds with subtle romance and high-spirited adventure," wrote a contributor in *Kirkus Reviews,* and *Library Journal* critic Cassada noted that the author "provides a wealth of action and a balanced cast of genuinely heroic and admirable characters." *Dark Moon Defender* centers on Justin, a member of the King's Riders who is sent on a covert mission to Lumanen Convent, where a noblewoman has been accused of persecuting mystics. "Once again," observed a *Publishers Weekly* reviewer, "Shinn expertly mixes romance with traditional fantasy for a satisfying read."

Rebellion looms in *Reader and Raelynx,* the fourth work in the "Twelve Houses" series. King Baryn decides to marry off his daughter, Amalie, inviting a group of suitors to the palace. Monitoring these events is Cammon, a telepathic reader who falls in love with the princess although such love is forbidden. A contributor in *Kirkus Reviews* wrote that Shinn's narrative in *Reader and Raelynx* includes "plenty of great twists, thrilling action sequences and long-awaited comeuppances along the way." In *Fortune and Fate* an elite warrior named Wren seeks to atone for her failure to protect King Baryn by rescuing the kidnapped daughter of a rebel leader, which act earns her the respect of Jasper, the girl's guardian. In reviewing this work, Cassada declared that Shinn "skillfully blends romance and adventure."

In addition to the "Samaria" and "Twelve Houses" series, Shinn has penned several stand-alone novels, including *Wrapt in Crystal, General Winston's Daughter,* and *Troubled Waters. Wrapt in Crystal* is a story of political and religious intrigue set on the small world of Semay. In the novel, Lt. Cowen Drake works for the Intergalactic Alliance of Federated Planets, an entity that has long been courting Semay in hopes that it will join the federation. Now Drake is assigned to investigate a series of murders in which all the victims are priestesses associated with one of Semay's two competing religions. "Shinn's flair for intriguing settings and sympathetic characters remains strong," complimented a critic for *Publishers Weekly,* while *Library Journal* reviewer Cassada described *Wrapt in Crystal* as "rich in detail and profound in spiritual underpinnings." Johnson, writing for *Booklist,* noted of the same novel that "Shinn skillfully combines suspense, sf, and romance while posting thoughtful questions on worship, faith, and sacrifice."

A young woman questions her nation's militaristic policies in *General Winston's Daughter,* a "powerful story" that is "entertaining and satisfying on many levels," according to *Kliatt* reviewer Claire Rosser. A wealthy heiress, Averie Winston travels to the conquered land of

Chiarrin to visit her father and fiancée, both who serve in the Aeberellen army. Once there, however, Averie's blossoming friendships with Lieutenant Du'Kai, an unorthodox soldier, and Jalessa, a Chiarrin villager, open her eyes to new ways of thinking. Although *General Winston's Daughter* "takes place in a fictionalized setting," Donna Rosenblum remarked in *School Library Journal*, "Shinn does an excellent job creating a parallel to the British Empire in its height of 19th-century imperialism."

In *Troubled Waters* a young woman escapes a forced marriage to the king and discovers her true destiny in a world governed by elemental substances. "This entertaining and suspenseful story is full of lively characters," a *Publishers Weekly* critic reported. Shinn has also garnered praise for *Quatrain,* a collection of four novellas "that affirms Shinn's skill with the shorter form," in the words of a *Publishers Weekly* reviewer.

Summers at Castle Auburn shifts from intrigue to romance in its story of Corie. The illegitimate daughter of

Cover of **Heart of Gold,** *in which Shinn mixes science fiction and romance in a story of a planet fraught with racial unrest.* (Ace Books, 2000. Cover design by Erika Fusari. All rights reserved. Reproduced by permission of Erika Fusari.)

a lord, Corie has been raised by her grandmother and trained in the healing arts. As a girl she formed a crush on the prince, but as now that she is older she realizes that he is self-centered and cruel. The prince hunts the Aliora, a magical race that Corie's people enslave, and Corie comes to realize that she has to make an effort to save these hunted folk. "While the story moves quickly in Shinn's seasoned hands, . . . fans may be left hungry for more substantive fare," a *Publishers Weekly* reviewer commented, noting the lack of substantive issues embedded within *Summers at Castle Auburn.* Luedtke found more to like, however, writing in *Booklist* that Shinn's novel is "a charmer for the romantically inclined."

With *Jenna Starborn* Shinn combines Regency romance with science fiction. Setting the plot of Charlotte Brontë's *Jane Eyre* in a futuristic world where children are sometimes raised in "gen-tanks," Shinn "is faithful to the original story but not slavishly so," Donna L. Scanlon noted in her *Kliatt* review. Half-citizen Jenna Starborn, created in one of these gen-tanks, is rejected by the woman who requested her creation. Sent off to a technical school, Jenna is eventually hired to perform nuclear-reactor maintenance at Thorrastone Park, the estate of Everett Ravenbeck. She and Ravenbeck fall in love and intend to marry until Jenna discovers that he has another wife. "Shinn fans will enjoy the way the author perfectly captures the tone and color of Brontë while maintaining Jenna's unique voice," praised a critic for *Publishers Weekly,* and *Booklist* reviewer Roberta Johnson proclaimed of *Jenna Starborn* that "Shinn's sf take on a great romantic tale succeeds."

Gateway centers on Daiyu, a Chinese-American adoptee living in St. Louis, who finds herself transported to an alternate version of the city after stepping through the Gateway Arch. In this unfamiliar world, one of many iterations created by the gods, America was colonized by Chinese settlers. Daiyu is recruited by the gods' servants to dispatch Chenglei, a rogue traveler who has assumed power in Shenglang. "Shinn is a prolific and skillful writer, and the world in which Daiyu finds herself is full of interesting detail," Barbara Scotto maintained in her *School Library Journal* review of *Gateway.*

As Shinn once told *SATA,* "I write science fiction/fantasy because I love the stories I can tell within these genres—stories of magic, glamour, and heroism that also include the smaller, intimate details of ordinary life." Discussing her role as a novelist on the *BSC Review* Web site, Shinn explained, "I know that there are magnificent books out there that flay the soul, that galvanize people into action, that change their perceptions of the world. I don't write those kinds of books. I want to write stories that other people can disappear into."

Biographical and Critical Sources

PERIODICALS

Booklist, May 1, 1996, Carl Hays, review of *Archangel,* p. 1492; May 15, 1999, review of *Wrapt in Crystal,* p.

Cover of Shinn's novel Gateway, *featuring cover art by Juliana* **Kolesova.** (Jacket art © 2009 by Juliana Kolesova. Reproduced by permission of Viking Children's Books, a division of Penguin Young Readers Group, a member of Penguin (USA) Inc., 345 Hudson St., NY 10014. All rights reserved.)

1684; April 15, 2001, Paula Luedtke, review of *Summers at Castle Auburn,* p. 1544; March 15, 2002, review of *Summers at Castle Auburn,* p. 1228; April 1, 2002, Roberta Johnson, review of *Jenna Starborn,* p. 1313; March 1, 2003, Roberta Johnson, review of *Angelica,* p. 1153; March 1, 2004, Regina Schroeder, review of *Angel-Seeker,* p. 1147; April 15, 2004, Gillian Engberg, review of *The Safe-keeper's Secret,* p. 1452; April 15, 2005, Jennifer Mattson, review of *The Truth-teller's Tale,* p. 1468; March 1, 2005, Paula Luedtke, review of *Mystic and Rider,* p. 1150; March 1, 2006, Paula Luedtke, review of *The Thirteenth House,* p. 77; May 15, 2006, Jennifer Mattson, review of *The Dream-maker's Magic,* p. 58; August, 2007, Anne O'Malley, review of *General Winston's Daughter,* p. 63; September 15, 2009, Courtney James, review of *Gateway,* p. 66; September 15, 2010, Rebecca Gerber, review of *Troubled Waters,* p. 38.

Bookwatch, May, 2004, review of *Angel-Seeker,* p. 5.

Bulletin of the Center for Children's Books, June, 2004, Timnah Card, review of *The Safe-keeper's Secret,* p. 437; November, 2009, Kate Quealy-Gainer, review of *Gateway,* p. 129.

Chronicle, April, 2005, Mike Jones, review of *The Truth-teller's Tale,* p. 19.

Kirkus Reviews, March 15, 1996, review of *Archangel,* p. 412; April 1, 1997, review of *Jovah's Angel,* p. 510; May 1, 2004, review of *The Safe-keeper's Secret,* p. 448; July 1, 2005, review of *The Truth-teller's Tale,* p. 743; January 1, 2006, review of *The Thirteenth House,* p. 21; May 15, 2006, review of *The Dream-maker's Magic,* p. 523; September 1, 2007, review of *General Winston's Daughter;* October 1, 2007, review of *Reader and Raelynx;* September 15, 2009, review of *Gateway.*

Kliatt, January, 1996, Gail E. Roberts, review of *The Shape-changer's Wife,* p. 18; September, 1997, Liz LaValley, review of *Jovah's Angel,* p. 23; July, 2002, Donna L. Scanlon, review of *Jenna Starborn,* p. 32; May, 2004, Michele Winship, review of *The Safe-keeper's Secret,* p. 13; July, 2005, Michele Winship, review of *The Truth-teller's Tale,* p. 16; September, 2007, Claire Rosser, review of *General Winston's Daughter,* p. 18.

Library Journal, May 15, 1997, p. 106; April 15, 1998, Jackie Cassada, review of *The Alleluia Files,* p. 119; May 15, 1999, Jackie Cassada, review of *Wrapt in Crystal,* p. 130; April 15, 2000, Jackie Cassada, review of *Heart of Gold,* p. 126; April 15, 2002, Jackie Cassada, review of *Jenna Starborn,* p. 127; March 15, 2004, Jackie Cassada, review of *Angel-Seeker,* p. 110; March 15, 2005, Jackie Cassada, review of *Mystic and Rider,* p. 75; February 15, 2006, Jackie Cassada, review of *The Thirteenth House,* p. 111; September 15, 2006, Jackie Cassada, review of *Dark Moon Defender,* p. 55; November 15, 2007, Jackie Cassada, review of *Reader and Raelynx,* p. 53; October 15, 2008, Jackie Cassada, review of *Fortune and Fate,* p. 61; September 15, 2009, Jackie Cassada, review of *Quatrain,* p. 53; September 15, 2010, Jackie Cassada, review of *Troubled Waters,* p. 65.

Magazine of Fantasy and Science Fiction, October, 2000, Michelle West, review of *Heart of Gold,* p. 44.

Publishers Weekly, April 12, 1999, review of *Wrapt in Crystal,* p. 59; March 20, 2000, review of *Heart of Gold,* p. 75, April 2, 2001, review of *Summers at Castle Auburn,* p. 44; March 4, 2002, review of *Jenna Starborn,* p. 62; February 17, 2003, review of *Angelica,* p. 61; January 26, 2004, review of *Angel-Seeker,* p. 236; February 7, 2005, review of *Mystic and Rider,* p. 46; January 9, 2006, review of *The Thirteenth House,* p. 36; August 14, 2006, review of *Dark Moon Defender,* p. 185; September 10, 2007, review of *Elemental Magic,* p. 45; October 1, 2007, review of *Reader and Raelynx,* p. 41; September 15, 2008, review of *Fortune and Fate,* p. 49; August 24, 2009, review of *Quatrain,* p. 46; October 19, 2009, review of *Gateway,* p. 53; August 16, 2010, review of *Troubled Waters,* p. 39.

St. Louis Post-Dispatch, April 2, 2006, J. Stephen Bolhafner, "St. Louis Writer Does Her Research," p. F9.

School Library Journal, June, 2004, Jane G. Connor, review of *The Safe-keeper's Secret,* p. 150; July, 2005, Cheri Dobbs, review of *The Safe-keeper's Secret* p. 108; July, 2006, Beth L. Meister, review of *The Dream-maker's Magic,* p. 112; January, 2008, Donnal Rosenblum, review of *General Winston's Daughter,* p. 126; December, 2009, Barbara Scotto, review of *Gateway,* p. 131.

Voice of Youth Advocates, April, 2000, review of *Wrapt in Crystal,* p. 13; August, 2001, review of *Summers at Castle Auburn,* p. 216; August, 2002, review of *Jenna Starborn,* p. 205; August, 2003, review of *Angelica,* p. 242; June, 2004, Kim Carter and Lillian Filliman, review of *The Safe-keeper's Secret,* p. 147; August, 2004, review of *Angel-Seeker,* p. 234; February, 2009, Beth Karpas, review of *Fortune and Fate,* p. 547; December, 2009, Diane Colson and Grace Zokovitch, review of *Gateway,* p. 423.

ONLINE

BSC Review Online, http://www.bscreview.com/ (October 7, 2009), Elena Nola, interview with Shinn; (October 16, 2009) Sharon Shinn, "Escaping into Fiction"; (November 16, 2010) Elena Nola, interview with Shinn.

Sharon Shinn Home Page, http://www.sharonshinn.net (April 15, 2011).

Writerspace.com, http://www.writerspace.com/ (December 20, 2005), Barbara Sheridan, interview with Shinn.

*   *   *

SKOVRON, Jon 1976-

Personal

Born 1976, in Columbus, OH; son of a dentist; married; children: two sons. *Education:* Carnegie Mellon University, B.A. (acting).

Addresses

Home—Metro-Washington, DC.

Career

Technical writer and novelist.

Writings

Struts and Frets, Amulet Books (New York, NY), 2009.
Misfits, Amulet Books (New York, NY), 2011.

Work included in anthologies *A Visitor's Guide to Mystic Falls,* SmartPop, 2010, and *Crush: 26 Real-life Stories of First Love,* edited by Andrea N. Richesin, Harlequin, 2011. Contributor to periodicals, including *Jim Baen's Universe, Chiaroscuro, Drexel Online Journal,* and *Internet Review of Science Fiction.*

Sidelights

Characterizing himself as a musical dilettante who can coax sound from eight different instruments, Jon Skovron works as a technical writer and dad by day. In his unoccupied time, Skovron writes young-adult fiction and has produced the novels *Struts and Frets* as well as

Misfit. While *Struts and Frets* draws on its author's own experiences as a creative-minded teen trying to balance his artistic muse with the demands of real life, *Misfits* fortunately does not. In Skovron's second novel, readers meet Jael, whose difficulty is attempting to reconcile the demonic tendency inherited from her 5,000-year-old mother with her life as a student at a Catholic high school.

Skovron grew up in Ohio, in a family where a creative career was strongly encouraged. While willing to please his parents in this regard, he was unsure what artistic path to take, and he dabbled in music, writing, and acting. Although he spent much of his time writing during junior high and high school, the life of an author did not seem tangible, and in college he majored in acting. Skovron realized that he was a mis-match with the demands of this vocation shortly after graduation. Turning to literature while trying to plot a new course, he found enlightenment in John Irving's popular novel *The World according to Garp,* which highlights the serendipity and elements of chance that can shape people's lives. In-

Cover of Jon Skovron's young-adult novel Struts and Frets, *which finds a young musician attempting to navigating the ups and downs of adolescence.* (Amulet Books, 2009. Jacket photograph by Jonathan Beckerman. Reproduced by permission of Amulet Books, and imprint of Harry N. Abrams, Inc.)

spired, he once again set to writing and, as he quipped on his home page, "a mere ten years later, *Struts and Frets* was published."

In *Struts and Frets* Sammy Bojar knows that he was destined to be a musician: after all, he has been raised carrying the family legacy of a grandfather who was a successful jazz musician. His indie rock band shows a lot of untapped promise, and an optimistic Sammy is determined to guide the group to a win at the upcoming Battle of the Bands concert. Although he valiantly works to inspire his fellow musicians with his own dedication to achieve musical stardom, the teen is continually confronted by obstacles, such as his grandfather's failing health, a frazzled mother, and the fact that his best friend Jen has started to view him as boyfriend material. "Good character development and solid pacing" were cited by a *Kirkus Reviews* writer in reviewing *Struts and Frets*, and a *Publishers Weekly* critic recommended Sammy as a teen many readers will relate to. Vivid "descriptions of what it's like to play and perform . . . add flourish to this coming-of-age story," the *Publishers Weekly* critic added. Citing Skovron's ability to craft "hilarious" scenes, *School Library Journal* contributor Ginny Gustin predicted that *Struts and Frets* "will find an audience not just with music fans, but also with those who appreciate a good coming-of-age story."

As a writer, "everything inspires me," Skovron explained in an online interview with Melissa Buron. "Everything I do feeds into it. Books, movies, music, visual art, of course. People I meet, old friends, strange encounters. Even the worst things that happen are grist for the mill. I can't tell you how many times I've been in some terrible or tragic situation and in the back of my head, thought, 'Well, at least this will make me a better writer. . . .' Richard Price said that a writer has to be constantly falling in love with life, and that is pretty true for me. Even when I'm miserable, I'm in love with it."

Biographical and Critical Sources

PERIODICALS

Bulletin of the Center for Children's Books, February, 2010, Elizabeth Bush, review of *Struts and Frets,* p. 260.
Kirkus Reviews, October 15, 2009, review of *Struts and Frets.*
Publishers Weekly, November 9, 2009, review of *Struts and Frets,* p. 48.
School Library Journal, January, 2010, Ginny Gustin, review of *Struts and Frets,* p. 113.
Voice of Youth Advocates, February, 2010, Caitlin Augusta, review of *Struts and Frets,* p. 501.

ONLINE

Jon Skovron Home Page, http://www.jonskovron.com. (April 20, 2011).
Melissa Buron Web log, http://melissaburon.livejournal.com/ (August 10, 2010), Melissa Buron, interview with Skovron.*

* * *

SNOW, Sarah

Personal

Married; children: two. *Education:* Rhode Island School of Design, B.F.A., 1992.

Addresses

Home—Hudson Valley, NY. *Agent*—Libby Ford Artist Representative, 320 E. 57th St., Ste. 10B, New York, NY 10022.

Career

Illustrator and collage artist. Former book designer. *Exhibitions:* Works exhibited at Ten Women Gallery, Santa Monica, then Venice, CA, 1998, 2001; Rhode Island School of Design Works gallery, Providence, RI, 2003; Mark Gruber Gallery, New Paltz, NY, 2005; Water Street Gallery, New York, NY, 2005, Cavalier Gallery, Nantucket, MA, 2006; and LaGalery, Ste. Paul, France, 2008.

Awards, Honors

Joseph LeFevere Memorial Award for Excellence in Illustration, 1992; Second Place award, New York Book Show, 1995.

Illustrator

Alison Formento, *This Tree Counts!,* Albert Whitman (Chicago, IL), 2010, abridged version published as *This Tree, 1, 2, 3,* 2011.
Alison Formento, *These Bees Count!,* Albert Whitman (Chicago, IL), 2012.
Alison Formento, *These Seas Count!,* Albert Whitman (Chicago, IL), 2013.

Contributor to periodicals, including *Travel & Leisure.*

Biographical and Critical Sources

PERIODICALS

Booklist, January 1, 2010, Julie Cummins, review of *This Tree Counts!,* p. 100.
Kirkus Reviews, February 15, 2010, review of *This Tree Counts!.*
School Library Journal, February, 2010, Linda L. Walkins, review of *This Tree Counts!,* p. 84.

ONLINE

Sarah Snow Home Page, http://www.sarahsnowcollage.com (April 24, 2011).

STOWER, Adam

Personal

Born in England; children: a daughter. *Education:* Norwich School of Art, B.A. (with honors); University of Brighton, M.A.

Addresses

Home—Brighton, England. *Agent*—Arena Agency, 31 Eleanor Rd., London E15 4AB, England. *E-mail*—adam@worldofadam.com.

Career

Illustrator and author.

Awards, Honors

Norfolk Library Silver Award for Children's Books, 2005, for *Slam!: A Tale of Consequences;* Red House Children's Book Award in younger-readers category, 2010, for *Bottoms Up!* by Jeanne Willis.

Writings

SELF-ILLUSTRATED

Two Left Feet, Bloomsbury (New York, NY), 2004.
The Den, Bloomsbury (London, England), 2005.
Slam!: A Tale of Consequences, Templar (Dorking, England), 2005.
(With Nick Denchfield) *The Diary of a Monster Catcher* (pop-up book), Alison Green/Scholastic (London, England), 2008.
Silly Doggy!, Templar (Dorking, England), 2011.

ILLUSTRATOR

(With Jonathon Heap) Robert Hull, reteller, *Norse Stories,* Thomson Learning (New York, NY), 1993.
(With Claire Robinson) Robert Hull, reteller, *Greek Stories,* Thomson Learning (New York, NY), 1994.
Chris Culshaw, *A Bit of a Drip, and The Letter,* Oxford University Press (Oxford, England), 1995.
Roger Norman, *Treetime,* Faber (London, England), 1997.
(With Tim Hayward and Robin Carter) Steve Parker, *It's an Ant's Life,* Reader's Digest Children's Books (Pleasantville, NY), 1999.
Emily Moore, *The Monarchy,* Hodder (London, England), 2000.
Sue Arengo, reteller, *The Shoemaker and the Elves,* Oxford University Press (Oxford, England), 2000.
Gillian Clements, *Romans Go Home!,* Pearson Education (Harlow, England), 2001.
Diane Mowat, reteller, *A Pair of Ghostly Hands and Other Stories,* Oxford University Press (Oxford, England), 2002.

John Escott, reteller, *William Tell and Other Stories,* Oxford University Press (Oxford, England), 2002.
Terence Blacker, *You Have Ghost Mail,* Macmillan (London, England), 2002.
Kate Saunders, *Cat and the Stinkwater War,* Macmillan (London, England), 2003.
Roger McGough, compiler, *Favourite Funny Stories,* Kingfisher (London, England), 2003, published as *More Funny Stories,* Kingfisher (Boston, MA), 2003.
Alan Temperley, *The Magician of Samarkand,* Macmillan (London, England), 2003.
Jane Bingham, adapter, *Around the World in Eighty Days,* Usborne (London, England), 2004.
Jimmy Fallon, *Snowball Fight!,* Dutton (New York, NY), 2005.
Roger McGough, compiler, *Comic Stories,* Kingfisher (London, England), 2005.
Timothy Knapman, *Mungo and the Picture Book Pirates,* Puffin (London, England), 2005.
Michael Lawrence, *The Griffin and Oliver Pie,* Orchard Books (London, England), 2006.
Jane Johnson, *The Secret Country* ("Eidolon Chronicles"), Simon & Schuster (New York, NY), 2006.
Jane Johnson, *The Shadow World* ("Eidolon Chronicles"), Simon & Schuster (New York, NY), 2007.
Jane Johnson, *Dragon's Fire* ("Eidolon Chronicles"), Simon & Schuster (New York, NY), 2007.
Lucy Bowman, *Antarctica,* Usborne (London, England), 2007.
Timothy Knapman, *Mungo and the Spiders from Space,* Puffin (London, England), 2007.
Timothy Knapman, *Mungo and the Dinosaur Island!,* Puffin (London, England), 2008.
Alison Green, *The Diary of a Monster Catcher,* paper models by Nick Denchfield, Scholastic (London, England), 2008.
Thomas Hardy, *The Three Strangers and Other Stories,* retold by Clare West, Oxford University Press (New York, NY), 2008.
Roger McGough, *Slapstick Poems,* Puffin (London, England), 2008.
Steve Cole and Linda Chapman, *Genie Us!,* Red Fox (London, England), 2008.
Steve Cole and Linda Chapman, *Genie and the Phoenix,* Red Fox (London, England), 2009.
Jeanne Willis, *Bottoms Up!,* Puffin (London, England), 2009.
Rob Stevens, *Vampanther Attack!* ("Mapmaker's Monsters" series), Macmillan Children's (London, England), 2009.
Rob Stevens, *Beware the Buffalogre!,* Macmillan Children's (London, England), 2009.
Debbie Dadey and Marcia Thornton Jones, *This Side of Magic,* Tor/Starscape (New York, NY), 2009.
Maureen Sherry, *Walls within Walls,* Katherine Tegen Books (New York, NY), 2010.
Neil Gaiman, *Odd and the Frost Giants,* Bloomsbury (London, England), 2010.
Jeanne Willis, *Sing a Song of Bottoms!,* Puffin (London, England), 2010.

Jane Johnson, *Legends of the Shadow World,* Simon & Schuster Books for Young Readers (New York, NY), 2010.

ILLUSTRATOR; "ED MOUSE" SERIES BY HONOR HEAD

Ed Mouse Finds out about Size and Shape, Belitha (London, England), 1997, Raintree Steck-Vaughn (Austin, TX), 1999.

Ed Mouse Finds out about Direction, Belitha (London, England), 1997, Raintree Steck-Vaughn (Austin, TX), 1999.

Ed Mouse Finds out about Opposites, Belitha (London, England), 1998, Raintree Steck-Vaughn (Austin, TX), 1999.

Ed Mouse Finds out about Times of Day, Belitha (London, England), 1998, Raintree Steck-Vaughn (Austin, TX), 1999.

ILLUSTRATOR; "SPY MICE" SERIES BY HEATHER VOGEL FREDERICK

For Your Paws Only, Puffin (London, England), 2006.
The Black Paw, Puffin (London, England), 2006.
Goldwhiskers, Puffin (London, England), 2007.

ILLUSTRATOR; "DRAGONS OF WAYWARD CRESCENT" SERIES BY CHRIS D'LACEY

Gruffen, Orchard (London, England), 2009.
Gauge, Orchard (London, England), 2009.
Grabber, Orchard (London, England), 2010.
Glade, Orchard (London, England), 2010.

ILLUSTRATOR; "BENJAMIN PRATT AND THE KEEPERS OF THE SCHOOL" SERIES

Andrew Clements, *Fear Itself,* Atheneum Books for Young Readers (New York, NY), 2010.
Andrew Clements, *We the Children,* Atheneum Books for Young Readers (New York, NY), 2010.

Sidelights

Adam Stower is a British illustrator whose work has been influenced by such well-known picture-book artists as Heath Robinson, Edmund Dulac, and Arthur Rackham. A graduate of the Norwich School of Art and the University of Brighton, Stower has provided artwork for texts by Honor Head, Roger McGough, Andrew Clement, Timothy Knapman, Heather Vogel Frederick, and other authors. He has also written and illustrated his own children's stories, among them *Two Left Feet, The Den, Slam!: A Tale of Consequences, Silly Doggy!,* and the pop-up book *The Diary of a Monster Catcher.*

Stower introduces Rufus, a cheerful, blue-skinned monster, in *Two Left Feet,* his debut self-illustrated work. Although Rufus loves to dance with his friends, he inevitably winds up on the floor after tripping over his own feet, both of which are, quite literally, left ones. When a messenger from the Glittering Palace invites the monsters to attend a ballroom dancing competition, Rufus cannot find a partner who wants to pair off with him. Dejected, the monster prepares to sit out the contest but is approached by Maddie, a boggart with her own anatomical quirk: she has two right feet. In *School Library Journal* Bethany L.W. Hankinson cited "the subtle humor" in *Two Left Feet,* and a *Publishers Weekly* critic remarked that "the delicate ink lines and golden, shimmery colors at times give Stower's artwork the appearance of classic hand-tinted etchings." A *Kirkus Reviews* contributor dubbed *Two Left Feet* "a terpsichorean triumph that will send even younger readers into a twirl."

As an illustrator, Stower has contributed his talent to dozens of picture books and novels for younger readers. *Snowball Fight!,* a story by *Saturday Night Live* star Jimmy Fallon, follows a young boy as he dashes outside on a wintry day to construct a fort strong enough to withstand a snowy onslaught from his playful neighbors. Just when he runs out of ammunition and appears to be overrun, the boy receives much-needed assistance from his younger sister. "Stower's watercolors, featuring pugnosed, wide-eyed kids, exude an old-fashioned winter friskiness," remarked a contributor in *Publishers Weekly,* and Sally R. Dow noted in *School Library Journal* that Stower's "energetic cartoon-style illustrations" for *Snowball Fight!* "capture the action and humor."

Stower's detailed illustration style pairs well with fantasy stories, such as Chris d'Lacey's *Gruffen,* the story of a family that raises young dragons with magical powers. Noting the "cozy" elements in *Gruffen,* Amy Holland added in *School Library Journal* that the artist's "line drawings add visual interest; their cartoon style also enforces the light, upbeat mood." *This Side of Magic,* by the prolific writing team of Debbie Dadey and Marcia Thornton Jones, benefits from what *Booklist* critic Carolyn Phelan described as "appealing line drawings" by Stower that catpture the story of two children who discover a hidden dimension inhabited by magical creatures. "The brightly colored comic-style illustrations" that Stower contributes to Timothy Knapman's *Mungo and the Spiders from Space* "will appeal to young fans looking for action and adventure," predicted *School Library Journal* contributor Maura Bresnahan, and in *Booklist* Ian Chipman noted of the same work that Knapman and Stower's "dizzying mix of space-adventure superheroics and bedtime fantasy fulfillment plays a bit with picture-book conventions." *Walls within Walls,* a middle-grade novel by Maureen Sherry, serves up a "breathtaking romp" in which the journey of three siblings following hidden clues to discover a lost fortune is captured in Stower's "full-page illustrations," according to *School Library Journal* critic Caitlin Augusta.

Stower's art is a feature of a trio of linked stories by Jane Johnson: *The Secret Country, The Shadow World,*

and *Dragon's Fire,* which are part of Johnson's "Eidolon Chronicles." In *The Secret Country* Ben Arnold purchases a talking cat named Iggy from Mr. Dodds' Pet Emporium, and learns from his new pet that his ailing mother is the rightful queen of the mythic world of Eidolon. Hoping to restore order to that realm, the boy and his sisters must now prevent Dodd and evil Uncle Aleister from joining forces and kidnapping the magical animals that inhabit Eidolon. In *The Shadow World* Ben encounters a host of creatures—including a centaur, a mermaid, and several selkies—after he enters Eidolon in order to rescue his older sister from the clutches of the nefarious Dodman. Praising Stower's contributions to *The Shadow World, School Library Journal* reviewer Sharon Grover remarked that "a whimsical black-and-white drawing opens each chapter."

Other multi-book series that feature Stower's art include Andrew Clements' "Benjamin Pratt and the Keepers of the School" books. Featuring the novels *We the Children* and *Fear Itself,* the series finds middle-schooler Ben Pratt acquiring a gold coin that dates to the revolutionary era and encourages its owner to defend the school that Ben now attends. When he learns that a deal to sell the school to a theme-park developer is afoot, the boy decides to research the property's history to find out why the school's preservation was deemed so important. Ben's quest continues in *Fear Itself,* as the preteen is joined with classmate Jill to follow the ownership of the school building back to its original founder, Duncan Oakes, and stop its destruction. "Expressive, dynamic full-page and spot illustrations rendered in pen and ink heighten the action" and propel *We the Children* to "an exciting ending," according to *School Library Journal* contributor Debbie S. Hoskins. Along with Clements' "solid writing," Stower's "expressive pen-and-ink illustrations add detail and excitement to the [continuing] adventure," asserted Debbie Hoskins in her *School Library Journal* review of *Fear Itself.*

"I have been illustrating professionally since the early 1990s but I have enjoyed drawing for as long as I can remember," Stower told *SATA.* "My first published works were cartoons for my school magazine, done when I was nine years old. During the first few years of my career much of my work was commissioned by publishers of educational books. Illustrating school books may not have been the most exciting work but I was glad of it as it proved to be an excellent apprenticeship in the art of illustrating to a brief.

"In these early years I would take on any commissions I was offered—illustrating text books, packaging, leaflets, etc.—but I was always drawn to the more narrative commissions. As time has gone on, I have specialized in illustrating children's fiction dividing my time between picture books and young fiction, with the occasional editorial/packaging job thrown into the mix. I enjoy the different challenge each type of job presents.

"I am an avid keeper of sketchbooks, which I use partly as diaries (particularly when traveling) but mostly as somewhere to enjoy doodling and let new ideas and characters evolve. Sometimes it's good to enjoy activities away from my desk, particularly when I'm stuck on a story idea. I swim and play the guitar (not very well), and attend life-drawing sessions among other things. The ideas soon start flowing again. I love what I do and feel very lucky to have the opportunity to do it."

Biographical and Critical Sources

PERIODICALS

Booklist, June 1, 2006, Sally Estes, review of *The Secret Country,* p. 71; December 1, 2007, Sally Estes, review of *The Shadow World,* p. 42; February 1, 2009, Ian Chipman, review of *Mungo and the Spiders from Space,* p. 46; June 1, 2009, Carolyn Phelan, review of *This Side of Magic,* p. 57; September 15, 2010, Todd Morning, review of *Fear Itself,* p. 65.

Horn Book, January-February, 2010, Robin L. Smith, review of *Gruffen,* p. 85; May-June, 2010, Susan Love Lempke, review of *We the Children,* p. 78.

Kirkus Reviews, July 1, 2004, review of *Two Left Feet,* p. 638; April 15, 2006, review of *The Secret Country,* p. 408; April 1, 2009, review of *This Side of Magic.*

Publishers Weekly, August 9, 2004, review of *Two Left Feet,* p. 250; April 15, 2005, review of *Snowball Fight!,* p. 58; May 4, 2009, review of *This Side of Magic,* p. 50; March 22, 2010, review of *We the Children,* p. 70.

School Library Journal, October, 2004, Bethany L.W. Hankinson, review of *Two Left Feet,* p. 135; November, 2005, Sally R. Dow, review of *Snowball Fight!,* p. 90; April, 2006, Margaret A. Chang, review of *The Secret Country,* p. 141; November, 2007, Sharon Grover, review of *The Shadow World,* p. 126; April, 2009, Maura Bresnahan, review of *Mungo and the Spiders from Space,* p. 110; May, 2010, Amy Holland, review of *Gruffen,* p. 82, and Debbie S. Hoskins, review of *We the Children,* p. 107; September, 2010, Debbie Hoskins, review of *Fear Itself,* p. 148; October, 2010, Caitlin Augusta, review of *Walls within Walls,* p. 126.

ONLINE

Adam Stower Home Page, http://www.worldofadam.com (April 24, 2011).

*   *   *

SUMNER, William 1971-

Personal

Born 1971; married; children: two daughters. *Education:* M.A. (education and archaeology); postgraduate work in biodefence.

Addresses

Home—NE.

Career

Military officer and author. U.S. Army 354th Civil Affairs Brigade, attained rank of captain and served tour of duty in Iraq; U.S. Strategic Command, attained rank of major. Affiliated with U.S. Committee of the Blue Shield.

Writings

(With Kelly Milner Halls) *Saving the Baghdad Zoo: A True Story of Hope and Heroes,* Greenwillow Books (New York, NY), 2010.

Sidelights

Major William Sumner has dedicated his career to serving the United States, and is now assigned to the U.S. Strategic Command. Stationed in Baghdad during the Iraq War, as a captain of the 354th Civil Affairs Brigade, Sumner undertook a mission that is unusual for someone in his position. Teaming up with children's writer Kelly Milner Halls, he recounts this mission in his book *Saving the Baghdad Zoo: A True Story of Hope and Heroes.*

In *Saving the Baghdad Zoo* readers are transported to the al-Zawraa' Gardens, a region of Baghdad that is known for its beauty. Established in 1971 and covering 200 acres, the Baghdad Zoo housed over 600 animals by the time the Iraq war broke out in 2003. As Baghdad fell under attack, the zoo animals suffered, in part due to the fact that their living conditions were inadequate to begin with and the sanctions imposed by the U.N. had limited the facility's access to veterinary care for several years. When Captain Sumner arrived at the zoo to determine the facility's status, he found animals that were severely stressed for want of food, water, and medical care. Most were missing and many were dead; of the twenty-two lions that the zoo had housed prior to the war, only two females remained. Assembling a team of specialists that included veterinarians, zoologists, and a host of local volunteers, Sumner embarked on a new mission: to bring the remaining zoo animals back to good heath and then to improve their habitat.

Full of photographs documenting the efforts of Sumner's team, *Saving the Baghdad Zoo* chronicles the stories of both human helpers and the animals themselves, among them a brown bear named Saedia, who was given a new, grass-carpeted home; Lumpy the camel, who was found, nearly starved, and transported back to the zoo on roads infested with enemy sniper nests; a group of Arabian racehorses that had been abducted by thieves; new resident tigers Hope and Riley, whose trip to Baghdad extended almost 7,000 miles; and a menagerie of tortoises, palace cheetahs, and pelicans among various other birds. The "upbeat tone" of Sumner and Halls' text "will leave younger audiences more pleased than disturbed," asserted a *Kirkus Reviews* writer, and Hazel Rochman noted in *Booklist* that *Saving the Baghdad Zoo* is "bolstered with large, beautiful color photos and informative sidebars." Sumner's "emotional commentary" is paired with his "sobering and uplifting photographs," according to a *Publishers Weekly,* and Christine M. Heppermann wrote in *Horn Book* that "this moving photo essay reveals how Americans and Iraquis . . . worked together" on a common cause. Although Baghdad's zoo remains a less-than-"sterling example of what a modern zoological park ought to be," *School Library Journal* contributor Patricia Manning dubbed *Saving the Baghdad Zoo* "a shining example of human efforts to provide care and comfort to abandoned animals and . . . sanctuary to Iraqi residents whose lives have been drastically disrupted."

Biographical and Critical Sources

PERIODICALS

Booklist, February 15, 2010, Hazel Rochman, review of *Saving the Baghdad Zoo: A True Story of Hope and Heroes,* p. 75.
Bulletin of the Center for Children's Books, May, 2010, Deborah Stevenson, review of *Saving the Baghdad Zoo,* p. 379.
Horn Book, May-June, 2010, Christine M. Heppermann, review of *Saving the Baghdad Zoo,* p. 108.
Kirkus Reviews, January 15, 2010, review of *Saving the Baghdad Zoo.*
Publishers Weekly, January 11, 2010, review of *Saving the Baghdad Zoo,* p. 48.
School Library Journal, June, 2010, Patricia Manning, review of *Saving the Baghdad Zoo,* p. 130.*

T-Y

TELLEGEN, Toon 1941-

Personal

Born November 18, 1941, in Brielle, Netherlands; married. *Education:* University of Utrecht, medical degree.

Addresses

Home—Amsterdam, Netherlands.

Career

Poet, children's book author, and physician. General practitioner of medicine in Amsterdam, Netherlands.

Awards, Honors

ANV/Visser Neerlandia-prijs, 1969, for *Als moeder ergens ziek van wordt;* Gouden Griffel, 1988, for *Toen niemand iets te doen had,* 1994, for *Bijna iedereen kon omvallen;* Zilveren Griffel, 1990, for *Langzaam, zo snel zij konden,* 1994, for *Jannes,* 1997, for *Teunis,* 1999, for *De verjaardag van alle anderen;* Woutertje Pieterse Prijs, 1992, for *Juffrouw Kachel,* 1994, for *Bijna iedereen kon omvallen,* 2007, for *Bijna iedereen kon omvallen;* Jan Campertprijs, 1993, for *Een dansschool;* Theo Thijssenprijs, 1997, for body of work; Gouden Uil, 2000, for *De Genezing van de Krekell;* Hans Christian Andersen Award finalist, 2006; Constantijn Huygensprijs, 2007, for body of work.

Writings

POETRY

(With Hiel Goslinga) *Jimmy Walker. Spel geschreven ter gelegenheid van het Utrechtsch studenten corps,* De Bezige Bij (Amsterdam, Netherlands), 1966.
Als moeder ergens ziek van wordt, 1969.
De zin van een liguster, Querido (Amsterdam, Netherlands), 1980.

De aanzet tot een web, Querido (Amsterdam, Netherlands), 1981.
Beroemde scherven, Querido (Amsterdam, Netherlands), 1982.
De andere ridders, Querido (Amsterdam, Netherlands), 1984.
Ik en ik, Querido (Amsterdam, Netherlands), 1985.
Mijn winter, Querido (Amsterdam, Netherlands), 1987.
In N. en andere Gedichten, Querido (Amsterdam, Netherlands), 1989, translated as *In N,* Cross-Cultural Communications (New York, NY), 1993.
Een langzame val, Querido (Amsterdam, Netherlands), 1991.
Een dansschool, Querido (Amsterdam, Netherlands), 1992.
Tijger onder de slakken, Querido (Amsterdam, Netherlands), 1994.
Als we vlammen waren, Querido (Amsterdam, Netherlands), 1996.
Over liefde en niets anders, Querido (Amsterdam, Netherlands), 1997, translation published as *About Love and about Nothing Else,* Shoestring Press, 2008.
Gewone gedichten, Querido (Amsterdam, Netherlands), 1998.
Er ligt een appel op een schaal, Querido (Amsterdam, Netherlands), 1999.
Kruis en munt, Querido (Amsterdam, Netherlands), 2000.
Gedichten 1977-1999, Querido (Amsterdam, Netherlands), 2000.
De een en de ander, Querido (Amsterdam, Netherlands), 2001.
Een man en een engel, Querido (Amsterdam, Netherlands), 2001.
Alleen Liefde: Een Keuze, Querido (Amsterdam, Netherlands), 2002.
Wie a zegt, Querido (Amsterdam, Netherlands), 2002.
Minuscule oorlogen (niet met het blote oog zichtbaar), Querido (Amsterdam, Netherlands), 2004.
Daar zijn woorden: een keuze uit de gedichten, Querido (Amsterdam, Netherlands), 2004.
. . . m n o p q . . . , illustrated by Jan Jutte, Querido (Amsterdam, Netherlands), 2005.
Wachten op wonderen, Querido (Amsterdam, Netherlands), 2005.

Raafvogels, Querido (Amsterdam, Netherlands), 2006.

Daar zijn woorden voor: een keuze uit de gedichten, Mutinga Pockets (Amsterdam, Netherlands), 2007.

Hemels en vergeefs, Querido (Amsterdam, Netherlands), 2008.

Stof dat als een meisje: Variaties op een thema, Querido (Amsterdam, Netherlands), 2009.

FICTION

Twee oude vrouwtjes (stories), Querido (Amsterdam, Netherlands), 1994.

Dora: een liefdesgeschiedenis (young-adult novel), Querido (Amsterdam, Netherlands), 1998.

De trein naar Pavlovsk en Oostvoorne (stories), Querido (Amsterdam, Netherlands), 2000.

Brieven aan Doornroosje, Querido (Amsterdam, Netherlands), 2002.

Ik zal je nooit vergeten, Querido (Amsterdam, Netherlands), 2007.

Een nieuwe tijd, Grafische Cultuurstichting (Amstelveen, Netherlands), 2007.

Work included in anthology *Go Dutch!: Eight Writers from the Netherlands*, Foundation for the Production and Translation of Dutch Literature (Amsterdam, Netherlands), 2009.

FOR CHILDREN

Er ging geen dag voorbij: negenenveertig verhalen over de eekhoorn en de andere dieren, Querido (Amsterdam, Netherlands), 1984, reprinted, 2004.

Toen niemand iets te doen had, illustrated by Mance Post, Querido (Amsterdam, Netherlands), 1987, reprinted, Querido (Amsterdam, Netherlands), 2008.

Mijn vader, Querido (Amsterdam, Netherlands), 1987.

Langzaam, zo snel als zij konden, illustrated by Mance Post, Querido (Amsterdam, Netherlands), 1990.

Misschien waren zij nergens, Querido (Amsterdam, Netherlands), 1991.

Jannes, Querido (Amsterdam, Netherlands), 1993.

Juffrouw Kachel, [Netherlands], 1994.

Bijna iedereen kon omvallen, illustrated by Anne van Buul, Querido (Amsterdam, Netherlands), 1994, reprinted, Muntinga Pockets (Amsterdam, Netherlands), 2009.

Misschien wisten zij alles. 313 verhalen over de eekhoorn en de andere dieren, illustrated by Geerten ten Bosch, Querido (Amsterdam, Netherlands), 1995.

De verjaardag van de eekhoorn (also see below), illustrated by Geerten ten Bosch, Querido (Amsterdam, Netherlands), 1996, translation published as *The Squirrel's Birthday and Other Parties*, illustrated by Jessica Ahlberg, Sterling (New York, NY), 2010.

De ontdekking van de honing, Querido (Amsterdam, Netherlands), 1996.

Misschien wisten zij alles. Alle verhalen over de eekhoorn en de andere dieren, illustrated by Geerten ten Bosch, Querido (Amsterdam, Netherlands), 1996.

Dokter Deter, Querido (Amsterdam, Netherlands), 1997.

Teunis, illustrated by Jan Jutte, Querido (Amsterdam, Netherlands), 1997.

De verjaardag van alle anderen (also see below), illustrated by Geerten ten Bosch, Querido (Amsterdam, Netherlands), 1999.

De genezing van de krekel, Querido (Amsterdam, Netherlands), 1999.

(Author of narration) Klaas ten Holt, *Pikkuhenki* (musical work), illustrated by Marit Törnvist, Donemus (Amsterdam, Netherlands), 2000.

Maar niet uit het hart, Querido (Amsterdam, Netherlands), 2002.

Plotseling ging de olifant aan, illustrated by Annemarie van Haeringen, Querido (Amsterdam, Netherlands), 2004.

Na aan het hart: Dierenverhalen vol vriesdschap, Querido (Amsterdam, Netherlands), 2004.

Midden den nacht, Querido (Amsterdam, Netherlands), 2005.

De eenzaamheid van de egel, Querido (Amsterdam, Netherlands), 2006.

Pikko, die Hexe, illustrated by Marit Törnqvist, Sauerländer (Düseldorf, Germany), 2006.

Dutch writer Toon Tellegen's stories for young children include Letters to Anyone and Everyone, *which features Jessica Ahlberg's illustrations in its English-language edition.* (Illustration copyright © 2009 by Jessica Ahlberg. Reproduced by permission of Boxer Books.)

De almacht van de boktor, Querido (Amsterdam, Netherlands), 2007.

Post voor iedereen, illustrated by Mance Post, Querido (Amsterdam, Netherlands), 2007.

Ik zal je nooit vergeten, [Netherlands], 2007.

De verjaardag van de eekhoorn en andere verhalen, illustrated by Geerten ten Bosch, Querido (Amsterdam, Netherlands), 2007.

De verschrompeling van de olifant, Walewijn (Amsterdam, Netherlands), 2008.

Met hart en ziel: Dierenverhalen voor elk feest, Querido (Amsterdam, Netherlands), 2008.

De genezing van de krekel, Querido (Amsterdam, Netherlands), 2008.

Een hart onder de riem: Dierenverhalen vol troost, Querido (Amsterdam, Netherlands), 2008.

Morgen was het feest, Querido (Amsterdam, Netherlands), 2008.

Iedereen was er: meer verhalen over de eekhoorn en de andere dieren, Querido (Amsterdam, Netherlands), 2009.

Beterschap. Dierenverhalen over ziekte en gezondheid, Querido (Amsterdam, Netherlands), 2009.

Welterusten. Dierenverhalen over slaap en sluimer, Querido (Amsterdam, Netherlands), 2009.

Goede reis. Dierenverhalen over vertrek en aankomst, Querido (Amsterdam, Netherlands), 2009.

Houd moed. Dierenverhalen over verdriet en eenzaamheid, Querido (Amsterdam, Netherlands), 2009.

Het vertrek van de mier, Querido (Amsterdam, Netherlands), 2009.

Letters to Anyone and Everyone, translated by Martin Cleaver, illustrated by Jessica Ahlberg, Boxer Books (London, England), 2009.

Wat dansen we heerlijk, illustrated by Annemarie van Haeringen, Querido (Amsterdam, Netherlands), 2010.

Mano de brandweerjongen, Rubinstein (Amsterdam, Netherlands), 2010.

Waar is Mo?, Rubinstein (Amsterdam, Netherlands), 2010.

Als Feda slaapt, Rubinstein (Amsterdam, Netherlands), 2010.

De genezing van de krekel, Querido (Amsterdam, Netherlands), 2010.

Far Away across the Sea, translated by Martin Clever, illustrated by Jessica Ahlberg, Boxer Books (London, England), 2011.

Author's work has been translated into several languages, including German, Polish, Russian, and Spanish.

Biographical and Critical Sources

PERIODICALS

Booklist, May 15, 2010, Carolyn Phelan, review of *Letters to Anyone and Everyone,* p. 44.

Kirkus Reviews, December 15, 2009, review of *Letters to Anyone and Everyone.*

School Librarian, spring, 2010, Anna Griffin, review of *The Squirrel's Birthday and Other Parties,* p. 32.

School Library Journal, April, 2010, Shawn Brommer, review of *Letters to Anyone and Everyone,* p. 141; November, 2010, Lynn K. Vanca, review of *Far Away across the Sea,* p. 85.

World Literature Today, summer, 1996, Martinus A. Bakker, review of *Misschien wisten Zij alles: Alle verhalen over de eekhoorn en de andere dierren,* p. 712; autumn, 1997, Martins A. Bakker, review of *Over liefde en over niets anders,* p. 818; autumn, 1999, Fred J. Nichols, review of *Gwone gedichten,* p. 755; winter, 1999, Henri Kops, review of *Dora: een liefdesgeschiedenis,* p. 162.

ONLINE

Netherlands Poetry International Web site, http://netherlands.poetryinternationalweb.org/ (April 15, 2011), "Toon Tellegen."*

*   *   *

TIERNEY, Fiona

Personal

Born in Dublin, Ireland; married; children: four.

Addresses

Home—North Dublin, Ireland. *E-mail*—fionatierney@eircom.net.

Career

Author.

Writings

PICTURE BOOKS

Look What Blew into the Zoo, illustrated by Úna Healy, Brian Gilsenen (Ireland), 2006.

Peek at the Week in the Zoo, illustrated by Úna Healy, Primary ABC Publications (Ireland), 2007.

Lion's Lunch?, illustrated by Margaret Chamberlain, Chicken House (Frome, England), 2009, Chicken House (New York, NY), 2010.

Author's works have been translated into Catalan, Korean, and Spanish.

Biographical and Critical Sources

PERIODICALS

Booklist, December 1, 2009, Julie Cummins, review of *Lion's Lunch?,* p. 51.

Fiona Tierney (Reproduced by permission.)

Kirkus Reviews, December 15, 2009, review of *Lion's Lunch?*

Publishers Weekly, December 21, 2009, review of *Lion's Lunch?,* p. 59.

School Library Journal, February, 2010, Sarah Polace, review of *Lion's Lunch?,* p. 96.

ONLINE

Fiona Tierney Home Page, http://www.fionatierney.com (April 24, 2011).

*   *   *

TRIPLETT, Gina

Personal

Born in MN; married Matt Curtius (an artist); children: Juniper. *Education:* Attended art school.

Addresses

Home—Philadelphia, PA. *Agent*—Frank Sturges, frank@ sturgesreps.com. *E-mail*—gina@ginaandmatt.com.

Career

Illustrator and fine-art painter. Clients include Starbuck's, Target, Macy's, and America Express. *Exhibi-*

tions: Collaborative paintings have been exhibited in New York, NY, and Los Angeles, CA.

Illustrator

Barbara Summers, editor, *Open the Usual Door: True-life Stories of Challenge, Adventure, and Success by Black Americans,* Houghton/Graphia (Boston, MA), 2005.

Susan Korman, *P Is for Philadelphia,* Temple University Press (Philadelphia, PA), 2005.

Leslie Connor, *Dead on Town Line,* Dial (New York, NY), 2005.

Isabella Zaruni, *The Magic Fortune-Teller,* Chronicle Books (San Francisco, CA), 2007.

Alex Flinn, *Diva,* HarperTeen (New York, NY), 2007.

Rose Kent, *Kimchi and Calamari,* HarperCollins (New York, NY), 2007.

Sara Lorimer, *Pregnancy to-Do's: A Book of Lists for Moms-to-Be,* Chronicle Books (San Francisco, CA), 2007.

Viola Canales, *The Tequila Worm,* Wendy Lamb Books (New York, NY), 2007.

Daisy Whitney, *The Mockingbirds,* Little, Brown Books for Young Readers (New York, NY), 2010.

Contributor to periodicals, including *New York Times, Rolling Stone,* and *Step.* Illustrations featured in *American Illustration, Communication Arts Illustration Annual, Curvy, Illustration Now, Picture Book, Print Regional Design Annual,* and *Society of Illustrators Annual.*

Sidelights

Gina Triplett is a painter who frequently works in collaboration with her husband and fellow artist, Matt Curtius. Based in Philadelphia, the couple draws on their joint interest in color, pattern, and nature to produce colorful and detailed images that have found their way into galleries and onto everything from packaging to restaurant walls to snowboards and water skis. Triplett's solo work includes creating illustrations and spot art for books and magazines, among them Leslie Connor's young-adult novel *Dead on Town Line* and Barbara Summers' *Open the Unusual Door: True-life Stories of Challenge, Adventure, and Success by Black Americans,* the latter which was hailed by *School Library Journal* critic Carol Jones Collins as a "little gem of a book."

Praised by *Booklist* contributor Todd Morning as "captivating," *Dead on Town Line* is a verse novel narrated by the ghost of Cassie Devlin. Murdered and her body hidden amid the rocks at the town line, Cassie learns the stories of other murder victims as she waits for her own body to be discovered. Triplett's illustrations "of nature and symbolic objects extends the sense of shifting between worlds with strong lines and bold contrasts," according to Morning. The "ethereal quality" of Connor's story is strengthened by Triplett's "black-and-white drawings depicting images from Cassie's life and death," asserted Sonja Cole in her *School Library Journal* review of *Dead on Town Line,* while in *Kliatt* Myrna Marler dubbed the novel's artwork "haunting."

Biographical and Critical Sources

PERIODICALS

Booklist, July, 2005, Todd Morning, review of *Dead on Town Line*, p. 1915; January 1, 2006, Kay Weisman, review of *Open the Usual Door: True-life Stories of Challenge, Adventure, and Success by Black Americans*, p. 79.

Kirkus Reviews, May 15, 2005, review of *Dead on Town Line*, p. 586.

Kliatt, July, 2005, Myrna Marler, review of *Dead on Town Line*, p. 10.

School Library Journal, July, 2005, Sonja Cole, review of *Dead on Town Line*, p. 101; December, 2005, Carol Jones Collins, review of *Open the Usual Door*, p. 175.

ONLINE

Gina Triplett Home Page, http://www.ginaandmatt.com (April 24, 2011).

Gina Triplet Web log, http://ginatriplett.blogspot.com (April 24, 2011).

*   *   *

VELÁSQUEZ, Gloria 1949-

Personal

Born December 21, 1949, in Loveland, CO; daughter of John E. (a migrant farm worker) and Frances (a migrant farm worker) Velásquez; divorced; children: Brandi Lynn Treviño, Robert John Velásquez Treviño. *Education:* University of Northern Colorado, B.A. (Chicano and Spanish studies), 1978; Stanford University, M.A., 1980, Ph.D. (Spanish literature), 1985. *Politics:* Democrat. *Religion:* "Roman Catholic and Diné." *Hobbies and other interests:* Playing guitar, writing songs and performing in a rock band.

Addresses

Home—San Luis Obispo, CA. *E-mail*—glvelasque@gmail.com.

Career

Author, educator, and musician. Hewlett Packard, secretary, 1966-67; California Polytechnic State University, professor of modern languages and literature, beginning 1985. Member of board, Canto al Pueblo, 1979, and Koger Kamp Foundation, 1992-93. UNC Ambassador, beginning 1992; speaker and activist; presenter at schools and libraries.

Member

PEN.

Awards, Honors

University of Northern Colorado-Greeley alumni honor, 1987, induction into Hall of Fame, 1989; Chicano Literary Prize for short story, University of California—Irvine, 1985; honored by Texas House of Representatives, 2001, for outstanding contributions to literature.

Writings

"ROOSEVELT HIGH SCHOOL" YOUNG-ADULT NOVEL SERIES

Juanita Fights the School Board, Arte Público Press/Piñata Books (Houston, TX), 1994.

Maya's Divided World, Piñata Books (Houston, TX), 1995.

Tommy Stands Alone, Piñata Books (Houston, TX), 1995.

Rina's Family Secret, Piñata Books (Houston, TX), 1998.

Ankiza, Piñata Books (Houston, TX), 2000.

Teen Angel, Piñata Books (Houston, TX), 2003.

Tyrone's Betrayal, Piñata Books (Houston, TX), 2006.

Rudy's Memory Walk, Piñata Books (Houston, TX), 2009.

Tommy Stands Tall, Piñata Books (Houston, TX), 2011.

Author's books have been translated into French.

OTHER

Used to be a Superwoman (poetry), Arte Público Press (Houston, TX), 1997.

Xicana on the Run (memoir), Arte Público Press (Houston, TX), 2005.

Author's manuscripts are archived at Stanford University, Stanford, CA.

Sidelights

In her work, Chicana/Latina poet and novelist Gloria Velásquez often touches on the themes that have shaped her life. Born to migrant farm workers, Velásquez spent a good deal of her childhood traveling between Colorado and Texas. Like many other Hispanics, the Velásquez family lived in poverty and knew little stability in its search to make ends meet. Much of Gloria's poetry and short fiction reflects this reality and shows a deep yearning to change an environment that allows such widespread disparity. She also expresses her strong feminist viewpoint, rebelling against the domination of the Chicana (female Mexican American) in modern-day society. Although much of her early work was poetry, beginning in the 1990s Velásquez shifted her focus to teen readers with the first of her "Roosevelt High School" series. Beginning with *Juanita Fights the School Board*, these novels incorporate themes and topics that their author feels strongly about. Their emphasis on Chicano/Latino characters has also been cited as something rare in the young-adult genre.

Velásquez was born in 1949 in Loveland, Colorado, where she attended her first years of school. In the course of her family moves from one place to another,

she attended another school in Texas before her parents finally settled in Johnstown, Colorado. In Johnstown, Velásquez' parents were able to find other work outside of the farm industry, and it was here that she graduated from Roosevelt High School, a place that would become the model for her "Roosevelt High" books. After high school, Velásquez worked as a secretary for Hewlett-Packard and attended night classes at a local college. It was during these classes that the future author began to develop her craft.

A fellowship from the University of Northern Colorado allowed Velásquez to study full time, double majoring in Chicano and Spanish studies. After earning her B.A. at the University of Northern Colorado, she moved on to Stanford University where she won several literary awards and ultimately earned a Ph.D. in Spanish literature. During her graduate work she wrote a groundbreaking dissertation titled "Cultural Ambivalence in Early Chicana Prose Fiction," which concentrated on the writings of Chicana authors of the twentieth-century and set the tone for the themes she has since explored in her prose. "Born and raised in poverty, I truly be-

Cover of Gloria L. Velásquez's young-adult novel **Rudy's Memory Walk,** *part of her "Roosevelt High School" series.* (Copyright © 2009 Arte Público Press/University of Houston. Reproduced with permission from the publisher.)

lieve that when you are born with nothing you have everything," Velásquez once commented. "It is this gift from the divine spirits that I share in my writing with the world, with our youth, with society."

In her "Roosevelt High School" books Velásquez addresses many of the issues that plague the Chicano/Latino community: alcoholism, single-parent families, divorce, lack of self-identity, and violence. For critics, the series has been notable in that it features realistic Chicano teens, characters who have rarely appeared in the stories released by mainstream U.S. publishers. In novels such as *Juanita Fights the School Board, Maya's Divided World, Rina's Family Secret,* and *Teen Angel,* Velásquez features recurring characters, the most prominent of which is Sandra Martinez, a guidance counselor at Roosevelt. Throughout the series, Ms. Martinez gives assistance to her students, helping them cope with various problems and providing a listening ear whenever they need to talk.

Velásquez also uses Martinez to develop subplots in several of the stories. In *Maya's Divided World,* for instance, Martinez's life has many parallels with that of Maya, a Roosevelt High student whose seemingly charmed life comes unraveled because of problems at home. When the story begins, Maya seems to be the perfect student: she is good looking, with wealthy parents, and the envy of her classmates. When her parents separate and file for a divorce, however, their breakup comes as a tremendous blow to Maya. Her school work begins to suffer, and she isolates herself from all of her best friends, unable to face them for fear that they will find out about the divorce. Finally, Maya's best friend persuades her to talk with Ms. Martinez, who helps the girl cope with her problems. Velásquez uses multiple first-person narratives throughout the book, providing multi-faceted viewpoints of Maya's predicament. In *Booklist* Jeanne Triner enthused about the cast of Chicano characters in the novel and wrote that Velásquez does "a nice job of giving readers a window into the culture and providing some positive role models."

In *Tommy Stands Alone* Velásquez focuses on a friend of Maya's, a Chicano student at Roosevelt High who is gay. To his friends and classmates, Tommy seems just like everybody else because he tries to conceal his sexual identity. When a friend discovers a note in his pocket that was written by a well-known gay boy, everyone learns Tommy's secret. Alienated and hurt, Tommy turns to alcohol and even attempts suicide in the hopes that it will ease his pain. Ms. Martinez again intercedes and counsels the young man. Critic Merri Monks of *Booklist* called *Tommy Stands Alone* an "engaging story."

Rina's Family Secret features a girl named Rina whose father is an alcoholic and physically abusive, both to her mother and to her and her siblings. When Rina's father, in a night of rage, stabs her mother with a knife, Rina decides that she can no longer tolerate the man's

In Rina's Family Secret *Velásquez focuses on an Hispanic girl who worries over her parents' abusive relationship.* (Copyright © 1998 Arte Público Press/University of Houston. Reproduced with permission from the publisher.)

abusive ways, or her mother's passivity, and she moves in with her grandmother. Ms. Martinez, who shares a common past with Rina, again plays a large role in helping the Puerto Rican student with the dilemma. Reviewing *Rina's Family Secret* in *Booklist*, Debbie Carton dubbed Velásquez' novel "a believable portrait of a multiethnic high-school community" that "realistically captures the emotions and actions of the teenagers who are part of it."

Ankiza, the fifth "Roosevelt High" novel, finds an African-American teen dating a white classmate, Hunter, and the emotional reactions of the girl's friends cause her to rethink her social loyalties. *Teen Angel* finds high-school sophomore Celia distraught upon learning that she is pregnant, while in *Tyrone's Betrayal* another Roosevelt High student worries that his anger toward his alcoholic father may derail his dreams of a college education. Velásquez turns her attention to a multigenerational relationship in *Rudy's Memory Walk,* which finds a senior teen watching as Alzheimer's begins to affect the personality of his beloved abuela. Reviewing *Ankiza* in *School Library Journal,* Cathy Coff-

man applauded the author for addressing "a powerful social issue with compassion and honesty," while Mary N. Oluonye observed in the same periodical that *Tyrone's Betrayal* "will hold teens' attention, especially reluctant readers." The "compassionate" narrative voice in *Rudy's Memory Walk* "gives readers a glimpse into the life and traditions of a working-class family," wrote a *Kirkus Reviews* critic, the writer going on to praise Velásquez' teen novel as both "educational" and "compelling."

Biographical and Critical Sources

BOOKS

Day, Frances, *Latina and Latino Voices in Literature,* Heinemann, 1997, pp. 169-175.
Dictionary of Literary Biography, Volume 122: *Chicano Writers, Second Series,* edited by Francisco A. Lomeli and Carl R. Shirley, Gale (Detroit, MI), 1992.
Velásquez, Gloria, *Xicana on the Run* (memoir), Arte Público Press (Houston, TX), 2005.
York, Sherry, *100 History-making Ethnic Women,* Linworth Publishing, 2004.

PERIODICALS

Booklist, March 1, 1995, Jeanne Triner, review of *Maya's Divided World,* p. 1236; October 15, 1995, Merri Monks, review of *Tommy Stands Alone,* p. 397; August, 1998, Debbie Carton, review of *Rina's Family Secret,* p. 1992.
Book Report, November-December, 2002, Sherry York, profile of Velásquez, p. 34.
Kirkus Reviews, October 1, 2009, review of *Rudy's Memory Walk.*
Kliatt, January, 2004, Francisca Goldsmith, review of *Teen Angel,* p. 20.
MELUS, spring, 1997, Alexia Kosmider, review of *Tommy Stands Alone,* p. 129.
School Library Journal, April, 2001, Cathy Coffman, review of *Ankiza,* p. 151; August, 2003, Linda L. Plevak, review of *Teen Angel,* p. 168; October, 2006, Mary N. Oluonye, review of *Tyrone's Betrayal,* p. 175; November, 2009, Diana Pierce, review of *Rudy's Memory Walk,* p. 123.

ONLINE

Gloria Velásquez Home Page, http://www.gloriavelasquez. com (April 20, 2011).

OTHER

La Raza de Colorado (television documentary), Public Broadcasting System, 2006.*

WALLACE, Chad

Personal

Male. *Education:* Syracuse University, B.F.A., 1997; Fashion Institute of Technology, M.A. (illustration), 2007.

Addresses

Home—Amawalk, NY. *E-mail*—chadwstudio@gmail.com.

Career

Illustrator and fine-artist. Teacher of art. *Exhibitions:* Work included in numerous exhibitions, including at Society of Illustrators, New York, NY, and at galleries in New York State and Los Angeles, CA.

Awards, Honors

Stevan Dohanos Award, Society of Illustrators, 2008.

Illustrator

Henry Wadsworth Longfellow (collected poems), edited by Frances Schoonmaker, Sterling Publishing (New York, NY), 1998.

Barbara Shaw McKinney, *Pass the Energy, Please!*, Dawn Publications (Nevada City, CA), 1999.

Pattie Schnetzler, *Earth Day Birthday,* Dawn Publications (Nevada City, CA), 2003.

Sherry Bowen, *Little Panda,* Richard Owen (Katonah, NY), 2003.

Sherry Shahan, *Mirounga's Pup,* Richard Owen (Katonah, NY), 2005.

Chad Mason, *Wake up, Bertha Bear!,* Down East Books (Camden, ME), 2007.

Brenda Z. Guiberson, *Earth: Feeling the Heat,* Henry Holt (New York, NY), 2010.

Martha S. Campbell, *Hidden in the Midden,* Richard C. Owen (Katonah, NY), 2010.

Sidelights

Working as a professional illustrator since the late 1990s, Chad Wallace has found a niche in illustrating children's books that focus on animals and world ecology. Wallace's photorealistic landscapes place viewers in settings that seem familiar but reveal surreal elements on closer inspection. He also enjoys painting animals, and illustrating children's stories allows him to play with an animal's nature by giving it human characteristics. Wallace's illustrations projects include Barbara Shaw McKinney's *Pass the Energy, Please!*, Pattie Schnetzler's *Earth Day Birthday,* and Brenda Z. Guiberson's *Earth: Feeling the Heat,* all of which transmit adult concerns over ecological harm to young children. Although much of his time is spent in his studio, Wallace often retires to a woodland cabin that has been his second home for several years.

Wallace enjoyed spending time in nature as a child, and drawing provided the means through which he studied plants and animals in detail. In 1997 he completed his B.F.A. at Syracuse University, returning to school several years later to earn a master's degree in illustration. In his art, he begins with traditional media—pencil and brown-toned oil paint on board. After blocking out the composition visually, he scans the initial "sketch" into Photoshop, then uses color to determine the values of shadow and light that will focus the eyes of the viewer where he wants it. "Working digitally allows for a care free working environment," Wallace explained on his home page. "I don't have to worry about messing up, because anything can be undone. So it keeps me loose, and maybe I'll be more inclined to try something new." After the digital image has been crafted to his satisfaction, Wallace transfers it to canvas and then adds the painterly details that are characteristic of his work.

In *Pass the Energy, Please!* McKinney's rhyming text takes young children on a tour of the food chain. The accompanying oil paintings "are large and colorful, showing fine details of birds, mammals, insects, and plants in their natural surroundings," according to *School Library Journal* contributor Blair Christolon. Wallace's "dramatic" paintings for *Earth Day Birthday* "provide plenty of visual interest," according to a *Kirkus Reviews* writer, and Lynn K. Vanca observed in her *School Library Journal* review that the book's "vibrant double-page paintings . . . are large enough to be seen if shared with a group." With its focus on global climate change, Guiberson's *Earth* comes to life in realistic paintings that are "effective and lovely to look at," according to Eva Elizabeth VonAncken, although the *School Library Journal* reviewer worried that the author's "bleak outlook . . . may be too grim for the intended audience." The artist's use of "dark lighting and subtly modulated colors" adds "additional emotional resonance" to Guiberson's theme, noted a *Kirkus Reviews* writer, the critic predicting that *Earth* will likely be useful "in raising consciousness about climate issues."

Biographical and Critical Sources

PERIODICALS

Booklist, March 15, 1999, review of *Henry Wadsworth Longfellow,* p. 1343; November 1, 2009, Hazel Rochman, review of *Earth: Feeling the Heat,* p. 49.

Kirkus Reviews, February 15, 2004, review of *Earth Day Birthday,* p. 185; January 1, 2010, review of *Earth.*

Publishers Weekly, June 25, 2001, review of *Henry Wadsworth Longfellow,* p. 74.

School Library Journal, March, 1999, Patricia Manning, review of *Henry Wadsworth Longfellow,* p. 222; August, 2000, Blair Christolon, review of *Pass the Energy, Please!,* p. 172; July, 2004, Lynn K. Vanca, review of *Earth Day Birthday,* p. 96; March, 2010, Eva Elisabeth VonAncken, review of *Earth,* p. 140.

Chad Wallace draws on his knowledge of nature in his detailed paintings for Brenda Z. Guiberson's **Earth: Feeling the Heat.** (Illustration copyright © 2010 by Chad Wallace. Reproduced by permission of Henry Holt & Company, LLC.)

Chad Wallace Home Page, http://chadwallace.com (April 24, 2011).

Chad Wallace Web log, http://chadwallaceart.blogspot.com (April 24, 2011).*

*   *   *

WALLACE, Daisy
See CUYLER, Margery

*   *   *

WARD, Rachel 1964-

Personal

Born 1964, in England; married; children: two. *Education:* Degree (geography). *Hobbies and other interests:* Swimming, spending time with family, reading, watching films.

Addresses

Home—Bath, England. *E-mail*—rachelward@rachel wardbooks.com.

Career

Author. Presenter at schools.

Awards, Honors

Frome Festival writer's prize, 2006, for short story; Angus Book Award, Oxfordshire Book Award, Hounslow Book Award, Branford Boase Prize shortlist, Leeds Book Award, Blackpool Book Prize, and Carnegie Medal longlist, and Booktrust Teenage Prize longlist, all c. 2010, all for *Numbers.*

Writings

"NUMBERS" NOVEL TRILOGY

Numbers, Chicken House (London, England), 2009, Chicken House/Scholastic (New York, NY), 2010.

The Chaos, Chicken House/Scholastic (New York, NY), 2011.

Infinity, Chicken House (London, England), 2011.

Adaptations

Numbers was optioned for film by Warp Films, 2010, and was adapted for audiobook, narrated by Sarah Coomes, Brilliance Audio, 2010.

Sidelights

Rachel Ward began writing as a hobby, beginning with short stories and moving to longer fiction as her plots gained complexity. In 2006, when one of her short sto-

ries won an award at a local writer's festival, Ward began to take her hobby more seriously. Although the first two novels she submitted for publication were roundly rejected, the third novel changed her life. With its first chapter consisting of Ward's award-winning short story, *Numbers* was released in 2009 and attracted the attention of awards committees and readers alike. "Writing has been a hobby—done in splendid isolation without going on any courses or joining any writers' groups—which has turned into something rather wonderful," Ward noted in an online interview for the *Adventures in Children's Publishing* Web log. The first novel in a trilogy, *Numbers* has been followed by *The Chaos* and *Infinity.*

In *Numbers* Jem Marsh is fifteen and spending her adolescence moving from foster home to foster home now that her single mom has died from a drug overdose. While school days are spent in special-ed classes, Jem has a special kind of knowledge that she is afraid to share with anyone else: if she looks into the eyes of another person, she sees a number signifying the date on which that person will die. Unhappy with this knowledge, she avoids getting close to others until she meets Spider, a classmate who enjoys her company. Although one glance reveals the fact that their relationship will be short-lived, Jem decides to spend a day with Spider. While waiting to board a popular Ferris Wheel, Jem suddenly realizes that everyone in line has the same death date—including Spider—and that date is today. Fleeing from the area with Spider in tow, Jem saves both of them from a terrorist bomb. However, their flight has been noticed by the police, and soon the teens find themselves on the run again, this time as suspected terrorists.

Characterizing the teens' journey as one "filled with heartwarming encounters with helpful but realistically wary strangers," a *Kirkus Reviews* writer praised *Numbers* as a "lovely, bittersweet tearjerker about living life to its fullest." "Ward demonstrates exceptional control of her material," asserted a *Publishers Weekly* critic, and Jem and Spider "remain true to themselves and their bleak circumstances." Describing *Numbers* as "gritty, bold, and utterly unique," Jane Henriksen Baird added in her *School Library Journal* review that Ward's debut novel features an ending that "is a real shocker." "Perhaps more than anything else," wrote Donna L. Miller in *Journal of Adolescent & Adult Literacy,* the novel "is about human resilience, about how a curse might be viewed as a gift, and about how love is the most important aspect of life." "*Numbers* is a high-concept, it-could-go-anywhere idea taken down an unexpected and interesting route," concluded Philip Ardagh in his London *Guardian* review of the novel. "Seemingly downbeat, it is both intelligent and life-affirming. First-time author Rachel Ward is certainly one to watch."

Ward continues Jem's story in *The Chaos,* but this time the person haunted by the ability to "see" death dates is

Cover of Rachel Ward's young-adult mystery Numbers, *featuring artwork by Christopher Stengel.* (Illustration by Christopher Stengel. Chicken House, 2010. Reproduced by permission of Chicken House, an imprint of Scholastic, Inc.)

her son, Adam. Like Jem, Adam soon finds himself surrounded by people that share the same death date, although that date is several years in the future—in 2025. Determined to discover what deadly event might occur on that date, the teen immerses himself in the study of plagues, wars, biological weapons, and the possibility of a nuclear meltdown. As in *Numbers, The Chaos* finds a teen harboring a terrible secret about a future that he may or may not be able to change.

Biographical and Critical Sources

PERIODICALS

Booklist, December 15, 2009, Debbie Carton, review of *Numbers,* p. 36.
Bulletin of the Center of Children's Books, February, 2010, Kate Quealy-Gainer, review of *Numbers,* p. 265.
Guardian (London, England), February 7, 2009, Philip Ardagh, review of *Numbers,* p. 11.
Journal of Adolescent & Adult Literacy, May, 2010, Donna L. Miller, review of *Numbers,* p. 700.
Kirkus Reviews, January 15, 2010, review of *Numbers.*
Los Angeles Times, February 14, 2010, Susan Carpenter, review of *Numbers.*

Publishers Weekly, January 4, 2010, review of *Numbers,* p. 48.
School Library Journal, January 1, 2010, Rick Margolis, interview with Ward and review of *Numbers,* p. 115.
Voice of Youth Advocates, April, 2010, Jamie S. Hansen, review of *Numbers,* p. 77.

ONLINE

Adventures in Children's Publishing Web log, http://childrenspublishing.blogspot.com/ (February 28, 2011), interview with Ward.
Rachel Ward Home Page, http://www.rachelwardbooks.com (April 24, 2011).*

* * *

WENSELL, Ulises 1945-

Personal

Born 1945, in Madrid, Spain.

Addresses

Home—Madrid, Spain. *Agent*—BookStop Literary Agency, 67 Meadow View Rd., Orinda, CA 94563.

Career

Illustrator and painter. Worked as an engineer.

Awards, Honors

Premio Nacional de Ilustración (Spain), 1978; Lazarillo prize, 1979; Serra d'Or prize, 1985; Owl Prize (Japan), 1985; APIM award, 1993; Hans Christian Andersen Award nomination (Spain), 2008.

Illustrator

A. Vera González, *Construye tu acuario,* Santillana (Madrid, Spain), 1970.
María Puncel, *Operación pata de oso,* Doncel (Madrid, Spain), 1971.
Paulino Posada, *La máquina automática,* Doncel (Madrid, Spain), 1971.
Mark Twain (pen name of Samuel Clemens), *Las aventuras de Tom Sawyer,* Spanish translation by Aldo Berti, Edaf (Madrid, Spain), 1973.
E. Salgari, *Sandokan,,* Edaf (Madrid, Spain), 1974.
Fernando Alonso, *La visita de la primavera,* Santillana (Madrid, Spain), 1975, translation published as *Spring and the Forgotten City,* Santillana (Miami, FL), 1998.
J.L. García Sánchez and M.A. Pacheo, *El viaje de nunca acabar,* Ediciones Altea (Madrid, Spain), 1976.
Fernando Alonso, *El mandarin y los pájaros,* Santillana (Madrid, Spain), 1976, translated by Nancy Sokol Green as *The Mandarin's Birds,* 1989.
Martínez Vilariño, *La bruja Babayaga,* Marpol (Madrid, Spain), 1977.

Martínez Vilariño, *Cascanueces,* Marpol (Madrid, Spain), 1977.

J.L. García Sánchez and M.A. Pacheo, *Soy una estación,* Ediciones Altea (Madrid, Spain), 1977, translated by Ruth Thomas as *I Am a Railway Station,* Basil Blackwell (London, England), 1977.

J.L. García Sánchez and M.A. Pacheo, *Soy una tienda,* Ediciones Altea (Madrid, Spain), 1977, translated by Ruth Thomas as *I Am a Shop,* Basil Blackwell (London, England), 1977.

Fernando Alonso, *El hombrecito vestido de gris y otros cuentos,* Afaguara (Madrid, Spain), 1978, Hot, Rinehart & Winston (Austin, TX), 1990.

María Luisa Seco, *Don Blanquisucio,* Miñon (Valladolid, Spain), 1978.

J.L. García Sánchez and M.A. Pacheo, *La niña invisible,* Ediciones Altea (Madrid, Spain), 1978, translated as *Annie, the Invisible Girl,* Methuen (New York, NY), 1979.

J.L. García Sánchez and M.A. Pacheo, *El niño que tenía dos ojos,* Ediciones Altea (Madrid, Spain), 1978, translated as *The Boy with Two Eyes,* Methuen (New York, NY), 1979.

Charlotte Herman and D. Francis, adaptors, *Come to Our House,* Rand McNally (Chicago, IL), 1978.

Adriana d'Atria, *Asi? Es nuestro hermano pequeño,* Ediciones Altea (Madrid, Spain), 1978.

Gloria Fuertes, *Las tres reinas magas,* Escuela Española (Madrid, Spain), 1979.

María Puncel, *Cuando sea mayor seré enferma,* Altea (Madrid, Spain), 1979, translated as *I Want to Be a Nurse,* 1979.

Carmen Conde, *El monje y el pajarillo,* Escuela Española (Madrid, Spain), 1980.

Josep Ma. Paramón, *El otoño,* Instituto Parramón (Barcelona, Spain), 1980, translated as *Autumn,* Fontain Press (Windsor, England), 1984.

María Puncel, *El premio,* Ediciones Altea (Madrid, Spain), 1980, Laredo Pub. Co. (Beverly Hills, CA), 1995.

María Puncel, *El tesoro,* Ediciones Altea (Madrid, Spain), 1980.

María Puncel, *El perro perdido,* Ediciones Altea (Madrid, Spain), 1980.

María Puncel, *La tormenta,* Ediciones Altea (Madrid, Spain), 1981.

María Puncel, *El viejo teatro,* Ediciones Altea (Madrid, Spain), 1981.

María Puncel, *El amigo nuevo,* Ediciones Altea (Madrid, Spain), 1981, Laredo Pub. Co. (Beverly Hills, CA), 1995.

René Escudié, *Trois petites filles,* Bayard (Paris, France), 1981.

Fernando Alonso, *El duende y el robot,* Miñon (Valladolid, Spain), 1981.

Gloria Fuertes, *El libro loco: De todo un poco,* Escuela Española (Madrid, Spain), 1981.

Gloria Fuertes, *Piopío Lope, el pollito miope,* Escuela Española (Madrid, Spain), 1981.

Gloria Fuertes, *Coleta, la poeta,* Escuela Española (Madrid, Spain), 1982.

Barbro Lindgren, *Histoire du petit monsieur tout seul,* Bayard (Paris, France), 1982.

Gloria Fuertes, *Coleta, payasa ¿qué pasa?,* Miñon (Valladolid, Spain), 1983.

Antonio Robles, *Cuentos de el perro, el ratón y el gato,* Miñon (Valladolid, Spain), 1983.

Ursel Scheffler, *Spatzen brauchen keinin Schirm,* Maier (Ravensburg, Germany), 1983, translated by Andrea Mernan as *A Walk in the Rain,* Putnam's (New York, NY), 1986.

Howard Goldsmith, *Little Lost Dog,* Santillana (Northvale, NJ), 1983.

Howard Goldsmith, *Stormy Day Together,* Santillana Pub. Co. (Northvale, NJ), 1983.

Howard Goldsmith, *The Contest,* Santillana Pub. Co. (Northvale, NJ), 1983.

Howard Goldsmith, *Treasure Hunt,* Santillana Pub. Co. (Northvale, NJ), 1983.

Howard Goldsmith, *Welcome, Makoto!,* Santillana Pub. Co. (Northvale, NJ), 1983.

Anne-Marie Chapouton, *Ti Michou et Gros Cachou,* Centurión (Paris, France), 1984.

Anne-Marie Chapouton, *Ich wünsch mir einen Hund,* Maier (Ravensburg, Germany), 1984, translated by Andrea Mernan as *Ben Finds a Friend,* Putnam (New York, NY), 1986.

Paloma Martínez, *El Tragaldabas,* Gakken (Tokio, Japan), 1985, adapted and translated by Paula Franklin as *The Greedy Monster,* Silver Burdett (Morristown, NJ), 1985.

Gloria Fuertes, *Cocoloco, pocoloco: Princesas traviesas,* Escuela Española (Madrid, Spain), 1985.

Gloria Fuertes, *El pirata Mofeta y la jirafa coqueta,* Escuela Española (Madrid, Spain), 1986.

Anne-Marie Chapouton, *Melanie Pilou,* Bayard (Paris, France), 1986.

Genevéve Laurencin, *Ich wünscht, ich wär,* Maier (Ravensburg, Germany), 1986, translated by Andrea Mernan as *I Wish I Were,* Putnam (New York, NY), 1987.

Christa Baisch, *Der Strom ist weg,* Maier (Ravensburg, Germany), 1986, translated by Andrea Mernan as *When the Lights Went Out,* Putnam (New York, NY), 1987.

Paloma Marínez, *Valentin, wo willst du hin?,* Maier (Ravensburg, Germany), 1987.

Alma Flor Ada, *Una vez en el medio del mar,* Escuela Española (Madrid, Spain), 1987.

Alain Thomas, *Un petit monsieur très sérioux,* Gautier-Languereau (Paris, France), 1987, translated by Didi Charney as *The Paper Airplane,* Aladdin Books (New York, NY), 1988.

Sofía de Habsburgo, *Al final, un hogar,* Anaya (Madrid, Spain), 1987.

René Escudié, *Poulou et Sebastien,* 1987, translated by Roderick Townley as *Paul and Sebastian,* Kane/Miller (Brooklyn, NY), 1987.

Roselyn Morel, *Grand-mére chocolat,* Gautier-Languereau (Paris, France), 1988.

Alma Flor, *A la sombra de un ala,* Escuela Española (Madrid, Spain), 1988.

Paloma Marínez, *Valentin, pass auf dich auf!,* Maier (Ravensburg, Germany), 1988.

Winifried Wolf, *Warum die Eisbären schwarze Nasen haben und andere Geschichten,* Ravensburger (Ravensburg, Germany), 1988.

Irina Korschunow, *Bruno et le dragon,* Bayard (Paris, France), 1988.

Beatrice Schenk de Regniers, *Warten auf Mama,* Maier (Ravensburg, Germany), 1990.

Bernadette Garreta, adaptor, *A la santé du Roi,* Bayard (Paris, France), 1990.

Paloma Marínez, *Valentin, hab keine Angst!,* Maier (Ravensburg, Germany), 1990.

Paloma Marínez, *Valentin hilft seinen Freunden,* Maier (Ravensburg, Germany), 1990.

Marie-Hélène Delval, *Élouïse et les loups,* Bayard (Paris, France), 1991.

Anne Marie Chapouton and Marie-Hélène Delval, *Quique y Trufo,* SM & B Hispano Francesa (Madrid, Spain), 1991.

Marie Agnès Gaudrat, *Images pour prier à Pâques,* Centurion (Paris, France), 1991.

Paloma Marínez, *Valentin ist Krank,* Maier (Ravensburg, Germany), 1992.

Ana María Machado, *Warum der kleine Delphin Purzelbäume schlägt und andere Geschichten,* Maier (Ravensburg, Germany), 1992.

Marie Agnès Gaudrat, *Devine à quoi ressemble la foi en Dieu,* Centurion (Paris, France), 1992.

Marie Agnès Gaudrat, *Devine à quoi ressemble la prole de Dieu,* Centurion (Paris, France), 1992.

Marie Agnès Gaudrat, *Devine à quoi ressemble la présence de Dieu,* Centurion (Paris, France), 1992, translated as *What Is God Like?,* Liturgical Press (Collegeville, MN), 1998.

Marie Agnès Gaudrat, *Pour parler de Dieu je te dirais . . . ,* Centurion (Paris, France), 1992.

Jo Hoestlandt, *Emile, bille de clown,* Bayard (Paris, France), 1992.

René Escudié, *La dispute de Poulou et Sébastien,* Bayard (Paris, France), 1993.

Antón Garcia, *El peregrino valiente,* SM & B (Madrid, Spain), 1993.

Joan Alavedra, *Sie Folgten einem Hellen Stern,* Maier (Ravensburg, Germany), 1993, translated as *They Followed a Bright Star,* Putnam (New York, NY), 1994.

Paloma Wensell, *Valentin und seine Freunde,* Ravensberger (Ravensburg, Germany), 1994.

Michel Amelin, *Le petit empereur de Chine,* Bayard (Paris, France), 1994.

Josiane Strelczyk, *Le grand courage,* Bayard (Paris, France), 1995.

Marie-Hélène Delval, reteller, *La Bible. Les belles histories de l'Ancient du Noveau Testament,* Bayard (Paris, France), 1995, translated by Ronnie Apter and Mark Herman as *Reader's Digest Bible for Children: Timeless Stories from the Old and New Testaments,* Reader's Digest Young Families (Westport, CT), 1995.

Paloma Wensell, *Un mundo sin distancias: la telecomunicación,* Telefónica (Madrid, Spain), 1996.

Paloma Wensell, *Valentin sucht ein Zuhause,* Ravensburger (Ravensburg, Germany), 1996.

Ursel Scheffler, *Wer hat Zeit für kleinen Bären?,* Ravensburger (Ravensburg, Germany), 1996, translated as

Who Has Time for Little Bear?, Doubleday Books for Young Readers (New York, NY), 1998.

Ursel Scheffler, *Klein Kuss für Bärenschwester,* Ravensburger (Ravensburg, Germany), 1998, translated as *Taking Care of Sister Bear,* Doubleday Books for Young Readers (New York, NY), 1999.

Paloma Wensell, *Bobo ganz allein im Unwalde,* Ravensburger (Ravensburg, Germany), 1999.

Charles Perrault, *Le chat botté,* Bayard (Paris, France), 1999.

Charles Perrault, *Le petit Poucet,* Bayard (Paris, France), 1999.

Ursel Scheffler, *Bleib mein Freund, kleiner Bär!,* Ravensburger (Ravensburg, Germany), 1999.

Paloma Wensell, *Valentin was ist das?,* Ravensburger (Ravensburg, Germany), 2000.

Paloma Wensell, *Bobo und sein kleiner Bruder werden Freunde,* Ravensburger (Ravensburg, Germany), 2000.

Charles Perrault, *Le petit Chaperon Rouge,* Bayard (Paris, France), 2000.

Paloma Wensell, *Meine ersten Valentin-Geschichten,* Ravensburger (Ravensburg, Germany), 2000.

Jacob and Wilhelm Grimm, *Hänsel et Gretel,* Bayard (Paris, France), 2001.

Mes Contes à moi, Bayard (Paris, France), 2001.

Paloma Wensell, *Valentin feiert Geburtstag,* Ravensburger (Ravensburg, Germany), 2001.

Ursel Scheffler, *Ich mag dich sehr, kleiner Bär!,* Ravensburger (Ravensburg, Germany), 2001.

Paloma Wensell, *Meine ersten Bibel-Geschichten,* Ravensburger (Ravensburg, Germany), 2001.

Paloma Wensell, *Große Abenteuer mit Valentin,* Ravensburger (Ravensburg, Germany), 2002.

Anne-Marie Abitan, *Souriceau veut apprendre à lire,* Bayard (Paris, France), 2002.

Jacques Pévert, *Cartes imaginaires,* Bayard (Paris, France), 2002.

Rosemarie Künzler-Behncke, *Wo bist du, lieber Gott?,* Ravensburger (Ravensburg, Germany), 2003, translated as *Where in the World Is God?,* Liturgical Press (Collegeville, MN), 2006.

Paloma Wensell, *Ein Pinguin spazieren ging . . . und viele andere Geschichten von großen und kleinen Tieren,* Ravensburger (Ravensburg, Germany), 2003.

Ursel Scheffler, *Meine schönsten Geschichten vom kleinen Bären,* Ravensburger (Ravensburg, Germany), 2003.

Paloma Wensell, *Unsere Weihnachtgeschichte,* Ravensburger (Ravensburg, Germany), 2004, translated by Linda M. Maloney as *The Christmas Star,* Liturgical Press (Collegeville, MN), 2006.

Rosmarie Künzler-Behncke, *Die kleinen Enten entdecken den Mond,* Ravensburger (Ravensburg, Germany), 2004.

Wer hat die schönsten Schäfchen? (traditional folksong), Ravensburger (Ravensburg, Germany), 2004.

Marie Bataille, *La boîte aux mots interdits,* Bayard (Paris, France), 2005.

Carlos Reviejo, *Platero y Juan Ramón,* SM (Madrid, Spain), 2005, Lectorum Publications (New York, NY), 2006.

Paloma Wensell, *Kleiner Wal, wo schwimmst du hin?,* Ravensburger (Ravensburg, Germany), 2006.

Begoña Ibarrola, *¿Qué le pasa a Mugán,* SM (Madrid, Spain), 2006.

Santiago Roncagliolo, *Matias y los imposibles,* Siruela (Madrid, Spain), 2006.

Geneviève Laurencin, *Noél de rêve,* Gossau (Zurich, Switzerland), 2006.

Paloma Wensell, *Kiku, der kleine Marienkäfer,* Ravensburger (Ravensburg, Germany), 2007.

Paloma Wensell, *Der kleine BJH und der große Mond,* Ravensburger (Ravensburg, Germany), 2007.

José Luis Berenguer, *¡Espera, ya voy!,* Tilde (Valencia, Spain), 2007.

Le chat botté et autres contes de toujours, Bayard (Paris, France), 2007.

Susana López, *La meor familia del mundo,* SM (Madrid, Spain), 2008, translated as *The Best Family in the world,* Kane/Miller (), 2010.

Almudena Taboada, *Lola, la loba,* SM (Madrid, Spain), 2008.

Javier Sobrino, *Las nanas de Miguel,* SM (Boadilla del Monte, Spain), 2010.

Alma Flor Ada and F. Isabel Campoy, *Ten Little Puppies,* English text by Rosalma Zubizarreta, Rayo (New York, NY), 2011.

Also illustrator of readers in the "Libros para mirar" series by Maria Puncel, published by Altea, 1977.

Author's works have been translated into Catalan, Danish, Dutch, Finnish, French, German, Greek, Icelandic, Italian, Japanese, Korean, Norwegian, Portuguese, Swedish, and Turkish.

Biographical and Critical Sources

PERIODICALS

Bookbird, April, 2008, profile of Wensell, p. 56.

Booklist, August, 1994, Carolyn Phelan, review of *They Followed a Bright Star,* p. 2050; January 1, 1999, Kathy Broderick, review of *Who Has Time for Little Bear?,* p. 890; September 1, 1999, Ellen Mandel, review of *Taking Care of Sister Bear,* p. 143; April 1, 2010, Carolyn Phelan, review of *The Best Family in the World,* p. 45.

Horn Book, November-December, 1994, Mary M. Burns, review of *They Followed a Bright Star,* p. 714.

Kirkus Reviews, January 15, 2010, review of *The Best Family in the World.*

Publishers Weekly, September 19, 1994, review of *They Followed a Bright Star,* p. 27; October 12, 1998, review of *Who Has Time for Little Bear?,* p. 76; March 1, 2010, review of *The Best Family in the World,* p. 49.

School Library Journal, May, 2010, Deborah Vose, review of *The Best Family in the World,* p. 86.*

*　　*　　*

YOUNG, James
See GRAHAM, Ian

Illustrations Index

(In the following index, the number of the *volume* in which an illustrator's work appears is given *before* the colon, and the *page number* on which it appears is given *after* the colon. For example, a drawing by Adams, Adrienne appears in Volume 2 on page 6, another drawing by her appears in Volume 3 on page 80, another drawing in Volume 8 on page 1, and so on and so on. . . .)

YABC

Index references to *YABC* refer to listings appearing in the two-volume *Yesterday's Authors of Books for Children,* also published by Gale, Cengage Learning. *YABC* covers prominent authors and illustrators who died prior to 1960.

A

Aas, Ulf *5:* 174
Abbe, S. van
  See van Abbe, S.
Abel, Raymond *6:* 122; *7:* 195; *12:* 3; *21:* 86; *25:* 119
Abelliera, Aldo *71:* 120
Abolafia, Yossi *60:* 2; *93:* 163; *152:* 202
Abrahams, Hilary *26:* 205; *29:* 24, 25; *53:* 61
Abrams, Kathie *36:* 170
Abrams, Lester *49:* 26
Abulafia, Yossi *154:* 67; *177:* 3
Accardo, Anthony *191:* 3, 8
Accornero, Franco *184:* 8
Accorsi, William *11:* 198
Acs, Laszlo *14:* 156; *42:* 22
Acuna, Ed *198:* 79
Adams, Adrienne *2:* 6; *3:* 80; *8:* 1; *15:* 107; *16:* 180; *20:* 65; *22:* 134, 135; *33:* 75; *36:* 103, 112; *39:* 74; *86:* 54; *90:* 2, 3
Adams, Connie J. *129:* 68
Adams, John Wolcott *17:* 162
Adams, Kathryn *224:* 1
Adams, Lynn *96:* 44
Adams, Norman *55:* 82
Adams, Pam *112:* 1, 2
Adams, Sarah *98:* 126; *164:* 180
Adams, Steve *209:* 64
Adamson, George *30:* 23, 24; *69:* 64
Addams, Charles *55:* 5
Addison, Kenneth *192:* 173
Addy, Sean *180:* 8; *222:* 31
Ade, Rene *76:* 198; *195:* 162
Adinolfi, JoAnn *115:* 42; *176:* 2; *217:* 79
Adkins, Alta *22:* 250
Adkins, Jan *8:* 3; *69:* 4; *144:* 2, 3, 4; *210:* 11, 17, 18, 19
Adl, Shirin *225:* 2
Adler, Kelynn *195:* 47
Adler, Peggy *22:* 6; *29:* 31
Adler, Ruth *29:* 29
Adlerman, Daniel *163:* 2
Adragna, Robert *47:* 145
Agard, Nadema *18:* 1
Agee, Jon *116:* 8, 9, 10; *157:* 4; *196:* 3, 4, 5, 6, 7, 8
Agre, Patricia *47:* 195
Aguirre, Alfredo *152:* 218
Ahl, Anna Maria *32:* 24

Ahlberg, Allan *68:* 6, 7, 9; *165:* 5; *214:* 9
Ahlberg, Janet *68:* 6, 7, 9; *214:* 9
Ahlberg, Jessica *229:* 2, 191
Aicher-Scholl, Inge *63:* 127
Aichinger, Helga *4:* 5, 45
Aitken, Amy *31:* 34
Ajhar, Brian *207:* 126; *220:* 2
Akaba, Suekichi *46:* 23; *53:* 127
Akasaka, Miyoshi *YABC 2:* 261
Akib, Jamel *181:* 13; *182:* 99; *220:* 74
Akino, Fuku *6:* 144
Alain *40:* 41
Alajalov *2:* 226
Albert, Chris *200:* 64
Alborough, Jez *86:* 1, 2, 3; *149:* 3
Albrecht, Jan *37:* 176
Albright, Donn *1:* 91
Alcala, Alfredo *91:* 128
Alcantará, Felipe Ugalde *171:* 186
Alcorn, John *3:* 159; *7:* 165; *31:* 22; *44:* 127; *46:* 23, 170
Alcorn, Stephen *110:* 4; *125:* 106; *128:* 172; *150:* 97; *160:* 188; *165:* 48; *201:* 113; *203:* 39; *207:* 3; *226:* 25
Alcott, May *100:* 3
Alda, Arlene *44:* 24; *158:* 2
Alden, Albert *11:* 103
Aldridge, Andy *27:* 131
Aldridge, George *105:* 125
Aldridge, Sheila *192:* 4
Alejandro, Cliff *176:* 75
Alex, Ben *45:* 25, 26
Alexander, Claire *228:* 2
Alexander, Ellen *91:* 3
Alexander, Lloyd *49:* 34
Alexander, Martha *3:* 206; *11:* 103; *13:* 109; *25:* 100; *36:* 131; *70:* 6, 7; *136:* 3, 4, 5; *169:* 120
Alexander, Paul *85:* 57; *90:* 9
Alexeieff, Alexander *14:* 6; *26:* 199
Alfano, Wayne *80:* 69
Aliki
  See Brandenberg, Aliki
Alko, Selina *218:* 2
Allamand, Pascale *12:* 9
Allan, Judith *38:* 166
Alland, Alexandra *16:* 255
Allen, Gertrude *9:* 6
Allen, Graham *31:* 145
Allen, Jonathan *131:* 3, 4; *177:* 8, 9, 10
Allen, Joy *168:* 185; *217:* 6, 7

Allen, Pamela *50:* 25, 26, 27, 28; *81:* 9, 10; *123:* 4, 5
Allen, Raul *207:* 94
Allen, Rowena *47:* 75
Allen, Thomas B. *81:* 101; *82:* 248; *89:* 37; *104:* 9
Allen, Tom *85:* 176
Allender, David *73:* 223
Alley, R.W. *80:* 183; *95:* 187; *156:* 100, 153; *169:* 4, 5; *179:* 17
Allison, Linda *43:* 27
Allon, Jeffrey *119:* 174
Allport, Mike *71:* 55
Almquist, Don *11:* 8; *12:* 128; *17:* 46; *22:* 110
Aloise, Frank *5:* 38; *10:* 133; *30:* 92
Alsenas, Linas *186:* 2
Alter, Ann *206:* 4, 5
Althea
  See Braithwaite, Althea
Altschuler, Franz *11:* 185; *23:* 141; *40:* 48; *45:* 29; *57:* 181
Alvin, John *117:* 5
Ambrus, Victor G. *1:* 6, 7, 194; *3:* 69; *5:* 15; *6:* 44; *7:* 36; *8:* 210; *12:* 227; *14:* 213; *15:* 213; *22:* 209; *24:* 36; *28:* 179; *30:* 178; *32:* 44, 46; *38:* 143; *41:* 25, 26, 27, 28, 29, 30, 31, 32; *42:* 87; *44:* 190; *55:* 172; *62:* 30, 144, 145, 148; *86:* 99, 100, 101; *87:* 66, 137; *89:* 162; *134:* 160
Ames, Lee J. *3:* 12; *9:* 130; *10:* 69; *17:* 214; *22:* 124; *151:* 13; *223:* 69
Amini, Mehrdokht *211:* 119
Amon, Aline *9:* 9
Amoss, Berthe *5:* 5
Amstutz, André *152:* 102; *214:* 11, 16; *223:* 99
Amundsen, Dick *7:* 77
Amundsen, Richard E. *5:* 10; *24:* 122
Ancona, George *12:* 11; *55:* 144; *145:* 7; *208:* 13
Anderson, Alasdair *18:* 122
Andersen, Bethanne *116:* 167; *162:* 189; *175:* 17; *191:* 4, 5; *218:* 20
Anderson, Bob *139:* 16
Anderson, Brad *33:* 28
Anderson, Brian *211:* 8
Anderson, C.W. *11:* 10
Anderson, Carl *7:* 4
Anderson, Catherine Corley *72:* 2
Anderson, Cecil *127:* 152
Anderson, David Lee *118:* 176

Anderson, Derek *169:* 9; *174:* 180
Anderson, Doug *40:* 111
Anderson, Erica *23:* 65
Anderson, G.E. *223:* 181
Anderson, Laurie *12:* 153, 155
Anderson, Lena *99:* 26
Anderson, Peggy Perry *179:* 2
Anderson, Sara *173:* 3
Anderson, Scoular *138:* 13; *201:* 6
Anderson, Stephanie *225:* 3
Anderson, Susan *90:* 12
Anderson, Tara *188:* 132; *211:* 115
Anderson, Wayne *23:* 119; *41:* 239; *56:* 7; *62:* 26; *147:* 6; *202:* 4, 5
Andreasen, Daniel *86:* 157; *87:* 104; *103:* 201, 202; *159:* 75; *167:* 106, 107; *168:* 184; *180:* 247; *186:* 9; *212:* 101; *220:* 110, 111; *221:* 56; *227:* 3, 4, 5, 6
Andrew, Ian *111:* 37; *116:* 12; *166:* 2
Andrew, John *22:* 4
Andrews, Benny *14:* 251; *31:* 24; *57:* 6, 7; *183:* 8
Andrews, Vaughn *166:* 28
Anelay, Henry *57:* 173
Angel, Marie *47:* 22
Angelo, Valenti *14:* 8; *18:* 100; *20:* 232; *32:* 70
Anglund, Joan Walsh *2:* 7, 250, 251; *37:* 198, 199, 200
Anholt, Catherine *74:* 8; *131:* 7; *141:* 5
Anholt, Laurence *141:* 4
Anno, Mitsumasa *5:* 7; *38:* 25, 26, 27, 28, 29, 30, 31, 32; *77:* 3, 4; *157:* 10, 11
Antal, Andrew *1:* 124; *30:* 145
Antram, David *152:* 133
Apostolou, Christy Hale
  See Hale, Christy
Apple, Margot *33:* 25; *35:* 206; *46:* 81; *53:* 8; *61:* 109; *64:* 21, 22, 24, 25, 27; *71:* 176; *77:* 53; *82:* 245; *92:* 39; *94:* 180; *96:* 107; *152:* 4, 5; *162:* 192, 194; *173:* 44; *214:* 21, 22, 23, 24
Appleyard, Dev *2:* 192
Aragones, Sergio *48:* 23, 24, 25, 26, 27
Araneus *40:* 29
Arbo, Cris *103:* 4; *220:* 4, 5
Archambault, Matt *85:* 173; *138:* 19, 20; *143:* 33; *145:* 144; *179:* 103; *187:* 7; *219:* 2
Archer, Janet *16:* 69; *178:* 156
Ardizzone, Edward *1:* 11, 12; *2:* 105; *3:* 258; *4:* 78; *7:* 79; *10:* 100; *15:* 232; *20:* 69,178; *23:* 223; *24:* 125; *28:* 25, 26, 27, 28, 29, 30, 31,33, 34, 35, 36, 37; *31:* 192, 193; *34:* 215, 217; *60:* 173; *64:* 145; *87:* 176; *YABC 2:* 25
Arena, Jill *176:* 49
Arenella, Roy *14:* 9
Argemi, David *197:* 2
Argent, Kerry *103:* 56; *138:* 17; *158:* 134
Arihara, Shino *201:* 98
Arisman, Marshall *162:* 50
Armer, Austin *13:* 3
Armer, Laura Adams *13:* 3
Armer, Sidney *13:* 3
Armitage, David *47:* 23; *99:* 5; *155:* 4
Armitage, Eileen *4:* 16
Armstrong, George *10:* 6; *21:* 72
Armstrong, Shelagh *102:* 114; *224:* 4
Armstrong-Ellis, Carey *185:* 196
Arno, Enrico *1:* 217; *2:* 22, 210; *4:* 9; *5:* 43; *6:* 52; *29:* 217, 219; *33:* 152; *35:* 99; *43:* 31, 32, 33; *45:* 212, 213, 214; *72:* 72; *74:* 166; *100:* 169
Arnold, Alli *187:* 40, 41
Arnold, Andrew *219:* 155; *221:* 155
Arnold, Caroline *174:* 5
Arnold, Emily *76:* 7, 9, 10
Arnold, Katya *115:* 11; *168:* 2, 3
Arnold, Tedd *116:* 14; *133:* 152; *160:* 5; *208:* 24, 25, 26, 176

Arnosky, Jim *22:* 20; *70:* 9, 10, 11; *118:* 3, 5; *160:* 8, 10; *189:* 5, 7, 8, 9, 10; *217:* 11, 12, 13, 14
Arnsteen, Katy Keck *105:* 97; *116:* 145
Arsenault, Isabelle *207:* 7; *226:* 109
Arrowood, Clinton *12:* 193; *19:* 11; *65:* 210
Artell, Mike *89:* 8
Arting, Fred J. *41:* 63
Artzybasheff, Boris *13:* 143; *14:* 15; *40:* 152, 155
Aruego, Ariane *6:* 4
Aruego, José *4:* 140; *6:* 4; *7:* 64; *33:* 195; *35:* 208; *68:* 16, 17; *75:* 46; *93:* 91, 92; *94:* 197; *109:* 65, 67; *125:* 2, 3, 4, 5; *127:* 188; *143:* 25; *178:* 17, 19, 74; *188:* 166; *202:* 164
Arzoumanian, Alik *177:* 12; *194:* 115
Asare, Meshack *86:* 9; *139:* 19
Ascensios, Natalie *105:* 139
Asch, Frank *5:* 9; *66:* 2, 4, 6, 7, 9, 10; *102:* 18, 19,21; *154:* 12
Ashby, Gail *11:* 135
Ashby, Gil *146:* 4
Ashby, Gwynneth *44:* 26
Ashley, C.W. *19:* 197
Ashmead, Hal *8:* 70
Ashton, Tim *211:* 204
Aska, Warabe *56:* 10
Assel, Steven *44:* 153; *77:* 22, 97
Astrop, John *32:* 56
Atene, Ann *12:* 18
Atherton, Lisa *38:* 198
Atkinson, Allen *60:* 5
Atkinson, J. Priestman *17:* 275
Atkinson, Janet *86:* 147; *103:* 138
Atkinson, Mike *127:* 74
Atkinson, Wayne *40:* 46
Attard, Karl *196:* 22, 23
Attebery, Charles *38:* 170
Atwell, Debby *150:* 6
Atwood, Ann *7:* 9
Aubrey, Meg Kelleher *77:* 159
Auch, Herm *173:* 7, 8
Auch, Mary Jane *173:* 7
Augarde, Steve *25:* 22; *159:* 7; *210:* 43, 44
Austerman, Miriam *23:* 107
Austin, Margot *11:* 16
Austin, Robert *3:* 44
Austin, Virginia *81:* 205; *127:* 221
Auth, Tony *51:* 5; *192:* 18
Avendano, Dolores *158:* 74
Avedon, Richard *57:* 140
Averill, Esther *1:* 17; *28:* 39, 40, 41
Avilés, Martha *218:* 6
Axeman, Lois *2:* 32; *11:* 84; *13:* 165; *22:* 8; *23:* 49; *61:* 116; *101:* 124
Axtel, David *155:* 110
Ayer, Jacqueline *13:* 7
Ayer, Margaret *15:* 12; *50:* 120
Ayers, Alan *91:* 58; *107:* 169
Ayliffe, Alex *95:* 164
Ayto, Russell *111:* 5; *112:* 54; *206:* 7, 8; *213:* 56
Azarian, Mary *112:* 9, 10; *114:* 129; *117:* 171; *137:* 163; *171:* 4, 5; *181:* 161; *188:* 128

B

B.T.B.
  See Blackwell, Basil T.
Baasansuren, Bolormaa *216:* 40
Babbitt, Bradford *33:* 158
Babbitt, Natalie *6:* 6; *8:* 220; *68:* 20; *70:* 242, 243; *194:* 8, 9
Baca, Maria *104:* 5
Bacchus, Andy *94:* 87
Bacha, Andy *109:* 169
Bachelet, Gilles *196:* 18
Bachem, Paul *48:* 180; *67:* 65; *144:* 206
Back, Adam *63:* 125

Back, George *31:* 161
Backes, Nick *190:* 72
Backhouse, Colin *78:* 142
Bacon, Bruce *4:* 74
Bacon, Paul *7:* 155; *8:* 121; *31:* 55; *50:* 42; *56:* 175; *62:* 82, 84
Bacon, Peggy *2:* 11, 228; *46:* 44
Baek, Matthew J. *169:* 95; *202:* 8
Baer, Julie *161:* 2
Baicker-McKee, Carol *177:* 15; *180:* 215
Bailey, Peter *58:* 174; *87:* 221; *194:* 12
Bailey, Sheila *155:* 11
Baker, Alan *22:* 22; *61:* 134; *93:* 11, 12; *146:* 6, 7, 10
Baker, Charlotte *2:* 12
Baker, Garin *89:* 65
Baker, Jeannie *23:* 4; *88:* 18, 19, 20
Baker, Jim *22:* 24
Baker, Joe *82:* 188; *111:* 55; *124:* 70; *197:* 73
Baker, Keith *179:* 6, 7; *222:* 36
Baker, Leslie *112:* 214; *132:* 103, 246; *180:* 74, 246
Baker-Smith, Grahame *223:* 10; *225:* 132
Baldacci, Rudy *184:* 9
Baldridge, Cyrus LeRoy *19:* 69; *44:* 50
Baldus, Jackie *216:* 81
Baldus, Zachary *152:* 231; *187:* 60
Balet, Jan *11:* 22
Balian, Lorna *9:* 16; *91:* 16
Balit, Christina *102:* 24; *159:* 9; *162:* 118, 119; *212:* 2, 3
Ballantyne, R.M. *24:* 34
Ballis, George *14:* 199
Balouch, Kristen *176:* 11
Baltzer, Hans *40:* 30
Banbery, Fred *58:* 15
Bancroft, Bronwyn *216:* 42
Banfill, A. Scott *98:* 7; *112:* 59
Bang, Molly *24:* 37, 38; *69:* 8, 9, 10; *111:* 7,9, 10, 11; *140:* 11; *158:* 37, 38, 39; *195:* 3; *215:* 11, 12, 13, 14
Banik, Yvette Santiago *21:* 136
Banks, Erin Bennett *211:* 12
Banner, Angela
  See Maddison, Angela Mary
Bannerman, Helen *19:* 13, 14
Banning, Greg *202:* 98
Bannon, Laura *6:* 10; *23:* 8
Bantock, Nick *74:* 229; *95:* 6
Banyai, Istvan *185:* 209; *193:* 14, 16; *209:* 155; *223:* 166, 167
Baptist, Michael *37:* 208
Baracca, Sal *135:* 206
Baranaski, Marcin *182:* 113
Barasch, Lynne *126:* 16; *186:* 15
Barbarin, Lucien C., Jr. *89:* 88
Barbour, Karen *96:* 5; *74:* 209; *170:* 16
Bare, Arnold Edwin *16:* 31
Bare, Colleen Stanley *32:* 33
Barger, Jan *147:* 11
Bargery, Geoffrey *14:* 258
Barkat, Jonathan *149:* 177; *164:* 254; *181:* 106; *184:* 186; *196:* 11; *198:* 148
Barker, Carol *31:* 27
Barker, Cicely Mary *49:* 50, 51
Barkley, James *4:* 13; *6:* 11; *13:* 112
Barks, Carl *37:* 27, 28, 29, 30, 31, 32, 33, 34
Barling, Joy *62:* 148
Barling, Tom *9:* 23
Barlow, Gillian *62:* 20
Barlow, Perry *35:* 28
Barlowe, Dot *30:* 223
Barlowe, Wayne *37:* 72; *84:* 43; *105:* 5
Barnard, Bryn *88:* 53; *13:* 55; *169:* 13; *193:* 194
Barneda, David *206:* 11
Barner, Bob *29:* 37; *128:* 33; *136:* 19, 20; *177:* 27
Barnes, Hiram P. *20:* 28
Barnes, Tim *137:* 28
Barnes-Murphy, Rowan *88:* 22

Barnett, Charles II *175:* 150
Barnett, Ivan *70:* 14
Barnett, Moneta *16:* 89; *19:* 142; *31:* 102; *33:* 30, 31, 32; *41:* 153; *61:* 94, 97
Barney, Maginel Wright *39:* 32, 33, 34; *YABC 2:* 306
Barnum, Jay Hyde *11:* 224; *20:* 5; *37:* 189, 190
Baron, Alan *80:* 3; *89:* 123
Barr, George *60:* 74; *69:* 64
Barragán, Paula S. *134:* 116; *186:* 158; *216:* 43, 44, 197
Barrall, Tim *115:* 152
Barraud, Martin *189:* 38
Barrauds *33:* 114
Barrer-Russell, Gertrude *9:* 65; *27:* 31
Barret, Robert *85:* 134
Barrett, Angela *40:* 136, 137; *62:* 74; *75:* 10; *76:* 142; *144:* 137; *145:* 14; *223:* 14
Barrett, Jennifer *58:* 149
Barrett, John E. *43:* 119
Barrett, Moneta *74:* 10
Barrett, Peter *55:* 169; *86:* 111
Barrett, Robert *62:* 145; *77:* 146; *82:* 35
Barrett, Ron *14:* 24; *26:* 35
Barron, John N. *3:* 261; *5:* 101; *14:* 220
Barrow, Ann *136:* 27
Barrows, Walter *14:* 268
Barry, Ethelred B. *37:* 79; *YABC 1:* 229
Barry, James *14:* 25
Barry, Katharina *2:* 159; *4:* 22
Barry, Robert E. *6:* 12
Barry, Scott *32:* 35
Barshaw, Ruth McNally *203:* 9
Bartenbach, Jean *40:* 31
Barth, Ernest Kurt *2:* 172; *3:* 160; *8:* 26; *10:* 31
Bartholomew, Caty *208:* 153
Bartholomew, Marie *200:* 66
Bartlett, Alison *101:* 88; *165:* 93; *209:* 51
Barton, Byron *8:* 207; *9:* 18; *23:* 66; *80:* 181; *90:* 18, 19, 20, 21; *126:* 29, 30
Barton, Harriett *30:* 71
Barton, Jill *129:* 108; *135:* 120; *145:* 185, 189; *184:* 177; *224:* 142, 143
Barton, Patrice *226:* 14
Bartram, Robert *10:* 42
Bartram, Simon *218:* 8
Bartsch, Jochen *8:* 105; *39:* 38
Bascove, Barbara *45:* 73
Base, Graeme *101:* 15, 16, 17, 18; *162:* 8, 10, 12
Baseman, Gary *174:* 12
Bash, Barbara *132:* 9
Baskin, Leonard *30:* 42, 43, 46, 47; *49:* 125, 126, 128, 129,133; *173:* 120
Bass, Saul *49:* 192
Bassett, Jeni *40:* 99; *64:* 30
Basso, Bill *99:* 139; *189:* 134
Batchelor, Joy *29:* 41, 47, 48
Bate, Norman *5:* 16
Bates, Amy June *188:* 170; *189:* 27, 28
Bates, Leo *24:* 35
Batet, Carmen *39:* 134
Batherman, Muriel *31:* 79; *45:* 185
Battaglia, Aurelius *50:* 44
Batten, John D. *25:* 161, 162
Batten, Mary *162:* 14, 15
Battles, Asa *32:* 94, 95
Bauer, Carla *193:* 6
Bauer, Jutta *150:* 32
Bauernschmidt, Marjorie *15:* 15
Baum, Allyn *20:* 10
Baum, Willi *4:* 24, 25; *7:* 173
Bauman, Leslie *61:* 121
Baumann, Jill *34:* 170
Baumhauer, Hans *11:* 218; *15:* 163, 165, 167
Baxter, Glen *57:* 100
Baxter, Leon *59:* 102
Baxter, Robert *87:* 129
Bayer, Herbert *181:* 16

Bayley, Dorothy *37:* 195
Bayley, Nicola *40:* 104; *41:* 34, 35; *69:* 15; *129:* 33, 34, 35
Baylin, Mark *158:* 233
Baynes, Pauline *2:* 244; *3:* 149; *13:* 133, 135,137, 141; *19:* 18, 19, 20; *32:* 208, 213, 214; *36:* 105, 108; *59:* 12, 13, 14, 16, 17, 18, 20; *100:* 158, 159, 243; *133:* 3, 4
Beach, Lou *150:* 150; *207:* 117, 118
Beame, Rona *12:* 40
Bean, Jonathan *196:* 102
Bear's Heart *73:* 215
Beard, Alex *222:* 40
Beard, Dan *22:* 31, 32
Beard, J.H. *YABC 1:* 158
Bearden, Romare *9:* 7; *22:* 35
Beardshaw, Rosalind *169:* 22; *190:* 22; *224:* 12; *225:* 6, 7, 8; *226:* 71
Beardsley, Aubrey *17:* 14; *23:* 181; *59:* 130, 131
Bearman, Jane *29:* 38
Beaton, Cecil *24:* 208
Beaton, Clare *125:* 28; *208:* 67; *220:* 10, 11, 12
Beauce, J.A. *18:* 103
Beaujard, Sophie *81:* 54
Beavers, Ethen *225:* 9
Beccia, Carlyn *189:* 29
Bechtold, Lisze *208:* 29
Beck, Andrea *226:* 16
Beck, Charles *11:* 169; *51:* 173
Beck, Ian *138:* 27; *182:* 150; *190:* 25; *225:* 130
Beck, Melinda *203:* 112
Beck, Ruth *13:* 11
Becker, Harriet *12:* 211
Beckerman, Jonathan *208:* 194
Beckett, Sheilah *25:* 5; *33:* 37, 38
Beckhoff, Harry *1:* 78; *5:* 163
Beckhorn, Susan Williams *189:* 32
Beckman, Kaj *45:* 38, 39, 40, 41
Beckman, Per *45:* 42, 43
Beddows, Eric *72:* 70
Bedford, F.D. *20:* 118, 122; *33:* 170; *41:* 220, 221,230, 233
Bee, Joyce *19:* 62
Bee, William *188:* 6
Beeby, Betty *25:* 36
Beech, Carol *9:* 149
Beech, Mark *192:* 122
Beek *25:* 51, 55, 59
Beeke, Tiphanie *177:* 127; *204:* 140; *212:* 178; *218:* 102
Beekman, Doug *125:* 146, 148
Beerbohm, Max *24:* 208
Beeson, Bob *108:* 57
Begin, Mary Jane *82:* 13; *206:* 13
Beha, Philippe *172:* 85
Behr, Joyce *15:* 15; *21:* 132; *23:* 161
Behrens, Hans *5:* 97
Beier, Ellen *135:* 170; *139:* 47; *183:* 164; *221:* 177; *222:* 151
Beingessner, Laura *220:* 14
Beinicke, Steve *69:* 18
Beisner, Monika *46:* 128, 131; *112:* 127
Belden, Charles J. *12:* 182
Belina, Renate *39:* 132
Bell, Corydon *3:* 20
Bell, Graham *54:* 48
Bell, Julia *151:* 214
Bell, Julie *159:* 172; *165:* 18
Bell, Thomas P. *76:* 182
Bellamy, Glen *127:* 15
Beltran, Alberto *43:* 37
Bemelmans, Ludwig *15:* 19, 21; *100:* 27
Ben-Ami, Doron *75:* 96; *84:* 107; *108:* 132; *110:* 63; *159:* 157; *197:* 142
Bendall-Brunello, John *150:* 4; *157:* 163; *185:* 3, 4; *203:* 5
Benda, Wladyslaw T. *15:* 256; *30:* 76, 77; *44:* 182

Bender, Robert *77:* 162; *79:* 13; *160:* 23
Bendick, Jeanne *2:* 24; *68:* 27, 28
Benioff, Carol *121:* 42; *175:* 23
Benner, Cheryl *80:* 11
Bennett, Charles H. *64:* 6
Bennett, Erin Susanne *165:* 216
Bennett, F.I. *YABC 1:* 134
Bennett, James *146:* 240
Bennett, Jill *26:* 61; *41:* 38, 39; *45:* 54
Bennett, Rainey *15:* 26; *23:* 53
Bennett, Richard *15:* 45; *21:* 11, 12, 13; *25:* 175
Bennett, Susan *5:* 55
Benny, Mike *142:* 78; *203:* 13, 14; *207:* 85
Benoit, Elise *77:* 74
Benson, Linda *60:* 130; *62:* 91; *75:* 101; *79:* 156; *134:* 129
Benson, Patrick *68:* 162; *147:* 17, 18, 19, 20
Bentley, Carolyn *46:* 153
Bentley, James *149:* 30
Bentley, Roy *30:* 162
Benton, Jim *172:* 22
Benton, Thomas Hart *2:* 99
Bereal, JaeMe *228:* 16
Berelson, Howard *5:* 20; *16:* 58; *31:* 50
Berenstain, Jan *12:* 47; *64:* 33, 34, 36, 37, 38, 40, 42, 44; *135:* 25, 28, 31, 35
Berenstain, Stan *12:* 47; *64:* 33, 34, 36, 37, 38, 40, 42, 44; *135:* 25, 28, 31, 35
Berenzy, Alix *65:* 13; *73:* 6; *78:* 115
Berg, Joan *1:* 115; *3:* 156; *6:* 26, 58
Berg, Ron *36:* 48, 49; *48:* 37, 38; *67:* 72
Bergen, David *115:* 44; *207:* 34
Berger, Barbara *77:* 14
Berger, Carin *185:* 6
Berger, Joe *221:* 9
Berger, William M. *14:* 143; *YABC 1:* 204
Bergherr, Mary *74:* 170; *151:* 123
Bergin, Mark *114:* 8, 9; *143:* 95; *160:* 26, 27
Bergstreser, Douglas *69:* 76
Bergum, Constance R. *121:* 14, 15; *208:* 31, 32, 33; *209:* 176
Bering, Claus *13:* 14
Berkeley, Jon *139:* 218
Berkowitz, Jeanette *3:* 249
Berman, Paul *66:* 14
Berman, Rachel *217:* 26
Bernal, Richard *154:* 176
Bernadette
  See Watts, Bernadette
Bernard, Gary *216:* 71
Bernardin, James *112:* 24; *167:* 94; *227:* 14, 15
Bernasconi, Pablo *183:* 10, 11
Bernath, Stefen *32:* 76
Berner, Rotraut Susanne *214:* 32
Bernhard, Durga *80:* 13
Bernstein, Michel J. *51:* 71
Bernstein, Ted *38:* 183; *50:* 131
Bernstein, Zena *23:* 46
Berridge, Celia *86:* 63
Berrill, Jacquelyn *12:* 50
Berry, Erick
  See Best, Allena
Berry, Holly *205:* 116; *210:* 49, 50
Berry, William D. *14:* 29; *19:* 48
Berry, William A. *6:* 219
Berson, Harold *2:* 17, 18; *4:* 28, 29, 220; *9:* 10; *12:* 19; *17:* 45; *18:* 193; *22:* 85; *34:* 172; *44:* 120; *46:* 42; *80:* 240
Bertholf, Bret *187:* 9; *189:* 32, 33
Berton, Patsy *99:* 16
Bertschmann, Harry *16:* 1
Besco, Don *70:* 99
Beskow, Elsa *20:* 13, 14, 15
Bess, Clayton *63:* 94
Best, Allena *2:* 26; *34:* 76
Betera, Carol *74:* 68
Bethell, Thomas N. *61:* 169
Bethers, Ray *6:* 22
Betteridge, Deirdre *214:* 34

Bettina
See Ehrlich, Bettina
Betts, Ethel Franklin *17:* 161, 164, 165; *YABC 2:* 47
Betz, Rudolf *59:* 161
Bewick, Thomas *16:* 40, 41, 43, 44, 45, 47; *54:* 150; *YABC 1:* 107
Beyer, Paul J. III *74:* 24
Bezencon, Jacqueline *48:* 40
Biamonte, Daniel *40:* 90
Bianchi, John *91:* 19
Bianco, Pamela *15:* 31; *28:* 44, 45, 46
Bible, Charles *13:* 15
Bice, Clare *22:* 40
Biedrzycki, David *186:* 170; *219:* 7
Bierman, Don *57:* 184
Biggers, John *2:* 123
Biggs, Brian *192:* 38; *196:* 15; *207:* 170
Bikadoroff, Roxanna *201:* 74
Bileck, Marvin *3:* 102; *40:* 36, 37
Bilibin, Ivan *61:* 8, 9, 12, 13, 14, 15, 151, 152, 154, 162
Billington, Patrick *98:* 71
Billout, Guy *144:* 38, 39
Bimen, Levent *5:* 179
Binch, Caroline *81:* 18; *140:* 15, 16; *144:* 115; *211:* 82
Binder, Hannes *169:* 163
Bing, Christopher *126:* 34
Binger, Bill *121:* 46
Binks, Robert *25:* 150
Binzen, Bill *24:* 47
Birch, Reginald *15:* 150; *19:* 33, 34, 35, 36; *37:* 196,197; *44:* 182; *46:* 176; *YABC 1:* 84; *2:* 34, 39
Birch, Wendy *223:* 70
Birchall, Mark *123:* 188
Bird, Esther Brock *1:* 36; *25:* 66
Birdsong, Keith *167:* 85; *219:* 105
Birkett, Georgie *204:* 121
Birkett, Rachel *78:* 206
Birling, Paul *109:* 30
Birmingham, Christian *132:* 243; *143:* 114; *209:* 58; *220:* 20
Birmingham, Lloyd P. *12:* 51; *83:* 13
Biro, Val *1:* 26; *41:* 42; *60:* 178; *67:* 23, 24; *84:* 242, 243
Bischoff, Ilse *44:* 51
Bishop, Don *199:* 133
Bishop, Gavin *97:* 17, 18; *144:* 42, 44; *216:* 52, 55, 56, 57
Bishop, Kathleen Wong *115:* 67
Bishop, Rich *56:* 43
Bite, I. *60:* 14
Bittinger, Ned *93:* 117; *205:* 115
Bjorklund, Lorence *3:* 188, 252; *7:* 100; *9:* 113; *10:* 66; *19:* 178; *33:* 122, 123; *35:* 36, 37, 38, 39,41, 42, 43; *36:* 185; *38:* 93; *47:* 106; *66:* 194; *YABC 1:* 242
Björkman, Steve *91:* 199; *160:* 110; *198:* 18; *218:* 188; *223:* 20, 21
Blabey, Aaron *214:* 35
Black Sheep *164:* 100
Blackburn, Loren H. *63:* 10
Blackall, Sophie *194:* 140; *209:* 157
Blackford, John *137:* 105; *180:* 36
Blackwell, Basil T. *YABC 1:* 68, 69
Blackwood, Freya *199:* 9
Blackwood, Gary L. *118:* 17
Blades, Ann *16:* 52; *37:* 213; *50:* 41; *69:* 21; *99:* 215
Blair, Jay *45:* 46; *46:* 155
Blaisdell, Elinore *1:* 121; *3:* 134; *35:* 63
Blake, Anne Catharine *189:* 71
Blake, Francis *198:* 4
Blake, Quentin *3:* 170; *10:* 48; *13:* 38; *21:* 180; *26:* 60; *28:* 228; *30:* 29, 31; *40:* 108; *45:* 219; *46:* 165, 168; *48:* 196; *52:* 10, 11, 12,13, 14, 15, 16, 17; *73:* 41, 43; *78:* 84, 86;

80: 250, 251; *84:* 210, 211, 212; *87:* 177; *96:* 24, 26, 28; *124:* 79; *125:* 32, 34; *181:* 139; *211:* 26, 27; *227:* 176; *229:* 167
Blake, Robert J. *37:* 90; *53:* 67; *54:* 23; *160:* 28, 29
Blake, William *30:* 54, 56, 57, 58, 59, 60
Blakeslee, Lys *218:* 11, 105
Blanchard, N. Taylor *82:* 140
Blass, Jacqueline *8:* 215
Blazek, Scott R. *91:* 71
Bleck, Cathie *118:* 116
Bleck, Linda *204:* 124
Blegvad, Erik *2:* 59; *3:* 98; *5:* 117; *7:* 131; *11:* 149; *14:* 34, 35; *18:* 237; *32:* 219; *60:* 106; *66:* 16, 17, 18, 19; *70:* 233; *76:* 18; *82:* 106; *87:* 45; *100:* 188; *129:* 125; *132:* 17, 18, 19, 20; *176:* 14; *200:* 100; *YABC 1:* 201
Blessen, Karen *93:* 126
Bliss, Corinne Demas *37:* 38
Bliss, Harry *196:* 27, 28, 29
Blitt, Barry *179:* 199; *187:* 13; *225:* 198
Bloch, Lucienne *10:* 12
Blondon, Herve *129:* 48; *183:* 22
Bloom, Lloyd *35:* 180; *36:* 149; *47:* 99; *62:* 117; *68:* 231; *72:* 136; *75:* 185; *83:* 99; *108:* 19; *229:* 114
Bloom, Suzanne *172:* 23, 24
Blossom, Dave *34:* 29
Blumenschein, E.L. *YABC 1:* 113, 115
Blumer, Patt *29:* 214
Blundell, Kim *29:* 36
Bluthenthal, Diana Cain *93:* 32; *104:* 106; *177:* 26
Blythe, Benjamin *128:* 7
Blythe, Gary *112:* 52; *181:* 166; *182:* 64; *185:* 7; *186:* 116, 117
Boake, Kathy *176:* 185
Board, Perry *171:* 99
Boardman, Gwenn *12:* 60
Boase, Susan *224:* 53
Boatwright, Phil *211:* 195
Bober, Richard *125:* 145; *132:* 40
Bobri *30:* 138; *47:* 27
Bock, Vera *1:* 187; *21:* 41
Bock, William Sauts *8:* 7; *14:* 37; *16:* 120; *21:* 141; *36:* 177; *62:* 203
Bodecker, N(iels) M(ogens) *8:* 13; *14:* 2; *17:* 55, 56, 57; *73:* 22, 23, 24
Boehm, Linda *40:* 31
Bogacki, Tomek *138:* 31, 32; *144:* 123; *202:* 13
Bogan, Paulette *197:* 152; *201:* 17
Bogdan, Florentina *107:* 43
Bohdal, Susi *22:* 44; *101:* 20
Bohlen, Nina *58:* 13
Boies, Alex *96:* 53
Bok, Chip *205:* 16
Bolam, Emily *101:* 216; *159:* 12; *205:* 59
Bolian, Polly *3:* 270; *4:* 30; *13:* 77; *29:* 197
Bolle, Frank *87:* 100; *208:* 101
Bollen, Roger *79:* 186; *83:* 16
Bolling, Vickey *114:* 44
Bollinger, Peter *101:* 7; *128:* 198; *172:* 26
Bolognese, Don *2:* 147, 231; *4:* 176; *7:* 146; *17:* 43; *23:* 192; *24:* 50; *34:* 108; *36:* 133; *71:* 24, 25; *103:* 131; *129:* 39, 40
Bolster, Rob *186:* 169
Bolton, A.T. *57:* 158
Bond, Arnold *18:* 116
Bond, Barbara Higgins *21:* 102
Bond, Bruce *52:* 97
Bond, Felicia *38:* 197; *49:* 55, 56; *89:* 170; *90:* 171; *126:* 37
Bond, Higgins *177:* 22, 23; *209:* 175; *220:* 22, 23, 24
Bonn, Pat *43:* 40
Bonner, Hannah *197:* 13, 14
Bonners, Susan *41:* 40; *85:* 36; *94:* 99, 100; *151:* 105, 106
Bono, Mary *184:* 73
Bonsall, Crosby *23:* 6

Booker, Philip *225:* 16
Boon, Debbie *103:* 6; *144:* 188
Boon, Emilie *86:* 23, 24
Boone, Debbie *165:* 77
Boore, Sara *60:* 73
Bootman, Colin *155:* 13; *159:* 35; *174:* 192; *222:* 128
Booth, Franklin *YABC 2:* 76
Booth, George *191:* 13
Booth, Graham *32:* 193; *37:* 41, 42
Borda, Juliette *102:* 188
Bordier, Georgette *16:* 54
Borges, Jose Francisco *119:* 62
Borja, Robert *22:* 48
Born, Adolf *49:* 63
Bornstein, Ruth *14:* 44; *88:* 45, 46; *107:* 30
Borten, Helen *3:* 54; *5:* 24
Bosin, Blackbear *69:* 104
Bossom, Naomi *35:* 48
Bostock, Mike *83:* 221; *114:* 14; *188:* 205
Boston, Peter *19:* 42
Bosustow, Stephen *34:* 202
Boszko, Ron *75:* 47
Bottner, Barbara *14:* 46
Boucher, Joelle *41:* 138
Boulat, Pierre *44:* 40
Boulet, Susan Seddon *50:* 47
Bouma, Paddy *118:* 25; *128:* 16
Bour, Daniele *66:* 145
Bourke-White, Margaret *15:* 286, 287; *57:* 102
Boutavant, Marc *200:* 136
Boutet de Monvel, M. *30:* 61, 62, 63, 65
Bowen, Betsy *105:* 222
Bowen, Richard *42:* 134
Bowen, Ruth *31:* 188
Bower, Ron *29:* 33
Bowers, David *95:* 38; *115:* 20; *127:* 169, 170; *165:* 57; *207:* 11
Bowers, Tim *185:* 35; *201:* 41; *218:* 13
Bowman, Claire *174:* 177
Bowman, Eric *151:* 23
Bowman, Leslie *85:* 203; *105:* 108; *116:* 76; *128:* 234; *182:* 24, 25
Bowman, Peter *146:* 214, 215; *150:* 115
Bowser, Carolyn Ewing *22:* 253
Boxall, Ed *178:* 28
Boyd, Aaron *158:* 242
Boyd, Patti *45:* 31
Boyle, Eleanor Vere *28:* 50, 51
Boynton, Sandra *57:* 13, 14, 15; *107:* 36, 37; *152:* 12, 13, 14
Bozzo, Frank *4:* 154
Brabbs, Derry *55:* 170
Brace, Eric *132:* 193, 194; *152:* 71; *184:* 195; *197:* 6; *201:* 54
Brackers de Hugo, Pierre *115:* 21
Bradford, June *158:* 138
Bradford, Ron *7:* 157
Bradley, David P. *69:* 105
Bradley, Richard D. *26:* 182
Bradley, William *5:* 164
Brady, Irene *4:* 31; *42:* 37; *68:* 191
Bragg, Michael *32:* 78; *46:* 31
Bragg, Ruth Gembicki *77:* 18
Brainerd, John W. *65:* 19
Braithwaite, Althea *23:* 12, 13; *119:* 16
Brak, Syd *146:* 187
Bralds, Braldt *90:* 28; *91:* 151
Bram, Elizabeth *30:* 67
Bramley, Peter *4:* 3
Brandenberg, Aliki *2:* 36, 37; *24:* 222; *35:* 49, 50, 51,52, 53, 54, 56, 57; *75:* 15, 17; *92:* 205; *113:* 18, 19, 20; *157:* 28; *156:* 111
Brandenburg, Alexa *75:* 19
Brandenburg, Jim *47:* 58; *150:* 212
Brandi, Lillian *31:* 158
Brandon, Brumsic, Jr. *9:* 25
Brannen, Sarah S. *202:* 15; *216:* 199
Bransom, Paul *17:* 121; *43:* 44
Braren, Loretta Trezzo *87:* 193

Brassard, France *186:* 22
Braun, Wendy *80:* 17, 18; *213:* 14
Brautigam, Don *115:* 175, 176; *225:* 109
Brazell, Derek *75:* 105; *79:* 9
Breathed, Berkeley *86:* 27, 28, 29; *161:* 13, 14; *229:* 10, 11, 12
Breckenreid, Julia *192:* 209
Breen, Steve *186:* 23
Brennan, Steve *83:* 230; *101:* 184
Brenner, Fred *22:* 85; *36:* 34; *42:* 34
Brett, Bernard *22:* 54
Brett, Harold M. *26:* 98, 99, 100
Brett, Jan *30:* 135; *42:* 39; *71:* 31, 32; *130:* 23, 24, 25, 26, 27; *171:* 15, 16
Brewer, Paul *106:* 115; *145:* 202
Brewer, Sally King *33:* 44
Brewster, Patience *40:* 68; *45:* 22, 183; *51:* 20; *66:* 144; *89:* 4; *97:* 30, 31; *212:* 99
Brick, John *10:* 15
Brickman, Robin D. *131:* 88; *142:* 150; *155:* 18; *178:* 109; *184:* 32
Bridge, David R. *45:* 28
Bridgman, L.J. *37:* 77
Bridwell, Norman *4:* 37; *138:* 36, 37, 40
Brierley, Louise *91:* 22; *96:* 165; *183:* 51
Briggs, Harry *172:* 187
Briggs, Raymond *10:* 168; *23:* 20, 21; *66:* 29, 31, 32; *131:* 28, 29; *184:* 15, 16
Brigham, Grace A. *37:* 148
Bright, Robert *24:* 55
Brighton, Catherine *107:* 39; *206:* 23
Brinckloe, Julie *13:* 18; *24:* 79, 115; *29:* 35; *63:* 140; *81:* 131
Brion *47:* 116
Brisley, Joyce L. *22:* 57
Brisson, James F. *110:* 60
Brittingham, Geoffrey *88:* 37
Brix-Henker, Silke *81:* 194
Broadway, Hannah *208:* 104
Brock, Charles E. *15:* 97; *19:* 247, 249; *23:* 224, 225; *36:* 88; *42:* 41, 42, 43, 44, 45; *100:* 189; *YABC 1:* 194, 196, 203
Brock, Emma *7:* 21
Brock, Henry Matthew *15:* 81; *16:* 141; *19:* 71; *34:* 115; *40:* 164; *42:* 47, 48, 49; *49:* 66
Brocksopp, Arthur *57:* 157
Broda, Ron *136:* 180; *174:* 123
Brodkin, Gwen *34:* 135
Brodovitch, Alexi *52:* 22
Bromhall, Winifred *5:* 11; *26:* 38
Bromley, Lizzy *159:* 179
Bronson, Linda *150:* 210; *174:* 133; *203:* 16, 17; *225:* 178
Brooke, L. Leslie *16:* 181, 182, 183, 186; *17:* 15, 16, 17; *18:* 194
Brooker, Christopher *15:* 251
Brooker, Kyrsten *111:* 94; *140:* 28; *162:* 111; *175:* 108; *186:* 42, 225; *199:* 12; *201:* 30; *219:* 98
Brooks, Erik *166:* 52; *182:* 30
Brooks, Karen Stormer *186:* 110; *220:* 65
Brooks, Maya Itzna *92:* 153
Brooks, Ron *94:* 15; *197:* 188; *212:* 6, 7, 8, 9
Brooks, S.G. *178:* 127
Broomfield, Maurice *40:* 141
Brotman, Adolph E. *5:* 21
Brown, Buck *45:* 48
Brown, Calef *179:* 18; *210:* 206; *217:* 30, 31; *225:* 201
Brown, Christopher *62:* 124, 125, 127, 128
Brown, Craig *73:* 28; *84:* 65; *224:* 18
Brown, Dan *61:* 167; *115:* 183, 184; *116:* 28, 29; *193:* 190; *200:* 21, 23
Brown, David *7:* 47; *48:* 52
Brown, Denise *11:* 213
Brown, Don *172:* 29
Brown, Elbrite *195:* 39; *198:* 5
Brown, Ford Madox *48:* 74
Brown, Gayle *224:* 184
Brown, Hunter *191:* 111, 112

Brown, Judith Gwyn *1:* 45; *7:* 5; *8:* 167; *9:* 182, 190; *20:* 16, 17, 18; *23:* 142; *29:* 117; *33:* 97; *36:* 23, 26; *43:* 184; *48:* 201, 223; *49:* 69; *86:* 227; *110:* 188; *153:* 7
Brown, Kathryn *98:* 26
Brown, Lisa *187:* 175
Brown, Laurie Krasny *99:* 30
Brown, Leo *225:* 18
Brown, Marc (Tolon) *10:* 17, 197; *14:* 263; *51:* 18; *53:* 11, 12, 13, 15, 16, 17; *75:* 58; *80:* 24, 25, 26; *82:* 261; *99:* 29; *145:* 22, 23, 25, 27; *162:* 198; *224:* 136
Brown, Marcia *7:* 30; *25:* 203; *47:* 31, 32, 33, 34, 35,36, 37, 38, 39, 40, 42, 43, 44; *YABC 1:* 27
Brown, Margery W. *5:* 32, 33; *10:* 3
Brown, Martin *101:* 43
Brown, Mary Barrett *97:* 74
Brown, Palmer *36:* 40
Brown, Paul *25:* 26; *26:* 107
Brown, Richard *61:* 18; *67:* 30
Brown, Rick *78:* 71; *150:* 154; *224:* 16
Brown, Robert S. *85:* 33
Brown, Rod *157:* 142
Brown, Ruth *55:* 165; *86:* 112, 113; *105:* 16, 17, 18; *171:* 178
Brown, Trevor *99:* 160; *139:* 247; *189:* 206
Browne, Anthony *45:* 50, 51, 52; *61:* 21, 22, 23, 24, 25; *105:* 21, 22, 23, 25
Browne, Dik *8:* 212; *67:* 32, 33, 35, 37, 39
Browne, Gordon *16:* 97; *64:* 114, 116, 117, 119, 121
Browne, Hablot K. *15:* 65, 80; *21:* 14, 15, 16, 17, 18, 19,20; *24:* 25
Browne, Jane *165:* 222
Browning, Coleen *4:* 132
Browning, Mary Eleanor *24:* 84
Bruce, Robert *23:* 23
Brude, Dick *48:* 215
Bruel, Nick *166:* 41; *205:* 17, 18
Brule, Al *3:* 135
Brumbeau, Jeff *157:* 29
Bruna, Dick *43:* 48, 49, 50; *76:* 27, 28
Brundage, Frances *19:* 244
Brunhoff, Jean de *24:* 57, 58
Brunhoff, Laurent de *24:* 60; *71:* 35, 36, 37
Brunkus, Denise *84:* 50; *123:* 117; *178:* 209; *193:* 99; *204:* 10, 11, 12; *209:* 202
Brunson, Bob *43:* 135
Bryan, Ashley *31:* 44; *72:* 27, 28, 29; *107:* 92; *116:* 192; *132:* 24; *178:* 33, 34, 35; *208:* 83
Bryant, Laura J. *176:* 36; *183:* 168; *214:* 141; *222:* 49, 152
Bryant, Michael *93:* 74
Brychta, Alex *21:* 21
Bryer, Diana *107:* 121
Bryson, Bernarda *3:* 88, 146; *39:* 26; *44:* 185; *131:* 40
Buba, Joy *12:* 83; *30:* 226; *44:* 56
Buchanan, George *166:* 198
Buchanan, Lilian *13:* 16
Buchanan, Rachel *171:* 71
Bucholtz-Ross, Linda *44:* 137
Buchs, Thomas *40:* 38
Buck, Margaret Waring *3:* 30
Buckhardt, Marc *172:* 59
Buckley, Mike *166:* 180
Budwine, Greg *175:* 172
Buehner, Mark *104:* 12, 15; *105:* 160; *119:* 98; *157:* 188; *159:* 39, 40, 43; *192:* 111; *219:* 13, 14, 15, 16; *221:* 17, 18, 19
Buehr, Walter *3:* 31
Buell, Carl *222:* 68
Buff, Conrad *19:* 52, 53, 54
Buff, Mary *19:* 52, 53
Bull, Charles Livingston *18:* 207; *88:* 175, 176
Bullen, Anne *3:* 166, 167
Buller, Jon *205:* 21
Bullock, Kathleen *77:* 24
Bumgarner-Kirby, Claudia *77:* 194
Burbank, Addison *37:* 43

Burchard, Peter Duncan *3:* 197; *5:* 35; *6:* 158, 218; *143:* 17
Burckhardt, Marc *94:* 48; *110:* 89; *196:* 41; *199:* 116
Burden, Andrea *227:* 26
Burger, Carl *3:* 33; *45:* 160, 162
Burgeson, Marjorie *19:* 31
Burgess, Anne *76:* 252
Burgess, Gelett *32:* 39, 42
Burgess, Mark *157:* 31
Burke, Jim *179:* 19; *185:* 63
Burke, Phillip *95:* 117
Burkert, Nancy Ekholm *18:* 186; *22:* 140; *24:* 62, 63,64, 65; *26:* 53; *29:* 60, 61; *46:* 171; *YABC 1:* 46
Burkhardt, Bruce *142:* 86
Burkhardt, Melissa A. *142:* 86
Burleson, Joe *104:* 35; *172:* 139; *227:* 124
Burn, Doris *6:* 172
Burn, Jeffrey *89:* 125; *152:* 132
Burn, Ted
    See Burn, Thomas E.
Burn, Thomas E. *151:* 41
Burnard, Damon *115:* 23
Burnett, Lindy *210:* 59
Burnett, Virgil *44:* 42
Burningham, John *9:* 68; *16:* 60, 61; *59:* 28, 29, 30,31, 32, 33, 35; *111:* 18, 19, 21; *160:* 37; *225:* 21, 24
Burns, Howard M. *12:* 173
Burns, Jim *47:* 70; *86:* 32; *91:* 197; *123:* 16
Burns, M.F. *26:* 69
Burns, Raymond *9:* 29
Burns, Robert *24:* 106
Burr, Dan *65:* 28; *108:* 134; *164:* 203; *182:* 68
Burr, Dane *12:* 2
Burra, Edward *YABC 2:* 68
Burrell, Galen *56:* 76
Burri, Rene *41:* 143; *54:* 166
Burridge, Marge Opitz *14:* 42
Burris, Burmah *4:* 81
Burroughs, John Coleman *41:* 64
Burroughs, Studley O. *41:* 65
Burton, Marilee Robin *46:* 33
Burton, Virginia Lee *2:* 43; *44:* 49, 51; *100:* 46, 47; *YABC 1:* 24; *147:* 56
Bush, Timothy *228:* 138
Busoni, Rafaello *1:* 186; *3:* 224; *6:* 126; *14:* 5; *16:* 62, 63
Butchkes, Sidney *50:* 58
Butler, Geoff *94:* 20
Butler, Ralph *116:* 212
Butterfield, Ned *1:* 153; *27:* 128; *79:* 63
Butterworth, Ian *184:* 48, 49
Butterworth, Nick *106:* 43, 44; *149:* 34
Buxton, John *123:* 12
Buzelli, Christopher *105:* 149
Buzonas, Gail *29:* 88
Buzzell, Russ W. *12:* 177
Byard, Carole *39:* 44; *57:* 18, 19, 20; *60:* 60; *61:* 93, 96; *69:* 210; *78:* 246; *79:* 227
Byars, Betsy *46:* 35
Byfield, Barbara Ninde *8:* 18
Byfield, Graham *32:* 29
Bynum, Janie *176:* 50
Byrd, Robert *13:* 218; *33:* 46; *158:* 70; *212:* 100; *226:* 39, 40; *229:* 102
Byrd, Samuel *123:* 104

C

Cabat, Erni *74:* 38
Cabban, Vanessa *138:* 73; *176:* 39; *185:* 65; *227:* 70
Cabrera, Jane *103:* 24; *152:* 27; *182:* 33, 34
Caceres, Ana Palmero *198:* 106
Caddy, Alice *6:* 41
Cady, Harrison *17:* 21, 23; *19:* 57, 58
Caffrey, Aileen *72:* 223; *141:* 154

Cairns, Julia *177:* 37
Caldecott, Randolph *16:* 98, 103; *17:* 32, 33, 36, 38, 39; *26:* 90; *100:* 49, 50; *YABC 2:* 172
Calder, Alexander *18:* 168
Calderón, Gloria *179:* 5
Calderon, W. Frank *25:* 160
Caldwell, Ben *105:* 75; *149:* 60; *195:* 61
Caldwell, Clyde *98:* 100; *116:* 39; *208:* 145
Caldwell, Doreen *23:* 77; *71:* 41
Caldwell, John *46:* 225
Call, Greg *126:* 135; *165:* 49; *182:* 105, 163; *197:* 18, 19; *200:* 159; *209:* 166; *212:* 161; *229:* 122
Callahan, Kevin *22:* 42
Callahan, Philip S. *25:* 77
Callan, Jamie *59:* 37
Calvert, Rosemary *218:* 96
Calvin, James *61:* 92
Camburn-Bracalente, Carol A. *118:* 22
Cameron, Chad *190:* 144
Cameron, Julia Margaret *19:* 203
Cameron, Scott *99:* 18
Camm, Martin *140:* 208, 209, 210
Campbell, Ann *11:* 43; *123:* 182; *183:* 68
Campbell, Bill *89:* 39
Campbell, Ken *126:* 143; *205:* 162
Campbell, Robert *55:* 120
Campbell, Rod *51:* 27; *98:* 34
Campbell, Walter M. *YABC 2:* 158
Camps, Luis *28:* 120, 121; *66:* 35
Canga, C.B. *187:* 165
Caniglia, Jeremy *201:* 89
Cann, Helen *124:* 50; *141:* 78; *170:* 138; *179:* 22, 23
Cannell, Jon *196:* 43
Cannon, Janell *78:* 25; *128:* 40
Canright, David *36:* 162
Cantone, AnnaLaura *182:* 146; *196:* 80
Canty, Thomas *85:* 161; *92:* 47; *113:* 192; *134:* 60; *185:* 117
Canyon, Christopher *150:* 44; *151:* 112
Caparo, Antonio Javier *204:* 128; *218:* 88; *220:* 114; *221:* 167; *227:* 125
Caple, Laurie *228:* 9
Caporale, Wende *70:* 42
Capp, Al *61:* 28, 30, 31, 40, 41, 43, 44
Cappon, Manuela *154:* 64; *218:* 149
Caras, Peter *36:* 64
Caraway, Caren *57:* 22
Caraway, James *3:* 200, 201
Carbe, Nino *29:* 183
Cares, Linda *67:* 176
Carigiet, Alois *24:* 67
Carle, Eric *4:* 42; *11:* 121; *12:* 29; *65:* 32,33, 34, 36; *73:* 63, 65; *163:* 55, 56
Carling, Amelia Lau *164:* 46
Carlino, Angela *168:* 43; *188:* 20
Carlson, Nancy L. *41:* 116; *56:* 25; *90:* 45; *144:* 48, 50; *213:* 24, 25, 26
Carluccio, Maria *175:* 129; *221:* 119
Carmi, Giora *79:* 35; *149:* 40; *208:* 126
Carpenter, Nancy *76:* 128; *86:* 173; *89:* 171; *131:* 186; *134:* 8; *138:* 215; *153:* 204; *159:* 93; *165:* 232; *211:* 134; *216:* 113
Carr, Archie *37:* 225
Carrick, Donald *5:* 194; *39:* 97; *49:* 70; *53:* 156; *63:* 15, 16, 17, 18, 19, 21; *80:* 131; *86:* 151; *118:* 24
Carrick, Malcolm *28:* 59, 60
Carrick, Paul *118:* 26; *194:* 28
Carrick, Valery *21:* 47
Carrier, Lark *71:* 43
Carroll, Jim *88:* 211; *140:* 177; *153:* 99; *195:* 75
Carroll, Lewis
    See Dodgson, Charles L.
Carroll, Michael *72:* 5
Carroll, Pamela *84:* 68; *128:* 214; *199:* 130
Carroll, Ruth *7:* 41; *10:* 68

Carter, Abby *81:* 32; *97:* 121; *102:* 61; *163:* 139; *164:* 125; *184:* 22, 23; *191:* 85; *222:* 51
Carter, Barbara *47:* 167, 169
Carter, David A. *114:* 24, 25; *170:* 42, 43; *228:* 29
Carter, Don *124:* 54; *184:* 100; *192:* 43, 44, 45
Carter, Harry *22:* 179
Carter, Helene *15:* 38; *22:* 202, 203; *YABC 2:* 220, 221
Carter, Penny *173:* 91
Cartlidge, Michelle *49:* 65; *96:* 50, 51
Cartwright, Reg *63:* 61, 62; *78:* 26; *143:* 4
Cartwright, Shannon *176:* 81
Carty, Leo *4:* 196; *7:* 163; *58:* 131
Cary *4:* 133; *9:* 32; *20:* 2; *21:* 143
Cary, Page *12:* 41
Casale, Paul *71:* 63; *109:* 122; *136:* 28
Case, Chris *209:* 23
Case, Sandra E. *16:* 2
Caseley, Judith *87:* 36; *159:* 47, 48, 49
Casilla, Robert *78:* 7; *167:* 124; *211:* 41; *212:* 165
Casino, Steve *85:* 193
Cassel, Lili
    See Wronker, Lili Cassel
Cassel-Wronker, Lili
    See Wronker, Lili Cassel
Cassels, Jean *8:* 50; *150:* 119; *173:* 37; *186:* 182
Cassen, Melody *140:* 51
Cassity, Don *104:* 24
Cassler, Carl *75:* 137, 138; *82:* 162
Casson, Hugh *65:* 38, 40, 42, 43
Castellon, Federico *48:* 45, 46, 47, 48
Castle, Jane *4:* 80
Castro L., Antonio *84:* 71; *226:* 43
Casu, Danny "casroc" *201:* 10
Catalano, Dominic *94:* 79; *163:* 60, 61; *162:* 54
Catalanotto, Peter *63:* 170; *70:* 23; *71:* 182; *72:* 96; *74:* 114; *76:* 194, 195; *77:* 7; *79:* 157; *80:* 28, 67; *83:* 157; *85:* 27; *108:* 11; *113:* 30, 31, 33, 34, 36; *114:* 27, 28, 29; *117:* 53; *124:* 168; *159:* 54, 55; *195:* 19, 20, 21, 22, 24, 174; *200:* 156; *207:* 103; *209:* 184; *226:* 4
Catania, Tom *68:* 82
Cather, Carolyn *3:* 83; *15:* 203; *34:* 216
Catlin, George *214:* 172
Catrow, David *117:* 179; *152:* 31, 33; *173:* 24; *206:* 29
Catusanu, Mircea *222:* 53
Cauley, Lorinda Bryan *44:* 135; *46:* 49
Cayard, Bruce *38:* 67
Cazet, Denys *52:* 27; *99:* 39, 40; *163:* 65, 66; *191:* 25, 27, 28
Ceccoli, Nicoletta *181:* 39; *188:* 99; *199:* 118; *209:* 6
Cecil, Randy *127:* 132, 133; *187:* 16, 17; *191:* 168; *209:* 5; *223:* 37, 38; *224:* 83
Cellini, Joseph *2:* 73; *3:* 35; *16:* 116; *47:* 103
Cepeda, Joe *90:* 62; *109:* 91; *134:* 172; *159:* 57, 58, 164; *197:* 157; *203:* 69, 95; *215:* 38, 39, 40
Chabrian, Debbi *45:* 55
Chabrian, Deborah *51:* 182; *53:* 124; *63:* 107; *75:* 84; *79:* 85; *82:* 247; *89:* 93; *101:* 197; *212:* 13
Chagnon, Mary *37:* 158
Chalmers, Mary *3:* 145; *13:* 148; *33:* 125; *66:* 214
Chamberlain, Christopher *45:* 57
Chamberlain, Margaret *46:* 51; *106:* 89; *188:* 193; *212:* 16, 17; *224:* 181
Chamberlain, Nigel *78:* 140
Chambers, C.E. *17:* 230
Chambers, Dave *12:* 151
Chambers, Jill *134:* 110
Chambers, Mary *4:* 188

Chambliss, Maxie *42:* 186; *56:* 159; *93:* 163, 164; *103:* 178; *186:* 33, 34; *196:* 39; *223:* 182
Champlin, Dale *136:* 124
Chan, Harvey *96:* 236; *99:* 153; *143:* 218; *179:* 144; *211:* 219
Chan, Peter *207:* 21; *221:* 39
Chandler, David P. *28:* 62
Chaney, Howard *139:* 27
Chang, Warren *101:* 209
Chapel, Jody *68:* 20
Chapman, C.H. *13:* 83, 85, 87
Chapman, Frederick T. *6:* 27; *44:* 28
Chapman, Gaye *203:* 133
Chapman, Gaynor *32:* 52, 53
Chapman, Jane *145:* 186; *150:* 56; *166:* 220; *174:* 202; *176:* 43, 44; *179:* 131; *202:* 189; *212:* 20, 21, 22; *216:* 123, 225; *221:* 181, 182
Chapman, Lynne *175:* 31; *197:* 25; *208:* 44
Chapman-Crane, Jeff *220:* 101
Chappell, Warren *3:* 172; *21:* 56; *27:* 125
Charles, Donald *30:* 154, 155
Charlip, Remy *4:* 48; *34:* 138; *68:* 53, 54; *119:* 29, 30; *210:* 63, 64
Charlot, Jean *1:* 137, 138; *8:* 23; *14:* 31; *48:* 151; *56:* 21
Charlot, Martin *64:* 72
Charlton, Michael *34:* 50; *37:* 39
Charmatz, Bill *7:* 45
Chartier, Normand *9:* 36; *52:* 49; *66:* 40; *74:* 220; *145:* 169; *168:* 91; *177:* 108
Chase, Lynwood M. *14:* 4
Chast, Roz *97:* 39, 40; *212:* 25
Chastain, Madye Lee *4:* 50
Chateron, Ann *152:* 19
Chatterton, Martin *68:* 102; *152:* 19; *225:* 42
Chau, Tungwai *140:* 35
Chauncy, Francis *24:* 158
Chayka, Doug *145:* 97; *177:* 150; *196:* 46; *212:* 58
Chee, Cheng-Khee *79:* 42; *81:* 224; *180:* 245
Chen, Chih-sien *90:* 226
Chen, Tony *6:* 45; *19:* 131; *29:* 126; *34:* 160
Chen, Wendy *221:* 76
Chen, Yong *183:* 34
Cheney, T.A. *11:* 47
Cheng, Andrea *205:* 28
Cheng, Judith *36:* 45; *51:* 16
Chermayeff, Ivan *47:* 53
Cherry, David *93:* 40
Cherry, Lynne *34:* 52; *65:* 184; *87:* 111; *99:* 46, 47
Chesak, Lina *135:* 118
Chess, Victoria *12:* 6; *33:* 42, 48, 49; *40:* 194; *41:* 145; *69:* 80; *72:* 100; *92:* 33, 34; *104:* 167
Chessare, Michele *41:* 50; *56:* 48; *69:* 145
Chesterton, G.K. *27:* 43, 44, 45, 47
Chestnutt, David *47:* 217
Chesworth, Michael *75:* 24, 152; *88:* 136; *94:* 25; *98:* 155; *160:* 42; *207:* 23, 24, 25; *214:* 145
Chetham, Celia *134:* 34
Chetwin, Grace *86:* 40
Cheung, Irving *158:* 96
Chevalier, Christa *35:* 66
Chew, Ruth *7:* 46; *132:* 147
Chewning, Randy *92:* 206
Chichester Clark, Emma *72:* 121; *77:* 212; *78:* 209; *87:* 143; *117:* 37, 39, 40; *144:* 138; *156:* 24, 25; *209:* 26
Chifflart *47:* 113, 127
Child, Lauren *119:* 32; *183:* 30, 31
Chin, Alex *28:* 54
Chitwood, Susan Tanner *163:* 16
Cho, Shinta *8:* 126
Chodos-Irvine, Margaret *52:* 102, 103, 107; *152:* 44
Choi, Yangsook *171:* 134; *173:* 135; *178:* 38, 39, 40

Choksi, Nishant _222:_ 54
Chollat, Emilie _170:_ 203
Chollick, Jay _25:_ 175
Choma, Christina _99:_ 169
Chomey, Steve _188:_ 53
Chorao, Kay _7:_ 200, 201; _8:_ 25; _11:_ 234; _33:_
   187; _35:_ 239; _69:_ 35; _70:_ 235; _123:_ 174;
   _193:_ 179; _215:_ 43, 44, 45, 46; _229:_ 174
Chorney, Steve _221:_ 63
Chow, Frances J. Soo Ping _206:_ 36
Chowdhury, Subrata _62:_ 130; _162:_ 22, 23
Christelow, Eileen _38:_ 44; _83:_ 198, 199; _90:_
   57, 58; _184:_ 26
Christensen, Bonnie _93:_ 100; _153:_ 67; _213:_ 29,
   30
Christensen, Gardell Dano _1:_ 57
Christensen, James C. _140:_ 226
Christiana, David _90:_ 64; _135:_ 13; _171:_ 7;
   _195:_ 26, 27
Christiansen, Per _40:_ 24
Christie, R. Gregory _116:_ 107; _127:_ 20, 21;
   _162:_ 179; _164:_ 114; _165:_ 137; _174:_ 157;
   _179:_ 172; _185:_ 17, 18, 19; _200:_ 2; _204:_ 85;
   _215:_ 207; _218:_ 57; _220:_ 80, 130; _225:_ 45,
   46, 47; _226:_ 211
Christy, Howard Chandler _17:_ 163, 164, 165,
   168, 169; _19:_ 186, 187; _21:_ 22, 23, 24, 25
Christy, Jana _194:_ 21
Chronister, Robert _23:_ 138; _63:_ 27; _69:_ 167
Church, Caroline Jayne _179:_ 27; _219:_ 28, 29
Church, Frederick _YABC 1:_ 155
Chute, Marchette _1:_ 59
Chwast, Jacqueline _1:_ 63; _2:_ 275; _6:_ 46, 47;
   _11:_ 125; _12:_ 202; _14:_ 235
Chwast, Seymour _3:_ 128, 129; _18:_ 43; _27:_
   152; _92:_ 79; _96:_ 56, 57, 58; _146:_ 32, 33;
   _197:_ 99
Cieslawski, Steve _101:_ 142; _127:_ 116; _158:_
   169, 171; _190:_ 174; _212:_ 85; _228:_ 123
Cinelli, Lisa _146:_ 253
Cirlin, Edgard _2:_ 168
Clairin, Georges _53:_ 109
Clapp, John _105:_ 66; _109:_ 58; _126:_ 7; _129:_
   148; _130:_ 165; _195:_ 48; _220:_ 102
Clark, Brenda _119:_ 85; _153:_ 55
Clark, David _77:_ 164; _134:_ 144, 145; _216:_ 66,
   67
Clark, Emma Chichester
   See Chichester Clark, Emma
Clark, Robert _227:_ 170
Clark, Victoria _35:_ 159
Clarke, Greg _169:_ 134; _215:_ 47, 115
Clarke, Gus _72:_ 226; _134:_ 31
Clarke, Harry _23:_ 172, 173
Clarke, Peter _75:_ 102
Claverie, Jean _38:_ 46; _88:_ 29
Clavis, Philippe Goossens _182:_ 167
Clay, Wil _203:_ 29
Clayton, Elaine _159:_ 60; _209:_ 32
Clayton, Robert _9:_ 181
Cleary, Brian P. _186:_ 37
Cleaver, Elizabeth _8:_ 204; _23:_ 36
Cleland, Janet _225:_ 111; _226:_ 48
Cleland, T.M. _26:_ 92
Clemens, Peter _61:_ 125
Clement, Charles _20:_ 38
Clement, Gary _186:_ 79; _191:_ 32
Clement, Janet _182:_ 50
Clement, Nathan _200:_ 30
Clement, Rod _97:_ 42
Clement, Stephen _88:_ 3
Clementson, John _84:_ 213
Clemesha, David _192:_ 49, 50
Cleminson, Kate _221:_ 26
Clevin, Jorgen _7:_ 50
Clifford, Judy _34:_ 163; _45:_ 198
Clokey, Art _59:_ 44
Clouse, Dennis _187:_ 158
Clouse, James _84:_ 15
Clouse, Nancy L. _78:_ 31; _114:_ 90; _225:_ 117
Clover, Peter _152:_ 45

Cneut, Carll _156:_ 166; _165:_ 67; _197:_ 26
Coalson, Glo _9:_ 72, 85; _25:_ 155; _26:_ 42; _35:_
   212; _53:_ 31; _56:_ 154; _94:_ 37, 38, 193
Cober, Alan E. _17:_ 158; _32:_ 77; _49:_ 127
Cober-Gentry, Leslie _92:_ 111
Cocca-Leffler, Maryann _80:_ 46; _136:_ 60; _139:_
   193; _194:_ 31, 33, 34
Cochran, Bobbye _11:_ 52
Cochran, Josh _221:_ 27
CoConis, Ted _4:_ 41; _46:_ 41; _51:_ 104
Cocozza, Chris _87:_ 18; _110:_ 173; _111:_ 149
Cockroft, Jason _152:_ 20
Coerr, Eleanor _1:_ 64; _67:_ 52
Coes, Peter _35:_ 172
Cogancherry, Helen _52:_ 143; _69:_ 131; _77:_ 93;
   _78:_ 220; _109:_ 204; _110:_ 129, 203: 92
Coggins, Jack _2:_ 69
Cohen, Alix _7:_ 53
Cohen, Lisa _225:_ 49
Cohen, Miriam _155:_ 23, 24
Cohen, Nancy R. _165:_ 35
Cohen, Santiago _164:_ 26; _215:_ 52, 199
Cohen, Sheldon _105:_ 33, 34; _166:_ 46, 47
Cohen, Vincent O. _19:_ 243
Cohen, Vivien _11:_ 112
Coker, Paul _51:_ 172
Colbert, Anthony _15:_ 41; _20:_ 193
Colby, C.B. _3:_ 47
Cole, Babette _58:_ 172; _96:_ 63, 64; _155:_ 29
Cole, Brock _68:_ 223; _72:_ 36, 37, 38, 192; _127:_
   23; _136:_ 64, 65; _197:_
Cole, Gwen _87:_ 185
Cole, Henry _178:_ 120; _181:_ 42, 43; _189:_ 60;
   _213:_ 35, 36; _222:_ 139
Cole, Herbert _28:_ 104
Cole, Michael _59:_ 46
Cole, Olivia H.H. _1:_ 134; _3:_ 223; _9:_ 111; _38:_
   104
Cole, Rachael _209:_ 39
Colin, Paul _102:_ 59; _123:_ 118; _126:_ 152; _192:_
   129
Colley, Jacqui _202:_ 20
Collicott, Sharleen _98:_ 39; _143:_ 29, 30
Collier, Bryan _126:_ 54; _151:_ 166; _174:_ 16, 17,
   18; _204:_ 18, 19; _208:_ 84; _211:_ 143; _228:_ 128
Collier, David _13:_ 127
Collier, John _27:_ 179; _208:_ 154
Collier, Steven _50:_ 52
Collier-Morales, Roberta _168:_ 61
Collins, Heather _66:_ 84; _67:_ 68; _81:_ 40; _98:_
   192, 193; _129:_ 95, 96, 98
Collins, Matt _167:_ 90
Collins, Ross _140:_ 23, 24; _200:_ 36, 37; _209:_
   54
Colman, Audrey _146:_ 161
Colón, Raul _108:_ 112; _113:_ 5; _117:_ 167; _134:_
   112; _146:_ 23; _159:_ 92; _166:_ 73; _180:_ 107;
   _186:_ 156; _190:_ 6; _193:_ 24, 205; _202:_ 21, 22,
   23; _217:_ 68; _220:_ 126, 157; _226:_ 118; _227:_
   165
Colonna, Bernard _21:_ 50; _28:_ 103; _34:_ 140;
   _43:_ 180; _78:_ 150
Comport, Sally Wern _117:_ 169; _169:_ 104; _190:_
   42; _207:_ 50
Conahan, Carolyn _215:_ 17
Conde, J.M. _100:_ 120
Condon, Grattan _54:_ 85 Condon, Ken _161:_ 44;
   _195:_ 28, 29
Cone, Ferne Geller _39:_ 49
Cone, J. Morton _39:_ 49
Conklin, Paul _43:_ 62
Connelly, Gwen _212:_ 30
Connelly, James _198:_ 12
Connolly, Howard _67:_ 88
Connolly, Jerome P. _4:_ 128; _28:_ 52
Connolly, Peter _47:_ 60
Conoly, Walle _110:_ 224
Conover, Chris _31:_ 52; _40:_ 184; _41:_ 51; _44:_
   79; _213:_ 39
Conroy, Melissa _226:_ 54
Constantin, Pascale _207:_ 159

Contreras, Gerry _72:_ 9
Converse, James _38:_ 70
Conway _62:_ 62
Conway, Michael _69:_ 12; _81:_ 3; _92:_ 108
Cook, Ande _188:_ 135
Cook, G.R. _29:_ 165
Cook, Joel _108:_ 160
Cook, Lynette _228:_ 211
Cookburn, W.V. _29:_ 204
Cooke, Donald E. _2:_ 77
Cooke, Tom _52:_ 118
Coomaraswamy, A.K. _50:_ 100
Coombs, Charles _43:_ 65
Coombs, Deborah _139:_ 175
Coombs, Patricia _2:_ 82; _3:_ 52; _22:_ 119; _51:_
   32, 33, 34, 35, 36, 37, 38, 39, 40, 42, 43
Cooney, Barbara _6:_ 16, 17, 50; _12:_ 42; _13:_ 92;
   _15:_ 145; _16:_ 74, 111; _18:_ 189; _23:_ 38, 89,
   93; _32:_ 138; _38:_ 105; _59:_ 48, 49, 51, 52, 53;
   _74:_ 222; _81:_ 100; _91:_ 25; _96:_ 71, 72, 74;
   _100:_ 149; _YABC2:_ 10
Cooper, Elisha _157:_ 38, 39
Cooper, Floyd _79:_ 95; _81:_ 45; _84:_ 82; _85:_ 74;
   _91:_ 118; _96:_ 77, 78; _103:_ 149; _144:_ 54; _145:_
   151; _159:_ 198; _176:_ 133, 134; _187:_ 26, 27,
   28, 29; _188:_ 22; _199:_ 175; _219:_ 66; _227:_ 38,
   39, 40, 42
Cooper, Heather _50:_ 39
Cooper, Helen _102:_ 42, 43, 44
Cooper, Mario _24:_ 107
Cooper, Marjorie _7:_ 112
Cope, Jane _61:_ 201; _108_ 52
Copeland, Mark _180:_ 12
Copelman, Evelyn _8:_ 61; _18:_ 25
Copley, Heather _30:_ 86; _45:_ 57
Corace, Jen _208:_ 48
Corbett, Grahame _30:_ 114; _43:_ 67
Corbino, John _19:_ 248
Corcos, Lucille _2:_ 223; _10:_ 27; _34:_ 66
Cordell, Matthew _197:_ 93; _199:_ 20, 21
Córdova, Amy _220:_ 194
Corey, Robert _9:_ 34
Corlass, Heather _10:_ 7
Cornell, James _27:_ 60
Cornell, Jeff _11:_ 58
Cornell, Laura _94:_ 179; _95:_ 25
Corr, Christopher _204:_ 98
Corral, Ridrigs _212:_ 87
Corrigan, Barbara _8:_ 37
Corrigan, Patrick _145:_ 149
Corwin, Judith Hoffman _10:_ 28
Corwin, Oliver _191:_ 119
Cory, Fanny Y. _20:_ 113; _48:_ 29
Cosentino, Ralph _169:_ 32
Cosgrove, Margaret _3:_ 100; _47:_ 63; _82:_ 133
Costabel, Eva Deutsch _45:_ 66, 67
Costanza, John _58:_ 7, 8, 9
Costello, Chris _86:_ 78
Costello, David F. _23:_ 55
Côté, Geneviéve _184:_ 37, 39; _210:_ 256; _211:_
   151
Cote, Nancy _126:_ 139; _156:_ 101; _174:_ 101;
   _182:_ 53, 54, 55; _222:_ 49
Cottenden, Jeff _190:_ 45
Couch, Greg _94:_ 124; _110:_ 13; _162:_ 31; _168:_
   149; _199:_ 22; _216:_ 144; _229:_ 103
Councell, Ruth Tietjen _79:_ 29
Courtney, Cathy _58:_ 69, 144; _59:_ 15; _61:_ 20,
   87
Courtney, R. _35:_ 110
Counihan, Claire _133:_ 106
Cousineau, Normand _89:_ 180; _112:_ 76; _227:_
   75
Cousins, Lucy _172:_ 53, 54; _205:_ 34, 35
Couture, Christin _41:_ 209
Covarrubias, Miguel _35:_ 118, 119, 123, 124,
   125
Coville, Katherine _32:_ 57; _36:_ 167; _92:_ 38
Covington, Neverne _113:_ 87
Cowdrey, Richard _169:_ 170; _178:_ 205; _204:_
   22, 23; _215:_ 31

Cowell, Cressida 140: 39
Cowell, Lucinda 77: 54
Cowles, Rose 203: 164, 167
Cox 43: 93
Cox, Charles 8: 20
Cox, David 56: 37; 90: 63; 119: 38
Cox, Palmer 24: 76, 77
Cox, Paul 226: 57, 58
Cox, Steve 140: 96
Coxe, Molly 69: 44
Coxon, Michele 158: 80
Crabb, Gordon 70: 39
Crabtree, Judith 98: 42
Craft, Kinuko 22: 182; 36: 220; 53: 122, 123,
    148,149; 74: 12; 81: 129; 86: 31; 89: 139;
    127: 27, 28, 29; 132: 142; 139: 38
Craig, Daniel 177: 67; 180: 11; 185: 203; 211:
    212; 224: 27; 229: 59
Craig, David 136: 198; 205: 37
Craig, Helen 49: 76; 62: 70, 71, 72; 69: 141;
    94: 42, 43, 44; 112: 53; 135: 101, 102; 213:
    45, 46, 47, 55, 81, 82
Crane, Alan H. 1: 217
Crane, H.M. 13: 111
Crane, Jack 43: 183
Crane, Jordan 174: 21
Crane, Walter 18: 46, 47, 48, 49, 53, 54, 56,
    57, 59, 60, 61; 22: 128; 24: 210, 217; 100:
    70, 71
Cravath, Lynne Avril 98: 45; 182: 58, 59; 216:
    48; 219: 61; 220: 124; 224: 183; 228: 74;
    229: 89
Crawford, Allen 212: 181
Crawford, Denise 137: 213
Crawford, Will 43: 77
Credle, Ellis 1: 69
Czekaj, Jef 217: 44; 218: 77
Czernecki, Stefan 154: 104; 178: 68, 69
Crespi, Francesca 87: 90
Cressy, Michael 124: 55; 203: 132
Crews, Donald 32: 59, 60; 76: 42, 43, 44
Crews, Nina 97: 49
Crichlow, Ernest 74: 88; 83: 203
Crilley, Mark 210: 71
Croft, James 150: 57
Crofut, Bob 80: 87; 81: 47
Crofut, Susan 23: 61
Croll, Carolyn 80: 137; 102: 52
Cross, Peter 56: 78; 63: 60, 65
Crossman, David A. 219: 38
Crowe, Elizabeth 88: 144
Crowell, Pers 3: 125
Cruikshank, George 15: 76, 83; 22: 74, 75, 76,
    77, 78, 79,80, 81, 82, 84, 137; 24: 22, 23
Crump, Fred H. 11: 62
Cruz, Ray 6: 55; 70: 234; 123: 173; 172: 192
Csatari, Joe 44: 82; 55: 152; 63: 25, 28; 102:
    58
Cuetara, Mittie 158: 85
Cuffari, Richard 4: 75; 5: 98; 6: 56; 7: 13,84,
    153; 8: 148, 155; 9: 89; 11: 19; 12: 55,
    96,114; 15: 51, 202; 18: 5; 20: 139; 21: 197;
    22: 14, 192; 23: 15, 106; 25: 97; 27: 133;
    28: 196; 29: 54; 30: 85; 31: 35; 36: 101; 38:
    171; 42: 97; 44: 92, 192; 45: 212, 213; 46:
    36, 198; 50: 164; 54: 80, 136, 137, 145; 56:
    17; 60: 63; 66: 49, 50; 70: 41; 71: 132; 77:
    157; 78: 58, 149; 79: 120; 85: 2, 152
Cugat, Xavier 19: 120
Cumings, Art 35: 160
Cummings, Chris 29: 167
Cummings, Michael 159: 142
Cummings, Pat 42: 61; 61: 99; 69: 205; 71:
    57,58; 78: 24, 25; 93: 75; 107: 49, 50; 164:
    259; 203: 45, 46
Cummings, Richard 24: 119
Cummings, Terrance 227: 49, 172
Cunette, Lou 20: 93; 22: 125
Cunningham, Aline 25: 180
Cunningham, David 11: 13
Cunningham, Imogene 16: 122, 127

Cunningham, Kelley 176: 159
Cupples, Pat 107: 12; 126: 109; 182: 13; 198:
    68; 217: 21, 22
Curlee, Lynn 98: 48; 141: 39; 190: 48
Currey, Anna 190: 145; 202: 130, 132
Curry, John Steuart 2: 5; 19: 84; 34: 36; 144:
    126
Curry, Tom 127: 131; 185: 25, 26
Curtis, Bruce 23: 96; 30: 88; 36: 22
Curtis, Neil 167: 30
Curtis, Stacy 205: 38
Cusack, Margaret 58: 49, 50, 51
Cushman, Doug 65: 57; 101: 39, 40; 133: 179;
    157: 45; 186: 157; 210: 76, 77
Cutting, Ann 196: 194
Cyrus, Kurt 132: 39; 179: 36, 37
Czechowski, Alicia 95: 21; 171: 37
Czernecki, Stefan 117: 173

D

Dabcovich, Lydia 25: 105; 40: 114; 99: 75, 76
Dacey, Bob 82: 175; 152: 65
d'Achille, Gino 127: 175, 176
Daily, Don 78: 197; 220: 154
Dain, Martin J. 35: 75
Dale, Penny 127: 224; 151: 57; 160: 89; 197:
    75
Dale, Rae 72: 197
Daley, Joann 50: 22
Dalton, Anne 40: 62; 63: 119
Daly, Deborah M. 74: 213
Daly, Jim 103: 60; 150: 48
Daly, Jude 138: 118, 119; 213: 41; 222: 56, 57
Daly, Nicholas 37: 53; 76: 48, 49
Daly, Niki 107: 15; 114: 38, 39, 40; 164: 86;
    192: 53; 198: 26, 27
Daly, Paul 97: 205
Dalziel, Brothers 33: 113
D'Amato, Alex 9: 48; 20: 25
D'Amato, Janet 9: 48; 20: 25; 26: 118
D'Amico, Steve 170: 52
Danalis, Johnny 167: 27
D'Andrea, Domenick 183: 108
Daniel, Alan 23: 59; 29: 110; 76: 50, 53, 55,
    56; 153: 76 115: 74; 134: 70
Daniel, Lea 76: 53, 55; 153: 76
Daniel, Lewis C. 20: 216
Daniels, Beau 73: 4
Daniels, Steve 22: 16
Daniels, Stewart 56: 12
Dann, Bonnie 31: 83
Dann, Penny 82: 128
Danska, Herbert 24: 219
Danyell, Alice 20: 27
Darbyshire, Kristen 218: 41
Dardik, Helen 208: 200
Darley, F.O.C. 16: 145; 19: 79, 86, 88, 185;
    21: 28,36; 35: 76, 77, 78, 79, 80, 81; YABC
    2: 175
Darling, Lois 3: 59; 23: 30, 31
Darling, Louis 1: 40, 41; 2: 63; 3: 59; 23:
    30,31; 43: 54, 57, 59; 121: 53
Darnell, K.L. 210: 247
Darrow, David R. 84: 101
Darrow, Whitney, Jr. 13: 25; 38: 220, 221
Darwin, Beatrice 43: 54
Darwin, Len 24: 82
Dastolfo, Frank 33: 179
Dauber, Liz 1: 22; 3: 266; 30: 49
Daugherty, James 3: 66; 8: 178; 13: 27, 28,
    161; 18: 101; 19: 72; 29: 108; 32: 156; 42:
    84; YABC 1: 256; 2: 174
d'Aulaire, Edgar Parin 5: 51; 66: 53
d'Aulaire, Ingri Parin 5: 51; 66: 53
Davalos, Felipe 99: 197; 159: 66; 174: 163
Davenier, Christine 125: 88; 127: 32; 128:
    152; 179: 39, 40; 216: 84, 85, 86, 87; 218:
    62, 63; 224: 73

Davick, Linda 151: 124; 208: 187
David, Jacques-Louis 193: 22
David, Jonathan 19: 37
Davidson, Kevin 28: 154
Davidson, Raymond 32: 61
Davie, Helen K. 77: 48, 49
Davies, Andy Robert 205: 169
Davies, Lottie 214: 69
Davis, Allen 20: 11; 22: 45; 27: 222; 29: 157;
    41: 99; 47: 99; 50: 84; 52: 105
Davis, Bette J. 15: 53; 23: 95
Davis, Dimitris 45: 95
Davis, Eleanor 209: 33
Davis, Hendon 151: 122
Davis, Jack E. 145: 139; 175: 84, 85; 208:
    102; 210: 81, 82; 213: 151
Davis, Jim 32: 63, 64
Davis, Katie 152: 52, 53, 54; 208: 52
Davis, Lambert 110: 23, 24; 176: 58
Davis, Marguerite 31: 38; 34: 69, 70; 100: 34;
    YABC 1: 126, 230
Davis, Nelle 69: 191
Davis, Paul 78: 214
Davis, Rich 206: 38
Davis, Stuart 211: 69
Davis, Yvonne LeBrun 94: 144
Davisson, Virginia H. 44: 178
DaVolls, Andy 85: 53
Dawson, Diane 24: 127; 42: 126; 52: 130; 68:
    104
Dawson, Janine 215: 198
Dawson, Willow 208: 54; 216: 119
Day, Alexandra 67: 59; 97: 54; 166: 65; 169:
    40; 197: 50, 51, 52, 54
Day, Larry 169: 88; 185: 59; 227: 55
Day, Rob 94: 110; 127: 24; 197: 32
Dean, Bob 19: 211
Dean, David 192: 55
de Angeli, Marguerite 1: 77; 27: 62, 65, 66,
    67, 69, 70, 72; 100: 75, 76; YABC 1: 166
DeArmond, Dale 70: 47
Deas, Michael 27: 219, 221; 30: 156; 67: 134;
    72: 24; 75: 155; 84: 206; 88: 124
Deas, Rich 191: 87; 193: 10; 212: 79
deBarros, Jim 196: 60
Debon, Nicolas 151: 60; 177: 46
de Bosschere, Jean 19: 252; 21: 4; 186: 44, 45
De Bruyn, M(onica) G. 13: 30, 31
Decker, C.B. 172: 120; 215: 94
De Cuir, John F. 1: 28, 29
Deeter, Catherine 74: 110; 103: 150; 137: 50
Degen, Bruce 40: 227, 229; 57: 28, 29; 56:
    156; 75: 229; 76: 19; 81: 36, 37; 92: 26; 93:
    199; 97: 56, 58, 59; 124: 40; 147: 39, 40,
    41; 168: 23; 205: 45, 46
De Grazia 14: 59; 39: 56, 57
DeGrazio, George 88: 40
deGroat, Diane 9: 39; 18: 7; 23: 123; 28: 200,
    201; 31: 58, 59; 34: 151; 41: 152; 43: 88;
    46: 40, 200; 49: 163; 50: 89; 52: 30, 34; 54:
    43; 63: 5; 70: 136; 71: 99; 73: 117,156; 77:
    34; 85: 48; 86: 201; 87: 142; 90: 72, 73,
    143; 95: 182; 111: 123; 118: 160; 126: 8;
    130: 130; 138: 93, 94; 169: 46, 47
de Groot, Lee 6: 21
Deines, Brian 110: 139; 220: 36, 37
DeJohn, Marie 89: 78
Dekhteryov, B. 61: 158
de Kiefte, Kees 94: 107
Delacre, Lulu 36: 66; 156: 35; 202: 10, 53;
    209: 36
Delaney, A. 21: 78
Delaney, Michael 180: 16
Delaney, Molly 80: 43
Delaney, Ned 28: 68; 56: 80; 102: 11
DeLapine, Jim 79: 21
De La Roche Saint Andre, Anne 75: 37
de Larrea, Victoria 6: 119, 204; 29: 103; 72:
    203; 87: 199
Delehanty, Joan W. 223: 165
DeLeon, Melanie 210: 43

Delessert, Étienne 7: 140; 46: 61, 62, 63, 65, 67, 68; 130: 38, 39, 40, 41, 42; 179: 46, 47, 48, 49; YABC 2: 209
Delezenne, Christine 186: 126
Delinois, Alix 228: 40
Del Negro, Janice 196: 161
Delon, Melanie 216: 30
DeLorenzo, Christopher 154: 149
Delulio, John 15: 54
DeLuna, Tony 88: 95
Demarest, Chris L. 45: 68, 69, 70; 73: 172, 173, 176; 78: 106; 82: 48, 49; 89: 212; 92: 86; 128: 57, 58; 175: 46, 48
De Mejo, Oscar 40: 67
De Muth, Roger 205: 184; 221: 35
Demi 11: 135; 15: 245; 66: 129, 130; 89: 216; 102: 66, 67, 68; 210: 86, 87, 89
Denetsosie, Hoke 13: 126; 82: 34
Denise, Christopher 147: 43, 44; 176: 101; 193: 35, 36, 37; 201: 37
Dennis, Morgan 18: 68, 69; 64: 89
Dennis, Wesley 2: 87; 3: 111; 11: 132; 18: 71, 72, 73, 74; 22: 9; 24: 196, 200; 46: 178; 69: 94, 96; 129: 62
Denos, Julia 202: 26
Denslow, W.W. 16: 84, 85, 86, 87; 18: 19, 20, 24; 29: 211; 100: 21
Denton, Kady MacDonald 110: 82; 130: 70; 181: 54, 55, 56; 192: 75
Denton, Phil 220: 6
Denton, Terry 72: 163; 174: 26; 186: 52; 196: 83, 84
DePalma, Mary Newell 132: 114; 139: 75; 185: 30, 31; 186: 121; 213: 62
dePaola, Tomie 8: 95; 9: 93; 11: 69; 25; 103; 28: 157; 29: 80; 39: 52, 53; 40: 226; 46: 187; 59: 61, 62, 63, 64, 65, 66, 67, 68, 69, 71, 72, 74; 62: 19; 108: 63, 67, 68, 70; 155: 62, 64, 66; 180: 105; 200: 47, 48, 49, 50; 226: 116
Deraney, Michael J. 77: 35; 78: 148
deRosa, Dee 70: 48; 71: 210; 91: 78
Dervaux, Isabelle 111: 117
DeSaix, Deborah Durland 180: 15; 188: 24
De Saulles, Tony 119: 39
de Sève, Peter 146: 261; 207: 78; 219: 42
Deshaprabhu, Meera Dayal 86: 192
Desimini, Lisa 86: 68; 94: 47; 96: 7; 104: 107; 125: 194; 131: 180; 172: 56; 216: 89, 90
de St. Menin, Charles 70: 17
Detmold, Edward J. 22: 104, 105, 106, 107; 35: 120; 64: 5; YABC 2: 203
Detrich, Susan 20: 133
Deutermann, Diana 77: 175
DeVelasco, Joseph E. 21: 51
de Veyrac, Robert YABC 2: 19
DeVille, Edward A. 4: 235
de Visser, John 55: 119
Devito, Bert 12: 164
Devlin, Harry 11: 74; 74: 63, 65; 136: 77, 78
Dewan, Ted 108: 73; 157: 55; 165: 129; 226: 67, 68, 69
Dewar, Nick 133: 122
Dewdney, Anna 184: 43, 44
Dewey, Ariane 7: 64; 33: 195; 35: 208; 68: 16,17; 75: 46; 93: 91; 94: 197; 109: 65, 66, 67; 125: 2, 3, 4, 5; 127: 188; 143: 25; 178: 17, 19, 74; 188: 166; 202: 164
Dewey, Jennifer (Owings) 58: 54; 64: 214; 65: 207; 88: 169; 103: 45
Dewey, Kenneth 39: 62; 51: 23; 56: 163
de Zanger, Arie 30: 40
Diakité, Baba Wagué 174: 28
Diamond, Donna 21: 200; 23: 63; 26: 142; 35: 83, 84, 85, 86, 87, 88, 89; 38: 78; 40: 147; 44: 152; 50: 144; 53: 126; 69: 46, 47, 48, 201; 71: 133; 123: 19
Dias, Ron 71: 67

Diaz, David 80: 213; 96: 83, 84; 108: 228; 110: 29; 149: 106; 150: 63; 179: 160; 184: 95, 97; 189: 51, 52, 53; 221: 86; 229: 37, 38, 39, 40
di Bartolo, Jim 225: 53
Dibley, Glin 138: 83; 141: 128; 211: 162; 221: 61
DiCesare, Joe 70: 38; 71: 63, 106; 79: 214; 93: 147; 116: 217; 143: 111; 166: 57
Dick, John Henry 8: 181
Dickens, Frank 34: 131
Dickey, Robert L. 15: 279
Dickson, Mora 84: 21
Didier, Sam 166: 114
Dietz, James 128: 223; 193: 136
di Fate, Vincent 37: 70; 90: 11; 93: 60; 109: 219, 220
Di Fiori, Lawrence 10: 51; 12: 190; 27: 97; 40: 219; 93: 57; 130: 45
Digby, Desmond 97: 180
Dignan, James 196: 143
Di Grazia, Thomas 32: 66; 35: 241
Dillard, Annie 10: 32
Dillard, Sarah 136: 186; 217: 53
Dillon, Corinne B. 1: 139
Dillon, Diane 4: 104, 167; 6: 23; 13: 29; 15: 99; 26: 148; 27: 136, 201; 51: 29, 48, 51, 52, 53, 54,55, 56, 57, 58, 59, 60, 61, 62; 54: 155; 56: 69; 58: 127,128; 61: 95; 62: 27; 64: 46; 68: 3; 69: 209; 74: 89; 79: 92; 86: 89; 92: 28, 177; 93: 7, 210; 94: 239, 240; 97: 167; 106: 58, 59,61, 64; 107: 3; 139: 246; 167: 77; 189: 202; 191: 191; 194: 45, 46, 48, 49
Dillon, Leo 4: 104, 167; 6: 23; 13: 29; 15: 99; 26: 148; 27: 136, 201; 51: 29, 48, 51, 52, 53, 54,55, 56, 57, 58, 59, 60, 61, 62; 54: 155; 56: 69; 58: 127,128; 61: 95; 62: 27; 64: 46; 68: 3; 69: 209; 74: 89; 79: 92; 86: 89; 92: 28, 177; 93: 7, 210; 94: 239, 240; 97: 167; 106: 58, 59,61, 64; 107: 3; 139: 246; 167: 77; 189: 202; 191: 191; 194: 45, 46, 48, 49
Dillon, Sharon Saseen 59: 179, 188
DiMaccio, Gerald 121: 80
DiMaggio, Joe 36: 22
DiMassi, Gina 169: 17
Dinan, Carol 25: 169; 59: 75
Dines, Glen 7: 66, 67
Dinesen, Thomas 44: 37
Dinh, Pham Viet 167: 184
Dinnerstein, Harvey 42: 63, 64, 65, 66, 67, 68; 50: 146
Dinsdale, Mary 10: 65; 11: 171
Dinyer, Eric 86: 148; 109: 163; 110: 239; 124: 11; 150: 69; 170: 4; 171: 30
Dion, Nathalie 170: 124; 213: 52
DiRocco, Carl 181: 23
DiSalvo-Ryan, DyAnne 59: 77; 62: 185; 117: 46; 144: 64; 150: 153; 186: 162
Disney, Walt 28: 71, 72, 73, 76, 77, 78, 79, 80, 81, 87, 88, 89,90, 91, 94
DiTerlizzi, Tony 105: 7; 147: 22; 154: 31, 32, 33; 214: 74
Divito, Anna 83: 159
Dixon, Don 74: 17; 109: 196
Dixon, Larry 127: 125
Dixon, Maynard 20: 165
Doares, Robert G. 20: 39
Dob, Bob 205: 14
Dobias, Frank 22: 162
Dobrin, Arnold 4: 68
Dobson, Steven Gaston 102: 103
Docherty, Thomas 218: 45, 46
Dockray, Tracy 139: 77
Docktor, Irv 43: 70
Dodd, Ed 4: 69
Dodd, Emma 203: 57
Dodd, Julie 74: 73
Dodd, Lynley 35: 92; 86: 71; 132: 45, 46, 47
Dodge, Bill 96: 36; 118: 7, 8, 9; 133: 135

Dodgson, Charles L. 20: 148; 33: 146; YABC 2: 98
Dodson, Bert 9: 138; 14: 195; 42: 55; 54: 8; 60: 49; 101: 125
Dodson, Liz Brenner 105: 117; 111: 15
Dohanos, Stevan 16: 10
Dolce, J. Ellen 74: 147; 75: 41
Dolch, Marguerite P. 50: 64
Dolesch, Susanne 34: 49
Dollar, Diane 57: 32
Dolobowsky, Mena 81: 54
Dolson, Hildegarde 5: 57
Domanska, Janina 6: 66, 67; YABC 1: 166
Domi 134: 113
Dominguez, El 53: 94
Domjan, Joseph 25: 93
Domm, Jeffrey C. 84: 69; 135: 70
Donahey, William 68: 209
Donahue, Dorothy 76: 170
Donahue, Vic 2: 93; 3: 190; 9: 44
Donald, Elizabeth 4: 18
Donalty, Alison 149: 195, 196, 197
Donato 85: 59; 149: 204; 191: 19
Donato, Michael A. 200: 143
Doner, Kim 208: 57
Doney, Todd L.W. 87: 12; 93: 112; 98: 135; 101: 57; 104: 40; 118: 163; 135: 162, 163; 151: 18; 227: 79
Donna, Natalie 9: 52
Donohue, Dorothy 95: 2; 132: 30; 176: 54, 55; 178: 77, 78, 79
Dooling, Michael 82: 19; 105: 55; 106: 224; 125: 135; 171: 46; 172: 12; 176: 120; 197: 89; 220: 39, 40
Doran, Ben-Ami 128: 189
Doran, Colleen 211: 48
Dore, Gustave 18: 169, 172, 175; 19: 93, 94, 95, 96, 97, 98,99, 100, 101, 102, 103, 104, 105; 23: 188; 25: 197, 199
Doremus, Robert 6: 62; 13: 90; 30: 95, 96, 97; 38: 97
Dorfman, Ronald 11: 128
Doriau 86: 59; 91: 152
Dorman, Brandon 197: 35; 204: 6; 210: 104; 212: 95; 216: 156; 222: 133
Dormer, Frank W. 200: 55; 222: 48
Dorros, Arthur 78: 42, 43; 91: 28
Doruyter, Karel 165: 105
dos Santos, Joyce Audy 57: 187, 189
Doty, Roy 28: 98; 31: 32; 32: 224; 46: 157; 82: 71; 142: 7
Doucet, Bob 132: 238; 169: 159
Dougherty, Charles 16: 204; 18: 74
Doughty, Rebecca 177: 174; 222: 159
Doughty, Thomas 118: 31; 140: 60
Douglas, Aaron 31: 103
Douglas, Allen 223: 53
Douglas, Carole Nelson 73: 48
Douglas, Goray 13: 151
Dow, Brian 150: 92
Dowd, Jason 132: 51, 52; 164: 244
Dowd, Vic 3: 244; 10: 97
Dowden, Anne Ophelia 7: 70, 71; 13: 120
Dowdy, Mrs. Regera 29: 100
Downard, Barry 202: 32
Downes, Belinda 180: 29
Downing, Julie 60: 140; 81: 50; 86: 200; 99: 129
Doyle, Janet 56: 31
Doyle, Richard 21: 31, 32, 33; 23: 231; 24: 177; 31: 87
Draper, Angie 43: 84
Drath, Bill 26: 34
Drawson, Blair 17: 53; 126: 65
Dray, Matt 177: 47
Drescher, Henrik 105: 60, 62, 63; 172: 72
Drescher, Joan 30: 100, 101; 35: 245; 52: 168; 137: 52
Dressell, Peggy 186: 41
Drew, Janet 201: 177
Drew, Patricia 15: 100

Dronzek, Laura *199:* 28, 29; *207:* 69
Drummond, Allan *209:* 41
Drummond, V.H. *6:* 70
Drury, Christian Potter *105:* 97; *186:* 224
Dubanevich, Arlene *56:* 44
Dubin, Jill *205:* 56; *217:* 25
Dubois, Claude K. *196:* 2
Dubois, Gerard *182:* 9
DuBurke, Randy *187:* 89; *222:* 136; *224:* 35
Ducak, Danilo *99:* 130; *108:* 214
Duchesne, Janet *6:* 162; *79:* 8
Duda, Jana *102:* 155; *209:* 134
Dudash, C. Michael *32:* 122; *77:* 134; *82:* 149; *212:* 93, 94
Duer, Douglas *34:* 177
Duewell, Kristina *195:* 76
Duffy, Daniel Mark *76:* 37; *101:* 196; *108:* 147, 148
Duffy, Joseph *38:* 203
Duffy, Pat *28:* 153
Dugan, Karen *181:* 26; *202:* 35
Dugin, Andrej *77:* 60
Dugina, Olga *77:* 60
Duke, Chris *8:* 195; *139:* 164
Duke, Kate *87:* 186; *90:* 78, 79, 80, 81; *192:* 21, 59, 60, 61, 63
Duke, Marion *165:* 87
Dulac, Edmund *19:* 108, 109, 110, 111, 112, 113, 114, 115, 117; *23:* 187; *25:* 152; *YABC 1:* 37; *2:* 147
Dulac, Jean *13:* 64
Dumas, Philippe *52:* 36, 37, 38, 39, 40, 41, 42, 43, 45; *119:* 40, 41, 42
Dunaway, Nancy *108:* 161
Dunbar, James *76:* 63
Dunbar, Polly *181:* 60, 61; *211:* 51, 52, 53; *212:* 42
Duncan, Beverly *72:* 92
Duncan, John *116:* 94
Dunn, H.T. *62:* 196
Dunn, Harvey *34:* 78, 79, 80, 81
Dunn, Iris *5:* 175
Dunn, Phoebe *5:* 175
Dunne, Jeanette *72:* 57, 173, 222
Dunnick, Regan *176:* 51; *178:* 83, 84; *219:* 36; *224:* 144; *229:* 83
Dunnington, Tom *3:* 36; *18:* 281; *25:* 61; *31:* 159; *35:* 168; *48:* 195; *79:* 144; *82:* 230
Dunn-Ramsey, Marcy *117:* 131
Dunrea, Olivier *59:* 81; *118:* 53, 54; *124:* 43
Duntze, Dorothee *88:* 28; *160:* 76
Dupasquier, Philippe *86:* 75; *104:* 76; *151:* 63
duPont, Lindsay Harper *207:* 39
DuQuette, Keith *90:* 83; *155:* 73, 74
Durand, Delphine *200:* 56
Durham, Sarah *192:* 248
Durney, Ryan *208:* 122
Duroussy, Nathalie *146:* 150
Durrell, Julie *82:* 62; *94:* 62
Dusíková, Maja *223:* 49
Dutz *6:* 59
Duvoisin, Roger *2:* 95; *6:* 76, 77; *7:* 197; *28:* 125; *30:* 101, 102, 103, 104, 105, 107; *47:* 205; *84:* 254
Dyer, Dale *141:* 71
Dyer, Jane *75:* 219; *129:* 28; *147:* 49, 50, 51; *168:* 121; *190:* 4; *191:* 57, 59, 60; *203:* 4
Dyer, Sarah *212:* 40
Dypold, Pat *15:* 37

E

E.V.B.
  See Boyle, Eleanor Vere (Gordon)
Eachus, Jennifer *29:* 74; *82:* 201; *164:* 153
Eadie, Bob *63:* 36
Eagle, Bruce *95:* 119
Eagle, Ellen *82:* 121; *89:* 3
Eagle, Jeremy *141:* 71

Eagle, Michael *11:* 86; *20:* 9; *23:* 18; *27:* 122; *28:* 57; *34:* 201; *44:* 189; *73:* 9; *78:* 235; *85:* 43
Earl-Bridges, Michele *159:* 128
Earle, Edwin *56:* 27
Earle, Olive L. *7:* 75
Earle, Vana *27:* 99
Earley, Lori *132:* 2; *186:* 4; *195:* 8
Early, Margaret *72:* 59
East, Jacqueline *218:* 198; *224:* 38
East, Stella *131:* 223
Eastman, P.D. *33:* 57
Easton, Reginald *29:* 181
Eaton, Tom *4:* 62; *6:* 64; *22:* 99; *24:* 124
Eaves, Edward *224:* 13
Ebbeler, Jeffrey *193:* 62; *206:* 45
Ebel, Alex *11:* 89
Eberbach, Andrea *192:* 115
Eckersley, Maureen *48:* 62
Eckert, Horst *72:* 62
Ede, Janina *33:* 59
Edens, Cooper *49:* 81, 82, 83, 84, 85; *112:* 58
Edens, John *109:* 115
Edgar, Sarah E. *41:* 97
Edgerton, Perky *195:* 144
Edliq, Emily S. *131:* 107
Edrien *11:* 53
Edwards, Freya *45:* 102
Edwards, George Wharton *31:* 155
Edwards, Gunvor *2:* 71; *25:* 47; *32:* 71; *54:* 106
Edwards, Jeanne *29:* 257
Edwards, Linda Strauss *21:* 134; *39:* 123; *49:* 88, 89
Edwards, Michelle *152:* 62, 63
Edwards, Wallace *170:* 55
Egan, Tim *155:* 76, 77, 78
Egge, David *102:* 71
Eggenhofer, Nicholas *2:* 81
Eggleton, Bob *74:* 40; *81:* 190, 191; *105:* 6; *121:* 183; *149:* 203; *166:* 215
Egielski, Richard *11:* 90; *16:* 208; *33:* 236; *38:* 35; *49:* 91, 92, 93, 95, 212, 213, 214, 216; *79:* 122; *106:* 67, 68, 69; *134:* 135; *144:* 244; *163:* 82, 84; *207:* 125; *225:* 200
Ehlert, Lois *35:* 97; *69:* 51; *112:* 7; *113:* 208; *128:* 63, 64, 65; *172:* 77, 79, 80; *220:* 43, 44, 45, 46, 47, 48
Ehrlich, Bettina *1:* 83
Eitan, Ora *160:* 165
Eichenberg, Fritz *1:* 79; *9:* 54; *19:* 248; *23:* 170; *24:* 200; *26:* 208; *50:* 67, 68, 69, 70, 71, 72, 73,74, 75, 77, 79, 80, 81; *60:* 165; *100:* 137; *YABC 1:* 104, 105; *2:* 213
Einsel, Naiad *10:* 35; *29:* 136
Einsel, Walter *10:* 37
Einzig, Susan *3:* 77; *43:* 78; *67:* 155; *129:* 154
Eisner, Will *165:* 82, 83
Eitzen, Allan *9:* 56; *12:* 212; *14:* 226; *21:* 194; *38:* 162; *76:* 218
Eldridge, H. *54:* 109
Eldridge, Harold *43:* 83
Elgaard, Greta *19:* 241
Elgin, Kathleen *9:* 188; *39:* 69
Ellacott, S.E. *19:* 118
Elliot, David *192:* 26; *208:* 62, 63
Elliott, Mark *93:* 69; *105:* 108; *107:* 123; *140:* 53; *165:* 189; *173:* 67; *195:* 95; *203:* 67; *210:* 99; *221:* 57, 70
Elliott, Sarah M. *14:* 58
Ellis, Carson *216:* 210
Ellis, Dianne *130:* 208
Ellis, Jan Davey *88:* 50; *115:* 80
Ellis, Richard *130:* 47, 48
Ellison, Chris *196:* 66; *199:* 131; *207:* 193
Ellison, Pauline *55:* 21
Ellwand, David *213:* 60
Elmer, Richard *78:* 5

Elmore, Larry *90:* 8
Elschner, Géraldine *183:* 38
Elwell, Peter *195:* 150
Elwell, Tristan *110:* 39; *121:* 182; *127:* 46; *137:* 144; *141:* 173; *151:* 236; *158:* 264; *167:* 119, 120, 121; *169:* 20; *190:* 12; *202:* 16; *226:* 6
Elzbieta *88:* 80, 81
Ember, Kathi *214:* 147
Emberley, Ed *8:* 53; *70:* 53, 54; *146:* 65, 69, 70; *218:* 50
Emberley, Rebecca *218:* 50
Emberley, Michael *34:* 83; *80:* 72; *119:* 47, 48; *147:* 100; *158:* 115; *189:* 62, 64; *203:* 87, 89
Emerling, Dorothy *104:* 27
Emery, Leslie *49:* 187
Emmett, Bruce *49:* 147; *80:* 175; *101:* 206; *220:* 200
Emry-Perrott, Jennifer *61:* 57
Emshwiller, Ed *174:* 45
Endle, Kate *191:* 167; *207:* 41
Engel, Diana *70:* 57
Engle, Mort *38:* 64
Englebert, Victor *8:* 54
English, Mark *101:* 207; *220:* 201
Enik, Ted *142:* 39
Enos, Randall *20:* 183
Enright, Maginel Wright *19:* 240, 243; *39:* 31, 35, 36
Enrique, Romeo *34:* 135
Ensor, Barbara *180:* 30
Epstein, Stephen *50:* 142, 148
Erdogan, Buket *174:* 179
Erdrich, Louise *141:* 62
Erhard, Walter *1:* 152
Erickson, Jim *196:* 190
Erickson, Phoebe *11:* 83; *59:* 85
Erikson, Mel *31:* 69
Eriksson, Eva *63:* 88, 90, 92, 93; *203:* 99; *207:* 44
Ering, Timothy Basil *131:* 100; *176:* 63, 64; *202:* 29; *204:* 8
Erlbruch, Wolf *181:* 66
Ernst, Lisa Campbell *47:* 147; *95:* 47; *154:* 46, 47, 48; *164:* 88; *212:* 45
Esco, Jo *61:* 103
Escourido, Joseph *4:* 81
Escrivá, Viví *119:* 51; *181:* 36
Essakalli, Julie Klear *200:* 58
Este, Kirk *33:* 111
Estep, David *73:* 57
Estes, Eleanor *91:* 66
Estoril, Jean *32:* 27
Estrada, Pau *74:* 76
Estrada, Ric *5:* 52, 146; *13:* 174
Etchemendy, Teje *38:* 68
Etheredges, the *73:* 12
Etienne, Kirk-Albert *145:* 184
Ets, Marie Hall *2:* 102
Ettlinger, Doris *171:* 98; *186:* 106; *197:* 126; *214:* 125
Eulalie *YABC 2:* 315
Eustace, David *224:* 24
Evangelista, Theresa M. *213:* 67
Evans, Greg *73:* 54, 55, 56; *143:* 40, 41
Evans, Katherine *5:* 64
Evans, Leslie *144:* 227; *207:* 57; *214:* 88; *221:* 28
Evans, Shane W. *159:* 142; *160:* 190; *168:* 39; *188:* 88; *189:* 66, 67, 68; *229:* 150
Everitt, Betsy *151:* 110
Ewart, Claire *76:* 69; *145:* 59, 60
Ewing, Carolyn *66:* 143; *79:* 52
Ewing, Juliana Horatia *16:* 92
Eyolfson, Norman *98:* 154

F

Fabian, Limbert *136:* 114
Facklam, Paul *132:* 62
Falconer, Ian *125:* 66; *179:* 59
Falconer, Pearl *34:* 23
Falkenstern, Lisa *70:* 34; *76:* 133; *78:* 171; *127:* 16; *191:* 151
Falls, C.B. *1:* 19; *38:* 71, 72, 73, 74
Falter, John *40:* 169, 170
Falwell, Cathryn *118:* 77; *137:* 185; *196:* 71, 72
Fancher, Lou *138:* 219; *141:* 64; *144:* 199; *177:* 51; *214:* 95; *221:* 63; *228:* 42, 43, 44
Fanelli, Sara *89:* 63; *126:* 69
Faria, Rosana *150:* 143
Faricy, Patrick *185:* 182; *212:* 61
Farooqi, Musharraf Ali *207:* 46
Farmer, Andrew *49:* 102
Farmer, Peter *24:* 108; *38:* 75
Farnsworth, Bill *93:* 189; *116:* 147; *124:* 8; *135:* 52; *146:* 242, 243, 244; *182:* 176; *186:* 31, 83, 84, 85; *191:* 197; *222:* 2
Farquharson, Alexander *46:* 75
Farrell, Darren *228:* 45
Farrell, David *40:* 135
Farrell, Russell *196:* 38
Farris, David *74:* 42
Fasolino, Teresa *118:* 145
Fatigati, Evelyn *24:* 112
Fatus, Sophie *182:* 74; *190:* 218; *225:* 131
Faul-Jansen, Regina *22:* 117
Faulkner, Jack *6:* 169
Faulkner, Matt *161:* 174; *167:* 75
Fava, Rita *2:* 29
Fax, Elton C. *1:* 101; *4:* 2; *12:* 77; *25:* 107
Fay *43:* 93
Fearing, Mark *223:* 142; *224:* 39, 40
Fearnley, Jan *153:* 82, 83; *205:* 63, 64, 65
Fearrington, Ann *146:* 80
Federspiel, Marian *33:* 51
Fedorov, Nickolai Ivanovich *110:* 102
Feelings, Tom *5:* 22; *8:* 56; *12:* 153; *16:* 105; *30:* 196; *49:* 37; *61:* 101; *69:* 56, 57; *93:* 74; *105:* 88
Fehr, Terrence *21:* 87
Feiffer, Jules *3:* 91; *8:* 58; *61:* 66, 67, 70, 74, 76,77, 78; *111:* 47, 48, 49, 50; *132:* 122; *157:* 62; *201:* 48, 49, 50
Feigeles, Neil *41:* 242
Feldman, Elyse *86:* 7
Feller, Gene *33:* 130
Fellows, Muriel H. *10:* 42
Felstead, Cathie *116:* 85
Felts, Shirley *33:* 71; *48:* 59
Fennell, Tracy *171:* 69
Fennelli, Maureen *38:* 181
Fenton, Carroll Lane *5:* 66; *21:* 39
Fenton, Mildred Adams *5:* 66; *21:* 39
Ferguson, Peter *177:* 30, 31; *181:* 154; *197:* 4; *199:* 40; *215:* 104; *221:* 66; *229:* 15, 16
Ferguson, Walter W. *34:* 86
Fernandes, Eugenie *77:* 67; *205:* 68
Fernandes, Stanislaw *70:* 28
Fernandez, Fernando *77:* 57
Fernandez, Laura *77:* 153; *101:* 117; *131:* 222; *170:* 119; *175:* 182
Ferrari, Alex *188:* 121
Ferrington, Susan *172:* 22
Fetz, Ingrid *11:* 67; *12:* 52; *16:* 205; *17:* 59; *29:* 105; *30:* 108, 109; *32:* 149; *43:* 142; *56:* 29; *60:* 34; *85:* 48; *87:* 146
Fiammenghi, Gioia *9:* 66; *11:* 44; *12:* 206; *13:* 57, 59; *52:* 126, 129; *66:* 64; *85:* 83; *91:* 161; *166:* 169
Fiedler, Joseph Daniel *96:* 42; *113:* 173; *129:* 164; *146:* 17; *159:* 68; *162:* 104
Field, Rachel *15:* 113
Fielding, David *70:* 124
Fieser, Stephen *152:* 36

Fine, Howard *145:* 159; *159:* 64; *165:* 134; *174:* 129; *181:* 68
Fine, Peter K. *43:* 210
Finger, Helen *42:* 81
Fink, Sam *18:* 119
Finlay, Winifred *23:* 72
Finney, Pat *79:* 215
Fiore, Peter *99:* 196; *125:* 139; *144:* 225; *160:* 169; *180:* 72; *212:* 103
Fiorentino, Al *3:* 240
Firehammer, Karla *174:* 202; *221:* 183; *228:* 84
Firmin, Charlotte *29:* 75; *48:* 70
Firmin, Peter *58:* 63, 64, 65, 67, 68, 70, 71
Firth, Barbara *81:* 208; *127:* 218; *179:* 62
Fischel, Lillian *40:* 204
Fischer, Hans *25:* 202
Fischer, Scott M. *207:* 37; *217:* 29
Fischer-Nagel, Andreas *56:* 50
Fischer-Nagel, Heiderose *56:* 50
Fisher, Carolyn *154:* 50
Fisher, Chris *79:* 62; *158:* 248; *188:* 195
Fisher, Cynthia *117:* 45; *137:* 118; *195:* 40
Fisher, Jeffrey *142:* 80
Fisher, Leonard Everett *3:* 6; *4:* 72, 86; *6:* 197; *9:* 59; *16:* 151, 153; *23:* 44; *27:* 134; *29:* 26; *34:* 87, 89, 90, 91, 93, 94, 95, 96; *40:* 206; *50:* 150; *60:* 158; *73:* 68, 70, 71, 72, 73; *176:* 71, 72, 73; *208:* 131; *YABC 2:* 169
Fisher, Lois *20:* 62; *21:* 7
Fisher, Valorie *177:* 55; *214:* 92
Fisk, Nicholas *25:* 112
Fitschen, Marilyn *2:* 20, 21; *20:* 48
Fitz-Maurice, Jeff *175:* 2
Fitzgerald, F.A. *15:* 116; *25:* 86, 87
Fitzgerald, Joanne *157:* 153, 154; *198:* 34, 35
Fitzgerald, Royce *205:* 5
Fitzhugh, Louise *1:* 94; *9:* 163; *45:* 75, 78
Fitzhugh, Susie *11:* 117
Fitzpatrick, Jim *109:* 130
Fitzpatrick, Marie-Louise *125:* 69, 70; *189:* 72, 73
Fitzsimmons, Arthur *14:* 128
Fix, Philippe *26:* 102
Flack, Marjorie *21:* 67; *100:* 93; *YABC 2:* 122
Flagg, James Montgomery *17:* 227
Flavin, Teresa *132:* 115; *186:* 119
Flax, Zeona *2:* 245
Fleetwood, Tony *171:* 51
Fleishman, Seymour *14:* 232; *24:* 87
Fleming, Denise *71:* 179; *81:* 58; *126:* 71, 72, 73; *173:* 52, 53
Fleming, Guy *18:* 41
Flesher, Vivienne *85:* 55
Fletcher, Claire *80:* 106; *157:* 159
Flint, Russ *74:* 80
Floate, Helen *111:* 163
Floca, Brian *155:* 88, 89; *190:* 10, 66, 67
Floethe, Richard *3:* 131; *4:* 90
Floherty, John J., Jr. *5:* 68
Flook, Helen *160:* 81
Flora, James *1:* 96; *30:* 111, 112
Florczak, Robert *166:* 51
Florian, Douglas *19:* 122; *83:* 64, 65; *125:* 71, 72, 74, 76; *128:* 130; *177:* 58, 60; *226:* 119
Flory, Jane *22:* 111
Flower, Renee *125:* 109
Floyd, Gareth *1:* 74; *17:* 245; *48:* 63; *62:* 35,36, 37, 39, 40, 41; *74:* 245; *79:* 56
Fluchere, Henri A. *40:* 79
Flynn, Alice *183:* 2
Flynn, Barbara *7:* 31; *9:* 70
Fogarty, Thomas *15:* 89
Foley, Greg *190:* 69
Folger, Joseph *9:* 100
Folkard, Charles *22:* 132; *29:* 128, 257, 258
Foott, Jeff *42:* 202
Forberg, Ati *12:* 71, 205; *14:* 1; *22:* 113; *26:* 22; *48:* 64, 65

Ford, George *24:* 120; *31:* 70, 177; *58:* 126; *81:* 103; *107:* 91; *136:* 100; *194:* 47; *208:* 81; *218:* 56
Ford, Gilbert *199:* 10
Ford, H.J. *16:* 185, 186
Ford, Jason *174:* 119
Ford, Pamela Baldwin *27:* 104
Fordham, John *168:* 160, 161
Foreman, Michael *2:* 110, 111; *67:* 99; *73:* 78, 79, 80,81, 82; *93:* 146; *135:* 55, 56, 57; *184:* 58, 59; *216:* 100, 101, 102, 103; *225:* 144
Forrester, Victoria *40:* 83
Forsey, Chris *140:* 210
Fortnum, Peggy *6:* 29; *20:* 179; *24:* 211; *26:* 76, 77, 78; *39:* 78; *58:* 19, 21, 23, 27; *YABC 1:* 148
Fortune, Eric *191:* 52
Foster, Brad W. *34:* 99
Foster, Genevieve *2:* 112
Foster, Gerald L. *7:* 78; *198:* 40
Foster, Jon *146:* 18; *198:* 7
Foster, Laura Louise *6:* 79
Foster, Marian Curtis *23:* 74; *40:* 42
Foster, Sally *58:* 73, 74
Fotheringham, Edwin *219:* 32
Foucher, Adele *47:* 118
Foust, Mitch *168:* 50
Fowler, Jim *184:* 190
Fowler, Mel *36:* 127
Fowler, Richard *87:* 219
Fowles, Shelley *165:* 127; *205:* 72
Fox, Charles Phillip *12:* 84
Fox, Christyan *188:* 36
Fox, Jim *6:* 187
Fox, Nathan *208:* 64
Fox-Davies, Sarah *76:* 150; *182:* 63; *199:* 42, 43
Frace, Charles *15:* 118
Frailey, Joy *72:* 108
Frame, Paul *2:* 45, 145; *9:* 153; *10:* 124; *21:* 71; *23:* 62; *24:* 123; *27:* 106; *31:* 48; *32:* 159; *34:* 195; *38:* 136; *42:* 55; *44:* 139; *60:* 39, 40, 41, 42, 43, 44, 46; *73:* 183
Frampton, David *85:* 72; *102:* 33; *139:* 182; *152:* 37; *189:* 171
Francis, Guy *198:* 164; *224:* 91; *225:* 65
Francois, Andre *25:* 117
Francoise
See Seignobosc, Francoise
Frank, Lola Edick *2:* 199
Frank, Mary *4:* 54; *34:* 100
Franke, Phil *45:* 91
Frankel, Alona *66:* 70
Frankel, Julie *40:* 84, 85, 202
Frankenberg, Robert *22:* 116; *30:* 50; *38:* 92, 94, 95; *68:* 111
Frankfeldt, Gwen *84:* 223; *110:* 92
Frankland, David *169:* 137; *182:* 164; *201:* 159; *214:* 35
Franklin, Ashton *165:* 144; *225:* 107
Franklin, John *24:* 22
Franson, Leanne R. *111:* 57, 58; *151:* 7; *223:* 63, 64, 158
Frascino, Edward *9:* 133; *29:* 229; *33:* 190; *48:* 80, 81, 82, 83, 84, 85, 86
Frasconi, Antonio *6:* 80; *27:* 208; *53:* 41, 43, 45, 47,48; *68:* 145; *73:* 226; *131:* 68
Fraser, Betty *2:* 212; *6:* 185; *8:* 103; *31:* 72,73; *43:* 136; *111:* 76
Fraser, Eric *38:* 78; *41:* 149, 151
Fraser, F.A. *22:* 234
Fraser, James *171:* 68
Fraser, Mary Ann *137:* 63; *214:* 98
Frasier, Debra *69:* 60; *112:* 67; *182:* 81, 82, 83
Fraustino, Lisa Rowe *146:* 87
Frazee, Marla *72:* 98; *105:* 79, 80; *151:* 67, 68; *164:* 165; *171:* 190, 191; *187:* 53, 54, 55, 56, 143; *222:* 173; *225:* 68, 69, 70; *226:* 180
Frazetta, Frank *41:* 72; *58:* 77, 78, 79, 80, 81, 82, 83

Frazier, Craig *177:* 63; *221:* 47
Freas, John *25:* 207
Fredrickson, Mark *103:* 33
Freeland, Michael J. *118:* 115
Freeman, Don *2:* 15; *13:* 249; *17:* 62, 63, 65, 67, 68; *18:* 243; *20:* 195; *23:* 213, 217; *32:* 155; *55:* 129
Freeman, Irving *67:* 150
Freeman, Laura *144:* 111; *200:* 62, 63
Freeman, Pietri *140:* 223
Freeman, Tom *167:* 118
Freeman, Tor *164:* 93
Fregosi, Claudia *24:* 117
Fremaux, Charlotte Murray *138:* 29; *141:* 95
French, Fiona *6:* 82, 83; *75:* 61; *109:* 170; *132:* 79, 80, 81, 82
French, Martin *163:* 4
French, S. Terrell *216:* 106
Frendak, Rodney *126:* 97, 98
Freschet, Gina *175:* 73
Freynet, Gilbert *72:* 221
Fried, Janice *202:* 121
Frieden, Sarajo *213:* 119
Friedman, Judith *43:* 197; *131:* 221
Friedman, Marvin *19:* 59; *42:* 86
Frinta, Dagmar *36:* 42
Frith, Michael K. *15:* 138; *18:* 120
Fritz, Ronald *46:* 73; *82:* 124
Fromm, Lilo *29:* 85; *40:* 197
Frost, A.B. *17:* 6, 7; *19:* 123, 124, 125, 126, 127, 128, 129,130; *100:* 119; *YABC 1:* 156, 157, 160; *2:* 107
Frost, Helen *183:* 51
Frost, Kristi *118:* 113
Frost, Michael *151:* 209; *209:* 44; *212:* 70
Froud, Brian *150:* 82, 83
Froud, Wendy *151:* 237
Fry, Guy *2:* 224
Fry, Rosalie *3:* 72; *YABC 2:* 180, 181
Fry, Rosalind *21:* 153, 168
Fryer, Elmer *34:* 115
Fuchs, Bernie *110:* 10; *162:* 46
Fuchs, Erich *6:* 84
Fuchshuber, Annegert *43:* 96
Fucile, Tony *221:* 48
Fufuka, Mahiri *32:* 146
Fuge, Charles *144:* 91, 93
Fujikawa, Gyo *39:* 75, 76; *76:* 72, 73, 74
Fulford, Deborah *23:* 159
Fuller, Margaret *25:* 189
Fulweiler, John *93:* 99
Funai, Mamoru *38:* 105
Funfhausen, Christian *196:* 30
Funk, Tom *7:* 17, 99
Furchgott, Terry *29:* 86
Furness, William Henry, Jr. *94:* 18
Furukawa, Mel *25:* 42
Fusari, Erika *164:* 227

G

Gaadt, David *78:* 212; *121:* 166; *201:* 171
Gaadt, George *71:* 9
Gaber, Susan *99:* 33; *115:* 57, 58; *164:* 195; *169:* 61, 62, 63; *185:* 50, 51; *188:* 124
Gaberell, J. *19:* 236
Gable, Brian *195:* 68, 69
Gabler, Mirko *99:* 71; *195:* 32
Gabor, Tim *216:* 61
Gackenbach, Dick *19:* 168; *41:* 81; *48:* 89, 90, 91, 92,93, 94; *54:* 105; *79:* 75, 76, 77
Gad, Victor *87:* 161
Gaetano, Nicholas *23:* 209
Gaffney-Kessell, Walter *94:* 219; *174:* 188
Gag, Flavia *17:* 49, 52
Gag, Wanda *100:* 101, 102; *YABC 1:* 135, 137, 138, 141, 143
Gagnon, Cecile *11:* 77; *58:* 87
Gaillard, Jason *200:* 69; *204:* 74

Gal, Laszlo *14:* 127; *52:* 54, 55, 56; *65:* 142; *68:* 150; *81:* 185; *96:* 104, 105
Gal, Susan *228:* 58
Galazinski, Tom *55:* 13
Galbraith, Ben *200:* 70
Galdone, Paul *1:* 156, 181, 206; *2:* 40, 241; *3:* 42,144; *4:* 141; *10:* 109, 158; *11:* 21; *12:* 118, 210; *14:* 12; *16:* 36, 37; *17:* 70, 71, 72, 73, 74; *18:* 111, 230; *19:* 183; *21:* 154; *22:* 150, 245; *33:* 126; *39:* 136, 137; *42:* 57; *51:* 169; *55:* 110; *66:* 80, 82, 139; *72:* 73; *100:* 84
Gale, Cathy *140:* 22; *143:* 52; *213:* 166
Gall, Chris *176:* 79, 80
Gallagher, Jack *187:* 100
Gallagher, S. Saelig *105:* 154; *198:* 91
Gallagher, Sears *20:* 112Gallagher-Cole, Mernie *206:* 56
Galloway, Ewing *51:* 154
Galouchka, Annouchka Gravel *95:* 55; *182:* 40
Galster, Robert *1:* 66
Galsworthy, Gay John *35:* 232
Galvez, Daniel *125:* 182
Gamble, Kim *112:* 64, 65; *124:* 77; *183:* 40, 42, 43, 56, 57; *187:* 170
Gammell, Stephen *7:* 48; *13:* 149; *29:* 82; *33:* 209; *41:* 88; *50:* 185, 186, 187; *53:* 51, 52, 53, 54, 55, 56,57, 58; *54:* 24, 25; *56:* 147, 148, 150; *57:* 27, 66; *81:* 62, 63; *87:* 88; *89:* 10; *106:* 223; *126:* 2; *128:* 71, 73, 74, 77; *154:* 34; *211:* 210; *226:* 80, 81, 82
Gamper, Ruth *84:* 198
Gampert, John *58:* 94
Ganly, Helen *56:* 56
Gannett, Ruth Chrisman *3:* 74; *18:* 254; *33:* 77, 78
Gannon, Ned *205:* 6
Gantschev, Ivan *45:* 32
Garafano, Marie *73:* 33
Garbot, Dave *131:* 106
Garbutt, Bernard *23:* 68
Garcia *37:* 71
Garcia, Geronimo *222:* 73
Garcia, Manuel *74:* 145
Garcia-Franco, Rebecca *173:* 46
Gardiner, Lindsey *178:* 128; *186:* 137
Gardner, Earle *45:* 167
Gardner, Joan *40:* 87
Gardner, Joel *40:* 87, 92
Gardner, John *40:* 87
Gardner, Lucy *40:* 87
Gardner, Richard
    See Cummings, Richard
Gardner, Sally *171:* 177; *177:* 66, 68; *229:* 58
Gargiulo, Frank *84:* 158
Garland, Michael *36:* 29; *38:* 83; *44:* 168; *48:* 78, 221, 222; *49:* 161; *60:* 139; *71:* 6, 11; *72:* 229; *74:* 142; *89:* 187; *93:* 183; *104:* 110; *131:* 55; *139:* 209; *168:* 56; *208:* 72, 73, 75
Garland, Peggy *60:* 139
Garland, Sarah *62:* 45; *135:* 67, 68; *171:* 118
Garn, Aimee *75:* 47
Garner, Joan *128:* 170
Garneray, Ambroise Louis *59:* 140
Garnett, Eve *3:* 75
Garnett, Gary *39:* 184
Garns, Allen *80:* 125; *84:* 39; *165:* 231; *209:* 44
Garófoli, Viviana *186:* 123
Garraty, Gail *4:* 142; *52:* 106
Garrett, Agnes *46:* 110; *47:* 157
Garrett, Edmund H. *20:* 29
Garrett, Tom *107:* 194; *215:* 179
Garrick, Jacqueline *67:* 42, 43; *77:* 94
Garrison, Barbara *19:* 133; *104:* 146; *109:* 87
Garro, Mark *108:* 131; *128:* 210
Garvey, Robert *98:* 222
Garza, Carmen Lomas *80:* 211; *182:* 86
Garza, Xavier *184:* 64
Gates, Frieda *26:* 80

Gaughan, Jack *26:* 79; *43:* 185
Gaver, Becky *20:* 61
Gavril, David *211:* 196
Gawing, Toby *72:* 52
Gay, Marie-Louise *68:* 76, 77, 78; *102:* 136; *126:* 76, 78, 81, 83; *127:* 55, 56; *179:* 70, 72, 73, 74; *224:* 81
Gay, Zhenya *19:* 135, 136
Gaydos, Tim *62:* 201
Gazsi, Ed *80:* 48
Gazso, Gabriel *73:* 85
Geary, Clifford N. *1:* 122; *9:* 104; *51:* 74
Geary, Rick *142:* 44, 46
Gee, Frank *33:* 26
Geehan, Wayne *157:* 181
Geer, Charles *1:* 91; *3:* 179; *4:* 201; *6:* 168; *7:* 96; *9:* 58; *10:* 72; *12:* 127; *39:* 156,157, 158, 159, 160; *42:* 88, 89, 90, 91; *55:* 111, 116
Geerinck, Manuel *173:* 128
Gehm, Charlie *36:* 65; *57:* 117; *62:* 60, 138
Geis, Alissa Imre *189:* 77
Geisel, Theodor Seuss *1:* 104, 105, 106; *28:* 108, 109, 110,111, 112, 113; *75:* 67, 68, 69, 70, 71; *89:* 127, 128; *100:* 106, 107, 108
Geisert, Arthur *92:* 67, 68; *133:* 72, 73, 74; *165:* 97, 98; *171:* 64, 65
Geldart, William *15:* 121; *21:* 202
Genia *4:* 84
Gentry, Cyrille R. *12:* 66
Genzo, John Paul *136:* 74
George, Jean *2:* 113
George, Lindsay Barrett *95:* 57; *155:* 97, 98
Geraghty, Paul *130:* 60, 61
Gerard, Jean Ignace *45:* 80
Gerard, Rolf *27:* 147, 150
Gerber, Mark *61:* 105
Gerber, Mary Jane *112:* 124; *171:* 56
Gerber, Stephanie *71:* 195
Gerdstein, Mordecai *169:* 105
Gergely, Tibor *54:* 15, 16
Geritz, Franz *17:* 135
Gerlach, Geff *42:* 58
Gerrard, Roy *47:* 78; *90:* 96, 97, 98, 99
Gerritsen, Paula *177:* 69; *217:* 166
Gershinowitz, George *36:* 27
Gerstein, Mordicai *31:* 117; *47:* 80, 81, 82, 83, 84, 85, 86; *51:* 173; *69:* 134; *107:* 122; *142:* 49, 52; *165:* 209; *176:* 119; *178:* 95, 97, 99; *215:* 173; *222:* 76
Gervase *12:* 27
Geter, Tyrone *146:* 249; *150:* 86
Getz, Arthur *32:* 148
Gévry, Claudine *188:* 47
Gewirtz, Bina *61:* 81
Giancola, Donato *95:* 146; *164:* 226; *229:* 181
Gibala-Broxholm, Scott *205:* 76; *219:* 186
Gibbons, Gail *23:* 78; *72:* 77, 78, 79; *82:* 182; *104:* 65; *160:* 99, 100; *201:* 59, 60, 62
Gibbs, Tony *40:* 95
Gibran, Kahlil *32:* 116
Gibson, Barbara Leonard *205:* 77; *212:* 151
Gider, Iskender *81:* 193
Giebfried, Rosemary *170:* 135
Giesen, Rosemary *34:* 192, 193
Giffard, Hannah *83:* 70
Giguere, George *20:* 111
Gilbert, John *19:* 184; *54:* 115; *YABC 2:* 287
Gilbert, W.S. *36:* 83, 85, 96
Gilbert, Yvonne *116:* 70; *128:* 84; *149:* 119; *185:* 69; *192:* 25; *195:* 81
Gilchrist, Jan Spivey *72:* 82, 83, 84, 85, 87; *77:* 90; *105:* 89, 91; *130:* 63, 64; *155:* 105, 107; *182:* 67
Giles, Will *41:* 218
Gili, Phillida *70:* 73
Gill, Margery *4:* 57; *7:* 7; *22:* 122; *25:* 166; *26:* 146, 147
Gillen, Denver *28:* 216
Gillette, Henry J. *23:* 237
Gilliam, Stan *39:* 64, 81
Gillies, Chuck *62:* 31

Illustrations Index

Gilliland, Jillian *87:* 58
Gillman, Alec *98:* 105
Gilman, Esther *15:* 124
Gilman, Phoebe *104:* 70, 71
Gilpin, Stephen *213:* 68
Ginsberg, Sari *111:* 184
Ginsburg, Max *62:* 59; *68:* 194 *Girard, Roge 161:* 30
Girouard, Patrick *155:* 100; *218:* 165
Giovanopoulos, Paul *7:* 104; *60:* 36
Giovine, Sergio *79:* 12; *93:* 118; *139:* 118; *205:* 114
Gist, E.M. *206:* 60
Githens, Elizabeth M. *5:* 47
Gladden, Scott *99:* 108; *103:* 160; *193:* 46, 47
Gladstone, Gary *12:* 89; *13:* 190
Gladstone, Lise *15:* 273
Glanzman, Louis S. *2:* 177; *3:* 182; *36:* 97, 98; *38:* 120, 122; *52:* 141, 144; *71:* 191; *91:* 54, 56
Glaser, Byron *154:* 59, 60
Glaser, Milton *3:* 5; *5:* 156; *11:* 107; *30:* 26; *36:* 112; *54:* 141; *151:* 70
Glass, Andrew *36:* 38; *44:* 133; *48:* 205; *65:* 3; *68:* 43, 45; *90:* 104, 105; *150:* 89; *223:* 73, 74
Glass, Marvin *9:* 174
Glasser, Judy *41:* 156; *56:* 140; *69:* 79; *72:* 101
Glattauer, Ned *5:* 84; *13:* 224; *14:* 26
Glauber, Uta *17:* 76
Gleeson, J.M. *YABC 2:* 207
Glegg, Creina *36:* 100
Glienke, Amelie *63:* 150
Gliewe, Unada *3:* 78, 79; *21:* 73; *30:* 220
Gliori, Debi *72:* 91; *138:* 82; *162:* 37; *189:* 79, 81, 82
Glovach, Linda *7:* 105
Gobbato, Imero *3:* 180, 181; *6:* 213; *7:* 58; *9:* 150; *18:* 39; *21:* 167; *39:* 82, 83; *41:* 137, 251; *59:* 177
Goble, Paul *25:* 121; *26:* 86; *33:* 65; *69:* 68, 69; *131:* 79, 80
Goble, Warwick *46:* 78, 79; *194:* 143
Godal, Eric *36:* 93
Godbey, Cory *221:* 154
Godkin, Celia *145:* 84, 86
Godfrey, Michael *17:* 279
Godon, Ingrid *166:* 163; *186:* 99
Goede, Irene *208:* 87
Goembel, Ponder *42:* 124
Goffe, Toni *61:* 83, 84, 85; *89:* 11; *90:* 124; *178:* 118
Goffstein, M.B. *8:* 71; *70:* 75, 76, 77
Golbin, Andre *15:* 125
Gold, Robert *166:* 151, 152
Goldfeder, Cheryl *11:* 191
Goldfinger, Jennifer P. *185:* 71
Goldman, Todd H. *221:* 50, 51
Goldsborough, June *5:* 154, 155; *8:* 92, *14:* 226; *19:* 139; *54:* 165
Goldsmith, Robert *110:* 77
Goldstein, Barry *198:* 147
Goldstein, Leslie *5:* 8; *6:* 60; *10:* 106
Goldstein, Nathan *1:* 175; *2:* 79; *11:* 41, 232; *16:* 55
Goldstrom, Robert *98:* 36; *145:* 51, 52
Golembe, Carla *79:* 80, 81; *136:* 91; *144:* 113; *193:* 53
Golin, Carlo *74:* 112
Gomez, Elena *188:* 122; *191:* 72
Gomez, Elizabeth *127:* 70; *133:* 76
Gomi, Taro *64:* 102; *103:* 74, 76
Gon, Adriano *101:* 112
Gonsalves, Ron *178:* 213; *212:* 196
Gonzalez, Maya Christina *104:* 3; *136:* 92; *215:* 4, 5
Gonzalez, Thomas *226:* 157
Gonzalez, Yolanda *212:* 65
Good, Karen Hillard *212:* 143; *214:* 103

Goodall, John S. *4:* 92, 93; *10:* 132; *66:* 92, 93; *YABC 1:* 198
Goode, Diane *15:* 126; *50:* 183; *52:* 114, 115; *76:* 195; *84:* 94; *99:* 141; *114:* 76, 77, 78; *170:* 99, 101; *225:* 80, 81, 82, 83, 84
Goodelman, Aaron *40:* 203
Goodenow, Earle *40:* 97
Goodfellow, Peter *62:* 95; *94:* 202
Goodman, Joan Elizabeth *50:* 86
Goodman, Vivienne *82:* 251; *146:* 181, 182
Goodnow, Patti *117:* 33
Goodrich, Carter *221:* 52, 53
Goodwin, Harold *13:* 74
Goodwin, Philip R. *18:* 206
Goor, Nancy *39:* 85, 86
Goor, Ron *39:* 85, 86
Goossens, Philippe *195:* 71
Gorbachev, Valeri *89:* 96; *112:* 97; *143:* 63, 64; *184:* 66, 67, 68, 101; *222:* 84, 85, 86, 87
Gordon, David *216:* 159
Gordon, Gwen *12:* 151
Gordon, Margaret *4:* 147; *5:* 48, 49; *9:* 79
Gordon, Mike *101:* 62, 63, 64
Gordon, Russell *136:* 204; *137:* 214; *228:* 34
Gordon, Walter *138:* 9
Gore, Leonid *89:* 51; *94:* 74; *136:* 8; *158:* 117; *166:* 136; *168:* 36; *170:* 107; *181:* 94; *185:* 73; *222:* 89, 90, 91, 92
Gorecka-Egan, Erica *18:* 35
Gorey, Edward *1:* 60, 61; *13:* 169; *18:* 192; *20:* 201; *29:* 90, 91, 92, 93, 94, 95, 96, 97, 98, 99, 100; *30:* 129; *32:* 90; *34:* 200, *65:* 48; *68:* 24, 25; *69:* 79; *70:* 80, 82, 83, 84; *85:* 136; *127:* 62
Gorman, Mike *222:* 167
Gorsline, Douglas *1:* 98; *6:* 13; *11:* 113; *13:* 104; *15:* 14; *28:* 117, 118; *YABC 1:* 15
Gorton, Julia *108:* 94; *178:* 81, 82
Gosfield, Josh *118:* 165, 166; *149:* 67
Gosner, Kenneth *5:* 135
Gosney, Joy *167:* 142
Gotlieb, Jules *6:* 127
Goto, Scott *115:* 86; *136:* 69; *203:* 77, 78
Gott, Barry *197:* 95; *212:* 102
Gottlieb, Dale *67:* 162; *107:* 16; *149:* 6
Goudey, Ray *97:* 86
Gough, Alan *91:* 57
Gough, Philip *23:* 47; *45:* 90
Gould, Chester *49:* 112, 113, 114, 116, 117, 118
Gould, Jason *151:* 232
Gourbault, Martine *177:* 159
Govern, Elaine R. *26:* 94
Gower, Teri *102:* 184
Gowing, Toby *60:* 25; *63:* 33; *78:* 70, 252; *83:* 228; *86:* 187; *93:* 145; *108:* 133; *110:* 217; *184:* 125; *225:* 142
Grabianski *20:* 144
Grabianski, Janusz *39:* 92, 93, 94, 95
Graboff, Abner *35:* 103, 104
Graef, Renée *61:* 188; *72:* 207; *204:* 45; *210:* 249
Grafe, Max *156:* 173; *178:* 237; *192:* 240; *198:* 51
Graham, A.B. *11:* 61
Graham, Bob *101:* 66, 67, 68; *151:* 74, 75; *187:* 65, 67, 68, 70
Graham, Georgia *188:* 3; *190:* 75
Graham, L. *7:* 108
Graham, Margaret Bloy *11:* 120; *18:* 305, 307
Graham, Mark *88:* 208; *159:* 153; *182:* 3
Grahame-Johnstone, Janet *13:* 61
Grahame-Johnstone, Anne *13:* 61
Grainger, Sam *42:* 95
Gralley, Jean *166:* 86
Gramatky, Hardie *1:* 107; *30:* 116, 119, 120, 122, 123
Gran, Julie *168:* 118
Granahan, Julie *84:* 84

GrandPré, Mary *84:* 131; *109:* 199; *118:* 76; *180:* 65; *184:* 70, 71, 180; *192:* 87; *215:* 24; *229:* 68, 69, 70
Grandström, Brita *176:* 139
Grandville, J.J. *45:* 81, 82, 83, 84, 85, 86, 87, 88; *47:* 125; *64:* 10
Granger, Paul *39:* 153
Granström, Brita *162:* 35; *167:* 46; *224:* 56, 57
Grant, (Alice) Leigh *10:* 52; *15:* 131; *20:* 20; *26:* 119; *48:* 202
Grant, Gordon *17:* 230, 234; *25:* 123, 124, 125, 126; *52:* 69; *YABC 1:* 164
Grant, Melvyn *159:* 186, 187; *170:* 48, 49; *213:* 168, 169; *226:* 163
Grant, Michelle *210:* 95
Grant, Renee *77:* 40
Grant, Shirley *109:* 45
Graves, Elizabeth *45:* 101
Graves, Keith *167:* 89; *191:* 74; *216:* 34; *223:* 103
Gray, Harold *33:* 87, 88
Gray, Les *82:* 76; *83:* 232
Gray, Reginald *6:* 69
Gray, Steve *226:* 206
Greco, Tony *184:* 6
Greder, Armin *76:* 235
Green, Ann Canevari *62:* 48
Green, Eileen *6:* 97
Green, Elizabeth Shippen *139:* 109
Green, Jonathan *86:* 135; *105:* 109; *221:* 73
Green, Ken *111:* 68
Green, Michael *32:* 216
Green, Robina *87:* 138
Green, Jonathan *157:* 105
Greene, Jeffrey *117:* 93
Greenaway, Kate *17:* 275; *24:* 180; *26:* 107; *41:* 222, 232; *100:* 115, 116; *YABC 1:* 88, 89; *2:* 131, 133, 136,138, 139, 141
Greenberg, Melanie Hope *72:* 93; *80:* 125; *101:* 174; *133:* 180; *186:* 189; *214:* 105
Greenseid, Diane *178:* 106, 107
Greenstein, Elaine *150:* 100
Greenwald, Sheila *1:* 34; *3:* 99; *8:* 72
Greger, Carol *76:* 86
Gregorian, Joyce Ballou *30:* 125
Gregory, Emilian *177:* 146; *187:* 10
Gregory, Fran *130:* 4; *140:* 93
Gregory, Frank M. *29:* 107
Greiffenhagen, Maurice *16:* 137; *27:* 57; *YABC 2:* 288
Greiner, Robert *6:* 86
Gretter, J. Clemens *31:* 134
Gretz, Susanna *7:* 114
Gretzer, John *1:* 54; *3:* 26; *4:* 162; *7:* 125; *16:* 247; *18:* 117; *28:* 66; *30:* 85, 211; *33:* 235; *56:* 16
Grey, Mini *166:* 90; *192:* 71
Grey Owl *24:* 41
Gri *25:* 90
Grieder, Walter *9:* 84
Griesbach/Martucci *59:* 3
Grifalconi, Ann *2:* 126; *3:* 248; *11:* 18; *13:* 182; *46:* 38; *50:* 145; *66:* 99, 100, 101, 104, 106; *69:* 38; *70:* 64; *87:* 128; *90:* 53; *93:* 49; *128:* 48; *133:* 79, 81; *210:* 111
Griffin, Gillett Good *26:* 96
Griffin, James *30:* 166
Griffin, John Howard *59:* 186
Griffin, Rachel *131:* 23
Griffith, Gershom *94:* 214
Griffiths, Dave *29:* 76
Griffiths, Dean *168:* 180; *169:* 182
Grimly, Gris *186:* 102; *192:* 112; *197:* 86; *219:* 34
Grimsdell, Jeremy *83:* 75
Grimwood, Brian *82:* 89
Gringhuis, Dirk *6:* 98; *9:* 196
Gripe, Harald *2:* 127; *74:* 98
Grisha *3:* 71
Grobler, Piet *201:* 100
Grohmann, Susan *84:* 97

Gropper, William *27:* 93; *37:* 193
Gros *60:* 199
Grose, Helen Mason *YABC 1:* 260; *2:* 150
Grossman, Nancy *24:* 130; *29:* 101
Grossman, Robert *11:* 124; *46:* 39
Groth, John *15:* 79; *21:* 53, 54; *83:* 230
Grover, Lorie Ann *168:* 59
Grubb, Lisa *160:* 116
Grue, Lisa *187:* 193
Gruelle, Johnny *35:* 107
Gschwind, William *11:* 72
Guarnaccia, Steven *201:* 170, 173
Guay-Mitchell, Rebecca *110:* 95, 96; *135:* 240; *180:* 76; *181:* 71, 73; *216:* 77
Guback, Georgia *88:* 102
Gudeon, Karla *212:* 67
Guerguerion, Claudine *105:* 73
Guevara, Susan *97:* 87; *167:* 49; *194:* 54
Guggenheim, Hans *2:* 10; *3:* 37; *8:* 136
Guhathaakurta, Ajanta *183:* 199
Guida, Lisa Chauncy *172:* 188
Guilbeau, Honore *22:* 69
Guillette, Joseph *137:* 37
Guisewite, Cathy *57:* 52, 53, 54, 56, 57
Gukova, Julia *95:* 104; *154:* 103; *168:* 195
Gundersheimer, Karen *35:* 240; *82:* 100
Gunderson, Nick *57:* 120
Gunnella *192:* 144
Gurney, James *76:* 97; *86:* 32
Gurney, John Steven *75:* 39, 82; *110:* 175; *143:* 67, 68; *169:* 172; *217:* 50, 88; *227:* 86, 87, 88; *228:* 139, 140, 141
Gusman, Annie *38:* 62
Gustafson, Scott *34:* 111; *43:* 40
Gustavson, Adam *104:* 10; *171:* 183; *176:* 87; *197:* 94; *204:* 35; *219:* 187
Guthridge, Bettina *108:* 79; *186:* 92
Guthrie, R. Dale *64:* 143
Guthrie, Robin *20:* 122
Gutierrez, Akemi *172:* 87; *205:* 135
Gutierrez, Alan *136:* 31, 32
Gutierrez, Rudy *97:* 162; *203:* 79; *216:* 158
Gutmann, Bessie Pease *73:* 93, 94
Gwynne, Fred *41:* 94, 95
Gyberg, Bo-Erik *38:* 131

H

Haas, Irene *17:* 77; *87:* 46; *96:* 117
Hack, Konrad *51:* 127
Hader, Berta H. *16:* 126
Hader, Elmer S. *16:* 126
Haeffele, Deborah *76:* 99
Haemer, Alan *62:* 109
Hafner, Marylin *22:* 196, 216; *24:* 44; *30:* 51; *35:* 95; *51:* 25, 160, 164; *86:* 16; *105:* 196; *121:* 93, 94; *149:* 208, 209; *179:* 82, 83, 84, 115; *190:* 200; *201:* 29; *217:* 91
Hagerty, Sean *62:* 181
Hague, Michael *32:* 128; *48:* 98, 99, 100, 101, 103, 105,106, 107, 108, 109, 110; *49:* 121; *51:* 105; *64:* 14, 15; *79:* 134; *80:* 91, 92; *83:* 135; *100:* 241; *102:* 29; *129:* 101, 103, 104; *185:* 80, 81, 82; *215:* 89
Hair, Jonathan *115:* 135
Halas, John *29:* 41, 47, 48
Haldane, Roger *13:* 76; *14:* 202
Hale, Bruce *203:* 83
Hale, Christy *79:* 124; *84:* 200; *114:* 201; *128:* 2, 3; *146:* 203; *158:* 243; *167:* 99; *179:* 87
Hale, Irina *26:* 97
Hale, James Graham *88:* 207
Hale, Kathleen *17:* 79; *66:* 114, 116, 118
Hale, Nathan *210:* 115, 116; *214:* 179
Haley, Amanda *205:* 82, 83
Haley, Gail E. *43:* 102, 103, 104, 105; *78:* 65, 67; *136:* 106, 107
Hall, Amanda *96:* 110
Hall, Angus *224:* 192

Hall, August N. *217:* 74
Hall, Chuck *30:* 189
Hall, Douglas *15:* 184; *43:* 106, 107; *86:* 100; *87:* 82; *129:* 72
Hall, H. Tom *1:* 227; *30:* 210
Hall, Melanie *116:* 48, 49; *169:* 77, 78; *219:* 170; *228:* 65, 66, 67
Hall, Michael *228:* 69
Hall, Sydney P. *31:* 89
Hall, Tim *164:* 196; *202:* 41
Hall, Vicki *20:* 24
Hallinan, P.K. *39:* 98
Hallman, Tom *98:* 166
Hally, Greg *101:* 200; *151:* 224
Halperin, Wendy Anderson *96:* 151; *125:* 96, 97, 98, 99; *139:* 22; *140:* 84; *200:* 77, 78; *210:* 157; *215:* 65; *228:* 24, 76
Halpern, Joan *10:* 25
Halpern, Shari *174:* 172
Halsey, Megan *96:* 172; *114:* 185; *180:* 8; *185:* 85
Halstead, Virginia *125:* 105
Halverson, Janet *49:* 38, 42, 44
Hallensleben, Georg *134:* 5, 6; *172:* 17
Hallett, Mark *220:* 63
Hamanaka, Sheila *71:* 100
Hamann, Brad *78:* 151
Hamann, Sigune *104:* 115
Hamberger, John *6:* 8; *8:* 32; *14:* 79; *34:* 136; *88:* 78
Hamil, Tom *14:* 80; *43:* 163
Hamilton, Bill and Associates *26:* 215
Hamilton, Helen S. *2:* 238
Hamilton, J. *19:* 83, 85, 87
Hamilton, Laurie *116:* 210
Hamilton, Todd Cameron *84:* 15
Hamlin, Janet *97:* 136; *124:* 90; *137:* 157; *182:* 117
Hamlin, Louise *71:* 135
Hammill, Matt *206:* 65
Hammond, Chris *21:* 37
Hammond, Elizabeth *5:* 36, 203
Hampshire, Michael *5:* 187; *7:* 110, 111; *48:* 150; *51:* 129
Hampson, Denman *10:* 155; *15:* 130
Hampton, Blake *41:* 244
Handford, Martin *64:* 105, 106, 107, 109
Handforth, Thomas *42:* 100, 101, 102, 103, 104, 105, 107
Handville, Robert *1:* 89; *38:* 76; *45:* 108, 109
Hane, Roger *17:* 239; *44:* 54
Haney, Elizabeth Mathieu *34:* 84
Hanke, Ted *71:* 10
Hankinson, Phil *181:* 164
Hanley, Catherine *8:* 161
Hann, Jacquie *19:* 144
Hanna, Cheryl *91:* 133
Hanna, Wayne A. *67:* 145
Hannon, Mark *38:* 37
Hanrahan, Kelly-Anne *203:* 142
Hansen, Gaby *159:* 11; *186:* 25; *224:* 11
Hansen, Mia *149:* 76
Hanson, Glen *229:* 84
Hanson, Joan *8:* 76; *11:* 139
Hanson, Peter E. *52:* 47; *54:* 99, 100; *73:* 21; *84:* 79; *116:* 144
Hansson, Gunilla *64:* 111, 112
Harbour, Elizabeth *221:* 68
Hardcastle, Nick *121:* 82; *175:* 185; *222:* 135
Hardy, David A. *9:* 96; *119:* 74
Hardy, Paul *YABC 2:* 245
Hargis, Wes *219:* 70 *Haring, Keith 145:* 65
Harlan, Jerry *3:* 96
Harlin, Greg *89:* 194; *103:* 82; *118:* 161; *121:* 167; *182:* 76; *201:* 172; *215:* 76
Harman, Dominic *206:* 48
Harness, Cheryl *106:* 80; *131:* 87; *178:* 111; *200:* 39
Harnischfeger *18:* 121
Harper, Arthur *YABC 2:* 121
Harper, Betty *126:* 90

Harper, Jamie *174:* 71; *214:* 212
Harper, Piers *79:* 27; *105:* 102; *161:* 67
Harrington, Glenn *82:* 18; *94:* 66, 68; *185:* 118
Harrington, Jack *83:* 162
Harrington, Richard *5:* 81
Harris, Andrew N. *191:* 78
Harris, Jim *127:* 130; *183:* 4
Harris, John *83:* 25
Harris, Nick *86:* 177
Harris, Susan Yard *42:* 121
Harrison, Florence *20:* 150, 152
Harrison, Harry *4:* 103
Harrison, Jack *28:* 149
Harrison, Mark *105:* 157; *165:* 190
Harrison, Ted *56:* 73
Harsh, Fred *72:* 107
Harston, Jerry *105:* 143
Hart, Lewis *98:* 115
Hart, Thomas *181:* 165
Hart, William *13:* 72
Hartland, Jessie *171:* 80, 81; *186:* 165; *223:* 58
Hartung, Susan Kathleen *150:* 107, 108; *173:* 106; *175:* 106; *192:* 78; *211:* 19
Hartelius, Margaret *10:* 24
Hartshorn, Ruth *5:* 115; *11:* 129
Harvey, Amanda *145:* 44
Harvey, Bob *48:* 219
Harvey, Gerry *7:* 180
Harvey, Lisa *97:* 21
Harvey, Paul *88:* 74
Harvey, Roland *71:* 88; *123:* 63; *179:* 94; *218:* 94; *219:* 74
Haskamp, Steve *195:* 36; *229:* 29
Hassall, Joan *43:* 108, 109
Hassell, Hilton *YABC 1:* 187
Hassett, John *162:* 59
Hasselriis, Else *18:* 87; *YABC 1:* 96
Hastings, Glenn *89:* 183
Hastings, Ian *62:* 67
Hauman, Doris *2:* 184; *29:* 58, 59; *32:* 85, 86, 87
Hauman, George *2:* 184; *29:* 58, 59; *32:* 85, 86, 87
Hausherr, Rosmarie *15:* 29
Haverfield, Mary *225:* 87
Hawkes, Kevin *78:* 72; *104:* 198; *105:* 197; *112:* 109; *126:* 87; *144:* 88; *149:* 210; *150:* 110, 135; *156:* 94; *164:* 35; *186:* 18; *190:* 197; *198:* 152; *201:* 70, 71, 72; *220:* 99; *221:* 90, 92, 93
Hawkins, Jacqui *112:* 86; *162:* 64
Hawkinson, John *4:* 109; *7:* 83; *21:* 64
Hawkinson, Lucy *21:* 64
Hawthorne, Mike *140:* 228
Haxton, Elaine *28:* 131
Haydock, Robert *4:* 95
Hayes, Geoffrey *26:* 111; *44:* 133; *91:* 85; *207:* 63
Hayes, Karel *207:* 65
Haynes, Max *72:* 107
Hays, Michael *73:* 207; *83:* 93; *139:* 197; *146:* 202, 250; *202:* 47
Haywood, Carolyn *1:* 112; *29:* 104
Heale, Jonathan *104:* 117
Healy, Daty *12:* 143
Healy, Deborah *58:* 181, 182; *101:* 111
Heap, Sue *102:* 207; *150:* 113, 114; *187:* 84, 85, 87
Hearn, Diane Dawson *79:* 99; *113:* 13; *209:* 71, 72; *211:* 106
Hearon, Dorothy *34:* 69
Heaslip, William *57:* 24, 25
Hechtkopf, H. *11:* 110
Heck, Ed *173:* 81
Hector, Julian *205:* 85
Hedderwick, Mairi *30:* 127; *32:* 47; *36:* 104; *77:* 86; *145:* 91, 93, 95
Heffernan, Phil *146:* 197; *195:* 172; *218:* 123
Hefter, Richard *28:* 170; *31:* 81, 82; *33:* 183

Hehenberger, Shelly *126:* 91
Heigh, James *22:* 98
Heighway, Richard *25:* 160; *64:* 4
Heighway-Bury, Robin *159:* 89
Heine, Helme *67:* 86; *135:* 91, 92
Heinly, John *45:* 113
Hellard, Susan *81:* 21; *204:* 82; *209:* 92
Hellebrand, Nancy *26:* 57
Heller, Linda *46:* 86
Heller, Ruth M. *66:* 125; *77:* 30, 32
Hellmuth, Jim *38:* 164
Helms, Georgeann *33:* 62
Helquist, Brett *142:* 203; *146:* 133, 134; *156:*
    10; *173:* 25; *180:* 106; *187:* 90, 91; *193:* 12;
    224: 186; *226:* 117; *229:* 76, 77, 78
Helweg, Hans *41:* 118; *50:* 93; *58:* 22, 26
Hemingway, Edward *212:* 71
Hemphill, Helen *179:* 95
Henba, Bobbie *90:* 195
Henderling, Lisa *214:* 65
Henderson, Dave *73:* 76; *75:* 191, 192, 193,
    194; *82:* 4
Henderson, D.F. *216:* 77
Henderson, Douglas *103:* 68
Henderson, Kathy *55:* 32; *155:* 118
Henderson, Keith *35:* 122
Henderson, Meryl *127:* 58, 60; *169:* 81; *228:*
Hendrix, John *187:* 133; *208:* 106, 107, 108;
    216: 115
Hendry, Linda *80:* 104; *83:* 83; *164:* 216
Hengeveld, Dennis *142:* 86
Henkes, Kevin *43:* 111; *108:* 106, 107, 108
Henneberger, Robert *1:* 42; *2:* 237; *25:* 83
Henriksen, Harold *35:* 26; *48:* 68
Henriquez, Celeste *103:* 137
Henriquez, Elsa *82:* 260
Henriquez, Emile F. *89:* 88; *211:* 56
Henry, Everett *29:* 191
Henry, Matthew *117:* 58
Henry, Paul *93:* 121; *194:* 125
Henry, Rohan *217:* 77
Henry, Thomas *5:* 102
Hensel *27:* 119
Henshaw, Jacqui *141:* 127
Henstra, Friso *8:* 80; *36:* 70; *40:* 222; *41:* 250;
    73: 100, 101
Henterly, Jamichael *93:* 4
Heo, Yumi *89:* 85, 86; *94:* 89, 90; *146:* 40,
    137, 138; *163:* 227; *201:* 192
Hepple, Norman *28:* 198
Herbert, Helen *57:* 70
Herbert, Jennifer *189:* 47
Herbert, Wally *23:* 101
Herbster, Mary Lee *9:* 33
Herder, Edwin *182:* 104
Herge
    See Remi, Georges
Hermansen, Pal *133:* 113
Hermanson, Dennis *10:* 55
Hermes, Gertrude *54:* 161
Herr, Margo *57:* 191
Herr, Susan *83:* 163
Herriman, George *140:* 74, 75, 76, 77, 78
Herriman, Lisa *87:* 190
Herring, Michael *121:* 76; *182:* 103
Herrington, Roger *3:* 161
Herscovici, C. *165:* 240
Hescox, Richard *85:* 86; *90:* 30; *139:* 35
Heslop, Mike *38:* 60; *40:* 130
Hess, Lydia J. *85:* 17
Hess, Mark *111:* 146; *113:* 207
Hess, Paul *134:* 47; *166:* 133; *193:* 13
Hess, Richard *42:* 31
Hester, Ronnie *37:* 85
Heuser, Olga J. *121:* 116
Heusser, Sibylle *168:* 195
Heustis, Louise L. *20:* 28
Hewgill, Jody *201:* 90
Hewitson, Jennifer *74:* 119; *124:* 167
Hewitt, Kathryn *80:* 126; *149:* 105; *184:* 93;
    196: 36; *229:* 99

Hewitt, Margaret *84:* 112
Heyduck-Huth, Hilde *8:* 82
Heyer, Carol *74:* 122; *130:* 72, 73; *192:* 35;
    203: 78
Heyer, Hermann *20:* 114, 115
Heyer, Marilee *102:* 108
Heyman, Ken *8:* 33; *34:* 113
Heyne, Ulrike *146:* 151
Heywood, Karen *48:* 114
Hickling, P.B. *40:* 165
Hickman, Stephen *85:* 58; *136:* 33; *171:* 128
Hierstein, Judith *56:* 40; *162:* 168; *212:* 72;
    227: 46
Higashi, Sandra *154:* 59, 60
Higginbottom, J. Winslow *8:* 170; *29:* 105,
    106
Higgins, Chester *101:* 79
Higham, David *50:* 104
Hilb, Nora *176:* 8
Hild, Anja *215:* 194
Hildebrandt, Greg *8:* 191; *55:* 35, 36, 38, 39,
    40, 42, 46; *172:* 110
Hildebrandt, Tim *8:* 191; *55:* 44, 45, 46
Hilder, Rowland *19:* 207
Hill, Eric *66:* 127, 128; *133:* 91
Hill, Gregory *35:* 190
Hill, Pat *49:* 120
Hillenbrand, Will *84:* 115; *92:* 76, 80; *93:* 131;
    104: 168; *128:* 137; *145:* 187; *146:* 184;
    147: 105, 106, 107; *152:* 59; *184:* 179; *195:*
    34, 180; *196:* 125; *210:* 122, 123, 124; *217:*
    62; *224:* 145
Hilliard, Richard *183:* 74
Hillier, Matthew *45:* 205
Hillman, Priscilla *48:* 115
Hills, Tad *113:* 4; *137:* 147; *173:* 83; *208:* 199
Himler, Ronald *6:* 114; *7:* 162; *8:* 17, 84, 125;
    14: 76; *19:* 145; *26:* 160; *31:* 43; *38:* 116;
    41: 44, 79; *43:* 52; *45:* 120; *46:* 43; *54:* 44,
    83; *58:* 180; *59:* 38; *68:* 146; *69:* 231; *70:*
    98; *71:* 177, 178; *77:* 219; *79:* 212; *83:* 62;
    89: 5; *91:* 160; *92:* 91, 92, 93; *94:* 93; *95:*
    69, 174, 194; *99:* 99, 112; *113:* 92; *118:* 114;
    137: 73, 74, 77, 167; *163:* 99; *165:* 138;
    178: 9, 220; *183:* 77, 79, 80, 81; *184:* 80,
    83; *215:* 151
Himmelman, John *47:* 109; *65:* 87; *94:* 96, 97;
    159: 85; *221:* 79, 80, 81, 82
Hinds, Bill *37:* 127, 130
Hines, Anna Grossnickle *51:* 90; *74:* 124; *95:*
    78, 79,80, 81
Hines, Bob *135:* 149, 150
Hirao, Amiko *203:* 98
Hiroko *99:* 61
Hiroshige *25:* 71
Hirsh, Marilyn *7:* 126
Hiscock, Bruce *137:* 80, 81; *204:* 51, 53
Hissey, Jane *103:* 90; *130:* 81
Hitch, Jeff *99:* 206; *128:* 86
Hitz, Demi *11:* 135; *15:* 245; *66:* 129, 130;
    152: 94, 95
Hnizdovsky, Jacques *32:* 96; *76:* 187
Ho, David *227:* 32
Ho, Kwoncjan *15:* 132
Hoban, Lillian *1:* 114; *22:* 157; *26:* 72; *29:* 53;
    40: 105, 107, 195; *41:* 80; *69:* 107, 108; *71:*
    98; *77:* 168; *106:* 50; *113:* 86; *136:* 118
Hoban, Tana *22:* 159; *104:* 82, 83, 85
Hobbie, Holly *225:* 90, 91
Hobbie, Jocelyn *190:* 78; *196:* 92
Hobbie, Nathaniel *196:* 92
Hobbs, Leigh *166:* 95
Hoberman, Norman *5:* 82
Hobson, Sally *77:* 185
Hockerman, Dennis *39:* 22; *56:* 23
Hodgell, P.C. *42:* 114
Hodges, C. Walter *2:* 139; *11:* 15; *12:* 25; *23:*
    34; *25:* 96; *38:* 165; *44:* 197; *45:* 95; *100:*
    57; *YABC 2:* 62, 63
Hodges, David *9:* 98
Hodgetts, Victoria *43:* 132

Hofbauer, Imre *2:* 162
Hoff, Syd *9:* 107; *10:* 128; *33:* 94; *72:*
    115,116, 117, 118; *138:* 114, 115
Hoffman, Rosekrans *15:* 133; *50:* 219; *63:* 97
Hoffman, Sanford *38:* 208; *76:* 174; *88:* 160,
    161; *151:* 156
Hoffmann, Felix *9:* 109
Hoffnung, Gerard *66:* 76, 77
Hofsinde, Robert *21:* 70
Hogan, Inez *2:* 141
Hogan, Jamie *192:* 94; *198:* 177
Hogarth, Burne *41:* 58; *63:* 46, 48, 49, 50, 52,
    53, 54, 55,56
Hogarth, Paul *41:* 102, 103, 104; *YABC 1:* 16
Hogarth, William *42:* 33
Hogenbyl, Jan *1:* 35
Hogner, Nils *4:* 122; *25:* 144
Hogrogian, Nonny *3:* 221; *4:* 106, 107; *5:* 166;
    7: 129; *15:* 2; *16:* 176; *20:* 154; *22:* 146; *25:*
    217; *27:* 206; *74:* 127, 128, 129, 149, 152;
    127: 99; *YABC 2:* 84, 94
Hokanson, Lars *93:* 111; *172:* 137; *212:* 88
Hokusai *25:* 71
Hol, Colby *126:* 96
Holberg, Richard *2:* 51
Holbrook, Kathy *107:* 114
Holdcroft, Tina *38:* 109; *227:* 99, 100, 160
Holden, Caroline *55:* 159
Holder, Heidi *36:* 99; *64:* 9
Holder, Jim *204:* 163
Holder, Jimmy *151:* 224
Holderness, Grizelda *215:* 107
Hole, Stian *204:* 55
Holiday, Henry *YABC 2:* 107
Holl, F. *36:* 91
Holland, Brad *45:* 59, 159
Holland, Gay W. *128:* 105; *225:* 76
Holland, Janice *18:* 118
Holland, Marion *6:* 116
Holland, Richard *216:* 109, 124
Holldobler, Turid *26:* 120
Holliday, Keaf *144:* 236
Hollinger, Deanne *12:* 116
Holm, Sharon Lane *114:* 84; *115:* 52
Holmes, B. *3:* 82
Holmes, Bea *7:* 74; *24:* 156; *31:* 93
Holmes, Dave *54:* 22
Holmes, Lesley *135:* 96
Holmgren, George Ellen *45:* 112
Holmlund, Heather D. *150:* 140
Holt, Norma *44:* 106
Holt, Pater *151:* 188
Holtan, Gene *32:* 192
Holub, Joan *149:* 72; *229:* 82
Holyfield, John *149:* 231; *227:* 101
Holz, Loretta *17:* 81
Hom, Nancy *79:* 195
Homar, Lorenzo *6:* 2
Homer, Winslow *128:* 8; *YABC 2:* 87
Honey, Elizabeth *112:* 95, 96; *137:* 93, 94
Honeywood, Varnette P. *110:* 68, 70
Hong, Lily Toy *76:* 104
Honigman, Marian *3:* 2
Honore, Paul *42:* 77, 79, 81, 82
Hood, Alun *69:* 145, 218; *72:* 41; *80:* 226; *87:*
    4; *95:* 139
Hood, Susan *12:* 43
Hook, Christian *104:* 103
Hook, Frances *26:* 188; *27:* 127
Hook, Jeff *14:* 137; *103:* 105
Hook, Richard *26:* 188
Hooks *63:* 30
Hooper, Hadley *177:* 145
Hoover, Carol A. *21:* 77
Hoover, Russell *12:* 95; *17:* 2; *34:* 156
Hope, James *141:* 116
Hopkins, Chris *99:* 127
Hopkinson, Leigh *202:* 70
Hopman, Philip *178:* 184
Hoppe, Paul *209:* 85

Hoppin, Augustus *34:* 66
Horacek, Judy *211:* 86
Horacek, Petr *163:* 117; *214:* 113
Horder, Margaret *2:* 108; *73:* 75
Horen, Michael *45:* 121
Horne, Daniel *73:* 106; *91:* 153; *109:* 127; *110:* 232; *164:* 176
Horne, Richard *111:* 80
Horowitz, Dave *204:* 58
Horse, Harry *128:* 195; *169:* 86
Horstman, Lisa *219:* 79
Horton, Anthony *211:* 98
Horvat, Laurel *12:* 201
Horvath, David *192:* 95
Horvath, Ferdinand Kusati *24:* 176
Horvath, Maria *57:* 171
Horwitz, Richard *57:* 174
Hotchkiss, De Wolfe *20:* 49
Hough, Charlotte *9:* 112; *13:* 98; *17:* 83; *24:* 195
Houlihan, Ray *11:* 214
House, Caroline *183:* 121
Housman, Laurence *25:* 146, 147
Houston, James *13:* 107; *74:* 132, 134, 135
Hovland, Gary *88:* 172; *171:* 148
Hoyt, Eleanor *158:* 231
How, W.E. *20:* 47
Howard, Alan *16:* 80; *34:* 58; *45:* 114
Howard, Arthur *165:* 111, 112; *190:* 5; *229:* 30
Howard, J.N. *15:* 234
Howard, John *33:* 179
Howard, Kim *116:* 71
Howard, Paul *142:* 126, 129; *144:* 187
Howard, Rob *40:* 161
Howarth, Daniel *170:* 34; *222:* 97, 98; *224:* 20; *225:* 77
Howe, John *79:* 101; *80:* 150; *115:* 47; *176:* 106; *207:* 32, 35
Howe, Phillip *79:* 117; *175:* 115
Howe, Stephen *1:* 232
Howell, Karen *119:* 123
Howell, Pat *15:* 139
Howell, Troy *23:* 24; *31:* 61; *36:* 158; *37:* 184; *41:* 76, 235; *48:* 112; *56:* 13; *57:* 3; *59:* 174; *63:* 5; *74:* 46; *89:* 188; *90:* 231; *95:* 97; *98:* 130; *99:* 189; *153:* 156, 157, 158; *176:* 104; *199:* 96, 98; *222:* 65
Howells, Tania *229:* 87
Howes, Charles *22:* 17
Hoyt, Ard *145:* 141; *190:* 82; *207:* 148
Hranilovich, Barbara *127:* 51
Hu, Ying-Hwa *116:* 107; *152:* 236; *173:* 171
Huang, Benrei *137:* 55
Huang, Zhong-Yang *117:* 30, 32; *213:* 18
Hubbard, Woodleigh Marx *98:* 67; *115:* 79; *160:* 138; *214:* 120
Hubbell, Patricia *222:* 31
Hubley, Faith *48:* 120, 121, 125, 130, 131, 132, 134
Hubley, John *48:* 125, 130, 131, 132, 134
Hudak, Michal *143:* 74
Hudnut, Robin *14:* 62
Huerta, Catherine *76:* 178; *77:* 44, 45; *90:* 182; *210:* 202
Huffaker, Sandy *10:* 56
Huffman, Joan *13:* 33
Huffman, Tom *13:* 180; *17:* 212; *21:* 116; *24:* 132; *33:* 154; *38:* 59; *42:* 147
Hughes, Arthur *20:* 148, 149, 150; *33:* 114, 148, 149
Hughes, Darren *95:* 44
Hughes, David *36:* 197
Hughes, Shirley *1:* 20, 21; *7:* 3; *12:* 217; *16:* 163; *29:* 154; *63:* 118; *70:* 102, 103, 104; *73:* 169; *88:* 70; *110:* 118, 119; *159:* 103
Hugo, Victor *47:* 112
Huliska-Beith, Laura *204:* 108; *220:* 137
Hull, Cathy *78:* 29
Hull, Richard *95:* 120; *123:* 175; *172:* 195
Hulsmann, Eva *16:* 166
Hume, Lachie *189:* 93

Hummel, Berta *43:* 137, 138, 139
Hummel, Lisl *29:* 109; *YABC 2:* 333, 334
Humphrey, Henry *16:* 167
Humphreys, Graham *25:* 168
Humphries, Tudor *76:* 66; *80:* 4; *124:* 4, 5; *226:* 112
Huneck, Stephen *183:* 88, 89
Hunt, James *2:* 143
Hunt, Jonathan *84:* 120
Hunt, Paul *119:* 104; *129:* 135; *139:* 160; *173:* 112
Hunt, Robert *110:* 206, 235; *147:* 136, 137; *170:* 3; *211:* 76; *226:* 189
Hunt, Scott *190:* 143
Hunter, Anne *133:* 190; *178:* 150
Huntington, Amy *180:* 99
Hurd, Clement *2:* 148, 149; *64:* 127, 128, 129, 131, 133, 134,135, 136; *100:* 37, 38
Hurd, Peter *24:* 30, 31,; *YABC 2:* 56
Hurd, Thacher *46:* 88, 89; *94:* 114, 115, 116; *123:* 81, 82, 84; *219:* 82
Hurlimann, Ruth *32:* 99
Hurst, Carol Otis *185:* 92
Hurst, Elise *221:* 98
Hurst, Philip *196:* 79
Hurst, Tracey *192:* 238
Hussar, Michael *114:* 113; *117:* 159
Hustler, Tom *6:* 105
Hutchins, Laurence *55:* 22
Hutchins, Pat *15:* 142; *70:* 106, 107, 108; *178:* 131, 132
Hutchinson, Sascha *95:* 211
Hutchinson, William M. *6:* 3, 138; *46:* 70
Hutchison, Paula *23:* 10
Hutton, Clarke *YABC 2:* 335
Hutton, Kathryn *35:* 155; *89:* 91
Hutton, Warwick *20:* 91
Huyette, Marcia *29:* 188
Hyatt, John *54:* 7
Hyatt, Mitch *178:* 162
Hyde, Maureen *82:* 17; *121:* 145, 146
Hyman, David *117:* 64
Hyman, Miles *210:* 132
Hyman, Trina Schart *1:* 204; *2:* 194; *5:* 153; *6:* 106; *7:* 138, 145; *8:* 22; *10:* 196; *13:* 96; *14:* 114; *15:* 204; *16:* 234; *20:* 82; *22:* 133; *24:* 151; *25:* 79, 82; *26:* 82; *29:* 83; *31:* 37, 39; *34:* 104; *38:* 84, 100, 128; *41:* 49; *43:* 146; *46:* 91, 92, 93, 95, 96, 97, 98, 99, 100, 101, 102, 103, 104, 105,108, 109, 111, 197; *48:* 60, 61; *52:* 32; *60:* 168; *66:* 38; *67:* 214; *72:* 74; *75:* 92; *79:* 57; *82:* 95, 238; *89:* 46; *95:* 91, 92, 93; *100:* 33, 199; *132:* 12; *147:* 33, 35, 36; *167:* 58, 60; *177:* 189, 190; *211:* 188

I

Ibarra, Rosa *147:* 91
Ibatoulline, Bagram *156:* 48; *174:* 33, 82; *202:* 30; *211:* 213; *224:* 84; *225:* 98, 99
Ichikawa, Satomi *29:* 152; *41:* 52; *47:* 133, 134,135, 136; *78:* 93, 94; *80:* 81; *146:* 143, 145, 146; *208:* 117, 118, 119
Ide, Jacqueline *YABC 1:* 39
Idle, Molly Schaar *223:* 95
Ilsley, Velma *3:* 1; *7:* 55; *12:* 109; *37:* 62; *38:* 184
Imai, Ayano *190:* 85, 86
in den Bosch, Nicole *150:* 204
Inga *1:* 142
Ingman, Bruce *134:* 50; *182:* 91, 92; *214:* 10
Ingpen, Robert *109:* 103, 104; *132:* 138; *137:* 177; *166:* 103; *181:* 140; *229:* 169
Ingraham, Erick *21:* 177; *84:* 256; *103:* 66
Inkpen, Mick *99:* 104, 105; *106:* 44
Innerst, Stacy *149:* 104
Innocenti, Roberto *21:* 123; *96:* 122; *159:* 111, 197; *199:* 176

Inoue, Yosuke *24:* 118
Iofin, Michael *97:* 157
Iosa, Ann *63:* 189
Ipcar, Dahlov *1:* 124, 125; *49:* 137, 138, 139, 140, 141, 142,143, 144, 145; *147:* 122, 124, 126
Irvin, Fred *13:* 166; *15:* 143, 144; *27:* 175
Irving, Jay *45:* 72
Irving, Laurence *27:* 50
Isaac, Joanne *21:* 76
Isaacs, Gary *170:* 188
Isadora, Rachel *43:* 159, 160; *54:* 31; *79:* 106, 107,108; *121:* 100, 102; *165:* 116, 117; *204:* 61, 63, 64
Ishmael, Woodi *24:* 111; *31:* 99
Isol *220:* 73
Ives, Ruth *15:* 257
Iwai, Melissa *149:* 233; *183:* 92; *199:* 115
Iwamura, Kazuo *213:* 87

J

Jabar, Cynthia *101:* 201; *210:* 134, 135
Jackness, Andrew *94:* 237
Jackson, Julian *91:* 104, 106
Jackson, Michael *43:* 42
Jackson, Shelley *79:* 71; *99:* 109; *187:* 82
Jacob, Murv *89:* 30
Jacobi, Kathy *62:* 118
Jacobs, Barbara *9:* 136
Jacobs, Lou, Jr. *9:* 136; *15:* 128
Jacobsen, Laura *176:* 98; *177:* 85, 86
Jacobson, Rick *131:* 222; *170:* 119; *222:* 52
Jacobus, Tim *79:* 140; *109:* 126; *129:* 180
Jacques, Robin *1:* 70; *2:* 1; *8:* 46; *9:* 20; *15:* 187; *19:* 253; *32:* 102, 103, 104; *43:* 184; *73:* 135; *YABC 1:* 42
Jaeggi, Yoshiko *186:* 184
Jaffee, Al *66:* 131, 132
Jago *216:* 122
Jagr, Miloslav *13:* 197
Jahn-Clough, Lisa *88:* 114; *152:* 104; *193:* 70, 71
Jahnke, Robert *84:* 24
Jainschigg, Nicholas *80:* 64; *91:* 138; *95:* 63; *99:* 25; *108:* 50; *171:* 41
Jakesevic, Nenad *85:* 102; *226:* 215
Jakobsen, Kathy *116:* 83
Jakubowski, Charles *14:* 192
Jambor, Louis *YABC 1:* 11
James, Ann *73:* 50; *82:* 113; *158:* 61; *183:* 44
James, Brian *140:* 91
James, Curtis E. *182:* 93
James, Derek *35:* 187; *44:* 91; *61:* 133; *74:* 2; *80:* 57; *86:* 88; *130:* 30; *179:* 29; *218:* 31
James, Gilbert *YABC 1:* 43
James, Gordon C. *195:* 89
James, Harold *2:* 151; *3:* 62; *8:* 79; *29:* 113; *51:* 195; *74:* 90
James, Kennon *126:* 211
James, Robin *50:* 106; *53:* 32, 34, 35
James, Simon *202:* 73, 74
James, Will *19:* 150, 152, 153, 155, 163
Janosch
    See Eckert, Horst
Janovitch, Marilyn *68:* 168
Janovitz, Marilyn *87:* 187; *130:* 198; *194:* 91
Jansons, Inese *48:* 117
Jansson, Alexander *216:* 59
Jansson, Tove *3:* 90; *41:* 106, 108, 109, 110, 111, 113, 114
Jaques, Faith *7:* 11, 132, 133; *21:* 83, 84; *69:* 114,116; *73:* 170
Jaques, Frances Lee *29:* 224
Jarka, Jeff *221:* 94
Jarrett, Clare *201:* 77
Jarrie, Martin *219:* 86
Jauss, Anne Marie *1:* 139; *3:* 34; *10:* 57, 119; *11:* 205; *23:* 194

Jay, Alison *158:* 97, 98; *183:* 126, 127; *196:* 95, 96, 97, 98; *200:* 72, 73, 74; *212:* 39
Jeffers, Oliver *175:* 111; *213:* 89
Jeffers, Susan *17:* 86, 87; *25:* 164, 165; *26:* 112; *50:* 132, 134, 135; *70:* 111, 112, 113; *137:* 107, 108, 109, 110, 111; *202:* 77, 78
Jefferson, Louise E. *4:* 160
Jenkin-Pearce, Susie *78:* 16
Jenkins, Debra Reid *85:* 202; *114:* 89; *173:* 134; *225:* 116
Jenkins, Jean *98:* 79, 102
Jenkins, Leonard *157:* 169; *167:* 128; *189:* 96, 97; *190:* 89
Jenkins, Patrick *72:* 126
Jenkins, Steve *124:* 177; *154:* 90, 91, 92, 93; *185:* 194; *188:* 81, 82, 83, 84, 85, 86; *218:* 67, 69, 70, 71, 72
Jenks, Aleta *73:* 117; *124:* 225
Jenkyns, Chris *51:* 97
Jensen, Bruce *95:* 39
Jensinius, Kirsten *56:* 58
Jeram, Anita *89:* 135; *102:* 122, 123; *129:* 112; *154:* 96, 97, 98; *164:* 154; *203:* 123, 124; *219:* 88, 89, 90, 91
Jernigan, E. Wesley *85:* 92
Jerome, Elaine *227:* 45
Jerome, Karen A. *72:* 194
Jeruchim, Simon *6:* 173; *15:* 250
Jeschke, Susan *20:* 89; *39:* 161; *41:* 84; *42:* 120
Jessel, Camilla *29:* 115
Jessell, Tim *159:* 3; *177:* 87; *181:* 95; *205:* 4; *213:* 74; *223:* 187; *225:* 102; *226:* 190
Jeyaveeran, Ruth *182:* 100
Jiang, Cheng An *109:* 108
Jiang, Wei *109:* 108
Jimenez, Maria *77:* 158; *93:* 127
Jobling, Curtis *138:* 74
Jocelyn, Marthe *118:* 83; *137:* 219; *163:* 119, 120; *198:* 62
Joerns, Consuelo *38:* 36; *44:* 94
John, Diana *12:* 209
John, Helen *1:* 215; *28:* 204
Johns, Elizabeth *127:* 33
Johns, Jasper *61:* 172
Johns, Jeanne *24:* 114
Johnson, Adrian *143:* 50
Johnson, Bruce *9:* 47
Johnson, Cathy *92:* 136; *218:* 112
Johnson, Crockett
    See Leisk, David
Johnson, D. William *23:* 104
Johnson, D.B. *183:* 98, 139
Johnson, David A. *175:* 18; *191:* 91; *218:* 19
Johnson, Gillian *119:* 175; *164:* 217; *215:* 99
Johnson, Harper *1:* 27; *2:* 33; *18:* 302; *19:* 61; *31:* 181; *44:* 46, 50, 95
Johnson, Ingrid *37:* 118
Johnson, James Ralph *1:* 23, 127
Johnson, James David *12:* 195
Johnson, Jane *48:* 136
Johnson, Joel Peter *98:* 18; *128:* 111; *201:* 13; *213:* 189
Johnson, John E. *34:* 133
Johnson, Kevin *72:* 44
Johnson, Kevin Eugene *109:* 215
Johnson, Larry *47:* 56; *123:* 107; *159:* 203
Johnson, Layne *187:* 94; *209:* 63; *222:* 100, 101
Johnson, Margaret S. *35:* 131
Johnson, Meredith Merrell *71:* 181; *83:* 158; *89:* 103; *104:* 88
Johnson, Milton *1:* 67; *2:* 71; *26:* 45; *31:* 107; *60:* 112; *68:* 96
Johnson, Pamela *16:* 174; *52:* 145; *62:* 140; *73:* 116; *85:* 64
Johnson, Paul Brett *83:* 95; *132:* 119
Johnson, Stephen T. *80:* 15; *131:* 35; *141:* 96; *145:* 40; *164:* 187; *175:* 32; *189:* 99, 100; *208:* 43

Johnson, Steve *138:* 219; *141:* 64; *144:* 199; *177:* 51; *214:* 95; *221:* 63; *228:* 42, 43, 44
Johnson, William R. *38:* 91
Johnson-Petrov, Arden *115:* 206
Johnston, David McCall *50:* 131, 133
Johnston, Lynne *118:* 85, 87, 89; *216:* 127, 128, 131
Johnstone, Anne *8:* 120; *36:* 89
Johnstone, Janet Grahame *8:* 120; *36:* 89
Jonas, Ann *50:* 107, 108, 109; *135:* 113
Jones, Bob *71:* 5; *77:* 199
Jones, Carol *5:* 131; *72:* 185, 186; *153:* 111, 112
Jones, Chuck *53:* 70, 71
Jones, Curtis *211:* 144
Jones, Davy *89:* 176
Jones, Douglas B. *185:* 192; *202:* 82
Jones, Elizabeth Orton *18:* 124, 126, 128, 129
Jones, Harold *14:* 88; *52:* 50
Jones, Holly *127:* 3
Jones, Jeff *41:* 64
Jones, Laurian *25:* 24, 27
Jones, Margaret *74:* 57
Jones, Noah Z. *182:* 37; *203:* 159
Jones, Randy *131:* 104
Jones, Richard *127:* 222
Jones, Robert *25:* 67
Jones, Wilfred *35:* 115; *YABC 1:* 163
Jordan, Charles *89:* 58
Jordan, Jess *158:* 136; *203:* 111
Jordan, Martin George *84:* 127
Jordan, Richard *84:* 36
Jorgenson, Andrea *91:* 111
Jorisch, Stéphane *153:* 56, 193; *177:* 29; *178:* 138, 139; *187:* 23; *211:* 182
Joseph, James *53:* 88
Joudrey, Ken *64:* 145; *78:* 6
Joyce, William *72:* 131, 132, 133, 134; *73:* 227; *145:* 37
Joyner, Jerry *34:* 138
Joyner, Loraine M. *209:* 17
Joysmith, Brenda *210:* 237
Juan, Ana *175:* 38; *179:* 111, 112; *213:* 9
Jucker, Sita *5:* 93
Judge, Lita *192:* 99
Judkis, Jim *37:* 38
Juhasz, Victor *31:* 67
Jullian, Philippe *24:* 206; *25:* 203
Jung, Tom *91:* 217
Junge, Alexandra *183:* 37
Junge, Walter *67:* 150
Jupo, Frank *7:* 148, 149
Jurisch, Stephane *154:* 105
Justice, Martin *34:* 72

K

Kabatova-Taborska, Zdenka *107:* 153
Kachik, John *165:* 230
Kaczman, James *156:* 98
Kadair, Deborah Ousley *184:* 45, 89
Kahl, David *74:* 95; *97:* 35; *109:* 174; *110:* 213; *198:* 15
Kahl, M.P. *37:* 83
Kahl, Virginia *48:* 138
Kahn, Katherine Janus *90:* 135; *211:* 155; *218:* 75, 76; *220:* 89,90
Kakimoo, Kozo *11:* 148
Kalett, Jim *48:* 159, 160, 161
Kalin, Victor *39:* 186
Kalis, Jennifer *207:* 82; *219:* 62
Kalman, Maira *96:* 131, 132; *137:* 115
Kalmenoff, Matthew *22:* 191
Kalow, Gisela *32:* 105
Kamen, Gloria *1:* 41; *9:* 119; *10:* 178; *35:* 157; *78:* 236; *98:* 82
Kaminsky, Jef *102:* 153
Kandell, Alice *35:* 133
Kane, Henry B. *14:* 90; *18:* 219, 220

Kane, Robert *18:* 131
Kanfer, Larry *66:* 141
Kangas, Juli *200:* 88
Kappes, Alfred *28:* 104
Karalus, Bob *41:* 157
Karas, G. Brian *80:* 60; *99:* 179; *115:* 41; *118:* 50; *136:* 168; *145:* 166; *149:* 245; *159:* 65; *171:* 192; *178:* 142, 143; *202:* 38; *209:* 142; *222:* 106, 107, 108, 109; *225:* 62
Karasz, Ilonka *128:* 163
Karlin, Eugene *10:* 63; *20:* 131
Karlin, Nurit *63:* 78; *103:* 110
Karpinski, Tony *134:* 160
Kasamatsu, Shiro *139:* 155
Kasparavicius, Kestutis *139:* 210
Kassian, Olena *64:* 94
Kastner, Jill *79:* 135; *117:* 84, 85
Kasuya, Masahiro *41:* 206, 207; *51:* 100
Kasza, Keiko *191:* 99, 100, 101, 102, 103
Katona, Robert *21:* 85; *24:* 126
Katz, Avi *199:* 55
Katz, Karen *158:* 122
Kauffer, E. McKnight *33:* 103; *35:* 127; *63:* 67
Kaufman, Angelika *15:* 156
Kaufman, Joe *33:* 119
Kaufman, John *13:* 158
Kaufman, Stuart *62:* 64; *68:* 226; *137:* 44
Kaufmann, John *1:* 174; *4:* 159; *8:* 43, 1; *10:* 102; *18:* 133, 134; *22:* 251
Kaye, Graham *1:* 9; *67:* 7, 8
Kaye, M.M. *62:* 95
Kazalovski, Nata *40:* 205
Keane, Bil *4:* 135
Kearney, David *72:* 47; *121:* 83
Keating, Pamel T. *77:* 37
Keats, Ezra Jack *3:* 18, 105, 257; *14:* 101, 102; *33:* 129; *57:* 79, 80, 82, 83, 84, 87
Keegan, Charles *166:* 211
Keegan, Marcia *9:* 122; *32:* 93
Keeler, Patricia A. *81:* 56; *183:* 102, 103
Keely, Jack *119:* 95
Keely, John *26:* 104; *48:* 214
Keen, Eliot *25:* 213
Keep, Richard C. *170:* 122
Keeping, Charles *9:* 124, 185; *15:* 28, 134; *18:* 115; *44:* 194, 196; *47:* 25; *52:* 3; *54:* 156; *69:* 123, 124; *74:* 56; *155:* 9
Keeter, Susan *168:* 46; *183:* 192
Keith, Eros *4:* 98; *5:* 138; *31:* 29; *43:* 220; *52:* 91, 92, 93, 94; *56:* 64, 66; *60:* 37; *79:* 93
Keleinikov, Andrei *65:* 101, 102
Kelen, Emery *13:* 115
Keller, A.J. *62:* 198
Keller, Arthur I. *26:* 106
Keller, Dick *36:* 123, 125
Keller, Holly *45:* 79; *76:* 118, 119, 120, 121; *108:* 137, 138, 140; *157:* 117, 118, 119; *216:* 136
Keller, Katie *79:* 222; *93:* 108
Keller, Laurie *196:* 105, 106
Keller, Ronald *45:* 208
Kelley, Gary *183:* 105; *216:* 78; *217:* 95, 96, 97
Kelley, Marty *211:* 91
Kelley, True *41:* 114, 115; *42:* 137; *75:* 35; *92:* 104, 105; *124:* 62; *130:* 100, 101; *179:* 120, 121, 122; *192:* 251
Kellogg, Steven *8:* 96; *11:* 207; *14:* 130; *20:* ; *201:* 38 58; *29:* 140, 141; *30:* 35; *41:* 141; *57:* 89, 90, 92,93, 94, 96; *59:* 182; *73:* 141; *77:* 129; *130:* 105, 106; *177:* 94, 95, 96, 97; *199:* 57; *217:* 61; *YABC 1:* 65, 73
Kelly, Billy *158:* 143
Kelly, Geoff *97:* 196; *112:* 25
Kelly, Irene *147:* 134; *210:* 144, 145
Kelly, John *194:* 186
Kelly, Joseph *174:* 94
Kelly, Kathleen M. *71:* 109
Kelly, Laura *89:* 217
Kelly, True *163:* 87

Kelly, Walt *18:* 136, 137, 138, 139, 140, 141, 144, 145, 146, 148, 149
Kemble, E.W. *34:* 75; *44:* 178; *YABC 2:* 54, 59
Kemly, Kathleen *209:* 165
Kemp-Welsh, Lucy *24:* 197; *100:* 214
Kendall, Jane *150:* 105; *186:* 109
Kendall, Peter *152:* 85
Kendrick, Dennis *79:* 213
Kennaway, Adrienne *60:* 55, 56; *171:* 88, 89
Kennedy, Anne *212:* 34
Kennedy, Doug *189:* 104
Kennedy, Paul Edward *6:* 190; *8:* 132; *33:* 120
Kennedy, Richard *3:* 93; *12:* 179; *44:* 193; *100:* 15; *YABC 1:* 57
Kent, Jack *24:* 136; *37:* 37; *40:* 81; *84:* 89; *86:* 150; *88:* 77
Kent, Rockwell *5:* 166; *6:* 129; *20:* 225, 226, 227,229; *59:* 144
Kenyon, Tony *81:* 201; *127:* 74
Kepes, Juliet *13:* 119
Kerins, Anthony *76:* 84
Kerr, Judity *24:* 137
Kerr, Phyllis Forbes *72:* 141
Kessler, Leonard *1:* 108; *7:* 139; *14:* 107, 227; *22:* 101; *44:* 96; *67:* 79; *82:* 123
Kest, Kristin *168:* 99; *173:* 23
Kesteven, Peter *35:* 189
Ketcham, Hank *28:* 140, 141, 142
Kettelkamp, Larry *2:* 164
Key, Alexander *8:* 99
Khalsa, Dayal Kaur *62:* 99
Kiakshuk *8:* 59
Kid, Tom *207:* 54
Kidd, Chip *94:* 23
Kidd, Richard *152:* 110
Kidd, Tom *64:* 199; *81:* 189; *185:* 173
Kiddell-Monroe, Joan *19:* 201; *55:* 59, 60; *87:* 174; *121:* 112
Kidder, Harvey *9:* 105; *80:* 41
Kidwell, Carl *43:* 145
Kieffer, Christa *41:* 89
Kiesler, Kate *110:* 105; *136:* 142
Kiff, Ken *40:* 45
Kilaka, John *223:* 107
Kilbride, Robert *37:* 100
Kilby, Don *141:* 144
Kim, David *201:* 79; *202:* 97
Kim, Glenn *99:* 82
Kimball, Anton *78:* 114; *119:* 105
Kimball, Yeffe *23:* 116; *37:* 88
Kimber, Murray *171:* 91
Kimmel, Warren *176:* 112
Kincade, Orin *34:* 116
Kindersley, Barnabas *96:* 110
Kindred, Wendy *7:* 151
King, Colin *53:* 3
King, Robin *10:* 164, 165
King, Stephen Michael *141:* 31; *197:* 191; *218:* 81, 82
King, Tara Calahan *139:* 172
King, Tony *39:* 121
Kingman, Dong *16:* 287; *44:* 100, 102, 104
Kingsley, Charles *YABC 2:* 182
Kingston, Julie *147:* 14
Kingston, Maxine Hong *53:* 92
Kinney, Jeff *187:* 97
Kipling, John Lockwood *YABC 2:* 198
Kipling, Rudyard *YABC 2:* 196
Kipniss, Robert *29:* 59
Kirchherr, Astrid *55:* 23
Kirchhoff, Art *28:* 136
Kirk, Daniel *153:* 115, 116, 117; *173:* 101; *196:* 113, 114, 115, 116
Kirk, David *117:* 88, 89; *161:* 97, 98
Kirk, Ruth *5:* 96
Kirk, Steve *170:* 37
Kirk, Tim *32:* 209, 211; *72:* 89; *83:* 49
Kirmse, Marguerite *15:* 283; *18:* 153
Kirsch, Vincent X. *124:* 207
Kirschner, Ruth *22:* 154

Kirwan, Wednesday *198:* 73
Kish, Ely *73:* 119; *79:* 2
Kitamura, Satoshi *62:* 102; *98:* 91; *101:* 147; *138:* 2; *143:* 83, 85, 86; *201:* 83; *223:* 3, 4
Kiss, Andrew *168:* 115
Kitchel, JoAnn E. *133:* 32
Kitchen, Bert *70:* 126; *193:* 49
Kittelsen, Theodor *62:* 14
Kiuchi, Tatsuro *114:* 71
Kiwak, Barbara *172:* 135
Klahr, Susan *176:* 196
Klapholz, Mel *13:* 35
Klee, Jutte *209:* 136
Klein, Bill *89:* 105
Klein, Robert *55:* 77
Klein, Suzanna *63:* 104
Kleinman, Zalman *28:* 143
Kleven, Elisa *173:* 96, 97; *217:* 100, 102
Kliban, B. *35:* 137, 138
Kline, Michael *127:* 66
Klise, M. Sarah *180:* 117, 118; *181:* 97; *221:* 100, 102
Knabel, Lonnie *73:* 103; *75:* 187, 228; *194:* 216
Kneen, Maggie *140:* 139; *221:* 104, 105
Knight, Ann *34:* 143
Knight, Christopher *13:* 125
Knight, Hilary *1:* 233; *3:* 21; *15:* 92, 158, 159; *16:* 258, 259, 260; *18:* 235; *19:* 169; *35:* 242; *46:* 167; *52:* 116; *69:* 126, 127; *132:* 129; *YABC 1:* 168, 169, 172
Knorr, Laura *200:* 91
Knorr, Peter *126:* 92, 93
Knotts, Howard *20:* 4; *25:* 170; *36:* 163
Knutson, Barbara *112:* 134; *202:* 108
Knutson, Kimberley *115:* 90
Kobayashi, Ann *39:* 58
Kochalka, James *196:* 120, 121, 122
Kocsis, J.C.
    See Paul, James
Kodman, Stanislawa *201:* 85; *224:* 72
Koehler, Hanne Lore *176:* 203
Koehn, Ilse *34:* 198; *79:* 123
Koelsch, Michael *99:* 182; *107:* 164; *109:* 239; *138:* 142; *150:* 94; *176:* 105; *187:* 63; *198:* 63
Koering, Ursula *3:* 28; *4:* 14; *44:* 5; *64:* 140,141; *85:* 46
Koerner, Henry
    See Koerner, W.H.D.
Koerner, W.H.D. *14:* 216; *21:* 88, 89, 90, 91; *23:* 211
Koetsch, Mike *166:* 68
Koffler, Camilla *36:* 113
Kogan, Deborah Ray *161:* 101, 102
Koide, Yasuko *50:* 114
Kolado, Karen *102:* 228
Kolesova, Juliana *217:* 81; *222:* 185; *229:* 183
Komarck, Michael *227:* 48
Komoda, Kiyo *9:* 128; *13:* 214
Kompaneyets, Marc *169:* 92
Konashevich, Vladimir *61:* 160
Konashevicha, V. *YABC 1:* 26
Konigsburg, E.L. *4:* 138; *48:* 141, 142, 144, 145; *94:* 129, 130; *126:* 129, 130, 131; *194:* 95, 98
Kono, Erin Eitter *177:* 99
Kooiker, Leonie *48:* 148
Koonook, Simon *65:* 157
Koontz, Robin Michal *136:* 155
Koopmans, Loek *101:* 121
Kopelke, Lisa *154:* 107
Kopper, Lisa *72:* 152, 153; *105:* 135, 136
Korach, Mimi *1:* 128, 129; *2:* 52; *4:* 39; *5:* 159; *9:* 129; *10:* 21; *24:* 69
Koren, Edward *5:* 100; *65:* 65, 67
Kosaka, Fumi *164:* 130
Koscielniak, Bruce *99:* 122; *153:* 120, 121, 122
Koshkin, Alexander *92:* 180
Kossin, Sandy *10:* 71; *23:* 105

Kostin, Andrej *26:* 204
Kosturko, Bob *164:* 56
Kotzky, Brian *68:* 184
Kovacevic, Zivojin *13:* 247
Kovalski, Maryann *58:* 120; *84:* 88; *97:* 124, 125, 126; *158:* 3; *186:* 80
Kozjan, Drazen *209:* 99
Krahn, Fernando *2:* 257; *34:* 206; *49:* 152
Krall, Dan *218:* 84, 85
Kramer, Anthony *33:* 81
Kramer, David *96:* 162; *109:* 132; *150:* 220
Kramer, Frank *6:* 121
Krantz, Kathy *35:* 83
Kratter, Paul *139:* 65
Kraus, Robert *13:* 217; *65:* 113; *93:* 93, 94
Krause, Jon *176:* 62
Krauss, Trisha *174:* 10
Kredel, Fritz *6:* 35; *17:* 93, 94, 95, 96; *22:* 147; *24:* 175; *29:* 130; *35:* 77; *YABC 2:* 166, 300
Kreloff, Eliot *189:* 107, 108; *205:* 182
Krementz, Jill *17:* 98; *49:* 41
Krenina, Katya *117:* 106; *125:* 133; *176:* 117; *221:* 107
Kresin, Robert *23:* 19
Kretschmar, Sonia *226:* 97
Krieger, Salem *54:* 164
Kriegler, Lyn *73:* 29
Krinitz, Esther Nisenthal *193:* 196
Krommes, Beth *128:* 141; *149:* 136; *181:* 100, 101; *184:* 105; *188:* 125; *208:* 135; *209:* 185
Krone, Mike *101:* 71
Kronheimer, Ann *135:* 119
Krosoczka, Jarrett J. *155:* 142; *200:* 93, 94
Kruck, Gerald *88:* 181
Krudop, Walter Lyon *199:* 19
Krupinski, Loretta *67:* 104; *102:* 131; *161:* 105, 106
Krupp, Robin Rector *53:* 96, 98
Krush, Beth *1:* 51, 85; *2:* 233; *4:* 115; *9:* 61; *10:* 191; *11:* 196; *18:* 164, 165; *32:* 72; *37:* 203; *43:* 57; *60:* 102, 103, 107, 108, 109
Krush, Joe *2:* 233; *4:* 115; *9:* 61; *10:* 191; *11:* 196; *18:* 164, 165; *32:* 72, 91; *37:* 203; *43:* 57; *60:* 102, 103, 107, 108, 109
Krych, Duane *91:* 43
Krykorka, Vladyana *96:* 147; *143:* 90, 91; *168:* 14
Kubick, Dana *165:* 91; *212:* 104, 105, 212
Kubinyi, Laszlo *4:* 116; *6:* 113; *16:* 118; *17:* 100; *28:* 227; *30:* 172; *49:* 24, 28; *54:* 23; *167:* 149
Kubricht, Mary *73:* 118
Kucharik, Elena *139:* 31
Kuchera, Kathleen *84:* 5
Kuhn, Bob *17:* 91; *35:* 235
Kulikov, Boris *163:* 185; *185:* 23; *205:* 99, 100; *217:* 160
Kulka, Joe *188:* 110
Kukalis, Romas *90:* 27; *139:* 37
Kuklin, Susan *63:* 82, 83, 84
Kunhardt, Dorothy *53:* 101
Kunhardt, Edith *67:* 105, 106
Kunstler, Mort *10:* 73; *32:* 143
Kurchevsky, V. *34:* 61
Kurczok, Belinda *121:* 118
Kurelek, William *8:* 107
Kuriloff, Ron *13:* 19
Kurisu, Jane *160:* 120
Kuskin, Karla *2:* 170; *68:* 115, 116; *111:* 116
Kutzer, Ernst *19:* 249
Kuzma, Steve *57:* 8; *62:* 93
Kuznetsova, Berta *74:* 45
Kvasnosky, Laura McGee *93:* 103; *142:* 83; *182:* 108
Kwas, Susan Estelle *179:* 116; *217:* 90
Kyong, Yunmee *165:* 139

L

LaBlanc, Andre *24:* 146
Laboccetta, Mario *27:* 120
LaBrose, Darcie *157:* 134
Labrosse, Darcia *58:* 88; *108:* 77; *178:* 89
LaCava, Vince *95:* 118
Laceky, Adam *32:* 121
Lacis, Astra *85:* 117
Lacome, Julie *174:* 96, 97
La Croix *YABC 2:* 4
Ladd, London *206:* 50
Ladwig, Tim *98:* 212; *117:* 76; *215:* 32; *223:* 111, 112
La Farge, Margaret *47:* 141
LaFave, Kim *64:* 177; *72:* 39; *97:* 146; *99:* 172; *106:* 123; *149:* 126; *196:* 128, 129
Lafontaine, Roger *167:* 158
Lafrance, Marie *197:* 109
Lagarrigue, Jerome *136:* 102; *187:* 81
Laimgruber, Monika *11:* 153
Laínez, René Colato *226:* 50
Laio, Jimmy *213:* 57
Laite, Gordon *1:* 130, 131; *8:* 209; *31:* 113; *40:* 63; *46:* 117
Laliberté, Louise-Andrée *169:* 98
LaMarche, Jim *46:* 204; *61:* 56; *94:* 69; *114:* 22; *129:* 163; *162:* 78, 80
Lamb, Jim *10:* 117
Lambase, Barbara *101:* 185; *150:* 221; *166:* 234
Lambert, J.K. *38:* 129; *39:* 24
Lambert, Sally Anne *133:* 191
Lambert, Saul *23:* 112; *33:* 107; *54:* 136
Lambert, Stephen *109:* 33; *174:* 99
Lambo, Don *6:* 156; *35:* 115; *36:* 146
Lamontagne, Jacques *166:* 227
Lamut, Sonja *57:* 193
Lamut, Sonya *85:* 102
Landa, Peter *11:* 95; *13:* 177; *53:* 119
Landau, Jacob *38:* 111
Landis, Joan *104:* 23; *203:* 32
Landon, Lucinda *79:* 31
Landshoff, Ursula *13:* 124
Landström, Lena *146:* 165, 166
Landström, Olof *146:* 166, 168; *170:* 22
Lane, Daniel *112:* 60
Lane, John R. *8:* 145
Lane, John *15:* 176, 177; *30:* 146
Lane, Nancy *166:* 74
Lang, G.D. *48:* 56
Lang, Gary *73:* 75
Lang, Glenna *221:* 113
Lang, Jerry *18:* 295
Langdo, Bryan *186:* 187; *191:* 113, 114, 115
Lange, Dorothea *50:* 141
Langley, Jonathan *162:* 128
Langner, Nola *8:* 110; *42:* 36
Lanino, Deborah *105:* 148
Lantz, Paul *1:* 82, 102; *27:* 88; *34:* 102; *45:* 123
Larkin, Bob *84:* 225
Laroche, Giles *126:* 140; *146:* 81; *221:* 116, 117
LaRochelle, David *171:* 97
Larrañaga, Ana Martín *229:* 106
Larrecq, John *44:* 108; *68:* 56
Larsen, Suzanne *1:* 13
Larson, Gary *57:* 121, 122, 123, 124, 125, 126, 127
Larsson, Carl *35:* 144, 145, 146, 147, 148, 149, 150, 152, 153, 154
Larsson, Karl *19:* 177
Lartitegui, Ana G. *105:* 167
LaRue, Jenna *167:* 20
La Rue, Michael D. *13:* 215
Lasker, Joe *7:* 186, 187; *14:* 55; *38:* 115; *39:* 47; *83:* 113, 114, 115
Latham, Barbara *16:* 188, 189; *43:* 71

Lathrop, Dorothy *14:* 117, 118, 119; *15:* 109; *16:* 78, 79, 81; *32:* 201, 203; *33:* 112; *YABC 2:* 301
Lattimore, Eleanor Frances *7:* 156
Lauden, Claire *16:* 173
Lauden, George, Jr. *16:* 173
Laune, Paul *2:* 235; *34:* 31
Laure, Jason *49:* 53; *50:* 122
Lauter, Richard *63:* 29; *67:* 111; *77:* 198
Lavallee, Barbara *74:* 157; *92:* 154; *96:* 126; *145:* 193; *166:* 125, 126; *186:* 155; *192:* 172
Lave, Fitz Hugh *59:* 139
Lavis, Steve *43:* 143; *87:* 137, 164, 165; *222:* 161; *225:* 121
Layton, Neal *152:* 120, 121; *182:* 65; *187:* 103, 105, 106
Law, Jenny *201:* 31
Lawrason, June *168:* 30
Lawrence, John *25:* 131; *30:* 141; *44:* 198, 200; *214:* 7
Lawrence, Stephen *20:* 195
Lawson, Carol *6:* 38; *42:* 93, 131; *174:* 56; *189:* 89; *209:* 59
Lawson, George *17:* 280
Lawson, Robert *5:* 26; *6:* 94; *13:* 39; *16:* 11; *20:* 100, 102, 103; *54:* 3; *66:* 12; *100:* 144, 145; *YABC 2:* 222, 224, 225, 227, 228, 229, 230, 231, 232, 233, 234, 235, 237, 238, 239, 240, 241
Layfield, Kathie *60:* 194
Lazare, Jerry *44:* 109; *74:* 28
Lazarevich, Mila *17:* 118
Lazarus, Claire *103:* 30
Lazarus, Keo Felker *21:* 94
Lazzaro, Victor *11:* 126
Lea, Bob *166:* 208; *203:* 108
Lea, Tom *43:* 72, 74
Leacroft, Richard *6:* 140
Leaf, Munro *20:* 99
Leake, Donald *70:* 41
Leander, Patricia *23:* 27
Lear, Edward *18:* 183, 184, 185
Lear, Rebecca *149:* 46
Lebenson, Richard *6:* 209; *7:* 76; *23:* 145; *44:* 191; *87:* 153
Le Cain, Errol *6:* 141; *9:* 3; *22:* 142; *25:* 198; *28:* 173; *68:* 128, 129; *86:* 49
Lechon, Daniel *113:* 211
Leder, Dora *129:* 172
Ledger, Bill *181:* 58
Leduc, Bernard *102:* 36
Lee, Alan *62:* 25, 28
Lee, Bryce *99:* 60; *101:* 195; *196:* 53
Lee, Chinlun *181:* 138; *182:* 112
Lee, Declan *191:* 20
Lee, Dom *83:* 118, 120; *93:* 123; *121:* 121, 126; *146:* 174, 175, 206, 207; *174:* 204
Lee, Doris *13:* 246; *32:* 183; *44:* 111
Lee, Hector Viveros *115:* 96
Lee, Ho Baek *200:* 160
Lee, Huy Voun *217:* 106
Lee, Jeanne M. *158:* 56
Lee, Jared *93:* 200; *157:* 229; *215:* 113, 191, 192, 193; *228:* 177
Lee, Jody *81:* 121; *82:* 225; *91:* 155; *100:* 182
Lee, Jody A. *127:* 124, 126, 127
  See also Lee, Jody
Lee, Manning de V. *2:* 200; *17:* 12; *27:* 87; *37:* 102, 103, 104; *YABC 2:* 304
Lee, Margaret *213:* 179
Lee, Marie G. *138:* 157
Lee, Paul *97:* 100; *105:* 72, 209; *109:* 177; *128:* 113; *202:* 45
Lee, Robert J. *3:* 97; *67:* 124
Lee, Victor *96:* 228; *105:* 182; *140:* 196; *208:* 191
Lee, Virginia *208:* 139, 140; *218:* 28
Leech, Dorothy *98:* 76
Leech, John *15:* 59
Leedy, Loreen *84:* 142; *128:* 144, 145, 146; *175:* 125, 126, 127

Leeman, Michael *44:* 157
Leeming, Catherine *87:* 39
Lees, Harry *6:* 112
LeFever, Bill *88:* 220, 221
Legenisel *47:* 111
Legrand, Edy *18:* 89, 93
Lehman, Barbara *73:* 123; *170:* 130
Lehrman, Rosalie *2:* 180
Leichman, Seymour *5:* 107
Leick, Bonnie *205:* 104
Leighton, Clare *25:* 130; *33:* 168; *37:* 105, 106, 108,109
Leisk, David *1:* 140, 141; *11:* 54; *30:* 137, 142, 143,144
Leister, Bryan *89:* 45; *106:* 37; *114:* 67; *149:* 236; *222:* 181
Leloir, Maurice *18:* 77, 80, 83, 99
Lemaître, Pascal *144:* 175; *176:* 130; *189:* 135; *225:* 124, 125
Lemieux, Michele *100:* 148; *139:* 153
Lemke, Horst *14:* 98; *38:* 117, 118, 119
Lemke, R.W. *42:* 162
Lemon, David Gwynne *9:* 1
LeMoult, Adolph *82:* 116
Lenn, Michael *136:* 89
Lennon, John *114:* 100
Lennox, Elsie *95:* 163; *143:* 160
Lenski, Lois *1:* 144; *26:* 135, 137, 139, 141; *100:* 153, 154
Lent, Blair *1:* 116, 117; *2:* 174; *3:* 206, 207; *7:* 168, 169; *34:* 62; *68:* 217; *133:* 101; *183:* 60
Leon, Jana *226:* 214
Leonard, David *212:* 149
Leonard, Richard *91:* 128
Leonard, Tom *207:* 95; *219:* 55
Leone, Leonard *49:* 190
Lerner, Carol *86:* 140, 141, 142
Lerner, Judith *116:* 138
Lerner, Sharon *11:* 157; *22:* 56
Leroux-Hugon, Helene *132:* 139
Leslie, Cecil *19:* 244
Lessac, Frané *80:* 182, 207; *96:* 182; *202:* 58; *209:* 104
Lessing, Erich *167:* 52; *173:* 60
Lester, Alison *50:* 124; *90:* 147, 148; *129:* 130; *218:* 91, 93
Lester, Mike *208:* 50
Lethcoe, Jason *191:* 116, 117
Le Tord, Bijou *49:* 156; *95:* 112
Leutz, Emanuel *165:* 27
Levai, Blaise *39:* 130
Levert, Mireille *211:* 101
Levin, Ted *12:* 148
Levine, David *43:* 147, 149, 150, 151, 152; *64:* 11
Levine, Joe *71:* 88; *219:* 74
Levine, Marge *81:* 127
Levinson, David *178:* 232
Levit, Herschel *24:* 223
Levstek, Ljuba *131:* 192; *134:* 216; *149:* 65; *168:* 180
Levy, Jessica Ann *19:* 225; *39:* 191
Levy, Lina *117:* 126
Lewin, Betsy *32:* 114; *48:* 177; *90:* 151; *91:* 125; *92:* 85; *115:* 105; *169:* 110, 111; *178:* 47; *186:* 188; *194:* 201; *222:* 120; *226:* 139
Lewin, Ted *4:* 77; *8:* 168; *20:* 110; *21:* 99,100; *27:* 110; *28:* 96, 97; *31:* 49; *45:* 55; *48:* 223; *60:* 20, 119, 120; *62:* 139; *66:* 108; *71:* 12; *72:* 21; *74:* 226; *76:* 139, 140; *77:* 82; *79:* 87; *85:* 49, 177; *86:* 55; *88:* 182; *93:* 28, 29; *94:* 34, 182, 194; *99:* 156; *104:* 8; *115:* 123; *118:* 74; *119:* 114, 116; *131:* 54; *145:* 99; *165:* 151; *177:* 75; *178:* 42; *190:* 30; *192:* 86; *195:* 101, 102; *203:* 52; *222:* 119; *226:* 136, 137, 138, 139
Lewis, Allen *15:* 112
Lewis, Anthony *227:* 114

Lewis, E.B. *88:* 143; *93:* 109; *119:* 79; *124:* 113; *128:* 49; *151:* 167; *168:* 110; *173:* 121; *174:* 66; *176:* 7; *184:* 150; *185:* 191; *211:* 108, 109, 110, 111; *223:* 17
Lewis, H.B. *170:* 124
Lewis, J. Patrick *162:* 83
Lewis, Jan *81:* 22
Lewis, Kim *136:* 165; *217:* 109, 111
Lewis, Richard W. *52:* 25
Lewis, Robin Baird *98:* 193
Lew-Vriethoff, Joanne *225:* 181
Leydon, Rita Floden *21:* 101
Li, Xiojun *187:* 172
Liao, Jimmy *202:* 100
Lichtenheld, Tom *152:* 125, 126; *222:* 160; *224:* 9
Lieblich, Irene *22:* 173; *27:* 209, 214
Lieder, Rick *108:* 197; *199:* 58, 59, 60
Lies, Brian *92:* 40; *141:* 101; *150:* 138; *190:* 97, 98, 99
Liese, Charles *4:* 222
Liew, Sonny *219:* 108
Life, Kay *79:* 49
Lifton, Robert Jay *66:* 154
Lightburn, Ron *86:* 153; *91:* 122
Lightfoot, Norman R. *45:* 47
Lignell, Lois *37:* 114
Lill, Debra *121:* 70
Lilly, Charles *8:* 73; *20:* 127; *48:* 53; *72:* 9,16; *77:* 98; *102:* 94
Lilly, Ken *37:* 224
Lim, John *43:* 153
Limona, Mercedes *51:* 183
Lin, Grace *143:* 217; *162:* 86, 87; *174:* 185
Lincoln, Patricia Henderson *27:* 27; *78:* 127
Lindahn, Ron *84:* 17
Lindahn, Val *84:* 17
Lindberg, Howard *10:* 123; *16:* 190
Lindberg, Jeffrey *64:* 77; *77:* 71; *79:* 54; *80:* 149; *174:* 109; *179:* 52
Linden, Seymour *18:* 200, 201; *43:* 140
Lindenbaum, Pija *144:* 143; *183:* 113
Linder, Richard *27:* 119
Lindman, Maj *43:* 154
Lindsay, Norman *67:* 114
Lindsay, Vachel *40:* 118
Lindstrom, Jack *145:* 118
Line, Les *27:* 143
Linell
  See Smith, Linell
Lintern, Tom *228:* 101
Lionni, Leo *8:* 115; *72:* 159, 160, 161
Lipinsky, Lino *2:* 156; *22:* 175
Lippincott, Gary A. *70:* 35; *119:* 118; *220:* 105, 106, 107
Lippman, Peter *8:* 31; *31:* 119, 120, 160
Lisi, Victoria *89:* 145
Lisker, Emily *169:* 114
Lisker, Sonia O. *16:* 274; *31:* 31; *44:* 113, 114
Lisowski, Gabriel *47:* 144; *49:* 157
Lissim, Simon *17:* 138
Little, Ed *89:* 145; *151:* 53
Little, Harold *16:* 72
Little, Mary E. *28:* 146
Littlewood, Karen *165:* 126; *211:* 112
Litty, Julie *111:* 63
Litzinger, Rosanne *151:* 101; *176:* 118; *196:* 133, 134, 135; *208:* 129; *209:* 147
Liu, Lesley *143:* 72
Lively, Lorna *19:* 216
Livingston, Susan *95:* 22
Liwska, Renata *164:* 113; *199:* 25, 69; *220:* 79
Ljungkvist, Laura *180:* 120
Llerena, Carlos Antonio *19:* 181
Lloyd, Errol *11:* 39; *22:* 178
Lloyd, Megan *77:* 118; *80:* 113; *97:* 75; *117:* 94, 95; *189:* 121, 122; *208:* 128; *211:* 72
Lloyd, Sam *183:* 116, 117
Lo, Beth *165:* 154
Lo, Koon-chiu *7:* 134
Loates, Glen *63:* 76

Lobel, Anita *6:* 87; *9:* 141; *18:* 248; *55:* 85,86, 87, 88, 93, 104; *60:* 67; *78:* 263; *82:* 110; *96:* 157, 159; *101:* 84; *132:* 35; *162:* 93, 94
Lobel, Arnold *1:* 188, 189; *5:* 12; *6:* 147; *7:* 167, 209; *18:* 190, 191; *25:* 39, 43; *27:* 40; *29:* 174; *52:* 127; *55:* 89, 91, 94, 95, 97, 98, 99, 100, 101, 102,103, 105, 106; *60:* 18, 31; *66:* 181, 183; *75:* 57; *82:* 246; *136:* 146
Lobel, Gillian *190:* 21
Lobo, Jen *229:* 53
Locker, Thomas *109:* 134
Lodge, Bernard *107:* 125, 126; *153:* 93
Loeb, Jeph *153:* 177
Lodge, Jo *112:* 119
Loefgren, Ulf *3:* 108
Loescher, Ann *20:* 108
Loescher, Gil *20:* 108
Loew, David *93:* 184; *171:* 120; *211:* 187
Lofting, Hugh *15:* 182, 183; *100:* 161, 162
Lofts, Pamela *60:* 188
Loh, George *38:* 88
Lomberg, Jon *58:* 160
Lonette, Reisie *11:* 211; *12:* 168; *13:* 56; *36:* 122; *43:* 155
Long, Ethan *168:* 146; *178:* 12; *182:* 120, 121; *196:* 124; *223:* 116, 117
Long, Laurel *162:* 135; *190:* 11; *203:* 113, 114; *228:* 212
Long, Loren *99:* 176; *172:* 65; *182:* 78; *188:* 114, 115
Long, Melinda *152:* 128
Long, Miles *115:* 174
Long, Sally *42:* 184
Long, Sylvia *74:* 168; *132:* 63; *179:* 134
Longoni, Eduardo *73:* 85
Longtemps, Ken *17:* 123; *29:* 221; *69:* 82
Looser, Heinz *YABC 2:* 208
Lopez, Loretta *190:* 100
López, Rafael *197:* 160; *198:* 85
Lopshire, Robert *6:* 149; *21:* 117; *34:* 166; *73:* 13
Lord, John Vernon *21:* 104; *23:* 25; *51:* 22
Lorenz, Albert *40:* 146; *115:* 127
Lorenzen, Geoffrey *229:* 24
Loretta, Sister Mary *33:* 73
Lorraine, Walter H. *3:* 110; *4:* 123; *16:* 192; *103:* 119
Los, Marek *146:* 22; *193:* 23
Loss, Joan *11:* 163
Louderback, Walt *YABC 1:* 164
Loughridge, Stuart *214:* 131
Louis, Catherine *212:* 186
Lousada, Sandra *40:* 138
Louth, Jack *149:* 252; *151:* 191, 192
Love, Judy *173:* 43; *196:* 40
Lovelock, Brian *214:* 132, 197
Low, Joseph *14:* 124, 125; *18:* 68; *19:* 194; *31:* 166; *80:* 239
Low, William *62:* 175; *80:* 147; *112:* 194; *150:* 202; *169:* 175; *177:* 110; *192:* 27
Lowe, Vicky *177:* 130
Lowenheim, Alfred *13:* 65, 66
Lowenstein, Sallie *116:* 90, 91
Lowery, Mike *227:* 115
Lowitz, Anson *17:* 124; *18:* 215
Lowrey, Jo *8:* 133
Loxton, Daniel *229:* 109
Lubach, Vanessa *142:* 152
Lubell, Winifred *1:* 207; *3:* 15; *6:* 151
Lubin, Leonard B. *19:* 224; *36:* 79, 80; *45:* 128, 129,131, 132, 133, 134, 135, 136, 137, 139, 140, 141; *70:* 95; *YABC2:* 96
Lucas, David *208:* 148
Lucht, Irmgard *82:* 145
Ludwig, Helen *33:* 144, 145
Luebs, Robin *212:* 109
Lufkin, Raymond *38:* 138; *44:* 48
Luhrs, Henry *7:* 123; *11:* 120
Lujan, Tonita *82:* 33
Lupo, Dom *4:* 204

Lustig, Loretta *30:* 186; *46:* 134, 135, 136, 137
Lutes, Jason *210:* 163
Luthardt, Kevin *172:* 125, 126; *217:* 2
Luxbacher, Irene *153:* 145; *219:* 112, 113
Luzak, Dennis *52:* 121; *99:* 142
Lydbury, Jane *82:* 98
Lydecker, Laura *21:* 113; *42:* 53
Lynch, Charles *16:* 33
Lynch, Marietta *29:* 137; *30:* 171
Lynch, P.J. *126:* 228; *129:* 110; *132:* 247; *183:* 64; *207:* 184; *213:* 100, 101, 102
Lyne, Alison Davis *188:* 118, 198
Lyon, Carol *102:* 26
Lyon, Elinor *6:* 154
Lyon, Fred *14:* 16
Lyon, Lea *212:* 110
Lyon, Tammie *175:* 170
Lyons, Oren *8:* 193
Lyster, Michael *26:* 41

M

Maas, Dorothy *6:* 175
Maas, Julie *47:* 61
Macaulay, David *46:* 139, 140, 141, 142, 143, 144, 145, 147, 149, 150; *72:* 167, 168, 169; *137:* 129, 130, 131, 132
MacCarthy, Patricia *69:* 141
Macdonald, Alister *21:* 55
Macdonald, Roberta *19:* 237; *52:* 164
MacDonald, Norman *13:* 99
MacDonald, Ross *201:* 103
MacDonald, Suse *54:* 41; *109* 138; *130:* 156; *193:* 106, 107, 109, 110
Mace, Varian *49:* 159
MacEachern, Stephen *206:* 2
Macguire, Robert Reid *18:* 67
Machetanz, Fredrick *34:* 147, 148
MacInnes, Ian *35:* 59
MacIntyre, Elisabeth *17:* 127, 128
Mack, Jeff *161:* 128; *194:* 119, 120; *219:* 67; *225:* 135
Mack, Stan *17:* 129; *96:* 33
Mackay, Donald *17:* 60
MacKaye, Arvia *32:* 119
Mackenzie, Robert *204:* 78
Mackenzie, Stuart *73:* 213
MacKenzie, Garry *33:* 159
Mackie, Clare *87:* 134
Mackinlay, Miguel *27:* 22
MacKinstry, Elizabeth *15:* 110; *42:* 139, 140, 141, 142, 143,144, 145
MacLeod, Lee *91:* 167
Maclise, Daniel *YABC 2:* 257
Macnaughton, Tina *182:* 145; *218:* 106, 107
MacRae, Tom *181:* 112
Madden, Don *3:* 112, 113; *4:* 33, 108, 155; *7:* 193; *78:* 12; *YABC 2:* 211
Maddison, Angela Mary *10:* 83
Madrid, Erwin *229:* 117
Madsen, Jim *146:* 259; *152:* 237; *184:* 106; *197:* 21; *202:* 103, 104
Maestro, Giulio *8:* 124; *12:* 17; *13:* 108; *25:* 182; *54:* 147; *59:* 114, 115, 116, 117, 118, 121, 123, 124, 125,126, 127; *68:* 37, 38; *106:* 129, 130, 131, 136, 137, 138
Maffia, Daniel *60:* 200
Maggio, Viqui *58:* 136, 181; *74:* 150; *75:* 90; *85:* 159; *90:* 158; *109:* 184; *193:* 113
Magnus, Erica *77:* 123
Magnuson, Diana *28:* 102; *34:* 190; *41:* 175
Magoon, Scott *181:* 104; *217:* 165; *222:* 126
Magovern, Peg *103:* 123; *218:* 164
Maguire, Sheila *41:* 100
Magurn, Susan *91:* 30
Mahony, Will *37:* 120
Mahony, Will *85:* 116
Mahood, Kenneth *24:* 141

Mahurin, Matt *164:* 225; *175:* 95; *189:* 37; *196:* 14; *209:* 163; *229:* 179
Maik, Henri *9:* 102
Maione, Heather *106:* 5; *178:* 8; *189:* 126, 127; *193:* 58
Maisto, Carol *29:* 87
Maitland, Antony *1:* 100, 176; *8:* 41; *17:* 246; *24:* 46; *25:* 177, 178; *32:* 74; *60:* 65, 195; *67:* 156; *87:* 131; *101:* 110
Majewski, Dawn W. *169:* 95
Mak, Kam *72:* 25; *75:* 43; *87:* 186; *97:* 24; *102:* 154; *149:* 195; *186:* 28; *209:* 132
Makie, Pam *37:* 117
Maktima, Joe *116:* 191
Maland, Nick *99:* 77
Male, Alan *132:* 64
Malone, James Hiram *84:* 161
Malone, Nola Langner *82:* 239
Malone, Peter *191:* 121, 122, 123
Malsberg, Edward *51:* 175
Malvern, Corinne *2:* 13; *34:* 148, 149
Manchess, Gregory *165:* 241; *203:* 119
Mancusi, Stephen *63:* 198, 199
Mandelbaum, Ira *31:* 115
Manders, John *138:* 152, 155; *188:* 171; *190:* 92; *199:* 5; *217:* 52; *219:* 35; *219:* 115, 116, 117
Mandine, Selma *228:* 103
Manet, Edouard *23:* 170
Mangiat, Jeff *173:* 127
Mangurian, David *14:* 133
Manham, Allan *42:* 109; *77:* 180; *80:* 227
Manley, Matt *103:* 167; *117:* 98; *172:* 49; *212:* 207
Manna, Giovanni *178:* 44
Manniche, Lise *31:* 121
Manning, Jane *96:* 203
Manning, Jo *63:* 154
Manning, Lawrence *191:* 153
Manning, Maurie J. *211:* 116
Manning, Mick *176:* 139; *224:* 57
Manning, Samuel F. *5:* 75
Mantel, Richard *57:* 73; *63:* 106; *82:* 255
Mantha, John *205:* 164; *217:* 117
Maraja *15:* 86; *YABC 1:* 28; *2:* 115
Marcellino, Fred *20:* 125; *34:* 222; *53:* 125; *58:* 205; *61:* 64, 121, 122; *68:* 154, 156, 157, 158, 159; *72:* 25; *86:* 184; *98:* 181; *118:* 129, 130, 131; *149:* 218; *194:* 7
Marchesi, Stephen *34:* 140; *46:* 72; *50:* 147; *66:* 239; *70:* 33; *73:* 18, 114, 163; *77:* 47, 76,147; *78:* 79; *80:* 30; *81:* 6; *89:* 66; *93:* 21,130; *94:* 94; *97:* 66; *98:* 96; *114:* 115, 116
Marchiori, Carlos *14:* 60
Marciano, John Bemelmans *118:* 133; *167:* 110, 111, 112
Marconi, Guilherme *220:* 143
Marcus, Barry David *139:* 248; *145:* 18
Maren, Julie *199:* 73
Margules, Gabriele *21:* 120
Mariana
    See Foster, Marian Curtis
Mariano, Michael *52:* 108
Marino, Dorothy *6:* 37; *14:* 135
Mario, Heide Stetson *101:* 202
Maris, Ron *71:* 123
Maritz, Nicolaas *85:* 123
Mark, Mona *65:* 105; *68:* 205; *116:* 213
Markham, R.L. *17:* 240
Marklew, Gilly *211:* 118
Marks, Alan *104:* 104; *109:* 182; *164:* 92; *185:* 134; *187:* 120, 121, 122; *218:* 114, 115
Marks, Cara *54:* 9
Marks, Colin *203:* 129
Marokvia, Artur *31:* 122
Marquez, Susan *108:* 121; *219:* 95
Marrella, Maria Pia *62:* 116
Marriott, Pat *30:* 30; *34:* 39; *35:* 164, 165, 166; *44:* 170; *48:* 186, 187, 188, 189, 191, 192, 193; *91:* 92

Mars, W.T. *1:* 161; *3:* 115; *4:* 208, 225; *5:* 92, 105, 186; *8:* 214; *9:* 12; *13:* 121; *27:* 151; *31:* 180; *38:* 102; *48:* 66; *62:* 164, 165; *64:* 62; *68:* 229; *79:* 55
Marschall, Ken *85:* 29
Marsh, Christine *3:* 164
Marsh, James *73:* 137
Marsh, Reginald *17:* 5; *19:* 89; *22:* 90, 96
Marshall, Anthony D. *18:* 216
Marshall, Felicia *170:* 190
Marshall, James *6:* 160; *40:* 221; *42:* 24, 25, 29; *51:* 111, 112, 113, 114, 115, 116, 117, 118, 119, 120, 121; *64:* 13; *75:* 126, 127, 128, 129; *102:* 10, 12; *216:* 26, 28
Marshall, Janet *97:* 154
Marstall, Bob *55:* 145; *84:* 153, 170; *104:* 145; *154:* 166, 167, 168
Martchenko, Michael *50:* 129, 153, 155, 156, 157; *83:* 144,145; *154:* 137, 138, 139
Marten, Ruth *129:* 52
Martin, Brad *199:* 186
Martin, Charles E. *70:* 144
Martin, Courtney A. *214:* 28
Martin, David Stone *24:* 232; *62:* 4
Martin, Fletcher *18:* 213; *23:* 151
Martin, Rene *7:* 144; *42:* 148, 149, 150
Martin, Richard E. *51:* 157; *131:* 203
Martin, Ron *32:* 81
Martin, Stefan *8:* 68; *32:* 124, 126; *56:* 33
Martin, Whitney *166:* 137
Martinez, Ed *58:* 192; *72:* 231; *77:* 33; *80:* 214; *167:* 123
Martinez, John *6:* 113; *118:* 13; *139:* 143
Martinez, Sergio *158:* 190; *220:* 156
Martini, Angela *183:* 161; *226:* 195
Martiniere, Stephan *171:* 130
Marton, Jirina *95:* 127, 128; *144:* 145
Martorell, Antonio *84:* 6; *97:* 161
Martucci, Griesbach *52:* 106
Marvin, Frederic *83:* 86
Marx, Robert F. *24:* 143
Marzollo, Jean *190:* 127
Masefield, Judith *19:* 208, 209
Masheris, Robert *51:* 156
Masiello, Ralph *186:* 171; *214:* 134
Mason, George F. *14:* 139
Mason, Robert *84:* 96
Masse, Josée *208:* 45; *217:* 19; *221:* 134
Massey, Barbara *68:* 142
Massie, Diane Redfield *16:* 194
Massie, Kim *31:* 43
Massini, Sarah *213:* 79
Mataya, David *121:* 66
Mathers, Petra *119:* 135; *163:* 104; *176:* 143, 144; *187:* 142; *196:* 101
Mathewuse, James *51:* 143
Mathieu, Joseph *14:* 33; *39:* 206; *43:* 167; *56:* 180; *79:* 126; *94:* 147; *185:* 140
Matje, Martin *169:* 177, 178; *172:* 180
Matsubara, Naoko *12:* 121
Matsuda, Shizu *13:* 167
Matsuoka, Mei *192:* 135; *214:* 84
Matte, L'Enc *22:* 183
Mattelson, Marvin *36:* 50, 51
Matheson, Jenny *180:* 132; *222:* 153
Matthews, Elizabeth *194:* 128; *223:* 35
Matthews, F. Leslie *4:* 216
Matthews, Tina *190:* 130
Mattingly, David *71:* 76, 77; *82:* 64; *91:* 216, 217; *109:* 25
Matulay, Laszlo *5:* 18; *43:* 168
Matus, Greta *12:* 142
Maughan, Bill *181:* 31; *211:* 211
Mauldin, Bill *27:* 23
Mauterer, Erin Marie *119:* 5
Mawicke, Tran *9:* 137; *15:* 191; *47:* 100
Mawson, Matt *74:* 115
Max, Peter *45:* 146, 147, 148, 149, 150
Maxie, Betty *40:* 135
Maxwell, John Alan *1:* 148
May, Katie *225:* 128

May, Steve *204:* 30
Mayan, Earl *7:* 193
Maydak, Michael S. *220:* 117
Mayer, Bill *200:* 138
Mayer, Danuta *117:* 103
Mayer, Marianna *32:* 132
Mayer, Mercer *11:* 192; *16:* 195, 196; *20:* 55, 57; *32:* 129, 130, 132, 133, 134; *41:* 144, 248, 252; *58:* 186; *73:* 140, 142, 143; *137:* 137, 138
Mayforth, Hal *166:* 77
Mayhew, James *85:* 121; *138:* 187; *149:* 140; *204:* 81
Mayhew, Richard *3:* 106
Mayo, Gretchen Will *38:* 81; *84:* 166
Mays, Victor *5:* 127; *8:* 45, 153; *14:* 245; *23:* 50; *34:* 155; *40:* 79; *45:* 158; *54:* 91; *66:* 240
Mazal, Chanan *49:* 104
Maze, Deborah *71:* 83
Mazellan, Ron *75:* 97, 98; *210:* 169
Mazetti, Alan *112:* 72
Mazille, Capucine *96:* 168
Mazza, Adriana Saviozzi *19:* 215
Mazzella, Mary Jo *82:* 165
Mazzetti, Alan *45:* 210
McAfee, Steve *135:* 146; *167:* 176; *191:* 84; *210:* 117; *218:* 34
McAlinden, Paul *112:* 128
McBride, Angus *28:* 49; *103:* 40
McBride, Will *30:* 110
McCaffery, Janet *38:* 145
McCall, Bruce *209:* 119
McCallum, Graham *78:* 78
McCallum, Stephen *141:* 143; *156:* 5; *166:* 228
McCann, Gerald *3:* 50; *4:* 94; *7:* 54; *41:* 121
McCarthy, Dan *174:* 74
McCarthy, Linda *177:* 128; *218:* 104
McCarthy, Meghan *168:* 134; *199:* 74
McCauley, Adam *157:* 36; *184:* 199; *193:* 100; *209:* 122
McCay, Winsor *41:* 124, 126, 128, 129, 130, 131; *77:* 79
McClary, Nelson *1:* 111
McClements, George *196:* 146
McClennan, Connie *210:* 181
McClintock, Barbara *57:* 135; *95:* 130; *146:* 190; *213:* 3, 5, 107, 108
McClintock, Theodore *14:* 141
McCloskey, Robert *1:* 184, 185; *2:* 186, 187; *17:* 209; *39:* 139, 140, 141, 142, 143, 146, 147, 148; *85:* 150, 151; *100:* 172, 173, 174
McClung, Robert *2:* 189; *68:* 166, 167
McClure, Gillian *31:* 132; *150:* 53
McClure, Nikki *218:* 120
McConnel, Jerry *31:* 75, 187
McConnell, Mary *102:* 49
McCord, Kathleen Garry *78:* 236
McCormack, John *66:* 193
McCormick, A.D. *35:* 119
McCormick, Dell J. *19:* 216
McCoy, Glenn *212:* 132
McCrady, Lady *16:* 198; *39:* 127
McCrea, James *3:* 122; *33:* 216
McCrea, Ruth *3:* 122; *27:* 102; *33:* 216
McCue, Lisa *65:* 148, 149; *77:* 54; *80:* 132; *175:* 33; *177:* 133, 135; *212:* 136, 137, 138
McCully, Emily Arnold *2:* 89; *4:* 120, 121, 146, 197; *5:* 2, 129; *7:* 191; *11:* 122; *15:* 210; *33:* 23; *35:* 244; *37:* 122; *39:* 88; *40:* 103; *50:* 30,31, 32, 33, 34, 35, 36, 37; *52:* 89, 90; *57:* 6; *62:* 3; *70:* 195; *86:* 96; *96:* 192; *97:* 93; *110:* 143,144; *117:* 47; *167:* 96; *210:* 175, 176; *225:* 179
McCurdy, Michael *13:* 153; *24:* 85; *81:* 160; *82:* 157, 158; *86:* 125; *97:* 92; *117:* 178; *132:* 6; *147:* 159, 160
McCusker, Paul *99:* 19
McDaniel, Jerry *132:* 135
McDaniel, Preston *160:* 206; *170:* 139

McDermott, Beverly Brodsky *11:* 180
McDermott, Gerald *16:* 201; *74:* 174, 175; *163:* 150, 151
McDermott, Mike *96:* 187
McDonald, Jill *13:* 155; *26:* 128
McDonald, Mercedes *169:* 118
McDonald, Ralph J. *5:* 123, 195
McDonnell, Flora *146:* 199, 200
McDonnell, Patrick *179:* 153, 154; *221:* 136, 137, 138
McDonough, Don *10:* 163
McElligott, Matt *196:* 147
McElmurry, Jill *137:* 148; *163:* 141; *202:* 186
McElrath-Eslick, Lori *129:* 145; *142:* 21; *173:* 123; *202:* 194; *204:* 88, 89
McEntee, Dorothy *37:* 124
McEwan, Keith *88:* 116; *165:* 122, 123
McEwen, Katharine *169:* 34
McFall, Christie *12:* 144
McFeely, Daniel *160:* 213
McGaw, Laurie *109:* 243; *143:* 216; *211:* 218
McGee, Barbara *6:* 165
McGee, Marni *163:* 153
McGillvray, Kim *158:* 171; *165:* 213; *186:* 183; *190:* 175
McGinley-Nally, Sharon *131:* 19
McGinnis, Robert *110:* 113; *177:* 80
McGovern, Tara *98:* 171
McGraw, Sheila *83:* 146
McGregor, Barbara *200:* 155
McGregor, Malcolm *23:* 27
McGrory, Anik *193:* 120
McGuire, Robert *204:* 57; *209:* 86
McGuirk, Leslie *152:* 159
McHale, John *138:* 190
McHenry, E.B. *193:* 122
McHugh, Tom *23:* 64
McIntosh, Jon *42:* 56
McKay, Donald *2:* 118; *32:* 157; *45:* 151, 152
McKean, Dave *150:* 71; *174:* 156; *197:* 83, 118; *229:* 45, 46
McKeating, Eileen *44:* 58
McKee, David *10:* 48; *21:* 9; *70:* 154, 155; *107:* 139, 140, 141; *134:* 218; *158:* 148, 149, 150, 151; *228:* 171
McKee, Diana *109:* 185
McKelvey, Patrick *164:* 141
McKendry, Joe *170:* 136
McKeveny, Tom *164:* 60; *173:* 79
McKie, Roy *7:* 44
McKie, Todd *205:* 181
McKillip, Kathy *30:* 153
McKinney, Ena *26:* 39
McKinnon, James *136:* 75
McKowen, Scott *172:* 63; *202:* 49
McLachlan, Edward *5:* 89
McLaren, Chesley *133:* 53; *213:* 112; *219:* 31
McLaren, Kirsty *123:* 99; *124:* 226
Mclean, Andrew *113:* 117, 118, 120, 121; *172:* 130, 131
Mclean, Janet *172:* 130
McLean, Meg *94:* 196
McLean, Sammis *32:* 197
McLean, Wilson *90:* 29; *113:* 195
McLoughlin, John C. *47:* 149
McLoughlin, Wayne *102:* 230; *134:* 178; *216:* 196
McMahon, Robert *36:* 155; *69:* 169
McManus, Shawn *85:* 71
McMenemy, Sarah *156:* 139; *211:* 93; *224:* 139; *226:* 152
McMillan, Bruce *22:* 184
McMullan, James *40:* 33; *67:* 172; *87:* 142; *99:* 63, 64; *189:* 133; *196:* 51
McMullen, Nigel *146:* 177
McNeely, Tom *162:* 55
McNaught, Harry *12:* 80; *32:* 136
McNaughton, Colin *39:* 149; *40:* 108; *92:* 144, 145, 146; *134:* 104, 106; *211:* 122, 123, 124
McNicholas, Maureen *38:* 148
McNicholas, Shelagh *173:* 61; *191:* 125, 126

McPhail, David *14:* 105; *23:* 135; *37:* 217, 218, 220,221; *47:* 151, 152, 153, 154, 155, 156, 158, 159, 160, 162, 163, 164; *71:* 211; *81:* 139, 140, 142; *86:* 123; *132:* 150; *140:* 129, 131, 132; *183:* 134, 135, 137; *189:* 132; *219:* 121, 122, 123, 124, 125
McPhee, Richard B. *41:* 133
McPheeters, Neal *78:* 132; *86:* 90; *99:* 162; *111:* 141; *142:* 162
McQuade, Jacqueline *124:* 223
McQueen, Lucinda *28:* 149; *41:* 249; *46:* 206; *53:* 103
McQuillan, Mary *153:* 97; *200:* 140
McVay, Tracy *11:* 68
McVicker, Charles *39:* 150
McWilliam, Howard *219:* 135
Mead, Ben Carlton *43:* 75
Meade, Holly *90:* 102; *94:* 101; *149:* 8; *151:* 107
Mecray, John *33:* 62
Meddaugh, Susan *20:* 42; *29:* 143; *41:* 241; *77:* 50; *84:* 173, 174, 175, 176, 177, 178; *125:* 160, 161, 162; *176:* 148, 149, 150, 151
Meehan, Dennis B. *56:* 144
Meents, Len W. *73:* 147, 150
Meers, Tony *99:* 113
Meisel, Paul *98:* 137; *124:* 18; *162:* 180; *179:* 16; *181:* 22; *194:* 154; *221:* 5; *224:* 100, 101, 102, 133
Melanson, Luc *149:* 229; *198:* 97, 98; *221:* 166
Melendez, Francisco *72:* 180
Melling, David *202:* 199
Melnychuk, Monika *153:* 65
Melo, Esperança *196:* 90
Melo, John *16:* 285; *58:* 203
Meloni, Maria Teresa *98:* 62
Meltzer, Ericka
  See O'Rourke, Ericka
Menasco, Milton *43:* 85
Menchin, Scott *188:* 129
Mendelson, Steven T. *86:* 154
Mendelssohn, Felix *19:* 170
Mendola, Christopher *88:* 223
Meng, Heinz *13:* 158
Merian, Maria Sibylla *140:* 88
Mero, Lee *34:* 68
Merrell, David *205:* 3
Merrill, Frank T. *16:* 147; *19:* 71; *YABC 1:* 226, 229,273
Merriman, Rachel *98:* 108; *114:* 122; *149:* 142
Merveille, David *200:* 142
Meryman, Hope *27:* 41
Meryweather, Jack *10:* 179
Meseldzija, Petar *168:* 97
Meserve, Jessica *184:* 137; *211:* 127
Messick, Dale *64:* 150, 151, 152
Meth, Harold *24:* 203
Meyer, Alex Eben *226:* 60
Meyer, Herbert *19:* 189
Meyer, Renate *6:* 170
Meyers, Bob *11:* 136
Meyers, Nancy *172:* 124
Meynell, Louis *37:* 76
Micale, Albert *2:* 65; *22:* 185
Miccuci, Charles *82:* 163; *144:* 150
Micich, Paul *164:* 163
Middleton, Jeffrey *177:* 173; *222:* 157
Middleton, Joshua *208:* 146; *219:* 24
Middleton-Sandford, Betty *2:* 125
Mieke, Anne *45:* 74
Mighell, Patricia *43:* 134
Miglio, Paige *101:* 203; *151:* 223; *201:* 118, 119; *204:* 162
Mikec, Larry *204:* 125
Mikolaycak, Charles *9:* 144; *12:* 101; *13:* 212; *21:* 121; *22:* 168; *30:* 187; *34:* 103, 150; *37:* 183; *43:* 179; *44:* 90; *46:* 115, 118, 119; *49:* 25; *78:* 121, 122, 205, 207; *81:* 4
Milelli, Pascal *129:* 66; *135:* 153; *187:* 45
Miles, Elizabeth *117:* 77

Miles, Jennifer *17:* 278
Milgrim, David *158:* 157; *187:* 125, 126, 128; *223:* 124, 125, 126, 127
Milhous, Katherine *15:* 193; *17:* 51
Millais, John E. *22:* 230, 231
Millar, H.R. *YABC 1:* 194, 195, 203
Millard, C.E. *28:* 186
Millard, Kerry *105:* 124; *204:* 93, 94
Miller, Don *15:* 195; *16:* 71; *20:* 106; *31:* 178
Miller, Edna *29:* 148
Miller, Edward *115:* 64; *183:* 140, 141; *218:* 129, 130, 131
Miller, Frank J. *25:* 94
Miller, Grambs *18:* 38; *23:* 16
Miller, Ian *99:* 128
Miller, Jane *15:* 196
Miller, Marcia *13:* 233
Miller, Marilyn *1:* 87; *31:* 69; *33:* 157
Miller, Mitchell *28:* 183; *34:* 207
Miller, Phil *175:* 150
Miller, Shane *5:* 140
Miller, Virginia *81:* 206
Millman, Isaac *172:* 18
Mills, Elaine *72:* 181
Mills, Judith Christine *130:* 168, 169
Mills, Lauren *92:* 170
Mills, Yaroslava Surmach *35:* 169, 170; *46:* 114
Millsap, Darrel *51:* 102
Milone, Karen *89:* 169; *222:* 149
Milord, Susan *147:* 163, 164; *200:* 144
Milot, René *226:* 127
Milton, Debbie *162:* 161
Mims, Ashley *170:* 51
Min, Willemien *222:* 62
Miner, Julia *98:* 69
Minor, Wendell *39:* 188; *52:* 87; *56:* 171; *58:* 116; *62:* 56; *66:* 109; *74:* 93; *78:* 129; *94:* 67; *117:* 12, 13; *124:* 84, 86; *136:* 121; *164:* 168, 169; *170:* 71; *199:* 79, 80, 81, 82; *217:* 63; *223:* 149; *226:* 90, 91, 92
Minter, Daniel *176:* 154; *179:* 177
Mirocha, Paul *81:* 133; *192:* 148; *194:* 36
Misako Rocks! *192:* 149, 150
Mitchell, Judith *109:* 117
Mitchell, Mark *91:* 208
Mitchell, Tracy *190:* 15
Mitgutsch, Ali *76:* 161
Mitsuhashi, Yoko *45:* 153
Miyake, Yoshi *38:* 141
Mizumura, Kazue *10:* 143; *18:* 223; *36:* 159
Mochi, Ugo *8:* 122; *38:* 150
Mock, Paul *55:* 83; *123:* 32
Modarressi, Mitra *90:* 236; *126:* 168; *173:* 165, 166; *200:* 147, 148
Modell, Frank *39:* 152
Mogenson, Jan *74:* 183
Mohn, Susan *89:* 224
Mohr, Mark *133:* 201
Mohr, Nicholasa *8:* 139; *113:* 127
Molan, Christine *60:* 177; *84:* 183
Moldon, Peter L. *49:* 168
Molk, Laurel *92:* 150
Mollica, Gene *197:* 11
Momaday, N. Scott *48:* 159
Mombourquette, Paul *112:* 91; *126:* 142
Monk, Julie *165:* 231; *191:* 96
Monks, Lydia *189:* 136, 137
Monroe, Chris *219:* 133
Monroy, Manuel *199:* 192
Montgomery, Lucy *150:* 126
Montgomery, Michael G. *208:* 159
Montgomery-Higham, Amanda *169:* 131
Monteiel, David *201:* 95
Montiel, David *69:* 106; *84:* 145
Montijo, Rhode *193:* 164
Montresor, Beni *2:* 91; *3:* 138; *38:* 152, 153, 154,155, 156, 157, 158, 159, 160; *68:* 63
Montserrat, Pep *128:* 135; *181:* 119; *184:* 53
Moon, Carl *25:* 183, 184, 185
Moon, Eliza *14:* 40

Moon, Ivan *22:* 39; *38:* 140
Moore, Adrienne *67:* 147
Moore, Agnes Kay Randall *43:* 187
Moore, Cyd *117:* 107, 108; *159:* 137, 138; *186:* 148, 149, 151; *203:* 15; *214:* 138, 139
Moore, Gustav *127:* 181, 182; *170:* 162, 163
Moore, Jackie *128:* 79
Moore, Janet *63:* 153
Moore, Margie *176:* 156; *221:* 125; *224:* 106, 107
Moore, Mary *29:* 160
Moore, Patrick *184:* 121
Moore, Yvette *101:* 11, 12; *154:* 141
Mora, Giovanni *179:* 127; *184:* 11
Mora, Raul Mina *20:* 41
Moraes, Odilon *102:* 144
Morales, Magaly *225:* 137
Morales, Yuyi *154:* 144; *226:* 120
Moran, Rosslyn *111:* 26
Moran, Tom *60:* 100
Mordan, C.B. *193:* 115
Mordvinoff, Nicolas *15:* 179
Moreno, René King *169:* 59; *190:* 133, 209; *212:* 52
Morgan, Barbara *169:* 116
Morgan, Jacqui *58:* 57
Morgan, Mary *114:* 133, 134, 135; *123:* 11; *213:* 115, 116, 117
Morgan, Tom *42:* 157
Morgan, Pierr *173:* 148
Morgenstern, Michael *158:* 7, 57; *171:* 103; *174:* 60; *226:* 12
Morice, Dave *93:* 142
Morin, Paul *73:* 132; *79:* 130; *88:* 140; *137:* 143
Moriuchi, Mique *177:* 203
Morozumi, Atsuko *110:* 155; *217:* 126, 127
Morrill, Leslie *18:* 218; *29:* 177; *33:* 84; *38:* 147; *42:* 127; *44:* 93; *48:* 164, 165, 167, 168, 169, 170,171; *49:* 162; *63:* 136, 180; *70:* 72; *71:* 70, 91,92; *72:* 228; *80:* 163, 164, 165; *90:* 121; *121:* 88; *178:* 117
Morrill, Rowena A. *84:* 16; *98:* 163
Morris *47:* 91
Morris, Frank *55:* 133; *60:* 28; *76:* 2
Morris, Harry O. *119:* 138
Morris, Jackie *128:* 194; *144:* 119; *151:* 146; *202:* 126, 127; *204:* 83; *211:* 80; *214:* 163
Morris, Jennifer E. *179:* 157
Morris, Oradel Nolen *128:* 180
Morris, Tony *62:* 146; *70:* 97
Morrison, Bill *42:* 116; *66:* 170; *69:* 40
Morrison, Gordon *87:* 150; *113:* 93; *128:* 181, 182; *183:* 144, 145, 146
Morrison, Frank *169:* 162; *205:* 156; *224:* 121; *226:* 154
Morrison, Taylor *159:* 144, 145; *187:* 131
Morrow, Gray *2:* 64; *5:* 200; *10:* 103, 114; *14:* 175
Morse, Scott *200:* 149, 150
Morton, Lee Jack *32:* 140
Morton, Marian *3:* 185
Mosberg, Hilary *117:* 195; *118:* 164; *149:* 55
Moser, Barry *56:* 68, 117, 118, 119, 120, 121, 122, 123, 124; *59:* 141; *60:* 160; *79:* 91, 147, 149, 151, 152; *82:* 81; *90:* 118; *91:* 35; *95:* 210; *97:* 91, 93; *102:* 152; *126:* 4; *128:* 175; *133:* 141; *138:* 167, 171, 174; *153:* 205; *174:* 130; *185:* 152, 154; *195:* 163; *204:* 115; *209:* 201
Moser, Cara *90:* 118; *138:* 167
Moses, Grandma *18:* 228
Moses, Will *178:* 170, 171
Moskof, Martin Stephen *27:* 152
Mosley, Francis *57:* 144
Moss, Donald *11:* 184
Moss, Geoffrey *32:* 198
Moss, Marissa *71:* 130; *104:* 127; *163:* 156; *216:* 164, 165, 166
Most, Bernard *48:* 173; *91:* 142, 143; *134:* 120
Mourning, Tuesday *205:* 25; *220:* 68; *221:* 42

Mowll, Joshua *188:* 133
Mowry, Carmen *50:* 62
Moxley, Sheila *96:* 174; *169:* 26; *206:* 16
Moyers, William *21:* 65
Moyler, Alan *36:* 142
Mozley, Charles *9:* 87; *20:* 176, 192, 193; *22:* 228; *25:* 205; *33:* 150; *43:* 170, 171, 172, 173, 174; *YABC2:* 89
Mueller, Hans Alexander *26:* 64; *27:* 52, 53
Mugnaini, Joseph *11:* 35; *27:* 52, 53; *35:* 62
Mujica, Rick *72:* 67; *88:* 95; *111:* 53; *180:* 185; *197:* 70
Mullen, Douglas *180:* 178
Muller, Robin *86:* 161
Muller, Steven *32:* 167
Muller, Jorg *35:* 215; *67:* 138, 139
Mulock, Julie *163:* 112
Mullins, Edward S. *10:* 101
Mullins, Patricia *51:* 68
Multer, Scott *80:* 108
Munari, Bruno *15:* 200
Munch, Edvard *140:* 143
Munowitz, Ken *14:* 148; *72:* 178, 179
Muñoz, Claudio *208:* 161
Munoz, William *42:* 160
Munro, Roxie *58:* 134; *136:* 177; *137:* 218; *184:* 133, 134; *223:* 130, 132, 133
Munsinger, Lynn *33:* 161; *46:* 126; *71:* 92; *82:* 80; *89:* 218; *92:* 125; *94:* 157, 158, 159, 160; *98:* 196; *103:* 198; *142:* 143; *145:* 133, 134, 136; *153:* 203; *176:* 162; *177:* 140, 141, 142; *189:* 113, 114, 116, 117; *201:* 42; *221:* 148, 149,150
Munson, Russell *13:* 9
Munster, Sebastian *166:* 107
Munzar, Barbara *149:* 75
Murdocca, Salvatore *73:* 212; *98:* 132; *111:* 168; *157:* 228; *164:* 257
Murphy, Bill *5:* 138; *130:* 170
Murphy, Jill *37:* 142; *70:* 166; *142:* 132, 134
Murphy, Kelly *130:* 212; *143:* 119; *176:* 158; *190:* 135
Murphy, Liz *210:* 183; *212:* 157
Murphy, Mary *196:* 158
Murphy, Tom *192:* 40
Murr, Karl *20:* 62
Murray, Joe *175:* 37
Murray, Ossie *43:* 176
Mussino, Attilio *29:* 131; *100:* 164
Mutchler, Dwight *1:* 25
Myers, Bernice *9:* 147; *36:* 75; *81:* 146, 147, 148
Muth, Jon J. *165:* 169; *167:* 109; *190:* 227; *193:* 59; *228:* 206
Myers, Christopher *183:* 150; *193:* 139
Myers, Duane O. *99:* 145
Myers, Tim *147:* 168
Myers, V.G. *142:* 41
Myers, Lou *11:* 2

N

Nachreiner, Tom *29:* 182
Nacht, Merle *65:* 49
Nadler, Ellis *88:* 91
Nagle, Shane *180:* 223
Nagy, Ian *195:* 64
Najaka, Marlies *62:* 101
Nakai, Michael *30:* 217; *54:* 29
Nakata, Hiroe *157:* 156; *162:* 30; *205:* 124, 125
Nakatani, Chiyoko *12:* 124
Narahashi, Keiko *77:* 188; *82:* 213; *115:* 142, 143, 144
Nascimbene, Yan *133:* 128; *173:* 132, 133
Nash, Lesa *87:* 135
Nash, Linell *46:* 175
Nash, Scott *130:* 36; *188:* 196; *224:* 180
Naso, John *33:* 183

Nason, Thomas W. *14:* 68
Nasser, Muriel *48:* 74
Nast, Thomas *21:* 29; *28:* 23; *51:* 132, 133, 134, 135,136, 137, 138, 139, 141
Nasta, Vincent *78:* 185
Natale, Vincent *76:* 3; *78:* 125; *112:* 47; *166:* 81; *174:* 189; *185:* 212; *197:* 59; *218:* 35
Natchev, Alexi *96:* 177
Nathan, Charlott *125:* 151
Nathan, Cheryl *150:* 104; *186:* 112
Natti, Susanna *20:* 146; *32:* 141, 142; *35:* 178; *37:* 143; *71:* 49; *93:* 98; *125:* 166, 168; *126:* 228; *151:* 6; *178:* 8; *188:* 106
Navarra, Celeste Scala *8:* 142
Naylor, Penelope *10:* 104
Nazz, James *72:* 8
Nebel, M. *45:* 154
Neebe, William *7:* 93
Needham, Dave *196:* 85
Needler, Jerry *12:* 93
Neel, Alice *31:* 23
Neely, Beth *119:* 184
Neely, Keith R. *46:* 124
Neff, Leland *78:* 74
Negri, Rocco *3:* 213; *5:* 67; *6:* 91, 108; *12:* 159
Negrin, Fabian *174:* 125; *175:* 15; *223:* 91
Neidigh, Sherry *128:* 53; *204:* 101, 102, 103; *222:* 95
Neilan, Eujin Kim *180:* 241; *200:* 151, 152
Neill, John R. *18:* 8, 10, 11, 21, 30; *100:* 22
Neilsen, Cliff *158:* 131; *177:* 112, 121; *209:* 8; *215:* 150
Neilsen, Terese *116:* 74
Nelson, Craig *62:* 151; *153:* *183:* 86
Nelson, Gail White *68:* 140
Nelson, Jennifer *129:* 152; *199:* 132
Nelson, Kadir *151:* 185; *154:* 146, 147; *157:* 189, 222; *181:* 122, 124; *197:* 155; *213:* 122, 123, 124
Nelson, Melissa *224:* 87
Nelson, S.D. *131:* 34; *181:* 126, 127; *228:* 23
Ness, Evaline *1:* 164, 165; *2:* 39; *3:* 8; *10:* 147; *12:* 53; *26:* 150, 151, 152, 153; *49:* 30, 31, 32; *56:* 30; *60:* 113
Neubecker, Robert *170:* 143; *214:* 157
Neville, Vera *2:* 182
Nevins, Daniel *191:* 173
Nevwirth, Allan *79:* 168
Newberry, Clare Turlay *1:* 170
Newbold, Greg *108:* 125; *145:* 199; *151:* 23; *193:* 178; *197:* 10; *199:* 92, 93
Newfeld, Frank *14:* 121; *26:* 154
Newland, Gillian *220:* 132
Newman, Andy *149:* 61; *195:* 63
Newman, Ann *43:* 90
Newman, Barbara Johansen *191:* 137, 138
Newsham, Ian *143:* 162
Newsom, Carol *40:* 159; *44:* 60; *47:* 189; *65:* 29; *70:* 192; *80:* 36; *85:* 137, 138; *92:* 167; *191:* 82
Newsom, Tom *49:* 149; *71:* 13, 62; *75:* 156; *91:* 113
Newton, Jill *83:* 105; *200:* 154
Nez, John *218:* 136
Ng, Michael *29:* 171
Ng, Simon *167:* 7
Ngui, Marc *229:* 50
Nguyen, Vincent *189:* 49; *226:* 160; *229:* 172
Nichols, Sandy *219:* 103
Nicholson, William *15:* 33, 34; *16:* 48
Nickens, Bessie *104:* 153
Nicklaus, Carol *45:* 194; *62:* 132, 133
Nickle, John *181:* 128
Nickless, Will *16:* 139
Nicholas, Corasue *154:* 20
Nicolas *17:* 130, 132, 133; *YABC 2:* 215
Niebrugge, Jane *6:* 118
Nielsen, Cliff *95:* 207, 208; *105:* 58; *114:* 112; *124:* 12; *125:* 91, 92; *132:* 224; *135:* 187; *136:* 40; *137:* 168; *145:* 54; *149:* 28; *158:*

129; *165:* 64, 158; *168:* 169; *170:* 6; *175:*
114, 116; *187:* 75, 76; *194:* 107; *197:* 172;
201: 14; *208:* 192; *211:* 186; *216:* 215; *217:*
67; *224:* 61, 62
Nielsen, Jon *6:* 100; *24:* 202
Nielsen, Kay *15:* 7; *16:* 211, 212, 213, 215,
217; *22:* 143; *YABC 1:* 32, 33
Niemann, Christoph *191:* 141
Nikola-Lisa, W. *180:* 180
Niland, Deborah *25:* 191; *27:* 156; *135:* 50;
172: 143
Niland, Kilmeny *25:* 191; *75:* 143
Nino, Alex *59:* 145
Ninon *1:* 5; *38:* 101, 103, 108
Nissen, Rie *44:* 35
Nithael, Mark *158:* 237
Nivola, Claire A. *78:* 126; *140:* 147; *208:* 164
Nixon, K. *14:* 152
Nobati, Eugenia *194:* 118
Noble, Louise *61:* 170
Noble, Marty *97:* 168; *125:* 171
Noble, Trinka Hakes *39:* 162; *84:* 157
Nobles, Scott *226:* 159
Noda, Takayo *168:* 143
Noguchi, Yoshie *30:* 99
Nolan, Dennis *42:* 163; *67:* 163; *78:* 189; *82:*
225; *83:* 26; *92:* 169, 170; *103:* 166; *111:*
35; *112:* 213; *127:* 171; *166:* 161; *194:* 218
Noll, Sally *82:* 171
Nolte, Larry *121:* 63, 65
Nones, Eric Jon *61:* 111; *76:* 38; *77:* 177
Noonan, Daniel *100:* 224
Noonan, Julia *4:* 163; *7:* 207; *25:* 151; *91:* 29;
95: 149
Norcia, Ernie *108:* 155; *140:* 47
Nordenskjold, Birgitta *2:* 208
Noreika, Robert *173:* 20; *217:* 24
Norling, Beth *149:* 153, 154; *209:* 77
Norman, Elaine *77:* 72, 176; *94:* 35; *136:* 63;
178: 42
Norman, Mary *36:* 138, 147
Norman, Michael *12:* 117; *27:* 168
Normandin, Luc *227:* 180
Northway, Jennifer *85:* 96
Nostlinger, Christiana *162:* 131
Novak, Linda *166:* 205
Novak, Matt *104:* 132, 133; *165:* 173, 174;
204: 104, 106
Novelli, Luca *61:* 137
Novgorodoff, Danica *215:* 133
Nugent, Cynthia *106:* 189; *205:* 126, 127; *209:*
180
Numberman, Neil *220:* 133
Numeroff, Laura Joffe *28:* 161; *30:* 177
Nurse, Chris *164:* 91
Nussbaumer, Paul *16:* 219; *39:* 117
Nutt, Ken *72:* 69; *97:* 170
Nyce, Helene *19:* 219
Nygren, Tord *30:* 148; *127:* 164

O

Oakley, Graham *8:* 112; *30:* 164, 165; *84:*
188,189, 190, 191, 192
Oakley, Thornton *YABC 2:* 189
Oberheide, Heide *118:* 37
Obligado, Lilian *2:* 28, 66, 67; *6:* 30; *14:* 179;
15: 103; *25:* 84; *61:* 138, 139, 140, 141, 143
Oblinski, Rafael *190:* 139
Obrant, Susan *11:* 186
O'Brien, Anne Sibley *53:* 116, 117; *155:* 115;
213: 127; *224:* 71; *227:* 9
O'Brien, John *41:* 253; *72:* 12; *89:* 59, 60; *98:*
16; *161:* 185; *169:* 16; *180:* 196; *228:* 38
O'Brien, Patrick *193:* 142, 143, 144
O'Brien, Teresa *87:* 89
O'Brien, Tim *93:* 25; *136:* 94; *164:* 57; *169:*
57; *173:* 55; *175:* 86; *184:* 192; *191:* 134;
193: 137; *210:* 159; *224:* 28, 29; *229:* 140

O'Clair, Dennis *127:* 25
O'Connor, George *183:* 153; *228:* 113, 114
Odell, Carole *35:* 47
Odem, Mel *99:* 164; *167:* 84, 87
O'Donohue, Thomas *40:* 89
Oechsli, Kelly *5:* 144, 145; *7:* 115; *8:* 83, 183;
13: 117; *20:* 94; *81:* 199
Ofer, Avi *208:* 143
Offen, Hilda *42:* 207
Ogden, Bill *42:* 59; *47:* 55
Ogg, Oscar *33:* 34
Ogle, Nancy Gray *163:* 144
Ohi, Ruth *90:* 175, 177; *131:* 63; *135:* 106;
175: 107; *179:* 55
Ohlsson, Ib *4:* 152; *7:* 57; *10:* 20; *11:* 90; *19:*
217; *41:* 246; *82:* 106; *92:* 213
Ohtomo, Yasuo *37:* 146; *39:* 212, 213
O'Keefe, Jennifer *136:* 184
O'Kelley, Mattie Lou *36:* 150
Olbinski, Rafal *149:* 27; *158:* 77; *203:* 36
Oldland, Nicholas *223:* 136
O'Leary, Chris *208:* 166
Oleynikov, Igor *202:* 134
Oliver, Isaac *171:* 182
Oliver, Jenni *23:* 121; *35:* 112
Oliver, Narelle *152:* 192; *197:* 129, 130
Oller, Erika *128:* 186; *134:* 126
Olschewski, Alfred *7:* 172
Olsen, Ib Spang *6:* 178, 179; *81:* 164
Olson, Alan *77:* 229
Olson-Brown, Ellen *183:* 154
Olugebefola, Ademola *15:* 205
O'Malley, Kevin *94:* 180; *106:* 8; *113:* 108;
136: 70; *157:* 193; *191:* 146; *203:* 78; *217:*
84
O'Neil, Dan IV *7:* 176
O'Neill, Catharine *72:* 113; *84:* 78; *134:* 153
O'Neill, Jean *22:* 146
O'Neill, Martin *187:* 39; *203:* 118
O'Neill, Michael J. *54:* 172
O'Neill, Rose *48:* 30, 31
O'Neill, Steve *21:* 118
Ono, Chiyo *7:* 97
Orbaan, Albert *2:* 31; *5:* 65, 171; *9:* 8; *14:*
241; *20:* 109
Orbach, Ruth *21:* 112
Orback, Craig *197:* 132
Orfe, Joan *20:* 81
Org, Ed *119:* 93
Ormai, Stella *72:* 129
Ormerod, Jan *55:* 124; *70:* 170, 171; *90:* 39;
132: 172, 173, 174; *147:* 98
Ormsby, Virginia H. *11:* 187
O'Rourke, Ericka *108:* 216; *117:* 194; *111:*
142; *119:* 194; *137:* 152; *150:* 134; *167:* 64;
172: 164; *188:* 163; *191:* 172; *201:* 15; *203:*
75; *209:* 130; *219:* 99
O'Rourke, Ericka Meltzer
   See O'Rourke, Ericka
Orozco, Jose Clemente *9:* 177
Orr, Forrest W. *23:* 9
Orr, N. *19:* 70
Ortiz, Vilma *88:* 158
Osborn, Kathy *152:* 232; *199:* 101, 102; *206:*
67
Osborn, Robert *65:* 49
Osborne, Billie Jean *35:* 209
Osmond, Edward *10:* 111
Ostow, David *223:* 138
O'Sullivan, Tom *3:* 176; *4:* 55; *78:* 195
Otani, June *124:* 42; *156:* 53
Otis, Rebecca *185:* 92
Ottley, Matt *147:* 221; *171:* 133
Otto, Svend *22:* 130, 141; *67:* 188, 189
Oudry, J.B. *18:* 167
Oughton, Taylor *5:* 23; *104:* 136
Overeng, Johannes *44:* 36
Overlie, George *11:* 156
Owens, Carl *2:* 35; *23:* 521

Owens, Gail *10:* 170; *12:* 157; *19:* 16; *22:* 70;
25: 81; *28:* 203, 205; *32:* 221, 222; *36:* 132;
46: 40; *47:* 57; *54:* 66, 67, 68, 69, 70, 71,
72, 73; *71:* 100; *73:* 64; *77:* 157; *80:* 32; *82:*
3; *99:* 226; *224:* 198
Owens, Mary Beth *113:* 202, 203; *191:* 148,
149
Owens, Nubia *84:* 74
Oxenbury, Helen *3:* 150, 151; *24:* 81; *68:* 174,
175,176; *81:* 209; *84:* 213, 245; *129:* 56;
149: 159; *184:* 181; *224:* 147
Oz, Robin *88:* 167; *185:* 181

P

Padgett, Jim *12:* 165
Page, Gail *205:* 128
Page, Homer *14:* 145
Page, Mark *162:* 70
Paget, Sidney *24:* 90, 91, 93, 95, 97
Paget, Walter *64:* 122
Paillot, Jim *173:* 89
Pajouhesh, Noushin *160:* 121
Pak *12:* 76
Pak, Yu Cha *86:* 174
Paladino, Lance *134:* 30
Palazzo, Tony *3:* 152, 153
Palecek, Josef *56:* 136; *89:* 158
Palen, Debbie *135:* 88; *195:* 148, 149
Palencar, John Jude *84:* 12, 45; *85:* 87; *92:*
187; *99:* 128; *110:* 204; *150:* 122; *171:* 86;
207: 36
Palin, Nicki *81:* 201; *89:* 161
Palladini, David *4:* 113; *40:* 176, 177, 178,
179, 181,224, 225; *50:* 138; *78:* 186
Pallarito, Don *43:* 36
Palmer, Carol *158:* 230; *195:* 187
Palmer, Heidi *15:* 207; *29:* 102
Palmer, Jan *42:* 153; *82:* 161
Palmer, Judd *153:* 160, 161
Palmer, Juliette *6:* 89; *15:* 208
Palmer, Kate Salley *104:* 143; *154:* 169
Palmer, Lemuel *17:* 25, 29
Palmisciano, Diane *110:* 62; *162:* 26; *202:*
138, 139
Palmquist, Eric *38:* 133
Pamintuan, Macky *214:* 160
Panesis, Nicholas *3:* 127
Panter, Gary *182:* 191
Panton, Doug *52:* 99
Paparone, Pamela *129:* 174
Papas, William *11:* 223; *50:* 160
Papin, Joseph *26:* 113
Papish, Robin Lloyd *10:* 80
Papp, Robert *198:* 41; *205:* 130; *219:* 53
Paradis, Susan *40:* 216
Paraquin, Charles H. *18:* 166
Pardo DeLange, Alex *179:* 128; *211:* 135, 136
Paris, Peter *31:* 127
Parisi, Elizabeth B. *141:* 82; *164:* 57
Park, Nick *113:* 143
Park, Seho *39:* 110
Park, W.B. *22:* 189
Parker, Ant *82:* 87, 88; *104:* 121
Parker, Buzz *227:* 154
Parker, Jake *227:* 134
Parker, Lewis *2:* 179
Parker, Nancy Winslow *10:* 113; *22:* 164; *28:*
47, 144; *52:* 7; *69:* 153; *91:* 171, 174; *132:*
175
Parker, Robert *4:* 161; *5:* 74; *9:* 136; *29:* 39
Parker, Robert Andrew *11:* 81; *29:* 186; *39:*
165; *40:* 25; *41:* 78; *42:* 123; *43:* 144; *48:*
182; *54:* 140; *74:* 141; *91:* 24; *111:* 115;
151: 201; *154:* 156; *200:* 163, 164; *211:* 67
Parker-Rees, Guy *149:* 145; *193:* 149, 150
Parkin, Trevor *140:* 151
Parkins, David *114:* 123; *146:* 176; *176:* 168;
192: 107; *218:* 139, 140, 141, 148; *224:* 92

Parkinson, Kathy 71: 143; 144: 234
Parkinson, Keith 70: 66
Parks, Gordon, Jr. 33: 228
Parlato, Stephen 222: 137
Parnall, Peter 5: 137; 16: 221; 24: 70; 40: 78; 51: 130; 69: 17, 155; 136: 22, 23, 24
Parnall, Virginia 40: 78
Paros, Jennifer 210: 197
Parow, Lorraine 158: 127
Parr, Todd 134: 139, 140; 179: 163, 164, 165
Parra, John 225: 150
Parrish, Anne 27: 159, 160
Parrish, Dillwyn 27: 159
Parrish, Maxfield 14: 160, 161, 164, 165; 16: 109; 18: 12, 13; YABC 1: 149, 152, 267; 2: 146, 149
Parry, David 26: 156
Parry, Marian 13: 176; 19: 179
Parsons, Garry 197: 135
Partch, Virgil 45: 163, 165
Pascal, David 14: 174
Paschkis, Julie 177: 153, 154; 220: 140, 141
Pasquier, J.A. 16: 91
Pastel, Elyse 201: 123
Pasternak, Robert 119: 53
Paterson, Diane 13: 116; 39: 163; 59: 164, 165, 166,167; 72: 51, 53; 129: 175; 177: 156, 157
Paterson, Helen 16: 93
Patkau, Karen 112: 123
Paton, Jane 15: 271; 35: 176
Patricelli, Leslie 207: 129
Patrick, John 139: 190
Patrick, Pamela 90: 160; 93: 211; 105: 12
Patrick, Tom 190: 103
Patterson, Geoffrey 54: 75
Patterson, Robert 25: 118
Patti, Joyce 187: 145, 146
Patz, Nancy 111: 40; 154: 161; 214: 80
Paul, James 4: 130; 23: 161
Paul, Korky 102: 85
Paull, Grace 24: 157; 87: 127
Paulsen, Ruth Wright 79: 160, 164; 189: 146
Pavlov, Elena 80: 49
Payne, Adam S. 135: 166
Payne, C.F. 145: 138, 140; 179: 168
Payne, Joan Balfour 1: 118
Payne, Tom 170: 27
Payson, Dale 7: 34; 9: 151; 20: 140; 37: 22
Payzant, Charles 21: 147
Peacock, Ralph 64: 118
Peake, Mervyn 22: 136, 149; 23: 162, 163, 164; YABC2: 307
Pearce, Carl 228: 107; 229: 148
Pearson, Larry 38: 225
Pearson, Tracey Campbell 64: 163, 164, 167, 168, 169; 118: 51; 156: 169, 171, 172; 163: 140; 219: 140, 141, 142, 143
Peat, Fern B. 16: 115
Peck, Anne Merriman 18: 241; 24: 155
Peck, Beth 66: 242; 79: 166; 80: 136; 91: 34; 95: 9; 101: 77; 164: 197; 190: 170
Peddicord, Jane Ann 199: 106
Pedersen, Janet 193: 152; 217: 57; 218: 15; 228: 85
Pedersen, Judy 66: 217; 121: 36; 172: 67
Pedersen, Vilhelm YABC 1: 40
Pederson, Sharleen 12: 92
Pedlar, Elaine 161: 45
Peek, Merle 39: 168
Peet, Bill 2: 203; 41: 159, 160, 161, 162, 163; 78: 158, 159, 160, 161
Peguero, Adrian 116: 133
Peguero, Gerard 116: 133
Pels, Winslow Pinney 55: 126
Peltier, Leslie C. 13: 178
Peltzer, Marc 202: 92
Penberthy, Mark 171: 78
Pendle, Alexy 7: 159; 13: 34; 29: 161; 33: 215; 86: 62

Pendola, Joanne 76: 203; 81: 125; 105: 181; 178: 152, 153
Pene du Bois, William 4: 70; 10: 122; 26: 61; 27: 145, 211; 35: 243; 41: 216; 68: 180, 181; 73: 45
Penfound, David 102: 185
Pennington, Eunice 27: 162
Peppe, Mark 28: 142
Peppe, Rodney 4: 164, 165; 74: 187, 188, 189
Pepper, Hubert 64: 143
Percy, Graham 63: 2
Pericoli, Matteo 178: 177
Perini, Ben 173: 77
Perkins, David 60: 68
Perkins, Lucy Fitch 72: 199
Perkins, Lynne Rae 172: 146; 212: 153
Perl, Susan 2: 98; 4: 231; 5: 44, 45, 118; 6: 199; 8: 137; 12: 88; 22: 193; 34: 54, 55; 52: 128; YABC 1: 176
Perlman, Janet 222: 141
Perrone, Donna 78: 166
Perry, Marie Fritz 165: 180
Perry, Patricia 29: 137; 30: 171
Perry, Roger 27: 163
Perske, Martha 46: 83; 51: 108, 147
Persson, Stina 175: 166
Pesek, Ludek 15: 237
Petach, Heidi 149: 166; 200: 207
Peters, David 72: 205; 182: 116
Petersen, Jeff 181: 95
Petersham, Maud 17: 108, 147, 148, 149, 150, 151, 152, 153
Petersham, Miska 17: 108, 147, 148, 149, 150, 151, 152, 153
Peterson, Eric 109: 125
Peterson, Nisse 99: 27
Peterson, R.F. 7: 101
Peterson, Russell 7: 130
Petie, Haris 2: 3; 10: 41, 118; 11: 227; 12: 70
Petit-Roulet, Philippe 227: 12
Petricic, Dusan 153: 75, 76, 77; 170: 12; 172: 13; 176: 170; 179: 56
Petrides, Heidrun 19: 223
Petrone, Valeria 159: 160; 171: 92; 186: 173; 204: 49; 216: 208; 220: 98
Petrosino, Tamara 177: 40; 193: 154, 155
Petruccio, Steven James 67: 159; 127: 5
Pettingill, Ondre 64: 181; 70: 64; 222: 167, 168
Peyo 40: 56, 57
Peyton, K.M. 15: 212
Pfeifer, Herman 15: 262
Pfister, Marcus 83: 165, 166, 167; 146: 152; 150: 160; 207: 132, 134, 135, 136
Pfloog, Jan 124: 60
Pham, LeUyen 160: 48; 175: 154, 156; 179: 149; 201: 124, 125, 126, 127; 204: 28; 208: 206; 217: 92
Phelan, Matt 182: 160; 184: 222; 215: 140, 141; 221: 157
Phillipps, J.C. 218: 142
Phillips, Craig 70: 151; 207: 74; 221: 159; 229: 22
Phillips, Douglas 1: 19
Phillips, F.D. 6: 202
Phillips, Gary R. 223: 23
Phillips, Louise 133: 67
Phillips, Matt 184: 173
Phillips, Thomas 30: 55
Philpot, Glyn 54: 46
Phiz
See Browne, Hablot K.
Piatti, Celestino 16: 223
Pica, Steve 115: 181
Picarella, Joseph 13: 147
Picart, Gabriel 121: 165; 201: 169
Picasso, Pablo 228: 131
Pichon, Liz 174: 139
Pickard, Charles 12: 38; 18: 203; 36: 152
Picken, George A. 23: 150
Pickens, David 22: 156

Pickering, Jimmy 195: 152; 197: 163
Pien, Lark 222: 143, 144
Pienkowski, Jan 6: 183; 30: 32; 58: 140, 141, 142,143, 146, 147; 73: 3; 87: 156, 157; 131: 189
Pieper, Christiane 200: 168
Pignataro, Anna 163: 220; 223: 143 Pile, Emma 218: 156 Pileggi, Steve 145: 122
Pilkey, Dav 68: 186; 115: 164, 166; 166: 173, 174, 175
Pimlott, John 10: 205
Pincus, Harriet 4: 186; 8: 179; 22: 148; 27: 164, 165; 66: 202
Pini, Wendy 89: 166
Pinkett, Neil 60: 8
Pinkney, Brian 81: 184, 185; 94: 107; 113: 146, 147; 117: 121, 166; 132: 145; 158: 108, 191; 160: 189; 200: 8
Pinkney, Jerry 8: 218; 10: 40; 15: 276; 20: 66; 24: 121; 33: 109; 36: 222; 38: 200; 41: 165, 166, 167, 168, 169, 170, 171, 173, 174; 44: 198; 48: 51; 53: 20; 56: 61, 68; 58: 184; 60: 59; 61: 91; 71: 146, 148, 149; 72: 17; 73: 149; 74: 159,192; 75: 45; 80: 206; 81: 44; 85: 144; 95: 50; 107: 158, 159, 160; 108: 164; 112: 114, 115; 133: 58; 195: 140; 227: 131
Pinkwater, Daniel Manus 8: 156; 46: 180, 181, 182, 185, 188, 189, 190; 151: 161 76: 178, 179, 180; 210: 203
Pinkwater, Manus
See Pinkwater, Daniel Manus
Pinkwater, Jill 114: 160, 161; 158: 179; 188: 143, 145, 146
Pinto, Ralph 10: 131; 45: 93
Pinto, Sara 200: 165
Pinon, Mark 74: 22
Piven, Hanoch 173: 142
Pistolesi 73: 211
Pitcairn, Ansel 188: 10; 227: 20
Pittman, Helena Clare 71: 151
Pitz, Henry C. 4: 168; 19: 165; 35: 128; 42: 80; YABC 2: 95, 176
Pitzenberger, Lawrence J. 26: 94
Pitzer, Susanna 181: 131
Place, François 218: 42
Plant, Andrew 214: 166
Player, Stephen 82: 190
Plecas, Jennifer 84: 201; 106: 124; 149: 168; 205: 180; 220: 81; 229: 152, 153, 154
Ploog, Mike 180: 19
Plowden, David 52: 135, 136
Plume, Ilse 170: 149
Plummer, William 32: 31
Podevin, Jean François 184: 185
Podwal, Mark 56: 170, 173; 101: 154, 155, 157; 149: 176; 160: 194; 224: 127, 128, 129
Pogany, Willy 15: 46, 49; 19: 222, 256; 25: 214; 44: 142, 143, 144, 145, 146, 147, 148
Pohrt, Tom 67: 116; 104: 80; 152: 199; 195: 154; 199: 85
Poirson, V.A. 26: 89
Polacco, Patricia 74: 195, 196, 197, 198; 123: 121, 122, 123; 180: 189, 190, 191, 193, 194; 212: 168, 170, 171
Polgreen, John 21: 44
Polhemus, Coleman 210: 209
Politi, Leo 1: 178; 4: 53; 21: 48; 47: 173,174, 176, 178, 179, 180, 181
Pollack, Barbara 219: 60
Pollema-Cahill, Phyllis 123: 126
Pollen, Samson 64: 80
Polonsky, Arthur 34: 168
Polseno, Jo 1: 53; 3: 117; 5: 114; 17: 154; 20: 87; 32: 49; 41: 245
Pomaska, Anna 117: 148
Pons, Bernadette 184: 100
Ponter, James 5: 204
Poole, Colin 111: 27
Poortvliet, Rien 6: 212; 65: 165, 166, 167
Pope, Kevin 183: 158

Popp, Wendy *72:* 122; *158:* 68
Poppel, Hans *71:* 154, 155
Porfirio, Guy *76:* 134
Portal, Colette *6:* 186; *11:* 203
Porter, George *7:* 181
Porter, Janice Lee *136:* 175; *164:* 37
Porter, John *113:* 47
Porter, Pat Grant *84:* 112; *125:* 101
Porter, Sue *146:* 246, 247; *213:* 139, 140, 141; *221:* 91
Porter, Walter *124:* 175
Porto, James *221:* 14
Posada, Mia *187:* 151
Posen, Michael *175:* 82
Posthuma, Sieb *150:* 163
Postier, Jim *202:* 140; *204:* 25
Postma, Lidia *79:* 17
Potter, Beatrix *100:* 194, 195; *132:* 179, 180, 181, 182; *YABC 1:* 208, 209, 210, 212, 213
Potter, Giselle *117:* 123; *143:* 44; *144:* 170, 197; *149:* 7; *150:* 165; *187:* 152, 153; *190:* 198; *196:* 152; *200:* 12; *225:* 60; *227:* 105
Potter, Katherine *104:* 147; *171:* 135; *173:* 136; *217:* 130, 131
Potter, Miriam Clark *3:* 162
Poulin, Stephane *98:* 140, 141
Poullis, Nick *146:* 210
Powell, Constance Buffington *174:* 141
Powell, Gary *151:* 208
Powell, Ivan *67:* 219
Power, Margaret *105:* 122
Powers, Daniel *161:* 173
Powers, Richard M. *1:* 230; *3:* 218; *7:* 194; *26:* 186
Powledge, Fred *37:* 154
Powzyk, Joyce *74:* 214
Poydar, Nancy *96:* 149; *190:* 180, 181, 182
Pracher, Richard *91:* 166
Prachaticka, Marketa *126:* 126
Prange, Beckie *181:* 169
Prap, Lila *177:* 165
Prater, John *103:* 142, 143, 144; *149:* 172
Pratt, Charles *23:* 29
Pratt, Christine Joy *214:* 167
Pratt, George *116:* 208; *212:* 37
Pratt, Pierre *150:* 73; *166:* 183; *168:* 172; *201:* 27; *208:* 171, 172, 173
Prebenna, David *73:* 174
Preiss-Glasser, Robin *123:* 176; *152* 40; *172:* 194
Press, Jenny *116:* 95
Preston, Mark *152:* 162
Pretro, Korinna *91:* 126
Prevost, Mikela *209:* 111
Price, Christine *2:* 247; *3:* 163, 253; *8:* 166
Price, Cynthia *118:* 156
Price, Edward *33:* 34
Price, Garrett *1:* 76; *2:* 42
Price, Hattie Longstreet *17:* 13
Price, Nick *216:* 173; *220:* 7
Price, Norman *YABC 1:* 129
Price, Willard *48:* 184
Priceman, Marjorie *81:* 171; *136:* 169; *156:* 200; *168:* 153, 154; *188:* 45; *226:* 7
Priestley, Alice *168:* 33; *227:* 142
Priestley, Chris *198:* 144
Primavera, Elise *26:* 95; *58:* 151; *73:* 37; *80:* 79; *86:* 156; *105:* 161; *213:* 157
Primrose, Jean *36:* 109
Prince, Alison *86:* 188, 189
Prince, Leonora E. *7:* 170
Pritchett, Shelley *116:* 148
Prittie, Edwin J. *YABC 1:* 120
Proimos, James *176:* 4; *217:* 132, 133, 134
Proimos, John *173:* 144
Prosmitsky, Jenya *132:* 33
Provensen, Alice *37:* 204, 215, 222; *70:* 176, 177, 178, 180, *71:* 213; *147:* 184; *191:* 190
Provensen, Martin *37:* 204, 215, 222; *70:* 176, 177, 178, 180, *71:* 213; *191:* 190
Pucci, Albert John *44:* 154

Pudlo *8:* 59
Puggaard, Ulla *196:* 25
Pullen, Zachary *211:* 161
Pulver, Harry, Jr. *129:* 159
Pulver, Robin *160:* 4
Punchatz, Don *99:* 57
Purdy, Susan *8:* 162
Pursell, Weimer *55:* 18
Purston, Oliver *229:* 156
Purtscher, Alfons *97:* 6
Puskas, James *5:* 141
Pyk, Jan *7:* 26; *38:* 123
Pyle, Chuck *99:* 149; *191:* 83
Pyle, Howard *16:* 225, 226, 227, 228, 230, 231, 232, 235; *24:* 27; *34:* 124, 125, 127, 128; *59:* 132; *100:* 198

Q

Quackenbush, Robert *4:* 190; *6:* 166; *7:* 175, 178; *9:* 86; *11:* 65, 221; *41:* 154; *43:* 157; *70:* 185, 186; *71:* 137; *85:* 47; *92:* 148; *133:* 154, 164, 169
Qualls, Sean *177:* 167, 168; *193:* 43; *228:* 108
Quennell, Marjorie (Courtney) *29:* 163, 164
Quidor, John *19:* 82
Quirk, John *62:* 170
Quirk, Thomas *12:* 81

R

Rackham, Arthur *15:* 32, 78, 214-227; *17:* 105, 115; *18:* 233; *19:* 254; *20:* 151; *22:* 129, 131, 132, 133; *23:* 175; *24:* 161, 181; *26:* 91; *32:* 118; *64:* 18; *100:* 9, 16, 203, 204; *YABC 1:* 25, 45, 55, 147; *2:* 103, 142, 173, 210
Racz, Michael *56:* 134
Raczka, Bob *191:* 155, 156
Radcliffe, Andrew *82:* 215
Rader, Laura *101:* 219; *197:* 147; *203:* 53
Radunsky, Vladimir *177:* 170; *192:* 30
Radzinski, Kandy *212:* 174
Rafilson, Sidney *11:* 172
Raglin, Tim *125:* 24
Raible, Alton *1:* 202, 203; *28:* 193; *35:* 181; *110:* 207
Raine, Patricia *82:* 74; *88:* 154
Ramá, Sue *173:* 45; *185:* 186; *190:* 184
Ramhorst, John *117:* 11
Ramirez, Gladys *177:* 19
Ramirez, Jose *207:* 27
Ramsey, James *16:* 41
Ramsey, Marcy Dunn *82:* 11; *180:* 186
Ramus, Michael *51:* 171
Rand, Paul *6:* 188
Rand, Ted *67:* 9, 10, 121, 123; *74:* 190; *84:* 170; *103:* 170; *112:* 6; *114:* 73; *139:* 168; *143:* 194; *156:* 154; *161:* 9, 10; *200:* 38; *204:* 7
Randazzo, Tony *81:* 98
Randell, William *55:* 54
Rane, Walter *93:* 144; *143:* 109; *184:* 126
Rankin, Joan *163:* 40; *212:* 176
Rankin, Laura *176:* 173, 174; *179:* 150
Ransome, Arthur *22:* 201
Ransome, James E. *74:* 137; *75:* 80; *84:* 181; *94:* 108; *117:* 115; *123:* 128, 129, 130; *158:* 101, 102; *159:* 205; *178:* 188, 189, 190; *216:* 114; *227:* 146, 148, 149, 150
Rantz, Don *119:* 184
Rao, Anthony *28:* 126
Raphael, Elaine *23:* 192; *71:* 24, 25
Rappaport, Eva *6:* 190

Raschka, Chris *80:* 187, 189, 190; *97:* 211; *115:* 210; *117:* 151, 152, 153, 154; *143:* 195; *145:* 153; *166:* 190, 191; *170:* 114; *207:* 140, 143, 144, 145; *208:* 82; *220:* 85
Rash, Andy *158:* 178; *162:* 172; *210:* 204; *219:* 145; *226:* 194
Raskin, Ellen *2:* 208, 209; *4:* 142; *13:* 183; *22:* 68; *29:* 139; *36:* 134; *38:* 173, 174, 175, 176, 177, 178,179, 180, 181; *60:* 163; *86:* 81
Rathmann, Peggy *93:* 32; *94:* 168; *157:* 212, 214
Ratkus, Tony *77:* 133
Rattray, Gail *227:* 96
Ratzkin, Lawrence *40:* 143
Rau, Margaret *9:* 157
Raverat, Gwen *YABC 1:* 152
Ravid, Joyce *61:* 73
Ravielli, Anthony *1:* 198; *3:* 168; *11:* 143
Ravilious, Robin *77:* 169
Rawlins, Donna *72:* 198; *73:* 15, 129
Rawlins, Janet *76:* 79
Rawlings, Steve *143:* 139; *151:* 54; *208:* 150
Rawlinson, Debbie *75:* 132
Ray, Deborah Kogan *8:* 164; *29:* 238; *50:* 112, 113; *62:* 119; *78:* 191; *203:* 149, 150, 151
Ray, Jane *96:* 166; *97:* 104; *152:* 208; *190:* 221; *196:* 165
Ray, Ralph *2:* 239; *5:* 73
Rayann, Omar *162:* 205; *186:* 29, 30
Rayevsky, Robert *64:* 17; *70:* 173; *80:* 204; *117:* 79; *190:* 187, 188
Raymond, Larry *31:* 108; *97:* 109
Rayner, Hugh *151:* 170
Rayner, Mary *22:* 207; *47:* 140; *72:* 191; *87:* 171, 172; *192:* 104
Rayner, Shoo
    See Rayner, Hugh
Raynes, John *71:* 19
Raynor, Dorka *28:* 168
Raynor, Paul *24:* 73
Rayyan, Omar *110:* 222; *112:* 17; *125:* 131
Razzi, James *10:* 127
Read, Alexander D. *20:* 45
Reader, Dennis *71:* 157
Reasoner, Charles *53:* 33, 36, 37
Rebenschied, Shane *203:* 76; *215:* 124
Reczuch, Karen *115:* 132; *145:* 131
Redlich, Ben *163:* 221; *198:* 193
Reddy, Mike *203:* 67
Reed, Joseph *116:* 139
Reed, Lynn Rowe *115:* 173; *171:* 146; *208:* 177; *215:* 144, 145
Reed, Mike *211:* 147; *215:* 131
Reed, Tom *34:* 171
Reeder, Colin *74:* 202; *77:* 113
Rees, Mary *134:* 219
Reese, Bob *60:* 135
Reeve, Philip *171:* 50
Reeves, Eira B. *130:* 173, 174; *141:* 151
Reeves, Rick *181:* 179
Reeves, Rosie *202:* 200
Regan, Dana *117:* 116
Regan, Laura *103:* 198; *153:* 206
Reichert, Renée *169:* 127
Reid, Barbara *82:* 178; *92:* 17; *93:* 169, 170; *222:* 45
Reid, Stephen *19:* 213; *22:* 89
Reim, Melanie *104:* 151; *150:* 98
Reinert, Kirk *89:* 138; *195:* 129
Reinertson, Barbara *44:* 150; *62:* 103
Reiniger, Lotte *40:* 185
Reisberg, Mira *119:* 2
Reisch, Jesse *158:* 130
Reiser, Lynn *81:* 175; *138:* 184; *180:* 200
Reiss, John J. *23:* 193
Relf, Douglas *3:* 63
Relyea, C.M. *16:* 29; *31:* 153
Remi, Georges *13:* 184
Remington, Frederic *19:* 188; *41:* 178, 179, 180, 181, 183,184, 185, 186, 187, 188; *62:* 197

Remkiewicz, Frank *67:* 102; *77:* 171; *80:* 130; *113:* 107; *152:* 116; *152:* 211, 212; *157:* 148; *217:* 120, 138, 139, 140, 141
Rendon, Maria *116:* 141; *192:* 134: 152
Renfro, Ed *79:* 176
Renier, Aaron *202:* 141; *207:* 119
Renlie, Frank *11:* 200
Reschofsky, Jean *7:* 118
Rethi *60:* 181
Rethi, Lili *2:* 153; *36:* 156
Reusswig, William *3:* 267
Revell, Cindy *195:* 93
Rex, Adam *156:* 172; *169:* 91; *186:* 178, 179; *215:* 103; *223:* 11; *225:* 154
Rex, Michael *157:* 147; *191:* 159, 160; *221:* 124
Rey, H.A. *1:* 182; *26:* 163, 164, 166, 167, 169; *69:* 172, 173, 174, 175; *86:* 195, 196, 197; *100:* 211; *YABC 2:* 17
Rey, Luis V. *201:* 162
Reynish, Jenny *222:* 155
Reynolds, Adrian *192:* 159, 160
Reynolds, Doris *5:* 71; *31:* 77
Reynolds, Peter H. *142:* 12; *179:* 175, 176; *202:* 113, 114; *226:* 30, 166, 167; *228:* 132
Rhead, Louis *31:* 91; *100:* 228
Rhodes, Andrew *38:* 204; *50:* 163; *54:* 76; *61:* 123, 124; *87:* 200
Ribbons, Ian *3:* 10; *37:* 161; *40:* 76
Ricci, Regolo *93:* 22; *164:* 148
Rice, Elizabeth *2:* 53, 214
Rice, Eve *34:* 174, 175; *91:* 172
Rice, James *22:* 210; *93:* 173
Rich, Anna *212:* 180
Rich, Martha *195:* 16
Richards, Chuck *170:* 154
Richards, George *40:* 116, 119, 121; *44:* 179
Richards, Henry *YABC 1:* 228, 231
Richardson, Ernest *2:* 144
Richardson, Frederick *18:* 27, 31
Richardson, John *110:* 88
Richman, Hilda *26:* 132
Richmond, George *24:* 179
Riddell, Chris *114:* 170, 195; *166:* 179; *199:* 164, 166, 167; *218:* 146, 148; *219:* 149, 150, 152, 153; *228:* 125
Riddle, Tohby *74:* 204; *151:* 179; *223:* 154, 156
Riding, Peter *63:* 195
Rieniets, Judy King *14:* 28
Riger, Bob *2:* 166
Riggio, Anita *73:* 191; *85:* 63; *137:* 184; *172:* 165
Rigano, Giovanni *219:* 45
Riley, Jon *74:* 70
Riley, Kenneth *22:* 230
Riley, Terry *203:* 100
Riley-Webb, Charlotte *153:* 143
Rim, Sujean *225:* 157
Rinaldi, Angelo *165:* 60, 69; *227:* 53
Ringgold, Faith *71:* 162; *114:* 173, 174, 176; *187:* 160, 161, 163
Ringi, Kjell *12:* 171
Rios, Tere
　See Versace, Marie
Rioux, Jo *215:* 110; *226:* 170
Ripper, Charles L. *3:* 175
Ripplinger, Henry *117:* 31
Ritchie, Scot *217:* 145
Ritchie, William *74:* 183
Ritter, John *175:* 14
Ritz, Karen *41:* 117; *72:* 239; *87:* 125; *102:* 7; *106:* 6
Rivas, Victor *209:* 193; *226:* 144
Rivers, Ruth *178:* 193
Rivkin, Jay *15:* 230
Rivoche, Paul *45:* 125
Roach, Marilynne *9:* 158
Robbin, Jodi *44:* 156, 159
Robbins, Frank *42:* 167
Robbins, Ken *147:* 191, 192

Robbins, Ruth *52:* 102
Roberts, Cliff *4:* 126
Roberts, David *154:* 4, 6; *191:* 162; *196:* 184; *197:* 105; *210:* 257
Roberts, Doreen *4:* 230; *28:* 105
Roberts, Jim *22:* 166; *23:* 69; *31:* 110
Roberts, Tony *109:* 195, 214
Roberts, W. *22:* 2, 3
Robertson, M.P. *197:* 153
Robins, Arthur *137:* 172; *151:* 225; *204:* 161
Robinson, Aminah Brenda Lynn *86:* 205; *103:* 55; *159:* 175
Robinson, Charles [1870-1937] *17:* 157, 171, 172, 173, 175, 176; *24:* 207; *25:* 204; *YABC 2:* 308, 309, 310, 331
Robinson, Charles *3:* 53; *5:* 14; *6:* 193; *7:* 150; *7:* 183; *8:* 38; *9:* 81; *13:* 188; *14:* 248, 249; *23:* 149; *26:* 115; *27:* 48; *28:* 191; *32:* 28; *35:* 210; *36:* 37; *48:* 96; *52:* 33; *53:* 157; *56:* 15; *62:* 142; *77:* 41; *111:* 148
Robinson, Fiona *225:* 158
Robinson, Jerry *3:* 262
Robinson, Joan G. *7:* 184
Robinson, Lolly *90:* 227
Robinson, T.H. *17:* 179, 181, 182, 183; *29:* 254
Robinson, W. Heath *17:* 185, 187, 189, 191, 193, 195, 197, 199, 202; *23:* 167; *25:* 194; *29:* 150; *YABC 1:* 44; *2:* 183
Rocco, John *187:* 4; *188:* 151; *208:* 180, 181, 182; *213:* 94; *222:* 34
Roche, Christine *41:* 98
Roche, Denis *99:* 184; *180:* 32; *196:* 168
Roche, P.K. *57:* 151, 152
Rocker, Fermin *7:* 34; *13:* 21; *31:* 40; *40:* 190,191
Rocklen, Margot *101:* 181
Rockwell, Anne *5:* 147; *33:* 171, 173; *71:* 166, 167,168; *114:* 183, 184; *194:* 152, 155
Rockwell, Gail *7:* 186
Rockwell, Harlow *33:* 171, 173, 175
Rockwell, Lizzy *114:* 182; *162:* 182; *185:* 189
Rockwell, Norman *23:* 39, 196, 197, 199, 200, 203, 204, 207; *41:* 140, 143; *123:* 47; *YABC 2:* 60
Rockwood, Richard *119:* 75
Rodanas, Kristina *156:* 183, 184; *221:* 127
Rodegast, Roland *43:* 100
Rodgers, Frank *69:* 177
Rodriguez, Albert G. *182:* 50
Rodriguez, Christina *184:* 12; *225:* 94
Rodriguez, Edel *204:* 86
Rodriguez, Joel *16:* 65
Rodriguez, Robert *145:* 145; *212:* 33
Rodriguez-Howard, Pauline *177:* 18
Roe, Monika *210:* 94
Roeckelein, Katrina *134:* 223
Roennfeldt, Robert *66:* 243
Roever, J.M. *4:* 119; *26:* 170
Roffey, Maureen *33:* 142, 176, 177
Rogasky, Barbara *46:* 90
Rogé *173:* 160
Rogers, Carol *2:* 262; *6:* 164; *26:* 129
Rogers, Chris M. *150:* 59; *196:* 61
Rogers, Forest *87:* 160; *101:* 76
Rogers, Frances *10:* 130
Rogers, Gregory *104:* 76; *126:* 57; *171:* 26
Rogers, Jacqueline *78:* 249; *80:* 34; *86:* 54 *103:* 70; *115:* 72; *129:* 173; *131:* 57, 225; *143:* 211; *153:* 100; *193:* 186; *203:* 51; *213:* 144, 145, 146; *214:* 142
Rogers, Sherry *191:* 66
Rogers, Walter S. *31:* 135, 138; *67:* 65, 168; *100:* 81
Rogers, William A. *15:* 151, 153, 154; *33:* 35
Rogoff, Barbara *95:* 20
Rohmann, Eric *103:* 152; *198:* 151
Rojankovsky, Feodor *6:* 134, 136; *10:* 183; *21:* 128,129, 130; *25:* 110; *28:* 42; *68:* 120
Rolfsen, Alf *62:* 15
Rolston, Steve *209:* 154; *223:* 113

Romain, Trevor *134:* 157
Roman, Barbara J. *103:* 171
Romas *114:* 111; *165:* 63
Romano, Robert *64:* 68
Romero, Alejandro *187:* 185
Roos, Maryn *168:* 198; *225:* 160; *226:* 143
Root, Barry *80:* 212; *90:* 196; *146:* 78; *156:* 165; *159:* 161; *182:* 18, 172
Root, Kimberly Bulcken *86:* 72; *98:* 21; *108:* 111; *127:* 114; *159:* 162; *176:* 134; *192:* 163
Roper, Bob *65:* 153
Roraback, Robin *111:* 156
Rorer, Abigail *43:* 222; *85:* 155
Rosales, Melodye *80:* 35
Rosamilia, Patricia *36:* 120
Rose, Carl *5:* 62
Rose, David S. *29:* 109; *70:* 120
Rose, Gerald *68:* 200, 201; *86:* 48
Rose, Naomi C. *228:* 136
Rose, Ted *93:* 178
Rosen, Elizabeth *205:* 137
Rosenbaum, Jonathan *50:* 46
Rosenberg, Amye *74:* 207, 208
Rosenberry, Vera *87:* 22, 26; *144:* 212, 213; *158:* 120; *219:* 163, 164
Rosenblum, Richard *11:* 202; *18:* 18
Rosenstiehl, Agnès *203:* 153
Rosier, Lydia *16:* 236; *20:* 104; *21:* 109; *22:* 125; *30:* 151, 158; *42:* 128; *45:* 214; *77:* 227, 228
Rosing, Jens *85:* 142
Ross
　See Thomson, Ross
Ross, Christine *83:* 172, 173
Ross, Clare Romano *3:* 123; *21:* 45; *48:* 199
Ross, Dave *32:* 152; *57:* 108
Ross, Graham *199:* 4
Ross, Herbert *37:* 78
Ross, John *3:* 123; *21:* 45
Ross, Johnny *32:* 190
Ross, Larry *47:* 168; *60:* 62
Ross, Ruth *109:* 233
Ross, Tony *17:* 204; *56:* 132; *65:* 176, 177, 179; *90:* 123; *123:* 186, 187, 190; *130:* 188, 190, 191, 192; *132:* 242; *174:* 159; *176:* 181, 182, 183; *202:* 198; *225:* 168, 170
Rossetti, Dante Gabriel *20:* 151, 153
Rostant, Larry *180:* 221; *194:* 108; *195:* 96; *197:* 12; *207:* 53; *210:* 189; *226:* 22
Roth, Arnold *4:* 238; *21:* 133
Roth, Julie Jersild *180:* 206
Roth, Marci *135:* 223
Roth, R.G. *184:* 50
Roth, Rob *105:* 98; *146:* 41
Roth, Robert *176:* 159
Roth, Roger *61:* 128; *190:* 192
Roth, Ruby *216:* 185
Roth, Stephanie *136:* 171, 172
Roth, Susan L. *80:* 38; *93:* 78; *134:* 165, 166; *181:* 145, 146
Rothenberg, Joani Keller *162:* 190, 191
Rothman, Michael *139:* 62; *184:* 34 *Rotman, Jeffrey L. 145:* 30
Rotondo, Pat *32:* 158
Roughsey, Dick *35:* 186
Rouille, M. *11:* 96
Rounds, Glen *8:* 173; *9:* 171; *12:* 56; *32:* 194; *40:* 230; *51:* 161, 166; *56:* 149; *70:* 198, 199; *YABC 1:* 1, 2, 3; *112:* 163
Roundtree, Katherine *114:* 88; *168:* 102
Rovetch, Lissa *201:* 164
Rowan, Evadne *52:* 51
Rowe, Eric *111:* 161
Rowe, Gavin *27:* 144; *72:* 47; *88:* 201
Rowe, John *132:* 70, 71; *180:* 126
Rowell, Kenneth *40:* 72
Rowen, Amy *52:* 143
Rowena *116:* 101
Rowland, Andrew *164:* 136
Rowland, Jada *83:* 73
Rowles, Daphne *58:* 24

Roy, Jeroo 27: 229; 36: 110
Royo 118: 32; 144: 105, 106, 108; 165: 19; 166: 166
Rubbino, Salvatore 220: 147
Rubel, Nicole 18: 255; 20: 59; 81: 66, 67; 95: 169, 170; 119: 60; 135: 177, 179, 180; 169: 68; 181: 150
Rubel, Reina 33: 217
Rud, Borghild 6: 15
Ruddell, Gary 110: 238; 116: 207
Rudolph, Norman Guthrie 17: 13
Rue, Leonard Lee III 37: 164
Rueda, Claudia 183: 170, 171
Ruelle, Karen Gray 126: 193
Ruff, Donna 50: 173; 72: 203; 78: 49; 80: 120,121; 93: 162; 164: 121
Ruffins, Reynold 10: 134, 135; 41: 191, 192, 193, 194, 195, 196; 125: 187, 188, 189; 162: 197
Ruhlin, Roger 34: 44
Rui, Paolo 217: 115
Ruiz, Art 95: 154; 110: 91
Rumford, James 193: 167
Runnerstroem, Bengt Arne 75: 161
Ruse, Margaret 24: 155
Rush, Ken 98: 74
Rush, Peter 42: 75
Russell, Charles M. 167: 171
Russell, E.B. 18: 177, 182
Russell, Jim 53: 134
Russell, Natalie 218: 170, 171
Russell, P. Craig 80: 196; 146: 102; 162: 186
Russo, Marisabina 84: 51; 106: 164; 151: 183; 188: 153, 154, 155, 156
Russo, Susan 30: 182; 36: 144
Russon, Mary 87: 145
Ruth, Greg 183: 125
Ruth, Rod 9: 161
Rutherford, Alexa 110: 108
Rutherford, Jenny 78: 5
Rutherford, Meg 25: 174; 34: 178, 179; 69: 73; 72: 31
Rutland, Jonathan 31: 126
Ruurs, Margriet 147: 195
Ruzzier, Sergio 159: 176, 177; 163: 184; 210: 214, 216
Ryan, Amy 188: 50
Ryan, Will 86: 134
Rycroft, Nina 228: 143
Ryden, Hope 8: 176
Rylant, Cynthia 112: 170, 172
Rymer, Alta M. 34: 181
Ryniak, Christopher 178: 11
Rystedt, Rex 49: 80

S

Saaf, Chuck 49: 179
Saaf, Donald 101: 220; 124: 180
Sabaka, Donna R. 21: 172
Sabin, Robert 45: 35; 60: 30; 99: 161; 223: 29
Sabuda, Robert 170: 166, 167, 168
Sacker, Amy 16: 100
Saelig, S.M. 129: 73; 173: 59
Saffioti, Lino 36: 176; 48: 60; 223: 26
Saflund, Birgitta 94: 2
Sagsoorian, Paul 12: 183; 22: 154; 33: 106; 87: 152
Sahara, Tony 168: 106; 177: 181; 178: 228; 186: 132; 207: 89
Sahlberg, Myron 57: 165
Saidens, Amy 145: 162; 191: 131; 210: 129
Saint Exupery, Antoine de 20: 157
Saint James, Synthia 152: 220; 188: 90; 200: 7
Sakai, Komako 213: 148
Saldutti, Denise 39: 186; 57: 178
Sale, Morton YABC 2: 31
Sale, Tim 153: 177

Salerno, Steven 150: 79; 176: 188; 202: 39; 216: 190
Salter, George 72: 128, 130
Saltzberg, Barney 135: 184, 185; 194: 160
Saltzman, David 86: 209
Salwowski, Mark 71: 54
Salzman, Yuri 86: 12
Sambourne, Linley YABC 2: 181
Sampson, Katherine 9: 197
Samson, Anne S. 2: 216
San Souci, Daniel 40: 200; 96: 199, 200; 113: 171; 157: 149; 170: 69; 192: 167, 168; 220: 152; 221: 126
Sancha, Sheila 38: 185
Sanchez, Enrique O. 155: 84
Sand, George X. 45: 182
Sandberg, Lasse 15: 239, 241
Sanders, Beryl 39: 173
Sanderson, Ruth 21: 126; 24: 53; 28: 63; 33: 67; 41: 48, 198, 199, 200, 201, 202, 203; 43: 79; 46: 36,44; 47: 102; 49: 58; 62: 121, 122; 85: 3; 109: 207, 208, 209, 210; 172: 157, 158; 223: 85; 224: 152, 153, 154
Sandia 119: 74
Sandin, Joan 4: 36; 6: 194; 7: 177; 12: 145,185; 20: 43; 21: 74; 26: 144; 27: 142; 28: 224, 225; 38: 86; 41: 46; 42: 35; 59: 6; 80: 136; 94: 188; 140: 116; 153: 179, 180; 197: 168
Sandland, Reg 39: 215
Sandoz, Edouard 26: 45, 47
Sanford, John 66: 96, 97
Sanger, Amy Wilson 205: 140
Sankey, Tom 72: 103
Sano, Kazuhiko 153: 208; 195: 171; 203: 21; 221: 71
Santat, Dan 188: 160; 221: 62; 223: 163; 224: 157, 158, 159
Santiago, Wilfred 210: 48
Santore, Charles 54: 139; 200: 171, 172
Santoro, Christopher 74: 215
Santos, Jesse J. 99: 24
Sapieha, Christine 1: 180
Saport, Linda 123: 137, 138; 215: 29
Sara
    See De La Roche Saint Andre, Anne
Sarcone-Roach, Julia 215: 158
Sardinha, Rick 175: 151
Sarg, Tony YABC 2: 236
Sargent, Claudia 64: 181
Sargent, Robert 2: 217
Saris 1: 33
Sarony YABC 2: 170
Saroff, Phyllis V. 202: 160
Sasaki, Goro 170: 46
Sasaki, Ellen Joy 216: 49
Sasek, Miroslav 16: 239, 240, 241, 242
Sassman, David 9: 79
Sattler, Jennifer Gordon 218: 175
Satty 29: 203, 205
Sauber, Robert 40: 183; 76: 256; 78: 154; 87: 92
Saunders, Dave 85: 163, 164, 165
Savadier, Elivia 84: 50; 145: 45; 164: 206; 228: 146
Savage, Naomi 56: 172
Savage, Steele 10: 203; 20: 77; 35: 28
Savage, Stephen 174: 182
Savio 76: 4
Savitt, Sam 8: 66, 182; 15: 278; 20: 96; 24: 192; 28: 98
Sawyer, Kem Knapp 84: 228, 229
Say, Allen 28: 178; 69: 182, 183, 232; 110: 194, 195,196; 161: 154, 155
Sayles, Elizabeth 82: 93; 105: 155; 109: 116; 180: 64; 220: 160, 161
Scabrini, Janet 13: 191; 44: 128
Scalora, Suza 224: 160
Scanlan, Peter 83: 27; 153: 165; 187: 149
Scanlon, Paul 83: 87
Scannell, Reece 105: 105

Scarry, Huck 35: 204, 205
Scarry, Richard 2: 220, 221; 18: 20; 35: 193, 194, 195,196, 197, 198, 199, 200, 201, 202; 75: 165, 167, 168
Schachner, Judith Byron 88: 180; 92: 163; 93: 102; 142: 82; 178: 199, 200; 190: 140; 228: 83
Schade, Susan 205: 21
Schaeffer, Mead 18: 81, 94; 21: 137, 138, 139; 47: 128
Schaffer, Amanda 90: 206
Schallau, Daniel 222: 164
Schanzer, Rosalyn 138: 192, 193
Scharl, Josef 20: 132; 22: 128
Scheel, Lita 11: 230
Scheffler, Axel 180: 23, 24
Scheib, Ida 29: 28
Schermer, Judith 30: 184
Schick, Eleanor 82: 210, 211; 144: 222
Schick, Joel 16: 160; 17: 167; 22: 12; 27: 176; 31: 147, 148; 36: 23; 38: 64; 45: 116, 117; 52: 5, 85; 104: 159
Schields, Gretchen 75: 171, 203
Schindelman, Joseph 1: 74; 4: 101; 12: 49; 26: 51; 40: 146; 56: 158; 73: 40
Schindler, Edith 7: 22
Schindler, S.D. 38: 107; 46: 196; 74: 162; 75: 172, 173; 99: 133; 112: 177; 118: 185, 186; 121: 71; 136: 159; 143: 45; 149: 120; 156: 30; 169: 135; 171: 161, 162, 163; 172: 9; 186: 163; 194: 109; 195: 35; 198: 170, 171, 172
Schlesinger, Bret 7: 77
Schlossberg, Elisabeth 221: 161
Schmid, Eleanore 12: 188; 126: 196, 197
Schmiderer, Dorothy 19: 224
Schmidt, Bill 73: 34; 76: 220, 222, 224
Schmidt, Elizabeth 15: 242
Schmidt, George Paul 132: 122
Schmidt, Karen Lee 54: 12; 71: 174; 92: 56; 94: 190, 191; 127: 103
Schmidt, Lynette 76: 205
Schmitz, Tamara 207: 147
Schneider, Christine M. 171: 165
Schneider, Howie 181: 159
Schneider, Rex 29: 64; 44: 171
Schnurr, Edward 170: 62
Schoberle, Cecile 80: 200; 92: 134; 218: 113
Schoenherr, Ian 32: 83; 173: 41
Schoenherr, John 1: 146, 147, 173; 3: 39, 139; 17: 75; 29: 72; 32: 83; 37: 168, 169, 170; 43: 164, 165; 45: 160, 162; 51: 127; 66: 196, 197, 198; 68: 83; 72: 240; 75: 225; 88: 176
Scholder, Fritz 69: 103
Schomburg, Alex 13: 23
Schongut, Emanuel 4: 102; 15: 186; 47: 218, 219; 52: 147, 148, 149, 150; 185: 27
Schoonover, Frank 17: 107; 19: 81, 190, 233; 22: 88,129; 24: 189; 31: 88; 41: 69; YABC 2: 282, 316
Schories, Pat 164: 210
Schottland, Miriam 22: 172
Schramm, Ulrik 2: 16; 14: 112
Schreiber, Elizabeth Anne 13: 193
Schreiber, Ralph W. 13: 193
Schreiter, Rick 14: 97; 23: 171; 41: 247; 49: 131
Schroades, John 214: 129
Schroeder, Binette 56: 128, 129
Schroeder, E. Peter 12: 112
Schroeder, Ted 11: 160; 15: 189; 30: 91; 34: 43
Schrotter, Gustav 22: 212; 30: 225
Schubert, Dieter 101: 167, 168; 217: 151, 152, 153, 155
Schubert, Ingrid 217: 151, 152, 153, 155
Schubert-Gabrys, Ingrid 101: 167, 168
Schucker, James 31: 163
Schuett, Stacey 72: 137; 208: 204
Schulder, Lili 146: 29

Schulke, Debra *57:* 167
Schulke, Flip *57:* 167
Schulz, Barbara *167:* 24
Schulz, Charles M. *10:* 137, 138, 139, 140, 141, 142; *118:* 192, 193, 194, 196, 199
Schutzer, Dena *109:* 32
Schwark, Mary Beth *51:* 155; *72:* 175
Schwartz, Amy *47:* 191; *82:* 100; *83:* 178, 179, 180,181; *129:* 107; *131:* 197, 198; *189:* 166, 168; *226:* 174
Schwartz, Carol *124:* 41; *130:* 199
Schwartz, Charles *8:* 184
Schwartz, Daniel *46:* 37
Schwartz, Joanie *124:* 170
Schwartzberg, Joan *3:* 208
Schwarz, Viviane *204:* 132
Schweitzer, Iris *2:* 137; *6:* 207
Schweninger, Ann *29:* 172; *82:* 246; *159:* 202; *168:* 166; *211:* 193
Schwinger, Laurence *84:* 44; *91:* 61
Scofield, Penrod *61:* 107; *62:* 160
Scott, Anita Walker *7:* 38
Scott, Art *39:* 41
Scott, Frances Gruse *38:* 43
Scott, Jane Wooster *226:* 181
Scott, Julian *34:* 126
Scott, Roszel *33:* 238
Scott, Sally *87:* 27
Scott, Steve *166:* 230, 231; *171:* 93
Scott, Trudy *27:* 172
Scotton, Rob *214:* 183
Scrace, Carolyn *143:* 95, 96
Scrambly, Crab *198:* 196
Scribner, Joanne *14:* 236; *29:* 78; *33:* 185; *34:* 208; *78:* 75; *164:* 237; *203:* 73
Scrofani, Joseph *31:* 65; *74:* 225
Scroggs, Kirk *187:* 169
Seaman, Mary Lott *34:* 64
Searle, Ronald *24:* 98; *42:* 172, 173, 174, 176, 177, 179; *66:* 73, 74; *70:* 205, 206, 207
Searle, Townley *36:* 85
Sebree, Charles *18:* 65
Sedacca, Joseph M. *11:* 25; *22:* 36
Seder, Jason *108:* 102
Seeger, Laura Vaccaro *172:* 162
Seegmiller, Don *174:* 57
Seely, David *164:* 173
Seeley, Laura L. *97:* 105
Segal, John *178:* 202
Segar, E.C. *61:* 179, 181
Segur, Adrienne *27:* 121
Seibold, J. Otto *83:* 188, 190, 191; *149:* 212, 214, 215, 216; *196:* 177, 179; *215:* 204
Seignobosc, Françoise *21:* 145, 146
Sejima, Yoshimasa *8:* 187
Selig, Sylvie *13:* 199
Seltzer, Isadore *6:* 18; *133:* 59
Seltzer, Meyer *17:* 214
Selven, Maniam *144:* 133
Selway, Martina *169:* 157
Selznick, Brian *79:* 192; *104:* 25; *117:* 175; *126:* 156; *134:* 171; *158:* 76, 78; *169:* 70; *171:* 172, 173; *191:* 106; *192:* 130; *197:* 158; *203:* 35; *205:* 92; *210:* 219, 220, 221, 222
Sempe, Jean-Jacques *47:* 92; *YABC 2:* 109
Sendak, Maurice *1:* 135, 190; *3:* 204; *7:* 142; *15:* 199; *17:* 210; *27:* 181, 182, 183, 185, 186, 187, 189,190, 191, 192, 193, 194, 195, 197, 198, 199, 203; *28:* 181, 182; *32:* 108; *33:* 148, 149; *35:* 238; *44:* 180, 181; *45:* 97, 99; *46:* 174; *73:* 225; *91:* 10, 11 *YABC1:* 167; *113:* 163, 165, 167, 168; *118:* 153; *127:* 161
Senders, Marci *180:* 79
Sengler, Johanna *18:* 256
Senn, Steve *60:* 145
Seredy, Kate *1:* 192; *14:* 20, 21; *17:* 210
Sergeant, John *6:* 74
Serra, Sebastía *212:* 215

Servello, Joe *10:* 144; *24:* 139; *40:* 91; *70:* 130, 131; *146:* 159
Seton, Ernest Thompson *18:* 260-269, 271
Seuss, Dr.
　See Geisel, Theodor
Severin, John Powers *7:* 62
Sewall, Marcia *15:* 8; *22:* 170; *37:* 171, 172, 173; *39:* 73; *45:* 209; *62:* 117; *69:* 185, 186; *71:* 212; *90:* 232; *96:* 127; *102:* 101; *107:* 129; *119:* 176, 177, 178, 180
Seward, James *70:* 35
Seward, Prudence *16:* 243
Sewell, Helen *3:* 186; *15:* 308; *33:* 102; *38:* 189, 190, 191, 192
Seymour, Stephen *54:* 21
Sfar, Joann *182:* 183
Shachat, Andrew *82:* 179
Shadbolt, Robert *203:* 68
Shahn, Ben *39:* 178; *46:* 193
Shalansky, Len *38:* 167
Shanks, Anne Zane *10:* 149
Shannon, David *57:* 137; *107:* 184; *112:* 216; *135:* 12; *152:* 223, 224, 225; *158:* 192; *212:* 159, 160, 163; *228:* 162, 163, 164, 165
Sharkey, Niamh *213:* 152
Sharp, Paul *52:* 60
Sharp, William *6:* 131; *19:* 241; *20:* 112; *25:* 141
Sharratt, Nick *102:* 207, 208; *104:* 163; *153:* 198; *175:* 176; *192:* 208; *199:* 141, 142, 143, 184, 187, 188
Shaw, Barclay *74:* 14, 16; *118:* 138
Shaw, Charles *21:* 135; *38:* 187; *47:* 124; *126:* 219
Shaw, Charles G. *13:* 200
Shaw, Hannah *227:* 163, 164
Shaw-Smith, Emma *144:* 117
Shea, Edmund *56:* 19
Shearer, Ted *43:* 193, 194, 195, 196
Sheban, Chris *182:* 185; *190:* 102, 104; *202:* 28; *204:* 112, 114; *209:* 150; *210:* 107; *220:* 103; *224:* 185
Shecter, Ben *16:* 244; *25:* 109; *33:* 188, 191; *41:* 77
Shed, Greg *74:* 94; *84:* 204; *129:* 149, 167: 91; *179:* 192; *223:* 104
Sheeban, Chris *144:* 190; *158:* 163
Shefcik, James *48:* 221, 222; *60:* 141
Shefelman, Karl *58:* 168
Shefelman, Tom *204:* 137
Shefts, Joelle *48:* 210
Shein, Bob *139:* 189
Sheinkin, Stephen *204:* 139
Shekerjian, Haig *16:* 245
Shekerjian, Regina *16:* 245; *25:* 73
Sheldon, David *184:* 174; *185:* 204; *211:* 189
Shelley, John *186:* 223
Shemie, Bonnie *96:* 207
Shenton, Edward *45:* 187, 188, 189; *YABC 1:* 218, 219, 221
Shepard, Ernest H. *3:* 193; *4:* 74; *16:* 101; *17:* 109; *25:* 148; *33:* 152, 199, 200, 201, 202, 203, 204, 205, 206,207; *46:* 194; *98:* 114; *100:* 111, 178, 179, 217, 219, 220,221; *YABC 1:* 148, 153, 174, 176, 180, 181
Shepard, Mary *4:* 210; *22:* 205; *30:* 132, 133; *54:* 150, 152, 153, 157, 158; *59:* 108, 109, 111; *100:* 246
Shepherd, Amanda *198:* 14
Shepherd, Irana *171:* 112
Sheppard, Kate *195:* 176
Shepperson, Rob *96:* 153; *177:* 163; *178:* 204; *197:* 34; *205:* 108
Sheridan, Brian *196:* 193
Sherman, Theresa *27:* 167
Sherwan, Earl *3:* 196
Shields, Charles D. *150:* 150; *36:* 63
Shields, Leonard *13:* 83, 85, 87
Shiffman, Lena *139:* 167; *168:* 136
Shiga, Jason *228:* 168
Shigley, Neil K. *66:* 219

Shillabeer, Mary *35:* 74
Shilston, Arthur *49:* 61; *62:* 58
Shimin, Symeon *1:* 93; *2:* 128, 129; *3:* 202; *7:* 85; *11:* 177; *12:* 139; *13:* 202, 203; *27:* 138; *28:* 65; *35:* 129; *36:* 130; *48:* 151; *49:* 59; *56:* 63, 65, 153
Shimizu, Yuko *215:* 197
Shine, Andrea *104:* 165; *128:* 34
Shinn, Everett *16:* 148; *18:* 229; *21:* 149, 150, 151; *24:* 218
Shinn, Florence Scovel *63:* 133, 135
Shore, Robert *27:* 54; *39:* 192, 193; *YABC 2:* 200
Shortall, Leonard *4:* 144; *8:* 196; *10:* 166; *19:* 227, 228, 229, 230; *25:* 78; *28:* 66, 167; *33:* 127; *52:* 125; *73:* 12, 212
Shortt, T.M. *27:* 36
Shpitalnik, Vladimir *83:* 194
Shropshire, Sandy *170:* 191
Shtainments, Leon *32:* 161
Shulevitz, Uri *3:* 198, 199; *17:* 85; *22:* 204; *27:* 212; *28:* 184; *50:* 190, 191, 192, 193, 194, 195, 196,197, 198, 199, 201; *106:* 181, 182, 183; *165:* 203, 205; *166:* 138
Shulman, Dee *180:* 140
Shupe, Bobbi *139:* 80, 81
Shute, A.B. *67:* 196
Shute, Linda *46:* 59; *74:* 118
Siberell, Anne *29:* 193
Sibley, Don *1:* 39; *12:* 196; *31:* 47
Sibthorp, Fletcher *94:* 111, 112
Sidjakov, Nicolas *18:* 274
Siebel, Fritz *3:* 120; *17:* 145
Siebold, J. Otto *158:* 227
Siegel, Hal *74:* 246
Sieger, Ted *189:* 172
Siegl, Helen *12:* 166; *23:* 216; *34:* 185, 186
Silin-Palmer, Pamela *184:* 102
Sill, John *140:* 194; *141:* 157; *221:* 163; *222:* 171
Sills, Joyce *5:* 199
Silva, Simon *108:* 122
Silver, Maggie *85:* 210
Silveria, Gordon *96:* 44
Silverstein, Alvin *8:* 189
Silverstein, Shel *33:* 211; *92:* 209, 210
Silverstein, Virginia *8:* 189
Silvey, Joe *135:* 203
Simard, Rémy *95:* 156; *221:* 144
Siminovich, Laura *219:* 172
Simmons, Elly *110:* 2; *127:* 69; *134:* 181
Simon, Eric M. *7:* 82
Simon, Hilda *28:* 189
Simon, Howard *2:* 175; *5:* 132; *19:* 199; *32:* 163, 164, 165
Simont, Marc *2:* 119; *4:* 213; *9:* 168; *13:* 238,240; *14:* 262; *16:* 179; *18:* 221; *26:* 210; *33:* 189, 194; *44:* 132; *58:* 122; *68:* 117; *73:* 204, 205, 206; *74:* 221; *126:* 199, 200; *133:* 195; *163:* 40; *164:* 128; *223:* 28
Sims, Agnes *54:* 152
Sims, Blanche *44:* 116; *57:* 129; *75:* 179, 180; *77:* 92; *104:* 192; *152:* 117; *156:* 160; *160:* 70; *168:* 174, 175; *198:* 17
Singer, Edith G. *2:* 30
Singer, Gloria *34:* 56; *36:* 43
Singer, Julia *28:* 190
Singh, Jen *178:* 146
Sinquette, Jaclyn *215:* 83
Siomades, Lorianne *134:* 45; *204:* 48; *217:* 157
Siracusa, Catherine *68:* 135; *82:* 218
Sís, Peter *67:* 179, 181, 183, 184, 185; *96:* 96, 98; *106:* 193, 194, 195; *149:* 224, 226; *180:* 177; *192:* 180, 182; *222:* 64
Sivard, Robert *26:* 124
Sivertson, Liz *116:* 84
Skardinski, Stanley *23:* 144; *32:* 84; *66:* 122; *84:* 108
Slack, Michael *185:* 108; *189:* 173, 174
Slackman, Charles B. *12:* 201

Slade, Christian *193:* 187; *204:* 134
Slade, Paul *61:* 170
Slark, Albert *99:* 212; *205:* 161
Slater, Rod *25:* 167
Slavin, Bill *182:* 14, 15; *196:* 90; *199:* 148, 149, 150; *217:* 20
Sloan, Joseph *16:* 68
Sloane, Eric *21:* 3; *52:* 153, 154, 155, 156, 157, 158, 160
Sloat, Teri *164:* 231
Slobodkin, Louis *1:* 200; *3:* 232; *5:* 168; *13:* 251; *15:* 13, 88; *26:* 173, 174, 175, 176, 178, 179; *60:* 180
Slobodkina, Esphyr *1:* 201
Slonim, David *166:* 167, 168
Small, David *50:* 204, 205; *79:* 44; *95:* 189, 190, 191; *126:* 203, 204; *136:* 119; *143:* 201, 202, 203; *144:* 246; *150:* 5; *161:* 176; *183:* 181, 182, 183, 184; *200:* 211; *212:* 86; *216:* 202, 203, 204
Small, W. *33:* 113
Smalley, Janet *1:* 154
Smath, Jerry *198:* 179, 180
Smedley, William T. *34:* 129
Smee, David *14:* 78; *62:* 30
Smee, Nicola *167:* 156
Smith, A.G., Jr. *35:* 182
Smith, Ali *204:* 68
Smith, Alvin *1:* 31, 229; *13:* 187; *27:* 216; *28:* 226; *48:* 149; *49:* 60
Smith, Andy *188:* 20; *207:* 151
Smith, Anne *194:* 147
Smith, Anne Warren *41:* 212
Smith, Barry *75:* 183
Smith, Brian *200:* 183
Smith, Carl *36:* 41
Smith, Cat Bowman *146:* 39; *164:* 219; *201:* 55, 184
Smith, Craig *97:* 197; *172:* 175; *206:* 40; *215:* 19; *217:* 129; *220:* 145
Smith, Donald A. *178:* 7
Smith, Doris Susan *41:* 139
Smith, Douglas *189:* 159; *213:* 170
Smith, Duane *171:* 152; *208:* 97
Smith, E. Boyd *19:* 70; *22:* 89; *26:* 63; *YABC 1:* 4, 5, 240, 248, 249
Smith, Edward J. *4:* 224
Smith, Elwood H. *157:* 231; *181:* 79; *203:* 160, 161, 162
Smith, Eunice Young *5:* 170
Smith, Gary *113:* 216
Smith, George *102:* 169
Smith, Howard *19:* 196
Smith, J. Gerard *95:* 42
Smith, Jacqueline Bardner *27:* 108; *39:* 197
Smith, Jay J. *61:* 119
Smith, Jeff *93:* 191
Smith, Jessie Willcox *15:* 91; *16:* 95; *18:* 231; *19:* 57, 242; *21:* 29, 156, 157, 158, 159, 160, 161; *34:* 65; *100:* 223; *YABC 1:* 6; *2:* 180, 185, 191, 311, 325
Smith, Jos. A. *52:* 131; *72:* 120; *74:* 151; *84:* 147, 148; *85:* 146; *87:* 96; *94:* 219; *96:* 97; *104:* 33; *108:* 126, 127, 128; *111:* 140; *136:* 145; *181:* 173; *200:* 213; *201:* 94
Smith, Kenneth R. *47:* 182
Smith, Keri *216:* 60
Smith, Kevin Warren *89:* 112
Smith, Kristin *209:* 197
Smith, L.H. *35:* 174
Smith, Lane *76:* 211, 213; *88:* 115; *105:* 202, 203,204, 205; *131:* 207; *160:* 217, 221; *179:* 183, 184, 185, 186; *199:* 122, 123, 124, 126; *224:* 164
Smith, Lee *29:* 32
Smith, Linell Nash *2:* 195
Smith, Maggie Kaufman *13:* 205; *35:* 191; *110:* 158; *178:* 226; *190:* 204; *209:* 145
Smith, Mavis *101:* 219
Smith, Moishe *33:* 155
Smith, Philip *44:* 134; *46:* 203

Smith, Ralph Crosby *2:* 267; *49:* 203
Smith, Robert D. *5:* 63
Smith, Sally J. *84:* 55
Smith, Susan Carlton *12:* 208
Smith, Terry *12:* 106; *33:* 158
Smith, Virginia *3:* 157; *33:* 72
Smith, William A. *1:* 36; *10:* 154; *25:* 65
Smith-Moore, J.J. *98:* 147
Smolinski, Dick *84:* 217
Smoljan, Joe *112:* 201
Smollin, Mike *39:* 203
Smyth, Iain *105:* 207
Smyth, M. Jane *12:* 15
Smythe, Fiona *151:* 213
Smythe, Theresa *141:* 37
Snair, Andy *176:* 4
Sneed, Brad *125:* 25; *191:* 175, 176; *211:* 194
Snow, Sarah *228:* 47
Snyder, Andrew A. *30:* 212
Snyder, Jerome *13:* 207; *30:* 173
Snyder, Joel *28:* 163
So, Meilo *162:* 201; *208:* 188
Soentpiet, Chris K. *97:* 208; *110:* 33; *159:* 184; *161:* 10; *163:* 130
Sofia *1:* 62; *5:* 90; *32:* 166; *86:* 43
Sofilas, Mark *93:* 157
Sogabe, Aki *207:* 153; *221:* 110
Sohn, Jiho *182:* 78
Sokol, Bill *37:* 178; *49:* 23
Sokolov, Kirill *34:* 188
Solbert, Ronni *1:* 159; *2:* 232; *5:* 121; *6:* 34; *17:* 249
Solomon, Michael *174:* 115
Solonevich, George *15:* 246; *17:* 47
Soloviov, Michael *223:* 122
Soma, Liana *81:* 118
Soman, David *90:* 122; *102:* 126; *140:* 120, 93; *188:* 43, 89; *200:* 180, 181
Sommer, Robert *12:* 211
Song, Jae *203:* 27
Soo, Kean *201:* 185
Sorel, Edward *4:* 61; *36:* 82; *65:* 191, 193; *126:* 214
Sorensen, Henri *196:* 58
Sorensen, Henrik *62:* 16
Sorensen, Svend Otto *22:* 130, 141; *67:* 188, 189
Sorra, Kristin *155:* 80; *229:* 85
Sosa, Hernan *198:* 66
Sostre, Maria *187:* 36
Sotomayor, Antonio *11:* 215
Souhami, Jessica *112:* 128; *176:* 193
Sousa, Natalie C. *209:* 89
Souza, Diana *71:* 139
Sovak, Jan *115:* 190
Sowards, Ben *215:* 62
Soyer, Moses *20:* 177
Spaenkuch, August *16:* 28
Spafford, Suzy *160:* 228
Spain, Valerie *105:* 76
Spain, Sunday Sahara *133:* 204
Spalenka, Greg *149:* 69; *151:* 228; *184:* 195; *191:* 21; *196:* 12; *198:* 181, 182, 201; *208:* 92
Spanfeller, James *1:* 72, 149; *2:* 183; *19:* 230, 231,232; *22:* 66; *36:* 160, 161; *40:* 75; *52:* 166; *76:* 37
Spangler, Brie *212:* 188
Sparks, Mary Walker *15:* 247
Spearing, Craig J. *228:* 172
Spears, Rick *182:* 187; *220:* 67
Speidel, Sandra *78:* 233; *94:* 178; *134:* 180; *210:* 67
Speirs, John *67:* 178
Spence, Geraldine *21:* 163; *47:* 196
Spence, Jim *38:* 89; *50:* 102
Spencer, Laurie *113:* 12
Spencer, Mark *57:* 170
Spengler, Kenneth J. *146:* 256
Sperling, Andrea *133:* 182
Spiegel, Beth *184:* 203

Spiegel, Doris *29:* 111
Spiegelman, Art *109:* 227
Spier, Jo *10:* 30
Spier, Peter *3:* 155; *4:* 200; *7:* 61; *11:* 78; *38:* 106; *54:* 120, 121, 122, 123, 124, 125, 126, 127, 128, 129, 130,131, 132, 133, 134
Spilka, Arnold *5:* 120; *6:* 204; *8:* 131
Spirin, Gennady *95:* 196, 197; *113:* 172; *128:* 9; *129:* 49; *134:* 210; *153:* 9; *204:* 143, 144, 145; *220:* 153
Spiro, Ruth *208:* 197
Spivak, I. Howard *8:* 10; *13:* 172
Spohn, David *72:* 233
Spohn, Kate *87:* 195; *147:* 201, 202
Spollen, Christopher J. *12:* 214
Spooner, Malcolm *40:* 142
Spoor, Mike *220:* 92
Spowart, Robin *82:* 228; *92:* 149; *133:* 131; *176:* 163; *177:* 183, 184; *217:* 123, 124
Sprague, Kevin *150:* 60; *196:* 62
Spranger, Nina *201:* 199
Sprattler, Rob *12:* 176
Spring, Bob *5:* 60
Spring, Ira *5:* 60
Springer, Harriet *31:* 92
Spudvilas, Anne *110:* 74; *197:* 192; *199:* 154
Spurll, Barbara *78:* 199; *88:* 141, 142; *99:* 215
Spurrier, Steven *28:* 198
Spuvilas, Anne *85:* 114
Spy
See Ward, Leslie
Squires, Stuart *127:* 74
St. Aubin, Bruno *179:* 54
St. John, J. Allen *41:* 62
Staake, Bob *209:* 168, 169; *229:* 132
Stabin, Victor *101:* 131; *164:* 158
Stadler, John *62:* 33; *204:* 149
Stadnyk, Greg *212:* 55
Staffan, Alvin E. *11:* 56; *12:* 187
Stahl, Ben *5:* 181; *12:* 91; *49:* 122; *71:* 128; *87:* 206; *112:* 107
Stair, Gobin *35:* 214
Stallwood, Karen *73:* 126
Stamaty, Mark Alan *12:* 215
Stammen, JoEllen McAllister *113:* 14
Stamp, Jørgen *225:* 184
Stampnick, Ken *51:* 142
Stanbridge, Joanne *150:* 91
Stanley, Diane *3:* 45; *37:* 180; *80:* 217, 219
Stanley, Sanna *145:* 228
Star, Lindsay *219:* 39
Starcke, Helmut *86:* 217
Stark, Ken *197:* 102
Starr, Branka *73:* 25
Stasiak, Krystyna *49:* 181; *64:* 194
Staub, Leslie *103:* 54
Stauffer, Brian *220:* 123
Staunton, Ted *112:* 192
Stawicki, Matt *164:* 250
Stead, L. *55:* 51, 56
Steadman, Broeck *97:* 185, 186; *99:* 56; *121:* 48; *208:* 190
Steadman, Henry *211:* 130
Steadman, Ralph *32:* 180; *123:* 143, 145
Stearn, Nick *183:* 26
Stearn, Todd *218:* 179
Steckler, June *90:* 178
Steele, Robert Gantt *169:* 174
Steichen, Edward *30:* 79
Steig, William *18:* 275, 276; *70:* 215, 216, 217, 218; *111:* 173, 174, 175, 176, 177
Stein, David Ezra *211:* 168
Stein, Harve *1:* 109
Steinberg, Saul *47:* 193
Steinel, William *23:* 146
Steiner, Charlotte *45:* 196
Steiner, Joan *110:* 219; *199:* 160, 161
Steirnagel, Michael *80:* 56
Stemp, Eric *60:* 184
Stengel, Christopher *229:* 200
Stephens, Alice Barber *66:* 208, 209

Stephens, Charles H. *YABC 2:* 279
Stephens, Pam *198:* 69
Stephens, Pat *126:* 110; *128:* 101
Stephens, William M. *21:* 165
Stephenson, Kristina *224:* 169
Steptoe, Javaka *151:* 203, 204; *190:* 169; *213:* 163, 164
Steptoe, John *8:* 197; *57:* 9; *63:* 158, 159, 160, 161,163, 164, 165, 166, 167; *96:* 4; *105:* 87
Stern, Simon *15:* 249, 250; *17:* 58; *34:* 192, 193
Sterret, Jane *53:* 27
Stetsios, Debbie *165:* 108, 109
Steven, Kat *158:* 237
Stevens, David *62:* 44
Stevens, Helen *189:* 31; *207:* 83
Stevens, Janet *40:* 126; *57:* 10, 11; *80:* 112; *90:* 221, 222; *109:* 156; *130:* 34; *166:* 202; *176:* 53, 116; *193:* 199, 200, 202; *208:* 127; *212:* 182
Stevens, Mary *11:* 193; *13:* 129; *43:* 95
Stevenson, Harvey *66:* 143; *80:* 201, 221; *153:* 60; *191:* 166
Stevenson, James *42:* 182, 183; *51:* 163; *66:* 184; *71:* 185, 187, 188; *78:* 262; *87:* 97; *113:* 182, 183,184, 185; *161:* 182, 183
Stevenson, Sucie *92:* 27; *104:* 194, 195; *112:* 168; *160:* 202; *194:* 172, 173; *195:* 166
Stewart, April Blair *75:* 210
Stewart, Arvis *33:* 98; *36:* 69; *60:* 118; *75:* 91; *127:* 4
Stewart, Charles *2:* 205
Stewart, Joel *151:* 205; *211:* 170, 171; *229:* 168
Stieg, William *172:* 58
Stiles, Fran *26:* 85; *78:* 56; *82:* 150
Stillman, Susan *44:* 130; *76:* 83
Stimpson, Tom *49:* 171
Stimson, James *208:* 46
Stinemetz, Morgan *40:* 151
Stinson, Paul *110:* 86
Stirnweis, Shannon *10:* 164
Stites, Joe *86:* 96
Stobbs, William *1:* 48, 49; *3:* 68; *6:* 20; *17:* 117, 217; *24:* 150; *29:* 250; *60:* 179; *87:* 204, 205,206
Stock, Catherine *37:* 55; *65:* 198; *72:* 7; *99:* 225; *114:* 197, 198, 199; *126:* 3; *145:* 161; *161:* 82; *173:* 149; *208:* 210; *214:* 192, 194; *224:* 196, 197
Stockman, Jack *113:* 24
Stoeke, Janet Morgan *90:* 225; *136:* 196; *202:* 182, 183
Stoerrle, Tom *55:* 147
Stolp, Jaap *49:* 98
Stolp, Todd *89:* 195
Stone, David L. *87:* 154
Stone, David *9:* 173
Stone, David K. *4:* 38; *6:* 124; *9:* 180; *43:* 182; *60:* 70
Stone, Helen V. *6:* 209
Stone, Helen *44:* 121, 122, 126
Stone, Kazuko G. *134:* 43
Stone, Kyle M. *202:* 185
Stone, Phoebe *86:* 212; *134:* 213; *162:* 188; *205:* 145
Stone, Steve *166:* 213; *208:* 185; *220:* 57,58; *224:* 124
Stone, Tony *150:* 34, 35
Storms, Patricia *217:* 163
Storrings, Michael *191:* 108; *216:* 217
Stoud, Virginia A. *89:* 31
Stover, Jill *82:* 234
Stower, Adam *217:* 89; *227:* 53
Strachan, Bruce *205:* 146
Stratton, Helen *33:* 151
Stratton-Porter, Gene *15:* 254, 259, 263, 264, 268, 269
Straub, Matt *192:* 176; *229:* 176
Straub, Phillip *197:* 22
Streano, Vince *20:* 173

Street, Janet Travell *84:* 235
Streeter, Clive *121:* 2
Strickland, Shadra *209:* 179
Stringer, Lauren *129:* 187; *154:* 172, 173; *161:* 127; *183:* 187, 188
Strodl, Daniel *47:* 95
Strogart, Alexander *63:* 139
Stromoski, Rick *111:* 179; *124:* 161, 190
Strong, Joseph D., Jr. *YABC 2:* 330
Stroyer, Poul *13:* 221
Strugnell, Ann *27:* 38
Struzan, Drew *117:* 6
Stubbs, William *73:* 196
Stubis, Talivaldis *5:* 182, 183; *10:* 45; *11:* 9; *18:* 304; *20:* 127
Stubley, Trevor *14:* 43; *22:* 219; *23:* 37; *28:* 61; *87:* 26
Stuck, Marion *104:* 44
Stuecklen, Karl W. *8:* 34, 65; *23:* 103
Stull, Betty *11:* 46
Stutzman, Mark *119:* 99
Stutzmann, Laura *73:* 185
Suarez, Maribel *162:* 208; *200:* 202
Suave, Gordon *209:* 66
Suba, Susanne *4:* 202, 203; *14:* 261; *23:* 134; *29:* 222; *32:* 30
Sue, Majella Lue *209:* 182; *212:* 146
Sueling, Barbara *98:* 185
Sueling, Gwenn *98:* 186
Sugarman, Tracy *3:* 76; *8:* 199; *37:* 181, 182
Sugimoto, Yugo *170:* 144; *223:* 137
Sugita, Yutaka *36:* 180, 181
Suh, John *80:* 157
Sullivan, Dorothy *89:* 113
Sullivan, Edmund J. *31:* 86
Sullivan, James F. *19:* 280; *20:* 192
Sully, Tom *104:* 199, 200; *182:* 77
Sumichrast, Jozef *14:* 253; *29:* 168, 213
Sumiko *46:* 57
Summers, Leo *1:* 177; *2:* 273; *13:* 22
Summers, Mark *118:* 144
Summers, Mike *190:* 176
Sutton, Judith *94:* 164
Svarez, Juan *56:* 113
Svendsen, Mark *181:* 176
Svolinsky, Karel *17:* 104
Swain, Carol *172:* 182
Swain, Su Zan Noguchi *21:* 170
Swan, Susan *22:* 220, 221; *37:* 66; *60:* 146; *145:* 205; *181:* 168
Swann, Susan *86:* 55
Swanson, Karl *79:* 65; *89:* 186
Swarner, Kristina *203:* 62; *215:* 184
Swayne, Sam *53:* 143, 145
Swayne, Zoa *53:* 143, 145
Swearingen, Greg *152:* 56; *165:* 135; *173:* 2; *224:* 32; *225:* 188
Sweat, Lynn *25:* 206; *57:* 176; *73:* 184; *168:* 178
Sweet, Darrell K. *60:* 9; *69:* 86; *74:* 15; *75:* 215; *76:* 130, 131; *81:* 96, 122; *82:* 253; *83:* 11; *84:* 14; *85:* 37; *89:* 140; *90:* 6; *91:* 137,139; *95:* 160, 161; *126:* 25; *185:* 175; *195:* 132
Sweet, Darrell K. *1:* 163; *4:* 136; *164:* 175
Sweet, Melissa *71:* 94; *72:* 172; *111:* 82; *139:* 53, 58; *141:* 88; *142:* 231; *155:* 121; *159:* 121, 122; *172:* 185; *188:* 127; *209:* 81; *211:* 174, 175; *218:* 21
Sweet, Ozzie *31:* 149, 151, 152
Sweetland, Robert *12:* 194
Swiatkowska, Gabi *132:* 43; *175:* 139; *180:* 218; *183:* 176
Swope, Martha *43:* 160; *56:* 86, 87, 89
Sylvada, Peter *154:* 174
Sylvester, Natalie G. *22:* 222
Szafran, Gene *24:* 144
Szasz, Susanne *13:* 55, 226; *14:* 48

Szekeres, Cyndy *2:* 218; *5:* 185; *8:* 85; *11:* 166; *14:* 19; *16:* 57, 159; *26:* 49, 214; *34:* 205; *60:* 150, 151, 152, 153, 154; *73:* 224; *74:* 218; *131:* 213, 215
Szpura, Beata *81:* 68; *119:* 65; *168:* 201
Szuc, Jeff *220:* 188

T

Taback, Simms *40:* 207; *52:* 120; *57:* 34; *80:* 241; *104:* 202, 203; *170:* 176, 177; *205:* 183
Taber, Patricia *75:* 124
Tabor, Nancy Maria Grande *89:* 210; *161:* 188
Taddei, Richard *112:* 13, 14
Tadgell, Nicole *150:* 77; *161:* 20; *177:* 186; *209:* 16; *220:* 190, 191
Tadiello, Ed *133:* 200
Tafuri, Nancy *39:* 210; *75:* 199, 200; *92:* 75; *130:* 215, 216, 217
Tailfeathers, Gerald *86:* 85
Tait, Douglas *12:* 220; *74:* 105, 106
Takabayashi, Mari *113:* 112; *130:* 22; *156:* 169
Takahashi, Hideko *136:* 160; *187:* 6; *209:* 152, 187
Takakjian, Portia *15:* 274
Takashima, Shizuye *13:* 228
Talarczyk, June *4:* 173
Talbott, Hudson *84:* 240; *163:* 100; *212:* 191, 192, 193
Tallarico, Tony *116:* 197
Tallec, Olivier *218:* 4
Tallon, Robert *2:* 228; *43:* 200, 201, 202, 203, 204, 205,206, 207, 209
Tamaki, Jillian *201:* 188
Tamas, Szecsko *29:* 135
Tamburine, Jean *12:* 222
Tanaka, Yoko *215:* 187
Tancredi, Sharon *215:* 127
Tandy, H.R. *13:* 69
Tandy, Russell H. *65:* 9; *100:* 30, 131
Tang, Charles *81:* 202; *90:* 192
Tang, Susan *80:* 174; *108:* 158
Tang, You-shan *63:* 100
Tankersley, Paul *69:* 206; *133:* 219
Tannenbaum, Robert *48:* 181
Tanner, Jane *87:* 13; *97:* 37
Tanner, Tim *72:* 192; *84:* 35
Tanobe, Miyuki *23:* 221
Tarabay, Sharif *110:* 149; *113:* 123; *169:* 83
Tarkington, Booth *17:* 224, 225
Tarlow, Phyllis *61:* 198
Tate, Don *159:* 141, 191; *183:* 69; *186:* 120
Tauss, Herbert *95:* 179
Tauss, Marc *117:* 160; *126:* 155; *178:* 221; *197:* 7; *223:* 168
Tavares, Matt *159:* 192, 193; *198:* 188, 189, 190; *199:* 86
Taylor, Ann *41:* 226
Taylor, Dahl *129:* 157
Taylor, Geoff *93:* 156; *197:* 173, 175; *204:* 151, 152
Taylor, Isaac *41:* 228
Taylor, Jennifer *226:* 128
Taylor, Mike *143:* 99, 100
Teague, Mark *83:* 6; *139:* 241; *170:* 180, 181; *205:* 150, 151
Teale, Edwin Way *7:* 196
Teason, James *1:* 14
Teckentrup, Britta *200:* 191, 192
Teeple, Lyn *33:* 147
Tee-Van, Helen Damrosch *10:* 176; *11:* 182
Teevee, Ningeokuluk *223:* 173
Teicher, Dick *50:* 211
Teichman, Mary *77:* 220; *124:* 208; *127:* 22; *197:* 33
Telgemeier, Raina *228:* 180, 181, 182
Temertey, Ludmilla *96:* 232; *104:* 43, 45; *109:* 244
Tempest, Margaret *3:* 237, 238; *88:* 200

Temple, Frances *85:* 185, 186, 187
Temple, Herbert *45:* 201
Templeton, Owen *11:* 77
ten Cate, Marijke *183:* 193
Tenggren, Gustaf *18:* 277, 278, 279; *19:* 15; *28:* 86; *YABC2:* 145
Tennent, Julie *81:* 105
Tenneson, Joyce *153:* 166
Tenney, Gordon *24:* 204
Tenniel, John *74:* 234, 235; *100:* 89; *YABC 2:* 99; *153:* 63
Tepper, Matt *116:* 80
Terkel, Ari *103:* 162
Terry, Michael *180:* 209
Terry, Will *131:* 73; *205:* 155; *223:* 105
Teskey, Donald *71:* 51
Tessler, Manya *200:* 193
Thacher, Mary M. *30:* 72
Thackeray, William Makepeace *23:* 224, 228
Thamer, Katie *42:* 187
Tharlet, Eve *146:* 149
Thelwell, Norman *14:* 201
Theobalds, Prue *40:* 23
Theurer, Marilyn Churchill *39:* 195
Thiesing, Lisa *89:* 134; *95:* 202; *156:* 190; *159:* 195
Thiewes, Sam *133:* 114
Thisdale, François *223:* 55
Thistlethwaite, Miles *12:* 224
Thollander, Earl *11:* 47; *18:* 112; *22:* 224
Thomas, Allan *22:* 13
Thomas, Art *48:* 217
Thomas, Eric *28:* 49
Thomas, Harold *20:* 98
Thomas, Jacqui *125:* 95
Thomas, Jan *197:* 180; *226:* 198
Thomas, Mark *42:* 136
Thomas, Martin *14:* 255
Thomas, Middy *177:* 114
Thompson, Arthur *34:* 107
Thompson, Carol *85:* 189; *95:* 75; *102:* 86; *147:* 166; *189:* 179, 180, 181; *190:* 84; *207:* 18
Thompson, Colin *95:* 204
Thompson, Ellen *51:* 88, 151; *60:* 33; *67:* 42; *77:* 148; *78:* 75, 219; *79:* 122, 170; *84:* 219; *85:* 97; *87:* 37; *88:* 192, 194; *89:* 80; *93:* 37; *98:* 59; *132:* 14
Thompson, George W. *22:* 18; *28:* 150; *33:* 135
Thompson, John *58:* 201; *102:* 226; *124:* 154; *128:* 228; *129:* 157; *150:* 49; *185:* 160; *191:* 192; *224:* 110
Thompson, Julie *44:* 158
Thompson, Katherine *132:* 146
Thompson, K. Dyble *84:* 6
Thompson, Miles *152:* 77
Thompson, Sharon *74:* 113; *158:* 60; *165:* 87
Thomson, Arline K. *3:* 264
Thomson, Bill *186:* 160
Thomson, Hugh *26:* 88
Thomson, Ross *36:* 179
Thorkelson, Gregg *95:* 183, 184; *98:* 58; *165:* 30, 31; *225:* 31, 32
Thorn, Lori *189:* 119
Thornberg, Dan *104:* 125
Thornburgh, Rebecca McKillip *143:* 37
Thorne, Diana *25:* 212
Thornhill, Jan *77:* 213
Thorpe, Peter *58:* 109
Thorvall, Kerstin *13:* 235
Threadgall, Colin *77:* 215
Thurber, James *13:* 239, 242, 243, 245, 248, 249
Thurman, Mark *63:* 173; *168:* 116
Tibbles, Jean-Paul *115:* 200
Tibbles, Paul *45:* 23
Tibo, Gilles *67:* 207; *107:* 199, 201
Tichenor, Tom *14:* 207
Tichnor, Richard *90:* 218

Tiegreen, Alan *36:* 143; *43:* 55, 56, 58; *77:* 200; *94:* 216, 217; *121:* 54, 59
Tierney, Tom *113:* 198, 200, 201
Tildes, Phyllis Limbacher *210:* 240
Tilley, Debbie *102:* 134; *133:* 226; *137:* 101; *159:* 96; *190:* 211, 212; *213:* 51
Tillman, Nancy *211:* 129, 178
Tillotson, Katherine *224:* 175
Tilney, F.C. *22:* 231
Timbs, Gloria *36:* 90
Timmins, Harry *2:* 171
Timmons, Bonnie *194:* 189
Tinkelman, Murray *12:* 225; *35:* 44
Titherington, Jeanne *39:* 90; *58:* 138; *75:* 79; *135:* 161
Tjader, Ella *209:* 14
Tobin, Nancy *145:* 197
Toddy, Irving *172:* 144
Tokunbo, Dimitrea *181:* 183; *187:* 182, 183; *226:* 209
Tolbert, Jeff *128:* 69
Toledo, Francisco *197:* 182; *198:* 199
Toledo, Natalia *197:* 182
Tolford, Joshua *1:* 221
Tolkien, J.R.R. *2:* 243; *32:* 215
Tolman, Marije *195:* 43
Tolmie, Ken *15:* 292
Tomei, Lorna *47:* 168, 171
Tomes, Jacqueline *2:* 117; *12:* 139
Tomes, Margot *1:* 224; *2:* 120, 121; *16:* 207; *18:* 250; *20:* 7; *25:* 62; *27:* 78, 79; *29:* 81, 199; *33:* 82; *36:* 186, 187, 188, 189, 190; *46:* 129; *56:* 71; *58:* 183; *70:* 228; *75:* 73, 75; *80:* 80; *83:* 97; *90:* 205
Tommaso, Rich *200:* 198
Tommorow, Tom *223:* 176
Toner, Raymond John *10:* 179
Tong, Gary *66:* 215
Tongier, Stephen *82:* 32
Tooke, Susan *173:* 162
Toothill, Harry *54:* 54; *7:* 49; *25:* 219; *42:* 192
Toothill, Ilse *6:* 54
Topaz, Ksenia *224:* 94
Topolski, Feliks *44:* 48
Torbert, Floyd James *22:* 226
Torgersen, Don *55:* 157
Torline, Kevin *169:* 171
Tormey, Bertram M. *75:* 3, 4
Torrecilla, Pablo *176:* 207
Torres, Leyla *156:* 199, 201
Torrey, Helen *87:* 41
Torrey, Marjorie *34:* 105
Torrey, Richard *189:* 182; *205:* 24
Toschik, Larry *6:* 102
Totten, Bob *13:* 93
Toy, Julie *128:* 112
Trachok, Cathy *131:* 16; *228:* 10
Tracy, Libba *82:* 24
Trago, Keith *158:* 253
Trail, Lee *55:* 157
Trang, To Ngoc *167:* 180
Trang, Winson *89:* 151
Trapani, Iza *116:* 202; *214:* 203
Travers, Bob *49:* 100; *63:* 145
Treatner, Meryl *95:* 180
Tremain, Ruthven *17:* 238
Tresilian, Stuart *25:* 53; *40:* 212
Trez, Alain *17:* 236
Trezzo, Loretta *86:* 45
Trier, Walter *14:* 96
Trimby, Elisa *47:* 199
Trinkle, Sally *53:* 27
Triplett, Gina *182:* 193; *188:* 100; *198:* 38
Tripp, F.J. *24:* 167
Tripp, Wallace *2:* 48; *7:* 28; *8:* 94; *10:* 54,76; *11:* 92; *31:* 170, 171; *34:* 203; *42:* 57; *60:* 157; *73:* 182
Trivas, Irene *53:* 4; *54:* 168; *82:* 46, 101
Trnka, Jiri *22:* 151; *43:* 212, 213, 214, 215; *YABC 1:* 30, 31
Trondheim, Lewis *182:* 183

Troughton, Joanna *37:* 186; *48:* 72
Troyer, Johannes *3:* 16; *7:* 18
Trudeau, G.B. *35:* 220, 221, 222; *48:* 119, 123, 126, 127,128, 129, 133; *168:* 189
Trueman, Matthew *165:* 208; *183:* 191; *220:* 61; *222:* 174
Truesdell, Sue *55:* 142; *108:* 219, 220; *212:* 202; *220:* 78
Tryon, Leslie *84:* 7; *139:* 214; *143:* 10; *181:* 10
Tseng, Jean *72:* 195; *94:* 102; *119:* 126; *151:* 106; *173:* 138, 139; *200:* 158
Tseng, Mou-sien *72:* 195; *94:* 102; *119:* 126; *151:* 106; *173:* 138, 139; *200:* 158
Tsinajinie, Andy *2:* 62
Tsinganos, Jim *180:* 142
Tsugami, Kyuzo *18:* 198, 199
Tucker, Ezra *156:* 31
Tuckwell, Jennifer *17:* 205
Tudor, Bethany *7:* 103
Tudor, Tasha *18:* 227; *20:* 185, 186, 187; *36:* 111; *69:* 196, 198; *100:* 44; *YABC 2:* 46, 314; *160:* 234
Tuerk, Hanne *71:* 201
Tugeau, Jeremy *199:* 170; *203:* 96
Tulloch, Maurice *24:* 79
Tunis, Edwin *1:* 218, 219; *28:* 209, 210, 211, 212
Tunnicliffe, C.F. *62:* 176; *177; *178; *179; *181
Turkle, Brinton *1:* 211, 213; *2:* 249; *3:* 226; *11:* 3; *16:* 209; *20:* 22; *50:* 23; *67:* 50; *68:* 65; *79:* 205, 206, 207; *128:* 47; *YABC 1:* 79
Turnbull, Christopher J. *143:* 99, 100
Turner, Gwenda *59:* 195
Turner, Helen *203:* 154
Turska, Krystyna *12:* 103; *31:* 173, 174, 175; *56:* 32,34; *100:* 66
Tusa, Tricia *72:* 242; *111:* 180, 181; *157:* 165; *164:* 186; *189:* 40; *201:* 9; *207:* 163, 164
Tusan, Stan *6:* 58; *22:* 236, 237
Tuschman, Richard *219:* 100; *224:* 188; *225:* 175
Tworkov, Jack *47:* 207
Tyers, Jenny *89:* 220
Tylden-Wright, Jenny *114:* 119
Tyrol, Adelaide Murphy *103:* 27
Tyrrell, Frances *107:* 204
Tzimoulis, Paul *12:* 104

U

Uchida, Yoshiko *1:* 220
Uderzo *47:* 88
Udovic, David *189:* 185; *195:* 201
Ueno, Noriko *59:* 155
Ugliano, Natascia *196:* 186
Ulm, Robert *17:* 238
Ulrich, George *73:* 15; *75:* 136, 139; *99:* 150
Ulriksen, Mark *101:* 58; *182:* 43; *210:* 243
Unada *84:* 67; *227:* 80
    See Gliewe, Unada
Underhill, Liz *53:* 159
Underwood, Beck *192:* 36
Underwood, Clarence *40:* 166
Unger, Jim *67:* 208
Ungerer, Tomi *5:* 188; *9:* 40; *18:* 188; *29:* 175; *33:* 221, 222, 223, 225; *71:* 48; *106:* 209, 210, 211, 212
Unwin, Nora S. *3:* 65, 234, 235; *4:* 237; *44:* 173, 174; *YABC 1:* 59; *2:* 301
Upitis, Alvis *145:* 179
Urban, Helle *149:* 243
Urbanovic, Jackie *86:* 86; *189:* 186, 187
Urberuaga, Emilio *219:* 110, 175
U'ren, Andrea *213:* 177
Uris, Jill *49:* 188, 197
Ursell, Martin *50:* 51
Utpatel, Frank *18:* 114
Utz, Lois *5:* 190

V

Vagin, Vladimir 66: 10; 142: 215
Vaillancourt, Francois 107: 199
Vainio, Pirkko 123: 157, 158
Valério, Geraldo 180: 225; 194: 116
Vallejo, Boris 62: 130; 72: 212; 91: 38; 93: 61
Van Abbe, S. 16: 142; 18: 282; 31: 90; YABC 2: 157, 161
Van Allsburg, Chris 37: 205, 206; 53: 161, 162, 163, 165,166, 167, 168, 169, 170, 171; 105: 215, 216, 217, 218; 156: 176, 177, 178
Vance, James 65: 28
Van Der Linde, Henry 99: 17
van der Meer, Ron 98: 204, 205
van der Meer, Atie 98: 204, 205
Vandivert, William 21: 175
Van Dongen, H.R. 81: 97
Van Dusen, Chris W. 173: 169; 228: 192
Vane, Mitch 210: 160; 218: 152
Van Everen, Jay 13: 160; YABC 1: 121
Van Fleet, John 165: 12, 13
Van Frankenhuyzen, Gijsbert 145: 230; 149: 164; 184: 151; 210: 248
van Genechten, Guido 165: 226
van Haeringen, Annemarie 193: 206
Van Horn, William 43: 218
van Hout, Mies 195: 191; 207: 58
van Kampen, Vlasta 194: 217
van Lawick, Hugo 62: 76, 79
Van Lieshout, Maria 201: 196; 223: 119
Van Loon, Hendrik Willem 18: 285, 289, 291
Van Munching, Paul 83: 85
van Ommen, Sylvia 186: 192
Van Patter, Bruce 183: 195
Van Rynbach, Iris 102: 192
Van Sciver, Ruth 37: 162
VanSeveren, Joe 63: 182
Van Stockum, Hilda 5: 193
Van Vleet, John 213: 180
Van Wassenhove, Sue 202: 193
Van Wely, Babs 16: 50; 79: 16
Van Wright, Cornelius 72: 18; 102: 208; 116: 107; 152: 236; 173: 170, 171; 199: 185
Van Zyle, Jon 103: 125; 160: 181, 182; 176: 199, 200; 221: 128
Vardzigulyants, Ruben 90: 54
Varga, Judy 29: 196
Vargo, Kurt 79: 224
Varley, Susan 61: 199; 63: 176, 177; 101: 148; 134: 220
Varon, Sara 195: 208
Vasconcellos, Daniel 80: 42
Vasiliu, Mircea 2: 166, 253; 9: 166; 13: 58; 68: 42
Vaughn, Frank 34: 157
Vavra, Robert 8: 206
Vawter, Will 17: 163
Vayas, Diana 71: 61
Vazquez, Carlos 125: 184
Veeder, Larry 18: 4
Velasquez, Eric 45: 217; 61: 45; 63: 110, 111; 88: 162; 90: 34, 144; 94: 213; 107: 147; 132: 192; 138: 213; 159: 126; 181: 184; 184: 96; 191: 16; 192: 234; 208: 37; 214: 81; 226: 201, 203, 212
Velasquez, Jose A. 63: 73
Velez, Walter 71: 75; 91: 154; 121: 181; 168: 49; 207: 52
Velthuijs, Max 110: 228, 229
Vendrell, Carme Sole 42: 205
Venezia, Mike 54: 17
Venti, Anthony Bacon 124: 103; 126: 26
Venturo, Piero 61: 194, 195
Ver Beck, Frank 18: 16, 17
Verling, John 71: 27
Verney, John 14: 225; 75: 8
Vernon, Ursula 204: 157
Verrier, Suzanne 5: 20; 23: 212

Verroken, Sarah 223: 178
Versace, Marie 2: 255
Verstraete, Randy 108: 193
Vess, Charles 215: 201
Vestal, H.B. 9: 134; 11: 101; 27: 25; 34: 158
Vestergaard, Hope 190: 203
Vicatan 59: 146
Vickrey, Robert 45: 59, 64
Victor, Joan Berg 30: 193
Vieceli, Emma 210: 245
Viereck, Ellen 3: 242; 14: 229
Vigna, Judith 15: 293; 102: 194, 195, 196, 197
Vila, Laura 207: 172
Vilato, Gaspar E. 5: 41
Villiard, Paul 51: 178
Vimnera, A. 23: 154
Vincent, Eric 34: 98
Vincent, Felix 41: 237
Vincent, Gabrielle 121: 175
Vip 45: 164
Viskupic, Gary 83: 48
Vitale, Stefano 109: 71, 107; 114: 219, 220; 123: 106; 138: 232; 180: 228, 229; 212: 38; 225: 191, 192, 193
Vivas, Julie 51: 67, 69; 96: 225; 197: 190; 199: 71
Voake, Charlotte 114: 221, 222; 180: 232
Vo-Dinh, Mai 16: 272; 60: 191
Vogel, Ilse-Margret 14: 230
Voigt, Erna 35: 228
Vojnar, Kamil 95: 31; 114: 4; 115: 62; 121: 90; 124: 72; 130: 31; 141: 81; 146: 196; 150: 123; 158: 5, 6; 158: 154; 171: 119, 188; 179: 15; 180: 112; 203: 74; 223: 30; 229: 43
Vojtech, Anna 42: 190; 108: 222, 223; 150: 203; 174: 173; 228: 21
von Buhler, Cynthia 149: 237; 162: 177; 177: 205; 180: 77; 185: 214, 215, 216
von Roehl, Angela 126: 191
von Schmidt, Eric 8: 62; 50: 209, 210
von Schmidt, Harold 30: 80
Vosburgh, Leonard 1: 161; 7: 32; 15: 295, 296; 23: 110; 30: 214; 43: 181
Voss, Tom 127: 104
Voter, Thomas W. 19: 3, 9
Vroman, Tom 10: 29
Vulliamy, Clara 72: 65
Vyner, Tim 228: 198

W

Waber, Bernard 47: 209, 210, 211, 212, 213, 214; 95: 215, 216, 217; 156: 203, 205, 206, 207
Wachenje, Benjamin 194: 170
Wack, Jeff 95: 140; 110: 90
Wagner, John 8: 200; 52: 104
Wagner, Ken 2: 59
Wagner, Michael 211: 159
Wahman, Wendy 218: 186
Waide, Jan 29: 225; 36: 139
Wainwright, Jerry 14: 85
Waites, Joan 171: 2; 226: 184
Wakeen, Sandra 47: 97
Wakiyama, Hanako 171: 96; 192: 236; 200: 16
Waldherr, Kris 81: 186
Waldman, Bruce 15: 297; 43: 178
Waldman, Neil 35: 141; 50: 163; 51: 180; 54: 78; 77: 112; 79: 162; 82: 174; 84: 5, 56, 106; 94: 232, 233, 234; 96: 41; 111: 139; 113: 9; 118: 30; 142: 220, 223; 203: 173, 174
Waldrep, Richard 111: 147; 198: 202
Walker, Brian 144: 128
Walker, Charles 1: 46; 4: 59; 5: 177; 11: 115; 19: 45; 34: 74; 62: 168; 72: 218
Walker, Dugald Stewart 15: 47; 32: 202; 33: 112

Walker, Gil 8: 49; 23: 132; 34: 42
Walker, Jeff 55: 154; 123: 116
Walker, Jim 10: 94
Walker, Mort 8: 213
Walker, Norman 41: 37; 45: 58
Walker, Stephen 12: 229; 21: 174
Wallace, Beverly Dobrin 19: 259
Wallace, Chad 229: 198
Wallace, Cly 87: 93
Wallace, Ian 53: 176, 177; 56: 165, 166; 58: 4; 98: 4; 101: 191; 112: 124; 141: 197, 198, 199, 200; 151: 212; 219: 180, 182
Wallace, John 105: 228
Wallace, Nancy Elizabeth 141: 204; 186: 195, 197, 199; 222: 191, 192, 193, 194
Wallenta, Adam 123: 180
Waller, S.E. 24: 36
Wallner, Alexandra 15: 120; 156: 183
Wallner, John C. 9: 77; 10: 188; 11: 28; 14: 209; 31: 56, 118; 37: 64; 51: 186, 187, 188, 189, 190, 191,192, 193, 194, 195; 52: 96; 53: 23, 26; 71: 99; 73: 158; 89: 215; 141: 9
Wallner, John 162: 17
Wallower, Lucille 11: 226
Walotsky, Ron 93: 87
Walsh, Ellen Stoll 99: 209; 147: 219; 194: 194, 195, 196
Walsh, Rebecca 158: 193; 217: 169, 170
Walsh, Vivian 149: 215; 158: 227
Walters, Anita 205: 163
Walters, Audrey 18: 294
Walther, Tom 31: 179
Walton, Garry 69: 149
Walton, Tony 11: 164; 24: 209; 153: 8; 177: 73
Waltrip, Lela 9: 195
Waltrip, Mildred 3: 209; 37: 211
Waltrip, Rufus 9: 195
Wan 12: 76
Wan, Shelly 212: 131
Wang, Lin 221: 179
Wang, Shaoli 216: 220
Wang, Suling 191: 183; 213: 194
Warburton, Sarah 154: 187
Wappers, G. 121: 40
Ward, Chad Michael 217: 121
Ward, Fred 52: 19
Ward, Helen 72: 244; 144: 240, 242
Ward, John 42: 191; 96: 54; 97: 110; 123: 105; 124: 71; 173: 66; 221: 55
Ward, Keith 2: 107; 132: 69
Ward, Leslie 34: 126; 36: 87
Ward, Lynd 1: 99, 132, 133, 150; 2: 108, 158, 196, 216; 18: 86; 27: 56; 29: 79, 187, 253, 255; 36: 199,200, 201, 202, 203, 204, 205, 206, 207, 209; 43: 34; 56: 28; 60: 116; 100: 65
Ward, Peter 37: 116
Waring, Geoff 172: 84
Warhola, James 92: 5; 115: 85, 87; 118: 174, 175, 177; 176: 84; 187: 189, 190; 223: 102
Warner, Ben 159: 171
Warner, Peter 14: 87
Warner, Sally 214: 210
Warnes, Tim 175: 159; 202: 188; 216: 224
Warnick, Elsa 113: 223
Warren, Betsy 2: 101
Warren, Jim 85: 81
Warren, Marion Cray 14: 215
Warshaw, Jerry 30: 197, 198; 42: 165
Wasden, Kevin 102: 162
Washington, Nevin 20: 123
Washington, Phyllis 20: 123
Wasserman, Amy L. 92: 110; 209: 95
Waterman, Stan 11: 76
Watkins-Pitchford, D.J. 6: 215, 217
Watling, James 67: 210; 78: 112; 101: 81; 117: 189, 190; 127: 119, 120
Watson, Aldren A. 2: 267; 5: 94; 13: 71; 19: 253; 32: 220; 42: 193, 194, 195, 196, 197, 198, 199, 200, 201; YABC 2: 202

Watson, G. *83:* 162
Watson, Gary *19:* 147; *36:* 68; *41:* 122; *47:* 139
Watson, J.D. *22:* 86
Watson, Jesse Joshua *197:* 124; *199:* 181; *202:* 136
Watson, Karen *11:* 26
Watson, Mary *117:* 193
Watson, Richard Jesse *62:* 188, 189; *211:* 201
Watson, Wendy *5:* 197; *13:* 101; *33:* 116; *46:* 163; *64:* 12; *74:* 242, 243; *91:* 21; *142:* 228; *215:* 79
Watt, Mélanie *136:* 206; *193:* 211
Wattenberg, Jane *174:* 200; *185:* 46; *187:* 108
Watterson, Bill *66:* 223, 225, 226
Watts, Bernadette *4:* 227; *103:* 182, 183
Watts, James *59:* 197; *74:* 145; *86:* 124
Watts, John *37:* 149
Watts, Leslie Elizabeth *150:* 207; *165:* 106; *209:* 67
Watts, Stan *116:* 205
Weatherby, Mark Alan *77:* 141
Web, Hannah *228:* 215
Webb, Jennifer *110:* 79
Webb, Lanny *142:* 175
Webb, Sophie *135:* 214
Webber, Helen *3:* 141
Webber, Irma E. *14:* 238
Weber, Erik *56:* 19, 20
Weber, Florence *40:* 153
Weber, Jill *127:* 227, 228; *189:* 163; *208:* 157; *209:* 190, 191; *216:* 46
Weber, Roland *61:* 204
Weber, Sam *190:* 227
Weber, William J. *14:* 239
Webster, Jean *17:* 241
Weeks, Sarah *162:* 39
Wegman, William *78:* 243
Wegner, Fritz *14:* 250; *20:* 189; *44:* 165; *86:* 62
Weidenear, Reynold H. *21:* 122
Weigel, Jeff *170:* 193
Weihs, Erika *4:* 21; *15:* 299; *72:* 201; *107:* 207, 208
Weil, Lisl *7:* 203; *10:* 58; *21:* 95; *22:* 188,217; *33:* 193
Weiman, Jon *50:* 162, 165; *52:* 103; *54:* 78, 79, 81; *78:* 80; *82:* 107; *93:* 82; *97:* 69; *105:* 179; *193:* 65
Weiner, Greg *215:* 21
Weiner, Sandra *14:* 240
Weiner, Scott *55:* 27
Weinhaus, Karen Ann *53:* 90; *71:* 50; *86:* 124
Weinman, Brad *197:* 20
Weinstock, Robert *204:* 165, 166
Weisgard, Leonard *1:* 65; *2:* 191, 197, 204, 264, 265; *5:* 108; *21:* 42; *30:* 200, 201, 203, 204; *41:* 47; *44:* 125; *53:* 25; *85:* 196, 198, 200, 201; *100:* 139,207; *YABC 2:* 13
Weisman, David *173:* 47
Weiss, Ellen *44:* 202
Weiss, Emil *1:* 168; *7:* 60
Weiss, Harvey *1:* 145, 223; *27:* 224, 227; *68:* 214; *76:* 245, 246, 247
Weiss, Nicki *33:* 229
Weissman, Bari *49:* 72; *90:* 125; *139:* 142
Weitzman, David L. *172:* 199
Welch, Sheila Kelly *130:* 221
Welkes, Allen *68:* 218
Wellington, Monica *99:* 223; *157:* 259, 260, 261; *222:* 197, 198, 199, 200
Welliver, Norma *76:* 94
Wellner, Fred *127:* 53
Wells, Frances *1:* 183
Wells, H.G. *20:* 194, 200
Wells, Haru *53:* 120, 121
Wells, Robert E. *184:* 208
Wells, Rosemary *6:* 49; *18:* 297; *60:* 32; *66:* 203; *69:* 215, 216; *114:* 227; *118:* 149, 150; *156:* 188, 189, 190, 191; *207:* 180, 181, 182, 183

Wells, Rufus III *56:* 111, 113
Wells, Susan *22:* 43
Wendelin, Rudolph *23:* 234
Wengenroth, Stow *37:* 47
Weninger, Brigitte *189:* 192, 194
Werenskiold, Erik *15:* 6; *62:* 17
Werner, Honi *24:* 110; *33:* 41; *88:* 122
Werth, Kurt *7:* 122; *14:* 157; *20:* 214; *39:* 128
Wesson,
West, Harry A. *124:* 38; *227:* 16
Westcott, Nadine Bernard *68:* 46; *84:* 49; *86:* 133; *106:* 199; *111:* 78; *113:* 111; *130:* 224; *139:* 54; *158:* 256; *194:* 199
Westerberg, Christine *29:* 226
Westerduin, Anne *105:* 229
Westerman, Johanna *162:* 206
Weston, Martha *29:* 116; *30:* 213; *33:* 85, 100; *53:* 181, 182, 183, 184; *77:* 95; *80:* 152; *119:* 196,197, 198, 199; *127:* 189; *133:* 196; *209:* 199
Wetherbee, Margaret *5:* 3
Wexler, Jerome *49:* 73; *150:* 129
Whalley, Peter *50:* 49
Whamond, Dave *222:* 203
Whatley, Bruce *186:* 93, 95; *207:* 127; *213:* 183, 184
Wheatley, Arabelle *11:* 231; *16:* 276
Wheeler, Cindy *49:* 205
Wheeler, Dora *44:* 179
Wheelright, Rowland *15:* 81; *YABC 2:* 286
Whelan, Michael *56:* 108; *70:* 27, 29, 67, 68, 148; *74:* 18; *84:* 14; *91:* 195, 196; *95:* 147; *98:* 150, 151; *106:* 157; *113:* 218, 220; *116:* 99, 100
Whelan, Patrick *135:* 145
Whistler, Rex *16:* 75; *30:* 207, 208
White, Beth *216:* 139
White, Craig *110:* 130; *119:* 193; *130:* 33; *179:* 31
White, David Omar *5:* 56; *18:* 6
White, Joan *83:* 225
White, Lee *221:* 176; *223:* 188, 189, 190
White, Martin *51:* 197; *85:* 127
Whitear *32:* 26
Whitehead, Beck *86:* 171
Whitehead, Jenny *221:* 16
Whitehead, S.B. *154:* 132
Whithorne, H.S. *7:* 49
Whitman, Candace *208:* 208
Whitney, George Gillett *3:* 24
Whitney, Jean *99:* 53
Whitson, Paul *102:* 161
Whittam, Geoffrey *30:* 191
Whyte, Mary *96:* 127
Wiberg, Harald *38:* 127; *93:* 215
Wick, Walter *77:* 128
Wickstrom, Sylvie *106:* 87; *169:* 180; *214:* 110
Wickstrom, Thor *200:* 205
Widener, Terry *105:* 230; *106:* 7; *163:* 23; *200:* 17; *209:* 195
Wiese, Kurt *3:* 255; *4:* 206; *14:* 17; *17:* 18, 19; *19:* 47; *24:* 152; *25:* 212; *32:* 184; *36:* 211,213, 214, 215, 216, 217, 218; *45:* 161; *100:* 92
Wiesner, David *33:* 47; *51:* 106; *57:* 67; *58:* 55; *64:* 78, 79, 81; *69:* 233; *72:* 247, 248, 249, 251,252, 253, 254; *83:* 134; *104:* 31; *117:* 197, 199, 200, 202; *139:* 223, 224; *151:* 51; *181:* 189, 190
Wiesner, William *4:* 100; *5:* 200, 201; *14:* 262
Wight, Eric *218:* 190
Wiggins, George *6:* 133
Wijngaard, Juan *111:* 36; *114:* 124; *227:* 136
Wikkelsoe, Otto *45:* 25, 26
Wikland, Ilon *5:* 113; *8:* 150; *38:* 124, 125, 130; *127:* 162
Wikler, Madeline *114:* 233
Wilbur, C. Keith, M.D. *27:* 228
Wilburn, Kathy *53:* 102; *68:* 234
Wilcox, Cathy *105:* 123

Wilcox, J.A.J. *34:* 122
Wilcox, Lydia *207:* 187
Wilcox, R. Turner *36:* 219
Wild, Jocelyn *46:* 220, 221, 222; *80:* 117
Wilde, George *7:* 139
Wildsmith, Brian *16:* 281, 282; *18:* 170, 171; *66:* 25; *69:* 224, 225, 227; *77:* 103; *83:* 218; *124:* 214,217, 219
Wildsmith, Mike *140:* 229
Wilhelm, Hans *58:* 189, 191; *73:* 157; *77:* 127; *135:* 229, 230, 233, 234; *196:* 209
Wilkin, Eloise *36:* 173; *49:* 208, 209, 210
Wilkinson, Barry *50:* 213
Wilkinson, Gerald *3:* 40
Wilkon, Jozef *31:* 183, 184; *71:* 206, 207, 209; *133:* 222
Wilks, Mike *34:* 24; *44:* 203; *224:* 193
Willems, Mo *154:* 245, 246, 247; *180:* 236, 237, 239; *228:* 204, 208
Willey, Bee *103:* 129; *139:* 159; *173:* 115
Willhoite, Michael A. *71:* 214
William, Maria *168:* 51
Williams, Berkeley, Jr. *64:* 75
Williams, Ferelith Eccles *22:* 238
Williams, Garth *1:* 197; *2:* 49, 270; *4:* 205; *15:* 198, 302, 304, 307; *16:* 34; *18:* 283, 298, 299, 300, 301; *29:* 177, 178, 179, 232, 233, 241, 242, 243, 244, 245, 248; *40:* 106; *66:* 229, 230, 231, 233, 234; *71:* 192; *73:* 218, 219, 220; *78:* 261; *100:* 251, 252, 255; *136:* 117; *YABC 2:* 15, 16, 19
Williams, J. Scott *48:* 28
Williams, Jennifer *102:* 201
Williams, Jenny *60:* 202; *81:* 21; *88:* 71
Williams, Kent *180:* 18
Williams, Kit *44:* 206, 207, 208, 209, 211, 212
Williams, Marcia *97:* 214; *159:* 208, 209
Williams, Maureen *12:* 238
Williams, Patrick *14:* 218
Williams, Richard *44:* 93; *72:* 229; *74:* 133; *78:* 155, 237; *91:* 178; *110:* 212; *136:* 201, 202, 203; *152:* 115
Williams, Sam *124:* 222; *153:* 11; *177:* 201, 202; *180:* 34; *212:* 49
Williams, Sophy *135:* 236
Williams, Vera B. *53:* 186, 187, 188, 189; *102:* 201, 202, 203; *210:* 65
Williamson, Alex *177:* 180; *205:* 50
Williamson, Mel *60:* 9
Willingham, Fred *104:* 206; *154:* 157
Willis, Adam *181:* 75; *209:* 11
Willmore, J.T. *54:* 113, 114
Wilsdorf, Anne *180:* 122; *189:* 124; *191:* 195
Wilson, Anne *160:* 114; *224:* 199, 200
Wilson, Charles Banks *17:* 92; *43:* 73
Wilson, Connie *113:* 179
Wilson, Dagmar *10:* 47
Wilson, Dawn *67:* 161; *81:* 120; *113:* 158
Wilson, Edward A. *6:* 24; *16:* 149; *20:* 220, 221; *22:* 87; *26:* 67; *38:* 212, 214, 215, 216, 217
Wilson, Forrest *27:* 231
Wilson, Gahan *35:* 234; *41:* 136
Wilson, George *76:* 87
Wilson, Helen Miranda *140:* 61
Wilson, Jack *17:* 139
Wilson, Janet *77:* 154; *96:* 114; *99:* 219, 220; *153:* 64 *106:* 122; *130:* 210; *145:* 178; *173:* 64
Wilson, John *22:* 240
Wilson, Maurice *46:* 224
Wilson, Patten *35:* 61
Wilson, Peggy *15:* 4; *84:* 20
Wilson, Phil *181:* 29
Wilson, Rowland B. *30:* 170
Wilson, Sarah *50:* 215
Wilson, Tom *33:* 232
Wilson, W.N. *22:* 26
Wilson-Max, Ken *170:* 196; *180:* 181
Wilton, Nicholas *103:* 52; *183:* 111
Wilwerding, Walter J. *9:* 202

Wimmer, Mike *63:* 6; *70:* 121; *75:* 186; *76:* 21,22, 23; *91:* 114; *97:* 45, 68; *98:* 28; *107:* 130; *146:* 21; *149:* 47; *173:* 126; *193:* 21, 25; *194:* 204, 205
Winborn, Marsha *78:* 34; *99:* 70; *192:* 20
Winch, John *165:* 233
Winchester, Linda *13:* 231
Wind, Betty *28:* 158
Windham, Kathryn Tucker *14:* 260
Windham, Sophie *184:* 212
Winfield, Alison *115:* 78; *214:* 121
Winfield, Wayne *72:* 23
Wing, Gary *64:* 147
Wing, Ron *50:* 85
Wingerter, Linda S. *132:* 199; *174:* 181; *200:* 196
Winick, Judd *124:* 227, 228, 229
Winn-Lederer, Ilene *202:* 91
Winnick, Karen B. *211:* 207
Winslow, Will *21:* 124
Winstead, Rosie *180:* 243
Winsten, Melanie Willa *41:* 41
Winter, Jeanette *151:* 240, 241, 242; *184:* 215, 217, 218, 219
Winter, Milo *15:* 97; *19:* 221; *21:* 181, 203, 204, 205; *64:* 19; *YABC 2:* 144
Winter, Paula *48:* 227
Winter, Susan *163:* 177; *182:* 201; *226:* 173
Winters, Greg *70:* 117
Winters, Nina *62:* 194
Wise, Louis *13:* 68
Wiseman, Ann *31:* 187
Wiseman, B. *4:* 233
Wishnefsky, Phillip *3:* 14
Wiskur, Darrell *5:* 72; *10:* 50; *18:* 246
Wisniewski, David *95:* 220, 221
Wisniewski, Robert *95:* 10; *119:* 192
Withee, Maureen *225:* 42
Witschonke, Alan *153:* 149, 150
Witt, Dick *80:* 244
Wittmann, Patrick *162:* 204
Wittman, Sally *30:* 219
Wittner, Dale *99:* 43
Wittwer, Hala *158:* 267; *195:* 80
Woehr, Lois *12:* 5
Wohlberg, Meg *12:* 100; *14:* 197; *41:* 255
Wohnoutka, Mike *137:* 68; *190:* 199; *195:* 218; *205:* 132; *221:* 6
Wojtowycz, David *167:* 168
Woldin, Beth Weiner *34:* 211
Wolf, Elizabeth *133:* 151; *208:* 175
Wolf, J. *16:* 91
Wolf, Janet *78:* 254
Wolf, Linda *33:* 163
Wolfe, Corey *72:* 213
Wolfe, Frances *216:* 227
Wolfe, Gillian *199:* 193
Wolff, Ashley *50:* 217; *81:* 216; *156:* 216, 217; *170:* 57; *174:* 174; *184:* 72; *203:* 181, 182, 183, 184
Wolff, Glenn *178:* 230
Wolff, Jason *213:* 186
Wolfsgruber, Linda *166:* 61
Wondriska, William *6:* 220
Wong, Janet S. *98:* 225; *152:* 43
Wong, Ken *224:* 23
Wong, Nicole *174:* 13; *214:* 216; *215:* 25
Wonsetler, John C. *5:* 168
Wood, Audrey *50:* 221, 222, 223; *81:* 219, 221; *198:* 206
Wood, Don *50:* 220, 225, 226, 228, 229; *81:* 218, 220; *139:* 239, 240
Wood, Grant *19:* 198
Wood, Heather *133:* 108
Wood, Ivor *58:* 17
Wood, Jakki *211:* 209
Wood, Muriel *36:* 119; *77:* 167; *171:* 55; *187:* 46
Wood, Myron *6:* 220
Wood, Owen *18:* 187; *64:* 202, 204, 205, 206, 208, 210

Wood, Rob *193:* 48
Wood, Ruth *8:* 11
Woodbridge, Curtis *133:* 138; *204:* 113
Wooding, Sharon L. *66:* 237
Woodruff, Liza *132:* 239; *182:* 46, 204
Woodruff, Thomas *171:* 73
Woods, John, Jr. *109:* 142
Woods, Maria *227:* 69
Woodson, Jack *10:* 201
Woodson, Jacqueline *94:* 242
Woodward, Alice *26:* 89; *36:* 81
Wool, David *26:* 27
Wooley, Janet *112:* 75; *227:* 74
Woolman, Steven *106:* 47; *163:* 73
Wooten, Vernon *23:* 70; *51:* 170
Worboys, Evelyn *1:* 166, 167
Word, Reagan *103:* 204
Wormell, Christopher *154:* 251; *202:* 206
Worth, Jo *34:* 143
Worth, Wendy *4:* 133
Wosmek, Frances *29:* 251
Wrenn, Charles L. *38:* 96; *YABC 1:* 20, 21
Wright, Barbara Mullarney *98:* 161
Wright, Cliff *168:* 203
Wright, Dare *21:* 206
Wright-Frierson, Virginia *58:* 194; *110:* 246
Wright, George *YABC 1:* 268
Wright, Joseph *30:* 160
Wronker, Lili Cassel *3:* 247; *10:* 204; *21:* 10
Wu, Donald *200:* 18
Wummer, Amy *154:* 181; *168:* 150; *176:* 85; *201:* 202, 203; *218:* 154
Wyant, Alexander Helwig *110:* 19
Wyatt, David *97:* 9; *101:* 44; *114:* 194; *140:* 20; *167:* 13; *188:* 48; *227:* 60
Wyatt, Stanley *46:* 210
Wyeth, Andrew *13:* 40; *YABC 1:* 133, 134
Wyeth, Jamie *41:* 257
Wyeth, N.C. *13:* 41; *17:* 252, 253, 254, 255, 256, 257, 258, 259, 264, 265, 266, 267, 268; *18:* 181; *19:* 80, 191, 200; *21:* 57, 183; *22:* 91; *23:* 152; *24:* 28, 99; *35:* 61; *41:* 65; *100:* 206; *YABC1:* 133, 223; *2:* 53, 75, 171, 187, 317
Wyman, Cherie R. *91:* 42
Wynne, Patricia J. *210:* 260; *223:* 184

X

Xuan, YongSheng *119:* 202, 207, 208; *140:* 36; *187:* 21; *226:* 221, 227, 230, 232, 233

Y

Yaccarino, Dan *141:* 208, 209; *147:* 171; *192:* 244, 245; *207:* 168
Yakovetic, Joe *59:* 202; *75:* 85
Yalowitz, Paul *93:* 33; *211:* 92
Yamaguchi, Marianne *85:* 118
Yamasaki, James *167:* 93
Yang, Belle *170:* 198
Yang, Jay *1:* 8; *12:* 239
Yap, Weda *6:* 176
Yaroslava
    See Mills, Yaroslava Surmach
Yashima, Taro *14:* 84
Yates, John *74:* 249, 250
Yates, Kelly *208:* 214
Yayo *178:* 88; *226:* 235
Yeatts, Tabatha *215:* 210
Yee, Cora *166:* 233
Yee, Wong Herbert *115:* 216, 217; *172:* 204, 205; *194:* 59
Yelchin, Eugene *204:* 4
Yeo, Brad *135:* 121; *192:* 106
Yerxa, Leo *181:* 195

Yezerski, Thomas F. *162:* 29
Ylla
    See Koffler, Camilla
Yohn, F.C. *23:* 128; *YABC 1:* 269
Yoo, Taeeun *191:* 198
Yorinks, Adrienne *144:* 248; *200:* 214
Yorke, David *80:* 178
Yoshida, Toshi *77:* 231
Yoshikawa, Sachiko *168:* 104; *177:* 28; *181:* 196, 197; *225:* 115
Youll, Paul *91:* 218
Youll, Stephen *92:* 227; *118:* 136, 137; *164:* 248; *202:* 92
Young, Amy L. *185:* 218; *190:* 46
Young, Cybéle *167:* 9
Young, Ed *7:* 205; *10:* 206; *40:* 124; *63:* 142; *74:* 250, 251, 252, 253; *75:* 227; *81:* 159; *83:* 98; *94:* 154; *115:* 160; *137:* 162; *YABC 2:* 242; *173:* 174, 175, 176; *205:* 29; *212:* 82; *221:* 72
Young, Mary O'Keefe *77:* 95; *80:* 247; *134:* 214; *140:* 213; *211:* 223, 225
Young, Noela *8:* 221; *89:* 231; *97:* 195
Young, Paul *190:* 222; *225:* 38
Young, Selina *153:* 12; *201:* 204, 205
Yuen, Sammy *223:* 46
Yum, Hyewon *211:* 228
Yun, Cheng Mung *60:* 143
Yung, Jennifer *220:* 136

Z

Zacharow, Christopher *88:* 98
Zacks, Lewis *10:* 161
Zadig *50:* 58
Zaffo, George *42:* 208
Zagwyn, Deborah Turney *138:* 227
Zahares, Wade *193:* 219
Zaid, Barry *50:* 127; *51:* 201
Zaidenberg, Arthur *34:* 218, 219, 220
Zalben, Jane Breskin *7:* 211; *79:* 230, 231, 233; *170:* 202
Zallinger, Jean *4:* 192; *8:* 8, 129; *14:* 273; *68:* 36; *80:* 254; *115:* 219, 220, 222
Zallinger, Rudolph F. *3:* 245
Zakrajsek, Molly *177:* 146
Zappa, Ahmet *180:* 250
Zebot, George *83:* 214
Zecca, Katherine *207:* 195
Zeck, Gerry *40:* 232
Zeff, Joe *181:* 98; *221:* 101
Zeifert, Harriet *154:* 265, 267
Zeiring, Bob *42:* 130
Zeldich, Arieh *49:* 124; *62:* 120
Zeldis, Malcah *86:* 239; *94:* 198; *146:* 265, 266
Zelinsky, Paul O. *14:* 269; *43:* 56; *49:* 218-223; *53:* 111; *68:* 195; *102:* 219, 222, 221, 222; *154:* 255, 256, 257; *171:* 141; *185:* 96
Zelvin, Diana *72:* 190; *76:* 101; *93:* 207
Zemach, Kaethe *149:* 250
Zemach, Margot *3:* 270; *8:* 201; *21:* 210, 211; *27:* 204, 205, 210; *28:* 185; *49:* 22, 183, 224; *53:* 151; *56:* 146; *70:* 245, 246; *92:* 74
Zeman, Ludmila *153:* 212
Zemsky, Jessica *10:* 62
Zepelinsky, Paul *35:* 93
Zerbetz, Evon *127:* 34; *158:* 109
Zezejl, Daniel *197:* 74
Zhang, Ange *101:* 190; *172:* 41
Zhang, Son Nang *163:* 113; *170:* 206
Ziegler, Jack *84:* 134
Zimdars, Berta *129:* 155
Zimet, Jay *147:* 94; *152:* 74; *196:* 75
Zimic, Tricia *72:* 95
Zimmer, Dirk *38:* 195; *49:* 71; *56:* 151; *65:* 214; *84:* 159; *89:* 26; *147:* 224
Zimmer, Tracie Vaughn *169:* 183

Zimmerman, Andrea *192:* 49, 50
Zimmermann, H. Werner *101:* 223; *112:* 197
Zimnik, Reiner *36:* 224
Zingone, Robin *180:* 134
Zinkeisen, Anna *13:* 106
Zinn, David *97:* 97
Zoellick, Scott *33:* 231

Zollars, Jaime *190:* 190
Zonia, Dhimitri *20:* 234, 235
Zorn, Peter A., Jr. *142:* 157
Zudeck, Darryl *58:* 129; *63:* 98; *80:* 52
Zug, Mark *88:* 131; *204:* 169
Zulewski, Tim *164:* 95
Zuma *99:* 36

Zvorykin, Boris *61:* 155
Zweifel, Francis *14:* 274; *28:* 187
Zwerger, Lisbeth *54:* 176, 178; *66:* 246, 247, 248; *130:* 230, 231, 232, 233; *181:* 92; *194:* 224, 225, 226
Zwinger, Herman H. *46:* 227
Zwolak, Paul *67:* 69, 71, 73, 74

Author Index

The following index gives the number of the volume in which an author's biographical sketch, Autobiography Feature, Brief Entry, or Obituary appears.

This index includes references to all entries in the following series, which are also published by The Gale Group.

YABC—*Yesterday's Authors of Books for Children: Facts and Pictures about Authors and Illustrators of Books for Young People from Early Times to 1960*
CLR—*Children's Literature Review: Excerpts from Reviews, Criticism, and Commentary on Books for Children*
SAAS—*Something about the Author Autobiography Series*

A

Aardema, Verna 1911-2000 .... *107*
  Obituary *119*
  Earlier sketches in SATA *:4, 68*
  See also CLR *17*
  See also SAAS *8*
Aaron, Chester 1923- *216*
  Autobiography Feature *216*
  Earlier sketches in SATA *9, 74*
  See also SAAS *12*
Aaseng, Nate
  See Aaseng, Nathan
Aaseng, Nathan 1953- *172*
  Brief entry *38*
  Earlier sketches in SATA *51, 88*
  See also CLR *54*
  See also SAAS *12*
Abadzis, Nick 1965- *193*
Abalos, Rafael 1956-
  See Abalos, Rafael
Abalos, Rafael 1956- *197*
Abbas, Jailan 1952- *91*
Abbey, Lynn
  See Abbey, Marilyn Lorraine
Abbey, Marilyn Lorraine 1948- *156*
Abbott, Alice
  See Borland, Kathryn Kilby
  and Speicher, Helen Ross S(mith)
Abbott, Jacob 1803-1879 .... *22*
Abbott, Manager Henry
  See Stratemeyer, Edward L.
Abbott, R(obert) Tucker 1919-1995 .... *61*
  Obituary *87*
Abbott, Sarah
  See Zolotow, Charlotte
Abbott, Tony 1952- *205*
  Earlier sketch in SATA *159*
Abdelsayed, Cindy 1962- *123*
Abdul, Raoul 1929- *12*
Abeele, Veronique van den *196*
Abel, Raymond 1911- *12*
Abell, Kathleen 1938- *9*
Abelove, Joan *110*
Abels, Harriette S(heffer) 1926- *50*
Abercrombie, Barbara 1939- *182*
  Earlier sketch in SATA *16*
Abercrombie, Barbara Mattes
  See Abercrombie, Barbara

Abercrombie, Lynn
  See Sorrells, Walter
Abernethy, Robert G(ordon) 1927- *5*
Abisch, Roslyn Kroop 1927- *9*
Abisch, Roz
  See Abisch, Roslyn Kroop
Ablow, Gail 1962- *198*
Abodaher, David J. (Naiph) 1919- *17*
Abolafia, Yossi 1944-
  See Abulafia, Yossi
Abolivier, Aurelie *219*
Abouzeid, Chris *175*
Abrahall, Clare Hoskyns
  See Hoskyns-Abrahall, Clare (Constance Drury)
Abrahams, Hilary (Ruth) 1938- *29*
Abrahams, Peter 1947- *194*
Abrahams, Robert David 1905-1998 .... *4*
Abramovitz, Anita (Zeltner Brooks) 1914- *5*
Abrams, Joy 1941- *16*
Abrams, Lawrence F. *58*
  Brief entry *47*
Abrashkin, Raymond 1911-1960 .... *50*
Abulafia, Yossi 1944- *177*
  Brief entry *46*
  Earlier sketch in SATA *60*
Acampora, Paul *175*
Accardo, Anthony *191*
Acer, David *206*
Achebe, Albert Chinualumogu
  See Achebe, Chinua
Achebe, Chinua 1930- *40*
  Brief entry *38*
  Earlier sketch in SATA *38*
  See also CLR *156*
Acheson, Alison 1964- *222*
Ackerman, Diane 1948- *102*
Ackerman, Eugene (Francis) 1888-1974 .... *10*
Ackerman, Karen 1951- *126*
Ackerman, Susan Yoder 1945- *92*
Ackison, Wendy Wassink 1956- *103*
Ackley, Peggy Jo 1955- *58*
Ackroyd, Peter 1949- *153*
Acorn, John (Harrison) 1958- *79*
Acredolo, Linda (Potter) 1947- *159*
Acs, Laszlo (Bela) 1931- *42*
  Brief entry *32*
Acuff, Selma Boyd 1924- *45*

Ada, Alma Flor 1938- *222*
  Autobiography Feature *222*
  Earlier sketches in SATA *43, 84, 143, 181*
  See also CLR *62*
Adair, Gilbert 1944- *98*
Adair, Ian 1942- *53*
Adair, Margaret Weeks (?)-1971 .... *10*
Adam, Cornel
  See Lengyel, Cornel Adam
Adam, Mark
  See Alexander, Marc
Adam, Robert 1948- *93*
Adams, Adrienne 1906- *90*
  Earlier sketch in SATA *8*
  See also CLR *73*
Adams, Andy 1859-1935
  See YABC *1*
Adams, Barbara Johnston 1943- *60*
Adams, Bruin
  See Ellis, Edward S.
Adams, Captain Bruin
  See Ellis, Edward S.
Adams, Captain J. F. C.
  See Ellis, Edward S.
Adams, Dale
  See Quinn, Elisabeth
Adams, Daniel
  See Nicole, Christopher
Adams, Debra
  See Speregen, Devra Newberger
Adams, Diane 1960- *217*
Adams, Douglas 1952-2001 .... *116*
  Obituary *128*
Adams, Douglas Noel
  See Adams, Douglas
Adams, Edith
  See Shine, Deborah
Adams, Florence 1932- *61*
Adams, Georgie 1945- *216*
Adams, Harriet S(tratemeyer) 1892(?)-1982 .... *1*
  Obituary *29*
Adams, Harrison
  See Rathborne, St. George (Henry)
  and Stratemeyer, Edward L.
Adams, Hazard 1926- *6*
Adams, Hazard Simeon
  See Adams, Hazard
Adams, John Anthony 1944- *67*
Adams, Kathryn *224*

Adams, Laurie 1941- *33*
Adams, Lowell
  See Joseph, James (Herz)
Adams, Nicholas
  See Pine, Nicholas
Adams, Nicholas
  See Smith, Sherwood
Adams, Nicholas
  See Doyle, Debra
  and Macdonald, James D.
Adams, Pam 1919- *112*
Adams, Pamela
  See Adams, Pam
Adams, Richard 1920- *69*
  Earlier sketch in SATA 7
  See also CLR *121*
Adams, Richard George
  See Adams, Richard
Adams, Ruth Joyce *14*
Adams, S.J.
  See Selzer, Adam
Adams, Tricia
  See Kite, Pat
Adams, William Taylor 1822-1897 .... *28*
Adam Smith, Janet (Buchanan) 1905-1999 .. *63*
Adamson, Gareth 1925-1982(?) *46*
  Obituary *30*
Adamson, George 1906-1989
  Obituary *63*
Adamson, George (Worsley) 1913-2005 ...... *30*
Adamson, Graham
  See Groom, Arthur William
Adamson, Joy(-Friederike Victoria)
  1910-1980 .... *11*
  Obituary *22*
Adamson, Wendy Writson 1942- *22*
Addasi, Maha 1968- *205*
Addison, Kenneth 1949(?)-2005 .... *187*
Addison, Kenneth L.
  See Addison, Kenneth
Addona, Angelo F. 1925- *14*
Addy, Sean 1976- *222*
Addy, Sharon Hart 1943- *192*
  Earlier sketch in SATA *108*
Addy, Ted
  See Winterbotham, R(ussell) R(obert)
Adelberg, Doris
  See Orgel, Doris
Adelson, Leone 1908- *11*
Adinolfi, JoAnn *176*
Adkins, Jan 1944- *210*
  Autobiography Feature *210*
  Earlier sketches in SATA 8, 69, 144
  See also CLR 77
  See also SAAS 19
Adl, Shirin 1975- *225*
Adler, C. S. 1932- *126*
  Earlier sketches in SATA 26, 63, 102
  See also CLR 78
  See also SAAS 15
Adler, Carole Schwerdtfeger
  See Adler, C. S.
Adler, David A. 1947- *178*
  Earlier sketches in SATA 14, 70, 106, 151
  See also CLR 108
Adler, Irene
  See Penzler, Otto
  and Storr, Catherine (Cole)
Adler, Irving 1913- *29*
  Autobiography Feature *164*
  Earlier sketch in SATA *1*
  See also CLR 27
  See also SAAS 15
Adler, Larry 1939- *36*
Adler, Peggy *22*
Adler, Ruth 1915-1968 .... *1*
Adlerman, Daniel (Ezra) 1963- *163*
  Earlier sketch in SATA 96
Adlerman, Kim
  See Adlerman, Kimberly M(arie)

Adlerman, Kimberly M(arie) 1964- *163*
  Earlier sketch in SATA 96
Adoff, Arnold 1935- *96*
  Earlier sketches in SATA 5, 57
  See also CLR 7
  See also SAAS 15
Adoff, Jaime *163*
Adoff, Jaime Levi
  See Adoff, Jaime
Adorjan, Carol (Madden) 1934- *71*
  Earlier sketch in SATA 10
Adrian, Frances
  See Polland, Madeleine A(ngela Cahill)
Adrian, Mary
  See Jorgensen, Mary Venn
Adshead, Gladys L(ucy) 1896-1985 .... *3*
Aesop 620(?)B.C.-560(?)B.C. *64*
  See also CLR *14*
Aesop, Abraham
  See Newbery, John
Affabee, Eric
  See Stine, R.L.
Agapida, Fray Antonio
  See Irving, Washington
Agard, John 1949- *223*
  Earlier sketch in SATA *138*
Agard, Nadema 1948- *18*
Agarwal, Deepa 1947- *141*
Agee, Jon 1960- *196*
  Earlier sketches in SATA *116, 157*
Agell, Charlotte 1959- *214*
  Earlier sketches in SATA 99, 150
Agent Orange
  See Moseley, James W(illett)
Aghill, Gordon
  See Garrett, Randall
  and Silverberg, Robert
Agle, Nan Hayden 1905- *3*
  See also SAAS 10
Agnew, Edith J(osephine) 1897-1988 .... *11*
Agnew, Lincoln *222*
Agonito, Joseph *177*
Agonito, Rosemary 1937- *177*
Aguilar, David *214*
Aguilar, David A.
  See Aguilar, David
Ahern, Margaret McCrohan 1921- *10*
Ahl, Anna Maria 1926- *32*
Ahlberg, Allan 1938- *214*
  Brief entry *35*
  Earlier sketches in SATA 68, 120, 165
  See also CLR 18
Ahlberg, Janet 1944-1994 .... *120*
  Brief entry *32*
  Obituary *83*
  Earlier sketch in SATA 68
  See also CLR 18
Ahlberg, Jessica 1980- *229*
Aho, Julia Kay
  See Kay, Julia
Aichinger, Helga 1937- *4*
Aiken, Clarissa (M.) Lorenz 1899-1992 .... *12*
  Obituary *109*
Aiken, Conrad 1889-1973 .... *30*
  Earlier sketch in SATA 3
Aiken, Conrad Potter
  See Aiken, Conrad
Aiken, Joan (Delano) 1924-2004 .... *73*
  Autobiography Feature *109*
  Obituary *152*
  Earlier sketches in SATA 2, 30
  See also CLR 90
  See also SAAS 1
Aillaud, Cindy Lou 1955- *184*
Ainsley, Alix
  See Steiner, Barbara A(nnette)
Ainsworth, Catherine Harris 1910- *56*
Ainsworth, Norma 1911-1987 .... *9*
Ainsworth, Ruth (Gallard) 1908- *73*
  Earlier sketch in SATA 7
Ainsworth, William Harrison 1805-1882 ..... *24*

Aistrop, Jack 1916- *14*
Aitken, Amy 1952- *54*
  Brief entry *40*
Aitken, Dorothy 1916- *10*
Aitmatov, Chingiz 1928-2008 .... *56*
Aitmatov, Chingiz Torekulovich
  See Aitmatov, Chingiz
Ajhar, Brian 1957- *220*
Akaba, Suekichi 1910- *46*
Akers, Floyd
  See Baum, L. Frank
Akib, Jamel *181*
Aks, Patricia 1926-1994 .... *68*
Alagoa, Ebiegberi Joe 1933- *108*
Alain
  See Brustlein, Daniel
Alajalov, Constantin 1900-1987
  Obituary *53*
Alalou, Ali *203*
Alalou, Elizabeth *203*
Alan, David
  See Horsfield, Alan
Alan, Robert
  See Silverstein, Robert Alan
Alarcon, Francisco X. 1954- *215*
  Earlier sketch in SATA *104*
Alarcon, Francisco Xavier
  See Alarcon, Francisco X.
Alarcon, Karen Beaumont
  See Beaumont, Karen
Albert, Burton 1936- *22*
Albert, Louise 1928- *157*
Albert, Michael 1966- *202*
Albert, Richard E. 1909-1999 .... *82*
Albert, Susan Wittig 1940- *107*
Alberts, Frances Jacobs 1907-1989 .... *14*
Albertson, Susan
  See Wojciechowski, Susan
Albion, Lee Smith *29*
Alborough, Jez 1959- *149*
  Earlier sketch in SATA 86
Albrecht, Lillie (Vanderveer H.)
  1894-1985 .... *12*
Albyn, Carole Lisa 1955- *83*
Alchemy, Jack
  See Gershator, David
Alcock, Gudrun 1908- *56*
  Brief entry *33*
Alcock, Vivien (Dolores) 1924-2003 .... *76*
  Brief entry *38*
  Obituary *148*
  Earlier sketch in SATA 45
  See also CLR 26
Alcorn, John 1935- *31*
  Brief entry *30*
Alcorn, Stephen 1958- *207*
  Earlier sketch in SATA *110*
Alcott, Louisa May 1832-1888 .... *100*
  See also YABC *1*
  See also CLR *109*
Alda, Arlene 1933- *205*
  Brief entry *36*
  Earlier sketches in SATA 44, 106, 158
  See also CLR 93
Alden, Isabella (Macdonald) 1841-1930 ..... *115*
  See also YABC *2*
Alden, Sue
  See Francis, Dorothy
Alderman, Clifford Lindsey 1902-1988 .... *3*
Alderson, Sue Ann 1940- *59*
  Brief entry *48*
Alding, Peter
  See Jeffries, Roderic
Aldis, Dorothy (Keeley) 1896-1966 .... *2*
Aldiss, Brian W. 1925- *34*
Aldiss, Brian Wilson
  See Aldiss, Brian W.
Aldon, Adair
  See Meigs, Cornelia Lynde
Aldous, Allan (Charles) 1911- *27*

Aldrich, Ann
  See Meaker, Marijane
Aldrich, Bess Streeter 1881-1954
  See CLR 70
Aldrich, Thomas (Bailey) 1836-1907 .... *114*
  Earlier sketch in SATA *17*
Aldridge, (Harold Edward) James 1918- *87*
Aldridge, Josephine Haskell *14*
Aldridge, Sheila 1974- *192*
Aleas, Richard
  See Ardai, Charles
Alegria, Malin 1974(?)- *190*
Alegria, Ricardo E(nrique) 1921- *6*
Aleksin, Anatolii Georgievich 1924- *36*
Alenov, Lydia 1948- *61*
Alex, Ben (a pseudonym) 1946- *45*
Alex, Marlee (a pseudonym) 1948- *45*
Alexander, Alma 1963- *217*
Alexander, Anna B(arbara Cooke) 1913- *1*
Alexander, Anne
  See Alexander, Anna B(arbara Cooke)
Alexander, Claire *228*
Alexander, Ellen 1938- *91*
Alexander, Frances (Laura) 1888-1979 .... *4*
Alexander, Janet 1907-1994 .... *97*
  Earlier sketch in SATA *1*
Alexander, Jill S. 1964- *223*
Alexander, Jill Shurbet
  See Alexander, Jill S.
Alexander, Jocelyn Anne Arundel 1930- *22*
Alexander, Linda 1935- *2*
Alexander, Lloyd 1924-2007 .... *135*
  Obituary *182*
  Earlier sketches in SATA *3, 49, 81, 129*
  See also CLR 48
  See also SAAS 19
Alexander, Lloyd Chudley
  See Alexander, Lloyd
Alexander, Marc 1929- *117*
Alexander, Martha 1920- *136*
  Earlier sketches in SATA *11, 70*
Alexander, Rae Pace
  See Alexander, Raymond Pace
Alexander, Raymond Pace 1898-1974 .... *22*
Alexander, Robert *200*
Alexander, Rod
  See Pellowski, Michael (Joseph)
Alexander, Sally Hobart 1943- *84*
Alexander, Sue 1933-2008 .... *136*
  Obituary *195*
  Earlier sketches in SATA *12, 89*
  See also SAAS 15
Alexander, Vincent Arthur 1925-1980
  Obituary *23*
Alexeieff, Alexandre A. 1901-1979 .... *14*
Alger, Horatio, Jr.
  See Stratemeyer, Edward L.
Alger, Horatio, Jr. 1832-1899 .... *16*
  See also CLR 87
Alger, Leclaire (Gowans) 1898-1969 .... *15*
Aliki
  See Brandenberg, Aliki
Alkema, Chester Jay 1932- *12*
Al-Khalili, Jim 1962- *124*
Alkiviades, Alkis 1953- *105*
Alko, Selina 1968- *218*
Alkouatli, Claire *186*
Allaby, John Michael
  See Allaby, Michael
Allaby, Michael 1933- *167*
Allamand, Pascale 1942- *12*
Allan, Mabel Esther 1915-1998 .... *75*
  Earlier sketches in SATA *5, 32*
  See also CLR 43
  See also SAAS *11*
Allan, Nicholas 1956- *123*
  Earlier sketch in SATA *79*
Allan-Meyer, Kathleen 1918- *51*
  Brief entry *46*
Allard, Harry
  See Allard, Harry G., Jr.

Allard, Harry G.
  See Allard, Harry G., Jr.
Allard, Harry G., Jr. 1928- *216*
  Earlier sketches in SATA *42, 102*
  See also CLR 85
Allee, Marjorie Hill 1890-1945 .... *17*
Allen, Adam
  See Epstein, Beryl
  and Epstein, Samuel
Allen, Alex B.
  See Heide, Florence Parry
Allen, Allyn
  See Eberle, Irmengarde
Allen, Betsy
  See Harrison, Elizabeth (Allen) Cavanna
Allen, Bob 1961- *76*
Allen, Gertrude E(lizabeth) 1888-1984 .... *9*
Allen, Grace
  See Hogarth, Grace (Weston Allen)
Allen, Jeffrey (Yale) 1948- *42*
Allen, John
  See Perry, Ritchie (John Allen)
Allen, Jonathan 1957- *177*
  Earlier sketch in SATA *131*
Allen, Jonathan Dean
  See Allen, Jonathan
Allen, Joy 1948- *217*
Allen, Judy (Christina) 1941- *124*
  Earlier sketch in SATA *80*
Allen, Kenneth S. 1913-1981 .... *56*
Allen, Leroy 1912- *11*
Allen, Linda 1925- *33*
Allen, Marjorie 1931- *22*
Allen, Maury 1932-2010 .... *26*
Allen, Merritt Parmelee 1892-1954 .... *22*
Allen, Nancy Kelly 1949- *171*
  Earlier sketch in SATA *127*
Allen, Nina (Stroemgren) 1935- *22*
Allen, Pamela (Kay) 1934- *123*
  Earlier sketches in SATA *50, 81*
  See also CLR 44
Allen, Raul *205*
Allen, Rodney F. 1938-1999 .... *27*
Allen, Roger MacBride 1957- *105*
Allen, Ruth
  See Peterson, Esther (Allen)
Allen, Samuel W(ashington) 1917- *9*
Allen, T. D.
  See Allen, Terril Diener
Allen, Terril Diener 1908- *35*
Allen, Terry D.
  See Allen, Terril Diener
Allen, Thomas B. 1929- *193*
  Earlier sketches in SATA *45, 140*
Allen, Thomas Benton
  See Allen, Thomas B.
Allen, Tom
  See Allen, Thomas B.
Allende, Isabel 1942- *163*
  See also CLR 99
Allerton, Mary
  See Govan, (Mary) Christine Noble
Alley, Robert W.
  See Alley, R.W.
Alley, R.W. *211*
  Earlier sketch in SATA *169*
Alley, Zoe B. *214*
Alleyn, Ellen
  See Rossetti, Christina
Allington, Richard L(loyd) 1947- *39*
  Brief entry *35*
Allison, Amy 1956- *138*
Allison, Bob *14*
Allison, Diane Worfolk *78*
Allison, Jennifer *173*
Allison, Linda 1948- *43*
Allison, Margaret
  See Klam, Cheryl
Allman, Barbara 1950- *137*
Allmendinger, David F(rederick), Jr. 1938- . *35*
Allred, Alexandra Powe 1965- *144*

Allred, Gordon T(hatcher) 1930- *10*
Allsop, Kenneth 1920-1973 .... *17*
Allsopp, Sophie *188*
Alma, Ann 1946- *201*
Almedingen, E. M.
  See Almedingen, Martha Edith von
Almedingen, Martha Edith von 1898-1971 .... *3*
Almon, Russell
  See Clevenger, William R.
  and Downing, David A(lmon)
Almond, David 1951- *158*
  Earlier sketch in SATA *114*
  See also CLR 85
Almond, Linda Stevens 1881(?)-1987
  Obituary *50*
Almquist, Don 1929- *11*
Alonzo, Sandra *199*
Alphin, Elaine Marie 1955- *139*
  Autobiography Feature *139*
  Earlier sketches in SATA *80, 130*
Alsenas, Linas 1979- *186*
Alsop, Mary O'Hara 1885-1980 .... *34*
  Obituary *24*
  Earlier sketch in SATA *2*
Alter, Anna 1974- *206*
  Earlier sketch in SATA *135*
Alter, Judith 1938- *101*
  Earlier sketch in SATA *52*
Alter, Judith MacBain
  See Alter, Judith
Alter, Judy
  See Alter, Judith
Alter, Robert Edmond 1925-1965 .... *9*
Alter, Stephen 1956- *187*
Althea
  See Braithwaite, Althea
Altman, Linda Jacobs 1943- *21*
Altman, Suzanne
  See Orgel, Doris
  and Schecter, Ellen
Alton, Steve *169*
Altschuler, Franz 1923- *45*
Altsheler, Joseph A(lexander) 1862-1919
  See YABC 1
Alvarez, John
  See del Rey, Lester
Alvarez, Joseph A. 1930- *18*
Alvarez, Julia 1950- *129*
al-Windawi, Thura
  See Windawi, Thura al-
Alyer, Philip A.
  See Stratemeyer, Edward L.
Amado, Elisa *193*
Amann, Janet 1951- *79*
Amato, Carol A. 1942- *92*
Amato, Mary 1961- *178*
  Earlier sketch in SATA *140*
Ambrose, Stephen E. 1936-2002 .... *138*
  Earlier sketch in SATA *40*
Ambrose, Stephen Edward
  See Ambrose, Stephen E.
Ambrus, Gyozo Laszlo 1935- *1*
  See also SAAS 4
Ambrus, Victor G.
  See Ambrus, Gyozo Laszlo
Amend, Bill 1962- *147*
Amerman, Lockhart 1911-1969 .... *3*
Ames, Evelyn 1908-1990 .... *13*
  Obituary *64*
Ames, Gerald 1906-1993 .... *11*
  Obituary *74*
Ames, Lee J(udah) 1921- *151*
  Earlier sketch in SATA *3*
Ames, Mildred 1919-1994 .... *85*
  Earlier sketches in SATA *22, 81*
Amico, Tom 1960(?)- *176*
Amit, Ofra 1966- *205*
Ammon, Richard 1942- *124*
Amon, Aline 1928- *9*
Amory, Jay
  See Lovegrove, James

Author Index

Amoss, Berthe 1925- 112
Earlier sketch in SATA 5
Amstutz, Andre 1925- 214
Anastasio, Dina 1941- 94
Brief entry 30
Earlier sketch in SATA 37
Anaya, Rudolfo 1937-
See CLR 129
Anaya, Rudolfo A.
See Anaya, Rudolfo
Anaya, Rudolpho Alfonso
See Anaya, Rudolfo
Anckarsvard, Karin Inez Maria 1915-1969 6
Ancona, George 1929- 208
Autobiography Feature 208
Earlier sketches in SATA 12, 85, 145, 192
See also SAAS 18
Anders, C. J.
See Bennett, Cherie
Anders, Isabel 1946- 101
Anders, Lou 176
Andersdatter, Karla M. 1938- 34
Andersen, Bethanne 1954- 191
Andersen, Hans Christian 1805-1875 100
See also YABC 1
See also CLR 113
Andersen, Ted
See Boyd, Waldo T.
Andersen, Yvonne 1932- 27
Anderson, Bernice G(oudy) 1894-1997 33
Anderson, Bob 1944- 139
Earlier sketch in SATA 136
Anderson, Brad 1924- 33
Brief entry 31
Anderson, Bradley Jay
See Anderson, Brad
Anderson, Brian 1974- 211
Anderson, C. C.
See Anderson, Catherine Corley
Anderson, C(larence) W(illiam) 1891-1971 . 11
Anderson, Carolyn Dunn
See Dunn, Carolyn
Anderson, Catherine C.
See Anderson, Catherine Corley
Anderson, Catherine Corley 1909-2001 72
See Lee, Cora
Anderson, Clifford
See Gardner, Richard (M.)
Anderson, Daryl Shon 1963- 93
Anderson, Dave
See Anderson, David
Anderson, David 1929- 60
Anderson, Derek 1969- 169
Anderson, Eloise Adell 1927- 9
Anderson, George
See Groom, Arthur William
Anderson, Grace Fox 1932- 43
Anderson, J(ohn) R(ichard) L(ane)
1911-1981 15
Obituary 27
Anderson, Jessica Lee 1980- 224
Anderson, Jodi Lynn 182
Anderson, John David 197
Anderson, John L. 1905- 2
Anderson, Joy 1928- 1
Anderson, Kevin J. 1962- 117
Earlier sketch in SATA 74
Anderson, Kevin James
See Anderson, Kevin J.
Anderson, Kirsty 1978- 108
Anderson, K.J.
See Moesta, Rebecca
Anderson, Laurie Halse 1961- 186
Earlier sketches in SATA 95, 132
See also CLR 138
Anderson, LaVere Francis Shoenfelt
1907-1998 27
Anderson, Leone Castell 1923- 53
Brief entry 49
Anderson, Lisa G. 1963- 108

Anderson, Lonzo
See Anderson, John L.
Anderson, Lucia (Lewis) 1922- 10
Anderson, Madelyn Klein 1926-2005 28
Anderson, Margaret J(ean) 1931- 27
See also SAAS 8
Anderson, Marilyn D. 1943- 144
Anderson, Mary 1939- 82
Earlier sketch in SATA 7
See also SAAS 23
Anderson, Matthew Tobin
See Anderson, M.T.
Anderson, Mona 1910-2004 40
Anderson, Mrs. Melvin
See Anderson, Catherine Corley
Anderson, M.T. 1968- 182
Earlier sketches in SATA 97, 146
Anderson, Norman Dean 1928- 22
Anderson, Peggy Perry 1953- 179
Earlier sketch in SATA 84
Anderson, Poul 1926-2001 90
Autobiography Feature 106
Brief entry 39
See also CLR 58
Anderson, Poul William
See Anderson, Poul
Anderson, Rachel 1943- 86
Earlier sketch in SATA 34
See also SAAS 18
Anderson, Rebecca J.
See Anderson, R.J.
Anderson, Rebecca M.
See Moesta, Rebecca
Anderson, Rebecca Moesta
See Moesta, Rebecca
Anderson, Richard
See Anderson, J(ohn) R(ichard) L(ane)
Anderson, R.J. 1970(?)- 216
Anderson, Sara 173
Anderson, Scoular 201
Anderson, (Tom) Scoular 138
Anderson, Stephanie 1976- 225
Anderson, Susan 1952- 90
Anderson, Thomas Scoular
See Anderson, Scoular
Anderson, W. B.
See Schultz, James Willard
Anderson, Wayne 1946- 202
Earlier sketches in SATA 56, 147
Andersson, Kenneth 1970- 200
Andre, Evelyn M. 1924- 27
Andre, Evelyn Marie
See Andre, Evelyn M.
Andreasen, Dan 227
Earlier sketch in SATA 186
Andreassen, Karl
See Boyd, Waldo T.
Andreassi, K. Robert
See DeCandido, Keith R.A.
Andree, Louise
See Coury, Louise Andree
Andrew, Ian 1962- 166
Earlier sketch in SATA 116
Andrew, Ian Peter
See Andrew, Ian
Andrew, Prudence (Hastings) 1924- 87
Andrews, Benny 1930-2006 31
Obituary 178
Andrews, Eleanor Lattimore
See Lattimore, Eleanor Frances
Andrews, Elton V.
See Pohl, Frederik
Andrews, F(rank) Emerson 1902-1978 22
Andrews, J(ames) S(ydney) 1934- 4
Andrews, Jan 1942- 167
Brief entry 49
Earlier sketches in SATA 58, 98
Andrews, Julie 1935- 153
Earlier sketch in SATA 7
See also CLR 85

Andrews, Laura
See Coury, Louise Andree
Andrews, Roy Chapman 1884-1960 19
Andrews, Tamra 1959- 129
Andrews, V(irginia) C(leo) 1924(?)-1986
Obituary 50
Andrews, Wendy
See Sharmat, Marjorie Weinman
Andrews, William G. 1930- 74
Andrews, William George
See Andrews, William G.
Andrezel, Pierre
See Blixen, Karen
Andriani, Renee
See Williams-Andriani, Renee
Andriola, Alfred J. 1912-1983
Obituary 34
Andrist, Ralph K. 1914-2004 45
Andronik, Catherine M. 189
Andryszewski, Tricia 1956- 148
Earlier sketch in SATA 88
Anelli, Melissa 1979- 215
Angaramo, Roberta 1974- 229
Angel, Ann 1952- 192
Angel, Carl 178
Angel, Marie 1923- 47
Angeles, Peter A. 1931- 40
Angeletti, Roberta 1964- 124
Angeli, Marguerite (Lofft) de
See de Angeli, Marguerite (Lofft)
Angell, Judie 1937- 78
Earlier sketch in SATA 22
See also CLR 33
Angell, Madeline 1919- 18
Angelo, Valenti 1897- 14
Angelou, Maya 1928- 136
Earlier sketch in SATA 49
See also CLR 53
Angier, Bradford -1997 12
Angle, Kimberly Greene 203
Angle, Paul M(cClelland) 1900-1975
Obituary 20
Anglund, Joan Walsh 1926- 2
See also CLR 94
Ango, Fan D.
See Longyear, Barry B(rookes)
Angrist, Stanley W(olff) 1933- 4
Anhalt, Ariela 1990(?)- 227
Anholt, Catherine 1958- 131
Earlier sketch in SATA 74
Anholt, Laurence 1959- 141
Earlier sketch in SATA 74
Aninno, J.G.
See Annino, Jan Godown
Anita
See Daniel, Anita
Anmar, Frank
See Nolan, William F.
Annett, Cora
See Scott, Cora Annett (Pipitone)
Annie-Jo
See Blanchard, Patricia
and Suhr, Joanne
Annino, Jan Godown 1952- 228
Annixter, Jane
See Sturtzel, Jane Levington
Annixter, Paul
See Sturtzel, Howard A(llison)
Anno, Mitsumasa 1926- 157
Earlier sketches in SATA 5, 38, 77
See also CLR 122
Anrooy, Francine Van
See Van Anrooy, Francine
Ansary, Mir Tamim 1948- 140
Anstey, Caroline 1958- 81
Antell, Will D. 1935- 31
Anthony, Barbara
See Barber, Antonia
Anthony, C. L.
See Smith, Dorothy Gladys
Anthony, Edward 1895-1971 21

Anthony, John
  See Beckett, Ronald Brymer
    and Ciardi, John (Anthony)
    and Sabini, John Anthony
Anthony, Joseph Patrick 1964- *103*
Anthony, Patricia 1947- *109*
Anthony, Piers 1934- *129*
  Autobiography Feature *129*
  Earlier sketch in SATA *84*
  See also CLR *118*
  See also SAAS *22*
Anthony, Susan C(arol) 1953- *87*
Anticaglia, Elizabeth 1939- *12*
Antieau, Kim *214*
Antilles, Kem
  See Moesta, Rebecca
Antle, Nancy 1955- *102*
Antolini, Margaret Fishback 1904-1985
  Obituary *45*
Anton, Michael J(ames) 1940- *12*
Antonacci, Robert J(oseph) 1916- *45*
  Brief entry *37*
Anvil, Christopher 1925-2009 .... *102*
Anzaldua, Gloria (Evanjelina) 1942-2004
  Obituary *154*
Aoki, Hisako 1942- *45*
Aoyagi, Nora *229*
Apfel, Necia H(alpern) 1930- *51*
  Brief entry *41*
Aphrodite, J.
  See Livingston, Carole
Apikuni
  See Schultz, James Willard
Apostolina, M. *184*
Apostolina, Michael
  See Apostolina, M.
Apostolou, Christine Hale 1955- *179*
  Earlier sketches in SATA *82, 128*
Appel, Allen (R.) 1945- *115*
Appel, Benjamin 1907-1977 .... *39*
  Obituary *21*
Appel, Martin 1948- *45*
Appel, Martin Eliot
  See Appel, Martin
Appel, Marty
  See Appel, Martin
Appelbaum, Diana Muir Karter 1953- *132*
Appelt, Kathi 1954- *190*
  Earlier sketches in SATA *83, 129*
Apperley, Dawn 1969- *135*
Appiah, Peggy 1921-2006 .... *84*
  Earlier sketch in SATA *15*
  See also SAAS *19*
Apple, Margot *214*
  Brief entry *42*
  Earlier sketches in SATA *64, 152*
Applebaum, Stan 1922- *45*
Applegate, K.A.
  See Applegate, Katherine
Applegate, Katherine 1956- *196*
  Earlier sketches in SATA *109, 162*
  See also CLR *90*
Applegate, Katherine Alice
  See Applegate, Katherine
Appleton, Victor
  See Barrett, Neal, Jr.
    and Doyle, Debra
    and Stratemeyer, Edward L.
    and Vardeman, Robert E.
Appollo 1969- *214*
Appollodorus, Olivier
  See Appollo
Apsler, Alfred 1907-1982 .... *10*
Aragones, Sergio 1937- *48*
  Brief entry *39*
Araujo, Frank P. 1937- *86*
Arbo, Cris 1950- *220*
  Earlier sketch in SATA *103*
Arbuckle, Dorothy Fry 1910-1982
  Obituary *33*
Arbuthnot, May Hill 1884-1969 .... *2*

Archambault, John *163*
  Earlier sketches in SATA *67, 112*
Archambault, Matthew 1968- *219*
Archbold, Rick 1950- *97*
Archer, Colleen Rutherford 1949- *164*
Archer, Frank
  See O'Connor, Richard
Archer, Jules 1915- *85*
  Earlier sketch in SATA *4*
  See also SAAS *5*
Archer, Lily 1981- *193*
Archer, Marion Fuller 1917- *11*
Archer, Nathan
  See Watt-Evans, Lawrence
Archer, Peggy 1947- *199*
Archibald, Joe
  See Archibald, Joseph S(topford)
Archibald, Joseph S(topford) 1898-1986 .... *3*
  Obituary *47*
Ard, William
  See Jakes, John
Ardagh, Philip 1961- *154*
Ardai, Charles 1969- *85*
Arden, Barbi
  See Stoutenburg, Adrien (Pearl)
Arden, William
  See Lynds, Dennis
Ardizzone, Edward (Jeffrey Irving)
  1900-1979 .... *28*
  Obituary *21*
  Earlier sketch in SATA *1*
  See also CLR *3*
Ardley, Neil 1937- *121*
  Earlier sketch in SATA *43*
Ardley, Neil Richard
  See Ardley, Neil
Arehart-Treichel, Joan 1942- *22*
Arena, Felice 1968- *151*
Arenella, Roy 1939- *14*
Argent, Kerry 1960- *138*
Arguelles, Francisco Xavier
  See Stork, Francisco X.
Argueta, Jorge *179*
Arihara, Shino 1973- *201*
Arkin, Alan 1934- *59*
  Brief entry *32*
Arkin, Alan Wolf
  See Arkin, Alan
Arksey, Neil *158*
Arlen, Leslie
  See Nicole, Christopher
Arley, Robert
  See Jackson, Mike
Armer, Alberta (Roller) 1904-1986 .... *9*
Armer, Laura Adams 1874-1963 .... *13*
Armistead, John 1941- *130*
Armitage, David 1943- *155*
  Brief entry *38*
  Earlier sketch in SATA *99*
Armitage, Frank
  See Carpenter, John
Armitage, Ronda (Jacqueline) 1943- *155*
  Brief entry *38*
  Earlier sketches in SATA *47, 99*
Armour, Richard (Willard) 1906-1989 .... *14*
  Obituary *61*
Armstrong, Alan 1939- *172*
Armstrong, Alan W.
  See Armstrong, Alan
Armstrong, George D. 1927- *10*
Armstrong, Gerry (Breen) 1929- *10*
Armstrong, Jeannette (C.) 1948- *102*
Armstrong, Jennifer 1961- *165*
  Autobiography Feature *120*
  Earlier sketches in SATA *77, 111*
  See also CLR *66*
  See also SAAS *24*
Armstrong, Louise *43*
  Brief entry *33*
Armstrong, Martin Donisthorpe
  1882-1974 .... *115*

Armstrong, Matthew 1975- *188*
Armstrong, Matthew S.
  See Armstrong, Matthew
Armstrong, Ralph Richard
  See Armstrong, Richard
Armstrong, Richard 1903-1986 .... *11*
Armstrong, Shelagh 1961- *224*
Armstrong, William H(oward) 1914-1999 ..... *4*
  Obituary *111*
  See also CLR *117*
  See also SAAS *7*
Armstrong-Ellis, Carey (Fraser) 1956- *145*
Armstrong-Hodgson, Shelagh
  See Armstrong, Shelagh
Arndt, Ursula (Martha H.) *56*
  Brief entry *39*
Arneson, D(on) J(on) 1935- *37*
Arnett, Caroline
  See Cole, Lois Dwight
Arnett, Jack
  See Goulart, Ron
Arnette, Robert
  See Silverberg, Robert
Arno, Enrico 1913-1981 .... *43*
  Obituary *28*
Arnold, Ann 1953(?)- *207*
Arnold, Caroline 1944- *228*
  Brief entry *34*
  Earlier sketches in SATA *36, 85, 131, 174*
  See also CLR *61*
  See also SAAS *23*
Arnold, Elizabeth 1944- *164*
Arnold, Elliott 1912-1980 .... *5*
  Obituary *22*
Arnold, Emily 1939- *210*
  Autobiography Feature *134*
  Earlier sketches in SATA *5, 50, 76, 110, 134*
  See also CLR *46*
  See also SAAS *7*
Arnold, Gillian Clare
  See Cross, Gillian
Arnold, Katya 1947- *168*
  Earlier sketches in SATA *82, 115*
Arnold, Louise *175*
Arnold, Louise Claire
  See Arnold, Louise
Arnold, Marsha Diane 1948- *147*
  Earlier sketch in SATA *93*
Arnold, Nick 1961- *113*
Arnold, Oren 1900-1980 .... *4*
Arnold, Susan (Riser) 1951- *58*
Arnold, Tedd 1949- *208*
  Earlier sketches in SATA *69, 116, 160*
Arnoldy, Julie
  See Bischoff, Julia Bristol
Arnosky, James Edward 1946- *189*
  Earlier sketches in SATA *70, 118*
  See also CLR *93*
Arnosky, Jim
  See Arnosky, James Edward
Arnott, Kathleen 1914- *20*
Arnov, Boris, Jr. 1926- *12*
Arnow, Harriette (Louisa) Simpson
  1908-1986 .... *42*
  Obituary *47*
Arnsteen, Katy Keck 1934- *68*
Arnstein, Helene S(olomon) 1915- *12*
Arntson, Herbert E(dward) 1911-1982 .... *12*
Aroner, Miriam *82*
Aronin, Ben 1904-1980
  Obituary *25*
Aronson, Marc 1950- *189*
  Autobiography Feature *189*
  Earlier sketches in SATA *126, 175*
Aronson, Marc Henry
  See Aronson, Marc
Aronson, Sarah *196*
Aronson, Virginia 1954- *122*
Arora, Shirley (Lease) 1930- *2*
Arrasmith, Patrick *176*

Arrick, Fran
   See Angell, Judie
Arrigan, Mary 1943- 142
Arrington, Aileen 183
Arrington, Stephen L. 1948- 97
Arrington, Stephen Lee
   See Arrington, Stephen L.
Arrley, Richmond
   See Delany, Samuel R., Jr.
Arrou-Vignod, Jean-Philippe 1958- 218
Arrowood, (McKendrick Lee) Clinton
   1939- 19
Arrowsmith, Pat 1930- 59
Arsenault, Isabelle 1978- 207
Artell, Mike 1948- 183
   Earlier sketches in SATA 89, 134
Arthur, Robert (Andrew) 1909-1969
   See Arthur, Robert, (Jr.)
Arthur, Robert, (Jr.) 1909-1969 118
Arthur, Ruth M(abel) 1905-1979 26
   Earlier sketch in SATA 7
Artis, Vicki Kimmel 1945- 12
Artzybasheff, Boris (Miklailovich)
   1899-1965 14
Aruego, Ariane
   See Dewey, Ariane
Aruego, Jose 1932- 178
   Earlier sketches in SATA 6, 68, 125
   See also CLR 5
Aruego, Jose Espiritu
   See Aruego, Jose
Arundel, Honor (Morfydd) 1919-1973 4
   Obituary 24
   See also CLR 35
Arundel, Jocelyn
   See Alexander, Jocelyn Anne Arundel
Arvey, Michael 1948- 79
Arzoumanian, Alik 177
Asare, Meshack (Yaw) 1945- 139
   Earlier sketch in SATA 86
Asaro, Catherine 1955- 165
   Earlier sketch in SATA 101
Asaro, Catherine Ann 1955-
   See Asaro, Catherine
Asay, Donna Day 1945- 127
Asbjornsen, Peter Christen 1812-1885 15
   See also CLR 104
Asch, Frank 1946- 154
   Earlier sketches in SATA 5, 66, 102
Ash, Jutta 1942- 38
Ashabranner, Brent 1921- 166
   Earlier sketches in SATA 1, 67, 130
   See also CLR 28
   See also SAAS 14
Ashabranner, Brent Kenneth
   See Ashabranner, Brent
Ashbless, William
   See Blaylock, James P.
   and Powers, Tim
Ashby, Gil 1958- 146
Ashby, Gwynneth 1922- 44
Ashby, Ruth 170
Ashby, Yvonne 1955- 121
Ashe, Arthur (Robert, Jr.) 1943-1993 65
   Obituary 87
Ashe, Geoffrey (Thomas) 1923- 17
   Autobiography Feature 125
Ashe, Mary Ann
   See Lewis, Mary
Asher, Bridget
   See Baggott, Julianna
Asher, Sandra Fenichel
   See Asher, Sandy
Asher, Sandy 1942- 71
   Autobiography Feature 158
   Brief entry 34
   Earlier sketch in SATA 36
   See also SAAS 13
Asheron, Sara
   See Moore, Lilian

Ashey, Bella
   See Breinburg, Petronella
Ashford, Daisy
   See Ashford, Margaret Mary
Ashford, Jeffrey
   See Jeffries, Roderic
Ashford, Margaret Mary 1881-1972 10
Ashland, Monk 1972- 207
Ashley, Bernard (John) 1935- 155
   Brief entry 39
   Earlier sketches in SATA 47, 79
   See also CLR 4
Ashley, Elizabeth
   See Salmon, Annie Elizabeth
Ashley, Ray
   See Abrashkin, Raymond
Ashman, Linda 1960- 203
   Earlier sketch in SATA 150
Ashton, Lorayne
   See Gottfried, Theodore Mark
Ashton, Warren T.
   See Adams, William Taylor
Asimov, Isaac 1920-1992 74
   Earlier sketches in SATA 1, 26
   See also CLR 79
Asinof, Eliot 1919-2008 6
Asinof, Eliot Tager
   See Asinof, Eliot
Aska, Warabe
   See Masuda, Takeshi
Askani, Tanja 1962- 227
Asprin, Robert 1946-2008 92
Asprin, Robert L.
   See Asprin, Robert
Asprin, Robert Lynn
   See Asprin, Robert
Asquith, Cynthia Mary Evelyn (Charteris)
   1887-1960 107
Asquith, Ros 153
Astley, Juliet
   See Lofts, Norah (Robinson)
Aston, Dianna Hutts 1964- 176
Aston, James
   See White, T(erence) H(anbury)
Ata, Te 1895-1995 119
Atene, Ann
   See Atene, (Rita) Anna
Atene, (Rita) Anna 1922- 12
Atheling, William, Jr.
   See Blish, James
Atkins, Catherine 160
Atkins, Jeannine 1953- 172
   Earlier sketch in SATA 113
Atkinson, Allen G. 1953(?)-1987 60
   Brief entry 46
   Obituary 55
Atkinson, Elizabeth 215
Atkinson, M. E.
   See Frankau, Mary Evelyn Atkinson
Atkinson, Margaret Fleming 14
Atteberry, Kevan J. 186
Attema, Martha 1949- 156
   Earlier sketch in SATA 94
Atticus
   See Davies, Hunter
   and Fleming, Ian
   and Pawle, Gerald Strachan
   and Wilson, (Thomas) Woodrow
Atwater, Florence (Hasseltine Carroll)
   1896-1979 66
   Earlier sketch in SATA 16
   See also CLR 19
Atwater, Montgomery Meigs 1904-1976 15
Atwater, Richard (Tupper) 1892-1948 66
   Brief entry 27
   Earlier sketch in SATA 54
   See also CLR 19
Atwater-Rhodes, Amelia 1984- 170
   Earlier sketch in SATA 124
Atwell, Debby 1953- 150
   Earlier sketch in SATA 87

Atwood, Ann (Margaret) 1913-1992 7
Atwood, Margaret 1939- 170
   Earlier sketch in SATA 50
Atwood, Margaret Eleanor
   See Atwood, Margaret
Aubrey, Meg Kelleher 1963- 83
Aubry, Claude B. 1914-1984 29
   Obituary 40
Auch, Herm 173
Auch, Mary Jane 173
   Earlier sketch in SATA 138
Auch, M.J.
   See Auch, Mary Jane
Auclair, Joan 1960- 68
Auel, Jean 1936- 91
Auel, Jean M.
   See Auel, Jean
Auel, Jean Marie
   See Auel, Jean
Auer, Martin 1951- 77
Augarde, Steve 1950- 210
   Earlier sketches in SATA 25, 159
Augarde, Steven Andre
   See Augarde, Steve
Augelli, John P(at) 1921- 46
Augustine, Mildred
   See Benson, Mildred
Ault, Phil
   See Ault, Phillip H(alliday)
Ault, Phillip H(alliday) 1914- 23
Ault, Rosalie Sain 1942- 38
Ault, Roz
   See Ault, Rosalie Sain
Aung, (Maung) Htin 1909- 21
Auntie Deb
   See Coury, Louise Andree
Auntie Louise
   See Coury, Louise Andree
Aunt Weedy
   See Alcott, Louisa May
Auseon, Andrew 1976- 217
   Earlier sketch in SATA 166
Austen, Carrie
   See Bennett, Cherie
Austen, Catherine 1965- 223
Austin, Carrie
   See Seuling, Barbara
Austin, Elizabeth S. 1907-1977 5
Austin, Harry
   See McInerny, Ralph
Austin, Margot 1909(?)-1990 11
   Obituary 66
Austin, Michael 178
Austin, Oliver L(uther), Jr. 1903-1988 7
   Obituary 59
Austin, Patricia 1950- 137
Austin, R. G.
   See Gelman, Rita Golden
   and Lamb, Nancy
Austin, Virginia 1951- 152
   Earlier sketch in SATA 80
Auteur, Hillary
   See Gottfried, Theodore Mark
Auth, Tony
   See Auth, William Anthony, Jr.
Auth, William Anthony, Jr. 1942- 192
Autry, Gloria Diener
   See Allen, Terril Diener
Auvil, Peggy A 1954- 122
Auvil, Peggy Appleby
   See Auvil, Peggy A
Aveni, Anthony F. 1938- 181
Aveni, Anthony Francis
   See Aveni, Anthony F.
Averbeck, Jim 1963- 201
Averill, Esther (Holden) 1902-1992 28
   Obituary 72
   Earlier sketch in SATA 1
Avery, A. A.
   See Montgomery, Rutherford George

Avery, Al
  See Montgomery, Rutherford George
Avery, Gillian 1926- 137
  Autobiography Feature 137
  Earlier sketches in SATA 7, 75
  See also SAAS 6
Avery, Gillian Elise
  See Avery, Gillian
Avery, Kay 1908- 5
Avery, Lorraine
  See Older, Effin
  and Older, Jules
Avery, Lynn
  See Cole, Lois Dwight
Avi 1937- 226
  Earlier sketches in SATA 14, 71, 108, 156, 190
  See also CLR 68
Aviles, Martha 218
Avishai, Susan 1949- 82
Avraham, Kate Aver 227
Avril, Francois 1961- 191
Avril, Lynne
  See Cravath, Lynne W.
Awdry, Christopher Vere 1940- 67
Awdry, Wilbert Vere 1911-1997 94
  See also CLR 23
Axelrod, Amy 131
Axelsen, Stephen 1953- 165
Axton, David
  See Koontz, Dean
Ayars, James S(terling) 1898-1986 4
Aye, A. K.
  See Edwards, Hazel (Eileen)
Ayer, Eleanor H. 1947-1998 121
  Earlier sketch in SATA 78
Ayer, Jacqueline 1930- 13
Ayer, Margaret (?)-1981 15
Aylesworth, Jim 1943- 213
  Earlier sketches in SATA 38, 89, 139
  See also CLR 89
Aylesworth, Thomas G(ibbons) 1927-1995 .. 88
  Earlier sketch in SATA 4
  See also CLR 6
  See also SAAS 17
Ayliffe, Alex 190
Aylward, Marcus
  See Alexander, Marc
Aymar, Brandt 1911- 22
Ayme, Marcel (Andre) 1902-1967 91
  See also CLR 25
Ayres, Becky
  See Hickox, Rebecca (Ayres)
Ayres, Katherine 1947- 187
Ayres, Pam 1947- 90
Ayres, Patricia Miller 1923-1985
  Obituary 46
Aytmatov, Chingiz
  See Aitmatov, Chingiz
Ayto, Russell 1960- 206
  Earlier sketches in SATA 111, 166
Azaid
  See Zaidenberg, Arthur
Azar, Penny 1952- 121
Azarian, Mary 1940- 171
  Earlier sketch in SATA 112
Azore, Barbara 1934- 188

B

Baasansuren, Bolormaa 1982- 216
Baastad, Babbis Friis
  See Friis-Baastad, Babbis Ellinor
Bab
  See Gilbert, W(illiam) S(chwenck)
Babbis, Eleanor
  See Friis-Baastad, Babbis Ellinor
Babbitt, Lucy Cullyford 1960- 85

Babbitt, Natalie 1932- 194
  Earlier sketches in SATA 6, 68, 106
  See also CLR 141
  See also SAAS 5
Babbitt, Natalie Zane Moore
  See Babbitt, Natalie
Babcock, Chris 1963- 83
Babcock, Dennis 1948- 22
Babcock, Dennis Arthur
  See Babcock, Dennis
Baber, Carolyn Stonnell 1936- 96
Baboni, Elena 198
Baca, Ana 1967- 191
Baca, Maria 1951- 104
Baccalario, Pierdomenico 1974- 222
Bach, Alice (Hendricks) 1942- 93
  Brief entry 27
  Earlier sketch in SATA 30
Bach, Bellamy
  See Windling, Terri
Bach, Mary 1960- 125
Bach, Richard 1936- 13
Bach, Richard David
  See Bach, Richard
Bache, Ellyn 1942- 124
Bachel, Beverly K. 1957- 142
Bachelet, Gilles 1952- 196
Bachman, Fred 1949- 12
Bachman, Richard
  See King, Stephen
Bachorz, Pam 1973- 226
Bachrach, Deborah 1943- 80
Backus, James Gilmore 1913-1989
  Obituary 63
Backus, Jim
  See Backus, James Gilmore
Bacmeister, Rhoda W(arner) 1893-1991 11
Bacon, Betty
  See Bacon, Elizabeth
Bacon, Elizabeth 1914-2001 3
  Obituary 131
Bacon, Joan Chase
  See Bowden, Joan Chase
Bacon, Josephine Dodge (Daskam)
  1876-1961 48
Bacon, Margaret Frances
  See Bacon, Peggy
Bacon, Margaret Hope 1921- 6
Bacon, Martha Sherman 1917-1981 18
  Obituary 27
  See also CLR 3
Bacon, Melvin 1950- 93
Bacon, Melvin L.
  See Bacon, Melvin
Bacon, Peggy 1895-1987 50
Bacon, R(onald) L(eonard) 1924- 84
  Earlier sketch in SATA 26
Baddiel, Ivor 1963- 210
Baden, Robert 1936- 70
Baden-Powell, Robert (Stephenson Smyth)
  1857-1941 16
Badt, Karin L(uisa) 1963- 91
Bae, Hyun-Joo 186
Baehr, Kingsley M. 1937- 89
Baehr, Patricia 1952- 65
Baehr, Patricia Goehner
  See Baehr, Patricia
Baek, Matthew J. 1971- 202
Baer, Jill
  See Gilbert, (Agnes) Joan (Sewell)
Baer, Judy 1951- 71
Baer, Julie 1960- 161
Baer-Block, Roxanna 172
Baerg, Harry J(ohn) 1909-1996 12
Baeten, Lieve 1954- 83
Bagert, Brod 1947- 191
  Earlier sketch in SATA 80
Baggette, Susan K. 1942- 126
Baggott, Julianna 1969- 197
Bagnold, Enid 1889-1981 25
  Earlier sketch in SATA 1

Baguley, Elizabeth 1959- 199
Bahlke, Valerie Worth -1994
  See Worth, Valerie
Bahous, Sally 1939- 86
Bahr, Mary (Madelyn) 1946- 95
Bahr, Robert 1940- 38
Bahti, Tom 1926-1972 57
  Brief entry 31
Bai, Durga 211
Baicker-McKee, Carol 1958- 177
Bailey, Alice Cooper 1890-1978 12
Bailey, Anne 1958- 71
Bailey, Bernadine (Freeman) 1901-1995 14
Bailey, Carolyn Sherwin 1875-1961 14
Bailey, Debbie 1954- 123
Bailey, Donna (Veronica Anne) 1938- 68
Bailey, Jane H(orton) 1916- 12
Bailey, John (Robert) 1940- 52
Bailey, Len 193
Bailey, Linda 1948- 217
  Earlier sketches in SATA 107, 182
Bailey, Maralyn Collins (Harrison) 1941- 12
Bailey, Matilda
  See Radford, Ruby L(orraine)
Bailey, Maurice Charles 1932- 12
Bailey, Pearl (Mae) 1918-1990 81
Bailey, Peter 1946- 194
Bailey, Ralph Edgar 1893-1982 11
Bailey, Sheila (Lucas) 1960- 155
Baillie, Allan 1943- 151
  Earlier sketch in SATA 87
  See also CLR 49
  See also SAAS 21
Baillie, Allan Stuart
  See Baillie, Allan
Baines, John (David) 1943- 71
Bains, Larry
  See Sabin, Louis
Baird, Alison 1963- 138
Baird, Bil 1904-1987 30
  Obituary 52
Baird, Thomas (P.) 1923-1990 45
  Brief entry 39
  Obituary 64
Baird, William Britton
  See Baird, Bil
Baity, Elizabeth Chesley 1907-1989 1
Baiul, Oksana 1977- 108
Bajoria, Paul 1964- 187
Bakeless, John (Edwin) 1894-1978 9
Bakeless, Katherine Little 1895-1992 9
Baker, Alan 1951- 146
  Earlier sketches in SATA 22, 93
Baker, Augusta 1911-1998 3
Baker, Barbara 1947- 192
Baker, Betty Lou 1928-1987 73
  Obituary 54
  Earlier sketch in SATA 5
Baker, Carin Greenberg 1959- 79
Baker, Charlotte 1910- 2
Baker, Christina
  See Kline, Christina Baker
Baker, Christopher W. 1952- 144
Baker, Deirdre 1955- 195
Baker, E.D. 190
Baker, (Mary) Elizabeth (Gillette) 1923- 7
Baker, Gayle Cunningham 1950- 39
Baker, James W. 1924- 65
  Earlier sketch in SATA 22
Baker, James W. 1926- 122
Baker, Janice E(dla) 1941- 22
Baker, Jeanette 178
Baker, Jeannie 1950- 156
  Earlier sketches in SATA 23, 88
  See also CLR 28
Baker, Jeffrey J(ohn) W(heeler) 1931- 5
Baker, Jim
  See Baker, James W.
Baker, Keith 1953- 222
  Earlier sketch in SATA 179
Baker, Ken 1962- 133

Baker, Laura Nelson 1911- 3
Baker, Margaret 1890-1965 4
Baker, Margaret J(oyce) 1918- 12
See also SAAS 8
Baker, Mary Gladys Steel 1892-1974 12
Baker, (Robert) Michael (Graham) 1938- 4
Baker, Nina (Brown) 1888-1957 15
Baker, Pamela J. 1947- 66
Baker, Rachel 1904-1978 2
Obituary 26
Baker, Roberta 206
Baker, Rosalie F. 1945- 166
Baker, Samm Sinclair 1909-1997 12
Obituary 96
Baker, Sharon Reiss 1962- 207
Baker, Susan (Catherine) 1942-1991 29
Baker-Smith, Grahame 223
Balaam
See Lamb, G(eoffrey) F(rederick)
Balan, Bruce 1959- 113
Balcavage, Dynise 1965- 137
Balch, Glenn 1902-1989 3
Obituary 83
See also SAAS 11
Baldacci, David 1960- 184
Baldacci, David G.
See Baldacci, David
and Baldacci, David
Balderose, Nancy Ward 1952- 93
Balderson, Margaret 1935- 151
Baldini, Michelle 205
Baldry, Cherith 1947- 167
Earlier sketch in SATA 72
Balducci, Carolyn 1946- 5
Balducci, Carolyn Feleppa
See Balducci, Carolyn
Baldwin, Alex
See Griffin, W. E. B.
Baldwin, Anne Norris 1938- 5
Baldwin, Clara 11
Baldwin, Gordo
See Baldwin, Gordon C(ortis)
Baldwin, Gordon C(ortis) 1908-1983 12
Baldwin, James 1841-1925 24
Baldwin, James 1924-1987 9
Obituary 54
Baldwin, Louis 1919- 110
Baldwin, Margaret
See Weis, Margaret
Baldwin, Stan(ley C.) 1929- 62
Brief entry 28
Bales, Carol Ann 1940- 57
Brief entry 29
Balet, Jan (Bernard) 1913- 11
Balgassi, Haemi 1971- 131
Balian, Lorna 1929- 91
Earlier sketch in SATA 9
Balit, Christina 1961- 212
Earlier sketches in SATA 102, 159
Ball, Duncan 1941- 73
Ball, Zachary
See Janas, Frankie-Lee
and Masters, Kelly R(ay)
Ballantine, Lesley Frost
See Frost, Lesley
Ballantyne, R(obert) M(ichael) 1825-1894 ... 24
See also CLR 137
Ballard, James G.
See Ballard, J.G.
Ballard, James Graham
See Ballard, J.G.
Ballard, Jane
See Gorman, Carol
Ballard, J.G. 1930-2009 93
Obituary 203
Ballard, Jim G.
See Ballard, J.G.
Ballard, John 1945- 110
Ballard, Lowell C(lyne) 1904-1986 12
Obituary 49
Ballard, (Charles) Martin 1929- 1

Ballard, Mignon F. 1934- 64
Brief entry 49
Ballard, Mignon Franklin
See Ballard, Mignon F.
Ballard, Robert D(uane) 1942- 85
See also CLR 60
Ballard, Robin 1965- 126
Balliett, Blue 1955- 156
Ballinger, Bryan 1968- 161
Ballouhey, Pierre 1944- 90
Balog, Cyn 221
Balogh, Penelope 1916-1975 1
Obituary 34
Balouch, Kristen 176
Balow, Tom 1931- 12
Baltazzi, Evan S(erge) 1921- 90
Balterman, Marcia Ridlon 1942- 22
Baltimore, J.
See Catherall, Arthur
Baltzer, Hans (Adolf) 1900- 40
Balzano, Jeanne (Koppel) 1912- 7
Bambara, Toni Cade 1939-1995 112
Bamfylde, Walter
See Bevan, Tom
Bamman, Henry A. 1918- 12
Banat, D. R.
See Bradbury, Ray
Bancroft, Bronwyn 1958- 216
Bancroft, Griffing 1907-1999 6
Bancroft, Laura
See Baum, L. Frank
Bandel, Betty 1912- 47
Baner, Skulda Vanadis 1897-1964 10
Banerjee, Anjali 174
Banfill, A. Scott 1956- 98
Bang, Betsy 1912- 48
Brief entry 37
Bang, Garrett
See Bang, Molly
Bang, Molly 1943- 215
Earlier sketches in SATA 24, 69, 111, 158
See also CLR 8
Bang, Molly Garrett
See Bang, Molly
Bang-Campbell, Monika 1975(?)- 195
Earlier sketch in SATA 140
Banjo, The
See Paterson, A(ndrew) B(arton)
Banke, Cecile de
See de Banke, Cecile
Banks, Erin Bennett 1978- 211
Banks, Kate 1960- 200
Earlier sketches in SATA 134, 172
Banks, Laura Stockton Voorhees 1908(?)-1980
Obituary 23
Banks, Lynne Reid
See Reid Banks, Lynne
Banks, Merry 197
Banks, Michael A. 1951- 101
Banks, Paul 1952- 174
Banks, Sara
See Harrell, Sara Gordon
Banks, Sara Jeanne Gordon Harrell
See Harrell, Sara Gordon
Bannatyne-Cugnet, Elizabeth Jo-Anne
See Bannatyne-Cugnet, Jo
Bannatyne-Cugnet, Jo 1951- 101
Banner, Angela
See Maddison, Angela Mary
Bannerman, Helen (Brodie Cowan Watson)
1862(?)-1946 19
See also CLR 144
Banning, Evelyn I. 1903-1993 36
Bannon, Laura (?)-1963 6
Bannor, Brett 1959- 143
Bansch, Helga 1957- 224
Banta, Susan 181
Bantock, Nick 1950(?)- 95
Banyai, Istvan 193
Barakat, Ibtisam 1963- 186

Barasch, Lynne 1939- 186
Earlier sketches in SATA 74, 126
Barbalet, Margaret 1949- 77
Barbary, James
See Baumann, Amy Beeching
and Beeching, Jack
Barbash, Shepard 1957- 84
Barbauld, Anna Laetitia 1743-1825
See CLR 160
Barbe, Walter Burke 1926- 45
Barber, Alison 222
Barber, Antonia 1932- 163
Earlier sketch in SATA 29
Barber, Atiim Kiambu
See Barber, Tiki
Barber, Lynda
See Graham-Barber, Lynda
Barber, Lynda Graham
See Graham-Barber, Lynda
Barber, Richard (William) 1941- 35
Barber, Ronde 1975- 182
Barber, Tiki 1975- 182
Barbera, Joe 1911-2006 51
Obituary 179
Barbera, Joseph
See Barbera, Joe
Barbera, Joseph Roland
See Barbera, Joe
Barberis, Juan C(arlos) 1920- 61
Barbour, Karen 1956- 170
Earlier sketches in SATA 63, 121
Barbour, Ralph Henry 1870-1944 16
Barclay, Bill
See Moorcock, Michael
Barclay, Isabel
See Dobell, I(sabel) M(arian) B(arclay)
Barclay, William Ewert
See Moorcock, Michael
Barclay, William Ewert
See Moorcock, Michael
Bardhan-Quallen, Sudipta 1977- 214
Earlier sketch in SATA 168
Bardoe, Cheryl 181
Bare, Arnold Edwin 1920- 16
Bare, Colleen Stanley 32
Bar-el, Dan 199
Barenholtz, Bernard 1914-1989
Obituary 64
Bargar, Gary W. 1947-1985 63
Barger, Jan 1948- 147
Barish, Matthew 1907-2000 12
Barkan, Joanne 127
Earlier sketch in SATA 77
Barker, Albert W. 1900- 8
Barker, Carol (Minturn) 1938- 31
Barker, Cicely Mary 1895-1973 49
Brief entry 39
See also CLR 88
Barker, Melvern 1907-1989 11
Barker, S. Omar 1894-1985 10
Barker, Squire Omar
See Barker, S. Omar
Barker, Will 1913-1983 8
Barkin, Carol 1944- 52
Earlier sketch in SATA 42
Barklem, Jill 1951- 96
See also CLR 31
Barkley, Brad 178
Barkley, James Edward 1941- 6
Barks, Carl 1901-2000 37
Barley, Janet Crane 1934- 95
Barlow, Steve 1952- 211
Barnaby, Ralph S(tanton) 1893-1986 9
Barnard, A. M.
See Alcott, Louisa May
Barnard, Bryn 1956- 169
Earlier sketch in SATA 115
Barne, Kitty
See Barne, Marion Catherine
Barne, Marion Catherine 1883-1957 97
Barneda, David 206

Barner, Bob 1947- *136*
  Earlier sketch in SATA *29*
Barnes, Dawn 1957- *175*
Barnes, Derrick *191*
Barnes, Derrick D.
  See Barnes, Derrick
Barnes, (Frank) Eric Wollencott 1907-1962 . *22*
Barnes, Joyce Annette 1958- *85*
Barnes, Laura T. 1958- *119*
Barnes, Loutricia
  See Barnes-Svarney, Patricia L(ou)
Barnes, Malcolm 1909(?)-1984
  Obituary *41*
Barnes, Michael 1934- *55*
Barnes-Murphy, Frances 1951- *88*
Barnes-Murphy, Rowan 1952- *88*
Barnes-Svarney, Patricia L(ou) 1953- *67*
Barnet, Nancy 1954- *84*
Barnett, Ivan 1947- *70*
Barnett, Lincoln (Kinnear) 1909-1979 .... *36*
Barnett, Mac *223*
Barnett, Moneta 1922-1976 .... *33*
Barnett, Naomi 1927- *40*
Barney, Maginel Wright 1881(?)-1966 .... *39*
  Brief entry *32*
Barnhart, Clarence L(ewis) 1900-1993 .... *48*
  Obituary *78*
Barnhouse, Rebecca 1961- *225*
Barnouw, Adriaan Jacob 1877-1968
  Obituary *27*
Barnouw, Victor 1915-1989 .... *43*
  Brief entry *28*
Barnstone, Willis 1927- *20*
Barnum, Jay Hyde 1888(?)-1962 .... *20*
Barnum, P. T., Jr.
  See Stratemeyer, Edward L.
Barnum, Richard *67*
  Earlier sketch in SATA *1*
Barnum, Theodore
  See Stratemeyer, Edward L.
Barnwell, Ysaye M. 1946- *200*
Baron, Kathi 1956- *226*
Baron, Kathy 1954- *90*
Baron, Virginia Olsen 1931- *46*
  Brief entry *28*
Barr, Donald 1921-2004 .... *20*
  Obituary *152*
Barr, George 1907-1992 .... *2*
Barr, Jene 1922-1985 .... *16*
  Obituary *42*
Barr, Nevada 1952- *126*
  Earlier sketch in SATA *115*
Barragan, Paula 1963- *216*
Barratt, Mark 1954- *224*
Barrer, Gertrude
  See Barrer-Russell, Gertrude
Barrer-Russell, Gertrude 1921- *27*
Barrett, Angela 1955- *223*
Barrett, Angela (Jane) 1955- *145*
  Earlier sketch in SATA *75*
Barrett, Ethel *87*
  Brief entry *44*
Barrett, Joyce Durham 1943- *138*
Barrett, Judi
  See Barrett, Judith
Barrett, Judith 1941- *204*
  Earlier sketch in SATA *26*
  See also CLR *98*
Barrett, Robert T(heodore) 1949- *92*
Barrett, Ron 1937- *14*
Barrett, Susan (Mary) 1938- *113*
Barrett, Tracy 1955- *207*
  Earlier sketches in SATA *84, 115, 156*
Barrett, William E(dmund) 1900-1986
  Obituary *49*
Barretta, Gene *214*
  Earlier sketch in SATA *176*
Barretton, Grandall
  See Garrett, Randall
Barrie, Baronet
  See Barrie, J. M.

Barrie, J. M. 1860-1937 .... *100*
  See also YABC *1*
  See also CLR *124*
Barrie, James Matthew
  See Barrie, J. M.
Barringer, William 1940-1996 .... *153*
Barrington, Michael
  See Moorcock, Michael
Barris, George 1925- *47*
Barrol, Grady
  See Bograd, Larry
Barron, Rex 1951- *84*
Barron, T.A. 1952- *192*
  Earlier sketches in SATA *83, 126*
  See also CLR *86*
Barron, Thomas Archibald
  See Barron, T.A.
Barron, Tom
  See Barron, T.A.
Barrow, Lloyd H. 1942- *73*
Barrows, Annie 1962- *180*
Barry, Dan 1958- *177*
Barry, Dana (Marie Malloy) 1949- *139*
Barry, James P(otvin) 1918- *14*
Barry, Katharina Watjen 1936- *4*
Barry, Robert 1931- *6*
Barry, Robert Everett
  See Barry, Robert
Barry, Scott 1952- *32*
Barry, Sheila Anne -2003 .... *91*
Barshaw, Ruth McNally *203*
Bartell, Susan S. *175*
Bartenbach, Jean 1918- *40*
Barth, Edna 1914-1980 .... *7*
  Obituary *24*
Barth, Kelly L. 1964- *152*
Barthelme, Donald 1931-1989 .... *7*
  Obituary *62*
Barth-Grozinger, Inge 1950- *185*
Bartholomew, Barbara 1941- *86*
  Brief entry *42*
Bartholomew, Jean
  See Beatty, Patricia (Robbins)
Bartlett, Alison *153*
Bartlett, Philip A. *1*
Bartlett, Robert Merrill 1899-1995 .... *12*
Bartoletti, Susan Campbell 1958- *173*
  Earlier sketches in SATA *88, 129, 135*
Barton, Byron 1930- *126*
  Earlier sketches in SATA *9, 90*
Barton, Chris *224*
Barton, Jill(ian) 1940- *75*
Barton, May Hollis *67*
  Earlier sketch in SATA *1*
Barton, Pat
  See Arrowsmith, Pat
Barton, Patrice 1955- *226*
Bartos-Hoeppner, Barbara 1923- *5*
Bartram, Simon *218*
  Earlier sketch in SATA *156*
Bartsch, Jochen 1906- *39*
Baruch, Dorothy W(alter) 1899-1962 .... *21*
Barunga, Albert 1912(?)-1977 .... *120*
Baryshnikov, Mikhail 1948- *192*
Bas, Rutger
  See Rutgers van der Loeff-Basenau, An(na)
  Maria Margaretha
Base, Graeme 1958- *162*
  Earlier sketches in SATA *67, 101*
  See also CLR *22*
Base, Graeme Rowland
  See Base, Graeme
Baseman, Gary 1960- *174*
Bash, Barbara 1948- *132*
Bashevis, Isaac
  See Singer, Isaac Bashevis
Bashevis, Yitskhok
  See Singer, Isaac Bashevis
Bashista, Adrienne Ehlert *203*
Basile, Gloria Vitanza 1929- *180*

Baskin, Leonard 1922-2000 .... *120*
  Brief entry *27*
  Earlier sketch in SATA *30*
Baskin, Nora Raleigh 1961- *189*
  Earlier sketch in SATA *129*
Bason, Lillian 1913- *20*
Bass, Hester 1956- *223*
Bass, L. G.
  See Geringer, Laura
Bassett, Jeni 1959- *64*
  Brief entry *43*
Bassett, John Keith
  See Keating, Lawrence A.
Bassett, Lisa 1958- *61*
Bassil, Andrea
  See Nilsen, Anna
Bastyra, Judy *108*
Basye, Dale E. *205*
Bataille, Marion 1963- *209*
Bat-Ami, Miriam 1950- *150*
  Autobiography Feature *150*
  Earlier sketches in SATA *82, 122*
Bate, Lucy 1939-1993 .... *18*
Bate, Norman (Arthur) 1916- *5*
Bateman, Colin 1962- *172*
Bateman, Donna M. *190*
Bateman, Teresa 1957- *216*
  Earlier sketches in SATA *112, 168*
Bates, Amy June *189*
Bates, Barbara S(nedeker) 1919- *12*
Bates, Betty
  See Bates, Elizabeth
Bates, Dianne 1948- *147*
Bates, Elizabeth 1921- *19*
Bates, Ivan *175*
Bates, Katharine Lee 1859-1929 .... *113*
Bates, Martine
  See Leavitt, Martine
Bateson, Catherine 1960- *197*
  Earlier sketch in SATA *157*
Batey, Tom 1946- *52*
  Brief entry *41*
Bath, Kevin P.
  See Bath, K.P.
Bath, K.P. 1959- *171*
Batherman, Muriel
  See Sheldon, Muriel
Batson, Larry 1930- *35*
Batt, Tanya Robyn 1970- *131*
Battaglia, Aurelius 1910- *50*
  Brief entry *33*
Batten, H(arry) Mortimer 1888-1958 .... *25*
Batten, Mary 1937- *162*
  Earlier sketches in SATA *5, 102*
Batterberry, Ariane Ruskin 1935- *13*
Batterberry, Michael Carver 1932-2010 .... *32*
Battle-Lavert, Gwendolyn 1951- *155*
  Earlier sketches in SATA *85, 131*
Battles, (Roxy) Edith 1921- *7*
Baudouy, Michel-Aime 1909- *7*
Bauer, A.C.E. *201*
Bauer, Caroline Feller 1935- *98*
  Brief entry *46*
  Earlier sketch in SATA *52*
  See also SAAS *24*
Bauer, Fred 1934- *36*
Bauer, Helen 1900-1988 .... *2*
Bauer, Joan 1951- *160*
  Earlier sketch in SATA *117*
Bauer, Jutta 1955- *150*
Bauer, Marion Dane 1938- *192*
  Autobiography Feature *144*
  Earlier sketches in SATA *20, 69, 113, 144*
  See also SAAS *9*
Bauer, Michael Gerard 1955(?)- *167*
Bauer, Steven 1948- *125*
Bauerschmidt, Marjorie 1926- *15*
Baughman, Dorothy 1940- *61*
Baum, Allyn Z(elton) 1924-1997 .... *98*
  Earlier sketch in SATA *20*

Baum, L. Frank
  See Thompson, Ruth Plumly
Baum, L. Frank 1856-1919 .... *100*
  Earlier sketch in SATA *18*
  See also CLR *107*
Baum, Louis 1948- *182*
  Brief entry *52*
  Earlier sketch in SATA *64*
Baum, Louis F.
  See Baum, L. Frank
Baum, Lyman Frank
  See Baum, L. Frank
Baum, Maxie *188*
Baum, Willi 1931- *4*
Bauman, Beth Ann 1964- *220*
Baumann, Amy Beeching 1922- *10*
Baumann, Amy Brown Beeching
  See Baumann, Amy Beeching
Baumann, Hans 1914- *2*
  See also CLR *35*
Baumann, Kurt 1935- *21*
Baumgartner, Barbara 1939- *86*
Baurys, Flo 1938- *122*
Baurys, Florence
  See Baurys, Flo
Bausum, Ann *173*
Bawden, Nina 1925- *132*
  Earlier sketches in SATA *4, 72*
  See also CLR *51*
  See also SAAS *16*
Bawden, Nina Mary Mabey
  See Bawden, Nina
Baxter, Andy
  See Dakin, Glenn
Baxter, Roberta 1952- *219*
Baxter, Valerie
  See Meynell, Laurence Walter
Bay, Jeanette Graham 1928- *88*
Bayer, Harold
  See Gregg, Andrew K.
Bayer, Jane E. (?)-1985
  Obituary *44*
Bayley, Nicola 1949- *129*
  Earlier sketches in SATA *41, 69*
Baylor, Byrd 1924- *136*
  Earlier sketches in SATA *16, 69*
  See also CLR *3*
Baynes, Pauline 1922-2008 .... *133*
  Obituary *196*
  Earlier sketches in SATA *19, 59*
Baynes, Pauline Diana
  See Baynes, Pauline
Bayoc, Cbabi *186*
Bayrock, Fiona *215*
BB
  See Watkins-Pitchford, Denys James
Beach, Charles
  See Reid, (Thomas) Mayne
Beach, Charles Amory *1*
Beach, Edward L. 1918-2002 .... *12*
  Obituary *140*
Beach, Edward Latimer
  See Beach, Edward L.
Beach, Lisa 1957- *111*
Beach, Lynn
  See Lance, Kathryn
Beach, Stewart T(aft) 1899-1979 .... *23*
Beachcroft, Nina 1931- *18*
Beagle, Peter S. 1939- *130*
  Earlier sketch in SATA *60*
Beagle, Peter Soyer
  See Beagle, Peter S.
Beaglehole, Helen 1946- *117*
Beake, Lesley 1949- *209*
Beale, Fleur *107*
Bealer, Alex W(inkler III) 1921-1980 .... *8*
  Obituary *22*
Beales, Valerie 1915- *74*
Beals, Carleton 1893-1979 .... *12*
Beals, Frank Lee 1881-1972
  Obituary *26*

Beam, Matt 1970- *187*
Beame, Rona 1934- *12*
Beamer, Charles 1942- *43*
Beamer, George Charles, Jr.
  See Beamer, Charles
Bean, Jonathan 1979- *194*
Bean, Normal
  See Burroughs, Edgar Rice
Beaney, Jan
  See Udall, Jan Beaney
Beaney, Jane
  See Udall, Jan Beaney
Bear, Carolyn
  See Rayban, Chloe
Bear, Greg 1951- *105*
  Earlier sketch in SATA *65*
Bear, Gregory Dale
  See Bear, Greg
Bearanger, Marie
  See Messier, Claire
Beard, Alex 1970- *222*
Beard, Charles A(ustin) 1874-1948 .... *18*
Beard, Dan(iel Carter) 1850-1941 .... *22*
Beard, Darleen Bailey 1961- *96*
Bearden, Romare (Howard) 1914(?)-1988 ... *22*
  Obituary *56*
Beardmore, Cedric
  See Beardmore, George
Beardmore, George 1908-1979 .... *20*
Beardshaw, Rosalind 1969- *225*
  Earlier sketch in SATA *190*
Beardsley, Martyn R. 1957- *150*
Bearman, Jane (Ruth) 1917- *29*
Bearn, Emily *220*
Beaton, Clare 1947- *220*
  Earlier sketch in SATA *125*
Beatty, Elizabeth
  See Holloway, Teresa (Bragunier)
Beatty, Hetty Burlingame 1907-1971 .... *5*
Beatty, Jerome, Jr. 1918- *5*
Beatty, John (Louis) 1922-1975 .... *6*
  Obituary *25*
Beatty, Patricia (Robbins) 1922-1991 .... *73*
  Obituary *68*
  Earlier sketches in SATA *1, 30*
  See also SAAS *4*
Beaty, Andrea *186*
Beaty, Mary (T.) 1947- *146*
Beaudoin, Sean *210*
Beauford, Jhenne Tyler
  See Beauford, Tyler
Beauford, Tyler 1990- *225*
Beaumont, Karen 1954- *204*
Beavers, Ethen 1971- *225*
Beccia, Carlyn *189*
Bechard, Margaret 1953- *164*
  Earlier sketch in SATA *85*
Bechtel, Louise Seaman 1894-1985 .... *4*
  Obituary *43*
Bechtold, Lisze *208*
Beck, Andrea 1956- *226*
Beck, Barbara L. 1927- *12*
Beck, Ian 1947- *190*
  Earlier sketch in SATA *138*
  See Beck, Ian Archibald
Beck, Peggy 1949- *171*
Beck, Scott *197*
Becker, Beril 1901-1999 .... *11*
Becker, Bonny *184*
Becker, Deborah Zimmett 1955- *138*
Becker, Helaine 1961- *142*
Becker, John (Leonard) 1901- *12*
Becker, John E(mil) 1942- *148*
Becker, Joyce 1936- *39*
Becker, May Lamberton 1873-1958 .... *33*
Becker, Neesa 1951- *123*
Becker, Shari *174*
Beckerman, Chad W. *198*
Beckett, Sheilah 1913- *33*
Beckhorn, Susan Williams 1953- *189*
Beckles Willson, Robina 1930- *27*

Beckman, Delores 1914-1994 .... *51*
Beckman, Gunnel 1910- *6*
  See also CLR *25*
  See also SAAS *9*
Beckman, Kaj
  See Beckman, Karin
Beckman, Karin 1913- *45*
Beckman, Per (Frithiof) 1913- *45*
Bedard, Michael 1949- *154*
  Earlier sketch in SATA *93*
  See also CLR *35*
Beddor, Frank *194*
Beddows, Eric
  See Nutt, Ken
Bedford, A. N.
  See Watson, Jane Werner
Bedford, Annie North
  See Watson, Jane Werner
Bedford, David *224*
  Earlier sketch in SATA *159*
Bedford, David J.
  See Bedford, David
Bedoukian, Kerop 1907-1981 .... *53*
Bee, Jay
  See Brainerd, John W(hiting)
Bee, William *188*
Beebe, B. F.
  See Johnson, B. F.
Beebe, (Charles) William 1877-1962 .... *19*
Beeby, Betty 1923- *25*
Beech, Mark 1971- *191*
Beech, Webb
  See Griffin, W. E. B.
Beecham, Jahnna *161*
Beechcroft, William
  See Hallstead, William F(inn III)
Beeching, Jack 1922- *14*
Beeke, Tiphanie *219*
  Earlier sketch in SATA *163*
Beeler, Janet
  See Shaw, Janet
Beeler, Nelson F(rederick) 1910-1978 .... *13*
Beere, Peter 1951- *97*
Beers, Dorothy Sands 1917- *9*
Beers, Lorna 1897-1989 .... *14*
Beers, V(ictor) Gilbert 1928- *130*
  Earlier sketch in SATA *9*
Beeton, Max
  See Redding, Robert Hull
Begay, Shonto 1954- *137*
Begaye, Lisa Shook
  See Beach, Lisa
Begin, Mary Jane 1963- *82*
Begin-Callanan, Mary Jane
  See Begin, Mary Jane
Begley, Kathleen A. 1948- *21*
Begley, Kathleen Anne
  See Begley, Kathleen A.
Beguine, Anna
  See Saintcrow, Lilith
Beha, Eileen *221*
Beha, Philippe *211*
Behan, Leslie
  See Gottfried, Theodore Mark
Behler, Deborah A. 1947- *145*
Behler, John L. 1943-2006 .... *145*
  Obituary *173*
Behler, John Luther
  See Behler, John L.
Behn, Harry 1898-1973 .... *2*
  Obituary *34*
Behnke, Frances L. *8*
Behr, Joyce 1929- *15*
Behrens, Andy *228*
Behrens, June York 1925- *19*
Behrman, Carol H(elen) 1925- *144*
  Earlier sketch in SATA *14*
Beifuss, John, (Jr.) 1959- *92*
Beil, Karen Magnuson 1950- *221*
  Earlier sketch in SATA *124*
Beil, Michael D. *226*

Beiler, Edna 1923- *61*
Beingessner, Laura 1965- *220*
Beinicke, Steve 1956- *69*
Beirne, Barbara 1933- *71*
Beiser, Arthur 1931- *22*
Beiser, Germaine 1931- *11*
Belair, Richard L. 1934- *45*
Belaney, Archibald Stansfeld 1888-1938 ...... *24*
　See also CLR 32
Belasen, Amy 1983- *213*
Belbin, David 1958- *164*
　Earlier sketch in SATA 106
Belden, Wilanne Schneider 1925- *56*
Belfrage, Sally 1936-1994 .... *65*
　Obituary *79*
Belknap, B. H.
　See Ellis, Edward S.
Belknap, Boynton
　See Ellis, Edward S.
Belknap, Boynton M.D.
　See Ellis, Edward S.
Bell, Anthea 1936- *148*
　Earlier sketch in SATA 88
Bell, Cathleen Davitt 1971- *203*
Bell, Cece *202*
Bell, Clare (Louise) 1952- *99*
Bell, Corydon Whitten 1894-1980 .... *3*
Bell, David Owen 1949- *99*
Bell, Emerson
　See Stratemeyer, Edward L.
Bell, Emily Mary
　See Cason, Mabel Earp
Bell, Frank
　See Benson, Mildred
Bell, Gertrude (Wood) 1911-1987 .... *12*
Bell, Gina
　See Balzano, Jeanne (Koppel)
Bell, Hilari 1958- *226*
　Earlier sketches in SATA 151, 197
Bell, Jadrien
　See Golden, Christie
Bell, Janet
　See Clymer, Eleanor
Bell, Janet Cheatham 1937- *127*
Bell, Krista 1950- *215*
　Earlier sketch in SATA 126
Bell, Krista Anne Blakeney
　See Bell, Krista
Bell, Margaret E(lizabeth) 1898-1990 .... *2*
Bell, Mary Reeves 1946- *88*
Bell, Norman (Edward) 1899- *11*
Bell, Raymond Martin 1907-1999 .... *13*
Bell, Siobhan *177*
Bell, Thelma Harrington 1896-1985 .... *3*
Bell, William 1945- *90*
　See also CLR 91
Bellairs, John (Anthony) 1938-1991 .... *160*
　Obituary *66*
　Earlier sketches in SATA 2, 68
　See also CLR 37
Beller, Susan Provost 1949- *128*
　Earlier sketch in SATA 84
　See also CLR 106
Bellingham, Brenda 1931- *99*
　Brief entry *51*
Bello, Rosario de
　See De Bello, Rosario
Belloc, Hilaire 1870-1953 .... *112*
　See also YABC 1
　See also CLR 102
Belloc, Joseph Hilaire Pierre Sebastien Rene
　Swanton
　See Belloc, Hilaire
Belloc, Joseph Peter Rene Hilaire
　See Belloc, Hilaire
Belloc, Joseph Pierre Hilaire
　See Belloc, Hilaire
Belloli, Andrea P. A. 1947- *86*
Bell-Rehwoldt, Sheri 1962- *199*
Bellville, Cheryl Walsh 1944- *54*
　Brief entry *49*

Bell-Zano, Gina
　See Balzano, Jeanne (Koppel)
Belpre, Pura 1899-1982 .... *16*
　Obituary *30*
Belting, Natalia Maree 1915-1997 .... *6*
Belton, John Raynor 1931- *22*
Belton, Sandra 1939- *186*
　Earlier sketches in SATA 85, 134
Belton, Sandra Yvonne
　See Belton, Sandra
Beltran, Alberto 1923- *43*
Beltran-Hernandez, Irene 1945- *74*
Belvedere, Lee
　See Grayland, Valerie (Merle Spanner)
Bemelmans, Ludwig 1898-1962 .... *100*
　Earlier sketch in SATA 15
　See also CLR 93
Benander, Carl D. 1941- *74*
Benary, Margot
　See Benary-Isbert, Margot
Benary-Isbert, Margot 1889-1979 .... *2*
　Obituary *21*
　See also CLR 12
Benasutti, Marion 1908-1992 .... *6*
Benatar, Raquel 1955- *167*
Benchley, Nathaniel (Goddard) 1915-1981 .. *25*
　Obituary *28*
　Earlier sketch in SATA 3
Benchley, Peter 1940-2006 .... *164*
　Earlier sketches in SATA 3, 89
Benchley, Peter Bradford
　See Benchley, Peter
Bendall-Brunello, John *185*
Bender, Edna 1941- *92*
Bender, Esther 1942- *88*
Bender, Lucy Ellen 1942- *22*
Bender, Robert 1962- *160*
　Earlier sketch in SATA 79
Bendick, Jeanne 1919- *135*
　Earlier sketches in SATA 2, 68
　See also CLR 5
　See also SAAS 4
Bendick, Robert L(ouis) 1917- *11*
Benedetto, William R. 1928- *180*
Benedetto, William Ralph
　See Benedetto, William R.
Benedict, Andrew
　See Arthur, Robert, (Jr.)
Benedict, Dorothy Potter 1889-1979 .... *11*
　Obituary *23*
Benedict, Lois Trimble 1902-1967 .... *12*
Benedict, Rex 1920-1995 .... *8*
Benedict, Stewart H(urd) 1924- *26*
Beneduce, Ann Keay *128*
Benet, Laura 1884-1979 .... *3*
　Obituary *23*
Benet, Stephen Vincent 1898-1943
　See YABC 1
Benet, Sula 1906-1982 .... *21*
　Obituary *33*
Ben-Ezer, Ehud 1936- *122*
Benezra, Barbara (Beardsley) 1921- *10*
Benham, Leslie 1922- *48*
Benham, Lois (Dakin) 1924- *48*
Benham, Mary Lile 1914-1991 .... *55*
Benjamin, E. M. J.
　See Bache, Ellyn
Benjamin, Floella 1949- *206*
Benjamin, Nora
　See Kubie, Nora Gottheil Benjamin
Benjamin, Saragail Katzman 1953- *86*
Benner, Cheryl 1962- *80*
Benner, Judith Ann 1942- *94*
Bennett, Alice
　See Ziner, Florence
Bennett, Artie *227*
Bennett, Cherie 1960- *158*
　Earlier sketch in SATA 97
Bennett, Dorothea
　See Young, Dorothea Bennett

Bennett, Erin Susanne
　See Banks, Erin Bennett
Bennett, Holly 1957- *181*
Bennett, James (W.) 1942- *153*
　Autobiography Feature *153*
　Earlier sketches in SATA 93, 148
Bennett, Jay 1912- *87*
　Brief entry *27*
　Earlier sketch in SATA 41
　See also SAAS 4
Bennett, Jill (Crawford) 1934- *41*
Bennett, John 1865-1956
　See YABC 1
Bennett, Penelope (Agnes) 1938- *94*
Bennett, Rachel
　See Hill, Margaret (Ohler)
Bennett, Rainey 1907-1998 .... *15*
　Obituary *111*
Bennett, Richard 1899- *21*
Bennett, Russell H(oradley) 1896- *25*
Bennett, Veronica 1953- *178*
Bennett, William (John) 1943- *102*
Benning, Elizabeth
　See Rice, Bebe Faas
Benny, Mike 1964- *203*
Benson, Elizabeth P(olk) 1924- *65*
Benson, Kathleen 1947- *183*
　Earlier sketches in SATA 62, 111
Benson, Linda M(aria) 1959- *84*
Benson, Mildred 1905-2002 .... *100*
　Obituary *135*
　Earlier sketches in SATA 1, 65, 67
Benson, Mildred Augustine Wirt
　See Benson, Mildred
Benson, Mildred Wirt
　See Benson, Mildred
Benson, Millie
　See Benson, Mildred
Benson, Patrick 1956- *147*
Benson, Sally 1900-1972 .... *35*
　Obituary *27*
　Earlier sketch in SATA 1
Bentley, Judith (McBride) 1945- *89*
　Earlier sketch in SATA 40
Bentley, Karen
　See Taschek, Karen
Bentley, Nancy (L.) 1946- *78*
Bentley, Nicolas Clerihew 1907-1978
　Obituary *24*
Bentley, Phyllis Eleanor 1894-1977 .... *6*
　Obituary *25*
Bentley, Roy 1947- *46*
Bentley, William (George) 1916- *84*
Bently, Peter 1960- *221*
Benton, Jim 1963- *172*
ben Uzair, Salem
　See Horne, Richard Henry Hengist
Ben-Zvi, Rebeccca Tova
　See O'Connell, Rebecca
Bercaw, Edna Coe 1961- *124*
Berck, Judith 1960- *75*
Bereal, JaeMe 1959(?)- *228*
Berelson, Howard 1940- *5*
Berends, Polly Berrien 1939- *50*
　Brief entry *38*
Berenstain, Jan 1923- *135*
　Earlier sketches in SATA 12, 64, 129
　See also CLR 150
　See also SAAS 20
Berenstain, Janice
　See Berenstain, Jan
Berenstain, Michael 1951- *220*
　Earlier sketch in SATA 45
Berenstain, Mike
　See Berenstain, Michael
Berenstain, Stan 1923-2005 .... *135*
　Obituary *169*
　Earlier sketches in SATA 12, 64, 129
　See also CLR 150
　See also SAAS 20

Berenstain, Stanley
See Berenstain, Stan
Berenzy, Alix 1957- 168
Earlier sketch in SATA 65
Beresford, Elisabeth 1928-2010 141
Earlier sketches in SATA 25, 86
See also SAAS 20
Berg, Adriane G(ilda) 1948- 152
Berg, Dave
See Berg, David
Berg, David 1920-2002 27
Obituary 137
Berg, Elizabeth 1948- 104
Berg, Jean Horton 1913-1995 6
Berg, Joan
See Victor, Joan Berg
Berg, Ron 1952- 48
Bergaust, Erik 1925-1978 20
Bergel, Colin J. 1963- 137
Bergen, Joyce 1949- 95
Berger, Barbara (Helen) 1945- 77
Berger, Carin 185
Berger, Gilda 1935- 88
Brief entry 42
Berger, Joe 1970- 221
Berger, Josef 1903-1971 36
Berger, Lou 213
Berger, Melvin H. 1927- 158
Autobiography Feature 124
Earlier sketches in SATA 5, 88
See also CLR 32
See also SAAS 2
Berger, Phil 1942-2001 62
Berger, Samantha 1969- 140
Berger, Samantha Allison
See Berger, Samantha
Berger, Terry 1933- 8
Bergey, Alyce 1934- 45
Bergey, Alyce Mae
See Bergey, Alyce
Bergin, Mark 1961- 160
Earlier sketch in SATA 114
Berglin, Ruth Marie 1970- 181
Bergman, Donna 1934- 73
Bergman, Mara 1956- 196
Bergman, Tamar 1939- 95
Bergren, Lisa T.
See Bergren, Lisa Tawn
Bergren, Lisa Tawn 200
Bergsma, Jody Lynn 163
Bergstein, Rita M. 211
Bergum, Constance R. 1952- 208
Earlier sketch in SATA 121
Berk, Ari 208
Berk, Josh 1976- 227
Berkebile, Fred D(onovan) 1900-1978
Obituary 26
Berkeley, Jon 1962- 204
Berkes, Marianne 217
Earlier sketch in SATA 173
Berkey, Barry Robert 1935- 24
Berkowitz, Freda Pastor 1908-1994 12
Berkus, Clara Widess 1909- 78
Berlan, Kathryn Hook 1946- 78
Berlfein, Judy Reiss 1958- 79
Berlin, Eric 1968- 195
Berliner, Don 1930- 33
Berliner, Franz 1930- 13
Berlitz, Charles (L. Frambach) 1914-2003 ... 32
Obituary 151
Berman, Len 1947- 229
Berman, Linda 1948- 38
Berman, Paul (Lawrence) 1949- 66
Berman, Rachel 1946- 217
Berna, Paul 1910-1994 15
Obituary 78
See also CLR 19
Bernadette
See Watts, (Anna) Bernadette
Bernard, Bruce 1928-2000 78
Obituary 124

Bernard, George I. 1949- 39
Bernard, Jacqueline (de Sieyes) 1921-1983 ... 8
Obituary 45
Bernard, Patricia 1942- 181
Earlier sketch in SATA 106
Bernard, Trish
See Bernard, Patricia
Bernardin, James 1966- 227
Earlier sketch in SATA 112
Bernardo, Anilu 184
Bernards, Neal 1963- 71
Bernasconi, Pablo 1973- 183
Bernays, Anne 1930- 32
Berner, Rotraut Susanne 1948- 214
Bernhard, Durga T. 1961- 80
Bernhard, Emery 1950- 80
Bernheimer, Kate 201
Bernier-Grand, Carmen T. 1947- 202
Bernstein, Daryl (Evan) 1976- 81
Bernstein, Joanne E(ckstein) 1943- 15
Bernstein, Jonathan 217
Bernstein, Margery 1933- 114
Bernstein, Nina 1949- 180
Bernstein, Theodore M(enline) 1904-1979 ... 12
Obituary 27
Berrien, Edith Heal
See Heal, Edith
Berrill, Jacquelyn (Batsel) 1905- 12
Berrington, John
See Brownjohn, Alan
Berry, B. J.
See Berry, Barbara J.
Berry, Barbara J. 1937- 7
Berry, Erick
See Best, (Evangel) Allena Champlin
Berry, Holly 1957- 210
Berry, James 1924- 110
Earlier sketch in SATA 67
See also CLR 143
Berry, Jane Cobb 1915(?)-1979
Obituary 22
Berry, Joy 1944- 58
Brief entry 46
Berry, Joy Wilt
See Berry, Joy
Berry, Julie 1974- 218
Berry, Lynne 190
Berry, William D(avid) 1926- 14
Bersani, Shennen 1961- 164
Berson, Harold 1926- 4
Bertagna, Julie 1962- 151
Bertholf, Bret 189
Bertin, Charles-Francois
See Berlitz, Charles (L. Frambach)
Bertolet, Paul
See McLaughlin, Frank
Berton, Pierre (Francis de Marigny)
1920-2004 99
Obituary 158
Bertrand, Cecile 1953- 76
Bertrand, Diane Gonzales 1956- 177
Earlier sketch in SATA 106
Bertrand, Lynne 1963- 164
Earlier sketch in SATA 81
Beskow, Elsa (Maartman) 1874-1953 20
See also CLR 17
Bess, Clayton
See Locke, Robert
Besson, Luc 1959- 199
Best, (Evangel) Allena Champlin 1892-1974 . 2
Obituary 25
Best, Cari 1951- 200
Earlier sketches in SATA 107, 149
Best, (Oswald) Herbert 1894-1980 2
Bestall, A(lfred) E(dmeades) 1892-1986 97
Obituary 48
Betancourt, Jeanne 1941- 148
Brief entry 43
Earlier sketches in SATA 55, 96
Beth, Mary
See Miller, Mary Beth

Bethancourt, T. Ernesto
See Paisley, Tom
Bethel, Dell 1929- 52
Bethell, Jean (Frankenberry) 1922- 8
Bethers, Ray 1902-1973 6
Bethke, Bruce Raymond 1955- 114
Bethlen, T.D.
See Silverberg, Robert
Bethune, J. G.
See Ellis, Edward S.
Bethune, J. H.
See Ellis, Edward S.
Betteridge, Anne
See Potter, Margaret
Betteridge, Deirdre 214
Bettina
See Ehrlich, Bettina Bauer
Bettmann, Otto Ludwig 1903-1998 46
Bettoli, Delana 187
Betts, James
See Haynes, Betsy
Betz, Eva Kelly 1897-1968 10
Bevan, Tom 1868-1930(?)
See YABC 2
Bevis, Mary 1939- 202
Bewick, Thomas 1753-1828 16
Beyer, Audrey White 1916- 9
Beyer, Paul J. III 1950- 74
Beynon, John
See Harris, John (Wyndham Parkes Lucas)
Beynon
Bezencon, Jacqueline (Buxcel) 1924- 48
Bhatia, Jamunadevi 1919- 48
Bhatia, June
See Bhatia, Jamunadevi
Bial, Morrison David 1917- 62
Bial, Raymond 1948- 225
Earlier sketches in SATA 76, 116, 165
Biala
See Brustlein, Janice Tworkov
Biale, Rachel 1952- 99
Bialk, Elisa
See Krautter, Elisa (Bialk)
Bianchi, John 1947- 91
Bianchi, Robert S(teven) 1943- 92
Bianco, Margery
See Bianco, Margery Williams
Bianco, Margery Williams 1881-1944 15
See also CLR 146
Bianco, Pamela 1906- 28
Bibby, Violet 1908-1996 24
Bible, Charles 1937- 13
Bibo, Bobette
See Gugliotta, Bobette
Bice, Clare 1909-1976 22
Bickerstaff, Isaac
See Swift, Jonathan
Bidner, Jenni 1963- 193
Biedrzycki, David 1955- 219
Biegel, Paul 1925- 79
Earlier sketch in SATA 16
See also CLR 27
See also SAAS 18
Biemiller, Carl L(udwig), Jr. 1912-1979 40
Obituary 21
Bienenfeld, Florence L(ucille) 1929- 39
Bierhorst, John (William) 1936- 149
Autobiography Feature 149
Earlier sketches in SATA 6, 91
See also SAAS 10
Biggar, Joan R. 1936- 120
Biggar, Joan Rawlins
See Biggar, Joan R.
Biggle, Lloyd, Jr. 1923-2002 65
Biggs, Brian 1968- 192
Bilal, Abdel W(ahab) 1970- 92
Bilbrough, Norman 1941- 111
Bildner, Phil 173
Bileck, Marvin 1920- 40
Bilibin, Ivan (Iakolevich) 1876-1942 61
Bill, Alfred Hoyt 1879-1964 44

Bill, Tannis 228
Billam, Rosemary 1952- 61
Billings, Charlene W(interer) 1941- 41
Billingsley, Franny 1954- 132
Billington, Elizabeth T(hain) 50
  Brief entry 43
Billout, Guy (Rene) 1941- 144
  Earlier sketch in SATA 10
  See also CLR 33
Bilson, Geoffrey 1938-1987 99
Binch, Caroline (Lesley) 1947- 140
  Earlier sketch in SATA 81
Bing, Christopher (H.) 126
Bingham, Caroline 1962- 158
Bingham, Jane M. 1941- 163
Bingham, Jane Marie
  See Bingham, Jane M.
Bingham, Janet 1959- 200
Bingham, Kelly 1967- 207
Bingham, Sam 1944- 96
Bingham, Samuel A.
  See Bingham, Sam
Bingley, Margaret (Jane Kirby) 1947- 72
Binkley, Anne
  See Rand, Ann (Binkley)
Binzen, Bill
  See Binzen, William
Binzen, William 24
Birch, David (W.) 1913-1996 89
Birch, Reginald B(athurst) 1856-1943 19
Birchman, David 1949- 72
Birchmore, Daniel A. 1951- 92
Bird, Carmel 1940- 124
Bird, E(lzy) J(ay) 1911- 58
Birdsall, Jeanne 1952(?)- 170
Birdseye, Tom 1951- 148
  Earlier sketches in SATA 66, 98
Birenbaum, Barbara 1941- 65
Birmingham, Christian 1970- 220
Birmingham, Lloyd P(aul) 1924- 83
  Earlier sketch in SATA 12
Birmingham, Ruth
  See Sorrells, Walter
Birney, Betty G. 1947- 169
  Earlier sketch in SATA 98
Biro, B.
  See Biro, B. S.
Biro, B. S. 1921- 1
  See also CLR 28
  See also SAAS 13
Biro, Val
  See Biro, B. S.
Birtha, Becky 1948- 229
Bischoff, Julia Bristol 1899-1970 12
Bishop, Bonnie 1943- 37
Bishop, Claire Huchet 1899(?)-1993 14
  Obituary 74
  See also CLR 80
Bishop, Courtney
  See Ruemmler, John D(avid)
Bishop, Curtis (Kent) 1912-1967 6
Bishop, Elizabeth 1911-1979
  Obituary 24
Bishop, Gavin 1946- 216
  Earlier sketches in SATA 97, 144
Bishop, Kathleen Wong 1954- 120
Bishop, Kathy
  See Bishop, Kathleen Wong
Bishop, Nic 1955- 161
  Earlier sketch in SATA 107
Bishop, Rudine Sims 224
Bisset, Donald 1910-1995 86
  Earlier sketch in SATA 7
Bisson, Terry 1942- 99
Bisson, Terry Ballantine
  See Bisson, Terry
Bitter, Gary G(len) 1940- 22
Bixby, William (Courtney) 1920-1986 6
  Obituary 47

Bjoerk, Christina 1938- 99
  Earlier sketch in SATA 67
  See also CLR 22
Bjork, Christina
  See Bjoerk, Christina
Bjorklund, Lorence F. 1913-1978 35
  Brief entry 32
Bjorkman, Lauren 222
Bjorkman, Steve 223
  Earlier sketch in SATA 163
Blabey, Aaron 1975(?)- 214
Black, Algernon David 1900-1993 12
  Obituary 76
Black, Holly 1971- 210
  Earlier sketch in SATA 147
Black, Irma Simonton 1906-1972 2
  Obituary 25
Black, Joe 1959- 224
Black, Rabbi Joe
  See Black, Joe
Black, Kat 217
Black, Katherine
  See Black, Kat
Black, Mansell
  See Trevor, Elleston
Black, MaryAnn
  See Easley, MaryAnn
Black, Susan Adams 1953- 40
Blackall, Bernie 1956- 126
Blackall, Sophie 182
Blackburn, Claire
  See Altman, Linda Jacobs
Blackburn, John(ny) Brewton 1952- 15
Blackburn, Joyce Knight 1920- 29
Blacker, Terence 1948- 194
Blacker, Tina
  See Louise, Tina
Blackett, Veronica Heath 1927- 12
Blackie, Jean Cutler 1943- 79
Blacklin, Malcolm
  See Chambers, Aidan
Blacklock, Dyan 1951- 112
Blackman, Malorie 1962- 196
  Earlier sketches in SATA 83, 128
Blackton, Peter
  See Wilson, Lionel
Blackwood, Alan 1932- 70
Blackwood, Freya 199
Blackwood, Gary
  See Blackwood, Gary L.
Blackwood, Gary L. 1945- 226
  Earlier sketches in SATA 72, 118, 169
Blade, Alexander
  See Garrett, Randall
  and Hamilton, Edmond
  and Silverberg, Robert
Blades, Ann (Sager) 1947- 69
  Earlier sketch in SATA 16
  See also CLR 15
Bladow, Suzanne Wilson 1937- 14
Blaine, Chris
  See Gardner, Craig Shaw
Blaine, John
  See Goodwin, Harold L(eland)
Blaine, Marge
  See Blaine, Margery Kay
Blaine, Margery Kay 1937- 11
Blair, Alison
  See Lerangis, Peter
Blair, Anne Denton 1914-1993 46
Blair, David Nelson 1954- 80
Blair, Eric
  See Orwell, George
Blair, Jay 1953- 45
Blair, Lucile
  See Yeakley, Marjory Hall
Blair, Margaret Whitman 1951- 227
  Earlier sketch in SATA 124
Blair, Mary 1911-1978 195
Blair, Pauline Hunter
  See Clarke, Pauline

Blair, Ruth Van Ness 1912-1999 12
Blair, Shannon
  See Kaye, Marilyn
Blair, Walter 1900-1992 12
  Obituary 72
Blaisdell, Bob
  See Blaisdell, Robert
Blaisdell, Robert 1959- 105
Blake, Bronwyn 1940- 149
Blake, Francis 198
Blake, Jon 1954- 171
  Earlier sketch in SATA 78
Blake, Olive
  See Supraner, Robyn
Blake, Quentin 1932- 211
  Earlier sketches in SATA 9, 52, 96, 125
  See also CLR 31
Blake, Robert 1949- 42
Blake, Robert J. 160
Blake, Walker E.
  See Griffin, W. E. B.
Blake, William 1757-1827 30
  See also CLR 52
Blakely, Gloria 1950- 139
Blakely, Roger K. 1922- 82
Blakeney, Jay D.
  See Chester, Deborah
Blakeslee, Lys 1985- 218
Blakey, Nancy 1955- 94
Blanc, Esther S. 1913-1997 66
Blanc, Mel 1908-1989
  Obituary 64
Blanchard, Patricia 125
Blanchet, M(uriel) Wylie 1891-1961 106
Blanco, Richard L(idio) 1926- 63
Bland, E.
  See Nesbit, E.
Bland, Edith Nesbit
  See Nesbit, E.
Bland, Fabian
  See Nesbit, E.
Blane, Gertrude
  See Blumenthal, Gertrude
Blank, Clarissa Mabel 1915-1965 62
Blankenship, LeeAnn 1944- 181
Blassingame, Wyatt Rainey 1909-1985 34
  Obituary 41
  Earlier sketch in SATA 1
Blatchford, Claire H. 1944- 94
Blauer, Ettagale 1940- 49
Bleck, Linda 207
Bledsoe, Glen L. 1951- 108
Bledsoe, Glen Leonard
  See Bledsoe, Glen L.
Bledsoe, Karen E. 1962- 167
  Earlier sketch in SATA 108
Bledsoe, Karen Elizabeth
  See Bledsoe, Karen E.
Bledsoe, Lucy Jane 1957- 162
  Earlier sketch in SATA 97
Bleeker, Sonia
  See Zim, Sonia Bleeker
Blegen, Daniel M. 1950- 92
Blegvad, Erik 1923- 132
  Earlier sketches in SATA 14, 66
Blegvad, Lenore 1926- 176
  Earlier sketches in SATA 14, 66
Blessing, Charlotte 223
Bley, Anette 1967- 188
Blish, James 1921-1975 66
Blish, James Benjamin
  See Blish, James
Blishen, Edward (William) 1920-1996 66
  Obituary 93
  Earlier sketch in SATA 8
Bliss, Corinne Demas 1947- 203
  Earlier sketches in SATA 37, 131
Bliss, Frederick
  See Card, Orson Scott
Bliss, Gillian
  See Paton Walsh, Jill

Bliss, Harry 1964- *196*
Earlier sketch in SATA *156*
Bliss, Reginald
See Wells, H. G.
Bliss, Ronald G(ene) 1942- *12*
Blitt, Barry *187*
Bliven, Bruce, Jr. 1916-2002 .... *2*
Blixen, Karen 1885-1962 .... *44*
Blizzard, Gladys S. (?)-1992 .... *79*
Blobaum, Cindy 1966- *123*
Bloch, Lucienne 1909-1999 .... *10*
Bloch, Marie Halun 1910-1998 .... *6*
See also SAAS *9*
Bloch, Robert (Albert) 1917-1994 .... *12*
Obituary *82*
Bloch, Serge 1956- *213*
Blochman, Lawrence G(oldtree)
1900-1975 .... *22*
Block, Francesca Lia 1962- *213*
Earlier sketches in SATA *80, 116, 158*
See also CLR *116*
See also SAAS *21*
Block, Irvin 1917- *12*
Blomgren, Jennifer (Alice) 1954- *136*
Blonder, Terry Joyce
See Golson, Terry
Blood, Charles Lewis 1929- *28*
Bloom, Barbara Lee 1943- *146*
Bloom, Freddy 1914-2000 .... *37*
Obituary *121*
Bloom, Lloyd 1947- *108*
Brief entry *43*
Bloom, Suzanne 1950- *172*
Bloomfield, Michaela 1966- *70*
Bloor, Edward 1950- *201*
Earlier sketches in SATA *98, 155*
Bloor, Edward William
See Bloor, Edward
Blos, Joan W. 1928- *153*
Autobiography Feature *153*
Brief entry *27*
Earlier sketches in SATA *33, 69, 109*
See also CLR *18*
See also SAAS *11*
Blos, Joan Winsor
See Blos, Joan W.
Blough, Glenn O(rlando) 1907-1995 .... *1*
Blue, Rose 1931- *166*
Autobiography Feature *117*
Earlier sketches in SATA *5, 91, 93*
See also SAAS *24*
Blue, Zachary
See Stine, R.L.
Bluemle, Elizabeth *209*
Bluggage, Oranthy
See Alcott, Louisa May
Blumberg, Leda 1956- *59*
Blumberg, Rhoda 1917- *123*
Earlier sketches in SATA *35, 70*
See also CLR *21*
Blume, Judy 1938- *195*
Earlier sketches in SATA *2, 31, 79, 142*
See also CLR *69*
Blume, Judy Sussman
See Blume, Judy
Blume, Lesley M.M. 1975- *180*
Blumenthal, Deborah *204*
Earlier sketch in SATA *161*
Blumenthal, Gertrude 1907-1971
Obituary *27*
Blumenthal, Shirley 1943- *46*
Blutig, Eduard
See Gorey, Edward (St. John)
Bly, Janet 1945- *43*
Bly, Janet Chester
See Bly, Janet
Bly, Stephen A(rthur) 1944- *116*
Earlier sketch in SATA *43*
Blyler, Allison Lee 1966- *74*
Blythe, Gary 1959- *185*

Blyton, Carey 1932-2002 .... *9*
Obituary *138*
Blyton, Enid 1897-1968 .... *25*
See also CLR *31*
Blyton, Enid Mary
See Blyton, Enid
Bo, Ben
See Richardson, V.A.
Boardman, Fon Wyman, Jr. 1911-2000 .... *6*
Boardman, Gwenn R.
See Petersen, Gwenn Boardman
Boase, Susan *226*
Boase, Wendy 1944-1999 .... *28*
Obituary *110*
Boatner, Mark Mayo III 1921- *29*
Bobbe, Dorothie de Bear 1905-1975 .... *1*
Obituary *25*
Bober, Natalie S. 1930- *134*
Earlier sketch in SATA *87*
See also SAAS *23*
Bobette, Bibo
See Gugliotta, Bobette
Bobri, Vladimir V. 1898-1986 .... *47*
Brief entry *32*
Bobritsky, Vladimir
See Bobri, Vladimir V.
Bochak, Grayce 1956- *76*
Bock, Hal
See Bock, Harold I.
Bock, Harold I. 1939- *10*
Bock, William Sauts Netamux'we 1939- *14*
Bodanis, David *179*
Bode, Janet 1943-1999 .... *96*
Obituary *118*
Earlier sketch in SATA *60*
Bode, N.E.
See Baggott, Julianna
Bodecker, N(iels) M(ogens) 1922-1988 .... *73*
Obituary *54*
Earlier sketch in SATA *8*
Bodeen, S. A. 1965- *158*
Earlier sketch in SATA *114*
Boden, Hilda
See Bodenham, Hilda Morris
Bodenham, Hilda Morris 1901- *13*
Bodett, Thomas Edward 1955- *70*
Bodett, Tom
See Bodett, Thomas Edward
Bodie, Idella F(allaw) 1925- *89*
Earlier sketch in SATA *12*
Bodker, Cecil
See Bødker, Cecil
Bødker, Cecil 1927- *133*
Earlier sketch in SATA *14*
See also CLR *23*
Bodsworth, (Charles) Fred(erick) 1918- *27*
Boeckman, Charles 1920- *12*
Boegehold, Betty (Doyle) 1913-1985 .... *42*
Obituary *42*
Boelts, Maribeth 1964- *200*
Earlier sketches in SATA *78, 163*
Boerst, William J. 1939- *170*
Earlier sketch in SATA *121*
Boesch, Mark J(oseph) 1917- *12*
Boesen, Victor 1908- *16*
Bogacki, Tomek 1950- *214*
Earlier sketch in SATA *138*
Bogaerts, Gert 1965- *80*
Bogan, Paulette 1960- *201*
Earlier sketch in SATA *129*
Bogart, Jo Ellen 1945- *222*
Earlier sketch in SATA *92*
See also CLR *59*
Boggs, Ralph Steele 1901-1994 .... *7*
Bograd, Larry 1953- *89*
Earlier sketch in SATA *33*
See also SAAS *21*
Bogue, Gary 1938- *195*
Bogue, Gary L.
See Bogue, Gary

Bohdal, Susi 1951- *101*
Earlier sketch in SATA *22*
Bohlen, Nina 1931- *58*
Bohlmeijer, Arno 1956- *94*
Bohner, Charles (Henry) 1927- *62*
Bohnhoff, Maya Kaathryn 1954- *88*
Boie, Kirsten 1950- *221*
Boiger, Alexandra *178*
Boissard, Janine 1932- *59*
Bojunga, Lygia
See Nunes, Lygia Bojunga
Bojunga-Nunes, Lygia
See Nunes, Lygia Bojunga
Bok, Arthur
See Bok, Chip
Bok, Chip 1952- *205*
Bolam, Emily 1969- *206*
Boland, Janice *98*
Bolden, Tonya 1959- *227*
Earlier sketches in SATA *79, 138, 188*
Bolden, Tonya Wilyce
See Bolden, Tonya
Boles, Paul Darcy 1916-1984 .... *9*
Obituary *38*
Bolian, Polly 1925- *4*
Bollen, Roger 1941(?)- *83*
Brief entry *29*
Bolliger, Max 1929- *7*
Bollinger, Max 1929- *167*
Bollinger, Peter *172*
Bolognese, Don(ald Alan) 1934- *129*
Earlier sketches in SATA *24, 71*
Bolognese, Elaine 1933- *23*
Bolotin, Norman (Phillip) 1951- *93*
Bolton, Carole 1926- *6*
Bolton, Elizabeth
See St. John, Nicole
Bolton, Evelyn
See Bunting, Eve
Bonar, Veronica
See Bailey, Donna (Veronica Anne)
Bond, B. J.
See Heneghan, James
Bond, Bruce 1939- *61*
Bond, Felicia 1954- *219*
Earlier sketches in SATA *49, 126*
Bond, Gladys Baker 1912- *14*
Bond, Higgins 1951- *220*
Earlier sketches in SATA *83, 177*
Bond, J. Harvey
See Winterbotham, R(ussell) R(obert)
Bond, (Thomas) Michael 1926- *157*
Earlier sketches in SATA *6, 58*
See also CLR *95*
See also SAAS *3*
Bond, Nancy 1945- *159*
Autobiography Feature *159*
Earlier sketches in SATA *22, 82*
See also CLR *11*
See also SAAS *13*
Bond, Nancy Barbara
See Bond, Nancy
Bond, Rebecca 1972- *214*
Earlier sketch in SATA *130*
Bond, Ruskin 1934- *87*
Earlier sketch in SATA *14*
Bondie, J. D.
See Cunningham, Chet
Bondoux, Anne-Laure 1971- *175*
Bone, Ian 1956- *158*
Earlier sketch in SATA *117*
Bonehill, Captain Ralph
See Stratemeyer, Edward L.
Bonestell, Chesley 1888-1986
Obituary *48*
Bonham, Barbara Thomas 1926- *7*
Bonham, Frank 1914-1989 .... *49*
Obituary *62*
Earlier sketch in SATA *1*
See also SAAS *3*

Boniface, William 1963- *182*
Earlier sketch in SATA *102*
Bonino, Louise
See Williams, Louise Bonino
Bonk, John J. *189*
Bonn, Pat
See Bonn, Patricia Carolyn
Bonn, Patricia Carolyn 1948- *43*
Bonner, Hannah *197*
Bonner, Mary Graham 1890-1974 .... *19*
Bonner, Mike 1951- *121*
Bonners, Susan 1947- *85*
Brief entry *48*
Bonnet, Rosalinde 1978- *226*
Bonnett-Rampersaud, Louise *173*
Bonning, Tony 1948- *169*
Bonsall, Crosby Barbara (Newell)
1921-1995 .... *23*
Obituary *84*
Bonsall, Joseph S. 1948- *119*
Bonsignore, Joan 1959- *140*
Bontemps, Arna 1902-1973 .... *44*
Obituary *24*
Earlier sketch in SATA *2*
See also CLR *6*
Bontemps, Arnaud Wendell
See Bontemps, Arna
Bonzon, Paul-Jacques 1908-1978 .... *22*
Boock, Paula 1964- *134*
Booher, Dianna Daniels 1948- *33*
Book, Rick 1949- *119*
Book, Rita
See Holub, Joan
Bookman, Charlotte
See Zolotow, Charlotte
Boon, Debbie 1960- *103*
Boon, Emilie (Laetitia) 1958- *86*
Boone, Charles Eugene
See Boone, Pat
Boone, Pat 1934- *7*
Booraem, Ellen *211*
Boorman, Linda 1940- *46*
Boorman, Linda Kay
See Boorman, Linda
Boorstin, Daniel J(oseph) 1914-2004 .... *52*
Boos, Ben 1971- *206*
Booth, Coe *187*
Booth, Ernest Sheldon 1915-1984 .... *43*
Booth, George 1926- *191*
Booth, Graham (Charles) 1935- *37*
Bootman, Colin *159*
Borden, Louise 1949- *190*
Autobiography Feature *141*
Earlier sketches in SATA *68, 104, 141*
Bordier, Georgette 1924- *16*
Borgman, James
See Borgman, Jim
Borgman, James Mark
See Borgman, Jim
Borgman, Jim 1954- *122*
Borgo, Lacy Finn 1972- *194*
Boring, Mel 1939- *168*
Earlier sketch in SATA *35*
Borja, Corinne 1929- *22*
Borja, Robert 1923- *22*
Borland, Hal
See Borland, Harold Glen
Borland, Harold Glen 1900-1978 .... *5*
Obituary *24*
Borland, Kathryn Kilby 1916- *16*
Borlenghi, Patricia 1951- *79*
Born, Adolf 1930- *49*
Bornstein, Ruth Lercher
See Bornstein-Lercher, Ruth
Bornstein-Lercher, Ruth 1927- *88*
Autobiography Feature *107*
Earlier sketch in SATA *14*
Borris, Albert *221*
Borski, Lucia Merecka *18*
Borten, Helen Jacobson 1930- *5*
Bortolotti, Dan 1969- *157*

Borton, Elizabeth
See Trevino, Elizabeth B(orton) de
Borton, Lady 1942- *98*
Borton de Trevino, Elizabeth
See Trevino, Elizabeth B(orton) de
Bortstein, Larry 1942-2010 .... *16*
Bortz, Alfred B(enjamin) 1944- *139*
Earlier sketch in SATA *74*
Bortz, Fred
See Bortz, Alfred B(enjamin)
Bosch, Pseudonymous *199*
Bosco, Jack
See Holliday, Joseph
Bose, Mitali
See Perkins, Mitali
Boshell, Gordon 1908-1991 .... *15*
Boshinski, Blanche 1922- *10*
Bosman, Paul 1929- *107*
Bosse, Malcolm (Joseph, Jr.) 1926-2002 .... *136*
Earlier sketch in SATA *35*
Bosserman, Charles Phillip
See Bosserman, Phillip
Bosserman, Phillip 1931- *84*
Bossley, Michele Martin 1969- *219*
Bossom, Naomi 1933- *35*
Bostock, Mike 1962- *114*
Boston, L(ucy) M(aria Wood) 1892-1990 .... *19*
Obituary *64*
See also CLR *3*
Bostrom, Kathleen (Susan) Long 1954- *139*
Bostrom, Kathy
See Bostrom, Kathleen (Susan) Long
Boswell, Addie *208*
Boswell, Addie Kay
See Boswell, Addie
Bosworth, J. Allan 1925- *19*
Bothwell, Jean (?)-1977 .... *2*
Botkin, B(enjamin) A(lbert) 1901-1975 .... *40*
Botsford, Ward 1927-2004 .... *66*
Botting, Douglas (Scott) 1934- *43*
Bottner, Barbara 1943- *170*
Autobiography Feature *121*
Earlier sketches in SATA *14, 93*
See also SAAS *26*
Bottone, Frank G., Jr. 1969- *141*
Bouchard, David 1952- *213*
Earlier sketch in SATA *117*
Boucher, (Clarence) Carter 1954- *129*
Boudelang, Bob
See Pell, Ed(ward)
Boughton, Richard 1954- *75*
Boulet, Susan Seddon 1941- *50*
Boulle, Pierre (Francois Marie-Louis)
1912-1994 .... *22*
Obituary *78*
Boulton, Jane 1921- *91*
Bouma, Paddy 1947- *128*
Bour, Daniele 1939- *62*
Bourbonniere, Sylvie 1966- *182*
Bourdon, David 1934-1998 .... *46*
Bourgeois, Paulette 1951- *153*
Bourne, Lesley
See Marshall, Evelyn
Bourne, Miriam Anne 1931-1989 .... *16*
Obituary *63*
Boutavant, Marc 1970- *200*
Boutet de Monvel, (Louis) M(aurice)
1850(?)-1913 .... *30*
See also CLR *32*
Bouwman, Heather M.
See Bouwman, H.M.
Bouwman, H.M. *209*
Bova, Ben 1932- *133*
Earlier sketches in SATA *6, 68*
See also CLR *96*
Bova, Benjamin William
See Bova, Ben
Bovaird, Anne E(lizabeth) 1960- *90*
Bow, Patricia 1946- *168*
Bowden, Joan Chase 1925- *51*
Brief entry *38*

Bowe, Julie 1962- *194*
Bowen, Alexandria Russell *97*
Bowen, Andy Russell
See Bowen, Alexandria Russell
Bowen, Anne 1952- *202*
Earlier sketch in SATA *170*
Bowen, Betty Morgan
See West, Betty
Bowen, Catherine (Shober) Drinker
1897-1973 .... *7*
Bowen, David
See Bowen, Joshua David
Bowen, Fred 1953- *136*
Bowen, Joshua David 1930- *22*
Bowen, Rhys
See Quin-Harkin, Janet
Bowen, Robert Sydney 1900-1977 .... *52*
Obituary *21*
Bowermaster, Jon 1954- *135*
Earlier sketch in SATA *77*
Bowers, Richard J.
See Bowers, Rick
Bowers, Rick 1952- *227*
Bowers, Terrell L. 1945- *101*
Bowers, Terry
See Bowers, Terrell L.
Bowers, Tim *218*
Earlier sketch in SATA *185*
Bowie, C. W.
See Old, Wendie C(orbin)
and Wirths, Claudine (Turner) G(ibson)
Bowie, Jim
See Norwood, Victor G(eorge) C(harles)
and Stratemeyer, Edward L.
Bowkett, Stephen 1953- *67*
Bowler, Jan Brett
See Brett, Jan
Bowler, Tim 1953- *209*
Earlier sketch in SATA *149*
Bowman, Catherine
See Smith, Cat Bowman
Bowman, Crystal 1951- *105*
Bowman, James Cloyd 1880-1961 .... *23*
Bowman, John S(tewart) 1931- *16*
Bowman, Kathleen (Gill) 1942- *52*
Brief entry *40*
Bowman, Leslie
See Bowman, Leslie W.
Bowman, Leslie W. *182*
Bowsher, Melodie *195*
Boxall, Ed *178*
Boyce, Frank Cottrell *182*
Boyce, George A(rthur) 1898- *19*
Boyd, Candy Dawson 1946- *72*
See also CLR *50*
Boyd, Pauline
See Schock, Pauline
Boyd, Selma
See Acuff, Selma Boyd
Boyd, Waldo T. 1918- *18*
Boyden, Linda 1948- *143*
Boyer, Allen B. 1963- *153*
Boyer, Robert E(rnst) 1929- *22*
Boyes, Vivien 1952- *106*
Boyes, Vivien Elizabeth
See Boyes, Vivien
Boyle, Ann (Peters) 1916- *10*
Boyle, Eleanor Vere (Gordon) 1825-1916 .... *28*
Boyle, Robert H. 1928- *65*
Boylston, Helen Dore 1895-1984 .... *23*
Obituary *39*
Boyne, John 1971- *181*
Boynton, Sandra (Keith) 1953- *152*
Brief entry *38*
Earlier sketches in SATA *57, 107*
See also CLR *105*
Boz
See Dickens, Charles
Bozarth, Jan *227*
Braasch, Gary *201*

Bracken, Charles
  See Pellowski, Michael (Joseph)
Brackers de Hugo, Pierre 1960- *115*
Brackett, Dolli Tingle 1911-1993 .... *137*
Brackett, Virginia 1950- *166*
  Earlier sketch in SATA *121*
Brackett, Virginia Roberts Meredith
  See Brackett, Virginia
Bradbury, Bianca (Ryley) 1908-1982 .... *56*
  Earlier sketch in SATA *3*
Bradbury, Edward P.
  See Moorcock, Michael
Bradbury, Ray 1920- *123*
  Earlier sketches in SATA *11, 64*
Bradbury, Ray Douglas
  See Bradbury, Ray
Bradby, Marie *161*
Bradfield, Carl 1942- *91*
Bradford, Ann (Liddell) 1917- *56*
  Brief entry *38*
Bradford, Barbara Taylor 1933- *66*
Bradford, Chris 1974- *215*
Bradford, Emma
  See Perrin, Pat
Bradford, Karleen 1936- *96*
  Earlier sketch in SATA *48*
Bradford, Lois J(ean) 1936- *36*
Bradford, Richard (Roark) 1932-2002 .... *59*
  Obituary *135*
Bradford, Sally
  See Bradford, Barbara Taylor
Bradley, Duane
  See Sanborn, Duane
Bradley, Kimberly Brubaker 1967- *179*
Bradley, Marion Zimmer 1930-1999 .... *139*
  Obituary *116*
  Earlier sketch in SATA *90*
  See also CLR *158*
Bradley, Timothy J. *193*
Bradley, Virginia 1912- *23*
Bradley, Will
  See Strickland, Brad
Bradman, Tony 1954- *152*
  Earlier sketch in SATA *81*
Bradshaw, Gillian (Joan) 1949- *118*
Bradshaw, Gillian 1956- *127*
Bradshaw, Gillian Marucha
  See Bradshaw, Gillian
Bradstreet, T. J.
  See Thesman, Jean
Brady, Esther Wood 1905-1987 .... *31*
  Obituary *53*
Brady, Irene 1943- *4*
Brady, Kimberley S. 1953- *101*
Brady, Kimberley Smith
  See Brady, Kimberley S.
Brady, Lillian 1902- *28*
Bragdon, Elspeth MacDuffie 1897-1980 .... *6*
Bragdon, Lillian Jacot *24*
Brager, Bruce L. 1949- *146*
Bragg, Georgia *225*
Bragg, Mabel Caroline 1870-1945 .... *24*
Bragg, Michael 1948- *46*
Bragg, Ruth Gembicki 1943- *77*
Brahm, Sumishta 1954- *58*
Brailsford, Frances
  See Wosmek, Frances
Brainerd, John W(hiting) 1918- *65*
Braithwaite, Althea 1940- *23*
  Autobiography Feature *119*
  See also SAAS *24*
Brallier, Jess M. 1953- *226*
Bram, Elizabeth 1948- *30*
Bramsen, Carin *227*
Bramsen, Kirsten *228*
Brancato, Robin F. 1936- *97*
  See also CLR *32*
  See also SAAS *9*
Brancato, Robin Fidler
  See Brancato, Robin F.

Branch, Muriel Miller 1943- *152*
  Earlier sketch in SATA *94*
Brand, Christianna
  See Lewis, Mary
Brand, Rebecca
  See Charnas, Suzy McKee
Brande, Robin *194*
Brandel, Marc 1919- *71*
Brandenberg, Alexa (Demetria) 1966- *97*
Brandenberg, Aliki 1929- *157*
  Earlier sketches in SATA *2, 35, 75, 113*
  See also CLR *71*
Brandenberg, Franz 1932- *75*
  Earlier sketches in SATA *8, 35*
Brandenburg, Jim 1945- *87*
Brandhorst, Carl T(heodore) 1898-1988 .... *23*
Brandis, Marianne 1938- *149*
  Earlier sketches in SATA *59, 96*
Brandon, Brumsic, Jr. 1927- *9*
Brandon, Curt
  See Bishop, Curtis (Kent)
Brandreth, Gyles 1948- *28*
Brandreth, Gyles Daubeney
  See Brandreth, Gyles
Brandt, Catharine 1905-1997 .... *40*
Brandt, Keith
  See Sabin, Louis
Brandt, Sue R(eading) 1916- *59*
Branfield, John (Charles) 1931- *11*
Branford, Henrietta 1946-1999 .... *106*
Branley, Franklyn M(ansfield) 1915-2002 .. *136*
  Earlier sketches in SATA *4, 68*
  See also CLR *13*
  See also SAAS *16*
Brannen, Sarah S. *202*
Branscum, Robbie (Tilley) 1937-1997 .... *72*
  Obituary *96*
  Earlier sketch in SATA *23*
  See also SAAS *17*
Bransom, (John) Paul 1885-1979 .... *43*
Brashares, Ann 1967- *188*
  Earlier sketch in SATA *145*
  See also CLR *113*
Brassard, France 1963- *186*
Braswell, E.J.
  See Lynn, Tracy
Braswell, Elizabeth J.
  See Lynn, Tracy
Braswell, Liz
  See Lynn, Tracy
Bratton, Helen 1899-1986 .... *4*
Bratun, Katy 1950- *160*
  Earlier sketch in SATA *83*
Braude, Michael 1936- *23*
Braun, Lilian Jackson 1916(?)- *109*
Brautigan, Richard 1935-1984 .... *56*
Brautigan, Richard Gary
  See Brautigan, Richard
Bray, Libba *203*
  Earlier sketch in SATA *159*
Bray, Martha E.
  See Bray, Libba
Braymer, Marjorie Elizabeth 1911-1988 .... *6*
Brazil, Angela 1869(?)-1947
  See CLR *157*
Breathed, Berke 1957- *161*
  Earlier sketch in SATA *86*
  See Breathed, Berkeley
Breathed, Berkeley *229*
  See Breathed, Berke
Breathed, Guy Berkeley
  See Breathed, Berke
Brecht, Edith 1895-1975 .... *6*
  Obituary *25*
Breck, Vivian
  See Breckenfeld, Vivian Gurney
Breckenfeld, Vivian Gurney 1895-1992 .... *1*
Breda, Tjalmar
  See DeJong, David C(ornel)
Bredeson, Carmen 1944- *163*
  Earlier sketch in SATA *98*

Breen, M.E. *216*
Breen, Molly
  See Breen, M.E.
Breen, Steve 1970- *186*
Breinburg, Petronella 1927- *11*
  See also CLR *31*
Breisky, William J(ohn) 1928- *22*
Brenaman, Miriam *172*
Brenna, Beverley 1962- *226*
Brennan, Caitlin
  See Tarr, Judith
Brennan, Gale (Patrick) 1927- *64*
  Brief entry *53*
Brennan, Herbie 1940- *214*
  Autobiography Feature *214*
  Earlier sketches in SATA *140, 183*
Brennan, J. H.
  See Brennan, Herbie
Brennan, James Herbert
  See Brennan, Herbie
Brennan, Jan
  See Brennan, Herbie
Brennan, Joseph Lomas 1903-2000 .... *6*
Brennan, Linda Crotta 1952- *130*
Brennan, Sarah Rees 1983- *221*
Brennan, Tim
  See Conroy, John Wesley
Brennan-Nelson, Denise *203*
Brenner, Anita 1905-1974 .... *56*
Brenner, Barbara (Johnes) 1925- *124*
  Earlier sketches in SATA *4, 42, 76*
  See also SAAS *14*
Brenner, Fred 1920- *36*
  Brief entry *34*
Brent, Hope 1935(?)-1984
  Obituary *39*
Brent, Stuart 1912-2010 .... *14*
Breskin, Jane
  See Zalben, Jane Breskin
Breslin, Theresa *128*
  Autobiography Feature *128*
  Earlier sketch in SATA *70*
Breslow, Maurice 1935- *72*
Breslow, Maurice A
  See Breslow, Maurice
Breslow, Susan 1951- *69*
Brett, Bernard 1925- *22*
Brett, Grace N(eff) 1900-1975 .... *23*
Brett, Jan 1949- *171*
  Earlier sketches in SATA *42, 71, 130*
  See also CLR *27*
Brett, Jan Churchill
  See Brett, Jan
Brett Bowler, Jan
  See Brett, Jan
Brewer, Heather 1973- *196*
Brewer, James D. 1951- *108*
Brewer, Sally King 1947- *33*
Brewster, Benjamin
  See Folsom, Franklin (Brewster)
Brewster, Hugh 1950- *191*
  Earlier sketch in SATA *95*
Brewster, Patience 1952- *97*
Brewton, John E(dmund) 1898-1982 .... *5*
Breznak, Irene *218*
Brian, Dennis 1971- *229*
Brian, Janeen (Paulette) 1948- *141*
Briant, Ed *218*
  Earlier sketch in SATA *180*
Brick, John 1922-1973 .... *10*
Brickman, Robin D. 1954- *155*
Bride, Nadja
  See Nobisso, Josephine
Bridgers, Sue Ellen 1942- *90*
  Autobiography Feature *109*
  Earlier sketch in SATA *22*
  See also CLR *18*
  See also SAAS *1*
Bridges, Laurie
  See Bruck, Lorraine
Bridges, Ruby (Nell) 1954- *131*

Bridges, William (Andrew) 1901-1984 5
Bridwell, Norman (Ray) 1928- 138
    Earlier sketches in SATA 4, 68
    See also CLR 96
Brier, Howard M(axwell) 1903-1969 8
Brierley, (Louise) 1958- 59
Briggs, Katharine Mary 1898-1980 101
    Obituary 25
Briggs, Peter 1921-1975 39
    Obituary 31
Briggs, Raymond 1934- 184
    Earlier sketches in SATA 23, 66, 131
    See also CLR 10
Briggs, Raymond Redvers
    See Briggs, Raymond
Bright, Paul 1949- 182
Bright, Robert Sr.) 1902-1988 63
    Obituary 60
    Earlier sketch in SATA 24
Bright, Robert Douglas
    See Bright, Robert Sr.)
Bright, Sarah
    See Shine, Deborah
Brightfield, Richard 1927- 65
    Brief entry 53
Brightfield, Rick
    See Brightfield, Richard
Brighton, Catherine 1943- 206
    Earlier sketches in SATA 65, 107
Brill, Marlene Targ 1945- 124
    Earlier sketch in SATA 77
Brimberg, Stanlee 1947- 9
Brimner, Larry Dane 1949- 170
    Autobiography Feature 112
    Earlier sketch in SATA 79
Brin, David 1950- 65
Brin, Ruth Firestone 1921- 22
Brinckloe, Julie 1950- 13
Brinckloe, Julie Lorraine
    See Brinckloe, Julie
Brindel, June (Rachuy) 1919- 7
Brindle, Max
    See Fleischman, Sid
Brindze, Ruth 1903-1984 23
Brink, Carol Ryrie 1895-1981 100
    Obituary 27
    Earlier sketches in SATA 1, 31
    See also CLR 149
Brinsmead, H. F(ay)
    See Brinsmead, H(esba) F(ay)
Brinsmead, H. F.
    See Brinsmead, H(esba) F(ay)
Brinsmead, H(esba) F(ay) 1922- 78
    Earlier sketch in SATA 18
    See also CLR 47
    See also SAAS 5
Briquebec, John
    See Rowland-Entwistle, (Arthur) Theodore
    (Henry)
Brisbane, Henry R.
    See Ellis, Edward S.
Brisco, P. A.
    See Matthews, Patricia
Brisco, Patty
    See Matthews, Patricia
    and Matthews, Clayton (Hartley)
Briscoe, Jill (Pauline) 1935- 56
    Brief entry 47
Brisley, Joyce Lankester 1896-1978 22
    Obituary 84
Brissenden, Connie
    See Brissenden, Constance
Brissenden, Constance 1947- 150
Brisson, Pat 1951- 177
    Autobiography Feature 133
    Earlier sketches in SATA 67, 128, 133
Britt, Albert 1874-1969
    Obituary 28
Britt, Dell 1934- 1
Brittain, Bill
    See Brittain, William

Brittain, C. Dale 1948- 82
Brittain, William 1930- 76
    Earlier sketch in SATA 36
    See also SAAS 7
Brittingham, Geoffrey (Hugh) 1959- 76
Brittney, L. 209
Britton, Kate
    See Stegeman, Janet Allais
Britton, Louisa
    See McGuire, Leslie (Sarah)
Britton, Rick 1952- 82
Bro, Margueritte (Harmon) 1894-1977 19
    Obituary 27
Broach, Elise 1963- 173
Broadhead, Helen Cross 1913- 25
Broadway, Hannah 208
Brochmann, Elizabeth 1938- 41
Brock, Betty (Carter) 1923-2003 4
    Obituary 150
Brock, C(harles) E(dmund) 1870-1938 42
    Brief entry 32
Brock, Delia
    See Ephron, Delia
Brock, Emma L(illian) 1886-1974 8
Brock, H(enry) M(atthew) 1875-1960 42
Brockett, Eleanor Hall 1913-1967 10
Brockman, C(hristian) Frank 1902-1985 26
Brockmeier, Kevin 1972- 176
Broda, Ron 1954- 209
Broderick, Dorothy M. 1929- 5
Brodeur, Ruth Wallace
    See Wallace-Brodeur, Ruth
Brodie, Sally
    See Cavin, Ruth
Brodsky, Beverly
    See McDermott, Beverly Brodsky
Brody, Wendy
    See Staub, Wendy Corsi
Broekel, Rainer Lothar
    See Broekel, Ray
Broekel, Ray 1923- 38
Broekstra, Lorette 1964- 189
    Earlier sketch in SATA 124
Brogden, Sherryl
    See Jordan, Sherryl
Broger, Achim
    See Broger, Achim
Broger, Achim 1944- 31
Broida, Marian 154
Brokamp, Marilyn 1920- 10
Broman, Fred
    See Moseley, James W(illett)
Bromhall, Winifred 26
Brommer, Gerald F(rederick) 1927- 28
Brondfield, Jerome 1913-1998 22
Brondfield, Jerry
    See Brondfield, Jerome
Bronner, Stephen Eric 1949- 101
Bronowski, Jacob 1908-1974 55
Bronson, Alice
    See Watkins, Dawn L.
Bronson, Linda 203
Bronson, Lynn
    See Lampman, Evelyn Sibley
Bronson, Wilfrid Swancourt 1894-1985
    Obituary 43
Brook, Judith (Penelope) 1926- 59
    Brief entry 51
Brook, Judy
    See Brook, Judith (Penelope)
Brooke, L(eonard) Leslie 1862-1940 17
    See also CLR 20
Brooke, William J. 1946- 139
Brooke-Haven, P.
    See Wodehouse, P. G.
Brooker, Kyrsten 199
Brookins, Dana 1931- 28
Brooks, Anita
    See Abramovitz, Anita (Zeltner Brooks)
Brooks, Bill 1939- 59

Brooks, Bruce 1950- 112
    Brief entry 53
    Earlier sketch in SATA 72
    See also CLR 25
Brooks, Caryl 1924- 84
Brooks, Charlotte K(endrick) 1918-1998 24
    Obituary 112
Brooks, Erik 1972- 182
    Earlier sketch in SATA 152
Brooks, George
    See Baum, L. Frank
Brooks, Gwendolyn 1917-2000 6
    Obituary 123
    See also CLR 27
Brooks, Gwendolyn Elizabeth
    See Brooks, Gwendolyn
Brooks, Jerome 1931- 23
Brooks, Kevin 1959- 197
    Earlier sketch in SATA 150
Brooks, Kevin M.
    See Brooks, Kevin
Brooks, Laurie 209
Brooks, Lester 1924- 7
Brooks, Martha 1944- 134
    Autobiography Feature 134
    Earlier sketches in SATA 68, 121
Brooks, Maurice (Graham) 1900- 45
Brooks, Polly Schoyer 1912- 12
Brooks, Ron 1948- 212
    Brief entry 33
    Earlier sketch in SATA 94
Brooks, Ronald George
    See Brooks, Ron
Brooks, Terry 1944- 60
Brooks, Walter R(ollin) 1886-1958 17
Brooks-Hill, Helen (Mason) 1908-1994 59
Broome, Errol 1937- 158
    Earlier sketch in SATA 105
Brophy, Nannette 1963- 73
Brosnan, James Patrick 1929- 14
Brosnan, Jim
    See Brosnan, James Patrick
Brostoff, Anita 1931- 132
Brothers Grimm
    See Grimm, Jacob Ludwig Karl
    and Grimm, Wilhelm Karl
Brothers Hildebrandt, The
    See Hildebrandt, Greg
    and Hildebrandt, Tim
Broun, Emily
    See Sterne, Emma Gelders
Brouwer, S. W.
    See Brouwer, Sigmund (W.)
Brouwer, Sigmund (W.) 1959- 109
Brow, Thea 1934- 60
Brower, Millicent 8
Brower, Pauline 1929- 22
Browin, Frances Williams 1898-1986 5
Brown, Alexis
    See Baumann, Amy Beeching
Brown, Anne Ensign 1937- 61
Brown, Beverly Swerdlow 97
Brown, Bill
    See Brown, William L(ouis)
Brown, Billye Walker
    See Cutchen, Billye Walker
Brown, Bob
    See Brown, Robert Joseph
Brown, Buck 1936- 45
Brown, Calef 217
    Earlier sketch in SATA 179
Brown, Cassie 1919-1986 55
Brown, Charlotte Lewis 181
Brown, Conrad 1922- 31
Brown, Craig 1947- 224
Brown, Craig 1947- 224
    Earlier sketch in SATA 73
Brown, Craig McFarland
    See Brown, Craig

Brown, David
  See Brown, David A(lan)
  and Myller, Rolf
Brown, Dee 1908-2002 .... *110*
  Obituary *141*
  Earlier sketch in SATA *5*
Brown, Dee Alexander
  See Brown, Dee
Brown, Don 1949- *200*
  Earlier sketch in SATA *172*
Brown, Drew T. III 1955- *83*
Brown, Drollene P. 1939- *53*
Brown, Elbrite *198*
Brown, Eleanor Frances 1908-1987 .... *3*
Brown, Elizabeth Ferguson 1937- *153*
Brown, Elizabeth M(yers) 1915- *43*
Brown, Fern G. 1918- *34*
Brown, (Robert) Fletch 1923- *42*
Brown, Fornan 1901-1996 .... *71*
  Obituary *88*
Brown, George Earl 1883-1964 .... *11*
Brown, George Mackay 1921-1996 .... *35*
Brown, Irene Bennett 1932- *3*
Brown, Irving
  See Adams, William Taylor
Brown, Ivor (John Carnegie) 1891-1974 .... *5*
  Obituary *26*
Brown, Jane Clark 1930- *81*
Brown, Janet Mitsui *87*
Brown, Jennifer 1972- *227*
Brown, Jo 1964- *170*
Brown, Joanne 1933- *147*
Brown, Joe David 1915-1976 .... *44*
Brown, Joseph E(dward) 1929- *59*
  Brief entry *51*
Brown, Judith Gwyn 1933- *20*
Brown, Kathryn 1955- *168*
  Earlier sketch in SATA *98*
Brown, Kathy
  See Brown, Kathryn
Brown, Ken (James) *129*
Brown, Kevin 1960- *101*
Brown, Laurene Krasny 1945- *99*
  Earlier sketch in SATA *54*
Brown, Laurie Krasny
  See Brown, Laurene Krasny
Brown, Leo *225*
Brown, Lloyd Arnold 1907-1966 .... *36*
Brown, Mahlon A.
  See Ellis, Edward S.
Brown, Marc (Tolon) 1946- *145*
  Earlier sketches in SATA *10, 53, 80*
  See also CLR *29*
Brown, Marcia (Joan) 1918- *47*
  Earlier sketch in SATA *7*
  See also CLR *12*
Brown, Margaret Wise 1910-1952 .... *100*
  See also YABC *2*
  See also CLR *107*
Brown, Margery (Wheeler) *78*
  Earlier sketch in SATA *5*
Brown, Marion Marsh 1908-2001 .... *6*
Brown, Myra Berry 1918- *6*
Brown, Palmer 1919- *36*
Brown, Pamela (Beatrice) 1924-1989 .... *5*
  Obituary *61*
Brown, Paul 1942- *221*
Brown, Peter 1979- *178*
Brown, Rachel W.N. 1947- *203*
Brown, Reeve Lindbergh
  See Lindbergh, Reeve
Brown, Richard
  See Brown, Rick
Brown, Richard E.
  See Brown, Rick
Brown, Rick 1946- *226*
  Earlier sketch in SATA *61*
Brown, Robert Joseph 1907-1989 .... *14*
Brown, Roderick (Langmere) Haig-
  See Haig-Brown, Roderick (Langmere)

Brown, Rosalie
  See Moore, Rosalie (Gertrude)
Brown, Roswell
  See Webb, Jean Francis (III)
Brown, Roy (Frederick) 1921-1982 .... *51*
  Obituary *39*
Brown, Ruth 1941- *170*
  Earlier sketch in SATA *105*
Brown, Scott 1971- *134*
Brown, Sue Ellen 1954- *81*
Brown, Tricia 1954- *114*
Brown, Vinson 1912-1991 .... *19*
Brown, Walter R(eed) 1929- *19*
Brown, Will
  See Ainsworth, William Harrison
Brown, William L(ouis) 1910-1964 .... *5*
Browne, Anthony 1946- *163*
  Brief entry *44*
  Earlier sketches in SATA *45, 61, 105*
  See also CLR *156*
Browne, Anthony Edward Tudor
  See Browne, Anthony
Browne, Dik
  See Browne, Richard Arthur Allen
Browne, Hablot Knight 1815-1882 .... *21*
Browne, Matthew
  See Rands, William Brighty
Browne, Nicki M.
  See Browne, N.M.
Browne, Nicky Matthews
  See Browne, N.M.
Browne, N.M. 1960- *167*
Browne, Richard Arthur Allen 1917-1989 ... *67*
  Brief entry *38*
Browne, Vee F. 1956- *214*
  Earlier sketch in SATA *90*
Browning, Robert 1812-1889
  See YABC *1*
  See also CLR *97*
Browning, Tom 1949- *226*
Brownjohn, Alan 1931- *6*
Brownlee, Walter 1930- *62*
Brownlie, Betty 1946- *159*
Brownlow, Kevin 1938- *65*
Brownlow, Mike *183*
Brownridge, William R(oy) 1932- *94*
Broyles, Anne 1953- *201*
Bruce, Dorita Fairlie 1885-1970
  Obituary *27*
Bruce, Harry 1934- *77*
Bruce, Mary 1927- *1*
Bruchac, Joseph III
  See Bruchac, Joseph
Bruchac, Joseph 1942- *228*
  Autobiography Feature *176*
  Earlier sketches in SATA *42, 89, 131, 176*
  See also CLR *46*
Bruchac, Margaret M.
  See Bruchac, Marge
Bruchac, Marge *181*
Bruck, Lorraine 1921- *55*
  Brief entry *46*
Bruel, Nick *205*
  Earlier sketch in SATA *166*
Bruel, Robert O. 1929-2002 .... *189*
Bruemmer, Fred 1929- *47*
Brugman, Alyssa (F.) 1974- *152*
Brumbeau, Jeff 1955- *157*
Bruna, Dick 1927- *76*
  Brief entry *30*
  Earlier sketch in SATA *43*
  See also CLR *7*
Brunhoff, Jean de 1899-1937 .... *24*
  See also CLR *116*
Brunhoff, Laurent de 1925- *150*
  Earlier sketches in SATA *24, 71*
  See also CLR *116*
Brunkus, Denise *204*
Bruno, Elsa Knight 1935-2009 .... *221*
Brunskill, Elizabeth Ann Flatt
  See Flatt, Lizann

Brush, Karen A(lexandra) 1960- *85*
Brussel-Smith, Bernard 1914- *58*
Brust, Steven 1955- *121*
  Earlier sketch in SATA *86*
Brust, Steven Karl Zoltan
  See Brust, Steven
Brustlein, Daniel 1904- *40*
Brustlein, Janice Tworkov -2000 .... *40*
  Obituary *126*
Brutschy, Jennifer 1960- *84*
Bryan, Ashley 1923- *178*
  Earlier sketches in SATA *31, 72, 132*
  See also CLR *66*
Bryan, Ashley F.
  See Bryan, Ashley
Bryan, Dorothy M. 1896(?)-1984
  Obituary *39*
Bryan, Jennifer *190*
Bryan, Sean *192*
Bryant, Bernice (Morgan) 1908-1976 .... *11*
Bryant, Jen 1960- *218*
  Earlier sketches in SATA *94, 175*
Bryant, Jennifer
  See Bryant, Jen
Bryant, Jennifer Fisher
  See Bryant, Jen
Bryant, Laura J. *176*
Brychta, Alex 1956- *21*
Brynie, Faith H. 1946- *113*
Brynie, Faith Hickman
  See Brynie, Faith H.
Bryson, Bernarda 1903-2004 .... *9*
Buba, Joy Flinsch 1904- *44*
Buchan, Bryan 1945- *36*
Buchan, John 1875-1940
  See YABC *2*
Buchan, Stuart 1942-1987
  Obituary *54*
Buchanan, Debby 1952- *82*
Buchanan, Deborah Leevonne
  See Buchanan, Debby
Buchanan, Jane 1956- *160*
Buchanan, Paul 1959- *116*
Buchanan, Sue 1939- *139*
Buchheimer, Naomi Barnett
  See Barnett, Naomi
Buchignani, Walter 1965- *84*
Buchmann, Stephen L. *194*
Buchwald, Art 1925-2007 .... *10*
Buchwald, Arthur
  See Buchwald, Art
Buchwald, Emilie 1935- *7*
Buck, Gisela 1941- *101*
Buck, Lewis 1925- *18*
Buck, Margaret Waring 1905-1997 .... *3*
Buck, Nola
  See Godwin, Laura
Buck, Pearl S. 1892-1973 .... *25*
  Earlier sketch in SATA *1*
Buck, Pearl Sydenstricker
  See Buck, Pearl S.
Buck, Siegfried 1941- *101*
Buckalew, Clare B.
  See Dunkle, Clare B.
Buckeridge, Anthony (Malcolm)
  1912-2004 .... *85*
  Earlier sketch in SATA *6*
Buckholtz, Eileen (Garber) 1949- *54*
  Brief entry *47*
Buckingham, Royce 1966- *210*
Buckingham, Royce Scott
  See Buckingham, Royce
Buckler, Ernest 1908-1984 .... *47*
Buckless, Andrea K. 1968- *117*
Buckley, Helen E(lizabeth) 1918- *90*
  Earlier sketch in SATA *2*
Buckley, James, Jr. 1963- *166*
  Earlier sketch in SATA *114*
Buckley, Michael *229*
  Earlier sketch in SATA *177*
Buckley, Susan *184*

Buckley, Susan Washburn
  See Buckley, Susan
Buckley-Archer, Linda 185
Buckmaster, Henrietta
  See Stephens, Henrietta Henkle
Bucks, Brad
  See Holub, Joan
Budd, E. S.
  See Sirimarco, Elizabeth
Budd, Lillian (Peterson) 1897-1989 7
Budhos, Marina 173
Buehler, Stephanie Jona 1956- 83
Buehner, Caralyn 1963- 219
  Earlier sketches in SATA *104, 159*
Buehner, Mark 1959- 221
  Earlier sketches in SATA *104, 159*
Buehr, Walter Franklin 1897-1971 3
Buell, Ellen Lewis
  See Cash, Ellen Lewis Buell
Buell, Janet 1952- 185
  Earlier sketch in SATA *106*
Buergel, Paul-Hermann H. 1949- 83
Buettner, Dan 1960- 95
Buff, Conrad 1886-1975 19
Buff, Mary (E. Marsh) 1890-1970 19
Buffett, Jimmy 1946- 110
  Earlier sketch in SATA *76*
Buffie, Margaret 1945- 161
  Earlier sketches in SATA *71, 107*
  See also CLR *39*
Bugbee, Emma 1888(?)-1981
  Obituary 29
Bugni, Alice 1951- 122
Buhhos, Marina Tamar
  See Budhos, Marina
Bujold, Lois McMaster 1949- 136
Bulfinch, Thomas 1796-1867 35
Bulion, Leslie 1958- 209
  Earlier sketch in SATA *161*
Bull, Angela (Mary) 1936- 45
Bull, Emma 1954- 190
  Autobiography Feature 103
  Earlier sketch in SATA *99*
Bull, Norman John 1916- 41
Bull, Peter (Cecil) 1912-1984
  Obituary 39
Bull, Schuyler M. 1974- 138
Bulla, Clyde R. 1914-2007 139
  Obituary 182
  Earlier sketches in SATA *2, 41, 91*
  See also SAAS *6*
Bullard, Lisa 1961- 142
Bullen, Alexandra 227
Buller, Jon 205
Bullock, Kathleen (Mary) 1946- 77
Bullock, Robert (D.) 1947- 92
Bulpin, (Barbara) Vicki 92
Bulwer-Lytton, Edward 1803-1873 23
Bulwer-Lytton, Edward George Earle Lytton
  See Bulwer-Lytton, Edward
Bumstead, Kathleen Mary 1918-1987 53
Bundles, A'Lelia Perry 1952- 76
Bunge, Daniela 1973- 207
Bunin, Catherine 1967- 30
Bunin, Sherry 1925- 30
Bunkers, Suzanne L. 1950- 136
Bunting, A.E.
  See Bunting, Eve
Bunting, Anne Evelyn
  See Bunting, Eve
Bunting, Eve 1928- 196
  Earlier sketches in SATA *18, 64, 110, 158*
  See also CLR *82*
Bunting, Glenn (Davison) 1957- 22
Bunyan, John 1628-1688
  See CLR *124*
Bupp, Walter
  See Garrett, Randall
Burack, Sylvia K. 1916-2003 35
  Obituary 143
Burbank, Addison (Buswell) 1895-1961 37

Burch, Joann J(ohansen) 75
Burch, Robert J(oseph) 1925- 74
  Earlier sketch in SATA *1*
  See also CLR *63*
Burchard, Peter Duncan 1921- 143
  Earlier sketches in SATA *5, 74*
  See also SAAS *13*
Burchard, S. H.
  See Burchard, Sue
Burchard, Sue 1937- 22
Burchardt, Nellie 1921- 7
Burckhardt, Marc 1962- 196
Burden, Andrea 1969-2009 227
Burdett, Lois 117
Burdick, Eugene (Leonard) 1918-1965 22
Burford, Eleanor
  See Hibbert, Eleanor Alice Burford
Burg, Ann E. 1954- 217
Burg, Shana 1968- 204
Burgan, Michael 1960- 167
  Earlier sketch in SATA *118*
Burger, Carl 1888-1967 9
Burgess, Ann Marie
  See Gerson, Noel Bertram
Burgess, Barbara Hood 1926- 69
Burgess, Em
  See Burgess, Mary Wyche
Burgess, (Frank) Gelett 1866-1951 32
  Brief entry 30
Burgess, Mark 157
Burgess, Mary Wyche 1916- 18
Burgess, Melvin 1954- 198
  Earlier sketches in SATA *96, 146*
Burgess, Michael
  See Gerson, Noel Bertram
Burgess, Robert F(orrest) 1927- 4
Burgess, Starling
  See Tudor, Tasha
Burgess, Thornton Waldo 1874-1965 17
Burgess, Trevor
  See Trevor, Elleston
Burgwyn, Mebane Holoman 1914-1992 7
Burke, David 1927- 46
Burke, Diana G.
  See Gallagher, Diana G.
Burke, Diana Gallagher
  See Gallagher, Diana G.
Burke, Dianne O'Quinn 1940- 89
Burke, Janine 1952- 139
Burke, Jim 1973- 179
Burke, John
  See O'Connor, Richard
Burke, Katie 1953- 168
Burke, Patrick 1958- 114
Burke, Ralph
  See Garrett, Randall
  and Silverberg, Robert
Burkert, Nancy Ekholm 1933- 24
  See also SAAS *14*
Burkett, D. Brent 194
Burke-Weiner, Kimberly 1962- 95
Burks, Brian 1955- 95
Burland, Brian (Berkeley) 1931- 34
Burland, C. A.
  See Burland, Cottie (Arthur)
Burland, Cottie (Arthur) 1905-1983 5
Burleigh, Robert 1936- 193
  Earlier sketches in SATA *55, 98, 146*
Burlingame, (William) Roger 1889-1967 2
Burman, Alice Caddy 1896(?)-1977
  Obituary 24
Burman, Ben Lucien 1896-1984 6
  Obituary 40
Burn, Doris 1923- 1
Burn, Ted
  See Burn, Thomas E.
Burn, Thomas E. 1940- 150
Burnard, Damon 1963- 115
Burnett, Constance Buel 1893-1975 36
Burnett, Frances Eliza Hodgson
  See Burnett, Frances Hodgson

Burnett, Frances Hodgson 1849-1924 100
  See also YABC *2*
  See also CLR *122*
Burnett, Lindy 210
Burnett Bossi, Lisa 193
Burney, Anton
  See Hopkins, (Hector) Kenneth
Burnford, Sheila (Philip Cochrane Every)
  1918-1984 3
  Obituary 38
  See also CLR *2*
Burnham, Gretchen
  See Sprague, Gretchen
Burnham, Nicole 1970- 161
Burnham, Niki
  See Burnham, Nicole
Burnham, Sophy 1936- 65
Burningham, John 1936- 225
  Earlier sketches in SATA *16, 59, 111, 160*
  See also CLR *9*
Burningham, Robin Yoko
  See Racoma, Robin Yoko
Burningham, Sarah O'Leary 216
Burns, Diane L. 1950- 81
  See also SAAS *24*
Burns, Eloise Wilkin
  See Wilkin, Eloise
Burns, Florence M. 1905-1988 61
Burns, Khephra 1950- 92
Burns, Loree Griffin 193
Burns, Marilyn 1941- 96
  Brief entry 33
Burns, Olive Ann 1924-1990 65
Burns, Patrick 1968- 227
Burns, Paul C. 5
Burns, Ray
  See Burns, Raymond (Howard)
Burns, Raymond (Howard) 1924- 9
Burns, Theresa 1961- 84
Burns, William A. 1909-1999 5
Burr, Dan 1951- 65
Burr, Dan 1960- 219
Burr, Lonnie 1943- 47
Burrell, Roy E(ric) C(harles) 1923- 72
Burroughs, Edgar Rice 1875-1950 41
  See also CLR *157*
Burroughs, Jean Mitchell 1908- 28
Burroughs, Polly 1925- 2
Burroway, Janet 1936- 23
Burroway, Janet Gay
  See Burroway, Janet
Burstein, Chaya M(alamud) 1923- 64
Burstein, Fred 1950- 83
Burstein, John 1949- 54
  Brief entry 40
Burstein, Stanley M.
  See Burstein, Stanley Mayer
Burstein, Stanley Mayer 1941- 175
Bursztynski, Sue 1953- 114
Burt, Jesse Clifton 1921-1976 46
  Obituary 20
Burt, Olive Woolley 1894-1981 4
Burtinshaw, Julie 185
Burton, Gennett 1945- 95
Burton, Hester (Wood-Hill) 1913-2000 74
  Earlier sketch in SATA *7*
  See also CLR *1*
  See also SAAS *8*
Burton, Leslie
  See McGuire, Leslie (Sarah)
Burton, Marilee Robin 1950- 82
  Earlier sketch in SATA *46*
Burton, Maurice 1898-1992 23
Burton, Rebecca 1970- 183
Burton, Robert (Wellesley) 1941- 22
Burton, Virginia Lee 1909-1968 100
  Earlier sketch in SATA *2*
  See also CLR *11*
Burton, William H(enry) 1890-1964 11
Busby, Ailie 192
Busby, Cylin 1970- 118

Busby, Edith (A. Lake) (?)-1964
Obituary 29
Busby, John 1942- 209
Buscaglia, (Felice) Leo(nardo) 1924-1998 ... 65
Buscaglia, Leo F.
See Buscaglia, (Felice) Leo(nardo)
Busch, Phyllis S. 1909- 30
Bush, Anne Kelleher
See Kelleher, Anne
Bush, Catherine 1961- 128
Bush, Jenna 1981- 208
Bush, Laura 1946- 208
Bushmiller, Ernest Paul 1905-1982 31
Bushmiller, Ernie
See Bushmiller, Ernest Paul
Bushnell, Jack 1952- 86
Busoni, Rafaello 1900-1962 16
Buss, Helen M.
See Clarke, Margaret
Busse, Sarah Martin 194
Busselle, Rebecca 1941- 80
Bustard, Anne 1951- 173
Butcher, Kristin 1951- 140
Butenko, Bohdan 1931- 90
Butler, Beverly Kathleen 1932- 7
Butler, Bill
See Butler, William Vivian
and Butler, Ernest Alton
and Butler, William Huxford
Butler, Charles 1963- 175
Earlier sketch in SATA 121
Butler, Charles Cadman
See Butler, Charles
Butler, Dori Hillestad 1965- 207
Earlier sketch in SATA 164
Butler, Dorothy 1925- 73
Butler, Geoff 1945- 94
Butler, John 1952- 225
Butler, M. Christina 1934- 224
Earlier sketches in SATA 72, 170
Butler, Octavia 1947-2006 84
See also CLR 65
Butler, Octavia E.
See Butler, Octavia
Butler, Octavia Estelle
See Butler, Octavia
Butler, Vivian
See Butler, William Vivian
Butler, William
See Butler, William Vivian
Butler, William Vivian 1927-1987 79
Butterfield, Moira 1960- 219
Butters, Dorothy Gilman
See Gilman, Dorothy
Butterworth, Emma Macalik 1928- 43
Butterworth, Nick 1946- 149
Earlier sketch in SATA 106
Butterworth, Oliver 1915-1990 1
Obituary 66
Butterworth, W. E.
See Griffin, W. E. B.
Butterworth, William E.
See Griffin, W. E. B.
Butterworth, William Edmund III
See Griffin, W. E. B.
Button, Lana 1968- 229
Butts, Ed 1951- 177
Butts, Edward P.
See Butts, Ed
Butts, Ellen R. 1942- 93
Butts, Ellen Rubinstein
See Butts, Ellen R.
Butzer, C. M. 1974- 212
Buxton, Ralph
See Silverstein, Alvin
and Silverstein, Virginia B.
Buzzeo, Toni 1951- 215
Earlier sketch in SATA 135
Byalick, Marcia 1947- 141
Earlier sketch in SATA 97
Byard, Carole (Marie) 1941- 57

Byars, Betsy 1928- 223
Autobiography Feature 108
Earlier sketches in SATA 4, 46, 80, 163
See also CLR 72
See also SAAS 1
Byars, Betsy Cromer
See Byars, Betsy
Byfield, Barbara Ninde 1930-1988 8
Byman, Jeremy 1944- 129
Bynum, Janie 133
Byrd, Elizabeth 1912-1989 34
Byrd, Nicole
See Zach, Cheryl (Byrd)
Byrd, Robert 1942- 226
Earlier sketches in SATA 33, 112, 158
Byrd, Robert John
See Byrd, Robert
Byrd, Tim 1964- 216
Byrne, Gayle 218
Byrne, Mary Gregg 1951- 162

C

C. 3. 3.
See Wilde, Oscar
C. E. M.
See Mastrangelo, Charles E(lmer)
Cabaniss, J(ames) Allen 1911-1997 5
Cabat, Erni 1914- 74
Cabban, Vanessa 1971- 176
Cable, Mary 1920- 9
Cabot, Meg 1967- 217
Earlier sketches in SATA 127, 175
See also CLR 85
Cabot, Meggin
See Cabot, Meg
Cabot, Meggin Patricia
See Cabot, Meg
Cabot, Patricia
See Cabot, Meg
Cabral, O. M.
See Cabral, Olga
Cabral, Olga 1909- 46
Cabrera, Cozbi A. 1963- 177
Cabrera, Jane 1968- 182
Earlier sketches in SATA 103, 152
Cabrera, Marcela 1966- 90
Caddy, Alice
See Burman, Alice Caddy
Cade, Toni
See Bambara, Toni Cade
Cadena, Beth 222
Cadmus and Harmonia
See Buchan, John
Cadnum, Michael 1949- 225
Earlier sketches in SATA 87, 121, 165
See also CLR 78
Caduto, Michael J. 1955- 103
Cadwallader, Sharon 1936- 7
Cady, (Walter) Harrison 1877(?)-1970 19
Caffey, Donna (J.) 1954- 110
Cagle, Malcolm W(infield) 1918- 32
Cahn, Rhoda 1922- 37
Cahn, William 1912-1976 37
Cain, Arthur H(omer) 1913-1981 3
Cain, Christopher
See Fleming, Thomas
Cain, Sheridan 1952- 186
Caine, Geoffrey
See Walker, Robert W.
Caines, Jeannette (Franklin) 1938- 78
Brief entry 43
See also CLR 24
Cairns, Trevor 1922- 14
Calabro, Marian 1954- 79
Caldecott, Moyra 1927- 22
Caldecott, Randolph (J.) 1846-1886 100
Earlier sketch in SATA 17
See also CLR 110

Calder, Charlotte 1952- 125
Calder, David 1932-1997 105
Calder, Lyn
See Calmenson, Stephanie
Calder, Marie D(onais) 1948- 96
Calderone-Stewart, Lisa
See Calderone-Stewart, Lisa-Marie
Calderone-Stewart, Lisa-Marie 1958- 123
Caldwell, Doreen (Mary) 1942- 71
Caldwell, John C(ope) 1913-1984 7
Caletti, Deb 1963- 221
Earlier sketch in SATA 171
Calhoun, B. B. 1961- 98
Calhoun, Chad
See Barrett, Neal, Jr.
and Cunningham, Chet
and Goulart, Ron
Calhoun, Dia 1959- 183
Earlier sketch in SATA 129
Calhoun, Mary
See Wilkins, Mary Huiskamp
Calhoun, T.B.
See Bisson, Terry
Cali, Davide 1972- 190
Calif, Ruth 1922- 67
Calkhoven, Laurie 1959- 229
Calkins, Franklin
See Stratemeyer, Edward L.
Call, Greg 197
Call, Hughie Florence 1890-1969 1
Callahan, Dorothy M. 1934- 39
Brief entry 35
Callahan, Dorothy Monahan
See Callahan, Dorothy M.
Callahan, Philip Serna 1923- 25
Callahan, Sean 1965- 222
Callan, Jamie 1954- 59
Callan, Jim 1951- 181
Callaway, Bernice (Anne) 1923- 48
Callaway, Kathy 1943- 36
Callen, Larry
See Callen, Lawrence Willard, Jr.
Callen, Lawrence Willard, Jr. 1927- 19
Calley, Karin 1965- 92
Calmenson, Stephanie 1952- 211
Brief entry 37
Earlier sketches in SATA 51, 84, 139
Calonita, Jen 216
Calvert, Elinor H.
See Lasell, Elinor H.
Calvert, John
See Leaf, (Wilbur) Munro
Calvert, Pam 1966- 205
Calvert, Patricia 1931- 132
Earlier sketches in SATA 45, 69
See also SAAS 17
Camburn, Carol A.
See Camburn-Bracalente, Carol A.
Camburn-Bracalente, Carol A. 1962- 118
Cameron, Ann 1943- 129
Earlier sketches in SATA 27, 89
See also SAAS 20
Cameron, Edna M. 1905-1999 3
Cameron, Eleanor (Frances) 1912-1996 25
Obituary 93
Earlier sketch in SATA 1
See also CLR 72
See also SAAS 10
Cameron, Elizabeth
See Nowell, Elizabeth Cameron
Cameron, Elizabeth Jane 1910-1976 32
Obituary 30
Cameron, Ian
See Payne, Donald Gordon
Cameron, M(alcolm) G(ordon) Graham
See Graham-Cameron, M(alcolm) G(ordon)
Cameron, M. Graham
See Graham-Cameron, M(alcolm) G(ordon)
Cameron, Mike Graham
See Graham-Cameron, M(alcolm) G(ordon)

Cameron, Natalie Russell
　See Russell, Natalie
Cameron, Polly 1928- 2
Cameron, Scott 1962- 84
Camp, Charles L. 1893-1975
　Obituary 31
Camp, Lindsay 1957- 133
Camp, Madeleine L'Engle
　See L'Engle, Madeleine
Camp, Walter (Chauncey) 1859-1925
　See YABC 1
Campbell, (Elizabeth) Andrea 1963- 50
Campbell, Ann R. 1925- 11
Campbell, Bill 1960- 89
Campbell, Bruce
　See Epstein, Samuel
Campbell, Camilla 1905-1992 26
Campbell, Carole R. 1939- 125
Campbell, Hope 1925- 20
Campbell, Hugh 1930- 90
Campbell, Jane
　See Edwards, Jane Campbell
Campbell, Julie
　See Tatham, Julie Campbell
Campbell, Patricia J(ean) 1930- 45
Campbell, Patty
　See Campbell, Patricia J(ean)
Campbell, Peter A. 1948- 99
Campbell, R. W.
　See Campbell, Rosemae Wells
Campbell, Robin
　See Strachan, Ian
Campbell, Rod 1945- 98
　Brief entry 44
　Earlier sketch in SATA 51
Campbell, Rosemae Wells 1909- 1
Campbell, Sarah C. 1966- 207
Camper, Cathy 1956- 170
Campion, Nardi Reeder 1917-2007 22
Campling, Elizabeth 1948- 53
Campos, Maria de Fatima 229
Campoy, F. Isabel 1946- 181
　Earlier sketch in SATA 143
Camps, Luis 1928- 66
Canales, Viola 1957- 141
Candell, Victor 1903-1977
　Obituary 24
Canfield, Dorothea F.
　See Fisher, Dorothy (Frances) Canfield
Canfield, Dorothea Frances
　See Fisher, Dorothy (Frances) Canfield
Canfield, Dorothy
　See Fisher, Dorothy (Frances) Canfield
Canfield, Jack 1944- 164
Canfield, Jane White 1897-1984 32
　Obituary 38
Canfield, Muriel 1935- 94
Canga, C.B. 1976- 216
Canga, Chris
　See Canga, C.B.
Caniff, Milton 1907-1988
　Obituary 58
Caniff, Milton Arthur Paul
　See Caniff, Milton
Cann, Helen 1969- 179
　Earlier sketch in SATA 124
Cann, Kate 1954- 152
　Earlier sketch in SATA 103
Cannan, Joanna
　See Pullein-Thompson, Joanna Maxwell
Cannell, Jon 196
Cannell, Jonathan C.
　See Cannell, Jon
Cannon, A.E. 202
　Earlier sketches in SATA 93, 163
Cannon, Ann Edwards
　See Cannon, A.E.
Cannon, Bettie (Waddell) 1922- 59
Cannon, Curt
　See Hunter, Evan
Cannon, Eileen E(mily) 1948- 119

Cannon, Frank
　See Mayhar, Ardath
Cannon, Janell 1957- 128
　Earlier sketch in SATA 78
　See also CLR 120
Cannon, Marian G. 1923- 85
Cannon, Taffy
　See Cannon, Eileen E(mily)
Cantone, AnnaLaura 182
Cantrell, Julie 1973- 217
Canusi, Jose
　See Barker, S. Omar
Canyon, Christopher 1966- 150
　Earlier sketch in SATA 104
Caparo, Antonio
　See Caparo, Antonio Javier
Caparo, Antonio Javier 205
Capek, Michael 1947- 142
　Earlier sketch in SATA 96
Capes, Bernard (Edward Joseph)
　1854-1918 116
Caple, Kathy 193
Caple, Laurie 1958- 201
Caplin, Alfred Gerald 1909-1979 61
　Obituary 21
Caponigro, John Paul 1965- 84
Capote, Truman 1924-1984 91
Capp, Al
　See Caplin, Alfred Gerald
Cappel, Constance 1936- 22
Cappetta, Cynthia 1949- 125
Cappo, Nan Willard 1955- 143
Capps, Benjamin (Franklin) 1922- 9
Cappy Dick
　See Cleveland, George
Captain Kangaroo
　See Keeshan, Robert J.
Captain Wheeler
　See Ellis, Edward S.
Captain Young of Yale
　See Stratemeyer, Edward L.
Capucilli, Alyssa Satin 1957- 203
　Earlier sketches in SATA 115, 163
Capucine
　See Mazille, Capucine
Carafoli, Marci
　See Balterman, Marcia Ridlon
Caraher, Kim(berley Elizabeth) 1961- 105
Caraker, Mary 1929- 74
Caras, Roger A(ndrew) 1928-2001 12
　Obituary 127
Caravantes, Peggy 1935- 140
Caraway, Caren 1939- 57
Carbone, Elisa 1954- 173
　Earlier sketches in SATA 81, 137
Carbone, Elisa Lynn
　See Carbone, Elisa
Carbonnier, Jeanne 1894-1974 3
　Obituary 34
Card, Orson Scott 1951- 127
　Earlier sketch in SATA 83
　See also CLR 116
Care, Felicity
　See Coury, Louise Andree
Carew, Jan 1925- 51
　Brief entry 40
Carew, Jan Rynveld
　See Carew, Jan
Carey, Benedict 1960- 219
Carey, Bonnie
　See Marshall, Bonnie C.
Carey, Charles W., Jr. 1951- 170
Carey, Ernestine Gilbreth 1908-2006 2
　Obituary 177
Carey, Janet Lee 1954(?)- 225
　Earlier sketch in SATA 185
Carey, Lisa 110
Carey, M. V.
　See Carey, Mary V(irginia)
Carey, Mary V(irginia) 1925-1994 44
　Brief entry 39

Carey, Peter 1943- 94
Carey, Peter Philip
　See Carey, Peter
Carey, Valerie Scho 1949- 60
Carheden, Goorel Kristina
　See Naaslund, Goorel Kristina
Carigiet, Alois 1902-1985 24
　Obituary 47
　See also CLR 38
Carini, Edward 1923- 9
Carkeet, David 1946- 75
Carle, Eric 1929- 163
　Earlier sketches in SATA 4, 65, 120
　See also CLR 72
　See also SAAS 6
Carleton, Captain L. C.
　See Ellis, Edward S.
Carleton, Captain Latham C.
　See Ellis, Edward S.
Carleton, Latham C.
　See Ellis, Edward S.
Carley, V(an Ness) Royal 1906-1976
　Obituary 20
Carling, Amelia Lau 1949- 164
　Earlier sketch in SATA 119
Carlisle, Carolyn
　See Hawes, Louise
Carlisle, Clark
　See Holding, James (Clark Carlisle, Jr.)
Carlisle, Olga Andreyev 1930- 35
Carlock, Miriam
　See Eyerly, Jeannette
Carls, Claudia 1978- 198
Carlsen, G(eorge) Robert 1917- 30
Carlsen, Ruth C(hristoffer) 1918- 2
Carlson, Bernice Wells 1910- 8
Carlson, Christopher C. 202
Carlson, Dale (Bick) 1935- 1
Carlson, Daniel (Bick) 1960- 27
Carlson, Kirsten 1968- 192
Carlson, Kirsten M.
　See Carlson, Kirsten
Carlson, Laurie 1952- 173
　Earlier sketch in SATA 101
Carlson, Laurie Winn
　See Carlson, Laurie
Carlson, Melody 1956- 171
　Earlier sketch in SATA 113
Carlson, Nancy 1953- 213
　Brief entry 45
　Earlier sketches in SATA 56, 90, 144
Carlson, Nancy L.
　See Carlson, Nancy
Carlson, Natalie Savage 1906-1997 68
　Earlier sketch in SATA 2
　See also SAAS 4
Carlson, Susan Johnston 1953- 88
Carlson, Vada F. 1897- 16
Carlstrom, Nancy White 1948- 215
　Brief entry 48
　Earlier sketches in SATA 53, 92, 156
Carlton, Keith
　See Robertson, Keith (Carlton)
Carlton, Susan 1960- 195
Carlyon, Richard 55
Carman, Bill
　See Carman, William
Carman, Patrick 1966- 197
　Earlier sketch in SATA 161
Carman, William 223
Carmer, Carl (Lamson) 1893-1976 37
　Obituary 30
Carmer, Elizabeth Black 1904- 24
Carmi, Giora 1944- 149
　Earlier sketch in SATA 79
Carmichael, Carrie
　See Carmichael, Harriet
Carmichael, Clay 218
Carmichael, Harriet 40
Carmody, Isobelle 1958- 191
　Earlier sketch in SATA 161

Carmody, Isobelle Jane
    See Carmody, Isobelle
Carney, Elizabeth 1981- *199*
Carney, Jeff 1962- *196*
Carney, Mary Lou 1949- *170*
Carol, Bill J.
    See Knott, William C(ecil, Jr.)
Caron, Romi
    See Caron-Kyselkova', Romana
Caron-Kyselkova', Romana 1967- *94*
Caroselli, Remus F(rancis) 1916- *36*
Carpelan, Bo 1926- *8*
Carpelan, Bo Gustaf Bertelsson
    See Carpelan, Bo
Carpenter, (John) Allan 1917- *81*
    Earlier sketch in SATA *3*
Carpenter, Angelica Shirley 1945- *153*
    Earlier sketch in SATA *71*
Carpenter, Frances 1890-1972 .... *3*
    Obituary *27*
Carpenter, John 1948- *58*
Carpenter, John Howard
    See Carpenter, John
Carpenter, Johnny
    See Carpenter, John
Carpenter, Nancy *215*
Carpenter, Nancy Sippel
    See Carpenter, Nancy
Carpenter, Patricia (Healy Evans) 1920- *11*
Carr, Glyn
    See Styles, (Frank) Showell
Carr, Harriett H(elen) 1899-1977 .... *3*
Carr, Jan 1953- *132*
    Earlier sketch in SATA *89*
Carr, M. J.
    See Carr, Jan
Carr, Mary Jane 1899-1988 .... *2*
    Obituary *55*
Carr, Philippa
    See Hibbert, Eleanor Alice Burford
Carr, Roger Vaughan 1937- *95*
Carrel, Annette Felder 1929- *90*
Carrick, Carol (Hatfield) 1935- *118*
    Earlier sketches in SATA *7, 63*
    See also SAAS *18*
Carrick, Donald (F.) 1929-1989 .... *63*
    Earlier sketch in SATA *7*
Carrick, Malcolm 1945- *28*
Carrick, Paul 1972- *194*
Carrier, Lark 1947- *71*
    Brief entry *50*
Carrier, Roch 1937- *166*
    Earlier sketch in SATA *105*
Carrighar, Sally 1898-1985 .... *24*
Carrillo, Patricia S.
    See Carrillo, P.S.
Carrillo, P.S. *209*
Carrington, G. A.
    See Cunningham, Chet
Carrington, Marsha Gray 1954- *168*
    Earlier sketch in SATA *111*
Carris, Joan 1938- *182*
    Brief entry *42*
    Earlier sketch in SATA *44*
Carris, Joan Davenport
    See Carris, Joan
Carroll, Curt
    See Bishop, Curtis (Kent)
Carroll, Elizabeth
    See Barkin, Carol
    and James, Elizabeth
Carroll, Jaye
    See Carroll, Michael
Carroll, Jenny
    See Cabot, Meg
Carroll, (Archer) Latrobe 1894-1996 .... *7*
Carroll, Laura
    See Parr, Lucy
Carroll, Lewis 1832-1898 .... *100*
    See also YABC *2*
    See also CLR *108*

Carroll, Michael 1966- *203*
Carroll, Raymond 1924- *86*
    Brief entry *47*
Carruth, Hayden 1921-2008 .... *47*
    Obituary *197*
Carryl, Charles E. 1841-1920 .... *114*
Carryl, Charles Edward
    See Carryl, Charles E.
Carse, Robert 1902-1971 .... *5*
Carson, J(ohn) Franklin 1920-1981 .... *1*
    Obituary *107*
Carson, Mary Kay 1964- *200*
    Earlier sketch in SATA *150*
Carson, Rachel 1907-1964 .... *23*
Carson, Rachel Louise
    See Carson, Rachel
Carson, Rosalind
    See Chittenden, Margaret
Carson, S. M.
    See Gorsline, (Sally) Marie
Carson, William C. 1928- *154*
Carter, Abby *222*
    Earlier sketch in SATA *184*
Carter, Alden R 1947- *137*
    Earlier sketch in SATA *67*
    See also CLR *22*
    See also SAAS *18*
Carter, Alden Richardson
    See Carter, Alden R
Carter, Andy 1948- *134*
Carter, Angela 1940-1992 .... *66*
    Obituary *70*
Carter, Angela Olive
    See Carter, Angela
Carter, Anne Laurel 1953- *209*
    Earlier sketch in SATA *135*
Carter, Asa Earl
    See Carter, Forrest
Carter, Avis Murton
    See Allen, Kenneth S.
Carter, Bruce
    See Hough, Richard (Alexander)
Carter, Carol S(hadis) 1948- *124*
Carter, David A. 1957- *228*
    Earlier sketches in SATA *114, 170*
Carter, Don 1958- *192*
    Earlier sketch in SATA *124*
Carter, Dorothy Sharp 1921- *8*
Carter, Forrest 1927(?)-1979 .... *32*
Carter, Helene 1887-1960 .... *15*
Carter, (William) Hodding, Jr. 1907-1972 ...... *2*
    Obituary *27*
Carter, James Earl, Jr.
    See Carter, Jimmy
Carter, Jimmy 1924- *79*
Carter, Katharine J(ones) 1905-1984 .... *2*
Carter, Lin(wood Vrooman) 1930-1988 .... *91*
Carter, Mike 1936- *138*
Carter, Nick
    See Avallone, Michael (Angelo, Jr.)
    and Ballard, (Willis) Todhunter
    and Crider, Bill
    and Cassiday, Bruce (Bingham)
    and Chastain, Thomas
    and Dey, Frederic (Merrill) Van Rensselaer
    and Garside, Jack
    and Hayes, Ralph E(ugene)
    and Henderson, M(arilyn) R(uth)
    and Lynds, Dennis
    and Lynds, Gayle (Hallenbeck)
    and Randisi, Robert J.
    and Rasof, Henry
    and Stratemeyer, Edward L.
    and Smith, Martin Cruz
    and Swain, Dwight V(reeland)
    and Vardeman, Robert E.
    and Wallmann, Jeffrey M(iner)
    and White, Lionel
Carter, Peter 1929- *57*
Carter, Phyllis Ann
    See Eberle, Irmengarde

Carter, Samuel (Thomson) III 1904-1988 .... *37*
    Obituary *60*
Carter, Timothy 1972- *224*
Carter, William E. 1926-1983 .... *1*
    Obituary *35*
Cartlidge, Michelle 1950- *96*
    Brief entry *37*
    Earlier sketch in SATA *49*
Cartner, William Carruthers 1910- *11*
Cartwright, Ann 1940- *78*
Cartwright, Reg(inald Ainsley) 1938- *64*
Cartwright, Sally 1923- *9*
Carusone, Al 1949- *89*
Carvell, Marlene *172*
Carver, John
    See Gardner, Richard (M.)
Carwell, L'Ann
    See McKissack, Patricia C.
Cary
    See Cary, Louis F(avreau)
Cary, Barbara Knapp 1912(?)-1975
    Obituary *31*
Cary, Kate 1967(?)- *174*
Cary, Louis F(avreau) 1915- *9*
Caryl, Jean
    See Kaplan, Jean Caryl Korn
Casanova, Mary 1957- *186*
    Earlier sketches in SATA *94, 136*
Cascone, A.G.
    See Cascone, Annette
    and Cascone, Gina
Cascone, Annette 1960- *103*
Cascone, Gina 1955- *103*
Case, Chris 1976- *209*
Case, Marshal T(aylor) 1941- *9*
Case, Michael
    See Howard, Robert West
Caseley, Judith 1951- *159*
    Brief entry *53*
    Earlier sketch in SATA *87*
Casewit, Curtis W(erner) 1922-2002 .... *4*
Casey, Barbara (Louise) 1944- *147*
    Earlier sketch in SATA *79*
Casey, Brigid 1950- *9*
Casey, Tina 1959- *141*
Cash, Ellen Lewis Buell 1905-1989
    Obituary *64*
Cash, John Carter 1970- *218*
Cash, Megan Montague *160*
Cashore, Kristin 1976(?)- *206*
Casilla, Robert 1959- *211*
    Earlier sketches in SATA *75, 146*
Cason, Mabel Earp 1892-1965 .... *10*
Cass, Joan E(velyn) *1*
Cass-Beggs, Barbara 1904- *62*
Cassedy, Patrice (Rinaldo) 1953- *149*
Cassedy, Sylvia 1930-1989 .... *77*
    Obituary *61*
    Earlier sketch in SATA *27*
    See also CLR *26*
Cassel, Lili
    See Wronker, Lili Cassel
Cassels, Jean *173*
Cassidy, Anne 1952- *166*
Cassidy, Anne Josephine
    See Cassidy, Anne
Cassidy, Cathy 1962- *183*
Cassino, Mark *228*
Casson, Hugh Maxwell 1910-1999 .... *65*
    Obituary *115*
Cassutt, Michael 1954- *78*
Cassutt, Michael Joseph
    See Cassutt, Michael
Castaldi, Elicia *194*
Castaldo, Nancy Fusco 1962- *151*
    Earlier sketch in SATA *93*
Castaneda, Omar S. 1954- *71*
Castell, Megan
    See Williams, Jeanne
Castellanos, Jane Mollie Robinson
    1913-2001 .... *9*

Castellon, Federico 1914-1971 .... *48*
Castellucci, Cecil 1969- *176*
Castillo, Edmund L. 1924-2005 .... *1*
   Obituary *167*
Castillo, Lauren *195*
Castle, Lee
   See Ogan, George F.
   and Ogan, Margaret E. (Nettles)
Castle, Paul
   See Howard, Vernon (Linwood)
Castle, Robert
   See Hamilton, Edmond
Castro L., Antonio 1941- *226*
Castrovilla, Selene 1966- *186*
Caswell, Brian 1954- *171*
   Earlier sketch in SATA *97*
Caswell, Deanna *223*
Caswell, Helen (Rayburn) 1923- *12*
Catalano, Dominic 1956- *163*
   Earlier sketch in SATA *76*
Catalano, Grace (A.) 1961- *99*
Catalanotto, Peter 1959- *195*
   Autobiography Feature *113*
   Earlier sketches in SATA *70, 114, 159*
   See also CLR 68
   See also SAAS 25
Catanese, P.W. 1961- *227*
   Earlier sketch in SATA *179*
Cate, Annette LeBlanc *196*
Cate, Dick
   See Cate, Richard Edward Nelson
Cate, Richard Edward Nelson 1932- *28*
Cather, Willa 1873-1947 .... *30*
   See also CLR 98
Catherall, Arthur 1906-1980 .... *74*
   Earlier sketches in SATA *3, 4*
Cathon, Laura E(lizabeth) 1908-1991 .... *27*
Catlett, Elizabeth 1919(?)- *82*
Catlin, Wynelle 1930- *13*
Catlow, Nikalas
   See Catlow, Niki
Catlow, Niki 1975- *193*
Cato, Heather *105*
Cato, Sheila *114*
Catran, Ken 1944- *190*
Catrow, David
   See Catrow, David J. III
Catrow, David J. III *206*
   Earlier sketch in SATA *152*
Catt, Louis
   See French, Vivian
Cattell, James 1954- *123*
Catton, (Charles) Bruce 1899-1978 .... *2*
   Obituary *24*
Catusanu, Mircea *222*
Catz, Max
   See Glaser, Milton
Caudell, Marian 1930- *52*
Caudill, Rebecca 1899-1985 .... *1*
   Obituary *44*
Cauley, Lorinda Bryan 1951- *46*
   Brief entry *43*
Caulfield, Peggy F. 1926-1987
   Obituary *53*
Cauman, Samuel 1910-1971 .... *48*
Causley, Charles (Stanley) 1917-2003 .... *66*
   Obituary *149*
   Earlier sketch in SATA *3*
   See also CLR 30
Cavallaro, Ann (Abelson) 1918- *62*
Cavallo, Diana 1931- *7*
Cavanagh, Helen (Carol) 1939- *98*
   Brief entry *37*
   Earlier sketch in SATA *48*
Cavanah, Frances 1899-1982 .... *31*
   Earlier sketch in SATA *1*
Cavanna, Betty
   See Harrison, Elizabeth (Allen) Cavanna
Cavanna, Elizabeth
   See Harrison, Elizabeth (Allen) Cavanna

Cave, Kathryn 1948- *123*
   Earlier sketch in SATA *76*
Cavendish, Peter
   See Horler, Sydney
Caveney, Philip 1951- *219*
Caveney, Philip Richard
   See Caveney, Philip
Cavin, Ruth 1918-2011 .... *38*
Cavin, Ruth Brodie
   See Cavin, Ruth
Cavoukian, Raffi 1948- *68*
Cawley, Winifred 1915- *13*
Cazeau, Charles J(ay) 1931- *65*
Cazet, Denys 1938- *191*
   Brief entry *41*
   Earlier sketches in SATA *52, 99, 163*
Cazzola, Gus 1934- *73*
Cebulash, Mel 1937- *91*
   Earlier sketch in SATA *10*
Ceccoli, Nicoletta *181*
Cecil, Randy 1968- *223*
   Earlier sketch in SATA *187*
Cecka, Melanie *199*
Ceder, Georgiana Dorcas -1985 .... *10*
Celenza, Anna Harwell *133*
Celestino, Martha Laing
   See Laing, Martha
Cepeda, Joe *215*
   Earlier sketch in SATA *159*
Cerf, Bennett (Alfred) 1898-1971 .... *7*
Cerf, Christopher (Bennett) 1941- *2*
Cermak, Martin
   See Duchacek, Ivo D(uka)
Cerullo, Mary M. 1949- *145*
   Earlier sketch in SATA *86*
Cervon, Jacqueline
   See Moussard, Jacqueline
Cetin, Frank Stanley 1921- *2*
Chabon, Michael 1963- *145*
Chabrian, Deborah
   See Chabrian, Deborah L.
Chabrian, Deborah L. *212*
Chaconas, D.J.
   See Chaconas, Dori
Chaconas, Dori 1938- *208*
   Earlier sketches in SATA *145, 175*
Chaconas, Doris J.
   See Chaconas, Dori
Chadda, Sarwat *224*
Chadwick, Lester *67*
   Earlier sketch in SATA *1*
Chaffee, Allen *3*
Chaffin, Lillie D(orton) 1925- *4*
Chaikin, Miriam 1924- *152*
   Earlier sketches in SATA *24, 102*
Chall, Marsha Wilson *150*
Challand, Helen J(ean) 1921- *64*
Challans, Mary
   See Renault, Mary
Chalmers, Mary (Eileen) 1927- *6*
   See also SAAS 14
Chamberlain, Barbara A.
   See Azore, Barbara
Chamberlain, Margaret 1954- *212*
   Earlier sketch in SATA *46*
Chamberlin, Kate 1945- *105*
Chamberlin, Mary 1960- *177*
Chamberlin, Rich *177*
Chamberlin, Richard
   See Chamberlin, Rich
Chambers, Aidan 1934- *171*
   Earlier sketches in SATA *1, 69, 108*
   See also CLR 151
   See also SAAS 12
Chambers, Bradford 1922-1984
   Obituary *39*
Chambers, Catherine E.
   See St. John, Nicole
Chambers, John W. 1933- *57*
   Brief entry *46*

Chambers, Kate
   See St. John, Nicole
Chambers, Margaret Ada Eastwood 1911- *2*
Chambers, Peggy
   See Chambers, Margaret Ada Eastwood
Chambers, Robert W(illiam) 1865-1933 .... *107*
Chambliss, Maxie *186*
Champlin, Susan 1961- *225*
Chan, Gillian 1954- *147*
   Earlier sketch in SATA *102*
Chan, Peter 1980(?)- *207*
Chance, James T.
   See Carpenter, John
Chance, John T.
   See Carpenter, John
Chance, Stephen
   See Turner, Philip (William)
Chandler, Caroline A(ugusta) 1906-1979 ..... *22*
   Obituary *24*
Chandler, David P. 1933- *28*
Chandler, David Porter
   See Chandler, David P.
Chandler, Edna Walker 1908-1982 .... *11*
   Obituary *31*
Chandler, Jennifer
   See Westwood, Jennifer
Chandler, Karen 1959- *122*
Chandler, Linda S(mith) 1929- *39*
Chandler, Pauline *175*
Chandler, Robert 1953- *40*
Chandler, Ruth Forbes 1894-1978 .... *2*
   Obituary *26*
Chandonnet, Ann F. 1943- *92*
Chaney, Jill 1932- *87*
Chang, Chih-Wei 1966- *111*
Chang, Cindy 1968- *90*
Chang, Grace 1961- *226*
Chang, Margaret 1941- *71*
Chang, Margaret Scrogin
   See Chang, Margaret
Chang, Raymond 1939- *142*
   Earlier sketches in SATA *71, 142 PEN*
Chanin, Michael 1952- *84*
Channel, A. R.
   See Catherall, Arthur
Chapian, Marie 1938- *29*
Chapin, Alene Olsen Dalton 1915(?)-1986
   Obituary *47*
Chapin, Tom 1945- *83*
Chapman, Allen *67*
   Earlier sketch in SATA *1*
Chapman, Cheryl O(rth) 1948- *80*
Chapman, (Constance) Elizabeth (Mann)
   1919- *10*
Chapman, Gaye 1970- *200*
Chapman, Gaye Coralie
   See Chapman, Gaye
Chapman, Gaynor 1935- *32*
Chapman, Gillian 1955- *120*
Chapman, Jane 1970- *212*
   Earlier sketches in SATA *122, 176*
Chapman, Jean *104*
   Earlier sketch in SATA *34*
   See also CLR 65
Chapman, John Stanton Higham 1891-1972
   Obituary *27*
Chapman, Lee
   See Bradley, Marion Zimmer
Chapman, Linda 1969- *223*
Chapman, Lynne 1960- *197*
Chapman, Lynne F(erguson) 1963- *150*
   Earlier sketch in SATA *94*
Chapman, Maristan
   See Chapman, John Stanton Higham
Chapman, Vera (Ivy May) 1898-1996 .... *33*
Chapman, Walker
   See Silverberg, Robert
Chappell, Audrey 1954- *72*
Chappell, Crissa-Jean *198*

Chappell, Warren 1904-1991 68
  Obituary 67
  Earlier sketch in SATA 6
  See also SAAS 10
Chapra, Mimi 182
Charbonneau, Eileen 1951- 118
  Earlier sketch in SATA 84
Charbonnet, Gabrielle 1961- 227
  Earlier sketch in SATA 81
Chardiet, Bernice 1927(?)- 27
Chardiet, Bernice Kroll
  See Chardiet, Bernice
Charest, Emily MacLachlan 198
Charles, Donald
  See Meighan, Donald Charles
Charles, Louis
  See Stratemeyer, Edward L.
Charles, Nicholas
  See Kuskin, Karla
Charles, Nicholas J.
  See Kuskin, Karla
Charles, Norma 153
Charles, Veronika Martenova 182
Charlip, Remy 1929- 119
  Earlier sketches in SATA 4, 68
  See also CLR 8
Charlot, Jean 1898-1979 8
  Obituary 31
Charlot, Martin 1944- 64
Charlot, Martin Day
  See Charlot, Martin
Charlton, Michael (Alan) 1923- 34
Charlton-Trujillo, e.E. 189
Charmatz, Bill 1925-2005 7
Charnas, Suzy McKee 1939- 110
  Earlier sketch in SATA 61
Charosh, Mannis 1906- 5
Chartier, Normand L. 1945- 66
Chase, Alice
  See McHargue, Georgess
Chase, Alyssa 1965- 92
Chase, Andra 1942- 91
Chase, Emily
  See Aks, Patricia
  and Garwood, Julie
  and Sachs, Judith
  and White, Carol
Chase, Mary (Coyle) 1907-1981 17
  Obituary 29
Chase, Mary Ellen 1887-1973 10
Chase, Paula 214
Chase, Richard 1904-1988 64
  Obituary 56
Chase, Samantha
  See Glick, Ruth
Chast, Roz 1954- 212
  Earlier sketch in SATA 97
Chastain, Madye Lee 1908-1989 4
Chataway, Carol 1955- 140
Chatterjee, Debjani 1952- 83
Chatterton, Martin 1961- 225
Chauncy, Nan(cen Beryl Masterman)
  1900-1970 6
  See also CLR 6
Chaundler, Christine 1887-1972 1
  Obituary 25
Chayka, Doug 196
Chbosky, Stephen 1972- 164
Cheaney, Janie B.
  See Cheaney, J.B.
Cheaney, J.B. 1950- 188
Chee, Cheng-Khee 1934- 79
Cheese, Chloe 1952- 118
Chekhonte, Antosha
  See Chekhov, Anton
Chekhov, Anton 1860-1904 90
Chekhov, Anton Pavlovich
  See Chekhov, Anton
Chelushkin, Kirill 1968- 186
Chen, Anthony 1929- 6

Chen, Chih-Yuan 1975- 216
  Earlier sketch in SATA 155
Chen, Ju-Hong 1941- 78
Chen, Pauline 1966- 202
Chen, Sara
  See Odgers, Sally Farrell
Chen, Tony
  See Chen, Anthony
Chen, Yong 1963- 183
Chen, Yuan-tsung 1932- 65
Chen, Zhiyuan
  See Chen, Chih-Yuan
Chenault, Nell
  See Smith, Linell Nash
Chen Chih-Yuan
  See Chen, Chih-Yuan
Chenery, Janet (Dai) 1923- 25
Cheney, Cora 1916-1999 3
  Obituary 110
Cheney, Glenn (Alan) 1951- 99
Cheney, Lynne V. 1941- 152
Cheney, Lynne Vincent
  See Cheney, Lynne V.
Cheney, Ted
  See Cheney, Theodore Albert
Cheney, Theodore A. Rees
  See Cheney, Theodore Albert
Cheney, Theodore Albert 1928- 11
Cheng, Andrea 1957- 205
  Earlier sketches in SATA 128, 172
Cheng, Christopher 1959- 173
  Earlier sketch in SATA 106
Cheng, Judith 1955- 36
Cheng, Shan
  See Jiang, Cheng An
Cheripko, Jan 1951- 155
  Earlier sketch in SATA 83
Chermayeff, Ivan 1932- 47
Chernenko, Dan
  See Turtledove, Harry
Chernett, Dan 224
Chernoff, Dorothy A.
  See Ernst, (Lyman) John
Chernoff, Goldie Taub 1909- 10
Cherry, Carolyn Janice
  See Cherryh, C.J.
Cherry, Lynne 1952- 99
  Earlier sketch in SATA 34
Cherryh, C.J. 1942- 172
  Earlier sketch in SATA 93
Cherryholmes, Anne
  See Price, Olive
Cheshire, Simon 172
Chesler, Bernice 1932-2002 59
Chess, Victoria (Dickerson) 1939- 92
  Earlier sketch in SATA 33
Chessa, Francesca 191
Chester, Deborah 1957- 85
Chester, Kate
  See Guccione, Leslie Davis
Chesterton, G. K. 1874-1936 27
Chesterton, Gilbert Keith
  See Chesterton, G. K.
Chesworth, Michael 207
  Earlier sketch in SATA 160
Chetin, Helen 1922- 6
Chetwin, Grace 86
  Brief entry 50
Chevalier, Christa 1937- 35
Chevalier, Tracy 1962- 128
Chew, Ruth 1920-2010 7
Chichester Clark, Emma 1955- 209
  Earlier sketches in SATA 117, 156, 69
Chidsey, Donald Barr 1902-1981 3
  Obituary 27
Chiefari, Janet D. 1942- 58
Chien, Catia 193
Chien-min, Lin
  See Rumford, James
Child, L. Maria
  See Child, Lydia Maria

Child, Lauren 1965- 183
  Earlier sketches in SATA 119, 160
Child, Lincoln 1957- 113
Child, Lincoln B.
  See Child, Lincoln
Child, Lydia Maria 1802-1880 67
Child, Mrs.
  See Child, Lydia Maria
Child, Philip 1898-1978 47
Children's Shepherd, The
  See Westphal, Arnold Carl
Childress, Alice 1920-1994 81
  Earlier sketches in SATA 7, 48
  See also CLR 14
Childs, H(alla) Fay (Cochrane) 1890-1971 1
  Obituary 25
Chilton, Charles (Frederick William)
  1917- 102
Chima, Cinda Williams 226
  Earlier sketch in SATA 192
Chimaera
  See Farjeon, Eleanor
Chin, Jason 1978- 218
Chin, Richard (M.) 1946- 52
Chinery, Michael 1938- 26
Chin-Lee, Cynthia 1958- 102
Chin-Lee D., Cynthia
  See Chin-Lee, Cynthia
Chippendale, Lisa A. 158
Chipperfield, Joseph Eugene 1912-1980(?) .. 87
  Earlier sketch in SATA 2
Chisholm, P. F.
  See Finney, Patricia
Chislett, Gail (Elaine) 1948- 58
Chittenden, Elizabeth F. 1903-1999 9
Chittenden, Margaret 1935- 28
Chittum, Ida 1918- 7
Chitwood, Suzanne Tanner 1958- 160
Chmielarz, Sharon Lee 1940- 72
Choate, Judith (Newkirk) 1940- 30
Chocolate, Debbi 1954- 223
  Earlier sketch in SATA 96
Chocolate, Deborah H. Newton
  See Chocolate, Debbi
Chodos-Irvine, Margaret 211
  Earlier sketch in SATA 152
Choi, Sook Nyul 1937- 73
  Autobiography Feature 126
  See also CLR 53
Choi, Yangsook 178
Choksi, Nishant 1975- 222
Choldenko, Gennifer 1957- 182
  Earlier sketch in SATA 135
Chorao, Kay 1936- 215
Chorao, (Ann Mc)Kay (Sproat) 1936- 162
  Earlier sketches in SATA 8, 69
Choron, Sandra (Zena Samelson) 1950- 146
Choung, Eun-hee 199
Chown, Marcus 1959- 137
Choyce, Lesley 1951- 165
  Earlier sketch in SATA 94
Choyce, Lesley Willis
  See Choyce, Lesley
Chrisman, Arthur Bowie 1889-1953 124
  See also YABC 1
Christelow, Eileen 1943- 184
  Autobiography Feature 120
  Brief entry 35
  Earlier sketches in SATA 38, 90
Christensen, Bonnie 1951- 213
  Earlier sketches in SATA 110, 157
Christensen, Gardell Dano 1907-1991 1
Christensen, Laurie
  See Steding, Laurie
Christesen, Barbara 1940- 40
Christgau, Alice Erickson 1902-1977 13
Christian, Mary Blount 1933- 9
Christiana, David 195
Christie, Agatha 1890-1976 36
Christie, Agatha Mary Clarissa
  See Christie, Agatha

Christie, Ann Philippa
    See Pearce, Philippa
Christie, Gregory
    See Christie, R. Gregory
Christie, Philippa
    See Pearce, Philippa
Christie, R. Gregory 1971- 225
    Earlier sketches in SATA *127, 185*
Christopher, John
    See Youd, Samuel
Christopher, Louise
    See Hale, Arlene
Christopher, Matt(hew Frederick)
    1917-1997 80
    Obituary 99
    Earlier sketches in SATA *2, 47*
    See also CLR *119*
    See also SAAS *9*
Christopher, Milbourne 1914(?)-1984 46
Christy, Howard Chandler 1873-1952 21
Chrustowski, Rick 176
Chrystie, Frances N(icholson) 1904-1986 60
Chu, Daniel 1933- 11
Chukovsky, Kornei (Ivanovich) 1882-1969 . 34
    Earlier sketch in SATA *5*
Church, Caroline Jayne 219
    Earlier sketch in SATA *179*
Church, Richard 1893-1972 3
Churchill, E(lmer) Richard 1937- 11
Churchill, Elizabeth
    See Hough, Richard (Alexander)
Chute, B(eatrice) J(oy) 1913-1987 2
    Obituary 53
Chute, Marchette (Gaylord) 1909-1994 1
Chwast, Jacqueline 1932- 6
Chwast, Seymour 1931- 146
    Earlier sketches in SATA *18, 96*
Ciardi, John (Anthony) 1916-1986 65
    Obituary 46
    Earlier sketch in SATA *1*
    See also CLR *19*
    See also SAAS *26*
Ciccone, Madonna Louise Veronica
    See Madonna
Ciddor, Anna 1957- 213
Ciment, James D. 1958- 140
Cirrone, Dorian 182
Cisneros, Sandra 1954-
    See CLR *123*
Citra, Becky 1954- 137
Citrin, Michael 1965(?)- 183
Claflin, Willy 1944- 208
Clair, Andree 19
Clampett, Bob 1914(?)-1985 44
    Obituary 38
Clampett, Robert
    See Clampett, Bob
Clapp, John 1968- 109
Clapp, Patricia 1912- 74
    Earlier sketch in SATA *4*
    See also SAAS *4*
Clare, Ellen
    See Sinclair, Olga
Clare, Helen
    See Clarke, Pauline
Claremont, Chris 1950- 87
Claremont, Christopher Simon
    See Claremont, Chris
Clark, Ann Nolan 1896-1995 82
    Obituary 87
    Earlier sketch in SATA *4*
    See also CLR *16*
    See also SAAS *16*
Clark, Champ 1923-2002 47
Clark, Christopher (Anthony) Stuart
    See Stuart-Clark, Christopher (Anthony)
Clark, Clara Gillow 1951- 154
    Earlier sketch in SATA *84*
Clark, David
    See Hardcastle, Michael

Clark, David Allen
    See Ernst, (Lyman) John
Clark, Emma Chichester
    See Chichester Clark, Emma
Clark, Frank J(ames) 1922- 18
Clark, Garel
    See Garelick, May
Clark, Halsey
    See Deming, Richard
Clark, Joan
    See Benson, Mildred
Clark, Joan 1934- 182
    Earlier sketches in SATA *59, 96*
Clark, Leonard 1905-1981 30
    Obituary 29
Clark, M. R.
    See Clark, Mavis Thorpe
Clark, Margaret (D.) 1943- 126
Clark, Margaret Goff 1913- 82
    Earlier sketch in SATA *8*
Clark, Mary Higgins 1929- 46
Clark, Mavis Thorpe 1909-1999 74
    Earlier sketch in SATA *8*
    See also CLR *30*
    See also SAAS *5*
Clark, Merle
    See Gessner, Lynne
Clark, Patricia Denise
    See Robins, Patricia
Clark, Patricia Finrow 1929- 11
Clark, Ronald Harry 1904-1999 193
Clark, Ronald William 1916-1987 2
    Obituary 52
Clark, Sherryl 1956- 149
Clark, Van D(eusen) 1909-1974 2
Clark, Virginia
    See Gray, Patricia (Clark)
Clark, Walter Van Tilburg 1909-1971 8
Clarke, Arthur
    See Clarke, Arthur C.
Clarke, Arthur C. 1917-2008 115
    Obituary 191
    Earlier sketches in SATA *13, 70*
    See also CLR *119*
Clarke, Arthur Charles
    See Clarke, Arthur C.
Clarke, Clorinda 1917- 7
Clarke, Elizabeth L. 1934- 103
Clarke, Greg 1959- 215
Clarke, Gus 1948- 134
Clarke, J.
    See Clarke, Judith
Clarke, James Hall
    See Rowland-Entwistle, (Arthur) Theodore
    (Henry)
Clarke, Joan B. 1921- 42
    Brief entry 27
Clarke, John
    See Laklan, Carli
    and Sontup, Dan(iel)
Clarke, Judith 1943- 164
    Earlier sketches in SATA *75, 110*
    See also CLR *61*
Clarke, Julia 1950- 138
Clarke, Kenneth 1957- 107
Clarke, Lea
    See Rowland-Entwistle, (Arthur) Theodore
    (Henry)
Clarke, Margaret 1941-
    See CLR *99*
Clarke, Mary Stetson 1911-1994 5
Clarke, Michael
    See Newlon, (Frank) Clarke
Clarke, Pauline 1921- 131
    Earlier sketch in SATA *3*
    See also CLR *28*
Clarkson, E(dith) Margaret 1915- 37
Clarkson, Ewan 1929- 9
Claudia, Susan
    See Goulart, Ron
    and Johnston, William

Claverie, Jean 1946- 38
Clay, Patrice 1947- 47
Clay, Wil 203
Clayman, Deborah Paula
    See Da Costa, Deborah
Claypool, Jane
    See Miner, Jane Claypool
Clayton, Elaine 1961- 209
    Earlier sketches in SATA *94, 159*
Clayton, Lawrence (Otto, Jr.) 1945- 75
Clayton, Sally Pomme 218
Clayton, Sandra 1951- 110
Cle, Troy 202
Clea, Super
    See Hantman, Clea
Cleary, Beverly 1916- 121
    Earlier sketches in SATA *2, 43, 79*
    See also CLR *72*
    See also SAAS *20*
Cleary, Beverly Atlee Bunn
    See Cleary, Beverly
Cleary, Brian P. 1959- 186
    Earlier sketches in SATA *93, 132*
Cleaver, Bill
    See Cleaver, William J.
Cleaver, Carole 1934- 6
Cleaver, Elizabeth (Ann Mrazik)
    1939-1985 23
    Obituary 43
    See also CLR *13*
Cleaver, Hylton Reginald 1891-1961 49
Cleaver, Vera 1919-1993 76
    Earlier sketch in SATA *22*
    See also CLR *6*
Cleaver, Vera Allen
    See Cleaver, Vera
Cleaver, William J. 1920-1981 22
    Obituary 27
    See also CLR *6*
Cleishbotham, Jebediah
    See Scott, Sir Walter
Cleland, Janet 226
Cleland, Mabel
    See Widdemer, Mabel Cleland
Clem, Margaret H(ollingsworth) 1923- 90
Clemens, James
    See Rollins, James
Clemens, Samuel
    See Twain, Mark
Clemens, Samuel Langhorne
    See Twain, Mark
Clemens, Virginia Phelps 1941- 35
Clement, Gary 191
Clement, Janet 182
Clement, Nathan 1966- 200
Clement, Priscilla Ferguson 1942- 171
Clement, Rod 97
Clement-Moore, Rosemary 229
    Earlier sketch in SATA *188*
Clements, Andrew 1949- 203
    Earlier sketches in SATA *104, 158*
Clements, Bruce 1931- 178
    Earlier sketches in SATA *27, 94*
Clemesha, David 192
Cleminson, Katie 221
Clemons, Elizabeth
    See Nowell, Elizabeth Cameron
Clerk, N. W.
    See Lewis, C. S.
Cleveland, Bob
    See Cleveland, George
Cleveland, George 1903(?)-1985
    Obituary 43
Cleveland-Peck, Patricia 80
Cleven, Cathrine
    See Cleven, Kathryn Seward
Cleven, Kathryn Seward 2
Clevenger, William R. 1954- 84
Clevenger, William Russell
    See Clevenger, William R.
Clevin, Joergen 1920- 7

Clevin, Jorgen
    See Clevin, Joergen
Clewes, Dorothy (Mary) 1907-2003 86
    Obituary 138
    Earlier sketch in SATA *1*
Clifford, David
    See Rosenberg, Eth Clifford
Clifford, Eth
    See Rosenberg, Eth Clifford
Clifford, Harold B(urton) 1893-1988 .... *10*
Clifford, Margaret Cort 1929- *1*
Clifford, Martin
    See Hamilton, Charles (Harold St. John)
Clifford, Mary Louise Beneway 1926- 23
Clifford, Peggy
    See Clifford, Margaret Cort
Clifford, Rachel Mark
    See Lewis, Brenda Ralph
Clifton, Lucille 1936-2010 128
    Earlier sketches in SATA *20, 69*
    See also CLR *5*
Clifton, Thelma Lucille
    See Clifton, Lucille
Climo, Shirley 1928- *166*
    Autobiography Feature *110*
    Brief entry 35
    Earlier sketches in SATA *39, 77*
    See also CLR *69*
Cline-Ransome, Lesa 201
Clinton, Catherine 1952- 203
Clinton, Cathryn 1957- 136
Clinton, Dirk
    See Silverberg, Robert
Clinton, Jon
    See Prince, J(ack) H(arvey)
Clippinger, Carol 193
Clish, (Lee) Marian 1946- 43
Clive, Clifford
    See Hamilton, Charles (Harold St. John)
Clokey, Art 1921- 59
Cloudsley-Thompson, J(ohn) L(eonard)
    1921- *19*
Clouse, Nancy L. 1938- 78
Clover, Peter 1952- 215
    Earlier sketch in SATA *152*
Clutha, Janet
    See Frame, Janet
Clutha, Janet Paterson Frame
    See Frame, Janet
Clymer, Eleanor 1906-2001 85
    Obituary 126
    Earlier sketch in SATA *9*
    See also SAAS *17*
Clyne, Patricia (Edwards) *31*
Cneut, Carll 1969- 197
Coalson, Glo 1946- 94
    Earlier sketch in SATA *26*
Coates, Anna 1958- 73
Coates, Belle 1896-1986 .... *2*
Coates, Ruth Allison 1915- *11*
Coats, Alice M(argaret) 1905-1976 .... *11*
Coatsworth, Elizabeth (Jane) 1893-1986 100
    Obituary 49
    Earlier sketches in SATA *2, 56*
    See also CLR *2*
Cobalt, Martin
    See Mayne, William
Cobb, Jane
    See Berry, Jane Cobb
Cobb, Mary 1931- 88
Cobb, Vicki 1938- 136
    Autobiography Feature 136
    Earlier sketches in SATA *8, 69, 131*
    See also CLR *2*
    See also SAAS *6*
Cobbett, Richard
    See Pluckrose, Henry
Cober, Alan E(dwin) 1935-1998 7
    Obituary *101*
Cobham, Sir Alan
    See Hamilton, Charles (Harold St. John)

Coburn, Jake 1978- *155*
Cocagnac, Augustin Maurice(-Jean) 1924- 7
Cocca-Leffler, Maryann 1958- *194*
    Earlier sketches in SATA *80, 136*
Cochran, Bill 187
Cochran, Bobbye A. 1949- *11*
Cochran, Josh 221
Cochran, Thomas 1955- 198
Cochrane, Hamilton E.
    See Cochrane, Mick
Cochrane, Mick 1956- 215
Cockcroft, Jason 217
Cockett, Mary *3*
Cocks, Peter 204
Cocovini, Abby 202
Coddell, Esme Raji
    See Codell, Esme Raji
Codell, Esme Raji 1968- 160
Cody, C. S.
    See Waller, Leslie
Cody, Jess
    See Cunningham, Chet
Cody, Matthew 229
Coe, Anne (E.) 1949- 95
Coe, Douglas
    See Epstein, Beryl
    and Epstein, Samuel
Coe, Lloyd 1899(?)-1976
    Obituary 30
Coen, Rena Neumann 1925- 20
Coerr, Eleanor (Beatrice) 1922- 67
    Earlier sketch in SATA *1*
Cofer, Judith Ortiz 1952- 164
    Earlier sketch in SATA *110*
Coffelt, Nancy 1961- 189
Coffey, Brian
    See Koontz, Dean
Coffin, Geoffrey
    See Mason, F(rancis) van Wyck
Coffin, M. T.
    See Stanley, George Edward
Coffin, M.T.
    See Stanley, George Edward
Coffman, Ramon Peyton 1896-1989 4
Cogan, Karen 1954- 125
Coggins, Jack (Banham) 1911-2006 .... *2*
Cohagan, Carolyn 1972- 228
Cohen, Barbara 1932-1992 77
    Obituary 74
    Earlier sketch in SATA *10*
    See also SAAS *7*
Cohen, Daniel (E.) 1936- 70
    Earlier sketch in SATA *8*
    See also CLR *43*
    See also SAAS *4*
Cohen, Deborah Bodin 1968- 180
Cohen, Jan Barger
    See Barger, Jan
Cohen, Jene Barr
    See Barr, Jene
Cohen, Joan Lebold 1932- 4
Cohen, Judith Love 1933- 78
Cohen, Lisa 1963- 225
Cohen, Miriam 1926-1955 155
    Earlier sketches in SATA *29, 106*
    See also SAAS *11*
Cohen, Nora 75
Cohen, Paul 1945- 58
Cohen, Paul S.
    See Cohen, Paul
Cohen, Peter Zachary 1931- 150
    Earlier sketch in SATA *4*
Cohen, Robert Carl 1930- 8
Cohen, Santiago 1954- 215
Cohen, Sholom 1951- 94
Cohn, Angelo 1914-1997 .... *19*
Cohn, Diana 194
Cohn, Rachel 1968- 228
    Earlier sketch in SATA *161*
Coit, Margaret Louise 1922-2003 .... *2*
    Obituary 142

Colasanti, Susane 1973- 214
Colato Lainez, Rene 1970- 226
    Earlier sketch in SATA *176*
Colbert, Anthony 1934-2007 .... *15*
Colbert, Nancy A. 1936- *139*
Colby, C(arroll) B(urleigh) 1904-1977 35
    Earlier sketch in SATA *3*
Colby, Jean Poindexter 1909-1993 23
Cole, Annette
    See Steiner, Barbara A(nnette)
Cole, Babette 1949- *155*
    Earlier sketches in SATA *61, 96*
Cole, Betsy 1940- 83
Cole, Brock 1938- 200
    Earlier sketches in SATA *72, 136*
    See also CLR *18*
Cole, Davis
    See Elting, Mary
Cole, Hannah 1954- 74
Cole, Henry 1955- 213
    Earlier sketch in SATA *181*
Cole, Jack -1974
    See Stewart, John
Cole, Jackson
    See Curry, Thomas Albert
    and Germano, Peter B.
    and Heckelmann, Charles N(ewman)
    and Newton, D(wight) B(ennett)
    and Schisgall, Oscar
Cole, Jennifer
    See Zach, Cheryl (Byrd)
Cole, Joanna 1944- *168*
    Brief entry 37
    Earlier sketches in SATA *49, 81, 120*
    See also CLR *40*
Cole, Lois Dwight 1903-1979 .... *10*
    Obituary 26
Cole, Michael 1947- 59
Cole, Samantha
    See Cole, Stephen
Cole, Sheila 1939- *171*
    Earlier sketches in SATA *24, 95*
Cole, Sheila R.
    See Cole, Sheila
Cole, Sheila Rotenberg
    See Cole, Sheila
Cole, Stephen 1971- *161*
Cole, William (Rossa) 1919-2000 71
    Earlier sketch in SATA *9*
    See also SAAS *9*
Coleman, Andrew
    See Pine, Nicholas
Coleman, Clare
    See Bell, Clare (Louise)
    and Easton, M(alcolm) Coleman
Coleman, Janet Wyman 184
Coleman, Loren 1947- *164*
Coleman, Loren Elwood, Jr.
    See Coleman, Loren
Coleman, Mary Ann 1928- 83
Coleman, Michael
    See Jones, Allan Frewin
Coleman, Michael 1946- 199
    Autobiography Feature *133*
    Earlier sketches in SATA *108, 133*
Coleman, Rowan 187
Coleman, William L(eRoy) 1938- 49
    Brief entry 34
Coleman, Wim 1926- 212
Coles, Robert (Martin) 1929- 23
Colfer, Eoin 1965- 197
    Earlier sketch in SATA *148*
    See also CLR *112*
Colin, Ann
    See Ure, Jean
Collard, Sneed B. III 1959- 184
    Earlier sketches in SATA *84, 139*
Colledge, Anne 1939- 142
Colley, Jacqui 1965- 202
Collicott, Sharleen 1937- 143
    Earlier sketch in SATA *98*

Collicutt, Paul *229*
Collier, Bryan *204*
  Earlier sketches in SATA *126, 174*
Collier, Christopher 1930- *70*
  Earlier sketch in SATA *16*
  See also CLR *126*
Collier, Ethel 1903-1999 .... *22*
Collier, James Lincoln 1928- *166*
  Earlier sketches in SATA *8, 70*
  See also CLR *126*
  See also SAAS *21*
Collier, Jane
  See Collier, Zena
Collier, Kristi *182*
Collier, Steven 1942- *61*
Collier, Zena 1926- *23*
Collings, Gillian 1939- *102*
Collington, Peter 1948- *99*
  Earlier sketch in SATA *59*
Collins, Ace 1953- *82*
Collins, Andrew J.
  See Collins, Ace
Collins, B. R. 1981- *214*
Collins, David R(aymond) 1940-2001 .... *121*
  Earlier sketch in SATA *7*
Collins, Heather 1946- *81*
Collins, Hunt
  See Hunter, Evan
Collins, Michael
  See Lynds, Dennis
Collins, Michael 1930- *58*
Collins, Pat Lowery 1932- *217*
  Earlier sketches in SATA *31, 151*
Collins, Paul 1954- *126*
Collins, Ross 1972- *200*
Collins, Ruth Philpott 1890-1975
  Obituary *30*
Collins, Suzanne *224*
  Earlier sketch in SATA *180*
Collins, Yvonne *194*
Collinson, A. S.
  See Collinson, Alan S.
Collinson, Alan S. 1934- *80*
Collinson, Roger (Alfred) 1936- *133*
Collison, Linda 1953- *185*
Collodi, Carlo 1826-1890 .... *100*
  Earlier sketch in SATA *29*
  See also CLR *120*
Colloms, Brenda 1919- *40*
Colman, Hila 1909-2008 .... *53*
  Earlier sketch in SATA *1*
  See also SAAS *14*
Colman, Morris 1899(?)-1981
  Obituary *25*
Colman, Penny (Morgan) 1944- *160*
  Autobiography Feature *160*
  Earlier sketches in SATA *77, 114*
Colman, Warren (David) 1944- *67*
Coloma, Cindy
  See Martinusen-Coloma, Cindy
Colombo, John Robert 1936- *50*
Colon, Raul *156*
Colon, Raul 1952- *202*
Colonius, Lillian 1911-1992 .... *3*
Colorado, Antonio J.
  See Colorado (Capella), Antonio J(ulio)
Colorado (Capella), Antonio J(ulio)
  1903-1994 .... *23*
  Obituary *79*
Colquhoun, Glenn 1964- *165*
Colston, Fifi E. 1960- *150*
Colt, Martin
  See Epstein, Beryl
  and Epstein, Samuel
Colum, Padraic 1881-1972 .... *15*
  See also CLR *36*
Columbus, Chris 1959- *97*
Columbus, Christopher
  See Columbus, Chris
Columella
  See Moore, Clement Clarke

Colver, Anne 1908- *7*
Colvin, James
  See Moorcock, Michael
Colwell, Eileen (Hilda) 1904-2002 .... *2*
Colwyn, Stewart
  See Pepper, Frank S.
Coman, Carolyn 1951- *197*
  Earlier sketch in SATA *127*
Combres, Elisabeth 1967- *226*
Combs, Lisa M.
  See McCourt, Lisa
Combs, Robert
  See Murray, John
Comfort, Jane Levington
  See Sturtzel, Jane Levington
Comfort, Mildred Houghton 1886-1976 .... *3*
Comins, Ethel M(ae) *11*
Comins, Jeremy 1933- *28*
Commager, Henry Steele 1902-1998 .... *23*
  Obituary *102*
Comora, Madeleine *190*
Compere, Mickie
  See Davidson, Margaret
Compestine, Ying Chang 1963- *187*
  Earlier sketch in SATA *140*
Comport, Sally Wern *190*
Compton, Patricia A. 1936- *75*
Comte, The Great
  See Hawkesworth, Eric
Comus
  See Ballantyne, R(obert) M(ichael)
Comyns, Nance
  See Comyns-Toohey, Nantz
Comyns-Toohey, Nantz 1956- *86*
Conahan, Carolyn
  See Conahan, Carolyn Digby
Conahan, Carolyn Digby 1961- *216*
Conan Doyle, Arthur
  See Doyle, Sir Arthur Conan
Condie, Ally *204*
Condie, Allyson B.
  See Condie, Ally
Condit, Martha Olson 1913- *28*
Condon, Bill 1949- *142*
Condon, Judith *83*
Condon, Ken *195*
Condy, Roy 1942- *96*
Cone, Ferne Geller 1921- *39*
Cone, Molly (Lamken) 1918- *151*
  Autobiography Feature *151*
  Earlier sketches in SATA *1, 28, 115*
  See also SAAS *11*
Cone, Patrick 1954- *89*
Coney, Michael G. 1932-2005 .... *61*
  Obituary *170*
Coney, Michael Greatrex
  See Coney, Michael G.
Coney, Mike
  See Coney, Michael G.
Conford, Ellen 1942- *162*
  Earlier sketches in SATA *6, 68, 110*
  See also CLR *71*
Conger, Lesley
  See Suttles, Shirley (Smith)
Conklin, Gladys Plemon 1903- *2*
Conklin, Paul S. 1929(?)-2003 .... *43*
  Brief entry *33*
  Obituary *147*
Conkling, Hilda 1910-1986 .... *23*
Conlan, Kathleen Elizabeth 1950- *145*
Conlan, Kathy
  See Conlan, Kathleen Elizabeth
Conley, Robyn 1963- *125*
Conley-Weaver, Robyn
  See Conley, Robyn
Conlon-McKenna, Marita 1956- *71*
Conly, Jane Leslie 1948- *164*
  Earlier sketches in SATA *80, 112*
Conly, Robert Leslie 1918(?)-1973 .... *23*
  See also CLR *2*

Connell, Kirk
  See Chapman, John Stanton Higham
Connell, Tom *206*
Connelly, Gwen 1952- *212*
Connelly, Marc(us Cook) 1890-1980
  Obituary *25*
Connolly, Jerome P(atrick) 1931- *8*
Connolly, Pat 1943- *74*
Connolly, Peter 1935- *105*
  Earlier sketch in SATA *47*
Conover, Chris 1950- *213*
  Earlier sketch in SATA *31*
Conquest, Owen
  See Hamilton, Charles (Harold St. John)
Conrad, Joseph 1857-1924 .... *27*
Conrad, Pam 1947-1996 .... *133*
  Brief entry *49*
  Obituary *90*
  Earlier sketches in SATA *52, 80*
  See also CLR *18*
  See also SAAS *19*
Conroy, Jack
  See Conroy, John Wesley
Conroy, John Wesley 1899-1990 .... *19*
  Obituary *65*
Conroy, Melissa 1969- *226*
Conroy, Robert
  See Goldston, Robert (Conroy)
Constable, Kate 1966- *172*
Constant, Alberta Wilson 1908-1981 .... *22*
  Obituary *28*
Constantin, Pascale *185*
Conway, Celeste *210*
Conway, David 1970- *213*
Conway, Diana C. 1943- *91*
Conway, Diana Cohen
  See Conway, Diana C.
Conway, Gordon
  See Hamilton, Charles (Harold St. John)
Cook, Ande *192*
Cook, Bernadine 1924- *11*
Cook, Fred J(ames) 1911-2003 .... *2*
  Obituary *145*
Cook, Glen 1944- *171*
  Earlier sketch in SATA *108*
Cook, Glen Charles
  See Cook, Glen
Cook, Hugh 1956- *85*
Cook, Hugh, Walter Gilbert
  See Cook, Hugh
Cook, Jean Thor 1930- *94*
Cook, Joel 1934- *79*
Cook, Joseph Jay 1924- *8*
Cook, Lisa Broadie *157*
Cook, Lyn
  See Waddell, Evelyn Margaret
Cook, Roy
  See Silverberg, Robert
Cook, Sally *207*
Cook, Trish *175*
Cooke, Ann
  See Cole, Joanna
Cooke, Arthur
  See Lowndes, Robert A(ugustine) W(ard)
Cooke, Barbara
  See Alexander, Anna B(arbara Cooke)
Cooke, David Coxe 1917- *2*
Cooke, Donald Ewin 1916-1985 .... *2*
  Obituary *45*
Cooke, Frank E. 1920- *87*
Cooke, Jean (Isobel Esther) 1929- *74*
Cooke, John Estes
  See Baum, L. Frank
Cooke, Trish 1962- *129*
Cookson, Catherine (McMullen) 1906-1998 .. *9*
  Obituary *116*
Cooley, Beth *210*
Cooley, Elizabeth
  See Cooley, Beth
Cooley, Regina Francoise 1940- *177*

Coolidge, Olivia E(nsor) 1908- 26
    Earlier sketch in SATA *1*
Cooling, Wendy 169
    Earlier sketch in SATA *111*
Coombs, Charles I(ra) 1914-1994 43
    Earlier sketch in SATA *3*
    See also SAAS *15*
Coombs, Chick
    See Coombs, Charles I(ra)
Coombs, Jonathan 204
Coombs, Kate 190
Coombs, Patricia 1926- 51
    Earlier sketch in SATA *3*
    See also SAAS *22*
Cooney, Barbara 1917-2000 96
    Obituary 123
    Earlier sketches in SATA *6, 59*
    See also CLR *23*
Cooney, Caroline B. 1947- 218
    Brief entry 41
    Earlier sketches in SATA *48, 80, 113, 130, 179*
Cooney, Doug 181
Cooney, Nancy Evans 1932- 42
Coontz, Otto 1946- 33
Cooper, Ann (Catharine) 1939- 104
Cooper, Dutch
    See Kuyper, Sjoerd
Cooper, Elisha 1971- 157
    Earlier sketch in SATA *99*
Cooper, Elizabeth Keyser -1992 47
Cooper, Floyd 227
    Earlier sketches in SATA *96, 144, 187*
    See also CLR *60*
Cooper, Gordon 1932- 23
Cooper, Helen 1963- 169
    Earlier sketch in SATA *102*
Cooper, Henry S. F., Jr. 1933- 65
Cooper, Henry Spotswood Fenimore, Jr.
    See Cooper, Henry S. F., Jr.
Cooper, Ilene 1948- 145
    Earlier sketches in SATA *66, 97*
Cooper, James Fenimore 1789-1851 19
    See also CLR *105*
Cooper, John R. *1*
Cooper, Kay 1941- *11*
Cooper, Lee Pelham 1926- 5
Cooper, Lester (Irving) 1919-1985 32
    Obituary 43
Cooper, Lettice (Ulpha) 1897-1994 35
    Obituary 82
Cooper, Louise 1952-2009 152
Cooper, M.E.
    See Davis, Maggie S.
Cooper, M.E.
    See Lerangis, Peter
Cooper, Melrose
    See Kroll, Virginia L.
Cooper, Michael L. 1950- 181
    Earlier sketches in SATA *79, 117*
Cooper, Michelle 1969- 226
Cooper, Patrick 1949- 134
Cooper, Susan 1935- 151
    Earlier sketches in SATA *4, 64, 104*
    See also CLR *161*
    See also SAAS *6*
Cooper, Susan Mary
    See Cooper, Susan
Cope, Jane U(rsula) 1949- 108
Copeland, Helen 1920- 4
Copeland, Mark 1956- 180
Copeland, Paul W. 23
Coplans, Peta 1951- 84
Copley (Diana) Heather Pickering 1918- 45
Coppard, A(lfred) E(dgar) 1878-1957
    See YABC *1*
Copper, Melinda 1952- 172
Copper, Melinda McConnaughey
    See Copper, Melinda
Corace, Jen 208

Coralie
    See Anderson, Catherine Corley
Corbett, Grahame 43
    Brief entry 36
Corbett, Scott 1913- 42
    Earlier sketch in SATA *2*
    See also CLR *1*
    See also SAAS *2*
Corbett, Sue 174
Corbett, W(illiam) J(esse) 1938- 102
    Brief entry 44
    Earlier sketch in SATA *50*
    See also CLR *19*
Corbin, Sabra Lee
    See Malvern, Gladys
Corbin, William
    See McGraw, William Corbin
Corbman, Marjorie 1987- 179
Corby, Dan
    See Catherall, Arthur
Corcoran, Barbara (Asenath) 1911-2003 77
    Autobiography Feature 125
    Earlier sketch in SATA *3*
    See also CLR *50*
    See also SAAS *20*
Corcos, Lucille 1908-1973 10
Cordell, Alexander
    See Graber, Alexander
Cordell, Matthew 1975- 199
Corder, Zizou
    See Young, Louisa
Corella, Joseph
    See Odgers, Sally Farrell
Coren, Alan 1938-2007 32
    Obituary 187
Corey, Dorothy 23
Corey, Shana 1974- 219
    Earlier sketch in SATA *133*
Corfe, Thomas Howell 1928- 27
Corfe, Tom
    See Corfe, Thomas Howell
Corfield, Robin Bell 1952- 74
Corke, Estelle 1969- 220
Corlett, William 1938-2005 46
    Brief entry 39
Cormack, M(argaret) Grant 1913- 11
Cormack, Maribelle B. 1902-1984 39
Cormier, Robert 1925-2000 83
    Obituary 122
    Earlier sketches in SATA *10, 45*
    See also CLR *55*
Cormier, Robert Edmund
    See Cormier, Robert
Cornelius, Carol 1942- 40
Cornelius, Kay 1933- 157
Cornell, J.
    See Cornell, Jeffrey
Cornell, James (Clayton, Jr.) 1938- 27
Cornell, Jean Gay 1920- 23
Cornell, Jeffrey 1945- 11
Cornell, Laura 189
Cornish, D.M. 1972- 185
Cornish, Sam(uel James) 1935- 23
Cornwall, Nellie
    See Sloggett, Nellie
Cornwell, Autumn 195
Corr, Christopher 1955- 189
Correy, Lee
    See Stine, G(eorge) Harry
Corrick, James A. 1945- 76
Corrigan, (Helen) Adeline 1909- 23
Corrigan, Barbara 1922- 8
Corrigan, Eireann 1977- 163
Corrin, Sara 1918- 86
    Brief entry 48
Corrin, Stephen 86
    Brief entry 48
Corsi, Wendy
    See Staub, Wendy Corsi
Cort, M. C.
    See Clifford, Margaret Cort

Cort, Margaret
    See Clifford, Margaret Cort
Corwin, Judith H(offman) 1946- 10
Corwin, Oliver
    See Corwin, Oliver J.
Corwin, Oliver J. 206
Cory, Rowena
    See Lindquist, Rowena Cory
Cosby, Bill 1937- 110
    Earlier sketch in SATA *66*
Cosby, William Henry, Jr.
    See Cosby, Bill
    and Cosby, Bill
Cosentino, Ralph 169
Cosgrave, John O'Hara II 1908-1968
    Obituary 21
Cosgrove, Margaret (Leota) 1926- 47
Cosgrove, Stephen E(dward) 1945- 53
    Brief entry 40
Coskey, Evelyn 1932- 7
Cosner, Shaaron 1940- 43
Cossi, Olga 1921- 216
    Earlier sketches in SATA *67, 102*
Costabel, Eva Deutsch 1924- 45
Costabel-Deutsch, Eva
    See Costabel, Eva Deutsch
Costales, Amy 1974- 227
Coste, Marion 1938- 183
Costello, David 174
Costello, David F(rancis) 1904-1990 23
Cte, Genevieve 1964- 184
Cote, Nancy 1952- 182
Cott, Jonathan 1942- 23
Cottam, Clarence 1899-1974 25
Cotten, Cynthia 188
Cottin, Menena 1950- 213
Cottle, Joan 1960- 135
Cottler, Joseph 1899-1996 22
Cottonwood, Joe 1947- 92
Cottrell, Leonard 1913-1974 24
Cottringer, Anne 1952- 150
    Earlier sketch in SATA *97*
Couch, Greg 199
Coulman, Valerie 1969- 161
Couloumbis, Akila 1932-2009 225
Couloumbis, Audrey 173
Counsel, June 1926- 70
Countryman, The
    See Whitlock, Ralph
Courlander, Harold 1908-1996 6
    Obituary 88
Coursen, Valerie 1965(?)- 102
Courtis, Stuart Appleton 1874-1969
    Obituary 29
Courtland, Tyler
    See Stevens, Serita
Courtney, Dayle
    See Goldsmith, Howard
Coury, Louise Andree 1895(?)-1983
    Obituary 34
Cousins, Linda 1946- 90
Cousins, Lucy 1964- 205
    Earlier sketch in SATA *172*
Cousins, Margaret 1905-1996 2
    Obituary 92
Cousteau, Jacques 1910-1997 98
    Earlier sketch in SATA *38*
Cousteau, Jacques-Yves
    See Cousteau, Jacques
Couture, Christin 1951- 73
Couvillon, Jacques 195
Coverly, Dave 1964- 223
Covert, Ralph 1968- 197
Coville, Bruce 1950- 216
    Autobiography Feature 155
    Earlier sketches in SATA *32, 77, 118, 155*
Covington, Dennis 109
Covington, Linda
    See Windsor, Linda
Cowan, Catherine 121

Cowan, Rebecca M.
  See Moesta, Rebecca
Cowan, Rebecca Moesta
  See Moesta, Rebecca
Coward, Fiona 1963- 178
Cowdrey, Richard 1959- 204
Cowell, Cressida 1966- 140
Cowen, Eve
  See Werner, Herma
Cowen, Ida 1898-1993 64
Cowie, Leonard W(allace) 1919- 4
Cowles, Kathleen
  See Krull, Kathleen
Cowley, Cassia Joy
  See Cowley, Joy
Cowley, Joy 1936- 164
  Autobiography Feature 118
  Earlier sketches in SATA *4, 90*
  See also CLR 55
  See also SAAS 26
Cowley, Marjorie 1925- 111
Cox, (Christopher) Barry 1931- 62
Cox, Clinton 1934- 108
  Earlier sketch in SATA *74*
Cox, David 1933- 56
Cox, David Dundas
  See Cox, David
Cox, Donald William 1921- 23
Cox, Jack
  See Cox, John Roberts
Cox, John Roberts 1915-1981 9
Cox, Judy 1954- 198
  Earlier sketches in SATA *117, 160*
Cox, Marion Monroe 1898-1983
  Obituary 34
Cox, Palmer 1840-1924 24
  See also CLR 24
Cox, Paul 1957- 226
Cox, Vic 1942- 88
Cox, Vicki 1945- 158
Cox, Victoria 1945- 44
Cox, Wallace 1924-1973 25
Cox, Wally
  See Cox, Wallace
Cox, William R(obert) 1901-1988 46
  Brief entry 31
  Obituary 57
Coxe, Molly 1959- 101
  Earlier sketch in SATA *69*
Coxon, Michele 1950- 158
  Earlier sketch in SATA *76*
Coy, Harold 1902-1986 3
Coy, John 1958- 171
  Earlier sketch in SATA *120*
Craats, Rennay 1973- 131
Crabtree, Judith 1928- 98
  Earlier sketch in SATA *63*
Crabtree, Julie 1970- 214
Cracker, Edward E.B.
  See Odgers, Sally Farrell
Craft, Elizabeth 1971(?)- 204
Craft, K. Y.
  See Craft, Kinuko Y.
Craft, Kinuko Y. 1940- 127
  Earlier sketch in SATA *65*
Craft, Kinuko Yamabe
  See Craft, Kinuko Y.
Craft, Ruth 1935- 87
  Brief entry 31
Craig, A. A.
  See Anderson, Poul
Craig, Alisa
  See MacLeod, Charlotte (Matilda)
Craig, David
  See James, Bill
Craig, Helen 1934- 213
  Earlier sketches in SATA *46, 49, 94*
Craig, Joe 1979- 198
Craig, Joe Alexander
  See Craig, Joe

Craig, John Eland
  See Chipperfield, Joseph Eugene
Craig, John Ernest 1921- 23
Craig, Kit
  See Reed, Kit
Craig, M. F.
  See Craig, Mary (Francis) Shura
Craig, M. Jean 17
Craig, M. S.
  See Craig, Mary (Francis) Shura
Craig, Margaret (Maze) 1911-1964 9
Craig, Mary
  See Craig, Mary (Francis) Shura
Craig, Mary Shura
  See Craig, Mary (Francis) Shura
Craig, Mary (Francis) Shura 1923-1991 86
  Obituary 65
  Earlier sketch in SATA *6*
  See also SAAS 7
Craig, Ruth 1922- 95
Craik, Mrs.
  See Craik, Dinah Maria (Mulock)
Craik, Dinah Maria (Mulock) 1826-1887 34
Crandall, Court 1965- 175
Crandell, Rachel 1943- 152
Crane, Barbara (Joyce) 1934- 31
Crane, Caroline 1930- 11
Crane, Jordan 1973- 174
Crane, M. A.
  See Wartski, Maureen (Ann Crane)
Crane, Royston Campbell 1901-1977
  Obituary 22
Crane, Stephen 1871-1900
  See YABC 2
  See also CLR *132*
Crane, Stephen Townley
  See Crane, Stephen
Crane, Walter 1845-1915 100
  Earlier sketch in SATA *18*
  See also CLR 56
Crane, William D(wight) 1892-1976 1
Cranfield, Ingrid 1945- 74
Cranshaw, Stanley
  See Fisher, Dorothy (Frances) Canfield
Crary, Elizabeth (Ann) 1942- 99
  Brief entry 43
Crary, Margaret (Coleman) 1906-1986 9
Craste, Marc 201
Cravath, Lynne Avril
  See Cravath, Lynne W.
Cravath, Lynne W. 1951- 182
  Earlier sketches in SATA *98, 148*
Craven, Thomas 1889-1969 22
Crawford, Brent 1975- 220
Crawford, Charles P. 1945- 28
Crawford, Deborah 1922- 6
Crawford, John E(dmund) 1904-1971 3
Crawford, K(aren) Michael 1959- 155
Crawford, Laura 1977(?)- 227
Crawford, Mel 1925- 44
  Brief entry 33
Crawford, Phyllis 1899- 3
Crawley, Dave 177
Cray, Roberta
  See Emerson, Ru
Crayder, Dorothy 7
Crayder, Teresa
  See Colman, Hila
Crayon, Geoffrey
  See Irving, Washington
Craz, Albert G. 1926- 24
Crebbin, June 1938- 169
  Earlier sketch in SATA *80*
Crecy, Jeanne
  See Williams, Jeanne
Credle, Ellis 1902-1998 1
Creech, Sharon 1945- 226
  Earlier sketches in SATA *94, 139, 172*
  See also CLR *164*
Creeden, Sharon 1938- 91
Creel, Ann Howard 1953- 187

Creighton, (Mary) Helen 1899-1989
  Obituary 64
Creighton, Jill 1949- 96
Crelin, Bob 1959(?)- 221
Crenson, Victoria 1952- 159
  Earlier sketch in SATA *88*
Cresp, Gael 1954- 119
Crespo, George 1962- 82
Cresswell, Helen 1934-2005 79
  Obituary 168
  Earlier sketches in SATA *1, 48*
  See also CLR 18
  See also SAAS 20
Cressy, Michael 1955- 124
Cressy, Mike
  See Cressy, Michael
Cretan, Gladys (Yessayan) 1921- 2
Cretzmeyer, Stacy (Megan) 1959- 124
Crew, Gary 1947- 163
  Earlier sketches in SATA *75, 110*
  See also CLR 42
Crew, Helen (Cecilia) Coale 1866-1941
  See YABC 2
Crew, Linda (Jean) 1951- 137
  Earlier sketch in SATA *71*
Crewe, Megan 1980- 225
Crews, Donald 1938- 76
  Brief entry 30
  Earlier sketch in SATA *32*
  See also CLR 7
Crews, Nina 1963- 158
  Earlier sketch in SATA *97*
Crichton, John Michael
  See Crichton, Michael
Crichton, Michael 1942-2008 88
  Obituary 199
  Earlier sketch in SATA *9*
Crider, Allen Billy
  See Crider, Bill
Crider, Bill 1941- 99
Crilley, Mark 1966- 210
  Autobiography Feature 148
  Earlier sketches in SATA *120, 148*
Crilley, Paul 1975- 227
Crimi, Carolyn 1959- 219
  Earlier sketch in SATA *176*
Cripps, Enid Margaret
  See Appiah, Peggy
Crisler, Curtis L. 188
Crisman, Ruth 1914- 73
Crisp, Marta Marie
  See Crisp, Marty
Crisp, Marty 1947- 128
Crispin, A(nn) C(arol) 1950- 86
Crist, James J. 1961- 168
Cristall, Barbara 79
Crist-Evans, Craig 1954- 153
Crocker, Carter 193
Crocker, Nancy 1956- 185
Crofford, Emily (Ardell) 1927- 61
Crofut, William E. III 1934- 23
Croggon, Alison 1962- 194
Croll, Carolyn 1945- 102
  Brief entry 52
  Earlier sketch in SATA *56*
Croman, Dorothy Young
  See Rosenberg, Dorothy
Cromie, Alice Hamilton 1914-2000 24
Cromie, William J(oseph) 1930- 4
Crompton, Anne Eliot 1930- 73
  Earlier sketch in SATA *23*
Crompton, Richmal
  See Lamburn, Richmal Crompton
Cronbach, Abraham 1882-1965 11
Crone, Ruth 1919-2003 4
Cronin, A(rchibald) J(oseph) 1896-1981 47
  Obituary 25
Cronin, Doreen (A.) 125
Cronin, Doreen 1966(?)- 178
  See also CLR *136*

Cronin, Doreen A.
See Cronin, Doreen
Cronn-Mills, Kirstin 1968- 224
Crook, Beverly Courtney 38
Brief entry 35
Crook, Connie Brummel 1930- 168
Earlier sketch in SATA 98
Crook, Constance
See Crook, Connie Brummel
Crosby, Alexander L. 1906-1980 2
Obituary 23
Crosby, Harry C.
See Anvil, Christopher
Crosby, Margaret
See Rathmann, Peggy
Crosher, G. R. 14
Cross, Gilbert B. 1939- 60
Brief entry 51
Cross, Gillian 1945- 178
Autobiography Feature 178
Earlier sketches in SATA 38, 71, 110, 165
See also CLR 28
Cross, Gillian Clare
See Cross, Gillian
Cross, Helen Reeder
See Broadhead, Helen Cross
Cross, Peter 1951- 95
Cross, Sarah 216
Cross, Shauna 1976(?)- 196
Cross, Tom 1954- 146
Cross, Verda 1914- 75
Cross, Wilbur Lucius III 1918- 2
Crossingham, John 1974- 226
Crossland, Caroline 1964- 83
Crossley-Holland, Kevin 1941- 165
Earlier sketches in SATA 5, 74, 120
See also CLR 84
See also SAAS 20
Crossley-Holland, Kevin John William
See Crossley-Holland, Kevin
Crossman, David A. 1951- 219
Crouch, Karen Hillard
See Good, Karen Hillard
Crouch, Marcus 1913-1996 4
Crout, George C(lement) 1917- 11
Crow, Donna Fletcher 1941- 40
Crow, Francis Luther
See Luther, Frank
Crow, Kristyn 208
Crowe, Andrew 111
Crowe, Carole 1943- 204
Crowe, Chris 206
Crowe, Ellie 203
Crowe, John
See Lynds, Dennis
Crowe, (Bettina) Peter Lum 1911- 6
Crowell, Grace Noll 1877-1969 34
Crowell, Pers 1910-1990 2
Crowell, Robert Leland 1909-2001 63
Crowfield, Christopher
See Stowe, Harriet Beecher
Crowley, Arthur 1945- 38
Crowley, Arthur McBlair
See Crowley, Arthur
Crowley, John 1942- 140
Earlier sketch in SATA 65
Crowley, Suzanne 1963- 196
Crowley, Suzanne Carlisle
See Crowley, Suzanne
Crownfield, Gertrude 1867-1945
See YABC 1
Crowther, James Gerald 1899-1983 14
Crowther, Kitty 1970- 220
Crowther, Robert 1948- 163
Cruikshank, George 1792-1878 22
See also CLR 63
Cruise, Robin 1951- 179
Crum, Shutta 192
Earlier sketch in SATA 134
Crummel, Susan Stevens 1949- 176
Earlier sketch in SATA 130

Crump, Fred H., Jr. 1931- 76
Earlier sketch in SATA 11
Crump, J(ames) Irving 1887-1979 57
Obituary 21
Crump, William D(rake) 1949- 138
Crunden, Reginald
See Cleaver, Hylton Reginald
Crunk, T.
See Crunk, Tony
Crunk, Tony 1956- 130
Crutcher, Chris 1946- 196
Earlier sketches in SATA 52, 99, 153
See also CLR 159
Crutcher, Christopher C.
See Crutcher, Chris
Cruz, Ray(mond) 1933- 6
Cruz Martinez, Alejandro (?)-1987 74
Crystal, Billy 1947- 154
Crystal, William
See Crystal, Billy
Ctvrtek, Vaclav 1911-1976
Obituary 27
Cuate, Melodie A. 219
Cuetara, Mittie 1957- 158
Earlier sketch in SATA 106
Cuffari, Richard 1925-1978 66
Obituary 25
Earlier sketch in SATA 6
Cuffe-Perez, Mary 1946- 199
Cullen, Countee 1903-1946 18
Cullen, Lynn 190
Culliford, Pierre 1928-1992 40
Obituary 74
Cullinan, Bernice E(llinger) 1926- 135
Culp, Louanna McNary 1901-1965 2
Culper, Felix
See McCaughrean, Geraldine
Cumbaa, Stephen 1947- 72
Cumming, Peter 1951- 168
Cumming, Primrose Amy 1915- 24
Cumming, Robert 1945- 65
Cummings, Betty Sue 1918- 15
See also SAAS 9
Cummings, John Michael 1963(?)- 216
Cummings, Mary 1951- 185
Cummings, Parke 1902-1987 2
Obituary 53
Cummings, Pat 1950- 203
Earlier sketches in SATA 42, 71, 107
See also CLR 48
See also SAAS 13
Cummings, Phil 1957- 123
Earlier sketch in SATA 74
Cummings, Priscilla 1951- 170
Earlier sketch in SATA 129
Cummings, Richard
See Gardner, Richard (M.)
Cummings, Terrance 227
Cummins, Julie 200
Cummins, Maria Susanna 1827-1866
See YABC 1
Cumpliano, Ina 207
Cuneo, Mary Louise -2001 85
Cunliffe, John Arthur 1933- 86
Earlier sketch in SATA 11
Cunliffe, Marcus (Falkner) 1922-1990 37
Obituary 66
Cunnane, Kelly 175
Cunningham, Bob
See May, Julian
Cunningham, Captain Frank
See Glick, Carl (Cannon)
Cunningham, Cathy
See Cunningham, Chet
Cunningham, Chet 1928- 23
Cunningham, Dale S(peers) 1932- 11
Cunningham, Dru 91
Cunningham, E. V.
See Fast, Howard

Cunningham, Julia (Woolfolk) 1916- 132
Earlier sketches in SATA 1, 26
See also SAAS 2
Cunningham, Lawrence J. 1943- 125
Cunningham, Virginia
See Holmgren, Virginia C(unningham)
Cunxin, Li 1961- 220
Curiae, Amicus
See Fuller, Edmund (Maybank)
Curie, Eve 1904-2007 1
Obituary 188
Curlee, Lynn 1947- 190
Earlier sketches in SATA 98, 141
Curley, Daniel 1918-1988 23
Obituary 61
Curley, Marianne 1959- 175
Earlier sketch in SATA 131
Currey, Anna 194
Currie, Robin 1948- 120
Currie, Stephen 1960- 132
Earlier sketch in SATA 82
Curry, Ann (Gabrielle) 1934- 72
Curry, Jane L(ouise) 1932- 138
Autobiography Feature 138
Earlier sketches in SATA 1, 52, 90
See also CLR 31
See also SAAS 6
Curry, Peggy Simson 1911-1987 8
Obituary 50
Curry, Tom 185
Curtis, Bruce (Richard) 1944- 30
Curtis, Chara M(ahar) 1950- 78
Curtis, Christopher Paul 1953- 187
Earlier sketches in SATA 93, 140
See also CLR 68
Curtis, Gavin 1965- 107
Curtis, Jamie Lee 1958- 144
Earlier sketch in SATA 95
See also CLR 88
Curtis, Jennifer Keats 185
Curtis, Marci 160
Curtis, Munzee
See Caseley, Judith
Curtis, Neil 1950-2006 202
Curtis, Patricia 1921- 101
Earlier sketch in SATA 23
Curtis, Peter
See Lofts, Norah (Robinson)
Curtis, Philip (Delacourt) 1920- 62
Curtis, Richard 1937- 29
Curtis, Richard Alan
See Curtis, Richard
Curtis, Richard Hale
See Deming, Richard
and Levinson, Leonard
and Rothweiler, Paul Roger
Curtis, Stacy 205
Curtis, Wade
See Pournelle, Jerry
Curtiss, A(rlene) B. 1934- 90
Cusack, Margaret 1945- 58
Cushman, Doug 1953- 210
Earlier sketches in SATA 65, 101, 157
Cushman, Jerome 2
Cushman, Karen 1941- 147
Earlier sketch in SATA 89
See also CLR 55
Cusick, Richie Tankersley 1952- 140
Earlier sketch in SATA 67
Cusimano, Maryann K.
See Love, Maryann Cusimano
Cutbill, Andy 1972- 201
Cutchen, Billye Walker 1930- 15
Cutchins, Judy 1947- 59
Cutler, Daniel S. 1951- 78
Cutler, Daniel Solomon
See Cutler, Daniel S.
Cutler, Ebbitt 1923- 9
Cutler, Ivor 1923-2006 24
Obituary 174

Cutler, Jane 1936- 162
  Earlier sketches in SATA 75, 118
Cutler, May Ebbitt
  See Cutler, Ebbitt
Cutler, Samuel
  See Folsom, Franklin (Brewster)
Cutlip, Kimbra L(eigh-Ann) 1964- 128
Cutrate, Joe
  See Spiegelman, Art
Cutt, W(illiam) Towrie 1898-1981 16
  Obituary 85
Cuyler, Margery 1948- 229
  Earlier sketches in SATA 39, 99, 156, 195
Cuyler, Margery Stuyvesant
  See Cuyler, Margery
Cuyler, Stephen
  See Bates, Barbara S(nedeker)
Cyrus, Kurt 1954- 179
  Earlier sketch in SATA 132
Czajkowski, James
  See Rollins, James
Czekaj, Jef 1969- 217
Czernecki, Stefan 1946- 178

D

Daagnese, Joseph 228
Dabba Smith, Frank 174
Dabcovich, Lydia 99
  Brief entry 47
  Earlier sketch in SATA 58
Dace, Dolores B(oelens) 1929- 89
Da Costa, Deborah 193
Daddo, Andrew 1967- 198
Dadey, Debbie 1959- 217
  Earlier sketches in SATA 73, 136
Dahl, Borghild (Margarethe) 1890-1984 7
  Obituary 37
Dahl, Roald 1916-1990 73
  Obituary 65
  Earlier sketches in SATA 1, 26
  See also CLR 111
Dahlberg, Maurine F. 1951- 171
Dahlstedt, Marden (Stewart) 1921-1983 8
  Obituary 110
Dahme, Joanne 206
Dain, Martin J. 1924-2000 35
Dakin, Glenn 1960- 224
Dakos, Kalli 1950- 115
  Earlier sketch in SATA 80
Dale, Anna 1971- 170
Dale, Gary
  See Reece, Colleen L.
Dale, George E.
  See Asimov, Isaac
Dale, Jack
  See Holliday, Joseph
Dale, Kim 1957- 123
Dale, Margaret J(essy) Miller 1911- 39
Dale, Mitzi
  See Hemstock, Gillian
Dale, Norman
  See Denny, Norman (George)
Dale, Penny 1954- 151
  Earlier sketch in SATA 70
Daley, Michael J. 170
Dalgliesh, Alice 1893-1979 17
  Obituary 21
  See also CLR 62
Dalkey, Kara 1953- 132
Dalkey, Kara Mia
  See Dalkey, Kara
Dallas, Ruth 1919- 86
Dalmas, John
  See Jones, John R(obert)
Dalton, Alene
  See Chapin, Alene Olsen Dalton
Dalton, Annie 1948- 140
  Earlier sketch in SATA 40

Dalton, Kit
  See Cunningham, Chet
Dalton, Pamela
  See Johnson, Pamela
Dalton, Sean
  See Chester, Deborah
Dalton, Sheila 1949- 108
D'Aluisio, Faith 1957- 205
Daly, James 217
Daly, Jim
  See Stratemeyer, Edward L.
Daly, Jude 1951- 222
  Earlier sketch in SATA 177
Daly, Kathleen N(orah) 124
  Brief entry 37
Daly, Maureen 1921-2006 129
  Obituary 176
  Earlier sketch in SATA 2
  See also CLR 96
  See also SAAS 1
Daly, Nicholas
  See Daly, Niki
Daly, Niki 1946- 198
  Earlier sketches in SATA 37, 76, 114, 164
  See also CLR 41
  See also SAAS 21
D'Amato, Alex 1919- 20
D'Amato, Janet (Potter) 1925- 9
Damerow, Gail 1944- 83
Damerow, Gail Jane
  See Damerow, Gail
D'Amico, Carmela 170
D'Amico, Steve 170
Damrell, Liz 1956- 77
Damrosch, Helen
  See Tee-Van, Helen Damrosch
Dana, Barbara 1940- 218
  Earlier sketch in SATA 22
Dana, Richard Henry, Jr. 1815-1882 26
Danachair, Caoimhin O
  See Danaher, Kevin
Danaher, Kevin 1913-2002 22
Danakas, John 1963- 94
Dandi
  See Mackall, Dandi Daley
D'Andrea, Kate
  See Steiner, Barbara A(nnette)
Dangerfield, Balfour
  See McCloskey, (John) Robert
Daniel, Alan 1939- 76
  Brief entry 53
Daniel, Anita 1893(?)-1978 23
  Obituary 24
Daniel, Anne
  See Steiner, Barbara A(nnette)
Daniel, Becky 1947- 56
Daniel, Claire 1949- 164
Daniel, Colin
  See Windsor, Patricia
Daniel, Hawthorne 1890- 8
Daniel, (Donna) Lee 1944- 76
Daniel, Rebecca
  See Daniel, Becky
Daniels, Guy 1919-1989 11
  Obituary 62
Daniels, Kit
  See Diver, Lucienne
Daniels, Lucy
  See Oldfield, Jenny
Daniels, Max
  See Gellis, Roberta
Daniels, Olga
  See Sinclair, Olga
Daniels, Patricia 1955- 93
Daniels, Zoe
  See Laux, Constance
Dank, Gloria Rand 1955- 56
  Brief entry 46
Dank, Leonard D(ewey) 1929- 44
Dank, Milton 1920- 31
Dann, Max 1955- 62

Danneberg, Julie 1958- 173
Dantz, William R.
  See Philbrick, Rodman
Danzig, Dianne 213
Danziger, Paula 1944-2004 149
  Brief entry 30
  Obituary 155
  Earlier sketches in SATA 36, 63, 102
  See also CLR 20
Darby, Gene Kegley
  See Darby, Jean (Kegley)
Darby, J. N.
  See Govan, (Mary) Christine Noble
Darby, Jean (Kegley) 1921- 68
Darby, Patricia (Paulsen) 14
Darby, Ray(mond) 1912-1982 7
Darbyshire, Kristen 218
d'Arcy, Willard
  See Cox, William R(obert)
Dare, Geena
  See McNicoll, Sylvia (Marilyn)
D'arge, Mackie 218
Darian, Shea 1959- 97
Daringer, Helen Fern 1892-1986 1
Darke, Marjorie 1929- 87
  Earlier sketch in SATA 16
Darley, F(elix) O(ctavius) C(arr)
  1822-1888 35
Darling, David J. 1953- 60
  Brief entry 44
Darling, Kathy
  See Darling, Mary Kathleen
Darling, Lois (MacIntyre) 1917-1989 3
  Obituary 64
Darling, Louis, (Jr.) 1916-1970 3
  Obituary 23
Darling, Mary Kathleen 1943- 124
  Earlier sketches in SATA 9, 79
Darling, Sandra Louise Woodward
  See Day, Alexandra
Darnell, K(athryn) L(ynne) 1955- 150
Darroll, Sally
  See Odgers, Sally Farrell
Darrow, Sharon 181
Darrow, Whitney, (Jr.) 1909-1999 13
  Obituary 115
Darwin, Len
  See Darwin, Leonard
Darwin, Leonard 1916- 24
Dasent, Sir George Webbe 1817-1896 62
  Brief entry 29
Dash, Joan 1925- 142
Daskam, Josephine Dodge
  See Bacon, Josephine Dodge (Daskam)
D'ath, Justin 1953- 174
  Earlier sketch in SATA 106
Dauer, Rosamond 1934- 23
Daugherty, Charles Michael 1914- 16
Daugherty, James (Henry) 1889-1974 13
  See also CLR 78
Daugherty, Richard D(eo) 1922- 35
Daugherty, Sonia Medwedeff (?)-1971
  Obituary 27
d'Aulaire, Edgar Parin 1898-1986 66
  Obituary 47
  Earlier sketch in SATA 5
  See also CLR 21
d'Aulaire, Ingri 1904-1980 66
  Obituary 24
  Earlier sketch in SATA 5
  See also CLR 21
d'Aulaire, Ingri Mortenson Parin
  See d'Aulaire, Ingri
Dave, Dave
  See Berg, David
Daveluy, Paule Cloutier 1919- 11
Davenier, Christine 1961- 216
  Earlier sketches in SATA 127, 179
Davenport, John 1960- 156
Daves, Michael 1938- 40

David, A. R.
    See David, A(nn) Rosalie
David, A(nn) Rosalie 1946- *103*
David, Jonathan
    See Ames, Lee J(udah)
David, Lawrence 1963- *165*
    Earlier sketch in SATA *111*
David, Peter 1956- *72*
David, Peter Allen
    See David, Peter
David, Rosalie
    See David, A(nn) Rosalie
Davidson, Alice Joyce 1932- *54*
    Brief entry *45*
Davidson, Basil 1914-2010 .... *13*
Davidson, (Marie) Diane 1924- *91*
Davidson, Hugh
    See Hamilton, Edmond
Davidson, Jessica 1915-1986 .... *5*
Davidson, Judith 1953- *40*
Davidson, Lionel 1922-2009 .... *87*
Davidson, Margaret 1936- *5*
Davidson, Marion
    See Garis, Howard R.
Davidson, Mary R. 1885-1973 .... *9*
Davidson, Mary S. 1940- *61*
Davidson, Mickie
    See Davidson, Margaret
Davidson, Nicole
    See Jensen, Kathryn
Davidson, R.
    See Davidson, Raymond
Davidson, Raymond 1926- *32*
Davidson, Rosalie 1921- *23*
Davie, Helen K(ay) 1952- *148*
    Earlier sketch in SATA *77*
Davies, Andrew (Wynford) 1936- *27*
Davies, Andy Robert *200*
Davies, Bettilu D(onna) 1942- *33*
Davies, Hunter 1936- *55*
    Brief entry *45*
Davies, Jacqueline 1962- *186*
    Earlier sketch in SATA *155*
Davies, Joan 1934- *50*
    Brief entry *47*
Davies, Nicola 1958- *182*
    Earlier sketches in SATA *99, 150*
Davies, Peter J(oseph) 1937- *52*
Davies, Sumiko 1942- *46*
Davis, (A.) Aubrey 1949- *153*
Davis, Barbara Steincrohn
    See Davis, Maggie S.
Davis, Bette J. 1923- *15*
Davis, Burke 1913- *4*
Davis, Christopher 1928- *6*
Davis, D(elbert) Dwight 1908-1965 .... *33*
Davis, Daniel S(heldon) 1936- *12*
Davis, David R. 1948- *106*
Davis, Donald 1944- *169*
    Earlier sketch in SATA *93*
Davis, Donald D.
    See Davis, Donald
Davis, Eleanor 1983(?)- *209*
Davis, Emma
    See Davis, Maggie S.
Davis, Gibbs 1953- *102*
    Brief entry *41*
    Earlier sketch in SATA *46*
Davis, Grania 1943- *88*
    Brief entry *50*
Davis, H(arold) L(enoir) 1896-1960 .... *114*
Davis, Heather 1970- *221*
Davis, Hubert J(ackson) 1904-1997 .... *31*
Davis, Jack E. *210*
Davis, Jacky *204*
Davis, James Robert 1945- *32*
Davis, Jenny 1953- *74*
Davis, Jim
    See Davis, James Robert
Davis, Julia 1900(?)-1993 .... *6*
    Obituary *75*

Davis, Karen (Elizabeth) 1944- *109*
Davis, Katie 1959(?)- *208*
    Earlier sketch in SATA *152*
Davis, Lambert *176*
Davis, Leslie
    See Guccione, Leslie Davis
Davis, Louise Littleton 1921- *25*
Davis, Maggie S. 1943- *57*
Davis, Marguerite 1889- *34*
Davis, Mary L(ee) 1935- *9*
Davis, Mary Octavia 1901-1976 .... *6*
Davis, Nancy 1958(?)- *229*
Davis, Nelle 1958- *73*
Davis, Ossie 1917-2005 .... *81*
    See also CLR *56*
Davis, Paxton 1925-1994 .... *16*
Davis, Rich 1958- *206*
Davis, Robert 1881-1949
    See YABC *1*
Davis, Robin W(orks) 1962- *87*
Davis, Russell Gerard 1922- *3*
Davis, Tanita S. *212*
Davis, Tim(othy N.) 1957- *94*
Davis, Tony 1961- *222*
Davis, Verne Theodore 1889-1973 .... *6*
Davis, Yvonne 1927- *115*
Davol, Marguerite W. 1928- *146*
    Earlier sketch in SATA *82*
DaVolls, Andy (P.) 1967- *85*
DaVolls, Linda 1966- *85*
Davys, Sarah
    See Manning, Rosemary
Dawes, Claiborne 1935- *111*
Dawson, Arthur L. *207*
Dawson, Elmer A. *67*
    Earlier sketch in SATA *1*
Dawson, Imogen (Zoe) 1948- *126*
    Earlier sketch in SATA *90*
Dawson, Janine 1957- *196*
Dawson, Mary 1919- *11*
Dawson, Willow 1975- *208*
Day, A(rthur) Grove 1904-1994 .... *59*
Day, Alexandra 1941- *197*
    Autobiography Feature *197*
    Earlier sketches in SATA *67, 97, 169*
    See also CLR *22*
    See also SAAS *19*
Day, Beth (Feagles) 1924- *33*
Day, Donna
    See Asay, Donna Day
Day, Edward C. 1932- *72*
Day, Jon 1936(?)- *79*
Day, Karen *187*
Day, Larry 1956- *227*
    Earlier sketch in SATA *181*
Day, Nancy 1953- *140*
Day, Nancy Raines 1951- *148*
    Earlier sketch in SATA *93*
Day, Shirley 1962- *94*
Day, Thomas 1748-1789
    See YABC *1*
Day, Trevor 1955- *124*
Dazey, Agnes J(ohnston) *2*
Dazey, Frank M. *2*
Deacon, Alexis 1978- *139*
Deacon, Eileen
    See Geipel, Eileen
Deacon, Richard
    See McCormick, (George) Donald (King)
Deadman, Ronald 1919-1988(?)
    Obituary *56*
Deak, Erzsi 1959- *152*
Dean, Anabel 1915- *12*
Dean, Carolee 1962- *148*
Dean, Claire *215*
Dean, David 1976- *192*
Dean, Karen Strickler 1923- *49*
Dean, Ruth (Brigham) 1947- *145*
Dean, Zoey
    See Bennett, Cherie

de Angeli, Marguerite (Lofft) 1889-1987 ... *100*
    Obituary *51*
    Earlier sketches in SATA *1, 27*
    See also CLR *1*
Deans, Karen *195*
Deans, Sis Boulos 1955- *136*
    Earlier sketch in SATA *78*
DeArmand, Frances Ullmann 1904(?)-1984 . *10*
    Obituary *38*
DeArmond, Dale 1914- *70*
DeArmond, Dale Burlison
    See DeArmond, Dale
Deary, Terry 1946- *171*
    Brief entry *41*
    Earlier sketches in SATA *51, 101*
Deaver, Julie Reece 1953- *68*
de Banke, Cecile 1889-1965 .... *11*
De Bello, Rosario 1923- *89*
Debon, Nicolas *186*
    Earlier sketch in SATA *151*
de Bono, Edward 1933- *66*
de Brissac, Malcolm
    See Dickinson, Peter
de Brunhoff, Jean
    See Brunhoff, Jean de
De Brunhoff, Laurent
    See Brunhoff, Laurent de
De Bruyn, Monica G. 1952- *13*
De Bruyn, Monica Jean Grembowicz
    See De Bruyn, Monica G.
DeBry, Roger K. 1942- *91*
de Camp, Catherine Crook 1907-2000 .... *83*
    Earlier sketch in SATA *12*
de Camp, L. Sprague 1907-2000 .... *83*
    Earlier sketch in SATA *9*
de Camp, Lyon Sprague
    See de Camp, L. Sprague
DeCandido, Keith R.A. *112*
Dechausay, Sonia E. *94*
Decker, C.B. *172*
Decker, Cynthia B.
    See Decker, C.B.
Decker, Duane 1910-1964 .... *5*
Decker, Timothy 1974- *197*
DeClements, Barthe 1920- *131*
    Earlier sketches in SATA *35, 71*
    See also CLR *23*
DeClements, Barthe Faith
    See DeClements, Barthe
de Clercq Zubli, Rita la Fontaine 1929- *199*
de Conte, Sieur Louis
    See Twain, Mark
Dedman, Stephen *108*
Dee, Barbara 1958- *220*
Dee, Catherine 1964- *138*
Dee, Ruby
    See Wallace, Ruby Ann
Deeble, Jason 1979- *221*
Deedy, Carmen Agra 1960- *196*
Deedy, John 1923- *24*
Deegan, Paul Joseph 1937- *48*
    Brief entry *38*
Deem, James M. 1950- *191*
    Autobiography Feature *191*
    Earlier sketches in SATA *75, 134*
Deem, James Morgan
    See Deem, James M.
Deeter, Catherine 1947- *137*
DeFelice, Cynthia 1951- *165*
    Earlier sketches in SATA *79, 121*
DeFelice, Cynthia C.
    See DeFelice, Cynthia
Defoe, Daniel 1660(?)-1731 .... *22*
    See also CLR *164*
de Fombelle, Timothee
    See Fombelle, Timothee de
DeFord, Deborah H. *123*
deFrance, Anthony
    See DiFranco, Anthony (Mario)

Degen, Bruce 1945- 205
　Brief entry 47
　Earlier sketches in SATA *57, 97, 147*
DeGering, Etta (Belle) Fowler 1898-1996 7
De Goldi, Kate 1959- 123
De Goldi, Kathleen Domenica
　See De Goldi, Kate
de Goursac, Olivier 1959- 184
De Grazia, Ettore 1909-1982 39
De Grazia, Ted
　See De Grazia, Ettore
deGroat, Diane 1947- 169
　Earlier sketches in SATA *31, 90*
deGros, J. H.
　See Villiard, Paul
de Grummond, Lena Young 62
　Earlier sketch in SATA *6*
de Hamel, Joan Littledale 1924- 86
De Haven, Tom 1949- 72
de Hugo, Pierre
　See Brackers de Hugo, Pierre
Deines, Brian 1955- 220
Deiss, Joseph Jay 1912-1999 12
de Jenkins, Lyll Becerra 1925-1997 102
DeJong, David C(ornel) 1905-1967 10
de Jong, Dola
　See de Jong, Dorothea Rosalie
de Jong, Dorothea Rosalie 1911-2003 7
　Obituary 149
DeJong, Meindert 1906-1991 2
　Obituary 68
　See also CLR *73*
DeJonge, Joanne E. 1943- 56
Deka, Connie
　See Laux, Constance
de Kay, Ormonde (Jr.) 1923-1998 7
　Obituary 106
DeKeyser, Stacy 1959- 214
de Kiriline, Louise
　See Lawrence, Louise de Kiriline
Dekker, Carl
　See Laffin, John (Alfred Charles)
　and Lynds, Dennis
deKruif, Paul (Henry) 1890-1971 50
　Earlier sketch in SATA *5*
Delacre, Lulu 1957- 209
　Earlier sketches in SATA *36, 156*
DeLaCroix, Alice 1940- 195
　Earlier sketch in SATA *75*
de la Cruz, Melissa 1971- 179
De la Garza, Phyllis 1942- 169
De Lage, Ida 1918- 11
de la Mare, Walter (John) 1873-1956 16
　See also CLR *148*
Delaney, Harry 1932- 3
Delaney, Joseph 1945- 172
Delaney, M.C.
　See Delaney, Michael
Delaney, Michael 1955- 180
　Earlier sketch in SATA *96*
Delaney, Michael Clark
　See Delaney, Michael
Delaney, Ned 1951- 28
Delaney, Thomas Nicholas III
　See Delaney, Ned
DeLange, Alex Pardo
　See Pardo DeLange, Alex
Delano, Hugh 1933- 20
Delano, Marfe Ferguson 215
Delany, Samuel R., Jr. 1942- 92
Delany, Samuel Ray
　See Delany, Samuel R., Jr.
de la Pena, Matt 205
De La Ramee, Marie Louise 1839-1908 20
de la Roche, Mazo 1879-1961 64
De La Roche Saint Andre, Anne 1950- 75
de Las Casas, Dianne 1970- 221
Delaune, (Jewel) Lynn (de Grummond) 7
DeLaurentis, Louise Budde 1920- 12
del Barco, Lucy Salamanca 1900(?)-1989
　Obituary 64

Delderfield, Eric R(aymond) 1909-1995 ...... *14*
Delderfield, Ronald Frederick 1912-1972 ... *20*
DeLeeuw, Adele (Louise) 1899-1988 30
　Obituary 56
　Earlier sketch in SATA *1*
De Leon, Nephtali 1945- 97
Delessert, Etienne 1941- 179
　Brief entry 27
　Earlier sketches in SATA *46, 130*
　See also CLR *81*
Delgado, James P. 1958- 122
Delinois, Alix 228
de Lint, Charles 1951- 207
　Earlier sketches in SATA *115, 157*
de Lint, Charles Henri Diederick Hofsmit
　See de Lint, Charles
Delmar, Roy
　See Wexler, Jerome (LeRoy)
Del Negro, Janice M. 197
Deloria, Vine, Jr. 1933-2005 21
　Obituary 171
Deloria, Vine Victor, Jr.
　See Deloria, Vine, Jr.
del Rey, Lester 1915-1993 22
　Obituary 76
Delrio, Martin
　See Doyle, Debra
　and Macdonald, James D.
Delton, Judy 1931-2001 77
　Obituary 130
　Earlier sketch in SATA *14*
　See also SAAS *9*
Delulio, John 1938- 15
Delving, Michael
　See Williams, Jay
de Marcken, Gail 186
Demarest, Chris L. 1951- 175
　Brief entry 44
　Earlier sketches in SATA *45, 82, 128*
Demarest, Christopher Lynn
　See Demarest, Chris L.
Demarest, Doug
　See Barker, Will
De Mari, Silvana 1953- 193
Demas, Corinne
　See Bliss, Corinne Demas
Demas, Vida 1927- 9
Dematons, Charlotte 1957- 203
DeMatteis, J.M. 1953- 180
DeMatteis, John Marc
　See DeMatteis, J.M.
De Mejo, Oscar 1911-1992 40
Demers, Dominique 1956- 177
de Messieres, Nicole 1930- 39
Demi 1942- 210
　Earlier sketches in SATA *11, 66, 102, 152*
　See also CLR *58*
Demijohn, Thom
　See Disch, Thomas M.
　and Sladek, John
Deming, Richard 1915-1983 24
Deming, Sarah 191
de Monfreid, Dorothee 1973- 189
Demuth, Patricia Brennan 1948- 84
　Brief entry 51
De Muth, Roger 1948- 221
Dendinger, Roger E. 1952- 158
Denenberg, Barry 1940- 175
Dengler, Marianna (Herron) 1935- 103
Dengler, Sandy 1939- 54
　Brief entry 40
Denim, Sue
　See Pilkey, Dav
Denise, Anika 210
Denise, Christopher 1968- 193
　Earlier sketch in SATA *147*
Denman, K.L. 1957- 186
Denmark, Harrison
　See Zelazny, Roger
Dennard, Deborah 1953- 136
　Earlier sketch in SATA *78*

Denney, Diana 1910-2000 25
　Obituary 120
Dennis, Morgan 1891(?)-1960 .... *18*
Dennis, Wesley 1903-1966 .... *18*
Denniston, Elinore 1900-1978
　Obituary 24
Denny, Norman (George) 1901-1982 43
Denos, Julia 202
Denslow, Sharon Phillips 1947- 142
　Earlier sketch in SATA *68*
Denslow, W(illiam) W(allace) 1856-1915 .... *16*
　See also CLR *15*
Dent, Grace 1973- 187
Denton, Kady MacDonald 181
　Earlier sketches in SATA *66, 110*
　See also CLR *71*
Denton, Terry 1950- 186
Denver, Walt
　See Redding, Robert Hull
　and Sherman, Jory (Tecumseh)
Denzel, Justin F(rancis) 1917-1999 46
　Brief entry 38
Denzer, Ann Wiseman
　See Wiseman, Ann (Sayre)
DePalma, Mary Newell 1961- 185
　Earlier sketch in SATA *139*
De Palma, Toni 199
dePaola, Thomas Anthony 1934- 200
　Earlier sketches in SATA *11, 59, 108, 155*
　See also CLR *81*
　See also SAAS *15*
dePaola, Tomie
　See dePaola, Thomas Anthony
deParrie, Paul 1949- 74
DePauw, Linda Grant 1940- 24
De Pretto, Lorenzo 1966- 225
DeRan, David 1946- 76
Derby, Ken 1956- 181
Derby, Kenneth R.
　See Derby, Ken
Derby, Pat 1942- 172
Derby, Sally 1934- 189
　Earlier sketches in SATA *89, 132*
de Regniers, Beatrice Schenk (Freedman)
　1914-2000 68
　Obituary 123
　Earlier sketch in SATA *2*
　See also SAAS *6*
Dereske, Jo 1947- 72
Deriso, Christine Hurley 1961- 210
Derleth, August (William) 1909-1971 5
Derman, Martha (Winn) 74
Derman, Sarah Audrey 1915- 11
DeRoberts, Lyndon
　See Silverstein, Robert Alan
Derom, Dirk 1980- 224
de Roo, Anne Louise 1931-1997 84
　Earlier sketch in SATA *25*
　See also CLR *63*
deRosa, Dee 70
Derrick, Lionel
　See Cunningham, Chet
Derrickson, Jim 1959- *141*
Derry Down Derry
　See Lear, Edward
Dervaux, Isabelle 1961- 106
Derwent, Lavinia 14
Desai, Anita 1937- 126
　Earlier sketch in SATA *63*
DeSaix, Deborah Durland 188
De Saulles, Tony 1958- 119
Desbarats, Peter 1933- 39
de Selincourt, Aubrey 1894-1962 14
de Seve, Peter 1958- 219
de Seve, Randall 198
Deshpande, Chris 1950- 69
Desimini, Lisa 1964- 216
　Earlier sketches in SATA *86, 148*
Desjarlais, John 1953- 71
Desjarlais, John J.
　See Desjarlais, John

Desmoinaux, Christel 1967- *149*
    Earlier sketch in SATA *103*
Desmond, Adrian 1947- *51*
Desmond, Adrian J.
    See Desmond, Adrian
Desmond, Adrian John
    See Desmond, Adrian
Desmond, Alice Curtis 1897-1990 .... *8*
Desnoettes, Caroline *183*
DeSpain, Pleasant 1943- *87*
Desputeaux, Helene 1959- *95*
Dessen, Sarah 1970- *172*
    Earlier sketch in SATA *120*
Detine, Padre
    See Olsen, Ib Spang
de Trevino, Elizabeth B.
    See Trevino, Elizabeth B(orton) de
de Trevino, Elizabeth Borton
    See Trevino, Elizabeth B(orton) de
Detwiler, Susan Dill 1956- *58*
Deuker, Carl 1950- *196*
    Earlier sketches in SATA *82, 150*
Deutsch, Babette 1895-1982 .... *1*
    Obituary *33*
Deutsch, Eva Costabel
    See Costabel, Eva Deutsch
Deutsch, Helen 1906-1992 .... *76*
Deutsch, Kurt
    See Singer, Kurt D.
De Valera, Sinead 1879(?)-1975
    Obituary *30*
Devaney, John 1926-1994 .... *12*
de Varennes, Monique 1947- *168*
de Varona, Frank J. 1943- *83*
Devereux, Frederick L(eonard), Jr.
    1914-1993 .... *9*
Devi, Nila
    See Woody, Regina Jones
DeVillers, Julia 1967- *227*
deVinck, Christopher 1951- *85*
DeVita, James *195*
DeVito, Cara 1956- *80*
Devlin, Dorothy Wende
    See Devlin, Wende
Devlin, Harry 1918-2001 .... *136*
    Earlier sketches in SATA *11, 74*
Devlin, Wende 1918-2002 .... *74*
    Earlier sketch in SATA *11*
Devon, Paddie 1953- *92*
Devons, Sonia 1974- *72*
Devorah-Leah *111*
de Vos, Gail 1949- *122*
de Vries, Anke 1936- *222*
DeVries, Douglas 1933- *122*
De Waard, E(lliott) John 1935- *7*
Dewan, Ted 1961- *226*
    Earlier sketches in SATA *108, 157*
Dewdney, Anna *184*
Dewdney, Selwyn (Hanington) 1909-1979 ... *64*
DeWeese, Gene
    See DeWeese, Thomas Eugene
DeWeese, Jean
    See DeWeese, Thomas Eugene
DeWeese, Thomas Eugene 1934- *46*
    Brief entry *45*
Dewey, Ariane 1937- *178*
    Earlier sketches in SATA *7, 109*
Dewey, Jennifer (Owings) 1941- *103*
    Brief entry *48*
    Earlier sketch in SATA *58*
Dewey, Kenneth Francis 1940- *39*
Dewin, Howie
    See Howie, Betsy
De Wire, Elinor 1953- *180*
deWit, Dorothy (May Knowles) 1916-1980 . *39*
    Obituary *28*
Dexter, Alison 1966- *125*
Dexter, John
    See Bradley, Marion Zimmer
Deyneka, Anita 1943- *24*
Deyrup, Astrith Johnson 1923- *24*

Dezern, Chad *201*
de Zubizarreta, Alma
    See Ada, Alma Flor
Dhami, Narinder 1958- *152*
Dhondy, Farrukh 1944- *152*
    Earlier sketch in SATA *65*
    See also CLR *41*
Diakite, Baba Wague 1961- *174*
Diakite, Penda 1993(?)- *174*
Diamand, Emily 1971- *227*
Diamond, Arthur 1957- *76*
Diamond, Donna 1950- *69*
    Brief entry *30*
    Earlier sketch in SATA *35*
Diamond, Petra
    See Sachs, Judith
Diamond, Rebecca
    See Sachs, Judith
Dias, Earl Joseph 1916- *41*
Dias, Ron 1937- *71*
Diaz, David 1959(?)- *229*
    Earlier sketches in SATA *96, 150, 189*
    See also CLR *65*
di Bartolo, Jim *225*
Dibley, Glin *188*
DiCamillo, Kate 1964- *202*
    Earlier sketches in SATA *121, 163*
    See also CLR *117*
Di Certo, J(oseph) J(ohn) 1933- *60*
DiCianni, Ron 1952- *107*
Dick, Trella Lamson 1889-1974 .... *9*
Dickens, Charles 1812-1870 .... *15*
    See also CLR *162*
Dickens, Charles John Huffam
    See Dickens, Charles
Dickens, Frank
    See Huline-Dickens, Frank William
Dickens, Monica (Enid) 1915-1992 .... *4*
    Obituary *74*
Dickerson, Roy Ernest 1886-1965
    Obituary *26*
Dickinson, Emily 1830-1886 .... *29*
Dickinson, Emily Elizabeth
    See Dickinson, Emily
Dickinson, Mary 1949- *48*
    Brief entry *41*
Dickinson, Mary-Anne
    See Rodda, Emily
Dickinson, Peter 1927- *229*
    Earlier sketches in SATA *5, 62, 95, 150*
    See also CLR *125*
Dickinson, Peter Malcolm de Brissac
    See Dickinson, Peter
Dickinson, Susan 1931- *8*
Dickinson, Terence 1943- *102*
Dickinson, W(illiam) Croft 1897-1963 .... *13*
Dickson, Gordon R. 1923-2001 .... *77*
Dickson, Gordon Rupert
    See Dickson, Gordon R.
Dickson, Helen
    See Reynolds, Helen Mary Greenwood Campbell
Dickson, Naida 1916- *8*
Diehn, Gwen 1943- *80*
Dierssen, Andreas 1962- *190*
Diesen, Deborah 1967- *200*
Dieterich, Michele M. 1962- *78*
Dietz, David H(enry) 1897-1984 .... *10*
    Obituary *41*
Dietz, Lew 1907-1997 .... *11*
    Obituary *95*
Diffily, Deborah *159*
Di Fiori, Larry
    See Di Fiori, Lawrence
Di Fiori, Lawrence 1934- *130*
DiFranco, Anthony (Mario) 1945- *42*
Digby, Anne 1935- *72*
Digges, Jeremiah
    See Berger, Josef
Digman, Kristina 1959- *176*

D'Ignazio, Fred 1949- *39*
    Brief entry *35*
D'Ignazio, Frederick
    See D'Ignazio, Fred
Di Grazia, Thomas (?)-1983 .... *32*
Dijkstra, Lida 1961- *195*
Dikty, Julian May
    See May, Julian
Dillard, Annie 1945- *140*
    Earlier sketch in SATA *10*
Dillard, Kristine 1964- *113*
Dillard, Polly Hargis 1916- *24*
Dillard, Sarah 1961- *217*
Diller, Harriett 1953- *78*
Dillon, Anna
    See Scott, Michael
Dillon, Barbara 1927- *44*
    Brief entry *39*
Dillon, Diane 1933- *194*
    Earlier sketches in SATA *15, 51, 106*
    See also CLR *44*
Dillon, Diane Claire
    See Dillon, Diane
Dillon, Eilis 1920-1994 .... *74*
    Autobiography Feature *105*
    Obituary *83*
    Earlier sketch in SATA *2*
    See also CLR *26*
Dillon, Jana (a pseudonym) 1952- *117*
Dillon, Leo 1933- *194*
    Earlier sketches in SATA *15, 51, 106*
    See also CLR *44*
Dillon, Sharon Saseen
    See Saseen, Sharon (Dillon)
Dils, Tracey E. 1958- *83*
Dilson, Jesse 1914-1988 .... *24*
Dinan, Carolyn *59*
    Brief entry *47*
Dines, Carol 1956- *175*
Dines, (Harry) Glen 1925-1996 .... *7*
Dinesen, Isak
    See Blixen, Karen
Dinessi, Alex
    See Schembri, Jim
Dinneen, Betty 1929- *61*
Dinnerstein, Harvey 1928- *42*
Dinsdale, Tim(othy Kay) 1924-1987 .... *11*
Dion, Nathalie 1964- *213*
Dionne, Erin 1975- *217*
Diop, Birago (Ismael) 1906-1989
    Obituary *64*
Diouf, Sylviane A. *168*
Diouf, Sylviane Anna
    See Diouf, Sylviane A.
DiPucchio, Kelly *204*
    Earlier sketch in SATA *159*
Dirk
    See Gringhuis, Richard H.
Dirks, Wilhelmina 1916- *59*
Dirks, Willy
    See Dirks, Wilhelmina
Dirtmeister
    See Tomecek, Steve
DiSalvo, DyAnne 1960- *144*
    Earlier sketch in SATA *59*
DiSalvo-Ryan, DyAnne
    See DiSalvo, DyAnne
Disch, Thomas M. 1940-2008 .... *92*
    Obituary *195*
    See also CLR *18*
    See also SAAS *15*
Disch, Thomas Michael
    See Disch, Thomas M.
Disch, Tom
    See Disch, Thomas M.
Disher, Garry 1949- *125*
    Earlier sketch in SATA *81*
Disney, Walt(er Elias) 1901-1966 .... *28*
    Brief entry *27*
Ditchfield, Christin 1973- *226*
    Earlier sketch in SATA *189*

DiTerlizzi, Tony 1969- 214
Earlier sketch in SATA 154
DiTerlooney, Tiny
See DiTerlizzi, Tony
Divakaruni, Chitra Banerjee 1956- 222
Earlier sketch in SATA 160
Di Valentin, Maria (Amelia) Messuri
1911-1985 7
Diver, Lucienne 1971- 218
Divine, Arthur Durham 1904-1987
Obituary 52
Divine, David
See Divine, Arthur Durham
Divine, L. 229
Dixon, Ann 1954- 212
Earlier sketches in SATA 77, 127
Dixon, Ann Renee
See Dixon, Ann
Dixon, Dougal 1947- 190
Earlier sketches in SATA 45, 127
Dixon, Franklin W.
See Barrett, Neal, Jr.
and Goulart, Ron
and Lantz, Francess L(in)
and Lerangis, Peter
and McFarlane, Leslie
and Stanley, George Edward
and Stratemeyer, Edward L.
Dixon, Jeanne 1936- 31
Dixon, Paige
See Corcoran, Barbara (Asenath)
Dixon, Peter L(ee) 1931- 6
Dixon, Rachel 1952- 74
Djoleto, (Solomon Alexander) Amu 1929- ... 80
d'Lacey, Chris 1949- 227
Earlier sketch in SATA 165
Doak, Annie
See Dillard, Annie
Doane, Pelagie 1906-1966 7
Dob, Bob 207
Dobell, I(sabel) M(arian) B(arclay)
1909-1998 11
Dobie, J(ames) Frank 1888-1964 43
Dobkin, Alexander 1908-1975
Obituary 30
Dobler, Lavinia G. 1910- 6
Dobrin, Arnold 1928- 4
Dobson, Jill 1969- 140
Dobson, Julia 1941- 48
Dobson, Mary 1954- 117
DoCampo, Valeria 1976- 217
Docherty, James
See Docherty, Jimmy
Docherty, Jimmy 1976- 204
Docherty, Thomas 1955- 218
Dockery, Wallene T. 1941- 27
Dockray, Tracy 1962- 139
Dockrey, Karen 1955- 103
Doctor, Bernard
See Doctor, Bernard Aquina
Doctor, Bernard Aquina 1950- 81
Doctor X
See Nourse, Alan E(dward)
Dodd, Ed(ward Benton) 1902-1991 4
Obituary 68
Dodd, Emma 1969- 203
Dodd, Lynley (Stuart) 1941- 132
Earlier sketches in SATA 35, 86
See also CLR 62
Dodd, Marty 1921- 142
Dodd, Quentin 1972- 137
Dodds, Bill 1952- 78
Dodds, Dayle Ann 1952- 201
Earlier sketches in SATA 75, 150
Doder, Josh 1968- 187
Dodge, Bertha S(anford) 1902-1995 8
Dodge, Fremont
See Grimes, Lee
Dodge, Gil
See Hano, Arnold

Dodge, Mary (Elizabeth) Mapes
1831(?)-1905 100
Earlier sketch in SATA 21
See also CLR 62
Dodgson, Charles Lutwidge
See Carroll, Lewis
Dodson, Kenneth MacKenzie 1907-1999 11
Dodson, Susan 1941- 50
Brief entry 40
Doerrfeld, Cori 1964- 214
Dogar, Sharon 1962- 211
Dogyear, Drew
See Gorey, Edward (St. John)
Doherty, Berlie 1943- 111
Earlier sketch in SATA 72
See also CLR 21
See also SAAS 16
Doherty, Charles Hugh 1913- 6
Doherty, Craig A. 1951- 169
Earlier sketch in SATA 83
Doherty, Katherine M(ann) 1951- 83
Doherty, Kieran 1945- 164
Dokas, Dara 1968- 216
Dokey, Cameron 1956- 97
Dolamore, Jaclyn 1982- 227
Dolan, Edward F(rancis), Jr. 1924- 94
Brief entry 31
Earlier sketch in SATA 45
Dolan, Ellen M(eara) 1929-1998 88
Dolan, Sean J. 1958- 74
Dolce, J. Ellen 1948- 75
Dolch, Edward William 1889-1961 50
Dolch, Marguerite Pierce 1891-1978 50
Dollar, Diane (Hills) 1933- 57
Dolson, Hildegarde
See Lockridge, Hildegarde (Dolson)
Domanska, Janina 1913(?)-1995 68
Obituary 84
Earlier sketch in SATA 6
See also CLR 40
See also SAAS 18
Dominguez, Angel 1953- 76
Dominguez, Angela N. 1982- 219
Domino, John
See Averill, Esther (Holden)
Domjan, Joseph (Spiri) 1907-1992 25
Domm, Jeffrey C. 1958- 84
Donahue, Dorothy 178
Donald, Rhonda Lucas 1962- 147
Donalds, Gordon
See Shirreffs, Gordon D(onald)
Donaldson, Bryna
See Stevens, Bryna
Donaldson, Gordon 1913-1993 64
Obituary 76
Donaldson, Joan 1953- 227
Earlier sketch in SATA 78
Donaldson, Julia 1948- 226
Earlier sketches in SATA 82, 132, 180
Donaldson, Stephen R. 1947- 121
Donaldson, Stephen Reeder
See Donaldson, Stephen R.
Doner, Kim 1955- 208
Earlier sketch in SATA 91
Doney, Todd L. W. 1959- 104
Dong-Sung, Kim 1970- 195
Dong-Sung Kim
See Dong-Sung, Kim
Donkin, Andrew 219
Donkin, Nance (Clare) 1915- 95
Donna, Natalie 1934-1979 9
Donnelly, Elfie 1950-
See CLR 104
Donnelly, Jennifer 1963- 154
Donnelly, Matt 1972- 148
Donnio, Sylviane 188
Donofrio, Beverly 1950- 209
Donoghue, Emma 1969- 101
Donohue, Moira Rose 1954- 201
Donoughue, Carol 1935- 139

Donovan, Frank (Robert) 1906-1975
Obituary 30
Donovan, Gail 1962- 217
Donovan, John 1928-1992 72
Brief entry 29
See also CLR 3
Donovan, Mary Lee 1961- 86
Donovan, William
See Berkebile, Fred D(onovan)
Donze, Mary Terese 1911- 89
Doob, Leonard W(illiam) 1909-2000 8
Doodler, Todd H.
See Goldman, Todd Harris
Dooley, Norah 1953- 74
Dooling, Michael 1958- 220
Earlier sketch in SATA 105
Dor, Ana
See Ceder, Georgiana Dorcas
Doran, Colleen 1963- 211
Dore, (Louis Christophe Paul) Gustave
1832-1883 19
Doremus, Robert 1913-2010 30
Doren, Marion (Walker) 1928- 57
Dorenkamp, Michelle 1957- 89
Dorflinger, Carolyn 1953- 91
Dorfman, Joaquin 1979- 180
Dorfman, Joaquin Emiliano
See Dorfman, Joaquin
Dorian, Edith M(cEwen) 1900-1983 5
Dorian, Harry
See Hamilton, Charles (Harold St. John)
Dorian, Marguerite 7
Dorin, Patrick C(arberry) 1939- 59
Brief entry 52
Dorman, Brandon 194
Dorman, Michael 1932- 7
Dorman, N. B. 1927- 39
Dormer, Frank W. 200
Dorris, Michael 1945-1997 75
Obituary 94
See also CLR 58
Dorris, Michael A.
See Dorris, Michael
Dorris, Michael Anthony
See Dorris, Michael
Dorritt, Susan
See Schlein, Miriam
Dorros, Alex 1991- 194
Dorros, Arthur 1950- 168
Earlier sketches in SATA 78, 122
See also CLR 42
See also SAAS 20
Dorros, Arthur M.
See Dorros, Arthur
Dorson, Richard M(ercer) 1916-1981 30
Doss, Helen (Grigsby) 1918- 20
Doss, Margot Patterson 6
dos Santos, Joyce Audy 1949- 57
Brief entry 42
Dothers, Anne
See Chess, Victoria (Dickerson)
Dotlich, Rebecca Kai 1951- 182
Dottig
See Grider, Dorothy
Dotts, Maryann J. 1933- 35
Doty, Jean Slaughter 1929- 28
Doty, Roy 1922- 28
Doubtfire, Dianne (Abrams) 1918- 29
Doucet, Sharon Arms 1951- 144
Autobiography Feature 144
Earlier sketch in SATA 125
Dougherty, Charles 1922- 18
Dougherty, Terri (L.) 1964- 146
Doughty, Rebecca 1955- 174
Douglas, Allen 223
Douglas, Blaise 1960- 101
Douglas, Carole Nelson 1944- 73
Douglas, Garry
See Kilworth, Garry
Douglas, James McM.
See Griffin, W. E. B.

Douglas, Kathryn
  See Ewing, Kathryn
Douglas, Leonard
  See Bradbury, Ray
Douglas, Lola
  See Zeises, Lara M.
Douglas, Marjory Stoneman 1890-1998 .... *10*
Douglas, Michael
  See Crichton, Michael
Douglas, Michael
  See Bright, Robert Sr.)
Douglas, Shirley Stewart
  See Tepper, Sheri S.
Douglass, Barbara 1930- *40*
Douglass, Frederick 1817(?)-1895 .... *29*
Douglass, Keith
  See Cunningham, Chet
Douty, Esther M(orris) 1909-1978 .... *8*
  Obituary *23*
Dow, Emily R. 1904-1987 .... *10*
Dow, Vicki
  See McVey, Vicki
Dowd, John David 1945- *78*
Dowd, Siobhan 1960-2007 .... *204*
Dowdell, Dorothy (Florence) Karns 1910- ... *12*
Dowden, Anne Ophelia Todd 1907-2007 .... *7*
  Obituary *180*
  See also SAAS *10*
Dowdey, Landon Gerald 1923- *11*
Dowdy, Mrs. Regera
  See Gorey, Edward (St. John)
Dowell, Frances O'Roark 1964- *205*
  Earlier sketch in SATA *157*
Dower, Laura 1967- *185*
Dowling, Terry 1947- *101*
Downard, Barry 1956- *202*
Downer, Ann 1960- *155*
Downer, Marion 1892(?)-1971 .... *25*
Downes, Belinda 1962- *180*
Downey, Fairfax D(avis) 1893-1990 .... *3*
  Obituary *66*
Downey, Lisa *214*
Downey, Lynn 1961- *185*
Downham, Jenny 1964- *192*
Downie, John 1931- *87*
Downie, Mary Alice 1934- *171*
  Earlier sketches in SATA *13, 87*
Downie, Mary Alice Dawe
  See Downie, Mary Alice
Downing, David A(lmon) 1958- *84*
Downing, Johnette *184*
Downing, Julie 1956- *148*
  Earlier sketch in SATA *81*
Downing, Paula E. 1951- *80*
Downing, Warwick
  See Downing, Wick
Downing, Wick 1931- *138*
Dowswell, Paul 1957- *184*
Doyle, A. Conan
  See Doyle, Sir Arthur Conan
Doyle, Sir Arthur Conan 1859-1930 .... *24*
  See also CLR *106*
Doyle, Brian 1935- *156*
  Earlier sketches in SATA *67, 104*
  See also CLR *22*
  See also SAAS *16*
Doyle, Charlotte 1937- *178*
  Earlier sketch in SATA *94*
Doyle, Charlotte Lackner
  See Doyle, Charlotte
Doyle, Conan
  See Doyle, Sir Arthur Conan
Doyle, Debra 1952- *165*
  Earlier sketch in SATA *105*
Doyle, Donovan
  See Boegehold, Betty (Doyle)
Doyle, Eugenie 1952- *225*
Doyle, John
  See Graves, Robert

Doyle, Malachy 1954- *165*
  Earlier sketch in SATA *120*
  See also CLR *83*
Doyle, Richard 1824-1883 .... *21*
Doyle, Sir A. Conan
  See Doyle, Sir Arthur Conan
Dr. A
  See Asimov, Isaac
  and Silverstein, Alvin
  and Silverstein, Virginia B.
Dr. Alphabet
  See Morice, Dave
Dr. Fred
  See Bortz, Alfred B(enjamin)
Dr. Laura
  See Schlessinger, Laura (Catherine)
Dr. Seuss 1904-1991 .... *100*
  Obituary *67*
  Earlier sketches in SATA *1, 28, 75*
  See also CLR *100*
Dr. Zed
  See Penrose, Gordon
Drabble, Margaret 1939- *48*
Drackett, Phil(ip Arthur) 1922- *53*
Draco, F.
  See Davis, Julia
Dracup, Angela 1943- *74*
Dragisic, Patricia *116*
Dragonwagon, Crescent 1952- *186*
  Autobiography Feature *186*
  Earlier sketches in SATA *11, 41, 75, 133*
  See also SAAS *14*
Drake, David 1945- *85*
Drake, David Allen
  See Drake, David
Drake, Frank
  See Hamilton, Charles (Harold St. John)
Drake, Jane 1954- *82*
Drake, Salamanda
  See Barlow, Steve
Drakeford, Dale B 1952- *113*
Drakeford, Dale Benjamin
  See Drakeford, Dale B
Draper, Hastings
  See Jeffries, Roderic
Draper, Sharon
  See Draper, Sharon M.
Draper, Sharon M. 1948- *195*
  Autobiography Feature *146*
  Earlier sketches in SATA *98, 146*
  See also CLR *57*
Draper, Sharon Mills
  See Draper, Sharon M.
Drapier, M. B.
  See Swift, Jonathan
Drawson, Blair 1943- *126*
  Earlier sketch in SATA *17*
Dray, Matt 1967- *177*
Dray, Matthew Frederick
  See Dray, Matt
Dresang, Eliza (Carolyn Timberlake) 1941- . *19*
Drescher, Henrik 1955- *172*
  Earlier sketches in SATA *67, 105*
  See also CLR *20*
Drescher, Joan E(lizabeth) 1939- *137*
  Earlier sketch in SATA *30*
Dressen-McQueen, Stacey *191*
Dreves, Veronica R. 1927-1986
  Obituary *50*
Drew, Patricia 1938- *15*
Drew, Patricia Mary
  See Drew, Patricia
Drewery, Mary 1918- *6*
Drewery, Melanie 1970- *165*
Drewry, Henry N(athaniel) 1924- *138*
Dreyer, Ellen *177*
Drial, J. E.
  See Laird, Jean E(louise)
Drimmer, Frederick 1916-2000 .... *60*
  Obituary *124*
Driskill, J. Lawrence 1920- *90*

Driskill, Larry
  See Driskill, J. Lawrence
Driving Hawk, Virginia
  See Sneve, Virginia Driving Hawk
Dron, Laura
  See Matthews, L. S.
Dronzek, Laura *199*
Drucker, Malka 1945- *214*
  Brief entry *29*
  Earlier sketches in SATA *39, 111*
Drucker, Olga Levy 1927- *79*
Druitt, Tobias
  See Purkiss, Diane
Drummond, Allan 1957- *209*
Drummond, Karona 1965- *220*
Drummond, V(iolet) H(ilda) 1911-2000 .... *6*
Drummond, Walter
  See Silverberg, Robert
Drury, Clare Marie
  See Hoskyns-Abrahall, Clare (Constance Drury)
Drury, Roger W(olcott) 1914-1996 .... *15*
Druse, Eleanor
  See King, Stephen
Dryden, Pamela
  See St. John, Nicole
D.T., Hughes
  See Hughes, Dean
Duane, Diane (Elizabeth) 1952- *145*
  Brief entry *46*
  Earlier sketches in SATA *58, 95*
Dubanevich, Arlene 1950- *56*
Dubelaar, Thea 1947- *60*
Dubin, Jill *205*
du Blanc, Daphne
  See Groom, Arthur William
Duble, Kathleen Benner 1958- *164*
Dubois, Claude K. 1960- *196*
DuBois, Rochelle Holt 1946- *41*
Du Bois, Shirley Graham 1907(?)-1977 .... *24*
  See Graham, Shirley
Du Bois, W. E. B. 1868-1963 .... *42*
Du Bois, William Edward Burghardt
  See Du Bois, W. E. B.
du Bois, William Pene
  See Pene du Bois, William (Sherman)
Duboise, Novella 1911-1999 .... *88*
Dubosarsky, Ursula 1961- *193*
  Earlier sketches in SATA *107, 147*
DuBose, LaRocque (Russ) 1926- *2*
Dubrovin, Vivian 1931- *139*
  Earlier sketch in SATA *65*
DuBurke, Randy *224*
  Earlier sketch in SATA *172*
Ducey, Jean Sparks 1915- *93*
Duchacek, Ivo D(uka) 1913-1988
  Obituary *55*
Du Chaillu, Paul (Belloni) 1835(?)-1903 ..... *26*
Ducharme, Dede Fox
  See Ducharme, Lilian Fox
Ducharme, Lilian Fox 1950- *122*
Ducornet, Erica 1943- *7*
Ducornet, Rikki
  See Ducornet, Erica
Duddle, Jonny 1971(?)- *219*
Duden, Jane 1947- *136*
Duder, Tessa 1940- *117*
  Earlier sketch in SATA *80*
  See also CLR *43*
  See also SAAS *23*
Dudley, Helen
  See Hope Simpson, Jacynth
Dudley, Martha Ward 1909(?)-1985
  Obituary *45*
Dudley, Nancy
  See Cole, Lois Dwight
Dudley, Robert
  See Baldwin, James
Dudley, Ruth H(ubbell) 1905-2001 .... *11*
Dudley-Smith, T.
  See Trevor, Elleston

Due, Linnea A. 1948- *64*
Dueck, Adele 1955- *97*
Dueland, Joy V(ivian) *27*
Duerr, Gisela 1968- *89*
Duey, Kathleen 1950- *199*
　Earlier sketch in SATA *132*
Dufault, Joseph Ernest Nephtali
　See James, Will(iam Roderick)
Duff, Annis (James) 1904(?)-1986
　Obituary *49*
Duff, Maggie
　See Duff, Margaret K(app)
Duff, Margaret K(app) 1916-2003 .... *37*
　Obituary *144*
Duffey, Betsy (Byars) 1953- *131*
　Earlier sketch in SATA *80*
Duffie, Charles 1960- *144*
Duffield, Katy S. 1961- *147*
Duffy, Carol Ann 1955- *165*
　Earlier sketch in SATA *95*
Duffy Stone, Heather *217*
Dugan, Jack
　See Griffin, W. E. B.
Dugan, John Kevin
　See Griffin, W. E. B.
Dugan, Karen *202*
Dugan, Karen M.
　See Dugan, Karen
Dugan, Michael (Gray) 1947- *15*
Duggan, Alfred Leo 1903-1964 .... *25*
Duggan, Maurice 1922-1974 .... *40*
　Obituary *30*
Duggan, Maurice Noel
　See Duggan, Maurice
Dugger, Elizabeth L.
　See Kanell, Beth
Duggleby, John 1952- *94*
Dugin, Andrej 1955- *77*
Dugina, Olga 1964- *77*
du Jardin, Rosamond Neal 1902-1963 .... *2*
Duka, Ivo
　See Duchacek, Ivo D(uka)
Duke, Kate 1956- *192*
　Earlier sketches in SATA *90, 148*
　See also CLR *51*
Duke, Will
　See Gault, William Campbell
Dulac, Edmund 1882-1953 .... *19*
Dumas, Alexandre (pere) 1802-1870 .... *18*
　See also CLR *134*
Dumas, Jacqueline 1946- *55*
Dumas, Philippe 1940- *119*
　Earlier sketch in SATA *52*
du Maurier, Daphne 1907-1989 .... *27*
　Obituary *60*
Dumbleton, Mike 1948- *206*
　Earlier sketches in SATA *73, 124*
Dunbar, Fiona 1961- *167*
Dunbar, Joyce 1944- *213*
　Earlier sketches in SATA *76, 112, 162*
Dunbar, Paul Laurence 1872-1906 .... *34*
Dunbar, Polly 1980(?)- *211*
　Earlier sketch in SATA *181*
Dunbar, Robert E(verett) 1926- *32*
Duncan, Alexandra
　See Moore, Ishbel (Lindsay)
Duncan, Alice Faye 1967- *168*
　Earlier sketch in SATA *95*
Duncan, Gregory
　See McClintock, Marshall
Duncan, Jane
　See Cameron, Elizabeth Jane
Duncan, Julia K.
　See Benson, Mildred
Duncan, Lois 1934- *219*
　Autobiography Feature *141*
　Earlier sketches in SATA *1, 36, 75, 133, 141*
　See also CLR *129*
　See also SAAS *2*
Duncan, Norman 1871-1916
　See YABC *1*

Duncan, Terence
　See Nolan, William F.
Duncombe, Frances (Riker) 1900-1994 .... *25*
　Obituary *82*
Dungy, Anthony
　See Dungy, Tony
Dungy, Tony 1955- *206*
Dunham, Montrew 1919- *162*
Dunham, Montrew Goetz
　See Dunham, Montrew
Dunkle, Clare B. 1964- *223*
　Earlier sketch in SATA *155*
Dunlap, Julie 1958- *84*
Dunleavy, Deborah 1951- *133*
Dunlop, Agnes M. R. (?)-1982 .... *87*
Dunlop, Eileen (Rhona) 1938- *76*
　Earlier sketch in SATA *24*
　See also SAAS *12*
Dunmore, Helen 1952- *201*
Dunn, Anne M. 1940- *107*
Dunn, Carolyn 1965- *208*
Dunn, Harvey T(homas) 1884-1952 .... *34*
Dunn, Herb
　See Gutman, Dan
Dunn, John M. (III) 1949- *93*
Dunn, Judy
　See Spangenberg, Judith Dunn
Dunn, Mary Lois 1930- *6*
Dunnahoo, Terry Janson 1927- *7*
Dunne, Jeanette 1952- *72*
Dunne, Kathleen 1933- *126*
Dunne, Marie
　See Clark, Ann Nolan
Dunne, Mary Collins 1914- *11*
Dunne, Mary Jo
　See Dunne, Mary Collins
Dunnett, Kaitlyn
　See Emerson, Kathy Lynn
Dunnett, Margaret (Rosalind) 1909-1977 ..... *42*
Dunnick, Regan *178*
Dunphy, Madeleine 1962- *219*
Dunrea, Olivier 1953- *160*
　Brief entry *46*
　Earlier sketches in SATA *59, 118*
Dunrea, Olivier Jean-Paul Dominique
　See Dunrea, Olivier
Dunstan Muller, Rachel *221*
Dunton, Dorothy 1912- *92*
Dupasquier, Philippe 1955- *151*
　Earlier sketch in SATA *86*
duPont, Lindsay *207*
duPont, Lindsay Harper
　See duPont, Lindsay
DuPrau, Jeanne 1944- *215*
　Earlier sketch in SATA *144*
Dupuy, T(revor) N(evitt) 1916-1995 .... *4*
　Obituary *86*
DuQuette, Keith 1960- *155*
　Earlier sketch in SATA *90*
Duran, Gloria 1924- *171*
Duran, Gloria Bradley
　See Duran, Gloria
Duranceau, Suzanne 1952- *162*
Durand, Delphine 1971- *200*
Durand, Hallie 1964(?)- *216*
Durango, Julia 1967- *215*
　Earlier sketch in SATA *173*
Durant, Alan 1958- *214*
　Earlier sketches in SATA *121, 165*
Durant, John 1902- *27*
Durbin, William 1951- *174*
　Earlier sketch in SATA *143*
Durell, Ann 1930- *66*
Durkee, Sarah *173*
Durney, Ryan *205*
Durrant, Lynda 1954- *212*
　Earlier sketches in SATA *96, 148*
Durrant, Sabine *210*
Durrell, Gerald (Malcolm) 1925-1995 .... *8*
　Obituary *84*
Durrell, Julie 1955- *94*

Durrett, Deanne 1940- *144*
　Earlier sketch in SATA *92*
Durst, Sarah Beth 1974- *203*
Dusikova, Maja 1946- *223*
Du Soe, Robert C. 1892-1958
　See YABC *2*
Dussling, Jennifer 1970- *143*
　Earlier sketch in SATA *96*
DuTemple, Lesley A. 1952- *113*
Dutton, Sandra *191*
Dutz
　See Davis, Mary Octavia
Duval, Katherine
　See James, Elizabeth
Duval, Kathy 1946- *181*
Duvall, Aimee
　See Thurlo, Aimee
　　and Thurlo, David
Duvall, Evelyn Millis 1906- *9*
Duvall, Jill D. 1932- *102*
Duvall, Jill Donovan
　See Duvall, Jill D.
Duvoisin, Roger (Antoine) 1904-1980 .... *30*
　Obituary *23*
　Earlier sketch in SATA *2*
　See also CLR *23*
Dwiggins, Don(ald J.) 1913-1988 .... *4*
　Obituary *60*
Dwight, Allan
　See Cole, Lois Dwight
Dwyer, Deanna
　See Koontz, Dean
Dwyer, K.R.
　See Koontz, Dean
Dyck, Peter J. 1914- *75*
Dyer, Alan 1953- *218*
Dyer, Hadley 1973- *229*
Dyer, James (Frederick) 1934- *37*
Dyer, Jane *191*
　Earlier sketch in SATA *147*
Dyer, Sarah 1978- *212*
Dyer, Sarah L.
　See Dyer, Sarah
Dyess, John (Foster) 1939- *76*
Dygard, Thomas J. 1931-1996 .... *97*
　Obituary *92*
　Earlier sketch in SATA *24*
　See also SAAS *15*
Dyke, John 1935- *35*

E

E. V. L.
　See Lucas, E(dward) V(errall)
Eagar, Frances (Elisabeth Stuart)
　1940-1978 .... *11*
　Obituary *55*
Eager, Edward (McMaken) 1911-1964 .... *17*
　See also CLR *43*
Eager, George 1921- *56*
Eager, George B.
　See Eager, George
Eagle, Ellen 1953- *61*
Eagle, Kin
　See Adlerman, Daniel (Ezra)
　　and Adlerman, Kimberly M(arie)
Eagle, Mike 1942- *11*
Eamer, Claire 1947- *222*
Earle, Olive L(ydia) 1888-1982 .... *7*
Earle, William
　See Johns, W(illiam) E(arle)
Earls, Nick 1963- *156*
　Earlier sketch in SATA *95*
Early, Jack
　See Scoppettone, Sandra
Early, Jon
　See Johns, W(illiam) E(arle)
Early, Margaret 1951- *72*
Earnest, Peter 1934- *222*

Earnshaw, Brian 1929- *17*
Earnshaw, Micky 1939- *88*
Earnshaw, Spencer Wright
  See Earnshaw, Micky
Easley, MaryAnn *94*
Eason, Alethea 1957- *197*
East, Jacqueline *224*
Eastman, Charles A(lexander) 1858-1939
  See YABC *1*
Eastman, P(hilip) D(ey) 1909-1986 .... *33*
  Obituary *46*
Easton, Kelly 1960- *192*
  Earlier sketch in SATA *141*
Eastwick, Ivy (Ethel) O(live) *3*
Eaton, Anne T(haxter) 1881-1971 .... *32*
Eaton, Anthony 1971- *167*
Eaton, George L.
  See Verral, Charles Spain
Eaton, Janet
  See Givens, Janet E(aton)
Eaton, Jeanette 1886-1968 .... *24*
Eaton, Maxwell III 1981- *199*
Eaton, Tom 1940- *22*
Ebbeler, Jeff
  See Ebbeler, Jeffrey
Ebbeler, Jeffrey 1974- *206*
Ebbitt, Carolyn Q. 1974(?)- *225*
Ebel, Alex 1927- *11*
Eber, Dorothy (Margaret) Harley 1930- *27*
Eberhart, Sheri S.
  See Tepper, Sheri S.
Eberle, Irmengarde 1898-1979 .... *2*
  Obituary *23*
Eble, Diane 1956- *74*
Eboch, Chris *113*
Eccles Williams, Ferelith 1920- *22*
Echeverria-Bis, Olivia *217*
Echeverria Gyorkos, Charmaine *216*
Echlin, Kim 1955- *166*
Eckblad, Edith Berven 1923- *23*
Ecke, Wolfgang 1927-1983
  Obituary *37*
Eckert, Allan W. 1931- *91*
  Brief entry *27*
  Earlier sketch in SATA *29*
  See also SAAS *21*
Eckert, Horst 1931- *72*
  Earlier sketch in SATA *8*
  See also CLR *26*
Ecklar, Julia (Marie) 1964- *112*
Eddings, David 1931-2009 .... *91*
Eddings, David Carroll
  See Eddings, David
Ede, Janina 1937- *33*
Edell, Celeste *12*
Edelman, Lily (Judith) 1915-1981 .... *22*
Edelson, Edward 1932- *51*
Edens, Cooper 1945- *166*
  Earlier sketches in SATA *49, 112*
Edens, (Bishop) David 1926- *39*
Edey, Maitland A(rmstrong) 1910-1992 .... *25*
  Obituary *71*
Edgerton, Perky *196*
Edgeworth, Maria 1768-1849 .... *21*
  See also CLR *153*
Edgson, Alison *211*
Edgy, Wardore
  See Gorey, Edward (St. John)
Edison, Theodore
  See Stratemeyer, Edward L.
Edler, Tim(othy) 1948- *56*
Edmiston, Jim 1948- *80*
Edmonds, I(vy) G(ordon) 1917- *8*
Edmonds, Walter D(umaux) 1903-1998 .... *27*
  Obituary *99*
  Earlier sketch in SATA *1*
  See also SAAS *4*
Edmund, Sean
  See Pringle, Laurence
Edsall, Marian (Stickney) 1920- *8*

Edwards, Al
  See Nourse, Alan E(dward)
Edwards, Anne 1927- *35*
Edwards, Audrey 1947- *52*
  Brief entry *31*
Edwards, Becky (Jane) 1966- *125*
Edwards, Bertram
  See Edwards, Herbert Charles
Edwards, Bronwen Elizabeth
  See Rose, Wendy
Edwards, Cecile Pepin 1916- *25*
Edwards, David 1962- *198*
Edwards, Dorothy 1914-1982 .... *88*
  Obituary *31*
  Earlier sketch in SATA *4*
Edwards, F. E.
  See Nolan, William F.
Edwards, Frank B. 1952- *93*
Edwards, Gunvor *32*
Edwards, Harvey 1929- *5*
Edwards, Hazel (Eileen) 1945- *135*
Edwards, Herbert Charles 1912- *12*
Edwards, Jane Campbell 1932- *10*
Edwards, Julia
  See Stratemeyer, Edward L.
Edwards, Julie
  See Andrews, Julie
Edwards, Julie Andrews
  See Andrews, Julie
Edwards, June
  See Bhatia, Jamunadevi
Edwards, Linda Strauss 1948- *49*
  Brief entry *42*
Edwards, Margaret (Alexander) 1902-1988
  Obituary *56*
Edwards, Michelle 1955- *152*
  Earlier sketch in SATA *70*
Edwards, Monica le Doux Newton
  1912-1998 .... *12*
Edwards, Olwen
  See Gater, Dilys
Edwards, Page (Lawrence, Jr.) 1941-1999 ... *59*
Edwards, Pamela Duncan *189*
Edwards, R. T.
  See Goulart, Ron
Edwards, Sally (Cary) 1929- *7*
Edwards, Samuel
  See Gerson, Noel Bertram
Edwards, Wallace 1957(?)- *170*
Edwardson, Debby Dahl *223*
Eeckhout, Emmanuelle 1976- *208*
Egan, E. W. 1922- *35*
Egan, Edward Welstead
  See Egan, E. W.
Egan, Kerry *175*
Egan, Lorraine Hopping 1960- *134*
  Earlier sketch in SATA *91*
Egan, Tim 1957- *191*
  Earlier sketches in SATA *89, 155*
Egermeier, Elsie E(milie) 1890-1986 .... *65*
Eggenberger, David 1918- *6*
Eggleston, Edward 1837-1902 .... *27*
Egielski, Richard 1952- *220*
  Earlier sketches in SATA *11, 49, 106, 163*
Egypt, Ophelia Settle 1903-1984 .... *16*
  Obituary *38*
Ehlert, Lois 1934- *172*
  Earlier sketches in SATA *35, 69, 128*
  See also CLR *28*
Ehlert, Lois Jane
  See Ehlert, Lois
Ehling, Katalin Olah 1941- *93*
Ehrenberg, Pamela 1972- *219*
Ehrenfreund, Norbert 1921- *86*
Ehrenhaft, Daniel 1970- *185*
Ehrenhaft, Daniel Parker
  See Ehrenhaft, Daniel
Ehrhardt, Karen 1963- *184*
Ehrlich, Amy 1942- *217*
  Earlier sketches in SATA *25, 65, 96, 132*
Ehrlich, Bettina Bauer 1903-1985 .... *1*

Ehrlich, Fred *205*
Ehrlich, Fred M.D.
  See Ehrlich, Fred
Ehrlich, H. M.
  See Ziefert, Harriet
Eichenberg, Fritz 1901-1990 .... *50*
  Earlier sketch in SATA *9*
Eichler, Margrit 1942- *35*
Eichner, James A. 1927- *4*
Eidson, Thomas 1944- *112*
Eifert, Virginia (Louise) S(nider) 1911-1966 . *2*
Eige, (Elizabeth) Lillian 1915- *65*
Eiken, J. Melia 1967- *125*
Einhorn, Edward 1970- *204*
Einsel, Naiad *10*
Einsel, Walter 1926- *10*
Einzig, Susan 1922- *43*
Eiseman, Alberta 1925- *15*
Eisenberg, Azriel (Louis) 1903-1985 .... *12*
Eisenberg, Lisa 1949- *155*
  Brief entry *50*
  Earlier sketch in SATA *57*
Eisenberg, Phyllis Rose 1924- *41*
Eisner, Vivienne
  See Margolis, Vivienne
Eisner, Will 1917-2005 .... *165*
  Earlier sketch in SATA *31*
Eisner, William Erwin
  See Eisner, Will
Eitzen, Allan 1928- *9*
Eitzen, Ruth (Carper) 1924- *9*
Ekwensi, C. O. D.
  See Ekwensi, Cyprian
Ekwensi, Cyprian 1921-2007 .... *66*
Ekwensi, Cyprian Odiatu Duaka
  See Ekwensi, Cyprian
Elam, Richard M(ace, Jr.) 1920- *9*
Elborn, Andrew
  See Clements, Andrew
  and Clements, Andrew
Elboz, Stephen 1956- *152*
Eldin, Peter 1939- *154*
Eldon, Kathy 1946- *107*
Eldridge, Marion *199*
Eley, Robin *219*
Elfman, Blossom 1925- *8*
Elgin, Kathleen 1923- *39*
Elia
  See Lamb, Charles
Eliot, A. D.
  See Jewett, Sarah Orne
Eliot, Alice
  See Jewett, Sarah Orne
Eliot, Anne
  See Cole, Lois Dwight
Eliot, Dan
  See Silverberg, Robert
Elish, Dan 1960- *204*
  Earlier sketches in SATA *68, 129*
Elisha, Ron 1951- *104*
Elisofon, Eliot 1911-1973
  Obituary *21*
Elkeles, Simone 1970- *187*
Elkin, Benjamin 1911-1995 .... *3*
Elkins, Dov Peretz 1937- *5*
Ellacott, S(amuel) E(rnest) 1911- *19*
Elleman, Barbara 1934- *147*
Ellen, Jaye
  See Nixon, Joan Lowery
Eller, Scott
  See Holinger, William (Jacques)
  and Shepard, Jim
Ellery, Amanda *216*
Ellestad, Myrvin
  See Ellestad, Myrvin H.
Ellestad, Myrvin H. 1921- *120*
Elliot, Bruce
  See Field, Edward
Elliot, David 1952- *208*
  Earlier sketch in SATA *122*

Elliott, Bruce
  See Field, Edward
Elliott, David 1947- 201
  Earlier sketch in SATA *163*
Elliott, Don
  See Silverberg, Robert
Elliott, Elizabeth Shippen Green
  See Green, Elizabeth Shippen
Elliott, Janice 1931-1995 .... *119*
Elliott, Joey
  See Houk, Randy
Elliott, Laura Malone 1957- *197*
Elliott, L.M.
  See Elliott, Laura Malone
Elliott, Louise *111*
Elliott, Mark 1949- *210*
Elliott, Odette 1939- *75*
Elliott, Patricia 1946- *176*
Elliott, Sarah M(cCarn) 1930- *14*
Elliott, (Robert) Scott 1970- *153*
Elliott, William
  See Bradbury, Ray
Elliott, Zetta *206*
Ellis, (Mary) Amabel (Nassau Strachey)
    Williams
  See Williams-Ellis, (Mary) Amabel (Nassau
    Strachey)
Ellis, Ann Dee *210*
Ellis, Anyon
  See Rowland-Entwistle, (Arthur) Theodore
    (Henry)
Ellis, Carson 1975- *190*
Ellis, Carson Friedman
  See Ellis, Carson
Ellis, Deborah 1960- *187*
  Earlier sketch in SATA *129*
Ellis, E. S.
  See Ellis, Edward S.
Ellis, Edward S. 1840-1916
  See YABC *1*
Ellis, Edward Sylvester
  See Ellis, Edward S.
Ellis, Ella Thorp 1928- *127*
  Earlier sketch in SATA *7*
  See also SAAS *9*
Ellis, Harry Bearse 1921-2004 .... *9*
Ellis, Herbert
  See Wilson, Lionel
Ellis, Julie 1961- *227*
Ellis, Mel(vin Richard) 1912-1984 .... *7*
  Obituary *39*
Ellis, Richard 1938- *130*
Ellis, Sarah 1952- *179*
  Earlier sketches in SATA *68, 131*
  See also CLR *42*
Ellison, Chris *196*
Ellison, Elizabeth Stow 1970- *209*
Ellison, Emily *114*
Ellison, Lucile Watkins 1907(?)-1979 .... *50*
  Obituary *22*
Ellison, Virginia H(owell) 1910- *4*
Ellsberg, Edward 1891-1983 .... *7*
Ellsworth, Loretta 1954- *199*
Ellsworth, Mary Ellen (Tressel) 1940- *146*
Ellwand, David 1965(?)- *213*
Elmer, Robert 1958- *154*
  Earlier sketch in SATA *99*
Elmore, (Carolyn) Patricia 1933- *38*
  Brief entry *35*
El-Moslimany, Ann P(axton) 1937- *90*
Elschner, Geraldine 1954- *183*
Elspeth
  See Bragdon, Elspeth MacDuffie
Elster, Jean Alicia 1953- *150*
Elting, Mary 1906- *88*
  Earlier sketch in SATA *2*
  See also SAAS *20*
Elvgren, Jennifer Riesmeyer *179*
Elwart, Joan Potter 1927- *2*
Elwell, Peter *220*

Elwood, Ann 1931- *55*
  Brief entry *52*
Elwood, Roger 1943-2007 .... *58*
Ely, Lesley *212*
Elya, Susan Middleton 1955- *202*
  Earlier sketches in SATA *106, 159*
Elzbieta *88*
Ember, Kathi *190*
Emberley, Barbara A. 1932- *146*
  Earlier sketches in SATA *8, 70*
  See also CLR *5*
Emberley, Barbara Anne
  See Emberley, Barbara A.
Emberley, Ed 1931- *146*
  Earlier sketches in SATA *8, 70*
  See also CLR *81*
Emberley, Edward Randolph
  See Emberley, Ed
Emberley, Michael 1960- *189*
  Earlier sketches in SATA *34, 80, 119*
Emberley, Rebecca 1958- *218*
Embry, Margaret Jacob 1919-1975 .... *5*
Emecheta, Buchi 1944- *66*
  See also CLR *158*
Emecheta, Florence Onye Buchi
  See Emecheta, Buchi
Emerson, Alice B.
  See Benson, Mildred
Emerson, Kate
  See Emerson, Kathy Lynn
Emerson, Kathy Lynn 1947- *63*
Emerson, Kevin *209*
Emerson, Ru 1944- *107*
  Earlier sketch in SATA *70*
Emerson, Sally 1952- *111*
Emerson, William K(eith) 1925- *25*
Emert, Phyllis R. 1947- *93*
Emert, Phyllis Raybin
  See Emert, Phyllis R.
Emery, Anne (McGuigan) 1907- *33*
  Earlier sketch in SATA *1*
Emmens, Carol Ann 1944- *39*
Emmett, Jonathan 1965- *188*
  Earlier sketch in SATA *138*
Emmons, Della (Florence) Gould 1890-1983
  Obituary *39*
Emory, Jerry 1957- *96*
Emrich, Duncan (Black Macdonald)
    1908-1970(?) *11*
Emshwiller, Carol 1921- *174*
  Autobiography Feature *174*
Emshwiller, Carol Fries
  See Emshwiller, Carol
Emslie, M. L.
  See Simpson, Myrtle L(illias)
Ende, Michael (Andreas Helmuth)
    1929-1995 .... *130*
  Brief entry *42*
  Obituary *86*
  Earlier sketch in SATA *61*
  See also CLR *138*
Enderle, Dotti 1954- *203*
  Earlier sketch in SATA *145*
Enderle, Judith (Ann) Ross 1941- *89*
  Autobiography Feature *114*
  Earlier sketch in SATA *38*
  See also SAAS *26*
Endle, Kate *207*
Enell, Trinka (Gochenour) 1951- *79*
Enfield, Carrie
  See Smith, Susan Vernon
Engdahl, Sylvia Louise 1933- *4*
  Autobiography Feature *122*
  See also CLR *2*
  See also SAAS *5*
Engel, Diana 1947- *70*
Engelbreit, Mary 1952- *169*
Engelhart, Margaret S. 1924- *59*
Engelmann, Kim (V.) 1959- *87*
England, George Allan 1877-1936 .... *102*
Englart, Mindi Rose 1965- *146*

Engle, Eloise
  See Paananen, Eloise (Katherine)
Engle, Margarita 1951- *193*
Englebert, Victor 1933- *8*
English, James W(ilson) 1915- *37*
English, Karen *202*
Engstrom, Elizabeth 1951- *110*
Enright, D(ennis) J(oseph) 1920-2002 .... *25*
  Obituary *140*
Enright, Dominique *194*
Enright, Elizabeth (Wright) 1909-1968 .... *9*
  See also CLR *4*
Ensor, Barbara *180*
Ensor, Robert (T.) 1922- *93*
Enthoven, Sam 1974- *187*
Entwistle, (Arthur) Theodore (Henry) Rowland
  See Rowland-Entwistle, (Arthur) Theodore
    (Henry)
Enys, Sarah L.
  See Sloggett, Nellie
Epanya, Christian A(rthur Kingue) 1956- *91*
Ephraim, Shelly S(chonebaum) 1952- *97*
Ephron, Delia 1944- *197*
  Brief entry *50*
  Earlier sketch in SATA *65*
Epler, Doris M. 1928- *73*
Epp, Margaret A(gnes) 1913- *20*
Eppenstein, Louise (Kohn) 1892-1987
  Obituary *54*
Epple, Anne Orth 1927- *20*
Epstein, Anne Merrick 1931- *20*
Epstein, Beryl 1910- *31*
  Earlier sketch in SATA *1*
  See also CLR *26*
  See also SAAS *17*
Epstein, Beryl M. Williams
  See Epstein, Beryl
Epstein, Perle S(herry) 1938- *27*
Epstein, Rachel S. 1941- *102*
Epstein, Samuel 1909-2000 .... *31*
  Earlier sketch in SATA *1*
  See also CLR *26*
  See also SAAS *17*
Erdman, Loula Grace 1905(?)-1976 .... *1*
Erdoes, Richard 1912- *33*
  Brief entry *28*
Erdogan, Buket *187*
Erdrich, Karen Louise
  See Erdrich, Louise
Erdrich, Louise 1954- *141*
  Earlier sketch in SATA *94*
Erickson, Betty J. 1923- *97*
Erickson, Betty Jean
  See Erickson, Betty J.
Erickson, John R. 1943- *136*
  Earlier sketch in SATA *70*
Erickson, Jon 1948- *141*
Erickson, Phoebe *59*
Erickson, Russell E(verett) 1932- *27*
Erickson, Sabra Rollins 1912-1995 .... *35*
Erickson, Walter
  See Fast, Howard
Ericson, Walter
  See Fast, Howard
Ericsson, Jennifer A. *170*
Erikson, Mel 1937- *31*
Eriksson, Eva 1949- *207*
Ering, Timothy Basil *176*
Erlanger, Baba
  See Trahey, Jane
Erlbach, Arlene 1948- *160*
  Earlier sketches in SATA *78, 115*
Erlbruch, Wolf 1948- *181*
Erlich, Lillian (Feldman) 1910-1983 .... *10*
Erlings, Fridrik 1962- *196*
Erlingsson, Friorik
  See Erlings, Fridrik
Ermatinger, James W. 1959- *170*
Ernest, William
  See Berkebile, Fred D(onovan)
Ernst, (Lyman) John 1940- *39*

Ernst, Kathleen
See Ernst, Kathleen A.
Ernst, Kathleen A. 1959- 162
Ernst, Kathryn (Fitzgerald) 1942- 25
Ernst, Lisa Campbell 1957- 212
Brief entry 44
Earlier sketches in SATA 55, 95, 154
Erskine, Kathryn 193
Ervin, Janet Halliday 1923- 4
Erwin, Will
See Eisner, Will
Esbaum, Jill 213
Earlier sketch in SATA 174
Esbensen, Barbara J(uster) 1925-1996 97
Brief entry 53
Earlier sketch in SATA 62
Eschbacher, Roger 160
Eschmeyer, R. E. 1898-1989 29
Escriva, Vivi 182
Eseki, Bruno
See Mphahlele, Es'kia
Esekie, Bruno
See Mphahlele, Es'kia
Eshmeyer, Reinhart Ernst
See Eschmeyer, R. E.
Eskridge, Ann E. 1949- 84
Espeland, Pamela (Lee) 1951- 128
Brief entry 38
Earlier sketch in SATA 52
Espinosa, Laura 203
Espinosa, Leo 203
Espriella, Don Manuel Alvarez
See Southey, Robert
Espy, Willard R(ichardson) 1910-1999 38
Obituary 113
Essakalli, Julie Klear 200
Essrig, Harry 1912- 66
Estep, Irene Compton 5
Esterl, Arnica 1933- 77
Estes, Eleanor (Ruth) 1906-1988 91
Obituary 56
Earlier sketch in SATA 7
See also CLR 70
Estoril, Jean
See Allan, Mabel Esther
Estrada, Pau 1961- 200
Earlier sketch in SATA 74
Etchemendy, Nancy 1952- 166
Earlier sketch in SATA 38
Etchemendy, Nancy Elise Howell
See Etchemendy, Nancy
Etchison, Birdie L(ee) 1937- 38
Etchison, Craig 1945- 133
Etherington, Frank 1945- 58
Etnier, Jennifer L. 227
Eton, Robert
See Meynell, Laurence Walter
Ets, Marie Hall 1893-1984 2
See also CLR 33
Ettlinger, Doris 1950- 173
Eugnia, Maria 222
Eulberg, Elizabeth 1975- 227
Eunson, (John) Dale 1904-2002 5
Obituary 132
Evan, Frances Y. 1951- 167
Evanoff, Vlad 1916- 59
Evans, Cambria 1981- 178
Evans, Douglas 1953- 144
Earlier sketch in SATA 93
Evans, Eva (Knox) 1905-1998 27
Evans, Freddi Williams 1957- 211
Earlier sketch in SATA 134
Evans, Greg 1947- 143
Earlier sketch in SATA 73
Evans, Hubert Reginald 1892-1986 118
Obituary 48
Evans, Katherine (Floyd) 1901-1964 5
Evans, Larry
See Evans, Laurence Chubb
Evans, Laurence Chubb 1939- 88

Evans, Lawrence Watt
See Watt-Evans, Lawrence
Evans, Leslie 1953- 214
Evans, Lezlie 180
Evans, Mari 1923- 10
Evans, Mark 19
Evans, Nancy 1950- 65
Evans, Nate 201
Evans, Patricia Healy
See Carpenter, Patricia (Healy Evans)
Evans, (Alice) Pearl 1927- 83
Evans, Shane W. 189
Evans, Shirlee 1931- 58
Evans, Tabor
See Cameron, Lou
and Knott, William C(ecil, Jr.)
and Wallmann, Jeffrey M(iner)
and Whittington, Harry (Benjamin)
Evarts, Esther
See Benson, Sally
Evarts, Hal G., (Jr.) 1915-1989 6
Everett, Gail
See Hale, Arlene
Evernden, Margery 1916- 5
Eversole, Robyn 1971- 74
Eversole, Robyn H.
See Eversole, Robyn
Eversole, Robyn Harbert
See Eversole, Robyn
Evslin, Bernard 1922-1993 83
Brief entry 28
Obituary 77
Earlier sketch in SATA 45
Ewart, Claire 1958- 145
Earlier sketch in SATA 76
Ewart, Franzeska G. 1950- 205
Ewen, David 1907-1985 4
Obituary 47
Ewing, Juliana (Horatia Gatty) 1841-1885 ... 16
See also CLR 78
Ewing, Kathryn 1921- 20
Eyerly, Jeannette 1908-2008 86
Obituary 196
Earlier sketch in SATA 4
See also SAAS 10
Eyerly, Jeannette Hyde
See Eyerly, Jeannette
Eyre, Dorothy
See McGuire, Leslie (Sarah)
Eyre, Frank 1910-1988
Obituary 62
Eyre, Katherine Wigmore 1901-1970 26
Ezzell, Marilyn 1937- 42
Brief entry 38

F

Fabe, Maxene 1943- 15
Faber, Doris (Greenberg) 1924- 78
Earlier sketch in SATA 3
Faber, Harold 1919-2010 5
Fabre, Jean Henri (Casimir) 1823-1915 22
Fabry, Glenn 1961- 205
Facklam, Margaret
See Thomas, Peggy
Facklam, Margery (Metz) 1927- 132
Earlier sketches in SATA 20, 85
Fadden, David Kanietakeron 196
Fadiman, Clifton (Paul) 1904-1999 11
Obituary 115
Fagan, Cary 1957- 186
Fagan, Deva 220
Fahs, Sophia Blanche Lyon 1876-1978 102
Failing, Barbara Larmon 182
Fain, Sarah 1971- 204
Fair, David 1952- 96
Fair, Sylvia 1933- 13

Fairfax-Lucy, Brian (Fulke Cameron-Ramsay)
1898-1974 6
Obituary 26
Fairfield, Flora
See Alcott, Louisa May
Fairlie, Gerard 1899-1983
Obituary 34
Fairman, Joan A(lexandra) 1935- 10
Faithfull, Gail 1936- 8
Falcone, L(ucy) M. 1951- 155
Falconer, Ian 1959- 179
Earlier sketch in SATA 125
See also CLR 146
Falconer, James
See Kirkup, James
Falconer, Lee N.
See May, Julian
Falkner, Brian 1962- 206
Falkner, Leonard 1900-1977 12
Fall, Andrew
See Arthur, Robert, (Jr.)
Fall, Thomas
See Snow, Donald Clifford
Faller, Regis 1968- 187
Falls, C(harles) B(uckles) 1874-1960 38
Brief entry 27
Falstein, Louis 1909-1995 37
Falvey, David 1982- 222
Falwell, Cathryn 1952- 196
Fancher, Lou 1960- 228
Earlier sketch in SATA 177
Fanelli, Sara 1969- 126
Earlier sketch in SATA 89
Fanning, Leonard M(ulliken) 1888-1967 5
Fantaskey, Beth 1965- 217
Faralla, Dana 1909- 9
Faralla, Dorothy W.
See Faralla, Dana
Farb, Peter 1929-1980 12
Obituary 22
Farber, Norma 1909-1984 75
Obituary 38
Earlier sketch in SATA 25
Fardell, John 1967- 195
Fardell, John William
See Fardell, John
Faria, Rosana 213
Farish, Terry 1947- 146
Earlier sketch in SATA 82
Farjeon, (Eve) Annabel 1919-2004 11
Obituary 153
Farjeon, Eleanor 1881-1965 2
See also CLR 34
Farley, Carol (J.) 1936- 137
Earlier sketch in SATA 4
Farley, Terri 165
Farley, Walter (Lorimer) 1915-1989 132
Earlier sketches in SATA 2, 43
Farlow, James O(rville, Jr.) 1951- 75
Farmer, Jacqueline 210
Farmer, Nancy 1941- 161
Earlier sketches in SATA 79, 117
Farmer, Patti 1948- 79
Farmer, Penelope (Jane) 1939- 105
Brief entry 39
Earlier sketch in SATA 40
See also CLR 8
See also SAAS 22
Farmer, Peter 1950- 38
Farmer, Philip Jose
See Farmer, Philip Jose
Farmer, Philip Jose 1918-2009 93
Obituary 201
Farmer, Philipe Jos
See Farmer, Philip Jose
Farnham, Burt
See Clifford, Harold B(urton)
Farnsworth, Bill 1958- 186
Earlier sketches in SATA 84, 135
Farooqi, Musharraf Ali 1968- 207
Farquhar, Margaret C(utting) 1905-1988 13

Farquharson, Alexander 1944- 46
Farquharson, Martha
  See Finley, Martha
Farr, Diana 82
  Earlier sketch in SATA 3
Farr, Finis (King) 1904-1982 10
Farr, Richard 1960- 209
Farrar, Jill
  See Morris, Jill
Farrar, Susan Clement 1917- 33
Farrell, Ben
  See Cebulash, Mel
Farrell, Darren 228
Farrell, John 1951- 204
Farrell, Patrick
  See Odgers, Sally Farrell
Farrell, Sally
  See Odgers, Sally Farrell
Farrer, Vashti 167
Farrington, Benjamin 1891-1974
  Obituary 20
Farrington, S(elwyn) Kip, Jr. 1904-1983 20
Farris, Christine King 1927- 206
Farshtey, Greg(ory T.) 1965- 148
Farthing, Alison 1936- 45
  Brief entry 36
Farthing-Knight, Catherine 1933- 92
Fassler, Joan (Grace) 1931- 11
Fast, Howard 1914-2003 7
  Autobiography Feature 107
Fast, Howard Melvin
  See Fast, Howard
Fasulo, Michael 1963- 83
Fatchen, Max 1920- 84
  Earlier sketch in SATA 20
  See also SAAS 20
Fate, Marilyn
  See Collins, Paul
Father Goose
  See Ghigna, Charles
Fatigati, Evelyn 1948- 24
Fatigati, Frances Evelyn
  See Fatigati, Evelyn
Fatio, Louise 1904-1993 6
Fatus, Sophie 1957- 182
Faulhaber, Martha 1926- 7
Faulkner, Anne Irvin 1906- 23
Faulkner, Frank
  See Ellis, Edward S.
Faulkner, Nancy
  See Faulkner, Anne Irvin
Faulknor, Cliff(ord Vernon) 1913- 86
Favole, Robert J(ames) 1950- 125
Fawcett, Katie Pickard 229
Fax, Elton Clay 1909-1993 25
Faxon, Lavinia
  See Russ, Lavinia (Faxon)
Feagles, Anita M.
  See Feagles, Anita MacRae
Feagles, Anita MacRae 1927- 9
Feagles, Elizabeth
  See Day, Beth (Feagles)
Feague, Mildred H. 1915- 14
Fearing, Mark 1968- 224
Fearnley, Jan 1965- 205
  Earlier sketch in SATA 153
Fearrington, Ann (Peyton) 1945- 146
Fecher, Constance
  See Heaven, Constance (Christina)
Feder, Chris Welles 1938- 81
Feder, Harriet K. 1928- 73
Feder, Paula (Kurzband) 1935- 26
Federici, Debbie 1965- 175
Federici, Debbie Tanner
  See Federici, Debbie
Feelings, Muriel 1938- 16
  See also CLR 5
  See also SAAS 8
Feelings, Muriel Lavita Grey
  See Feelings, Muriel

Feelings, Thomas 1933-2003 69
  Obituary 148
  Earlier sketch in SATA 8
  See also CLR 58
  See also SAAS 19
Feelings, Tom
  See Feelings, Thomas
Fehler, Gene 1940- 201
  Earlier sketch in SATA 74
Fehrenbach, T(heodore) R(eed, Jr.) 1925- 33
Feiffer, Jules 1929- 201
  Earlier sketches in SATA 8, 61, 111, 157
Feiffer, Jules Ralph
  See Feiffer, Jules
Feiffer, Kate 1964- 206
  Earlier sketch in SATA 170
Feig, Barbara Krane 1937- 34
Feig, Paul 221
Feikema, Feike
  See Manfred, Frederick (Feikema)
Feil, Hila 1942- 12
Feilen, John
  See May, Julian
Feinberg, Barbara Jane 1938- 123
  Earlier sketch in SATA 58
Feinberg, Barbara Silberdick
  See Feinberg, Barbara Jane
Feinstein, John 1956- 195
  Earlier sketch in SATA 163
Feldman, Anne (Rodgers) 1939- 19
Feldman, Elane 79
Feldman, Eve B. 221
Feldman, Jody 200
Felin, M. Sindy 194
Felix
  See Vincent, Felix
Fell, Derek 1939- 167
Fell, Derek John
  See Fell, Derek
Fellowes, Julian 1950- 198
Fellows, Muriel H. 10
Fellows, Stan 1957- 177
Fellows, Stanley
  See Fellows, Stan
Felsen, Henry Gregor 1916-1995 1
  See also SAAS 2
Felstead, Cathie 1954- 192
Feltenstein, Arlene 1934- 119
Feltenstine, Arlene H.
  See Feltenstein, Arlene
Felton, Harold William 1902-1991 1
Felton, Ronald Oliver 1909- 3
Felts, Shirley 1934- 33
Felts, Susannah 1973- 214
Fenderson, Lewis H., Jr. 1907-1983 47
  Obituary 37
Fenner, Carol (Elizabeth) 1929-2002 89
  Obituary 132
  Earlier sketch in SATA 7
  See also SAAS 24
Fenner, Phyllis R(eid) 1899-1982 1
  Obituary 29
Fensham, Elizabeth 169
Fenten, Barbara D(oris) 1935- 26
Fenten, D(onald) X. 1932- 4
Fenton, Carroll Lane 1900-1969 5
Fenton, Edward 1917-1995 7
  Obituary 89
Fenton, Joe 213
Fenton, Mildred Adams 1899-1995 21
Fenwick, Patti
  See Grider, Dorothy
Feravolo, Rocco Vincent 1922- 10
Ferber, Brenda A. 1967- 184
Ferber, Edna 1887-1968 7
Fergus, Charles 114
Ferguson, Alane 1957- 182
  Earlier sketch in SATA 85
Ferguson, Bob
  See Ferguson, Robert Bruce
Ferguson, Cecil 1931- 45

Ferguson, Peter 1968- 199
Ferguson, Robert Bruce 1927-2001 13
Ferguson, Sarah 1959- 180
  Earlier sketches in SATA 66, 110
Ferguson, Sarah Margaret
  See Ferguson, Sarah
Ferguson, Walter (W.) 1930- 34
Fergusson, Erna 1888-1964 5
Fermi, Laura 1907-1977 6
  Obituary 28
Fern, Eugene A. 1919-1987 10
  Obituary 54
Fern, Tracey E. 202
Fernandes, Eugenie 1943- 205
  Earlier sketches in SATA 77, 139
Fernandez, Laura 1960- 171
Ferraiolo, Jack D. 208
Ferrari, Maria 123
Ferrari, Michael 223
Ferrari, Michael J.
  See Ferrari, Michael
Ferreiro, Carmen 1958- 158
Ferrell, Nancy Warren 1932- 70
Ferrer, Isabel
  See Riu, Isabel Ferrer
Ferri, Giuliano 1965- 197
Ferrier, Lucy
  See Penzler, Otto
Ferris, Helen Josephine 1890-1969 21
Ferris, James Cody
  See McFarlane, Leslie
Ferris, Jean 1939- 202
  Brief entry 50
  Earlier sketches in SATA 56, 105, 149
Ferris, Jeri Chase 1937- 84
Ferry, Charles 1927- 92
  Earlier sketch in SATA 43
  See also CLR 34
  See also SAAS 20
Fetz, Ingrid 1915- 30
Feydy, Anne Lindbergh
  See Sapieyevski, Anne Lindbergh
Fiammenghi, Gioia 1929- 66
  Earlier sketch in SATA 9
Fiarotta, Noel
  See Ficarotta, Noel
Fiarotta, Phyllis
  See Ficarotta, Phyllis
Ficarotta, Noel 1944- 15
Ficarotta, Phyllis 1942- 15
Fichter, George S. 1922-1993 7
Ficocelli, Elizabeth 189
Fidler, Kathleen (Annie) 1899-1980 87
  Obituary 45
  Earlier sketch in SATA 3
Fiedler, Jean(nette Feldman) 4
Fiedler, Joseph Daniel 159
Fiedler, Lisa 185
Field, Dorothy 1944- 97
Field, Edward 1924- 109
  Earlier sketch in SATA 8
Field, Elinor Whitney 1889-1980
  Obituary 28
Field, Eugene 1850-1895 16
Field, Gans T.
  See Wellman, Manly Wade
Field, James 1959- 113
Field, Peter
  See Drago, Harry Sinclair
  and Dresser, Davis
  and Mann, E(dward) B(everly)
Field, Rachel (Lyman) 1894-1942 15
  See also CLR 21
Fielding, Kate
  See Oldfield, Jenny
Fields, Bryan W. 1958(?)- 188
Fields, Lisa 1984(?)- 216
Fields, Terri 1948- 191
Fields, T.S.
  See Fields, Terri

Fienberg, Anna 1956- 183
Earlier sketch in SATA *112*
Fiery, Ann
See Barrows, Annie
Fife, Dale (Odile Hollerbach) 1901- *18*
Fighter Pilot, A
See Johnston, H(ugh) A(nthony) S(tephen)
Figler, Jeanie 1949- 123
Figley, Marty Rhodes 1948- 158
Earlier sketch in SATA *88*
Figueredo, D(anilo) H. 1951- 155
Figueroa, Pablo 1938- 9
Fijan, Carol 1918- 12
Filderman, Diane E(lizabeth) 1959- 87
Files, Meg 1946- 107
Fillmore, Parker H(oysted) 1878-1944
See YABC *1*
Filstrup, Chris
See Filstrup, E(dward) Christian
Filstrup, E(dward) Christian 1942- 43
Filstrup, Janie
See Merrill, Jane
Finbarr, Desmond
See Zobel Nolan, Allia
Finchler, Judy 1943- 93
Finder, Martin
See Salzmann, Siegmund
Findlay, Jamieson 1958- 169
Findon, Joanne 1957- 161
Fine, Anne 1947- 197
Earlier sketches in SATA *29, 72, 111, 160*
See also CLR *25*
See also SAAS *15*
Fine, Edith Hope 169
Fine, Howard 1961- 181
Fine, Jane
See Ziefert, Harriet
Finger, Charles J(oseph) 1869(?)-1941 42
Fink, William B(ertrand) 1916- 22
Finke, Blythe Foote 1922- 26
Finkel, George (Irvine) 1909-1975 8
Finkelstein, Norman H. 1941- 220
Earlier sketches in SATA *73, 137*
Finkelstein, Norman Henry
See Finkelstein, Norman H.
Finlay, Alice Sullivan 1946- 82
Finlay, Winifred Lindsay Crawford
(McKissack) 1910-1989 23
Finlayson, Ann 1925- 8
Finley, Martha 1828-1909 43
See also CLR *148*
Finley, Mary Peace 1942- 83
Finn, Mary 208
Finney, Jack 1911-1995 109
Finney, Patricia 1958- 163
Finney, Shan 1944- 65
Finney, Walter Braden
See Finney, Jack
Firer, Ben Zion
See Firer, Benzion
Firer, Benzion 1914- 64
Fireside, Bryna J. 1932- 73
Firmin, Charlotte 1954- 29
Firmin, Peter 1928- 58
Earlier sketch in SATA *15*
Firth, Barbara 179
Fischbach, Julius 1894-1988 10
Fischer, John
See Fluke, Joanne
Fischer, R.J.
See Fluke, Joanne
Fischer, Scott M. 1971- 195
Fischer-Nagel, Andreas 1951- 56
Fischer-Nagel, Heiderose 1956- 56
Fischler, Shirley (Walton) 66
Fischler, Stan(ley I.) 66
Brief entry 36
Fischtrom, Harvey 1933-1974 3
Fishback, Margaret
See Antolini, Margaret Fishback
Fishbone, Greg R. 195

Fisher, Aileen (Lucia) 1906-2002 73
Obituary 143
Earlier sketches in SATA *1, 25*
See also CLR *49*
Fisher, Barbara 1940- 44
Brief entry 34
Fisher, Carolyn 1968- 154
Fisher, Catherine 1957- 155
Fisher, Chris 1958- 80
Fisher, Clavin C(argill) 1912- 24
Fisher, Cynthia 195
Fisher, Dorothy (Frances) Canfield 1879-1958
See YABC *1*
See also CLR *71*
Fisher, Gary L. 1949- 86
Fisher, John 1909-1996 15
Fisher, John Oswald Hamilton
See Fisher, John
Fisher, Laura Harrison 1934- 5
Fisher, Leonard Everett 1924- 176
Autobiography Feature 122
Earlier sketches in SATA *4, 34, 73, 120*
See also CLR *18*
See also SAAS *1*
Fisher, Lois I. 1948- 38
Brief entry 35
Fisher, Margery (Turner) 1913-1992 20
Obituary 74
Fisher, Marshall Jon 1963- 113
Fisher, Nikki
See Strachan, Ian
Fisher, Robert (Tempest) 1943- 47
Fisher, Suzanne
See Staples, Suzanne Fisher
Fisher, Valorie 214
Earlier sketch in SATA *177*
Fishman, Cathy Goldberg 1951- 106
Fisk, Nicholas
See Higginbottom, David
Fisk, Pauline 1948- 160
Earlier sketch in SATA *66*
Fiske, Tarleton
See Bloch, Robert (Albert)
Fisscher, Catharina G. M. 1958- 142
Fisscher, Tiny
See Fisscher, Catharina G. M.
Fitch, Clarke
See Sinclair, Upton
Fitch, John IV
See Cormier, Robert
Fitch, Sheree 1956- 178
Earlier sketch in SATA *108*
Fitschen, Dale 1937- 20
Fitzalan, Roger
See Trevor, Elleston
Fitzgerald, Captain Hugh
See Baum, L. Frank
FitzGerald, Cathleen 1932-1987
Obituary 50
Fitzgerald, Dawn 175
Fitzgerald, Edward Earl 1919-2001 20
Fitzgerald, F(rancis) A(nthony) 1940- 15
Fitzgerald, Joanne 1956- 198
Fitzgerald, John D(ennis) 1907(?)-1988 20
Obituary 56
See also CLR *1*
Fitzgerald, Merni Ingrassia 1955- 53
Fitzgibbon, Terry 1948- 121
Fitzhardinge, Joan Margaret 1912- 73
Earlier sketch in SATA *2*
See also CLR *5*
See also SAAS *3*
Fitzhugh, Louise (Perkins) 1928-1974 45
Obituary 24
Earlier sketch in SATA *1*
See also CLR *72*
Fitzhugh, Percy Keese 1876-1950 65
Fitzmaurice, Kathryn 217
Fitzpatrick, Becca 1979- 224
Fitzpatrick, Marie-Louise 1962- 189
Earlier sketch in SATA *125*

FitzRalph, Matthew
See McInerny, Ralph
Fitz-Randolph, Jane (Currens) 1915- 51
Fitzsimons, Cecilia 1952- 97
Fitzsimons, Cecilia A.L.
See Fitzsimons, Cecilia
Flack, Marjorie 1897-1958 100
See also YABC *2*
See also CLR *28*
Flack, Naomi John White -1999 40
Brief entry 35
Flake, Sharon G. 166
Flanagan, John 1944- 180
Flanagan, John Anthony
See Flanagan, John
Flannery, Kate
See De Goldi, Kate
Flatt, Lizann 1966- 88
Fleagle, Gail S(hatto) 1940- 117
Fleetwood, Jenni 1947- 80
Fleischer, Jane
See Oppenheim, Joanne
Fleischhauer-Hardt, Helga 1936- 30
Fleischman, Albert Sidney
See Fleischman, Sid
Fleischman, John 1948- 145
Fleischman, Paul 1952- 156
Brief entry 32
Earlier sketches in SATA *39, 72, 110*
See also CLR *66*
See also SAAS *20*
Fleischman, Sid 1920-2010 185
Earlier sketches in SATA *8, 59, 96, 148*
See also CLR *15*
Fleischner, Jennifer 1956- 188
Earlier sketch in SATA *93*
Fleisher, Paul 1948- 132
Earlier sketch in SATA *81*
Fleisher, Robbin 1951-1977 52
Brief entry 49
Fleishman, Seymour 1918- 66
Brief entry 32
Fleming, A. A.
See Arthur, Robert, (Jr.)
Fleming, Alice Mulcahey 1928- 9
Fleming, Candace 1962- 225
Earlier sketches in SATA *94, 143, 190*
Fleming, Denise 1950- 173
Earlier sketches in SATA *81, 126*
Fleming, Elizabeth P. 1888-1985
Obituary 48
Fleming, Ian 1908-1964 9
Fleming, Ian Lancaster
See Fleming, Ian
Fleming, Ronald Lee 1941- 56
Fleming, Sally
See Walker, Sally M.
Fleming, Stuart
See Knight, Damon (Francis)
Fleming, Susan 1932- 32
Fleming, Thomas 1927- 8
Fleming, Thomas James
See Fleming, Thomas
Fleming, Virginia (Edwards) 1923- 84
Flesch, Y.
See Flesch, Yolande
Flesch, Yolande 1950- 55
Flesch, Yolande Catarina
See Flesch, Yolande
Fletcher, Charlie 220
Fletcher, Charlie May Hogue 1897-1977 3
Fletcher, Colin 1922-2007 28
Fletcher, Dirk
See Cunningham, Chet
Fletcher, George U.
See Pratt, (Murray) Fletcher
Fletcher, Helen Jill 1910- 13
Fletcher, Ralph 1953- 195
Earlier sketches in SATA *105, 149*
See also CLR *104*

Fletcher, Ralph J.
  See Fletcher, Ralph
Fletcher, Richard E. 1917(?)-1983
  Obituary 34
Fletcher, Rick
  See Fletcher, Richard E.
Fletcher, Susan 1951- 181
  Earlier sketches in SATA 70, 110
Fletcher, Susan Clemens
  See Fletcher, Susan
Fleur, Paul
  See Pohl, Frederik
Flexner, James Thomas 1908-2003 9
Flinn, Alex 1966- 198
  Earlier sketch in SATA 159
Flint, Helen 1952- 102
Flint, Russ 1944- 74
Flitner, David, Jr. 1949- 7
Flitner, David Perkins
  See Flitner, David, Jr.
Floca, Brian 190
  Earlier sketch in SATA 155
Floethe, Louise Lee 1913-1988 4
Floethe, Richard 1901-1998 4
Floherty, John Joseph 1882-1964 25
Flood, Bo
  See Flood, Nancy Bo
Flood, Nancy Bo 1945- 130
Flood, Pansie Hart 1964- 140
Flood, William 1942- 129
Flooglebuckle, Al
  See Spiegelman, Art
Flora, James (Royer) 1914-1998 30
  Obituary 103
  Earlier sketch in SATA 1
  See also SAAS 6
Flores-Galbis, Enrique 1952- 186
Florian, Douglas 1950- 177
  Earlier sketches in SATA 19, 83, 125
Flory, Jane Trescott 1917- 22
Flournoy, Valerie 1952- 95
Flournoy, Valerie Rose
  See Flournoy, Valerie
Flowerdew, Phyllis -1994 33
Flowers, Pam 1946- 136
Flowers, Sarah 1952- 98
Floyd, Gareth 1940- 62
  Brief entry 31
Fluchere, Henri 1914-1991 40
Fluke, Joanne 1943- 88
Flutsztejn-Gruda, Ilona 1930- 170
Flynn, Barbara 1928- 9
Flynn, Jackson
  See Bensen, Donald R.
  and Shirreffs, Gordon D(onald)
Flynn, Nicholas
  See Odgers, Sally Farrell
Flynn, Pat 1968- 214
Flynn, Patrick
  See Flynn, Pat
Flynn, Rachel 1953- 171
  Earlier sketch in SATA 109
Flynn, Warren (G.) 1950- 154
Fodor, R. V. 1944- 25
Fodor, Ronald Victor
  See Fodor, R. V.
Fogelin, Adrian 1951- 175
  Earlier sketch in SATA 129
Foley, (Anna) Bernice Williams 1902-1987 . 28
Foley, Greg E. 1969- 190
Foley, June 1944- 44
Foley, (Mary) Louise Munro 1933- 106
  Brief entry 40
  Earlier sketch in SATA 54
Foley, Rae
  See Denniston, Elinore
Folke, Will
  See Bloch, Robert (Albert)
Follett, Helen Thomas 1884(?)-1970
  Obituary 27

Folsom, Franklin (Brewster) 1907-1995 5
  Obituary 88
Folsom, Michael (Brewster) 1938-1990 40
  Obituary 88
Fombelle, Timothee de 1973- 218
Fontenot, Mary Alice 1910-2003 91
  Obituary 209
  Earlier sketch in SATA 34
Fontes, Justine 172
Fontes, Ron 1952- 183
Foon, Dennis 1951- 119
Fooner, Michael 22
Foote, Timothy (Gilson) 1926- 52
Forberg, Ati
  See Forberg, Beate Gropius
Forberg, Beate Gropius 1925- 22
Forbes, Anna 1954- 101
Forbes, Bryan 1926- 37
Forbes, Cabot L.
  See Hoyt, Edwin P(almer), Jr.
Forbes, Esther 1891-1967 100
  Earlier sketch in SATA 2
  See also CLR 147
Forbes, Graham B. 1
Forbes, Kathryn
  See McLean, Kathryn (Anderson)
Forbes, Robert
  See Arthur, Robert, (Jr.)
Ford, Albert Lee
  See Stratemeyer, Edward L.
Ford, Barbara 56
  Brief entry 34
Ford, Bernette 212
Ford, Bernette G.
  See Ford, Bernette
Ford, B.G.
  See Ford, Bernette
Ford, Brian J(ohn) 1939- 49
Ford, Carolyn 1938- 98
Ford, Carolyn Mott
  See Ford, Carolyn
Ford, Christine 1953- 176
Ford, David
  See Baldacci, David
  and Baldacci, David
Ford, David B.
  See Baldacci, David
Ford, David Baldacci
  See Baldacci, David
Ford, Elbur
  See Hibbert, Eleanor Alice Burford
Ford, Ellen 1949- 89
Ford, George (Jr.) 31
Ford, Hilary
  See Youd, Samuel
Ford, Hildegarde
  See Morrison, Velma Ford
Ford, Jerome W. 1949- 78
Ford, Jerry
  See Ford, Jerome W.
Ford, John C. 1971- 221
Ford, Juwanda G(ertrude) 1967- 102
Ford, Marcia
  See Radford, Ruby L(orraine)
Ford, Nancy K(effer) 1906-1961
  Obituary 29
Ford, Peter 1936- 59
Ford, S. M.
  See Uhlig, Susan
Forde, Catherine 1961- 170
Foreman, Mark 199
Foreman, Michael 1938- 216
  Earlier sketches in SATA 2, 73, 129, 135, 184
  See also CLR 32
  See also SAAS 21
Foreman, Wilmoth 1939- 153
Forest, Antonia 1915-2003 29
  Obituary 149
Forest, Dial
  See Gault, William Campbell

Forest, Heather 1948- 185
  Earlier sketch in SATA 120
Forester, C. S. 1899-1966 13
Forester, Cecil Scott
  See Forester, C. S.
Forester, Victoria 214
Forler, Nan 223
Forman, Brenda 1936- 4
Forman, James
  See Forman, James D.
Forman, James D. 1932-2009 70
  Earlier sketch in SATA 8
Forman, James Douglas
  See Forman, James D.
Forman, Mark L.
  See Forman, M.L.
Forman, M.L. 1964- 215
Forman, Ruth 1970- 186
Formento, Alison 228
Forrest, Elizabeth
  See Salsitz, Rhondi Vilott
Forrest, Mary
  See Pausacker, Jenny
Forrest, Sybil
  See Markun, Patricia Maloney
Forrestal, Elaine 1941- 165
  Earlier sketch in SATA 117
Forrester, Frank H. 1919(?)-1986
  Obituary 52
Forrester, Helen
  See Bhatia, Jamunadevi
Forrester, Jade
  See Pausacker, Jenny
Forrester, Marian
  See Schachtel, Roger
Forrester, Sandra 1949- 166
  Earlier sketch in SATA 90
Forrester, Victoria 1940- 40
  Brief entry 35
Forsee, (Frances) Aylesa -1986 1
Forsey, Chris 1950- 59
Forshay-Lunsford, Cin 1965- 60
Forster, E. M. 1879-1970 57
Forster, Edward Morgan
  See Forster, E. M.
Forsyth, Kate 1966- 154
Fort, Paul
  See Stockton, Francis Richard
Forte, Maurizio 1961- 110
Fortey, Richard 1946- 109
Fortey, Richard A.
  See Fortey, Richard
Fortey, Richard Alan
  See Fortey, Richard
Forth, Melissa D(eal) 96
Fortnum, Peggy
  See Nuttall-Smith, Margaret Emily Noel
Fortune, Eric 182
Forward, Robert L(ull) 1932-2002 82
Foster, Alan Dean 1946- 70
Foster, Brad W. 1955- 34
Foster, Doris Van Liew 1899-1993 10
Foster, E(lizabeth) C(onnell) 1902- 9
Foster, Elizabeth 1902- 12
Foster, Elizabeth 1905-1963 10
Foster, F. Blanche 1919- 11
Foster, G(eorge) Allen 1907-1969 26
Foster, Genevieve (Stump) 1893-1979 2
  Obituary 23
  See also CLR 7
Foster, Gerald L. 198
Foster, Hal
  See Foster, Harold
Foster, Harold 1892-1982 31
Foster, Jeanne
  See Williams, Jeanne
Foster, John
  See Foster, John L(ouis)
  and Furcolo, Foster
Foster, John (Thomas) 1925- 8
Foster, John L(ouis) 1941- 102

Foster, Juliana *196*
Foster, Laura Louise (James) 1918- *6*
Foster, Leila Merrell 1929- *73*
Foster, Lynne 1937- *74*
Foster, Margaret Lesser 1899(?)-1979
    Obituary *21*
Foster, Marian Curtis 1909-1978 .... *23*
Foster, Mark 1961- *197*
Foster, Sally *58*
Fotheringham, Edwin *201*
Foulds, E. V.
    See Foulds, Elfrida Vipont
Foulds, Elfrida Vipont 1902-1992 .... *52*
Fountas, Angela Jane *180*
Fourie, Corlia 1944- *91*
Fourth Brother, The
    See Aung, (Maung) Htin
Fowke, Edith (Margaret) 1913-1996 .... *14*
Fowles, John 1926-2005 .... *22*
    Obituary *171*
Fowles, John Robert
    See Fowles, John
Fowles, Shelley 1956- *205*
Fox, Aileen 1907-2005 .... *58*
    Obituary *170*
Fox, Aileen Mary
    See Fox, Aileen
Fox, Annie 1950- *175*
Fox, Charles Philip 1913-2003 .... *12*
    Obituary *150*
Fox, Christyan *188*
Fox, Diane *188*
Fox, Eleanor
    See St. John, Wylly Folk
Fox, Fontaine Talbot, Jr. 1884-1964
    Obituary *23*
Fox, Fred 1903(?)-1981
    Obituary *27*
Fox, Freeman
    See Hamilton, Charles (Harold St. John)
Fox, Geoffrey 1941- *73*
Fox, Grace
    See Anderson, Grace Fox
Fox, Helen 1962- *181*
Fox, Karen C. 1969- *229*
Fox, Larry *30*
Fox, Lee 1958- *227*
Fox, Lorraine 1922-1976 .... *27*
    Earlier sketch in SATA *11*
Fox, Louisa
    See Kroll, Virginia L.
Fox, Mary Virginia 1919- *152*
    Brief entry *39*
    Earlier sketches in SATA *44, 88*
Fox, Mem 1946- *211*
    Earlier sketches in SATA *51, 103, 155*
    See also CLR *80*
Fox, Merrion Frances
    See Fox, Mem
Fox, Michael W(ilson) 1937- *15*
Fox, Norma Diane
    See Mazer, Norma Fox
Fox, Paula 1923- *167*
    Earlier sketches in SATA *17, 60, 120*
    See also CLR *96*
Fox, Robert J. 1927- *33*
Fox, Robert Joseph
    See Fox, Robert J.
Fox-Davies, Sarah 1956- *199*
Foyt, Victoria .... *187.*
Fradin, Dennis
    See Fradin, Dennis Brindell
Fradin, Dennis Brindell 1945- *185*
    Earlier sketches in SATA *29, 90, 135*
Fradin, Judith Bloom 1945- *185*
    Earlier sketches in SATA *90, 152*
Frailey, Paige (Menefee) 1965- *82*
Frame, Janet 1924-2004 .... *119*
Frame, Janet Paterson
    See Frame, Janet

Frame, Paul 1913-1994 .... *60*
    Brief entry *33*
    Obituary *83*
Frances, Miss
    See Horwich, Frances R(appaport)
Franchere, Ruth *18*
Francis, Charles
    See Holme, Bryan
Francis, Dee
    See Haas, Dorothy F.
Francis, Dorothy 1926- *127*
    Earlier sketch in SATA *10*
Francis, Dorothy B.
    See Francis, Dorothy
Francis, Dorothy Brenner
    See Francis, Dorothy
Francis, Guy *225*
Francis, Jaye
    See Pausacker, Jenny
Francis, Pamela (Mary) 1926- *11*
Franck, Eddie
    See Cooke, Frank E.
Franco, Betsy *223*
    Earlier sketches in SATA *150, 188*
Franco, Eloise (Bauder) 1910- *62*
Franco, Johan (Henri Gustave) 1908-1988 ... *62*
Franco, Marjorie *38*
Franco, Tom *224*
Francois, Andre 1915-2005 .... *25*
Francoise
    See Seignobosc, Francoise
Frank, Anne 1929-1945 .... *87*
    Brief entry *42*
    See also CLR *101*
Frank, Annelies Marie
    See Frank, Anne
Frank, Daniel B. 1956- *55*
Frank, Emily R.
    See Frank, E.R.
Frank, E.R. 1967- *157*
Frank, Helene
    See Vautier, Ghislaine
Frank, Hillary 1976- *148*
Frank, John *199*
Frank, Josette 1893-1989 .... *10*
    Obituary *63*
Frank, Lucy 1947- *166*
    Earlier sketch in SATA *94*
Frank, Mary 1933- *34*
Frank, R., Jr.
    See Ross, Frank (Xavier), Jr.
Frankau, Mary Evelyn Atkinson 1899-1974 .. *4*
Frankel, Alona 1937- *66*
Frankel, Bernice *9*
Frankel, Edward 1910- *44*
Frankel, Ellen 1951- *78*
Frankel, Julie 1947- *40*
    Brief entry *34*
Frankenberg, Robert 1911- *22*
Frankland, David *207*
Franklin, Cheryl J. 1955- *70*
Franklin, Harold 1926- *13*
Franklin, Kristine L. 1958- *124*
    Earlier sketch in SATA *80*
Franklin, Lance
    See Lantz, Francess L(in)
Franklin, Madeleine
    See L'Engle, Madeleine
Franklin, Madeleine L'Engle
    See L'Engle, Madeleine
Franklin, Madeleine L'Engle Camp
    See L'Engle, Madeleine
Franklin, Max
    See Deming, Richard
Franklin, Steve
    See Stevens, Franklin
Franson, Leanne 1963- *223*
    Earlier sketch in SATA *111*
Franson, Scott E. 1966- *192*
Franzen, Nils-Olof 1916- *10*

Frascino, Edward *48*
    Brief entry *33*
    See also SAAS *9*
Frasconi, Antonio 1919- *131*
    Earlier sketches in SATA *6, 53*
    See also SAAS *11*
Fraser, Betty
    See Fraser, Elizabeth Marr
Fraser, Elizabeth Marr 1928- *31*
Fraser, Eric (George) 1902-1983 .... *38*
Fraser, Mary Ann 1959- *214*
    Earlier sketches in SATA *76, 137*
    See also SAAS *23*
Fraser, Wynnette (McFaddin) 1925- *90*
Frasier, Debra 1953- *182*
    Earlier sketches in SATA *69, 112*
Fraustino, Lisa Rowe 1961- *146*
    Autobiography Feature *146*
    Earlier sketch in SATA *84*
Frazee, Marla 1958- *225*
    Earlier sketches in SATA *105, 151, 187*
Frazer, Megan 1977- *221*
Frazetta, Frank 1928-2010 .... *58*
Frazier, Craig 1955- *221*
    Earlier sketch in SATA *177*
Frazier, Neta (Osborn) Lohnes 1890-1990 ..... *7*
Frazier, Sundee T. 1968- *198*
Frazier, Sundee Tucker
    See Frazier, Sundee T.
Frederic, Mike
    See Cox, William R(obert)
Frederick, Heather Vogel *207*
Fredericks, Anthony D. 1947- *113*
Freed, Alvyn M. 1913-1993 .... *22*
Freedman, Benedict 1919- *27*
Freedman, Claire *227*
    Earlier sketch in SATA *185*
Freedman, Deborah 1960- *191*
Freedman, Jeff 1953- *90*
Freedman, Nancy 1920-2010 .... *27*
Freedman, Russell 1929- *175*
    Earlier sketches in SATA *16, 71, 123*
    See also CLR *71*
Freedman, Russell Bruce
    See Freedman, Russell
Freeman, Barbara C. 1906-1999 .... *28*
Freeman, Barbara Constance
    See Freeman, Barbara C.
Freeman, Bill
    See Freeman, William Bradford
Freeman, Don 1908-1978 .... *17*
    See also CLR *90*
Freeman, Ira Maximilian 1905-1987 .... *21*
Freeman, Kimberley
    See Wilkins, Kim
Freeman, Laura *200*
Freeman, Lucy (Greenbaum) 1916-2004 ...... *24*
Freeman, Mae 1907-1985 .... *25*
Freeman, Mae Blacker
    See Freeman, Mae
Freeman, Marcia S. 1937- *102*
Freeman, Marcia Sheehan
    See Freeman, Marcia S.
Freeman, Martha 1956- *201*
    Earlier sketches in SATA *101, 152*
Freeman, Nancy 1932- *61*
Freeman, Peter J.
    See Calvert, Patricia
Freeman, Sarah (Caroline) 1940- *66*
Freeman, Tor 1977- *164*
Freeman, VicToria
    See Freeman, Tor
Freeman, William Bradford 1938- *58*
    Brief entry *48*
Fregosi, Claudia (Anne Marie) 1946- *24*
Freitas, Donna 1972- *205*
French, Allen 1870-1946
    See YABC *1*
French, Dorothy Kayser 1926- *5*

French, Fiona 1944- *132*
  Earlier sketches in SATA *6, 75*
  See also CLR 37
  See also SAAS 21
French, Jackie *186*
  Autobiography Feature *139*
  Earlier sketches in SATA *108, 139*
  See French, Jackie Anne
  and French, Jacqueline Anne
French, Kathryn
  See Mosesson, Gloria R(ubin)
French, Martin *176*
French, Michael 1944- *49*
  Brief entry *38*
French, Paul
  See Asimov, Isaac
French, S. Terrell *216*
French, Simon 1957- *147*
  Earlier sketch in SATA *86*
French, Vivian *209*
  Earlier sketch in SATA *165*
Frenette, Liza *126*
Freschet, Gina 1960- *175*
  Earlier sketch in SATA *139*
Frewer, Glyn (M.) 1931- *11*
Frey, Darcy *98*
Freymann, Saxton 1958(?)- *178*
Freymann-Weyr, Garret 1965- *145*
Freymann-Weyr, Rhoda Garret Michaela
  See Freymann-Weyr, Garret
Frick, C. H.
  See Irwin, Constance (H.) Frick
Frick, Constance
  See Irwin, Constance (H.) Frick
Fricke, Aaron 1962- *89*
Fridell, Ron 1943- *124*
Fried, Janice *197*
Friedlander, Joanne K(ohn) 1930- *9*
Friedman, Aimee 1979- *189*
Friedman, D. Dina 1957- *180*
Friedman, Debra 1955- *150*
Friedman, Estelle (Ehrenwald) 1920- *7*
Friedman, Frieda 1905- *43*
Friedman, Ina R(osen) 1926- *136*
  Brief entry *41*
  Earlier sketch in SATA *49*
Friedman, Jerrold David
  See Gerrold, David
Friedman, Judi 1935- *59*
Friedman, Laurie 1964- *219*
  Earlier sketches in SATA *138, 179*
Friedman, Marvin 1930- *42*
  Brief entry *33*
Friedman, Robin 1968- *219*
  Earlier sketch in SATA *162*
Friedmann, Stan 1953- *80*
Friedrich, Otto (Alva) 1929-1995 .... *33*
Friedrich, Priscilla 1927- *39*
Friend, Catherine 1957(?)- *194*
Friend, David Michael 1975- *195*
Friend, Natasha 1972- *184*
Friendlich, Dick
  See Friendlich, Richard J.
Friendlich, Richard J. 1909- *11*
Friermood, Elisabeth Hamilton 1903-1992 .... *5*
Friesen, Bernice (Sarah Anne) 1966- *105*
Friesen, Gayle 1960- *200*
  Earlier sketch in SATA *109*
Friesen, Jonathan 1967(?)- *206*
Friesner, Esther 1951- *207*
  Earlier sketches in SATA *71, 168*
Friesner, Esther M.
  See Friesner, Esther
Friis-Baastad, Babbis Ellinor 1921-1970 .... *7*
Frimmer, Steven 1928- *31*
Frischmuth, Barbara 1941- *114*
Friskey, Margaret (Richards) 1901-1995 .... *5*
Fritts, Mary Bahr
  See Bahr, Mary (Madelyn)

Fritz, Jean (Guttery) 1915- *163*
  Autobiography Feature *122*
  Earlier sketches in SATA *1, 29, 72, 119*
  See also CLR 96
  See also SAAS 2
Froehlich, Margaret W(alden) 1930- *56*
Frois, Jeanne 1953- *73*
Froissart, Jean 1338(?)-1410(?) *28*
Froman, Elizabeth Hull 1920-1975 .... *10*
Froman, Robert (Winslow) 1917- *8*
Fromm, Lilo 1928- *29*
Frommer, Harvey 1937- *41*
Frost, A(rthur) B(urdett) 1851-1928 .... *19*
Frost, Elizabeth
  See Frost-Knappman, Elizabeth
Frost, Erica
  See Supraner, Robyn
Frost, Helen 1949- *194*
  Autobiography Feature *194*
  Earlier sketches in SATA *157, 183*
Frost, Helen Marie
  See Frost, Helen
Frost, Lesley 1899-1983 .... *14*
  Obituary *34*
Frost, Robert 1874-1963 .... *14*
  See also CLR 67
Frost, Robert Lee
  See Frost, Robert
Frost, Shelley 1960- *138*
Frost-Knappman, Elizabeth 1943- *179*
Froud, Brian 1947- *150*
Fry, Annette R(iley) *89*
Fry, Christopher 1907-2005 .... *66*
Fry, Edward Bernard 1925- *35*
Fry, Rosalie Kingsmill 1911-1992 .... *3*
  See also SAAS 11
Fry, Virginia Lynn 1952- *95*
Frye, Sally
  See Moore, Elaine
Fuchs, Bernie 1932- *162*
  Earlier sketch in SATA *95*
Fuchs, Erich 1916- *6*
Fuchshuber, Annegert 1940- *43*
Fucile, Tony *221*
Fuerst, Jeffrey B. 1956- *143*
Fuertes, Gloria 1918-1998 .... *115*
Fuge, Charles 1966- *144*
  Earlier sketch in SATA *74*
Fujikawa, Gyo 1908-1998 .... *76*
  Brief entry *30*
  Obituary *110*
  Earlier sketch in SATA *39*
  See also CLR 25
  See also SAAS 16
Fujita, Tamao 1905-1999 .... *7*
Fujiwara, Kim 1957- *81*
Fujiwara, Michiko 1946- *15*
Fuka, Vladimir 1926-1977
  Obituary *27*
Fulcher, Jennifer
  See Westwood, Jennifer
Fuller, Catherine Leuthold 1916- *9*
Fuller, Edmund (Maybank) 1914- *21*
Fuller, Iola
  See McCoy, Iola Fuller
Fuller, John G(rant, Jr.) 1913-1990 .... *65*
Fuller, Kathleen
  See Gottfried, Theodore Mark
Fuller, Lois Hamilton 1915- *11*
Fuller, Margaret 1810-1850 .... *25*
Fuller, Maud
  See Petersham, Maud
Fuller, Roy (Broadbent) 1912-1991 .... *87*
Fuller, Sarah Margaret
  See Fuller, Margaret
Fults, John Lee 1932- *33*
Funk, Thompson 1911- *7*
Funk, Tom
  See Funk, Thompson

Funke, Cornelia 1958- *209*
  Earlier sketches in SATA *154, 174*
  See also CLR 145
Funke, Cornelia Caroline
  See Funke, Cornelia
Funke, Lewis 1912-1992 .... *11*
Fuqua, Jonathon Scott 1966- *141*
Furbee, Mary R.
  See Furbee, Mary Rodd
Furbee, Mary Rodd 1954- *138*
Furchgott, Terry 1948- *29*
Furlong, Monica (Mavis) 1930-2003 .... *86*
  Obituary *142*
Furlonger, Patricia
  See Wrightson, Patricia
Furman, Gertrude Lerner Kerman 1909- *21*
Furniss, Tim 1948- *49*
Furrow, Robert 1985- *172*
Furukawa, Toshi 1924- *24*
Fusillo, Archimede 1962- *137*
Futcher, Jane P. 1947- *76*
Futehali, Zahida
  See Whitaker, Zai
Fyleman, Rose (Amy) 1877-1957 .... *21*
Fyson, Jenny Grace
  See Fyson, J.G.
Fyson, J.G. 1904-1998 .... *42*

G

Gaan, Margaret 1914- *65*
Gaber, Susan 1956- *169*
  Earlier sketch in SATA *115*
Gaberman, Judie Angell
  See Angell, Judie
Gabhart, Ann
  See Gabhart, Ann H.
Gabhart, Ann H. 1947- *75*
Gable, Brian 1949- *195*
Gabler, Mirko 1951- *77*
Gabriel, Adriana
  See Rojany, Lisa
Gabrys, Ingrid Schubert
  See Schubert-Gabrys, Ingrid
Gackenbach, Dick 1927- *79*
  Brief entry *30*
  Earlier sketch in SATA *48*
Gadd, Jeremy 1949- *116*
Gaddis, Vincent H. 1913-1997 .... *35*
Gadler, Steve J. 1905-1985 .... *36*
Gaeddert, Lou Ann (Bigge) 1931- *103*
  Earlier sketch in SATA *20*
Gaeddert, Louann
  See Gaeddert, Lou Ann (Bigge)
Gaer, Joseph 1897-1969 .... *118*
Gaer, Yossef
  See Gaer, Joseph
Gaetz, Dayle Campbell 1947- *138*
Gaffney, Timothy R. 1951- *170*
  Earlier sketch in SATA *69*
Gaffron, Norma 1931- *97*
Gaffron, Norma Bondeson
  See Gaffron, Norma
Gag, Flavia 1907-1979
  Obituary *24*
Gag, Wanda (Hazel) 1893-1946 .... *100*
  See also YABC *1*
  See also CLR *150*
Gage, Brian *162*
Gage, Wilson
  See Steele, Mary Q(uintard Govan)
Gagliano, Eugene M. 1946- *150*
Gagliardo, Ruth Garver 1895(?)-1980
  Obituary *22*
Gagnon, Cecile 1936- *58*
Gaillard, Jason 1965- *200*
Gaiman, Neil 1960- *228*
  Earlier sketches in SATA *85, 146, 197*
  See also CLR 109

Gaiman, Neil Richard
  See Gaiman, Neil
Gainer, Cindy 1962- 74
Gaines, Ernest J. 1933- 86
  See also CLR 62
Gaines, Ernest James
  See Gaines, Ernest J.
Gaither, Gloria 1942- 127
Gal, Laszlo 1933- 96
  Brief entry 32
  Earlier sketch in SATA 52
  See also CLR 61
Gal, Susan 228
Galbraith, Ben 1980- 200
Galbraith, Kathryn O. 1945- 219
  Earlier sketch in SATA 85
Galbraith, Kathryn Osebold
  See Galbraith, Kathryn O.
Galdone, Paul 1907(?)-1986 66
  Obituary 49
  Earlier sketch in SATA 17
  See also CLR 16
Galindo, Claudia 1979- 203
Galinsky, Ellen 1942- 23
Gall, Chris 1961- 176
Gallagher, Diana G. 1946- 153
Gallagher, Lurlene Nora
  See McDaniel, Lurlene
Gallagher-Cole, Mernie 1958- 206
Gallant, Roy A(rthur) 1924- 110
  Earlier sketches in SATA 4, 68
  See also CLR 30
Gallardo, Evelyn 1948- 78
Gallaz, Christophe 1948- 162
  See also CLR 126
Gallego Garcia, Laura 1977- 173
Gallico, Paul 1897-1976 13
Gallico, Paul William
  See Gallico, Paul
Gallo, Donald R. 1938- 112
  Autobiography Feature 104
Gallo, Donald Robert
  See Gallo, Donald R.
Galloway, Owateka (S.) 1981- 121
Galloway, Priscilla 1930- 227
  Earlier sketches in SATA 66, 112
Gallup, Joan 1957- 128
Galouchko, Annouchka Gravel 1960- 95
Galt, Thomas Franklin, Jr. 1908-1989 5
Galt, Tom
  See Galt, Thomas Franklin, Jr.
Galvin, Matthew R. 1950- 93
Galvin, Matthew Reppert
  See Galvin, Matthew R.
Gamble, Kim 1952- 183
  Earlier sketches in SATA 81, 124
Gambrell, Jamey 82
Gamerman, Martha 1941- 15
Gammell, Stephen 1943- 226
  Earlier sketches in SATA 53, 81, 128
  See also CLR 83
Ganly, Helen (Mary) 1940- 56
Gannett, Ruth Chrisman (Arens)
  1896-1979 33
Gannett, Ruth Stiles 1923- 3
Gannij, Joan 208
Gannij, Joan Levine
  See Gannij, Joan
Gannon, Ned 1974- 205
Gannon, Robert Haines 1931- 8
Gano, Lila 1949- 76
Gans, Roma 1894-1996 45
  Obituary 93
Gant, Matthew
  See Hano, Arnold
Gantner, Susan (Verble) 1939- 63
Gantos, Jack 1951- 169
  Earlier sketches in SATA 20, 81, 119
  See also CLR 85
Gantos, John Bryan, Jr.
  See Gantos, Jack

Ganz, Yaffa 1938- 61
  Brief entry 52
Garafano, Marie 1942- 84
Garant, Andre J. 1968- 123
Garbe, Ruth Moore
  See Moore, Ruth (Ellen)
Garber, Esther
  See Lee, Tanith
Garcia, Cristina 1958- 208
Garcia, Emma 1969- 198
Garcia, Geronimo 1960- 222
Garcia, Kami 1972- 229
Garcia, Yolanda P. 1952- 113
Garcia, Yolanda Pacheco
  See Garcia, Yolanda P.
Gard, Janice
  See Latham, Jean Lee
Gard, Joyce
  See Reeves, Joyce
Gard, Robert Edward 1910-1992 18
  Obituary 74
Gard, (Sanford) Wayne 1899-1986
  Obituary 49
Gardam, Jane 1928- 130
  Brief entry 28
  Earlier sketches in SATA 39, 76
  See also CLR 12
  See also SAAS 9
Gardam, Jane Mary
  See Gardam, Jane
Gardella, Tricia 1944- 96
Garden, Nancy 1938- 147
  Autobiography Feature 147
  Earlier sketches in SATA 12, 77, 114
  See also CLR 51
  See also SAAS 8
Gardiner, John Reynolds 1944-2006 64
  Obituary 174
Gardiner, Lindsey 1971- 144
Gardner, Craig Shaw 1949- 99
Gardner, Dic
  See Gardner, Richard (M.)
Gardner, Graham 159
Gardner, Hugh 1910-1986
  Obituary 49
Gardner, Jane Mylum 1946- 83
Gardner, Jeanne LeMonnier 1925- 5
Gardner, John, Jr. 1933-1982 40
  Obituary 31
Gardner, John Champlin, Jr.
  See Gardner, John, Jr.
Gardner, John E(dward) 1917- 192
Gardner, Lyn 192
Gardner, Martin 1914-2010 142
  Earlier sketch in SATA 16
Gardner, Miriam
  See Bradley, Marion Zimmer
Gardner, Richard (M.) 1931- 24
Gardner, Richard A(lan) 1931-2003 13
  Obituary 144
Gardner, Sally 229
  Earlier sketch in SATA 177
Gardner, Sandra 1940- 70
Gardner, Scot 1968- 143
Gardner, Sheldon 1934- 33
Gardner, Ted
  See Gardner, Theodore Roosevelt II
Gardner, Theodore Roosevelt
  See Gardner, Theodore Roosevelt II
Gardner, Theodore Roosevelt II 1934- 84
Garelick, May 1910-1989 19
Garfield, James B. 1881-1984 6
  Obituary 38
Garfield, Leon 1921-1996 76
  Obituary 90
  Earlier sketches in SATA 1, 32
  See also CLR 166
Garfinkle, Debra L.
  See Garfinkle, D.L.
Garfinkle, D.L. 187
Garis, Howard R. 1873-1962 13

Garis, Howard Roger
  See Garis, Howard R.
Garland, Mark 1953- 79
Garland, Mark A.
  See Garland, Mark
Garland, Michael 1952- 208
  Earlier sketch in SATA 168
Garland, Sarah 1944- 135
  Earlier sketch in SATA 62
Garland, Sherry 1948- 145
  Autobiography Feature 145
  Earlier sketches in SATA 73, 114
Garner, Alan 1934- 69
  Autobiography Feature 108
  Earlier sketch in SATA 18
  See also CLR 130
Garner, David 1958- 78
Garner, Eleanor Ramrath 1930- 122
Garner, James Finn 1960(?)- 92
Garnet, A. H.
  See Slote, Alfred
Garnett, Eve C. R. 1900-1991 3
  Obituary 70
Garofoli, Viviana 1970- 186
Garou, Louis P.
  See Bowkett, Stephen
Garraty, John A. 1920-2007 23
  Obituary 189
Garraty, John Arthur
  See Garraty, John A.
Garren, Devorah-Leah
  See Devorah-Leah
Garret, Maxwell R. 1917- 39
Garretson, Victoria Diane
  See Cox, Victoria
Garrett, Helen 1895- 21
Garrett, Randall 1927-1987 180
Garrett, Richard 1920- 82
Garrigue, Sheila 1931- 21
Garrison, Barbara 1931- 163
  Earlier sketch in SATA 19
Garrison, Frederick
  See Sinclair, Upton
Garrison, Mary 1952- 146
Garrison, Peter
  See Gardner, Craig Shaw
Garrison, Webb B(lack) 1919-2000 25
Garrity, Jennifer Johnson 1961- 124
Garrity, Linda K. 1947- 128
Garsee, Jeannine 199
Garst, Doris Shannon 1894-1981 1
Garst, Shannon
  See Garst, Doris Shannon
Garth, Will
  See Hamilton, Edmond
  and Kuttner, Henry
Garthwaite, Marion H(ook) 1893-1981 7
Garton, Malinda D(ean) (?)-1976
  Obituary 26
Garvie, Maureen 1944- 175
Garvie, Maureen McCallum
  See Garvie, Maureen
Garza, Carmen Lomas 1948- 182
Garza, Xavier 184
Gascoigne, Bamber 1935- 62
Gaskins, Pearl Fuyo 1957- 134
Gasperini, Jim 1952- 54
  Brief entry 49
Gater, Dilys 1944- 41
Gates, Doris 1901-1987 34
  Obituary 54
  Earlier sketch in SATA 1
  See also SAAS 1
Gates, Frieda 1933- 26
Gates, Susan 1950- 153
Gates, Viola R. 1931- 101
Gathorne-Hardy, Jonathan G. 1933- 124
  Earlier sketch in SATA 26
Gatti, Anne 1952- 103
Gatty, Juliana Horatia
  See Ewing, Juliana (Horatia Gatty)

Gauch, Patricia Lee 1934- 228
    Earlier sketches in SATA 26, 80
    See also CLR 56
    See also SAAS 21
Gauch, Sarah 223
Gaudasinska, Elzbieta 1943- 190
Gaul, Randy 1959- 63
Gault, Clare 1925- 36
Gault, Frank 1926-1982 36
    Brief entry 30
Gault, William Campbell 1910-1995 8
Gauthier, Gail 1953- 203
    Earlier sketches in SATA 118, 160
Gaver, Becky
    See Gaver, Rebecca
Gaver, Rebecca 1952- 20
Gavin, Jamila 1941- 223
    Earlier sketches in SATA 96, 125
Gay, Amelia
    See Hogarth, Grace (Weston Allen)
Gay, Francis
    See Gee, H(erbert) L(eslie)
Gay, Kathlyn 1930- 144
    Earlier sketch in SATA 9
Gay, Marie-Louise 1952- 179
    Earlier sketches in SATA 68, 126
    See also CLR 27
    See also SAAS 21
Gay, Michel 1947- 162
Gay, Zhenya 1906-1978 19
Gaze, Gillian
    See Barklem, Jill
Gear, Kathleen M. O'Neal
    See Gear, Kathleen O'Neal
Gear, Kathleen O'Neal 1954- 224
    Earlier sketches in SATA 71, 166
Gear, W. Michael 1955- 224
    Earlier sketches in SATA 71, 166
Geary, Rick 1946- 142
Geason, Susan 1946- 122
Gedalof, Robin
    See McGrath, Robin
Gedge, Pauline (Alice) 1945- 101
Gee, H(erbert) L(eslie) 1901-1977
    Obituary 26
Gee, Maurice 1931- 227
    Earlier sketches in SATA 46, 101
    See also CLR 56
Gee, Maurice Gough
    See Gee, Maurice
Geehan, Wayne (E.) 1947- 107
Geer, Charles 1922- 42
    Brief entry 32
Geeslin, Campbell 1925- 163
    Earlier sketch in SATA 107
Gehman, Mary W. 1923- 86
Gehr, Mary 1910(?)-1997 32
    Obituary 99
Geipel, Eileen 1932- 30
Geis, Alissa Imre 1976- 189
Geis, Darlene Stern 1918(?)-1999 7
    Obituary 111
Geisel, Helen 1898-1967 26
Geisel, Theodor Seuss
    See Dr. Seuss
Geisert, Arthur 1941- 171
    Brief entry 52
    Earlier sketches in SATA 56, 92, 133
    See also CLR 87
    See also SAAS 23
Geisert, Arthur Frederick
    See Geisert, Arthur
Geisert, Bonnie 1942- 165
    Earlier sketch in SATA 92
Geist, Ken 191
Gelber, Lisa 210
Geldart, William 1936- 15
Gelinas, Paul J. 1904-1996 10
Gellis, Roberta 1927- 128
Gellis, Roberta Leah Jacobs
    See Gellis, Roberta

Gellman, Marc 112
Gelman, Amy 1961- 72
Gelman, Jan 1963- 58
Gelman, Rita Golden 1937- 131
    Brief entry 51
    Earlier sketch in SATA 84
Gelman, Steve 1934- 3
Gemignani, Tony 1973- 220
Gemming, Elizabeth 1932- 11
Gendel, Evelyn W. 1916(?)-1977
    Obituary 27
Gennaro, Joseph F., Jr. 1924- 53
Gennaro, Joseph Francis, Jr.
    See Gennaro, Joseph F., Jr.
Gentieu, Penny 204
Gentile, Petrina 1969- 91
Gentle, Mary 1956- 48
Gentleman, David (William) 1930- 7
Gentry, Marita 215
Geoghegan, Adrienne 1962- 143
George, Barbara
    See Katz, Bobbi
George, Emily
    See Katz, Bobbi
George, Gail
    See Katz, Bobbi
George, Jean
    See George, Jean Craighead
George, Jean C.
    See George, Jean Craighead
George, Jean Craighead 1919- 226
    Earlier sketches in SATA 2, 68, 124, 170
    See also CLR 136
George, Jessica Day 1976- 210
George, John L(othar) 1916- 2
George, Kristine O'Connell 1954- 156
    Earlier sketch in SATA 110
George, Lindsay Barrett 1952- 206
    Earlier sketches in SATA 95, 155
George, S. C. 1898- 11
George, Sally
    See Orr, Wendy
George, Sidney Charles
    See George, S. C.
George, Twig C. 1950- 114
George, W(illiam) Lloyd 1900(?)-1975
    Obituary 30
Georgiou, Constantine 1927- 7
Georgiou, Theo
    See Odgers, Sally Farrell
Geraghty, Paul 1959- 130
Gerard, Jean Ignace Isidore 1803-1847 45
Geras, Adele 1944- 180
    Autobiography Feature 180
    Earlier sketches in SATA 23, 87, 129, 173
    See also SAAS 21
Geras, Adele Daphne Weston
    See Geras, Adele
Gerber, Carole 1947- 207
Gerber, Linda 213
Gerber, Merrill Joan 1938- 170
    Autobiography Feature 170
    Earlier sketches in SATA 64, 127
Gerber, Perren 1933- 104
Gerberg, Mort 1931- 64
Gergely, Tibor 1900-1978 54
    Obituary 20
Geringer, Laura 1948- 164
    Earlier sketches in SATA 29, 94
Gerler, William R(obert) 1917-1996 47
Gerrard, Jean 1933- 51
Gerrard, Roy 1935-1997 90
    Brief entry 45
    Obituary 99
    Earlier sketch in SATA 47
    See also CLR 23
Gerritsen, Paula 1956- 177
Gerrold, David 1944- 144
    Earlier sketch in SATA 66
Gershator, David 1937- 180

Gershator, Phillis 1942- 188
    Earlier sketches in SATA 90, 158
Gershon, Dann 1955- 187
Gershon, Gina 1962- 187
Gerson, Corinne 1927- 37
Gerson, Mary-Joan 136
    Earlier sketch in SATA 79
Gerson, Noel Bertram 1914-1988 22
    Obituary 60
Gerstein, Mordicai 1935- 222
    Brief entry 36
    Earlier sketches in SATA 47, 81, 142, 178
    See also CLR 102
Gertridge, Allison 1967- 132
Gervais, Bernadette 1959- 80
Gervay, Susanne 183
Gesner, Clark 1938-2002 40
    Obituary 143
Gessner, Lynne 1919- 16
Geter, Tyrone 150
Getz, David 1957- 91
Getzinger, Donna 1968- 128
Geus, Mireille 1964- 207
Gevirtz, Eliezer 1950- 49
Gevry, Claudine 188
Gewe, Raddory
    See Gorey, Edward (St. John)
Ghan, Linda (R.) 1947- 77
Ghent, Natale 1962- 148
Gherman, Beverly 1934- 123
    Earlier sketch in SATA 68
Ghigna, Charles 1946- 153
    Earlier sketch in SATA 108
Giacobbe, Beppe 1953- 174
Giambastiani, Kurt R. A. 1958- 141
Giannini, Enzo 1946- 68
Gibala-Broxholm, Scott 1959(?)- 205
Gibbons, Alan 1953- 198
    Earlier sketch in SATA 124
Gibbons, Faye 1938- 103
    Earlier sketch in SATA 65
Gibbons, Gail 1944- 201
    Earlier sketches in SATA 23, 72, 104, 160
    See also CLR 8
    See also SAAS 12
Gibbons, Gail Gretchen
    See Gibbons, Gail
Gibbons, Kaye 1960- 117
Gibbs, Adrea 1960- 126
Gibbs, Alonzo (Lawrence) 1915-1992 5
Gibbs, (Cecilia) May 1877-1969
    Obituary 27
Gibbs, Tony
    See Gibbs, Wolcott, Jr.
Gibbs, Wolcott, Jr. 1935- 40
Giblin, James Cross 1933- 197
    Earlier sketches in SATA 33, 75, 122
    See also CLR 29
    See also SAAS 12
Gibson, Andrew (William) 1949- 72
Gibson, Barbara L. 205
Gibson, Barbara Leonard
    See Gibson, Barbara L.
Gibson, Betty 1911- 75
Gibson, Jo
    See Fluke, Joanne
Gibson, Josephine
    See Hine, Sesyle Joslin
    and Hine, Al(fred Blakelee)
Gibson, Marley 1966- 225
Gibson, Sarah P. 1962- 211
Gibson, William 1914-2008 66
    Obituary 199
Gibson, William Ford
    See Gibson, William
Gidal, Nachum
    See Gidal, Tim Nachum
Gidal, Sonia (Epstein) 1922- 2
Gidal, Tim Nachum 1909-1996 2
Gidalewitsch, Nachum
    See Gidal, Tim Nachum

Gideon, Melanie 1963- 175
Giegling, John A(llan) 1935- 17
Gifaldi, David 1950- 209
   Earlier sketch in SATA 76
Giff, Patricia Reilly 1935- 203
   Earlier sketches in SATA 33, 70, 121, 160
Giffard, Hannah 1962- 83
Gifford, Carrie 224
Gifford, Clive 1966- 198
Gifford, Griselda 1931- 171
   Earlier sketch in SATA 42
Gifford, Kerri 1961- 91
Gifford, Peggy 1952- 191
Gilbert, Ann
   See Taylor, Ann
Gilbert, Anne Yvonne 1951- 185
Gilbert, Barbara Snow 1954- 97
Gilbert, Catherine
   See Murdock, Catherine Gilbert
Gilbert, Frances
   See Collings, Gillian
Gilbert, Harriett 1948- 30
Gilbert, (Agnes) Joan (Sewell) 1931- 10
Gilbert, John (Raphael) 1926- 36
Gilbert, Nan
   See Gilbertson, Mildred Geiger
Gilbert, Roby Goodale 1966- 90
Gilbert, Ruth Gallard Ainsworth
   See Ainsworth, Ruth (Gallard)
Gilbert, Sara (Dulaney) 1943- 82
   Earlier sketch in SATA 11
Gilbert, Sheri L. 157
Gilbert, Suzie 1956- 97
Gilbert, W(illiam) S(chwenck) 1836-1911 ... 36
Gilbert, Yvonne
   See Gilbert, Anne Yvonne
Gilbertson, Mildred Geiger 1908-1988 2
Gilbreath, Alice 1921- 12
Gilbreth, Frank B., Jr. 1911-2001 2
Gilbreth, Frank Bunker
   See Gilbreth, Frank B., Jr.
Gilchrist, Jan Spivey 1949- 130
   Earlier sketch in SATA 72
Gilden, Mel 1947- 97
Giles, Gail 196
   Earlier sketch in SATA 152
Gilfond, Henry 2
Gilge, Jeanette 1924- 22
Gili, Phillida 1944- 70
Gill, Derek (Lewis Theodore) 1919-1997 9
Gill, Margery Jean 1925- 22
Gill, Shelley 176
Gill, Stephen 1932- 63
Gillespie, Carol Ann 1951- 158
Gillett, Mary (Bledsoe) 7
Gillette, Henry Sampson 1915- 14
Gillette, J. Lynett 1946- 103
Gillette, Jan Lynett
   See Gillette, J. Lynett
Gilley, Jeremy 1969- 174
Gillham, Bill
   See Gillham, W(illiam) E(dwin) C(harles)
Gillham, W(illiam) E(dwin) C(harles)
   1936- 42
Gilliam, Stan 1946- 39
   Brief entry 35
Gilliland, Alexis A. 1931- 72
Gilliland, Alexis Arnaldus
   See Gilliland, Alexis A.
Gilliland, (Cleburne) Hap 1918- 92
Gilliland, Judith Heide 180
Gillmor, Don 1954- 127
Gilman, Dorothy 1923- 5
Gilman, Esther 1925- 15
Gilman, Laura Anne 178
Gilman, Phoebe 1940-2002 104
   Obituary 141
   Earlier sketch in SATA 58
Gilmore, Iris 1900-1982 22
Gilmore, Kate 1931- 87
Gilmore, Mary (Jean Cameron) 1865-1962 . 49

Gilmore, Rachna 1953- 209
Gilmore, Susan 1954- 59
Gilpin, Stephen 213
   Earlier sketch in SATA 177
Gilroy, Beryl (Agatha) 1924- 80
Gilson, Barbara
   See Gilson, Charles James Louis
Gilson, Charles James Louis 1878-1943
   See YABC 2
Gilson, Jamie 1933- 176
   Brief entry 34
   Earlier sketches in SATA 37, 91
Gimpel, Carolyn
   See Hart, Carolyn
Ginsberg, Blaze 1987- 222
Ginsburg, Mirra 1909-2000 92
   Earlier sketch in SATA 6
   See also CLR 45
Giovanni, Nikki 1943- 208
   Earlier sketches in SATA 24, 107
   See also CLR 73
Giovanni, Yolanda Cornelia
   See Giovanni, Nikki
Giovanni, Yolande Cornelia
   See Giovanni, Nikki
Giovanni, Yolande Cornelia, Jr.
   See Giovanni, Nikki
Giovanopoulos, Paul (Arthur) 1939- 7
Gipson, Billie
   See Letts, Billie
Gipson, Fred(erick Benjamin) 1908-1973 2
   Obituary 24
Girard, Linda (Walvoord) 1942- 41
Giraudon, David 1975- 215
Girion, Barbara 1937- 78
   Earlier sketch in SATA 26
   See also SAAS 14
Girl, Nerdy
   See Castellucci, Cecil
Girouard, Patrick 1957- 155
Girzone, Joseph F. 1930- 76
Girzone, Joseph Francis
   See Girzone, Joseph F.
Gise, Joanne
   See Mattern, Joanne
Gist, E.M. 206
Gittings, Jo (Grenville) Manton 1919- 3
Gittings, Robert (William Victor) 1911-1992 . 6
   Obituary 70
Givens, Janet E(aton) 1932- 60
Givner, Joan 1936- 171
Givner, Joan Mary
   See Givner, Joan
Gladstone, Eve
   See Werner, Herma
Gladstone, Gary 1935- 12
Gladstone, M(yron) J. 1923- 37
Glanville, Brian (Lester) 1931- 42
Glanzman, Louis S. 1922- 36
Glaser, Byron 1954- 154
Glaser, Dianne E(lizabeth) 1937- 50
   Brief entry 31
Glaser, Isabel Joshlin 1929- 94
Glaser, Linda 225
Glaser, Milton 1929- 151
   Earlier sketch in SATA 11
Glaser, Shirley 151
Glaspell, Susan 1882(?)-1948
   See YABC 2
Glass, Andrew 1949- 223
   Brief entry 46
   Earlier sketches in SATA 90, 150
Glass, Linzi 175
Glass, Linzi Alex
   See Glass, Linzi
Glasscock, Amnesia
   See Steinbeck, John
Glassman, Bruce 1961- 76
Glatt, Lisa 1963- 217
Glauber, Uta (Heil) 1936- 17
Glazer, Thomas (Zachariah) 1914-2003 9

Glazer, Tom
   See Glazer, Thomas (Zachariah)
Gleasner, Diana (Cottle) 1936- 29
Gleason, Judith 1929- 24
Gleason, Katherine (A.) 1960- 104
Gleeson, Libby 1950- 142
   Autobiography Feature 142
   Earlier sketches in SATA 82, 118
Gleiter, Jan 1947- 111
Gleitzman, Morris 1953- 156
   Earlier sketch in SATA 88
   See also CLR 88
Glen, Maggie 1944- 88
Glendinning, Richard 1917-1988 24
Glendinning, Sally
   See Glendinning, Sara W(ilson)
Glendinning, Sara W(ilson) 1913-1993 24
Glenn, John W. 195
Glenn, Mel 1943- 93
   Brief entry 45
   Earlier sketch in SATA 51
   See also CLR 51
Glenn, Patricia Brown 1953- 86
Glenn, Sharlee 159
Glenn, Sharlee Mullins
   See Glenn, Sharlee
Glennon, Karen M. 1946- 85
Gles, Margaret Breitmaier 1940- 22
Glick, Carl (Cannon) 1890-1971 14
Glick, Ruth 1942- 125
Glick, Ruth Burtnick
   See Glick, Ruth
Glick, Virginia Kirkus 1893-1980
   Obituary 23
Gliewe, Unada (Grace) 1927- 3
Glimmerveen, Ulco 1958- 85
Glines, Carroll V(ane), Jr. 1920- 19
Gliori, Debi 1959- 189
   Earlier sketches in SATA 72, 138
Globe, Leah Ain 1900- 41
Glori Ann
   See Blakely, Gloria
Glovach, Linda 1947- 105
   Earlier sketch in SATA 7
Glover, Denis (James Matthews) 1912-1980 . 7
Glubok, Shirley (Astor) 146
   Autobiography Feature 146
   Earlier sketches in SATA 6, 68
   See also CLR 1
   See also SAAS 7
Gluck, Felix 1923-1981
   Obituary 25
Glyman, Caroline A. 1967- 103
Glynne-Jones, William 1907-1977 11
Gobbato, Imero 1923- 39
Gobbletree, Richard
   See Quackenbush, Robert M(ead)
Goble, Dorothy 26
Goble, Paul 1933- 131
   Earlier sketches in SATA 25, 69
   See also CLR 21
Goble, Warwick (?)-1943 46
Godden, (Margaret) Rumer 1907-1998 36
   Obituary 109
   Earlier sketch in SATA 3
   See also CLR 20
   See also SAAS 12
Gode, Alexander
   See Gode von Aesch, Alexander (Gottfried
   Friedrich)
Gode von Aesch, Alexander (Gottfried
   Friedrich) 1906-1970 14
Godfrey, Jane
   See Bowden, Joan Chase
Godfrey, Martyn
   See Godfrey, Martyn N.
   and Godfrey, Martyn N.
Godfrey, Martyn N. 1949-2000 95
   See also CLR 57
Godfrey, William
   See Youd, Samuel

Godkin, Celia 1948- 145
   Earlier sketch in SATA 66
Godkin, Celia Marilyn
   See Godkin, Celia
Godon, Ingrid 1958- 186
Godown, Jan
   See Annino, Jan Godown
Godwin, Laura 1956- 179
Godwin, Sam
   See Pirotta, Saviour
Godwin, Sarah Massini
   See Massini, Sarah
Goede, Irene 1966- 208
Goedecke, Christopher (John) 1951- 81
Goekler, Susan
   See Wooley, Susan Frelick
Goembel, Ponder 204
Goertzen, Glenda 172
Goettel, Elinor 1930- 12
Goetz, Delia 1898-1996 22
   Obituary 91
Goffe, Toni 1936- 61
Goffstein, Brooke
   See Goffstein, Marilyn Brooke
Goffstein, M. B.
   See Goffstein, Marilyn Brooke
Goffstein, Marilyn Brooke 1940- 70
   Earlier sketch in SATA 8
   See also CLR 3
Goforth, Ellen
   See Francis, Dorothy
Gogol, Sara 1948-2004 80
Goh, Chan Hon 1969- 145
Going, Kelly L.
   See Going, K.L.
Going, Kelly Louise
   See Going, K.L.
Going, K.L. 199
   Earlier sketch in SATA 156
Golann, Cecil Paige 1921-1995 11
Golbin, Andree 1923- 15
Gold, Alison Leslie 1945- 104
Gold, August 1955- 215
Gold, Bernice 150
Gold, Phyllis
   See Goldberg, Phyllis
Gold, Robert S(tanley) 1924- 63
Gold, Sharlya 9
Gold, Susan
   See Gold, Susan Dudley
Gold, Susan Dudley 1949- 147
Goldbach, Veronica 1980- 220
Goldberg, Grace 1956- 78
Goldberg, Herbert S. 1926- 25
Goldberg, Jacob 1943- 94
Goldberg, Jake
   See Goldberg, Jacob
Goldberg, Myla 1972(?)- 210
Goldberg, Phyllis 1941- 21
Goldberg, Stan J. 1939- 26
Goldberg, Susan 1948- 71
Goldberg, Whoopi 1955- 119
Goldberger, Judith M. 1948- 80
Goldblatt, Stacey 1969(?)- 191
Golden, Christie 1963- 167
   Earlier sketch in SATA 116
Goldentyer, Debra 1960- 84
Goldfeder, Cheryl
   See Pahz, Cheryl Suzanne
Goldfeder, James
   See Pahz, James Alon
Goldfeder, Jim
   See Pahz, James Alon
Goldfinger, Jennifer P. 1963- 185
Goldfrank, Helen Colodny 1912- 6
Goldin, Augusta 1906-1999 13
Goldin, Barbara Diamond 1946- 129
   Autobiography Feature 129
   Earlier sketch in SATA 92
   See also SAAS 26
Goldin, David 1963- 101

Golding, Julia 1969- 188
Golding, Theresa Martin 1960- 150
Golding, William 1911-1993
   See CLR 130
Golding, William Gerald
   See Golding, William
Goldman, Alex J. 1917- 65
Goldman, E. M. 1943- 103
Goldman, Eleanor Maureen
   See Goldman, E. M.
Goldman, Elizabeth 1949- 90
Goldman, Judy 1955- 212
Goldman, Steven 1964- 207
Goldman, Todd Harris 221
Goldring, Ann 1937- 149
Golds, Cassandra 1962- 226
Goldsborough, June 1923- 19
Goldschmidt, Judy 202
Goldsmith, Connie 1945- 147
Goldsmith, Howard 1943- 108
   Earlier sketch in SATA 24
Goldsmith, John Herman Thorburn 1903-1987
   Obituary 52
Goldsmith, Oliver 1730(?)-1774 26
Goldsmith, Ruth M. 1919- 62
Goldstein, Nathan 1927- 47
Goldstein, Philip 1910-1997 23
Goldston, Robert (Conroy) 1927- 6
Goldstone, Bruce 183
Goldstone, Lawrence A.
   See Treat, Lawrence
Goldszmit, Henryk 1878-1942 65
   See also CLR 152
Golembe, Carla 1951- 79
Golenbock, Peter 1946- 99
Goll, Reinhold W(eimar) 1897-1993 26
Gollub, Matthew 1960- 134
   Earlier sketch in SATA 83
Golson, Terry 213
Golson, Terry Blonder
   See Golson, Terry
Gomes, Filomena 1965- 183
Gomez, Elena 191
Gomez, Elizabeth 133
Gomez-Freer, Elizabeth
   See Gomez, Elizabeth
Gomi, Taro 1945- 103
   Earlier sketch in SATA 64
   See also CLR 57
Gondosch, Linda 1944- 58
Gonsalves, Rob 1959- 209
Gonyea, Mark 194
Gonzalez, Catherine Troxell 1917-2000 87
Gonzalez, Christina
   See Gonzalez, Maya Christina
Gonzalez, Gloria 1940- 23
Gonzalez, Julie 1958- 174
Gonzalez, Julie Sehers
   See Gonzalez, Julie
Gonzalez, Lucia M. 1957- 202
Gonzalez, Maya
   See Gonzalez, Maya Christina
Gonzalez, Maya Christina 1964- 175
   Earlier sketch in SATA 115
Gonzalez, Rigoberto 1970- 147
Goobie, Beth 1959- 128
Good, Alice 1950- 73
Good, Clare
   See Romano, Clare
Good, Karen Hillard 214
Goodall, Daphne Machin
   See Machin Goodall, Daphne (Edith)
Goodall, Jane 1934- 111
Goodall, John S(trickland) 1908-1996 66
   Obituary 91
   Earlier sketch in SATA 4
   See also CLR 25
Goodbody, Slim
   See Burstein, John
Goode, Diane 1949- 225
   Earlier sketches in SATA 15, 84, 114, 170

Goode, Diane Capuozzo
   See Goode, Diane
Goode, Stephen Ray 1943- 55
   Brief entry 40
Goodenow, Earle 1913- 40
Goodhart, Pippa 1958- 196
   Earlier sketch in SATA 153
Goodhue, Thomas W. 1949- 143
Goodin, Sallie (Brown) 1953- 74
Goodman, Alison 1966- 111
Goodman, Deborah Lerme 1956- 50
   Brief entry 49
Goodman, Elaine 1930- 9
Goodman, Emily 217
Goodman, Joan Elizabeth 1950- 162
   Earlier sketches in SATA 50, 94
Goodman, Susan E. 1952- 181
Goodman, Walter 1927-2002 9
Goodman Koz, Paula 211
Goodrich, Carter 1959(?)- 221
Goodrich, Samuel Griswold 1793-1860 23
Goodsell, Jane Neuberger 1921(?)-1988
   Obituary 56
Goodweather, Hartley
   See King, Thomas
GoodWeather, Hartley
   See King, Thomas
Goodwin, Hal
   See Goodwin, Harold L(eland)
Goodwin, Harold L(eland) 1914-1990 51
   Obituary 65
   Earlier sketch in SATA 13
Goodwin, William 1943- 117
Goor, Nancy (Ruth Miller) 1944- 39
   Brief entry 34
Goor, Ron(ald Stephen) 1940- 39
   Brief entry 34
Goossen, Agnes
   See Epp, Margaret A(gnes)
Goossens, Philippe 1963- 195
Gootman, Marilyn E. 1944- 179
Gopnik, Adam 1956- 171
Gorbachev, Valeri 1944- 222
   Autobiography Feature 143
   Earlier sketches in SATA 98, 143, 184
Gordion, Mark
   See Turtledove, Harry
Gordon, Ad
   See Hano, Arnold
Gordon, Amy 1949- 197
   Earlier sketches in SATA 115, 156
Gordon, Bernard Ludwig 1931-2010 27
Gordon, Colonel H. R.
   See Ellis, Edward S.
Gordon, David
   See Garrett, Randall
Gordon, Donald
   See Payne, Donald Gordon
Gordon, Dorothy 1893-1970 20
Gordon, Esther S(aranga) 1935- 10
Gordon, Frederick 1
Gordon, Gaelyn 1939-1997
   See CLR 75
Gordon, Garrett
   See Garrett, Randall
Gordon, Gary
   See Edmonds, I(vy) G(ordon)
Gordon, Hal
   See Goodwin, Harold L(eland)
Gordon, Jeffie Ross
   See Enderle, Judith (Ann) Ross
   and Gordon, Stephanie Jacob
Gordon, John
   See Gesner, Clark
Gordon, John (William) 1925- 84
Gordon, Lew
   See Baldwin, Gordon C(ortis)
Gordon, Margaret (Anna) 1939- 9
Gordon, Mike 1948- 101
Gordon, Mildred 1912-1979
   Obituary 24

Gordon, Selma
    See Lanes, Selma G.
Gordon, Sheila 1927- 88
    See also CLR 27
Gordon, Shirley 1921- 48
    Brief entry 41
Gordon, Sol 1923- 11
Gordon, Stephanie Jacob 1940- 89
    Autobiography Feature 114
    Earlier sketch in SATA 64
    See also SAAS 26
Gordon, Stewart
    See Shirreffs, Gordon D(onald)
Gordons, The
    See Gordon, Mildred
    and Gordon, Gordon
Gore, Leonid 222
    Earlier sketch in SATA 185
Gorelick, Molly C(hernow) 1920-2003 9
    Obituary 153
Gorey, Edward (St. John) 1925-2000 70
    Brief entry 27
    Obituary 118
    Earlier sketch in SATA 29
    See also CLR 36
Gorham, Charles Orson 1868-1936 36
Gorham, Michael
    See Folsom, Franklin (Brewster)
Gorman, Carol 187
    Earlier sketch in SATA 150
Gorman, Jacqueline Laks 1955- 148
Gorman, Mike 206
Gormley, Beatrice 1942- 202
    Brief entry 35
    Earlier sketches in SATA 39, 127
Gorog, Judith (Katharine Allen) 1938- 75
    Earlier sketch in SATA 39
Gorrell, Gena K. 1946- 170
Gorsline, Douglas (Warner) 1913-1985 11
    Obituary 43
Gorsline, (Sally) Marie 1928- 28
Gorsline, S. M.
    See Gorsline, (Sally) Marie
Gorton, Julia 218
Gorton, Kaitlyn
    See Emerson, Kathy Lynn
Gorton, Kathy Lynn
    See Emerson, Kathy Lynn
Goryan, Sirak
    See Saroyan, William
Goschke, Julia 1973- 208
Goscinny, Rene 1926-1977 47
    Brief entry 39
    See also CLR 37
Goss, Clay(ton E.) 1946- 82
Goss, Gary 1947- 124
Goss, Mini 1963- 186
Goto, Scott 203
Gott, Barry 197
Gottesman, S. D.
    See Kornbluth, C(yril) M.
    and Lowndes, Robert A(ugustine) W(ard)
    and Pohl, Frederik
Gottfried, Ted
    See Gottfried, Theodore Mark
Gottfried, Theodore Mark 1928- 150
    Earlier sketch in SATA 85
Gottlieb, Gerald 1923- 7
Gottlieb, William P. 1917-2006 24
Gottlieb, William Paul
    See Gottlieb, William P.
Goudey, Alice E(dwards) 1898-1993 20
Goudge, Eileen 1950- 88
Goudge, Elizabeth (de Beauchamp)
    1900-1984 2
    Obituary 38
    See also CLR 94
Gough, Catherine
    See Mulgan, Catherine
Gough, Philip 1908-1986 45
Gough, Sue 1940- 106

Goulart, Ron 1933- 67
    Earlier sketch in SATA 1
Goulart, Ronald Joseph
    See Goulart, Ron
Gould, Alberta 1945- 96
Gould, Chester 1900-1985 49
    Obituary 43
Gould, Jean R(osalind) 1909-1993 11
    Obituary 77
Gould, Lilian 6
Gould, Marilyn 1928- 76
    Earlier sketch in SATA 15
Gould, Robert 154
Gould, Steven 1955- 95
Gould, Steven Charles
    See Gould, Steven
Gourley, Catherine 1950- 190
    Earlier sketch in SATA 95
Gourse, Leslie 1939-2004 89
Govan, (Mary) Christine Noble 1898-1985 9
Gove, Doris 1944- 72
Govenar, Alan 1952- 189
Govenar, Alan Bruce
    See Govenar, Alan
Govern, Elaine 1939- 26
Gowen, L. Kris 1968- 156
Graaf, Peter
    See Youd, Samuel
Graber, Alexander 1914-1997 98
    Earlier sketch in SATA 7
Graber, George Alexander
    See Graber, Alexander
Graber, Janet 1942- 170
Graber, Richard (Fredrick) 1927- 26
Grabianski, Janusz 1928-1976 39
    Obituary 30
Graboff, Abner 1919-1986 35
Grace, Fran(ces Jane) 45
Grace, N.B.
    See Harper, Suzanne
Grace, Theresa
    See Mattern, Joanne
Gracza, Margaret Young 1928- 56
Graduate of Oxford, A
    See Ruskin, John
Grady, Denise 1952- 189
Graeber, Charlotte Towner 106
    Brief entry 44
    Earlier sketch in SATA 56
Graef, Renee 1956- 204
Graeme, Roderic
    See Jeffries, Roderic
Graf, Michael
    See Graf, Mike
Graf, Mike 1960- 164
Grafe, Max 198
Graff, Lisa 1981- 188
Graff, Polly Anne Colver
    See Colver, Anne
Graff, (S.) Stewart 1908-2009 9
Graham, Ada 1931- 11
Graham, Alastair 1945- 74
Graham, Arthur Kennon
    See Harrison, David L.
Graham, Bob 1942- 187
    Earlier sketches in SATA 63, 101, 151
    See also CLR 31
Graham, Brenda Knight 1942- 32
Graham, Charlotte
    See Bowden, Joan Chase
Graham, Christine 1952- 224
Graham, Eleanor 1896-1984 18
    Obituary 38
Graham, Ennis
    See Molesworth, Mary Louisa
Graham, Frank, Jr. 1925- 11
Graham, Georgia 1959- 190
Graham, Ian 1953- 229
    Earlier sketch in SATA 112
Graham, John 1926-2007 11

Graham, Kennon
    See Harrison, David L.
Graham, Larry
    See Graham, Lawrence
Graham, Lawrence 1962- 63
Graham, Lawrence Otis
    See Graham, Lawrence
Graham, Linda
    See Graham-Barber, Lynda
Graham, Lorenz (Bell) 1902-1989 74
    Obituary 63
    Earlier sketch in SATA 2
    See also CLR 10
    See also SAAS 5
Graham, Margaret Bloy 1920- 11
Graham, Robin Lee 1949- 7
Graham, Shirley 1896(?)-1977
    See Du Bois, Shirley Graham
Graham-Barber, Lynda 1944- 159
    Earlier sketch in SATA 42
Graham-Cameron, M.
    See Graham-Cameron, M(alcolm) G(ordon)
Graham-Cameron, M(alcolm) G(ordon)
    1931- 53
    Brief entry 45
Graham-Cameron, Mike
    See Graham-Cameron, M(alcolm) G(ordon)
Grahame, Kenneth 1859-1932 100
    See also YABC 1
    See also CLR 135
Gralley, Jean 166
Gramatky, Hardie 1907-1979 30
    Obituary 23
    Earlier sketch in SATA 1
    See also CLR 22
Grambling, Lois G. 1927- 206
    Earlier sketches in SATA 71, 148
Grambo, Rebecca L(ynn) 1963- 109
Grammer, June Amos 1927- 58
Grand, Samuel 1912-1988 42
Grandits, John 1949- 192
GrandPre, Mary 1954- 229
    Earlier sketch in SATA 184
Grandville, J. J.
    See Gerard, Jean Ignace Isidore
Grandville, Jean Ignace Isidore Gerard
    See Gerard, Jean Ignace Isidore
Granfield, Linda 1950- 160
    Earlier sketch in SATA 96
Grange, Peter
    See Nicole, Christopher
Granger, Margaret Jane 1925(?)-1977
    Obituary 27
Granger, Michele 1949- 88
Granger, Peggy
    See Granger, Margaret Jane
Granowsky, Alvin 1936- 101
Granstaff, Bill 1925- 10
Granstrom, Brita 1969- 224
    Earlier sketches in SATA 111, 167
Grant, Bruce 1893-1977 5
    Obituary 25
Grant, Cynthia D. 1950- 147
    Earlier sketches in SATA 33, 77
Grant, Eva 1907-1996 7
Grant, Evva H. 1913-1977
    Obituary 27
Grant, Gordon 1875-1962 25
Grant, Gwen(doline Ellen) 1940- 47
Grant, Judyann Ackerman 211
Grant, Katie M.
    See Grant, K.M.
Grant, K.M. 175
Grant, (Alice) Leigh 1947- 10
Grant, Matthew G.
    See May, Julian
Grant, Maxwell
    See Gibson, Walter B(rown)
    and Lynds, Dennis
Grant, Melvyn 183
Grant, Myrna (Lois) 1934- 21

Grant, Neil 1938- *154*
Earlier sketch in SATA *14*
Grant, Nicholas
See Nicole, Christopher
Grant, Richard 1948- *80*
Grant, Skeeter
See Spiegelman, Art
Grater, Michael 1923- *57*
Gratz, Alan 1972- *212*
Graullera, Fabiola
See Graullera Ramirez, Fabiola
Graullera Ramirez, Fabiola *225*
Gravel, Fern
See Hall, James Norman
Gravelle, Karen 1942- *166*
Earlier sketch in SATA *78*
Graves, Charles Parlin 1911-1972 .... *4*
Graves, Keith *191*
Earlier sketch in SATA *156*
Graves, Robert 1895-1985 .... *45*
Graves, Robert von Ranke
See Graves, Robert
Graves, Valerie
See Bradley, Marion Zimmer
Gravett, Emily 1972(?)- *189*
Gray, Betsy
See Poole, Gray Johnson
Gray, Caroline
See Nicole, Christopher
Gray, Claudia *213*
Gray, Dianne E. *183*
Gray, Elizabeth Janet
See Vining, Elizabeth Gray
Gray, Genevieve S(tuck) 1920-1995 .... *4*
Gray, Harold (Lincoln) 1894-1968 .... *33*
Brief entry *32*
Gray, Jenny
See Gray, Genevieve S(tuck)
Gray, John Lee
See Jakes, John
Gray, Judith A. 1949- *93*
Gray, Judith Anne
See Gray, Judith A.
Gray, Keith *151*
Gray, Kes 1960- *153*
Gray, Les 1929- *82*
Gray, Libba Moore 1937- *83*
Gray, Luli 1945- *149*
Earlier sketch in SATA *90*
Gray, Marian
See Pierce, Edith Gray
Gray, Nicholas Stuart 1922-1981 .... *4*
Obituary *27*
Gray, Nigel 1941- *104*
Earlier sketch in SATA *33*
Gray, (Lucy) Noel (Clervaux) 1898-1983 .... *47*
Gray, Patricia (Clark) *7*
Gray, Patsey
See Gray, Patricia (Clark)
Gray, Rita *184*
Graydon, Shari 1958- *158*
Grayland, V. Merle
See Grayland, Valerie (Merle Spanner)
Grayland, Valerie (Merle Spanner) *7*
Grayson, Devin (Kalile) 1970- *119*
Grayson, Kristine
See Rusch, Kristine Kathryn
Grayson, Paul 1946- *79*
Graystone, Lynn
See Brennan, Joseph Lomas
Great Comte, The
See Hawkesworth, Eric
Greaves, Margaret 1914-1995 .... *87*
Earlier sketch in SATA *7*
Greaves, Nick 1955- *77*
Greban, Quentin 1977- *223*
Gree, Alain 1936- *28*
Green, Adam
See Weisgard, Leonard (Joseph)
Green, Anne Canevari 1943- *62*

Green, Brian
See Card, Orson Scott
Green, Cliff(ord) 1934- *126*
Green, Connie Jordan 1938- *80*
Green, D.
See Casewit, Curtis W(erner)
Green, Elizabeth Shippen 1871-1954 .... *139*
Green, Hannah
See Greenberg, Joanne (Goldenberg)
Green, Jane 1937- *9*
Green, Jessica *211*
Green, John 1977(?)- *170*
Green, Mary Moore 1906- *11*
Green, Morton 1937- *8*
Green, Norma B(erger) 1925- *11*
Green, Phyllis 1932- *20*
Green, Roger (Gilbert) Lancelyn 1918-1987 . *2*
Obituary *53*
Green, (James Le)Roy 1948- *89*
Green, Sheila Ellen 1934- *148*
Earlier sketches in SATA *8, 87*
Green, Timothy 1953- *91*
Greenaway, Kate 1846-1901 .... *100*
See also YABC *2*
See also CLR *111*
Greenbank, Anthony Hunt 1933- *39*
Greenberg, David 1954- *171*
Greenberg, David T.
See Greenberg, David
Greenberg, Harvey R. 1935- *5*
Greenberg, Jan 1942- *211*
Earlier sketches in SATA *61, 125*
Greenberg, Joanne (Goldenberg) 1932- *25*
Greenberg, Melanie Hope 1954- *214*
Earlier sketch in SATA *72*
Greenberg, Polly 1932- *52*
Brief entry *43*
Greenblat, Rodney Alan 1960- *106*
Greenburg, Dan 1936- *175*
Earlier sketch in SATA *102*
Greene, Bette 1934- *161*
Earlier sketches in SATA *8, 102*
See also CLR *140*
See also SAAS *16*
Greene, Carla 1916- *67*
Earlier sketch in SATA *1*
Greene, Carol *102*
Brief entry *44*
Earlier sketch in SATA *66*
Greene, Constance C(larke) 1924- *72*
Earlier sketch in SATA *11*
See also CLR *62*
See also SAAS *11*
Greene, Edgar
See Papademetriou, Lisa
Greene, Ellin 1927- *23*
Greene, Graham 1904-1991 .... *20*
Greene, Graham Henry
See Greene, Graham
Greene, Jacqueline Dembar 1946- *212*
Earlier sketches in SATA *76, 131*
Greene, Laura Offenhartz 1935- *38*
Greene, Meg
See Malvasi, Meg Greene
Greene, Michele 1962- *178*
Greene, Michele Dominguez
See Greene, Michele
Greene, Rhonda Gowler 1955- *160*
Earlier sketch in SATA *101*
Greene, Stephanie 1950- *221*
Earlier sketches in SATA *127, 173*
Greene, Wade 1933- *11*
Greene, Yvonne
See Flesch, Yolande
Greenfeld, Howard (Scheinman) 1928- *140*
Earlier sketch in SATA *19*
Greenfeld, Josh(ua Joseph) 1928- *62*
Greenfield, Eloise 1929- *155*
Earlier sketches in SATA *19, 61, 105*
See also CLR *38*
See also SAAS *16*

Greenhaus, Thelma Nurenberg 1903-1984
Obituary *45*
Greenhut, Josh
See Mercer, Sienna
Greening, Hamilton
See Hamilton, Charles (Harold St. John)
Greenlaw, M. Jean 1941- *107*
Greenleaf, Barbara Kaye 1942- *6*
Greenleaf, Peter 1910-1997 .... *33*
Greenlee, Sharon 1935- *77*
Greeno, Gayle 1949- *81*
Greenseid, Diane 1948- *178*
Earlier sketch in SATA *93*
Greenspun, Adele Aron 1938- *142*
Earlier sketch in SATA *76*
Greenstein, Elaine 1959- *150*
Earlier sketch in SATA *82*
Greenwald, Sheila
See Green, Sheila Ellen
Greenwood, Barbara 1940- *129*
Earlier sketch in SATA *90*
Greenwood, Mark 1958- *202*
Greenwood, Pamela D. 1944- *115*
Greer, Richard
See Garrett, Randall
and Silverberg, Robert
Gregg, Andrew K. 1929- *81*
Gregg, Charles T(hornton) 1927- *65*
Gregg, Walter H(arold) 1919- *20*
Gregor, Arthur 1923- *36*
Gregor, Lee
See Pohl, Frederik
Gregori, Leon 1919- *15*
Gregorian, Joyce Ballou 1946-1991 .... *30*
Obituary *83*
Gregorich, Barbara 1943- *184*
Earlier sketch in SATA *66*
Gregorowski, Christopher 1940- *30*
Gregory, Diana (Jean) 1933- *49*
Brief entry *42*
Gregory, Harry
See Gottfried, Theodore Mark
Gregory, Jean
See Ure, Jean
Gregory, Kristiana 1951- *212*
Earlier sketches in SATA *74, 136*
Gregory, Nan 1944- *192*
Earlier sketch in SATA *148*
Gregory, Philippa 1954- *122*
Gregory, Stephen
See Penzler, Otto
Gregory, Valiska 1940- *82*
Greif, Jean-Jacques 1944- *195*
Greisman, Joan Ruth 1937- *31*
Grendon, Stephen
See Derleth, August (William)
Grenville, Pelham
See Wodehouse, P. G.
Gretz, Susanna 1937- *7*
Gretzer, John *18*
Grewdead, Roy
See Gorey, Edward (St. John)
Grey, Carol
See Lowndes, Robert A(ugustine) W(ard)
Grey, Christopher *191*
Grey, Christopher Peter
See Grey, Christopher
Grey, Jerry 1926- *11*
Grey, Mini *205*
Earlier sketch in SATA *166*
Greybeard the Pirate
See Macintosh, Brownie
Grey Owl
See Belaney, Archibald Stansfeld
Gri
See Denney, Diana
Gribbin, John 1946- *159*
Gribbin, John R.
See Gribbin, John
Grice, Frederick 1910-1983 .... *6*
Grider, Dorothy 1915- *31*

Gridley, Marion E(leanor) 1906-1974 35
  Obituary 26
Grieco-Tiso, Pina 1954- 108
Grieder, Walter 1924- 9
Griego, Tony A. 1955- 77
Griese, Arnold A(lfred) 1921- 9
Griessman, Annette 1962- 170
  Earlier sketch in SATA 116
Grieve, James 1934- 146
Grifalconi, Ann 1929- 210
  Earlier sketches in SATA 2, 66, 133
  See also CLR 35
  See also SAAS 16
Griffin, Adele 1970- 195
  Earlier sketches in SATA 105, 153
Griffin, Elizabeth May 1985- 89
Griffin, Gillett Good 1928- 26
Griffin, Judith Berry 34
Griffin, Kitty 1951- 137
Griffin, Peni R. 1961- 193
  Earlier sketches in SATA 67, 99
Griffin, Steven A. 1953- 89
Griffin, Steven Arthur
  See Griffin, Steven A.
Griffin, W. E. B. 1929- 5
Griffith, Connie 1946- 89
Griffith, Gershom 1960- 85
Griffith, Helen V. 1934- 87
  Autobiography Feature 107
  Earlier sketch in SATA 39
Griffith, Helen Virginia
  See Griffith, Helen V.
Griffith, Jeannette
  See Eyerly, Jeannette
Griffith, Saul 1974- 200
Griffiths, Andy 1961- 196
  Earlier sketch in SATA 152
Griffiths, G(ordon) D(ouglas) 1910-1973
  Obituary 20
Griffiths, Helen 1939- 86
  Earlier sketch in SATA 5
  See also CLR 75
  See also SAAS 5
Grigson, Jane (McIntire) 1928-1990 63
Grimes, Lee 1920- 68
Grimes, Nikki 1950- 218
  Earlier sketches in SATA 93, 136, 174
  See also CLR 42
Grimly, Gris 186
Grimm, Jacob Ludwig Karl 1785-1863 22
  See also CLR 112
Grimm, Wilhelm Karl 1786-1859 22
  See also CLR 112
Grimm, William C(arey) 1907-1992 14
Grimm and Grim
  See Grimm, Jacob Ludwig Karl
  and Grimm, Wilhelm Karl
Grimm Brothers
  See Grimm, Jacob Ludwig Karl
  and Grimm, Wilhelm Karl
Grimsdell, Jeremy 1942- 83
Grimshaw, Nigel (Gilroy) 1925- 23
Grimsley, Gordon
  See Groom, Arthur William
Grindley, Jane Sally
  See Grindley, Sally
Grindley, Sally 1953- 148
Gringhuis, Dirk
  See Gringhuis, Richard H.
Gringhuis, Richard H. 1918-1974 6
  Obituary 25
Grinnell, David
  See Wollheim, Donald A(llen)
Grinnell, George Bird 1849-1938 16
Grinspoon, David
  See Grinspoon, David H.
Grinspoon, David H. 1959- 156
Grinspoon, David Harry
  See Grinspoon, David H.

Gripe, Maria 1923- 74
  Earlier sketch in SATA 2
  See also CLR 5
Gripe, Maria Kristina
  See Gripe, Maria
Gritton, Steve 223
Grobler, Piet 1959- 201
Groch, Judith (Goldstein) 1929- 25
Grode, Redway
  See Gorey, Edward (St. John)
Groener, Carl
  See Lowndes, Robert A(ugustine) W(ard)
Groening, Matt 1954- 116
  Earlier sketch in SATA 81
Grohmann, Susan 1948- 84
Grohskopf, Bernice 7
Grol, Lini R(icharda) 1913- 9
Grollman, Earl A. 1925- 22
Groom, Arthur William 1898-1964 10
Grooms, Duffy 1964- 169
Gross, Alan 1947- 54
  Brief entry 43
Gross, Ernie 1913- 67
Gross, Philip 1952- 164
  Earlier sketch in SATA 84
Gross, Philip John
  See Gross, Philip
Gross, Ruth Belov 1929- 33
Gross, Sarah Chokla 1906-1976 9
  Obituary 26
Grosser, Morton 1931- 74
Grosser, Vicky 1958- 83
Grossman, Bill 1948- 126
  Earlier sketch in SATA 72
Grossman, Nancy 1940- 29
Grossman, Patricia 1951- 73
Grossman, Robert 1940- 11
Grossmann-Hensel, Katharina 1973- 219
Grote, JoAnn A. 1951- 113
Groten, Dallas 1951- 64
Groth, John (August) 1908-1988 21
  Obituary 56
Groth-Fleming, Candace
  See Fleming, Candace
Grove, Vicki 1948- 151
  Autobiography Feature 151
  Earlier sketch in SATA 122
Grover, Lorie Ann 1964- 168
Grover, Wayne 1934- 69
Groves, Georgina
  See Symons, (Dorothy) Geraldine
Groves, Maketa 1950- 107
Groves, Seli 77
Grubb, Lisa 160
Gruber, Michael 1940- 173
Gruber, Terry (deRoy) 1953- 66
Gruelle, John 1880-1938 35
  Brief entry 32
  See also CLR 34
Gruelle, Johnny
  See Gruelle, John
Gruenberg, Sidonie Matsner 1881-1974 2
  Obituary 27
Gruhzit-Hoyt, Olga (Margaret) 1922- 127
  Earlier sketch in SATA 16
Grummer, Arnold E(dward) 1923- 49
Grunewalt, Pine
  See Kunhardt, Edith
Grunwell, Jeanne Marie 1971- 147
Grupper, Jonathan 137
Gryski, Camilla 1948- 72
Guarino, Dagmar
  See Guarino, Deborah
Guarino, Deborah 1954- 68
Guay, Georgette (Marie Jeanne) 1952- 54
Guay, Rebecca 209
Guay-Mitchell, Rebecca
  See Guay, Rebecca
Guback, Georgia 88
Guccione, Leslie Davis 1946- 111
  Earlier sketch in SATA 72

Guck, Dorothy 1913-2002 27
Gudeon, Karla 212
Guerny, Gene
  See Gurney, Gene
Guest, Elissa Haden 1953- 218
  Earlier sketch in SATA 125
Guest, Jacqueline 1952- 135
Guevara, Susan 167
  Earlier sketch in SATA 97
Gugler, Laurel Dee 95
Gugliotta, Bobette 1918-1994 7
Guianan, Eve 1965- 102
Guiberson, Brenda Z. 1946- 211
  Earlier sketches in SATA 71, 124
Guibert, Emmanuel 1964- 181
Guile, Melanie 1949- 152
  Earlier sketch in SATA 104
Guillaume, Jeanette G. Flierl 1899-1990 8
Guillot, Rene 1900-1969 7
  See also CLR 22
Guisewite, Cathy 1950- 57
Guisewite, Cathy Lee
  See Guisewite, Cathy
Gulbis, Stephen 1959- 142
Gulley, Judie 1942- 58
Gump, P. Q.
  See Card, Orson Scott
Gundrey, Elizabeth 1924- 23
Gunn, James E. 1923- 35
Gunn, James Edwin
  See Gunn, James E.
Gunn, Robin Jones 1955- 84
Gunnella 1956- 197
Gunning, Monica Olwen 1930- 161
Gunston, Bill
  See Gunston, William Tudor
Gunston, William Tudor 1927- 9
Gunterman, Bertha Lisette 1886(?)-1975
  Obituary 27
Gunther, John 1901-1970
Guravich, Dan 1918- 74
Gurko, Leo 1914- 9
Gurko, Miriam 1910(?)-1988 9
  Obituary 58
Gurney, Gene 1924- 65
Gurney, James 1958- 120
  Earlier sketch in SATA 76
Gurney, John Steven 1962- 227
  Earlier sketches in SATA 75, 143
Gustafson, Sarah R.
  See Riedman, Sarah R(egal)
Gustafson, Scott 1956- 34
Gustavson, Adam 1974- 214
  Earlier sketch in SATA 176
Guthrie, A(lfred) B(ertram), Jr. 1901-1991 .. 62
  Obituary 67
Guthrie, Anne 1890-1979 28
Guthrie, Donna W. 1946- 105
  Earlier sketch in SATA 63
Gutierrez, Akemi 172
Gutierrez, Rudy 203
Gutman, Bill 128
  Brief entry 43
  Earlier sketch in SATA 67
Gutman, Dan 1955- 221
  Earlier sketches in SATA 77, 139, 188
Gutman, Naham 1899(?)-1981
  Obituary 25
Gutmann, Bessie Pease 1876-1960 73
Guy, Geoffrey 1942- 153
Guy, Ginger Foglesong 1954- 171
Guy, Rosa 1925- 122
  Earlier sketches in SATA 14, 62
  See also CLR 137
Guy, Rosa Cuthbert
  See Guy, Rosa
Guy, Susan 1948- 149
Guymer, (Wilhelmina) Mary 1909- 50
Guzman, Lila 1952- 168
Guzman, Rick 1957- 168
Gwaltney, Doris 1932- 181

Gwynne, Fred(erick Hubbard) 1926-1993 .... *41*
  Brief entry *27*
  Obituary *75*
Gwynne, Oscar A.
  See Ellis, Edward S.
Gwynne, Oswald A.
  See Ellis, Edward S.
Gyorkos, Charmaine Echeverria
  See Echeverria Gyorkos, Charmaine

H

Haab, Sherri 1964- *169*
  Earlier sketch in SATA *91*
Haar, Jaap ter
  See ter Haar, Jaap
Haarsma, P.J. *183*
Haas, Carolyn Buhai 1926- *43*
Haas, Dan 1957- *105*
Haas, Dorothy F. *46*
  Brief entry *43*
  See also SAAS *17*
Haas, Irene 1929- *96*
  Earlier sketch in SATA *17*
Haas, James E. 1943- *40*
Haas, James Edward
  See Haas, James E.
Haas, Jessie 1959- *215*
Haas, (Katherine) Jessie 1959- *135*
  Autobiography Feature *135*
  Earlier sketch in SATA *98*
Haas, Merle S. 1896(?)-1985
  Obituary *41*
Habenstreit, Barbara 1937- *5*
Haber, Karen 1955- *78*
Haber, Louis 1910-1988 .... *12*
Hacker, Randi 1951- *185*
Hacker, Randi Dawn
  See Hacker, Randi
Hackett, John Winthrop 1910-1997 .... *65*
Hacks, Peter 1928-2003
  Obituary *151*
Haddix, Margaret Peterson 1964- *224*
  Earlier sketches in SATA *94, 125, 187*
Haddon, Mark 1962- *223*
  Earlier sketch in SATA *155*
Hader, Berta (Hoerner) 1891(?)-1976 .... *16*
Hader, Elmer (Stanley) 1889-1973 .... *16*
Hadithi, Mwenye
  See Hobson, Bruce
Hadley, Franklin
  See Winterbotham, R(ussell) R(obert)
Hadley, Lee 1934-1995 .... *89*
  Brief entry *38*
  Obituary *86*
  Earlier sketch in SATA *47*
  See also CLR *40*
  See also SAAS *14*
Haeffele, Deborah 1954- *76*
Haenel, Wolfram 1956- *89*
  See also CLR *64*
Hafner, Marylin 1925- *179*
  Earlier sketches in SATA *7, 121*
Haft, Erin
  See Ehrenhaft, Daniel
Hager, Alan 1940- *176*
Hager, Alice Rogers 1894-1969
  Obituary *26*
Hager, Betty 1923- *89*
Hager, Jenna Bush
  See Bush, Jenna
Hager, Sarah *171*
Hager, Thomas 1953- *119*
Hager, Tom
  See Hager, Thomas
Hagerup, Klaus 1946- *186*
Haggard, H(enry) Rider 1856-1925 .... *16*
Haggerty, James J(oseph) 1920- *5*

Hagon, Priscilla
  See Allan, Mabel Esther
Hague, Kathleen 1949- *49*
  Brief entry *45*
Hague, Michael 1948- *185*
  Brief entry *32*
  Earlier sketches in SATA *48, 80, 129*
Hague, Michael R.
  See Hague, Michael
Hague, Susan Kathleen
  See Hague, Kathleen
Hahn, Emily 1905-1997 .... *3*
  Obituary *96*
Hahn, Hannelore *8*
Hahn, James (Sage) 1947- *9*
Hahn, Lynn 1949- *9*
Hahn, Mary Downing 1937- *208*
  Autobiography Feature *157*
  Brief entry *44*
  Earlier sketches in SATA *50, 81, 138, 157*
  See also SAAS *12*
Hahn, Michael T. 1953- *92*
Hahn, Mona Lynn
  See Hahn, Lynn
Haig, Matt 1975- *221*
Haig-Brown, Roderick (Langmere)
  1908-1976 .... *12*
  See also CLR *31*
Haight, Anne Lyon 1895-1977
  Obituary *30*
Haight, Rip
  See Carpenter, John
Haight, Sandy 1949- *79*
Haij, Vera
  See Jansson, Tove (Marika)
Hailstone, Ruth *219*
Haines, Gail Kay 1943- *11*
Haines, Margaret Ann Beck
  See Beck, Peggy
Haining, Peter 1940-2007 .... *14*
  Obituary *188*
Haining, Peter Alexander
  See Haining, Peter
Hains, Harriet
  See Watson, Carol
Hajdusiewicz, Babs Bell *163*
Hakim, Joy 1931- *173*
  Earlier sketch in SATA *83*
Halacy, D. S., Jr. 1919-2002 .... *36*
  See also SAAS *8*
Halacy, Dan
  See Halacy, D. S., Jr.
Halam, Ann
  See Jones, Gwyneth A.
Haldane, Roger John 1945- *13*
Hale, Arlene 1924-1982 .... *49*
Hale, Bruce 1957- *203*
  Earlier sketch in SATA *123*
Hale, Christy
  See Apostolou, Christine Hale
Hale, Dean 1972- *227*
Hale, Edward Everett 1822-1909 .... *16*
Hale, Glenn
  See Walker, Robert W.
Hale, Helen
  See Mulcahy, Lucille Burnett
Hale, Irina 1932- *26*
Hale, Kathleen 1898-2000 .... *66*
  Obituary *121*
  Earlier sketch in SATA *17*
Hale, Linda (Howe) 1929- *6*
Hale, Lucretia P.
  See Hale, Lucretia Peabody
Hale, Lucretia Peabody 1820-1900 .... *26*
  See also CLR *105*
Hale, Marian *194*
Hale, Nancy 1908-1988 .... *31*
  Obituary *57*
Hale, Nathan 1976- *210*
Hale, Shannon *200*
  Earlier sketch in SATA *158*

Haley, Amanda *205*
Haley, Gail E(inhart) 1939- *161*
  Autobiography Feature *161*
  Brief entry *28*
  Earlier sketches in SATA *43, 78, 136*
  See also CLR *21*
  See also SAAS *13*
Haley, Neale *52*
Halfmann, Janet 1944- *208*
Hall, Adam
  See Trevor, Elleston
Hall, Adele 1910- *7*
Hall, Anna Gertrude 1882-1967 .... *8*
Hall, August *207*
Hall, Barbara 1961- *68*
Hall, Becky 1950- *186*
Hall, Beverly B. 1918- *95*
Hall, Borden
  See Yates, Raymond F(rancis)
Hall, Brian P(atrick) 1935- *31*
Hall, Cameron
  See del Rey, Lester
Hall, Caryl
  See Hansen, Caryl (Hall)
Hall, Donald 1928- *97*
  Earlier sketch in SATA *23*
Hall, Donald Andrew, Jr.
  See Hall, Donald
Hall, Douglas 1931- *43*
Hall, Elizabeth 1929- *77*
Hall, Elvajean 1910-1984 .... *6*
Hall, Francie 1940- *166*
Hall, James Norman 1887-1951 .... *21*
Hall, Jesse
  See Boesen, Victor
Hall, Katy
  See McMullan, Kate
Hall, Kirsten Marie 1974- *67*
Hall, Lynn 1937- *79*
  Earlier sketches in SATA *2, 47*
  See also SAAS *4*
Hall, Malcolm 1945- *7*
Hall, Marcellus *203*
Hall, Marjory
  See Yeakley, Marjory Hall
Hall, Melanie 1949- *228*
  Earlier sketches in SATA *78, 116, 169*
Hall, Michael 1954- *228*
Hall, Patricia 1940- *136*
Hall, Rosalys Haskell 1914- *7*
Hall, Teri *229*
Hall, Willis 1929-2005 .... *66*
Hallard, Peter
  See Catherall, Arthur
Hallas, Richard
  See Knight, Eric
Hall-Clarke, James
  See Rowland-Entwistle, (Arthur) Theodore
  (Henry)
Hallensleben, Georg 1958- *173*
Haller, Dorcas Woodbury 1946- *46*
Hallett, Mark 1947- *220*
  Earlier sketch in SATA *83*
Halliburton, Richard 1900-1939(?) *81*
Halliburton, Warren J. 1924- *19*
Halliday, Brett
  See Dresser, Davis
  and Johnson, (Walter) Ryerson
  and Terrall, Robert
Halliday, William R(oss) 1926- *52*
Hallin, Emily Watson 1916-1995 .... *6*
Hallinan, P. K. 1944- *39*
  Brief entry *37*
Hallinan, Patrick Kenneth
  See Hallinan, P. K.
Hallman, Ruth 1929- *43*
  Brief entry *28*
Hallowell, Tommy
  See Hill, Thomas

Hall-Quest, (Edna) Olga W(ilbourne)
  1899-1986 11
  Obituary 47
Halls, Kelly Milner 1957- 220
  Earlier sketch in SATA 131
Hallstead, William F(inn III) 1924- 11
Hallward, Michael 1889-1982 12
Halperin, Michael 156
Halperin, Wendy Anderson 1952- 200
  Earlier sketches in SATA 80, 125
Halpern, Julie 1975- 198
Halpin, Brendan 1968- 193
Halpin, Marlene 1927- 88
Halse, Laurie Beth
  See Anderson, Laurie Halse
Halsell, Grace (Eleanor) 1923-2000 13
Halsey, Megan 185
Halsted, Anna Roosevelt 1906-1975
  Obituary 30
Halter, Jon C(harles) 1941- 22
Halverson, Deborah 202
Halvorson, Adeline 218
Halvorson, Marilyn 1948- 123
Hamalian, Leo 1920- 41
Hamberger, John 1934- 14
Hamblin, Dora Jane 1920- 36
Hambly, Barbara 1951- 108
Hambly, Barbara Joan
  See Hambly, Barbara
Hamer, Martyn
  See Eldin, Peter
Hamerstrom, Frances 1907-1998 24
Hamil, Thomas Arthur 1928- 14
Hamill, Ethel
  See Webb, Jean Francis (III)
Hamilton, (John) Alan 1943- 66
Hamilton, Alice
  See Cromie, Alice Hamilton
Hamilton, Anita 1919- 92
Hamilton, Buzz
  See Hemming, Roy G.
Hamilton, Carol (Jean Barber) 1935- 94
Hamilton, Charles (Harold St. John)
  1876-1961 13
Hamilton, Charles 1913-1996 65
  Obituary 93
Hamilton, Clive
  See Lewis, C. S.
Hamilton, Dorothy (Drumm) 1906-1983 12
  Obituary 35
Hamilton, Edith 1867-1963 20
Hamilton, Edmond 1904-1977 118
Hamilton, (Muriel) Elizabeth (Mollie)
  1906- 23
Hamilton, Emma Walton 1962- 177
Hamilton, Franklin
  See Silverberg, Robert
Hamilton, Gail
  See Corcoran, Barbara (Asenath)
  and Dodge, Mary Abigail
Hamilton, Kersten 1958- 204
  Earlier sketch in SATA 134
Hamilton, K.R.
  See Hamilton, Kersten
Hamilton, Martha 1953- 183
  Earlier sketch in SATA 123
Hamilton, Mary (E.) 1927- 55
Hamilton, Mollie
  See Kaye, M.M.
Hamilton, Morse 1943-1998 101
  Earlier sketch in SATA 35
Hamilton, Peter F. 1960- 109
Hamilton, Priscilla
  See Gellis, Roberta
Hamilton, Ralph
  See Stratemeyer, Edward L.
Hamilton, Virginia 1936-2002 123
  Obituary 132
  Earlier sketches in SATA 4, 56, 79
  See also CLR 127

Hamilton, Virginia Esther
  See Hamilton, Virginia
Hamilton-Paterson, James 1941- 82
Hamlet, Ova
  See Lupoff, Richard A(llen)
Hamley, D. C.
  See Hamley, Dennis
Hamley, Dennis 1935- 69
  Earlier sketch in SATA 39
  See also CLR 47
  See also SAAS 22
Hamley, Dennis C.
  See Hamley, Dennis
Hamlin, Peter J. 1970- 84
Hamm, Diane Johnston 1949- 78
Hammer, Charles 1934- 58
Hammer, Richard 1928- 6
Hammerman, Gay M(orenus) 1926- 9
Hammill, Matt 1982- 206
Hammond, Andrew 1970- 181
Hammond, Ralph
  See Hammond Innes, Ralph
Hammond, Winifred G(raham) 1899-1992 ... 29
  Obituary 107
Hammond Innes, Ralph 1913-1998 116
Hammontree, Marie (Gertrude) 1913- 13
Hample, Zack 1977- 161
Hampshire, Joyce Gregorian
  See Gregorian, Joyce Ballou
Hampshire, Susan 1942- 98
Hampson, (Richard) Denman 1929- 15
Hampson, Frank 1918(?)-1985
  Obituary 46
Hampton, Wilborn 1940- 196
  Earlier sketch in SATA 156
Hamre, Leif 1914- 5
Hamsa, Bobbie 1944- 52
  Brief entry 38
Han, Jenny 1981- 175
Han, Lu
  See Stickler, Soma Han
Han, Soma
  See Stickler, Soma Han
Han, Suzanne Crowder 1953- 89
Hancock, Mary A. 1923- 31
Hancock, Sibyl 1940- 9
Hand, Elizabeth 1957- 167
  Earlier sketch in SATA 118
Handford, Martin (John) 1956- 64
  See also CLR 22
Handforth, Thomas (Schofield) 1897-1948 .. 42
Handleman, Philip 1951- 222
Handler, Daniel
  See Snicket, Lemony
Handville, Robert (Tompkins) 1924- 45
Hane, Roger 1940-1974
  Obituary 20
Hanel, Wolfram
  See Haenel, Wolfram
Haney, Lynn 1941- 23
Hanff, Helene 1916-1997 97
  Earlier sketch in SATA 11
Hanft, Josh 1956- 197
Hanft, Joshua E.
  See Hanft, Josh
Hanley, Boniface Francis 1924- 65
Hanlon, Emily 1945- 15
Hann, Jacquie 1951- 19
Hann, Judith 1942- 77
Hanna, Bill
  See Hanna, William (Denby)
Hanna, Cheryl 1951- 84
Hanna, Dan 200
Hanna, Jack (Bushnell) 1947- 74
Hanna, Nell(ie L.) 1908- 55
Hanna, Paul R(obert) 1902-1988 9
Hanna, William (Denby) 1910-2001 51
  Obituary 126
Hannam, Charles 1925- 50
Hannan, Peter 1954- 187
Hannigan, Katherine 170

Hannon, Ezra
  See Hunter, Evan
Hann-Syme, Marguerite 127
Hano, Arnold 1922- 12
Hano, Renee Roth
  See Roth-Hano, Renee
Hanover, Terri
  See Huff, Tanya
Hansen, Amy S. 229
Hansen, Ann Larkin 1958- 96
Hansen, Brooks 1965- 104
Hansen, Caryl (Hall) 1929- 39
Hansen, Ian V. 1929- 113
Hansen, Jennifer 1972- 156
Hansen, Joyce 1942- 172
  Autobiography Feature 172
  Brief entry 39
  Earlier sketches in SATA 46, 101
  See also CLR 21
  See also SAAS 15
Hansen, Joyce Viola
  See Hansen, Joyce
Hansen, Mark Victor 112
Hansen, Ron 1947- 56
Hansen, Ronald Thomas
  See Hansen, Ron
Hansen, Thore 1942- 224
Hanser, Richard (Frederick) 1909-1981 13
Hanson, Joan 1938- 8
Hanson, Joseph E. 1894(?)-1971
  Obituary 27
Hanson, Mary Elizabeth 188
Hanson, Warren 1949- 155
Hansson, Gunilla 1939- 64
Hantman, Clea 200
Hapka, C.A.
  See Hapka, Catherine
Hapka, Catherine 223
Hapka, Cathy
  See Hapka, Catherine
Harald, Eric
  See Boesen, Victor
Harazin, S. A. 210
Harbour, Elizabeth 1968- 221
Harcourt, Ellen Knowles 1890(?)-1984
  Obituary 36
Hard, Charlotte (Ann) 1969- 98
Hardcastle, Michael 1933- 216
  Brief entry 38
  Earlier sketch in SATA 47
Harding, Lee 1937- 32
  Brief entry 31
Hardinge, Frances 1973- 210
Hardt, Helga Fleischhauer
  See Fleischhauer-Hardt, Helga
Hardwick, Richard Holmes, Jr. 1923- 12
Hardy, Alice Dale 67
  Earlier sketch in SATA 1
Hardy, David A(ndrews) 1936- 9
Hardy, Janice 222
Hardy, Jon 1958- 53
Hardy, LeAnne 1951- 154
Hardy, Stuart
  See Schisgall, Oscar
Hare, Norma Q(uarles) 1924- 46
  Brief entry 41
Harel, Nira 1936- 154
Harford, Henry
  See Hudson, W(illiam) H(enry)
Hargis, Wes 219
Hargrave, Leonie
  See Disch, Thomas M.
Hargreaves, (Charles) Roger 1935-1988
  Obituary 56
Hargrove, James 1947- 57
  Brief entry 50
Hargrove, Jim
  See Hargrove, James
Harik, Elsa
  See Marston, Elsa

Harik, Elsa M.
  See Marston, Elsa
Harik, Elsa Marston
  See Marston, Elsa
Hariton, Anca I. 1955- 79
Hark, Mildred
  See McQueen, Mildred Hark
Harkaway, Hal
  See Stratemeyer, Edward L.
Harkins, Philip 1912-1997 6
  Obituary 129
Harlan, Elizabeth 1945- 41
  Brief entry 35
Harlan, Glen
  See Cebulash, Mel
Harlan, Judith 1949- 135
  Earlier sketch in SATA 74
  See also CLR 81
Harland, Richard 1947- 152
Harlee, J. V.
  See Leese, Jennifer L.B.
Harler, Ann
  See Van Steenwyk, Elizabeth (Ann)
Harley, Avis 183
Harley, Bill 1954- 208
  Earlier sketch in SATA 87
Harlow, Joan Hiatt 1932- 226
  Earlier sketch in SATA 157
Harman, Fred 1902(?)-1982
  Obituary 30
Harman, Hugh 1903-1982
  Obituary 33
Harmelink, Barbara (Mary) 9
Harmer, Mabel 1894-1992 45
Harmon, Dan
  See Harmon, Daniel E(lton)
Harmon, Daniel E(lton) 1949- 157
Harmon, Margaret 1906- 20
Harmon, Michael 1969- 189
Harmon, Michael B.
  See Harmon, Michael
Harmon, William (Ruth) 1938- 65
Harnan, Terry 1920- 12
Harness, Cheryl 1951- 178
  Earlier sketch in SATA 131
Harnett, Cynthia (Mary) 1893-1981 5
  Obituary 32
Harper, Anita 1943- 41
Harper, Betty 1946- 126
Harper, Charise
  See Harper, Charise Mericle
Harper, Charise Mericle 226
  Earlier sketch in SATA 179
Harper, Elaine
  See Hallin, Emily Watson
Harper, Ellen
  See Noble, Marty
Harper, Jamie 174
Harper, Jessica 1949- 148
Harper, Jo 1932- 169
  Earlier sketch in SATA 97
Harper, Lee 201
Harper, Mary Wood
  See Dixon, Jeanne
Harper, Piers 1966- 161
  Earlier sketch in SATA 105
Harper, Suzanne 194
Harper, Wilhelmina 1884-1973 4
  Obituary 26
Harrah, Madge 1931- 154
Harrah, Michael 1940- 41
Harrah, Monique
  See Harrah, Madge
Harrar, George E. 1949- 124
Harrell, Beatrice Orcutt 1943- 93
Harrell, Janice 1945- 70
Harrell, Sara Gordon 1940- 26
Harrell, Sara Jeanne Gordon
  See Harrell, Sara Gordon
Harries, Joan 1922- 39
Harrill, Ronald 1950- 90

Harrington, Denis J(ames) 1932- 88
Harrington, Evelyn Davis 1911- 5
Harrington, Janice N. 1956- 187
Harrington, Lyn
  See Harrington, Evelyn Davis
Harris, Alan 1944- 71
Harris, Aurand 1915-1996 37
  Obituary 91
Harris, Bob
  See Harris, Robert J.
Harris, Carol Flynn 1933- 135
Harris, Catherine
  See Ainsworth, Catherine Harris
Harris, Christie
  See Harris, Christie (Lucy) Irwin
Harris, Christie (Lucy) Irwin 1907-2002 74
  Autobiography Feature 116
  Earlier sketch in SATA 6
  See also CLR 47
  See also SAAS 10
Harris, Christine 1955- 105
Harris, Colver
  See Colver, Anne
Harris, David 1942- 118
Harris, David William
  See Harris, David
Harris, Dorothy Joan 1931- 153
  Earlier sketch in SATA 13
Harris, Geraldine 1951- 54
Harris, Geraldine Rachel
  See Harris, Geraldine
Harris, Jacqueline L. 1929- 62
Harris, Janet 1932-1979 4
  Obituary 23
Harris, Jesse
  See Standiford, Natalie
Harris, Joan 1946- 146
Harris, Joe 1928- 201
Harris, Joel Chandler 1848-1908 100
  See also YABC 1
  See also CLR 128
Harris, John (Wyndham Parkes Lucas) Beynon
  1903-1969 118
Harris, Johnson
  See Harris, John (Wyndham Parkes Lucas)
  Beynon
Harris, Jonathan 1921-1997 52
Harris, Larry Vincent 1939- 59
Harris, Lavinia
  See St. John, Nicole
Harris, Leon A., Jr. 1926-2000 4
Harris, Lois V. 199
Harris, Lorle K(empe) 1912-2001 22
Harris, Marilyn
  See Springer, Marilyn Harris
Harris, Mark Jonathan 1941- 84
  Earlier sketch in SATA 32
Harris, Mary K(athleen) 1905-1966 119
Harris, Robert J. 1955- 195
Harris, Robie H. 1940- 203
  Brief entry 53
  Earlier sketches in SATA 90, 147
Harris, Robin
  See Shine, Deborah
Harris, Rosemary (Jeanne) 82
  Earlier sketch in SATA 4
  See also CLR 30
  See also SAAS 7
Harris, Ruth Elwin 1935- 164
Harris, Sherwood 1932-2009 25
Harris, Steven Michael 1957- 55
Harris, Trudy 1949- 191
  Earlier sketch in SATA 128
Harris-Filderman, Diane
  See Filderman, Diane E(lizabeth)
Harrison, C(hester) William 1913-1994 35
Harrison, Carol
  See Harrison, Carol Thompson
Harrison, Carol Thompson 113
Harrison, David L. 1937- 186
  Earlier sketches in SATA 26, 92, 150

Harrison, Deloris 1938- 9
Harrison, Edward Hardy 1926- 56
Harrison, Elizabeth (Allen) Cavanna
  1909-2001 30
  Earlier sketch in SATA 1
  See also SAAS 4
Harrison, Harry 1925- 4
Harrison, Harry Max
  See Harrison, Harry
Harrison, Mette Ivie 1970- 202
  Earlier sketch in SATA 149
Harrison, Michael 1939- 106
Harrison, Molly (Hodgett) 1909-2002 41
Harrison, Sarah 1946- 63
Harrison, Ted
  See Harrison, Edward Hardy
Harsh, Fred (T.) 1925- 72
Harshaw, Ruth H(etzel) 1890-1968 27
Harshman, Marc 1950- 109
  Earlier sketch in SATA 71
Hart, Alexandra 1939- 14
Hart, Alison
  See Leonhardt, Alice
Hart, Bruce 1938-2006 57
  Brief entry 39
Hart, Carole 1943- 57
  Brief entry 39
Hart, Carolyn 1936- 74
Hart, Carolyn G.
  See Hart, Carolyn
Hart, Carolyn Gimpel
  See Hart, Carolyn
Hart, Jan Siegel 1940- 79
Hart, Joyce 1954- 148
Hart, Karen 185
Hart, Lenore 171
Hart, Philip S. 1944- 180
Hart, Virginia 1949- 83
Harte, Bret 1836(?)-1902 26
Harte, Francis Brett
  See Harte, Bret
Harter, Debbie 1963- 107
Hartfield, Claire 1957- 147
Hartinger, Brent 1964- 217
  Earlier sketches in SATA 145, 174
Hartland, Jessie 171
Hartley, Ellen (Raphael) 1915-1980 23
Hartley, Fred Allan III 1953- 41
Hartley, William B(rown) 1913-1980 23
Hartling, Peter
  See Hartling, Peter
Hartling, Peter 1933- 66
  See also CLR 29
Hartman, Bob 1955- 224
Hartman, Carrie 226
Hartman, Cassie 202
Hartman, Dan 1955- 202
Hartman, Evert 1937- 38
  Brief entry 35
Hartman, Jane E. 1928- 47
Hartman, Jane Evangeline
  See Hartman, Jane E.
Hartman, Louis F(rancis) 1901-1970 22
Hartman, Rachel 174
Hartman, Victoria 1942- 91
Hartnett, Sonya 1968- 176
  Earlier sketches in SATA 93, 130
Hartry, Nancy 219
Hartshorn, Ruth M. 1928- 11
Hartung, Susan Kathleen 192
  Earlier sketch in SATA 150
Hartwig, Manfred 1950- 81
Harvey, Alyxandra 1974- 227
  Earlier sketch in SATA 189
Harvey, Brett 1936- 61
Harvey, Edith 1908(?)-1972
  Obituary 27
Harvey, Gill 189
Harvey, Karen D. 1935- 88
Harvey, Roland 1945- 219
  Earlier sketches in SATA 71, 123, 179

Harvey-Fitzhenry, Alyxandra
  See Harvey, Alyxandra
Harwick, B. L.
  See Keller, Beverly L(ou)
Harwin, Brian
  See Henderson, LeGrand
Harwood, Pearl Augusta (Bragdon)
  1903-1998 9
Haseley, Dennis 1950- *221*
  Brief entry 44
  Earlier sketches in SATA *57, 105, 157*
Hashmi, Kerri 1955- *108*
Haskell, Arnold L(ionel) 1903-1981(?) 6
Haskins, James
  See Haskins, James S.
Haskins, James S. 1941-2005 .... *132*
  Autobiography Feature *132*
  Earlier sketches in SATA *9, 69, 105*
  See also CLR *39*
  See also SAAS *4*
Haskins, Jim
  See Haskins, James S.
Hasler, Eveline 1933- *181*
Hasler, Joan 1931- 28
Hass, Robert 1941- 94
Hassall, Joan 1906-1988 43
  Obituary 56
Hassett, Ann 1958- *162*
Hassett, John *162*
Hassler, Jon 1933-2008 .... *19*
  Obituary *191*
Hassler, Jon Francis
  See Hassler, Jon
Hastings, Beverly
  See Barkin, Carol
  and James, Elizabeth
Hastings, Graham
  See Jeffries, Roderic
Hastings, Ian 1912- 62
Hastings, Victor
  See Disch, Thomas M.
Haszard, Patricia Moyes 1923-2000 63
Hatch, Lynda S. 1950- 90
Hathaway, Barbara *164*
Hathorn, Elizabeth
  See Hathorn, Libby
Hathorn, Elizabeth Helen
  See Hathorn, Libby
Hathorn, Libby 1943- *156*
  Autobiography Feature *156*
  Earlier sketches in SATA *74, 120*
Hatkoff, Craig 1954- *192*
Hatlo, Jimmy 1898-1963
  Obituary 23
Hatton, Caroline 1957- *205*
Hauff, Wilhelm 1802-1827
  See CLR *155*
Haugaard, Erik Christian 1923- 68
  Earlier sketch in SATA *4*
  See also CLR *11*
  See also SAAS *12*
Haugaard, Kay *117*
Haugen, Hayley Mitchell 1968- *172*
Haugen, Tormod 1945- 66
Hauman, Doris 1898-1984 32
Hauman, George 1890-1961 32
Hauptly, Denis J. 1945- 57
Hauptly, Denis James
  See Hauptly, Denis J.
Hauser, Jill Frankel 1950- *127*
Hauser, Margaret L(ouise) 1909- 10
Hausherr, Rosmarie 1943- 86
Hausman, Gerald 1945- *180*
  Earlier sketches in SATA *13, 90, 132*
  See also CLR *89*
Hausman, Gerry
  See Hausman, Gerald
Hauth, Katherine B. 1940- 99
Hautman, Pete 1952- *173*
  Earlier sketches in SATA *82, 128*

Hautman, Peter Murray
  See Hautman, Pete
Hautzig, Deborah 1956- *106*
  Earlier sketch in SATA *31*
Hautzig, Esther Rudomin 1930-2009 .... *148*
  Earlier sketches in SATA *4, 68*
  See also CLR *22*
  See also SAAS *15*
Havel, Geoff 1955- *152*
Havel, Jennifer
  See Havill, Juanita
Havelin, Kate 1961- *143*
Haven, Paul 1971(?)- *213*
Haverfield, Mary *225*
Havighurst, Walter (Edwin) 1901-1994 .... *1*
  Obituary 79
Haviland, Virginia 1911-1988 6
  Obituary 54
Havill, Juanita 1949- *224*
  Earlier sketches in SATA *74, 155*
Hawes, Judy 1913- 4
Hawes, Louise 1943- *180*
  Earlier sketch in SATA *60*
Hawk, Fran *222*
Hawke, Rosanne 1953- *165*
  Earlier sketch in SATA *124*
Hawke, Rosanne Joy
  See Hawke, Rosanne
Hawkes, Kevin 1959- *201*
  Earlier sketches in SATA *78, 150*
Hawkes, Nigel 1943- *119*
Hawkesworth, Eric 1921- *13*
Hawking, Lucy 1969- *197*
Hawkins, Arthur 1903-1985 .... *19*
Hawkins, Colin 1945- *162*
  Earlier sketch in SATA *112*
Hawkins, Jacqui *162*
  Earlier sketch in SATA *112*
Hawkins, Jimmy 1941- *188*
Hawkins, Laura 1951- 74
Hawkins, (Helena Ann) Quail 1905-2002 6
  Obituary *141*
Hawkins, Rachel 1979- *228*
Hawkinson, John (Samuel) 1912-1994 4
Hawkinson, Lucy (Ozone) 1924-1971 21
Hawks, Robert 1961- 85
Hawley, Mabel C. 67
  Earlier sketch in SATA *1*
Haworth, Danette *207*
Haworth-Attard, Barbara 1953- *215*
Hawthorne, Captain R. M.
  See Ellis, Edward S.
Hawthorne, Nathaniel 1804-1864
  See YABC *2*
  See also CLR *163*
Hay, Jeff T. *154*
Hay, John 1915-2011 .... *13*
Hay, Samantha *213*
Hay, Timothy
  See Brown, Margaret Wise
Hayashi, Leslie Ann 1954- *115*
Hayashi, Nancy 1939- *186*
  Earlier sketch in SATA *80*
Haycak, Cara 1961- *180*
Haycock, Kate 1962- 77
Haycraft, Howard 1905-1991 6
  Obituary 70
Haycraft, Molly Costain 1911- 6
Hayden, Gwendolen Lampshire 1904- 35
Hayden, Robert
  See Hayden, Robert Earl
Hayden, Robert C(arter), Jr. 1937- 47
  Brief entry 28
Hayden, Robert E.
  See Hayden, Robert Earl
Hayden, Robert Earl 1913-1980 .... *19*
  Obituary 26
Hayden, Torey L. 1951- *163*
  Earlier sketch in SATA *65*
Hayden, Torey Lynn
  See Hayden, Torey L.

Hayes, Carlton J(oseph) H(untley)
  1882-1964 .... *11*
Hayes, Daniel 1952- *109*
  Earlier sketch in SATA *73*
Hayes, Geoffrey 1947- *207*
  Earlier sketches in SATA *26, 91*
Hayes, Joe 1945- *131*
  Earlier sketch in SATA *88*
Hayes, John F. 1904-1980 .... *11*
Hayes, Karel 1949- *207*
Hayes, Rosemary *227*
  Earlier sketch in SATA *158*
Hayes, Sarah 1945- *208*
Hayes, Sheila 1937- 51
  Brief entry 50
Hayes, Will 7
Hayes, William D(imitt) 1913-1976 8
Haynes, Betsy 1937- 94
  Brief entry 37
  Earlier sketch in SATA *48*
  See also CLR *90*
Haynes, David 1955- 97
Haynes, Linda
  See Swinford, Betty (June Wells)
Haynes, Mary 1938- 65
Haynes, Max 1956- 72
Hays, Anna Jane *214*
Hays, H(offmann) R(eynolds) 1904-1980 26
Hays, Thomas A.
  See Hays, Tony
Hays, Thomas Anthony
  See Hays, Tony
Hays, Tony 1957- 84
Hays, Wilma Pitchford 1909- 28
  Earlier sketch in SATA *1*
  See also CLR *59*
  See also SAAS *3*
Hayward, Linda 1943- *185*
  Brief entry 39
  Earlier sketch in SATA *101*
Haywood, Carolyn 1898-1990 75
  Obituary 64
  Earlier sketches in SATA *1, 29*
  See also CLR *22*
Hazelaar, Cor *217*
Hazell, Rebecca (Eileen) 1947- *141*
Hazen, Barbara Shook 1930- *178*
  Earlier sketches in SATA *27, 90*
Hazen, Lynn E. *202*
Head, Gay
  See Hauser, Margaret L(ouise)
Head, Tom 1978- *167*
Headley, Elizabeth
  See Harrison, Elizabeth (Allen) Cavanna
Headley, Justina Chen 1968- *176*
Headstrom, (Birger) Richard 1902-1985 8
Heady, Eleanor B(utler) 1917-1979 8
Heagy, William D. 1964- 76
Heal, Edith 1903-1995 7
Heal, Gillian 1934- 89
Heale, Jay (Jeremy Peter Wingfield) 1937- .. 84
Healey, Brooks
  See Albert, Burton
Healey, Larry 1927- 44
  Brief entry 42
Heap, Sue 1954- *187*
  Earlier sketch in SATA *150*
Heaps, Willard A(llison) 1908-1987 26
Hearn, Diane Dawson 1952- *209*
  Earlier sketch in SATA *79*
Hearn, Emily
  See Valleau, Emily
Hearn, Julie 1958- *212*
  Earlier sketch in SATA *152*
Hearn, Lian
  See Rubinstein, Gillian
Hearn, Sneed
  See Gregg, Andrew K.
Hearne, Betsy 1942- *146*
  Earlier sketches in SATA *38, 95*
Heath, Charles D(ickinson) 1941- 46

Heath, Veronica
　See Blackett, Veronica Heath
Heaven, Constance (Christina) 1911- 7
Hebert-Collins, Sheila 1948- *111*
Hecht, George J(oseph) 1895-1980
　Obituary 22
Hecht, Henri Joseph 1922- 9
Hechtkopf, Henryk 1910- *17*
Heck, Bessie (Mildred) Holland 1911-1995 . 26
Heck, Ed 1963- *173*
Heckert, Connie K(aye Delp) 1948- 82
Hector, Julian 205
Hedderwick, Mairi 1939- 145
　Earlier sketches in SATA *30, 77*
Hedges, Sid(ney) G(eorge) 1897-1974 28
Hedrick, Irene Hope 1920- *175*
Heelan, Jamee Riggio 1965- 146
Heerboth, Sharon
　See Leon, Sharon
Heffernan, John 1949- *168*
　Earlier sketch in SATA *121*
Heffron, Dorris 1944- 68
Hefter, Richard 1942- *31*
Hegamin, Tonya C. 1975- 209
Hegarty, Reginald Beaton 1906-1973 10
Hehenberger, Shelly 1968- *126*
Heidbreder, Robert 1947- *196*
　Earlier sketch in SATA *130*
Heidbreder, Robert K.
　See Heidbreder, Robert
Heide, Florence Parry 1919- *192*
　Earlier sketches in SATA *32, 69, 118*
　See also CLR *60*
　See also SAAS *6*
Heiderstadt, Dorothy 1907-2001 6
Heidi Louise
　See Erdrich, Louise
Heidler, David S(tephen) 1955- *132*
Heidler, Jeanne T. 1956- *132*
Heilbroner, Joan Knapp 1922- 63
Heilbrun, Lois Hussey 1922(?)-1987
　Obituary 54
Heiligman, Deborah 1958- *193*
　Earlier sketches in SATA *90, 144*
Heilman, Joan Rattner 50
Heimann, Rolf 1940- *164*
　Earlier sketch in SATA *120*
Hein, Lucille Eleanor 1915-1994 20
Heine, Helme 1941- *135*
　Earlier sketch in SATA *67*
　See also CLR *18*
Heinlein, Robert A. 1907-1988 69
　Obituary 56
　Earlier sketch in SATA *9*
　See also CLR *75*
Heinlein, Robert Anson
　See Heinlein, Robert A.
Heins, Ethel L(eah) 1918-1997 .... *101*
Heins, Paul 1909- *13*
Heintze, Carl 1922- 26
Heinz, Bill
　See Heinz, W. C.
Heinz, Brian J. 1946- *181*
　Earlier sketch in SATA *95*
Heinz, Brian James
　See Heinz, Brian J.
Heinz, W. C. 1915-2008 26
Heinz, Wilfred Charles
　See Heinz, W. C.
Heinzen, Mildred
　See Masters, Mildred
Heisel, Sharon E(laine) 1941- *125*
　Earlier sketch in SATA *84*
Heitzmann, William Ray 1948- 73
Heitzmann, Wm. Ray
　See Heitzmann, William Ray
Helakoski, Leslie *178*
Helberg, Shirley Adelaide Holden 1919- ... 138
Heldring, Thatcher 229
Helfer, Andrew *187*
Helfer, Ralph 1937- *177*

Helfman, Elizabeth S(eaver) 1911-2001 .... *3*
Helfman, Harry Carmozin 1910-1995 .... *3*
Helgerson, Joseph 1950- *181*
Hellard, Susan 182
Hellberg, Hans-Eric 1927- 38
Heller, Linda 1944- 46
　Brief entry 40
Heller, Mike
　See Hano, Arnold
Heller, Ruth M. 1924- *112*
　Earlier sketch in SATA *66*
Hellman, Hal
　See Hellman, Harold
Hellman, Harold 1927- *4*
Helman, Andrea (Jean) 1946- 160
　Earlier sketch in SATA *107*
Helmer, Diana Star 1962- 86
Helmer, Marilyn 160
　Earlier sketch in SATA *112*
Helps, Racey 1913-1971 2
　Obituary 25
Helquist, Brett 229
　Earlier sketches in SATA *146, 187*
Helweg, Hans H. 1917- 50
　Brief entry 33
Helyar, Jane Penelope Josephine 1933- *5*
　Autobiography Feature 138
　See also SAAS *2*
Hemingway, Edith M. 1950- 223
Hemingway, Edith Morris
　See Hemingway, Edith M.
Hemingway, Edward 1969(?)- 212
Hemmant, Lynette 1938- 69
Hemming, Roy G. 1928-1995 .... *11*
　Obituary 86
Hemphill, Helen 1955- *179*
Hemphill, Kris (Harrison) 1963- *118*
Hemphill, Martha Locke 1904-1973 37
Hemphill, Michael 220
Hemphill, Stephanie 190
Hemstock, Gillian 1956- *173*
Henba, Bobbie 1926- 87
Henbest, Nigel 1951- 55
　Brief entry 52
Henderley, Brooks *1*
Henderson, Aileen Kilgore 1921- 178
Henderson, Aileen Mary
　See Fox, Aileen
Henderson, Gordon 1950- 53
Henderson, Kathy 1949- 155
　Brief entry 53
　Earlier sketches in SATA *55, 95*
Henderson, Lauren 1966- 201
Henderson, LeGrand 1901-1965 9
Henderson, Nancy Wallace 1916- 22
Henderson, Zenna (Chlarson) 1917-1983 .... *5*
Hendrickson, Walter Brookfield, Jr. 1936- 9
Hendrix, John 1976- 208
Hendry, Diana 1941- 213
　Earlier sketches in SATA *68, 106*
Hendry, Frances Mary 1941- *171*
　Earlier sketch in SATA *110*
Hendry, Linda (Gail) 1961- 83
Heneghan, James 1930- 160
　Earlier sketches in SATA *53, 97*
Henkes, Kevin 1960- 207
　Earlier sketches in SATA *43, 76, 108, 154*
　See also CLR *108*
Henn, Astrid 214
Hennessy, Barbara G.
　See Hennessy, B.G.
Hennessy, Barbara Gulbrandsen
　See Hennessy, B.G.
Hennessy, B.G. 1951- *175*
Hennesy, Carolyn 1962- 221
Henney, Carolee Wells 1928- 102
Henriod, Lorraine 1925- 26
Henriquez, Emile F. 1937- 170
　Earlier sketch in SATA *89*
Henry, April 1959- *174*
Henry, Ernest 1948- 107

Henry, Joanne Landers 1927- 6
Henry, Maeve 1960- 75
Henry, Marguerite 1902-1997 .... *100*
　Obituary 99
　See also CLR *4*
　See also SAAS *7*
Henry, Marie H. 1935- 65
Henry, Marilyn 1939- *117*
Henry, Marion
　See del Rey, Lester
Henry, O. 1862-1910
　See YABC *2*
Henry, Oliver
　See Henry, O.
Henry, Rohan 217
Henry, T. E.
　See Rowland-Entwistle, (Arthur) Theodore
　(Henry)
Henschel, Elizabeth Georgie 56
Henson, Heather 206
Henson, James Maury
　See Henson, Jim
Henson, Jim 1936-1990 43
　Obituary 65
Henstra, Friso 1928- 73
　Earlier sketch in SATA *8*
　See also SAAS *14*
Hentoff, Nat(han Irving) 1925- *133*
　Brief entry 27
　Earlier sketches in SATA *42, 69*
　See also CLR *52*
Henty, G(eorge) A(lfred) 1832-1902 64
　See also CLR *76*
Heo, Yumi 1964- 206
　Earlier sketches in SATA *94, 146*
Hepler, Heather *177*
Herald, Kathleen
　See Peyton, Kathleen Wendy
Herb, Angela M. 1970- 92
Herbert, Cecil
　See Hamilton, Charles (Harold St. John)
Herbert, Don 1917-2007 2
　Obituary *184*
Herbert, Donald Jeffrey
　See Herbert, Don
Herbert, Frank 1920-1986 37
　Obituary 47
　Earlier sketch in SATA *9*
Herbert, Frank Patrick
　See Herbert, Frank
Herbert, Helen (Jean) 1947- 57
Herbert, Janis 1956- *139*
Herbert, Wally 1934-2007 23
Herbert, Walter William
　See Herbert, Wally
Herbst, Judith 1947- 74
Herda, D.J. 1948- 80
Herge
　See Remi, Georges
Heritage, Martin
　See Horler, Sydney
Herkimer, L(awrence) R(ussell) 1925(?)- 42
Herlihy, Dirlie Anne 1935- 73
Herlong, Madaline
　See Herlong, M.H.
Herlong, M.H. *211*
Herman, Charlotte 1937- *203*
　Earlier sketches in SATA *20, 99*
Hermanson, Dennis (Everett) 1947- 10
Hermes, Jules 1962- 92
Hermes, Patricia 1936- *191*
　Earlier sketches in SATA *31, 78, 141*
Hermes, Patricia Mary
　See Hermes, Patricia
Hernandez, Natalie Nelson 1929- *123*
Herndon, Ernest 91
Herold, Ann Bixby 1937- 72
Herrera, Diego
　See Yayo
Herrera, Juan Felipe 1948- *127*

Herrick, Steven 1958- *209*
Earlier sketches in SATA *103, 156*
Herriman, George (Joseph) 1880-1944 .... *140*
Herriot, James 1916-1995 .... *135*
Brief entry *44*
Earlier sketch in SATA *86*
See also CLR *80*
Herrmanns, Ralph 1933- *11*
Herrold, Tracey
See Dils, Tracey E.
Herron, Carolivia 1947- *203*
Herron, Edward A(lbert) 1912- *4*
Herschler, Mildred Barger *130*
Hersey, John 1914-1993 .... *25*
Obituary *76*
Hersey, John Richard
See Hersey, John
Hershberger, Priscilla (Gorman) 1951- *81*
Hershenhorn, Esther 1945- *151*
Hershey, Kathleen M. 1934- *80*
Hershey, Mary *173*
Hershey, Mary L.
See Hershey, Mary
Hersom, Kathleen 1911- *73*
Hertz, Grete Janus 1915- *23*
Herxheimer, Sophie 1963- *220*
Herzig, Alison Cragin 1935- *87*
Herzog, Brad 1968- *131*
Heslewood, Juliet 1951- *82*
Hess, Lilo 1916- *4*
Hess, Paul 1961- *134*
Hesse, Hermann 1877-1962 .... *50*
Hesse, Karen 1952- *215*
Autobiography Feature *113*
Earlier sketches in SATA *74, 103, 158*
See also CLR *141*
See also SAAS *25*
Hest, Amy 1950- *193*
Earlier sketches in SATA *55, 82, 129*
Heuer, Karsten 1968(?)- *202*
Heuer, Kenneth John 1927- *44*
Heuman, William 1912-1971 .... *21*
Heuston, Kimberley 1960- *167*
Heuston, Kimberley Burton
See Heuston, Kimberley
Heuvel, Eric 1960- *224*
Hewes, Agnes Danforth 1874-1963 .... *35*
Hewett, Anita 1918-1989 .... *13*
Hewett, Joan 1930- *140*
Earlier sketch in SATA *81*
Hewett, Richard 1929- *81*
Hewitson, Jennifer 1961- *97*
Hewitt, Margaret 1961- *84*
Hewitt, Sally 1949- *127*
Hext, Harrington
See Phillpotts, Eden
Hey, Nigel S(tewart) 1936- *20*
Heyduck-Huth, Hilde 1929- *8*
Heyer, Carol 1950- *130*
Earlier sketch in SATA *74*
Heyer, Marilee 1942- *102*
Earlier sketch in SATA *64*
Heyerdahl, Thor 1914-2002 .... *52*
Earlier sketch in SATA *2*
Heyes, (Nancy) Eileen 1956- *150*
Earlier sketch in SATA *80*
Heyliger, William 1884-1955
See YABC *1*
Heyman, Ken(neth Louis) 1930- *114*
Earlier sketch in SATA *34*
Heyward, (Edwin) DuBose 1885-1940 .... *21*
Heywood, Karen 1946- *48*
Hezlep, William (Earl) 1936- *88*
Hiaasen, Carl 1953- *208*
Hiatt, Shelby *226*
Hibbert, Arthur Raymond
See Hibbert, Christopher
Hibbert, Christopher 1924-2008 .... *4*
Obituary *201*
Hibbert, Eleanor Alice Burford 1906-1993 .... *2*
Obituary *74*

Hickman, Estella (Lee) 1942- *111*
Hickman, Janet 1940- *127*
Earlier sketch in SATA *12*
Hickman, Martha Whitmore 1925- *26*
Hickman, Pamela 1958- *186*
Earlier sketch in SATA *128*
Hickock, Will
See Harrison, C(hester) William
Hickok, Lorena A. 1893-1968 .... *20*
Hickox, Rebecca (Ayres) *116*
Hicks, Barbara Jean 1953- *165*
Hicks, Betty *191*
Hicks, Clifford B. 1920- *50*
Hicks, Eleanor B.
See Coerr, Eleanor (Beatrice)
Hicks, Harvey
See Stratemeyer, Edward L.
Hicks, Peter 1952- *111*
Hicyilmaz, Gaye 1947- *157*
Earlier sketch in SATA *77*
Hieatt, Constance B(artlett) 1928- *4*
Hiebert, Ray Eldon 1932- *13*
Hierstein, Judith *212*
Hierstein, Judy
See Hierstein, Judith
Higdon, Hal 1931- *4*
Higginbottom, David 1923- *87*
Earlier sketch in SATA *25*
Higginbottom, J(effrey) Winslow 1945- *29*
Higgins, Dalton *223*
Higgins, F.E. *219*
Higgins, Fiona
See Higgins, F.E.
Higgins, Joanna 1945- *125*
Higgins, Simon (Richard) 1958- *105*
Higginsen, Vy *79*
High, Linda Oatman 1958- *188*
Autobiography Feature *188*
Earlier sketches in SATA *94, 145*
High, Philip E. 1914- *119*
High, Philip Empson
See High, Philip E.
Higham, David 1949- *50*
Higham, David Michael
See Higham, David
Higham, Jon Atlas
See Higham, Jonathan Huw
Higham, Jonathan Huw 1960- *59*
Highet, Helen
See MacInnes, Helen (Clark)
Hightman, Jason 1971(?)- *189*
Hightman, J.P.
See Hightman, Jason
Hightower, Florence Cole 1916-1981 .... *4*
Obituary *27*
Highwater, Jamake (Mamake)
1942(?)-2001 .... *69*
Brief entry *30*
Earlier sketch in SATA *32*
See also CLR *17*
Hilb, Nora 1953- *178*
Hildebrandt, Greg, Jr. 1970- *228*
Hildebrandt, Greg 1939- *172*
Brief entry *33*
Earlier sketch in SATA *55*
Hildebrandt, Tim 1939-2006 .... *55*
Brief entry *33*
Hildebrandt, Timothy
See Hildebrandt, Tim
Hildebrandts, The
See Hildebrandt, Greg
and Hildebrandt, Tim
Hilder, Rowland 1905-1993 .... *36*
Obituary *77*
Hildick, E. W.
See Hildick, Wallace
Hildick, Wallace 1925-2001 .... *68*
Earlier sketch in SATA *2*
See also SAAS *6*
Hilgartner, Beth 1957- *58*

Hill, Alexis
See Craig, Mary (Francis) Shura
and Glick, Ruth
Hill, Anthony R. 1942- *164*
Earlier sketch in SATA *91*
Hill, Anthony Robert
See Hill, Anthony R.
Hill, David 1942- *152*
Earlier sketch in SATA *103*
Hill, Donna (Marie) 1921- *124*
Earlier sketch in SATA *24*
Hill, Douglas 1935-2007 .... *78*
Earlier sketch in SATA *39*
Hill, Douglas Arthur
See Hill, Douglas
Hill, Elizabeth Starr 1925- *143*
Earlier sketch in SATA *24*
Hill, Eric 1927- *133*
Brief entry *53*
Earlier sketch in SATA *66*
See also CLR *13*
Hill, Gordon
See Eldin, Peter
Hill, Grace Brooks *67*
Earlier sketch in SATA *1*
Hill, Grace Livingston 1865-1947
See YABC *2*
Hill, Helen M(orey) 1915- *27*
Hill, Isabel *225*
Hill, Isabel T.
See Hill, Isabel
Hill, John
See Koontz, Dean
Hill, Johnson
See Kunhardt, Edith
Hill, Judy I. R.
See Roberts, Judy I.
Hill, Kathleen Louise 1917- *4*
Hill, Kay
See Hill, Kathleen Louise
Hill, Kirkpatrick 1938- *188*
Earlier sketches in SATA *72, 126*
Hill, Laban
See Hill, Laban Carrick
Hill, Laban Carrick *170*
Hill, Lee Sullivan 1958- *96*
Hill, Lorna 1902-1991 .... *12*
Hill, Margaret (Ohler) 1915- *36*
Hill, Meg
See Hill, Margaret (Ohler)
Hill, Meredith
See Craig, Mary (Francis) Shura
Hill, Monica
See Watson, Jane Werner
Hill, Pamela Smith 1954- *112*
Hill, Ralph Nading 1917-1987 .... *65*
Hill, Robert W(hite) 1919-1982 .... *12*
Obituary *31*
Hill, Ruth A.
See Viguers, Ruth Hill
Hill, Ruth Livingston
See Munce, Ruth Hill
Hill, Stuart 1958- *186*
Hill, Susan 1942- *183*
Hill, Susan Elizabeth
See Hill, Susan
Hill, Susanna Leonard 1965- *193*
Hill, Thomas 1960- *82*
Hillcourt, William 1900-1992 .... *27*
Hillenbrand, Will 1960- *210*
Earlier sketches in SATA *84, 147*
Hiller, Ilo (Ann) 1938- *59*
Hillerman, Anthony Grove
See Hillerman, Tony
Hillerman, Tony 1925-2008 .... *6*
Obituary *198*
Hillert, Margaret 1920- *91*
Earlier sketch in SATA *8*
Hilliard, Richard *183*
Hillman, Ben 1957- *202*
Hillman, Elizabeth 1942- *75*

Hillman, John 1952- 120
Hillman, Martin
    See Hill, Douglas
Hillman, Priscilla 1940- 48
    Brief entry 39
Hillman, Shane 200
Hills, C.A.R. 1955- 39
Hills, Charles Albert Reis
    See Hills, C.A.R.
Hills, Tad 173
Hilton, Irene Pothus -1979 7
Hilton, James 1900-1954 34
Hilton, Margaret Lynette 1946- 105
    Earlier sketch in SATA 68
    See also CLR 25
    See also SAAS 21
Hilton, Nette
    See Hilton, Margaret Lynette
Hilton, Ralph 1907-1982 8
Hilton, Suzanne 1922- 4
Hilton-Bruce, Anne
    See Hilton, Margaret Lynette
Him, George 1937-1982
    Obituary 30
Himelblau, Linda -2005 179
Himelstein, Shmuel 1940- 83
Himler, Ann 1946- 8
Himler, Ronald 1937- 183
    Earlier sketches in SATA 6, 92, 137
Himler, Ronald Norbert
    See Himler, Ronald
Himmelman, John 1959- 221
    Earlier sketches in SATA 47, 94, 159
Himmelman, John C.
    See Himmelman, John
Hinckley, Helen
    See Jones, Helen Hinckley
Hind, Dolores (Ellen) 1931- 53
    Brief entry 49
Hindin, Nathan
    See Bloch, Robert (Albert)
Hindley, Judy 1940- 179
    Earlier sketch in SATA 120
Hinds, P. Mignon 98
Hinds, Patricia Mignon
    See Hinds, P. Mignon
Hine, Sesyle Joslin 1929- 2
Hines, Anna Grossnickle 1946- 209
    Brief entry 45
    Earlier sketches in SATA 51, 95, 141
    See also SAAS 16
Hines, Gary (Roger) 1944- 136
    Earlier sketch in SATA 74
Hinman, Bonnie 1950- 216
Hinojosa, Maria (de Lourdes) 1961- 88
Hinton, Nigel 1941- 166
Hinton, S. E. 1950- 160
    Earlier sketches in SATA 19, 58, 115
    See also CLR 23
Hinton, Sam 1917-2009 43
Hinton, Susan Eloise
    See Hinton, S. E.
Hintz, Martin 1945- 128
    Brief entry 39
    Earlier sketch in SATA 47
Hintz, Stephen V. 1975- 129
Hippopotamus, Eugene H.
    See Kraus, (Herman) Robert
Hirano, Cathy 1957- 68
Hirao, Amiko 203
Hirsch, Karen 1941- 61
Hirsch, Odo 157
    Earlier sketch in SATA 111
Hirsch, Phil 1926- 35
Hirsch, S. Carl 1913-1990 2
    See also SAAS 7
Hirschfelder, Arlene B. 1943- 227
    Earlier sketches in SATA 80, 138
Hirschi, Ron 1948- 192
    Earlier sketches in SATA 56, 95
Hirschmann, Linda (Ann) 1941- 40

Hirsh, Marilyn 1944-1988 7
    Obituary 58
Hirshberg, Al(bert Simon) 1909-1973 38
Hiscock, Bruce 1940- 204
    Earlier sketches in SATA 57, 137
Hiser, Constance 1950- 71
Hiser, Iona Seibert -1998 4
Hislop, Julia Rose Catherine 1962- 74
Hissey, Jane 1952- 130
    Autobiography Feature 130
    Earlier sketches in SATA 58, 103
Hissey, Jane Elizabeth
    See Hissey, Jane
Hitchcock, Alfred (Joseph) 1899-1980 27
    Obituary 24
Hite, Sid 1954- 175
    Earlier sketches in SATA 75, 136
Hitte, Kathryn 1919- 16
Hitz, Demi
    See Demi
Hitzeroth, Deborah L. 1961- 78
Hnizdovsky, Jacques 1915- 32
Ho, Jannie 226
Ho, Louise 185
Ho, Minfong 1951- 151
    Earlier sketches in SATA 15, 94
    See also CLR 28
Hoagland, Edward (Morley) 1932- 51
Hoare, Robert J(ohn) 1921-1975 38
Hoban, Julia 217
Hoban, Lillian 1925-1998 69
    Obituary 104
    Earlier sketch in SATA 22
    See also CLR 67
Hoban, Russell 1925- 136
    Earlier sketches in SATA 1, 40, 78
    See also CLR 139
Hoban, Russell Conwell
    See Hoban, Russell
Hoban, Tana 1917(?)-2006 104
    Obituary 173
    Earlier sketches in SATA 22, 70
    See also CLR 76
    See also SAAS 12
Hobart, Lois (Elaine) 7
Hobbie, Holly 1942- 225
    Earlier sketch in SATA 178
    See also CLR 88
Hobbie, Jocelyn 190
Hobbie, Nathaniel 196
Hobbs, Leigh 1953- 166
Hobbs, Valerie 1941- 193
    Autobiography Feature 145
    Earlier sketches in SATA 93, 145
    See also CLR 148
Hobbs, Will 1947- 177
    Autobiography Feature 127
    Earlier sketches in SATA 72, 110
    See also CLR 59
Hobbs, William Carl
    See Hobbs, Will
Hoberman, Mary Ann 1930- 228
    Earlier sketches in SATA 5, 72, 111, 158
    See also CLR 22
    See also SAAS 18
Hobson, Bruce 1950- 62
Hobson, Burton (Harold) 1933- 28
Hobson, Laura Z(ametkin) 1900-1986 52
Hobson, Sally 1967- 172
    Earlier sketch in SATA 84
Hoce, Charley E. 174
Hochman, David 202
Hochschild, Arlie Russell 1940- 11
Hockaby, Stephen
    See Mitchell, Gladys (Maude Winifred)
Hockenberry, Hope
    See Newell, Hope Hockenberry
Hodge, Deborah 1954- 163
    Earlier sketch in SATA 122
Hodge, P. W.
    See Hodge, Paul W(illiam)

Hodge, Paul W(illiam) 1934- 12
Hodgell, P(atricia) C(hristine) 1951- 42
Hodges, C. Walter 1909-2004 2
    Obituary 158
Hodges, Carl G. 1902-1964 10
Hodges, Cyril Walter
    See Hodges, C. Walter
Hodges, Elizabeth Jamison 1
Hodges, Margaret 1911-2005 167
    Obituary 172
    Earlier sketches in SATA 1, 33, 75, 117
    See also SAAS 9
Hodges, Margaret Moore
    See Hodges, Margaret
Hodgetts, Blake Christopher 1967- 43
Hodgkins, Fran 1964- 199
Hodgkinson, Leigh 1975- 202
Hodgman, Ann 1956- 198
Hodgson, Harriet (W.) 1935- 84
Hoehne, Marcia 1951- 89
Hoellwarth, Cathryn Clinton
    See Clinton, Cathryn
Hoestlandt, Jo 1948- 221
    Earlier sketch in SATA 94
Hoestlandt, Jocelyne
    See Hoestlandt, Jo
Hoexter, Corinne K. 1927- 6
Hoeye, Michael 1947- 136
Hof, Marjolijn 1956- 226
Hoff, Carol 1900-1979 11
Hoff, Mary (King) 1956- 157
    Earlier sketch in SATA 74
Hoff, Syd(ney) 1912-2004 138
    Obituary 154
    Earlier sketches in SATA 9, 72
    See also CLR 83
    See also SAAS 4
Hoffman, Edwin D. 49
Hoffman, Elizabeth P(arkinson) 1921-2003
    Obituary 153
Hoffman, Mary 1945- 211
    Earlier sketches in SATA 59, 97, 144
    See also SAAS 24
Hoffman, Mat 1972- 150
Hoffman, Nina Kiriki 1955- 160
Hoffman, Phyllis M. 1944- 4
Hoffman, Phyllis Miriam
    See Hoffman, Phyllis M.
Hoffman, Rosekrans 1926- 15
Hoffmann, E(rnst) T(heodor) A(madeus)
    1776-1822 27
    See also CLR 133
Hoffmann, Felix 1911-1975 9
Hoffmann, Heinrich 1809-1894
    See CLR 122
Hoffmann, Margaret Jones 1910- 48
Hoffmann, Peggy
    See Hoffmann, Margaret Jones
Hofher, Catherine Baxley 1954- 130
Hofher, Cathy
    See Hofher, Catherine Baxley
Hofmeyr, Dianne (Louise) 138
Hofsepian, Sylvia A. 1932- 74
Hofsinde, Robert 1902-1973 21
Hogan, Bernice Harris 1929- 12
Hogan, Inez 1895-1973 2
Hogan, James P. 1941-2010 81
Hogan, James Patrick
    See Hogan, James P.
Hogan, Jamie 192
Hogan, Linda 1947- 132
Hogan, Mary 1957- 210
Hogarth, Burne 1911-1996 89
    Earlier sketch in SATA 63
Hogarth, Grace (Weston Allen) 1905-1995 .. 91
Hogarth, Jr.
    See Kent, Rockwell
Hogarth, (Arthur) Paul 1917-2001 41
Hogg, Garry 1902-1976 2
Hogg, Gary 1957- 172
    Earlier sketch in SATA 105

Hogner, Dorothy Childs 4
Hogner, Nils 1893-1970 25
Hogrogian, Nonny 1932- 74
    Autobiography Feature 127
    Earlier sketch in SATA 7
    See also CLR 95
    See also SAAS 1
Hoh, Diane 1937- 102
    Brief entry 48
    Earlier sketch in SATA 52
Hoke, Helen
    See Watts, Helen L. Hoke
Hoke, Helen L.
    See Watts, Helen L. Hoke
Hoke, John 1925-2011 7
Hoke, John Lindsay
    See Hoke, John
Hokenson, Terry 1948- 193
Hol, Coby 1943- 126
Holabird, Katharine 1948- 213
    Earlier sketches in SATA 62, 135
Holaday, Bobbie 1922- 153
Holbeach, Henry
    See Rands, William Brighty
Holberg, Ruth L(angland) 1889-1984 1
Holbrook, Kathy 1963- 107
Holbrook, Peter
    See Glick, Carl (Cannon)
Holbrook, Sabra
    See Erickson, Sabra Rollins
Holbrook, Sara 131
Holbrook, Stewart Hall 1893-1964 2
Holcomb, Jerry (Leona) Kimble 1927- 113
Holcomb, Nan
    See McPhee, Norma H.
Holdcroft, Tina 227
Holden, Elizabeth Rhoda
    See Lawrence, Louise
Holding, James (Clark Carlisle, Jr.)
    1907-1997 3
Hole, Stian 1969- 204
Holeman, Linda 1949- 136
    Autobiography Feature 136
    Earlier sketch in SATA 102
Holgate, Doug 225
Holinger, William (Jacques) 1944- 90
Holisher, Desider 1901-1972 6
Holl, Adelaide Hinkle 1910- 8
Holl, Kristi
    See Holl, Kristi D.
Holl, Kristi D. 1951- 51
Holl, Kristi Diane
    See Holl, Kristi D.
Holland, Gay W. 1941- 128
Holland, Isabelle (Christian) 1920-2002 70
    Autobiography Feature 103
    Obituary 132
    Earlier sketch in SATA 8
    See also CLR 57
Holland, Janice 1913-1962 18
Holland, John L(ewis) 1919- 20
Holland, Joyce
    See Morice, Dave
Holland, Julia 1954- 106
Holland, Lynda (H.) 1959- 77
Holland, Lys
    See Gater, Dilys
Holland, Marion 1908-1989 6
    Obituary 61
Holland, Richard 1976- 216
Holland, Trish 221
Hollander, John 1929- 13
Hollander, Nicole 1940(?)- 101
Hollander, Paul
    See Silverberg, Robert
Hollander, Phyllis 1928- 39
Hollander, Zander 1923- 63
Holldobler, Turid 1939- 26
Holliday, Joe
    See Holliday, Joseph
Holliday, Joseph 1910- 11

Holling, Holling C(lancy) 1900-1973 15
    Obituary 26
    See also CLR 50
Hollingsworth, Alvin C(arl) 1930- 39
Hollingsworth, Mary 1947- 166
    Earlier sketch in SATA 91
Holloway, Teresa (Bragunier) 1906- 26
Hollyer, Beatrice 1957- 226
Hollyer, Belinda 204
Holm, (Else) Anne (Lise) 1922-1998 1
    See also CLR 75
    See also SAAS 7
Holm, Jennifer L. 1968(?)- 183
    Earlier sketches in SATA 120, 163
Holm, Matthew 1974- 174
Holm, Sharon Lane 1955- 114
    Earlier sketch in SATA 78
Holman, Felice 1919- 82
    Earlier sketch in SATA 7
    See also SAAS 17
Holm and Hamel
    See Holm, Jennifer L.
Holmberg, Bo R. 1945- 203
Holme, Bryan 1913-1990 26
    Obituary 66
Holmes, Barbara Ware 1945- 127
    Earlier sketch in SATA 65
Holmes, Elizabeth 1957- 191
Holmes, Elizabeth Ann
    See Holmes, Elizabeth
Holmes, John
    See Souster, (Holmes) Raymond
Holmes, Marjorie (Rose) 1910-2002 43
Holmes, Martha 1961- 72
Holmes, Mary Tavener 1954- 199
Holmes, Mary Z(astrow) 1943- 80
Holmes, Oliver Wendell 1809-1894 34
Holmes, Peggy 1898- 60
Holmes, Raymond
    See Souster, (Holmes) Raymond
Holmes, Rick
    See Hardwick, Richard Holmes, Jr.
Holmes, Sara Lewis 186
Holmgren, Helen Jean 1930- 45
Holmgren, Sister George Ellen
    See Holmgren, Helen Jean
Holmgren, Virginia C(unningham) 1909- 26
Holmquist, Eve 1921- 11
Holt, K.A.
    See Roy, Kari Anne
Holt, Kimberly Willis 1960- 223
    Earlier sketches in SATA 122, 179
Holt, Margaret 1937- 4
Holt, Margaret Van Vechten (Saunders)
    1899-1963 32
Holt, Michael (Paul) 1929- 13
Holt, Rackham
    See Holt, Margaret Van Vechten (Saunders)
Holt, Rochelle L.
    See DuBois, Rochelle Holt
Holt, Stephen
    See Thompson, Harlan
Holt, Victoria
    See Hibbert, Eleanor Alice Burford
Holtei, Christa 1953- 214
Holton, Leonard
    See Wibberley, Leonard
Holtz, Thomas R., Jr. 1965- 203
Holtze, Sally Holmes 1952- 64
Holtzman, Jerome 1926-2008 57
    Obituary 194
Holub, Joan 1956- 229
    Earlier sketches in SATA 99, 149
Holub, Josef 1926- 175
Holubitsky, Katherine 1955- 165
    Earlier sketch in SATA 121
Holyer, Erna Maria 1925- 22
Holyer, Ernie
    See Holyer, Erna Maria
Holyfield, John 1969- 227
Holz, Loretta 1943- 17

Holz, Loretta Marie
    See Holz, Loretta
Homel, David 1952- 97
Homze, Alma C. 1932- 17
Honey, Elizabeth 1947- 137
    Autobiography Feature 137
    Earlier sketch in SATA 112
Honeycutt, Natalie 1945- 97
Hong, Lily Toy 1958- 76
Hong, Maxine Ting Ting
    See Kingston, Maxine Hong
Honig, Donald 1931- 18
Honig, Donald Martin
    See Honig, Donald
Honness, Elizabeth H. 1904- 2
Hoobler, Dorothy 1941- 161
    Earlier sketches in SATA 28, 109
Hoobler, Thomas 161
    Earlier sketches in SATA 28, 109
Hood, Joseph F. 1925- 4
Hood, Robert E. 1926- 21
Hood, Sarah
    See Killough, (Karen) Lee
Hook, Brendan 1963- 105
Hook, Frances 1912-1983 27
Hook, Geoffrey R(aynor) 1928- 103
Hook, Jeff
    See Hook, Geoffrey R(aynor)
Hook, Martha 1936- 27
Hooker, Richard
    See Heinz, W. C.
Hooker, Ruth 1920-1998 21
hooks, bell 1952(?)- 170
    Earlier sketch in SATA 115
Hooks, William H(arris) 1921- 94
    Earlier sketch in SATA 16
Hoon, Patricia Easterly 1954- 90
Hooper, Byrd
    See St. Clair, Byrd Hooper
Hooper, Mary 1948- 205
    Earlier sketch in SATA 160
Hooper, Maureen Brett 1927- 76
Hooper, Meredith 1939- 159
    Earlier sketches in SATA 28, 101
Hooper, Meredith Jean
    See Hooper, Meredith
Hooper, Patricia 1941- 95
Hoopes, Lyn Littlefield 1953- 49
    Brief entry 44
Hoopes, Ned E(dward) 1932- 21
Hoopes, Roy 1922-2009 11
Hoose, Phillip 1947- 215
    Earlier sketch in SATA 137
Hoover, H(elen) M(ary) 1935- 132
    Brief entry 33
    Earlier sketches in SATA 44, 83
    See also SAAS 8
Hoover, Helen (Drusilla Blackburn)
    1910-1984 12
    Obituary 39
Hope, Christopher 1944- 62
Hope, Christopher David Tully
    See Hope, Christopher
Hope, Laura Lee
    See Goulart, Ron
    and Stanley, George Edward
Hope Simpson, Jacynth 1930- 12
Hopf, Alice (Martha) L(ightner) 1904-1988 ... 5
    Obituary 55
Hopgood, Tim 1961- 224
Hopkins, A. T.
    See Turngren, Annette
Hopkins, C. M.
    See Hopkins, Cathy
Hopkins, Cathy 1953- 165
Hopkins, Cathy M.
    See Hopkins, Cathy
Hopkins, Clark 1895-1976
    Obituary 34
Hopkins, Ellen 1955- 128

Hopkins, Ellen L.
See Hopkins, Ellen
Hopkins, Jackie
See Hopkins, Jackie Mims
Hopkins, Jackie Mims 1952- 178
Earlier sketch in SATA 92
Hopkins, Joseph G(erard) E(dward) 1909- ... 11
Hopkins, (Hector) Kenneth 1914-1988
Obituary 58
Hopkins, Lee Bennett 1938- 215
Earlier sketches in SATA 3, 68, 125, 168
See also CLR 44
See also SAAS 4
Hopkins, Lyman
See Folsom, Franklin (Brewster)
Hopkins, Marjorie 1911-1999 9
Hopkins, Mary R(ice) 1956- 97
Hopkinson, Amanda 1948- 84
Hopkinson, Deborah 1952- 216
Autobiography Feature 180
Earlier sketches in SATA 76, 108, 159, 180
See also CLR 118
Hopman, Philip 1961- 177
Hoppe, Joanne 1932- 42
Hoppe, Matthias 1952- 76
Hoppe, Paul 209
Hopper, Nancy J. 1937- 38
Brief entry 35
Hoppey, Tim 1958- 225
Hopping, Lorraine Jean
See Egan, Lorraine Hopping
Horacek, Judy 1961- 211
Horaek, Petr 214
Earlier sketch in SATA 163
Horenstein, Henry 1947- 108
Horgan, Paul (George Vincent O'Shaughnessy)
1903-1995 13
Obituary 84
Horlak, E.E.
See Tepper, Sheri S.
Horler, Sydney 1888-1954 102
Horley, Alex 1970- 229
Horn, Sandra Ann 1944- 154
Hornblow, Arthur, Jr. 1893-1976 15
Hornblow, Leonora 1920-2005 18
Obituary 171
Hornblow, Leonora Schinasi
See Hornblow, Leonora
Horne, Constance 1927- 149
Horne, Richard 1960-2007 169
Obituary 180
Earlier sketch in SATA 111
Horne, Richard Henry Hengist
1802(?)-1884 29
Horner, Althea (Jane) 1926- 36
Horner, Dave 1934- 12
Horner, Jack 1946- 106
Horner, John R.
See Horner, Jack
Horner, John Robert
See Horner, Jack
Hornik, Laurie Miller 159
Horniman, Joanne 1951- 167
Earlier sketch in SATA 98
Hornos, Axel 1907-1994 20
Hornstein, Reuben Aaron 1912- 64
Horowitz, Anthony 1955- 195
Earlier sketch in SATA 137
Horowitz, Dave 1970- 204
Earlier sketch in SATA 172
Horowitz, Ruth 1957- 136
Horrocks, Anita 1958- 169
Horse, Harry
See Horne, Richard
Horsfield, Alan 1939- 153
Horstman, Lisa 1964- 219
Hort, Lenny 179
Horton, James O. 1943- 173
Horton, James Oliver
See Horton, James O.
Horton, Joan 217

Horton, Madelyn (Stacey) 1962- 77
Horvath, Betty 1927- 4
Horvath, David 1972(?)- 192
Horvath, Polly 1957- 194
Earlier sketches in SATA 85, 140
See also CLR 90
Horwich, Frances R(appaport) 1908-2001 11
Obituary 130
Horwitz, Elinor Lander 45
Brief entry 33
Horwood, William 1944- 85
Hosford, Dorothy (Grant) 1900-1952 22
Hosford, Jessie 1892-1990 5
Hoshi, Shin'ichi 1926- 101
Hoshino, Felicia 1968- 189
Hoskyns-Abrahall, Clare (Constance
Drury) 13
Hosler, Danamarie 1978- 184
Hossack, Sylvia 1939- 83
Hossack, Sylvie Adams
See Hossack, Sylvia
Hosseini, Khaled 1965- 156
Hossell, Karen Price
See Price, Karen
Hosta, Dar 192
Hostetler, Marian 1932- 91
Hostetter, Joyce Moyer 1952- 228
Houck, Carter 1924- 22
Hough, Charlotte 1924-2008 9
Obituary 202
Hough, Helen Charlotte
See Hough, Charlotte
Hough, Judy Taylor 1932- 63
Brief entry 51
Earlier sketch in SATA 56
Hough, Richard (Alexander) 1922-1999 17
Houghton, Eric 1930- 7
Houk, Randy 1944- 97
Houlehen, Robert J. 1918- 18
Houlton, Peggy Mann 1925(?)-1990 6
Household, Geoffrey 1900-1988 14
Obituary 59
Housman, Laurence 1865-1959 25
Houston, Dick 1943- 74
Houston, Gloria 138
Autobiography Feature 138
Earlier sketch in SATA 81
Houston, James A(rchibald) 1921-2005 74
Obituary 163
Earlier sketch in SATA 13
See also CLR 3
See also SAAS 17
Houston, James D. 1933-2009 78
Obituary 203
Houston, James Dudley
See Houston, James D.
Houston, James Dudley
See Houston, James D.
Houston, Jeanne Toyo Wakatsuki
See Houston, Jeanne Wakatsuki
Houston, Jeanne Wakatsuki 1934- 168
Autobiography Feature 168
Earlier sketch in SATA 78
Houston, Juanita C. 1921- 129
Houton, Kathleen
See Kilgore, Kathleen
Houts, Amy F. 164
Houts, Michelle 219
Hovey, Kate 158
Howard, Alan 1922- 45
Howard, Alyssa
See Buckholtz, Eileen (Garber)
and Glick, Ruth
and Titchener, Louise
Howard, Arthur 1948- 212
Earlier sketch in SATA 165
Howard, Arthur Charles
See Howard, Arthur
Howard, Elizabeth Fitzgerald 1927- 119
Earlier sketch in SATA 74

Howard, Ellen 1943- 184
Earlier sketches in SATA 67, 99
Howard, Jane R(uble) 1924- 87
Howard, Norman Barry 1949- 90
Howard, P. M.
See Howard, Pauline Rodriguez
Howard, Paul 1967- 190
Earlier sketch in SATA 118
Howard, Pauline Rodriguez 1951- 124
Howard, Prosper
See Hamilton, Charles (Harold St. John)
Howard, Robert West 1908-1988 5
Howard, Todd 1964- 135
Howard, Tristan
See Currie, Stephen
Howard, Vernon (Linwood) 1918-1992 40
Obituary 73
Howard, Warren F.
See Pohl, Frederik
Howarth, Daniel 222
Earlier sketch in SATA 188
Howarth, David (Armine) 1912-1991 6
Obituary 68
Howarth, Lesley 1952- 94
Howe, Deborah 1946-1978 29
Howe, James 1946- 224
Earlier sketches in SATA 29, 71, 111, 161
See also CLR 9
Howe, John F. 1957- 79
Howe, Norma 1930- 126
Howe, Peter 1942- 214
Howell, Pat 1947- 15
Howell, S.
See Styles, (Frank) Showell
Howell, Simmone 1971- 214
Howell, Virginia
See Ellison, Virginia H(owell)
Howells, Tania 229
Howes, Barbara 1914-1996 5
Howie, Betsy 1962- 215
Howie, Diana 1945- 122
Howie, Diana Melson
See Howie, Diana
Howker, Janni 1957- 72
Brief entry 46
See also CLR 14
See also SAAS 13
Howland, Ethan 1963- 131
Hoy, Linda 1946- 65
Hoy, Nina
See Roth, Arthur J(oseph)
Hoyle, Geoffrey 1942- 18
Hoyt, Ard 190
Hoyt, Edwin P(almer), Jr. 1923- 28
Hoyt, Erich 1950- 140
Earlier sketch in SATA 65
Hoyt, Olga
See Gruhzit-Hoyt, Olga (Margaret)
Hrdlitschka, Shelley 1956- 167
Earlier sketch in SATA 111
Hrdlitschka, Shelley Joanne
See Hrdlitschka, Shelley
Hromic, Alma A.
See Alexander, Alma
Htin Aung, U.
See Aung, (Maung) Htin
Hu, Ying-Hwa 173
Huang, Benrei 1959- 86
Huang, Nathan 1982(?)- 228
Hubalek, Linda K. 1954- 111
Hubbard, Crystal 209
Hubbard, Jennifer R. 227
Hubbard, Margaret Ann
See Priley, Margaret (Ann) Hubbard
Hubbard, Michelle Calabro 1953- 122
Hubbard, Patricia 1945- 124
Hubbard, Woodleigh Marx 160
Earlier sketch in SATA 98
Hubbell, Patricia 1928- 186
Earlier sketches in SATA 8, 132
Hubery, Julia 195

Hubley, Faith Elliot 1924-2001 .... *48*
  Obituary *133*
Hubley, John 1914-1977 .... *48*
  Obituary *24*
Huck, Charlotte S. 1922- *136*
  Earlier sketch in SATA *82*
Hucke, Johannes 1966- *218*
Hudak, Michal 1956- *143*
Hudson, Cheryl Willis 1948- *160*
  Earlier sketch in SATA *81*
Hudson, Jan 1954-1990 .... *77*
  See also CLR *40*
Hudson, Jeffery
  See Crichton, Michael
Hudson, Jeffrey
  See Crichton, Michael
Hudson, (Margaret) Kirsty 1947- *32*
Hudson, Margaret
  See Shuter, Jane (Margaret)
Hudson, W(illiam) H(enry) 1841-1922 .... *35*
Hudson, Wade 1946- *162*
  Earlier sketch in SATA *74*
Huelsmann, Eva 1928- *16*
Huerlimann, Bettina 1909-1983 .... *39*
  Obituary *34*
Huerlimann, Ruth 1939- *32*
  Brief entry *31*
Huff, Barbara A. 1929- *67*
Huff, Tanya 1957- *171*
  Earlier sketch in SATA *85*
Huff, Tanya Sue
  See Huff, Tanya
Huff, T.S.
  See Huff, Tanya
Huff, Vivian 1948- *59*
Huffaker, Sandy 1943- *10*
Huffman, Tom *24*
Huggins, Nathan Irvin 1927-1989 .... *63*
Huggins, Peter 1951- *178*
Hughes, Carol 1955- *217*
  Earlier sketch in SATA *108*
Hughes, Dean 1943- *139*
  Earlier sketches in SATA *33, 77*
  See also CLR *76*
Hughes, Eden
  See Griffin, W. E. B.
Hughes, Edward James
  See Hughes, Ted
Hughes, James Langston
  See Hughes, Langston
Hughes, Langston 1902-1967 .... *33*
  Earlier sketch in SATA *4*
  See also CLR *17*
Hughes, Libby *71*
Hughes, Matilda
  See MacLeod, Charlotte (Matilda)
Hughes, Monica 1925-2003 .... *162*
  Earlier sketches in SATA *15, 70, 119*
  See also CLR *60*
  See also SAAS *11*
Hughes, Monica Ince
  See Hughes, Monica
Hughes, Pat *197*
Hughes, Richard (Arthur Warren)
  1900-1976 .... *8*
  Obituary *25*
Hughes, Sara
  See Saunders, Susan
Hughes, Shirley 1927- *159*
  Earlier sketches in SATA *16, 70, 110*
  See also CLR *15*
Hughes, Susan 1960- *216*
Hughes, Ted 1930-1998 .... *49*
  Brief entry *27*
  Obituary *107*
  See also CLR *131*
Hughes, Thomas 1822-1896 .... *31*
  See also CLR *160*
Hughes, Virginia
  See Campbell, Hope
Hughes, Walter (Llewellyn) 1910-1993 .... *26*

Hughey, Roberta 1942- *61*
Hugo, Pierre Brackers de
  See Brackers de Hugo, Pierre
Hugo, Victor 1802-1885 .... *47*
Hugo, Victor Marie
  See Hugo, Victor
Huline-Dickens, Frank William 1931- *34*
Huling, Jan *172*
Huliska-Beith, Laura *175*
Hull, Eleanor (Means) 1913- *21*
Hull, Eric Traviss
  See Harnan, Terry
Hull, H. Braxton
  See Jacobs, Helen Hull
Hull, Jesse Redding
  See Hull, Jessie Redding
Hull, Jessie Redding 1932- *51*
Hull, Katharine 1921-1977 .... *23*
Hull, Lise (E.) 1954- *148*
Hull, Maureen 1949- *142*
Hulme, Joy N. 1922- *161*
  Earlier sketches in SATA *74, 112*
Hults, Dorothy Niebrugge 1898-2000 .... *6*
Humble, Richard 1945- *60*
Hume, Lachie *189*
Hume, Lotta Carswell *7*
Hume, Ruth Fox 1922-1980 .... *26*
  Obituary *22*
Hume, Stephen Eaton 1947- *136*
Hummel, Berta 1909-1946 .... *43*
Hummel, Sister Maria Innocentia
  See Hummel, Berta
Hummon, Marcus 1960- *213*
Humphrey, Carol Sue 1956- *167*
Humphrey, Henry (III) 1930- *16*
Humphrey, Kate
  See Forsyth, Kate
Humphrey, Sandra McLeod 1936- *95*
Humphreys, Martha 1943- *71*
Humphreys, Susan L.
  See Lowell, Susan
Humphries, Tudor 1953- *226*
Hundal, Nancy 1957- *128*
Huneck, Stephen 1949- *183*
  Earlier sketch in SATA *129*
Hungerford, Hesba Fay
  See Brinsmead, H(esba) F(ay)
Hungerford, Pixie
  See Brinsmead, H(esba) F(ay)
Hunkin, Tim 1950- *53*
Hunkin, Timothy Mark Trelawney
  See Hunkin, Tim
Hunt, Angela Elwell 1957- *159*
  Earlier sketch in SATA *75*
Hunt, Bernice 1920- *4*
Hunt, Charlotte Dumaresq
  See Demi
Hunt, Francesca
  See Holland, Isabelle (Christian)
Hunt, Irene 1907-2001 .... *91*
  Earlier sketch in SATA *2*
  See also CLR *1*
Hunt, Janie Louise 1963- *102*
Hunt, Jonathan 1966- *84*
Hunt, Joyce 1927- *31*
Hunt, Linda 1940- *39*
Hunt, Lisa B(ehnke) 1967- *84*
Hunt, Mabel Leigh 1892-1971 .... *1*
  Obituary *26*
Hunt, Morton M(agill) 1920- *22*
Hunt, Nigel
  See Greenbank, Anthony Hunt
Hunt, Peter (Leonard) 1945- *76*
Hunter, Anne B. 1966- *118*
Hunter, Bernice Thurman 1922-2002 .... *85*
  Brief entry *45*
Hunter, Bobbi Dooley 1945- *89*
Hunter, Captain Marcy
  See Ellis, Edward S.
Hunter, Chris
  See Fluke, Joanne

Hunter, Clingham M.D.
  See Adams, William Taylor
Hunter, Edith Fisher 1919- *31*
Hunter, Erin
  See Cary, Kate
Hunter, Evan 1926-2005 .... *25*
  Obituary *167*
Hunter, George E.
  See Ellis, Edward S.
Hunter, Hilda 1921- *7*
Hunter, Jana
  See Hunter, Jana Novotny
Hunter, Jana Novotny *190*
Hunter, Jim 1939- *65*
Hunter, Kristin
  See Lattany, Kristin Hunter
Hunter, Leigh
  See Etchison, Birdie L(ee)
Hunter, Lieutenant Ned
  See Ellis, Edward S.
Hunter, Linzie 1979- *227*
Hunter, Mel 1927-2004 .... *39*
Hunter, Mollie 1922- *139*
  Autobiography Feature *139*
  Earlier sketches in SATA *2, 54, 106*
  See also CLR *25*
  See also SAAS *7*
Hunter, Ned
  See Ellis, Edward S.
Hunter, Norman (George Lorimer)
  1899-1995 .... *84*
  Earlier sketch in SATA *26*
Hunter, Ryan Ann
  See Greenwood, Pamela D.
  and Macalaster, Elizabeth G.
Hunter, Sara Hoagland 1954- *98*
Hunter Blair, Pauline
  See Clarke, Pauline
Huntington, Amy 1956- *180*
  Earlier sketch in SATA *138*
Huntington, Geoffrey *145*
Huntington, Harriet E(lizabeth) 1909- *1*
Huntley, Amy *225*
Huntsberry, William E(mery) 1916- *5*
Hurd, Clement (G.) 1908-1988 .... *64*
  Obituary *54*
  Earlier sketch in SATA *2*
  See also CLR *49*
Hurd, Edith Thacher 1910-1997 .... *64*
  Obituary *95*
  Earlier sketch in SATA *2*
  See also CLR *49*
  See also SAAS *13*
Hurd, John Thacher
  See Hurd, Thacher
Hurd, Thacher 1949- *219*
  Autobiography Feature *123*
  Brief entry *45*
  Earlier sketches in SATA *46, 94*
Hurley, Jo
  See Dower, Laura
Hurley, Tonya *207*
Hurlimann, Bettina
  See Huerlimann, Bettina
Hurlimann, Ruth
  See Huerlimann, Ruth
Hurmence, Belinda 1921- *77*
  See also CLR *25*
  See also SAAS *20*
Hurst, Carol Otis 1933-2007 .... *185*
  Earlier sketch in SATA *130*
Hurt-Newton, Tania 1968- *84*
Hurwin, Davida Wills 1950- *180*
Hurwitz, Johanna 1937- *175*
  Earlier sketches in SATA *20, 71, 113*
  See also SAAS *18*
Hurwood, Bernhardt J. 1926-1987 .... *12*
  Obituary *50*
Husain, Shahrukh 1950- *108*
Huser, Glen 1943- *151*
Hutchens, Paul 1902-1977 .... *31*

Hutchins, Carleen M.
  See Hutchins, Carleen Maley
Hutchins, Carleen Maley 1911-2009 9
  Obituary 206
Hutchins, Hazel J. 1952- 175
  Brief entry 51
  Earlier sketches in SATA *81, 135*
  See also SAAS 24
Hutchins, Pat 1942- 178
  Earlier sketches in SATA *15, 70, 111*
  See also CLR 20
  See also SAAS 16
Hutchins, Ross Elliott 1906- 4
Hutchison, Linda 1942- 152
Huthmacher, J. Joseph 1929- 5
Hutto, Nelson (Allen) 1904-1985 20
Hutton, Kathryn 1915- 89
Hutton, Sam
  See Jones, Allan Frewin
Hutton, Warwick 1939-1994 20
  Obituary 83
  See also SAAS 17
Huxley, Aldous 1894-1963 63
  See also CLR 151
Huxley, Aldous Leonard
  See Huxley, Aldous
Huxley, Elspeth (Josceline Grant)
    1907-1997 62
  Obituary 95
Hyde, Catherine R.
  See Hyde, Catherine Ryan
Hyde, Catherine Ryan 1955- 224
  Earlier sketch in SATA *141*
Hyde, Dayton O(gden) 9
Hyde, Hawk
  See Hyde, Dayton O(gden)
Hyde, Jeannette
  See Eyerly, Jeannette
Hyde, Margaret O. 1917- 139
  Earlier sketches in SATA *1, 42, 76*
  See also CLR 23
  See also SAAS 8
Hyde, Margaret Oldroyd
  See Hyde, Margaret O.
Hyde, Shelley
  See Reed, Kit
Hyde, Wayne Frederick 1922- 7
Hylander, Clarence J(ohn) 1897-1964 7
Hyman, Miles 1962- 210
Hyman, Paula Chase
  See Chase, Paula
Hyman, Robin 1931- 12
Hyman, Robin Phiilip
  See Hyman, Robin
Hyman, Trina Schart 1939-2004 95
  Obituary 158
  Earlier sketches in SATA *7, 46*
  See also CLR 50
Hymes, Lucia M(anley) 1907-1998 7
Hyndman, Jane Andrews Lee 1912-1978 46
  Obituary 23
  Earlier sketch in SATA *1*
Hyndman, Robert Utley 1906-1973 18
Hynes, Pat 98

I

Iannone, Jeanne
  See Balzano, Jeanne (Koppel)
Ibatoulline, Bagram 1965(?)- 225
  Earlier sketch in SATA *174*
Ibbitson, John Perrie 1955- 102
Ibbotson, Eva 1925-2010 221
  Earlier sketches in SATA *13, 103, 156*
Ibbotson, M. C(hristine) 1930- 5
Icenoggle, Jodi 1967- 168
Icenoggle, Jodi O.
  See Icenoggle, Jodi

Ichikawa, Satomi 1949- 208
  Brief entry 36
  Earlier sketches in SATA *47, 78, 146*
  See also CLR 62
Idle, Molly Schaar 223
Iggulden, Hal 1972- 196
Ignoffo, Matthew 1945- 92
Igus, Toyomi 1953- 112
  Earlier sketch in SATA *76*
Ihimaera, Witi (Tame) 1944- 148
Ikeda, Daisaku 1928- 77
Ilowite, Sheldon A. 1931- 27
Ilsey, Dent
  See Chapman, John Stanton Higham
Ilsley, Dent
  See Chapman, John Stanton Higham
Ilsey, Velma (Elizabeth) 1918- 12
Imai, Ayano 1980- 190
Imai, Miko 1963- 90
Imershein, Betsy 1953- 62
Immel, Mary Blair 1930- 28
Immell, Myra H. 1941- 92
Impey, Rose 1947- 223
  Earlier sketches in SATA *69, 152*
Ingalls, Ann 227
Ingelow, Jean 1820-1897 33
Ingermanson, Randall 1958- 134
Ingermanson, Randy
  See Ingermanson, Randall
Ingersoll, Norman 1928- 79
Ingham, Colonel Frederic
  See Hale, Edward Everett
Ingman, Bruce 1963- 182
  Earlier sketch in SATA *134*
Ingman, Nicholas 1948- 52
Ingold, Jeanette 128
Ingpen, Robert 1936- 166
  Earlier sketch in SATA *109*
Ingpen, Robert Roger
  See Ingpen, Robert
Ingraham, Erick 1950- 145
Ingraham, Leonard W(illiam) 1913-2003 4
Ingram, Scott 1948- 167
  Earlier sketch in SATA *92*
Ingram, W. Scott
  See Ingram, Scott
Ingrams, Doreen 1906-1997 97
  Earlier sketch in SATA *20*
Ingrid, Charles
  See Salsitz, Rhondi Vilott
Ingves, Gunilla 1939- 101
Ingves, Gunilla Anna Maria Folkesdotter
  See Ingves, Gunilla
Inkpen, Mick 1952- 154
  Earlier sketch in SATA *99*
Innes, (Ralph) Hammond
  See Hammond Innes, Ralph
Innes, Ralph Hammond
  See Hammond Innes, Ralph
Innes, Stephanie 220
Innocenti, Roberto 1940- 159
  Earlier sketch in SATA *96*
  See also CLR 126
Innocenti and Gallaz
  See Gallaz, Christophe
  and Innocenti, Roberto
Inns, Chris 212
Inyart, Gene
  See Namovicz, Gene Inyart
Ionesco, Eugene 1909-1994 7
  Obituary 79
Ipcar, Dahlov (Zorach) 1917- 147
  Autobiography Feature 147
  Earlier sketches in SATA *1, 49*
  See also SAAS 8
Ireland, Karin 151
  Earlier sketch in SATA *101*
Ironside, Jetske 1940- 60
Irvin, Fred 1914- 15
Irvine, Georgeanne 1955- 72
Irvine, Joan 1951- 80

Irving, Alexander
  See Hume, Ruth Fox
Irving, Robert
  See Adler, Irving
Irving, Washington 1783-1859
  See YABC 2
  See also CLR 97
Irwin, Ann(abelle Bowen) 1915-1998 89
  Brief entry 38
  Obituary 106
  Earlier sketch in SATA *44*
  See also CLR 40
  See also SAAS 14
Irwin, Constance (H.) Frick 1913-1995 6
Irwin, Hadley
  See Hadley, Lee
  and Irwin, Ann(abelle Bowen)
Irwin, Keith Gordon 1885-1964 11
Isaac, Joanne 1934- 21
Isaacs, Anne 1949- 185
  Earlier sketch in SATA *90*
Isaacs, Jacob
  See Kranzler, George G(ershon)
Isaacson, Philip M(arshall) 1924- 87
Isadora, Rachel 1953(?)- 204
  Brief entry 32
  Earlier sketches in SATA *54, 79, 121, 165*
  See also CLR 7
Isbell, Rebecca T(emple) 1942- 125
Isham, Charlotte H(ickock) 1912- 21
Ishida, Jui 176
Ish-Kishor, Judith 1892-1972 11
Ish-Kishor, Sulamith 1896-1977 17
Ishmael, Woodi 1914-1995 31
  Obituary 109
Isle, Sue 1963- 105
Isol 1972- 220
Israel, Elaine 1945- 12
Israel, Marion Louise 1882-1973
  Obituary 26
Iterson, S(iny) R(ose) Van
  See Van Iterson, S(iny) R(ose)
Ivanko, John D. 1966- 111
Ivanko, John Duane
  See Ivanko, John D.
Iversen, Jeremy 1980(?)- 174
Iversen, Jeremy Watt
  See Iversen, Jeremy
Iverson, Carol (L.) 1941- 145
Iverson, Diane 1950- 122
Iverson, Eric G.
  See Turtledove, Harry
Ivery, Martha M. 1948- 124
Ives, David 1951- 173
Ives, Morgan
  See Bradley, Marion Zimmer
Ives, Penny 1956- 215
Iwai, Melissa 183
Iwamatsu, Jun Atsushi 1908-1994 81
  Earlier sketch in SATA *14*
  See also CLR 4
Iwamura, Kazuo 1939- 213
Iwasaki (Matsumoto), Chihiro 1918-1974
  See CLR 18
Iyengar, Malathi Michelle 1954- 220

J

Jabar, Cynthia 210
Jablonski, Carla 184
Jac, Lee
  See Morton, Lee Jack, Jr.
Jacka, Martin 1943- 72
Jackson, Alison 1953- 228
  Earlier sketches in SATA *73, 108, 160*
Jackson, Anne 1896(?)-1984
  Obituary 37
Jackson, Barry
  See Jackson, Barry E.

Jackson, Barry E. 200
Jackson, C(aary) Paul 1902-1991 6
Jackson, Caary
See Jackson, C(aary) Paul
Jackson, Charlotte E. (Cobden) 1903(?)-1989
Obituary 62
Jackson, Dave
See Jackson, J. David
Jackson, Donna M. 1959- 206
Jackson, Ellen 1943- 214
Earlier sketches in SATA 75, 115, 167
Jackson, Ellen B.
See Jackson, Ellen
Jackson, Garnet Nelson 1944- 87
Jackson, Geoffrey (Holt Seymour) 1915-1987
Obituary 53
Jackson, Gina
See Fluke, Joanne
Jackson, Guida M. 1930- 71
Jackson, J. David 1944- 91
Jackson, Jacqueline 1928- 65
Jackson, Jacqueline Dougan
See Jackson, Jacqueline
Jackson, Jesse 1908-1983 29
Obituary 48
Earlier sketch in SATA 2
See also CLR 28
Jackson, Marjorie 1928- 127
Jackson, Melanie 1956- 141
Jackson, Mike 1946- 91
Jackson, Neta J. 1944- 91
Jackson, O. B.
See Jackson, C(aary) Paul
Jackson, Rob 1961- 176
Jackson, Robert B(lake) 1926- 8
Jackson, Robert Bradley
See Jackson, Rob
Jackson, Sally
See Kellogg, Jean (Defrees)
Jackson, Shirley 1919-1965 2
Jackson, Woody 1948- 92
Jackson Issa, Kai 205
Jacob, Helen Pierce 1927- 21
Jacobin
See Bisson, Terry
Jacobs, Deborah Lynn 187
Jacobs, Flora Gill 1918-2006 5
Obituary 178
Jacobs, Francine 1935- 150
Brief entry 42
Earlier sketch in SATA 43
Jacobs, Frank 1929- 30
Jacobs, Helen Hull 1908-1997 12
Jacobs, Joseph 1854-1916 25
Jacobs, Judy 1952- 69
Jacobs, Laurie A. 1956- 89
Jacobs, Leah
See Gellis, Roberta
Jacobs, Lee
See Stone, Tanya Lee
Jacobs, Leland Blair 1907-1992 20
Obituary 71
Jacobs, Linda
See Altman, Linda Jacobs
Jacobs, Lou(is), Jr. 1921- 2
Jacobs, Shannon K. 1947- 77
Jacobs, Susan
See Quinn, Susan
Jacobs, William Jay 1933- 89
Earlier sketch in SATA 28
Jacobsen, Laura 177
Jacobson, Daniel 1923- 12
Jacobson, Jennifer
See Jacobson, Jennifer Richard
Jacobson, Jennifer Richard 1958- 170
Jacobson, Morris K(arl) 1906- 21
Jacobson, Rick 170
Jacopetti, Alexandra
See Hart, Alexandra

Jacques, Brian 1939-2011 176
Earlier sketches in SATA 62, 95, 138
See also CLR 21
Jacques, Robin 1920-1995 32
Brief entry 30
Obituary 86
See also SAAS 5
Jaekel, Susan M. 1948- 89
Jaffe, Michele 179
Jaffe, Michele Sharon
See Jaffe, Michele
Jaffee, Al(lan) 1921- 66
Earlier sketch in SATA 37
Jagendorf, Moritz (Adolf) 1888-1981 2
Obituary 24
Jago 1979- 216
Jahn, Joseph Michael
See Jahn, Michael
Jahn, Michael 1943- 28
Jahn, Mike
See Jahn, Michael
Jahn-Clough, Lisa 1967- 193
Earlier sketches in SATA 88, 152
Jahsmann, Allan Hart 1916- 28
Jakes, John 1932- 62
Jakes, John William
See Jakes, John
James, Andrew
See Kirkup, James
James, Ann 1952- 168
Earlier sketches in SATA 82, 117
James, Betsy 183
James, Bill 1929- 205
James, B.J.
See James, Brian
James, Brian 1976- 212
Earlier sketch in SATA 140
James, Bronte
See Nash, Renea Denise
James, Captain Lew
See Stratemeyer, Edward L.
James, Charlie 1961- 185
James, Curtis E. 182
James, Dynely
See Mayne, William
James, Edwin
See Gunn, James E.
James, Elizabeth 1942- 97
Earlier sketches in SATA 39, 45, 52
James, Emily
See Standiford, Natalie
James, Gordon C. 1973- 195
James, Harry Clebourne 1896-1978 11
James, J. Alison 1962- 146
Earlier sketch in SATA 83
James, Josephine
See Sterne, Emma Gelders
James, Mary
See Meaker, Marijane
James, Matt 201
James, Philip
See del Rey, Lester
and Moorcock, Michael
James, Robin 1953- 50
James, Robin Irene
See James, Robin
James, Simon 1961- 202
James, T. F.
See Fleming, Thomas
James, Tegan
See Odgers, Sally Farrell
James, Will(iam Roderick) 1892-1942 19
Jameson, W. C. 1942- 93
Jamieson, Ian R.
See Goulart, Ron
Jamieson, Victoria 218
Jamiolkowski, Raymond M. 1953- 81
Jane, Mary Childs 1909-1991 6
Jane, Pamela 158

Janeczko, Paul B(ryan) 1945- 155
Earlier sketches in SATA 53, 98
See also CLR 47
See also SAAS 18
Janes, Edward C. 1908-1984 25
Janes, Edward Clarence
See Janes, Edward C.
Janes, J(oseph) Robert 1935- 148
Brief entry 50
Earlier sketch in SATA 101
Janeway, Elizabeth (Hall) 1913-2005 19
Janger, Kathleen N. 1940- 66
Jango-Cohen, Judith 1955- 208
Janice
See Brustlein, Janice Tworkov
Janisch, Heinz 1960- 181
Janni, Rebecca 229
Janosch
See Eckert, Horst
Janover, Caroline (Davis) 1943- 141
Earlier sketch in SATA 89
Janovitz, Marilyn 194
Jansen, Jared
See Cebulash, Mel
Janson, Dora Jane (Heineberg) 1916- 31
Janson, H(orst) W(oldemar) 1913-1982 9
Jansson, Tove (Marika) 1914-2001 41
Earlier sketch in SATA 3
See also CLR 125
Janus, Grete
See Hertz, Grete Janus
Jaques, Faith 1923-1997 97
Earlier sketches in SATA 21, 69
Jaquith, Priscilla 1908- 51
Jaramillo, Mari-Luci 1928- 139
Jarka, Jeff 221
Jarman, Julia 1946- 198
Earlier sketch in SATA 133
Jarman, Rosemary Hawley 1935- 7
Jarrell, Mary Von Schrader 1914- 35
Jarrell, Randall 1914-1965 7
See also CLR 111
Jarrett, Clare 1952- 201
Jarrett, Roxanne
See Werner, Herma
Jarrie, Martin 1953- 219
Jarrow, Gail 1952- 185
Earlier sketch in SATA 84
Jarvis, E.K.
See Ellison, Harlan
and Silverberg, Robert
Jarvis, Robin 1963- 181
Jarzab, Anna 1984- 227
Jaskol, Julie 1958- 127
Jasner, W. K.
See Watson, Jane Werner
Jassem, Kate
See Oppenheim, Joanne
Jauss, Anne Marie 1902(?)-1991 10
Obituary 69
Javernick, Ellen 1938- 217
Earlier sketch in SATA 89
Javins, Marie 1966- 212
Jay, Alison 196
Jayne, Lieutenant R. H.
See Ellis, Edward S.
Jaynes, Clare
See Mayer, Jane Rothschild
Jeake, Samuel, Jr.
See Aiken, Conrad
Jean-Bart, Leslie 1954- 121
Jeapes, Ben 1965- 174
Jecan, Gavriel 1962- 200
Jefferds, Vincent H(arris) 1916- 59
Brief entry 49
Jefferies, (John) Richard 1848-1887 16
Jeffers, Dawn 189
Jeffers, Oliver 1977- 213
Earlier sketch in SATA 175

Jeffers, Susan 1942- 202
  Earlier sketches in SATA *17, 70, 129, 137*
  See also CLR *30*
Jefferson, Sarah
  See Farjeon, (Eve) Annabel
Jeffries, Roderic 1926- *4*
Jeffries, Roderic Graeme
  See Jeffries, Roderic
Jenkin-Pearce, Susie 1943- *80*
Jenkins, A. M. 1961- *174*
Jenkins, Amanda McRaney
  See Jenkins, A. M.
Jenkins, Debra Reid
  See Reid Jenkins, Debra
Jenkins, Emily 1967- *174*
  Earlier sketch in SATA *144*
Jenkins, Jean *98*
Jenkins, Jerry B. 1949- *149*
Jenkins, Jerry Bruce
  See Jenkins, Jerry B.
Jenkins, Leonard *189*
Jenkins, Marie M(agdalen) 1909- *7*
Jenkins, Martin 1959- *216*
Jenkins, M.D.
  See Jenkins, Martin
Jenkins, Patrick 1955- *72*
Jenkins, Steve 1952- *218*
  Earlier sketches in SATA *154, 188*
Jenkins, William A(twell) 1922-1998 .... *9*
Jenkyns, Chris 1924- *51*
Jennewein, James *215*
Jennewein, Jim
  See Jennewein, James
Jennings, Christopher S. 1971(?)- *201*
Jennings, Coleman A(lonzo) 1933- *64*
Jennings, C.S.
  See Jennings, Christopher S.
Jennings, Dana Andrew 1957- *93*
Jennings, Elizabeth (Joan) 1926-2001 .... *66*
Jennings, Gary 1928-1999 .... *9*
  Obituary *117*
Jennings, Gary Gayne
  See Jennings, Gary
Jennings, Linda 1937- *211*
Jennings, Linda M.
  See Jennings, Linda
Jennings, Patrick 1962- *205*
  Earlier sketches in SATA *96, 160*
Jennings, Paul 1943- *165*
  Earlier sketch in SATA *88*
  See also CLR *40*
Jennings, Richard W. 1945- *185*
  Earlier sketch in SATA *136*
Jennings, Robert
  See Hamilton, Charles (Harold St. John)
Jennings, S. M.
  See Meyer, Jerome Sydney
Jennings, Sharon 1954- *95*
Jennings, Sharon Elizabeth
  See Jennings, Sharon
Jennison, C. S.
  See Starbird, Kaye
Jennison, Keith Warren 1911-1995 .... *14*
Jensen, Kathryn 1949- *81*
Jensen, Kristine Mary 1961- *78*
Jensen, Niels 1927- *25*
Jensen, Vickie (Dee) 1946- *81*
Jensen, Virginia Allen 1927- *8*
Jenson-Elliott, Cynthia L(ouise) 1962- *143*
Jeram, Anita 1965- *219*
  Earlier sketches in SATA *71, 102, 154*
Jerman, Jerry 1949- *89*
Jernigan, E. Wesley 1940- *85*
Jernigan, Gisela (Evelyn) 1948- *85*
Jerome, Elaine *228*
Jeschke, Susan 1942- *42*
  Brief entry *27*
Jessel, Camilla (Ruth) 1937- *143*
  Earlier sketch in SATA *29*
Jessell, Tim *225*
  Earlier sketch in SATA *177*

Jessey, Cornelia
  See Sussman, Cornelia Silver
Jewel
  See Kilcher, Jewel
Jewell, Nancy 1940- *109*
  Brief entry *41*
Jewett, Eleanore Myers 1890-1967 .... *5*
Jewett, Sarah Orne 1849-1909 .... *15*
Jewett, Theodora Sarah Orne
  See Jewett, Sarah Orne
Jezard, Alison 1919- *57*
  Brief entry *34*
Jiang, Cheng An 1943- *109*
Jiang, Ji-li 1954- *101*
Jiang, Zheng An
  See Jiang, Cheng An
Jiler, John 1946- *42*
  Brief entry *35*
Jimenez, Francisco 1943- *219*
  Earlier sketch in SATA *108*
Jinks, Catherine 1963- *207*
  Earlier sketches in SATA *94, 155*
Jobb, Jamie 1945- *29*
Jobling, Curtis *131*
Jocelyn, Ann Henning 1948- *92*
Jocelyn, Marthe 1956- *198*
  Earlier sketches in SATA *118, 163*
Joerns, Consuelo *44*
  Brief entry *33*
Joey D
  See Macaulay, Teresa
Johansen, Krista V.
  See Johansen, K.V.
Johansen, K.V 1968- *186*
Johansen, K.V. 1968- *186*
  Earlier sketch in SATA *129*
Johansson, Philip *163*
John, Antony 1972- *206*
John, Joyce *59*
Johns, Avery
  See Cousins, Margaret
Johns, Elizabeth 1943- *88*
Johns, Janetta
  See Quin-Harkin, Janet
Johns, Linda 1945- *173*
Johns, W(illiam) E(arle) 1893-1968 .... *55*
Johns, Captain W. E.
  See Johns, W(illiam) E(arle)
Johnson, A.
  See Johnson, Annabell
Johnson, A. E.
  See Johnson, Annabell
  and Johnson, Edgar (Raymond)
Johnson, Angela 1961- *188*
  Earlier sketches in SATA *69, 102, 150*
  See also CLR *33*
Johnson, Annabel
  See Johnson, Annabell
Johnson, Annabell 1921- *72*
  Earlier sketch in SATA *2*
Johnson, Art 1946- *123*
Johnson, B. F. 1920- *1*
Johnson, Benjamin F., of Boone
  See Riley, James Whitcomb
Johnson, Bettye 1858-1919
  See Rogers, Bettye
Johnson, Caryn
  See Goldberg, Whoopi
Johnson, Caryn E.
  See Goldberg, Whoopi
Johnson, Caryn Elaine
  See Goldberg, Whoopi
Johnson, Charles R. 1925- *11*
Johnson, Charlotte Buel
  See von Wodtke, Charlotte Buel Johnson
Johnson, Chuck
  See Johnson, Charles R.
Johnson, Crockett
  See Leisk, David (Johnson)
Johnson, D(ana) William 1945- *23*
Johnson, Daniel Shahid 1954- *73*

Johnson, David
  See Johnson, David A.
Johnson, David A. 1951- *191*
Johnson, D.B. 1944- *183*
  Earlier sketch in SATA *146*
Johnson, Dianne 1960- *130*
Johnson, Dinah
  See Johnson, Dianne
Johnson, Dolores 1949- *69*
Johnson, Donald B.
  See Johnson, D.B.
Johnson, Dorothy M(arie) 1905-1984 .... *6*
  Obituary *40*
Johnson, E(ugene) Harper *44*
Johnson, Edgar (Raymond) 1912-1990 .... *72*
  Earlier sketch in SATA *2*
Johnson, Eleanor Murdock 1892-1987
  Obituary *54*
Johnson, Elizabeth 1911-1984 .... *7*
  Obituary *39*
Johnson, Eric W(arner) 1918-1994 ....
  Obituary *82*
  Earlier sketch in SATA *8*
Johnson, Evelyne 1922- *20*
Johnson, Fred 19(?)-1982 .... *63*
Johnson, Gaylord 1884-1972 .... *7*
Johnson, Gerald White 1890-1980 .... *19*
  Obituary *28*
Johnson, Gillian 1963- *215*
Johnson, Harper
  See Johnson, E(ugene) Harper
Johnson, Harriett 1908-1987
  Obituary *53*
Johnson, James Ralph 1922- *1*
Johnson, James Weldon 1871-1938 .... *31*
  See also CLR *32*
Johnson, Jane 1951- *48*
Johnson, Joan J. 1942- *59*
Johnson, John E(mil) 1929- *34*
Johnson, Johnny 1901-1995
  See Johnson, (Walter) Ryerson
Johnson, Kathleen Jeffrie 1950- *186*
Johnson, La Verne B(ravo) 1925- *13*
Johnson, Layne *222*
  Earlier sketch in SATA *187*
Johnson, Lee Kaiser 1962- *78*
Johnson, Lissa H(alls) 1955- *65*
Johnson, Lois Smith 1894-1993 .... *6*
Johnson, Lois Walfrid 1936- *130*
  Earlier sketches in SATA *22, 91*
Johnson, Margaret S(weet) 1893-1964 .... *35*
Johnson, Marguerite Annie
  See Angelou, Maya
Johnson, Mary Frances K. 1929(?)-1979
  Obituary *27*
Johnson, Maud Battle 1918(?)-1985
  Obituary *46*
Johnson, Maureen 1973- *200*
Johnson, Meredith Merrell 1952- *104*
Johnson, Milton 1932- *31*
Johnson, Neil 1954- *135*
  Earlier sketch in SATA *73*
Johnson, Pamela 1949- *71*
Johnson, Patricia Polin 1956- *84*
Johnson, Paul Brett 1947- *132*
  Earlier sketch in SATA *83*
Johnson, Rebecca L. 1956- *147*
  Earlier sketch in SATA *67*
Johnson, Rick L. 1954- *79*
Johnson, (Walter) Ryerson 1901-1995 .... *10*
  Obituary *106*
Johnson, Scott 1952- *119*
  Earlier sketch in SATA *76*
Johnson, Sherrie 1948- *87*
Johnson, Shirley K(ing) 1927- *10*
Johnson, Siddie Joe 1905-1977
  Obituary *20*
Johnson, Spencer 1938- *145*
  Brief entry *38*
Johnson, Stacie
  See Myers, Walter Dean

Johnson, Stephen T. 1964- *189*
  Earlier sketches in SATA *84, 141*
Johnson, Steve 1960- *177*
Johnson, Sue Kaiser 1963- *78*
Johnson, Sylvia A. *166*
  Brief entry *52*
  Earlier sketch in SATA *104*
Johnson, Varian 1977- *229*
Johnson, William R. *38*
Johnson, William Weber 1909-1992 .... *7*
Johnson-Feelings, Dianne
  See Johnson, Dianne
Johnston, Agnes Christine
  See Dazey, Agnes J(ohnston)
Johnston, Annie Fellows 1863-1931 .... *37*
Johnston, Dorothy Grunbock 1915-1979 ...... *54*
Johnston, Ginny 1946- *60*
Johnston, H(ugh) A(nthony) S(tephen)
  1913-1967 .... *14*
Johnston, Janet 1944- *71*
Johnston, Jeffry W. *188*
Johnston, Johanna 1914(?)-1982 .... *12*
  Obituary *33*
Johnston, Julie 1941- *110*
  Autobiography Feature *128*
  Earlier sketch in SATA *78*
  See also CLR *41*
  See also SAAS *24*
Johnston, Lynn 1947- *216*
  Earlier sketch in SATA *118*
Johnston, Lynn Beverley
  See Johnston, Lynn
Johnston, Mark *194*
Johnston, Norma
  See St. John, Nicole
Johnston, Portia
  See Takakjian, Portia
Johnston, Susan Taylor 1942- *180*
  Earlier sketches in SATA *8, 83, 128*
  See Johnston, Tony
Johnston, Tim(othy Patrick) 1962- *146*
Johnston, Tony *226*
  See Johnston, Susan Taylor
Joinson, Carla *160*
Jolin, Paula *186*
Jolivet, Joelle 1965- *221*
Jonas, Ann 1932- *135*
  Brief entry *42*
  Earlier sketch in SATA *50*
  See also CLR *74*
Jonell, Lynne 1956- *196*
  Earlier sketch in SATA *109*
Jones, Adrienne 1915-2000 .... *82*
  Earlier sketch in SATA *7*
  See also SAAS *10*
Jones, Allan Frewin 1954- *204*
Jones, Annabel
  See Lewis, Mary
Jones, Betty Millsaps 1940- *54*
Jones, Carol 1942- *153*
  Earlier sketch in SATA *79*
Jones, Carrie 1971- *229*
  Earlier sketch in SATA *191*
Jones, Charles M.
  See Jones, Chuck
Jones, Charlotte Foltz 1945- *122*
  Earlier sketch in SATA *77*
Jones, Chuck 1912-2002 .... *53*
  Obituary *133*
Jones, Constance *112*
Jones, Constance A.
  See Jones, Constance
Jones, David 1956- *202*
Jones, Diana Wynne 1934-2011 .... *160*
  Earlier sketches in SATA *9, 70, 108*
  See also CLR *120*
  See also SAAS *7*
Jones, Douglas B. *202*
Jones, Douglas C(lyde) 1924-1998 .... *52*
Jones, Elizabeth McDavid *155*

Jones, Elizabeth Orton 1910-2005 .... *18*
  Obituary *164*
Jones, Evan 1915-1996 .... *3*
Jones, Frewin
  See Jones, Allan Frewin
Jones, Geraldine
  See McCaughrean, Geraldine
Jones, Gillingham
  See Hamilton, Charles (Harold St. John)
Jones, Gwyneth A. 1952- *159*
Jones, Gwyneth Ann
  See Jones, Gwyneth A.
Jones, Harold 1904-1992 .... *14*
  Obituary *72*
Jones, Helen Hinckley 1903-1991 .... *26*
Jones, Helen L(ouise) 1903-1973
  Obituary *22*
Jones, Hettie 1934- *42*
  Brief entry *27*
Jones, Hortense P. 1918- *9*
Jones, J. Sydney 1948- *101*
Jones, Jasmine
  See Papademetriou, Lisa
Jones, Jennifer (Berry) 1947- *90*
Jones, Jessie Mae Orton 1887(?)-1983
  Obituary *37*
Jones, John R(obert) 1926- *76*
Jones, Jon Sydney
  See Jones, J. Sydney
Jones, Judith
  See James, Bill
Jones, Kimberly K. 1957- *187*
Jones, Marcia Thornton 1958- *217*
  Earlier sketches in SATA *73, 115*
Jones, Martha T(annery) 1931- *130*
Jones, Mary Alice 1898(?)-1980 .... *6*
Jones, McClure *34*
Jones, Noah Z. *182*
Jones, Patrick 1961- *210*
  Earlier sketch in SATA *136*
Jones, Penelope 1938- *31*
Jones, Rebecca C(astaldi) 1947- *99*
  Earlier sketch in SATA *33*
Jones, Robin D(orothy) 1959- *80*
Jones, Sanford W.
  See Thorn, John
Jones, Sylvie *185*
Jones, Sylvie Michelle
  See Jones, Sylvie
Jones, Terence Graham Parry 1942- *127*
  Brief entry *51*
  Earlier sketch in SATA *67*
Jones, Terry
  See Jones, Terence Graham Parry
Jones, Tim Wynne
  See Wynne-Jones, Tim
Jones, Traci L. *186*
Jones, V. M. 1958- *147*
Jones, Veda Boyd 1948- *119*
Jones, Victoria Mary
  See Jones, V. M.
Jones, Volcano
  See Mitchell, Adrian
Jones, Weyman (B.) 1928- *4*
  See also SAAS *11*
Jones, William Glynne
  See Glynne-Jones, William
Jonk, Clarence 1906-1987 .... *10*
Jonsberg, Barry 1951- *168*
Joos, Francoise 1956- *78*
Joos, Frederic 1953- *78*
Joosse, Barbara 1949- *220*
  Earlier sketches in SATA *52, 96, 164*
Joosse, Barbara M.
  See Joosse, Barbara
Joosse, Barbara Monnot
  See Joosse, Barbara
Jordan, Alexis Hill
  See Glick, Ruth
  and Titchener, Louise
Jordan, Anne Devereaux 1943- *80*

Jordan, Chris
  See Philbrick, Rodman
Jordan, Deloris *191*
Jordan, Devin *221*
Jordan, Don
  See Howard, Vernon (Linwood)
Jordan, Hope Dahle 1905-1995 .... *15*
Jordan, Jael (Michal) 1949- *30*
Jordan, June 1936-2002 .... *136*
  Earlier sketch in SATA *4*
  See also CLR *10*
Jordan, June Meyer
  See Jordan, June
Jordan, Lee
  See Scholefield, Alan
Jordan, Martin George 1944- *84*
Jordan, Robert 1948-2007 .... *95*
Jordan, Robert K.
  See Jordan, Robert
Jordan, Rosa 1939- *191*
Jordan, Roslyn M. *189*
Jordan, Sherryl 1949- *122*
  Earlier sketch in SATA *71*
  See also SAAS *23*
Jordan, Shirley 1930- *154*
Jordan, Tanis 1946- *84*
Jorgensen, Ivar
  See Ellison, Harlan
  and Garrett, Randall
Jorgensen, Mary Venn -1995 .... *36*
Jorgensen, Norman 1954- *157*
Jorgenson, Ivar
  See Silverberg, Robert
Jorisch, Stephane *178*
Joseph, Anne
  See Coates, Anna
Joseph, James (Herz) 1924- *53*
Joseph, Joan 1939- *34*
Joseph, Joseph M(aron) 1903-1979 .... *22*
Joseph, Patrick
  See O'Malley, Kevin
Josephs, Rebecca
  See Talbot, Toby
Josephson, Judith Pinkerton 1943- *198*
Josh
  See Twain, Mark
Joshua, Peter
  See Stone, Peter
Joslin, Mary 1953- *176*
Joslin, Sesyle
  See Hine, Sesyle Joslin
Joubert, Beverly 1957- *204*
Joubert, Dereck *204*
Journet, Mireille
  See Marokvia, Mireille
Joyce, Bill
  See Joyce, William
Joyce, J(ames) Avery 1902-1987 .... *11*
  Obituary *50*
Joyce, Peter 1937- *127*
Joyce, William 1957- *118*
  Brief entry *46*
  Earlier sketch in SATA *72*
  See also CLR *26*
Joyner, Jerry 1938- *34*
Juan, Ana 1961- *179*
Jubb, Sophie *210*
Jubert, Herve *185*
Juby, Susan 1969- *202*
  Earlier sketch in SATA *156*
Jucker, Sita 1921- *5*
Judah, Aaron 1923- *118*
Judd, Cyril
  See Kornbluth, C(yril) M.
  and Merril, Judith
  and Pohl, Frederik
Judd, Denis (O'Nan) 1938- *33*
Judd, Frances K.
  See Benson, Mildred
Jude, Conny *81*
Judge, Lita *192*

Judson, Clara Ingram 1879-1960 .... *38*
   Brief entry *27*
Judy, Stephen
   See Tchudi, Stephen N.
Judy, Stephen N.
   See Tchudi, Stephen N.
Juhasz, Victor 1954- *177*
Jukes, Mavis 1947- *219*
   Brief entry *43*
   Earlier sketches in SATA *72, 111*
   See also SAAS *12*
Jules, Jacqueline 1956- *218*
   Earlier sketches in SATA *148, 183*
Julesberg, Elizabeth Rider Montgomery
   1902-1985 .... *34*
   Obituary *41*
   Earlier sketch in SATA *3*
Julian, Jane
   See Wiseman, David
Jumpp, Hugo
   See MacPeek, Walter G.
Junco, Martha Aviles
   See Aviles, Martha
Jungman, Ann *165*
Jupo, Frank J. 1904-1981 .... *7*
Jurmain, Suzanne 1945- *169*
   Earlier sketch in SATA *72*
Jurmain, Suzanne Tripp
   See Jurmain, Suzanne
Juster, Norton 1929- *220*
   Earlier sketches in SATA *3, 132*
   See also CLR *112*
Justus, May 1898-1989 .... *1*
   Obituary *106*
Juvenilia
   See Taylor, Ann

K

Kaaberbol, Lene
   See Kaaberbol, Lene
Kaaberbol, Lene 1960- *159*
Kabdebo, Tamas
   See Kabdebo, Thomas
Kabdebo, Thomas 1934- *10*
Kabibble, Osh
   See Jobb, Jamie
Kacer, Kathy 1954- *184*
   Earlier sketch in SATA *142*
Kaczman, James *156*
Kadair, Deborah Ousley *184*
Kadefors, Sara 1965- *218*
Kadesch, Robert R(udstone) 1922- *31*
Kadohata, Cynthia 1956(?)- *228*
   Earlier sketches in SATA *155, 180*
   See also CLR *121*
Kadohata, Cynthia L.
   See Kadohata, Cynthia
Kaempfert, Wade
   See del Rey, Lester
Kaestner, Erich 1899-1974 .... *14*
   See also CLR *153*
Kagawa, Julie *228*
Kahl, Jonathan (D.) 1959- *77*
Kahl, M(arvin) P(hilip) 1934- *37*
Kahl, Virginia (Caroline) 1919-2004 .... *48*
   Brief entry *38*
   Obituary *158*
Kahn, Joan 1914-1994 .... *48*
   Obituary *82*
Kahn, Katherine Janus 1942- *220*
   Earlier sketches in SATA *90, 167*
Kahn, Peggy
   See Katz, Bobbi
Kahn, Roger 1927- *37*
Kahukiwa, Robyn 1940- *134*
Kains, Josephine
   See Goulart, Ron
Kaizuki, Kiyonori 1950- *72*

Kajikawa, Kimiko *212*
Kakimoto, Kozo 1915- *11*
Kalashnikoff, Nicholas 1888-1961 .... *16*
Kalb, Jonah 1926- *23*
Kalbacken, Joan 1925- *96*
Kalechofsky, Roberta 1931- *92*
Kaler, James Otis 1848-1912 .... *15*
Kalis, Jennifer *207*
Kalish, Claire M. 1947- *92*
Kallen, Stuart A. 1955- *126*
   Earlier sketch in SATA *86*
Kallen, Stuart Arnold
   See Kallen, Stuart A.
Kallevig, Christine Petrell 1955- *164*
Kalman, Bobbie 1947- *63*
Kalman, Maira 1949- *137*
   Earlier sketch in SATA *96*
   See also CLR *32*
Kalnay, Francis 1899-1992 .... *7*
Kaloustian, Rosanne 1955- *93*
Kalow, Gisela 1946- *32*
Kalstein, Dave *175*
Kamara, Mariatu *214*
Kamen, Gloria 1923- *98*
   Earlier sketch in SATA *9*
Kamerman, Sylvia E.
   See Burack, Sylvia K.
Kamm, Josephine (Hart) 1905-1989 .... *24*
Kammerman, Sylvia K.
   See Burack, Sylvia K.
Kandel, Michael 1941- *93*
Kandell, Alice S. 1938- *35*
Kane, Bob 1916-1998 .... *120*
Kane, Henry Bugbee 1902-1971 .... *14*
Kane, Kim 1973(?)- *221*
Kane, L. A.
   See Mannetti, Lisa
Kane, Robert W. 1910- *18*
Kane, Wilson
   See Bloch, Robert (Albert)
Kanefield, Teri 1960- *135*
Kanell, Beth *215*
Kaner, Etta 1947- *198*
   Earlier sketch in SATA *126*
Kanetzke, Howard W(illiam) 1932- *38*
Kangas, Juli 1958- *200*
Kann, Elizabeth *180*
Kann, Victoria *180*
Kanninen, Barbara *196*
Kanninen, Barbara J.
   See Kanninen, Barbara
Kanoza, Muriel Canfield
   See Canfield, Muriel
Kantner, Seth 1965- *179*
Kanzawa, Toshiko
   See Furukawa, Toshi
Kanzler, John 1963- *188*
Kaplan, Andrew 1960- *78*
Kaplan, Anne Bernays
   See Bernays, Anne
Kaplan, Bess 1927- *22*
Kaplan, Boche 1926- *24*
Kaplan, Elizabeth 1956- *83*
Kaplan, Elizabeth A.
   See Kaplan, Elizabeth
Kaplan, Irma 1900- *10*
Kaplan, Jean Caryl Korn 1926- *10*
Kaplow, Robert 1954- *70*
Karageorge, Michael
   See Anderson, Poul
Karas, G. Brian 1957- *222*
   Earlier sketch in SATA *178*
Karas, George Brian
   See Karas, G. Brian
Karasz, Ilonka 1896-1981
   Obituary *29*
Karen, Ruth 1922-1987 .... *9*
   Obituary *54*
Kark, Nina Mary
   See Bawden, Nina
Karl, Herb 1938- *73*

Karl, Jean E(dna) 1927-2000 .... *122*
   Earlier sketch in SATA *34*
   See also SAAS *10*
Karlin, Bernie 1927- *68*
Karlin, Eugene 1918- *10*
Karlin, Nurit *103*
   Earlier sketch in SATA *63*
Karlins, Mark 1947- *219*
Karnes, Frances A. 1937- *110*
Karp, Naomi J. 1926- *16*
Karpinski, J. Rick
   See Karpinski, John Eric
Karpinski, John Eric 1952- *81*
Karpinski, Rick
   See Karpinski, John Eric
Karr, Kathleen 1946- *212*
   Earlier sketches in SATA *82, 127*
Karr, Phyllis Ann 1944- *119*
Karwoski, Gail 1949- *127*
Karwoski, Gail Langer
   See Karwoski, Gail
Kashiwagi, Isami 1925- *10*
Kaslik, Ibi
   See Kaslik, Ibolya Emma
Kaslik, Ibolya Emma 1973- *185*
Kassem, Lou 1931- *62*
   Brief entry *51*
Kastel, Warren
   See Silverberg, Robert
Kastner, Erich
   See Kaestner, Erich
Kastner, Jill (Marie) 1964- *117*
   Earlier sketch in SATA *70*
Kasuya, Masahiro 1937- *51*
Kasza, Keiko 1951- *191*
   Earlier sketch in SATA *124*
Kataphusin
   See Ruskin, John
Katchen, Carole 1944- *9*
Katcher, Brian 1975- *203*
Kathryn
   See Searle, Kathryn Adrienne
Kato, Aya 1982- *202*
Katona, Robert 1949- *21*
Katsarakis, Joan Harries
   See Harries, Joan
Katz, Alan *185*
Katz, Avi 1949- *199*
Katz, Avner 1939- *103*
Katz, Bobbi 1933- *217*
   Earlier sketches in SATA *12, 179*
Katz, Fred(eric Phillip) 1938- *6*
Katz, Jane B(resler) 1934- *33*
Katz, Karen 1947- *195*
   Earlier sketch in SATA *158*
Katz, Marjorie P.
   See Weiser, Marjorie P(hillis) K(atz)
Katz, Susan 1945- *156*
Katz, Welwyn Wilton 1948- *96*
   Autobiography Feature *118*
   Earlier sketch in SATA *62*
   See also CLR *45*
Katz, William 1940- *98*
Katz, William Loren 1927- *13*
Kaufman, Bel *57*
Kaufman, Jeff 1955- *84*
Kaufman, Joe 1911-2001 .... *33*
Kaufman, Joseph
   See Kaufman, Joe
Kaufman, Mervyn D. 1932- *4*
Kaufmann, Angelika 1935- *15*
Kaufmann, John 1931- *18*
Kaula, Edna Mason 1906-1987 .... *13*
Kaur Khalsa, Dayal
   See Khalsa, Dayal Kaur
Kavaler, Lucy 1930- *23*
Kavanagh, Jack 1920- *85*
Kavanagh, P(atrick) J(oseph Gregory)
   1931- *122*
Kavanaugh, Ian
   See Webb, Jean Francis (III)

Kay, Alan N. 1965- 144
Kay, Elizabeth 1949- 165
Kay, Guy Gavriel 1954- 167
  Earlier sketch in SATA *121*
Kay, Helen
  See Goldfrank, Helen Colodny
Kay, Jackie 1961- 165
  Earlier sketch in SATA *97*
Kay, Jacqueline Margaret
  See Kay, Jackie
Kay, Julia 205
Kay, Mara 13
Kay, Verla 1946- 210
  Earlier sketch in SATA *120*
Kaye, Danny 1913-1987
  Obituary 50
Kaye, Geraldine (Hughesdon) 1925- 85
  Earlier sketch in SATA *10*
Kaye, Judy
  See Baer, Judy
Kaye, Marilyn 1949- 110
  Earlier sketch in SATA *56*
Kaye, Mary Margaret
  See Kaye, M.M.
Kaye, M.M. 1908-2004 62
  Obituary 152
Kaye, Mollie
  See Kaye, M.M.
Kaye, Peggy 1948- 143
Keach, James P. 1950- 125
Keams, Geri 1951- 117
Keane, Bil 1922- 4
Keane, Dave 1965- 216
Keaney, Brian 1954- 188
  Earlier sketch in SATA *106*
Kearney, Meg 1964- 178
Kearny, Jillian
  See Goulart, Ron
Keat, Nawuth 1964- 222
Keating, Bern
  See Keating, Leo Bernard
Keating, Frank 1944- 143
Keating, Lawrence A. 1903-1966 23
Keating, Leo Bernard 1915- 10
Keats, Emma 1899(?)-1979(?) 68
Keats, Ezra Jack 1916-1983 57
  Obituary 34
  Earlier sketch in SATA *14*
  See also CLR *35*
Keefer, Catherine
  See Ogan, George F.
  and Ogan, Margaret E. (Nettles)
Keefer, Janice Kulyk
  See Kulyk Keefer, Janice
Keegan, Marcia 1943- 104
  Earlier sketch in SATA *9*
Keehn, Sally M. 1947- 165
  Earlier sketch in SATA *87*
Keel, Frank
  See Keeler, Ronald F(ranklin)
Keeler, Patricia 183
Keeler, Patricia A.
  See Keeler, Patricia
Keeler, Ronald F(ranklin) 1913-1983 47
Keely, Jack 1951- 119
Keen, Martin L. 1913-1992 4
Keenan, Sheila 1953- 95
Keene, Ann T. 1940- 86
Keene, Ann Todd
  See Keene, Ann T.
Keene, Carolyn
  See Benson, Mildred
  and Goulart, Ron
  and Lerangis, Peter
  and McFarlane, Leslie
  and Stanley, George Edward
  and Stratemeyer, Edward L.
Keens-Douglas, Richardo 1953- 154
  Earlier sketch in SATA *95*
Keep, Linda Lowery
  See Lowery, Linda

Keep, Richard 1949- 170
Keep, Richard Cleminson
  See Keep, Richard
Keeping, Charles (William James)
  1924-1988 69
  Obituary 56
  Earlier sketch in SATA *9*
  See also CLR *34*
Keeshan, Robert J. 1927-2004 32
  Obituary 151
Kehlenbeck, Angela 1959- 186
Kehoe, Tim 1970- 224
Kehret, Peg 1936- 212
  Autobiography Feature 149
  Earlier sketches in SATA *73, 108, 149*
Keillor, Garrison 1942- 58
Keillor, Gary Edward
  See Keillor, Garrison
Keir, Christine
  See Pullein-Thompson, Christine
Keiser, Paige 220
Keister, Douglas 1948- 88
Keith, Doug 1952- 81
Keith, Eros 1942- 52
Keith, Hal 1934- 36
Keith, Harold (Verne) 1903-1998 74
  Earlier sketch in SATA *2*
Keith, Robert
  See Applebaum, Stan
Keleinikov, Andrei 1924- 65
Kelemen, Julie 1959- 78
Kelen, Emery 1896-1978 13
  Obituary 26
Kelleam, Joseph E(veridge) 1913-1975 31
Kelleher, Anne 1959- 97
Kelleher, Annette 1950- 122
Kelleher, Daria Valerian 1955- 79
Kelleher, Victor (Michael Kitchener)
  1939- 129
  Brief entry 52
  Earlier sketch in SATA *75*
  See also CLR *36*
Keller, Beverly L(ou) 91
  Earlier sketch in SATA *13*
Keller, Charles 1942- 82
  Earlier sketch in SATA *8*
Keller, Debra 1958- 94
Keller, Dick 1923- 36
Keller, Emily 96
Keller, Gail Faithfull
  See Faithfull, Gail
Keller, Holly 1942- 216
  Brief entry 42
  Earlier sketches in SATA *76, 108, 157*
  See also CLR *45*
Keller, Irene (Barron) 1927-2002 36
  Obituary 139
Keller, Laurie 1961(?)- 196
Kelley, Ann 1941- 217
Kelley, Ellen A. 185
Kelley, Ellen Chavez
  See Kelley, Ellen A.
Kelley, Gary 1945- 217
  Earlier sketch in SATA *183*
Kelley, Leo P(atrick) 1928- 32
  Brief entry 31
Kelley, Marty 1971- 211
Kelley, Patrick (G.) 1963- 129
Kelley, Patte 1947- 93
Kelley, True 1946- 179
Kelley, True (Adelaide) 1946- 130
  Brief entry 39
  Earlier sketches in SATA *41, 92*
Kelley, True Adelaide
  See Kelley, True
Kellin, Sally Moffet 1932- 9
Kelling, Furn L. 1914-2000 37
Kellogg, Gene
  See Kellogg, Jean (Defrees)
Kellogg, Jean (Defrees) 1916-1978 10

Kellogg, Steven 1941- 177
  Earlier sketches in SATA *8, 57, 130*
  See also CLR *6*
Kellogg, Steven Castle
  See Kellogg, Steven
Kellow, Kathleen
  See Hibbert, Eleanor Alice Burford
Kelly, C. M. O.
  See Gibbs, (Cecilia) May
Kelly, Clint 1950- 140
Kelly, Eric P(hilbrook) 1884-1960
  See YABC *1*
Kelly, Fiona
  See Coleman, Michael
  and Hendry, Frances Mary
  and Jones, Allan Frewin
  and Oldfield, Jenny
  and Welford, Sue
Kelly, Irene 1957- 210
  Earlier sketch in SATA *147*
Kelly, Jacqueline 216
Kelly, Jeff
  See Kelly, Jeffrey
Kelly, Jeffrey 1946- 65
Kelly, Joanne (W.) 1934- 87
Kelly, Kate 1958- 91
Kelly, Kathleen M. 1964- 71
Kelly, Katy 1955- 215
  Earlier sketch in SATA *169*
Kelly, Lauren
  See Oates, Joyce Carol
Kelly, Laurene 1954- 123
Kelly, Martha Rose 1914-1983 37
Kelly, Marty
  See Kelly, Martha Rose
Kelly, Mij 166
Kelly, Ralph
  See Geis, Darlene Stern
Kelly, Regina Z(immerman) 1898-1986 5
Kelly, Rosalie (Ruth) 43
Kelly, Tom 1961- 191
Kelly, Walt(er Crawford) 1913-1973 18
Kelsey, Alice Geer 1896-1982 1
Kelsey, Elin 1961- 159
Kelsey, Marybeth 216
Kemly, Kathleen 1958- 197
Kemnitz, Thomas Milton, Jr. 1984- 152
Kemnitz, Tom, Jr.
  See Kemnitz, Thomas Milton, Jr.
Kemp, Gene 1926- 75
  Earlier sketch in SATA *25*
  See also CLR *29*
Kempner, Mary Jean 1913-1969 10
Kempter, Christa 1945- 187
Kempton, Jean Welch 1914- 10
Kenah, Katharine 1949- 182
Kenda, Margaret 1942- 71
Kendall, Carol (Seeger) 1917- 74
  Earlier sketch in SATA *11*
  See also SAAS *7*
Kendall, Gideon 1966- 215
Kendall, Katherine
  See Applegate, Katherine
Kendall, Lace
  See Stoutenburg, Adrien (Pearl)
Kendall, Martha E. 87
Kendall, Russ 1957- 83
Kenealy, James P. 1927- 52
  Brief entry 29
Kenealy, Jim
  See Kenealy, James P.
Kennaway, Adrienne 1945- 171
  Earlier sketch in SATA *60*
Kennedy, Anne 1955- 198
Kennedy, Anne Vittur
  See Kennedy, Anne
Kennedy, Brendan 1970- 57
Kennedy, Dana Forrest 1917- 74
Kennedy, Dorothy M(intzlaff) 1931- 53
Kennedy, Doug 1963- 189
  Earlier sketch in SATA *122*

Kennedy, Frances 1937- *192*
Kennedy, James *214*
Kennedy, John F. 1917-1963 .... *11*
Kennedy, John Fitzgerald
See Kennedy, John F.
Kennedy, Joseph Charles
See Kennedy, X. J.
Kennedy, Kim *189*
Kennedy, Marlane 1962- *210*
Kennedy, Pamela (J.) 1946- *87*
Kennedy, Paul E(dward) 1929- *113*
Earlier sketch in SATA *33*
Kennedy, Richard (Pitt) 1910-1989
Obituary *60*
Kennedy, (Jerome) Richard 1932- *22*
Kennedy, Robert 1938- *63*
Kennedy, T.A. 1953- *42*
Brief entry *35*
Kennedy, Teresa
See Kennedy, T.A.
Kennedy, Teresa A.
See Kennedy, T.A.
Kennedy, William 1928- *57*
Kennedy, William Joseph
See Kennedy, William
Kennedy, X. J. 1929- *130*
Autobiography Feature *130*
Earlier sketches in SATA *14, 86*
See also CLR *27*
See also SAAS *22*
Kennell, Ruth Epperson 1893-1977 .... *6*
Obituary *25*
Kennemore, Tim 1957- *220*
Earlier sketch in SATA *133*
Kennen, Ally *190*
Kennett, David 1959- *206*
Earlier sketch in SATA *121*
Kennison, Ruth *202*
Kenny, Ellsworth Newcomb 1909-1971
Obituary *26*
Kenny, Herbert Andrew 1912-2002 .... *13*
Kenny, Jude
See Daly, Jude
Kenny, Kathryn
See Bowden, Joan Chase
and Krull, Kathleen
and Sanderlin, Owenita (Harrah)
and Stack, Nicolete Meredith
Kenny, Kevin
See Krull, Kathleen
Kensinger, George
See Fichter, George S.
Kensington, Kathryn Wesley
See Rusch, Kristine Kathryn
Kent, Alexander
See Reeman, Douglas Edward
Kent, David
See Lambert, David
Kent, Deborah Ann 1948- *155*
Brief entry *41*
Earlier sketches in SATA *47, 104*
Kent, Jack
See Kent, John Wellington
Kent, John Wellington 1920-1985 .... *24*
Obituary *45*
Kent, Lisa 1942- *90*
Kent, Mallory
See Lowndes, Robert A(ugustine) W(ard)
Kent, Margaret 1894- *2*
Kent, Rockwell 1882-1971 .... *6*
Kent, Rose *188*
Kent, Sherman 1903-1986 .... *20*
Obituary *47*
Kenward, Jean 1920- *42*
Kenworthy, Leonard S. 1912-1991 .... *6*
Kenyon, Karen (Smith) 1938- *145*
Kenyon, Kate
See Adorjan, Carol (Madden)
and Ransom, Candice
Kenyon, Ley 1913-1990 .... *6*
Keown, Elizabeth *78*

Kepes, Juliet A(ppleby) 1919-1999 .... *13*
Kephart, Beth 1960- *196*
Kerby, Mona 1951- *202*
Earlier sketch in SATA *75*
Kerigan, Florence 1896-1984 .... *12*
Kerley, Barbara 1960- *191*
Earlier sketch in SATA *138*
Kerman, Gertrude
See Furman, Gertrude Lerner Kerman
Kerns, Thelma 1929- *116*
Kerr, Anne Louise
See Mackey, Weezie Kerr
Kerr, Bob 1951- *120*
Kerr, Jessica 1901-1991 .... *13*
Kerr, (Anne-)Judith 1923-1970 .... *24*
Kerr, M. E.
See Meaker, Marijane
Kerr, P.B.
See Kerr, Philip
Kerr, Philip 1956- *168*
Kerr, Phyllis Forbes 1942- *72*
Kerr, Tom 1950- *77*
Kerrin, Jessica Scott *174*
Kerry, Frances
See Kerigan, Florence
Kerry, Lois
See Duncan, Lois
Kershen, (L.) Michael 1982- *82*
Kerven, Rosalind 1954- *83*
Ker Wilson, Barbara 1929- *121*
Earlier sketches in SATA *20, 70*
See also SAAS *18*
Kerz, Anna 1947- *220*
Keselman, Gabriela 1953- *128*
Kesey, Ken 1935-2001 .... *66*
Obituary *131*
Kesey, Ken Elton
See Kesey, Ken
Kesler, Jay 1935- *65*
Kessel, Joyce Karen 1937- *41*
Kessler, Cristina *190*
Kessler, Ethel 1922- *44*
Brief entry *37*
Kessler, Leonard P. 1921- *14*
Kessler, Liz 1966- *206*
Kest, Kristin 1967- *168*
Earlier sketch in SATA *118*
Kesteven, G. R.
See Crosher, G. R.
Ketcham, Hank
See Ketcham, Henry King
Ketcham, Henry King 1920-2001 .... *28*
Brief entry *27*
Obituary *128*
Ketcham, Sallie 1963- *124*
Ketchum, Liza 1946- *132*
Earlier sketch in SATA *78*
Ketner, Mary Grace 1946- *75*
Kettelkamp, Larry (Dale) 1933- *2*
See also SAAS *3*
Ketteman, Helen 1945- *223*
Earlier sketches in SATA *73, 115, 167*
Kettle, Peter
See Glover, Denis (James Matthews)
Kevles, Bettyann Holtzmann 1938- *23*
Key, Alexander (Hill) 1904-1979 .... *8*
Obituary *23*
Key, Samuel M.
See de Lint, Charles
Key, Watt 1970- *189*
Keyes, Daniel 1927- *37*
Keyes, Diane *207*
Keyes, Fenton 1915-1999 .... *34*
Keyes, Greg 1963- *116*
Keyes, J. Gregory
See Keyes, Greg
Keyser, Marcia 1933- *42*
Keyser, Sarah
See McGuire, Leslie (Sarah)
Khalid, Mohamed Nor
See Lat

Khalsa, Dayal Kaur 1943-1989 .... *62*
See also CLR *30*
Khan, Hena *214*
Khan, Rukhsana 1962- *165*
Earlier sketch in SATA *118*
Khanshendel, Chiron
See Rose, Wendy
Kheirabadi, Masoud 1951- *158*
Khemir, Sabiha *87*
Kherdian, David 1931- *74*
Autobiography Feature *125*
Earlier sketch in SATA *16*
See also CLR *24*
Khing, T.T. 1933- *192*
Kibbe, Pat (Hosley) *60*
Kidd, Diana 1933-2000 .... *150*
Kidd, Richard 1952-2008 .... *152*
Obituary *194*
Kidd, Ronald 1948- *173*
Earlier sketches in SATA *42, 92*
Kiddell, John 1922- *3*
Kiddell-Monroe, Joan 1908-1972 .... *55*
Kidwell, Carl 1910- *43*
Kiefer, Irene 1926- *21*
Kiefer, Kathleen Balmes 1957- *142*
Kiepper, Shirley Morgan 1933- *10*
Kierstead, Vera M.
See Kierstead-Farber, Vera M.
Kierstead-Farber, Vera M. 1913- *121*
Kierstead-Farber, Vera May
See Kierstead-Farber, Vera M.
Kiesel, Stanley 1925- *35*
Kiesler, Kate (A.) 1971- *152*
Earlier sketch in SATA *90*
Kihn, Greg 1952- *110*
Kikukawa, Cecily H(arder) 1919- *44*
Brief entry *35*
Kilaka, John 1966- *223*
Kilcher, Jewel 1974- *109*
Kile, Joan 1940- *78*
Kilgore, Kathleen 1946- *42*
Kilian, Crawford 1941- *35*
Killdeer, John
See Mayhar, Ardath
Killien, Christi 1956- *73*
Killilea, Marie (Lyons) 1913-1991 .... *2*
Killingback, Julia 1944- *63*
Killough, (Karen) Lee 1942- *64*
Kilpatrick, Don *206*
Kilreon, Beth
See Walker, Barbara (Jeanne) K(erlin)
Kilworth, Garry 1941- *216*
Earlier sketch in SATA *94*
Kilworth, Garry D.
See Kilworth, Garry
Kilworth, Garry Douglas
See Kilworth, Garry
Kim, David 1977- *201*
Kim, Dong-hwa 1950- *225*
Kim, Helen 1899-1970 .... *98*
Kim, Joung Un 1970- *205*
Kimball, Gayle 1943- *90*
Kimball, Violet T(ew) 1932- *126*
Kimball, Yeffe 1914-1978 .... *37*
Kimber, Murray 1964- *171*
Kimble, Warren *176*
Kimbrough, Emily 1899-1989 .... *2*
Obituary *59*
Kimeldorf, Martin 1948- *121*
Kimeldorf, Martin R.
See Kimeldorf, Martin
Kimenye, Barbara 1940(?)- *121*
Kimmel, Elizabeth Cody *209*
Earlier sketch in SATA *170*
Kimmel, Eric A. 1946- *208*
Earlier sketches in SATA *13, 80, 125, 176*
Kimmel, Margaret Mary 1938- *43*
Brief entry *33*
Kimmelman, Burt 1947- *180*
Kimmelman, Leslie 1958- *211*
Earlier sketches in SATA *85, 156*

Kincaid, Jamaica 1949-
　See CLR 63
Kincher, Jonni 1949- 79
Kindl, Patrice 1951- 128
　Earlier sketch in SATA 82
　See also CLR 132
Kindred, Wendy (Good) 1937- 7
Kinerk, Robert 199
Kines, Pat Decker 1937- 12
King, Adam
　See Hoare, Robert J(ohn)
King, Alison
　See Martini, Teri
King, (Maria) Anna 1964- 72
King, A.S. 1970- 217
King, Billie Jean 1943- 12
King, Christine
　See Farris, Christine King
King, Christopher (L.) 1945- 84
King, (David) Clive 1924- 144
　Earlier sketch in SATA 28
King, Colin 1943- 76
King, Cynthia 1925- 7
King, Daniel (John) 1963- 130
King, Daren 1972- 197
King, Elizabeth 1953- 83
King, Frank O. 1883-1969
　Obituary 22
King, Frank R. 1904-1999 127
King, Jane
　See Currie, Stephen
King, Jeanette (Margaret) 1959- 105
King, Larry L. 1929- 66
King, Laurie R. 1952- 88
King, Marian 1900(?)-1986 23
　Obituary 47
King, Martin Luther, Jr. 1929-1968 14
King, Mary Ellen 1958- 93
King, Paul
　See Drackett, Phil(ip Arthur)
King, Paula
　See Downing, Paula E.
King, Stephen 1947- 161
　Earlier sketches in SATA 9, 55
　See also CLR 124
King, Stephen Edwin
　See King, Stephen
King, Stephen Michael 218
　Earlier sketch in SATA 157
King, Steve
　See King, Stephen
King, Thomas 1943- 96
King, Thomas Hunt
　See King, Thomas
King, Tony 1947- 39
King, Willie Christine
　See Farris, Christine King
Kingfisher, Rupert 209
Kingman, Dong (Moy Shu) 1911-2000 44
Kingman, Lee
　See Natti, Lee
Kingsbury, Evan
　See Walker, Robert W.
Kingsland, Leslie William 1912- 13
Kingsley, Charles 1819-1875
　See YABC 2
　See also CLR 77
Kingsley, Emily Perl 1940- 33
Kingsley, Kaza 193
King-Smith, Dick 1922-2011 192
　Brief entry 38
　Earlier sketches in SATA 47, 80, 135
　See also CLR 40
Kingston, Maxine Hong 1940- 53
Kingston, Maxine Ting Ting Hong
　See Kingston, Maxine Hong
Kinkade, Sheila 1962- 229
Kinney, C. Cle(land) 1915- 6
Kinney, Harrison 1921- 13
Kinney, Jean Stout 1912- 12
Kinney, Jeff 1971- 187

Kinsey, Elizabeth
　See Clymer, Eleanor
Kinsey, Helen 1948- 82
Kinsey-Warnock, Natalie 1956- 167
　Earlier sketches in SATA 71, 116
Kinzel, Dorothy 1950- 57
Kinzel, Dottie
　See Kinzel, Dorothy
Kipling, Joseph Rudyard
　See Kipling, Rudyard
Kipling, Rudyard 1865-1936 100
　See also YABC 2
　See also CLR 65
Kippax, Frank
　See Needle, Jan
Kirby, David 1944- 78
Kirby, David K.
　See Kirby, David
Kirby, David Kirk
　See Kirby, David
Kirby, Margaret
　See Bingley, Margaret (Jane Kirby)
Kirby, Pamela F. 1952- 220
Kirby, Susan E. 1949- 62
Kirk, Connie Ann 1957- 167
Kirk, Daniel 1952- 196
　Earlier sketches in SATA 107, 153
Kirk, David 1955- 161
　Earlier sketch in SATA 117
Kirk, Heather 1949- 166
Kirk, Ruth (Kratz) 1925- 5
Kirkham, Dinah
　See Card, Orson Scott
Kirkland, Will
　See Hale, Arlene
Kirkpatrick, Katherine (Anne) 1964- 113
Kirkup, James 1918-2009 12
Kirkus, Virginia
　See Glick, Virginia Kirkus
Kirkwood, Kathryn
　See Fluke, Joanne
Kirsch, Vincent X. 211
Kirshenbaum, Binnie 79
Kirshner, David S. 1958- 123
Kirtland, G. B.
　See Hine, Sesyle Joslin
　and Hine, Al(fred Blakelee)
Kirwan, Wednesday 198
Kish, Eleanor M(ary) 1924- 73
Kish, Ely
　See Kish, Eleanor M(ary)
Kishida, Eriko 1929- 12
Kisinger, Grace Gelvin (Maze) 1913-1965 .. 10
Kissel, Richard 209
Kissin, Eva H. 1923- 10
Kissinger, Rosemary K.
　See Updyke, Rosemary K.
Kistler, John M. 1967- 160
Kitamura, Satoshi 1956- 201
　Earlier sketches in SATA 62, 98, 143
　See also CLR 60
Kitchen, Bert
　See Kitchen, Herbert Thomas
Kitchen, Herbert Thomas 1940- 70
Kite, L. Patricia
　See Kite, Pat
Kite, Pat 1940- 78
Kitt, Tamara
　See de Regniers, Beatrice Schenk (Freedman)
Kittinger, Jo S(usenbach) 1955- 148
　Earlier sketch in SATA 96
Kituomba
　See Odaga, Asenath (Bole)
Kitzinger, Sheila 1929- 57
Kiwak, Barbara 1966- 103
Kjelgaard, James Arthur 1910-1959 17
　See also CLR 81
Kjelgaard, Jim
　See Kjelgaard, James Arthur
Kjelle, Marylou Morano 1954- 146
Klages, Ellen 1954- 196

Klagsbrun, Francine (Lifton) 36
Klaits, Barrie 1944- 52
Klam, Cheryl 191
Klaperman, Gilbert 1921- 33
Klaperman, Libby Mindlin 1921-1982 33
　Obituary 31
Klass, David 1960- 207
　Earlier sketches in SATA 88, 142
Klass, Morton 1927-2001 11
Klass, Sheila Solomon 1927- 219
　Autobiography Feature 126
　Earlier sketches in SATA 45, 99
　See also SAAS 26
Klause, Annette Curtis 1953- 175
　Earlier sketch in SATA 79
　See also CLR 104
Klaveness, Jan O'Donnell 1939- 86
Kleberger, Ilse 1921- 5
Kleeberg, Irene (Flitner) Cumming 1932- 65
Klein, Aaron E. 1930-1998 45
　Brief entry 28
Klein, Bill 1945- 89
Klein, David 1919-2001 59
Klein, Frederick C. 1938- 154
Klein, Gerda Weissmann 1924- 44
Klein, H(erbert) Arthur 8
Klein, James 1932- 115
Klein, Leonore (Glotzer) 1916- 6
Klein, Lisa 1958- 211
Klein, Lisa M.
　See Klein, Lisa
Klein, Mina C(ooper) 1906-1979 8
Klein, Norma 1938-1989 57
　Earlier sketch in SATA 7
　See also CLR 162
　See also SAAS 1
Klein, Rachel S. 1953- 105
Klein, Robin 1936- 164
　Brief entry 45
　Earlier sketches in SATA 55, 80
　See also CLR 21
Klemin, Diana 65
Klemm, Barry 1945- 104
Klemm, Edward G., Jr. 1910-2001 30
Klemm, Roberta K(ohnhorst) 1884-1975 30
Kleven, Elisa 1958- 217
　Earlier sketches in SATA 76, 173
　See also CLR 85
Klevin, Jill Ross 1935- 39
　Brief entry 38
Kliban, B(ernard) 1935-1990 35
　Obituary 66
Klier, Kimberly Wagner 208
Klimo, Kate 214
Klimowicz, Barbara 1927- 10
Kline, Christina Baker 1964- 101
Kline, James
　See Klein, James
Kline, Jim
　See Kline, Jim
Kline, Lisa Williams 1954- 143
Kline, Suzy 1943- 193
　Autobiography Feature 193
　Brief entry 48
　Earlier sketches in SATA 67, 99, 152
Kliros, Thea 1935- 106
Klise, Kate 221
　Earlier sketch in SATA 181
Klise, M. Sarah 1961- 180
　Earlier sketch in SATA 128
Klots, Alexander Barrett 1903-1989
　Obituary 62
Klug, Ron(ald) 1939- 31
Knaak, Richard A. 1961- 166
　Earlier sketch in SATA 86
Knaak, Richard Allen
　See Knaak, Richard A.
Knapman, Timothy 200
Knapp, Edward
　See Kunhardt, Edith
Knapp, Ron 1952- 34

Knebel, Fletcher 1911-1993 .... *36*
  Obituary *75*
Kneeland, Linda Clarke 1947- *94*
Kneen, Maggie 1957- *221*
Knickerbocker, Diedrich
  See Irving, Washington
Knifesmith
  See Cutler, Ivor
Knigge, Robert (R.) 1921(?)-1987 .... *50*
Knight, Anne (Katherine) 1946- *34*
Knight, Brenda *112*
Knight, Christopher G. 1943- *96*
Knight, Damon (Francis) 1922-2002 .... *9*
  Obituary *139*
Knight, David C(arpenter) 1925-1984 .... *14*
  See also CLR 38
Knight, Eric 1897-1943 .... *18*
Knight, Eric Mowbray
  See Knight, Eric
Knight, Francis Edgar 1905- *14*
Knight, Frank
  See Knight, Francis Edgar
Knight, Hilary 1926- *132*
  Earlier sketches in SATA *15, 69*
Knight, Joan
  See Knight, Joan (MacPhail)
Knight, Joan (MacPhail) *159*
  Earlier sketch in SATA *82*
Knight, Kathryn Lasky
  See Lasky, Kathryn
Knight, Mallory T.
  See Hurwood, Bernhardt J.
Knight, Ruth Adams 1898-1974
  Obituary *20*
Knight, Theodore O. 1946- *77*
Knobloch, Dorothea 1951- *88*
Knoepfle, John (Ignatius) 1923- *66*
Knorr, Laura 1971- *200*
Knott, Bill
  See Knott, William C(ecil, Jr.)
Knott, William C(ecil, Jr.) 1927- *3*
Knotts, Howard (Clayton, Jr.) 1922- *25*
Knowles, Anne 1933- *37*
Knowles, Jo 1970- *197*
Knowles, Johanna Beth
  See Knowles, Jo
Knowles, John 1926-2001 .... *89*
  Obituary *134*
  Earlier sketch in SATA *8*
  See also CLR 98
Knox, Calvin M.
  See Silverberg, Robert
Knox, (Mary) Eleanor Jessie 1909-2000 ...... *59*
  Earlier sketch in SATA *30*
Knox, Elizabeth 1959- *176*
Knox, Elizabeth Fiona
  See Knox, Elizabeth
Knox, James
  See Brittain, William
Knox, Jolyne 1937- *76*
Knudsen, James 1950- *42*
Knudsen, Michelle 1974- *220*
  Earlier sketch in SATA *171*
Knudson, Mike 1965- *209*
Knudson, R. R.
  See Knudson, Rozanne
Knudson, Richard L(ewis) 1930- *34*
Knudson, Rozanne 1932-2008 .... *79*
  Earlier sketch in SATA *7*
  See also SAAS 18
Knutson, Barbara 1959-2005 .... *166*
Knutson, Kimberley *115*
Knye, Cassandra
  See Disch, Thomas M.
Kobayashi, Masako Matsuno 1935- *6*
Kober, Shahar 1979- *213*
Koch, Dorothy Clarke 1924- *6*
Koch, Kenneth 1925-2002 .... *65*
Koch, Kenneth Jay
  See Koch, Kenneth
Koch, Phyllis (Mae) McCallum 1911- *10*

Kochalka, James 1967- *196*
Kocsis, J. C.
  See Paul, James
Koda-Callan, Elizabeth 1944- *140*
  Earlier sketch in SATA 67
Kodera, Craig 1956- *222*
Kodman, Stanislawa *201*
Koehler, Phoebe 1955- *85*
Koehler-Pentacoff, Elizabeth 1957- *160*
  Earlier sketch in SATA 96
Koehn, Ilse
  See Van Zwienen, Ilse Charlotte Koehn
Koeller, Carol *192*
Koenig, Viviane 1950- *80*
Koering, Ursula 1921-1976 .... *64*
Koerner, W(illiam) H(enry) D(avid)
  1878-1938 .... *21*
Koertge, Ron 1940- *209*
  Earlier sketches in SATA *53, 92, 131*
Koestler-Grack, Rachel A. 1973- *156*
Koff, Richard Myram 1926- *62*
Koffinke, Carol 1949- *82*
Kogan, Deborah
  See Kogan Ray, Deborah
Kogan Ray, Deborah 1940- *203*
  Earlier sketches in SATA *8, 50, 161*
Kogawa, Joy 1935- *99*
Kogawa, Joy Nozomi
  See Kogawa, Joy
Kogler, Jennie
  See Kogler, Jennifer Anne
Kogler, Jennifer Anne 1982(?)- *174*
Kohara, Kazuno *207*
Kohl, Herbert 1937- *47*
Kohl, Herbert R.
  See Kohl, Herbert
Kohl, MaryAnn F(aubion) 1947- *144*
  Earlier sketch in SATA *74*
Kohler, Dean Ellis 1947- *226*
Kohler, Julilly H(ouse) 1908-1976
  Obituary *20*
Kohn, Bernice
  See Hunt, Bernice
Kohn, Rita (T.) 1933- *89*
Kohner, Frederick 1905-1986 .... *10*
  Obituary *48*
Koide, Tan 1938-1986 .... *50*
Koike, Kay 1940- *72*
Koja, Kathe 1960- *199*
  Earlier sketch in SATA *155*
Koja, Stephan *198*
Kolar, Bob 1960(?)- *206*
Kolb, Larry J. 1953- *175*
Kolba, St. Tamara *22*
Kolibalova, Marketa
  See Kolibalova, Marketa
Kolibalova, Marketa 1953- *126*
Koller, Jackie French 1948- *157*
  Earlier sketches in SATA *72, 109*
  See also CLR 68
Kolodny, Nancy J. 1946- *76*
Kolosov, Jacqueline 1967- *199*
Komaiko, Leah 1954- *164*
  Earlier sketch in SATA *97*
Komisar, Lucy 1942- *9*
Komoda, Beverly 1939- *25*
Komoda, Kiyo 1937- *9*
Kompaneyets, Marc 1974- *169*
Komroff, Manuel 1890-1974 .... *2*
  Obituary *20*
Konigsburg, Bill 1970- *207*
Konigsburg, E.L. 1930- *194*
  Earlier sketches in SATA *4, 48, 94, 126*
  See also CLR 81
Konigsburg, Elaine Lobl
  See Konigsburg, E.L.
Koning, Hans 1921-2007 .... *5*
  Obituary *182*
Koningsberger, Hans
  See Koning, Hans
Konkle, Janet Everest 1917- *12*

Kono, Erin Eitter 1973- *177*
Konrad, Marla Stewart *218*
Konzak, Burt 1946- *151*
Koob, Theodora (J. Foth) 1918- *23*
Kooiker, Leonie
  See Kooyker-Romijn, Johanna Maria
Koons, James
  See Pernu, Dennis
Koontz, Dean 1945- *165*
  Earlier sketch in SATA *92*
  See Koontz, Dean R.
Koontz, Dean R. *225*
  See Koontz, Dean
Koontz, Dean Ray
  See Koontz, Dean
Koontz, Robin Michal 1954- *136*
  Earlier sketch in SATA *70*
Kooyker, Leonie
  See Kooyker-Romijn, Johanna Maria
Kooyker-Romijn, Johanna Maria 1927- *48*
Kooyker-Romyn, Johanna Maria
  See Kooyker-Romijn, Johanna Maria
Kopelke, Lisa 1963- *154*
Kopper, Lisa 1950- *105*
  Brief entry *51*
Kopper, Lisa Esther
  See Kopper, Lisa
Koppes, Steven N. 1957- *169*
Koppes, Steven Nelson
  See Koppes, Steven N.
Korach, Mimi 1922- *9*
Koralek, Jenny 1934- *215*
  Earlier sketches in SATA *71, 140*
Korczak, Janusz
  See Goldszmit, Henryk
Koren, Edward (Benjamin) 1935- *148*
  Earlier sketch in SATA *5*
Koren, Edward 1935- *206*
Korinets, Iurii Iosifovich
  See Korinetz, Yuri (Iosifovich)
Korinetz, Yuri (Iosifovich) 1923- *9*
  See also CLR 4
Korman, Bernice 1937- *78*
Korman, Gordon 1963- *226*
  Brief entry *41*
  Earlier sketches in SATA *49, 81, 119, 167*
  See also CLR 25
Korman, Gordon Richard
  See Korman, Gordon
Korman, Justine 1958- *70*
Kornblatt, Marc 1954- *147*
  Earlier sketch in SATA *84*
Kornprobst, Jacques 1937- *177*
Korte, Gene J. 1950- *74*
Korthues, Barbara 1971- *203*
Korty, Carol 1937- *15*
Koscielniak, Bruce 1947- *153*
  Earlier sketches in SATA *67, 99*
Koshin, Alexander (A.) 1952- *86*
Kositsky, Lynne 1947- *158*
Koskenmaki, Rosalie
  See Maggio, Rosalie
Koss, Amy Goldman 1954- *158*
  Earlier sketch in SATA *115*
Kossin, Sandy (Sanford) 1926- *10*
Kossman, Nina 1959- *84*
Kostecki-Shaw, Jenny Sue *203*
Kostick, Conor 1964- *186*
Kotzwinkle, William 1938- *146*
  Earlier sketches in SATA *24, 70*
  See also CLR 6
Kouhi, Elizabeth 1917- *54*
  Brief entry *49*
Kouts, Anne 1945- *8*
Koutsky, Jan Dale 1955- *146*
Kovacs, Deborah 1954- *132*
  Earlier sketch in SATA *79*
Kovalski, Maryann 1951- *175*
  Earlier sketches in SATA *58, 97*
  See also CLR 34
  See also SAAS 21

Kowalski, Kathiann M. 1955- *151*
  Earlier sketch in SATA *96*
Koz, Paula G.
  See Goodman Koz, Paula
Kozjan, Drazen *209*
Kraft, Betsy Harvey 1937- *157*
Kraft, Erik P. *193*
Krahn, Fernando 1935- *49*
  Brief entry *31*
  See also CLR *3*
Krakauer, Hoong Yee Lee 1955- *86*
Krakauer, Jon 1954- *108*
Krall, Dan 1970- *218*
Kramer, George
  See Heuman, William
Kramer, Nora 1896(?)-1984 .... *26*
  Obituary *39*
Kramer, Remi (Thomas) 1935- *90*
Krantz, Hazel (Newman) *12*
Kranzler, George G(ershon) 1916- *28*
Kranzler, Gershon
  See Kranzler, George G(ershon)
Krasilovsky, Phyllis 1926- *38*
  Earlier sketch in SATA *1*
  See also CLR *83*
  See also SAAS *5*
Krasne, Betty
  See Levine, Betty K(rasne)
Krasner, Steven 1953- *154*
Krasnesky, Thad 1969(?)- *224*
Krasno, Rena 1923- *104*
Kratman, Tom *175*
Kraus, Joanna Halpert 1937- *87*
Kraus, (Herman) Robert 1925-2001 .... *93*
  Obituary *130*
  Earlier sketches in SATA *4, 65*
  See also SAAS *11*
Krauss, Ruth 1911-1993 .... *30*
  Obituary *75*
  Earlier sketch in SATA *1*
  See also CLR *42*
Krauss, Ruth Ida
  See Krauss, Ruth
Krautter, Elisa (Bialk) 1912(?)-1990 ...... *1*
  Obituary *65*
Krautwurst, Terry 1946- *79*
Kray, Robert Clement 1930- *82*
Krech, Bob 1956- *185*
Krech, Robert
  See Krech, Bob
Kredel, Fritz 1900-1973 .... *17*
Kreikemeier, Gregory Scott 1965- *85*
Kreloff, Elliot *189*
Krementz, Jill 1940- *134*
  Earlier sketches in SATA *17, 71*
  See also CLR *5*
  See also SAAS *8*
Kremer, Marcie
  See Sorenson, Margo
Krenina, Katya 1968- *221*
  Earlier sketch in SATA *101*
Krensky, Stephen 1953- *188*
  Brief entry *41*
  Earlier sketches in SATA *47, 93, 136*
Krensky, Stephen Alan
  See Krensky, Stephen
Kresh, Paul 1919-1997 .... *61*
  Obituary *94*
Kress, Nancy 1948- *147*
  Autobiography Feature *147*
  Earlier sketch in SATA *85*
Kricher, John C. 1944- *113*
Krieger, Melanie 1944- *96*
Krinitz, Esther Nisenthal 1927-2001 ...... *194*
Kripke, Dorothy Karp *30*
Krisher, Trudy 1946- *160*
  Earlier sketch in SATA *86*
Krisher, Trudy B.
  See Krisher, Trudy
Krishnaswami, Uma 1956- *182*
  Earlier sketch in SATA *144*

Kristiansen, Teddy 1964- *210*
Kristiansen, Teddy H.
  See Kristiansen, Teddy
Kristof, Jane 1932- *8*
Kroeber, Theodora (Kracaw) 1897-1979 ..... *1*
Kroeger, Mary Kay 1950- *92*
Krohn, Katherine E(lizabeth) 1961- *125*
  Earlier sketch in SATA *84*
Kroll, Francis Lynde 1904-1973 .... *10*
Kroll, Steven 1941-2011 .... *212*
  Autobiography Feature *135*
  Earlier sketches in SATA *19, 66, 125, 135*
  See also SAAS *7*
Kroll, Virginia L. 1948- *225*
  Earlier sketches in SATA *76, 114, 168*
Kroll, Virginia Louisa
  See Kroll, Virginia L.
Kromhout, Rindert 1958- *189*
Krommes, Beth 1956- *208*
  Earlier sketches in SATA *128, 181*
Kronenwetter, Michael 1943- *62*
Kroniuk, Lisa
  See Berton, Pierre (Francis de Marigny)
Kropp, Paul 1948- *38*
  Brief entry *34*
  See also CLR *96*
Kropp, Paul Stephan
  See Kropp, Paul
Krosoczka, Jarrett J. 1977- *200*
  Earlier sketch in SATA *155*
Krovatin, Christopher 1985- *171*
Krudop, Walter
  See Krudop, Walter Lyon
Krudop, Walter Lyon 1966- *210*
Kruess, James
  See Kruss, James
Kruglik, Gerald *187*
Krull, Kathleen 1952- *229*
  Autobiography Feature *106*
  Brief entry *39*
  Earlier sketches in SATA *52, 80, 149, 184*
  See also CLR *44*
Krumgold, Joseph (Quincy) 1908-1980 ...... *48*
  Obituary *23*
  Earlier sketch in SATA *1*
Krupinski, Loretta 1940- *161*
  Earlier sketches in SATA *67, 102*
Krupnick, Karen 1947- *89*
Krupp, E. C. 1944- *123*
  Earlier sketch in SATA *53*
Krupp, Edwin Charles
  See Krupp, E. C.
Krupp, Robin Rector 1946- *53*
Krush, Beth 1918- *18*
Krush, Joe 1918-
  See Krush, Joseph P.
Krush, Joseph P. 1918- *18*
Kruss, James 1926-1997 .... *8*
  See also CLR *9*
Kruusval, Catarina 1951- *201*
Krykorka, Vladyana 1945- *96*
Krystoforski, Andrej 1943- *196*
Kubick, Dana *212*
Kubie, Eleanor Gottheil
  See Kubie, Nora Gottheil Benjamin
Kubie, Nora Benjamin
  See Kubie, Nora Gottheil Benjamin
Kubie, Nora Gottheil Benjamin 1899-1988 . *39*
  Obituary *59*
Kubinyi, Laszlo 1937- *94*
  Earlier sketch in SATA *17*
Kudlinski, Kathleen V. 1950- *213*
  Earlier sketch in SATA *150*
Kuehnert, Stephanie 1979- *205*
Kuenstler, Morton 1927- *10*
Kuh, Charlotte 1892(?)-1985
  Obituary *43*
Kuharski, Janice 1947- *128*
Kuhn, Dwight *199*
Kuijer, Guus 1942- *179*

Kujoth, Jean Spealman 1935-1975
  Obituary *30*
Kuklin, Susan 1941- *163*
  Earlier sketches in SATA *63, 95*
  See also CLR *51*
Kulak, Jeff 1984(?)- *223*
Kulikov, Boris 1966- *205*
  Earlier sketch in SATA *170*
Kulka, Joe *188*
Kulling, Monica 1952- *89*
Kullman, Harry 1919-1982 .... *35*
Kulyk Keefer, Janice 1952- *132*
Kumin, Maxine 1925- *12*
Kumin, Maxine Winokur
  See Kumin, Maxine
Kunhardt, Dorothy (Meserve) 1901-1979 .... *53*
  Obituary *22*
Kunhardt, Edith 1937- *67*
Kunjufu, Jawanza 1953- *73*
Kunstler, Morton
  See Kuenstler, Morton
Kuntz, J(ohn) L. 1947- *91*
Kuntz, Jerry 1956- *133*
Kupferberg, Herbert 1918-2001 .... *19*
Kuratomi, Chizuko 1939- *12*
  See also CLR *32*
Kurczok, Belinda 1978- *121*
Kurelek, William 1927-1977 .... *8*
  Obituary *27*
  See also CLR *2*
Kurian, George 1928- *65*
Kurjian, Judi(th M.) 1944- *127*
Kurland, Gerald 1942- *13*
Kurland, Michael 1938- *118*
  Earlier sketch in SATA *48*
Kurland, Michael Joseph
  See Kurland, Michael
Kuroi, Ken 1947- *120*
Kurokawa, Mitsuhiro 1954- *88*
Kurten, Bjorn (Olof) 1924-1988 .... *64*
Kurtz, Jane 1952- *139*
  Earlier sketch in SATA *91*
  See also CLR *123*
Kurtz, Katherine 1944- *182*
  Earlier sketches in SATA *76, 126*
Kurtz, Katherine Irene
  See Kurtz, Katherine
Kurusa 1942- *226*
Kurz, Rudolf 1952- *95*
Kushner, Donn (J.) 1927- *52*
  See also CLR *55*
Kushner, Ellen 1955- *202*
  Earlier sketch in SATA *98*
Kushner, Ellen Ruth
  See Kushner, Ellen
Kushner, Jill Menkes 1951- *62*
Kushner, Lawrence 1943- *169*
  Earlier sketch in SATA *83*
Kushner, Tony 1956- *160*
Kuskin, Karla 1932-2009 .... *164*
  Obituary *206*
  Earlier sketches in SATA *2, 68, 111*
  See also CLR *4*
  See also SAAS *3*
Kuskin, Karla Seidman
  See Kuskin, Karla
Kusugak, Michael 1948- *143*
Kusugak, Michael Arvaarluk
  See Kusugak, Michael
Kutner, Merrily 1948- *196*
Kuttner, Paul 1922- *18*
Kuyper, Sjoerd 1952- *177*
Kuzma, Kay 1941- *39*
Kvale, Velma R(uth) 1898-1979 .... *8*
Kvasnosky, Laura McGee 1951- *182*
  Earlier sketches in SATA *93, 142*
Kwasney, Michelle D. 1960- *162*
Kyle, Benjamin
  See Gottfried, Theodore Mark
Kyle, Elisabeth
  See Dunlop, Agnes M. R.

Kyte, Kathy S. 1946- 50
  Brief entry 44

L

L., Barry
  See Longyear, Barry B(rookes)
L., Tommy
  See Lorkowski, Thomas V(incent)
Labatt, Mary 1944- 215
Labouisse, Eve Curie
  See Curie, Eve
Labouisse, Eve Denise
  See Curie, Eve
Lace, William W. 1942- 126
Lacey, Joshua
  See Doder, Josh
Lachenmeyer, Nathaniel 1969- 221
Lachner, Dorothea
  See Knobloch, Dorothea
Lachtman, Ofelia Dumas 1919- 179
Lackey, Mercedes
  See Lackey, Mercedes R.
Lackey, Mercedes R. 1950- 127
  Earlier sketch in SATA 81
Lackey, Mercedes Ritchie
  See Lackey, Mercedes R.
Lacoe, Addie 78
Lacombe, Benjamin 1982- 198
Lacome, Julie 1961- 174
  Earlier sketch in SATA 80
LaCour, Nina 1982- 222
Lacy, Leslie Alexander 1937- 6
Ladd, Cheryl (Jean) 1951- 113
Ladd, London 1972(?)- 206
Ladd, Louise 1943- 97
Ladd, Veronica
  See Miner, Jane Claypool
Laden, Nina 1962- 148
  Earlier sketch in SATA 85
Lader, Lawrence 1919-2006 6
  Obituary 178
LaDoux, Rita C. 1951- 74
Ladwig, Tim 1952- 223
Ladwig, Timothy
  See Ladwig, Tim
Lady, A
  See Taylor, Ann
Lady Mears
  See Tempest, Margaret Mary
Lady of Quality, A
  See Bagnold, Enid
La Farge, Oliver 1901-1963 19
La Farge, Oliver Hazard Perry
  See La Farge, Oliver
La Farge, Phyllis 14
LaFave, Kim 196
LaFaye, A. 1970- 220
  Earlier sketches in SATA 105, 156
LaFaye, Alexandria R.T.
  See LaFaye, A.
LaFevers, R.L. 191
LaFevers, Robin L.
  See LaFevers, R.L.
Lafferty, Mur 1973- 227
Laffin, John (Alfred Charles) 1922- 31
LaFleur, Suzanne 1983- 221
LaFontaine, Bruce 1948- 176
  Earlier sketch in SATA 114
La Fontaine, Jean de 1621-1695 18
Lafrance, Marie 1955- 197
Lager, Claude
  See Lapp, Christiane (Germain)
Lager, Marilyn 1939- 52
Lagercrantz, Rose (Elsa) 1947- 39
Lagerloef, Selma
  See Lagerlof, Selma
Lagerlof, Selma 1858-1940 15
  See also CLR 7

Laguna, Sofie 1968- 158
LaHaye, Tim 1926- 149
LaHaye, Timothy F.
  See LaHaye, Tim
Laidlaw, Rob 205
Laiken, Deirdre S. 1948- 48
  Brief entry 40
Laiken, Deirdre Susan
  See Laiken, Deirdre S.
Laimgruber, Monika 1946- 11
Lain, Anna
  See Lamb, Nancy
Laing, Alexander (Kinnan) 1903-1976 117
Laing, Martha 1951- 39
Laird, Christa 1944- 108
  Autobiography Feature 120
  See also SAAS 26
Laird, Elizabeth 1943- 228
  Earlier sketches in SATA 77, 114, 159
  See also CLR 65
Laird, Elizabeth Mary Risk
  See Laird, Elizabeth
Laird, Jean E(louise) 1930- 38
Laite, Gordon 1925- 31
Lake, Harriet
  See Taylor, Paula (Wright)
Lake, Nick 227
Lakeman, Victoria
  See Forester, Victoria
Lakin, Patricia 1944- 190
Laklan, Carli 1907-1988 5
Laliberte, Louise-Andree 1958- 169
Lalicki, Barbara 61
Lalicki, Tom 1949- 186
Lally, Soinbhe 1945- 119
LaMarche, Jim 162
Lamb, Albert 187
Lamb, Beatrice Pitney 1904-1997 21
Lamb, Charles 1775-1834 17
Lamb, Elizabeth Searle 1917- 31
Lamb, G(eoffrey) F(rederick) 10
Lamb, Harold (Albert) 1892-1962 53
Lamb, Lynton (Harold) 1907-1977 10
Lamb, Mary Ann 1764-1847 17
Lamb, Nancy 1939- 80
Lamb, Robert (Boyden) 1941- 13
Lamba, Marie 195
Lambert, David 1932- 84
  Brief entry 49
Lambert, David Compton
  See Lambert, David
Lambert, Janet 1895(?)-1973 25
Lambert, Martha L. 113
Lambert, Saul 1928- 23
Lambert, Stephen 174
Lamburn, Richmal Crompton 1890-1969 5
Lamensdorf, Len 1930- 120
Lamensdorf, Leonard
  See Lamensdorf, Len
Laminack, Lester L. 1956- 163
  Earlier sketch in SATA 120
Lammle, Leslie 1965- 213
Lamont, Priscilla 200
Lamorisse, Albert (Emmanuel) 1922-1970 ... 23
Lampert, Emily 1951- 52
  Brief entry 49
Lamplugh, Lois 1921- 17
Lampman, Evelyn Sibley 1907-1980 87
  Obituary 23
  Earlier sketch in SATA 4
Lamprey, Louise 1869-1951
  See YABC 2
Lampton, Chris
  See Lampton, Christopher F.
Lampton, Christopher
  See Lampton, Christopher F.
Lampton, Christopher F. 67
  Brief entry 47
Lamstein, Sarah 1943- 174
  Earlier sketch in SATA 126

Lamstein, Sarah Marwil
  See Lamstein, Sarah
Lanagan, Margo 1960- 201
  Earlier sketch in SATA 163
Lancaster, Bruce 1896-1963 9
Lancaster, Matthew 1973(?)-1983
  Obituary 45
Lance, Kathryn 1943- 76
Land, Barbara (Neblett) 1923- 16
Land, Jane
  See Borland, Kathryn Kilby
  and Speicher, Helen Ross S(mith)
Land, Myrick (Ebben) 1922-1998 15
Land, Ross
  See Borland, Kathryn Kilby
  and Speicher, Helen Ross S(mith)
Landa, Norbert 1952- 218
Landau, Elaine 1948- 141
  Earlier sketches in SATA 10, 94
Landau, Jacob 1917- 38
Landeck, Beatrice 1904-1978 15
Landin, Les 1923- 2
Landis, J. D. 1942- 60
  Brief entry 52
Landis, James D.
  See Landis, J. D.
Landis, James David
  See Landis, J. D.
Landis, Jill Marie 1948- 101
Landman, Tanya 207
Landmann, Bimba 1968- 176
Landon, Dena 1978(?)- 168
Landon, Lucinda 1950- 56
  Brief entry 51
Landon, Margaret (Dorothea Mortenson)
  1903-1993 50
Landowne, Youme 1970- 211
Landry, Leo 202
Landshoff, Ursula 1908-1989 13
Landstrom, Lena 1943- 206
  Earlier sketch in SATA 146
Landstrom, Olof 1943- 146
Landy, Derek 1974- 210
Lane, Alison Hoffman 215
Lane, Carolyn 1926-1993 10
Lane, Connie
  See Laux, Constance
Lane, Dakota 1959- 166
  Earlier sketch in SATA 105
Lane, Jerry
  See Martin, Patricia Miles
Lane, John (Richard) 1932- 15
Lane, Leena 199
Lane, Margaret 1907-1994 65
  Brief entry 38
  Obituary 79
Lane, Rose Wilder 1887-1968 29
  Brief entry 28
Lanes, Selma G. 1929- 3
Lanes, Selma Gordon
  See Lanes, Selma G.
Lanfredi, Judy 1964- 83
Lang, Andrew 1844-1912 16
  See also CLR 101
Lang, Aubrey 169
Lang, Glenna 1951- 221
Lang, Lang 1982- 208
Lang, Paul 1948- 83
Lang, Susan S. 1950- 68
Lang, T.T.
  See Taylor, Theodore
Langart, Darrell T.
  See Garrett, Randall
Langdo, Bryan 1973- 191
  Earlier sketch in SATA 138
Lange, John
  See Crichton, Michael
Lange, Karen E. 190
Lange, Suzanne 1945- 5
Langley, Andrew 1949- 166
  Earlier sketch in SATA 104

Langley, Charles P(itman) III 1949- 103
Langley, Jonathan 1952- 122
Langley, Noel 1911-1980
    Obituary 25
Langley, Wanda 173
Langner, Nola
    See Malone, Nola Langner
Langone, John (Michael) 1929- 46
    Brief entry 38
Langreuter, Jutta 1944- 122
Langrish, Katherine 177
Langsen, Richard C. 1953- 95
Langstaff, John 1920-2005 68
    Obituary 172
    Earlier sketch in SATA 6
    See also CLR 3
Langstaff, John Meredith
    See Langstaff, John
Langstaff, Launcelot
    See Irving, Washington
Langston, Laura 1958- 186
Langton, Jane 1922- 200
    Autobiography Feature 140
    Earlier sketches in SATA 3, 68, 129, 140
    See also CLR 33
    See also SAAS 5
Lanier, Sidney 1842-1881 18
Lanier, Sterling E. 1927-2007 109
Lanier, Sterling Edmund
    See Lanier, Sterling E.
Lanino, Deborah 1964- 123
Lankford, Mary D. 1932- 112
    Earlier sketch in SATA 77
Lannin, Joanne 1951- 121
Lannin, Joanne A.
    See Lannin, Joanne
Lansdale, Joe R. 1951- 116
Lansdale, Joe Richard
    See Lansdale, Joe R.
Lansing, Alfred 1921-1975 35
Lansing, Karen E. 1954- 71
Lansky, Vicki 1942- 177
Lanthier, Jennifer 1964- 204
Lantier-Sampon, Patricia 1952- 92
Lantz, Fran
    See Lantz, Francess L(in)
Lantz, Francess L(in) 1952-2004 153
    Autobiography Feature 153
    Obituary 159
    Earlier sketches in SATA 63, 109
Lantz, Paul 1908- 45
Lantz, Walter 1900-1994 37
    Obituary 79
Lanza, Barbara 1945- 101
Lapp, Christiane (Germain) 1948- 74
Lappin, Peter 1911-1999 32
Larbalestier, Justine 178
Lardy, Philippe 1963- 168
LaReau, Jenna 181
LaReau, Kara 181
Larios, Julie 1949- 178
Larios, Julie Hofstrand
    See Larios, Julie
Larkin, Amy
    See Burns, Olive Ann
Larkin, Maia
    See Wojciechowska, Maia (Teresa)
Larkspur, Penelope
    See Wyatt, Valerie
Laroche, Giles 1956- 221
    Earlier sketches in SATA 71, 126
LaRochelle, David 1960- 171
    Earlier sketch in SATA 115
Larom, Henry V. 1903(?)-1975
    Obituary 30
LaRose, Linda 125
Larrabee, Lisa 1947- 84
Larranaga, Ana Martin 1969- 229
Larrecq, John M(aurice) 1926-1980 44
    Obituary 25
Larrick (Crosby), Nancy 1910-2004 4

Larsen, Anita 1942- 78
Larsen, Egon 1904- 14
Larsen, Rebecca 1944- 54
Larson, Eve
    See St. John, Wylly Folk
Larson, Gary 1950- 57
Larson, Hope 1982- 205
Larson, Ingrid D(ana) 1965- 92
Larson, Jean Russell 1930- 121
Larson, Kirby 1954- 181
    Earlier sketch in SATA 96
Larson, Norita D. 1944- 29
Larson, Norita Dittberner
    See Larson, Norita D.
Larson, William H. 1938- 10
Larsson, Carl (Olof) 1853-1919 35
LaSalle, Charles A.
    See Ellis, Edward S.
LaSalle, Charles E.
    See Ellis, Edward S.
Lasell, Elinor H. 1929- 19
Lasell, Fen H.
    See Lasell, Elinor H.
Lasenby, Jack 1931- 172
    Earlier sketches in SATA 65, 103
Laser, Michael 1954- 117
Lash, Joseph P. 1909-1987 43
Lasher, Faith B. 1921- 12
Lasker, David 1950- 38
Lasker, Joe
    See Lasker, Joseph Leon
Lasker, Joseph Leon 1919- 83
    Earlier sketch in SATA 9
    See also SAAS 17
Laski, Marghanita 1915-1988 55
Laskin, Pamela L. 1954- 75
Lasky, Kathryn 1944- 210
    Earlier sketches in SATA 13, 69, 112, 157
    See also CLR 140
Lasky Knight, Kathryn
    See Lasky, Kathryn
Lass, Bonnie 131
Lassalle, C. E.
    See Ellis, Edward S.
Lassiter, Mary
    See Hoffman, Mary
Lassiter, Rhiannon 1977- 157
Lat 1951- 196
Latham, Barbara 1896- 16
Latham, Frank B(rown) 1910-2000 6
Latham, Irene 1971- 228
Latham, Jean Lee 1902-1995 68
    Earlier sketch in SATA 2
    See also CLR 50
Latham, Mavis
    See Clark, Mavis Thorpe
Latham, Philip
    See Richardson, Robert S(hirley)
Lathrop, Dorothy P(ulis) 1891-1980 14
    Obituary 24
Lathrop, Francis
    See Leiber, Fritz (Reuter, Jr.)
Latimer, Jim 1943- 80
Latta, Rich
    See Latta, Richard
Latta, Richard 1946- 113
Latta, Sara L. 1960- 174
Lattany, Kristin
    See Lattany, Kristin Hunter
Lattany, Kristin (Eggleston) Hunter 1931- . 154
    Autobiography Feature 154
    Earlier sketch in SATA 132
Lattany, Kristin Hunter 1931-2008 132
    Earlier sketch in SATA 12
    See also CLR 3
    See also SAAS 10
Lattimore, Eleanor Frances 1904-1986 7
    Obituary 48
Lattin, Ann
    See Cole, Lois Dwight

Lauber, Patricia (Grace) 1924- 138
    Earlier sketches in SATA 1, 33, 75
    See also CLR 16
Laugesen, Malene 207
Laugesen, Malene Reynolds
    See Laugesen, Malene
Laugesen, Mary E(akin) 1906-1995 5
Laughbaum, Steve 1945- 12
Laughlin, Florence Young 1910-2001 3
Laughlin, Rosemary 1941- 123
Launder, Sally 206
Laure, Ettagale
    See Blauer, Ettagale
Laure, Jason 1940- 50
    Brief entry 44
Laurence, Ester Hauser 1935- 7
Laurence, Jean Margaret Wemyss
    See Laurence, Margaret
Laurence, Margaret 1926-1987
    Obituary 50
Laurie, Rona 1916- 55
Laurie, Victoria 218
Laurin, Anne
    See McLaurin, Anne
Lauritzen, Jonreed 1902-1979 13
Lauscher, Hermann
    See Hesse, Hermann
Lauture, Denize 1946- 86
Laux, Connie
    See Laux, Constance
Laux, Constance 1952- 97
Laux, Dorothy 1920- 49
Lavallee, Barbara 1941- 166
    Earlier sketch in SATA 74
Lavender, David (Sievert) 1910-2003 97
    Obituary 145
    Earlier sketch in SATA 64
Lavender, William D. 1921- 143
Laverne, Christine 175
Lavert, Gwendolyn Battle 1951-
    See Battle-Lavert, Gwendolyn
Laverty, Donald
    See Blish, James
    and Knight, Damon (Francis)
Lavigne, Louis-Dominique 1949- 107
Lavine, David 1928- 31
Lavine, Sigmund Arnold 1908-1986 82
    Earlier sketch in SATA 3
    See also CLR 35
Lavis, Steve 225
Lavond, Paul Dennis
    See Kornbluth, C(yril) M.
    and Lowndes, Robert A(ugustine) W(ard)
    and Pohl, Frederik
Law, Stephen 225
Law, Stephen
    See Law, Stephen
Lawford, Paula Jane 1960- 57
    Brief entry 53
Lawhead, Stephen R. 1950- 109
Lawhead, Steve
    See Lawhead, Stephen R.
Lawler, Janet 222
Lawlor, Laurie 1953- 137
    Earlier sketch in SATA 80
Lawlor, William
    See Lawlor, William T.
Lawlor, William T. 1951- 183
Lawrence, Ann (Margaret) 1942-1987 41
    Obituary 54
Lawrence, Caroline 1954- 203
Lawrence, Iain 1955- 183
    Earlier sketch in SATA 135
Lawrence, J. T.
    See Rowland-Entwistle, (Arthur) Theodore
    (Henry)
Lawrence, Jerome 1915-2004 65
Lawrence, John 1933- 30
Lawrence, Josephine 1890(?)-1978
    Obituary 24

Lawrence, Louise 1943- *119*
Earlier sketches in SATA *38, 78*
Lawrence, Louise de Kiriline 1894-1992 ..... *13*
Lawrence, Lynn
See Garland, Sherry
Lawrence, Margery H. 1889-1969 .... *120*
Lawrence, Michael 1943- *132*
Lawrence, Mildred Elwood 1907-1997 .... *3*
Lawrence, R(onald) D(ouglas) 1921- *55*
Lawrinson, Julia 1969- *141*
Lawson, Amy
See Gordon, Amy
Lawson, Carol (Antell) 1946- *42*
Lawson, Don(ald Elmer) 1917-1990 .... *9*
Lawson, Joan 1906- *55*
Lawson, Julie 1947- *126*
Earlier sketch in SATA *79*
See also CLR *89*
Lawson, Marion Tubbs 1896-1994 .... *22*
Lawson, Robert 1892-1957 .... *100*
See also YABC *2*
See also CLR *73*
Lawton, Clive A. 1951- *145*
Laxdal, Vivienne 1962- *112*
Laybourn, Emma *193*
Layburn, Joe *228*
Laycock, George (Edwin) 1921- *5*
Layne, Laura
See Knott, William C(ecil, Jr.)
Layne, Steven L. *171*
Layson, Annelex Hofstra 1938(?)- *211*
Layton, Neal 1971- *187*
Earlier sketch in SATA *152*
Layton, Neal Andrew
See Layton, Neal
Lazare, Gerald John 1927- *44*
Lazare, Jerry
See Lazare, Gerald John
Lazarevich, Mila 1942- *17*
Lazarus, Keo Felker 1913-1993 .... *21*
Obituary *129*
Lea, Alec 1907- *19*
Lea, Bob 1952- *203*
Lea, Joan
See Neufeld, John (Arthur)
Leach, Maria 1892-1977 .... *39*
Brief entry *28*
Leacock, Elspeth 1946- *131*
Leacroft, Helen (Mabel Beal) 1919- *6*
Leacroft, Richard (Vallance Becher) 1914- *6*
Leaf, Margaret P. 1909(?)-1988
Obituary *55*
Leaf, (Wilbur) Munro 1905-1976 .... *20*
See also CLR *25*
Leaf, VaDonna Jean 1929- *26*
Leah, Devorah
See Devorah-Leah
Leakey, Richard E(rskine Frere) 1944- *42*
Leal, Ann Haywood *216*
Leander, Ed
See Richelson, Geraldine
Lear, Edward 1812-1888 .... *100*
Earlier sketch in SATA *18*
See also CLR *75*
Lears, Laurie 1955- *127*
Leasor, James 1923-2007 .... *54*
Leasor, Thomas James
See Leasor, James
Leavitt, Jerome E(dward) 1916- *23*
Leavitt, Martine 1953- *170*
LeBar, Mary E(velyn) 1910-1982 .... *35*
LeBlanc, Annette M. 1965- *68*
LeBlanc, L(ee) 1913- *54*
LeBox, Annette 1943- *145*
Lebrun, Claude 1929- *66*
Le Cain, Errol (John) 1941-1989 .... *68*
Obituary *60*
Earlier sketch in SATA *6*
Lechner, Jack *201*
Lechner, John 1966- *200*
Leck, James 1973- *229*

Lecourt, Nancy (Hoyt) 1951- *73*
Ledbetter, Suzann 1953- *119*
Leder, Jane Mersky 1945- *61*
Brief entry *51*
Lederer, Muriel 1929- *48*
Lederer, William J. 1912-2009 .... *62*
Lederer, William Julius
See Lederer, William J.
Lee, Amanda
See Baggett, Nancy
and Buckholtz, Eileen (Garber)
and Glick, Ruth
Lee, Benjamin 1921- *27*
Lee, Betsy 1949- *37*
Lee, Carol
See Fletcher, Helen Jill
Lee, Carol Ann 1969- *185*
Lee, Chinlun *182*
Lee, Cora *223*
See Anderson, Catherine Corley
Lee, Dennis (Beynon) 1939- *102*
Earlier sketch in SATA *14*
See also CLR *3*
Lee, Dom 1959- *146*
Autobiography Feature *121*
Earlier sketch in SATA *83*
See also SAAS *26*
Lee, Doris Emrick 1905-1983 .... *44*
Obituary *35*
Lee, Edward
See Lee, J. Edward
Lee, Elizabeth Rogers 1940- *90*
Lee, Harper 1926- *11*
Lee, Hector Viveros 1962- *115*
Lee, Howard N.
See Goulart, Ron
Lee, Huy Voun 1969- *217*
Earlier sketch in SATA *129*
Lee, Insu *213*
Lee, J. Edward 1953- *130*
Lee, Jared 1943- *215*
Lee, Jared D.
See Lee, Jared
Lee, Jeanne M. 1943- *138*
Lee, John R(obert) 1923-1976 .... *27*
Lee, Jordan
See Scholefield, Alan
Lee, Joseph Edward
See Lee, J. Edward
Lee, Julian
See Latham, Jean Lee
Lee, Linda
See Eyerly, Jeannette
Lee, Liz
See Lee, Elizabeth Rogers
Lee, Lucy
See Talbot, Charlene Joy
Lee, Lyn 1953- *128*
Lee, Manning de Villeneuve 1894-1980 ...... *37*
Obituary *22*
Lee, Marian
See Clish, (Lee) Marian
Lee, Marie G. 1964- *178*
Earlier sketches in SATA *81, 130*
Lee, Marie Myung-Ok
See Lee, Marie G.
Lee, Mary Price 1934- *82*
Earlier sketch in SATA *8*
Lee, Mildred
See Scudder, Mildred Lee
Lee, Nelle Harper
See Lee, Harper
Lee, Richard S. 1927- *82*
Lee, Robert C. 1931- *20*
Lee, Robert Edwin 1918-1994 .... *65*
Obituary *82*
Lee, Robert J. 1921- *10*
Lee, Roy
See Hopkins, Clark
Lee, Sally 1943- *67*
Lee, Suzy *193*

Lee, Tammie
See Townsend, Thomas L.
Lee, Tanith 1947- *185*
Earlier sketches in SATA *8, 88, 134*
Lee, Virginia 1976- *208*
Leech, Ben
See Bowkett, Stephen
Leeds, Contance *188*
Leedy, Loreen 1959- *175*
Brief entry *50*
Earlier sketches in SATA *54, 84, 128*
Leedy, Loreen Janelle
See Leedy, Loreen
Lee-Hostetler, Jeri 1940- *63*
Leekley, Thomas B(riggs) 1910-2001 .... *23*
Leeming, Jo Ann
See Leeming, Joseph
Leeming, Joseph 1897-1968 .... *26*
Leemis, Ralph B. 1954- *72*
Leese, Jennifer L.B. 1970- *163*
Leeson, Muriel 1920- *54*
Leeson, R. A.
See Leeson, Robert (Arthur)
Leeson, Robert (Arthur) 1928- *76*
Earlier sketch in SATA *42*
Lee Tae-Jun 1904-1956(?) *194*
Lee-Tai, Amy 1964- *189*
Leffland, Ella 1931- *65*
Leffler, Silke *197*
Lefler, Irene (Whitney) 1917- *12*
LeFrak, Karen *182*
Le Gallienne, Eva 1899-1991 .... *9*
Obituary *68*
Legg, Gerald 1947- *143*
Legg, Sarah Martha Ross Bruggeman (?)-1982
Obituary *40*
LeGrand
See Henderson, LeGrand
Le Guin, Ursula K. 1929- *194*
Earlier sketches in SATA *4, 52, 99, 149*
See also CLR *91*
Le Guin, Ursula Kroeber
See Le Guin, Ursula K.
Legum, Colin 1919-2003 .... *10*
Lehman, Barbara 1963- *170*
Earlier sketch in SATA *115*
Lehman, Bob *91*
Lehman, Elaine *91*
Lehmann, Debra Lynn
See Vanasse, Deb
Lehman-Wilzig, Tami 1950- *224*
Lehn, Cornelia 1920- *46*
Lehne, Judith Logan 1947- *93*
Lehr, Delores 1920- *10*
Lehr, Norma 1930- *71*
Leiber, Fritz (Reuter, Jr.) 1910-1992 .... *45*
Obituary *73*
Leibold, Jay 1957- *57*
Brief entry *52*
Leichman, Seymour 1933- *5*
Leick, Bonnie *205*
Leigh, Nila K. 1981- *81*
Leigh, Tom 1947- *46*
Leigh-Pemberton, John 1911-1997 .... *35*
Leighton, Clare (Veronica Hope)
1899-1989 .... *37*
Leighton, Margaret (Carver) 1896-1987 .... *1*
Obituary *52*
Leijten, Aileen *216*
Leiner, Al(an) 1938- *83*
Leiner, Katherine 1949- *93*
Leipold, L. Edmond 1902-1983 .... *16*
Leisk, David (Johnson) 1906-1975 .... *30*
Obituary *26*
Earlier sketch in SATA *1*
See also CLR *98*
Leist, Christina *226*
Leister, Mary 1917- *29*
Leitch, Patricia 1933- *98*
Earlier sketch in SATA *11*
Leitner, Isabella 1924- *86*

Lekich, John 202
Leland, Bob 1956- 92
Leland, Robert E.
    See Leland, Bob
Lematre, Pascal 1967- 225
    Earlier sketch in SATA *176*
Lember, Barbara Hirsch 1941- 92
LeMieux, A.C. 1954- 125
    Earlier sketch in SATA *90*
LeMieux, Anne
    See LeMieux, A.C.
LeMieux, Anne Connelly
    See LeMieux, A.C.
Lemieux, Michele 1955- 139
Lemke, Horst 1922- 38
Lemna, Don 1936- 216
Lenain, Thierry 1959- 201
Lenanton, Carola Mary Anima Oman
    See Oman, Carola (Mary Anima)
Lenard, Alexander 1910-1972
    Obituary 21
Lendroth, Susan 207
L'Engle, Madeleine 1918-2007 128
    Obituary 186
    Earlier sketches in SATA *1, 27, 75*
    See also CLR *57*
    See also SAAS *15*
L'Engle, Madeleine Camp Franklin
    See L'Engle, Madeleine
Lengyel, Cornel Adam 1915- 27
Lengyel, Emil 1895-1985 3
    Obituary 42
Lennon, John 1940-1980 114
Lennon, John Ono
    See Lennon, John
Leno, Jay 1950- 154
LeNoir, Janice 1941- 89
Lens, Sidney 1912-1986 13
    Obituary 48
Lenski, Lois 1893-1974 100
    Earlier sketches in SATA *1, 26*
    See also CLR *26*
Lent, Blair 1930-2009 133
    Obituary 200
    Earlier sketch in SATA *2*
Lent, Henry Bolles 1901-1973 17
Lent, John 1948- 108
Leodhas, Sorche Nic
    See Alger, Leclaire (Gowans)
Leokum, Arkady 1916(?)- 45
Leon, Carol Boyd 212
Leon, Sharon 1959- 79
Leonard, Alison 1944- 70
Leonard, Anna
    See Gilman, Laura Anne
Leonard, Constance (Brink) 1923- 42
    Brief entry 40
Leonard, Dutch
    See Leonard, Elmore
Leonard, Elmore 1925- 163
Leonard, Elmore John, Jr.
    See Leonard, Elmore
Leonard, Jonathan N(orton) 1903-1975 36
Leonard, Laura 1923- 75
Leonard, Tom 1955- 207
Leonetti, Mike 1958- 202
Leong, Gor Yun
    See Ellison, Virginia H(owell)
Leonhard, Herb 217
Leonhardt, Alice 1950- 152
Lerangis, Peter 1955- 171
    Earlier sketch in SATA *72*
Lerman, Josh 215
Lerner, Aaron 1920-2007 35
    Obituary 179
Lerner, Aaron Bunsen
    See Lerner, Aaron
Lerner, Carol 1927- 86
    Earlier sketch in SATA *33*
    See also CLR *34*
    See also SAAS *12*

Lerner, Gerda 1920- 65
Lerner, Harriet 1944- 101
Lerner, Marguerite Rush 1924-1987 11
    Obituary 51
Lerner, Sharon (Ruth) 1938-1982 11
    Obituary 29
Leroe, Ellen 1949- 99
    Brief entry 51
    Earlier sketch in SATA *61*
Leroe, Ellen W.
    See Leroe, Ellen
Leroe, Ellen Whitney
    See Leroe, Ellen
Leroux, Gaston 1868-1927 65
Leroux-Hugon, Helene 1955- 132
LeRoy, Gen 52
    Brief entry 36
Lerrigo, Marion Olive 1898-1968
    Obituary 29
LeShan, Eda J(oan) 1922-2002 21
    See also CLR *6*
Leshem, Yossi 1947- 222
LeSieg, Theo.
    See Dr. Seuss
Lesinski, Jeanne M. 1960- 120
Leslie, Robert Franklin 1911-1990 7
Leslie, Roger 1961- 168
Leslie, Roger James
    See Leslie, Roger
Leslie, Sarah
    See McGuire, Leslie (Sarah)
LeSourd, Catherine
    See Marshall, (Sarah) Catherine (Wood)
Lessac, Frane
    See Lessac, Frane
Lessac, Frane 1954- 209
    Earlier sketches in SATA *61, 148*
Lessem, Dino Don
    See Lessem, Don
Lessem, Don 1951- 182
    Earlier sketches in SATA *97, 155*
Lesser, Margaret 1899(?)-1979
    Obituary 22
Lesser, Rika 1953- 53
Lester, Alison 1952- 218
    Earlier sketches in SATA *50, 90, 129*
Lester, Helen 1936- 189
    Earlier sketches in SATA *46, 92, 145*
Lester, Julius 1939- 157
    Earlier sketches in SATA *12, 74, 112*
    See also CLR *143*
Lester, Julius Bernard
    See Lester, Julius
Lester, Mike 1955- 206
    Earlier sketch in SATA *131*
Le Sueur, Meridel 1900-1996 6
Leszczynski, Diana 211
Lethcoe, Jason 191
Le Tord, Bijou 1945- 95
    Earlier sketch in SATA *49*
Letts, Billie 1938- 121
Letts, Elizabeth
    See Alalou, Elizabeth
Leuck, Laura 1962- 192
    Earlier sketches in SATA *85, 146*
Leung, Hilary 1975- 225
Leutscher, Alfred (George) 1913- 23
Levai, Blaise 1919- 39
Levchuk, Lisa 215
Levenkron, Steven 1941- 86
Leverich, Kathleen 1948- 103
LeVert, John 1946- 55
Levert, Mireille 1956- 211
LeVert, William John
    See LeVert, John
Levete, Sarah 1961- 153
Levin, Betty 1927- 201
    Earlier sketches in SATA *19, 84, 137*
    See also SAAS *11*
Levin, Ira 1929-2007 66
    Obituary 187

Levin, Ira Marvin
    See Levin, Ira
Levin, Marcia Obrasky 1918- 13
Levin, Meyer 1905-1981 21
    Obituary 27
Levin, Miriam (Ramsfelder) 1962- 97
Levine, Abby 1943- 54
    Brief entry 52
Levine, Anna 212
Levine, Betty K(rasne) 1933- 66
Levine, David 1926-2009 43
    Brief entry 35
Levine, Edna S(imon) 35
Levine, Ellen 1939- 190
Levine, Evan 1962- 77
    Earlier sketch in SATA *74*
Levine, Gail Carson 1947- 195
    Earlier sketches in SATA *98, 161*
    See also CLR *85*
Levine, I(srael) E. 1923-2003 12
    Obituary 146
Levine, Joan Goldman 11
Levine, Joseph 1910- 33
Levine, Kristin 1974- 213
Levine, Marge 1934- 81
Levine, Rhoda 14
Levine, Sarah 1970- 57
Levine, Shar 1953- 131
Levine-Freidus, Gail
    See Provost, Gail Levine
Levinson, Nancy Smiler 1938- 211
    Earlier sketches in SATA *33, 80, 140*
Levinson, Riki 99
    Brief entry 49
    Earlier sketch in SATA *52*
Levithan, David 1972- 166
Levitin, Sonia 1934- 192
    Autobiography Feature 131
    Earlier sketches in SATA *4, 68, 119, 131*
    See also CLR *53*
    See also SAAS *2*
Levitt, Sidney (Mark) 1947- 68
Levon, O. U.
    See Kesey, Ken
Levoy, Myron 1930- 49
    Brief entry 37
Levy, Barrie 112
Levy, Constance 1931- 140
    Earlier sketch in SATA *73*
    See also SAAS *22*
Levy, Elizabeth 1942- 169
    Earlier sketches in SATA *31, 69, 107*
    See also SAAS *18*
Levy, Janice 172
Levy, Marilyn 1937- 67
Levy, Nathan 1945- 63
Levy, Robert 1945- 82
Lewees, John
    See Stockton, Francis Richard
Lewin, Betsy 1937- 222
    Autobiography Feature 115
    Earlier sketches in SATA *32, 90, 169*
Lewin, Hugh 1939- 72
    Brief entry 40
    See also CLR *9*
Lewin, Ted 1935- 226
    Autobiography Feature 115
    Earlier sketches in SATA *21, 76, 119, 165,
    195*
Lewis, Alice C. 1936- 46
Lewis, Alice Hudson 1895(?)-1971
    Obituary 29
Lewis, Amanda 1955- 80
Lewis, Anthony 1927- 27
Lewis, Anthony 1966- 227
    Earlier sketch in SATA *120*
Lewis, Barbara A. 1943- 73
Lewis, Beverly 1949- 80
Lewis, Brenda Ralph 1932- 72
Lewis, Brian 1963- 128

Lewis, C. S. 1898-1963 .... *100*
  Earlier sketch in SATA *13*
  See also CLR *109*
Lewis, Claudia (Louise) 1907-2001 .... *5*
Lewis, Clive Staples
  See Lewis, C. S.
Lewis, Cynthia Copeland 1960- *111*
Lewis, E. M. *123*
  Earlier sketch in SATA *20*
Lewis, Earl Bradley
  See Lewis, E.B.
Lewis, E.B. 1956- *211*
  Earlier sketches in SATA *93, 124, 168*
Lewis, Elizabeth Foreman 1892-1958 .... *121*
  See also YABC *2*
Lewis, Francine
  See Wells, Helen
Lewis, Harry Sinclair
  See Lewis, Sinclair
Lewis, Hilda (Winifred) 1896-1974
  Obituary *20*
Lewis, J. Patrick 1942- *205*
  Earlier sketches in SATA *69, 104, 162*
Lewis, Jack P(earl) 1919- *65*
Lewis, Jean 1924- *61*
Lewis, Jon Samuel
  See Lewis, J.S.
Lewis, Joseph Anthony
  See Lewis, Anthony
Lewis, J.S. 1972- *203*
Lewis, Julinda
  See Lewis-Ferguson, Julinda
Lewis, Kevin *173*
Lewis, Kim 1951- *217*
  Earlier sketches in SATA *84, 136*
Lewis, Linda (Joy) 1946- *67*
Lewis, Lucia Z.
  See Anderson, Lucia (Lewis)
Lewis, Marjorie 1929- *40*
  Brief entry *35*
Lewis, Mary 1907(?)-1988 .... *64*
  Obituary *56*
Lewis, Mervyn
  See Frewer, Glyn (M.)
Lewis, Michael
  See Untermeyer, Louis
Lewis, Naomi 1911-2009 .... *144*
  Earlier sketch in SATA *76*
Lewis, Paeony 1960- *173*
Lewis, Paul
  See Gerson, Noel Bertram
Lewis, Richard 1935- *3*
Lewis, Richard 1956- *209*
Lewis, Rob 1962- *72*
Lewis, Roger
  See Zarchy, Harry
Lewis, Rose *209*
Lewis, Rose A.
  See Lewis, Rose
Lewis, Shannon
  See Llywelyn, Morgan
Lewis, Shari 1934-1998 .... *35*
  Brief entry *30*
  Obituary *104*
Lewis, Sylvan R.
  See Aronson, Virginia
Lewis, Thomas P(arker) 1936- *27*
Lewis, Wendy A. 1966- *150*
Lewis-Ferguson, Julinda 1955- *85*
Lewison, Wendy Cheyette *177*
Lewiton, Mina 1904-1970 .... *2*
Lew-Vriethoff, Joanne *186*
Lexau, Joan M. *130*
  Earlier sketches in SATA *1, 36*
Ley, Willy 1906-1969 .... *2*
Leydon, Rita (Floden) 1949- *21*
Leyland, Eric (Arthur) 1911- *37*
L'Hommedieu, Dorothy Keasley 1885-1961
  Obituary *29*
Li, Xiao Jun 1952- *86*
Liao, Jimmy 1958- *202*

Liatsos, Sandra Olson 1942- *103*
Libby, Alisa M. *189*
Libby, Barbara M. *153*
Libby, Bill
  See Libby, William M.
Libby, William M. 1927-1984 .... *5*
  Obituary *39*
Liberty, Gene 1924- *3*
Lichtenheld, Tom *208*
  Earlier sketch in SATA *152*
Lichtman, Wendy 1946- *193*
Liddell, Kenneth 1912-1975 .... *63*
Liddiment, Carol *224*
Lidz, Jane *120*
Lieb, Josh 1972- *224*
Lieberman, E(dwin) James 1934- *62*
Liebers, Arthur 1913-1984 .... *12*
Lieblich, Irene 1923- *22*
Liers, Emil E(rnest) 1890-1975 .... *37*
Lies, Brian 1963- *190*
  Earlier sketch in SATA *131*
Lieshout, Elle van
  See van Lieshout, Elle
Liestman, Vicki 1961- *72*
Lietz, Gerald S. 1918- *11*
Liew, Sonny 1974- *219*
Life, Kay (Guinn) 1930- *83*
Lifton, Betty Jean 1926-2010 .... *118*
  Earlier sketch in SATA *6*
Lifton, Robert Jay 1926- *66*
Lightburn, Ron 1954- *91*
Lightburn, Sandra 1955- *91*
Lightner, A. M.
  See Hopf, Alice (Martha) L(ightner)
Lightner, Alice
  See Hopf, Alice (Martha) L(ightner)
Lignell, Lois 1911- *37*
Liles, Maurine Walpole 1935- *81*
Lillegard, Dee *184*
Lilley, Stephen R. 1950- *97*
Lilley, Stephen Ray
  See Lilley, Stephen R.
Lillington, Kenneth (James) 1916-1998 .... *39*
Lilly, Nate *182*
Lilly, Ray
  See Curtis, Richard
Lim, John 1932- *43*
Liman, Ellen (Fogelson) 1936- *22*
Limb, Sue 1946- *203*
  Earlier sketch in SATA *158*
Limburg, Peter R(ichard) 1929- *13*
Lin, Grace 1974- *198*
  Earlier sketches in SATA *111, 162*
Lincoln, C(harles) Eric 1924-2000 .... *5*
Lincoln, Christopher 1952- *208*
Lincoln, Hazel *187*
Lincoln, James
  See Bates, Katharine Lee
Lindbergh, Anne
  See Sapieyevski, Anne Lindbergh
Lindbergh, Anne Morrow 1906-2001 .... *33*
  Obituary *125*
Lindbergh, Anne Spencer Morrow
  See Lindbergh, Anne Morrow
Lindbergh, Charles A(ugustus, Jr.)
  1902-1974 .... *33*
Lindbergh, Reeve 1945- *163*
  Earlier sketch in SATA *116*
Lindblom, Steven (Winther) 1946- *94*
  Brief entry *39*
  Earlier sketch in SATA *42*
Linde, Gunnel 1924- *5*
Lindenbaum, Pija 1955- *183*
  Earlier sketches in SATA *77, 144*
Lindgren, Astrid (Anna Emilia Ericsson)
  1907-2002 .... *38*
  Obituary *128*
  Earlier sketch in SATA *2*
  See also CLR *119*

Lindgren, Barbro 1937- *207*
  Brief entry *46*
  Earlier sketches in SATA *63, 120*
  See also CLR *86*
Lindman, Maj (Jan) 1886-1972 .... *43*
Lindo, Elvira 1962- *219*
Lindop, Edmund 1925- *5*
Lindquist, Jennie Dorothea 1899-1977 .... *13*
Lindquist, Rowena Cory 1958- *98*
Lindquist, Willis 1908-1988 .... *20*
Lindsay, Nicholas Vachel
  See Lindsay, Vachel
Lindsay, Norman Alfred William
  1879-1969 .... *67*
  See also CLR *8*
Lindsay, Vachel 1879-1931 .... *40*
Lindsey, Kathleen D(orothy) 1949- *153*
Line, David
  See Davidson, Lionel
Line, Les 1935-2010 .... *27*
Lines, Kathleen Mary 1902-1988
  Obituary *61*
Linfield, Esther *40*
Lingard, Joan (Amelia) 1932- *130*
  Autobiography Feature *130*
  Earlier sketches in SATA *8, 74, 114*
  See also CLR *89*
  See also SAAS *5*
Link, Martin 1934- *28*
Linn, Margot
  See Ziefert, Harriet
Linnea, Sharon 1956- *82*
Lintern, Tom *228*
Lion, Melissa 1976- *176*
Lionni, Leo(nard) 1910-1999 .... *72*
  Obituary *118*
  Earlier sketch in SATA *8*
  See also CLR *71*
Lipinsky de Orlov, Lino S. 1908- *22*
Lipkind, William 1904-1974 .... *15*
Lipman, David 1931-2008 .... *21*
Lipman, Matthew 1923-2010 .... *14*
Lipp, Frederick *204*
Lippincott, Bertram 1898(?)-1985
  Obituary *42*
Lippincott, Gary A. 1953- *220*
  Earlier sketches in SATA *73, 119*
Lippincott, Joseph W(harton) 1887-1976 ..... *17*
Lippincott, Sarah Lee 1920- *22*
Lippman, Peter J. 1936- *31*
Lipsyte, Robert 1938- *198*
  Earlier sketches in SATA *5, 68, 113, 161*
  See also CLR *76*
Lipsyte, Robert Michael
  See Lipsyte, Robert
Lisandrelli, Elaine Slivinski 1951- *94*
Lisker, Sonia O. 1933- *44*
Lisle, Holly 1960- *208*
  Earlier sketch in SATA *98*
Lisle, Janet Taylor 1947- *150*
  Brief entry *47*
  Earlier sketches in SATA *59, 96*
  See also SAAS *14*
Lisle, Rebecca *162*
Lisle, Seward D.
  See Ellis, Edward S.
Lisowski, Gabriel 1946- *47*
  Brief entry *31*
Liss, Howard 1922-1995 .... *4*
  Obituary *84*
Lissiat, Amy
  See Thompson, Colin
Lisson, Deborah 1941- *110*
  Earlier sketch in SATA *71*
List, Ilka Katherine 1935- *6*
Liston, Robert A. 1927- *5*
Litchfield, Ada B(assett) 1916-1999 .... *5*
Litchfield, Jo 1973- *116*
Lithgow, John 1945- *145*
Lithgow, John Arthur
  See Lithgow, John

Litowinsky, Olga 1936- 26
Litowinsky, Olga Jean
  See Litowinsky, Olga
Littke, Lael J. 1929- *140*
  Earlier sketches in SATA *51, 83*
Little, A. Edward
  See Klein, Aaron E.
Little, Douglas 1942- *96*
Little, (Flora) Jean 1932- *149*
  Earlier sketches in SATA *2, 68, 106*
  See also CLR *4*
  See also SAAS *17*
Little, Lessie Jones 1906-1986 60
  Obituary 50
Little, Mary E. 1912-1999 28
Littlechild, George 1958- 85
Littledale, Freya (Lota) 1929-1992 74
  Earlier sketch in SATA *2*
Littlefield, Bill 1948- 83
Littlefield, Holly 1963- 97
Littlesugar, Amy 1953- *176*
  Earlier sketch in SATA *122*
Littleton, Mark R. 1950- *142*
  Earlier sketch in SATA *89*
Littlewood, Karin *211*
Littman, Sarah Darer *221*
  Earlier sketch in SATA *175*
Litty, Julie 1971- *181*
Litzinger, Rosanne 1948- *196*
Liu, Cynthea *221*
Lively, Penelope 1933- *164*
  Earlier sketches in SATA *7, 60, 101*
  See also CLR *159*
Lively, Penelope Margaret
  See Lively, Penelope
Liverakos, L. A.
  See Gilman, Laura Anne
Liversidge, (Henry) Douglas 1913- 8
Livesey, Claire (Warner) 1927- *127*
Livingston, Carole 1941- 42
Livingston, (M.) Irene 1932- *150*
Livingston, Myra Cohn 1926-1996 68
  Obituary 92
  Earlier sketch in SATA *5*
  See also CLR *7*
  See also SAAS *1*
Livingston, Richard R(oland) 1922- 8
Livo, Norma J. 1929- 76
Liwska, Renata *199*
Ljungkvist, Laura *180*
Llerena Aguirre, Carlos 1952- 19
Llerena Aguirre, Carlos Antonio
  See Llerena Aguirre, Carlos
Llewellyn, Claire 1954- *196*
  Earlier sketches in SATA *77, 143*
Llewellyn, Grace 1964- *110*
Llewellyn, Richard
  See Llewellyn Lloyd, Richard Dafydd Vivian
Llewellyn, Sam 1948- *185*
  Earlier sketch in SATA *95*
Llewellyn Lloyd, Richard Dafydd Vivian
  1906-1983 .... *11*
  Obituary 37
Llewelyn, T. Harcourt
  See Hamilton, Charles (Harold St. John)
Lloyd, Alan
  See Lloyd, A.R.
Lloyd, Alan Richard
  See Lloyd, A.R.
Lloyd, A.R. 1927- *168*
  Earlier sketch in SATA *97*
Lloyd, David
  See Lloyd, David T.
Lloyd, David T. 1954- *167*
Lloyd, E. James
  See James, Elizabeth
Lloyd, Errol 1943- 22
Lloyd, Hugh
  See Fitzhugh, Percy Keese
Lloyd, James
  See James, Elizabeth

Lloyd, Megan 1958- *189*
  Earlier sketches in SATA *77, 117*
Lloyd, Norman 1909-1980
  Obituary 23
Lloyd, (Mary) Norris 1908-1993 .... *10*
  Obituary 75
Lloyd, Saci 1967- *220*
Lloyd, Sam *183*
Lloyd-Jones, Sally 1960- *179*
Lloyd Webber, Andrew 1948- 56
Llywelyn, Morgan 1937- *109*
Lo, Ginnie *165*
Lo, Malinda 1974- *222*
Lo, Virginia M.
  See Lo, Ginnie
Lobato, Jose Bento Monteiro 1882-1948 ... *114*
Lobel, Anita (Kempler) 1934- *162*
  Earlier sketches in SATA *6, 55, 96*
Lobel, Arnold (Stark) 1933-1987 55
  Obituary 54
  Earlier sketch in SATA *6*
  See also CLR *5*
Lobel, Gillian *181*
Lobsenz, Amelia *12*
Lobsenz, Norman M(itchell) 1919- 6
Lochak, Michele 1936- 39
Lochlons, Colin
  See Jackson, C(aary) Paul
Locke, Clinton W. *1*
Locke, Elsie (Violet) 1912-2001 87
Locke, Gary 1963- *197*
Locke, Lucie 1904-1989 .... *10*
Locke, Robert 1944- 63
  See also CLR *39*
Locker, Thomas 1937- *109*
  Earlier sketch in SATA *59*
  See also CLR *14*
Lockhart, E.
  See Jenkins, Emily
Lockridge, Hildegarde (Dolson)
  1908-1981 .... *121*
  Earlier sketch in SATA *5*
Lockwood, Mary
  See Spelman, Mary
Lodge, Bernard 1933- *215*
  Earlier sketches in SATA *33, 107*
Lodge, Jo 1966- *173*
  Earlier sketch in SATA *112*
Loeb, Jeffrey 1946- 57
Loeb, Robert H., Jr. 1917- 21
Loefgren, Ulf 1931- *3*
Loehfelm, Bill 1969- *153*
Loehr, Mallory *184*
Loehr, Patrick 1968(?)- *194*
Loeper, John J(oseph) 1929- *118*
  Earlier sketch in SATA *10*
Loescher, Ann Dull 1942- 20
Loescher, Gil 1945- 20
Loescher, Gilburt Damian
  See Loescher, Gil
Loewer, Jean Jenkins
  See Jenkins, Jean
Loewer, (Henry) Peter 1934- 98
LoFaro, Jerry 1959- 77
Lofo
  See Heimann, Rolf
Lofthouse, Liz *199*
Lofting, Hugh (John) 1886-1947 .... *100*
  Earlier sketch in SATA *15*
  See also CLR *143*
Lofts, Norah (Robinson) 1904-1983 8
  Obituary 36
Logan, Alysia
  See Divine, L.
Logan, Jake
  See Knott, William C(ecil, Jr.)
  and Krepps, Robert W(ilson)
  and Pearl, Jacques Bain
  and Riefe, Alan
  and Rifkin, Shepard
  and Smith, Martin Cruz

Logan, Mark
  See Nicole, Christopher
Logan, Rochelle 1954- *169*
Logsted, Greg *221*
Logston, Anne 1962- *112*
Logue, Christopher 1926- 23
Logue, Mary 1952- *161*
  Earlier sketch in SATA *112*
Logue, Mary Louise
  See Logue, Mary
Loh, Morag 1935- 73
Lohans, Alison 1949- *101*
Loizeaux, William *185*
Loken, Newton Clayton 1919- 26
Lomas, Steve
  See Brennan, Joseph Lomas
Lomask, Milton (Nachman) 1909-1991 20
Lombard, Jenny *178*
Lombino, Salvatore
  See Hunter, Evan
LoMonaco, Palmyra 1932- *102*
London, Jack 1876-1916 18
  See also CLR *108*
London, Jane
  See Geis, Darlene Stern
London, John Griffith
  See London, Jack
London, Jonathan 1947- *221*
  Earlier sketches in SATA *74, 113, 157*
Lonergan, (Pauline) Joy (MacLean) 1909- ... *10*
Lonette, Reisie (Dominee) 1924- 43
Long, Cathryn J. 1946- 89
Long, Earlene (Roberta) 1938- 50
Long, Emmett
  See Leonard, Elmore
Long, Ethan 1968(?)- *223*
  Earlier sketch in SATA *182*
Long, Helen Beecher *1*
Long, Judith Elaine 1953- 20
Long, Judy
  See Long, Judith Elaine
Long, Kim 1949- 69
Long, Laura Mooney 1892-1967
  Obituary 29
Long, Laurel *203*
Long, Loren 1966(?)- *188*
  Earlier sketch in SATA *151*
Long, Melinda 1960- *152*
Long, Sylvia 1948- *179*
  Earlier sketch in SATA *120*
Longbeard, Frederick
  See Longyear, Barry B(rookes)
Longfellow, Henry Wadsworth 1807-1882 ... 19
  See also CLR *99*
Longfellow, Layne 1937- *102*
Longfellow, Layne A.
  See Longfellow, Layne
Longman, Harold S. 1919- 5
Longsworth, Polly 1933- 28
Longtemps, Kenneth 1933- 17
Longway, A. Hugh
  See Lang, Andrew
Longyear, Barry B(rookes) 1942- *117*
Look, Lenore *180*
Loomans, Diane 1955- 90
Loomis, Christine *160*
  Earlier sketch in SATA *113*
Loomis, Jennifer A. 1942- *101*
Loomis, Robert D. 5
Lopez, Angelo (Cayas) 1967- 83
Lopez, Antonio Castro
  See Castro L., Antonio
Lopez, Barry 1945- 67
Lopez, Barry Holstun
  See Lopez, Barry
Lopez, Jack 1950- *178*
Lopez, Loretta 1963- *190*
Lopez, Lorraine 1956- *181*
Lopez, Lorraine M.
  See Lopez, Lorraine
Lopez, Mario 1973- *226*

Lopez, Rafael 1961(?)- *198*
Lopshire, Robert M(artin) 1927- *6*
Loraine, Connie
  See Reece, Colleen L.
Lorbiecki, Marybeth 1959- *172*
  Earlier sketch in SATA *121*
Lord, Athena V. 1932- *39*
Lord, Beman 1924-1991 .... *5*
  Obituary *69*
Lord, Bette Bao 1938- *58*
  See also CLR *151*
Lord, Cynthia *182*
Lord, Doreen Mildred Douglas
  See Lord, Douglas
Lord, Douglas 1904-1992 .... *12*
Lord, Janet *204*
Lord, John Vernon 1939- *21*
Lord, Michele *201*
Lord, Nancy J.
  See Titus, Eve
Lord, Patricia C. 1927-1988
  Obituary *58*
Lord, Walter 1917-2002 .... *3*
Lorde, Diana
  See Reno, Dawn E(laine)
Lorenz, Albert 1941- *115*
Lorenzini, Carlo
  See Collodi, Carlo
Lorey, Dean 1967- *193*
Lorimer, Janet 1941- *60*
Loring, Emilie (Baker) 1864(?)-1951 .... *51*
Lorkowski, Thomas V(incent) 1950- *92*
Lorkowski, Tom
  See Lorkowski, Thomas V(incent)
Lorraine, Walter (Henry) 1929- *16*
Lorrimer, Claire
  See Robins, Patricia
Loss, Joan 1933- *11*
Lothrop, Harriet Mulford Stone 1844-1924 . *20*
Lottridge, Celia Barker 1936- *157*
  Earlier sketch in SATA *112*
LoTurco, Laura 1963- *84*
Lotz, Wolfgang 1912-1981 .... *65*
Loughridge, Stuart 1978- *214*
Louie, Ai-Ling 1949- *40*
  Brief entry *34*
Louis, Catherine 1963- *186*
Louis, Pat
  See Francis, Dorothy
Louisburgh, Sheila Burnford
  See Burnford, Sheila (Philip Cochrane Every)
Louise, Anita
  See Riggio, Anita
Louise, Tina 1934- *191*
Lourie, Helen
  See Storr, Catherine (Cole)
Lourie, Peter 1952- *183*
  Earlier sketches in SATA *82, 142*
Lourie, Peter King
  See Lourie, Peter
Love, Ann 1947- *168*
  Earlier sketch in SATA *79*
Love, D. Anne 1949- *180*
  Earlier sketches in SATA *96, 145*
Love, Douglas 1967- *92*
Love, Judith Dufour
  See Love, Judy
Love, Judy *188*
Love, Katherine (Isabel) 1907- *3*
Love, Kathleen Ann
  See Love, Ann
Love, Maryann Cusimano *223*
Love, Sandra (Weller) 1940- *26*
Lovegrove, James 1965- *216*
Lovegrove, J.M.H.
  See Lovegrove, James
Lovejoy, Jack 1937- *116*
Lovelace, Delos Wheeler 1894-1967 .... *7*
Lovelace, Maud Hart 1892-1980 .... *2*
  Obituary *23*

Lovell, Ingraham
  See Bacon, Josephine Dodge (Daskam)
Lovelock, Brian 1956- *214*
Loverseed, Amanda (Jane) 1965- *75*
Lovett, Margaret (Rose) 1915- *22*
Low, Alice 1926- *156*
  Earlier sketches in SATA *11, 76*
Low, Elizabeth Hammond 1898-1991 .... *5*
Low, Joseph 1911-2007 .... *14*
Low, Penelope Margaret
  See Lively, Penelope
Low, William *177*
Lowe, Helen 1961- *206*
Lowe, Jay, Jr.
  See Loeper, John J(oseph)
Lowell, Pamela *187*
Lowell, Susan 1950- *206*
  Earlier sketches in SATA *81, 127*
Lowenstein, Dyno 1914-1996 .... *6*
Lowenstein, Sallie 1949- *116*
Lowery, Linda 1949- *151*
  Earlier sketch in SATA *74*
Lowery, Mike *227*
Lowitz, Anson C. 1901(?)-1978 .... *18*
Lowitz, Sadyebeth Heath 1901-1969 .... *17*
Lowndes, Robert A(ugustine) W(ard)
  1916-1998 .... *117*
Lowrey, Janette Sebring 1892-1986 .... *43*
Lowry, Lois 1937- *177*
  Autobiography Feature *127*
  Earlier sketches in SATA *23, 70, 111*
  See also CLR *72*
  See also SAAS *3*
Lowry, Lois Hammersberg
  See Lowry, Lois
Lowry, Peter 1953- *7*
Lowther, George F. 1913-1975
  Obituary *30*
Loxton, Daniel 1975- *229*
Loyie, Larry 1933- *150*
Lozansky, Edward D. 1941- *62*
Lozier, Herbert 1915- *26*
Lubar, David 1954- *190*
  Earlier sketch in SATA *133*
Lubell, Cecil 1912-2000 .... *6*
Lubell, Winifred (A. Milius) 1914- *6*
Lubin, Leonard
  See Lubin, Leonard B.
Lubin, Leonard B. 1943-1994 .... *45*
  Brief entry *37*
Lubka, S. Ruth 1948- *154*
Lubner, Susan *185*
Luby, Thia 1954- *124*
Lucado, Max (Lee) 1955- *104*
Lucas, Cedric 1962- *101*
Lucas, David 1966- *208*
Lucas, E(dward) V(errall) 1868-1938 .... *20*
Lucas, Eileen 1956- *113*
  Earlier sketch in SATA *76*
Lucas, George 1944- *56*
Lucas, Jerry 1940- *33*
Lucas, Margeaux *186*
Lucas, Victoria
  See Plath, Sylvia
Lucashenko, Melissa 1967- *104*
Luccarelli, Vincent 1923- *90*
Luce, Celia (Geneva Larsen) 1914- *38*
Luce, Willard (Ray) 1914-1990 .... *38*
Lucht, Irmgard 1937- *82*
Lucke, Deb *202*
Luckett, Dave 1951- *220*
  Earlier sketches in SATA *106, 167*
Luckhardt, Mildred Corell 1898-1990 .... *5*
Ludden, Allen (Ellsworth) 1918(?)-1981
  Obituary *27*
Ludel, Jacqueline 1945- *64*
Ludlow, Geoffrey
  See Meynell, Laurence Walter
Ludlum, Mabel Cleland
  See Widdemer, Mabel Cleland
Ludwig, Helen *33*

Ludwig, Lyndell 1923- *63*
Ludwig, Trudy 1959- *209*
  Earlier sketch in SATA *166*
Luebs, Robin 1949- *212*
Lueders, Edward (George) 1923- *14*
Luenn, Nancy 1954- *79*
  Earlier sketch in SATA *51*
Lufkin, Raymond H. 1897- *38*
Lugard, Flora Louisa Shaw 1852-1929 .... *21*
Luger, Harriett Mandelay 1914- *23*
Luhrmann, Winifred B(ruce) 1934- *11*
Luis, Earlene W. 1929- *11*
Lujan, Jorge *201*
Luke, Pauline *178*
Luke, Pauline R.
  See Luke, Pauline
Lum, Kate *229*
Lum, Peter
  See Crowe, (Bettina) Peter Lum
Lumry, Amanda (R.) *159*
Lund, Deb *157*
Lund, Doris Herold 1919- *12*
Lunde, Darrin *202*
Lundebrek, Amy 1975- *213*
Lung, Chang
  See Jordan, Robert
Lunge-Larsen, Lise 1955- *184*
  Earlier sketch in SATA *138*
Lunn, Carolyn (Kowalczyk) 1960- *67*
Lunn, Janet (Louise Swoboda) 1928- *110*
  Earlier sketches in SATA *4, 68*
  See also CLR *18*
  See also SAAS *12*
Lunsford, Cin Forshay
  See Forshay-Lunsford, Cin
Lupica, Michael
  See Lupica, Mike
Lupica, Michael Thomas
  See Lupica, Mike
Lupica, Mike 1952- *177*
Lupoff, Dick
  See Lupoff, Richard A(llen)
Lupoff, Richard A(llen) 1935- *60*
Lurie, Alison 1926- *112*
  Earlier sketch in SATA *46*
Lurie, Morris 1938- *72*
Lussert, Anneliese 1929- *101*
Lusted, Marcia Amidon 1962- *143*
Lustig, Arnost 1926-2011 .... *56*
Lustig, Loretta 1944- *46*
Lutes, Jason 1967- *210*
Luthardt, Kevin 1973- *172*
Luther, Frank 1905-1980
  Obituary *25*
Luther, Rebekah (Lyn) S(tiles) 1960- *90*
Luttmann, Gail
  See Damerow, Gail
Luttrell, Guy L. 1938- *22*
Luttrell, Ida (Alleene) 1934- *91*
  Brief entry *35*
  Earlier sketch in SATA *40*
Luttrell, William (J. III) 1954- *149*
Lutz, John 1939- *180*
Lutz, John Thomas
  See Lutz, John
Lutz, Norma Jean 1943- *122*
Lutzeier, Elizabeth 1952- *72*
Lutzker, Edythe 1904-1991 .... *5*
Luxbacher, Irene 1970- *219*
  Earlier sketch in SATA *153*
Luzadder, Patrick 1954- *89*
Luzzati, Emanuele 1921-2007 .... *7*
Luzzatto, Paola Caboara 1938- *38*
Ly, Many 1977- *208*
Lybbert, Tyler 1970- *88*
Lydon, Michael 1942- *11*
Lyfick, Warren
  See Reeves, Lawrence F.
Lyle, Katie Letcher 1938- *8*

Lynch, Chris 1962- 209
  Earlier sketches in SATA 95, 131, 171
  See also CLR 58
Lynch, Janet Nichols 1952- 221
Lynch, Jay 1945- 204
Lynch, Lorenzo 1932- 7
Lynch, Marietta 1947- 29
Lynch, Patricia (Nora) 1898-1972 9
Lynch, Patrick James
  See Lynch, P.J.
Lynch, P.J. 1962- 213
  Earlier sketches in SATA 79, 122
Lynds, Dennis 1924-2005 47
  Brief entry 37
Lyne, Alison Davis 188
Lyngseth, Joan
  See Davies, Joan
Lynn, Elizabeth A(nne) 1946- 99
Lynn, Mary
  See Brokamp, Marilyn
Lynn, Patricia
  See Watts, Mabel Pizzey
Lynn, Tracy 175
Lyon, Elinor 1921-2008 6
  Obituary 192
Lyon, Elinor Bruce
  See Lyon, Elinor
Lyon, George Ella 1949- 207
  Autobiography Feature 148
  Earlier sketches in SATA 68, 119, 148
Lyon, Lea 1945- 212
Lyon, Lyman R.
  See de Camp, L. Sprague
Lyons, Dorothy M(arawee) 1907-1997 3
Lyons, Grant 1941- 30
Lyons, Jayne 226
Lyons, Marcus
  See Blish, James
Lyons, Mary E. 1947- 195
  Autobiography Feature 195
  Earlier sketches in SATA 93, 142
Lyons, Mary Evelyn
  See Lyons, Mary E.
Lystad, Mary (Hanemann) 1928- 11
Lytle, Elizabeth Stewart 1949- 79
Lytle, Robert A. 1944- 119
Lyttle, Richard B(ard) 1927- 23
Lytton, Deborah 1966- 218
Lytton, Edward G.E.L. Bulwer-Lytton Baron
  See Bulwer-Lytton, Edward
Lytton of Knebworth, Baron
  See Bulwer-Lytton, Edward

M

Ma, Wenhai 1954- 84
Maar, Leonard (Frank, Jr.) 1927- 30
Maartens, Maretha 1945- 73
Maas, Selve -1997 14
Maass, Robert 195
Mabie, Grace
  See Mattern, Joanne
Mac
  See MacManus, Seumas
  and Maccari, Ruggero
Macalaster, Elizabeth G. 1951- 115
MacAlister, Katie 159
MacAlister, V. A.
  See McKernan, Victoria
MacAllan, Andrew
  See Leasor, James
MacAodhagain, Eamon
  See Egan, E. W.
MacArthur-Onslow, Annette Rosemary
  1933- 26
Macaulay, David (Alexander) 1946- 137
  Brief entry 27
  Earlier sketches in SATA 46, 72
  See also CLR 14

Macaulay, Teresa 1947- 95
Macauley, Theresa E.
  See Macaulay, Teresa
Macavinta, Courtney 176
MacBeth, George (Mann) 1932-1992 4
  Obituary 70
MacBride, Roger Lea 1929-1995 85
MacCarter, Don 1944- 91
MacClintock, Dorcas 1932- 8
MacCready, Robin Merrow 1959(?)- 190
MacCullough, Carolyn 174
MacDonald, Alan 1958- 192
MacDonald, Amy 1951- 156
  Autobiography Feature 156
  Earlier sketches in SATA 76, 136
MacDonald, Anne Elizabeth Campbell Bard
  -1958
  See MacDonald, Betty
MacDonald, Anne Louise 1955- 217
MacDonald, Anson
  See Heinlein, Robert A.
Macdonald, Betty 1908-1958
  See YABC 1
Macdonald, Blackie
  See Emrich, Duncan (Black Macdonald)
Macdonald, Caroline 1948- 86
  Obituary 111
  See also CLR 60
Macdonald, Dwight 1906-1982 29
  Obituary 33
MacDonald, George 1824-1905 100
  Earlier sketch in SATA 33
  See also CLR 67
MacDonald, Golden
  See Brown, Margaret Wise
Macdonald, Guy 195
Macdonald, James D. 1954- 67
  Earlier sketches in SATA 81, 114, 165, 1
Macdonald, Marcia
  See Hill, Grace Livingston
MacDonald, Margaret Read 1940- 194
  Earlier sketches in SATA 94, 164
Macdonald, Marianne 1934- 113
Macdonald, Mary
  See Gifford, Griselda
Macdonald, Maryann 1947- 189
  Earlier sketch in SATA 72
MacDonald, Ross 1957- 201
Macdonald, Shelagh 1937- 25
MacDonald, Suse 1940- 193
  Brief entry 52
  Earlier sketches in SATA 54, 109
Macdonald, Wendy 217
Macdonald, Wendy M.
  See Macdonald, Wendy
Macdonald, Zillah K(atherine) 1885-1979 ... 11
MacDonnell, Megan
  See Stevens, Serita
MacDougal, John
  See Blish, James
Mace, Elisabeth 1933- 27
Mace, Varian 1938- 49
MacEachern, Stephen 206
MacEwen, Gwendolyn (Margaret)
  1941-1987 50
  Obituary 55
Macfarlan, Allan A. 1892-1982 35
MacFarlane, Iris 1922- 11
MacGill-Callahan, Sheila 1926-2000 78
MacGregor, Carol Lynn 153
MacGregor, Ellen 1906-1954 39
  Brief entry 27
MacGregor-Hastie, Roy (Alasdhair Niall)
  1929- 3
MacGrory, Yvonne 1948- 142
Machado, Ana Maria 1941- 150
MacHale, D.J. 1956- 175
MacHale, Donald James
  See MacHale, D.J.
Machetanz, Frederick 1908- 34

Machin, Sue
  See Williams, Sue
Machin Goodall, Daphne (Edith) 37
Macht, Norm
  See Macht, Norman L.
Macht, Norman L. 1929- 122
Macht, Norman Lee
  See Macht, Norman L.
Macht, Norman Lee
  See Macht, Norman L.
MacInnes, Helen (Clark) 1907-1985 22
  Obituary 44
Macintosh, Brownie 1950- 98
MacIntyre, Elisabeth 1916- 17
MacIntyre, Rod
  See MacIntyre, R.P.
MacIntyre, R.P. 1947- 203
MacIntyre, R.P. 1947- 203
MacIntyre, Wendy 1947- 196
Mack, Jeff 194
Mack, L.V.
  See Kimmelman, Burt
Mack, Stan(ley) 17
Mack, Todd 168
Mack, Tracy 1968- 183
  Earlier sketch in SATA 128
Mackall, Dandi D.
  See Mackall, Dandi Daley
Mackall, Dandi Daley 1949- 218
  Earlier sketches in SATA 118, 177, 182
Mackay, Claire 1930- 97
  Autobiography Feature 124
  Earlier sketch in SATA 40
  See also CLR 43
Mackay, Constance D'Arcy (?)-1966 125
Mackay, Donald 1914-2005 81
  Obituary 173
Mackay, Donald Alexander
  See Mackay, Donald
MacKaye, Percy (Wallace) 1875-1956 32
Mackel, Kathryn 1950- 162
Mackel, Kathy
  See Mackel, Kathryn
MacKellar, William 1914- 4
Macken, JoAnn Early 1953- 201
Macken, Walter 1915-1967 36
Mackenzie, Anna 1963- 212
MacKenzie, Jill (Kelly) 1947- 75
Mackenzie, Robert 1974- 204
Mackey, Ernan
  See McInerny, Ralph
Mackey, Weezie Kerr 188
Mackie, Maron
  See McNeely, Jeannette
Mackin, Edward
  See McInerny, Ralph
MacKinnon, Bernie 1957- 69
MacKinnon Groomer, Vera 1915- 57
MacKinstry, Elizabeth 1879-1956 42
Mackler, Carolyn 1973- 156
MacLachlan, Emily
  See Charest, Emily MacLachlan
MacLachlan, Patricia 1938- 229
  Brief entry 42
  Earlier sketches in SATA 62, 107, 168
  See also CLR 14
MacLane, Jack
  See Crider, Bill
MacLean, Alistair 1922(?)-1987 23
  Obituary 50
MacLean, Alistair Stuart
  See MacLean, Alistair
Maclean, Art
  See Shirreffs, Gordon D(onald)
MacLean, Christine Kole 1962- 177
MacLean, Glynne 1964- 150
MacLean, Jill 1941- 211
MacLeod, Beatrice 1910- 162
  Earlier sketch in SATA 10
MacLeod, Beatrice Beach
  See MacLeod, Beatrice

MacLeod, Charlotte (Matilda) 1922-2005 28
  Obituary 160
MacLeod, Doug 1959- 201
  Earlier sketch in SATA 60
MacLeod, Elizabeth 184
  Earlier sketch in SATA 158
MacLeod, Ellen Jane (Anderson) 1916- 14
MacManus, James
  See MacManus, Seumas
MacManus, Seumas 1869-1960 25
MacMaster, Eve (Ruth) B(owers) 1942- 46
MacMillan, Annabelle
  See Quick, Annabelle
MacMillan, Dianne M(arie) 1943- 125
  Earlier sketch in SATA 84
Macnaughton, Tina 218
  Earlier sketch in SATA 182
Macneill, Janet
  See McNeely, Jeannette
MacPeek, Walter G. 1902-1973 4
  Obituary 25
MacPhail, Catherine 1946- 197
  Earlier sketch in SATA 130
MacPherson, Margaret 1908-2001 9
  See also SAAS 4
MacPherson, Thomas George 1915-1976
  Obituary 30
MacPherson, Winnie 1930- 107
MacRae, Tom 1980- 181
Macrae, Travis
  See Feagles, Anita MacRae
MacRaois, Cormac 1944- 72
Macumber, Mari
  See Sandoz, Mari(e Susette)
Macy, Sue 1954- 227
  Earlier sketches in SATA 88, 134
Madaras, Lynda 1947- 151
Madden, Colleen 228
Madden, Colleen M.
  See Madden, Colleen
Madden, Don 1927- 3
Madden, Kerry 1961- 168
Madden-Lunsford, Kerry
  See Madden, Kerry
Maddern, Eric 1950- 166
Maddigan, Beth 1967- 174
Maddison, Angela Mary 1923- 10
  See also CLR 24
Maddock, Reginald (Bertram) 1912-1994 15
Maddox, Jake
  See Trumbauer, Lisa
Madenski, Melissa (Ann) 1949- 77
Madian, Jon 1941- 9
Madigan, Lisa Kay
  See Madigan, L.K.
Madigan, L.K. (?)-2011 224
Madison, Alan 182
Madison, Arnold 1937- 6
Madison, Bennett 220
Madison, Winifred 5
Madonna 1958- 149
Madsen, Gunnar 171
Madsen, Jim 1964- 202
Madsen, Ross Martin 1946- 82
Madsen, Susan A. 1954- 90
Madsen, Susan Arrington
  See Madsen, Susan A.
Maehlqvist, Stefan 1943- 30
Maestro, Betsy (Crippen) 1944- 106
  Brief entry 30
  Earlier sketch in SATA 59
  See also CLR 45
Maestro, Giulio 1942- 106
  Earlier sketches in SATA 8, 59
  See also CLR 45
Maeterlinck, Maurice 1862-1949 66
Magee, Doug 1947- 78
Magee, Wes 1939- 64
Maggio, Rosalie 1943- 69
Magid, Ken(neth Marshall) 65
Magnus, Erica 1946- 77

Magoon, Kekla 1980- 213
Magoon, Scott 222
  Earlier sketch in SATA 182
Magorian, James 1942- 92
  Earlier sketch in SATA 32
Magorian, Michelle 1947- 128
  Earlier sketch in SATA 67
Magorian, Michelle Jane
  See Magorian, Michelle
Magovern, Peg 103
Magsamen, Sandra 1959- 213
Maguire, Gregory
  See Nearing, Penny
Maguire, Gregory 1954- 200
  Autobiography Feature 200
  Earlier sketches in SATA 28, 84, 129
  See also SAAS 22
Maguire, Gregory Peter
  See Maguire, Gregory
Maguire, Jack 1920-2000 74
Maguire, Jesse
  See Smith, Sherwood
Maguire, Jessie
  See Smith, Sherwood
Maher, Ramona 1934- 13
Mahlqvist, Stefan
  See Maehlqvist, Stefan
Mahon, Julia C(unha) 1916- 11
Mahony, Elizabeth Winthrop
  See Winthrop, Elizabeth
Mahood, Kenneth 1930- 24
Mahy, Margaret 1936- 171
  Earlier sketches in SATA 14, 69, 119
  See also CLR 155
Mahy, Margaret May
  See Mahy, Margaret
Maiden, Cecil (Edward) 1902-1981 52
Maidoff, Ilka
  See List, Ilka Katherine
Maifair, Linda Lee 1947- 83
Maik, Henri
  See Hecht, Henri Joseph
Maillu, David G(ian) 1939- 111
Maine, Trevor
  See Catherall, Arthur
Mains, Randolph P. 1946- 80
Maione, Heather 189
Maiorano, Robert 1946- 43
Maisner, Heather 1947- 89
Maison, Della
  See Katz, Bobbi
Maitland, Antony Jasper 1935- 25
Maitland, Barbara 102
Mai-Wyss, Tatjana 1972- 187
Maizels, Jennie 210
Major, Kevin (Gerald) 1949- 134
  Earlier sketches in SATA 32, 82
  See also CLR 11
Majure, Janet 1954- 96
Makhijani, Pooja 188
Makie, Pam 1943- 37
Makowski, Silk
  See Sullivan, Silky
Makowski, Silvia Ann
  See Sullivan, Silky
Malam, John 1957- 152
  Earlier sketch in SATA 89
Maland, Nick 195
Malaspina, Ann 1957- 222
Malcolm, Dan
  See Silverberg, Robert
Malcolm, Jahnna N.
  See Beecham, Jahnna
Malcolmson, Anne
  See von Storch, Anne B.
Malcolmson, David 1899-1978 6
Maletta, Dr. Arlene
  See Feltenstein, Arlene
Maley, Carleen
  See Hutchins, Carleen Maley

Mali, Jane Lawrence 1937-1995 51
  Brief entry 44
  Obituary 86
Malkin, Nina 1959(?)- 179
Mallett, Jerry J. 1939- 76
Malley, Gemma 198
Malley, G.R.
  See Malley, Gemma
Mallory, Kenneth 1945- 185
  Earlier sketch in SATA 128
Mallowan, Agatha Christie
  See Christie, Agatha
Malmberg, Carl 1904-1979 9
Malmgren, Dallin 1949- 65
Malo, John W. 1911-2000 4
Malone, James Hiram 1930- 84
Malone, Marianne 229
Malone, Nola Langner 1930-2003 8
  Obituary 151
Malone, Patricia 1932- 155
Malone, Peter 1953- 191
Maloney, Pat
  See Markun, Patricia Maloney
Malory, Sir Thomas 1410(?)-1471(?) 59
  Brief entry 33
Maltese, Michael 1909(?)-1981
  Obituary 24
Malvasi, Meg Greene 143
Malvern, Corinne 1905-1956 34
Malvern, Gladys (?)-1962 23
Mama G.
  See Davis, Grania
Mammano, Julie 1962- 202
  Earlier sketch in SATA 107
Mamonova, Tatyana 1943- 93
Manchel, Frank 1935- 10
Manchess, Gregory 1955- 203
Manchester, William (Raymond)
  1922-2004 65
Mandabach, Brian 1962(?)- 197
Mandel, Brett H. 1969- 108
Mandel, Peter 1957- 87
Mandel, Sally (Elizabeth) 1944- 64
Mandell, Muriel (Hortense Levin) 1921- 63
Manders, John 1957- 219
  Earlier sketch in SATA 175
Mandine, Selma 1973- 228
Manes, Stephen 1949- 99
  Brief entry 40
  Earlier sketch in SATA 42
Manfred, Frederick (Feikema) 1912-1994 30
Mangin, Marie France 1940- 59
Mangione, Gerlando 1909-1998 6
  Obituary 104
Mangione, Jerre
  See Mangione, Gerlando
Mango, Karin N. 1936- 52
Mangurian, David 1938- 14
Mania, Cathy 1950- 102
Mania, Robert 1952- 102
Mania, Robert C., Jr.
  See Mania, Robert
Maniatty, Taramesha 1978- 92
Maniscalco, Joseph 1926- 10
Manivong, Laura 1967- 229
Manley, Deborah 1932- 28
Manley, Seon 1921- 15
  See also CLR 3
  See also SAAS 2
Mann, Elizabeth 1948- 153
Mann, Josephine
  See Pullein-Thompson, Josephine (Mary
    Wedderburn)
Mann, Kenny 1946- 91
Mann, Pamela 1946- 91
Mann, Patrick
  See Waller, Leslie
Mann, Peggy
  See Houlton, Peggy Mann
Mannetti, Lisa 1953- 57
  Brief entry 51

Mannheim, Grete (Salomon) 1909-1986 ...... *10*
Manniche, Lise 1943- *31*
Manning, Jane K. *185*
Manning, Maurie
    See Manning, Maurie J.
Manning, Maurie J. *211*
Manning, Maurie Jo
    See Manning, Maurie J.
Manning, Mick 1959- *176*
Manning, Rosemary 1911-1988 .... *10*
Manning, Sarra *162*
Manning-Sanders, Ruth (Vernon)
    1895(?)-1988 .... *73*
    Obituary *57*
    Earlier sketch in SATA *15*
Mannion, Diane
    See Paterson, Diane
Mannis, Celeste Davidson *173*
Mannon, Warwick
    See Hopkins, (Hector) Kenneth
Manos, Helen *199*
Mansir, A. Richard 1932- *170*
Manson, Ainslie Kertland 1938- *115*
Manson, Beverlie 1945- *57*
    Brief entry *44*
Mantchev, Lisa *221*
Mantha, John 1960- *217*
Manthorpe, Helen 1958- *122*
Mantinband, Gerda (B.) 1917- *74*
Manton, Jo
    See Gittings, Jo (Grenville) Manton
Manuel, Lynn 1948- *179*
    Earlier sketch in SATA *99*
Manushkin, Fran 1942- *205*
    Earlier sketches in SATA *7, 54, 93, 166*
Manushkin, Frances
    See Manushkin, Fran
Man Without a Spleen, A
    See Chekhov, Anton
Many, Paul 1947- *210*
Many, Paul A.
    See Many, Paul
Manzano, Sonia 1950- *167*
Mapes, Mary A.
    See Ellison, Virginia H(owell)
Maple, Marilyn 1931- *80*
Mappin, Strephyn 1956- *109*
Mara, Barney
    See Roth, Arthur J(oseph)
Mara, Jeanette
    See Cebulash, Mel
Mara, Rachna
    See Gilmore, Rachna
Marais, Josef 1905-1978
    Obituary *24*
Marasmus, Seymour
    See Rivoli, Mario
Marbach, Ethel
    See Pochocki, Ethel (Frances)
Marcal, Annette B.
    See Callaway, Bernice (Anne)
Marcelino
    See Agnew, Edith J(osephine)
Marcellino, Fred 1939-2001 .... *118*
    Obituary *127*
    Earlier sketch in SATA *68*
March, Carl
    See Fleischman, Sid
Marchant, Bessie 1862-1941
    See YABC *2*
Marchant, Catherine
    See Cookson, Catherine (McMullen)
Marcher, Marion Walden 1890-1987 .... *10*
Marchesi, Stephen 1951- *114*
Marchesi, Steve
    See Marchesi, Stephen
    and Older, Effin
    and Older, Jules
Marchetta, Melina 1965- *170*

Marciano, John Bemelmans 1970- *167*
    Earlier sketch in SATA *118*
    See also CLR *93*
Marco, Lou
    See Gottfried, Theodore Mark
Marcus, Leonard S. 1950- *187*
    Earlier sketch in SATA *133*
Marcus, Paul 1953- *82*
Marcus, Rebecca B(rian) 1907- *9*
Marcuse, Aida E. 1934- *89*
Marek, Margot L. 1934(?)-1987
    Obituary *54*
Maren, Julie 1970- *199*
Margaret, Karla
    See Andersdatter, Karla M.
Margolin, Harriet
    See Ziefert, Harriet
Margolis, Jeffrey A. 1948- *108*
Margolis, Leslie *187*
Margolis, Richard J(ules) 1929-1991 .... *86*
    Obituary *67*
    Earlier sketch in SATA *4*
Margolis, Vivienne 1922- *46*
Mariana
    See Foster, Marian Curtis
Marie, Geraldine 1949- *61*
Mariner, Scott
    See Pohl, Frederik
Marino, Dorothy Bronson 1912- *14*
Marino, Jan 1936- *114*
Marino, Nan *216*
Marino, Nick
    See Deming, Richard
Marino, Peter 1960- *179*
Marinsky, Jane *227*
Mario, Anna
    See Odgers, Sally Farrell
Marion, Henry
    See del Rey, Lester
Maris, Ron *71*
    Brief entry *45*
Mark, Jan 1943-2006 .... *164*
    Obituary *173*
    Earlier sketches in SATA *22, 69, 114*
    See also CLR *11*
Mark, Janet Marjorie
    See Mark, Jan
Mark, Joan T. 1937- *122*
Mark, Pauline (Dahlin) 1913-1997 .... *14*
Mark, Polly
    See Mark, Pauline (Dahlin)
Mark, Ted
    See Gottfried, Theodore Mark
Markel, Michelle *169*
Marker, Sherry 1941- *76*
Markert, Jennifer 1965- *83*
Markert, Jenny
    See Markert, Jennifer
Markey, Kevin 1965- *215*
Markham, Lynne 1947- *102*
Markham, Marion M. 1929- *60*
Markham, Wendy
    See Staub, Wendy Corsi
Markins, W. S.
    See Jenkins, Marie M(agdalen)
Markle, Sandra 1946- *218*
    Brief entry *41*
    Earlier sketches in SATA *57, 92, 148, 185*
Markle, Sandra L.
    See Markle, Sandra
Marklew, Gilly *211*
Marko, Katherine D(olores) *28*
Markoosie
    See Patsauq, Markoosie
Marks, Alan 1957- *187*
    Earlier sketch in SATA *77, 151*
Marks, Burton 1930- *47*
    Brief entry *43*
Marks, Graham *158*
Marks, Hannah K.
    See Trivelpiece, Laurel

Marks, J.
    See Highwater, Jamake (Mamake)
Marks, J(ames) M(acdonald) 1921- *13*
Marks, Laurie J. 1957- *68*
Marks, Margaret L. 1911(?)-1980
    Obituary *23*
Marks, Mickey Klar -1986 .... *12*
Marks, Peter
    See Smith, Robert Kimmel
Marks, Rita 1938- *47*
Marks, Stan(ley) *14*
Marks-Highwater, J.
    See Highwater, Jamake (Mamake)
Markun, Patricia Maloney 1924- *15*
Markusen, Bruce (Stanley Rodriguez)
    1965- *141*
Marley, Louise 1952- *173*
    Earlier sketch in SATA *120*
Marlin, Hilda
    See Van Stockum, Hilda
Marlow, Layne *204*
Marlow, Max
    See Nicole, Christopher
Marlow, Susan K. 1953- *178*
Marlowe, Amy Bell *67*
    Earlier sketch in SATA *1*
Marlowe, Jack
    See Deary, Terry
Marlowe, Tess
    See Glick, Ruth
Marney, Dean 1952- *90*
Marokvia, Artur 1909- *31*
Marokvia, Mireille 1908-2008 .... *5*
    Obituary *197*
Marokvia, Mireille Journet
    See Marokvia, Mireille
Marol, Jean-Claude 1946- *125*
Marr, John S(tuart) 1940- *48*
Marr, Melissa 1972- *189*
Marric, J. J.
    See Butler, William Vivian
    and Creasey, John
Marrin, Albert 1936- *193*
    Brief entry *43*
    Earlier sketches in SATA *53, 90, 126*
    See also CLR *53*
Marriott, Alice Lee 1910-1992 .... *31*
    Obituary *71*
Marriott, Janice 1946- *134*
Marriott, Pat(ricia) 1920- *35*
Marriott, Zoe 1982- *216*
Marriott, Zoe Davina
    See Marriott, Zoe
Marroquin, Patricio
    See Markun, Patricia Maloney
Mars, W. T.
    See Mars, Witold Tadeusz J.
Mars, Witold Tadeusz J. 1912-1985 .... *3*
Marsden, Carolyn 1950- *212*
    Autobiography Feature *212*
    Earlier sketches in SATA *140, 175*
Marsden, John 1950- *146*
    Earlier sketches in SATA *66, 97*
    See also CLR *34*
    See also SAAS *22*
Marsh, Carole 1946- *127*
Marsh, Dave 1950- *66*
Marsh, J. E.
    See Marshall, Evelyn
Marsh, James 1946- *73*
Marsh, Jean
    See Marshall, Evelyn
Marsh, Joan F. 1923- *83*
Marsh, Katherine 1974- *220*
Marsh, Paul
    See Hopkins, (Hector) Kenneth
Marsh, Valerie 1954- *89*
Marshall, Anthony D(ryden) 1924- *18*
Marshall, Bonnie C. 1941- *141*
    Earlier sketch in SATA *18*
Marshall, Bridget M(ary) 1974- *103*

Marshall, (Sarah) Catherine (Wood)
  1914-1983 2
  Obituary 34
Marshall, Douglas
  See McClintock, Marshall
Marshall, Edmund
  See Hopkins, (Hector) Kenneth
Marshall, Edward
  See Marshall, James
Marshall, Evelyn 1897-1991 11
Marshall, Felicity 1950- 116
Marshall, Garry 1934- 60
Marshall, H. H.
  See Jahn, Michael
Marshall, James 1942-1992 75
  Earlier sketches in SATA 6, 51
  See also CLR 21
Marshall, James Edward
  See Marshall, James
Marshall, James Vance
  See Payne, Donald Gordon
Marshall, Janet (Perry) 1938- 97
Marshall, Jeff
  See Laycock, George (Edwin)
Marshall, Kim
  See Marshall, Michael (Kimbrough)
Marshall, Michael (Kimbrough) 1948- 37
Marshall, Percy
  See Young, Percy M(arshall)
Marshall, S(amuel) L(yman) A(twood)
  1900-1977 21
Marsoli, Lisa Ann 1958- 101
  Brief entry 53
Marsten, Richard
  See Hunter, Evan
Marston, Elsa 1933- 156
Marston, Hope Irvin 1935- 127
  Earlier sketch in SATA 31
Marszalek, John F. 1939- 167
Marszalek, John Francis, Jr.
  See Marszalek, John F.
Marszalek, John Francis 1939-
  See Marszalek, John F.
Martchenko, Michael 1942- 154
  Earlier sketches in SATA 50, 95
Martel, Aimee
  See Thurlo, Aimee
  and Thurlo, David
Martel, Suzanne 1924- 99
Martignoni, Margaret E. 1908(?)-1974
  Obituary 27
Martin, Ann M. 1955- 192
  Brief entry 41
  Earlier sketches in SATA 44, 70, 126
  See also CLR 32
Martin, Bill, Jr. 1916-2004 145
  Brief entry 40
  Earlier sketches in SATA 40, 67
  See also CLR 97
Martin, Charles E(lmer)
  See Mastrangelo, Charles E(lmer)
Martin, Christopher
  See Hoyt, Edwin P(almer), Jr.
Martin, C.K. Kelly 207
Martin, Claire 1933- 76
Martin, Courtney Autumn 1984- 205
Martin, David Stone 1913-1992 39
Martin, Donald
  See Honig, Donald
Martin, Dorothy 1921- 47
Martin, Dorothy McKay
  See Martin, Dorothy
Martin, Eugene 1
Martin, Eva M. 1939- 65
Martin, Frances M(cEntee) 1906-1998 36
Martin, Francesca 1947- 101
Martin, Fred 1948- 119
Martin, Fredric
  See Christopher, Matt(hew Frederick)
Martin, George Raymond Richard
  See Martin, George R.R.

Martin, George R.R. 1948- 118
Martin, J(ohn) P(ercival) 1880(?)-1966 15
Martin, Jacqueline Briggs 1945- 188
  Earlier sketches in SATA 98, 149
Martin, Jane Read 1957- 84
Martin, Jeremy
  See Levin, Marcia Obrasky
Martin, Les
  See Schulman, L(ester) M(artin)
Martin, Linda 1961- 82
Martin, Lynne 1923- 21
Martin, Marcia
  See Levin, Marcia Obrasky
Martin, Marvin 1926- 126
Martin, Melanie
  See Pellowski, Michael (Joseph)
Martin, Nancy
  See Salmon, Annie Elizabeth
Martin, Patricia 200
Martin, Patricia A.
  See Martin, Patricia
Martin, Patricia Miles 1899-1986 43
  Obituary 48
  Earlier sketch in SATA 1
Martin, Peter
  See Chaundler, Christine
Martin, Rafe 1946- 175
Martin, Rene 1891-1977 42
  Obituary 20
Martin, Rupert (Claude) 1905- 31
Martin, S. R.
  See Mappin, Strephyn
Martin, Stefan 1936- 32
Martin, Vicky
  See Storey, Victoria Carolyn
Martin, Webber
  See Silverberg, Robert
Martin, Wendy
  See Martini, Teri
Martin, William Ivan, Jr.
  See Martin, Bill, Jr.
Martineau, Diane 1940- 178
Martineau, Harriet 1802-1876
  See YABC 2
Martinet, Jeanne 1958- 80
Martinez, Agnes 167
Martinez, Arturo O. 1933- 192
Martinez, Claudia Guadalupe 1978- 214
Martinez, Ed(ward) 1954- 98
Martinez, Elizabeth Coonrod 1954- 85
Martinez, Victor 1954-2011 95
Martini, Angela 1972(?)- 223
Martini, Teri 1930- 3
Martini, Therese
  See Martini, Teri
Martino, Alfred C. 1964- 174
Martinson, Janis
  See Herbert, Janis
Martinusen, Cindy
  See Martinusen-Coloma, Cindy
Martinusen, Cindy McCormick
  See Martinusen-Coloma, Cindy
Martinusen-Coloma, Cindy 1970- 218
Marton, Jirina 1946- 144
  Earlier sketch in SATA 95
Marton, Pierre
  See Stone, Peter
Martson, Del
  See Lupoff, Richard A(llen)
Martyr, Paula (Jane)
  See Lawford, Paula Jane
Maruki, Toshi 1912-2000 112
  See also CLR 19
Marvin, Isabel R(idout) 1924- 84
Marx, Patricia Windschill
  See Marx, Trish
Marx, Robert F(rank) 1936- 24
Marx, Trish 1948- 202
  Earlier sketches in SATA 112, 160
Marzani, Carl (Aldo) 1912-1994 12

Marzollo, Jean 1942- 190
  Autobiography Feature 190
  Earlier sketches in SATA 29, 77, 130
  See also SAAS 15
Masefield, John (Edward) 1878-1967 19
  See also CLR 164
Masiello, Ralph 1961- 214
Masoff, Joy 1951- 118
Mason, Adrienne 1962- 163
Mason, Cherie 170
Mason, Edwin A. 1905-1979
  Obituary 32
Mason, Ernst
  See Pohl, Frederik
Mason, F(rancis) van Wyck 1901-1978 3
  Obituary 26
Mason, Frank W.
  See Mason, F(rancis) van Wyck
Mason, George Frederick 1904-2000 14
Mason, Miriam E(vangeline) 1900-1973 2
  Obituary 26
Mason, Prue 195
Mason, Simon 1962- 178
Mason, Tally
  See Derleth, August (William)
Mason, Van Wyck
  See Mason, F(rancis) van Wyck
Mass, Wendy 1967- 196
  Earlier sketch in SATA 158
Mass, William
  See Gibson, William
Masse, Josee 221
Masselman, George 1897-1971 19
Massey, Misty 212
Massie, Dianne Redfield 1938- 125
  Earlier sketch in SATA 16
Massie, Elizabeth 108
Massini, Sarah 213
Masson, Sophie 1959- 179
  Earlier sketch in SATA 133
Masters, Anthony (Richard) 1940-2003 112
  Obituary 145
Masters, Kelly R(ay) 1897-1987 3
Masters, Mildred 1932- 42
Masters, William
  See Cousins, Margaret
Masters, Zeke
  See Bensen, Donald R.
  and Goulart, Ron
Mastrangelo, Charles E(lmer) 1910-1995 70
  Earlier sketch in SATA 69
Masuda, Takeshi 1944- 56
Matas, Carol 1949- 194
  Autobiography Feature 112
  Earlier sketch in SATA 93
  See also CLR 52
Matchette, Katharine E. 1941- 38
Math, Irwin 1940- 42
Mathabane, Mark 1960- 123
Mather, Kirtley F(letcher) 1888-1978 65
Mathers, Petra 1945- 176
  Earlier sketch in SATA 119
  See also CLR 76
Matheson, Richard (Christian) 1953- 119
Matheson, Shirlee Smith 1942- 155
Mathews, Eleanor
  See Mathews, Ellie
Mathews, Ellie 1946(?)- 193
Mathews, Janet 1914-1992 41
Mathews, Judith
  See Goldberger, Judith M.
Mathews, Louise
  See Tooke, Louise Mathews
Mathiesen, Egon 1907-1976
  Obituary 28
Mathieu, Joe 1949- 185
  Brief entry 36
  Earlier sketches in SATA 43, 94
Mathieu, Joseph P.
  See Mathieu, Joe

Mathis, Sharon Bell 1937- 58
    Earlier sketch in SATA 7
    See also CLR *147*
    See also SAAS *3*
Matlin, Marlee 1965- 181
Matlin, Marlee Beth
    See Matlin, Marlee
Matloff, Gregory 1945- 73
Matott, Justin 1961- 109
Matranga, Frances Carfi 1922- 78
Matray, James I. 1948- 161
Matray, James Irving
    See Matray, James I.
Matson, Emerson N(els) 1926- 12
Matsui, Tadashi 1926- 8
Matsuno, Masako
    See Kobayashi, Masako Matsuno
Matsuoka, Mei 1981- 192
Matte, (Encarnacion) L'Enc 1936- 22
Mattern, Joanne 1963- 122
Mattheson, Jenny 180
Matthew, James
    See Barrie, J. M.
Matthews, Aline
    See De Wire, Elinor
Matthews, Andrew 1948- 138
Matthews, Caitlin 1952- 122
Matthews, Cecily 1945- 221
Matthews, Downs 1925- 71
Matthews, Elizabeth 1978- 194
Matthews, Ellen
    See Bache, Ellyn
Matthews, Ellen 1950- 28
Matthews, Harold Downs
    See Matthews, Downs
Matthews, Jacklyn Meek
    See Meek, Jacklyn O'Hanlon
Matthews, John (Kentigern) 1948- 116
Matthews, L. S. 183
Matthews, Laura S.
    See Matthews, L. S.
Matthews, Liz
    See Pellowski, Michael (Joseph)
Matthews, Morgan
    See Pellowski, Michael (Joseph)
Matthews, Nicola
    See Browne, N.M.
Matthews, Patricia 1927-2006 28
Matthews, Patricia Anne
    See Matthews, Patricia
Matthews, Tina 1961- 190
Matthews, Tom L.
    See Lalicki, Tom
Matthews, William Henry III 1919- 45
    Brief entry 28
Matthiessen, Peter 1927- 27
Mattingley, Christobel (Rosemary) 1931- 85
    Earlier sketch in SATA 37
    See also CLR *24*
    See also SAAS *18*
Matulay, Laszlo 1912- 43
Matus, Greta 1938- 12
Matzigkeit, Philip 220
Maugham, W. S.
    See Maugham, W. Somerset
Maugham, W. Somerset 1874-1965 54
Maugham, William S.
    See Maugham, W. Somerset
Maugham, William Somerset
    See Maugham, W. Somerset
Maurer, Diane Philippoff
    See Maurer-Mathison, Diane V(ogel)
Maurer, Diane Vogel
    See Maurer-Mathison, Diane V(ogel)
Maurer-Mathison, Diane V(ogel) 1944- 89
Mauser, Pat Rhoads
    See McCord, Patricia
Mauser, Patricia Rhoads
    See McCord, Patricia
Maves, Mary Carolyn 1916- 10
Maves, Paul B(enjamin) 1913-1994 10

Mavor, Salley 1955- 125
Mawicke, Tran 1911- 15
Max 1906-1989
    See Diop, Birago (Ismael)
Max, Peter 1939- 45
Maxon, Anne
    See Best, (Evangel) Allena Champlin
Maxwell, Arthur S. 1896-1970 11
Maxwell, B.E. 1957- 211
Maxwell, Bruce E.
    See Maxwell, B.E.
Maxwell, Edith 1923- 7
Maxwell, Gavin 1914-1969 65
Maxwell, Katie
    See MacAlister, Katie
Maxwell, William (Keepers, Jr.) 1908-2000
    Obituary 128
Maxwell-Hyslop, Miranda 1968- 154
May, Charles Paul 1920- 4
May, Elaine Tyler 1947- 120
May, J. C.
    See May, Julian
May, Julian 1931- 11
May, Katie 225
May, Robert Lewis 1905-1976
    Obituary 27
May, Robert Stephen 1929-1996 46
May, Robin
    See May, Robert Stephen
Mayall, Beth 171
Mayberry, Florence V(irginia) Wilson 10
Maybury, Richard J. 1946- 72
Maybury, Rick
    See Maybury, Richard J.
Maydak, Michael S. 1952- 220
Mayer, Agatha
    See Maher, Ramona
Mayer, Albert Ignatius, Jr. 1906-1994
    Obituary 29
Mayer, Ann M(argaret) 1938- 14
Mayer, Bill 200
Mayer, Danuta 1958- 117
Mayer, Hannelore Valencak 1929- 42
Mayer, Jane Rothschild 1903-2001 38
Mayer, Marianna 1945- 132
    Earlier sketches in SATA 32, 83
Mayer, Mercer 1943- 137
    Earlier sketches in SATA 16, 32, 73, 129
    See also CLR *11*
Mayerson, Charlotte Leon 36
Mayerson, Evelyn Wilde 1935- 55
Mayfield, Katherine 1958- 118
Mayfield, Sue 1963- 146
    Earlier sketch in SATA 72
Mayhar, Ardath 1930- 38
Mayhew, James 1964- 204
    Earlier sketches in SATA 85, 149
Maynard, Olga 1920- 40
Mayne, William 1928-2010 122
    Earlier sketches in SATA 6, 68
    See also CLR *123*
    See also SAAS *11*
Mayne, William James Carter
    See Mayne, William
Maynes, J. O. Rocky, Jr.
    See Maynes, J. Oscar, Jr.
Maynes, J. Oscar, Jr. 1929- 38
Mayo, Gretchen Will 1936- 163
    Earlier sketch in SATA 84
Mayo, Margaret 1935- 165
    Earlier sketches in SATA 38, 96
Mayo, Margaret Mary
    See Mayo, Margaret
Mayr, Diane 1949- 197
Mays, Lucinda L(a Bella) 1924- 49
Mays, (Lewis) Victor (Jr.) 1927- 5
Mazellan, Ron 210
Mazer, Anne 1953- 192
    Earlier sketches in SATA 67, 105

Mazer, Harry 1925- 167
    Earlier sketches in SATA 31, 67, 105
    See also CLR *16*
    See also SAAS *11*
Mazer, Norma Fox 1931-2009 198
    Earlier sketches in SATA 24, 67, 105, 168
    See also CLR *23*
    See also SAAS *1*
Mazille, Capucine 1953- 96
Mazo, Michael 223
Mazza, Adriana 1928- 19
Mazzio, Joann 1926- 74
Mbugua, Kioi Wa 1962- 83
McAfee, Carol 1955- 81
McAllister, Amanda
    See Dowdell, Dorothy (Florence) Karns
    and Hager, Jean
    and Meaker, Eloise
McAllister, Angela 225
    Earlier sketch in SATA *182*
McAllister, Margaret I. 1956- 169
    Earlier sketch in SATA *117*
McAllister, M.I.
    See McAllister, Margaret I.
McArdle, Paula 1971- 198
McArthur, Nancy 96
McAvoy, Jim 1972- 142
McBain, Ed
    See Hunter, Evan
McBain, Georgina 189
McBratney, Sam 1943- 203
    Earlier sketches in SATA 89, 164
    See also CLR *44*
McBrier, Michael
    See Older, Effin
    and Older, Jules
McCafferty, Jim 1954- 84
McCaffery, Janet 1936- 38
McCaffrey, Anne 1926- 152
    Autobiography Feature 152
    Earlier sketches in SATA 8, 70, 116
    See also CLR *130*
    See also SAAS *11*
McCaffrey, Anne Inez
    See McCaffrey, Anne
McCaffrey, Kate 1970- 228
McCaffrey, Mary
    See Szudek, Agnes S(usan) P(hilomena)
McCain, Becky Ray 1954- 138
McCain, Murray (David, Jr.) 1926-1981 7
    Obituary 29
McCall, Bruce 1935(?)- 209
McCall, Edith (Sansom) 1911- 6
McCall, Virginia Nielsen 1909-2000 13
McCall, Wendell
    See Pearson, Ridley
McCall Smith, Alexander
    See Smith, Alexander McCall
McCallum, Phyllis
    See Koch, Phyllis (Mae) McCallum
McCallum, Stephen 1960- 91
McCampbell, Darlene Z. 1942- 83
McCann, Edson
    See del Rey, Lester
    and Pohl, Frederik
McCann, Gerald 1916- 41
McCann, Helen 1948- 75
McCannon, Dindga 41
McCants, William D. 1961- 82
McCarter, Neely Dixon 1929- 47
McCarthy, Agnes 1933- 4
McCarthy, Colin (John) 1951- 77
McCarthy, Mary 1951- 203
McCarthy, Meghan 199
    Earlier sketch in SATA *168*
McCarthy, Ralph F. 1950- 139
McCarthy-Tucker, Sherri N. 1958- 83
McCarty, Peter 1966- 182
McCarty, Rega Kramer 1904-1986 10
McCaslin, Nellie 1914-2005 12

McCaughrean, Geraldine 1951- *173*
  Earlier sketches in SATA *87, 139*
  See also CLR *38*
McCaughren, Tom 1936- *75*
McCauley, Adam 1965- *209*
  Earlier sketch in SATA *128*
McCay, (Zenas) Winsor 1869-1934 .... *134*
  Earlier sketch in SATA *41*
McClafferty, Carla Killough 1958- *137*
McClary, Jane Stevenson 1919-1990
  Obituary *64*
McCleery, Patsy R. 1925- *133*
  Earlier sketch in SATA *88*
McClelland, Susan *214*
McClements, George *196*
McClintock, Barbara 1955- *213*
  Earlier sketches in SATA *57, 95, 146*
McClintock, Marshall 1906-1967 .... *3*
McClintock, May Garelick
  See Garelick, May
McClintock, Mike
  See McClintock, Marshall
McClintock, Norah *226*
  Earlier sketch in SATA *178*
McClintock, Theodore 1902-1971 .... *14*
McClinton, Leon 1933- *11*
McCloskey, Kevin 1951- *79*
McCloskey, (John) Robert 1914-2003 .... *100*
  Obituary *146*
  Earlier sketches in SATA *2, 39*
  See also CLR *7*
McCloy, James F(loyd) 1941- *59*
McClung, Robert M(arshall) 1916- *135*
  Earlier sketches in SATA *2, 68*
  See also CLR *11*
  See also SAAS *15*
McClure, Gillian Mary 1948- *31*
McClure, Nikki *218*
McColley, Kevin 1961- *80*
  See also SAAS *23*
McConduit, Denise Walter 1950- *89*
McConnell, James Douglas Rutherford
  1915-1988 .... *40*
  Obituary *56*
McCord, Anne 1942- *41*
McCord, David (Thompson Watson)
  1897-1997 .... *18*
  Obituary *96*
  See also CLR *9*
McCord, Jean 1924- *34*
McCord, Pat Mauser
  See McCord, Patricia
McCord, Patricia 1943- *159*
  Earlier sketch in SATA *37*
McCord, Patricia Sue Rhoads Mauser
  See McCord, Patricia
McCormack, Caren McNelly *217*
McCormick, Brooks
  See Adams, William Taylor
McCormick, Dell J. 1892-1949 .... *19*
McCormick, (George) Donald (King)
  1911-1998 .... *14*
McCormick, Edith (Joan) 1934- *30*
McCormick, Kimberly A. 1960- *153*
McCormick, Patricia 1956- *181*
  Earlier sketch in SATA *128*
McCourt, Edward (Alexander) 1907-1972
  Obituary *28*
McCourt, Lisa 1964- *214*
  Earlier sketches in SATA *117, 159*
McCourt, Malachy 1931- *126*
McCoy, Glenn 1965- *212*
McCoy, Iola Fuller *3*
McCoy, J(oseph) J(erome) 1917- *8*
McCoy, Karen Kawamoto 1953- *82*
McCoy, Lois (Rich) 1941- *38*
McCrady, Lady 1951- *16*
McCrea, James (Craig, Jr.) 1920- *3*
McCrea, Ruth (Pirman) 1921- *3*
McCreigh, James
  See Pohl, Frederik

McCrumb, Sharyn 1948- *109*
McCue, Lisa 1959- *212*
  Earlier sketches in SATA *65, 177*
McCue, Lisa Emiline
  See McCue, Lisa
McCullen, Andrew
  See Arthur, Robert, (Jr.)
McCullers, Carson 1917-1967 .... *27*
McCullers, Lula Carson Smith
  See McCullers, Carson
McCulloch, Derek (Ivor Breashur) 1897-1967
  Obituary *29*
McCulloch, John Tyler
  See Burroughs, Edgar Rice
McCulloch, Sarah
  See Ure, Jean
McCullough, David 1933- *62*
McCullough, David Gaub
  See McCullough, David
McCullough, Frances Monson 1938- *8*
McCullough, Sharon Pierce 1943- *131*
McCully, Emily Arnold
  See Arnold, Emily
McCune, Dan
  See Haas, Dorothy F.
McCunn, Ruthanne Lum 1946- *63*
McCurdy, Michael (Charles) 1942- *147*
  Earlier sketches in SATA *13, 82*
McCusker, Paul 1958- *220*
McCutcheon, Elsie (Mary Jackson) 1937- ... *60*
McCutcheon, John 1952- *97*
McDaniel, Becky Bring 1953- *61*
McDaniel, Lurlene 1944- *218*
  Earlier sketches in SATA *71, 146*
McDaniels, Pellom III 1968- *121*
McDaniels, Preston 1952- *192*
McDearmon, Kay *20*
McDermott, Beverly Brodsky 1941- *11*
McDermott, Eleni *156*
McDermott, Gerald (Edward) 1941- *163*
  Earlier sketches in SATA *16, 74*
  See also CLR *9*
McDermott, Michael 1962- *76*
McDevitt, Jack 1935- *155*
  Earlier sketch in SATA *94*
McDevitt, John Charles
  See McDevitt, Jack
McDole, Carol
  See Farley, Carol (J.)
McDonald, Candice Hartsough 1982- *225*
McDonald, Collin 1943- *79*
McDonald, Gerald D(oan) 1905-1970 .... *3*
McDonald, Jamie
  See Heide, Florence Parry
McDonald, Janet 1953-2007 .... *204*
  Earlier sketch in SATA *148*
McDonald, Jill (Masefield) 1927-1982 .... *13*
  Obituary *29*
McDonald, Joyce 1946- *164*
  Earlier sketch in SATA *101*
McDonald, Lucile Saunders 1898-1992 .... *10*
McDonald, Mary Ann 1956- *84*
McDonald, Megan 1958- *202*
  Autobiography Feature *151*
  Earlier sketches in SATA *67, 99, 148, 151*
  See also CLR *94*
McDonald, Meme 1954- *112*
McDonald, Mercedes 1956- *169*
  Earlier sketch in SATA *97*
McDonald, Rae A. 1952- *201*
McDonell, Chris 1960- *138*
McDonnell, Christine 1949- *225*
  Earlier sketches in SATA *34, 115*
McDonnell, Flora (Mary) 1963- *146*
  Earlier sketch in SATA *90*
McDonnell, Kathleen 1947- *186*
McDonnell, Lois Eddy 1914-2001 .... *10*
McDonnell, Patrick 1956- *221*
  Earlier sketch in SATA *179*
McDonough, Yona Zeldis 1957- *73*
McDowell, Marilyn Taylor *217*

McElligott, Matt 1968- *196*
  Earlier sketch in SATA *135*
McElligott, Matthew
  See McElligott, Matt
McElmeel, Sharron L. 1942- *128*
McElmurry, Jill *198*
  Earlier sketch in SATA *159*
McElrath, William N. 1932- *65*
McElrath-Eslick, Lori 1960- *204*
  Earlier sketch in SATA *96*
McEntee, Dorothy (Layng) 1902- *37*
McEvoy, Anne *214*
McEwen, Katharine *183*
McEwen, Robert (Lindley) 1926-1980
  Obituary *23*
McFadden, Kevin Christopher
  See Pike, Christopher
McFall, Christie 1918- *12*
McFall, Gardner 1952- *183*
McFarlan, Donald M(aitland) 1915- *59*
McFarland, Henry "Hammer"
  See McFarland, Henry O.
McFarland, Henry O. 1934- *143*
McFarland, Kenton D(ean) 1920- *11*
McFarland, Martha
  See Smith-Ankrom, M. E.
McFarlane, Leslie 1902-1977 .... *100*
  Earlier sketches in SATA *31, 1, 65, 67*
  See also CLR *118*
McFarlane, Leslie Charles
  See McFarlane, Leslie
McFarlane, Peter 1940- *95*
McFarlane, Peter William
  See McFarlane, Peter
McFarlane, Sheryl P. 1954- *86*
McFarlane, Todd 1961- *117*
McGaw, Jessie Brewer 1913-1997 .... *10*
McGee, Barbara 1943- *6*
McGee, Marni *163*
McGhee, Alison 1960- *196*
McGhee, Alison R.
  See McGhee, Alison
McGhee, Holly M.
  See Durand, Hallie
McGiffin, (Lewis) Lee (Shaffer) 1908-1978 ... *1*
McGill, Alice *159*
McGill, Marci
  See Balterman, Marcia Ridlon
McGill, Marci Ridlon
  See Balterman, Marcia Ridlon
McGill, Ormond 1913- *92*
McGinley, Jerry 1948- *116*
McGinley, Phyllis 1905-1978 .... *44*
  Obituary *24*
  Earlier sketch in SATA *2*
McGinnis, Lila S(prague) 1924- *44*
McGinty, Alice B. 1963- *202*
  Earlier sketch in SATA *134*
McGivern, Justin 1985- *129*
McGivern, Maureen Daly
  See Daly, Maureen
McGivern, Maureen Patricia Daly
  See Daly, Maureen
McGough, Elizabeth (Hemmes) 1934- *33*
McGovern, Ann 1930- *132*
  Earlier sketches in SATA *8, 69, 70*
  See also CLR *50*
  See also SAAS *17*
McGowen, Thomas E. 1927- *109*
  Earlier sketch in SATA *2*
McGowen, Tom
  See McGowen, Thomas E.
McGrady, Mike 1933- *6*
McGrath, Barbara Barbieri 1953- *169*
  Earlier sketch in SATA *108*
McGrath, Robin 1949- *121*
McGrath, Thomas (Matthew) 1916-1990 ..... *41*
  Obituary *66*

McGraw, Eloise Jarvis 1915-2000 .... *67*
  Obituary *123*
  Earlier sketch in SATA *1*
  See also SAAS 6
McGraw, William Corbin 1916-1999 .... *3*
McGreal, Elizabeth
  See Yates, Elizabeth
McGregor, Barbara 1959- *82*
McGregor, Craig 1933- *8*
McGregor, Iona 1929- *25*
McGrory, Anik *193*
McGuffey, Alexander Hamilton 1816-1896 . *60*
McGuigan, Mary Ann 1949- *228*
  Earlier sketch in SATA *106*
McGuire, Edna 1899- *13*
McGuire, Leslie (Sarah) 1945- *94*
  Brief entry *45*
  Earlier sketch in SATA *52*
McGuire, Robert *187*
McGuirk, Leslie (A.) 1960- *152*
McGurk, Slater
  See Roth, Arthur J(oseph)
McHargue, Georgess 1941- *77*
  Earlier sketch in SATA *4*
  See also CLR *2*
  See also SAAS *5*
McHenry, E.B. 1963(?)- *193*
McHugh, (Berit) Elisabet 1941- *55*
  Brief entry *44*
McIlvaine, Jane
  See McClary, Jane Stevenson
McIlwraith, Maureen Mollie Hunter
  See Hunter, Mollie
McInerney, Judith W(hitelock) 1945- *49*
  Brief entry *46*
McInerny, Ralph 1929-2010 .... *93*
McInerny, Ralph Matthew
  See McInerny, Ralph
McKaughan, Larry (Scott) 1941- *75*
McKay, Donald 1895- *45*
McKay, Hilary 1959- *208*
  Earlier sketches in SATA *92, 145*
  See also SAAS 23
McKay, Hilary Jane
  See McKay, Hilary
McKay, Lawrence, Jr. 1948- *114*
McKay, Robert W. 1921- *15*
McKay, Sharon E. 1954- *165*
McKay, Simon
  See Nicole, Christopher
McKean, Dave 1963- *197*
McKean, David Jeff
  See McKean, Dave
McKeating, Eileen 1957- *81*
McKee, David (John) 1935- *158*
  Earlier sketches in SATA *70, 107*
  See also CLR *38*
McKee, Tim 1970- *111*
McKeever, Marcia
  See Laird, Jean E(louise)
McKellar, Danica 1975- *213*
McKelvey, Carole A. 1942- *78*
McKelvy, Charles 1950- *124*
McKendrick, Melveena (Christine) 1941- *55*
McKendry, Joe 1972- *170*
McKenna, Colleen O'Shaughnessy 1948- .. *136*
  Earlier sketch in SATA *76*
McKenzie, Dorothy Clayton 1910-1981
  Obituary *28*
McKenzie, Ellen Kindt 1928- *80*
McKernan, Victoria 1957- *171*
McKie, Robin *112*
McKillip, Patricia A. 1948- *174*
  Earlier sketches in SATA *30, 80, 126*
McKillip, Patricia Anne
  See McKillip, Patricia A.
McKim, Audrey Margaret 1909-1999 .... *47*
McKimmie, Chris *194*
McKinley, Jennifer Carolyn Robin
  See McKinley, Robin

McKinley, Robin 1952- *229*
  Brief entry *32*
  Earlier sketches in SATA *50, 89, 130, 195*
  See also CLR *127*
McKinney, Barbara Shaw 1951- *116*
McKinney, Nadine 1938- *91*
McKinty, Adrian *186*
McKissack, Fredrick L. 1939- *162*
  Brief entry *53*
  Earlier sketches in SATA *73, 117*
  See also CLR *55*
McKissack, Fredrick Lemuel
  See McKissack, Fredrick L.
McKissack, Patricia C. 1944- *195*
  Earlier sketches in SATA *51, 73, 117, 162*
  See also CLR *129*
McKissack, Patricia L'Ann Carwell
  See McKissack, Patricia C.
McKissack and McKissack
  See McKissack, Fredrick L.
  and McKissack, Patricia C.
McKown, Robin (?)-1976 .... *6*
McKy, Katie 1956- *184*
McLaren, Chesley *213*
McLaren, Clemence 1938- *158*
  Earlier sketch in SATA *105*
McLaughlin, Frank 1934- *73*
McLaughlin, Julie 1984- *226*
McLaughlin, Lauren *209*
McLaurin, Anne 1953- *27*
McLean, Andrew 1946- *172*
  Earlier sketch in SATA *113*
McLean, J. Sloan
  See Gillette, Virginia M(ary)
  and Wunsch, Josephine (McLean)
McLean, Jacqueline
  See Kolosov, Jacqueline
McLean, Janet 1946- *113*
McLean, Kathryn (Anderson) 1909-1966 .... *9*
McLean, Virginia Overton 1946- *90*
McLean-Carr, Carol 1948- *122*
McLeish, Kenneth 1940-1997 .... *35*
McLenighan, Valjean 1947- *46*
  Brief entry *40*
McLennan, Connie *171*
McLennan, Will
  See Wisler, G(ary) Clifton
McLeod, Bob 1951- *173*
McLeod, Chum 1955- *95*
McLeod, Emilie Warren 1926-1982 .... *23*
  Obituary *31*
McLeod, Kirsty
  See Hudson, (Margaret) Kirsty
McLeod, Margaret Vail
  See Holloway, Teresa (Bragunier)
McLerran, Alice 1933- *137*
  Earlier sketch in SATA *68*
McLimans, David 1949- *182*
McLoughlin, John C. 1949- *47*
McMahon, Bob 1956- *208*
McManus, Patrick F. 1933- *46*
McManus, Patrick Francis
  See McManus, Patrick F.
McMeekin, Clark
  See McMeekin, Isabel McLennan
McMeekin, Isabel McLennan 1895-1973 .... *3*
McMenemy, Sarah 1965- *226*
  Earlier sketch in SATA *156*
McMillan, Bruce 1947- *192*
  Earlier sketches in SATA *22, 70, 129*
  See also CLR *47*
McMillan, Naomi
  See Grimes, Nikki
McMorey, James L.
  See Moyer, Terry J.
McMorrow, Annalisa 1969- *104*
McMullan, Jim 1934- *150*
  Earlier sketch in SATA *87*
McMullan, K. H.
  See McMullan, Kate

McMullan, Kate 1947- *189*
  Brief entry *48*
  Earlier sketches in SATA *52, 87, 132*
McMullan, Kate Hall
  See McMullan, Kate
McMullan, Margaret 1960- *203*
McMurtrey, Martin A(loysius) 1921- *21*
McNabb, Linda 1963- *147*
McNair, Kate *3*
McNair, Sylvia 1924-2002 .... *74*
McNamara, Margaret C(raig) 1915-1981
  Obituary *24*
McNaught, Harry *32*
McNaughton, Colin 1951- *211*
  Earlier sketches in SATA *39, 92, 134*
  See also CLR *54*
McNaughton, Janet 1953- *162*
  Earlier sketch in SATA *110*
McNeal, Laura *194*
McNeal, Tom *194*
McNeely, Jeannette 1918- *25*
McNeer, May (Yonge) 1902-1994 .... *81*
  Earlier sketch in SATA *1*
McNeese, Tim 1953- *139*
McNeill, Janet
  See Alexander, Janet
McNicholas, Shelagh *191*
McNickle, D'Arcy 1904-1977
  Obituary *22*
McNickle, William D'Arcy
  See McNickle, D'Arcy
McNicoll, Sylvia (Marilyn) 1954- *113*
  See also CLR *99*
McNulty, Faith 1918-2005 .... *168*
  Earlier sketches in SATA *12, 84, 139*
McPhail, David 1940- *219*
  Brief entry *32*
  Earlier sketches in SATA *47, 81, 140, 183*
McPhail, David M.
  See McPhail, David
McPhail, David Michael
  See McPhail, David
McPhee, Norma H. 1928- *95*
McPhee, Peter 1957- *214*
McPhee, Richard B(yron) 1934- *41*
McPherson, James M. 1936- *141*
  Earlier sketch in SATA *16*
McPherson, James Munro
  See McPherson, James M.
McQueen, Lucinda 1950- *58*
  Brief entry *48*
McQueen, Mildred Hark 1908-1978 .... *12*
McQuillan, Mary *200*
McRae, Russell (William) 1934- *63*
McShean, Gordon 1936- *41*
Mc Swigan, Marie 1907-1962 .... *24*
McTavish, Sandy
  See Eyerly, Jeannette
McVeity, Jen *148*
McVey, Vicki 1946- *80*
McVicker, Charles (Taggart) 1930- *39*
McVicker, Chuck
  See McVicker, Charles (Taggart)
McVoy, Terra Elan *220*
McWhirter, A(lan) Ross 1925-1975 .... *37*
  Obituary *31*
McWhirter, Norris (Dewar) 1925-2004 .... *37*
McWilliam, Howard 1977- *219*
McWilliams, Karen 1943- *65*
Mdurvwa, Hajara E. 1962- *92*
Meacham, Margaret 1952- *203*
  Earlier sketch in SATA *95*
Meachum, Virginia 1918- *133*
  Earlier sketch in SATA *87*
Mead, Alice 1952- *146*
  Earlier sketch in SATA *94*
Mead, Margaret 1901-1978
  Obituary *20*
Mead, Russell (M., Jr.) 1935- *10*
Mead, Stella (?)-1981
  Obituary *27*

Meade, Elizabeth Thomasina 1854(?)-1914(?)
  See CLR 163
Meade, Ellen
  See Roddick, Ellen
Meade, Holly 207
Meade, L. T.
  See Meade, Elizabeth Thomasina
Meade, Marion 1934- 127
  Earlier sketch in SATA 23
Meader, Stephen W(arren) 1892-1977 1
Meadmore, Susan
  See Sallis, Susan (Diana)
Meadow, Charles T(roub) 1929- 23
Meadowcroft, Enid LaMonte
  See Wright, Enid Meadowcroft (LaMonte)
Meadows, Daisy
  See Chapman, Linda
Meadows, Graham (W.) 1934- 161
Meadows, Michelle 202
Meaker, M. J.
  See Meaker, Marijane
Meaker, Marijane 1927- 160
  Autobiography Feature 111
  Earlier sketches in SATA 20, 61, 99
  See also CLR 29
  See also SAAS 1
Meaker, Marijane Agnes
  See Meaker, Marijane
Means, Florence Crannell 1891-1980 1
  Obituary 25
  See also CLR 56
Mearian, Judy Frank 1936- 49
Mebus, Scott 1974- 216
Mecca, Judy Truesdell 1955- 127
Mechling, Lauren 1978(?)- 194
Mechling, Lauren 1978(?)- 194
Mechner, Jordan 1964- 205
Medary, Marjorie 1890-1980 14
Meddaugh, Susan 1944- 176
  Earlier sketches in SATA 29, 84, 125
Medearis, Angela Shelf 1956- 123
  Earlier sketch in SATA 72
Medearis, Mary 1915- 5
Medina, Jane 1953- 167
  Earlier sketch in SATA 122
Medina, Meg 1963- 212
Medina, Nico 1982- 193
Medlicott, Mary 1946- 88
Mee, Charles L., Jr. 1938- 72
  Earlier sketch in SATA 8
Meehan, Kierin 218
Meehl, Brian 204
Meek, Jacklyn O'Hanlon 1933- 51
  Brief entry 34
Meek, S(terner St.) P(aul) 1894-1972
  Obituary 28
Meeker, Clare Hodgson 1952- 96
Meeker, Oden 1919(?)-1976 14
Meeker, Richard
  See Brown, Fornan
Meeks, Esther MacBain 1
Meggs, Libby Phillips 1943- 130
Mehdevi, Alexander (Sinclair) 1947- 7
Mehdevi, Anne (Marie) Sinclair 1947- 8
Meidell, Sherry 1951- 73
Meier, Minta 1906- 55
Meighan, Donald Charles 1929- 30
Meigs, Cornelia Lynde 1884-1973 6
  See also CLR 55
Meilach, Dona Z(weigoron) 1926- 34
Meilman, Philip W(arren) 1951- 79
Meinstereifel, Ronald L. 1960- 134
Meisel, Paul 224
  Earlier sketch in SATA 184
Meister, Cari 204
Melanson, Luc 198
Melcher, Daniel 1912-1985
  Obituary 43
Melcher, Frederic Gershom 1879-1963
  Obituary 22
Melcher, Marguerite Fellows 1879-1969 10

Meldrum, Christina 206
Melendez, Francisco 1964- 72
Melhuish, Eva 199
Melin, Grace Hathaway 1892-1973 10
Mellersh, H(arold) E(dward) L(eslie)
  1897- 10
Melling, David 186
Melmed, Laura Krauss 212
Melmoth, Sebastian
  See Wilde, Oscar
Melnikoff, Pamela (Rita) 97
Meltzer, Amy 1968- 202
Meltzer, Milton 1915-2009 201
  Autobiography Feature 124
  Earlier sketches in SATA 1, 50, 80, 128
  See also CLR 13
  See also SAAS 1
Melville, Anne
  See Potter, Margaret
Melville, Herman 1819-1891 59
Melwood, Mary
  See Lewis, E. M.
Melzack, Ronald 1929- 5
Memling, Carl 1918-1969 6
Menchin, Scott 188
Mendel, Jo
  See Bond, Gladys Baker
  and Gilbertson, Mildred Geiger
Mendelson, Steven T. 1958-1995 86
Mendelson-Stevens, Serita Deborah
  See Stevens, Serita
Mendes, Valerie 1939- 157
Mendez, Raymond A. 1947- 66
Mendez, Simon 1975- 215
Mendonca, Susan
  See Smith, Susan Vernon
Mendoza, George 1934- 41
  Brief entry 39
  See also SAAS 7
Menendez, Shirley (C.) 1937- 146
Meng, Cece 194
Meng, Heinz (Karl) 1924- 13
Mennen, Ingrid 1954- 85
Menotti, Gian Carlo 1911-2007 29
  Obituary 180
Menuhin, Sir Yehudi 1916-1999 40
  Obituary 113
Menville, Douglas 1935- 64
Menzel, Barbara Jean 1946- 63
Menzel, Peter 1948- 207
Mercati, Cynthia 164
Mercati, Cynthia J.
  See Mercati, Cynthia
Mercer, Charles (Edward) 1917-1988 16
  Obituary 61
Mercer, Jessie 21
Mercer, Sienna 192
Meredith, Arnold
  See Hopkins, (Hector) Kenneth
Meredith, David William
  See Miers, Earl Schenck
Meringoff, Laurene Krasny
  See Brown, Laurene Krasny
Meriwether, Louise 1923- 52
  Brief entry 31
Merlin, Arthur
  See Blish, James
Merlin, Christina
  See Heaven, Constance (Christina)
Merrell, Billy 1982- 222
Merriam, Eve 1916-1992 73
  Earlier sketches in SATA 3, 40
  See also CLR 14
Merrill, Jane 1946- 42
Merrill, Jane Merrill
  See Merrill, Jane
Merrill, Jean (Fairbanks) 1923- 82
  Earlier sketch in SATA 1
  See also CLR 52
Merrill, Phil
  See Merrill, Jane

Merriman, Alex
  See Silverberg, Robert
Merriman, Rachel 1971- 149
  Earlier sketch in SATA 98
Merrit, Elizabeth
  See Goudge, Eileen
Merski, Patricia K.
  See Merski, P.K.
Merski, P.K. 172
Mertz, Barbara
  See Peters, Elizabeth
Mertz, Barbara Gross
  See Peters, Elizabeth
Merveille, David 200
Merz, Jennifer J. 196
Meschel, Susan V. 1936- 83
Meschenmoser, Sebastian 1980- 229
Meserve, Jessica 211
Messenger, Charles (Rynd Milles) 1942- 59
Messick, Dale 1906-2005 64
  Brief entry 48
Messier, Claire 1956- 103
Messieres, Nicole de
  See de Messieres, Nicole
Messinger, Carla 198
Messmer, Otto 1892(?)-1983 37
Messner, Kate 224
Mesta, Gabriel
  See Moesta, Rebecca
Metaxas, Eric 1963- 211
Metcalf, Doris H(unter) 91
Metcalf, Suzanne
  See Baum, L. Frank
Metos, Thomas H(arry) 1932- 37
Metter, Bert(ram Milton) 1927- 56
Metzenthen, David 1958- 167
  Earlier sketch in SATA 106
Meunier, Brian 1954- 195
Meyer, Barbara 1939- 77
Meyer, Carolyn 1935- 142
  Autobiography Feature 142
  Earlier sketches in SATA 9, 70, 118
  See also SAAS 9
Meyer, Carolyn Mae
  See Meyer, Carolyn
Meyer, Edith Patterson 1895-1993 5
Meyer, F(ranklyn) E(dward) 1932- 9
Meyer, Jean Shepherd 11
Meyer, Jerome Sydney 1895-1975 3
  Obituary 25
Meyer, June
  See Jordan, June
Meyer, Kerstin 1966- 190
Meyer, L.A. 1942- 221
  Earlier sketches in SATA 12, 144
Meyer, Louis A.
  See Meyer, L.A.
Meyer, Renate 1930- 6
Meyer, Stephenie 1973- 193
  See also CLR 142
Meyer, Susan E. 1940- 64
Meyerhoff, Jenny 1972- 208
Meyers, Susan 1942- 164
  Earlier sketches in SATA 19, 108
Meynell, Laurence Walter 1899-1989
  Obituary 61
Meynier, Yvonne (Pollet) 1908- 14
Mezey, Robert 1935- 33
Micale, Albert 1913- 22
Michael, James
  See Scagnetti, Jack
Michael, Jan 1947- 216
Michael, Livi 1960- 172
Michael, Manfred
  See Winterfeld, Henry
Michael, Olivia
  See Michael, Livi
Michaelis, Antonia 1979- 215
Michaels, Barbara
  See Peters, Elizabeth
Michaels, Jamie 195

Michaels, Joanne Louise
See Teitelbaum, Michael
Michaels, Kristin
See Williams, Jeanne
Michaels, Molly
See Untermeyer, Louis
Michaels, Neal
See Teitelbaum, Michael
Michaels, Rune 194
Michaels, Ski
See Pellowski, Michael (Joseph)
Michaels, Steve 1955- 71
Michaels, William M. 1917- 77
Michalak, Jamie 1973- 217
Michel, Anna 1943- 49
Brief entry 40
Michel, Francois 1948- 82
Michelin, Linda 183
Michelson, Richard 198
Earlier sketch in SATA 173
Micich, Paul 74
Mickelson, Scott 1963- 213
Micklish, Rita 1931- 12
Micklos, John, Jr. 1956- 173
Earlier sketch in SATA 129
Micklos J., John, Jr. 1956-
See Micklos, John, Jr.
Micucci, Charles (Patrick, Jr.) 1959- 144
Earlier sketch in SATA 82
Middleton, Haydn 1955- 152
Earlier sketch in SATA 85
Miers, Earl Schenck 1910-1972 1
Obituary 26
Migdale, Lawrence 1951- 89
Miglio, Paige 1966- 201
Mikaelsen, Ben 1952- 173
Earlier sketches in SATA 73, 107
Mikaelsen, Benjamin John
See Mikaelsen, Ben
Miklowitz, Gloria D. 1927- 129
Earlier sketches in SATA 4, 68
See also SAAS 17
Mikolaycak, Charles 1937-1993 78
Obituary 75
Earlier sketch in SATA 9
See also SAAS 4
Mild, Warren (Paul) 1922- 41
Milelli, Pascal 1965- 135
Miles, Betty 1928- 78
Earlier sketch in SATA 8
See also SAAS 9
Miles, Miska
See Martin, Patricia Miles
Miles, (Mary) Patricia 1930- 29
Miles, Patricia A.
See Martin, Patricia Miles
Miles, Victoria 1966- 188
Milgrim, David 223
Earlier sketches in SATA 158, 187
Milgrom, Harry 1912-1978 25
Milhous, Katherine 1894-1977 15
Milich, Zoran 174
Milios, Rita 1949- 79
Militant
See Sandburg, Carl
Millais, Raoul 1901- 77
Millar, Barbara F. 1924- 12
Millar, Margaret (Ellis Sturm) 1915-1994 61
Obituary 79
Millard, Glenda 203
Millard, Kerry 204
Millbank, Captain H. R.
See Ellis, Edward S.
Millen, C(ynthia) M. 1955- 114
Miller, Albert G(riffith) 1905-1982 12
Obituary 31
Miller, Alice Ann 1958- 150
Miller, Alice P(atricia McCarthy) 22
Miller, Allan 1978- 216
Miller, Christopher 1976- 215

Miller, Debbie 1951- 160
Earlier sketch in SATA 103
Miller, Debbie S.
See Miller, Debbie
Miller, Deborah Uchill 1944- 61
Miller, Don 1923- 15
Miller, Doris R.
See Mosesson, Gloria R(ubin)
Miller, Eddie
See Miller, Edward
Miller, Edna Anita 1920- 29
Miller, Edward 1905-1974 8
Miller, Edward 1964- 218
Earlier sketch in SATA 183
Miller, Elizabeth 1933- 41
Miller, Ellanita 1957- 87
Miller, Eugene 1925- 33
Miller, Frances A. 1937- 52
Brief entry 46
Miller, Heather Lynn 1971- 214
Miller, Helen M(arkley) -1984 5
Miller, Helen Topping 1884-1960
Obituary 29
Miller, Jane (Judith) 1925-1989 15
Miller, Jewel 1956- 73
Miller, John
See Samachson, Joseph
Miller, Judi 117
Miller, Karen 1949- 210
Miller, Karen Hokanson
See Miller, Karen
Miller, Kate 1948- 193
Miller, Kirsten 1973- 185
Miller, Louise (Rolfe) 1940- 76
Miller, M. L. 85
Miller, Madge 1918- 63
Miller, Margaret J.
See Dale, Margaret J(essy) Miller
Miller, Marilyn (Jean) 1925- 33
Miller, Marvin 65
Miller, Mary
See Northcott, (William) Cecil
Miller, Mary Beth 1942- 9
Miller, Mary Beth 1964- 185
Miller, Maryann 1943- 73
Miller, Natalie 1917-1976 35
Miller, Pat 1951- 214
Miller, Robert H. 1944- 91
Miller, Ron 1947- 185
Miller, Ruth White
See White, Ruth
Miller, Sandra
See Miller, Sandy
Miller, Sandra Peden
See Miller, Sandy
Miller, Sandy 1948- 41
Brief entry 35
Miller, Sarah 1969- 175
Miller, Virginia
See Austin, Virginia
Miller, William R. 1959- 116
Miller Brothers
See Miller, Allan
Milligan, Bryce 1953- 170
Milligan, Spike
See Milligan, Terence Alan
Milligan, Terence Alan 1918-2002 29
Obituary 134
See also CLR 92
Millington, Ada
See Deyneka, Anita
Millman, Isaac 1933- 140
Mills, Adam
See Stanley, George Edward
Mills, Claudia 1954- 191
Brief entry 41
Earlier sketches in SATA 44, 89, 145
Mills, Elaine (Rosemary) 1941- 72
Mills, G. Riley 196
Mills, Joyce C. 1944- 102
Mills, Judith Christine 1956- 130

Mills, Yaroslava Surmach 1925-2008 35
Millspaugh, Ben P. 1936- 77
Millstead, Thomas E. 30
Millward, Gwen 202
Milne, A. A. 1882-1956 100
See also YABC 1
See also CLR 108
Milne, Alan Alexander
See Milne, A. A.
Milne, Lorus J. 5
See also CLR 22
See also SAAS 18
Milne, Margery 5
See also CLR 22
See also SAAS 18
Milne, Terry
See Milne, Theresa Ann
Milne, Theresa Ann 1964- 84
Milnes, Irma McDonough 1924- 101
Milonas, Rolf
See Myller, Rolf
Milone, Karen
See Dugan, Karen
Milone-Dugan, Karen
See Dugan, Karen
Milord, Susan 1954- 200
Earlier sketches in SATA 74, 147
Milotte, Alfred G(eorge) 1904-1989 11
Obituary 62
Milstein, Linda 1954- 80
Milton, Ann 134
Milton, Hilary (Herbert) 1920- 23
Milton, John R(onald) 1924- 24
Milton, Joyce 1946- 101
Brief entry 41
Earlier sketch in SATA 52
Milusich, Janice 216
Milverton, Charles A.
See Penzler, Otto
Milway, Alex 1978- 215
Milway, Katie Smith 1960- 203
Minahan, John A. 1956- 92
Minar, Barbra (Goodyear) 1940- 79
Minard, Rosemary 1939- 63
Minarik, Else Holmelund 1920- 127
Earlier sketch in SATA 15
See also CLR 33
Miner, Jane Claypool 1933- 103
Brief entry 37
Earlier sketch in SATA 38
Miner, Lewis S. 1909-1971 11
Mines, Jeanette 1948- 61
Mines, Jeanette Marie
See Mines, Jeanette
Minier, Nelson
See Stoutenburg, Adrien (Pearl)
Minnitt, Ronda Jacqueline
See Armitage, David
Minor, Wendell 1944- 199
Earlier sketches in SATA 78, 109, 164
Minter, Daniel 1961- 176
Mintonye, Grace 4
Miranda, Anne 1954- 109
Earlier sketch in SATA 71
Miranda, Inaki 1983(?)- 207
Mirocha, Paul 192
Mirsky, Jeannette 1903-1987 8
Obituary 51
Mirsky, Reba Paeff 1902-1966 1
Misako Rocks! 192
Misenta, Marisol
See Innes, Stephanie
Mishica, Clare 1960- 91
Miskovits, Christine 1939- 10
Miss Frances
See Horwich, Frances R(appaport)
Miss Read
See Saint, Dora Jessie
Mister Rogers
See Rogers, Fred McFeely

Mitchard, Jacquelyn 1956- *219*
  Earlier sketches in SATA *98, 168*
Mitchell, Adrian 1932-2008 .... *166*
  Obituary *200*
  Earlier sketch in SATA *104*
Mitchell, Allison
  See Griffin, W. E. B.
Mitchell, Betty Jo
  See Mitchell, B.J.
Mitchell, B.J. 1931- *120*
Mitchell, Clyde
  See Ellison, Harlan
  and Silverberg, Robert
Mitchell, Cynthia 1922- *29*
Mitchell, (Sibyl) Elyne (Keith) 1913- *10*
Mitchell, Gladys (Maude Winifred)
  1901-1983 .... *46*
  Obituary *35*
Mitchell, Jay
  See Roberson, Jennifer
Mitchell, Joyce Slayton 1933- *142*
  Brief entry *43*
  Earlier sketch in SATA *46*
Mitchell, K. L.
  See Lamb, Elizabeth Searle
Mitchell, Kathy 1948- *59*
Mitchell, Lori 1961- *128*
Mitchell, Margaree King 1953- *84*
Mitchell, Marianne 1947- *145*
Mitchell, Rhonda *89*
Mitchell, Saundra 1974(?)- *217*
Mitchell, Stephen 1943- *199*
Mitchell, Susan
  See Mitchell, Susan K.
Mitchell, Susan K. 1972- *210*
Mitchell, Todd 1974- *191*
Mitchell, Yvonne 1925-1979
  Obituary *24*
Mitchelson, Mitch
  See Mitchelson, Peter Richard
Mitchelson, Peter Richard 1950- *104*
Mitchison, Naomi (Margaret Haldane)
  1897-1999 .... *24*
  Obituary *112*
Mitchnik, Helen 1901-1982 .... *41*
  Brief entry *35*
Mitchum, Hank
  See Knott, William C(ecil, Jr.)
  and Murray, Stuart A. P.
  and Newton, D(wight) B(ennett)
  and Sherman, Jory (Tecumseh)
Mitgutsch, Ali 1935- *76*
Mitsuhashi, Yoko *45*
  Brief entry *33*
Mitton, Jacqueline 1948- *162*
  Earlier sketches in SATA *66, 115*
Mitton, Simon 1946- *66*
Mitton, Tony 1951- *203*
  Earlier sketches in SATA *104, 149*
Miura, Taro 1968- *181*
Mizner, Elizabeth Howard 1907- *27*
Mizumura, Kazue *18*
Mlynowski, Sarah 1977(?)- *180*
Mobin-Uddin, Asma *216*
  Earlier sketch in SATA *172*
Mobley, Joe A. 1945- *91*
Moche, Dinah (Rachel) L(evine) 1936- *44*
  Brief entry *40*
Mochi, Ugo (A.) 1889-1977 .... *38*
Mochizuki, Ken 1954- *146*
  Earlier sketch in SATA *81*
  See also SAAS *22*
Modarressi, Mitra 1967- *200*
  Earlier sketch in SATA *126*
Modell, Frank B. 1917- *39*
  Brief entry *36*
Modesitt, Jeanne 1953- *217*
  Earlier sketches in SATA *92, 143*
Modesitt, L.E., Jr. 1943- *164*
  Earlier sketch in SATA *91*

Modesitt, Leland Exton, Jr.
  See Modesitt, L.E., Jr.
Modrell, Dolores 1933- *72*
Moe, Barbara 1937- *20*
Moe, Jorgen (Ingebretsen) 1813-1882
  See CLR *104*
Moed-Kass, Pnina *169*
Moerbeek, Kees 1955- *98*
Moeri, Louise 1924- *93*
  Earlier sketch in SATA *24*
  See also SAAS *10*
Moesta, Rebecca 1956- *182*
Moffett, Jami 1952- *84*
Moffett, Mark W. 1957(?)- *203*
Moffett, Martha (Leatherwood) 1934- *8*
Mogensen, Suzanne A(ncher) 1946- *129*
Mohammed, Khadra *197*
Mohanty, Raja *223*
Mohn, Peter B(urnet) 1934- *28*
Mohn, Viola Kohl 1914- *8*
Mohr, Nicholasa 1938- *97*
  Autobiography Feature *113*
  Earlier sketch in SATA *8*
  See also CLR *22*
  See also SAAS *8*
Mok, Esther 1953- *93*
Molan, Christine 1943- *84*
Molarsky, Osmond 1909- *16*
Moldon, Peter L(eonard) 1937- *49*
Mole, John 1941- *103*
  Earlier sketch in SATA *36*
  See also CLR *61*
Molesworth, Mary Louisa 1839-1921 .... *98*
  See also CLR *166*
Molin, Charles
  See Mayne, William
Molina, Silvia 1946- *97*
Molk, Laurel 1957- *162*
  Earlier sketch in SATA *92*
Mollel, Tololwa M. 1952- *88*
Molloy, Anne Baker 1907-1999 .... *32*
Molloy, Michael (John) 1940- *162*
Molloy, Paul (George) 1924- *5*
Moloney, James 1954- *202*
  Autobiography Feature *144*
  Earlier sketches in SATA *94, 144*
Molski, Carol *215*
Momaday, N. Scott 1934- *48*
  Brief entry *30*
Momaday, Navarre Scott
  See Momaday, N. Scott
Monaco, Octavia 1963- *169*
Monagle, Bernie 1957- *121*
Moncure, Jane Belk 1926- *23*
Monjo, F(erdinand) N(icholas III)
  1924-1978 .... *16*
  See also CLR *2*
Monk, Isabell 1952- *136*
Monks, Lydia *189*
Monroe, Chris 1962- *219*
Monroe, Christine
  See Monroe, Chris
Monroe, Lyle
  See Heinlein, Robert A.
Monroe, Marion
  See Cox, Marion Monroe
Monroy, Manuel 1970- *196*
Monsell, Helen Albee 1895-1971 .... *24*
Monson-Burton, Marianne 1975- *139*
Montana, Bob 1920-1975
  Obituary *21*
Montanari, Eva 1977- *209*
Montecalvo, Janet *177*
Montenegro, Laura Nyman 1953- *95*
Montero, Gloria 1933- *109*
Montes, Marisa 1951- *144*
Montgomerie, Norah (Mary) 1913- *26*
Montgomery, Constance
  See Cappel, Constance
Montgomery, Elizabeth
  See Julesberg, Elizabeth Rider Montgomery

Montgomery, Elizabeth Rider
  See Julesberg, Elizabeth Rider Montgomery
Montgomery, Hugh (Edward) 1962- *146*
Montgomery, L. M. 1874-1942 .... *100*
  See also YABC *1*
  See also CLR *145*
Montgomery, Lucy Maud
  See Montgomery, L. M.
Montgomery, Michael G. 1952- *208*
Montgomery, Raymond A. (Jr.) 1936- *39*
Montgomery, Rutherford George 1894-1985 . *3*
Montgomery, Sy 1958- *184*
  Autobiography Feature *132*
  Earlier sketches in SATA *114, 132*
Montgomery, Vivian *36*
Monthei, Betty *179*
Montijo, Rhode *179*
Montileaux, Donald F. 1948- *183*
Montpetit, Charles 1958- *101*
Montresor, Beni 1926-2001 .... *38*
  Earlier sketch in SATA *3*
  See also SAAS *4*
Montserrat, Pep *181*
Monty Python
  See Chapman, Graham
  and Cleese, John (Marwood)
  and Gilliam, Terry
  and Idle, Eric
  and Jones, Terence Graham Parry
  and Palin, Michael
Moodie, Craig 1956- *172*
Moodie, Fiona 1952- *133*
Moody, Minerva
  See Alcott, Louisa May
Moody, Ralph Owen 1898-1982 .... *1*
Moon, Carl 1879(?)-1948 .... *25*
Moon, Grace (Purdie) 1877(?)-1947 .... *25*
Moon, Lily
  See Warnes, Tim
Moon, Nicola 1952- *147*
  Earlier sketch in SATA *96*
Moon, Pat 1946- *113*
Moon, Sheila 1910-1991 .... *5*
  Obituary *114*
Moon, Sheila Elizabeth
  See Moon, Sheila
Mooney, Bel 1946- *95*
Mooney, Bill 1936- *122*
Mooney, Elizabeth C(omstock) 1918-1986
  Obituary *48*
Mooney, William
  See Mooney, Bill
Moor, Emily
  See Deming, Richard
Moorcock, Michael 1939- *166*
  Earlier sketch in SATA *93*
Moorcock, Michael John
  See Moorcock, Michael
Moorcock, Michael John
  See Moorcock, Michael
Moore, Anne Carroll 1871-1961 .... *13*
Moore, Cheri
  See Ladd, Cheryl (Jean)
Moore, Clement Clarke 1779-1863 .... *18*
Moore, Cyd 1957- *186*
  Earlier sketches in SATA *83, 133*
Moore, Don W. 1905(?)-1986
  Obituary *48*
Moore, Elaine 1944- *86*
Moore, Eva 1942- *103*
  Earlier sketch in SATA *20*
Moore, Ishbel (Lindsay) 1954- *140*
Moore, Jack (William) 1941- *46*
  Brief entry *32*
Moore, Janet Gaylord 1905-1992 .... *18*
Moore, Jim 1946- *42*
Moore, John Travers 1908- *12*
Moore, Lilian 1909-2004 .... *137*
  Obituary *155*
  Earlier sketch in SATA *52*
  See also CLR *15*

Moore, Liz
  See Moore, M. Elizabeth
Moore, M. Elizabeth 1959- *156*
Moore, Margaret R(umberger) 1903- *12*
Moore, Margie *224*
  Earlier sketch in SATA *176*
Moore, Marianne 1887-1972 .... *20*
Moore, Marianne Craig
  See Moore, Marianne
Moore, Patrick (Alfred Caldwell) 1923- *49*
  Brief entry *39*
  See also SAAS 8
Moore, Patrick 1959- *184*
Moore, Perry 1971-2011 .... *193*
Moore, Peter 1963- *175*
Moore, Peter G.
  See Moore, Peter
Moore, Raina 1970- *212*
Moore, Ray (S.) 1905(?)-1984
  Obituary *37*
Moore, Regina
  See Dunne, Mary Collins
Moore, Rosalie (Gertrude) 1910-2001 .... *9*
Moore, Ruth (Ellen) 1908-1989 .... *23*
Moore, Ruth Nulton 1923- *38*
Moore, S(arah) E. *23*
Moore, Sarah Margaret
  See Hodges, Margaret
Moore, Stephanie Perry 1969(?)- *214*
Moore, Tara 1950- *61*
Moore, Yvette 1958- *154*
  Earlier sketches in SATA *69, 70*
Moores, Dick
  See Moores, Richard (Arnold)
Moores, Richard (Arnold) 1909-1986
  Obituary *48*
Mooser, Stephen 1941- *75*
  Earlier sketch in SATA *28*
Mora, Francisco X(avier) 1952- *90*
Mora, Pat 1942- *186*
  Earlier sketches in SATA *92, 134*
  See also CLR 58
Mora, Patricia
  See Mora, Pat
Morais, Flavio *207*
Morales, Magaly *225*
Morales, Yuyi *180*
  Earlier sketch in SATA *154*
Moran, Tom 1943- *60*
Moranville, Sharelle Byars *196*
  Earlier sketch in SATA *152*
Moray Williams, Ursula 1911-2006 .... *3*
  Obituary *177*
  See also SAAS 9
Mordecai, Martin *220*
Morden, Simon 1966(?)- *211*
Mordhorst, Heidi 1964- *222*
Mordvinoff, Nicolas 1911-1973 .... *17*
More, Caroline
  See Cone, Molly (Lamken)
  and Strachan, Margaret Pitcairn
Moreau, Jean-Pierre
  See Jarrie, Martin
Moreno, Rene King *190*
Moreton, Andrew Esq.
  See Defoe, Daniel
Morey, Charles
  See Fletcher, Helen Jill
Morey, Walt(er Nelson) 1907-1992 .... *51*
  Obituary *70*
  Earlier sketch in SATA *3*
  See also SAAS 9
Morgan, Alfred P(owell) 1889-1972 .... *33*
Morgan, Alison (Mary) 1930- *85*
  Earlier sketch in SATA *30*
Morgan, Anne 1954- *121*
Morgan, Christopher 1956- *199*
Morgan, Clay 1950- *198*
Morgan, Douglas
  See Macdonald, James D.

Morgan, Ellen
  See Bumstead, Kathleen Mary
Morgan, Geoffrey 1916- *46*
Morgan, Helen (Gertrude Louise)
  1921-1990 .... *29*
Morgan, Jane
  See Cooper, James Fenimore
  and Franklin, Jane (Morgan)
  and Moren, Sally M(oore)
Morgan, Lenore H. 1908-1976 .... *8*
Morgan, Mary 1957- *213*
  Earlier sketches in SATA *81, 114*
Morgan, McKayla
  See Basile, Gloria Vitanza
Morgan, Michaela
  See Basile, Gloria Vitanza
Morgan, Nicola 1961- *161*
Morgan, Nina 1953- *110*
Morgan, Pierr 1952- *122*
  Earlier sketch in SATA *77*
Morgan, Robin (Evonne) 1941- *80*
Morgan, Roxanne
  See Gentle, Mary
Morgan, Sarah (Nicola) 1959- *68*
Morgan, Shirley
  See Kiepper, Shirley Morgan
Morgan, Stacy T(owle) 1959- *104*
Morgan, Stevie
  See Davies, Nicola
Morgan, Tom 1942- *42*
Morgan, Wendy
  See Staub, Wendy Corsi
Morgan-Vanroyen, Mary
  See Morgan, Mary
Morgenstern, Susie Hoch 1945- *133*
Mori, Hana 1909-1990(?) *88*
Mori, Kyoko 1957- *122*
  Autobiography Feature *126*
  See also CLR 64
  See also SAAS 26
Moriarty, Jaclyn 1968- *162*
Moriarty, William J. 1930- *127*
Morice, Dave 1946- *93*
Morin, Isobel V. 1928- *110*
Morine, Hoder
  See Conroy, John Wesley
Morley, Ben *228*
Morley, Taia *199*
Morley, Wilfred Owen
  See Lowndes, Robert A(ugustine) W(ard)
Morningstar, Mildred (Whaley) 1912-1997 .. *61*
  Obituary *114*
Morozumi, Atsuko *217*
  Earlier sketch in SATA *110*
Morpurgo, Michael 1943- *225*
  Earlier sketches in SATA *93, 143, 184*
  See also CLR 51
Morrah, Dave
  See Morrah, David Wardlaw, Jr.
Morrah, David Wardlaw, Jr. 1914-1991 .... *10*
Morreale-de la Garza, Phyllis
  See De la Garza, Phyllis
Morressy, John 1930-2006 .... *23*
Morrill, Leslie H(olt) 1934-2003 .... *48*
  Brief entry *33*
  Obituary *148*
  See also SAAS 22
Morris, Carla *210*
Morris, Carla D.
  See Morris, Carla
Morris, Chris(topher Crosby) 1946- *66*
Morris, Deborah 1956- *91*
Morris, Desmond 1928- *14*
Morris, Desmond John
  See Morris, Desmond
Morris, Don 1954- *83*
Morris, Gerald 1963- *207*
  Earlier sketches in SATA *107, 150*
Morris, Gerald Paul
  See Morris, Gerald
Morris, Gilbert (Leslie) 1929- *104*

Morris, Jackie *202*
  Earlier sketch in SATA *151*
Morris, Janet (Ellen) 1946- *66*
Morris, Jay
  See Tatham, Julie Campbell
Morris, (Margaret) Jean 1924- *98*
Morris, Jeffrey
  See Morris, Jeffrey Brandon
Morris, Jeffrey B.
  See Morris, Jeffrey Brandon
Morris, Jeffrey Brandon 1941- *92*
Morris, Jennifer E. 1969- *179*
Morris, Jill 1936- *165*
  Earlier sketch in SATA *119*
Morris, Juddi *85*
Morris, Judy K. 1936- *61*
Morris, Oradel Nolen *128*
Morris, Richard 1969- *224*
Morris, Robert A(da) 1933- *7*
Morris, William 1913-1994 .... *29*
Morrison, Angela *218*
Morrison, Bill 1935- *66*
  Brief entry *37*
Morrison, Chloe Anthony Wofford
  See Morrison, Toni
Morrison, Dorothy Nafus *29*
Morrison, Frank 1971- *226*
  Earlier sketch in SATA *185*
Morrison, Gordon 1944- *183*
  Earlier sketches in SATA *87, 128*
Morrison, Joan 1922- *65*
Morrison, Lillian 1917- *108*
  Earlier sketch in SATA *3*
Morrison, Lucile Phillips 1896- *17*
Morrison, Martha A. 1948- *77*
Morrison, Meighan 1966- *90*
Morrison, P.R. *196*
Morrison, Richard
  See Lowndes, Robert A(ugustine) W(ard)
Morrison, Robert
  See Lowndes, Robert A(ugustine) W(ard)
Morrison, Roberta
  See Webb, Jean Francis (III)
Morrison, Slade 1964-2010 .... *228*
Morrison, Susan Dudley
  See Gold, Susan Dudley
Morrison, Taylor 1971- *187*
  Earlier sketches in SATA *95, 159*
Morrison, Toni 1931- *144*
  Earlier sketch in SATA *57*
  See also CLR 99
Morrison, Velma Ford 1909- *21*
Morrison, Wilbur Howard 1915- *64*
Morrison, William
  See Samachson, Joseph
Morriss, James E(dward) 1932- *8*
Morrissey, Dean *183*
Morrow, Barbara Olenyik 1952- *167*
Morrow, Betty
  See Bacon, Elizabeth
Morrow, Sue Anne 1966- *218*
Morse, C. Scott
  See Morse, Scott
Morse, Carol
  See Yeakley, Marjory Hall
Morse, C.S.
  See Morse, Scott
Morse, Dorothy B(ayley) 1906-1979
  Obituary *24*
Morse, Flo 1921- *30*
Morse, Scott 1973- *200*
Morse, Tony 1953- *129*
Mort, Vivian
  See Cromie, Alice Hamilton
Mortensen, Denise Dowling *179*
Mortensen, Lori 1955- *221*
Mortimer, Anne 1958- *206*
  Earlier sketch in SATA *116*
Mortimer, Mary H.
  See Coury, Louise Andree
Morton, Alexandra (Hubbard) 1957- *144*

Morton, Anthony
See Arthur, Robert, (Jr.)
Morton, Christine
See Morton-Shaw, Christine
Morton, Jane 1931- 50
Morton, Joseph C. 1932- 156
Morton, Lee Jack, Jr. 1928- 32
Morton, Miriam 1918(?)-1985 9
Obituary 46
Morton-Shaw, Christine 1957- 211
Mosatche, Harriet 1949- 122
Mosatche, Harriet S.
See Mosatche, Harriet
Moscow, Alvin 1925- 3
Mosel, Arlene (Tichy) 1921-1996 7
Moseley, James W(illett) 1931- 139
Moseng, Elisabeth 1967- 90
Moser, Barry 1940- 185
Earlier sketches in SATA 56, 79, 138
See also CLR 49
See also SAAS 15
Moser, Don(ald Bruce) 1932- 31
Moser, Laura 194
Moser, Lisa 192
Moses, Sheila P. 1961- 168
Moses, Will 1956- 178
Earlier sketch in SATA 120
Mosesson, Gloria R(ubin) 24
Mosher, Richard 1949- 120
Moskin, Marietta D(unston) 1928- 23
Moskof, Martin Stephen 1930- 27
Mosley, Francis 1957- 57
Moss, Don(ald) 1920- 11
Moss, Elaine (Dora) 1924- 57
Brief entry 31
Moss, Jeff(rey) 1942-1998 73
Obituary 106
Moss, Marissa 1959- 216
Earlier sketches in SATA 71, 104, 163
See also CLR 134
Moss, Miriam 1955- 202
Earlier sketches in SATA 76, 140
Moss, Thylias 1954- 108
Moss, Thylias Rebecca Brasier
See Moss, Thylias
Most, Bernard 1937- 134
Brief entry 40
Earlier sketches in SATA 48, 91
Mosz, Gosia 1972- 194
Mott, Evelyn Clarke 1962- 133
Earlier sketch in SATA 75
Motz, Lloyd 1909-2004 20
Mould, Chris 205
Mould, Edwin
See Whitlock, Ralph
Moulton, Mark Kimball 212
Mouly, Francoise 155
Mountain, Robert
See Montgomery, Raymond A. (Jr.)
Mountfield, David
See Grant, Neil
Mourlevat, Jean-Claude 1952- 187
Mourning, Tuesday 206
Moussard, Jacqueline 1924- 24
Mowat, Claire 1933- 123
Mowat, Claire Angel Wheeler
See Mowat, Claire
Mowat, Farley 1921- 55
Earlier sketch in SATA 3
See also CLR 20
Mowat, Farley McGill
See Mowat, Farley
Mowll, Joshua 1970(?)- 188
Mowry, Jess 1960- 131
Autobiography Feature 131
Earlier sketch in SATA 109
See also CLR 65
Moxley, Sheila 1966- 96
Moyer, Terry J. 1937- 94
Moyes, Patricia
See Haszard, Patricia Moyes

Moyler, Alan (Frank Powell) 1926- 36
Mozelle, Shirley 179
Mozley, Charles 1915- 43
Brief entry 32
Mphahlele, Es'kia 1919-2008 119
Obituary 198
Mphahlele, Ezekiel
See Mphahlele, Es'kia
Mphahlele, Zeke
See Mphahlele, Es'kia
Mr. McGillicuddy
See Abisch, Roslyn Kroop
Mr. Sniff
See Abisch, Roslyn Kroop
Mr. Tivil
See Lorkowski, Thomas V(incent)
Mr. Wizard
See Herbert, Don
Mraz, David 1947- 219
Mrs. Fairstar
See Horne, Richard Henry Hengist
Muchamore, Robert 1972- 175
Muchmore, Jo Ann 1937- 103
Mude, O.
See Gorey, Edward (St. John)
Mudgeon, Apeman
See Mitchell, Adrian
Mueller, Jorg 1942- 67
See also CLR 43
Mueller, Miranda R. 201
Mueller, Virginia 1924- 28
Muggs
See Watkins, Lois
Muir, Diana
See Appelbaum, Diana Muir Karter
Muir, Frank (Herbert) 1920-1998 30
Muir, Helen 1937- 65
Muirhead, Margaret 220
Mukerji, Dhan Gopal 1890-1936 40
See also CLR 10
Mulcahy, Lucille Burnett 12
Muldrow, Diane 229
Mulford, Philippa 1948- 112
Earlier sketch in SATA 43
Mulford, Philippa Greene
See Mulford, Philippa G.
Mulgan, Catherine 1931- 24
Mulila, Vigad G.
See Maillu, David G(ian)
Mull, Brandon 1974- 190
Mullen, Michael 1937- 122
Muller, Billex
See Ellis, Edward S.
Muller, Birte 1973- 214
Muller, Jorg
See Mueller, Jorg
Muller, (Lester) Robin 1953- 86
Mullin, Caryl Cude 1969- 130
Mullins, Edward S(wift) 1922- 10
Mullins, Hilary 1962- 84
Mulock, Dinah Maria
See Craik, Dinah Maria (Mulock)
Mulvihill, William Patrick 1923- 8
Mumford, Ruth
See Dallas, Ruth
Mumy, Bill 1954- 112
Mun
See Leaf, (Wilbur) Munro
Munari, Bruno 1907-1998 15
See also CLR 9
Munce, Ruth Hill 1898- 12
Mundy, Simon 1954- 64
Mundy, Simon Andrew James Hainault
See Mundy, Simon
Munger, Nancy 170
Munowitz, Ken 1935-1977 14
Munoz, Claudio 208
Munoz, William 1949- 92
Earlier sketch in SATA 42
Munro, Alice 1931- 29

Munro, Alice Anne
See Munro, Alice
Munro, Eleanor 1928- 37
Munro, Roxie 1945- 223
Earlier sketches in SATA 58, 136, 184
Munsch, Bob
See Munsch, Robert (Norman)
Munsch, Robert (Norman) 1945- 120
Brief entry 48
Earlier sketches in SATA 50, 83
See also CLR 19
Munsinger, Lynn 1951- 221
Earlier sketches in SATA 33, 94, 177
Munson, Derek 1970- 139
Munson, R. W.
See Karl, Jean E(dna)
Munson-Benson, Tunie 1946- 15
Munsterberg, Peggy 1921- 102
Muntean, Michaela 182
Munthe, Nelly 1947- 53
Munves, James (Albert) 1922- 30
Munzer, Martha E. 1899-1999 4
Murawski, Darlyne A. 193
Murch, Mel
See Manes, Stephen
Murdoch, David H(amilton) 1937- 96
Murdoch, Patricia 1957- 192
Murdock, Catherine Gilbert 185
Murhall, J(acqueline) J(ane) 1964- 143
Murphy, Barbara Beasley 1933- 130
Earlier sketch in SATA 5
Murphy, Claire Rudolf 1951- 137
Earlier sketch in SATA 76
Murphy, E(mmett) Jefferson 1926- 4
Murphy, Elizabeth Ann Maureen
See Murphy, Liz
Murphy, Jill 1949- 214
Earlier sketches in SATA 37, 70, 142
See also CLR 39
Murphy, Jill Frances
See Murphy, Jill
Murphy, Jim 1947- 224
Brief entry 32
Earlier sketches in SATA 37, 77, 124, 185
See also CLR 53
Murphy, Joseph E., Jr. 1930- 65
Murphy, Kelly 1977- 190
Earlier sketch in SATA 143
Murphy, Liz 1964- 210
Murphy, Louise 1943- 155
Murphy, Mary 1961- 196
Murphy, Pat
See Murphy, E(mmett) Jefferson
Murphy, Patricia J. 1963- 132
Murphy, Rita 180
Murphy, Robert (William) 1902-1971 10
Murphy, Shirley Rousseau 1928- 126
Earlier sketches in SATA 36, 71
See also SAAS 18
Murphy, Stuart J. 1942- 157
Earlier sketch in SATA 115
Murphy, Thomas Basil, Jr. 1935- 191
Murphy, Tim
See Murphy, Jim
Murphy, Tom
See Murphy, Thomas Basil, Jr.
Murray, John 1923- 39
Murray, Kirsty 1960- 165
Earlier sketch in SATA 108
Murray, Marguerite 1917- 63
Murray, Marian 5
Murray, Martine 1965- 125
Murray, (Judith) Michele (Freedman)
1933-1974 7
Murray, Ossie 1938- 43
Murray, Peter
See Hautman, Pete
Murrow, Liza Ketchum
See Ketchum, Liza
Musgrave, Florence 1902-1999 3

Musgrove, Margaret W(ynkoop) 1943- 124
  Earlier sketch in SATA 26
Musgrove, Marianne 207
Mussey, Virginia Howell
  See Ellison, Virginia H(owell)
Mussey, Virginia T.H.
  See Ellison, Virginia H(owell)
Mussi, Sarah 206
Mutel, Cornelia F. 1947- 74
Muth, Jon J. 206
  Earlier sketch in SATA 165
Mutz
  See Kuenstler, Morton
Mwangi, Meja 1948- 174
My Brother's Brother
  See Chekhov, Anton
Myers, Anna 220
  Earlier sketch in SATA 160
Myers, Arthur 1917- 91
  Earlier sketch in SATA 35
Myers, Bernice 81
  Earlier sketch in SATA 9
Myers, Caroline Elizabeth Clark
  1887-1980 28
Myers, Christopher 1975- 183
  See also CLR 97
Myers, Edward 1950- 227
  Earlier sketches in SATA 96, 172
Myers, Elisabeth P(erkins) 1918- 36
Myers, (Mary) Hortense (Powner)
  1913-1987 10
Myers, Jack 1913-2006 83
  Obituary 178
Myers, Jack Edgar
  See Myers, Jack
Myers, Lou 1915-2005 81
  Obituary 171
Myers, Louis
  See Myers, Lou
Myers, R.E. 1924- 119
Myers, Robert Eugene
  See Myers, R.E.
Myers, Tim 1953- 176
  Earlier sketch in SATA 147
Myers, Timothy Joseph
  See Myers, Tim
Myers, Walter Dean 1937- 229
  Brief entry 27
  Earlier sketches in SATA 41, 71, 109, 157,
  193
  See also CLR 110
  See also SAAS 2
Myers, Walter M.
  See Myers, Walter Dean
Myller, Rolf 1926-2006 27
  Obituary 175
Myra, Harold L(awrence) 1939- 46
  Brief entry 42
Myracle, Lauren 1969- 204
  Earlier sketch in SATA 162
Myrus, Donald (Richard) 1927- 23
Mysterious Traveler, The
  See Arthur, Robert, (Jr.)

N

Na, An 149
Naaslund, Goorel Kristina 1940- 170
Nadel, Laurie 1948- 74
Naden, Corinne J. 1930- 166
  Earlier sketch in SATA 79
Nadimi, Suzan 188
Nadol, Jen 228
Nagda, Ann Whitehead 199
Nagel, Andreas Fischer
  See Fischer-Nagel, Andreas
Nagel, Heiderose Fischer
  See Fischer-Nagel, Heiderose
Nagle, Shane 176

Nahoko, Uehashi
  See Uehashi, Nahoko
Naidoo, Beverley 1943- 180
  Earlier sketches in SATA 63, 135
  See also CLR 29
Nails, Jennifer 213
Naiyomah, Wilson Kimeli 1977- 226
Nakae, Noriko 1940- 59
Nakata, Hiroe 205
Nakatani, Chiyoko 1930-1981 55
  Brief entry 40
  See also CLR 30
Nally, Susan W. 1947- 90
Namioka, Lensey 1929- 157
  Autobiography Feature 116
  Earlier sketches in SATA 27, 89
  See also CLR 48
  See also SAAS 24
Namovicz, Gene Inyart 1927- 6
Nance, Andrew 210
Nanji, Shenaaz 1954- 204
  Earlier sketch in SATA 131
Nanogak Agnes 1925- 61
Napier, Mark
  See Laffin, John (Alfred Charles)
Napoli, Donna Jo 1948- 190
  Earlier sketches in SATA 92, 137
  See also CLR 51
  See also SAAS 23
Napp, Daniel 1974- 204
Narahashi, Keiko 1959- 115
  Earlier sketch in SATA 79
Narayan, R. K. 1906-2001 62
Narayan, Rasipuram Krishnaswami
  See Narayan, R. K.
Nascimbene, Yan 1949- 173
  Earlier sketch in SATA 133
Nash, Bruce M(itchell) 1947- 34
Nash, Fredric Ogden
  See Nash, Ogden
Nash, Linell
  See Smith, Linell Nash
Nash, Mary (Hughes) 1925- 41
Nash, Ogden 1902-1971 46
  Earlier sketch in SATA 2
Nash, Renea Denise 1963- 81
Nast, Elsa Ruth
  See Watson, Jane Werner
Nast, Thomas 1840-1902 51
  Brief entry 33
Nastick, Sharon 1954- 41
Natale, Vince 196
Natalini, Sandro 1970- 222
Natarajan, Srividya 187
Nathan, Adele (Gutman) 1900(?)-1986
  Obituary 48
Nathan, Amy 155
  Earlier sketch in SATA 104
Nathan, Dorothy (Goldeen) (?)-1966 15
Nathan, Robert (Gruntal) 1894-1985 6
  Obituary 43
Nathanson, Laura Walther 1941- 57
Nation, Kaleb 1988- 222
Natti, Lee 1919- 67
  Earlier sketch in SATA 1
  See also SAAS 3
Natti, Susanna 1948- 125
  Earlier sketch in SATA 32
Nau, Thomas 186
Naughtie, Eleanor
  See Updale, Eleanor
Naughton, Bill
  See Naughton, William John (Francis)
Naughton, James Franklin 1957- 85
Naughton, Jim
  See Naughton, James Franklin
Naughton, William John (Francis)
  1910-1992 86
Navarra, John Gabriel 1927- 8
Nayeri, Dina 226
Naylor, Penelope 1941- 10

Naylor, Phyllis 1933-
  See Naylor, Phyllis Reynolds
Naylor, Phyllis Reynolds 1933- 209
  Autobiography Feature 152
  See also CLR 135
  See also SAAS 10
Nazarian, Nikki
  See Nichols, Cecilia Fawn
Nazaroff, Alexander I(vanovich) 1898-1981 .. 4
Nazoa, Aquiles 1920-1976 198
Neal, Harry Edward 1906-1993 5
  Obituary 76
Neal, Michael
  See Teitelbaum, Michael
Nearing, Penny 1916- 47
  Brief entry 42
Nebel, Gustave E. 45
  Brief entry 33
Nebel, Mimouca
  See Nebel, Gustave E.
Nee, Kay Bonner 10
Needham, Kate 1962- 95
Needle, Jan 1943- 98
  Earlier sketch in SATA 30
  See also CLR 43
  See also SAAS 23
Needleman, Jacob 1934- 6
Neel, David 1960- 82
Neel, Preston 1959- 93
Neff, Henry H. 1973- 221
Negri, Rocco 1932- 12
Negrin, Fabian 1963- 189
Neidigh, Sherry 1956- 204
Neier, Aryeh 1937- 59
Neigoff, Anne 13
Neigoff, Mike 1920- 13
Neilan, Eujin Kim 1969- 200
Neilson, Frances Fullerton (Jones)
  1910-2001 14
Neimark, Anne E. 1935- 145
  Earlier sketch in SATA 4
Neimark, Paul G. 1934- 80
  Brief entry 37
Neitzel, Shirley 1941- 134
  Earlier sketch in SATA 77
Nell
  See Hanna, Nell(ie L.)
Nelscott, Kris
  See Rusch, Kristine Kathryn
Nelson, Blake 1960- 177
Nelson, Catherine Chadwick 1926- 87
Nelson, Cordner 1918-2009 54
  Brief entry 29
Nelson, Cordner Bruce
  See Nelson, Cordner
Nelson, D.A. 1970- 215
Nelson, Dawn Ann
  See Nelson, D.A.
Nelson, Drew 1952- 77
Nelson, Esther L. 1928- 13
Nelson, Jandy 229
Nelson, Jim A.
  See Stotter, Mike
Nelson, Julie L. 1970- 117
Nelson, Kadir 213
  Earlier sketches in SATA 154, 181
Nelson, Kris
  See Rusch, Kristine Kathryn
Nelson, Lawrence E(rnest) 1928-1977
  Obituary 28
Nelson, Marilyn 1946- 60
  Autobiography Feature 180
Nelson, Mary Carroll 1929- 23
Nelson, O. Terry 1941- 62
Nelson, Peter 1953- 73
Nelson, Peter N.
  See Nelson, Peter
Nelson, R. A. 197
Nelson, Richard K(ing) 1941- 65
Nelson, Robin Laura 1971- 141
Nelson, Roy Paul 1923- 59

Nelson, S.D. *181*
Nelson, Sharlene (P.) 1933- *96*
Nelson, Suzanne 1976- *184*
Nelson, Ted (W.) 1931- *96*
Nelson, Theresa 1948- *143*
   Autobiography Feature *143*
   Earlier sketch in SATA *79*
Nelson, Vaunda Micheaux 1953- *220*
Nemeth, Sally *187*
Neri, G. *197*
Neri, Greg
   See Neri, G.
Neri, Gregory
   See Neri, G.
Nerlove, Miriam 1959- *53*
   Brief entry *49*
Nesbit, E. 1858-1924 .... *100*
   See also YABC *1*
   See also CLR *70*
Nesbit, Edith
   See Nesbit, E.
Nesbit, Troy
   See Folsom, Franklin (Brewster)
Nespojohn, Katherine V(eronica) 1912-1975 . *7*
Ness, Evaline (Michelow) 1911-1986 .... *26*
   Obituary *49*
   Earlier sketch in SATA *1*
   See also CLR *6*
   See also SAAS *1*
Ness, Patrick 1971- *207*
Nestor, Larry 1940- *149*
Nestor, William P(rodromos) 1947- *49*
Nethery, Mary *93*
Neubecker, Robert *214*
   Earlier sketch in SATA *170*
Neuberger, Julia (Babette Sarah) 1950- *142*
   Earlier sketch in SATA *78*
Neufeld, John (Arthur) 1938- *131*
   Autobiography Feature *131*
   Earlier sketches in SATA *6, 81*
   See also CLR *52*
   See also SAAS *3*
Neuhaus, David 1958- *83*
Neumeyer, Peter F(lorian) 1929- *13*
Neurath, Marie (Reidemeister) 1898-1986 ..... *1*
Neuschwander, Cindy 1953- *157*
   Earlier sketch in SATA *107*
Neusner, Jacob 1932- *38*
Neville, Charles
   See Bodsworth, (Charles) Fred(erick)
Neville, Emily Cheney 1919- *1*
   See also SAAS *2*
Neville, Mary
   See Woodrich, Mary Neville
Nevins, Albert (Francis) J(erome)
   1915-1997 .... *20*
Nevius, Carol 1955- *186*
Newberger, Devra
   See Speregen, Devra Newberger
Newberry, Clare Turlay 1903-1970 .... *1*
   Obituary *26*
Newbery, John 1713-1767 .... *20*
   See also CLR *147*
Newbery, Linda 1952- *184*
   Earlier sketch in SATA *142*
Newbigging, Martha *198*
Newbold, Greg *199*
Newcomb, Ellsworth
   See Kenny, Ellsworth Newcomb
Newcombe, Eugene A. 1923-1990 .... *45*
   Brief entry *33*
Newcombe, Jack
   See Newcombe, Eugene A.
Newcome, Robert 1955- *91*
Newcome, Zita 1959- *88*
Newell, Crosby
   See Bonsall, Crosby Barbara (Newell)
Newell, Edythe W(eatherford) 1910-1989 .... *11*
Newell, Hope Hockenberry 1896-1965 .... *24*
Newfeld, Frank 1928- *26*
Newgarden, Mark 1959- *194*

Newland, Gillian *220*
Newlon, (Frank) Clarke 1905(?)-1982 .... *6*
   Obituary *33*
Newman, Barbara Johansen *191*
Newman, C.J.
   See Newman, Coleman J.
Newman, Coleman J. 1935- *82*
Newman, Daisy 1904-1994 .... *27*
   Obituary *78*
Newman, Gerald 1939- *46*
   Brief entry *42*
Newman, Jeff 1976- *228*
Newman, Jerry
   See Newman, Coleman J.
Newman, Leslea 1955- *134*
   Earlier sketches in SATA *71, 128*
Newman, Margaret
   See Potter, Margaret
Newman, Marjorie *146*
Newman, Matthew (Harrison) 1955- *56*
Newman, Nanette 1934- *162*
Newman, Robert (Howard) 1909-1988 .... *87*
   Obituary *60*
   Earlier sketch in SATA *4*
Newman, Shirlee P(etkin) *144*
   Earlier sketches in SATA *10, 90*
Newsom, Carol 1948- *92*
   Earlier sketch in SATA *40*
Newsom, Tom 1944- *80*
Newth, Mette 1942- *140*
Newton, David E(dward) 1933- *67*
Newton, James R(obert) 1935- *23*
Newton, Jill 1964- *200*
Newton, Robert 1965- *191*
Newton, Suzanne 1936- *77*
   Earlier sketch in SATA *5*
Newton, Vanessa
   See Newton, Vanessa Brantley
Newton, Vanessa Brantley 1962(?)- *206*
Ney, John 1923- *43*
   Brief entry *33*
Nez, John *218*
   Earlier sketch in SATA *155*
Nez, John Abbott
   See Nez, John
Ng, Franklin *82*
Ngui, Marc 1972- *229*
Nguyen, Vincent *226*
   Earlier sketch in SATA *187*
Nichol, B(arrie) P(hillip) 1944-1988 .... *66*
Nicholas, Louise D.
   See Watkins, Dawn L.
Nicholls, Judith (Ann) 1941- *61*
Nicholls, Sally 1983- *209*
Nichols, Cecilia Fawn 1906-1987 .... *12*
Nichols, Grace 1950- *164*
   Earlier sketch in SATA *98*
Nichols, Janet (Louise) 1952- *67*
Nichols, Judy 1947- *124*
Nichols, Leigh
   See Koontz, Dean
Nichols, Michael 1952- *215*
Nichols, Nick
   See Nichols, Michael
Nichols, Paul
   See Hawks, Robert
Nichols, Peter
   See Youd, Samuel
Nichols, (Joanna) Ruth 1948- *15*
   See also CLR *149*
Nichols, Travis *206*
Nicholson, C. R.
   See Nicole, Christopher
Nicholson, Christina
   See Nicole, Christopher
Nicholson, Joyce Thorpe 1919-2011 .... *35*
Nicholson, Lois P. 1949- *88*
Nicholson, Robin
   See Nicole, Christopher
Nicholson, William *180*

Nicholson, William 1872-1949
   See CLR *76*
Nickel, Barbara 1966- *188*
Nickell, Joe 1944- *167*
   Earlier sketch in SATA *73*
Nickelsburg, Janet 1893-1983 .... *11*
Nickerson, Betty 1922- *14*
Nickerson, Elizabeth
   See Nickerson, Betty
Nickl, Barbara (Elisabeth) 1939- *56*
Nicklaus, Carol *62*
   Brief entry *33*
Nickle, John *181*
Nickless, Will 1902-1979(?) *66*
Nic Leodhas, Sorche
   See Alger, Leclaire (Gowans)
Nicol, Ann
   See Turnbull, Ann
Nicolas
   See Mordvinoff, Nicolas
Nicolay, Helen 1866-1954
   See YABC *1*
Nicole, Christopher 1930- *5*
Nicole, Christopher Robin
   See Nicole, Christopher
Nicoll, Helen 1937- *87*
Nicolson, Cynthia Pratt 1949- *141*
Ni Dhuibhne, Eilis 1954- *91*
Niehaus, Paddy Bouma
   See Bouma, Paddy
Nields, Nerissa 1967- *166*
Nielsen, Kay (Rasmus) 1886-1957 .... *16*
   See also CLR *16*
Nielsen, Laura F. 1960- *93*
Nielsen, Laura Farnsworth
   See Nielsen, Laura F.
Nielsen, Nancy J. 1951- *77*
Nielsen, Susin 1964- *195*
Nielsen, Virginia
   See McCall, Virginia Nielsen
Nielsen-Fernlund, Susin
   See Nielsen, Susin
Niemann, Christoph 1970- *191*
Nieuwsma, Milton J(ohn) 1941- *142*
Nightingale, Sandy 1953- *76*
Nikolajeva, Maria 1952- *127*
Nikola-Lisa, W. 1951- *180*
   Earlier sketch in SATA *71*
Niland, Deborah 1951- *172*
   Earlier sketch in SATA *27*
Niland, Kilmeny *75*
Nilsen, Anna 1948- *174*
   Earlier sketch in SATA *96*
Nilsson, Eleanor 1939- *117*
   Earlier sketch in SATA *81*
   See also SAAS *23*
Nilsson, Per 1954- *159*
Nimmo, Jenny 1944- *144*
   Earlier sketch in SATA *87*
   See also CLR *44*
Nishimura, Kae *196*
Niven, Larry 1938- *171*
   Earlier sketch in SATA *95*
Niven, Laurence Van Cott
   See Niven, Larry
Niven, Laurence VanCott
   See Niven, Larry
Nivola, Claire A. 1947- *208*
   Earlier sketches in SATA *84, 140*
Nix, Garth 1963- *210*
   Earlier sketches in SATA *97, 143*
   See also CLR *68*
Nixon, Hershell Howard 1923- *42*
Nixon, Joan Lowery 1927-2003 .... *115*
   Obituary *146*
   Earlier sketches in SATA *8, 44, 78*
   See also CLR *24*
   See also SAAS *9*
Nixon, K.
   See Nixon, Kathleen Irene (Blundell)

Nixon, Kathleen Irene (Blundell)
    1894-1988(?) *14*
    Obituary *59*
Nobati, Eugenia 1968- *201*
Nobisso, Josephine 1953- *121*
    Earlier sketch in SATA *78*
Noble, Iris (Davis) 1922-1986 .... *5*
    Obituary *49*
Noble, Marty 1947- *125*
    Earlier sketch in SATA *97*
Noble, Trinka Hakes 1944- *197*
    Brief entry *37*
    Earlier sketch in SATA *123*
Nobleman, Marc Tyler 1972- *203*
Noda, Takayo 1961- *168*
Nodelman, Perry 1942- *101*
Nodset, Joan L.
    See Lexau, Joan M.
Noel Hume, Ivor 1927- *65*
Noestlinger, Christine
    See Nostlinger, Christine
Noguere, Suzanne 1947- *34*
Nolan, Dennis 1945- *166*
    Brief entry *34*
    Earlier sketches in SATA *42, 92*
Nolan, Han 1956- *157*
    Earlier sketch in SATA *109*
Nolan, Janet 1956- *191*
    Earlier sketch in SATA *145*
Nolan, Jeannette Covert 1897-1974 .... *2*
    Obituary *27*
Nolan, Lucy *215*
Nolan, Paul T(homas) 1919- *48*
Nolan, William F. 1928- *88*
    Brief entry *28*
Nolan, William Francis
    See Nolan, William F.
Nolen, Jerdine 1953- *157*
    Earlier sketch in SATA *105*
Noll, Amanda *219*
Noll, Sally 1946- *82*
Noonan, Brandon 1979- *184*
Noonan, Diana 1960- *146*
Noonan, Julia 1946- *148*
    Earlier sketches in SATA *4, 95*
Norac, Carl 1960- *166*
Norcross, John
    See Conroy, John Wesley
Nordan, Robert W(arren) 1934-2004 .... *133*
Nordhoff, Charles Bernard 1887-1947 .... *23*
Nordlicht, Lillian *29*
Nordstrom, Ursula 1910-1988 .... *3*
    Obituary *57*
Nordtvedt, Matilda 1926- *67*
Norling, Beth 1969- *149*
Norman, Charles 1904-1996 .... *38*
    Obituary *92*
Norman, Geoffrey *223*
Norman, Howard
    See Norman, Howard A.
Norman, Howard A. 1949- *81*
Norman, James
    See Schmidt, James Norman
Norman, Jay
    See Arthur, Robert, (Jr.)
Norman, Lilith 1927- *120*
    Earlier sketch in SATA *86*
Norman, Mary 1931- *36*
Norman, Steve
    See Pashko, Stanley
Norment, Lisa 1966- *91*
Norris, Gunilla Brodde 1939- *20*
North, Andrew
    See Norton, Andre
North, Anthony
    See Koontz, Dean
North, Captain George
    See Stevenson, Robert Louis
North, Captain George
    See Stevenson, Robert Louis

North, Howard
    See Trevor, Elleston
North, Joan 1920- *16*
North, Milou
    See Erdrich, Louise
North, Robert
    See Withers, Carl A.
North, Sara
    See Bonham, Barbara Thomas
    and Hager, Jean
North, Sherry *201*
North, Sterling 1906-1974 .... *45*
    Obituary *26*
    Earlier sketch in SATA *1*
Northcott, (William) Cecil 1902-1987
    Obituary *55*
Northeast, Brenda V(ictoria) 1948- *106*
Northmore, Elizabeth Florence 1906-1974 . *122*
Norton, Alice Mary
    See Norton, Andre
Norton, Andre 1912-2005 .... *91*
    Earlier sketches in SATA *1, 43*
    See also CLR *50*
Norton, Browning
    See Norton, Frank R. B(rowning)
Norton, Frank R. B(rowning) 1909-1989 ..... *10*
Norton, Mary 1903-1992 .... *60*
    Obituary *72*
    Earlier sketch in SATA *18*
    See also CLR *140*
Nosredna, Trebor
    See Anderson, Bob
Nostlinger, Christine 1936- *162*
    Brief entry *37*
    Earlier sketch in SATA *64*
    See also CLR *12*
Nourse, Alan E(dward) 1928-1992 .... *48*
    See also CLR *33*
Novak, Matt 1962- *204*
    Brief entry *52*
    Earlier sketches in SATA *60, 104, 165*
Novelli, Luca 1947- *61*
Novgorodoff, Danica 1982(?)- *215*
Nowell, Elizabeth Cameron *12*
Noyes, Deborah 1965- *194*
    Earlier sketch in SATA *145*
Nugent, Cynthia 1954- *205*
Nugent, Nicholas 1949- *73*
Numberman, Neil 1981(?)- *220*
Numeroff, Laura 1953- *206*
    Earlier sketches in SATA *28, 90, 142*
    See also CLR *85*
Numeroff Joffe, Laura
    See Numeroff, Laura
Nunes, Lygia Bojunga 1932- *154*
    Earlier sketch in SATA *75*
Nunn, Laura (Donna) Silverstein 1968- *124*
Nurenberg, Thelma
    See Greenhaus, Thelma Nurenberg
Nurnberg, Maxwell 1897-1984 .... *27*
    Obituary *41*
Nussbaumer, Paul (Edmund) 1934- *16*
Nutt, Ken 1951- *163*
    Earlier sketch in SATA *97*
Nuttall-Smith, Margaret Emily Noel 1919- .. *26*
Nuygen, Mathieu 1967- *80*
Nuzum, K. A. *195*
Nuzum, Kathy A.
    See Nuzum, K. A.
Nwapa, Flora (Nwanzuruaha) 1931-1993
    See CLR *162*
Nyberg, (Everett Wayne) Morgan 1944- *87*
Nyce, (Nellie) Helene von Strecker
    1885-1969 .... *19*
Nyce, Vera 1862-1925 .... *19*
Nye, Naomi Shihab 1952- *198*
    Earlier sketches in SATA *86, 147*
    See also CLR *59*
Nye, Robert 1939- *6*
Nyeu, Tao *206*
Nyikos, Stacy A. 1969- *164*

Nystrom, Carolyn 1940- *130*
    Earlier sketch in SATA *67*

O

O. Henry
    See Henry, O.
Oakes, Elizabeth H. 1964- *132*
Oakes, Vanya 1909-1983 .... *6*
    Obituary *37*
Oakley, Don(ald G.) 1927- *8*
Oakley, Graham 1929- *84*
    Earlier sketch in SATA *30*
    See also CLR *7*
Oakley, Helen (McKelvey) 1906- *10*
Oaks, J. Adams *220*
Oana, Katherine 1929- *53*
    Brief entry *37*
Oates, Eddie H. 1943- *88*
Oates, Joyce Carol 1938- *159*
Oates, Stephen B(aery) 1936- *59*
Obed, Ellen Bryan 1944- *74*
Oberle, Joseph 1958- *69*
Oberman, Sheldon 1949-2004 .... *85*
    Autobiography Feature *114*
    Obituary *153*
    See also CLR *54*
    See also SAAS *26*
Obligado, Lilian (Isabel) 1931- *61*
    Brief entry *45*
Obrant, Susan 1946- *11*
O'Brian, E.G.
    See Clarke, Arthur C.
O'Brien, Anne Sibley 1952- *213*
    Brief entry *48*
    Earlier sketches in SATA *53, 80*
O'Brien, E.G.
    See Clarke, Arthur C.
O'Brien, Esse Forrester 1895(?)-1975
    Obituary *30*
O'Brien, Johnny *222*
O'Brien, Patrick 1960- *193*
O'Brien, Robert C.
    See Conly, Robert Leslie
O'Brien, Thomas C. 1938-2010 .... *29*
O'Brien, Thomas Clement
    See O'Brien, Thomas C.
O'Callaghan, Julie 1954- *113*
O'Callahan, Jay 1938- *88*
O'Carroll, Ryan
    See Markun, Patricia Maloney
Ochiltree, Dianne 1953- *117*
Ockham, Joan Price
    See Price, Joan
O'Connell, Margaret F(orster) 1935-1977 .... *30*
    Obituary *30*
O'Connell, Peg
    See Ahern, Margaret McCrohan
O'Connell, Rebecca 1968- *212*
    Earlier sketch in SATA *130*
O'Connor, Barbara 1950- *193*
    Earlier sketch in SATA *154*
O'Connor, Francine M(arie) 1930- *90*
O'Connor, Genevieve A. 1914- *75*
O'Connor, George *228*
    Earlier sketch in SATA *183*
O'Connor, Ian 1965- *188*
O'Connor, Jane 1947- *186*
    Brief entry *47*
    Earlier sketches in SATA *59, 103, 150*
O'Connor, Karen 1938- *89*
    Earlier sketch in SATA *34*
O'Connor, Patrick
    See Wibberley, Leonard
O'Connor, Richard 1915-1975
    Obituary *21*
O'Conor, Jane 1958- *78*

Odaga, Asenath (Bole) 1937- *130*
  Earlier sketch in SATA *67*
  See also SAAS *19*
O Danachair, Caoimhin
  See Danaher, Kevin
Odanaka, Barbara *159*
O'Daniel, Janet 1921- *24*
O'Day, Cathy
  See Crane, Barbara (Joyce)
O'Dell, Scott 1898-1989 .... *134*
  Earlier sketches in SATA *12, 60*
  See also CLR *126*
Odenwald, Robert P(aul) 1899-1965 .... *11*
Odgers, Sally
  See Odgers, Sally Farrell
Odgers, Sally Farrell 1957- *139*
  Earlier sketch in SATA *72*
Odone, Jamison 1980- *209*
O'Donnell, Dick
  See Lupoff, Richard A(llen)
  and Thompson, Don(ald Arthur)
O'Donnell, Liam 1970- *209*
Odriozola, Elena *186*
Oechsli, Kelly 1918-1999 .... *5*
Oesterle, Virginia Rorby
  See Rorby, Ginny
Ofek, Uriel 1926- *36*
  See also CLR *28*
Ofer, Avi 1975- *207*
Offenbacher, Ami 1958- *91*
Offill, Jenny 1968- *211*
Offit, Sidney 1928- *10*
Ofosu-Appiah, L(awrence) H(enry) 1920- ... *13*
Ogan, George F. 1912-1983 .... *13*
Ogan, M. G.
  See Ogan, George F.
  and Ogan, Margaret E. (Nettles)
Ogan, Margaret E. (Nettles) 1923-1979 .... *13*
Ogburn, Charlton (Jr.) 1911-1998 .... *3*
  Obituary *109*
Ogburn, Jacqueline K. *162*
Ogilvie, Elisabeth May 1917-2006 .... *40*
  Brief entry *29*
  Obituary *176*
Ogilvy, Gavin
  See Barrie, J. M.
Ogilvy, Ian 1943- *177*
Ogilvy, Ian Raymond
  See Ogilvy, Ian
Ogle, Lucille Edith 1904-1988
  Obituary *59*
Ogletree, Charles J. 1952- *175*
O'Green, Jennifer
  See Roberson, Jennifer
O'Green, Jennifer Roberson
  See Roberson, Jennifer
O'Hagan, Caroline 1946- *38*
O'Hanlon, Jacklyn
  See Meek, Jacklyn O'Hanlon
O'Hara, Elizabeth
  See Ni Dhuibhne, Eilis
O'Hara, Kenneth
  See Morris, (Margaret) Jean
O'Hara, Mary
  See Alsop, Mary O'Hara
O'Hara (Alsop), Mary
  See Alsop, Mary O'Hara
O'Hare, Jeff(rey A.) 1958- *105*
O'hearn, Kate *225*
Ohi, Ruth 1964- *95*
Ohiyesa
  See Eastman, Charles A(lexander)
Ohlsson, Ib 1935- *7*
Ohmi, Ayano 1959- *115*
Ohtomo, Yasuo 1946- *37*
o huigin, sean 1942- *138*
  See also CLR *75*
Oiseau
  See Moseley, James W(illett)
Oke, Janette 1935- *97*

O'Keefe, Susan Heyboer *176*
  Earlier sketch in SATA *133*
O'Keeffe, Frank 1938- *99*
O'Kelley, Mattie Lou 1908-1997 .... *97*
  Earlier sketch in SATA *36*
Okimoto, Jean Davies 1942- *103*
  Earlier sketch in SATA *34*
Okomfo, Amasewa
  See Cousins, Linda
olafsdottir, Gudrun Elin
  See Gunnella
Olaleye, Isaac O. 1941- *96*
  See also SAAS *23*
Olcott, Frances Jenkins 1872(?)-1963 .... *19*
Old, Wendie C(orbin) 1943- *154*
Old Boy
  See Hughes, Thomas
Oldenburg, E(gbert) William 1936-1974 ...... *35*
Older, Effin 1942- *114*
Older, Jules 1940- *156*
  Earlier sketch in SATA *114*
Oldfield, Jenny 1949- *140*
Oldfield, Margaret J(ean) 1932- *56*
Oldfield, Pamela 1931- *86*
Oldham, June *70*
Oldham, Mary 1944- *65*
Oldland, Nicholas 1972- *223*
Olds, Elizabeth 1896-1991 .... *3*
  Obituary *66*
Olds, Helen Diehl 1895-1981 .... *9*
  Obituary *25*
Oldstyle, Jonathan
  See Irving, Washington
O'Leary, Brian (Todd) 1940- *6*
O'Leary, Chris *208*
O'Leary, Patsy B. 1937- *97*
O'Leary, Patsy Baker
  See O'Leary, Patsy B.
Oleynikov, Igor 1953- *202*
Oliphant, B.J.
  See Tepper, Sheri S.
Oliver, Burton
  See Burt, Olive Woolley
Oliver, Chad
  See Oliver, Symmes C.
Oliver, John Edward 1933- *21*
Oliver, Lauren 1982- *228*
Oliver, Lin *202*
Oliver, Marilyn Tower 1935- *89*
Oliver, Mark 1960- *214*
Oliver, Narelle 1960- *197*
  Earlier sketch in SATA *152*
Oliver, Shirley (Louise Dawkins) 1958- *74*
Oliver, Symmes C. 1928-1993 .... *101*
Oliviero, Jamie 1950- *84*
Olmsted, Lorena Ann 1890-1989 .... *13*
Olney, Ross R. 1929- *13*
Olschewski, Alfred (Erich) 1920- *7*
Olsen, Barbara *148*
Olsen, Carol 1945- *89*
Olsen, Ib Spang 1921- *81*
  Earlier sketch in SATA *6*
Olsen, Violet (Mae) 1922-1991 .... *58*
Olson, Arielle North 1932- *67*
Olson, David J. 1974- *198*
Olson, Gene 1922- *32*
Olson, Gretchen *187*
Olson, Helen Kronberg *48*
Olson, Kay Melchisedech 1948- *175*
Olson, Marianne
  See Mitchell, Marianne
Olson-Brown, Ellen 1967- *183*
Olten, Manuela 1970- *197*
Olugebefola, Ademole 1941- *15*
Oluonye, Mary N(kechi) 1955- *111*
Om
  See Gorey, Edward (St. John)
O'Malley, Donough *208*
O'Malley, Kevin 1961- *191*
  Earlier sketch in SATA *157*
Oman, Carola (Mary Anima) 1897-1978 ..... *35*

O'Mara, Carmel 1965- *166*
O'Mara-Horwitz, Carmel
  See O'Mara, Carmel
O'Meara, Walter (Andrew) 1897-1989 .... *65*
Ommanney, F(rancis) D(ownes) 1903-1980 . *23*
Omololu, Cynthia Jaynes *222*
O Mude
  See Gorey, Edward (St. John)
Oneal, Elizabeth 1934- *82*
  Earlier sketch in SATA *30*
  See also CLR *13*
O'Neal, Katherine Pebley 1957- *204*
O'Neal, Reagan
  See Jordan, Robert
O'Neal, Regan
  See Jordan, Robert
Oneal, Zibby
  See Oneal, Elizabeth
O'neill, Alexis 1949- *220*
O'Neill, Amanda 1951- *111*
O'Neill, Catharine *203*
O'Neill, Gerard K(itchen) 1927-1992 .... *65*
O'Neill, Judith (Beatrice) 1930- *34*
O'Neill, Mary L(e Duc) 1908(?)-1990 .... *2*
  Obituary *64*
O'Neill, Reagan
  See Jordan, Robert
Onslow, Annette Rosemary MacArthur
  See MacArthur-Onslow, Annette Rosemary
Onslow, John 1906-1985
  Obituary *47*
Onyefulu, Ifeoma 1959- *157*
  Earlier sketches in SATA *81, 115*
Opie, Iona (Margaret Balfour) 1923- *118*
  Earlier sketches in SATA *3, 63*
  See also SAAS *6*
Opie, Peter (Mason) 1918-1982 .... *118*
  Obituary *28*
  Earlier sketches in SATA *3, 63*
Oppel, Kenneth 1967- *199*
  Earlier sketches in SATA *99, 153*
Oppel, Kenneth Kerry
  See Oppel, Kenneth
Oppenheim, Joanne 1934- *174*
  Earlier sketches in SATA *5, 82, 136*
Oppenheim, Shulamith Levey 1928- *177*
Oppenheimer, Joan L(etson) 1925- *28*
Oppong, Joseph Ransford 1953- *160*
Optic, Oliver
  See Adams, William Taylor
  and Stratemeyer, Edward L.
Oram, Hiawyn 1946- *101*
  Earlier sketch in SATA *56*
Orbach, Ruth Gary 1941- *21*
Orback, Craig *197*
Orczy, Emma
  See Orczy, Baroness Emmuska
Orczy, Emma Magdalena Rosalia Maria Josefa
  See Orczy, Baroness Emmuska
Orczy, Emmuska
  See Orczy, Baroness Emmuska
Orczy, Baroness Emmuska 1865-1947 .... *40*
Orde, A.J.
  See Tepper, Sheri S.
O'Reilly, Jackson
  See Jordan, Robert
Orenstein, Denise Gosliner 1950- *157*
Orgad, Dorit 1936- *199*
Orgel, Doris 1929- *148*
  Earlier sketches in SATA *7, 85*
  See also CLR *48*
  See also SAAS *19*
Orgill, Roxane *198*
Oriolo, Joe
  See Oriolo, Joseph D.
Oriolo, Joseph D. 1913-1985
  Obituary *46*
Orlandelli, Alessandro
  See Horley, Alex
Orlean, Susan 1955- *209*
Orleans, Ilo 1897-1962 .... *10*

Orlev, Uri 1931- *135*
  Earlier sketch in SATA *58*
  See also CLR *30*
  See also SAAS *19*
Ormai, Stella *57*
  Brief entry *48*
Ormerod, Jan 1946- *210*
  Brief entry *44*
  Earlier sketches in SATA *55, 70, 132*
  See also CLR *20*
Ormerod, Janette Louise
  See Ormerod, Jan
Ormes, Jackie
  See Ormes, Zelda J.
Ormes, Zelda J. 1914-1986
  Obituary *47*
Ormondroyd, Edward 1925- *14*
Ormsby, Virginia H(aire) 1906-1990 .... *11*
Orona-Ramirez, Kristy 1964- *189*
Orozco, Jose-Luis 1948- *179*
Orr, Katherine S(helley) 1950- *72*
Orr, Wendy 1953- *206*
  Earlier sketches in SATA *90, 141*
Orris
  See Ingelow, Jean
Orth, Richard
  See Gardner, Richard (M.)
Ortiz Cofer, Judith
  See Cofer, Judith Ortiz
Orwell, George 1903-1950 .... *29*
  See also CLR *68*
Orwin, Joanna 1944- *141*
Os, Eric van
  See van Os, Erik
Osborn, Elinor 1939- *145*
Osborn, Jacob 1981(?)- *215*
Osborn, Kathy 1955(?)- *199*
Osborn, Lois D(orothy) 1915- *61*
Osborne, Charles 1927- *59*
Osborne, Chester G(orham) 1915-1987 .... *11*
Osborne, David
  See Silverberg, Robert
Osborne, George
  See Silverberg, Robert
Osborne, Leone Neal 1914-1996 2
Osborne, Linda Barrett 1949- *215*
Osborne, Mary Pope 1949- *144*
  Earlier sketches in SATA *41, 55, 98*
  See also CLR *88*
Osceola
  See Blixen, Karen
Osgood, William E(dward) 1926- *37*
O'Shaughnessy, Darren
  See Shan, Darren
O'Shaughnessy, Ellen Cassels 1937- *78*
O'shaughnessy, Tam 1951- *221*
O'Shea, Catherine Patricia Shiels
  See O'Shea, Pat
O'Shea, Pat 1931-2007 .... *87*
  See also CLR *18*
Osmond, Edward 1900- *10*
Ossoli, Sarah Margaret
  See Fuller, Margaret
Ostendorf, (Arthur) Lloyd, (Jr.) 1921-2000 .. *65*
  Obituary *125*
Osterweil, Adam 1972- *217*
Ostow, Micol 1976- *223*
  Earlier sketch in SATA *170*
Otfinoski, Steven 1949- *116*
  Earlier sketch in SATA *56*
Otis, James
  See Kaler, James Otis
O'Toole, Thomas 1941- *71*
O'Trigger, Sir Lucius
  See Horne, Richard Henry Hengist
Otten, Charlotte
  See Otten, Charlotte F.
Otten, Charlotte F. 1926- *98*
Otten, Charlotte Fennema
  See Otten, Charlotte F.

Ottley, Matt 1962- *171*
  Earlier sketch in SATA *102*
Ottley, Reginald Leslie 1909-1985 .... *26*
  See also CLR *16*
Otto, Margaret Glover 1909-1976
  Obituary *30*
Otto, Svend
  See Soerensen, Svend Otto
Ouellet, Debbie 1954- *219*
Oughton, Jerrie (Preston) 1937- *131*
  Earlier sketch in SATA *76*
Oughton, (William) Taylor 1925- *104*
Ouida
  See De La Ramee, Marie Louise
Ousley, Odille 1896-1976 .... *10*
Outcalt, Todd 1960- *123*
Overmyer, James E. 1946- *88*
Overton, Jenny (Margaret Mary) 1942- *52*
  Brief entry *36*
Owen, Ann
  See Qualey, Marsha
Owen, Annie 1949- *75*
Owen, Caroline Dale
  See Snedeker, Caroline Dale (Parke)
Owen, Clifford
  See Hamilton, Charles (Harold St. John)
Owen, Dilys
  See Gater, Dilys
Owen, (Benjamin) Evan 1918-1984 .... *38*
Owen, (John) Gareth 1936-2002 .... *162*
  Earlier sketch in SATA *83*
  See also CLR *31*
  See also SAAS *14*
Owen, James A. *185*
Owens, Bryant 1968- *116*
Owens, Dana Elaine
  See Queen Latifah
Owens, Gail 1939- *54*
Owens, Mary Beth *191*
Owens, Thomas S(heldon) 1960- *86*
Owens, Tom
  See Owens, Thomas S(heldon)
Oxenbury, Helen 1938- *149*
  Earlier sketches in SATA *3, 68*
  See also CLR *70*
Oxendine, Bess Holland 1933- *90*
Oz, Frank (Richard) 1944- *60*
Ozer, Jerome S. 1927- *59*

P

Paananen, Eloise (Katherine) 1923-1993 9
Pace, Lorenzo 1943- *131*
Pace, Mildred Mastin 1907- *46*
  Brief entry *29*
Pachter, Hedwig (?)-1988 .... *63*
Pack, Janet 1952- *77*
Pack, Robert 1929- *118*
Packard, Edward 1931- *148*
  Earlier sketches in SATA *47, 90*
Packer, Kenneth L. 1946- *116*
Packer, Vin
  See Meaker, Marijane
Pad, Peter
  See Stratemeyer, Edward L.
Page, Eileen
  See Heal, Edith
Page, Eleanor
  See Coerr, Eleanor (Beatrice)
Page, Gail 1950- *205*
Page, Jake 1936- *81*
Page, James Keena, Jr.
  See Page, Jake
Page, Lou Williams 1912-1997 .... *38*
Page, Mary
  See Heal, Edith
Page, Robin 1943- *154*
Pagliarulo, Antonio 1977(?)- *212*
Pagnucci, Susan 1944- *90*

Pahlen, Kurt 1907-2003
  Obituary *147*
Pahz, Cheryl
  See Pahz, Cheryl Suzanne
Pahz, Cheryl Suzanne 1949- *11*
Pahz, James Alon 1943- *11*
Paice, Margaret 1920- *10*
Paige, Harry W(orthington) 1922- *41*
  Brief entry *35*
Paige, Richard
  See Koontz, Dean
Paige, Robin
  See Albert, Susan Wittig
Paine, Penelope Colville 1946- *87*
Paine, Roberta M. 1925- *13*
Paisley, Tom 1932- *11*
  See also CLR *3*
Palatini, Margie *207*
  Earlier sketches in SATA *134, 174*
Palazzo, Anthony D.
  See Palazzo, Tony
Palazzo, Tony 1905-1970 .... *3*
Palder, Edward L. 1922- *5*
Palecek, Josef 1932- *56*
Palecek, Libuse 1937- *89*
Palen, Debbie *195*
Palin, Michael 1943- *67*
Palin, Michael Edward
  See Palin, Michael
Palladini, David (Mario) 1946- *40*
  Brief entry *32*
Pallas, Norvin 1918-1983 .... *23*
Pallister, John C(lare) 1891-1980
  Obituary *26*
Pallotta, Gerard Larry
  See Pallotta, Jerry
Pallotta, Jerry 1953- *186*
Pallotta-Chiarolli, Maria 1960- *117*
Palmer, Bernard (Alvin) 1914-1998 .... *26*
Palmer, C. Everard 1930- *14*
Palmer, (Ruth) Candida 1926- *11*
Palmer, Cyril Everard
  See Palmer, C. Everard
Palmer, Don
  See Benson, Mildred
Palmer, Hap 1942- *68*
Palmer, Heidi 1948- *15*
Palmer, Helen Marion
  See Geisel, Helen
Palmer, Jessica 1953- *120*
Palmer, Judd 1972- *153*
Palmer, Juliette 1930- *15*
Palmer, Kate Salley 1946- *97*
Palmer, Maria
  See Strachan, Ian
Palmer, Maria
  See Brennan, Herbie
Palmer, Robin 1909-2000 .... *43*
Palmero Caceres, Ana *198*
Palmisciano, Diane *202*
Paltrowitz, Donna 1950- *61*
  Brief entry *50*
Paltrowitz, Donna Milman
  See Paltrowitz, Donna
Paltrowitz, Stuart 1946- *61*
  Brief entry *50*
Pamela, Todd 1950- *124*
Pamintuan, Macky *214*
  Earlier sketch in SATA *178*
Panagopoulos, Janie Lynn *149*
Panati, Charles 1943- *65*
Panchyk, Richard 1970- *138*
Panetta, George 1915-1969 .... *15*
Panetta, Joseph N. 1953- *96*
Pang, YaWen Ariel *206*
Panik, Sharon 1952- *82*
Panowski, Eileen Thompson 1920- *49*
Pansy
  See Alden, Isabella (Macdonald)
Pantell, Dora (Fuchs) *39*
Panter, Carol 1936- *9*

Paolini, Christopher 1983- *157*
  See also CLR *102*
Papademetriou, Lisa *175*
Paparone, Pam *185*
Paparone, Pamela
  See Paparone, Pam
Papas, Bill
  See Papas, William
Papas, William 1927-2000 .... *50*
Papashvily, George 1898-1978 .... *17*
Papashvily, Helen (Waite) 1906-1996 .... *17*
Pape, D. L.
  See Pape, Donna (Lugg)
Pape, Donna (Lugg) 1930- *82*
  Earlier sketch in SATA *2*
Paperny, Myra (Green) 1932- *51*
  Brief entry *33*
Papineau, Lucie 1962- *224*
Papp, Robert 1967- *205*
Paradis, Adrian A(lexis) 1912- *67*
  Earlier sketch in SATA *1*
  See also SAAS *8*
Paradis, Marjorie Bartholomew
  1886(?)-1970 .... *17*
Paradiz, Valerie 1963- *176*
Paratore, Coleen
  See Paratore, Coleen Murtagh
Paratore, Coleen Murtagh 1958- *200*
Pardo DeLange, Alex *211*
Parenteau, Shirley 1935- *199*
  Brief entry *40*
  Earlier sketch in SATA *47*
Parish, Margaret 1927-1988 .... *73*
  Obituary *59*
  Earlier sketch in SATA *17*
  See also CLR *22*
Parish, Margaret Holt
  See Holt, Margaret
Parish, Peggy
  See Parish, Margaret
Park, Barbara 1947- *123*
  Brief entry *35*
  Earlier sketches in SATA *40, 78*
  See also CLR *34*
Park, Bill
  See Park, W(illiam) B(ryan)
Park, Frances 1955- *171*
Park, Ginger *173*
Park, Janie Jaehyun *150*
Park, Jordan
  See Kornbluth, C(yril) M.
  and Pohl, Frederik
Park, Linda Sue 1960- *200*
  Earlier sketches in SATA *127, 173*
  See also CLR *84*
Park, Nick 1958- *113*
Park, Rosina Ruth Lucia
  See Park, Ruth
Park, Ruth 1917(?)-2010 .... *93*
  Earlier sketch in SATA *25*
  See also CLR *51*
Park, W(illiam) B(ryan) 1936- *22*
Parke, Marilyn 1928- *82*
Parker, Barbara Keevil 1938- *157*
Parker, Daniel
  See Ehrenhaft, Daniel
Parker, Elinor Milnor 1906- *3*
Parker, Jake 1977- *227*
Parker, Julie F. 1961- *92*
Parker, Kim 1963- *174*
Parker, Kristy 1957- *59*
Parker, Lois M(ay) 1912-1996 .... *30*
Parker, Margot M. 1937- *52*
Parker, Marjorie Blain 1960- *205*
  Earlier sketch in SATA *145*
Parker, Mary Jessie 1948- *71*
Parker, Nancy Winslow 1930- *132*
  Earlier sketches in SATA *10, 69*
  See also SAAS *20*
Parker, Richard 1915-1990 .... *14*

Parker, Robert
  See Boyd, Waldo T.
  and Parker, Robert Andrew
Parker, Robert Andrew 1927- *200*
Parker, Steve 1954- *213*
Parker, Tom S. *215*
Parker, Toni Trent 1947-2005 .... *142*
  Obituary *169*
Parker-Rees, Guy *193*
Parker-Rock, Michelle *214*
Parkes, Lucas
  See Harris, John (Wyndham Parkes Lucas)
  Beynon
Parkhill, John
  See Cox, William R(obert)
Parkins, David 1955- *218*
  Earlier sketch in SATA *176*
Parkinson, Curtis *219*
Parkinson, Ethelyn M(inerva) 1906-1999 ..... *11*
Parkinson, Kathryn N. 1954- *71*
Parkinson, Kathy
  See Parkinson, Kathryn N.
Parkinson, Siobhan
  See Parkinson, Siobhan
Parkinson, Siobhan 1954- *178*
Parks, Deborah A. 1948- *133*
  Earlier sketch in SATA *91*
Parks, Edd Winfield 1906-1968 .... *10*
Parks, Gordon 1912-2006 .... *108*
  Obituary *175*
  Earlier sketch in SATA *8*
Parks, Gordon Roger Alexander
  See Parks, Gordon
Parks, Peggy J. 1951- *143*
Parks, PJ
  See Parks, Peggy J.
Parks, Rosa 1913-2005 .... *83*
  Obituary *169*
Parks, Rosa Louise Lee
  See Parks, Rosa
Parks, Van Dyke 1943- *62*
Parlato, Stephen 1954- *222*
Parley, Peter
  See Goodrich, Samuel Griswold
Parlin, John
  See Graves, Charles Parlin
Parme, Fabrice 1966- *191*
Parnall, Peter 1936- *69*
  Earlier sketch in SATA *16*
  See also SAAS *11*
Paros, Jennifer *210*
Parotti, Phillip (Elliott) 1941- *109*
Parr, Ann 1943- *144*
Parr, Danny
  See Parr, Ann
Parr, Letitia (Evelyn) 1906-1985(?) *37*
Parr, Lucy 1924- *10*
Parr, Todd *179*
  Earlier sketch in SATA *134*
Parra, John 1972- *225*
Parrish, Anne 1888-1957 .... *27*
Parrish, Mary
  See Cousins, Margaret
Parrish, Maxfield
  See Parrish, (Frederick) Maxfield
Parrish, (Frederick) Maxfield 1870-1966 ..... *14*
Parry, Marian 1924- *13*
Parry, Rosanne *212*
Parson Lot
  See Kingsley, Charles
Parsons, Alexandra 1947- *92*
Parsons, Ellen
  See Dragonwagon, Crescent
Parsons, Garry 1951- *197*
Parsons, Martin 1951- *116*
Parsons, Martin Leslie
  See Parsons, Martin
Parsons, Tom
  See MacPherson, Thomas George
Parsons-Yazzi, Evangeline *172*

Partch, Virgil Franklin II 1916-1984 .... *39*
  Obituary *39*
Parton, Dolly 1946- *94*
Parton, Dolly Rebecca
  See Parton, Dolly
Partridge, Benjamin W., Jr. 1915-2005 .... *28*
  Obituary *163*
Partridge, Benjamin Waring, Jr.
  See Partridge, Benjamin W., Jr.
Partridge, Cora Cheney
  See Cheney, Cora
Partridge, Elizabeth *216*
  Earlier sketch in SATA *134*
Partridge, Jenny (Lilian) 1947- *52*
  Brief entry *37*
Pasachoff, Naomi 1947- *147*
Pascal, David 1918- *14*
Pascal, Francine 1938- *143*
  Brief entry *37*
  Earlier sketches in SATA *51, 80*
  See also CLR *25*
Paschal, Nancy
  See Trotter, Grace V(iolet)
Paschkis, Julie 1957- *220*
  Earlier sketch in SATA *177*
Pascudniak, Pascal
  See Lupoff, Richard A(llen)
Pashko, Stanley 1913-1982 .... *29*
Pasqualotto, Chiara 1976- *228*
Passailaigue, Thomas E.
  See Paisley, Tom
Pastel, Elyse *201*
Pateman, Robert 1954- *84*
Patent, Dorothy Hinshaw 1940- *162*
  Autobiography Feature *162*
  Earlier sketches in SATA *22, 69, 120*
  See also CLR *19*
  See also SAAS *13*
Paterson, A(ndrew) B(arton) 1864-1941 .... *97*
Paterson, Banjo
  See Paterson, A(ndrew) B(arton)
Paterson, Diane 1946- *177*
  Brief entry *33*
  Earlier sketch in SATA *59*
Paterson, John (Barstow) 1932- *114*
Paterson, Katherine 1932- *204*
  Earlier sketches in SATA *13, 53, 92, 133*
  See also CLR *127*
Paterson, Katherine Womeldorf
  See Paterson, Katherine
Patience, John 1949- *90*
Patneaude, David 1944- *159*
  Earlier sketch in SATA *85*
Paton, Alan 1903-1988 .... *11*
  Obituary *56*
Paton, Alan Stewart
  See Paton, Alan
Paton, Jane (Elizabeth) 1934- *35*
Paton, Priscilla 1952- *98*
Paton Walsh, Gillian
  See Paton Walsh, Jill
Paton Walsh, Jill 1937- *190*
  Autobiography Feature *190*
  Earlier sketches in SATA *4, 72, 109*
  See also CLR *128*
  See also SAAS *3*
Patricelli, Leslie *207*
Patrick, Susan
  See Robins, Patricia
Patron, Susan 1948- *182*
  Earlier sketch in SATA *76*
Patsauq, Markoosie 1942-
  See CLR *23*
Patschke, Steve 1955- *125*
Patten, Brian 1946- *152*
  Earlier sketch in SATA *29*
Patterson, Charles 1935- *59*
Patterson, Geoffrey 1943- *54*
  Brief entry *44*
Patterson, James 1947- *197*
  Earlier sketch in SATA *164*

Patterson, James B.
  See Patterson, James
Patterson, Lillie G. -1999 88
  Earlier sketch in SATA *14*
Patterson, Nancy Ruth 1944- 148
  Earlier sketch in SATA *72*
Patterson, Valerie O. 223
Pattison, Darcy (S.) 1954- 126
  Earlier sketch in SATA *72*
Pattou, Edith 164
Patz (Blaustein), Nancy 154
Paul, Aileen 1917- 12
Paul, Alison 196
Paul, Ann Whitford 1941- 209
  Earlier sketches in SATA *76, 110, 168*
Paul, Chris 1985- 224
Paul, David (Tyler) 1934-1988
  Obituary 56
Paul, Dominique 1973- 184
Paul, Elizabeth
  See Crow, Donna Fletcher
Paul, Hamish Vigne Christie 1951- 151
  See also CLR *87*
Paul, James 1936- 23
Paul, Korky
  See Paul, Hamish Vigne Christie
Paul, Robert
  See Roberts, John G(aither)
Paul, Tessa 1944- 103
Pauley, Kimberly 1973- 208
Pauli, Hertha (Ernestine) 1909-1973 3
  Obituary 26
Paull, Grace A. 1898- 24
Paulsen, Gary 1939- 189
  Earlier sketches in SATA *22, 50, 54, 79, 111,*
  158
  See also CLR *82*
Paulson, Jack
  See Jackson, C(aary) Paul
Pauquet, Gina Ruck
  See Ruck-Pauquet, Gina
Pausacker, Jenny 1948- 72
  See also SAAS *23*
Pausewang, Gudrun 1928- 165
  Earlier sketch in SATA *104*
Pavel, Frances 1907- 10
Paver, Michelle 215
  Earlier sketch in SATA *170*
Paxton
  See Barr, Nevada
Paxton, Thomas R. 1937- 70
Paxton, Tom
  See Paxton, Thomas R.
Paye, Won-Ldy 185
Payne, Alan
  See Jakes, John
Payne, Bernal C., Jr. 1941- 60
Payne, C. Douglas
  See Payne, C.D.
Payne, C.D. 1949- 133
Payne, C.F. 1956- 179
Payne, Chris Fox
  See Payne, C.F.
Payne, Donald Gordon 1924- 37
Payne, Emmy
  See West, Emily Govan
Payne, Nina 135
Payne, Rachel Ann
  See Jakes, John
Payson, Dale 1943- 9
Payzant, Charles 18
Paz, A.
  See Pahz, James Alon
Paz, Natalia Toledo
  See Toledo, Natalia
Paz, Zan
  See Pahz, Cheryl Suzanne
Peace, Mary
  See Finley, Mary Peace
Peacock, Louise 210
Peacock, Shane 1957- 192

Peake, Mervyn 1911-1968 23
Peale, Norman Vincent 1898-1993 20
  Obituary 78
Pearce, Ann Philippa
  See Pearce, Philippa
Pearce, Carl 229
Pearce, Emily Smith 1975- 199
Pearce, Jacqueline 1962- 146
Pearce, Margaret 104
Pearce, Philippa 1920-2006 129
  Obituary 179
  Earlier sketches in SATA *1, 67*
  See also CLR *9*
Peare, Catherine Owens 1911- 9
Pearle, Ida 207
Pearsall, Shelley 1966- 190
Pearson, Gayle 1947- 119
  Earlier sketch in SATA *53*
Pearson, Jean Mary
  See Gardam, Jane
Pearson, Kit 1947- 77
  Autobiography Feature 117
  See also CLR *26*
Pearson, Mary E. 1955- 211
  Earlier sketch in SATA *134*
Pearson, Michael Parker
  See Pearson, Mike Parker
Pearson, Mike Parker 1957- 228
Pearson, Ridley 1953- 182
Pearson, Susan 1946- 166
  Brief entry 27
  Earlier sketches in SATA *39, 91*
Pearson, Tracey Campbell 1956- 219
  Earlier sketches in SATA *64, 155*
Pease, (Clarence) Howard 1894-1974 2
  Obituary 25
Peavy, Linda 1943- 54
Peck, Anne Merriman 1884-1976 18
Peck, Beth 1957- 190
  Earlier sketch in SATA *79*
Peck, Jan 159
Peck, Jeanie J. 1967- 147
Peck, Marshall III 1951- 92
Peck, Richard 1934- 228
  Autobiography Feature 110
  Earlier sketches in SATA *18, 55, 97, 110, 158,*
  190
  See also CLR *142*
  See also SAAS *2*
Peck, Richard Wayne
  See Peck, Richard
Peck, Robert Newton 1928- 156
  Autobiography Feature 108
  Earlier sketches in SATA *21, 62, 111*
  See also CLR *163*
  See also SAAS *1*
Peck, Sylvia 1953- 133
Peck-Whiting, Jeanie J.
  See Peck, Jeanie J.
Peddicord, Jane Ann 199
Pedersen, Janet 193
Pederson, Sharleen
  See Collicott, Sharleen
Pedler, Caroline 197
Peebles, Anne
  See Galloway, Priscilla
Peek, Merle 1938- 39
Peel, John 1954- 79
Peel, Norman Lemon
  See Hirsch, Phil
Peeples, Edwin A(ugustus, Jr.) 1915-1994 6
Peers, Judi 1956- 119
Peers, Judith May West
  See Peers, Judi
Peet, Bill
  See Peet, William Bartlett
Peet, Creighton B. 1899-1977 30
Peet, Mal 227
  Earlier sketch in SATA *171*
Peet, Malcolm
  See Peet, Mal

Peet, William Bartlett 1915-2002 78
  Obituary 137
  Earlier sketches in SATA *2, 41*
  See also CLR *12*
Peete, Holly Robinson 1964- 229
Peguero, Leone 116
Pelaez, Jill 1924- 12
Pelham, David 1938- 70
Pelikan, Judy 1941- 219
Pell, Ed(ward) 1950- 157
Pelletier, Andrew T. 195
Pelletier, Andrew Thomas
  See Pelletier, Andrew T.
Pellowski, Anne 1933- 20
Pellowski, Michael (Joseph) 1949- 151
  Brief entry 48
  Earlier sketch in SATA *88*
Pellowski, Michael Morgan
  See Pellowski, Michael (Joseph)
Pelta, Kathy 1928- 18
Peltier, Leslie C(opus) 1900-1980 13
Pemberton, Bonnie 191
Pemberton, John Leigh
  See Leigh-Pemberton, John
Pembury, Bill
  See Groom, Arthur William
Pemsteen, Hans
  See Manes, Stephen
Pendennis, Arthur Esquir
  See Thackeray, William Makepeace
Pender, Lydia Podger 1907- 61
Pendery, Rosemary (Schmitz) 7
Pendle, Alexy 1943- 29
Pendle, George 1906-1977
  Obituary 28
Pendleton, Don
  See Cunningham, Chet
  and Garside, Jack
  and Jagninski, Tom
  and Krauzer, Steven M(ark)
  and Obstfeld, Raymond
Pendleton, Thomas 1965- 206
Pendziwol, Jean E. 1965- 177
Pene du Bois, William (Sherman)
  1916-1993 68
  Obituary 74
  Earlier sketch in SATA *4*
  See also CLR *1*
Penn, Audrey 1947- 212
Penn, Audrey 1950- 22
Penn, Ruth Bonn
  See Rosenberg, Eth Clifford
Pennac, Daniel 1944- 155
Pennage, E. M.
  See Finkel, George (Irvine)
Penner, Fred 1946- 169
  Earlier sketch in SATA *67*
Penner, Frederick Ralph Cornelius
  See Penner, Fred
Penner, Lucille Recht 1942- 226
Penney, Grace Jackson 1904-2000 35
Penney, Ian 1960- 76
Penney, Sue 1957- 152
  Earlier sketch in SATA *102*
Pennington, Eunice 1923- 27
Pennington, Lillian Boyer 1904-2003 45
Pennypacker, Sara 1951- 187
Penrose, Gordon 1925- 66
Penson, Mary E. 1917- 78
Penzler, Otto 1942- 38
Pepe, Phil 1935- 20
Pepe, Philip
  See Pepe, Phil
Peppe, Rodney (Darrell) 1934- 74
  Earlier sketch in SATA *4*
  See also SAAS *10*
Pepper, Frank S. 1910-1988
  Obituary 61
Percy, Charles Henry
  See Smith, Dorothy Gladys
Percy, Rachel 1930- 63

Perdomo, Willie *228*
Perdrizet, Marie-Pierre 1952- *79*
Perenyi, Constance 1954- *93*
Perenyi, Constance Marie
    See Perenyi, Constance
Perera, Hilda 1926- *105*
Perera, Thomas Biddle 1938- *13*
Peretti, Frank E. 1951- *141*
    Earlier sketch in SATA *80*
Perez, L. King 1940- *199*
Perez, Lana
    See Perez, Marlene
Perez, Lucia Angela 1973- *182*
Perez, Marlene *170*
Pericoli, Matteo 1968- *178*
Perkins, Al(bert Rogers) 1904-1975 .... *30*
Perkins, Dan
    See Tomorrow, Tom
Perkins, Lucy Fitch 1865-1937 .... *72*
Perkins, Lynne Rae 1956- *212*
    Earlier sketches in SATA *131, 172*
Perkins, (Richard) Marlin 1905-1986 .... *21*
    Obituary *48*
Perkins, Mitali 1963- *188*
    Earlier sketch in SATA *88*
Perks, Anne-Marie 1955- *122*
Perl, Erica S. *222*
    Earlier sketch in SATA *188*
Perl, Lila *72*
    Earlier sketch in SATA *6*
Perl, Susan 1922-1983 .... *22*
    Obituary *34*
Perlman, Janet 1954- *222*
Perlman, Rhea 1948- *183*
Perlmutter, O(scar) William 1920-1975 .... *8*
Pernu, Dennis 1970- *87*
Perrault, Charles 1628-1703 .... *25*
    See also CLR *134*
Perret, Delphine 1980- *190*
Perret, Gene (Richard) 1937- *76*
Perriman, Cole
    See Perrin, Pat
Perriman, Cole
    See Coleman, Wim
    and Perrin, Pat
Perrin, Pat *212*
Perrine, Mary 1913-1976 .... *2*
Perrins, Lesley 1953- *56*
Perrow, Angeli 1954- *121*
Perry, Andrea 1956- *190*
    Earlier sketch in SATA *148*
Perry, Barbara Fisher
    See Fisher, Barbara
Perry, Elizabeth 1959- *174*
Perry, Elizabeth Goodwin
    See Perry, Elizabeth
Perry, John 1967- *223*
Perry, Marie Fritz *165*
Perry, Patricia 1949- *30*
Perry, Phyllis J(ean) 1933- *152*
    Earlier sketches in SATA *60, 101*
Perry, Ritchie (John Allen) 1942- *105*
Perry, Roger 1933- *27*
Perry, Steve(n Carl) 1947- *76*
Pershall, Mary K. 1951- *172*
    Earlier sketch in SATA *70*
Pershing, Marie
    See Schultz, Pearle Henriksen
Perske, Robert 1927- *57*
Persun, Morgan Reed
    See Watkins, Dawn L.
Perversi, Margaret *213*
Petach, Heidi *149*
Peter
    See Stratemeyer, Edward L.
Peters, Alexander
    See Hollander, Zander
Peters, Andrew Fusek 1965- *169*
    Earlier sketch in SATA *107*
Peters, Bernadette 1948- *212*

Peters, Caroline
    See Betz, Eva Kelly
Peters, David
    See David, Peter
Peters, Elizabeth 1927- *49*
Peters, Emma
    See Price, Karen
Peters, Gabriel
    See Matott, Justin
Peters, Julie Anne 1952- *197*
    Earlier sketches in SATA *82, 128*
Peters, Linda
    See Catherall, Arthur
Peters, Lisa Westberg 1951- *161*
    Earlier sketches in SATA *74, 115*
Peters, Patricia 1953- *84*
Peters, Russell M. 1929- *78*
Peters, S. H.
    See Henry, O.
    and Proffitt, Nicholas
Peters, Stephanie True 1965- *224*
Petersen, David 1946- *109*
    Earlier sketch in SATA *62*
Petersen, Gwenn Boardman 1924- *12*
Petersen, P(eter) J(ames) 1941- *118*
    Brief entry *43*
    Earlier sketches in SATA *48, 83*
Petersen, Palle 1943- *85*
Petersham, Maud 1890-1971 .... *17*
    See also CLR *24*
Petersham, Maud Sylvia Fuller
    See Petersham, Maud
Petersham, Miska 1888-1960 .... *17*
    See also CLR *24*
Peterson, Cris 1952- *174*
    Earlier sketches in SATA *84, 145*
Peterson, Dawn 1934- *86*
Peterson, Esther (Allen) 1934- *35*
Peterson, Hans 1922- *8*
Peterson, Harold L(eslie) 1922-1978 .... *8*
Peterson, Helen Stone 1910- *8*
Peterson, Jean Sunde 1941- *108*
Peterson, Jeanne Whitehouse 1939- *159*
    Earlier sketch in SATA *29*
Peterson, Kathleen B. 1951- *119*
Peterson, Lorraine 1940- *56*
    Brief entry *44*
Peterson, Mary *215*
Peterson, Shelley 1952- *146*
Peterson, Will
    See Cocks, Peter
Petie, Haris
    See Petty, Roberta
Petricic, Dusan 1946- *176*
Petrides, Heidrun 1944- *19*
Petrie, Catherine 1947- *52*
    Brief entry *41*
Petrone, Valeria *186*
Petrosino, Tamara *193*
Petroski, Catherine (Ann Groom) 1939- *48*
Petrovich, Michael B(oro) 1922- *40*
Petrovskaya, Kyra
    See Wayne, Kyra Petrovskaya
Petruccio, Steven James 1961- *67*
Petrucha, Stefan 1959- *213*
Petry, Ann 1908-1997 .... *5*
    Obituary *94*
    See also CLR *12*
Petry, Ann Lane
    See Petry, Ann
Pettit, Jayne 1932- *108*
Petty, J.T. 1977- *189*
Petty, Kate 1951-2007 .... *204*
Petty, Roberta 1915- *10*
Pevsner, Stella *131*
    Earlier sketches in SATA *8, 77*
    See also SAAS *14*
Peyo
    See Culliford, Pierre
Peyton, K. M.
    See Peyton, Kathleen Wendy

Peyton, Kathleen Wendy 1929- *157*
    Earlier sketches in SATA *15, 62*
    See also CLR *3*
    See also SAAS *17*
Pfanner, (Anne) Louise 1955- *68*
Pfeffer, Susan Beth 1948- *180*
    Earlier sketches in SATA *4, 83*
    See also CLR *11*
    See also SAAS *17*
Pfeffer, Wendy 1929- *204*
    Earlier sketches in SATA *78, 142*
Pfeiffer, Janet (B.) 1949- *96*
Pfister, Marcus *207*
    Earlier sketches in SATA *83, 150*
    See also CLR *42*
Pfitsch, Patricia Curtis 1948- *148*
Pfitzenmaier, Audrey 1959- *220*
Pflieger, Pat 1955- *84*
Pham, LeUyen 1973- *201*
    Earlier sketch in SATA *175*
Phelan, Mary Kay 1914- *3*
Phelan, Matt 1970- *215*
    Earlier sketch in SATA *172*
Phelan, Terry Wolfe 1941- *56*
Phelps, Ethel Johnston 1914-1984 .... *35*
Philbrick, Rodman 1951- *163*
Philbrick, W. Rodman
    See Philbrick, Rodman
Philbrick, W.R.
    See Philbrick, Rodman
Philbrook, Clem(ent E.) 1917- *24*
Phillipps, J.C. *218*
Phillipps, Julie Christine
    See Phillipps, J.C.
Phillips, Aileen Paul
    See Paul, Aileen
Phillips, Betty Lou
    See Phillips, Elizabeth Louise
Phillips, Bob 1940- *95*
Phillips, Douglas A. 1949- *161*
Phillips, Elizabeth Louise *58*
    Brief entry *48*
Phillips, Gary R. *225*
Phillips, Irv(ing W.) 1905-2000 .... *11*
    Obituary *125*
Phillips, Jack
    See Sandburg, Carl
Phillips, Leon
    See Gerson, Noel Bertram
Phillips, Loretta (Hosey) 1893-1987 .... *10*
Phillips, Louis 1942- *102*
    Earlier sketch in SATA *8*
Phillips, Mark
    See Garrett, Randall
    and Janifer, Laurence M(ark)
Phillips, Mary Geisler 1881-1964 .... *10*
Phillips, Michael
    See Nolan, William F.
Phillips, (Woodward) Prentice 1894-1981 .... *10*
Phillpotts, Eden 1862-1960 .... *24*
Phin
    See Thayer, Ernest Lawrence
Phipson, Joan
    See Fitzhardinge, Joan Margaret
Phiz
    See Browne, Hablot Knight
Phleger, Fred B. 1909-1993 .... *34*
Phleger, Marjorie Temple 1908(?)-1986 .... *1*
    Obituary *47*
Piaget, Jean 1896-1980
    Obituary *23*
Piatti, Celestino 1922- *16*
Picard, Barbara Leonie 1917- *89*
    Earlier sketch in SATA *2*
    See also SAAS *10*
Pichon, Liz *174*
Pickard, Charles 1932- *36*
Pickering, James Sayre 1897-1969 .... *36*
    Obituary *28*
Pickering, Jimmy *195*
Pickering, Robert B. 1950- *93*

Pielichaty, Helena 1955- *142*
Pien, Lark *222*
Pienkowski, Jan (Michal) 1936- *131*
　Earlier sketches in SATA *6, 58*
　See also CLR *6*
Pierce, Edith Gray 1893-1977 .... *45*
Pierce, Katherine
　See St. John, Wylly Folk
Pierce, Meredith Ann 1958- *127*
　Brief entry *48*
　Earlier sketch in SATA *67*
　See also CLR *20*
Pierce, Ruth (Ireland) 1936- *5*
Pierce, Sharon
　See McCullough, Sharon Pierce
Pierce, Tamora 1954- *187*
　Brief entry *49*
　Earlier sketches in SATA *51, 96, 153*
Pierce, Terry *178*
Pierik, Robert 1921- *13*
Piernas-Davenport, Gail *199*
Piers, Robert
　See Anthony, Piers
Pig, Edward
　See Gorey, Edward (St. John)
Pignataro, Anna 1965- *223*
Pike, Aprilynne *218*
Pike, Bob
　See Pike, Robert W.
Pike, Christopher 1954(?)- *156*
　Earlier sketch in SATA *68*
　See also CLR *29*
Pike, Deborah 1951- *89*
Pike, E(dgar) Royston 1896-1980 .... *22*
　Obituary *56*
Pike, R. William 1956- *92*
Pike, Robert
　See Pike, Robert W.
Pike, Robert W. 1931- *102*
Pike, Robert Wilson
　See Pike, Robert W.
Pilarski, Laura 1926- *13*
Pilgrim, Anne
　See Allan, Mabel Esther
Pilkey, Dav 1966- *166*
　Earlier sketches in SATA *68, 115*
　See also CLR *160*
Pilkey, David Murray, Jr.
　See Pilkey, Dav
Pilkington, Francis Meredyth 1907-1993 .... *4*
Pilkington, Roger (Windle) 1915-2003 .... *10*
　Obituary *144*
Pilutti, Deb *208*
Pin, Isabel 1975- *183*
Pinchot, David 1914(?)-1983
　Obituary *34*
Pincus, Harriet 1938- *27*
Pinczes, Elinor J(ane) 1940- *81*
Pine, Nicholas 1951- *91*
Pine, Tillie S(chloss) 1896-1999 .... *13*
Pini, Richard (Alan) 1950- *89*
Pini, Wendy 1951- *89*
Pinkerton, Kathrene Sutherland (Gedney)
　1887-1967
　Obituary *26*
Pinkett, Jada
　See Smith, Jada Pinkett
Pinkney, Andrea Davis 1963- *160*
　Earlier sketch in SATA *113*
Pinkney, Brian 1961- *206*
　Earlier sketches in SATA *74, 148*
　See also CLR *54*
Pinkney, Gloria Jean 1941- *212*
　Earlier sketch in SATA *85*
Pinkney, J. Brian
　See Pinkney, Brian

Pinkney, Jerry 1939- *198*
　Autobiography Feature *198*
　Brief entry *32*
　Earlier sketches in SATA *41, 71, 107, 151*
　See also CLR *43*
　See also SAAS *12*
Pinkney, John *97*
Pinkney, Sandra L. *193*
　Earlier sketch in SATA *128*
Pinkwater, D. Manus
　See Pinkwater, Daniel
Pinkwater, Daniel 1941- *210*
　Earlier sketches in SATA *8, 46, 76, 114, 158*
　See also CLR *4*
　See also SAAS *3*
Pinkwater, Daniel M.
　See Pinkwater, Daniel
Pinkwater, Daniel Manus
　See Pinkwater, Daniel
Pinkwater, Jill *188*
Pinkwater, Manus
　See Pinkwater, Daniel
Pinner, Joma
　See Werner, Herma
Pinto, Sara *200*
Pioneer
　See Yates, Raymond F(rancis)
Piowaty, Kim Kennelly 1957- *49*
Piper, Roger
　See Fisher, John
Pirner, Connie White 1955- *72*
Piro, Richard 1934- *7*
Pirot, Alison Lohans
　See Lohans, Alison
Pirotta, Saviour *184*
Pirsig, Robert M(aynard) 1928- *39*
Pita
　See Rendon, Maria
Pitcher, C.
　See Pitcher, Caroline
Pitcher, Caroline 1948- *214*
　Earlier sketch in SATA *128*
Pitcher, Caroline Nell
　See Pitcher, Caroline
Pitman, (Isaac) James 1901-1985
　Obituary *46*
Pitre, Felix 1949- *84*
Pitrone, Jean Maddern 1920- *4*
Pittman, Helena Clare 1945- *71*
Pitz, Henry C(larence) 1895-1976 .... *4*
　Obituary *24*
Pitzer, Susanna 1958- *181*
Piven, Hanoch 1963- *173*
Pixley, Marcella *194*
Pizer, Vernon 1918- *21*
Place, Marian T(empleton) 1910- *3*
Place, Robin (Mary) 1926- *71*
Plaidy, Jean
　See Hibbert, Eleanor Alice Burford
Plain, Belva 1919-2010 .... *62*
Plaine, Alfred R. 1898(?)-1981
　Obituary *29*
Plant, Andrew *214*
Plath, Sylvia 1932-1963 .... *96*
Platt, Chris 1959- *185*
Platt, Kin 1911- *86*
　Earlier sketch in SATA *21*
　See also SAAS *17*
Platt, Randall 1948- *95*
Platt, Randall Beth
　See Platt, Randall
Platt, Richard 1953- *218*
　Earlier sketches in SATA *120, 166*
Playfellow, Robin
　See Ellis, Edward S.
Playsted, James
　See Wood, James Playsted
Plecas, Jennifer 1966- *229*
　Earlier sketches in SATA *84, 149*
Plimpton, George 1927-2003 .... *10*
　Obituary *150*

Plimpton, George Ames
　See Plimpton, George
Plomer, William Charles Franklin
　1903-1973 .... *24*
Plotz, Helen Ratnoff 1913-2000 .... *38*
Plourde, Lynn 1955- *218*
　Earlier sketches in SATA *122, 168*
Plowden, David 1932- *52*
Plowden, Martha Ward 1948- *98*
Plowhead, Ruth Gipson 1877-1967 .... *43*
Plowman, Stephanie 1922- *6*
Pluckrose, Henry 1931- *141*
　Earlier sketch in SATA *13*
Pluckrose, Henry Arthur
　See Pluckrose, Henry
Plum, J.
　See Wodehouse, P. G.
Plum, Jennifer
　See Kurland, Michael
Plumb, Charles P. 1900(?)-1982
　Obituary *29*
Plume, Ilse *170*
　Brief entry *43*
Plumme, Don E.
　See Katz, Bobbi
Plummer, Margaret 1911- *2*
Plum-Ucci, Carol *184*
Poblocki, Dan 1981- *224*
Pochocki, Ethel (Frances) 1925- *76*
Podendorf, Illa (E.) 1903(?)-1983 .... *18*
　Obituary *35*
Podwal, Mark 1945- *224*
　Earlier sketches in SATA *101, 160*
Podwal, Mark H.
　See Podwal, Mark
Poe, Edgar Allan 1809-1849 .... *23*
Poe, Ty (Christopher) 1975- *94*
Pogany, William Andrew 1882-1955 .... *44*
　Brief entry *30*
Pogany, Willy
　See Pogany, William Andrew
Pogue, Carolyn 1948- *223*
Pohl, Frederik 1919- *24*
Pohlmann, Lillian (Grenfell) 1902-1997 .... *11*
Pohrt, Tom 1953- *195*
　Earlier sketches in SATA *67, 152*
Pointon, Robert
　See Rooke, Daphne
Points, Larry G. 1945- *177*
　Earlier sketch in SATA *133*
Points, Larry Gene
　See Points, Larry G.
Pokeberry, P.J.
　See Mitchell, B.J.
POLA
　See Watson, Pauline
Polacco, Patricia 1944- *212*
　Earlier sketches in SATA *74, 123, 180*
　See also CLR *40*
Polacco, Patricia Ann
　See Polacco, Patricia
Polak, Monique 1960- *178*
Polatnick, Florence T. 1923- *5*
Polcovar, Jane 1948- *211*
Polder, Markus
　See Kruss, James
Polenghi, Evan 1961- *225*
Polese, Carolyn 1947- *58*
Polese, James 1914- *87*
Polette, Nancy (Jane) 1930- *42*
Polhamus, Jean Burt 1928- *21*
Polhemus, Coleman *210*
Policoff, Stephen Phillip 1948- *77*
Polikoff, Barbara G. 1929- *162*
　Earlier sketch in SATA *77*
Polikoff, Barbara Garland
　See Polikoff, Barbara G.
Polisar, Barry Louis 1954- *134*
　Earlier sketch in SATA *77*

Politi, Leo 1908-1996 47
    Obituary 88
    Earlier sketch in SATA *1*
    See also CLR 29
Polking, Kirk 1925- 5
Pollack, Jill S. 1963- 88
Pollack, Merrill S. 1924-1988
    Obituary 55
Polland, Barbara K(ay) 1939- 44
Polland, Madeleine A(ngela Cahill) 1918- ... 68
    Earlier sketch in SATA *6*
    See also SAAS 8
Pollema-Cahill, Phyllis 1958- 123
Pollock, Bruce 1945- 46
Pollock, Mary
    See Blyton, Enid
Pollock, Penny 1935- 137
    Brief entry 42
    Earlier sketch in SATA *44*
Pollowitz, Melinda Kilborn 1944- 26
Polner, Murray 1928- 64
Polonsky, Arthur 1925- 34
Polseno, Jo 17
Pomaska, Anna 1946- 117
Pomerantz, Charlotte 1930- 177
    Earlier sketch in SATA *20, 80*
Pomeroy, Pete
    See Roth, Arthur J(oseph)
Pon, Cindy 1973- 216
Pon, Cynthia 229
Pond, Alonzo W(illiam) 1894-1986 5
Pontiflet, Ted 1932- 32
Poole, Gray Johnson 1906- 1
Poole, Josephine
    See Helyar, Jane Penelope Josephine
Poole, (Jane Penelope) Josephine
    See Helyar, Jane Penelope Josephine
Poole, Lynn 1910-1969 1
Poole, Peggy 1925- 39
Poon, Janice 228
Poortvliet, Rien 1932- 65
    Brief entry 37
Pope, Elizabeth Marie 1917-1992 38
    Brief entry 36
Pope, Kevin 1958- 183
Popescu, Christine
    See Pullein-Thompson, Christine
Poploff, Michelle 1956- 67
Popp, K. Wendy 91
Poppel, Hans 1942- 71
Porfirio, Guy 1958- 197
Portal, Colette 1936- 6
Porte, Barbara Ann 1943- 152
    Brief entry 45
    Earlier sketches in SATA *57, 93*
Porter, A(nthony) P(eyton) 1945- 68
Porter, Connie (Rose) 1959(?)- 129
    Earlier sketch in SATA *81*
Porter, Donald Clayton
    See Gerson, Noel Bertram
Porter, Eleanor H(odgman) 1868-1920
    See CLR *110*
Porter, Gene Stratton
    See Stratton-Porter, Gene
Porter, Janice Lee 1953- 108
    Earlier sketch in SATA *68*
Porter, Katherine Anne 1890-1980 39
    Obituary 23
Porter, Kathryn
    See Swinford, Betty (June Wells)
Porter, Pamela 1956- 193
Porter, Sheena 1935- 24
    See also SAAS 10
Porter, Sue
    See Limb, Sue
Porter, Sue 1951- 213
    Earlier sketch in SATA *76*
Porter, Tracey 191
Porter, William Sydney
    See Henry, O.
Portis, Antoinette 189

Porto, Tony 1960- 153
Portteus, Eleanora Marie Manthei (?)-1983
    Obituary 36
Posada, Mia 187
Posell, Elsa Z(eigerman) -1995 3
Posesorski, Sherie 216
Posten, Margaret L(ois) 1915- 10
Postgate, Daniel 1964- 216
Posthuma, Sieb 1960- 150
Postier, Jim 1965- 202
Potok, Chaim 1929-2002 106
    Obituary 134
    Earlier sketch in SATA *33*
    See also CLR 92
Potok, Herbert Harold
    See Potok, Chaim
Potok, Herman Harold
    See Potok, Chaim
Potter, Alicia 216
Potter, Beatrix 1866-1943 132
    Earlier sketch in SATA *100*
    See also YABC *1*
    See also CLR 165
Potter, Ellen 1973- 218
Potter, Giselle 187
    Earlier sketch in SATA *150*
Potter, Helen Beatrix
    See Potter, Beatrix
Potter, Katherine 217
Potter, Margaret 1926-1998 21
    Obituary 104
Potter, Marian 1915- 9
Potter, Miriam Clark 1886-1965 3
Poulin, Stephane 1961- 98
    See also CLR 28
Poulton, Kimberly 1957(?)- 136
Pournelle, Jerry 1933- 161
    Earlier sketches in SATA *26, 91*
Pournelle, Jerry Eugene
    See Pournelle, Jerry
Povelite, Kay 1955- 102
Pow, Tom 1950- 163
Powe-Allred, Alexandra
    See Allred, Alexandra Powe
Powell, A. M.
    See Morgan, Alfred P(owell)
Powell, Consie 174
Powell, E. Sandy 1947- 72
Powell, E.S.
    See Powell, E. Sandy
Powell, Pamela 1960- 78
Powell, Patricia Hruby 1951- 136
Powell, Randy 1956- 118
Powell, Richard Stillman
    See Barbour, Ralph Henry
Powell, Robert (Stephenson Smyth) Baden
    See Baden-Powell, Robert (Stephenson
    Smyth)
Powell, Stephanie 1953- 93
Power, Margaret (M.) 1945- 125
    Earlier sketch in SATA *75*
Powers, Anne
    See Schwartz, Anne Powers
Powers, Bill 1931- 52
    Brief entry 31
Powers, Daniel 1959- 164
Powers, J. L. 195
Powers, Jessica
    See Powers, J. L.
Powers, Jessica Lynn
    See Powers, J. L.
Powers, Margaret
    See Heal, Edith
Powers, Tim 1952- 107
Powers, Timothy Thomas
    See Powers, Tim
Powledge, Fred 1935- 37
Poydar, Nancy 190
Poynter, Margaret 1927- 27
Prachaticka, Marketa
    See Kolibalova, Marketa

Prachatika, Marketa
    See Kolibalova, Marketa
Prager, Arthur 44
Prager, Ellen J. 1962- 136
Prange, Beckie 172
Prap, Lila 1955- 177
Praprotnik-Zupancic, Lilijana
    See Prap, Lila
Pratchett, Terence David John
    See Pratchett, Terry
Pratchett, Terry 1948- 185
    Earlier sketches in SATA *82, 139*
    See also CLR 64
Prater, John 1947- 149
    Earlier sketches in SATA *72, 103*
Prato, Rodica 184
Pratt, Christine Joy 214
Pratt, (Murray) Fletcher 1897-1956 102
Pratt, Kristin Joy 1976- 87
Pratt, Pierre 1962- 208
    Earlier sketches in SATA *95, 166*
Preiss, Byron 1953-2005 166
    Brief entry 42
    Earlier sketch in SATA *47*
Preiss, Byron Cary
    See Preiss, Byron
Preller, James 1961- 209
    Earlier sketch in SATA *88*
Prelutsky, Jack 1940- 171
    Earlier sketches in SATA *22, 66, 118*
    See also CLR 115
Prentice, Amy
    See Kaler, James Otis
Prescott, Casey
    See Morris, Chris(topher Crosby)
Presnall, Judith (Ann) Janda 1943- 96
Pressler, Mirjam 1940- 155
Preston, Douglas 1956- 113
Preston, Edna Mitchell 40
Preston, Lillian Elvira 1918- 47
Preus, Margi 209
Preussler, Otfried 1923- 24
Prevert, Jacques 1900-1977
    Obituary 30
Prevert, Jacques Henri Marie
    See Prevert, Jacques
Prevost, Guillaume 1964- 192
Prevost, Mikela 203
Price, Beverley Joan 1931- 98
Price, Charlie 187
Price, Christine (Hilda) 1928-1980 3
    Obituary 23
Price, Garrett 1896-1979
    Obituary 22
Price, Jennifer
    See Hoover, Helen (Drusilla Blackburn)
Price, Joan 1931- 124
Price, Jonathan (Reeve) 1941- 46
Price, Karen 1957- 125
Price, Kathy Z. 1957- 172
Price, Lucie Locke
    See Locke, Lucie
Price, Olive 1903-1991 8
Price, Susan 1955- 128
    Earlier sketches in SATA *25, 85*
Price, Willard 1887-1983 48
    Brief entry 38
Price-Groff, Claire 127
Priceman, Marjorie 1958- 168
    Earlier sketches in SATA *81, 120*
Prichard, Katharine Susannah 1883-1969 66
Priddy, Roger 227
Prideaux, Tom 1908-1993 37
    Obituary 76
Priestley, Alice 1962- 227
    Earlier sketch in SATA *95*
Priestley, Chris 1958- 198
Priestley, Lee (Shore) 1904-1999 27
Priestly, Doug 1954- 122
Priestly, Douglas Michael
    See Priestly, Doug

Prieto, Mariana Beeching 1912-1999 .... *8*
Priley, Margaret (Ann) Hubbard 1909-1992
  Obituary *130*
Primavera, Elise 1954- *185*
  Brief entry *48*
  Earlier sketches in SATA *58, 109*
Prime, Derek (James) 1931- *34*
Prince, Alison (Mary) 1931- *86*
  Earlier sketch in SATA *28*
Prince, April Jones 1975- *180*
Prince, J(ack) H(arvey) 1908- *17*
Prince, Joshua *188*
Prince, Maggie *102*
Prineas, Sarah *204*
Pringle, Eric *138*
Pringle, Laurence 1935- *201*
  Autobiography Feature *201*
  Earlier sketches in SATA *4, 68, 104, 154*
  See also CLR *57*
  See also SAAS *6*
Pringle, Laurence Patrick
  See Pringle, Laurence
Prinz, Yvonne 1960- *175*
Prior, Natalie Jane 1963- *106*
Pritchett, Elaine H(illyer) 1920- *36*
Pritchett, Laura 1971- *178*
Pritchett, Laura Rose
  See Pritchett, Laura
Pritts, Kim Derek 1953- *83*
Prochazkova, Iva 1953- *68*
Proctor, Everitt
  See Montgomery, Rutherford George
Proeysen, Alf 1914-1970 .... *67*
  See also CLR *24*
Professor Scribbler
  See Hollingsworth, Mary
Proimos, James 1955- *217*
  Earlier sketch in SATA *173*
Promitzer, Rebecca *229*
Prose, Francine 1947- *198*
  Earlier sketches in SATA *101, 149*
Prosek, James 1975- *216*
Protopopescu, Orel *186*
Protopopescu, Orel Odinov
  See Protopopescu, Orel
Provensen, Alice 1918- *147*
  Earlier sketches in SATA *9, 70*
  See also CLR *11*
Provensen, Martin 1916-1987 .... *70*
  Obituary *51*
  Earlier sketch in SATA *9*
  See also CLR *11*
Provensen, Martin Elias
  See Provensen, Martin
Provenzo, Eugene (F., Jr.) 1949- *142*
  Earlier sketch in SATA *78*
Provist, d'Alain 1906-1989
  See Diop, Birago (Ismael)
Provost, Gail Levine 1944- *65*
Provost, Gary (Richard) 1944-1995 .... *66*
Proysen, Alf
  See Proeysen, Alf
Pruett, Candace (J.) 1968- *157*
Pryor, Bonnie H. 1942- *69*
Pryor, Boori (Monty) 1950- *112*
Pryor, Helen Brenton 1897-1972 .... *4*
Pryor, Michael 1957- *153*
Pucci, Albert John 1920- *44*
Pudney, John (Sleigh) 1909-1977 .... *24*
Pugh, Ellen (Tiffany) 1920- *7*
Pullein-Thompson, Christine 1925-2005 ...... *82*
  Obituary *172*
  Earlier sketch in SATA *3*
Pullein-Thompson, Diana
  See Farr, Diana
Pullein-Thompson, Joanna Maxwell
  1898-1961 .... *82*
Pullein-Thompson, Josephine (Mary
  Wedderburn) *82*
  Earlier sketch in SATA *3*
Pullen, Zachary *189*

Pullman, Philip 1946- *198*
  Earlier sketches in SATA *65, 103, 150*
  See also CLR *84*
  See also SAAS *17*
Pullman, Philip Nicholas
  See Pullman, Philip
Pulver, Harry, Jr. 1960- *129*
Pulver, Robin 1945- *208*
  Earlier sketches in SATA *76, 133*
Puner, Helen W(alker) 1915-1989 .... *37*
  Obituary *63*
Purdy, Carol 1943- *120*
  Earlier sketch in SATA *66*
Purdy, Susan G(old) 1939- *8*
Purkiss, Diane 1961- *194*
Purmell, Ann 1953- *206*
  Earlier sketch in SATA *147*
Purnell, Idella 1901-1982 .... *120*
Purscell, Phyllis 1934- *7*
Purtill, Richard L. 1931- *53*
Pushker, Gloria 1927- *162*
  Earlier sketch in SATA *75*
Pushker, Gloria Teles
  See Pushker, Gloria
Pushkin, Aleksandr Sergeevich
  See Pushkin, Alexander
Pushkin, Alexander 1799-1837 .... *61*
Putnam, Alice 1916- *61*
Putnam, Arthur Lee
  See Alger, Horatio, Jr.
Putnam, Peter B(rock) 1920-1998 .... *30*
  Obituary *106*
Puttapipat, Niroot *199*
Puttock, Simon *178*
Puvilland, Alex *205*
Puvilland, Alexandre
  See Puvilland, Alex
Puybaret, Eric 1976- *299*
  Earlier sketch in SATA *195*
Pyle, Charles S. 1954(?)- *229*
Pyle, Chuck
  See Pyle, Charles S.
Pyle, Howard 1853-1911 .... *100*
  Earlier sketch in SATA *16*
  See also CLR *117*
Pyle, Katharine 1863-1938 .... *66*
Pyne, Mable Mandeville 1903-1969 .... *9*
Pyrnelle, Louise-Clarke 1850-1907 .... *114*

Q

Quackenbush, Robert M(ead) 1929- *133*
  Autobiography Feature *133*
  Earlier sketches in SATA *7, 70*
  See also CLR *122*
  See also SAAS *7*
Qualey, Marsha 1953- *124*
  Earlier sketch in SATA *79*
Qualls, Sean *177*
Quammen, David 1948- *7*
Quark, Jason
  See Eldin, Peter
Quarles, Benjamin 1904-1996 .... *12*
Quarles, Benjamin Arthur
  See Quarles, Benjamin
Quatermass, Martin
  See Carpenter, John
Quattlebaum, Mary 1958- *185*
  Earlier sketches in SATA *88, 134*
Quay, Emma *173*
  Earlier sketch in SATA *119*

Queen, Ellery
  See Deming, Richard
  and Dannay, Frederic
  and Davidson, Avram (James)
  and Fairman, Paul W.
  and Flora, Fletcher
  and Holding, James (Clark Carlisle, Jr.)
  and Hoch, Edward D.
  and Kane, Henry
  and Lee, Manfred B.
  and Marlowe, Stephen
  and Powell, (Oval) Talmage
  and Sheldon, Walter J(ames)
  and Sturgeon, Theodore (Hamilton)
  and Tracy, Don(ald Fiske)
  and Vance, Jack
Queen Latifah 1970- *185*
Quennell, Marjorie Courtney 1884-1972 ...... *29*
Quentin
  See Sheldon, David
Quentin, Brad
  See Bisson, Terry
Quest, (Edna) Olga W(ilbourne) Hall
  See Hall-Quest, (Edna) Olga W(ilbourne)
Quick, Annabelle 1922-1986 .... *2*
Quigg, Jane (Hulda) (?)-1986
  Obituary *49*
Quigley, Sarah 1976- *220*
Quill, Monica
  See McInerny, Ralph
Quin-Harkin, Janet 1941- *165*
  Earlier sketches in SATA *18, 90, 119*
Quin-Harkin, Janet Elizabeth
  See Quin-Harkin, Janet
Quinlan, Susan E. 1954- *88*
Quinlan, Susan Elizabeth
  See Quinlan, Susan E.
Quinn, Elisabeth 1881-1962 .... *22*
Quinn, Pat 1947- *130*
Quinn, Patrick 1950- *73*
Quinn, Rob 1972- *138*
Quinn, Susan 1940- *30*
Quinn, Susan Taft
  See Quinn, Susan
Quinn, Theodora K.
  See Kroeber, Theodora (Kracaw)
Quinn, Vernon
  See Quinn, Elisabeth
Quirk, Anne (E.) 1956- *99*
Quixley, Jim 1931- *56*
Quyth, Gabriel
  See Jennings, Gary

R

Ra, Carol F. 1939- *76*
Raab, Evelyn 1951- *129*
Rabb, Margo 1972- *188*
Rabb, M.E.
  See Rabb, Margo
Rabe, Berniece (Louise) 1928- *148*
  Autobiography Feature *148*
  Earlier sketches in SATA *7, 77*
  See also SAAS *10*
Rabe, Olive H(anson) (?)-1968 .... *13*
Rabin, Staton 1958- *162*
  Earlier sketch in SATA *84*
Rabinowich, Ellen 1946- *29*
Rabinowitz, Sandy 1954- *52*
  Brief entry *39*
Rachlin, Carol K(ing) 1919- *64*
Rachlin, Harvey 1951- *47*
Rachlin, Harvey Brant
  See Rachlin, Harvey
Rachlin, Nahid *64*
Rachlis, Eugene (Jacob) 1920-1986
  Obituary *50*

Rackham, Arthur 1867-1939 .... *100*
   Earlier sketch in SATA *15*
   See also CLR *57*
Racoma, Robin Yoko 1953- *207*
Raczka, Bob 1963- *228*
   Earlier sketches in SATA *163, 191*
Radencich, Marguerite C. 1952-1998 .... *79*
Rader, Laura *197*
Radford, Ruby L(orraine) 1891-1971 .... *6*
Radin, Ruth Yaffe 1938- *107*
   Brief entry *52*
   Earlier sketch in SATA *56*
Radlauer, David 1952- *28*
Radlauer, Edward 1921- *15*
Radlauer, Ruth Shaw 1926- *98*
   Earlier sketch in SATA *15*
Radley, Gail 1951- *112*
   Earlier sketch in SATA *25*
Radunsky, Vladimir *177*
Radzinski, Kandy 1948- *212*
Rae, Gwynedd 1892-1977 .... *37*
Raebeck, Lois 1921- *5*
Rael, Elsa Okon 1927-
   See CLR *84*
Raffi
   See Cavoukian, Raffi
Raftery, Gerald (Bransfield) 1905-1986 .... *11*
Ragan-Reid, Gale 1956- *90*
Rahaman, Vashanti 1953- *98*
Rahn, Joan Elma 1929- *27*
Rai, Bali 1971- *152*
Raible, Alton (Robert) 1918- *35*
Raiff, Stan 1930- *11*
Raines, Shirley C(arol) 1945- *128*
Rainey, W. B.
   See Blassingame, Wyatt Rainey
Rake, Jody 1961- *157*
Rallison, Janette 1966- *183*
Ralston, Jan
   See Dunlop, Agnes M. R.
Rama, Sue *190*
Ramal, Walter
   See de la Mare, Walter (John)
Ramanujan, A(ttipat) K(rishnaswami)
   1929-1993 .... *86*
Rame, David
   See Divine, Arthur Durham
Ramirez, Jose 1967- *198*
Ramirez, Orlando L. 1972- *194*
Ramos, Jorge 1958- *205*
Ramstad, Ralph L. 1919- *115*
Ramthun, Bonnie *214*
Rana, Indi
   See Rana, Indira Higham
Rana, Indira Higham 1944- *82*
Rana, J.
   See Bhatia, Jamunadevi
Ranadive, Gail 1944- *10*
Rand, Ann (Binkley) *30*
Rand, Gloria 1925- *156*
   Earlier sketch in SATA *101*
Rand, Paul 1914-1996 .... *6*
Randall, Carrie
   See Ransom, Candice
Randall, David 1972- *167*
Randall, Florence Engel 1917-1997 .... *5*
Randall, Janet
   See Young, Janet Randall
   and Young, Robert W(illiam)
Randall, Robert
   See Garrett, Randall
   and Silverberg, Robert
Randall, Ruth (Elaine) Painter 1892-1971 ..... *3*
Randell, Beverley
   See Price, Beverley Joan
Randle, Kristen D. 1952- *92*
   Autobiography Feature *119*
   See also SAAS *24*
Randle, Kristen Downey
   See Randle, Kristen D.

Randolph, Boynton M.D.
   See Ellis, Edward S.
Randolph, Ellen
   See Rawn, Melanie
Randolph, Geoffrey
   See Ellis, Edward S.
Randolph, J. H.
   See Ellis, Edward S.
Randolph, Lieutenant J. H.
   See Ellis, Edward S.
Rands, William Brighty 1823-1882 .... *17*
Raney, Ken 1953- *74*
Rankin, Joan 1940- *212*
   Earlier sketches in SATA *88, 148*
Rankin, Laura 1953(?)- *176*
Ranney, Agnes V. 1916-1985 .... *6*
Ransom, Candice 1952- *222*
   Brief entry *49*
   Earlier sketches in SATA *52, 89, 135, 183*
Ransom, Jeanie Franz 1957- *187*
Ransome, Arthur (Michell) 1884-1967 .... *22*
   See also CLR *8*
Ransome, James E. 1961- *227*
   Earlier sketches in SATA *76, 123, 178*
   See also CLR *86*
Rant, Tol E.
   See Longyear, Barry B(rookes)
Rao, Rohitash *218*
Raphael, Elaine
   See Bolognese, Elaine
Raposo, Joseph Guilherme 1938-1989
   Obituary *61*
Rapp, Adam 1968- *148*
Rappaport, Doreen *211*
   Earlier sketch in SATA *151*
Rappaport, Eva 1924- *6*
Rappoport, Ken 1935- *167*
   Earlier sketch in SATA *89*
Rarick, Carrie 1911-2002 .... *41*
Raschka, Chris 1959- *207*
   Earlier sketches in SATA *80, 117, 166*
Raschka, Christopher
   See Raschka, Chris
Rascol, Sabina I. *159*
Rash, Andy *219*
   Earlier sketch in SATA *162*
Raskin, Edith Lefkowitz 1908-1987 .... *9*
Raskin, Ellen 1928-1984 .... *139*
   Earlier sketches in SATA *2, 38*
   See also CLR *12*
Raskin, Joseph 1897-1982 .... *12*
   Obituary *29*
Rathjen, Carl Henry 1909-1984 .... *11*
Rathmann, Peggy 1953- *157*
   Earlier sketch in SATA *94*
   See also CLR *77*
Ratliff, Thomas M. 1948- *118*
Ratner, Sue Lynn
   See Alexander, Sue
Rattigan, Jama Kim 1951- *99*
Ratto, Linda Lee 1952- *79*
Rattray, Simon
   See Trevor, Elleston
Ratz de Tagyos, Paul 1958- *198*
   Earlier sketch in SATA *76*
Rau, Dana Meachen 1971- *218*
   Earlier sketches in SATA *94, 167*
Rau, Margaret 1913- *168*
   Earlier sketch in SATA *9*
   See also CLR *8*
Rauch, Mabel Thompson 1888-1972
   Obituary *26*
Raucher, Herman 1928- *8*
Raude, Karina *199*
Rauh, Sherry
   See North, Sherry
Raum, Elizabeth 1949- *155*
Raut, Radhashyam *222*
Raven, Margot Theis *184*
RavenWolf, Silver 1956- *155*

Ravielli, Anthony 1916-1997 .... *3*
   Obituary *95*
Ravilious, Robin 1944- *77*
Ravishankar, Anushka 1961- *200*
Rawding, F(rederick) W(illiam) 1930- *55*
Rawlings, Marjorie Kinnan 1896-1953 ...... *100*
   See also YABC *1*
   See also CLR *63*
Rawlins, Donna 1956- *206*
Rawlinson, Julia *212*
   Earlier sketch in SATA *175*
Rawls, (Woodrow) Wilson 1913-1984 .... *22*
   See also CLR *81*
Rawlyk, George Alexander 1935- *64*
Rawn, Melanie 1954- *98*
Rawn, Melanie Robin
   See Rawn, Melanie
Rawson, Katherine 1955- *190*
Ray, Carl 1943-1978 .... *63*
Ray, Deborah
   See Kogan Ray, Deborah
Ray, Delia 1963- *179*
   Earlier sketch in SATA *70*
Ray, Irene
   See Sutton, Margaret Beebe
Ray, Jane 1960- *196*
   Earlier sketches in SATA *72, 152*
Ray, JoAnne 1935- *9*
Ray, Mary (Eva Pedder) 1932- *127*
   Earlier sketch in SATA *2*
Ray, Mary Lyn 1946- *154*
   Earlier sketch in SATA *90*
Rayban, Chloe 1944- *167*
Rayevsky, Robert 1955- *190*
   Earlier sketch in SATA *81*
Raymond, James Crossley 1917-1981
   Obituary *29*
Raymond, Robert
   See Alter, Robert Edmond
Rayner, Catherine *204*
Rayner, Hugh *151*
Rayner, Mary 1933- *87*
   Earlier sketch in SATA *22*
   See also CLR *41*
Rayner, Shoo
   See Rayner, Hugh
Rayner, William 1929- *55*
   Brief entry *36*
Raynor, Dorka *28*
Raynor, Gemma 1985- *216*
Rayson, Steven 1932- *30*
Rayyan, Omar 1968- *216*
Razzell, Arthur (George) 1925- *11*
Razzell, Mary (Catherine) 1930- *102*
Razzi, James 1931- *10*
Read, Elfreida 1920- *2*
Read, Nicholas 1956- *146*
Read, Piers Paul 1941- *21*
Reade, Deborah 1949- *69*
Reader, Dennis 1929- *71*
Reading, Richard P(atrick) 1962- *161*
Readman, Jo 1958- *89*
Ready, Kirk L(ewis) 1943- *39*
Reaney, James 1926-2008 .... *43*
Reaney, James Crerar
   See Reaney, James
Reardon, Joyce
   See Pearson, Ridley
Reaver, Chap 1935-1993 .... *69*
   Obituary *77*
Reaver, Herbert R.
   See Reaver, Chap
Reaves, J. Michael
   See Reaves, (James) Michael
Reaves, (James) Michael 1950- *99*
Reber, Deborah *189*
Recorvits, Helen *191*
Redding, Robert Hull 1919- *2*
Redekopp, Elsa *61*
Redlich, Ben 1977- *181*
Redsand, Anna 1948- *184*

Redway, Ralph
  See Hamilton, Charles (Harold St. John)
Redway, Ridley
  See Hamilton, Charles (Harold St. John)
Reece, Colleen L. 1935- *116*
Reece, Gabrielle 1970- *108*
Reed, Amy 1979- *223*
Reed, Betty Jane 1921- *4*
Reed, Dallas
  See Pendleton, Thomas
Reed, E.
  See Evans, Mari
Reed, Gwendolyn E(lizabeth) 1932- *21*
Reed, Kit 1932- *184*
  Autobiography Feature *184*
  Earlier sketches in SATA *34, 116*
Reed, Lynn Rowe *215*
  Earlier sketch in SATA *171*
Reed, Mike 1951- *211*
Reed, Neil 1961- *99*
Reed, Talbot Baines 1852-1893
  See CLR *76*
Reed, Thomas (James) 1947- *34*
Reed, William Maxwell 1871-1962 .... *15*
Reeder, Carolyn 1937- *97*
  Earlier sketch in SATA *66*
  See also CLR *69*
Reeder, Colin (Dawson) 1938- *74*
Reeder, Colonel Red
  See Reeder, Russell P(otter), Jr.
Reeder, Russell P(otter), Jr. 1902-1998 .... *4*
  Obituary *101*
Reeder, Stephanie Owen 1951- *102*
Reed-Jones, Carol 1955- *112*
Reef, Catherine 1951- *223*
  Earlier sketches in SATA *73, 128, 189*
Reekie, Jocelyn (Margaret) 1947- *145*
Reeman, Douglas Edward 1924- *63*
  Brief entry *28*
Rees, Celia 1949- *124*
Rees, David (Bartlett) 1936-1993 .... *69*
  Obituary *76*
  Earlier sketch in SATA *36*
  See also SAAS *5*
Rees, Douglas 1947- *169*
Rees, Ennis (Samuel, Jr.) 1925-2009 .... *3*
Rees, (George) Leslie (Clarence)
  1905-2000 .... *105*
  Obituary *135*
Reese, Bob
  See Reese, Robert A.
Reese, Carolyn Johnson 1938- *64*
Reese, Della 1931(?)- *114*
Reese, Lyn
  See Reese, Carolyn Johnson
Reese, Robert A. 1938- *60*
  Brief entry *53*
Reese, (John) Terence 1913-1996 .... *59*
Reeve, Joel
  See Cox, William R(obert)
Reeve, Kirk 1934- *117*
Reeve, Philip *201*
  Earlier sketch in SATA *170*
Reeve, Rosie *188*
  Earlier sketch in SATA *186*
Reeves, Dia 1977- *227*
Reeves, Faye Couch 1953- *76*
Reeves, James
  See Reeves, John Morris
Reeves, Jeni 1947- *111*
Reeves, John Morris 1909-1978 .... *87*
  Earlier sketch in SATA *15*
Reeves, Joyce 1911- *17*
Reeves, Lawrence F. 1926- *29*
Reeves, Ruth Ellen
  See Ranney, Agnes V.
Regan, Dian Curtis 1950- *224*
  Autobiography Feature *149*
  Earlier sketches in SATA *75, 133, 149*
Regehr, Lydia 1903-1991 .... *37*
Reger, James P. 1952- *106*

Reger, Rob 1969- *227*
Reggiani, Renee 1925- *18*
Rehm, Karl M. 1935- *72*
Reibstein, Mark *211*
Reich, Ali
  See Katz, Bobbi
Reich, Susanna 1954- *214*
  Earlier sketch in SATA *113*
Reiche, Dietlof 1941- *159*
Reichert, Edwin C(lark) 1909-1988
  Obituary *57*
Reichert, Mickey Zucker
  See Reichert, Miriam Zucker
Reichert, Miriam Zucker 1962- *85*
Reichert, Renee *172*
Reichhold, Jane(t E.) 1937- *147*
Reid, Alastair 1926- *46*
Reid, Barbara 1922- *21*
Reid, Barbara (Jane) 1957- *93*
  See also CLR *64*
Reid, Desmond
  See Moorcock, Michael
  and McNeilly, Wilfred (Glassford)
Reid, Eugenie Chazal 1924- *12*
Reid, John Calvin *21*
Reid, (Thomas) Mayne 1818-1883 .... *24*
Reid, Meta Mayne 1905-1991 .... *58*
  Brief entry *36*
Reid, Robin (Nicole) 1969- *145*
Reid Banks, Lynne 1929- *165*
  Earlier sketches in SATA *22, 75, 111*
  See also CLR *86*
Reider, Katja 1960- *126*
Reid Jenkins, Debra 1955- *87*
Reidy, Jean *228*
Reiff, Stephanie Ann 1948- *47*
  Brief entry *28*
Reig, June 1933- *30*
Reigot, Betty Polisar 1924- *55*
  Brief entry *41*
Reilly, Joan *195*
Reim, Melanie (K.) 1956- *104*
Reinach, Jacquelyn (Krasne) 1930-2000 ...... *28*
Reiner, Carl 1922- *151*
Reiner, William B(uck) 1910-1976 .... *46*
  Obituary *30*
Reinfeld, Fred 1910-1964 .... *3*
Reinhardt, Dana 1971- *175*
Reinhart, Matthew 1971- *197*
  Earlier sketch in SATA *161*
Reiniger, Lotte 1899-1981 .... *40*
  Obituary *33*
Reinsma, Carol 1949- *91*
Reinstedt, Randall A. 1935- *101*
Reinstedt, Randy
  See Reinstedt, Randall A.
Reisberg, Mira 1955- *82*
Reisberg, Veg
  See Reisberg, Mira
Reiser, Lynn 1944- *180*
  Earlier sketches in SATA *81, 138*
Reiser, Lynn Whisnant
  See Reiser, Lynn
Reisgies, Teresa (Maria) 1966- *74*
Reiss, Johanna 1929(?)- *18*
  See also CLR *19*
Reiss, Johanna de Leeuw
  See Reiss, Johanna
Reiss, John J. *23*
Reiss, Kathryn 1957- *144*
  Earlier sketch in SATA *76*
Reit, Seymour Victory 1918-2001 .... *21*
  Obituary *133*
Reit, Sy
  See Reit, Seymour Victory
Relf, Patricia 1954- *134*
  Earlier sketch in SATA *71*
Remark, Erich Paul
  See Remarque, Erich Maria
Remarque, Erich Maria 1898-1970
  See CLR *159*

Remi, Georges 1907-1983 .... *13*
  Obituary *32*
  See also CLR *114*
Remington, Frederic S(ackrider)
  1861-1909 .... *41*
Remkiewicz, Frank 1939- *217*
  Earlier sketches in SATA *77, 152*
Rempt, Fiona 1973- *198*
Remy, Georges
  See Remi, Georges
Renaud, Anne 1957- *211*
Renaud, Bernadette 1945- *66*
Renault, Mary 1905-1983 .... *23*
  Obituary *36*
Rendell, Joan *28*
Rendina, Laura (Jones) Cooper 1902- *10*
Rendon, Marcie R. 1952- *97*
Rendon, Maria 1965- *116*
Renee, Janina 1956- *140*
Renfro, Ed 1924- *79*
Renick, Marion (Lewis) 1905-1983 .... *1*
Renier, Aaron 1977- *202*
Renken, Aleda 1907- *27*
Renlie, Frank H. 1936- *11*
Rennert, Laura Joy *224*
Rennert, Richard Scott 1956- *67*
Rennison, Louise 1951- *149*
Reno, Dawn E(laine) 1953- *130*
Rensie, Willis
  See Eisner, Will
Renton, Cam
  See Armstrong, Richard
Renvoize, Jean *5*
Resau, Laura 1973- *190*
Resciniti, Angelo G. 1952- *75*
Resnick, Michael David
  See Resnick, Mike
Resnick, Mike 1942- *159*
  Earlier sketches in SATA *38, 106*
Resnick, Seymour 1920- *23*
Retla, Robert
  See Alter, Robert Edmond
Rettig, Liz *199*
Rettstatt, Chris
  See Ashland, Monk
Reuter, Bjarne (B.) 1950- *142*
  Earlier sketch in SATA *68*
Reuter, Carol (Joan) 1931- *2*
Revena
  See Wright, Betty Ren
Revsbech, Vicki
  See Liestman, Vicki
Rex, Adam *225*
  Earlier sketch in SATA *186*
Rex, Michael *191*
Rey, H. A. 1898-1977 .... *100*
  Earlier sketches in SATA *1, 26, 69*
  See also CLR *93*
Rey, Hans Augusto
  See Rey, H. A.
Rey, Luis V. 1955- *201*
Rey, Margret 1906-1996 .... *86*
  Obituary *93*
  Earlier sketch in SATA *26*
  See also CLR *93*
Rey, Margret Elisabeth
  See Rey, Margret
Reyher, Becky
  See Reyher, Rebecca Hourwich
Reyher, Rebecca Hourwich 1897-1987 .... *18*
  Obituary *50*
Reynish, Jenny *222*
Reynold, Ann
  See Bernardo, Anilu
Reynolds, Aaron 1970- *197*
Reynolds, Adrian 1963- *192*
Reynolds, C. Buck 1957- *107*
Reynolds, Dickson
  See Reynolds, Helen Mary Greenwood Campbell

Reynolds, Helen Mary Greenwood Campbell
1884-1969
  Obituary 26
Reynolds, Jan 1956- 180
Reynolds, John
  See Whitlock, Ralph
Reynolds, Madge
  See Whitlock, Ralph
Reynolds, Malvina 1900-1978 44
  Obituary 24
Reynolds, Marilyn 1935- 121
  See also SAAS 23
Reynolds, Marilyn M.
  See Reynolds, Marilyn
Reynolds, Marilynn 1940- 141
  Earlier sketch in SATA 80
Reynolds, Pamela 1923- 34
Reynolds, Peter H. 1961- 226
  Earlier sketch in SATA 128
Reynolds, Peter J. 1961- 179
Reynolds, Susan 179
Rhine, Richard
  See Silverstein, Alvin
  and Silverstein, Virginia B.
Rhoades, Diane 1952- 90
Rhodes, Bennie (Loran) 1927- 35
Rhodes, Donna McKee 1962- 87
Rhodes, Frank Harold Trevor 1926- 37
Rhuday-Perkovich, Olugbemisola 227
Rhue, Morton
  See Strasser, Todd
Rhyne, Nancy 1926- 66
Rhynes, Martha E. 1939- 141
Ribbons, Ian 1924- 37
  Brief entry 30
  See also SAAS 3
Ricciuti, Edward R(aphael) 1938- 10
Rice, Alice (Caldwell) Hegan 1870-1942 63
Rice, Bebe Faas 1932- 89
Rice, Charles D(uane) 1910-1971
  Obituary 27
Rice, Dale R. 1948- 42
Rice, Dale Richard
  See Rice, Dale R.
Rice, Dick
  See Rice, R. Hugh
Rice, Earle (Wilmont), Jr. 1928- 151
  Earlier sketch in SATA 92
Rice, Edward 1918-2001 47
  Brief entry 42
Rice, Elizabeth 1913-1976 2
Rice, Eve 1951- 91
  Earlier sketch in SATA 34
Rice, Eve Hart
  See Rice, Eve
Rice, Inez 1907- 13
Rice, James 1934- 93
  Earlier sketch in SATA 22
Rice, John F. 1958- 82
Rice, R. Hugh 1929- 115
Rice, Richard H.
  See Rice, R. Hugh
Rich, Anna 1956- 212
Rich, Barbara
  See Graves, Robert
Rich, Elaine Sommers 1926- 6
Rich, Josephine Bouchard 1912- 10
Rich, Louise Dickinson 1903-1991 54
  Obituary 67
Rich, Naomi 217
Richard, Adrienne 1921- 5
  See also SAAS 9
Richard, James Robert
  See Bowen, Robert Sydney
Richards, Chuck 1957- 170
Richards, Frank
  See Hamilton, Charles (Harold St. John)
Richards, Hilda
  See Hamilton, Charles (Harold St. John)
Richards, Jackie 1925- 102
Richards, Jean 1940- 135

Richards, Justin 169
Richards, Kay
  See Baker, Susan (Catherine)
Richards, Laura E(lizabeth Howe) 1850-1943
  See YABC 1
  See also CLR 54
Richards, Leigh
  See King, Laurie R.
Richards, Marlee
  See Brill, Marlene Targ
Richards, Norman 1932- 48
Richards, R(onald) C(harles) W(illiam)
1923- 59
  Brief entry 43
Richards, Walter Alden (Jr.) 1907-1988
  Obituary 56
Richardson, Andrew (William) 1986- 120
Richardson, Carol 1932- 58
Richardson, Frank Howard 1882-1970
  Obituary 27
Richardson, Grace Lee
  See Dickson, Naida
Richardson, Jean (Mary) 59
Richardson, Judith Benet 1941- 77
Richardson, Nigel 1957- 187
Richardson, Robert S(hirley) 1902-1981 8
Richardson, Sandy 1949- 116
Richardson, V.A. 189
Richardson, Willis 1889-1977 60
Richelson, Geraldine 1922- 29
Richemont, Enid 1940- 82
Richler, Mordecai 1931-2001 98
  Brief entry 27
  Earlier sketch in SATA 44
  See also CLR 17
Richman, Sophia 1941- 142
Rich-McCoy, Lois
  See McCoy, Lois (Rich)
Richmond, Robin 1951- 75
Richoux, Pat(ricia) 1927- 7
Richter, Alice 1941- 30
Richter, Conrad (Michael) 1890-1968 3
Richter, Hans Peter 1925-1993 6
  See also CLR 21
  See also SAAS 11
Richter, Jutta 1955- 184
Rickard, Graham 1949- 71
Rico, Don(ato) 1917-1985
  Obituary 43
Riddell, Chris 1962- 219
  Earlier sketches in SATA 114, 166
Riddell, Christopher Barry
  See Riddell, Chris
Riddell, Edwina 1955- 82
Ridden, Brian 1934- 123
  See Ridden, Brian John
Riddle, Tohby 1965- 223
  Earlier sketches in SATA 74, 151
Riddleburger, Sam 202
Riddles, Libby 1956- 140
Ride, Sally 1951- 219
Ride, Sally Kristen
  See Ride, Sally
Rideout, Sandy 194
Rider, D. F.
  See Perrin, Pat
Rider, David F.
  See Perrin, Pat
Ridge, Antonia (Florence) (?)-1981 7
  Obituary 27
Ridge, Martin 1923-2003 43
Ridley, Philip 171
  Earlier sketch in SATA 88
Ridlon, Marci
  See Balterman, Marcia Ridlon
Riedman, Sarah R(egal) 1902-1995 1
Riehecky, Janet 1953- 164
Ries, Lori 185
Riesenberg, Felix, Jr. 1913-1962 23
Rieu, E(mile) V(ictor) 1887-1972 46
  Obituary 26

Riffenburgh, Beau 1955- 175
Rigg, Sharon
  See Creech, Sharon
Riggenbach, Holly
  See Black, Holly
Riggio, Anita 1952- 148
  Earlier sketch in SATA 73
Riggs, Shannon 190
Riggs, Sidney Noyes 1892-1975
  Obituary 28
Riggs, Stephanie 1964- 138
Riglietti, Serena 1969- 189
Rigney, James Oliver, Jr.
  See Jordan, Robert
Rikhoff, Jean 1928- 9
Rikki
  See Ducornet, Erica
Riley, James A. 1939- 97
Riley, James Whitcomb 1849-1916 17
Riley, Jocelyn 1949- 60
  Brief entry 50
Riley, Jocelyn Carol
  See Riley, Jocelyn
Riley, Linda Capus 1950- 85
Riley, Martin 1948- 81
Rim, Sujean 225
Rimbauer, Steven
  See Pearson, Ridley
Rimes, (Margaret) LeAnn 1982- 154
Rinaldi, Ann 1934- 202
  Brief entry 50
  Earlier sketches in SATA 51, 78, 117, 161
  See also CLR 46
Rinard, Judith E(llen) 1947- 140
  Earlier sketch in SATA 44
Rinck, Maranke 1976- 214
Rinder, Lenore 1949- 92
Ring, Elizabeth 1920- 79
Ringdahl, Mark
  See Longyear, Barry B(rookes)
Ringgold, Faith 1930- 187
  Earlier sketches in SATA 71, 114
  See also CLR 30
Ringi, Kjell (Arne Soerensen) 1939- 12
Rinkoff, Barbara Jean (Rich) 1923-1975 4
  Obituary 27
Rinn, Miriam 1946- 127
Riordan, James 1936- 95
Riordan, Rick 208
  Earlier sketch in SATA 174
Rios, Tere
  See Versace, Marie Teresa Rios
Rioux, Jo 226
Rioux, Jo-Anne
  See Rioux, Jo
Ripken, Cal, Jr. 1960- 215
  Earlier sketch in SATA 114
Ripken, Calvin Edward, Jr.
  See Ripken, Cal, Jr.
Ripley, Catherine 1957- 82
Ripley, Elizabeth Blake 1906-1969 5
Ripper, Charles L(ewis) 1929- 3
Ripper, Chuck
  See Ripper, Charles L(ewis)
Rippin, Sally 220
Riq
  See Atwater, Richard (Tupper)
Rish, David 1955- 110
Riskind, Mary 1944- 60
Rissinger, Matt 1956- 93
Rissman, Art
  See Sussman, Susan
Rissman, Susan
  See Sussman, Susan
Ritchie, Barbara Gibbons 14
Ritchie, Scot 1954- 217
Ritter, Felix
  See Kruss, James
Ritter, John H. 1951- 215
  Earlier sketches in SATA 129, 137

Ritter, Lawrence S(tanley) 1922-2004 .... *58*
 Obituary *152*
Ritthaler, Shelly 1955- *91*
Ritts, Paul 1920(?)-1980
 Obituary *25*
Ritz, Karen 1957- *202*
 Earlier sketch in SATA *80*
Riu, Isabel Ferrer 1969- *222*
Rivera, Geraldo (Miguel) 1943- *54*
 Brief entry *28*
Rivera, Guadalupe
 See Rivera Marin, Guadalupe
Rivera Marin, Guadalupe 1924- *224*
Rivers, Elfrida
 See Bradley, Marion Zimmer
Rivers, Karen 1970- *131*
Riverside, John
 See Heinlein, Robert A.
Rivkin, Ann 1920- *41*
Rivoli, Mario 1943- *10*
Roach, Marilynne K. 1946- *9*
Roach, Marilynne Kathleen
 See Roach, Marilynne K.
Roach, Portia
 See Takakjian, Portia
Robb, Don 1937- *194*
Robb, Laura 1937- *95*
Robberecht, Thierry 1960- *182*
Robbins, Frank 1917-1994(?) *42*
 Brief entry *32*
Robbins, Jacqui *221*
Robbins, Ken 1945- *219*
 Brief entry *53*
 Earlier sketches in SATA *94, 147*
Robbins, Raleigh
 See Hamilton, Charles (Harold St. John)
Robbins, Ruth 1917(?)- *14*
Robbins, Tony
 See Pashko, Stanley
Robbins, Wayne
 See Cox, William R(obert)
Robel, S. L.
 See Fraustino, Lisa Rowe
Roberson, Jennifer 1953- *72*
Roberson, John R(oyster) 1930- *53*
Robert, Adrian
 See St. John, Nicole
Roberts, Bethany *202*
 Earlier sketch in SATA *133*
Roberts, Bruce (Stuart) 1930- *47*
 Brief entry *39*
Roberts, Charles G(eorge) D(ouglas)
 1860-1943 .... *88*
 Brief entry *29*
 See also CLR *33*
Roberts, David
 See Cox, John Roberts
Roberts, David 1970- *191*
Roberts, Diane 1937- *184*
Roberts, Elizabeth 1944- *80*
Roberts, Elizabeth Madox 1886-1941 .... *33*
 Brief entry *27*
 See also CLR *100*
Roberts, Jim
 See Bates, Barbara S(nedeker)
Roberts, Jody *218*
Roberts, John G(aither) 1913-1993 .... *27*
Roberts, Judy I. 1957- *93*
Roberts, Katherine 1962- *152*
Roberts, Ken *223*
 See Lake, Kenneth R(obert)
Roberts, M. L.
 See Mattern, Joanne
Roberts, Marion 1966- *212*
Roberts, Nancy Correll 1924- *52*
 Brief entry *28*
Roberts, Priscilla 1955- *184*
Roberts, Terence
 See Sanderson, Ivan T(erence)

Roberts, Willo Davis 1928-2004 .... *150*
 Autobiography Feature *150*
 Obituary *160*
 Earlier sketches in SATA *21, 70, 133*
 See also CLR *95*
 See also SAAS *8*
Robertson, Barbara (Anne) 1931- *12*
Robertson, Don 1929-1999 .... *8*
 Obituary *113*
Robertson, Dorothy Lewis 1912- *12*
Robertson, Ellis
 See Ellison, Harlan
 and Silverberg, Robert
Robertson, James I., Jr. 1930- *182*
Robertson, James Irvin
 See Robertson, James I., Jr.
Robertson, Janet (E.) 1935- *68*
Robertson, Jennifer Sinclair 1942-1998 ...... *12*
Robertson, Jenny
 See Robertson, Jennifer Sinclair
Robertson, Keith (Carlton) 1914-1991 .... *85*
 Obituary *69*
 Earlier sketch in SATA *1*
 See also SAAS *15*
Robertson, Mark
 See Robertson, M.P.
Robertson, M.P. 1965- *197*
Robertson, Stephen
 See Walker, Robert W.
Robertus, Polly M. 1948- *212*
 Earlier sketch in SATA *73*
Robeson, Kenneth
 See Dent, Lester
 and Goulart, Ron
Robeson, Kenneth
 See Johnson, (Walter) Ryerson
Robinet, Harriette Gillem 1931- *104*
 Earlier sketch in SATA *27*
 See also CLR *64*
Robins, Deri 1958- *166*
 Earlier sketch in SATA *117*
Robins, Patricia 1921- *117*
Robins, Rollo, Jr.
 See Ellis, Edward S.
Robins, Seelin
 See Ellis, Edward S.
Robinson, Adjai 1932- *8*
Robinson, Aminah Brenda Lynn 1940- *159*
 Earlier sketch in SATA *77*
Robinson, Barbara (Webb) 1927- *84*
 Earlier sketch in SATA *8*
Robinson, C(harles) A(lexander), Jr.
 1900-1965 .... *36*
Robinson, Charles 1870-1937 .... *17*
Robinson, Charles 1931- *6*
Robinson, Dorothy W. 1929- *54*
Robinson, Elizabeth Keeler 1959- *204*
Robinson, Eve
 See Tanselle, Eve
Robinson, Fiona 1965- *225*
Robinson, Glen 1953- *92*
Robinson, Glendal P.
 See Robinson, Glen
Robinson, Jan M. 1933- *6*
Robinson, Jean O. 1934- *7*
Robinson, Joan (Mary) G(ale Thomas)
 1910-1988 .... *7*
Robinson, Kim Stanley 1952- *109*
Robinson, Lee 1948- *110*
Robinson, Lloyd
 See Silverberg, Robert
Robinson, Lynda S(uzanne) 1951- *107*
Robinson, Marileta 1942- *32*
Robinson, Maudie Millian Oller 1914- *11*
Robinson, Maurice R(ichard) 1895-1982
 Obituary *29*
Robinson, Nancy K(onheim) 1942-1994 ...... *91*
 Brief entry *31*
 Obituary *79*
 Earlier sketch in SATA *32*
Robinson, Ray 1920- *23*

Robinson, Raymond Kenneth
 See Robinson, Ray
Robinson, Shari
 See McGuire, Leslie (Sarah)
Robinson, Sharon 1950- *197*
 Earlier sketch in SATA *162*
Robinson, Spider 1948- *118*
Robinson, Sue
 See Robinson, Susan Maria
Robinson, Susan Maria 1955- *105*
Robinson, Susan Patricia
 See Gates, Susan
Robinson, Suzanne
 See Robinson, Lynda S(uzanne)
Robinson, T(homas) H(eath) 1869-1950 ...... *17*
Robinson, Tim 1963- *205*
Robinson, (Wanda) Veronica 1926- *30*
Robinson, W(illiam) Heath 1872-1944 .... *17*
Robison, Bonnie 1924- *12*
Robison, Nancy L(ouise) 1934- *32*
Robles, Harold E. 1948- *87*
Robottom, John 1934- *7*
Robson, Eric 1939- *82*
Roca, Francois 1971- *200*
Rocco, John 1967- *188*
Roche, A. K.
 See Abisch, Roslyn Kroop
 and Kaplan, Boche
Roche, Denis 1967- *196*
 Earlier sketch in SATA *99*
Roche, Denis Mary
 See Roche, Denis
Roche, Luane 1937- *170*
Roche, P(atricia) K. 1935- *57*
 Brief entry *34*
Roche, Terry
 See Poole, Peggy
Rochman, Hazel 1938- *105*
Rock, Lois
 See Joslin, Mary
Rock, Maxine 1940- *108*
Rocker, Fermin 1907- *40*
Rockliff, Mara *224*
Rocklin, Joanne 1946- *134*
 Earlier sketch in SATA *86*
Rockwell, Anne F. 1934- *194*
 Earlier sketches in SATA *33, 71, 114, 162*
 See also SAAS *19*
Rockwell, Anne Foote
 See Rockwell, Anne F.
Rockwell, Bart
 See Pellowski, Michael (Joseph)
Rockwell, Harlow 1910-1988 .... *33*
 Obituary *56*
Rockwell, Lizzy 1961- *185*
Rockwell, Norman (Percevel) 1894-1978 .... *23*
Rockwell, Thomas 1933- *70*
 Earlier sketch in SATA *7*
 See also CLR *6*
Rockwood, Joyce 1947- *39*
Rockwood, Roy
 See McFarlane, Leslie
 and Stratemeyer, Edward L.
Rodanas, Kristina 1952- *155*
Rodari, Gianni 1920-1980
 See CLR *24*
Rodd, Kathleen Tennant
 See Rodd, Kylie Tennant
Rodd, Kylie Tennant 1912-1988 .... *57*
 Obituary *55*
 Earlier sketch in SATA *6*
Rodda, Emily 1948- *146*
 Earlier sketch in SATA *97*
 See also CLR *32*
Roddenberry, Eugene Wesley 1921-1991 ..... *45*
 Obituary *69*
Roddenberry, Gene
 See Roddenberry, Eugene Wesley
Roddick, Ellen 1936- *5*
Roddie, Shen *153*
Roddy, Lee 1921- *57*

Rodenas, Paula *73*
Rodgers, Frank 1944- *69*
Rodgers, Mary 1931- *130*
  Earlier sketch in SATA *8*
  See also CLR *20*
Rodman, Emerson
  See Ellis, Edward S.
Rodman, Eric
  See Silverberg, Robert
Rodman, Maia
  See Wojciechowska, Maia (Teresa)
Rodman, Mary Ann *185*
Rodman, (Cary) Selden 1909-2002 .... *9*
Rodowsky, Colby 1932- *164*
  Earlier sketches in SATA *21, 77, 120*
  See also SAAS *22*
Rodowsky, Colby F.
  See Rodowsky, Colby
Rodriguez, Alejo 1941- *83*
Rodriguez, Alex 1975- *189*
Rodriguez, Christina 1981- *177*
Rodriguez, Edel 1971- *196*
Rodriguez, Luis J. 1954- *125*
Rodriguez, Rachel *180*
Rodriguez, Rachel Victoria
  See Rodriguez, Rachel
Roeder, Virginia Marsh 1926- *98*
Roehrig, Catharine H. 1949- *67*
Roennfeldt, Robert 1953- *78*
Roessel-Waugh, C. C.
  See Waugh, Carol-Lynn Rossel
  and Waugh, Charles G(ordon)
Roets, Lois F. 1937- *91*
Roever, J(oan) M(arilyn) 1935- *26*
Rofes, Eric 1954-2006 .... *52*
Rofes, Eric Edward 1954-2006
  See Rofes, Eric
Roffey, Maureen 1936- *33*
Rogak, Lisa 1962- *80*
Rogak, Lisa Angowski
  See Rogak, Lisa
Rogan, S. Jones *199*
Rogan, Sally Jones
  See Rogan, S. Jones
Rogasky, Barbara 1933- *144*
  Earlier sketch in SATA *86*
Rogers, (Thomas) Alan (Stinchcombe)
  1937- *81*
  Earlier sketch in SATA *2*
Rogers, Bettye 1858-1919 .... *103*
Rogers, Cindy 1950- *89*
Rogers, Emma 1951- *74*
Rogers, Frances 1888-1974 .... *10*
Rogers, Fred McFeely 1928-2003 .... *33*
  Obituary *138*
Rogers, Gregory 1957- *211*
Rogers, Hal
  See Sirimarco, Elizabeth
Rogers, Jacqueline 1958- *213*
Rogers, Jean 1919- *55*
  Brief entry *47*
Rogers, Matilda 1894-1976 .... *5*
  Obituary *34*
Rogers, Pamela 1927- *9*
Rogers, Paul 1950- *98*
  Earlier sketch in SATA *54*
Rogers, Robert
  See Hamilton, Charles (Harold St. John)
Rogers, Sherry *193*
Rogers, W(illiam) G(arland) 1896-1978 .... *23*
Rohan, M. S.
  See Rohan, Michael Scott
Rohan, Michael Scott 1951- *98*
Rohan, Mike Scott
  See Rohan, Michael Scott
Rohmann, Eric 1957- *171*
  See also CLR *100*
Rohmer, Harriet 1938- *56*
Rohrer, Doug 1962- *89*
Rojan
  See Rojankovsky, Feodor (Stepanovich)

Rojankovsky, Feodor (Stepanovich)
  1891-1970 .... *21*
Rojany, Lisa *94*
Rokeby-Thomas, Anna E(lma) 1911- *15*
Roland, Albert 1925-2002 .... *11*
Roland, Mary
  See Lewis, Mary
Roleff, Tamara L. 1959- *143*
Rolerson, Darrell A(llen) 1946- *8*
Roll, Winifred 1909-1998 .... *6*
Rollins, Charlemae Hill 1897-1979 .... *3*
  Obituary *26*
Rollins, James 1961- *216*
Rollock, Barbara T(herese) 1924- *64*
Rolston, Steve 1978- *209*
Romack, Janice Reed
  See LeNoir, Janice
Romain, Trevor *134*
Romanenko, Vitaliy 1962- *101*
Romano, Christy
  See Romano, Christy Carlson
Romano, Christy Carlson 1984- *210*
Romano, Clare 1922- *111*
  Earlier sketch in SATA *48*
Romano, Louis G. 1921- *35*
Romano, Melora A. 1966- *118*
Romano, Ray 1957- *170*
Romano, Raymond
  See Romano, Ray
Romijn, Johanna Maria Kooyker
  See Kooyker-Romijn, Johanna Maria
Romyn, Johanna Maria Kooyker
  See Kooyker-Romijn, Johanna Maria
Rong, Yu 1970- *174*
Rongen, Bjoern 1906- *10*
Rongen, Bjorn
  See Rongen, Bjoern
Ronson, Mark
  See Alexander, Marc
Rood, Ronald (N.) 1920- *12*
Rook, Sebastian
  See Jeapes, Ben
Rooke, Daphne 1914-2009 .... *12*
Rooke, Daphne Marie
  See Rooke, Daphne
Rooney, Ronnie 1970- *212*
Roop, Connie 1951- *167*
  Brief entry *49*
  Earlier sketches in SATA *54, 116*
Roop, Constance Betzer
  See Roop, Connie
Roop, Peter 1951- *167*
  Brief entry *49*
  Earlier sketches in SATA *54, 116*
Roop, Peter G.
  See Roop, Peter
Roop, Peter Geiger
  See Roop, Peter
Roos, Maryn *225*
Roos, Stephen 1945- *128*
  Brief entry *41*
  Earlier sketches in SATA *47, 77*
Roosa, Karen 1961- *218*
Roose-Evans, James 1927- *65*
Roosevelt, Eleanor 1884-1962 .... *50*
Root, Barry *182*
Root, Betty *84*
Root, Kimberly Bulcken *192*
Root, Phyllis 1949- *224*
  Brief entry *48*
  Earlier sketches in SATA *55, 94, 145, 184*
Root, Shelton L., Jr. 1923-1986
  Obituary *51*
Roper, Laura (Newbold) Wood 1911-2003 .. *34*
  Obituary *150*
Roper, Robert 1946- *142*
  Earlier sketch in SATA *78*
Roraback, Robin (Ellan) 1964- *111*
Rorby, Ginny 1944- *94*
Rorer, Abigail 1949- *85*
Rosaler, Maxine *208*

Rosamel, Godeleine de 1968- *151*
Roscoe, D(onald) T(homas) 1934- *42*
Rose, Anne *8*
Rose, Deborah Lee 1955- *185*
  Earlier sketches in SATA *71, 124*
Rose, Elizabeth (Jane Pretty) 1933- *68*
  Brief entry *28*
Rose, Florella
  See Carlson, Vada F.
Rose, Gerald (Hembdon Seymour) 1935- *68*
  Brief entry *30*
Rose, Malcolm 1953- *168*
  Earlier sketch in SATA *107*
Rose, Nancy A.
  See Sweetland, Nancy A(nn)
Rose, Naomi C. *228*
Rose, Ted 1940- *93*
Rose, Wendy 1948- *12*
Rosen, Elizabeth 1961- *205*
Rosen, Lillian (Diamond) 1928- *63*
Rosen, Marvin 1933- *161*
Rosen, Michael 1946- *229*
  Brief entry *40*
  Earlier sketches in SATA *48, 84, 137, 181*
  See also CLR *45*
Rosen, Michael J. 1954- *199*
  Earlier sketch in SATA *86*
Rosen, Michael Wayne
  See Rosen, Michael
Rosen, Sidney 1916- *1*
Rosen, Winifred 1943- *8*
Rosenbaum, Maurice 1907-1987 .... *6*
Rosenberg, Amye 1950- *74*
Rosenberg, Dorothy 1906- *40*
Rosenberg, Eth Clifford 1915- *92*
  See also SAAS *22*
Rosenberg, Jane 1949- *58*
Rosenberg, Liz 1958- *129*
  Earlier sketch in SATA *75*
Rosenberg, Maxine B(erta) 1939- *93*
  Brief entry *47*
  Earlier sketch in SATA *55*
Rosenberg, Nancy (Sherman) 1931- *4*
  See Sherman, Nancy
Rosenberg, Sharon 1942- *8*
Rosenberry, Vera 1948- *219*
  Earlier sketches in SATA *83, 144*
Rosenblatt, Arthur
  See Rosenblatt, Arthur S.
Rosenblatt, Arthur S. 1938- *68*
  Brief entry *45*
Rosenblatt, Lily 1956- *90*
Rosenbloom, Joseph 1928- *21*
Rosenblum, Richard 1928- *11*
Rosenburg, John M. 1918- *6*
Rosenfeld, Dina 1962- *99*
Rosenstiehl, Agnes 1941- *203*
Rosenthal, Amy Krouse 1965- *222*
  Earlier sketch in SATA *177*
Rosenthal, Betsy R. 1957- *178*
Rosenthal, Harold 1914-1999 .... *35*
Rosenthal, M(acha) L(ouis) 1917-1996 .... *59*
Rosenthal, Marc 1949- *193*
Rosenthal, Mark A(lan) 1946- *64*
Rosing, Norbert 1953- *196*
Rosman, Steven M 1956- *81*
Rosman, Steven Michael
  See Rosman, Steven M
Rosoff, Meg 1956- *209*
  Earlier sketch in SATA *160*
Ross, Alan
  See Warwick, Alan R(oss)
Ross, Christine 1950- *172*
  Earlier sketch in SATA *83*
Ross, Clare
  See Romano, Clare
Ross, Dana Fuller
  See Cockrell, Amanda
  and Gerson, Noel Bertram
Ross, Dave
  See Ross, David

Ross, David 1896-1975 .... *49*
    Obituary *20*
Ross, David 1949- *133*
    Earlier sketch in SATA *32*
Ross, Deborah J.
    See Wheeler, Deborah
Ross, Diana
    See Denney, Diana
Ross, Edward S(hearman) 1915- *85*
Ross, Eileen 1950- *115*
Ross, Frank (Xavier), Jr. 1914- *28*
Ross, Jane 1961- *79*
Ross, John 1921- *45*
Ross, Judy 1942- *54*
Ross, Katharine Reynolds
    See Ross, Kathy
Ross, Kathy 1948- *169*
    Earlier sketch in SATA *89*
Ross, Kent 1956- *91*
Ross, Lillian Hammer 1925- *72*
Ross, Michael Elsohn 1952- *170*
    Earlier sketches in SATA *80, 127*
Ross, Pat(ricia Kienzle) 1943- *53*
    Brief entry *48*
Ross, Ramon R(oyal) 1930- *62*
Ross, Stewart 1947- *134*
    Earlier sketch in SATA *92*
    See also SAAS 23
Ross, Tom 1958- *84*
Ross, Tony 1938- *225*
    Earlier sketches in SATA *17, 65, 130, 176*
Ross, Wilda 1915- *51*
    Brief entry *39*
Rossel, Seymour 1945- *28*
Rossell, Judith 1953- *187*
Rossel-Waugh, C. C.
    See Waugh, Carol-Lynn Rossel
Rossetti, Christina 1830-1894 .... *20*
    See also CLR *115*
Rossetti, Christina Georgina
    See Rossetti, Christina
Rossi, Joyce 1943- *116*
Rossotti, Hazel Swaine 1930- *95*
Rostkowski, Margaret I. 1945- *59*
Rostoker-Gruber, Karen *229*
Roth, Arnold 1929- *21*
Roth, Arthur J(oseph) 1925-1993 .... *43*
    Brief entry *28*
    Obituary *75*
    See also SAAS 11
Roth, Carol *222*
Roth, David 1940- *36*
Roth, Julie Jersild *180*
Roth, Matthue 1978(?)- *174*
Roth, Roger 1990- *190*
Roth, Ruby 1983(?)- *216*
Roth, Stephanie *202*
Roth, Susan L. *181*
    Earlier sketch in SATA *134*
Rothberg, Abraham 1922-2011 .... *59*
Roth-Hano, Renee 1931- *85*
Rothkopf, Carol Z. 1929- *4*
Rothman, Joel 1938- *7*
Rotner, Shelley 1951- *169*
    Earlier sketch in SATA *76*
Rottman, S.L. 1970- *157*
    Earlier sketch in SATA *106*
Rottman, Susan Lynn
    See Rottman, S.L.
Roueche, Berton 1911-1994 .... *28*
Roughsey, Dick 1921(?)-1985 .... *35*
    See also CLR *41*
Roughsey, Goobalathaldin
    See Roughsey, Dick
Rounds, Glen (Harold) 1906-2002 .... *112*
    Obituary *141*
    Earlier sketches in SATA *8, 70*
Rourke, Constance Mayfield 1885-1941
    See YABC *1*
Rouss, Sylvia *211*
Rovetch, Gerda 1925(?)- *202*

Rovetch, L. Bob
    See Rovetch, Lissa
Rovetch, Lissa *201*
Rowan, Deirdre
    See Williams, Jeanne
Rowe, Jennifer
    See Rodda, Emily
Rowe, John A. 1949- *198*
    Earlier sketch in SATA *146*
Rowe, Viola Carson 1903-1969
    Obituary *26*
Rowh, Mark 1952- *90*
Rowland, Florence Wightman 1900-1997 ...... *8*
    Obituary *108*
Rowland-Entwistle, (Arthur) Theodore (Henry)
    1925- *94*
    Earlier sketch in SATA *31*
Rowling, J.K. 1965- *174*
    Earlier sketch in SATA *109*
    See also CLR *112*
Rowling, Joanne Kathleen
    See Rowling, J.K.
Rowsome, Frank (Howard), Jr. 1914-1983 .. *36*
Roy, Gabrielle 1909-1983 .... *104*
Roy, Jacqueline 1954- *74*
Roy, James 1968- *218*
Roy, Jennifer
    See Roy, Jennifer Rozines
Roy, Jennifer Rozines 1967- *178*
Roy, Jessie Hailstalk 1895-1986
    Obituary *51*
Roy, Kari Anne 1977(?)- *221*
Roy, Liam
    See Scarry, Patricia (Murphy)
Roy, Ron 1940- *228*
    Brief entry *35*
    Earlier sketches in SATA *40, 110*
Roybal, Laura 1956- *85*
Roybal, Laura Husby
    See Roybal, Laura
Royds, Caroline 1953- *55*
Royston, Angela 1945- *169*
    Earlier sketch in SATA *120*
Rozakis, Laurie E. 1952- *84*
Rozen, Anna 1960- *206*
Rubbino, Salvatore 1970- *220*
Rubel, David 1961- *223*
Rubel, Nicole 1953- *181*
    Earlier sketches in SATA *18, 95, 135*
Rubin, Eva Johanna 1925- *38*
Rubin, Susan Goldman 1939- *182*
    Earlier sketches in SATA *84, 132*
Rubin, Vicky 1964- *193*
Rubinetti, Donald 1947- *92*
Rubinger, Ami 1953- *225*
Rubinstein, Gillian 1942- *158*
    Autobiography Feature *116*
    Earlier sketches in SATA *68, 105*
    See also CLR *35*
    See also SAAS 25
Rubinstein, Gillian Margaret
    See Rubinstein, Gillian
Rubinstein, Patricia -2003
    See Forest, Antonia
Rubinstein, Patricia Giulia Caulfield Kate
    See Forest, Antonia
Rubinstein, Robert E(dward) 1943- *49*
Rublowsky, John M(artin) 1928- *62*
Rubright, Lynn 1936- *171*
Ruby, Laura *227*
    Earlier sketches in SATA *155, 181*
Ruby, Lois 1942- *184*
    Autobiography Feature *105*
    Brief entry *34*
    Earlier sketches in SATA *35, 95*
Ruby, Lois F.
    See Ruby, Lois
Ruchlis, Hy(man) 1913-1992 .... *3*
    Obituary *72*
Ruckdeschel, Liz *214*
Rucker, Mike 1940- *91*

Ruckman, Ivy 1931- *93*
    Earlier sketch in SATA *37*
Ruck-Pauquet, Gina 1931- *40*
    Brief entry *37*
Ruddell, Deborah 1949- *210*
Ruditis, Paul *190*
Rudley, Stephen 1946- *30*
Rudolph, Marguerita 1908- *21*
Rudomin, Esther
    See Hautzig, Esther Rudomin
Rue, Leonard Lee III 1926- *142*
    Earlier sketch in SATA *37*
Rueda, Claudia *183*
Ruedi, Norma Paul
    See Ainsworth, Norma
Ruelle, Karen Gray 1957- *209*
    Earlier sketches in SATA *84, 126*
Ruemmler, John D(avid) 1948- *78*
Ruepp, Krista 1947- *143*
Ruffell, Ann 1941- *30*
Ruffins, Reynold 1930- *125*
    Earlier sketch in SATA *41*
Rugg, Jim *206*
Ruggles, Lucy
    See Williams, Kathryn
Rugoff, Milton 1913- *30*
Ruhen, Olaf 1911-1989 .... *17*
Rui, Paolo 1962- *217*
Rukeyser, Muriel 1913-1980
    Obituary *22*
Rumbaut, Hendle 1949- *84*
Rumford, James 1948- *193*
    Earlier sketch in SATA *116*
Rumsey, Marian (Barritt) 1928- *16*
Rumstuckle, Cornelius
    See Brennan, Herbie
Runholt, Susan *216*
Runnerstroem, Bengt Arne 1944- *75*
Runyan, John
    See Palmer, Bernard (Alvin)
Runyon, Brent *217*
Runyon, Catherine 1947- *62*
Ruoff, A. LaVonne Brown 1930- *76*
Rupp, Rebecca *185*
Rusch, Elizabeth 1966- *198*
Rusch, Kris
    See Rusch, Kristine Kathryn
Rusch, Kristine Kathryn 1960- *113*
Rush, Alison 1951- *41*
Rush, Peter 1937- *32*
Rushdie, Ahmed Salman
    See Rushdie, Salman
Rushdie, Salman 1947-
    See CLR *125*
Rushford, Patricia H(elen) 1943- *134*
Rushmore, Helen 1898-1994 .... *3*
Rushmore, Robert (William) 1926-1986 .... *8*
    Obituary *49*
Ruskin, Ariane
    See Batterberry, Ariane Ruskin
Ruskin, John 1819-1900 .... *24*
Russ, Lavinia (Faxon) 1904-1992 .... *74*
Russell, Charlotte
    See Rathjen, Carl Henry
Russell, Ching Yeung 1946- *107*
Russell, Don(ald Bert) 1899-1986
    Obituary *47*
Russell, Franklin (Alexander) 1926- *11*
Russell, Gertrude Barrer
    See Barrer-Russell, Gertrude
Russell, Helen Ross 1915- *8*
Russell, James 1933- *53*
Russell, Jim
    See Russell, James
Russell, Joan Plummer 1930- *139*
Russell, Natalie 1972- *218*
Russell, P(hilip) Craig 1951- *162*
    Earlier sketch in SATA *80*
Russell, Patrick
    See Sammis, John
Russell, Paul (Gary) 1942- *57*

Russell, Sarah
  See Laski, Marghanita
Russell, Sharman Apt 1954- 123
Russell, Solveig Paulson 1904-1985 3
Russo, Marisabina 1950- 188
  Earlier sketches in SATA *106, 151*
Russo, Monica J. 1950- 83
Russo, Susan 1947- 30
Russon, Penni 1974- 179
Rutgers van der Loeff, An
  See Rutgers van der Loeff-Basenau, An(na)
  Maria Margaretha
Rutgers van der Loeff-Basenau, An(na) Maria
  Margaretha 1910- 22
Ruth, Rod 1912-1987 9
Rutherford, Douglas
  See McConnell, James Douglas Rutherford
Rutherford, Meg 1932- 34
Ruthin, Margaret
  See Catherall, Arthur
Rutkoski, Marie 1977- 219
Rutledge, Jill Zimmerman 1951- 155
Rutz, Viola Larkin 1932- 12
Ruurs, Margriet 1952- 215
  Earlier sketches in SATA *97, 147*
Ruzicka, Rudolph 1883-1978
  Obituary 24
Ruzzier, Sergio 1966- 210
  Earlier sketch in SATA *159*
Ryan, Betsy
  See Ryan, Elizabeth (Anne)
Ryan, Cheli Duran 20
Ryan, Darlene 1958- 176
Ryan, Elizabeth (Anne) 1943- 30
Ryan, Jeanette
  See Mines, Jeanette
Ryan, John 1921-2009 22
Ryan, John Gerald Christopher
  See Ryan, John
Ryan, Margaret 1950- 166
  Earlier sketch in SATA *78*
Ryan, Mary E. 1953- 61
Ryan, Mary Elizabeth
  See Ryan, Mary E.
Ryan, Pam Munoz 1951- 197
  Earlier sketch in SATA *134*
Ryan, Patrick 1957- 138
Ryan, Peter (Charles) 1939- 15
Ryan-Lush, Geraldine 1949- 89
Rybakov, Anatoli (Naumovich) 1911-1998 .. 79
  Obituary 108
Rybakov, Anatolii (Naumovich)
  See Rybakov, Anatoli (Naumovich)
Rybolt, Thomas R. 1954- 62
Rybolt, Thomas Roy
  See Rybolt, Thomas R.
Rybolt, Tom
  See Rybolt, Thomas R.
Rycroft, Nina 228
Rydberg, Ernest E(mil) 1901-1993 21
Rydberg, Lou(isa Hampton) 1908- 27
Rydell, Katy 1942- 91
Rydell, Wendell
  See Rydell, Wendy
Rydell, Wendy 4
Ryden, Hope 91
  Earlier sketch in SATA *8*
Ryder, Joanne 1946- 226
  Brief entry 34
  Earlier sketches in SATA *65, 122, 163*
  See also CLR *37*
Ryder, Pamela
  See Lamb, Nancy
Rye, Anthony
  See Youd, Samuel
Rylant, Cynthia 1954- 195
  Brief entry 44
  Earlier sketches in SATA *50, 76, 112, 160*
  See also CLR *86*
  See also SAAS *13*

Rymer, Alta May 1925- 34
Rymond, Lynda Gene 199

S

S. L. C.
  See Twain, Mark
S., Svend Otto
  See Soerensen, Svend Otto
Saaf, Donald W(illiam) 1961- 124
Saal, Jocelyn
  See Sachs, Judith
Sabbeth, Carol (Landstrom) 1957- 125
Saberhagen, Fred 1930-2007 89
  Obituary 184
  Earlier sketch in SATA *37*
Saberhagen, Fred T.
  See Saberhagen, Fred
Saberhagen, Fred Thomas
  See Saberhagen, Fred
Saberhagen, Frederick Thomas
  See Saberhagen, Fred
Sabin, Edwin L(egrand) 1870-1952
  See YABC *2*
Sabin, Francene 27
Sabin, Lou
  See Sabin, Louis
Sabin, Louis 1930- 27
Sabre, Dirk
  See Laffin, John (Alfred Charles)
Sabuda, Robert (James) 1965- 120
  Earlier sketch in SATA *81*
Sabuda, Robert 1965- 170
Sabuda, Robert James
  See Sabuda, Robert
Sachar, Louis 1954- 154
  Brief entry 50
  Earlier sketches in SATA *63, 104*
  See also CLR *161*
Sachs, Elizabeth-Ann 1946- 48
Sachs, Judith 1947- 52
  Brief entry 51
Sachs, Marilyn 1927- 164
  Autobiography Feature 110
  Earlier sketches in SATA *3, 68*
  See also CLR *2*
  See also SAAS *2*
Sachs, Marilyn Stickle
  See Sachs, Marilyn
Sackett, S(amuel) J(ohn) 1928- 12
Sackson, Sid 1920- 16
Sacre, Antonio 1968- 152
Saddler, Allen
  See Richards, R(onald) C(harles) W(illiam)
Saddler, K. Allen
  See Richards, R(onald) C(harles) W(illiam)
Sadie, Stanley 1930-2005 14
Sadie, Stanley John
  See Sadie, Stanley
Sadiq, Nazneen
  See Sheikh, Nazneen
Sadler, Catherine Edwards 1952- 60
  Brief entry 45
Sadler, Marilyn (June) 1950- 79
Sadler, Mark
  See Lynds, Dennis
Saffer, Barbara 144
Sagan, Carl 1934-1996 58
  Obituary 94
Sagan, Carl Edward
  See Sagan, Carl
Sage, Angie 1952- 197
Sage, Juniper
  See Brown, Margaret Wise
  and Hurd, Edith Thacher
Sagsoorian, Paul 1923- 12
Said, S.F. 1967- 174
Saidman, Anne 1952- 75
Saint, Dora Jessie 1913- 10

St. Anthony, Jane 175
St. Antoine, Sara L. 1966- 84
St. Clair, Byrd Hooper 1905-1976
  Obituary 28
St. Crow, Lili
  See Saintcrow, Lilith
Saintcrow, Lilith 1976- 221
Saint-Exupery, Antoine de 1900-1944 20
  See also CLR *142*
Saint-Exupery, Antoine Jean Baptiste Marie
  Roger de
  See Saint-Exupery, Antoine de
St. George, Judith 1931- 161
  Earlier sketches in SATA *13, 99*
  See also CLR *57*
  See also SAAS *12*
St. George, Judith Alexander
  See St. George, Judith
St. James, Blakely
  See Gottfried, Theodore Mark
  and Platt, Charles
St. James, Blakely
  See Griffin, W. E. B.
St. James, Sierra
  See Rallison, Janette
Saint James, Synthia 1949- 152
  Earlier sketch in SATA *84*
St. John, Lauren 1966- 214
St. John, Nicole 143
  Autobiography Feature 143
  Earlier sketches in SATA *29, 89*
  See also CLR *46*
  See also SAAS *7*
St. John, Patricia Mary 1919-1993
  Obituary 79
St. John, Philip
  See del Rey, Lester
St. John, Wylly Folk 1908-1985 10
  Obituary 45
St. Max, E. S.
  See Ellis, Edward S.
St. Meyer, Ned
  See Stratemeyer, Edward L.
St. Mox, E. A.
  See Ellis, Edward S.
St. Myer, Ned
  See Stratemeyer, Edward L.
St. Tamara
  See Kolba, St. Tamara
Saito, Michiko
  See Fujiwara, Michiko
Sakai, Komako 1966- 213
Sakaki, Ichiro 1969- 192
Sakamoto, Miki 198
Sakers, Don 1958- 72
Sakharnov, S.
  See Sakharnov, Svyatoslav
Sakharnov, Svyatoslav 1923- 65
Sakharnov, Svyatoslav Vladimirovich
  See Sakharnov, Svyatoslav
Saksena, Kate 148
Sakurai, Gail 1952- 153
  Earlier sketch in SATA *87*
Salamanca, Lucy
  See del Barco, Lucy Salamanca
Salas, Laura Purdie 1966- 216
Salassi, Otto R(ussell) 1939-1993 38
  Obituary 77
Salat, Cristina 82
Saldana, Rene, Jr. 186
Saldutti, Denise 1953- 39
Sale, Tim 1956- 153
Salem, Kay 1952- 92
Salerno, Steven 176
Salinger, J.D. 1919-2010 67
  See also CLR *18*
Salinger, Jerome David
  See Salinger, J.D.
Salisbury, Graham 1944- 195
  Earlier sketches in SATA *76, 108, 161*
Salisbury, Joyce E(llen) 1944- 138

Salkey, (Felix) Andrew (Alexander)
1928-1995 118
Earlier sketch in SATA 35
Salley, Coleen 166
Sallis, Susan (Diana) 1929- 55
Salmieri, Daniel 1983- 208
Salmon, Annie Elizabeth 1899- 13
Salmon, Dena K. 1959(?)- 219
Salonen, Roxane Beauclair 1968- 184
Salsi, Lynn 1947- 130
Salsitz, R. A. V.
See Salsitz, Rhondi Vilott
Salsitz, Rhondi Vilott 115
Salten, Felix
See Salzmann, Siegmund
Salter, Cedric
See Knight, Francis Edgar
Salter, Sydney 220
Saltman, Judith 1947- 64
Saltzberg, Barney 1955- 194
Earlier sketch in SATA 135
Saltzman, David (Charles Laertes)
1967-1990 86
Salvadori, Mario (George) 1907-1997 97
Earlier sketch in SATA 40
Salwood, F.K.
See Kilworth, Garry
Salzer, L. E.
See Wilson, Lionel
Salzman, Marian 1959- 77
Salzmann, Siegmund 1869-1945 25
Samachson, Dorothy (Mirkin) 1914-1997 3
Samachson, Joseph 1906-1980 3
Obituary 52
Sammis, John 1942- 4
Sampson, Emma (Keats) Speed 1868-1947 . 68
Sampson, Fay 1935- 151
Brief entry 40
Earlier sketch in SATA 42
Sampson, Fay Elizabeth
See Sampson, Fay
Sampson, Michael 1952- 143
Earlier sketch in SATA 95
Samson, Anne S(tringer) 1933- 2
Samson, Joan 1937-1976 13
Samson, Suzanne M. 1959- 91
Samuels, Barbara 199
Samuels, Charles 1902-1982 12
Samuels, Cynthia K(alish) 1946- 79
Samuels, Gertrude 1910(?)-2003 17
Obituary 147
Sanborn, Duane 1914-1996 38
Sancha, Sheila 1924- 38
Sanchez, Alex 1957- 151
Sanchez, Anita 1956- 209
Sanchez, Sonia 1934- 136
Earlier sketch in SATA 22
See also CLR 18
Sanchez-Silva, Jose Maria 1911- 132
Earlier sketch in SATA 16
See also CLR 12
Sand, George X. 45
Sandak, Cass R(obert) 1950-2001 51
Brief entry 37
Sandberg, (Karin) Inger 1930- 15
Sandberg, Karl C. 1931- 35
Sandberg, Lasse (E. M.) 1924- 15
Sandburg, Carl 1878-1967 8
See also CLR 67
Sandburg, Carl August
See Sandburg, Carl
Sandburg, Charles
See Sandburg, Carl
Sandburg, Charles A.
See Sandburg, Carl
Sandburg, Helga 1918- 3
See also SAAS 10
Sandell, Lisa Ann 1977- 175
Sandemose, Iben 1950- 211
Sander, Heather L. 1947- 157
Sanderlin, George 1915- 4

Sanderlin, Owenita (Harrah) 1916- 11
Sanders, Betty Jane
See Monthei, Betty
Sanders, Nancy I. 1960- 141
Earlier sketch in SATA 90
Sanders, Scott Russell 1945- 109
Earlier sketch in SATA 56
Sanders, Winston P.
See Anderson, Poul
Sanderson, Irma 1912- 66
Sanderson, Ivan T(erence) 1911-1973 6
Sanderson, Margaret Love
See Keats, Emma
and Sampson, Emma (Keats) Speed
Sanderson, Ruth 1951- 224
Earlier sketches in SATA 41, 109, 172
Sanderson, Ruth L.
See Sanderson, Ruth
Sanders-Wells, Linda 220
Sand-Eveland, Cyndi 211
Sandin, Joan 1942- 197
Earlier sketches in SATA 12, 94, 153
Sandison, Janet
See Cameron, Elizabeth Jane
Sandler, Martin W. 216
Earlier sketch in SATA 160
Sandom, J. Gregory
See Welsh, T.K.
Sandom, J.G.
See Welsh, T.K.
Sandoz, Mari(e Susette) 1900-1966 5
Sanford, Agnes (White) 1897-1976 61
Sanford, Doris 1937- 69
Sanford, Rose
See Simmonds, Posy
Sanger, Amy Wilson 1967- 205
Sanger, Marjory Bartlett 1920- 8
San Jose, Christine 1929- 167
Sankey, Alice (Ann-Susan) 1910- 27
San Souci, Daniel 192
Earlier sketch in SATA 96
San Souci, Robert D. 1946- 220
Earlier sketches in SATA 40, 81, 117, 158
See also CLR 43
Santamaria, Benjamin 1955- 184
Santat, Dan 224
Earlier sketch in SATA 188
Santesson, Hans Stefan 1914(?)-1975
Obituary 30
Santiago, Esmeralda 1948- 129
Santopolo, Jill 214
Santore, Charles 1935- 200
Santoro, C.
See Santoro, Christopher
Santoro, Christopher 218
Santos, Helen
See Griffiths, Helen
Santrey, Louis
See Sabin, Louis
Santucci, Barbara 1948- 130
Sapergia, Barbara 1943- 181
Sapet, Kerrily 1972- 214
Sapieyevski, Anne Lindbergh 1940-1993 81
Brief entry 32
Earlier sketches in SATA 35, 78
Saport, Linda 1954- 123
Sapp, Allen 1929- 151
Sarac, Roger
See Caras, Roger A(ndrew)
Sarah, Duchess of York
See Ferguson, Sarah
Sarasin, Jennifer
See Sachs, Judith
Sarcone-Roach, Julia 215
Sardinha, Rick 192
Sarg, Anthony Frederick
See Sarg, Tony
Sarg, Tony 1882-1942
See YABC 1
Sargent, Pamela 1948- 78
Earlier sketch in SATA 29

Sargent, Robert 1933- 2
Sargent, Sarah 1937- 44
Brief entry 41
Sargent, Shirley 1927-2004 11
Sarnoff, Jane 1937- 10
Saroff, Phyllis V. 202
Saroyan, William 1908-1981 23
Obituary 24
Sartell, Debra 229
Sarton, Eleanor May
See Sarton, May
Sarton, May 1912-1995 36
Obituary 86
Sasaki, Chris 182
Sasaki, Ellen Joy 206
Saseen, Sharon (Dillon) 1949- 59
Sasek, Miroslav 1916-1980 16
Obituary 23
See also CLR 4
Sasso, Sandy Eisenberg 1947- 162
Earlier sketches in SATA 86, 116
Sathre, Vivian 1952- 133
Earlier sketch in SATA 79
Satterfield, Charles
See del Rey, Lester
and Pohl, Frederik
Sattgast, L. J.
See Sattgast, Linda J.
Sattgast, Linda J. 1953- 91
Sattler, Helen Roney 1921-1992 74
Earlier sketch in SATA 4
See also CLR 24
Sattler, Jennifer
See Sattler, Jennifer Gordon
Sattler, Jennifer Gordon 218
Sauer, Julia Lina 1891-1983 32
Obituary 36
Sauer, Tammi 1972- 223
Sauerwein, Leigh 1944- 155
Saul, Carol P. 1947- 117
Earlier sketch in SATA 78
Saul, John III
See Saul, John
Saul, John 1942- 98
Saul, John W.
See Saul, John
Saul, John W. III
See Saul, John
Saul, John Woodruff III
See Saul, John
Saul, (Ellen) Wendy 1946- 42
Saulnier, Karen Luczak 1940- 80
Saunders, Caleb
See Heinlein, Robert A.
Saunders, Dave 1939- 85
Saunders, Julie 1939- 85
Saunders, (William) Keith 1910-1994 12
Saunders, Rubie (Agnes) 1929- 21
Saunders, Steven
See Jones, Allan Frewin
Saunders, Susan 1945- 96
Brief entry 41
Earlier sketch in SATA 46
Saunders-Smith, Gail 1952- 169
Sauvain, Philip Arthur 1933- 111
Savadier, Elivia 1950- 228
Earlier sketches in SATA 79, 164
Savage, Alan
See Nicole, Christopher
Savage, Blake
See Goodwin, Harold L(eland)
Savage, Candace 1949- 142
Savage, Deborah 1955- 76
Savage, Jeff 1961- 97
Savage, Katharine James 1905-1989
Obituary 61
Savage, Stephen 1965- 194
Savage, Thomas 1915-2003
Obituary 147
Savageau, Cheryl 1950- 96
Savery, Constance (Winifred) 1897-1999 1

Saville, Andrew
  See Taylor, Andrew
Saville, (Leonard) Malcolm 1901-1982 23
  Obituary 31
Saviozzi, Adriana
  See Mazza, Adriana
Savitt, Sam 1917-2000 8
  Obituary 126
Savitz, Harriet May 1933-2008 72
  Earlier sketch in SATA 5
  See also SAAS 26
Sawicki, Mary 1950- 90
Sawyer, (Frederick) Don(ald) 1947- 72
Sawyer, Kem Knapp 1953- 84
Sawyer, Robert J. 1960- 149
  Earlier sketch in SATA 81
Sawyer, Robert James
  See Sawyer, Robert J.
Sawyer, Ruth 1880-1970 17
  See also CLR 36
Saxby, H.M.
  See Saxby, (Henry) Maurice
Saxby, (Henry) Maurice 1924- 71
Saxon, Andrew
  See Arthur, Robert, (Jr.)
Saxon, Antonia
  See Sachs, Judith
Say, Allen 1937- 161
  Earlier sketches in SATA 28, 69, 110
  See also CLR 135
Sayers, Frances Clarke 1897-1989 3
  Obituary 62
Sayles, Elizabeth 1956- 220
  Earlier sketches in SATA 108, 163
Saylor-Marchant, Linda 1963- 82
Sayre, April Pulley 1966- 191
  Earlier sketches in SATA 88, 131
Sazer, Nina 1949- 13
Scabrini, Janet 1953- 13
Scagell, Robin 1946- 107
Scagnetti, Jack 1924- 7
Scaletta, Kurtis 1968- 215
Scalora, Suza 224
Scamander, Newt
  See Rowling, J.K.
Scamell, Ragnhild 1940- 180
  Earlier sketch in SATA 77
Scandiffio, Laura 227
Scanlon, Elizabeth Garton
  See Scanlon, Liz Garton
Scanlon, Liz Garton 226
Scanlon, Marion Stephany 11
Scannel, John Vernon
  See Scannell, Vernon
Scannell, Vernon 1922-2007 59
  Obituary 188
Scarborough, Elizabeth
  See Scarborough, Elizabeth Ann
Scarborough, Elizabeth Ann 1947- 171
  Earlier sketch in SATA 98
Scarf, Maggi
  See Scarf, Maggie
Scarf, Maggie 1932- 5
Scariano, Margaret M. 1924- 86
Scarlett, Susan
  See Streatfeild, Noel
Scarry, Huck
  See Scarry, Richard McClure, Jr.
Scarry, Patricia (Murphy) 1924- 2
Scarry, Patsy
  See Scarry, Patricia (Murphy)
Scarry, Richard (McClure) 1919-1994 75
  Obituary 90
  Earlier sketches in SATA 2, 35
  See also CLR 41
Scarry, Richard McClure, Jr. 1953- 35
Schachner, Judith Byron 1951- 178
  Earlier sketch in SATA 88
Schachner, Judy
  See Schachner, Judith Byron
Schachtel, Roger 1949- 38

Schachtel, Roger Bernard
  See Schachtel, Roger
Schade, Susan 189
Schaedler, Sally 116
Schaefer, Carole Lexa 173
Schaefer, Jack (Warner) 1907-1991 66
  Obituary 65
  Earlier sketch in SATA 3
Schaefer, Lola M. 1950- 183
  Earlier sketches in SATA 91, 144
Schaeffer, Mead 1898- 21
Schaeffer, Susan Fromberg 1941- 22
Schaer, Brigitte 1958- 112
Schallau, Daniel 1966- 222
Schaller, George
  See Schaller, George B.
Schaller, George B. 1933- 30
Schaller, George Beals
  See Schaller, George B.
Schanzer, Rosalyn (Good) 1942- 138
  Earlier sketch in SATA 77
Schatell, Brian 66
  Brief entry 47
Schechter, Betty (Goodstein) 1921- 5
Schechter, Simone
  See Elkeles, Simone
Schecter, Ellen 1944- 85
Scheeder, Louis 1946- 141
Scheer, Julian (Weisel) 1926-2001 8
Scheffer, Victor B(lanchard) 1906- 6
Scheffler, Axel 1957- 180
Scheffler, Ursel 1938- 81
Scheffrin-Falk, Gladys 1928- 76
Scheidl, Gerda Marie 1913- 85
Scheier, Michael 1943- 40
  Brief entry 36
Schell, Mildred 1922- 41
Schell, Orville (Hickok) 1940- 10
Scheller, Melanie 1953- 77
Schellie, Don 1932- 29
Schembri, Jim 1962- 124
Schembri, Pamela 1969- 195
Schemm, Mildred Walker 1905-1998 21
  Obituary 103
Schenker, Dona 1947- 133
  Earlier sketch in SATA 68
Scher, Paula 1948- 47
Scherer, Jeffrey 194
Scherf, Margaret 1908-1979 10
Schermer, Judith (Denise) 1941- 30
Schertle, Alice 1941- 192
  Earlier sketches in SATA 36, 90, 145
Schick, Alice 1946- 27
Schick, Eleanor 1942- 144
  Earlier sketches in SATA 9, 82
Schick, Joel 1945- 31
  Brief entry 30
Schields, Gretchen 1948- 75
Schiff, Ken(neth Roy) 1942- 7
Schiller, Andrew 1919- 21
Schiller, Barbara (Heyman) 1928- 21
Schiller, Pamela (Byrne) 127
Schindel, John 1955- 213
  Earlier sketches in SATA 77, 115
Schindelman, Joseph 1923- 67
  Brief entry 32
Schindler, S.D. 1952- 198
  Brief entry 50
  Earlier sketches in SATA 75, 118, 171
Schindler, Steven D.
  See Schindler, S.D.
Schinto, Jeanne 1951- 93
Schisgall, Oscar 1901-1984 12
  Obituary 38
Schlaepfer, Gloria G. 1931- 154
Schlee, Ann 1934- 44
  Brief entry 36
Schleichert, Elizabeth 1945- 77

Schlein, Miriam 1926-2004 130
  Obituary 159
  Earlier sketches in SATA 2, 87
  See also CLR 41
Schlesinger, Arthur M., Jr. 1917-2007 61
  Obituary 181
  See Schlesinger, Arthur Meier
Schlesinger, Arthur Meier 1888-1965
Schlessinger, Laura (Catherine) 1947- 160
  Earlier sketch in SATA 110
Schlitz, Laura Amy 184
Schloat, G. Warren, Jr. 1914-2000 4
Schlossberg, Elisabeth 221
Schmais, Libby 227
Schmatz, Pat 197
Schmid, Eleonore 1939- 126
  Earlier sketches in SATA 12, 84
Schmid, Susan Maupin 208
Schmiderer, Dorothy 1940- 19
Schmidt, Annie M. G. 1911-1995 67
  Obituary 91
  See also CLR 22
Schmidt, C.A. 196
Schmidt, Diane 1953- 70
Schmidt, Elizabeth 1915- 15
Schmidt, Gary D. 1957- 193
  Earlier sketches in SATA 93, 135
Schmidt, James Norman 1912-1983 21
Schmidt, Karen Lee 1953- 185
  Earlier sketch in SATA 94
Schmidt, Lynette 1952- 76
Schmitz, Tamara 207
Schneider, Antonie 1954- 167
  Earlier sketch in SATA 89
Schneider, Christine M. 1972(?)- 171
  Earlier sketch in SATA 120
Schneider, Dick
  See Schneider, Richard H.
Schneider, Elisa
  See Kleven, Elisa
Schneider, Herman 1905-2003 7
  Obituary 148
Schneider, Howie -2007 181
Schneider, Josh 1980- 196
Schneider, Laurie
  See Adams, Laurie
Schneider, Nina 1913-2007 2
  Obituary 186
Schneider, Nina Zimet
  See Schneider, Nina
Schneider, Rex 1937- 44
Schneider, Richard H. 1922- 171
Schneider, Richard Henry
  See Schneider, Richard H.
Schneider, Robyn 1986- 187
Schnirel, James R. 1931- 14
Schnitter, Jane T. 1958- 88
Schnitzlein, Danny 134
Schnur, Steven 1952- 144
  Earlier sketch in SATA 95
Schnurre, Wolfdietrich 1920-1989
  Obituary 63
Schoberle, Cecile 1949- 80
Schock, Pauline 1928- 45
Schoell, William 1951- 160
Schoen, Barbara (Taylor) 1924-1993 13
Schoenherr, Ian 177
Schoenherr, John 1935-2010 66
  Earlier sketch in SATA 37
  See also SAAS 13
Schoenherr, John Carl
  See Schoenherr, John
Schofield, Sandy
  See Rusch, Kristine Kathryn
Scholastica, Sister Mary
  See Jenkins, Marie M(agdalen)
Scholefield, A. T.
  See Scholefield, Alan
Scholefield, Alan 1931- 66
Scholefield, Edmund O.
  See Griffin, W. E. B.

Scholey, Arthur 1932- 28
Scholz, Jackson Volney 1897-1986
   Obituary 49
Schon, Nick 1955- 223
Schone, Virginia 22
Schongut, Emanuel 1936- 184
   Brief entry 36
   Earlier sketch in SATA 52
Schoonover, Frank (Earle) 1877-1972 24
Schoor, Gene 1921- 3
Schories, Pat 1952- 164
   Earlier sketch in SATA 116
Schorr, Melissa 1972- 194
Schorr, Melissa Robin
   See Schorr, Melissa
Schott, Jane A. 1946- 172
Schotter, Roni 190
   Earlier sketches in SATA 105, 149
Schrader, Dave 1967(?)- 225
Schraff, Anne E(laine) 1939- 92
   Earlier sketch in SATA 27
Schram, Penninah 1934- 219
   Earlier sketch in SATA 119
Schrank, Joseph 1900-1984
   Obituary 38
Schrecengost, Maity 1938- 118
Schrecengost, S. Maitland
   See Schrecengost, Maity
Schreck, Karen
   See Schreck, Karen Halvorsen
Schreck, Karen Halvorsen 1962- 185
Schrecker, Judie 1954- 90
Schreiber, Elizabeth Anne (Ferguson)
   1947- 13
Schreiber, Ralph W(alter) 1942- 13
Schreiner, Samuel A(gnew), Jr. 1921- 70
Schroades, John 214
Schroder, Monika 1965- 229
Schroeder, Alan 1961- 98
   Earlier sketch in SATA 66
Schroeder, Binette
   See Nickl, Barbara (Elisabeth)
Schroeder, Russell (K.) 1943- 146
Schroeder, Ted 1931(?)-1973
   Obituary 20
Schubert, Dieter 1947- 217
   Earlier sketches in SATA 62, 101
Schubert, Ingrid 1953- 217
Schubert, Leda 1950(?)- 181
Schubert-Gabrys, Ingrid 1953- 101
   Earlier sketch in SATA 62
Schuelein-Steel, Danielle
   See Steel, Danielle
Schuelein-Steel, Danielle Fernande
   See Steel, Danielle
Schuerger, Michele R. 110
Schuett, Stacey 1960- 168
   Earlier sketch in SATA 75
Schulke, Flip Phelps Graeme 1930- 57
Schulman, Arlene 1961- 105
Schulman, Janet 1933- 208
   Earlier sketches in SATA 22, 137
Schulman, L(ester) M(artin) 1934- 13
Schulte, Elaine L(ouise) 1934- 36
Schultz, Betty K(epka) 1932- 125
Schultz, Gwendolyn 21
Schultz, James Willard 1859-1947
   See YABC 1
Schultz, Pearle Henriksen 1918- 21
Schulz, Charles M. 1922-2000 10
   Obituary 118
Schulz, Charles Monroe
   See Schulz, Charles M.
Schumacher, Julie 1958- 191
Schumaker, Ward 1943- 96
Schuman, Michael A. 1953- 134
   Earlier sketch in SATA 85
Schur, Maxine
   See Schur, Maxine Rose

Schur, Maxine Rose 1948- 135
   Autobiography Feature 135
   Brief entry 49
   Earlier sketches in SATA 53, 98
Schurfranz, Vivian 1925- 13
Schutzer, A. I. 1922- 13
Schuyler, Pamela R. 1948- 30
Schwabach, Karen 185
Schwager, Tina 1964- 110
Schwandt, Stephen (William) 1947- 61
Schwark, Mary Beth 1954- 51
Schwartz, Alvin 1927-1992 56
   Obituary 71
   Earlier sketch in SATA 4
   See also CLR 89
Schwartz, Amy 1954- 189
   Brief entry 41
   Earlier sketches in SATA 47, 83, 131
   See also CLR 25
   See also SAAS 18
Schwartz, Anne Powers 1913-1987 10
Schwartz, Carol 1954- 77
Schwartz, Charles W(alsh) 1914- 8
Schwartz, David M. 1951- 110
   Earlier sketch in SATA 59
Schwartz, David Martin
   See Schwartz, David M.
Schwartz, Elizabeth Reeder 1912- 8
Schwartz, Ellen 1949- 117
Schwartz, Jerome L.
   See Lawrence, Jerome
Schwartz, Joanne 1960- 220
Schwartz, Joel L. 1940- 54
   Brief entry 51
Schwartz, Joyce R. 1950- 93
Schwartz, Julius 1907-2004 45
Schwartz, Perry 1942- 75
Schwartz, Sheila (Ruth) 1929- 27
Schwartz, Stephen (Lawrence) 1948- 19
Schwartz, Virginia Frances 1950- 184
   Earlier sketch in SATA 131
Schwarz, Silvia Tessa Viviane
   See Schwarz, Viviane
Schwarz, Viviane 1977- 204
Schwarz, (Silvia Tessa) Viviane 1977- 141
Schweitzer, Byrd Baylor
   See Baylor, Byrd
Schweitzer, Iris 59
   Brief entry 36
Schweninger, Ann 1951- 168
   Earlier sketches in SATA 29, 98
Schwerin, Doris H(alpern) 1922- 64
Schy, Yael 197
Scieszka, Jon 1954- 199
   Earlier sketches in SATA 68, 105, 160
   See also CLR 107
Scillian, Devin 199
   Earlier sketch in SATA 128
Scioscia, Mary (Hershey) 1926- 63
Sciurba, Katie 1957- 196
Scofield, Penrod 1933- 62
   Obituary 78
Scoggin, Margaret C(lara) 1905-1968 47
   Brief entry 28
Scoltock, Jack 1942- 141
   Earlier sketch in SATA 72
Scoppettone, Sandra 1936- 92
   Earlier sketch in SATA 9
Scot, Michael
   See Rohan, Michael Scott
Scot-Bernard, P.
   See Bernard, Patricia
Scotland, Jay
   See Jakes, John
Scott, Alastair
   See Allen, Kenneth S.
Scott, Ann Herbert 1926- 140
   Autobiography Feature 140
   Brief entry 29
   Earlier sketches in SATA 56, 94

Scott, Bill
   See Scott, William N(eville)
Scott, Bill 1920(?)-1985
   Obituary 46
Scott, Cora Annett (Pipitone) 1931- 11
Scott, Dan
   See Barker, S. Omar
Scott, Elaine 1940- 198
   Earlier sketches in SATA 36, 90, 164
Scott, Elizabeth 1972- 194
Scott, Jack Denton 1915-1995 83
   Earlier sketch in SATA 31
   See also CLR 20
   See also SAAS 14
Scott, Jane (Harrington) 1931- 55
Scott, Jane Wooster 1939- 226
Scott, Jessica
   See De Wire, Elinor
Scott, John 1912-1976 14
Scott, John Anthony 1916- 23
Scott, John M(artin) 1913- 12
Scott, Mary
   See Mattern, Joanne
Scott, Melissa 1960- 109
Scott, Michael 1959- 211
Scott, Michael Peter
   See Scott, Michael
Scott, Mike
   See Scott, Michael
Scott, Richard
   See Rennert, Richard Scott
Scott, Roney
   See Gault, William Campbell
Scott, Sally 1909-1978 43
Scott, Sally 1948- 44
Scott, Sally Elisabeth
   See Scott, Sally
Scott, W. N.
   See Scott, William N(eville)
Scott, Sir Walter 1771-1832
   See YABC 2
   See also CLR 154
Scott, Warwick
   See Trevor, Elleston
Scott, William N(eville) 1923- 87
Scotti, Anna
   See Coates, Anna
Scotton, Rob 1960- 214
   Earlier sketch in SATA 177
Scribner, Charles, Jr. 1921-1995 13
   Obituary 87
Scribner, Joanne L. 1949- 33
Scribner, Kimball 1917- 63
Scrimger, Richard 1957- 164
   Earlier sketch in SATA 119
Scrimsher, Lila Gravatt 1897-1974
   Obituary 28
Scroder, Walter K. 1928- 82
Scroggs, Kirk 187
Scruggs, Sandy 1961- 89
Scudder, Brooke 1959- 154
Scudder, Mildred Lee 1908- 6
   See also SAAS 12
Scull, Marie-Louise 1943-1993 77
Scuro, Vincent 1951- 21
Seabrooke, Brenda 1941- 148
   Earlier sketches in SATA 30, 88
Seagraves, D.B.
   See Seagraves, Donny Bailey
Seagraves, Donny
   See Seagraves, Donny Bailey
Seagraves, Donny Bailey 1951- 224
Seaman, Augusta Huiell 1879-1950 31
Seamands, Ruth 1916- 9
Searcy, Margaret Zehmer 1926- 54
   Brief entry 39
Searight, Mary W(illiams) 1918- 17
Searle, Kathryn Adrienne 1942- 10
Searle, Ronald (William Fordham) 1920- 70
   Earlier sketch in SATA 42
Sears, Stephen W. 1932- 4

Seaskull, Cecil
  See Castellucci, Cecil
Sebastian, Lee
  See Silverberg, Robert
Sebestyen, Igen
  See Sebestyen, Ouida
Sebestyen, Ouida 1924- *140*
  Earlier sketch in SATA *39*
  See also CLR *17*
  See also SAAS *10*
Sebrey, Mary Ann 1951- *62*
Sechrist, Elizabeth Hough 1903-1991 .... *2*
Sederman, Marty *211*
Sedges, John
  See Buck, Pearl S.
Sedgwick, Marcus 1968- *197*
  Earlier sketch in SATA *160*
Seed, Cecile Eugenie 1930- *86*
  Earlier sketch in SATA *8*
  See also CLR *76*
Seed, Jenny
  See Seed, Cecile Eugenie
Seed, Sheila Turner 1937(?)-1979
  Obituary *23*
Seeger, Elizabeth 1889-1973
  Obituary *20*
Seeger, Laura Vaccaro *200*
  Earlier sketch in SATA *172*
Seeger, Pete 1919- *139*
  Earlier sketch in SATA *13*
Seeger, Peter R.
  See Seeger, Pete
Seeley, Laura L. 1958- *71*
Seever, R.
  See Reeves, Lawrence F.
Sefozo, Mary 1925- *82*
Sefton, Catherine
  See Waddell, Martin
Segal, John *178*
Segal, Joyce 1940- *35*
Segal, Lore 1928- *228*
  Autobiography Feature *228*
  Earlier sketches in SATA *4, 66, 163*
  See also SAAS *11*
Segal, Lore Groszmann
  See Segal, Lore
Segar, E(lzie) C(risler) 1894-1938 .... *61*
Segovia, Andres 1893(?)-1987
  Obituary *52*
Seguin, Marilyn W(eymouth) 1951- *91*
Seguin-Fontes, Marthe 1924- *109*
Seibold, J. Otto 1960- *196*
  Earlier sketches in SATA *83, 149*
  See also SAAS *22*
Seidel, Ross *95*
Seidelman, James Edward 1926- *6*
Seiden, Art(hur) *107*
  Brief entry *42*
Seidensticker, John 1944- *200*
Seidler, Ann (G.) 1925- *131*
Seidler, Tor 1952- *149*
  Brief entry *46*
  Earlier sketches in SATA *52, 98*
Seidman, Karla
  See Kuskin, Karla
Seidman, Laurence Ivan 1925- *15*
Seigel, Kalman 1917-1998 .... *12*
  Obituary *103*
Seignobosc, Francoise 1897-1961 .... *21*
Seinfeld, Jerry 1954- *146*
Seitz, Jacqueline 1931- *50*
Seixas, Judith S. 1922- *17*
Sejima, Yoshimasa 1913- *8*
Selberg, Ingrid (Maria) 1950- *68*
Selden, George
  See Thompson, George Selden
Selden, Neil R(oy) 1931- *61*
Self, Margaret Cabell 1902-1996 .... *24*
Selfors, Suzanne 1963- *193*
Selick, Henry 1952- *183*
Selig, Sylvie 1942- *13*

Selkirk, Jane
  See Chapman, John Stanton Higham
Sellers, Naomi
  See Flack, Naomi John White
Sellier, Marie 1953- *212*
Selman, LaRue W. 1927- *55*
Selsam, Millicent E(llis) 1912-1996 .... *29*
  Obituary *92*
  Earlier sketch in SATA *1*
  See also CLR *1*
Seltzer, Meyer 1932- *17*
Seltzer, Richard 1946- *41*
Seltzer, Richard Warren, Jr.
  See Seltzer, Richard
Selvadurai, Shyam 1965(?)- *171*
Selway, Martina 1940- *169*
  Earlier sketch in SATA *74*
Selzer, Adam 1980- *229*
  Earlier sketch in SATA *192*
Selznick, Brian 1966- *210*
  Earlier sketches in SATA *79, 117, 171*
Semel, Nava 1954- *107*
Semloh
  See Holmes, Peggy
Sendak, Jack 1924(?)-1995 .... *28*
Sendak, Maurice 1928- *165*
  Earlier sketches in SATA *1, 27, 113*
  See also CLR *131*
Sendak, Maurice Bernard
  See Sendak, Maurice
Sender, Ruth M(insky) 1926- *62*
Sengler, Johanna 1924- *18*
Senir, Mirik
  See Snir, Mirik
Senisi, Ellen B. 1951- *116*
Senisi, Ellen Babinec
  See Senisi, Ellen B.
Senn, J(oyce) A(nn) 1941- *115*
Senn, Steve 1950- *60*
  Brief entry *48*
Sensel, Joni 1962- *204*
Serafini, Frank *201*
Serage, Nancy 1924- *10*
Seredy, Kate 1899-1975 .... *1*
  Obituary *24*
  See also CLR *10*
Serfozo, Mary 1925- *194*
Seroff, Victor I(lyitch) 1902-1979 .... *12*
  Obituary *26*
Serra, Sebastia 1966- *202*
Serraillier, Ian (Lucien) 1912-1994 .... *73*
  Obituary *83*
  Earlier sketch in SATA *1*
  See also CLR *2*
  See also SAAS *3*
Serros, Michele *175*
Serros, Michele M.
  See Serros, Michele
Servello, Joe 1932- *10*
Service, Pamela F. 1945- *222*
  Earlier sketch in SATA *64*
Service, Robert
  See Service, Robert W.
Service, Robert W. 1874(?)-1958 .... *20*
Serwadda, W(illiam) Moses 1931- *27*
Serwer-Bernstein, Blanche L(uria)
  1910-1997 .... *10*
Sescoe, Vincent E. 1938- *123*
Seskin, Steve 1953- *211*
Seth, Mary
  See Lexau, Joan M.
Seton, Anya 1904(?)-1990 .... *3*
  Obituary *66*
Seton, Ernest (Evan) Thompson 1860-1946 . *18*
  See also CLR *59*
Seton-Thompson, Ernest
  See Seton, Ernest (Evan) Thompson
Seuling, Barbara 1937- *220*
  Autobiography Feature *220*
  Earlier sketches in SATA *10, 98, 145, 193*
  See also SAAS *24*

Seuss, Dr.
  See Dr. Seuss
Severn, Bill
  See Severn, William Irving
Severn, David
  See Unwin, David S.
Severn, William Irving 1914- *1*
Sewall, Marcia 1935- *119*
  Earlier sketches in SATA *37, 69*
Seward, Prudence 1926- *16*
Sewell, Anna 1820-1878 .... *100*
  Earlier sketch in SATA *24*
  See also CLR *17*
Sewell, Helen (Moore) 1896-1957 .... *38*
Sexton, Anne 1928-1974 .... *10*
Sexton, Anne Harvey
  See Sexton, Anne
Seymour, Alta Halverson *10*
Seymour, Jane 1951- *139*
Seymour, Tres 1966- *164*
  Earlier sketch in SATA *82*
Sfar, Joann 1971- *182*
Shachtman, Tom 1942- *49*
Shackleton, C.C.
  See Aldiss, Brian W.
Shader, Rachel
  See Sofer, Barbara
Shadow, Jak
  See Sutherland, Jon
Shadyland, Sal
  See Cooper, Louise
Shafer, Audrey *183*
Shafer, Robert E(ugene) 1925- *9*
Shaffer, Terea 1968- *79*
Shahan, Sherry 1949- *216*
  Earlier sketches in SATA *92, 134*
Shahn, Ben(jamin) 1898-1969
  Obituary *21*
Shahn, Bernarda Bryson
  See Bryson, Bernarda
Shaik, Fatima *114*
Shalant, Phyllis 1949- *150*
Shan, Darren 1972- *199*
  Earlier sketches in SATA *129, 168*
Shan, D.B.
  See Shan, Darren
Shanahan, Lisa *199*
Shanberg, Karen
  See Shragg, Karen (I.)
Shane, Harold Gray 1914-1993 .... *36*
  Obituary *76*
Shange, Ntozake 1948- *157*
Shanks, Ann Zane (Kushner) *10*
Shannon, David 1959- *228*
  Earlier sketches in SATA *107, 152*
  See also CLR *87*
Shannon, George 1952- *202*
  Earlier sketches in SATA *35, 94, 143*
Shannon, George William Bones
  See Shannon, George
Shannon, Jacqueline *63*
Shannon, Margaret
  See Silverwood, Margaret Shannon
Shannon, Monica 1905(?)-1965 .... *28*
Shannon, Terry
  See Mercer, Jessie
Shannon, Terry Miller 1951- *148*
Shapiro, Irwin 1911-1981 .... *32*
Shapiro, Jody Fickes 1940- *193*
Shapiro, Karen Jo 1964- *186*
Shapiro, Michelle 1961- *196*
Shapiro, Milton J. 1926- *32*
Shapiro, Tricia
  See Andryszewski, Tricia
Shapiro, Zachary 1970- *213*
Shapp, Charles M(orris) 1906-1989
  Obituary *61*
Shapp, Martha Glauber 1910- *3*
Sharenow, Robert *193*
Sharfman, Amalie *14*
Sharkey, Niamh *213*

Sharma, Partap 1939- *15*
Sharma, Rashmi
    See Singh, Rashmi Sharma
Sharman, Alison
    See Leonard, Alison
Sharmat, Marjorie Weinman 1928- *133*
    Earlier sketches in SATA *4, 33, 74*
Sharmat, Mitchell 1927- *127*
    Earlier sketch in SATA *33*
Sharp, Anne Wallace 1947- *144*
Sharp, Luke
    See Alkiviades, Alkis
Sharp, Margery 1905-1991 .... *29*
    Obituary *67*
    Earlier sketch in SATA *1*
    See also CLR *27*
Sharp, Zerna A. 1889-1981
    Obituary *27*
Sharpe, Jon
    See Duncan, Alice
    and Knott, William C(ecil, Jr.)
    and Messman, Jon
Sharpe, Mitchell R(aymond) 1924- *12*
Sharpe, Susan 1946- *71*
Sharratt, Nick 1962- *199*
    Earlier sketches in SATA *104, 153*
Shasha, Mark 1961- *80*
Shattuck, Roger 1923-2005 .... *64*
    Obituary *174*
Shattuck, Roger Whitney
    See Shattuck, Roger
Shaw, Arnold 1909-1989 .... *4*
    Obituary *63*
Shaw, Carolyn V. 1934- *91*
Shaw, Charles (Green) 1892-1974 .... *13*
Shaw, Evelyn S. 1927- *28*
Shaw, Flora Louisa
    See Lugard, Flora Louisa Shaw
Shaw, Hannah 1982(?)- *227*
Shaw, Janet 1937- *146*
    Earlier sketch in SATA *61*
    See also CLR *96*
Shaw, Janet Beeler
    See Shaw, Janet
Shaw, Liane 1959- *222*
Shaw, Lisa
    See Rogak, Lisa
Shaw, Margret 1940- *68*
Shaw, Mary 1965- *180*
Shaw, Nancy 1946- *162*
    Earlier sketch in SATA *71*
Shaw, Ray *7*
Shaw, Richard 1923- *12*
Shawn, Frank S.
    See Goulart, Ron
Shay, Art
    See Shay, Arthur
Shay, Arthur 1922- *4*
Shay, Lacey
    See Shebar, Sharon Sigmond
Shea, Bob *188*
Shea, George 1940- *54*
    Brief entry *42*
Shea, Pegi Deitz 1960- *172*
    Earlier sketches in SATA *77, 137*
Shearer, Alex 1949- *204*
Shearer, John 1947- *43*
    Brief entry *27*
    See also CLR *34*
Shearer, Ted 1919- *43*
Shearing, Leonie 1972- *184*
Sheban, Chris *182*
Shebar, Sharon Sigmond 1945- *36*
Shecter, Ben 1935- *16*
Shedd, Warner 1934- *147*
    Earlier sketch in SATA *87*
Sheedy, Alexandra Elizabeth 1962- *39*
    Earlier sketch in SATA *19*
Sheehan, Ethna 1908-2000 .... *9*
Sheehan, Patty 1945- *77*

Sheehan, Sean 1951- *154*
    Earlier sketch in SATA *86*
Sheen, Barbara 1949- *143*
Shefelman, Janice 1930- *205*
    Earlier sketches in SATA *58, 129*
Shefelman, Janice Jordan
    See Shefelman, Janice
Shefelman, Tom 1927- *204*
    Earlier sketch in SATA *58*
Sheffer, H. R.
    See Abels, Harriette S(heffer)
Sheffield, Charles 1935-2002 .... *109*
Sheffield, Janet N. 1926- *26*
Sheikh, Nazneen 1944- *101*
Sheinkin, Steve 1968- *204*
Sheinmel, Courtney 1977- *211*
Shekerjian, Regina Tor *16*
Shelby, Anne 1948- *85*
    Autobiography Feature *121*
    See also SAAS *26*
Sheldon, Ann
    See Antle, Nancy
Sheldon, Ann *67*
    Earlier sketch in SATA *1*
Sheldon, Aure 1917-1976 .... *12*
Sheldon, David *185*
Sheldon, Deyan *181*
Sheldon, John
    See Bloch, Robert (Albert)
Sheldon, Muriel 1926- *45*
    Brief entry *39*
Shell, Barry 1951- *176*
Shelley, Frances
    See Wees, Frances Shelley
Shelley, John 1959- *202*
Shelley, Mary
    See Shelley, Mary Wollstonecraft
Shelley, Mary Wollstonecraft 1797-1851 ..... *29*
    See also CLR *133*
Shelton, Paula Young 1961- *227*
Shelton, William Roy 1919-1995 .... *5*
    Obituary *129*
Shemie, Bonnie (Jean Brenner) 1949- *96*
Shemin, Margaretha (Hoeneveld) 1928- *4*
Shen, Michele 1953- *173*
Shenker, Michele
    See Shen, Michele
Shenton, Edward 1895-1977 .... *45*
Shepard, Aaron 1950- *187*
    Earlier sketches in SATA *75, 113*
Shepard, Ernest Howard 1879-1976 .... *100*
    Obituary *24*
    Earlier sketches in SATA *3, 33*
    See also CLR *27*
Shepard, James R.
    See Shepard, Jim
Shepard, Jim 1956- *164*
    Earlier sketch in SATA *90*
Shepard, Mary
    See Knox, (Mary) Eleanor Jessie
Shephard, Esther 1891-1975 .... *5*
    Obituary *26*
Shepherd, Amanda *201*
Shepherd, Donna Walsh
    See Walsh Shepherd, Donna
Shepherd, Elizabeth *4*
Shepherd, Irana *173*
Shepherd, Roni
    See Shepherd, Irana
Sheppard, Kate *195*
Shepperson, Rob *178*
Sherburne, Zoa (Lillian Morin) 1912-1995 .... *3*
    See also SAAS *18*
Sherk-Savage, Candace
    See Savage, Candace
Sherlock, Patti *71*
Sherman, D(enis) R(onald) 1934- *48*
    Brief entry *29*
Sherman, Diane (Finn) 1928- *12*
Sherman, Elizabeth
    See Friskey, Margaret (Richards)

Sherman, Harold (Morrow) 1898-1987 .... *37*
    Obituary *137*
Sherman, Josepha *163*
    Earlier sketch in SATA *75*
Sherman, Michael
    See Lowndes, Robert A(ugustine) W(ard)
Sherman, Nancy
    See Rosenberg, Nancy (Sherman)
Sherman, Pat *174*
Sherman, Peter Michael
    See Lowndes, Robert A(ugustine) W(ard)
Sherrard, Valerie (Anne) 1957- *141*
Sherrod, Jane
    See Singer, Jane Sherrod
Sherry, Clifford J. 1943- *84*
Sherry, (Dulcie) Sylvia 1932- *122*
    Earlier sketch in SATA *8*
Sherwan, Earl 1917- *3*
Sherwood, Jonathan
    See London, Jonathan
Sheth, Kashmira *186*
Shetterly, Will 1955- *78*
    Autobiography Feature *106*
Shetterly, William Howard
    See Shetterly, Will
Shiefman, Vicky 1942- *22*
Shields, Brenda Desmond (Armstrong)
    1914- *37*
Shields, Carol Diggory *174*
Shields, Charles 1944- *10*
Shields, Gillian *203*
Shiels, Barbara
    See Adams, Barbara Johnston
Shiffman, Lena 1957- *101*
Shiga, Jason 1976- *228*
Shiina, Makoto 1944- *83*
Shimin, Symeon 1902-1984 .... *13*
Shimko, Bonnie 1941- *191*
Shine, Andrea 1955- *104*
Shine, Deborah 1932- *71*
Shinn, Everett 1876-1953 .... *21*
Shinn, Sharon 1957- *229*
    Earlier sketches in SATA *110, 164*
Shippen, Katherine B(inney) 1892-1980 .... *1*
    Obituary *23*
    See also CLR *36*
Shippey, T. A. 1943- *143*
Shippey, Thomas Alan
    See Shippey, T. A.
Shipton, Eric Earle 1907-1977 .... *10*
Shipton, Jonathan 1948- *215*
Shipton, Paul 1963- *196*
Shiraz, Yasmin *173*
Shirer, William L(awrence) 1904-1993 .... *45*
    Obituary *78*
Shirley, Debra *203*
Shirley, Gayle C 1955- *96*
Shirley, Gayle Corbett
    See Shirley, Gayle C
Shirley, Jean 1919- *70*
Shirreffs, Gordon D(onald) 1914-1996 .... *11*
Shirts, Morris A(lpine) 1922- *63*
Shlichta, Joe 1968- *84*
Shmurak, Carole B. 1944- *118*
Sholokhov, Mikhail 1905-1984
    Obituary *36*
Sholokhov, Mikhail Aleksandrovich
    See Sholokhov, Mikhail
Shore, Diane Z. *215*
    Earlier sketch in SATA *179*
Shore, Diane ZuHone
    See Shore, Diane Z.
Shore, June Lewis *30*
Shore, Nancy 1960- *124*
Shore, Robert 1924- *39*
Short, Michael 1937- *65*
Short, Roger
    See Arkin, Alan
Shortall, Leonard W. *19*
Shortt, Tim(othy Donald) 1961- *96*
Shotwell, Louisa Rossiter 1902-1993 .... *3*

Shoulders, Michael 1954- 216
Shoup, Barbara 1947- 156
    Earlier sketch in SATA 86
    See also SAAS 24
Shoveller, Herb 184
Showalter, Jean B(reckinridge) 12
Showell, Ellen Harvey 1934- 33
Showers, Paul C. 1910-1999 92
    Obituary 114
    Earlier sketch in SATA 21
    See also CLR 6
    See also SAAS 7
Shpakow, Tanya 1959(?)- 94
Shpitalnik, Vladimir 1964- 83
Shragg, Karen (I.) 1954- 142
Shreeve, Elizabeth 1956- 156
Shreve, Susan
    See Shreve, Susan Richards
Shreve, Susan Richards 1939- 152
    Brief entry 41
    Earlier sketches in SATA 46, 95
Shriver, Jean Adair 1932- 75
Shriver, Maria 1955- 134
Shriver, Maria Owings
    See Shriver, Maria
Shrode, Mary
    See Hollingsworth, Mary
Shtainmets, Leon 32
Shub, Elizabeth 1915(?)-2004 5
Shuken, Julia 1948- 84
Shulevitz, Uri 1935- 165
    Earlier sketches in SATA 3, 50, 106
    See also CLR 61
Shulman, Alix Kates 1932- 7
Shulman, Dee 1957- 146
Shulman, Irving 1913-1995 13
Shulman, Lisa 202
Shulman, Mark 1962- 184
Shulman, Max 1919-1988
    Obituary 59
Shulman, Milton 1913-2004
    Obituary 154
Shulman, Neil B(arnett) 1945- 89
Shumsky, Zena
    See Collier, Zena
Shura, Mary Francis
    See Craig, Mary (Francis) Shura
Shusterman, Neal 1962- 201
    Autobiography Feature 140
    Earlier sketches in SATA 85, 121, 140
Shuter, Jane (Margaret) 1955- 151
    Earlier sketch in SATA 90
Shuttlesworth, Dorothy Edwards 3
Shwartz, Susan (Martha) 1949- 94
Shyer, Christopher 1961- 98
Shyer, Marlene Fanta 13
Siberell, Anne 29
Sibley, Don 1922- 12
Siburt, Ruth 1951- 121
Siculan, Daniel 1922- 12
Siddon, Barbara
    See Bradford, Barbara Taylor
Sidgwick, Ethel 1877-1970 116
Sidjakov, Nicolas 1924- 18
Sidman, Joyce 1956- 181
    Earlier sketch in SATA 145
Sidney, Frank
    See Warwick, Alan R(oss)
Sidney, Margaret
    See Lothrop, Harriet Mulford Stone
Siebert, Diane 1948- 189
Siegal, Aranka 1930- 88
    Brief entry 37
Siegel, Beatrice 36
Siegel, Helen
    See Siegl, Helen
Siegel, Robert 1939- 39
Siegel, Robert Harold
    See Siegel, Robert
Siegel, Siena Cherson 1967(?)- 185
Siegelson, Kim L. 1962- 114

Sieger, Ted 1958- 189
Siegl, Helen 1924- 34
Siepmann, Mary Aline
    See Wesley, Mary (Aline)
Sierra, Judy 1945- 195
    Earlier sketches in SATA 104, 162
Sieswerda, Paul L. 1942- 147
Sievert, Terri
    See Dougherty, Terri (L.)
Sigsawa, Keiichi 1972- 211
Silas
    See McCay, (Zenas) Winsor
Silcock, Sara Lesley 1947- 12
Silin-Palmer, Pamela 184
Sill, Cathryn 1953- 221
    Earlier sketches in SATA 74, 141
Sill, John 1947- 222
    Earlier sketches in SATA 74, 140
Sillitoe, Alan 1928-2010 61
Sills, Leslie (Elka) 1948- 129
Silly, E. S.
    See Kraus, (Herman) Robert
Silsbe, Brenda 1953- 73
Silva, Joseph
    See Goulart, Ron
Silvano, Wendi 1962- 223
Silver, Jago
    See Jago
Silver, Maggie 216
Silver, Ruth
    See Chew, Ruth
Silverberg, Robert 1935- 91
    Autobiography Feature 104
    Earlier sketch in SATA 13
    See also CLR 59
Silverman, Erica 1955- 222
    Earlier sketches in SATA 78, 112, 165
Silverman, Janis L. 1946- 127
Silverman, Mel(vin Frank) 1931-1966 9
Silverman, Robin L. 1954- 96
Silverman, Robin Landew
    See Silverman, Robin L.
Silverstein, Alvin 1933- 124
    Earlier sketches in SATA 8, 69
    See also CLR 25
Silverstein, Herma 1945- 106
Silverstein, Robert Alan 1959- 124
    Earlier sketch in SATA 77
Silverstein, Shel 1932-1999 92
    Brief entry 27
    Obituary 116
    Earlier sketch in SATA 33
    See also CLR 96
Silverstein, Sheldon Allan
    See Silverstein, Shel
Silverstein, Virginia B. 1937- 124
    Earlier sketches in SATA 8, 69
    See also CLR 25
Silverstein, Virginia Barbara Opshelor
    See Silverstein, Virginia B.
Silverthorne, Elizabeth 1930- 35
Silverwood, Margaret Shannon 1966- 137
    Earlier sketch in SATA 83
Silvey, Diane F. 1946- 135
Sim, David 1953- 162
Sim, Dorrith M. 1931- 96
Simak, Clifford D(onald) 1904-1988
    Obituary 56
Simard, Remy 1959- 168
Siminovich, Lorena 1976(?)- 219
Simmie, Lois (Ann) 1932- 106
    See also CLR 23
Simmonds, Posy 1945- 130
Simmonds, Rosemary Elizabeth
    See Simmonds, Posy
Simmons, Andra 1939- 141
Simmons, Elly 1955- 134
Simmons, Michael 1970- 185
Simms, Laura 1947- 117
Simner, Janni Lee 113

Simon, Charlie May
    See Fletcher, Charlie May Hogue
Simon, Francesca 1955- 111
Simon, Gabriel 1972- 118
Simon, Hilda Rita 1921- 28
    See also CLR 39
Simon, Howard 1903-1979 32
    Obituary 21
Simon, Joe
    See Simon, Joseph H.
Simon, Joseph H. 1913- 7
Simon, Martin P(aul William) 1903-1969 12
Simon, Mina Lewiton
    See Lewiton, Mina
Simon, Norma (Feldstein) 1927- 129
    Earlier sketches in SATA 3, 68
Simon, Seymour 1931- 202
    Earlier sketches in SATA 4, 73, 138
    See also CLR 63
Simon, Shirley (Schwartz) 1921- 11
Simon, Solomon 1895-1970 40
Simonetta, Linda 1948- 14
Simonetta, Sam 1936- 14
Simons, Barbara B(rooks) 1934- 41
Simont, Marc 1915- 126
    Earlier sketches in SATA 9, 73
Simpson, Colin 1908-1983 14
Simpson, Harriette
    See Arnow, Harriette (Louisa) Simpson
Simpson, Jacynth Hope
    See Hope Simpson, Jacynth
Simpson, Lesley 1963- 150
Simpson, Margaret 1943- 128
Simpson, Myrtle L(illias) 1931- 14
Sims, Blanche 168
    Earlier sketch in SATA 75
Sims, Blanche L.
    See Sims, Blanche
Sims, Rudine
    See Bishop, Rudine Sims
Simundsson, Elva 1950- 63
Sinclair, Clover
    See Gater, Dilys
Sinclair, Emil
    See Hesse, Hermann
Sinclair, Jeff 1958- 77
Sinclair, Olga 1923- 121
Sinclair, Rose
    See Smith, Susan Vernon
Sinclair, Upton 1878-1968 9
Sinclair, Upton Beall
    See Sinclair, Upton
Singer, A.L.
    See Lerangis, Peter
Singer, Arthur 1917-1990 64
Singer, Isaac
    See Singer, Isaac Bashevis
Singer, Isaac Bashevis 1904-1991 27
    Obituary 68
    Earlier sketch in SATA 3
    See also CLR 1
Singer, Jane Sherrod 1917-1985 4
    Obituary 42
Singer, Julia 1917- 28
Singer, Kurt D. 1911-2005 38
    Obituary 172
Singer, Marilyn 1948- 201
    Autobiography Feature 158
    Brief entry 38
    Earlier sketches in SATA 48, 80, 125, 158
    See also CLR 48
    See also SAAS 13
Singer, Muff 1942-2005 104
    Obituary 160
Singer, Nicky 1956- 194
Singer, Susan (Mahler) 1941- 9
Singh, Rashmi Sharma 1952- 90
Singleton, Linda Joy 1957- 166
    Earlier sketch in SATA 88
Singleton, L.J.
    See Singleton, Linda Joy

Singleton, Sarah 1966- *214*
Sinykin, Sheri
  See Sinykin, Sheri Cooper
Sinykin, Sheri Cooper 1950- *142*
  Autobiography Feature *142*
  Earlier sketches in SATA *72, 133*
Sinykin, Sheril Terri Cooper
  See Sinykin, Sheri Cooper
Siomades, Lorianne *217*
Sipiera, Paul P., (Jr.) 1948- *144*
  Earlier sketch in SATA *89*
Siracusa, Catherine (Jane) 1947- *82*
Sirett, Dawn (Karen) 1966- *88*
Sirimarco, Elizabeth 1966- *158*
Sirof, Harriet 1930- *94*
  Earlier sketch in SATA *37*
Sirois, Allen L. 1950- *76*
Sirvaitis (Chernyaev), Karen (Ann) 1961- ... *79*
Sis, Peter 1949- *192*
  Earlier sketch in SATA *149*
  See also CLR *110*
Sisson, Rosemary Anne 1923- *11*
Sister Mary Terese
  See Donze, Mary Terese
Sita, Lisa 1962- *87*
Sitarski, Anita *200*
Sitomer, Alan Lawrence *174*
Sitomer, Harry 1903-1985 .... *31*
Sitomer, Mindel 1903-1987 .... *31*
Sittenfeld, Curtis 1975(?)- *164*
Sive, Helen R(obinson) 1951- *30*
Sivulich, Sandra (Jeanne) Stroner 1941- *9*
Siy, Alexandra *193*
Skarmeta, Antonio 1940- *57*
Skeers, Linda 1958- *207*
Skelly, James R(ichard) 1927- *17*
Skelton, Matthew 1971- *185*
Skinner, Constance Lindsay 1877-1939
  See YABC *1*
Skinner, Cornelia Otis 1901-1979 .... *2*
Skipper, G. C. 1939- *46*
  Brief entry *38*
Sklansky, Amy E(dgar) 1971- *145*
Sklansky, Amy E. 1971- *204*
Skofield, James *95*
  Brief entry *44*
Skold, Betty Westrom 1923- *41*
Skorpen, Liesel Moak 1935- *3*
Skott, Maria
  See Nikolajeva, Maria
Skovron, Jon 1976- *229*
Skrypuch, Marsha Forchuk 1954- *134*
Skultety, Nancy Laney 1960- *175*
Skurzynski, Gloria 1930- *145*
  Autobiography Feature *145*
  Earlier sketches in SATA *8, 74, 122*
  See also SAAS *9*
Skurzynski, Gloria Joan
  See Skurzynski, Gloria
Skutch, Robert 1925- *89*
Skye, Maggie
  See Werner, Herma
Skye, Obert *200*
  Earlier sketch in SATA *170*
Slack, Michael 1969- *189*
Slackman, Charles B. 1934- *12*
Slade, Arthur G. 1967- *221*
  Earlier sketches in SATA *106, 149*
Slade, Arthur Gregory
  See Slade, Arthur G.
Slade, Christian 1974- *193*
Slade, Richard 1910-1971 .... *9*
Slade, Suzanne 1964- *226*
Slangerup, Erik Jon 1969- *130*
Slate, Joseph 1928- *174*
  Earlier sketches in SATA *38, 122*
Slate, Joseph Frank
  See Slate, Joseph
Slater, Dashka 1963- *179*
Slater, David Michael 1970- *212*

Slater, Ray
  See Lansdale, Joe R.
Slaughter, Hope 1940- *84*
Slaughter, Jean
  See Doty, Jean Slaughter
Slaughter, Tom 1955- *152*
Slavicek, Louise Chipley 1956- *144*
Slavin, Bill 1959- *199*
  Earlier sketches in SATA *76, 148*
Slaymaker, Melissa Eskridge 1958- *158*
Slayton, Fran Cannon *221*
Sleator, William 1945- *208*
  Earlier sketches in SATA *3, 68, 118, 161*
  See also CLR *128*
Sleator, William Warner III
  See Sleator, William
Slegers, Liesbet 1975- *154*
Sleigh, Barbara 1906-1982 .... *86*
  Obituary *30*
  Earlier sketch in SATA *3*
Slepian, Jan 1921- *85*
  Brief entry *45*
  Earlier sketch in SATA *51*
  See also SAAS *8*
Slepian, Janice B.
  See Slepian, Jan
Slicer, Margaret O. 1920- *4*
Slier, Debby
  See Shine, Deborah
Sloan, Brian 1966- *172*
Sloan, Carolyn 1937- *116*
  Earlier sketch in SATA *58*
Sloan, Glenna 1930- *120*
Sloan, Glenna Davis
  See Sloan, Glenna
Sloane, Eric 1910(?)-1985 .... *52*
  Obituary *42*
Sloane, Todd 1955- *88*
Sloat, Teri 1948- *164*
  Earlier sketches in SATA *70, 106*
Slobodkin, Florence Gersh 1905-1994 .... *5*
  Obituary *107*
Slobodkin, Louis 1903-1975 .... *26*
  Earlier sketch in SATA *1*
Slobodkina, Esphyr 1908-2002 .... *1*
  Obituary *135*
  See also SAAS *8*
Sloggett, Nellie 1851-1923 .... *44*
Slonim, David 1966- *207*
Sloss, Lesley Lord 1965- *72*
Slote, Alfred 1926- *72*
  Earlier sketch in SATA *8*
  See also CLR *4*
  See also SAAS *21*
Slote, Elizabeth 1956- *80*
Small, Charlie
  See Ward, Nick
Small, David 1945- *216*
  Brief entry *46*
  Earlier sketches in SATA *50, 95, 126, 183*
  See also CLR *53*
Small, Ernest
  See Lent, Blair
Small, Mary 1932- *165*
Small, Terry 1942- *75*
Smallcomb, Pam 1954- *159*
Smallman, Steve *227*
  Earlier sketch in SATA *197*
Smalls, Irene
  See Smalls-Hector, Irene
Smalls-Hector, Irene 1950- *146*
  Earlier sketch in SATA *73*
  See also CLR *103*
Smallwood, Norah (Evelyn) 1910(?)-1984
  Obituary *41*
Smaridge, Norah (Antoinette) 1903-1994 ...... *6*
Smath, Jerry 1933- *198*
Smee, Nicola 1948- *167*
  Earlier sketch in SATA *76*
Smiley, Virginia Kester 1923- *2*
Smit, Noelle 1972- *199*

Smith, Alexander McCall 1948- *179*
  Earlier sketch in SATA *73*
Smith, Andrew 1959- *209*
Smith, Andrew Anselmo
  See Smith, Andrew
Smith, Andy J. 1975- *207*
Smith, Anne Warren 1938- *41*
  Brief entry *34*
Smith, Barry (Edward Jervis) 1943- *75*
Smith, Beatrice S(chillinger) *12*
Smith, Betsy Covington 1937- *55*
  Earlier sketch in SATA *43*
Smith, Betty (Wehner) 1904-1972 .... *6*
Smith, Bradford 1909-1964 .... *5*
Smith, Brenda 1946- *82*
Smith, C. Pritchard
  See Hoyt, Edwin P(almer), Jr.
Smith, Caesar
  See Trevor, Elleston
Smith, Cat Bowman 1939- *201*
Smith, Charles R., Jr. 1969- *203*
  Earlier sketch in SATA *159*
Smith, Craig 1955- *172*
  Earlier sketches in SATA *81, 117*
Smith, Cynthia Leitich 1967- *215*
  Earlier sketch in SATA *152*
Smith, D. James 1955- *176*
Smith, Danna *216*
Smith, Danna Kessimakis
  See Smith, Danna
Smith, Datus C(lifford), Jr. 1907-1999 .... *13*
  Obituary *116*
Smith, Debra 1955- *89*
Smith, Derek 1943- *141*
Smith, Dick King
  See King-Smith, Dick
Smith, D.J.
  See Smith, D. James
Smith, Dodie
  See Smith, Dorothy Gladys
Smith, Doris Buchanan 1934-2002 .... *75*
  Obituary *140*
  Earlier sketch in SATA *28*
  See also SAAS *10*
Smith, Dorothy Gladys 1896-1990 .... *82*
  Obituary *65*
Smith, Dorothy Stafford 1905- *6*
Smith, Duane 1974- *202*
Smith, E(lmer) Boyd 1860-1943
  See YABC *1*
Smith, E(dric) Brooks 1917- *40*
Smith, Elwood H. 1941- *203*
Smith, Emily Wing 1980- *215*
Smith, Emma 1923- *52*
  Brief entry *36*
Smith, (Katherine) Eunice (Young)
  1902-1993 .... *5*
Smith, Frances C(hristine) 1904-1986 .... *3*
Smith, Gary R. 1932- *14*
Smith, Geof 1969- *102*
Smith, George Harmon 1920- *5*
Smith, Gordon 1951- *184*
Smith, Greg Leitich *152*
Smith, H(arry) Allen 1907-1976
  Obituary *20*
Smith, Helene 1937- *142*
Smith, Hope Anita *202*
Smith, Howard E(verett), Jr. 1927- *12*
Smith, Hugh L(etcher) 1921-1968 .... *5*
Smith, Icy 1966- *228*
Smith, Imogene Henderson 1922- *12*
Smith, Jacqueline B. 1937- *39*
Smith, Jada Pinkett 1971- *161*
Smith, James Noel 1950- *193*
Smith, Janet (Buchanan) Adam
  See Adam Smith, Janet (Buchanan)
Smith, Janice Lee 1949- *155*
  Earlier sketch in SATA *54*
Smith, Jean
  See Smith, Frances C(hristine)
Smith, Jean Pajot 1945- *10*

Smith, Jeff 1958- *161*
  Earlier sketch in SATA *93*
Smith, Jeff Allen
  See Smith, Jeff
Smith, Jeffrey Alan
  See Smith, Jeff
Smith, Jenny 1963- *90*
Smith, Jessie
  See Kunhardt, Edith
Smith, Jessie Willcox 1863-1935 .... *21*
  See also CLR *59*
Smith, Joan (Mary) 1933- *54*
  Brief entry *46*
Smith, Johnston
  See Crane, Stephen
Smith, Jos A. 1936- *181*
  Earlier sketches in SATA *73, 120*
Smith, Joseph Arthur
  See Smith, Jos A.
Smith, Judie R. 1936- *80*
Smith, Kirsten 1970- *210*
Smith, Lafayette
  See Higdon, Hal
Smith, Lane 1959- *224*
  Earlier sketches in SATA *76, 131, 179*
  See also CLR *47*
Smith, Lee
  See Albion, Lee Smith
Smith, Lendon H(oward) 1921- *64*
Smith, Lillian H(elena) 1887-1983
  Obituary *32*
Smith, Linda 1949- *177*
Smith, Linell Nash 1932- *2*
Smith, Lucia B. 1943- *30*
Smith, Maggie 1965- *190*
Smith, Margaret Emily Noel Nuttall
  See Nuttall-Smith, Margaret Emily Noel
Smith, Marion Hagens 1913- *12*
Smith, Marion Jaques 1899-1987 .... *13*
Smith, Mary Ellen *10*
Smith, Marya 1945- *78*
Smith, Mike
  See Smith, Mary Ellen
Smith, Nancy Covert 1935- *12*
Smith, Norman F. 1920- *70*
  Earlier sketch in SATA *5*
Smith, Patricia Clark 1943- *96*
Smith, Pauline C.
  See Arthur, Robert, (Jr.)
Smith, Pauline C(oggeshall) 1908-1994 .... *27*
Smith, Philip Warren 1936- *46*
Smith, R. Alexander McCall
  See Smith, Alexander McCall
Smith, Rebecca 1946- *123*
Smith, Robert Kimmel 1930- *77*
  Earlier sketch in SATA *12*
Smith, Robert Paul 1915-1977 .... *52*
  Obituary *30*
Smith, Roland 1951- *193*
  Earlier sketches in SATA *115, 161*
Smith, Rosamond
  See Oates, Joyce Carol
Smith, Ruth Leslie 1902- *2*
Smith, Samantha 1972-1985
  Obituary *45*
Smith, Sandra Lee 1945- *75*
Smith, Sarah Stafford
  See Smith, Dorothy Stafford
Smith, Sharon 1947- *82*
Smith, Sherri L. 1971- *156*
Smith, Sherwood 1951- *206*
  Autobiography Feature *206*
  Earlier sketches in SATA *82, 140*
Smith, Shirley Raines
  See Raines, Shirley C(arol)
Smith, Susan Carlton 1923- *12*
Smith, Susan Mathias 1950- *43*
  Brief entry *35*
Smith, Susan Vernon 1950- *48*
  Brief entry *45*
Smith, Tim(othy R.) 1945- *151*

Smith, Ursula 1934- *54*
Smith, Vian (Crocker) 1920-1969 .... *11*
Smith, Wanda VanHoy 1926- *65*
Smith, Ward
  See Goldsmith, Howard
Smith, William A. 1918- *10*
Smith, William Jay 1918- *154*
  Autobiography Feature *154*
  Earlier sketches in SATA *2, 68*
  See also SAAS *22*
Smith, Winsome 1935- *45*
Smith, Z.Z.
  See Westheimer, David
Smith-Ankrom, M. E. 1942- *130*
Smith-Griswold, Wendy 1955- *88*
Smith-Rex, Susan J. 1950- *94*
Smithsen, Richard
  See Pellowski, Michael (Joseph)
Smithson, Ryan 1985- *216*
Smits, Teo
  See Smits, Theodore R(ichard)
Smits, Theodore R(ichard) 1905-1996 .... *45*
  Brief entry *28*
Smolinski, Dick 1932- *86*
Smothers, Ethel Footman 1944- *149*
  Earlier sketch in SATA *76*
Smucker, Anna Egan 1948- *209*
Smucker, Barbara 1915-2003 .... *130*
  Earlier sketches in SATA *29, 76*
  See also CLR *10*
  See also SAAS *11*
Smucker, Barbara Claassen
  See Smucker, Barbara
Smyth, Iain 1959- *105*
Snedeker, Caroline Dale (Parke) 1871-1956
  See YABC *2*
Sneed, Brad *191*
Sneider, Marian 1932-2005 .... *197*
Snell, Gordon 1933(?)- *228*
Snell, Nigel (Edward Creagh) 1936- *57*
  Brief entry *40*
Snellgrove, L(aurence) E(rnest) 1928- *53*
Snelling, Dennis (Wayne) 1958- *84*
Sneve, Virginia Driving Hawk 1933- *95*
  Earlier sketch in SATA *8*
  See also CLR *2*
Snicket, Lemony 1970- *215*
  Earlier sketches in SATA *126, 187*
  See also CLR *79*
Sniegoski, Thomas E. *195*
Sniegoski, Tom
  See Sniegoski, Thomas E.
Snir, Eleyor *225*
Snir, Mirik 1948- *226*
Snodgrass, Mary Ellen 1944- *75*
Snodgrass, Quentin Curtius
  See Twain, Mark
Snodgrass, Thomas Jefferson
  See Twain, Mark
Snook, Barbara (Lillian) 1913-1976 .... *34*
Snow, Alan 1959- *190*
Snow, Carol 1965- *208*
Snow, Donald Clifford 1917-1979 .... *16*
Snow, Dorothea J(ohnston) 1909- *9*
Snow, Richard F(olger) 1947- *52*
  Brief entry *37*
Snow, Sarah *229*
Snyder, Anne 1922-2001 .... *4*
  Obituary *125*
Snyder, Bernadette McCarver 1930- *97*
Snyder, Carol 1941- *35*
Snyder, Gerald S(eymour) 1933- *48*
  Brief entry *34*
Snyder, Jerome 1916-1976
  Obituary *20*
Snyder, Laurel 1974- *209*
Snyder, Midori 1954- *106*
Snyder, Paul A. 1946- *125*

Snyder, Zilpha Keatley 1927- *226*
  Autobiography Feature *163*
  Earlier sketches in SATA *1, 28, 75, 110, 163*
  See also CLR *121*
  See also SAAS *2*
Snyderman, Reuven K. 1922- *5*
So, Meilo *162*
Sobel, June 1950- *149*
Soble, Jennie
  See Cavin, Ruth
Sobol, Donald J. 1924- *132*
  Earlier sketches in SATA *1, 31, 73*
  See also CLR *4*
Sobol, Harriet Langsam 1936- *47*
  Brief entry *34*
Sobol, Richard *211*
Sobol, Rose 1931- *76*
Sobott-Mogwe, Gaele 1956- *97*
Soderlind, Arthur E(dwin) 1920- *14*
Soentpiet, Chris K. 1970- *159*
  Earlier sketch in SATA *97*
Soerensen, Svend Otto 1916- *67*
Sofer, Barbara 1949- *109*
Sofer, Rachel
  See Sofer, Barbara
Softly, Barbara Frewin 1924- *12*
Sogabe, Aki *207*
Soglow, Otto 1900-1975
  Obituary *30*
Sohl, Frederic J(ohn) 1916- *10*
Sohr, Daniel 1973- *190*
Sokol, Bill
  See Sokol, William
Sokol, William 1923- *37*
Sokolov, Kirill 1930- *34*
Solbert, Romaine G. 1925- *2*
Solbert, Ronni
  See Solbert, Romaine G.
Solheim, James *133*
Solomon, Heather M. *188*
Solomon, Joan 1930- *51*
  Brief entry *40*
Solomons, Ikey Esquir
  See Thackeray, William Makepeace
Solonevich, George 1915-2003 .... *15*
Solot, Mary Lynn 1939- *12*
Solov'ev, Mikhail
  See Soloviov, Michael
Soloviov, Michael 1972- *222*
Soman, David 1965- *200*
Somerlott, Robert 1928-2001 .... *62*
Somers, Kevin *205*
Somervill, Barbara A(nn) 1948- *140*
Sommer, Angela
  See Sommer-Bodenburg, Angela
Sommer, Carl 1930- *175*
  Earlier sketch in SATA *126*
Sommer, Elyse 1929- *7*
Sommer, Robert 1929- *12*
Sommer-Bodenburg, Angela 1948- *113*
  Earlier sketch in SATA *63*
Sommerdorf, Norma 1926- *131*
Sommerdorf, Norma Jean
  See Sommerdorf, Norma
Sommerfelt, Aimee 1892-1975 .... *5*
Son, John *160*
Sones, Sonya *131*
Sonneborn, Ruth (Cantor) 1899-1974 .... *4*
  Obituary *27*
Sonnenblick, Jordan 1969- *223*
  Earlier sketch in SATA *185*
  See also CLR *144*
Sonnenmark, Laura A. 1958- *73*
Soo, Kean *201*
Sopko, Eugen 1949- *58*
Sorel, Edward 1929- *126*
  Brief entry *37*
  Earlier sketch in SATA *65*
Sorensen, Henri 1950- *115*
  Earlier sketch in SATA *77*

Sorensen, Svend Otto
    See Soerensen, Svend Otto
Sorensen, Virginia 1912-1991 2
    Obituary 72
    See also SAAS 15
Sorenson, Jane 1926- 63
Sorenson, Margo 1946- 96
Sorley Walker, Kathrine 41
Sorra, Kristin 185
Sorrells, Walter 177
Sorrentino, Joseph N. 1937- 6
Sortor, June Elizabeth 1939- 12
Sortor, Toni
    See Sortor, June Elizabeth
Sosa, Hernan 1977- 203
Soskin, V. H.
    See Ellison, Virginia H(owell)
Soto, Gary 1952- 174
    Earlier sketches in SATA 80, 120
    See also CLR 38
Sotomayor, Antonio 1902-1985 11
Souci, Robert D. San
    See San Souci, Robert D.
Soudley, Henry
    See Wood, James Playsted
Souhami, Jessica 176
Soule, Gardner (Bosworth) 1913-2000 14
Soule, Jean Conder 1919- 10
Soup, Cuthbert
    See Swallow, Gerry
Souster, (Holmes) Raymond 1921- 63
South, Sheri Cobb 1959- 82
Southall, Ivan 1921-2008 134
    Autobiography Feature 134
    Earlier sketches in SATA 3, 68
    See also CLR 165
    See also SAAS 3
Southall, Ivan Francis
    See Southall, Ivan
Southey, Robert 1774-1843 54
Southgate, Vera 54
Souza, Janet
    See Tashjian, Janet
Sovak, Jan 1953- 115
Sowden, Celeste
    See Walters, Celeste
Sowter, Nita 69
Spafford, Suzy 1945- 160
Spagnoli, Cathy 1950- 134
    Earlier sketch in SATA 79
Spain, Sahara Sunday 1991- 133
Spain, Susan Rosson 185
Spalding, Andrea 1944- 150
    Earlier sketch in SATA 101
Spalenka, Greg 1958- 198
Spanfeller, James J. 1930- 19
    See also SAAS 8
Spanfeller, Jim
    See Spanfeller, James J.
Spangenberg, Judith Dunn 1942- 5
Spangler, Brie 212
Spanyol, Jessica 1965- 206
    Earlier sketch in SATA 137
Spar, Jerome 1918- 10
Sparks, Barbara 1942- 78
Sparks, Beatrice (Mathews) 1918- 44
    Brief entry 28
    See also CLR 139
Sparks, Mary W. 1920- 15
Spaulding, Douglas
    See Bradbury, Ray
Spaulding, Leonard
    See Bradbury, Ray
Spaulding, Norma 107
Speare, Elizabeth George 1908-1994 62
    Obituary 83
    Earlier sketch in SATA 5
    See also CLR 8
Spearing, Craig J. 228
Spearing, Judith (Mary Harlow) 1922- 9
Spears, Rick 182

Speck, Katie 196
Speck, Nancy 1959- 104
Specking, Inez 1890-1960(?) 11
Speed, Nell
    See Keats, Emma
    and Sampson, Emma (Keats) Speed
Speed, Nell (Ewing) 1878-1913 68
Speer, Bonnie Stahlman 1929- 113
Speer-Lyon, Tammie L. 1965- 89
Speicher, Helen Ross S(mith) 1915- 8
Speir, Nancy 1958- 210
    Earlier sketch in SATA 81
Spellman, John W(illard) 1934- 14
Spellman, Roger G.
    See Cox, William R(obert)
Spelman, Cornelia Maude 1946- 144
    Earlier sketch in SATA 96
Spelman, Mary 1934- 28
Spelvin, George
    See Lerangis, Peter
    and Phillips, David Atlee
Spence, Cynthia
    See Eble, Diane
Spence, Eleanor (Rachel) 1928- 21
    See also CLR 26
Spence, Geraldine 1931- 47
Spencer, Ann 1918- 10
Spencer, Britt 206
Spencer, Cornelia
    See Yaukey, Grace S(ydenstricker)
Spencer, Donald D(ean) 1931- 41
Spencer, Elizabeth 1921- 14
Spencer, Leonard G.
    See Garrett, Randall
    and Silverberg, Robert
Spencer, William 1922- 9
Spencer, Zane A(nn) 1935- 35
Spengler, Margaret 223
Sper, Emily 1957- 142
Speregen, Devra Newberger 1964- 84
Sperling, Dan(iel Lee) 1949- 65
Sperry, Armstrong W. 1897-1976 1
    Obituary 27
Sperry, Raymond
    See Garis, Howard R.
Sperry, Raymond, Jr. 1
Spetter, Jung-Hee 1969- 134
Spicer, Dorothy Gladys -1975 32
Spiegel, Beth 184
Spiegelman, Art 1948- 158
    Earlier sketch in SATA 109
Spiegelman, Judith M. 5
Spielberg, Steven 1947- 32
Spier, Peter (Edward) 1927- 54
    Earlier sketch in SATA 4
    See also CLR 5
Spilhaus, Athelstan (Frederick) 1911-1998 .. 13
    Obituary 102
Spilka, Arnold 1917- 6
Spillane, Frank Morrison
    See Spillane, Mickey
Spillane, Mickey 1918-2006 66
    Obituary 176
Spillebeen, Geert 1956- 225
Spinelli, Eileen 1942- 225
    Earlier sketches in SATA 38, 101, 150, 186
Spinelli, Jerry 1941- 195
    Earlier sketches in SATA 39, 71, 110, 158
    See also CLR 82
Spink, Reginald (William) 1905-1994 11
Spinka, Penina Keen 1945- 72
Spinner, Stephanie 1943- 132
    Earlier sketches in SATA 38, 91
Spinossimus
    See White, William, Jr.
Spiotta-DiMare, Loren 173
Spires, Ashley 1978- 183
Spires, Elizabeth 1952- 215
    Earlier sketch in SATA 71, 111
Spiridellis, Gregg 1971(?)- 199

Spirin, Gennadii
    See Spirin, Gennady
Spirin, Gennadij
    See Spirin, Gennady
Spirin, Gennady 1948- 204
    Earlier sketches in SATA 95, 134
    See also CLR 88
Spiro, Ruth 208
Spivak, Dawnine 101
Spizman, Robyn Freedman 194
Spohn, David 1948- 72
Spohn, Kate 1962- 147
    Earlier sketch in SATA 87
Spollen, Christopher 1952- 12
Spooner, Michael (Tim) 1954- 92
Spoor, Mike 218
Spowart, Robin 1947- 177
    Earlier sketch in SATA 82
Spradlin, Michael P. 204
Sprague, Gretchen 1926-2003 27
Spranger, Nina 1969- 203
Sprengel, Artie
    See Lerangis, Peter
Sprigge, Elizabeth (Miriam Squire)
    1900-1974 10
Spring, (Robert) Howard 1889-1965 28
Springer, Kristina 226
Springer, Margaret 1941- 78
Springer, Marilyn Harris 1931- 47
Springer, Nancy 1948- 222
    Earlier sketches in SATA 65, 110, 172
Springstubb, Tricia 1950- 78
    Brief entry 40
    Earlier sketch in SATA 46
Spudvilas, Anne 1951- 199
    Earlier sketch in SATA 94
Spurll, Barbara 1952- 78
Spurr, Elizabeth 172
Spykman, E(lizabeth) C(hoate) 1896-1965 .. 10
    See also CLR 35
Spyri, Johanna (Heusser) 1827-1901 100
    Earlier sketch in SATA 19
    See also CLR 115
Squires, Janet 215
Squires, Phil
    See Barker, S. Omar
Srba, Lynne 98
Sreenivasan, Jyotsna 1964- 101
S-Ringi, Kjell
    See Ringi, Kjell (Arne Soerensen)
Staake, Bob 1957- 209
Stacey, Cherylyn 1945- 96
Stacy, Donald
    See Pohl, Frederik
Stadler, John 204
Stadtler, Bea 1921- 17
Stafford, Jean 1915-1979
    Obituary 22
Stafford, Liliana 1950- 141
Stafford, Paul 1966- 116
Stahl, Ben(jamin) 1910-1987 5
    Obituary 54
Stahl, Hilda 1938-1993 48
    Obituary 77
Stahler, David, Jr. 218
    Earlier sketch in SATA 162
Staines, Bill 1949- 213
Stainton, Sue 187
Stair, Gobin (John) 1912- 35
Stalder, Valerie 27
Stamaty, Mark Alan 1947- 12
Stambler, Irwin 1924- 5
Stamp, Jorgen 1969- 225
Stampler, Ann Redisch 209
Standiford, Natalie 1961- 169
    Earlier sketch in SATA 81
Stanek, Lou Willett 1931- 63
Stang, Judit 1921-1977 29
Stang, Judy
    See Stang, Judit
Stangl, (Mary) Jean 1928- 67

Stanhope, Eric
  See Hamilton, Charles (Harold St. John)
Stankevich, Boris 1928- 2
Stanley, Diane 1943- 213
  Brief entry 32
  Earlier sketches in SATA *37, 80, 115, 164*
  See also CLR *46*
  See also SAAS *15*
Stanley, Elizabeth 1947- 206
Stanley, George Edward 1942-2011 228
  Earlier sketches in SATA *53, 111, 157, 1, 67*
Stanley, Jerry 1941- 127
  Earlier sketch in SATA *79*
Stanley, Mandy 165
Stanley, Robert
  See Hamilton, Charles (Harold St. John)
Stanley, Sanna 1962- 145
Stanli, Sue
  See Meilach, Dona Z(weigoron)
Stanstead, John
  See Groom, Arthur William
Stanton, Karen 1960- 190
Stanton, Schuyler
  See Baum, L. Frank
Staples, Suzanne Fisher 1945- 207
  Earlier sketches in SATA *70, 105, 151*
  See also CLR *137*
Stapleton, Marjorie (Winifred) 1932- 28
Stapp, Arthur D(onald) 1906-1972 4
Starbird, Kaye 1916- 6
  See also CLR *60*
Stark, Evan 1942- 78
Stark, James
  See Goldston, Robert (Conroy)
Stark, Ken 1943- 199
Stark, Ulf 1944- 124
Starke, Ruth (Elaine) 1946- 129
Starkey, Marion L(ena) 1901-1991 13
Starmer, Aaron 1976- 226
Starr, Ward
  See Manes, Stephen
Starret, William
  See McClintock, Marshall
Starr Taylor, Bridget 1959- 99
Stasiak, Krystyna 49
Staub, Frank 1949- 116
Staub, Frank Jacob
  See Staub, Frank
Staub, Wendy Corsi 1964- 114
Stauffacher, Sue 1961- 199
  Earlier sketch in SATA *155*
Stauffer, Don
  See Berkebile, Fred D(onovan)
Staunton, Schuyler
  See Baum, L. Frank
Staunton, Ted 1956- 167
  Earlier sketch in SATA *112*
Stead, Judy 210
Stead, Philip C.
  See Stringer, Helen
Stead, Philip Christian 225
Stead, Rebecca 1968(?)- 228
  Earlier sketch in SATA *188*
Steadman, Ralph 1936- 123
  Earlier sketch in SATA *32*
Steadman, Ralph Idris
  See Steadman, Ralph
Stearman, Kaye 1951- 118
Stearn, Ted 1961- 218
Stearns, Monroe (Mather) 1913-1987 5
  Obituary 55
Steckler, Arthur 1921-1985 65
Steding, Laurie 1953- 119
Steel, Danielle 1947- 66
Steel, Danielle Fernande
  See Steel, Danielle
Steele, Addison II
  See Lupoff, Richard A(llen)
Steele, Alexander 1958- 116
Steele, Henry Maxwell
  See Steele, Max

Steele, Mary 1930- 94
Steele, Mary Q(uintard Govan) 1922-1992 .. 51
  Obituary 72
  Earlier sketch in SATA *3*
Steele, Max 1922-2005 168
  Earlier sketch in SATA *10*
Steele, Philip 1948- 140
  Earlier sketch in SATA *81*
Steele, William O(wen) 1917-1979 51
  Obituary 27
  Earlier sketch in SATA *1*
Steelhammer, Ilona 1952- 98
Steelsmith, Shari 1962- 72
Stefanik, Alfred T. 1939- 55
Steffanson, Con
  See Cassiday, Bruce (Bingham)
  and Goulart, Ron
Steffens, Bradley 1955- 166
  Earlier sketch in SATA *77*
Steffensmeier, Alexander 1977- 195
Stegeman, Janet Allais 1923- 49
  Brief entry 49
Steggall, Susan 1967- 182
Steig, William 1907-2003 111
  Obituary 149
  Earlier sketches in SATA *18, 70*
  See also CLR *103*
Steig, William H.
  See Steig, William
Stein, David Ezra 211
  Earlier sketch in SATA *180*
Stein, Janet 1955- 218
Stein, M(eyer) L(ewis) 1920- 6
Stein, Mathilde 1969- 195
Stein, Mini 2
Stein, R(ichard) Conrad 1937- 154
  Earlier sketches in SATA *31, 82*
Stein, Wendy 1951- 77
Steinbeck, John 1902-1968 9
Steinbeck, John Ernst
  See Steinbeck, John
Steinberg, Alfred 1917-1995 9
Steinberg, David 1962- 200
Steinberg, D.J.
  See Steinberg, David
Steinberg, Fannie 1899-1990 43
Steinberg, Fred J. 1933- 4
Steinberg, Phillip Orso 1921- 34
Steinberg, Rafael (Mark) 1927- 45
Steinberg, Saul 1914-1999 67
Steincrohn, Maggie
  See Davis, Maggie S.
Steiner, Barbara A(nnette) 1934- 83
  Earlier sketch in SATA *13*
  See also SAAS *13*
Steiner, Charlotte 1900-1981 45
Steiner, George 1929- 62
Steiner, Joan 199
  Earlier sketch in SATA *110*
Steiner, Jorg
  See Steiner, Jorg
Steiner, Jorg 1930- 35
Steiner, K. Leslie
  See Delany, Samuel R., Jr.
Steiner, Stan(ley) 1925-1987 14
  Obituary 50
Steins, Richard 1942- 79
Stem, Jacqueline 1931- 110
Stemple, Heidi E.Y. 1966- 214
Stemple, Jason 179
Steneman, Shep 1945- 132
Stengel, Joyce A. 1938- 158
Stephanie, Gordon
  See Gordon, Stephanie Jacob
Stephens, Alice Barber 1858-1932 66
Stephens, Casey
  See Wagner, Sharon B.
Stephens, Henrietta Henkle 1909-1993 6
Stephens, J.B.
  See Lynn, Tracy
Stephens, Mary Jo 1935- 8

Stephens, Rebecca 1961- 141
Stephens, Reed
  See Donaldson, Stephen R.
Stephens, Suzanne
  See Kirby, Susan E.
Stephens, William M(cLain) 1925- 21
Stephensen, A. M.
  See Manes, Stephen
Stephenson, Kristina 224
Stephenson, Lynda 1941- 179
Stephenson, Lynda A.
  See Stephenson, Lynda
Stepp, Ann 1935- 29
Stepto, Michele 1946- 61
Steptoe, Javaka 1971- 213
  Earlier sketch in SATA *151*
Steptoe, John (Lewis) 1950-1989 63
  Earlier sketch in SATA *8*
  See also CLR *12*
Sterling, Brett
  See Bradbury, Ray
  and Hamilton, Edmond
  and Samachson, Joseph
Sterling, Dorothy 1913-2008 83
  Autobiography Feature 127
  Obituary 200
  Earlier sketch in SATA *1*
  See also CLR *1*
  See also SAAS *2*
Sterling, Helen
  See Watts, Helen L. Hoke
Sterling, Philip 1907-1989 8
  Obituary 63
Sterling, Shirley (Anne) 1948- 101
Stern, Ellen Norman 1927- 26
Stern, Judith M. 1951- 75
Stern, Madeleine
  See Stern, Madeleine B.
Stern, Madeleine B. 1912-2007 14
Stern, Madeleine Bettina
  See Stern, Madeleine B.
Stern, Maggie 1953- 156
Stern, Philip Van Doren 1900-1984 13
  Obituary 39
Stern, Simon 1943- 15
Sterne, Emma Gelders 1894- 6
Steurt, Marjorie Rankin 1888-1978 10
Stevens, April 1963- 208
Stevens, Bryna 1924- 65
Stevens, Carla M(cBride) 1928- 13
Stevens, Chambers 1968- 128
Stevens, Diane 1939- 94
Stevens, Franklin 1933- 6
Stevens, Greg
  See Cook, Glen
Stevens, Gwendolyn 1944- 33
Stevens, Helen 209
Stevens, Jan Romero 1953- 95
Stevens, Janet 1953- 193
  Earlier sketches in SATA *90, 148*
Stevens, Kathleen 1936- 49
Stevens, Leonard A. 1920- 67
Stevens, Lucile Vernon 1899-1994 59
Stevens, Margaret Dean
  See Aldrich, Bess Streeter
Stevens, Patricia Bunning 1931- 27
Stevens, Peter
  See Geis, Darlene Stern
Stevens, Serita 1949- 70
Stevens, Serita Deborah
  See Stevens, Serita
Stevens, Serita Mendelson
  See Stevens, Serita
Stevens, Shira
  See Stevens, Serita
Stevenson, Anna (M.) 1905- 12
Stevenson, Augusta 1869(?)-1976 2
  Obituary 26
Stevenson, Burton Egbert 1872-1962 25
Stevenson, Drew 1947- 60
Stevenson, Emma 207

Stevenson, Harvey 1960- *148*
    Earlier sketch in SATA *80*
Stevenson, James 1929- *195*
    Brief entry *34*
    Earlier sketches in SATA *42, 71, 113, 161*
    See also CLR *17*
Stevenson, Janet 1913- *8*
Stevenson, Robert Louis 1850-1894 .... *100*
    See also YABC *2*
    See also CLR *107*
Stevenson, Robert Louis Balfour
    See Stevenson, Robert Louis
Stevenson, Sucie
    See Stevenson, Sucie
Stevenson, Sucie 1956- *194*
    Earlier sketch in SATA *104*
Stewart, A(gnes) C(harlotte) *15*
Stewart, Amber *181*
Stewart, Chantal 1945- *173*
    Earlier sketch in SATA *121*
Stewart, Charles
    See Zurhorst, Charles (Stewart, Jr.)
Stewart, Eleanor
    See Porter, Eleanor H(odgman)
Stewart, Elisabeth J(ane) 1927- *93*
Stewart, Elizabeth Laing 1907- *6*
Stewart, Gail B. 1949- *141*
Stewart, George Rippey 1895-1980 .... *3*
    Obituary *23*
Stewart, Jennifer J. 1960- *128*
Stewart, Jennifer Jenkins
    See Stewart, Jennifer J.
Stewart, Joel *211*
    Earlier sketch in SATA *151*
Stewart, John 1920- *14*
Stewart, Mary (Florence Elinor) 1916- *12*
Stewart, Mary Rainbow
    See Stewart, Mary (Florence Elinor)
Stewart, Melissa 1968- *209*
    Earlier sketches in SATA *111, 167*
Stewart, Paul 1955- *199*
    Earlier sketches in SATA *114, 163*
Stewart, Robert Neil 1891-1972 .... *7*
Stewart, Sarah *143*
Stewart, Scott
    See Zaffo, George J.
Stewart, Trenton Lee 1970- *216*
Stewart, W(alter) P. 1924- *53*
Stewart, Whitney 1959- *167*
    Earlier sketch in SATA *92*
Stewig, John Warren 1937- *162*
    Earlier sketches in SATA *26, 110*
Stickler, Soma Han 1942- *128*
Stidworthy, John 1943- *63*
Stiegemeyer, Julie *180*
Stier, Catherine *198*
Stiles, Martha Bennett *108*
    Earlier sketch in SATA *6*
Still, James 1906-2001 .... *29*
    Obituary *127*
Stille, Darlene R. 1942- *170*
    Earlier sketch in SATA *126*
Stille, Darlene Ruth
    See Stille, Darlene R.
Stillerman, Marci *104*
Stillerman, Robbie 1947- *12*
Stilley, Frank 1918- *29*
Stilton, Geronimo *158*
Stimpson, Gerald
    See Mitchell, Adrian
Stimson, James 1964- *213*
Stine, Catherine *165*
Stine, G(eorge) Harry 1928-1997 .... *136*
    Earlier sketch in SATA *10*
Stine, Jovial Bob
    See Stine, R.L.
Stine, R.L. 1943- *194*
    Earlier sketches in SATA *31, 76, 129*
    See also CLR *111*
Stine, Robert Lawrence
    See Stine, R.L.

Stinetorf, Louise (Allender) 1900-1992 .... *10*
Stinson, Kathy 1952- *98*
Stirling, Arthur
    See Sinclair, Upton
Stirling, Ian 1941- *77*
Stirling, Nora B(romley) 1900-1997 .... *3*
Stirnweis, Shannon 1931- *10*
Stobbs, William 1914-2000 .... *17*
    Obituary *120*
Stock, Carolmarie 1951- *75*
Stock, Catherine 1952- *214*
    Earlier sketches in SATA *65, 114, 158*
Stockdale, Susan 1954- *206*
    Earlier sketch in SATA *98*
Stockham, Peter (Alan) 1928- *57*
Stockton, Francis Richard 1834-1902 .... *44*
    Brief entry *32*
Stockton, Frank R.
    See Stockton, Francis Richard
Stockwell-Moniz, Marc J. 1954- *164*
Stoddard, Edward G. 1923- *10*
Stoddard, Hope 1900-1987 .... *6*
Stoddard, Sandol 1927- *98*
    Earlier sketch in SATA *14*
Stoehr, Shelley 1969- *107*
Stoeke, Janet Morgan 1957- *202*
    Earlier sketches in SATA *90, 136*
Stohl, Margaret *227*
Stohner, Anu 1952- *179*
Stoiko, Michael 1919- *14*
Stojic, Manya 1967- *156*
Stoker, Abraham
    See Stoker, Bram
Stoker, Bram 1847-1912 .... *29*
Stokes, Cedric
    See Beardmore, George
Stokes, Jack (Tilden) 1923- *13*
Stokes, Olivia Pearl 1916- *32*
Stolarz, Laurie Faria 1972- *203*
Stolz, Mary 1920-2006 .... *133*
    Obituary *180*
    Earlier sketches in SATA *10, 71*
    See also SAAS *3*
Stolz, Mary Slattery
    See Stolz, Mary
Stone, Alan
    See Svenson, Andrew E(dward)
Stone, David K(arl) 1922- *9*
Stone, David Lee 1978- *166*
Stone, Eugenia 1879-1971 .... *7*
Stone, Gene
    See Stone, Eugenia
Stone, Helen V(irginia) *6*
Stone, Idella Purnell
    See Purnell, Idella
Stone, Ikey
    See Purnell, Idella
Stone, Irving 1903-1989 .... *3*
    Obituary *64*
Stone, Jeff *178*
Stone, Jon 1931-1997 .... *39*
    Obituary *95*
Stone, Josephine Rector
    See Dixon, Jeanne
Stone, Kyle M. 1972- *202*
Stone, Lesley
    See Trevor, Elleston
Stone, Peter 1930-2003 .... *65*
    Obituary *143*
Stone, Phoebe *205*
    Earlier sketch in SATA *134*
Stone, Raymond *1*
Stone, Rosetta
    See Dr. Seuss
Stone, Tanya Lee 1965- *217*
    Earlier sketch in SATA *182*
Stonehouse, Bernard 1926- *140*
    Earlier sketches in SATA *13, 80*
Stones, (Cyril) Anthony 1934- *72*
Stong, Phil(ip Duffield) 1899-1957 .... *32*

Stoops, Erik D(aniel) 1966- *142*
    Earlier sketch in SATA *78*
Stoppelmoore, Cheryl Jean
    See Ladd, Cheryl (Jean)
Stops, Sue 1936- *86*
Storace, Patricia *193*
Storad, Conrad J. 1957- *119*
Storey, Margaret 1926- *9*
Storey, Victoria Carolyn 1945- *16*
Stork, Francisco
    See Stork, Francisco X.
Stork, Francisco X. 1953- *210*
Storme, Peter
    See Stern, Philip Van Doren
Storms, Patricia 1963- *217*
Storr, Catherine (Cole) 1913-2001 .... *87*
    Obituary *122*
    Earlier sketch in SATA *9*
Story, Josephine
    See Loring, Emilie (Baker)
Stotko, Mary-Ann 1960- *154*
Stott, Ann *219*
Stott, Dorothy (M.) 1958- *99*
    Earlier sketch in SATA *67*
Stott, Dot
    See Stott, Dorothy (M.)
Stotter, Mike 1957- *108*
Stotts, Stuart *227*
Stout, Shawn K. *226*
Stout, William 1949- *132*
Stoutenburg, Adrien (Pearl) 1916-1982 .... *3*
Stoutland, Allison 1963- *130*
Stover, Allan C(arl) 1938- *14*
Stover, Jill (Griffin) 1958- *82*
Stover, Marjorie Filley 1914- *9*
Stowe, Harriet Beecher 1811-1896
    See YABC *1*
    See also CLR *131*
Stowe, Harriet Elizabeth Beecher
    See Stowe, Harriet Beecher
Stowe, Leland 1899-1994 .... *60*
    Obituary *78*
Stowe, Rosetta
    See Ogan, George F.
    and Ogan, Margaret E. (Nettles)
Stower, Adam *229*
    Earlier sketch in SATA *195*
Strachan, Bruce 1959- *205*
Strachan, Ian 1938- *85*
Strachan, Linda *167*
Strachan, Margaret Pitcairn 1908-1998 .... *14*
Strahinich, H. C.
    See Strahinich, Helen C.
Strahinich, Helen C. 1949- *78*
Strait, Treva Adams 1909-2002 .... *35*
Strand, Mark 1934- *41*
Strange, Philippa
    See Coury, Louise Andree
Stranger, Joyce
    See Wilson, Joyce M.
Strangis, Joel 1948- *124*
Strannigan, Shawn 1956- *93*
Strannigan, Shawn Alyne
    See Strannigan, Shawn
Strasnick, Lauren *222*
Strasser, Todd 1950- *215*
    Earlier sketches in SATA *41, 45, 71, 107, 153*
    See also CLR *11*
Stratemeyer, Edward L. 1862-1930 .... *100*
    Earlier sketches in SATA *1, 67*
    See also CLR *166*
    See Adams, Harrison
Stratford, Philip 1927- *47*
Stratton, Allan 1951- *178*
Stratton, J. M.
    See Whitlock, Ralph
Stratton, Thomas
    See Coulson, Robert S(tratton)
    and DeWeese, Thomas Eugene
Stratton-Porter, Gene 1863-1924 .... *15*
    See also CLR *87*

Strauss, Gwen 1963- 77
Strauss, Joyce 1936- 53
Strauss, Linda Leopold 1942- 127
Strauss, Susan (Elizabeth) 1954- 75
Strayer, E. Ward
See Stratemeyer, Edward L.
Streano, Vince(nt Catello) 1945- 20
Streatfeild, Mary Noel
See Streatfeild, Noel
Streatfeild, Noel 1897(?)-1986 20
Obituary 48
See also CLR 83
Street, Janet Travell 1959- 84
Street, Julia Montgomery 1898-1993 11
Streissguth, Thomas 1958- 116
Strelkoff, Tatiana 1957- 89
Stren, Patti 1949- 88
Brief entry 41
See also CLR 5
Strete, Craig Kee 1950- 96
Earlier sketch in SATA *44*
Stretton, Barbara (Humphrey) 1936- 43
Brief entry 35
Strickland, Brad 1947- 200
Earlier sketches in SATA *83, 137, 142*
Strickland, Craig (A.) 1956- 102
Strickland, Dorothy S(alley) 1933- 89
Strickland, Michael R. 1965- 144
Earlier sketch in SATA *83*
Strickland, Shadra 209
Strickland, Tessa 173
Strickland, William Bradley
See Strickland, Brad
Striegel, Jana 1955- 140
Striegel-Wilson, Jana
See Striegel, Jana
Striker, Lee
See Clark, Margaret (D.)
Striker, Susan 1942- 63
Stringer, Helen 225
Stringer, Lauren 1957- 183
Earlier sketch in SATA *129*
Stroeyer, Poul 1923- 13
Stromoski, Rick 1958- 111
Strong, Charles
See Epstein, Beryl
and Epstein, Samuel
Strong, David
See McGuire, Leslie (Sarah)
Strong, Jeremy 1949- 175
Earlier sketches in SATA *36, 105*
Strong, J.J.
See Strong, Jeremy
Strong, Pat
See Hough, Richard (Alexander)
Strong, Stacie 1965- 74
Stroud, Bettye 1939- 165
Earlier sketch in SATA *96*
Stroud, Jonathan 1970- 213
Earlier sketches in SATA *102, 159*
See also CLR *134*
Stroyer, Poul
See Stroeyer, Poul
Strug, Kerri 1977- 108
Stryer, Andrea Stenn 1938- 192
Stryker, Daniel
See Morris, Chris(topher Crosby)
and Stump, Jane Barr
Stuart, David
See Hoyt, Edwin P(almer), Jr.
Stuart, Derek
See Foster, John L(ouis)
Stuart, Forbes 1924- 13
Stuart, Ian
See MacLean, Alistair
Stuart, Jesse (Hilton) 1906-1984 2
Obituary 36
Stuart, Ruth McEnery 1849(?)-1917 116
Stuart, Sheila
See Baker, Mary Gladys Steel
Stuart-Clark, Christopher (Anthony) 1940- .. 32

Stubis, Talivaldis 1926- 5
Stubley, Trevor (Hugh) 1932- 22
Stuchner, Joan Betty 209
Stucky, Naomi R. 1922- 72
Stucley, Elizabeth
See Northmore, Elizabeth Florence
Stultifer, Morton
See Curtis, Richard
Sture-Vasa, Mary
See Alsop, Mary O'Hara
Sturges, Philemon 174
Sturtevant, Katherine 1950- 180
Earlier sketch in SATA *130*
Sturton, Hugh
See Johnston, H(ugh) A(nthony) S(tephen)
Sturtzel, Howard A(llison) 1894-1985 1
Sturtzel, Jane Levington 1903-1996 1
Stutley, D(oris) J(ean) 1959- 142
Stutson, Caroline 1940- 104
Stuve-Bodeen, Stephanie
See Bodeen, S. A.
Stux, Erica 1929- 140
Styles, (Frank) Showell 1908- 10
Stynes, Barbara White 133
Suarez, Maribel 1952- 201
Suba, Susanne 4
Suber, Melissa 213
Subond, Valerie
See Grayland, Valerie (Merle Spanner)
Sudbery, Rodie 1943- 42
Sudyka, Diana 208
Sue, Majella Lue 209
Suen, Anastasia 1956(?)- 157
Sufrin, Mark 1925- 76
Sugarman, Joan G. 1917- 64
Sugarman, Tracy 1921- 37
Sugita, Yutaka 1930- 36
Suhl, Yuri (Menachem) 1908-1986 8
Obituary 50
See also CLR 2
See also SAAS *1*
Suhr, Joanne 129
Suid, Murray 1942- 27
Sullivan, Edward T. 206
Sullivan, George (Edward) 1927- 147
Earlier sketches in SATA *4, 89*
Sullivan, Jacqueline Levering 203
Sullivan, Jody
See Rake, Jody
Sullivan, Kathryn A. 1954- 141
Sullivan, Mary Ann 1954- 63
Sullivan, Mary W(ilson) 1907- 13
Sullivan, Pat
See Messmer, Otto
Sullivan, Paul 1939- 106
Sullivan, Sarah G. 1953- 179
Sullivan, Silky 1940- 101
Sullivan, Sue
See Sullivan, Susan E.
Sullivan, Susan E. 1962- 123
Sullivan, Thomas Joseph, Jr. 1947- 16
Sullivan, Tom
See Sullivan, Thomas Joseph, Jr.
Sully, Tom 1959- 104
Suma, Nova Ren 223
Sumichrast, Jozef 1948- 29
Sumiko
See Davies, Sumiko
Summerforest, Ivy B.
See Kirkup, James
Summers, Barbara 1944- 182
Summers, Cassia Joy
See Cowley, Joy
Summers, James L(evingston) 1910-1973 57
Brief entry 28
Summertree, Katonah
See Windsor, Patricia
Summy, Barrie 208
Sumner, William 1971- 229
Sun, Chyng Feng 1959- 90

Sunderlin, Sylvia (S.) 1911-1997 28
Obituary 99
Sung, Betty Lee 26
Supeene, Shelagh Lynne 1952- 153
Supplee, Suzanne 204
Supraner, Robyn 1930- 101
Earlier sketch in SATA *20*
Supree, Burt(on) 1941-1992 73
Surface, Mary Hall 1958- 126
Surge, Frank 1931- 13
Susac, Andrew 1929- 5
Susi, Geraldine Lee 1942- 98
Sussman, Cornelia Silver 1914-1999 59
Sussman, Irving 1908-1996 59
Sussman, Michael 1953- 217
Sussman, Michael B.
See Sussman, Michael
Sussman, Susan 1942- 48
Sutcliff, Rosemary 1920-1992 78
Obituary 73
Earlier sketches in SATA *6, 44*
See also CLR *138*
Sutcliffe, Jane 1957- 138
Sutherland, Colleen 1944- 79
Sutherland, Efua (Theodora Morgue)
1924-1996 25
Sutherland, Jon 1958- 167
Sutherland, Jonathan D.
See Sutherland, Jon
Sutherland, Jonathan David
See Sutherland, Jon
Sutherland, Margaret 1941- 15
Sutherland, Zena Bailey 1915-2002 37
Obituary 137
Suttles, Shirley (Smith) 1922- 21
Sutton, Ann (Livesay) 1923- 31
Sutton, Eve(lyn Mary) 1906-1992 26
Sutton, Felix 1910(?)-1973 31
Sutton, Jane 1950- 52
Brief entry 43
Sutton, Larry M(atthew) 1931- 29
Sutton, Margaret Beebe 1903-2001 1
Obituary 131
Sutton, Myron Daniel 1925- 31
Sutton, Roger 1956- 93
Sutton, Sally 1973- 214
Suzanne, Jamie
See Hawes, Louise
and Lantz, Francess L(in)
and Singleton, Linda Joy
and Zach, Cheryl (Byrd)
Suzuki, David 1936- 138
Suzuki, David Takayoshi
See Suzuki, David
Svendsen, Mark 1962- 181
Earlier sketch in SATA *120*
Svendsen, Mark Nestor
See Svendsen, Mark
Svenson, Andrew E(dward) 1910-1975 2
Obituary 26
Swaab, Neil 1978- 191
Swaim, Jessica 1950- 202
Swain, Carol 1962- 172
Swain, Gwenyth 1961- 134
Earlier sketch in SATA *84*
Swain, Ruth
See Swain, Ruth Freeman
Swain, Ruth Freeman 1951- 161
Earlier sketch in SATA *119*
Swain, Su Zan (Noguchi) 1916- 21
Swain, Wilson 1976- 225
Swallow, Gerry 227
Swallow, Pamela Curtis 178
Swamp, Jake 1941- 98
Swan, Susan 1944- 108
Earlier sketch in SATA *22*
Swann, Brian (Stanley Frank) 1940- 116
Swann, E.L.
See Lasky, Kathryn
Swann, Ruth Rice 1920- 84
Swanson, Diane 1944- 203

Swanson, Helen M(cKendry) 1919- *94*
Swanson, June 1931- *76*
Swanson, Susan Marie *209*
Swanson, Wayne 1942- *167*
Swarner, Kristina 1965- *215*
Swarthout, Glendon (Fred) 1918-1992 .... *26*
Swarthout, Kathryn 1919- *7*
Swayne, Sam(uel F.) 1907- *53*
Swayne, Zoa (Lourana) 1905- *53*
Swearingen, Greg 1976- *225*
Sweat, Lynn 1934- *168*
    Earlier sketch in SATA 57
Swede, George 1940- *67*
Sweeney, James B(artholomew) 1910-1999 . *21*
Sweeney, Joyce 1955- *167*
    Earlier sketches in SATA 65, 68, 108
Sweeney, Joyce Kay
    See Sweeney, Joyce
Sweeney, Karen O'Connor
    See O'Connor, Karen
Sweeney, Matthew (Gerard) 1952- *156*
Sweet, Melissa 1956- *211*
    Earlier sketch in SATA 172
Sweet, Sarah C.
    See Jewett, Sarah Orne
Sweetland, Nancy A(nn) 1934- *48*
Swenson, Allan A(rmstrong) 1933- *21*
Swenson, May 1919-1989 .... *15*
Swentzell, Rina 1939- *79*
Swiatkowska, Gabi 1971(?)- *180*
Swift, Bryan
    See Knott, William C(ecil, Jr.)
Swift, David
    See Kaufmann, John
Swift, Hildegarde Hoyt 1890(?)-1977
    Obituary *20*
Swift, Jonathan 1667-1745 .... *19*
    See also CLR 161
Swift, Merlin
    See Leeming, Joseph
Swiger, Elinor Porter 1927- *8*
Swinburne, Laurence (Joseph) 1924- *9*
Swinburne, Stephen R. 1952- *188*
    Earlier sketch in SATA 150
Swinburne, Steve
    See Swinburne, Stephen R.
Swindells, Robert (Edward) 1939- *150*
    Brief entry *34*
    Earlier sketches in SATA 50, 80
    See also SAAS 14
Swinford, Betty (June Wells) 1927- *58*
Swinford, Bob
    See Swinford, Betty (June Wells)
Swithen, John
    See King, Stephen
Switzer, Ellen 1923- *48*
Swope, Sam *156*
Swope, Samuel
    See Swope, Sam
Sybesma, Jetske
    See Ironside, Jetske
Sydney, Frank
    See Warwick, Alan R(oss)
Sydor, Colleen 1960- *207*
Sykes, Julie 1963- *202*
Sylvada, Peter 1964- *202*
Sylvester, Natalie G(abry) 1922- *22*
Syme, (Neville) Ronald 1913-1992 .... *87*
    Earlier sketch in SATA 2
Symes, R. F. *77*
Symes, Ruth Louise 1962- *179*
Symons, (Dorothy) Geraldine 1909- *33*
Symons, Stuart
    See Stanley, George Edward
Symynkywicz, Jeffrey B. 1954- *87*
Symynkywicz, Jeffrey Bruce
    See Symynkywicz, Jeffrey B.
Synge, (Phyllis) Ursula 1930- *9*
Sypher, Lucy Johnston 1907- *7*
Szasz, Suzanne (Shorr) 1915-1997 .... *13*
    Obituary *99*

Szekeres, Cyndy 1933- *157*
    Autobiography Feature *157*
    Earlier sketches in SATA 5, 60, 131
    See also SAAS 13
Szekessy, Tanja *98*
Szpura, Beata 1961- *93*
Szuc, Jeff 1975- *220*
Szudek, Agnes S(usan) P(hilomena) *57*
    Brief entry *49*
Szulc, Tad 1926-2001 .... *26*
Szydlow, Jarl
    See Szydlowski, Mary Vigliante
Szydlowski, Mary Vigliante 1946- *94*
Szymanski, Lois 1957- *91*

T

Taback, Simms 1932- *170*
    Brief entry *36*
    Earlier sketches in SATA 40, 104
    See also CLR 100
Taber, Gladys (Bagg) 1899-1980
    Obituary *22*
Tabor, Nancy Maria Grande 1949- *161*
    Earlier sketch in SATA 89
Tabrah, Ruth Milander 1921- *14*
Tacang, Brian *213*
Tackach, James 1953- *123*
Tackach, James M.
    See Tackach, James
Tadgell, Nicole 1969- *220*
    Earlier sketch in SATA 177
Tafolla, Carmen 1951- *220*
Tafolla, Mary Carmen
    See Tafolla, Carmen
Tafuri, Nancy 1946- *192*
    Autobiography Feature *192*
    Earlier sketches in SATA 39, 75, 130
    See also CLR 74
    See also SAAS 14
Tagg, Christine Elizabeth 1962- *138*
Tagliaferro, Linda *173*
Taha, Karen T(erry) 1942- *156*
    Earlier sketch in SATA 71
Tai, Sharon O. 1963- *153*
Tait, Douglas 1944- *12*
Takabayashi, Mari 1960- *156*
    Earlier sketch in SATA 115
Takahashi, Hideko *209*
Takahashi, Rumiko 1957- *163*
Takakjian, Portia 1930- *15*
Takashima, Misako
    See Misako Rocks!
Takashima, Shizuye 1928- *13*
Takayama, Sandi 1962- *106*
Takeda, Pete(r M.) 1964- *148*
Tal, Eve 1947- *176*
Talbert, Marc (Alan) 1953- *154*
    Autobiography Feature *154*
    Earlier sketches in SATA 68, 99
Talbot, Charlene Joy 1928- *10*
Talbot, Toby 1928- *14*
Talbott, Hudson 1949- *212*
    Earlier sketches in SATA 84, 131
Talifero, Gerald 1950- *75*
Talker, T.
    See Rands, William Brighty
Tallarico, Tony 1933- *116*
Tallcott, Emogene *10*
Tallec, Olivier 1970- *197*
Tallis, Robyn
    See Smith, Sherwood
Tallon, Robert 1939- *43*
    Brief entry *28*
Talmadge, Marian *14*
Tamaki, Jillian 1980- *201*
Tamar, Erika 1934- *150*
    Earlier sketches in SATA 62, 101
Tamarin, Alfred H. 1913-1980 .... *13*

Tamburine, Jean 1930- *12*
Tames, Richard (Lawrence) 1946- *102*
    Earlier sketch in SATA 67
Tamminga, Frederick W(illiam) 1934- *66*
Tammuz, Benjamin 1919-1989
    Obituary *63*
Tan, Amy 1952- *75*
Tan, Amy Ruth
    See Tan, Amy
Tan, Shaun 1974- *198*
Tanaka, Beatrice 1932- *76*
Tanaka, Shelley *214*
    Earlier sketch in SATA 136
Tanaka, Yoko 1947- *215*
Tang, Charles 1948- *81*
Tang, Greg *172*
Tang, You-Shan 1946- *53*
Tania B.
    See Blixen, Karen
Tankard, Jeremy 1973- *191*
Tannen, Mary 1943- *37*
Tannenbaum, Beulah Goldstein 1916- *3*
Tannenbaum, D(onald) Leb 1948- *42*
Tanner, Jane 1946- *74*
Tanner, Louise S(tickney) 1922-2000 .... *9*
Tanobe, Miyuki 1937- *23*
Tanselle, Eve 1933- *125*
Tapio, Pat Decker
    See Kines, Pat Decker
Tapp, Kathy Kennedy 1949- *88*
    Brief entry *50*
Tarbescu, Edith 1939- *107*
Tarkington, (Newton) Booth 1869-1946 .... *17*
Tarpley, Natasha A(nastasia) 1971- *147*
Tarr, Judith 1955- *149*
    Earlier sketch in SATA 64
Tarry, Ellen 1906-2008 .... *16*
    See also CLR 26
    See also SAAS 16
Tarshis, Jerome 1936- *9*
Tarshis, Lauren *187*
Tarsky, Sue 1946- *41*
Taschek, Karen 1956- *185*
Tashjian, Janet 1956- *151*
    Earlier sketch in SATA 102
Tashjian, Virginia A. 1921-2008 .... *3*
Tasker, James 1908- *9*
Tate, Don(ald E.) *159*
Tate, Eleanora E. 1948- *191*
    Earlier sketches in SATA 38, 94
    See also CLR 37
Tate, Eleanora Elaine
    See Tate, Eleanora E.
Tate, Ellalice
    See Hibbert, Eleanor Alice Burford
Tate, Joan 1922- *86*
    Earlier sketch in SATA 9
    See also SAAS 20
Tate, Mary Anne
    See Hale, Arlene
Tate, Nikki *134*
Tate, Richard
    See Masters, Anthony (Richard)
Tate, Suzanne 1930- *91*
Tatham, Betty *142*
Tatham, Campbell
    See Elting, Mary
Tatham, Julie
    See Tatham, Julie Campbell
Tatham, Julie Campbell 1908-1999 .... *80*
Tavares, Matt *198*
    Earlier sketch in SATA 159
Tavares, Victor 1971- *176*
Taves, Isabella 1915- *27*
Tayleur, Karen 1961- *213*
Taylor, Alastair 1959- *130*
Taylor, Andrew 1951- *70*
Taylor, Andrew John Robert
    See Taylor, Andrew
Taylor, Ann 1782-1866 .... *41*
    Brief entry *35*

Taylor, Audilee Boyd 1931- .... _59_
Taylor, Barbara J. 1927- .... _10_
Taylor, Ben
  See Strachan, Ian
Taylor, Brooke .... _205_
Taylor, Carl 1937-2010 .... _14_
Taylor, Carrie-Jo
  See Taylor, C.J.
Taylor, Cheryl Munro 1957- .... _96_
Taylor, C.J. 1952- .... _224_
Taylor, Cora (Lorraine) 1936- .... _103_
  Earlier sketch in SATA _64_
  See also CLR _63_
Taylor, Dave 1948- .... _78_
Taylor, David
  See Taylor, Dave
Taylor, David 1900-1965 .... _10_
Taylor, Debbie A. 1955- .... _169_
Taylor, Eleanor 1969- .... _206_
Taylor, Elizabeth 1912-1975 .... _13_
Taylor, Florance Walton .... _9_
Taylor, Florence M(arian Tompkins)
  1892-1983 .... _9_
Taylor, Gage 1942-2000 .... _87_
Taylor, Geoff 1946- .... _204_
Taylor, G.P. 1958(?)- .... _216_
  Earlier sketch in SATA _156_
Taylor, Graham Peter
  See Taylor, G.P.
Taylor, Greg 1951- .... _221_
Taylor, Herb(ert Norman, Jr.) 1942-1987 ..... _22_
  Obituary .... _54_
Taylor, J. David
  See Taylor, Dave
Taylor, Jane 1783-1824 .... _41_
  Brief entry .... _35_
Taylor, Jerry D(uncan) 1938- .... _47_
Taylor, John Robert
  See Taylor, Andrew
Taylor, Judy
  See Hough, Judy Taylor
Taylor, Kenneth N. 1917-2005 .... _26_
Taylor, Kenneth Nathaniel
  See Taylor, Kenneth N.
Taylor, Kim .... _180_
Taylor, L(ester) B(arbour), Jr. 1932- .... _27_
Taylor, Lois Dwight Cole
  See Cole, Lois Dwight
Taylor, Louise Todd 1939- .... _47_
Taylor, Margaret 1950- .... _106_
Taylor, Mark 1927- .... _32_
  Brief entry .... _28_
Taylor, Mildred D. 1943- .... _135_
  See also CLR _144_
  See also SAAS _5_
Taylor, Mildred Delois
  See Taylor, Mildred D.
Taylor, Paula (Wright) 1942- .... _48_
  Brief entry .... _33_
Taylor, Peter Lane .... _210_
Taylor, Robert Lewis 1912-1998 .... _10_
Taylor, Sean 1965- .... _192_
Taylor, Susan Champlin
  See Champlin, Susan
Taylor, Sydney (Brenner) 1904(?)-1978 .... _28_
  Obituary .... _26_
  Earlier sketch in SATA _1_
Taylor, Theodore 1921-2006 .... _128_
  Obituary .... _177_
  Earlier sketches in SATA _5, 54, 83_
  See also CLR _30_
  See also SAAS _4_
Taylor, William 1938- .... _164_
  Earlier sketches in SATA _78, 113_
  See also CLR _63_
Taylor-Butler, Christine 1959- .... _218_
Tazewell, Charles 1900-1972 .... _74_
Tchana, Katrin
  See Tchana, Katrin Hyman
Tchana, Katrin H.
  See Tchana, Katrin Hyman

Tchana, Katrin Hyman 1963- .... _177_
  Earlier sketch in SATA _125_
Tchekhov, Anton
  See Chekhov, Anton
Tchen, Richard .... _120_
Tchudi, Stephen N. 1942- .... _55_
Teague, Bob
  See Teague, Robert
Teague, Mark 1963- .... _205_
  Earlier sketches in SATA _68, 99, 170_
Teague, Mark Christopher
  See Teague, Mark
Teague, Robert 1929- .... _32_
  Brief entry .... _31_
Teal, Val 1902-1997 .... _10_
  Obituary .... _114_
Teal, Valentine M.
  See Teal, Val
Teale, Edwin Way 1899-1980 .... _7_
  Obituary .... _25_
Teasdale, Sara 1884-1933 .... _32_
Tebbel, John (William) 1912-2004 .... _26_
Teckentrup, Britta 1969- .... _200_
Tedesco, P.R.
  See Naylor, Phyllis Reynolds
Teensma, Lynne Bertrand
  See Bertrand, Lynne
Tee-Van, Helen Damrosch 1893-1976 .... _10_
  Obituary .... _27_
Teevee, Ningeokuluk 1963- .... _223_
Tegner, Bruce 1928- .... _62_
Teitelbaum, Michael 1953- .... _116_
  Earlier sketch in SATA _59_
Tejima
  See Tejima, Keizaburo
Tejima, Keizaburo 1931- .... _139_
  See also CLR _20_
Telander, Todd (G.) 1967- .... _88_
Teleki, Geza 1943- .... _45_
Telemaque, Eleanor Wong 1934- .... _43_
Telescope, Tom
  See Newbery, John
Telgemeier, Raina 1977- .... _228_
Tellegen, Toon 1941- .... _229_
Tellis, Annabel 1967- .... _191_
Temkin, Sara Anne Schlossberg 1913-1996 . _26_
Temko, Florence .... _13_
Tempest, Margaret Mary 1892-1982
  Obituary .... _33_
Templar, Maurice
  See Groom, Arthur William
Temple, Arthur
  See Northcott, (William) Cecil
Temple, Charles 1947- .... _79_
Temple, Frances (Nolting) 1945-1995 .... _85_
Temple, Herbert 1919- .... _45_
Temple, Paul
  See McConnell, James Douglas Rutherford
Temple, William F(rederick) 1914-1989 .... _107_
Tenggren, Gustaf 1896-1970 .... _18_
  Obituary .... _26_
Tennant, Kylie
  See Rodd, Kylie Tennant
Tennant, Veronica 1947- .... _36_
Tenneshaw, S.M.
  See Beaumont, Charles
  and Garrett, Randall
  and Silverberg, Robert
Tenniel, John 1820-1914 .... _74_
  Brief entry .... _27_
  See also CLR _146_
Tepper, Sheri S. 1929- .... _113_
Tepper, Yona 1941- .... _228_
Terada, Alice M. 1928- .... _90_
Terban, Marvin 1940- .... _54_
  Brief entry .... _45_
Teresi, Judith M.
  See Goldberger, Judith M.
ter Haar, Jaap 1922- .... _6_
  See also CLR _15_
Terhune, Albert Payson 1872-1942 .... _15_

Terkel, Susan N(eiburg) 1948- .... _103_
  Earlier sketch in SATA _59_
Terlouw, Jan (Cornelis) 1931- .... _30_
Terrazzini, Daniela Jaglenka .... _218_
Terrell, John Upton 1900-1988
  Obituary .... _60_
Terrill, Beth .... _198_
Terrill, Elizabeth
  See Terrill, Beth
Terris, Susan 1937- .... _77_
  Earlier sketch in SATA _3_
Terry, Luther L(eonidas) 1911-1985 .... _11_
  Obituary .... _42_
Terry, Margaret
  See Dunnahoo, Terry Janson
Terry, Walter 1913-1982 .... _14_
Terry, Will 1966- .... _205_
Terzian, James P. 1915- .... _14_
Tessendorf, K(enneth) C(harles) 1925-2003 . _75_
  Obituary .... _142_
Tessler, Manya .... _200_
Tessler, Stephanie Gordon
  See Gordon, Stephanie Jacob
Testa, Dom .... _208_
Tester, Sylvia Root 1939- .... _64_
  Brief entry .... _37_
Tether, (Cynthia) Graham 1950- .... _46_
  Brief entry .... _36_
Tetzner, Lisa 1894-1963 .... _169_
Thach, James Otis 1969- .... _195_
Thacher, Mary McGrath 1933- .... _9_
Thackeray, William Makepeace 1811-1863 .. _23_
Thaler, Michael C.
  See Thaler, Mike
Thaler, Mike 1936- .... _215_
  Brief entry .... _47_
  Earlier sketches in SATA _56, 93_
Thaler, Shmuel 1958- .... _126_
  Earlier sketch in SATA _72_
Thamer, Katie 1955- .... _42_
Thane, Elswyth 1900-1984(?) .... _32_
Tharp, Louise (Marshall) Hall 1898-1992 ...... _3_
  Obituary .... _129_
Tharp, Tim 1957- .... _189_
Thayer, Ernest Lawrence 1863-1940 .... _60_
Thayer, Jane
  See Woolley, Catherine
Thayer, Marjorie 1908-1992 .... _74_
  Brief entry .... _37_
Thayer, Peter
  See Wyler, Rose
Thelwell, Norman 1923-2004 .... _14_
Themerson, Stefan 1910-1988 .... _65_
Thermes, Jennifer 1966- .... _155_
Theroux, Paul 1941- .... _109_
  Earlier sketch in SATA _44_
Theroux, Paul Edward
  See Theroux, Paul
Thesman, Jean .... _124_
  Earlier sketch in SATA _74_
The Tjong-Khing
  See Khing, T.T.
Thieda, Shirley Ann 1943- .... _13_
Thiele, Colin 1920-2006 .... _125_
  Earlier sketches in SATA _14, 72_
  See also CLR _27_
  See also SAAS _2_
Thiele, Colin Milton
  See Thiele, Colin
Thiesing, Lisa 1958- .... _159_
  Earlier sketch in SATA _95_
Thimmesh, Catherine .... _189_
Thiry, Joan (Marie) 1926- .... _45_
Thisdale, Francois 1964- .... _222_
Thistlethwaite, Miles 1945- .... _12_
Thollander, Earl 1922- .... _22_
Thomas, Abigail 1941- .... _112_
Thomas, Andrea
  See Hill, Margaret (Ohler)
Thomas, Art(hur Lawrence) 1952- .... _48_
  Brief entry .... _38_

Thomas, Carroll
  See Ratliff, Thomas M.
  and Shmurak, Carole B.
Thomas, Dylan 1914-1953 60
Thomas, Dylan Marlais
  See Thomas, Dylan
Thomas, Egbert S.
  See Ellis, Edward S.
Thomas, Estelle Webb 1899-1982 26
Thomas, Frances 1943- 171
  Earlier sketch in SATA 92
Thomas, Garen 213
Thomas, H. C.
  See Keating, Lawrence A.
Thomas, Ianthe 1951- 139
  Brief entry 42
  See also CLR 8
Thomas, J. F.
  See Fleming, Thomas
Thomas, Jan 1958- 226
  Earlier sketch in SATA 197
Thomas, Jane Resh 1936- 171
  Earlier sketches in SATA 38, 90
Thomas, Jerry D. 1959- 91
Thomas, Joan Gale
  See Robinson, Joan (Mary) G(ale Thomas)
Thomas, Joyce Carol 1938- 210
  Autobiography Feature 137
  Earlier sketches in SATA 40, 78, 123, 137
  See also CLR 19
  See also SAAS 7
Thomas, Lee
  See Floren, Lee
  and Pendleton, Thomas
Thomas, Lowell Jackson, Jr. 1923- 15
Thomas, Margaret
  See Thomas, Peggy
Thomas, Meredith 1963- 119
Thomas, Michael
  See Wilks, Michael Thomas
Thomas, Middy 1931- 191
Thomas, Patricia 1934- 199
  Earlier sketch in SATA 51
Thomas, Peggy 174
Thomas, Rob 1965- 97
Thomas, Scott 1959- 147
Thomas, Velma Maia 1955- 171
Thomas, Vernon (Arthur) 1934- 56
Thomas, Victoria
  See DeWeese, Thomas Eugene
  and Kugi, Constance Todd
Thomasma, Kenneth R. 1930- 90
Thomason, Mark 215
Thomassie, Tynia 1959- 92
Thompson, Alicia 1984- 224
Thompson, Brenda 1935- 34
Thompson, Carol 1951- 189
  Earlier sketch in SATA 85
Thompson, China
  See Lewis, Mary
Thompson, Colin 1942- 198
  Earlier sketches in SATA 95, 163
Thompson, David H(ugh) 1941- 17
Thompson, Eileen
  See Panowski, Eileen Thompson
Thompson, George Selden 1929-1989 73
  Obituary 63
  Earlier sketch in SATA 4
  See also CLR 8
Thompson, Harlan 1894-1987 10
  Obituary 53
Thompson, Hilary 1943- 56
  Brief entry 49
Thompson, Joanna Maxwell Pullein
  See Pullein-Thompson, Joanna Maxwell
Thompson, Julian F(rancis) 1927- 155
  Brief entry 40
  Earlier sketches in SATA 55, 99
  See also CLR 24
  See also SAAS 13

Thompson, K(athryn Carolyn) Dyble
  1952- 82
Thompson, Kate 1956- 204
Thompson, Kay 1912(?)-1998 16
  See also CLR 22
Thompson, Lauren 1962- 200
  Earlier sketches in SATA 132, 174
Thompson, Lauren Stevens
  See Thompson, Lauren
Thompson, Megan Lloyd
  See Lloyd, Megan
Thompson, Richard 1951- 184
Thompson, Ruth Plumly 1891-1976 66
Thompson, Sharon 1952- 119
Thompson, Sharon Elaine
  See Thompson, Sharon
Thompson, Stith 1885-1976 57
  Obituary 20
Thompson, Vivian L(aubach) 1911- 3
Thomson, Bill 1963- 187
Thomson, Celia
  See Lynn, Tracy
Thomson, David (Robert Alexander)
  1914-1988 40
  Obituary 55
Thomson, Melissa 1979- 205
Thomson, Pat 1939- 122
  Earlier sketch in SATA 77
Thomson, Peggy 1922- 31
Thomson, Sarah L. 212
  Earlier sketch in SATA 178
Thon, Melanie Rae 1957- 132
Thong, Roseanne 174
Thor, Annika 1950- 222
Thorburn, John
  See Goldsmith, John Herman Thorburn
Thorn, John 1947- 59
Thorndyke, Helen Louise
  See Benson, Mildred
Thorne, Ian
  See May, Julian
Thorne, Jean Wright
  See May, Julian
Thornhill, Jan 1955- 148
  Earlier sketch in SATA 77
Thornton, Hall
  See Silverberg, Robert
Thornton, W. B.
  See Burgess, Thornton Waldo
Thornton, Yvonne S. 1947- 96
Thornton, Yvonne Shirley
  See Thornton, Yvonne S.
Thorpe, E(ustace) G(eorge) 1916- 21
Thorpe, J. K.
  See Nathanson, Laura Walther
Thorvall, Kerstin 1925- 13
Thorvall-Falk, Kerstin
  See Thorvall, Kerstin
Thrasher, Crystal (Faye) 1921- 27
Threadgall, Colin 1941- 77
Three Little Pigs
  See Lantz, Francess L(in)
Thum, Gladys 1920- 26
Thum, Marcella 28
  Earlier sketch in SATA 3
Thundercloud, Katherine
  See Witt, Shirley Hill
Thurber, James 1894-1961 13
Thurber, James Grover
  See Thurber, James
Thurlo, Aimee 161
Thurlo, David 161
Thurman, Judith 1946- 33
Thurman, Mark (Gordon Ian) 1948- 63
Thwaite, Ann (Barbara Harrop) 1932- 14
Tibbets, Peggy 127
Tibbles, Jean-Paul 1958- 115
Tibo, Gilles 1951- 107
  Earlier sketch in SATA 67
Tiburzi, Bonnie 1948- 65

Ticheburn, Cheviot
  See Ainsworth, William Harrison
Tichenor, Tom 1923-1992 14
Tichnor, Richard 1959- 90
Tichy, William 1924- 31
Tickle, Jack
  See Chapman, Jane
Tidholm, Anna-Clara 1946- 223
Tiegreen, Alan F. 1935- 94
  Brief entry 36
Tierney, Fiona 229
Tierney, Frank M. 1930- 54
Tierney, Tom 1928- 113
Tiffault, Benette W. 1955- 77
Tildes, Phyllis Limbacher 1945- 210
Tiller, Ruth L. 1949- 83
Tilley, Debbie 190
Tillman, Nancy 211
Tillotson, Katherine 224
Tilly, Nancy 1935- 62
Tilton, Madonna Elaine 1929- 41
Tilton, Rafael
  See Tilton, Madonna Elaine
Timberlake, Amy 156
Timberlake, Carolyn
  See Dresang, Eliza (Carolyn Timberlake)
Timmers, Leo 1970- 190
Timmins, Jeffrey Stewart 1979- 227
Timmins, William F(rederick) 10
Tinbergen, Niko(laas) 1907-1988
  Obituary 60
Tincknell, Cathy 194
Tiner, John Hudson 1944- 32
Tingle, Dolli (?)-
  See Brackett, Dolli Tingle
Tingle, Rebecca 174
Tingle, Tim 208
Tingum, Janice 1958- 91
Tinkelman, Murray 1933- 12
Tinkham, Kelly A. 188
Tinkle, (Julien) Lon 1906-1980 36
Tinling, Marion (Rose) 1904- 140
Tipene, Tim 1972- 141
Tippett, James S(terling) 1885-1958 66
Tirone Smith, Mary-Ann 1944- 143
Titlebaum, Ellen 195
Titler, Dale M(ilton) 1926- 35
  Brief entry 28
Titmarsh, Michael Angelo
  See Thackeray, William Makepeace
Titus, Eve 1922- 2
Tjia, Sherwin 1975- 204
Tjong Khing, The 1933- 76
Tobias, Katherine
  See Gottfried, Theodore Mark
Tobias, Tobi 1938- 82
  Earlier sketch in SATA 5
  See also CLR 4
Tobin, James 226
Tocci, C. Lee 1958- 220
Tocci, Cynthia Lee
  See Tocci, C. Lee
Tocher, Timothy 228
Todd, Anne Ophelia
  See Dowden, Anne Ophelia Todd
Todd, Barbara 1961- 173
Todd, Barbara K(eith) 1917- 10
Todd, Chuck 195
Todd, H(erbert) E(atton) 1908-1988 84
  Earlier sketch in SATA 11
Todd, Loreto 1942- 30
Todd, Pamela 212
Todd, Peter
  See Hamilton, Charles (Harold St. John)
Toews, Miriam 1964- 165
Tofel, Richard J. 1957- 140
Toft, Kim Michelle 1960- 170
Tokunbo, Dimitrea 187
Tolan, Stephanie S. 1942- 142
  Earlier sketches in SATA 38, 78
Toland, John (Willard) 1912-2004 38

Tolbert, Steve 1944- *143*
Toledo, Francisco 1940- *198*
Toledo, Natalia 1967- *197*
Tolkien, J. R. R. 1892-1973 .... *100*
  Obituary *24*
  Earlier sketches in SATA *2, 32*
  See also CLR *152*
Tolkien, John Ronald Reuel
  See Tolkien, J. R. R.
Toll, Emily
  See Cannon, Eileen E(mily)
Toll, Nelly S. 1935- *78*
Tolland, W. R.
  See Heitzmann, William Ray
Tolles, Martha 1921- *76*
  Earlier sketch in SATA *8*
Tolliver, Ruby C(hangos) 1922- *110*
  Brief entry *41*
  Earlier sketch in SATA *55*
Tolmie, Kenneth Donald 1941- *15*
Tolstoi, Lev
  See Tolstoy, Leo
Tolstoy, Leo 1828-1910 .... *26*
Tolstoy, Count Leo
  See Tolstoy, Leo
Tolstoy, Leo Nikolaevich
  See Tolstoy, Leo
Tomalin, Ruth *29*
Tomaselli, Rosa
  See Pausacker, Jenny
Tomecek, Steve *172*
Tomes, Margot (Ladd) 1917-1991 .... *70*
  Brief entry *27*
  Obituary *69*
  Earlier sketch in SATA *36*
Tomey, Ingrid 1943- *77*
Tomfool
  See Farjeon, Eleanor
Tomic, Tomislav 1977- *202*
Tomkins, Jasper
  See Batey, Tom
Tomline, F. Latour
  See Gilbert, W(illiam) S(chwenck)
Tomlinson, Heather *192*
Tomlinson, Jill 1931-1976 .... *3*
  Obituary *24*
Tomlinson, Reginald R(obert) 1885-1979(?)
  Obituary *27*
Tomlinson, Theresa 1946- *165*
  Earlier sketch in SATA *103*
  See also CLR *60*
Tommaso, Rich 1970(?)- *200*
Tomorrow, Tom 1961- *223*
Tompert, Ann 1918- *139*
  Earlier sketches in SATA *14, 89*
Tompkins, Troy
  See Cle, Troy
Toner, Raymond John 1908-1986 .... *10*
Tong, Gary S. 1942- *66*
Tong, Paul *188*
Took, Belladonna
  See Chapman, Vera (Ivy May)
Tooke, Louise Mathews 1950- *38*
Tooke, Susan *173*
Toonder, Martin
  See Groom, Arthur William
Toothaker, Roy Eugene 1928- *18*
Tooze, Ruth (Anderson) 1892-1972 .... *4*
Topaz, Ksenia *212*
Topek, Susan Remick 1955- *78*
Topping, Audrey R(onning) 1928- *14*
Tor, Regina
  See Shekerjian, Regina Tor
Torbert, Floyd James 1922- *22*
Torgersen, Don Arthur 1934- *55*
  Brief entry *41*
Torley, Luke
  See Blish, James
Torrecilla, Pablo 1967- *206*
Torres, Andres Segovia
  See Segovia, Andres

Torres, Daniel 1958- *102*
Torres, John A. 1965- *163*
  Earlier sketch in SATA *94*
Torres, John Albert
  See Torres, John A.
Torres, Laura 1967- *146*
  Earlier sketch in SATA *87*
Torres, Leyla 1960- *155*
Torrey, Rich
  See Torrey, Richard
Torrey, Richard *189*
Torrie, Malcolm
  See Mitchell, Gladys (Maude Winifred)
Toten, Teresa 1955- *99*
Totham, Mary
  See Breinburg, Petronella
Touponce, William F. 1948- *114*
Tournier, Michel 1924- *23*
Tournier, Michel Edouard
  See Tournier, Michel
Towle, Ben 1970- *228*
Towle, Wendy 1963- *79*
Towne, Mary
  See Spelman, Mary
Townley, Rod
  See Townley, Roderick
Townley, Roderick 1942- *177*
Townsend, Brad W. 1962- *91*
Townsend, John Rowe 1922- *132*
  Autobiography Feature *132*
  Earlier sketches in SATA *4, 68*
  See also CLR *2*
  See also SAAS *2*
Townsend, Michael 1981- *194*
Townsend, Sue 1946- *93*
  Brief entry *48*
  Earlier sketch in SATA *55*
Townsend, Susan Lilian
  See Townsend, Sue
Townsend, Thomas L. 1944- *59*
Townsend, Tom
  See Townsend, Thomas L.
Townsend, Wendy 1962- *201*
Townson, Hazel *134*
Toye, William Eldred 1926- *8*
Traherne, Michael
  See Watkins-Pitchford, Denys James
Trahey, Jane 1923-2000 .... *36*
  Obituary *120*
Trapani, Iza 1954- *214*
  Earlier sketches in SATA *80, 116*
Trapp, Maria Augusta von
  See von Trapp, Maria Augusta
Travers, P(amela) L(yndon) 1899-1996 ...... *100*
  Obituary *90*
  Earlier sketches in SATA *4, 54*
  See also CLR *93*
  See also SAAS *2*
Travis, Lucille *133*
  Earlier sketch in SATA *88*
Treadgold, Mary 1910-2005 .... *49*
Trease, (Robert) Geoffrey 1909-1998 .... *60*
  Obituary *101*
  Earlier sketch in SATA *2*
  See also CLR *42*
  See also SAAS *6*
Treat, Lawrence 1903-1998 .... *59*
Tredez, Alain 1926- *17*
Tredez, Denise 1930- *50*
Treece, Henry 1912-1966 .... *2*
  See also CLR *2*
Tregarthen, Enys
  See Sloggett, Nellie
Tregaskis, Richard 1916-1973 .... *3*
  Obituary *26*
Treherne, Katie Thamer 1955- *76*
Trell, Max 1900-1996 .... *14*
  Obituary *108*
Tremain, Ruthven 1922- *17*
Trembath, Don 1963- *168*
  Earlier sketch in SATA *96*

Tremens, Del
  See MacDonald, Amy
Trent, Robbie 1894-1988 .... *26*
Trent, Timothy
  See Malmberg, Carl
Treseder, Terry Walton 1956- *68*
Tresilian, (Cecil) Stuart 1891-(?) *40*
Tresselt, Alvin 1916-2000 .... *7*
  See also CLR *30*
Trevino, Elizabeth B(orton) de 1904- *29*
  Earlier sketch in SATA *1*
  See also SAAS *5*
Trevor, Elleston 1920-1995 .... *28*
Trevor, Frances
  See Teasdale, Sara
Trevor, Glen
  See Hilton, James
Trevor, (Lucy) Meriol 1919-2000 .... *113*
  Obituary *122*
  Earlier sketch in SATA *10*
Trewellard, J.M. *195*
Trewellard, Juliet
  See Trewellard, J.M.
Trez, Alain
  See Tredez, Alain
Trez, Denise
  See Tredez, Denise
Trezise, Percy 1923-
  See CLR *41*
Trezise, Percy James
  See Trezise, Percy
Triggs, Tony D. 1946- *70*
Trimble, Marshall I(ra) 1939- *93*
Trimby, Elisa 1948- *47*
  Brief entry *40*
Tring, A. Stephen
  See Meynell, Laurence Walter
Triplett, Gina *229*
Tripp, Eleanor B(aldwin) 1936- *4*
Tripp, Janet 1942- *108*
Tripp, Jenny *188*
Tripp, John
  See Moore, John Travers
Tripp, Nathaniel 1944- *101*
Tripp, Paul 1916-2002 .... *8*
  Obituary *139*
Tripp, Valerie 1951- *168*
  Earlier sketch in SATA *78*
Tripp, Wallace (Whitney) 1940- *31*
Trivelpiece, Laurel 1926- *56*
  Brief entry *46*
Trivett, Daphne Harwood 1940- *22*
Trivizas, Eugene 1946- *84*
Trnka, Jiri 1912-1969 .... *43*
  Brief entry *32*
Trollope, Anthony 1815-1882 .... *22*
Trost, Lucille W(ood) 1938- *149*
  Earlier sketch in SATA *12*
Trott, Betty 1933- *91*
Trotter, Deborah W. *184*
Trotter, Grace V(iolet) 1900-1991 .... *10*
Trottier, Maxine 1950- *175*
  Earlier sketch in SATA *131*
Troughton, Joanna (Margaret) 1947- *37*
Trout, Kilgore
  See Farmer, Philip Jose
Trout, Richard E. *123*
Trudeau, Garretson Beekman
  See Trudeau, G.B.
Trudeau, Garry
  See Trudeau, G.B.
Trudeau, Garry B.
  See Trudeau, G.B.
Trudeau, G.B. 1948- *168*
  Earlier sketch in SATA *35*
Trueit, Trudi
  See Trueit, Trudi Strain
Trueit, Trudi Strain 1963- *179*
Trueman, Matthew *183*
Trueman, Terry 1947- *178*
  Earlier sketch in SATA *132*

Truesdell, Judy
  See Mecca, Judy Truesdell
Truesdell, Sue
  See Truesdell, Susan G.
Truesdell, Susan G. 212
  Brief entry 45
  Earlier sketch in SATA *108*
Trumbauer, Lisa 1963- 228
  Earlier sketch in SATA *149*
Trumbauer, Lisa Trutkoff
  See Trumbauer, Lisa
Truss, Jan 1925- 35
Truss, Lynne 1955(?)- 194
Tryon, Leslie 194
  Earlier sketch in SATA *139*
Tubb, Jonathan N. 1951- 78
Tubb, Kristin O'Donnell 1971- 209
Tubby, I. M.
  See Kraus, (Herman) Robert
Tucker, Allan James
  See James, Bill
Tucker, Caroline
  See Nolan, Jeannette Covert
Tucker, James
  See James, Bill
Tudor, Edward
  See Browne, Anthony
Tudor, Tasha 1915-2008 160
  Obituary 205
  Earlier sketches in SATA *20, 69*
  See also CLR *13*
Tuerk, Hanne 1951- 71
Tugeau, Jeremy 199
Tulloch, Richard 1949- 180
  Earlier sketch in SATA *76*
Tulloch, Richard George
  See Tulloch, Richard
Tulloch, Shirley 169
Tully, John (Kimberley) 1923- 14
Tumanov, Vladimir A. 1961- 138
Tung, Angela 1972- 109
Tunis, Edwin (Burdett) 1897-1973 28
  Obituary 24
  Earlier sketch in SATA *1*
  See also CLR *2*
Tunis, John R(oberts) 1889-1975 37
  Brief entry 30
Tunnell, Michael
  See Tunnell, Michael O.
Tunnell, Michael O. 1950- 157
  Earlier sketch in SATA *103*
Tunnell, Michael O'Grady
  See Tunnell, Michael O.
Tunnicliffe, C(harles) F(rederick)
  1901-1979 62
Turck, Mary C. 1950- 144
Turk, Hanne
  See Tuerk, Hanne
Turk, Ruth 1917- 82
Turkle, Brinton 1915- 79
  Earlier sketch in SATA *2*
Turlington, Bayly 1919-1977 5
  Obituary 52
Turnbull, Agnes Sligh 1888-1982 14
Turnbull, Ann 1943- 160
  Earlier sketch in SATA *18*
Turnbull, Ann Christine
  See Turnbull, Ann
Turnbull, Susan 222
Turner, Alice K. 1940- 10
Turner, Ann 1945- 188
  Autobiography Feature 188
  Earlier sketches in SATA *14, 77, 113, 178*
Turner, Ann Warren
  See Turner, Ann
Turner, Bonnie 1932- 75
Turner, Elizabeth 1774-1846
  See YABC *2*
Turner, Glennette Tilley 1933- 183
  Earlier sketch in SATA *71*

Turner, Josie
  See Crawford, Phyllis
Turner, Megan Whalen 1965- 174
  Earlier sketch in SATA *94*
Turner, Pamela S. 1957- 211
Turner, Philip (William) 1925- 83
  Earlier sketch in SATA *11*
  See also CLR *89*
  See also SAAS *6*
Turner, Robyn 1947- 77
Turner, Sheila R.
  See Seed, Sheila Turner
Turngren, Annette 1902(?)-1980
  Obituary 23
Turngren, Ellen (?)-1964 3
Turska, Krystyna (Zofia) 1933- 31
  Brief entry 27
Turteltaub, H. N.
  See Turtledove, Harry
Turtledove, Harry 1949- 166
  Earlier sketch in SATA *116*
Turtledove, Harry Norman
  See Turtledove, Harry
Tusa, Tricia 1960- 207
  Earlier sketches in SATA *72, 111*
Tusiani, Joseph 1924- 45
Twain, Mark 1835-1910 100
  See also YABC *2*
  See also CLR *156*
Tweit, Susan J 1956- 94
Tweit, Susan Joan
  See Tweit, Susan J
Tweton, D. Jerome 1933- 48
Twinem, Neecy 1958- 92
Twohill, Maggie
  See Angell, Judie
Tworkov, Jack 1900-1982 47
  Obituary 31
Tyche
  See Papademetriou, Lisa
Tyers, Jenny 1969- 89
Tyers, Kathy 1952- 82
Tyler, Anne 1941- 173
  Earlier sketches in SATA *7, 90*
Tyler, Linda
  See Tyler, Linda W(agner)
Tyler, Linda W(agner) 1952- 65
Tyler, Vicki 1952- 64
Tyne, Joel
  See Schembri, Jim
Tyrrell, Frances 1959- 107

                    U

Ubell, Earl 1926-2007 4
  Obituary 182
Uchida, Yoshiko 1921-1992 53
  Obituary 72
  Earlier sketch in SATA *1*
  See also CLR *56*
  See also SAAS *1*
Udall, Jan Beaney 1938- 10
Uden, (Bernard Gilbert) Grant 1910- 26
Uderzo, Albert 1927-
  See CLR *37*
Udovic, David 1950- 189
Udovic, Jane Morris 1947- 224
Udry, Janice May 1928- 152
  Earlier sketch in SATA *4*
Uegaki, Chieri 1969- 211
  Earlier sketch in SATA *153*
Uehashi, Nahoko 1962- 215
Ueno, Noriko
  See Nakae, Noriko
Ugliano, Natascia 196
Uhlberg, Myron 174
Uhlig, Richard 1970- 195
Uhlig, Susan 1955- 129
Ulam, S(tanislaw) M(arcin) 1909-1984 51

Ullman, Barb Bentler 210
Ullman, James Ramsey 1907-1971 7
Ulm, Robert 1934-1977 17
Ulmer, Louise 1943- 53
Ulmer, Wendy K. 1950- 201
Ulrich, Maureen 1958- 206
Ulriksen, Mark 1957- 210
Ulyatt, Kenneth 1920- 14
Umansky, Kaye 1946- 224
  Earlier sketches in SATA *158, 188*
Unada
  See Gliewe, Unada (Grace)
Uncle Carter
  See Boucher, (Clarence) Carter
Uncle Eric
  See Maybury, Richard J.
Uncle Gus
  See Rey, H. A.
Uncle Mac
  See McCulloch, Derek (Ivor Breashur)
Uncle Ray
  See Coffman, Ramon Peyton
Uncle Shelby
  See Silverstein, Shel
Underhill, Alice Mertie (Waterman)
  1900-1971 10
Underhill, Liz 1948- 53
  Brief entry 49
Underwood, Deborah 1962- 206
Unger, Harlow G. 1931- 75
Unger, Harlow Giles
  See Unger, Harlow G.
Unger, Jim 1937- 67
Ungerer, (Jean) Thomas 1931- 106
  Earlier sketches in SATA *5, 33*
  See also CLR *77*
Ungerer, Tomi 1931-
  See Ungerer, (Jean) Thomas
Unkelbach, Kurt 1913-1992 4
Unnerstad, Edith (Totterman) 1900-1982 3
  See also CLR *36*
Unobagha, Uzo 139
Unrau, Ruth 1922- 9
Unstead, R(obert) J(ohn) 1915-1988 12
  Obituary 56
Unsworth, Walt(er) 1928- 4
Untermeyer, Bryna Ivens 1909-1985 61
Untermeyer, Louis 1885-1977 37
  Obituary 26
  Earlier sketch in SATA *2*
Unwin, David S. 1918-2010 14
Unwin, David Storr
  See Unwin, David S.
Unwin, Nora S(picer) 1907-1982 3
  Obituary 49
Unzner, Christa 1958- 141
  Earlier sketch in SATA *80*
Unzner-Fischer, Christa
  See Unzner, Christa
Updale, Eleanor 1953- 175
Updyke, Rosemary K. 1924- 103
Upitis, Alvis 109
Urbain, Cat 1956- 211
Urbain, Catherine
  See Urbain, Cat
Urban, Helle (Denise) 1957- 149
Urban, Linda 199
Urbanovic, Jackie 189
Urberuaga, Emilio 1954- 219
Urbigkit, Cat 1965- 196
Urdahl, Catherine 215
Ure, Jean 1943- 192
  Autobiography Feature 192
  Earlier sketches in SATA *48, 78, 129*
  See also CLR *34*
  See also SAAS *14*
U'Ren, Andrea 1968- 213
  Earlier sketch in SATA *142*
Uris, Leon 1924-2003 49
  Obituary 146

Uris, Leon Marcus
　See Uris, Leon
Ursu, Anne 177
Ury, Allen B. 1954- 98
Uschan, Michael V. 1948- 129
Usher, Margo Scegge
　See McHargue, Georgess
Usher, Mark David
　See Usher, M.D.
Usher, M.D. 1966- 221
Uslan, Michael E. 1951- 169
Uston, Ken(neth Senzo) 1935-1987 65
Uttley, Alice Jane 1884-1976 88
　Obituary 26
　Earlier sketch in SATA 3
Uttley, Alison
　See Uttley, Alice Jane
Utz, Lois (Marie) 1932-1986 5
　Obituary 50

V

Vaeth, J. Gordon 1921- 17
Vaeth, Joseph Gordon
　See Vaeth, J. Gordon
Vagin, Vladimir (Vasilevich) 1937- 142
Vail, Rachel 1966- 201
　Earlier sketches in SATA 94, 163
Vainio, Pirkko 1957- 123
　Earlier sketch in SATA 76
Valen, Nanine 1950- 21
Valencak, Hannelore
　See Mayer, Hannelore Valencak
Valens, Amy 1946- 70
Valens, E(vans) G(ladstone), Jr. 1920-1992 ... 1
Valentine, Johnny 72
Valerio, Geraldo 1970- 180
Valgardson, W. D. 1939- 151
　Earlier sketch in SATA 101
Valgardson, William Dempsey
　See Valgardson, W. D.
Valleau, Emily 1925- 51
Vamos, Samantha R. 215
Van Abbe, Salaman 1883-1955 18
Van Allsburg, Chris 1949- 156
　Earlier sketches in SATA 37, 53, 105
　See also CLR 113
Van Anrooy, Francine 1924- 2
Van Anrooy, Frans
　See Van Anrooy, Francine
Vanasse, Deb 1957- 170
Van Buren, David 203
Van Camp, Katie 1981- 222
Vance, Cynthia 207
Vance, Eleanor Graham 1908-1985 11
Vance, Gerald
　See Garrett, Randall
　and Silverberg, Robert
Vance, Marguerite 1889-1965 29
Vance-Abrams, Cynthia
　See Vance, Cynthia
VanCleave, Janice 1942- 116
　Autobiography Feature 123
　Earlier sketch in SATA 75
Vandenburg, Mary Lou 1943- 17
Vander Boom, Mae M. 14
Vander-Els, Betty 1936- 63
van der Heide, Iris 1970- 183
van der Linde, Laurel 1952- 78
van der Linden, Martijn 1979- 214
van der Meer, Ron 1945- 98
van de Ruit, John 1975- 199
Van de Veer, Judy 1912-1982 4
　Obituary 33
Vanderwal, Andrew H. 1956- 219
Vanderwerff, Corrine 1939- 117
Vander Zee, Ruth 199
　Earlier sketch in SATA 159

Vande Velde, Vivian 1951- 211
　Earlier sketches in SATA 62, 95, 141
　See also CLR 145
Vandivert, Rita (Andre) 1905-1986 21
Van Draanen, Wendelin 207
　Earlier sketch in SATA 122
Van Dusen, Chris 228
　Earlier sketch in SATA 173
Van Duyn, Janet 1910- 18
Van Dyne, Edith
　See Baum, L. Frank
　and Sampson, Emma (Keats) Speed
　and van Zantwijk, Rudolf (Alexander
　Marinus)
Vane, Mitch
　See Vane, Mitchelle
Vane, Mitchelle 176
van Frankenhuyzen, Gijsbert 1951- 132
Van Genechten, Guido 1957- 165
van Haeringen, Annemarie 193
Van Hook, Beverly 1941- 99
Van Hook, Beverly H.
　See Van Hook, Beverly
Van Hook, Beverly Hennen
　See Van Hook, Beverly
Van Horn, William 1939- 43
van Hout, Mies 1962- 178
Van Iterson, S(iny) R(ose) 26
Van Kampen, Vlasta 1943- 163
　Earlier sketch in SATA 54
Van Laan, Nancy 1939- 214
　Earlier sketch in SATA 105
van Lawick-Goodall, Jane
　See Goodall, Jane
Van Leeuwen, Jean 1937- 211
　Autobiography Feature 141
　Earlier sketches in SATA 6, 82, 132, 141
　See also SAAS 8
van Lhin, Erik
　See del Rey, Lester
van Lieshout, Elle 1963- 217
van Lieshout, Maria 201
Van Loon, Hendrik Willem 1882-1944 18
van Ommen, Sylvia 1978- 186
VanOosting, James 1951- 170
Van Orden, M(erton) D(ick) 1921- 4
van Os, Erik 1963- 217
Van Patter, Bruce 183
Van Reek, Wouter 204
Van Rensselaer, Alexander (Taylor Mason)
　1892-1962 14
Van Riper, Guernsey, Jr. 1909-1995 3
van Rossum, Heleen 1962- 174
Van Rynbach, Iris 1952- 102
Vansant, Rhonda Joy Edwards 1950- 92
Van Steenwyk, Elizabeth (Ann) 1928- 89
　Earlier sketch in SATA 34
Van Stockum, Hilda 1908-2006 5
　Obituary 179
van Straaten, Harmen 1961- 218
　Earlier sketch in SATA 195
Van Tuyl, Barbara 1940- 11
van Vogt, A(lfred) E(lton) 1912-2000 14
　Obituary 124
Van Wassenhove, Sue 1951- 202
Van Woerkom, Dorothy (O'Brien)
　1924-1996 21
Van Wormer, Joe
　See Van Wormer, Joseph Edward
Van Wormer, Joseph Edward 1913-1998 35
Van Wright, Cornelius 173
Van Zwienen, Ilse Charlotte Koehn
　1929-1991 34
　Brief entry 28
　Obituary 67
Van Zyle, Jon 1942- 176
　Earlier sketch in SATA 84
Varela, Barry 180
Varga, Judy
　See Stang, Judit
Varley, Dimitry V. 1906-1984 10

Varley, Susan 1961- 134
　Earlier sketch in SATA 63
Varon, Sara 195
Vasileva, Tatiana
　See Wassiljewa, Tatjana
Vasiliev, Valery 1949- 80
Vasilieva, Tatiana
　See Wassiljewa, Tatjana
Vasiliu, Mircea 1920- 2
Vass, George 1927- 57
　Brief entry 31
Vaughan, Carter A.
　See Gerson, Noel Bertram
Vaughan, Harold Cecil 1923- 14
Vaughan, Marcia (K.) 1951- 159
　Earlier sketches in SATA 60, 95
Vaughan, Richard 1947- 87
Vaughan, Sam(uel) 1928- 14
Vaughn, Ruth 1935- 14
Vaught, Susan 1965- 195
Vaupel, Robin 198
Vautier, Ghislaine 1932- 53
Vavra, Robert James 1935- 8
Vecsey, George Spencer 1939- 9
Vedral, Joyce L(auretta) 1943- 65
Vega, Denise 216
　Earlier sketch in SATA 174
Vega, Denise B.
　See Vega, Denise
Vega, Diego
　See Adkins, Jan
Veglahn, Nancy (Crary) 1937- 5
Vejjajiva, Jane 1963- 189
Velasquez, Crystal 228
Velasquez, Eric 226
　Earlier sketch in SATA 192
Velasquez, Gloria 1949- 229
　Earlier sketch in SATA 113
Velthuijs, Max 1923-2005 110
　Obituary 160
　Earlier sketch in SATA 53
Venable, Alan (Hudson) 1944- 8
Venezia, Mike 1945- 150
Venner, Grace Chang
　See Chang, Grace
Ventura, Anthony
　See Pellowski, Michael (Joseph)
Ventura, Piero (Luigi) 1937- 61
　Brief entry 43
　See also CLR 16
Vequin, Capini
　See Quinn, Elisabeth
Verba, Joan Marie 1953- 78
Verboven, Agnes 1951- 103
verDorn, Bethea (Stewart) 1952- 76
Vere, Ed 197
Verissimo, Erico (Lopes) 1905-1975 113
Verne, Jules 1828-1905 21
　See also CLR 88
Verne, Jules Gabriel
　See Verne, Jules
Verner, Gerald 1897(?)-1980
　Obituary 25
Verney, John 1913-1993 14
　Obituary 75
Verniero, Joan C. 1949- 181
Vernon, (Elda) Louise A(nderson) 1914- 14
Vernon, Rosemary
　See Smith, Susan Vernon
Vernon, Ursula 204
Vernor, D.
　See Casewit, Curtis W(erner)
Verr, Harry Coe
　See Kunhardt, Edith
Verral, Charles Spain 1904-1990 11
　Obituary 65
Verrillo, Erica 1953- 199
Verrillo, Erica F.
　See Verrillo, Erica
Verroken, Sarah 1982- 223

Verrone, Robert J. 1935(?)-1984
  Obituary 39
Versace, Marie Teresa Rios 1917- 2
Vertreace, Martha M(odena) 1945- 78
Vesey, A(manda) 1939- 62
Vesey, Mark (David) 1958- 123
Vesey, Paul
  See Allen, Samuel W(ashington)
Vess, Charles 1951- 215
Vestergaard, Hope 178
Vestly, Anne-Cath(arina) 1920-2008 14
  See also CLR 99
Vevers, (Henry) Gwynne 1916-1988 45
  Obituary 57
Viator, Vacuus
  See Hughes, Thomas
Viau, Nancy 208
Vicar, Henry
  See Felsen, Henry Gregor
Vick, Helen Hughes 1950- 88
Vicker, Angus
  See Felsen, Henry Gregor
Vickers, Sheena 1960- 94
Vickery, Kate
  See Kennedy, T.A.
Victor, Edward 1914- 3
Victor, Joan Berg 1942- 30
Vidrine, Beverly Barras 1938- 188
  Earlier sketch in SATA 103
Vieceli, Emma 1979- 210
Viereck, Ellen K. 1928- 14
Viereck, Phillip 1925- 3
Viergutz, Dina Nayeri
  See Nayeri, Dina
Viertel, Janet 1915- 10
Vigliante, Mary
  See Szydlowski, Mary Vigliante
Vigna, Judith 1936- 102
  Earlier sketch in SATA 15
Viguers, Ruth Hill 1903-1971 6
Vila, Laura 207
Vilela, Fernando 1973- 216
Villareal, Ray 187
Villasenor, Edmund
  See Villasenor, Victor E.
Villasenor, Edmundo
  See Villasenor, Victor E.
Villasenor, Victor
  See Villasenor, Victor E.
Villasenor, Victor E. 1940- 171
Villasenor, Victor Edmundo
  See Villasenor, Victor E.
Villiard, Paul 1910-1974 51
  Obituary 20
Villiers, Alan (John) 1903-1982 10
Vilott, Rhondi
  See Salsitz, Rhondi Vilott
Vincent, Amy
  See Gray, Claudia
Vincent, Eric Douglas 1953- 40
Vincent, Erin 1969- 188
Vincent, Felix 1946- 41
Vincent, Gabrielle 1928-2000 121
  Earlier sketch in SATA 61
  See also CLR 13
Vincent, Mary Keith
  See St. John, Wylly Folk
Vincent, Rachel 1978- 222
Vincent, William R.
  See Heitzmann, William Ray
Vinegar, Tom
  See Gregg, Andrew K.
Vinest, Shaw
  See Longyear, Barry B(rookes)
Vinge, Joan (Carol) D(ennison) 1948- 113
  Earlier sketch in SATA 36
Vining, Elizabeth Gray 1902-1999 6
  Obituary 117
Vinson, Kathryn 1911-1995 21
Vinton, Iris 1906(?)-1988 24
  Obituary 55

Viola, Herman J(oseph) 1938- 126
Viorst, Judith 1931- 172
  Earlier sketches in SATA 7, 70, 123
  See also CLR 90
Vip
  See Partch, Virgil Franklin II
Vipont, Charles
  See Foulds, Elfrida Vipont
Vipont, Elfrida
  See Foulds, Elfrida Vipont
Viramontes, Helena Maria 1954-
  See CLR 285
Viscott, David S(teven) 1938-1996 65
Visser, W(illem) F(rederik) H(endrik)
  1900-1968 10
Vitale, Stefano 1958- 225
  Earlier sketches in SATA 114, 180
Vivas, Julie 1947- 96
Vivelo, Jackie 1943- 63
Vivelo, Jacqueline J.
  See Vivelo, Jackie
Vivelo, Jacqueline Jean
  See Vivelo, Jackie
Vivian, Siobhan 1979(?)- 215
Vizzini, Ned 1981- 179
  Earlier sketch in SATA 125
Vlahos, Olivia 1924- 31
Vlasic, Bob
  See Hirsch, Phil
Voake, Charlotte 180
  Earlier sketch in SATA 114
Voake, Steve 1961- 178
Vo-Dinh, Mai 1933- 16
Vogel, Carole Garbuny 1951- 105
  Earlier sketch in SATA 70
Vogel, Ilse-Margret 1918- 14
Vogel, John H., Jr. 1950- 18
Vogt, Esther Loewen 1915-1999 14
Vogt, Gregory L. 94
Vogt, Marie Bollinger 1921- 45
Vohwinkel, Astrid 1969- 207
Voight, Virginia Frances 1909-1989 8
Voigt, Cynthia 1942- 160
  Brief entry 33
  Earlier sketches in SATA 48, 79, 116
  See also CLR 141
Voigt, Erna 1925- 35
Voigt-Rother, Erna
  See Voigt, Erna
Vojtech, Anna 1946- 108
  Earlier sketch in SATA 42
Vollstadt, Elizabeth Weiss 1942- 121
Volponi, Paul 228
  Earlier sketch in SATA 175
Volting, Dr. R.E.
  See Lerangis, Peter
Von Ahnen, Katherine 1922- 93
von Buhler, Cynthia 185
Vondra, J. Gert
  See Vondra, Josef
Vondra, Josef 1941- 121
Vondra, Josef Gert
  See Vondra, Josef
Von Gunden, Kenneth 1946- 113
Von Hagen, Victor Wolfgang 1908-1985 29
von Klopp, Vahrah
  See Malvern, Gladys
von Schmidt, Eric 1931-2007 50
  Brief entry 36
  Obituary 181
von Storch, Anne B. 1910- 1
von Trapp, Maria Augusta 1905-1987 16
von Wodtke, Charlotte Buel Johnson
  1918-1982 46
von Ziegesar, Cecily 1970- 161
Vos, Ida 1931-2006 121
  Earlier sketch in SATA 69
  See also CLR 85
Vosburgh, Leonard (W.) 1912- 15
Votaw, Carol 1961- 201

Voyle, Mary
  See Manning, Rosemary
Vrettos, Adrienne Maria 187
Vriens, Jacques 1946- 151
Vugteveen, Verna Aardema
  See Aardema, Verna
Vulture, Elizabeth T.
  See Gilbert, Suzie
Vuong, Lynette Dyer 1938- 110
  Earlier sketch in SATA 60
Vyner, Tim 1963- 228

W

Waas, Uli
  See Waas-Pommer, Ulrike
Waas-Pommer, Ulrike 1949- 85
Waber, Bernard 1924- 155
  Brief entry 40
  Earlier sketches in SATA 47, 95
  See also CLR 55
Wachtel, Shirley Russak 1951- 88
Wachter, Oralee (Roberts) 1935- 61
  Brief entry 51
Waddell, Evelyn Margaret 1918- 10
Waddell, Martin 1941- 129
  Autobiography Feature 129
  Earlier sketches in SATA 43, 81, 127
  See also CLR 31
  See also SAAS 15
Waddy, Lawrence 1912-2010 91
Waddy, Lawrence Heber
  See Waddy, Lawrence
Wade, Mary Dodson 1930- 151
  Earlier sketch in SATA 79
Wade, Suzanne
  See Kirby, Susan E.
Wade, Theodore E., Jr. 1936- 37
Wademan, Peter John 1946- 122
Wademan, Spike
  See Wademan, Peter John
Wadsworth, Ginger 1945- 223
  Earlier sketches in SATA 103, 157
Wagenheim, Kal 1935- 21
Wagner, Michele R. 1975- 157
Wagner, Sharon B. 1936- 4
Wagoner, David (Russell) 1926- 14
Wahl, Jan (Boyer) 1933- 132
  Earlier sketches in SATA 2, 34, 73
  See also SAAS 3
Wahl, Mats 1945- 186
Wahman, Wendy 218
Waide, Jan 1952- 29
Wainscott, John Milton 1910-1981 53
Wainwright, Debra 218
Wainwright, Richard M. 1935- 91
Wainwright, Ruth
  See Symes, Ruth Louise
Wait, Lea 1946- 137
Waite, Judy 174
Waite, Judy Bernard
  See Bernard, Patricia
Waite, Michael
  See Waite, Michael P.
Waite, Michael P. 1960- 101
Waite, P(eter) B(usby) 1922- 64
Waites, Joan C. 187
Waitley, Douglas 1927- 30
Wakefield, Jean L.
  See Laird, Jean E(louise)
Wakin, Daniel (Joseph) 1961- 84
Wakin, Edward 1927- 37
Wakiyama, Hanako 1966- 192
Walck, Henry Z. 1908(?)-1984
  Obituary 40
Walden, Amelia Elizabeth 3
Walden, Mark 188
Waldherr, Kris 1963- 76
Waldman, Bruce 1949- 15

Waldman, Neil 1947- *203*
  Earlier sketches in SATA *51, 94, 142*
Waldrep, Richard *198*
Waldron, Ann Wood 1924-2010 .... *16*
Waldron, Kathleen Cook *176*
Wales, Dirk 1931- *205*
Walgren, Judy 1963- *118*
Walker, Addison
  See Walker, Mort
Walker, Addison Mort
  See Walker, Mort
Walker, Alice 1944- *31*
Walker, Alice Malsenior
  See Walker, Alice
Walker, Anna *223*
Walker, Barbara (Jeanne) K(erlin) 1921- *80*
  Earlier sketch in SATA *4*
Walker, Barbara M(uhs) 1928- *57*
Walker, (James) Braz(elton) 1934-1983 .... *45*
Walker, David 1965- *197*
Walker, David G(ordon) 1926- *60*
Walker, David Harry 1911-1992 .... *8*
  Obituary *71*
Walker, Diana 1925- *9*
Walker, Diane Marie Catherine
  See Walker, Kate
Walker, Dick
  See Pellowski, Michael (Joseph)
Walker, Frank 1931-2000 .... *36*
Walker, Holly Beth
  See Bond, Gladys Baker
Walker, Kate 1950- *165*
  Earlier sketch in SATA *82*
Walker, Kathrine Sorley
  See Sorley Walker, Kathrine
Walker, Kristin *228*
Walker, Lou Ann 1952- *66*
  Brief entry *53*
Walker, Louise Jean 1891-1976
  Obituary *35*
Walker, Mary Alexander 1927- *61*
Walker, Mildred
  See Schemm, Mildred Walker
Walker, Mort 1923- *8*
Walker, Pamela 1948- *142*
  Earlier sketch in SATA *24*
Walker, Paul Robert 1953- *154*
Walker, Robert W. 1948- *66*
Walker, Robert Wayne
  See Walker, Robert W.
Walker, Sally M. 1954- *221*
  Earlier sketch in SATA *135*
Walker, Stephen J. 1951- *12*
Walker-Blondell, Becky 1951- *89*
Wallace, Barbara Brooks 1922- *136*
  Earlier sketches in SATA *4, 78*
  See also CLR *150*
  See also SAAS *17*
Wallace, Beverly Dobrin 1921- *19*
Wallace, Bill 1947- *169*
  Brief entry *47*
  Earlier sketches in SATA *53, 101*
Wallace, Carol 1948- *218*
Wallace, Chad *229*
Wallace, Daisy
  See Cuyler, Margery
Wallace, Ian 1950- *219*
  Earlier sketches in SATA *53, 56, 141*
  See also CLR *37*
Wallace, John 1966- *155*
  Earlier sketch in SATA *105*
Wallace, John A(dam) 1915-2004 .... *3*
  Obituary *155*
Wallace, Karen 1951- *188*
  Earlier sketches in SATA *83, 139*
Wallace, Nancy Elizabeth 1948- *222*
  Earlier sketches in SATA *141, 186*
Wallace, Nigel
  See Hamilton, Charles (Harold St. John)
Wallace, Paula S. *153*

Wallace, Rich 1957- *196*
  Earlier sketches in SATA *117, 158*
Wallace, Robert 1932-1999 .... *47*
  Brief entry *37*
Wallace, Ruby Ann 1923(?)- *77*
Wallace, William Keith
  See Wallace, Bill
Wallace-Brodeur, Ruth 1941- *169*
  Brief entry *41*
  Earlier sketches in SATA *51, 88*
Wallenta, Adam 1974- *123*
Waller, Leslie 1923-2007 .... *20*
Walley, Byron
  See Card, Orson Scott
Walliams, David 1971- *227*
Wallis, Diz 1949- *77*
Wallis, G. McDonald
  See Campbell, Hope
Wallner, Alexandra 1946- *156*
  Brief entry *41*
  Earlier sketches in SATA *51, 98*
Wallner, John C. 1945- *133*
  Earlier sketches in SATA *10, 51*
Wallower, Lucille *11*
Walrod, Amy 1973(?)- *182*
Walsh, Ann 1942- *176*
  Earlier sketch in SATA *62*
Walsh, Ellen Stoll 1942- *194*
  Earlier sketches in SATA *49, 99, 147*
Walsh, George Johnston 1889-1981 .... *53*
Walsh, Gillian Paton
  See Paton Walsh, Jill
Walsh, Jill Paton
  See Paton Walsh, Jill
Walsh, Joanna 1970- *182*
Walsh, Lawrence 1942- *170*
Walsh, Marissa 1972- *195*
Walsh, Mary Caswell 1949- *118*
Walsh, Mitzy
  See Walsh, Marissa
Walsh, Rebecca *217*
Walsh, Suella *170*
Walsh, V. L.
  See Walsh, Vivian
Walsh, Vivian 1960- *120*
Walsh Shepherd, Donna 1948- *78*
Walter, Frances V. 1923- *71*
Walter, Mildred Pitts 1922- *133*
  Brief entry *45*
  Earlier sketch in SATA *69*
  See also CLR *61*
  See also SAAS *12*
Walter, Villiam Christian
  See Andersen, Hans Christian
Walter, Virginia
  See Walter, Virginia A.
Walter, Virginia A. *134*
Walters, Audrey 1929- *18*
Walters, Celeste 1938- *126*
Walters, Eric 1957- *205*
  Earlier sketches in SATA *99, 155*
Walters, Eric Robert
  See Walters, Eric
Walters, Gregory 1964- *213*
Walters, Helen B. (?)-1987
  Obituary *50*
Walters, Hugh
  See Hughes, Walter (Llewellyn)
Walther, Thomas A. 1950- *31*
Walther, Tom
  See Walther, Thomas A.
Waltner, Elma 1912-1987 .... *40*
Waltner, Willard H. 1909- *40*
Walton, Darwin McBeth 1926- *119*
Walton, Fiona L. M. 1959- *89*
Walton, Richard J. 1928- *4*
Walton, Rick 1957- *204*
  Earlier sketches in SATA *101, 151*
Waltrip, Lela (Kingston) 1904-1995 .... *9*
Waltrip, Mildred 1911- *37*
Waltrip, Rufus (Charles) 1898-1988 .... *9*

Walworth, Nancy Zinsser 1917- *14*
Wang, Gabrielle *212*
Wang, Lin 1973- *221*
Wang, Shaoli *216*
Wangerin, Walter, Jr. 1944- *98*
  Brief entry *37*
  Earlier sketch in SATA *45*
Waniek, Marilyn
  See Nelson, Marilyn
Waniek, Marilyn Nelson 1946-
  See Nelson, Marilyn
Wannamaker, Bruce
  See Moncure, Jane Belk
Warbler, J. M.
  See Cocagnac, Augustin Maurice(-Jean)
Warburg, Sandol Stoddard
  See Stoddard, Sandol
Warburton, Tom 1968(?)- *218*
Ward, David 1967- *213*
Ward, E. D.
  See Gorey, Edward (St. John)
  and Lucas, E(dward) V(errall)
Ward, Ed
  See Stratemeyer, Edward L.
Ward, Helen 1962- *206*
  Earlier sketches in SATA *72, 144*
Ward, Jay 1920-1989
  Obituary *63*
Ward, Jennifer 1963- *226*
  Earlier sketch in SATA *146*
Ward, John (Stanton) 1917- *42*
Ward, Jonas
  See Ard, William
  and Cox, William R(obert)
  and Garfield, Brian (Francis Wynne)
Ward, Lynd (Kendall) 1905-1985 .... *36*
  Obituary *42*
  Earlier sketch in SATA *2*
Ward, Martha (Eads) *5*
Ward, Melanie
  See Curtis, Richard
  and Lynch, Marilyn
Ward, Nicholas John
  See Ward, Nick
Ward, Nick 1955- *190*
Ward, Rachel 1964- *229*
Ward, Tom
  See Stratemeyer, Edward L.
Wardell, Dean
  See Prince, J(ack) H(arvey)
Wardlaw, Lee 1955- *115*
  Earlier sketch in SATA *79*
Ware, Cheryl 1963- *101*
Ware, Chris 1967- *140*
Ware, Leon (Vernon) 1909-1976 .... *4*
Wargin, Kathy-jo 1964- *210*
  Earlier sketch in SATA *145*
Warhola, James 1955- *187*
Warman, Jessica 1981- *225*
Warner, Frank A. *67*
  Earlier sketch in SATA *1*
Warner, Gertrude Chandler 1890-1979 .... *9*
  Obituary *73*
Warner, J(ohn) F. 1929- *75*
Warner, Lucille Schulberg *30*
Warner, Matt
  See Fichter, George S.
Warner, Oliver (Martin Wilson) 1903-1976 . *29*
Warner, Sally 1946- *214*
  Earlier sketch in SATA *131*
Warner, Sunny (B.) 1931- *108*
Warnes, Tim 1971- *216*
  Earlier sketches in SATA *116, 166*
Warnes, Timothy
  See Warnes, Tim
Warnick, Elsa 1942- *113*
Warren, Andrea 1946- *98*
Warren, Betsy
  See Warren, Elizabeth Avery
Warren, Billy
  See Warren, William Stephen

Warren, Cathy 1951- 62
    Brief entry 46
Warren, Elizabeth
    See Supraner, Robyn
Warren, Elizabeth Avery 1916- 46
    Brief entry 38
Warren, Jackie M. 1953- 135
Warren, Joshua P(aul) 1976- 107
Warren, Joyce W(illiams) 1935- 18
Warren, Mary Phraner 1929- 10
Warren, Robert Penn 1905-1989 46
    Obituary 63
Warren, Scott S. 1957- 79
Warren, William Stephen 1882-1968 9
Warrick, Patricia Scott 1925- 35
Warriner, John 1907(?)-1987
    Obituary 53
Warsh
    See Warshaw, Jerry
Warshaw, Jerry 1929- 30
Warshaw, Mary 1931- 89
Warshofsky, Fred 1931- 24
Warshofsky, Isaac
    See Singer, Isaac Bashevis
Wartski, Maureen (Ann Crane) 1940- 50
    Brief entry 37
Warwick, Alan R(oss) 1900-1973 42
Wa-Sha-Quon-Asin
    See Belaney, Archibald Stansfeld
Wa-sha-quon-asin
    See Belaney, Archibald Stansfeld
Washburn, Bradford 1910-2007 38
    Obituary 181
Washburn, Henry Bradford, Jr.
    See Washburn, Bradford
Washburn, Jan(ice) 1926- 63
Washburn, Lucia 193
Washburne, Carolyn Kott 1944- 86
Washburne, Heluiz Chandler 1892-1970 10
    Obituary 26
Washington, Booker T. 1856-1915 28
Washington, Donna L. 1967- 159
    Earlier sketch in SATA 98
Wasserman, Robin 1978- 207
Wasserstein, Wendy 1950-2006 94
    Obituary 174
Wassiljewa, Tatjana 1928- 106
Watanabe, Etsuko 1968- 219
Watanabe, Shigeo 1928- 131
    Brief entry 32
    Earlier sketch in SATA 39
    See also CLR 8
Waters, John F(rederick) 1930- 4
Waters, Summer
    See Sykes, Julie
Waters, Tony 1958- 75
Waterton, Betty 1923- 99
    Brief entry 34
    Earlier sketch in SATA 37
Waterton, Betty Marie
    See Waterton, Betty
Watkins, Dawn L. 126
Watkins, Gloria Jean
    See hooks, bell
Watkins, Lis
    See Watkins, Liselotte
Watkins, Liselotte 1971- 215
Watkins, Lois 1930- 88
Watkins, Peter 1934- 66
Watkins, Yoko Kawashima 1933- 93
Watkins-Pitchford, Denys James
    1905-1990 87
    Obituary 66
    Earlier sketch in SATA 6
    See also SAAS 4
Watling, James 1933- 117
    Earlier sketch in SATA 67
Watson, Aldren A(uld) 1917- 42
    Brief entry 36
Watson, Amy Zakrzewski 1965- 76

Watson, B. S.
    See Teitelbaum, Michael
Watson, Carol 1949- 78
Watson, C.G. 193
Watson, Clyde 1947- 68
    Earlier sketch in SATA 5
    See also CLR 3
Watson, Helen Orr 1892-1978
    Obituary 24
Watson, James 1936- 106
    Earlier sketch in SATA 10
Watson, Jane Werner 1915- 54
    Earlier sketch in SATA 3
Watson, Jesse Joshua 199
Watson, John H.
    See Farmer, Philip Jose
Watson, Mary 1953- 117
Watson, N. Cameron 1955- 81
Watson, Nancy Dingman 32
Watson, Pauline 1925- 14
Watson, Richard F.
    See Silverberg, Robert
Watson, Richard Jesse 1951- 211
    Earlier sketch in SATA 62
Watson, Sally (Lou) 1924- 3
Watson, Sasha 211
Watson, Wendy (McLeod) 1942- 142
    Earlier sketches in SATA 5, 74
Watson Taylor, Elizabeth 1915- 41
Watt, Melanie 1975- 193
    Earlier sketch in SATA 136
Watt, Thomas 1935- 4
Wattenberg, Jane 174
Watterson, Bill 1958- 66
Watt-Evans, Lawrence 1954- 121
Watts, (Anna) Bernadette 1942- 103
    Earlier sketch in SATA 4
Watts, Ephraim
    See Horne, Richard Henry Hengist
Watts, Franklin (Mowry) 1904-1978 46
    Obituary 21
Watts, Helen L. Hoke 1903-1990
    Obituary 65
Watts, Irene N(aemi) 1931- 111
    Earlier sketch in SATA 56
Watts, Isaac 1674-1748 52
Watts, James K(ennedy) M(offitt) 1955- 59
Watts, Jeri Hanel 1957- 170
Watts, Julia 1969- 103
Watts, Leander 1956- 146
Watts, Leslie Elizabeth 1961- 168
Watts, Mabel Pizzey 1906-1994 11
Watts, Nigel 1957-1999 121
Waugh, C. C. Roessel
    See Waugh, Carol-Lynn Rossel
    and Waugh, Charles G(ordon)
Waugh, Carol-Lynn Rossel 1947- 41
Waugh, Dorothy -1996 11
Waugh, Sylvia 1935- 169
Waugh, Virginia
    See Sorensen, Virginia
Wax, Wendy A. 1963- 219
    Earlier sketches in SATA 73, 163
Wayland, April Halprin 1954- 143
    Earlier sketch in SATA 78
    See also SAAS 26
Wayland, Patrick
    See O'Connor, Richard
Wayne, (Anne) Jenifer 1917-1982 32
Wayne, Kyra Petrovskaya 1918- 8
Wayne, Richard
    See Decker, Duane
Wayshak, Deborah Noyes
    See Noyes, Deborah
Waystaff, Simon
    See Swift, Jonathan
Weales, Gerald (Clifford) 1925- 11
Weary, Ogdred
    See Gorey, Edward (St. John)
Weatherford, Carole Boston 1956- 226
    Earlier sketches in SATA 138, 181

Weatherill, Cat 203
Weatherly, Lee 1967- 192
Weatherly, Myra 1926- 130
Weatherly, Myra S.
    See Weatherly, Myra
Weaver, Brian M.
    See Numberman, Neil
Weaver, Harriett E. 1908-1993 65
Weaver, John L. 1949- 42
Weaver, Robyn
    See Conley, Robyn
Weaver, Robyn M.
    See Conley, Robyn
Weaver, Tess 197
Weaver, Ward
    See Mason, F(rancis) van Wyck
Weaver, Will 1950- 217
    Earlier sketches in SATA 88, 109, 161
Weaver, William Weller
    See Weaver, Will
Weaver-Gelzer, Charlotte 1950- 79
Webb, Christopher
    See Wibberley, Leonard
Webb, Jacqueline
    See Pearce, Margaret
Webb, Jacquelyn
    See Pearce, Margaret
    and Pearce, Margaret
Webb, Jean Francis (III) 1910-1991 35
Webb, Kaye 1914- 60
Webb, Lois Sinaiko 1922- 82
Webb, Margot 1934- 67
Webb, Sharon 1936-2010 41
Webb, Sophie 1958- 135
Webber, Andrew Lloyd
    See Lloyd Webber, Andrew
Webber, Desiree Morrison 1956- 170
Webber, Irma E(leanor Schmidt)
    1904-1995 14
Weber, Alfons 1921- 8
Weber, Bruce 1942- 120
    Earlier sketch in SATA 73
Weber, Debora 1955- 58
Weber, EdNah New Rider 1919(?)- 168
Weber, Elka 1968- 219
Weber, Jill 1950- 209
    Earlier sketch in SATA 127
Weber, Judith E(ichler) 1938- 64
Weber, Ken(neth J.) 1940- 90
Weber, Lenora Mattingly 1895-1971 2
    Obituary 26
Weber, Lisa K. 217
Weber, Lori 1959- 220
Weber, Michael 1945- 87
Weber, Sandra 1961- 158
Weber, William J(ohn) 1927- 14
Webster, Alice Jane Chandler 1876-1916 17
Webster, David 1930- 11
Webster, Frank V. 67
    Earlier sketch in SATA 1
Webster, Gary
    See Garrison, Webb B(lack)
Webster, James 1925-1981 17
    Obituary 27
Webster, Jean
    See Webster, Alice Jane Chandler
Wechsler, Doug 189
Wechsler, Herman J. 1904-1976
    Obituary 20
Wechter, Nell (Carolyn) Wise 1913-1989 .. 127
    Earlier sketch in SATA 60
Weck, Thomas L. 1942- 62
Wedd, Kate
    See Gregory, Philippa
Weddle, Ethel Harshbarger 1897-1996 11
Wedekind, Annie 204
Weeks, Sarah 194
    Earlier sketch in SATA 158
Weems, David B(urnola) 1922- 80
Wees, Frances Shelley 1902-1982 58
Weevers, Peter 1944- 59

Wegen, Ronald 1946-1985 99
Wegman, William (George) 1943- 135
  Earlier sketches in SATA *78, 129*
Wegner, Fritz 1924- 20
Wehrman, Vicki 223
Weidhorn, Manfred 1931- 60
Weidt, Maryann N. 1944- 85
Weigel, Jeff 1958- 170
Weigelt, Udo 1960- 201
  Earlier sketch in SATA *168*
Weihs, Erika 1917-2010 107
  Earlier sketch in SATA *15*
Weik, Mary Hays 1898(?)-1979 3
  Obituary 23
Weil, Ann Yezner 1908-1969 9
Weil, Lisl 1910- 7
Weilerstein, Sadie Rose 1894-1993 3
  Obituary 75
Weill, Cynthia 1959- 167
Wein, Elizabeth E. 1964- 151
  Earlier sketch in SATA *82*
Wein, Elizabeth Eve
  See Wein, Elizabeth E.
Wein, Hallie
  See Zobel Nolan, Allia
Weinberg, Larry
  See Weinberg, Lawrence (E.)
Weinberg, Lawrence (E.) 92
  Brief entry 48
Weinberger, Tanya 1939- 84
Weiner, Sandra 1922- 14
Weingarten, Lynn 217
Weingarten, Violet (Brown) 1915-1976 3
  Obituary 27
Weingartner, Charles 1922- 5
Weinheimer, Beckie 1958- 186
Weinstein, Bruce 1960- 220
Weinstein, Bruce M.
  See Weinstein, Bruce
Weinstein, Ellen Slusky 1959- 200
Weinstein, Muriel Harris 215
Weinstein, Nina 1951- 73
Weinstock, Robert 1967- 204
Weir, Bob 1947- 76
Weir, Diana (R.) Loiewski 1958- 111
Weir, Joan S(herman) 1928- 99
Weir, LaVada 2
Weir, Rosemary (Green) 1905-1994 21
Weir, Wendy 1949- 76
Weis, Margaret 1948- 164
  Earlier sketches in SATA *38, 92*
Weisberger, Bernard A(llen) 1922- 21
Weisburd, Stefi 1957- 202
Weiser, Marjorie P(hillis) K(atz) 1934- 33
Weisgard, Leonard (Joseph) 1916-2000 85
  Obituary 122
  Earlier sketches in SATA *2, 30*
  See also SAAS *19*
Weiss, Adelle 1920- 18
Weiss, Ann E(dwards) 1943- 69
  Earlier sketch in SATA *30*
  See also SAAS *13*
Weiss, Edna
  See Barth, Edna
Weiss, Ellen 1953- 44
Weiss, Harvey 1922- 76
  Earlier sketches in SATA *1, 27*
  See also CLR *4*
  See also SAAS *19*
Weiss, Jaqueline Shachter 1926- 65
Weiss, Malcolm E. 1928- 3
Weiss, Margaret Edith
  See Weis, Margaret
Weiss, Miriam
  See Schlein, Miriam
Weiss, Mitch 1951- 183
  Earlier sketch in SATA *123*
Weiss, Nicki 1954- 86
  Earlier sketch in SATA *33*
Weiss, Renee Karol 1923- 5
Weissberger, Ela 1930- 181

Weissberger, Ela Stein
  See Weissberger, Ela
Weissenborn, Hellmuth 1898-1982
  Obituary 31
Weissman, Elissa Brent 217
Weitzman, David L. 1936- 172
  Earlier sketch in SATA *122*
Wekesser, Carol A. 1963- 76
Welber, Robert 26
Welch, Amanda (Jane) 1945- 75
Welch, D'Alte Aldridge 1907-1970
  Obituary 27
Welch, Holly 206
Welch, Jean-Louise
  See Kempton, Jean Welch
Welch, Pauline
  See Bodenham, Hilda Morris
Welch, Ronald
  See Felton, Ronald Oliver
Welch, Sheila Kelly 1945- 130
Welch, Willy 1952- 93
Weldin, Frauke 1969- 188
Welford, Sue 1942- 75
Weller, George 1907-2002 31
  Obituary 140
Weller, George Anthony
  See Weller, George
Welling, Peter J. 1947- 135
Wellington, Monica 1957- 222
  Earlier sketches in SATA *67, 99, 157*
Wellman, Alice 1900-1984 51
  Brief entry 36
Wellman, Manly Wade 1903-1986 6
  Obituary 47
Wellman, Paul I. 1898-1966 3
Wellman, Paul Iselin
  See Wellman, Paul I.
Wellman, Sam 1939- 122
Wellman, Samuel
  See Wellman, Sam
Wells, H. G. 1866-1946 20
  See also CLR *133*
Wells, Helen
  See Campbell, Hope
Wells, Helen 1910-1986 49
  Earlier sketch in SATA *2*
Wells, Herbert George
  See Wells, H. G.
Wells, J. Wellington
  See de Camp, L. Sprague
Wells, June
  See Swinford, Betty (June Wells)
Wells, Robert
  See Welsch, Roger L(ee)
Wells, Robert E. 184
Wells, Rosemary 1943- 207
  Earlier sketches in SATA *18, 69, 114, 156*
  See also CLR *69*
  See also SAAS *1*
Wells, Susan (Mary) 1951- 78
Wels, Byron G(erald) 1924-1993 9
Welsbacher, Anne 1955- 89
Welsch, Roger L(ee) 1936- 82
Welsh, David
  See Hills, C.A.R.
Welsh, Mary Flynn 1910(?)-1984
  Obituary 38
Welsh, T.K. 1956- 184
Weltevrede, Pieter 1957- 228
Weltner, Linda R(iverly) 1938- 38
Welton, Jude 1955- 143
  Earlier sketch in SATA *79*
Welty, S. F.
  See Welty, Susan F.
Welty, Susan F. 1905- 9
Wemmlinger, Raymond 190
Wendelin, Rudolph 1910-2000 23
Weninger, Brigitte 1960- 189
Wensell, Ulises 1945- 229
Wentworth, Robert
  See Hamilton, Edmond

Werlin, Nancy 1961- 161
  Earlier sketches in SATA *87, 119*
Werner, Elsa Jane
  See Watson, Jane Werner
Werner, Herma 1926- 47
  Brief entry 41
Werner, Jane
  See Watson, Jane Werner
Werner, K.
  See Casewit, Curtis W(erner)
Wersba, Barbara 1932- 58
  Autobiography Feature 103
  Earlier sketch in SATA *1*
  See also CLR *78*
  See also SAAS *2*
Werstein, Irving 1914(?)-1971 14
Werth, Kurt 1896-1983 20
Wesley, Alison
  See Barnes, Michael
Wesley, Kathryn
  See Rusch, Kristine Kathryn
Wesley, Mary (Aline) 1912-2002 66
Wesley, Valerie Wilson 1947- 168
  Earlier sketch in SATA *106*
West, Andrew
  See Arthur, Robert, (Jr.)
West, Anna 1938- 40
West, Barbara
  See Price, Olive
West, Betty 1921- 11
West, Bruce 1951- 63
West, C. P.
  See Wodehouse, P. G.
West, Dorothy
  See Benson, Mildred
West, Emily Govan 1919- 38
West, Emmy
  See West, Emily Govan
West, James
  See Withers, Carl A.
West, Jerry
  See Svenson, Andrew E(dward)
West, (Mary) Jessamyn 1902-1984
  Obituary 37
West, John
  See Arthur, Robert, (Jr.)
West, Owen
  See Koontz, Dean
West, Ward
  See Borland, Harold Glen
Westall, Robert (Atkinson) 1929-1993 69
  Obituary 75
  Earlier sketch in SATA *23*
  See also CLR *13*
  See also SAAS *2*
Westaway, Jane 1948- 121
Westcott, Nadine Bernard 1949- 130
Westera, Marleen 1962- 187
Westerberg, Christine 1950- 29
Westerduin, Anne 1945- 105
Westerfeld, Scott 1963- 161
Westervelt, Virginia Veeder 1914-2005 10
Westheimer, David 1917-2005 14
  Obituary 170
Westheimer, David Kaplan
  See Westheimer, David
Westmacott, Mary
  See Christie, Agatha
Westman, Barbara 70
Westman, Paul (Wendell) 1956- 39
Westmoreland, William C. 1914-2005 63
Westmoreland, William Childs
  See Westmoreland, William C.
Weston, Allen
  See Hogarth, Grace (Weston Allen)
  and Norton, Andre
Weston, Carol 1956- 135
Weston, Carrie 190
Weston, John (Harrison) 1932- 21
Weston, Martha 1947- 119
  Earlier sketch in SATA *53*

Weston, Robert Paul 209
Westphal, Arnold Carl 1897- 57
Westrup, Hugh 102
Westwood, Jennifer 1940-2008 10
  Obituary 192
Wexler, Jerome (LeRoy) 1923- 14
Weyland, Jack 1940- 81
Weyn, Suzanne 1955- 220
  Earlier sketches in SATA *63, 101, 164*
Weyr, Garret
  See Freymann-Weyr, Garret
Wezyk, Joanna 1966- 82
Whaley, Joyce Irene 1923- 61
Whalin, W. Terry 1953- 93
Whamond, Dave 222
Wharf, Michael
  See Weller, George
Wharmby, Margot 63
Wharton, Edith 1862-1937
  See CLR *136*
Wharton, Edith Newbold Jones
  See Wharton, Edith
Wharton, Thomas 1963- 223
Whatley, Bruce 1954- 213
  Earlier sketch in SATA *177*
Wheatley, Arabelle 1921- 16
Wheatley, Nadia 1949- 147
Wheeler, Cindy 1955- 49
  Brief entry 40
Wheeler, Deborah 1947- 83
Wheeler, Janet D. *1*
Wheeler, Jill C. 1964- 136
  Earlier sketch in SATA *86*
Wheeler, Jody 1952- 148
  Earlier sketch in SATA *84*
Wheeler, Lisa 1963- 200
  Earlier sketch in SATA *162*
Wheeler, Opal 1898- 23
Whelan, Elizabeth M(urphy) 1943- 14
Whelan, Gloria 1923- 224
  Earlier sketches in SATA *85, 128, 178*
  See also CLR *90*
Whelan, Gloria Ann
  See Whelan, Gloria
Whinnem, Reade Scott 224
Whipple, A(ddison) B(eecher) C(olvin)
  1918- 64
Whipple, Cal
  See Whipple, A(ddison) B(eecher) C(olvin)
Whisp, Kennilworthy
  See Rowling, J.K.
Whistler, Reginald John 1905-1944 30
Whistler, Rex
  See Whistler, Reginald John
Whitaker, Zai 183
Whitcher, Susan (Godsil) 1952- 96
Whitcomb, Jon 1906-1988 10
  Obituary 56
Whitcomb, Laura 1958- 214
  Earlier sketch in SATA *171*
White, Amy Brecount 228
White, Anne Terry 1896-1980 2
White, Bessie (Felstiner) 1892(?)-1986
  Obituary 50
White, Carolyn 1948- 130
White, Dale
  See Place, Marian T(empleton)
White, Dori 1919- 10
White, E. B. 1899-1985 100
  Obituary 44
  Earlier sketches in SATA *2, 29*
  See also CLR *107*
White, Eliza Orne 1856-1947
  See YABC *2*
White, Elwyn Brooks
  See White, E. B.
White, Florence M(eiman) 1910- 14
White, Laurence B(arton), Jr. 1935- 10
White, Lee 223
  Earlier sketch in SATA *176*
White, Martin 1943- 51

White, Nancy 1942- 126
White, Ramy Allison 67
  Earlier sketch in SATA *1*
White, Robb 1909-1990 83
  Earlier sketch in SATA *1*
  See also CLR *3*
  See also SAAS *1*
White, Ruth 1942- 186
  Autobiography Feature 186
  Earlier sketches in SATA *39, 117, 165*
White, Ruth C.
  See White, Ruth
White, T(erence) H(anbury) 1906-1964 12
  See also CLR *139*
White, Tekla N. 1934- 115
White, Timothy (Thomas Anthony)
  1952-2002 60
White, Tom 1923- 148
White, William, Jr. 1934- 16
Whitehead, Don(ald) F. 1908-1981 4
Whitehead, Jenny 1964- 191
Whitehead, Kathy 1957- 176
Whitehouse, Arch
  See Whitehouse, Arthur George Joseph
Whitehouse, Arthur George Joseph
  1895-1979 14
  Obituary 23
Whitehouse, Elizabeth S(cott) 1893-1968 35
Whitehouse, Jeanne
  See Peterson, Jeanne Whitehouse
Whitelaw, Nancy 1933- 166
  Earlier sketch in SATA *76*
Whitesel, Cheryl Aylward 162
Whiting, Sue 1960- 205
Whiting, Susan Allana
  See Whiting, Sue
Whitinger, R. D.
  See Place, Marian T(empleton)
Whitley, David 1984- 225
Whitley, Mary Ann
  See Sebrey, Mary Ann
Whitley, Peggy 1938- 140
Whitlock, Pamela 1921(?)-1982
  Obituary 31
Whitlock, Ralph 1914-1995 35
Whitman, Alice
  See Marker, Sherry
Whitman, Candace 1958- 208
Whitman, Sylvia (Choate) 1961- 135
  Earlier sketch in SATA *85*
Whitman, Walt 1819-1892 20
Whitman, Walter
  See Whitman, Walt
Whitmore, Arvella 1922- 125
Whitmore, Benette 1955- 203
Whitney, Alex(andra) 1922- 14
Whitney, David C(harles) 1921- 48
  Brief entry 29
Whitney, Kim Ablon 162
Whitney, Phyllis A. 1903-2008 30
  Obituary 189
  Earlier sketch in SATA *1*
  See also CLR *59*
Whitney, Phyllis Ayame
  See Whitney, Phyllis A.
Whitney, Sharon 1937- 63
Whitney, Thomas P. 1917-2007 25
  Obituary 189
Whitney, Thomas Porter
  See Whitney, Thomas P.
Whittington, Mary K(athrine) 1941- 75
Whitworth, John 1945- 123
Whybrow, Ian 202
  Earlier sketch in SATA *132*
Whyte, Mal(colm Kenneth, Jr.) 1933- 62
Whyte, Mary 1953- 148
  Earlier sketch in SATA *94*
Whyte, Ron 1942(?)-1989
  Obituary 63
Whytock, Cherry 177
Wiater, Stanley 1953- 84

Wibbelsman, Charles J(oseph) 1945- 59
Wibberley, Leonard 1915-1983 45
  Obituary 36
  Earlier sketch in SATA *2*
  See also CLR *3*
Wibberley, Leonard Patrick O'Connor
  See Wibberley, Leonard
Wiberg, Harald (Albin) 1908- 93
  Brief entry 40
Wick, Walter 1953- 148
Wickberg, Susan
  See Rottman, S.L.
Wickens, Elaine 86
Wicker, Ireene 1905(?)-1987
  Obituary 55
Wickstrom, Sylvie 1960- 169
Wickstrom, Thor 1960- 200
Widdemer, Mabel Cleland 1902-1964 5
Widener, Terry 1950- 209
  Earlier sketch in SATA *105*
Widerberg, Siv 1931- 10
Wiebe, Rudy 1934- 156
Wiebe, Rudy Henry
  See Wiebe, Rudy
Wieler, Diana (Jean) 1961- 109
Wiener, Lori 1956- 84
Wier, Ester (Alberti) 1910-2000 3
Wiese, Kurt 1887-1974 36
  Obituary 24
  Earlier sketch in SATA *3*
  See also CLR *86*
Wiesel, Elie 1928- 56
Wiesel, Eliezer
  See Wiesel, Elie
Wiesner, David 1956- 181
  Earlier sketches in SATA *72, 117, 139*
  See also CLR *84*
Wiesner, Portia
  See Takakjian, Portia
Wiesner, William 1899-1984 5
Wiggers, Raymond 1952- 82
Wiggin, Eric E. 1939- 167
  Earlier sketch in SATA *88*
Wiggin, Eric Ellsworth 1939-
  See Wiggin, Eric E.
Wiggin (Riggs), Kate Douglas (Smith)
  1856-1923
  See YABC *1*
  See also CLR *52*
Wiggins, VeraLee (Chesnut) 1928-1995 89
Wight, Eric 1974- 218
Wight, James Alfred
  See Herriot, James
Wignell, Edel 1936- 69
Wijnberg, Ellen 85
Wikland, Ilon 1930- 93
  Brief entry 32
Wikler, Madeline 1943- 114
Wilber, Donald N(ewton) 1907-1997 35
Wilbur, C. Keith 1923- 27
Wilbur, Frances 1921- 107
Wilbur, Helen L. 1948- 204
Wilbur, Richard 1921- 108
  Earlier sketch in SATA *9*
Wilbur, Richard Purdy
  See Wilbur, Richard
Wilburn, Kathy 1948- 68
Wilcox, Charlotte 1948- 72
Wilcox, Leah 1975(?)- 207
Wilcox, R(uth) Turner 1888-1970 36
Wilcox, Roger
  See Collins, Paul
Wild, Jocelyn 1941- 46
Wild, Kate 1954- 192
Wild, Margaret 1948- 197
  Earlier sketch in SATA *151*
Wild, Robin (Evans) 1936- 46
Wild, Robyn 1947- 117
Wilde, D. Gunther
  See Hurwood, Bernhardt J.

Wilde, Oscar 1854(?)-1900 24
  See also CLR *114*
Wilde, Oscar Fingal O'Flahertie Willis
  See Wilde, Oscar
Wilder, Buck
  See Smith, Tim(othy R.)
Wilder, Laura Elizabeth Ingalls
  See Wilder, Laura Ingalls
Wilder, Laura Ingalls 1867-1957 100
  Earlier sketches in SATA *15, 29*
  See also CLR *111*
Wildsmith, Brian 1930- 124
  Earlier sketches in SATA *16, 69*
  See also CLR *52*
  See also SAAS *5*
Wiles, Deborah 171
Wilhelm, Doug 1952- 190
Wilhelm, Hans 1945- 196
  Autobiography Feature 196
  Earlier sketches in SATA *58, 135*
  See also CLR *46*
  See also SAAS *21*
Wilkie, Katharine E(lliott) 1904-1980 31
Wilkin, Eloise 1904-1987 49
  Obituary 54
Wilkins, Frances 1923- 14
Wilkins, Kim 147
Wilkins, Marilyn (Ruth) 1926- 30
Wilkins, Marne
  See Wilkins, Marilyn (Ruth)
Wilkins, Mary Huiskamp 1926- 2
  See also CLR *42*
Wilkins, Mary Huiskamp Calhoun
  See Wilkins, Mary Huiskamp
Wilkins, Rose 180
Wilkinson, (Thomas) Barry 1923- 50
  Brief entry 32
Wilkinson, Beth 1925- 80
Wilkinson, Brenda 1946- 91
  Earlier sketch in SATA *14*
  See also CLR *20*
Wilkinson, (John) Burke 1913-2000 4
Wilkinson, Carole 1950- 210
Wilkinson, Sylvia 1940- 56
  Brief entry 39
Wilkon, Jozef 1930- 133
  Earlier sketches in SATA *31, 71*
Wilkowski, Sue 193
Wilks, Michael Thomas 1947- 44
  See Wilks, Mike
Wilks, Mike 224
  See Wilks, Michael Thomas
Will
  See Lipkind, William
Willard, Barbara (Mary) 1909-1994 74
  Earlier sketch in SATA *17*
  See also CLR *2*
  See also SAAS *5*
Willard, Elizabeth Kimmel
  See Kimmel, Elizabeth Cody
Willard, Mildred Wilds 1911-1978 14
Willard, Nancy 1936- 191
  Brief entry 30
  Earlier sketches in SATA *37, 71, 127*
  See also CLR *5*
Willcox, Isobel 1907-1996 42
Willems, Mo 228
  Earlier sketches in SATA *154, 180*
  See also CLR *114*
Willett, Edward 1959- 115
Willett, Edward C.
  See Willett, Edward
Willey, Bee 184
Willey, Margaret 1950- 226
  Earlier sketch in SATA *86*
Willey, Robert
  See Ley, Willy
Willhoite, Michael A. 1946- 71
William, Kate
  See Armstrong, Jennifer
Williams, Alex 1969- 209

Williams, Arlene 171
Williams, Barbara 1925- 107
  Earlier sketch in SATA *11*
  See also CLR *48*
  See also SAAS *16*
Williams, Barbara 1937- 62
Williams, Beryl
  See Epstein, Beryl
Williams, Brian (Peter) 1943- 54
Williams, Carol Lynch 1959- 212
  Earlier sketch in SATA *110*
Williams, Charles
  See Collier, James Lincoln
Williams, Clyde C. 1881-1974 8
  Obituary 27
Williams, Coe
  See Harrison, C(hester) William
Williams, Colleen Madonna Flood 1963- .. 156
Williams, Cynthia G. 1958- 123
Williams, Dar 1967- 168
Williams, Donna Reilly 1945- 83
Williams, Dorothy
  See Williams, Marcia
Williams, Dorothy Snowden
  See Williams, Dar
Williams, Eric (Ernest) 1911-1983 14
  Obituary 38
Williams, Ferelith Eccles
  See Eccles Williams, Ferelith
Williams, Frances B.
  See Browin, Frances Williams
Williams, Garth (Montgomery) 1912-1996 .. 66
  Obituary 90
  Earlier sketch in SATA *18*
  See also CLR *57*
  See also SAAS *7*
Williams, Guy R(ichard) 1920- 11
Williams, Hawley
  See Heyliger, William
Williams, Helen 1948- 77
Williams, J. R.
  See Williams, Jeanne
Williams, J. Walker
  See Wodehouse, P. G.
Williams, Jay 1914-1978 41
  Obituary 24
  Earlier sketch in SATA *3*
  See also CLR *8*
Williams, Jeanne 1930- 5
Williams, Jenny 1939- 60
Williams, Karen Lynn 1952- 224
  Earlier sketches in SATA *66, 99*
Williams, Kathryn 1981- 222
Williams, Kit 1946(?)- 44
  See also CLR *4*
Williams, L. E.
  See Williams, Laura E.
Williams, Laura E.
  See Williams, Laura Ellen
Williams, Laura Ellen 180
Williams, Leslie 1941- 42
Williams, Linda 1948- 59
Williams, Louise Bonino 1904(?)-1984
  Obituary 39
Williams, Lynn
  See Hale, Arlene
Williams, Marcia 1945- 159
  Earlier sketches in SATA *71, 97*
Williams, Marcia Dorothy
  See Williams, Marcia
Williams, Margery
  See Bianco, Margery Williams
Williams, Mark
  See Arthur, Robert, (Jr.)
Williams, Mark London 1959- 140
Williams, Maureen 1951- 12
Williams, Michael
  See St. John, Wylly Folk
Williams, Patrick J.
  See Griffin, W. E. B.

Williams, Paulette Linda
  See Shange, Ntozake
Williams, Pete
  See Faulknor, Cliff(ord Vernon)
Williams, S. P.
  See Hart, Virginia
Williams, Sam 177
  Earlier sketch in SATA *124*
Williams, Selma R(uth) 1925- 14
Williams, Sherley Anne 1944-1999 78
  Obituary 116
Williams, Sheron 1955- 77
Williams, Shirley
  See Williams, Sherley Anne
Williams, Slim
  See Williams, Clyde C.
Williams, Sophy 1965- 135
Williams, Sue 1948-2007 208
Williams, Susan
  See Beckhorn, Susan Williams
Williams, Suzanne
  See Williams, Suzanne Morgan
Williams, Suzanne 1953- 202
  Earlier sketch in SATA *71*
Williams, Suzanne M.
  See Williams, Suzanne Morgan
Williams, Suzanne Morgan 1949- 207
Williams, Ursula Moray
  See Moray Williams, Ursula
Williams, Vera B(aker) 1927- 102
  Brief entry 33
  Earlier sketch in SATA *53*
  See also CLR *9*
Williams-Andriani, Renee 1963- 98
Williams-Ellis, (Mary) Amabel (Nassau
  Strachey) 1894-1984 29
  Obituary 41
Williams-Garcia, Rita 1957- 160
  Earlier sketch in SATA *98*
  See also CLR *36*
Williamson, Gwyneth 1965- 109
Williamson, Henry (William) 1895-1977 37
  Obituary 30
Williamson, Joanne S(mall) 1926- 122
  Earlier sketch in SATA *3*
Williamson, Kate T. 1979- 215
Williamson, Melanie 196
Willis, Charles
  See Clarke, Arthur C.
Willis, Connie 1945- 110
  See also CLR *66*
Willis, Cynthia Chapman 215
Willis, Jeanne 1959- 195
  Earlier sketches in SATA *61, 123*
Willis, Jeanne Mary
  See Willis, Jeanne
Willis, Meredith Sue 1946- 101
Willis, Nancy Carol 1952- 139
  Earlier sketch in SATA *93*
Willis, Paul J. 1955- 113
Willms, Russ 95
Willoughby, Lee Davis
  See Avallone, Michael (Angelo, Jr.)
  and Brandner, Gary (Phil)
  and Deming, Richard
  and DeAndrea, William L(ouis)
  and Laymon, Richard (Carl)
  and Streib, Dan(iel Thomas)
  and Toombs, John
  and Webb, Jean Francis (III)
Willson, Robina Beckles
  See Beckles Willson, Robina
Wilma, Dana
  See Faralla, Dana
Wilsdorf, Anne 1954- 191
Wilson, Anne 1974- 224
Wilson, April 80
Wilson, Barbara Ker
  See Ker Wilson, Barbara
Wilson, Beth P(ierre) 8

Wilson, Budge 1927- *55*
   Brief entry *51*
Wilson, Carletta 1951- *81*
Wilson, Carter 1941- *6*
Wilson, Charles Morrow 1905-1977 .... *30*
Wilson, Christopher B. 1910(?)-1985
   Obituary *46*
Wilson, Darryl B(abe) 1939- *90*
Wilson, Diane Lee *172*
Wilson, Dirk
   See Pohl, Frederik
Wilson, Dorothy Clarke 1904-2003 .... *16*
Wilson, Edward A(rthur) 1886-1970 .... *38*
Wilson, Ellen (Janet Cameron) (?)-1976 ...... *9*
   Obituary *26*
Wilson, Eric (H.) 1940- *34*
   Brief entry *32*
Wilson, Erica *51*
Wilson, Forrest 1918- *27*
Wilson, Gahan 1930- *35*
   Brief entry *27*
Wilson, Gina 1943- *85*
   Brief entry *34*
   Earlier sketch in SATA *36*
Wilson, (Leslie) Granville 1912- *14*
Wilson, Hazel (Hutchins) 1898-1992 .... *3*
   Obituary *73*
Wilson, J(erry) M. 1964- *121*
Wilson, Jacqueline 1945- *199*
   Brief entry *52*
   Earlier sketches in SATA *61, 102, 153*
Wilson, John 1922- *22*
Wilson, John 1951- *227*
   Earlier sketch in SATA *182*
Wilson, John Alexander
   See Wilson, John
Wilson, Johnniece Marshall 1944- *75*
Wilson, Jonathan 1950- *181*
Wilson, Joyce M. *84*
   Earlier sketch in SATA *21*
   See also SAAS *24*
Wilson, Karma *221*
   Earlier sketch in SATA *174*
Wilson, Leslie 1952- *166*
Wilson, Linda Miller 1936- *116*
Wilson, Lionel 1924-2003 .... *33*
   Brief entry *31*
   Obituary *144*
Wilson, Marjorie
   See Wilson, Budge
Wilson, Martin 1973- *205*
Wilson, Maurice (Charles John) 1914- *46*
Wilson, Nancy Hope 1947- *138*
   Earlier sketch in SATA *81*
Wilson, Nathan D.
   See Wilson, N.D.
Wilson, N.D. 1978- *194*
Wilson, Nick
   See Ellis, Edward S.
Wilson, Phil 1948- *181*
Wilson, Ron(ald William) 1941- *38*
Wilson, Sarah 1934- *208*
   Earlier sketches in SATA *50, 142*
Wilson, Tom 1931- *33*
   Brief entry *30*
Wilson, Troy 1970- *169*
Wilson, Walt(er N.) 1939- *14*
Wilson-Max, Ken 1965- *170*
   Earlier sketch in SATA *93*
Wilton, Elizabeth 1937- *14*
Wilton, Hal
   See Pepper, Frank S.
Wilwerding, Walter Joseph 1891-1966 .... *9*
Wimmer, Mike 1961- *194*
   Earlier sketch in SATA *70*
Winborn, Marsha (Lynn) 1947- *75*
Winch, John 1944- *165*
   Earlier sketch in SATA *117*
Winchester, James H(ugh) 1917-1985 .... *30*
   Obituary *45*

Winchester, Stanley
   See Youd, Samuel
Windawi, Thura al- 1983(?)- *165*
Winders, Gertrude Hecker -1987 .... *3*
Windham, Basil
   See Wodehouse, P. G.
Windham, Kathryn T(ucker) 1918- *14*
Windham, Sophie *184*
Windling, Terri 1958- *151*
Windrow, Martin
   See Windrow, Martin Clive
Windrow, Martin C.
   See Windrow, Martin Clive
Windrow, Martin Clive 1944- *68*
Windsor, Claire
   See Hamerstrom, Frances
Windsor, Linda 1950- *124*
Windsor, Patricia 1938- *78*
   Earlier sketch in SATA *30*
   See also SAAS *19*
Wineman-Marcus, Irene 1952- *81*
Winer, Yvonne 1934- *120*
Winerip, Michael *175*
Winfield, Arthur M.
   See Stratemeyer, Edward L.
Winfield, Edna
   See Stratemeyer, Edward L.
Winfield, Julia
   See Armstrong, Jennifer
Wing, Natasha 1960- *200*
   Earlier sketch in SATA *82*
Wingerter, Linda S. 1973(?)- *207*
Winget, Susan *211*
Winick, Judd 1970- *124*
Winks, Robin William 1930-2003 .... *61*
Winn, Alison
   See Wharmby, Margot
Winn, Chris 1952- *42*
Winn, Janet Bruce 1928- *43*
Winn, Marie 1936(?)- *38*
Winnick, Karen B. 1946- *211*
Winnick, Karen B(eth) B(inkoff) 1946- *51*
Winn-Lederer, Ilene *198*
Winslow, Barbara 1947- *91*
Winstead, Rosie *180*
Winston, Clara 1921-1983 .... *54*
   Obituary *39*
Winston, Richard 1917-1979 .... *54*
Winston, Sherri 1964(?)- *201*
Winter, Janet 1926- *126*
Winter, Jeanette 1939- *184*
   Earlier sketch in SATA *151*
Winter, Jonah 1962- *225*
   Earlier sketch in SATA *179*
Winter, Milo (Kendall) 1888-1956 .... *21*
Winter, Paula Cecelia 1929- *48*
Winter, R. R.
   See Winterbotham, R(ussell) R(obert)
Winter, Susan *182*
Winterbotham, R(ussell) R(obert)
   1904-1971 .... *10*
Winterbotham, Russ
   See Winterbotham, R(ussell) R(obert)
Winterfeld, Henry 1901-1990 .... *55*
Winters, J. C.
   See Cross, Gilbert B.
Winters, Jon
   See Cross, Gilbert B.
Winters, Katherine
   See Winters, Kay
Winters, Kay 1936- *153*
   Earlier sketch in SATA *103*
Winters, Nina 1944- *62*
Winters, Paul A. 1965- *106*
Winterson, Jeanette 1959- *190*
Winterton, Gayle
   See Adams, William Taylor
Winthrop, Elizabeth 1948- *164*
   Autobiography Feature *116*
   Earlier sketches in SATA *8, 76*
   See also CLR *89*

Winton, Ian (Kenneth) 1960- *76*
Winton, Tim 1960- *98*
Wintz-Litty, Julie
   See Litty, Julie
Wirt, Ann
   See Benson, Mildred
Wirt, Mildred A.
   See Benson, Mildred
Wirtenberg, Patricia Z. 1932-2007 .... *10*
Wirtenberg, Patricia Zarrella
   See Wirtenberg, Patricia Z.
Wirth, Beverly 1938- *63*
Wirths, Claudine (Turner) G(ibson)
   1926-2000 .... *104*
   Earlier sketch in SATA *64*
Wise, Bill 1958- *191*
Wise, Lenny
   See Wise, Leonard
Wise, Leonard 1940- *167*
Wise, Leonard A.
   See Wise, Leonard
Wise, Leonard Allan
   See Wise, Leonard
Wise, William 1923- *163*
   Earlier sketch in SATA *4*
Wise, Winifred E. *2*
Wiseman, Ann (Sayre) 1926- *31*
Wiseman, B(ernard) 1922-1995 .... *4*
Wiseman, David 1916- *43*
   Brief entry *40*
Wiseman, Eva 1947- *210*
Wishinsky, Frieda 1948- *166*
   Earlier sketches in SATA *70, 112*
Wisler, G(ary) Clifton 1950- *103*
   Brief entry *46*
   Earlier sketch in SATA *58*
Wismer, Donald (Richard) 1946- *59*
Wisner, Bill
   See Wisner, William L.
Wisner, William L. 1914(?)-1983 .... *42*
Wisnewski, David 1953-2002
   See Wisniewski, David
Wisniewski, David 1953-2002 .... *95*
   Obituary *139*
   See also CLR *51*
Wister, Owen 1860-1938 .... *62*
Witham, (Phillip) Ross 1917- *37*
Withers, Carl A. 1900-1970 .... *14*
Withers, Pam 1956- *182*
Withrow, Sarah 1966- *199*
   Earlier sketch in SATA *124*
Witt, Dick 1948- *80*
Witt, Shirley Hill 1934- *17*
Wittanen, Etolin 1907- *55*
Wittels, Harriet Joan 1938- *31*
Wittenstein, Vicki Oransky 1954- *228*
Wittig, Susan
   See Albert, Susan Wittig
Wittlinger, Ellen 1948- *189*
   Autobiography Feature *128*
   Earlier sketches in SATA *83, 122*
Wittman, Sally (Anne Christensen) 1941- *30*
Witty, Paul 1898-1976 .... *50*
   Obituary *30*
Wodehouse, P. G. 1881-1975 .... *22*
Wodehouse, Pelham Grenville
   See Wodehouse, P. G.
Wodge, Dreary
   See Gorey, Edward (St. John)
Woelfle, Gretchen 1945- *145*
Wohlberg, Meg 1905-1990 .... *41*
   Obituary *66*
Wohlrabe, Raymond A. 1900-1977 .... *4*
Wohnoutka, Mike *195*
Wojciechowska, Maia (Teresa) 1927-2002 ... *83*
   Autobiography Feature *104*
   Obituary *134*
   Earlier sketches in SATA *1, 28*
   See also CLR *1*
   See also SAAS *1*

Wojciechowski, Susan 126
  Earlier sketch in SATA 78
Wojnarowski, Adrian 1970- 190
Wojtusik, Elizabeth 208
Wolcott, Patty 1929- 14
Wold, Allen L. 1943- 64
Wold, Jo Anne 1938- 30
Woldin, Beth Weiner 1955- 34
Wolf, Allan 1963- 192
Wolf, Bernard 1930- 102
  Brief entry 37
Wolf, Erica (Van Varick) 1978- 156
Wolf, Gita 1956- 101
Wolf, J. M.
  See Wolf, Joan M.
Wolf, Janet 1957- 78
Wolf, Joan M. 1966- 193
Wolf, Sallie 1950- 205
  Earlier sketch in SATA 80
Wolfe, Art 1952- 76
Wolfe, Burton H. 1932- 5
Wolfe, Frances 216
Wolfe, Gene 1931- 165
  Earlier sketch in SATA 118
Wolfe, Gene Rodman
  See Wolfe, Gene
Wolfe, Gillian 199
Wolfe, Louis 1905-1985 8
  Obituary 133
Wolfe, Rinna (Evelyn) 1925- 38
Wolfenden, George
  See Beardmore, George
Wolfer, Dianne 1961- 167
  Autobiography Feature 117
  Earlier sketch in SATA 104
Wolff, Alexander (Nikolaus) 1957- 137
  Earlier sketch in SATA 63
Wolff, Ashley 1956- 203
  Earlier sketches in SATA 50, 81, 155
Wolff, Diane 1945- 27
Wolff, Ferida 1946- 164
  Earlier sketch in SATA 79
Wolff, Jason 1972- 213
Wolff, Jennifer Ashley
  See Wolff, Ashley
Wolff, Nancy 202
Wolff, Robert Jay 1905-1977 10
Wolff, Sonia
  See Levitin, Sonia
Wolff, Virginia Euwer 1937- 137
  Earlier sketch in SATA 78
  See also CLR 62
Wolfman, Judy 1933- 138
Wolfson, Evelyn 1937- 62
Wolitzer, Hilma 1930- 31
Wolkoff, Judie (Edwards) 93
  Brief entry 37
Wolkstein, Diane 1942- 138
  Earlier sketches in SATA 7, 82
Wollheim, Donald A(llen) 1914-1990
  Obituary 69
Wolny, P.
  See Janeczko, Paul B(ryan)
Wolters, Richard A. 1920-1993 35
Wondriska, William 1931- 6
Wong, Jade Snow 1922-2006 112
  Obituary 175
Wong, Janet S. 1962- 210
  Earlier sketches in SATA 98, 148
  See also CLR 94
Wong, Marissa Lopez 226
Wong, Nicole 214
Woo, Howie 1974- 207
Wood, Addie Robinson
  See Wiggin, Eric E.
Wood, Anne (Savage) 1937- 64
Wood, Audrey 198
  Brief entry 44
  Earlier sketches in SATA 50, 81, 139
  See also CLR 26

Wood, Catherine
  See Etchison, Birdie L(ee)
Wood, David 1944- 212
  Earlier sketch in SATA 87
Wood, Don 1945- 50
  Brief entry 44
  See also CLR 26
Wood, Douglas 1951- 180
  Earlier sketches in SATA 81, 132
Wood, Douglas Eric
  See Wood, Douglas
Wood, Edgar A(llardyce) 1907-1998 14
Wood, Esther
  See Brady, Esther Wood
Wood, Frances Elizabeth 34
Wood, Frances M. 1951- 97
Wood, Jacqueline
  See Wood, Jakki
Wood, Jakki 1957- 211
Wood, James Playsted 1905- 1
Wood, Jenny 1955- 88
Wood, John Norris 1930- 85
Wood, June Rae 1946- 120
  Earlier sketch in SATA 79
  See also CLR 82
Wood, Kerry
  See Wood, Edgar A(llardyce)
Wood, Kim Marie 134
Wood, Laura N.
  See Roper, Laura (Newbold) Wood
Wood, Linda C(arol) 1945- 59
Wood, Marcia 1956- 80
Wood, Marcia Mae
  See Wood, Marcia
Wood, Nancy
  See Wood, Nancy C.
Wood, Nancy C. 1936- 178
  Earlier sketch in SATA 6
Wood, Nuria
  See Nobisso, Josephine
Wood, Owen 1929- 64
Wood, Phyllis Anderson 1923- 33
  Brief entry 30
Wood, Richard 1949- 110
Wood, Tim(othy William Russell) 1946- 88
Wood, Wallace 1927-1981
  Obituary 33
Woodard, Carol 1929- 14
Woodburn, John Henry 1914- 11
Woodbury, David Oakes 1896-1981 62
Woodford, Peggy 1937- 25
Woodhouse, Barbara (Blackburn)
  1910-1988 63
Woodhull, Ann Love 194
Wooding, Chris 1977- 166
Wooding, Sharon
  See Wooding, Sharon L(ouise)
Wooding, Sharon L(ouise) 1943- 66
Woodman, Allen 1954- 76
Woodrich, Mary Neville 1915- 2
Woodruff, Elvira 1951- 211
  Earlier sketches in SATA 70, 106, 162
Woodruff, Joan Leslie 1953- 104
Woodruff, Liza 1971(?)- 182
Woodruff, Marian
  See Goudge, Eileen
Woodruff, Noah 1977- 86
Woods, George A(llan) 1926-1988 30
  Obituary 57
Woods, Geraldine 1948- 111
  Brief entry 42
  Earlier sketch in SATA 56
Woods, Harold 1945- 56
  Brief entry 42
Woods, Lawrence
  See Lowndes, Robert A(ugustine) W(ard)
Woods, Margaret 1921- 2
Woods, Nat
  See Stratemeyer, Edward L.
Woods, Titania
  See Weatherly, Lee

Woodson, Jack
  See Woodson, John Waddie Jr.
Woodson, Jacqueline 1964- 189
  Earlier sketches in SATA 94, 139
  See also CLR 49
Woodson, Jacqueline Amanda
  See Woodson, Jacqueline
Woodson, John Waddie Jr. 1913- 10
Woodtor, Dee
  See Woodtor, Delores Parmer
Woodtor, Dee Parmer 1945(?)-2002
  See Woodtor, Delores Parmer
Woodtor, Delores Parmer 1945-2002 93
Wood-Trost, Lucille
  See Trost, Lucille W(ood)
Woodward, (Landon) Cleveland 1900-1986 . 10
  Obituary 48
Woodworth, Chris 1957- 168
Woodworth, Viki 1952- 127
Woody, Regina Jones 1894-1983 3
Woodyadd, Charlotte
  See Hough, Charlotte
Woog, Adam 1953- 125
  Earlier sketch in SATA 84
Wooldridge, Connie Nordhielm 1950- 143
  Earlier sketch in SATA 92
Wooldridge, Frosty 1947- 140
Wooldridge, Rhoda 1906-1988 22
Wooley, Susan Frelick 1945- 113
Woolf, Paula 1950- 104
Woolfe, Angela 1976- 169
Woolley, Catherine 1904-2005 3
  Obituary 166
Woolman, Steven 1969-2004 163
  Earlier sketch in SATA 90
Woolsey, Janette 1904-1989 3
  Obituary 131
Worcester, Donald E(mmet) 1915- 18
Word, Reagan 1944- 103
Work, Virginia 1946- 57
  Brief entry 45
Worline, Bonnie Bess 1914- 14
Wormell, Christopher 1955- 154
  Earlier sketch in SATA 103
Wormell, Mary 1959- 96
Wormser, Richard 1933- 106
  Autobiography Feature 118
  See also SAAS 26
Wormser, Sophie 1897-1979 22
Worth, Richard
  See Wiggin, Eric E.
Worth, Richard 1945- 59
  Brief entry 46
Worth, Valerie 1933-1994 81
  Earlier sketches in SATA 8, 70
  See also CLR 21
Worthington, Leonie 1956- 200
Wortis, Avi
  See Avi
Wortis, Edward Irving
  See Avi
Wosmek, Frances 1917- 29
Woychuk, Denis 1953- 71
Wrede, Patricia C(ollins) 1953- 146
  Earlier sketch in SATA 67
Wriggins, Sally Hovey 1922- 17
Wright, Alexandra 1979- 103
Wright, Betty Ren 1927- 109
  Brief entry 48
  Earlier sketch in SATA 63
Wright, Cliff 1963- 168
  Earlier sketch in SATA 76
Wright, Courtni
  See Wright, Courtni C(rump)
Wright, Courtni C(rump) 1950- 84
Wright, Courtni Crump
  See Wright, Courtni C(rump)
Wright, Dare 1914(?)-2001 21
  Obituary 124
Wright, David K. 1943- 112
  Earlier sketch in SATA 73

Wright, Elinor
    See Lyon, Elinor
Wright, Enid Meadowcroft (LaMonte)
    1898-1966 .... *3*
Wright, Esmond 1915-2003 .... *10*
Wright, Frances Fitzpatrick 1897-1982 .... *10*
Wright, J. B.
    See Barkan, Joanne
Wright, Johanna *220*
Wright, Judith 1915-2000 .... *14*
    Obituary *121*
Wright, Judith Arundell
    See Wright, Judith
Wright, Katrina
    See Gater, Dilys
Wright, Kenneth
    See del Rey, Lester
Wright, Kit 1944- *87*
Wright, Leslie B(ailey) 1959- *91*
Wright, Michael 1954- *198*
Wright, Nancy Means *38*
Wright, R(obert) H(amilton) 1906- *6*
Wright, Rachel *220*
    Earlier sketch in SATA *134*
Wright, Susan Kimmel 1950- *97*
Wrightfrierson
    See Wright-Frierson, Virginia (Marguerite)
Wright-Frierson, Virginia (Marguerite)
    1949- *110*
    Earlier sketch in SATA *58*
Wrightson, Alice Patricia
    See Wrightson, Patricia
Wrightson, Patricia 1921-2010 .... *112*
    Obituary *215*
    Earlier sketches in SATA *8, 66*
    See also CLR *154*
    See also SAAS *4*
Wroble, Lisa A. 1963- *134*
Wrongo, I.B.
    See Katz, Alan
Wronker, Lili
    See Wronker, Lili Cassel
Wronker, Lili Cassel 1924- *10*
Wryde, Dogear
    See Gorey, Edward (St. John)
Wu, Donald *212*
Wu, Elizabeth
    See Wu, Liz
Wu, Liz *184*
Wu, Norbert 1961- *155*
    Earlier sketch in SATA *101*
Wulf, Linda Press *205*
Wulffson, Don 1943- *155*
    Earlier sketches in SATA *32, 88*
Wulffson, Don L.
    See Wulffson, Don
Wummer, Amy 1955- *201*
Wunderli, Stephen 1958- *79*
Wunsch, Josephine (McLean) 1914- *64*
Wunsch, Marjory 1942- *220*
    Earlier sketch in SATA *82*
Wuorio, Eva-Lis 1918- *34*
    Brief entry *28*
Wurts, Janny 1953- *98*
Wyatt, B. D.
    See Robinson, Spider
Wyatt, David 1968- *185*
Wyatt, Jane
    See Bradbury, Bianca (Ryley)
Wyatt, Melissa 1963- *177*
Wyatt, Valerie *209*
Wyeth, Betsy James 1921- *41*
Wyeth, N(ewell) C(onvers) 1882-1945 .... *17*
    See also CLR *106*
Wyler, Rose 1909-2000 .... *18*
    Obituary *121*
Wylie, Betty Jane *48*
Wylie, Laura
    See Matthews, Patricia
Wylie, Laurie
    See Matthews, Patricia

Wyllie, Stephen *86*
Wyman, Andrea *75*
Wyman, Carolyn 1956- *83*
Wymer, Norman (George) 1911- *25*
Wynard, Talbot
    See Hamilton, Charles (Harold St. John)
Wyndham, John
    See Harris, John (Wyndham Parkes Lucas)
    Beynon
Wyndham, Lee
    See Hyndman, Jane Andrews Lee
Wyndham, Robert
    See Hyndman, Robert Utley
Wynne, Patricia J. *210*
Wynne-Jones, Tim 1948- *186*
    Autobiography Feature *136*
    Earlier sketches in SATA *67, 96, 136*
    See also CLR *58*
Wynne-Jones, Timothy
    See Wynne-Jones, Tim
Wynter, Edward (John) 1914- *14*
Wynyard, Talbot
    See Hamilton, Charles (Harold St. John)
Wyss, Johann David Von 1743-1818 .... *29*
    Brief entry *27*
    See also CLR *92*
Wyss, Thelma Hatch 1934- *202*
    Earlier sketches in SATA *10, 140*

                            X

Xavier, Father
    See Hurwood, Bernhardt J.
Xuan, YongSheng 1952- *226*
    Autobiography Feature *226*
    Earlier sketch in SATA *116*

                            Y

Yaccarino, Dan *192*
    Earlier sketch in SATA *141*
Yadin, (Rav-Aloof) Yigael 1917-1984 .... *55*
Yaffe, Alan
    See Yorinks, Arthur
Yagher, Kevin 1962- *143*
Yakovetic, (Joseph Sandy) 1952- *59*
Yakovetic, Joe
    See Yakovetic, (Joseph Sandy)
Yamada, Utako 1963- *188*
Yamaguchi, Marianne (Illenberger) 1936- *7*
Yamaka, Sara 1978- *92*
Yamanaka, Lois-Ann 1961- *166*
Yamasaki, Katie *206*
Yancey, Diane 1951- *138*
    Earlier sketch in SATA *81*
Yancey, Richard *193*
Yancey, Rick
    See Yancey, Richard
Yang, Belle 1960- *170*
Yang, James 1960- *190*
Yang, Jay 1941- *12*
Yang, Mingyi 1943- *72*
Yarbrough, Camille 1938- *79*
    See also CLR *29*
Yarbrough, Ira 1910(?)-1983
    Obituary *35*
Yaroslava
    See Mills, Yaroslava Surmach
Yarrow, Peter 1938- *195*
Yashima, Taro
    See Iwamatsu, Jun Atsushi
Yates, Elizabeth 1905-2001 .... *68*
    Obituary *128*
    Earlier sketch in SATA *4*
    See also SAAS *6*
Yates, Janelle K(aye) 1957- *77*
Yates, John 1939- *74*
Yates, Kelly 1971- *208*

Yates, Louise 1983(?)- *218*
Yates, Philip 1956- *212*
    Earlier sketches in SATA *92, 149*
Yates, Raymond F(rancis) 1895-1966 .... *31*
Yaukey, Grace S(ydenstricker) 1899-1994 ... *80*
    Earlier sketch in SATA *5*
Yayo 1961- *226*
Yazzie, Johnson 1946- *205*
Ye, Ting-xing 1952- *106*
Yeahpau, Thomas M. 1975- *187*
Yeakley, Marjory Hall 1908- *21*
Yeatman, Linda 1938- *42*
Yeatts, Tabatha 1970- *215*
Yee, Brenda Shannon *133*
Yee, Lisa 1959- *218*
    Earlier sketch in SATA *160*
Yee, Paul 1956- *211*
    Earlier sketches in SATA *67, 96, 143*
    See also CLR *44*
Yee, Tammy *206*
Yee, Wong Herbert 1953- *172*
    Earlier sketch in SATA *78, 115*
Yeh, Chun-Chan 1914- *79*
Ye Junjian
    See Yeh, Chun-Chan
Yelchin, Eugene 1956- *196*
Yenawine, Philip 1942- *85*
Yensid, Retlaw
    See Disney, Walt(er Elias)
Yeo, Wilma (Lethem) 1918-1994 .... *81*
    Earlier sketch in SATA *24*
Yeoman, John 1934- *80*
    Earlier sketch in SATA *28*
    See also CLR *46*
Yep, Kathleen S. *203*
Yep, Laurence 1948- *213*
    Earlier sketches in SATA *7, 69, 123, 176*
    See also CLR *132*
Yep, Laurence Michael
    See Yep, Laurence
Yepsen, Roger B(ennet), Jr. 1947- *59*
Yerian, Cameron John *21*
Yerian, Margaret A. *21*
Yerxa, Leo 1947- *181*
Yetska
    See Ironside, Jetske
Yezerski, Thomas F. 1969- *190*
Yin *194*
Ylvisaker, Anne 1965(?)- *172*
Yoder, Carolyn P. 1953- *149*
Yoder, Carolyn Patricia
    See Yoder, Carolyn P.
Yoder, Dorothy Meenen 1921- *96*
Yoder, Dot
    See Yoder, Dorothy Meenen
Yoder, Walter D. 1933- *88*
Yohalem, Eve *219*
Yolen, Jane 1939- *194*
    Autobiography Feature *111*
    Earlier sketches in SATA *4, 40, 75, 112, 158*
    See also CLR *149*
    See also SAAS *1*
Yolen, Jane Hyatt
    See Yolen, Jane
Yonezu, Yusuke *196*
Yonge, Charlotte 1823-1901 .... *17*
Yonge, Charlotte Mary
    See Yonge, Charlotte
Yoo, Paula 1969(?)- *174*
Yoo, Taeeun *191*
Yoon, Salina 1972- *204*
Yorinks, Adrienne 1956- *171*
Yorinks, Arthur 1953- *200*
    Earlier sketches in SATA *33, 49, 85, 144*
    See also CLR *20*
York, Alison
    See Nicole, Christopher
York, Andrew
    See Nicole, Christopher
York, Carol Beach 1928- *77*
    Earlier sketch in SATA *6*

York, Rebecca
  See Buckholtz, Eileen (Garber)
  and Glick, Ruth
York, Simon
  See Heinlein, Robert A.
Yoshida, Toshi 1911- 77
Yoshikawa, Sachiko 181
Yost, Edna 1889-1971
  Obituary 26
Youd, C. S.
  See Youd, Samuel
Youd, Samuel 1922- 135
  Brief entry 30
  Earlier sketch in SATA 47
  See also CLR 2
  See also SAAS 6
Youme
  See Landowne, Youme
Young, Amy L. 185
Young, Anne Mortimer
  See Mortimer, Anne
Young, Bob
  See Young, Robert W(illiam)
  and Young, James Robert
Young, Carol 1945- 102
Young, Catherine
  See Olds, Helen Diehl
Young, Clarence
  See Garis, Howard R.
  and Stratemeyer, Edward L.
Young, Collier
  See Bloch, Robert (Albert)
Young, Dan 1952- 126
Young, Dianne 1959- 88
Young, Dorothea Bennett 1924- 31
Young, Ed 1931- 211
  Earlier sketches in SATA 10, 74, 122, 173
  See also CLR 27
Young, Ed Tse-chun
  See Young, Ed
Young, Edward
  See Reinfeld, Fred
Young, E.L. 1973- 219
Young, Elaine L.
  See Schulte, Elaine L(ouise)
Young, Emma L.
  See Young, E.L.
Young, James
  See Graham, Ian
Young, Jan
  See Young, Janet Randall
Young, Janet 1957- 188
Young, Janet Randall 1919-1994 3
Young, Janet Ruth
  See Young, Janet
Young, Jeff C. 1948- 132
Young, John
  See Macintosh, Brownie
Young, Judy 1956- 207
  Earlier sketch in SATA 155
Young, Judy (Elaine) Dockrey 1949- 72
Young, Karen Romano 1959- 168
  Earlier sketch in SATA 116
Young, Ken 1956- 86
Young, Lois Horton 1911-1981 26
Young, Louisa 161
Young, Louise B. 1919- 64
Young, Margaret B. 1922-2009 2
Young, Margaret Buckner
  See Young, Margaret B.
Young, Mary 1940- 89
Young, Miriam 1913-1974 7
Young, Noela 1930- 89
Young, (Rodney Lee) Patrick (Jr.) 1937- 22
Young, Percy M(arshall) 1912-2004 31
  Obituary 154
Young, Richard Alan 1946- 72
Young, Robert W(illiam) 1916-1969 3
Young, Ross B. 1955- 150
Young, Ruth 1946- 67

Young, Sara
  See Pennypacker, Sara
Young, Scott A. 1918-2005 5
Young, Scott Alexander
  See Young, Scott A.
Young, Selina 1971-2006 201
Young, Vivien
  See Gater, Dilys
Younger, Barbara 1954- 108
Youngs, Betty 1934-1985 53
  Obituary 42
Younkin, Paula 1942- 77
Yount, Lisa (Ann) 1944- 124
  Earlier sketch in SATA 74
Yourgrau, Barry 179
Yuditskaya, Tatyana 1964- 75
Yum, Hyewon 211
Yumoto, Kazumi 1959- 153

Z

Zach, Cheryl (Byrd) 1947- 98
  Brief entry 51
  Earlier sketch in SATA 58
  See also SAAS 24
Zacharias, Gary L. 1946- 153
Zadoff, Allen 1967- 224
Zaffo, George J. (?)-1984 42
Zagarenski, Pamela 1969(?)- 183
Zagwyn, Deborah Turney 1953- 138
  Earlier sketch in SATA 78
Zahares, Wade 193
Zahler, Diane 228
Zahn, Timothy 1951- 156
  Earlier sketch in SATA 91
Zaid, Barry 1938- 51
Zaidenberg, Arthur 1908(?)-1990 34
  Obituary 66
Zalben, Jane Breskin 1950- 170
  Earlier sketches in SATA 7, 79, 120
  See also CLR 84
Zallinger, Jean (Day) 1918- 115
  Earlier sketches in SATA 14, 80
Zallinger, Peter Franz 1943- 49
Zambreno, Mary Frances 1954- 140
  Earlier sketch in SATA 75
Zanderbergen, George
  See May, Julian
Zappa, Ahmet 1974- 180
Zappa, Ahmet Emuukha Rodan
  See Zappa, Ahmet
Zappler, Lisbeth 1930- 10
Zarchy, Harry 1912-1987 34
Zarin, Cynthia 1959- 192
  Earlier sketch in SATA 108
Zaring, Jane (Thomas) 1936- 40
Zarins, Joyce Audy
  See dos Santos, Joyce Audy
Zaslavsky, Claudia 1917- 36
Zaugg, Sandra L. 1938- 118
Zaugg, Sandy
  See Zaugg, Sandra L.
Zaunders, Bo 1939- 137
Zawadzki, Marek 1958- 97
Zebra, A.
  See Scoltock, Jack
Zebrowski, George 1945- 67
Zebrowski, George T.
  See Zebrowski, George
Zecca, Katherine 207
Zeck, Gerald Anthony 1939- 40
Zeck, Gerry
  See Zeck, Gerald Anthony
Zed, Dr.
  See Penrose, Gordon
Zei, Alki 1925- 24
  See also CLR 6
Zeier, Joan T(heresa) 1931- 81

Zeinert, Karen 1942-2002 137
  Earlier sketch in SATA 79
Zeises, Lara M. 1976- 184
  Earlier sketch in SATA 145
Zelazny, Roger 1937-1995 57
  Brief entry 39
Zelazny, Roger Joseph
  See Zelazny, Roger
Zeldis, Malcah 1931- 146
  Earlier sketch in SATA 86
Zelinsky, Paul O. 1953- 154
  Brief entry 33
  Earlier sketches in SATA 49, 102
  See also CLR 55
Zellan, Audrey Penn
  See Penn, Audrey
Zemach, Harve
  See Fischtrom, Harvey
Zemach, Kaethe 1958- 149
  Brief entry 39
  Earlier sketch in SATA 49
Zemach, Margot 1931-1989 70
  Obituary 59
  Earlier sketch in SATA 21
Zemach-Bersin, Kaethe
  See Zemach, Kaethe
Zeman, Ludmila 1947- 153
Zepeda, Gwendolyn 1971- 206
Zephaniah, Benjamin 1958- 189
  Earlier sketches in SATA 86, 140
Zephaniah, Benjamin Obadiah Iqbal
  See Zephaniah, Benjamin
Zephaniah, Benjamin Pbadiah Iqubal
  See Zephaniah, Benjamin
Zerman, Melvyn Bernard 1930-2010 46
Zettner, Pat 1940- 70
Zevin, Gabrielle 176
Zhang, Christopher Zhong-Yuan 1954- 91
Zhang, Song Nan 1942- 170
  Earlier sketch in SATA 85
Ziefert, Harriet 1941- 205
  Earlier sketches in SATA 101, 154
Ziegler, Jack (Denmore) 1942- 60
Ziemienski, Dennis (Theodore) 1947- 10
Ziliox, Marc
  See Fichter, George S.
Zillah
  See Macdonald, Zillah K(atherine)
Zim, Herbert S(pencer) 1909-1994 30
  Obituary 85
  Earlier sketch in SATA 1
  See also CLR 2
  See also SAAS 2
Zim, Sonia Bleeker 1909-1971 2
  Obituary 26
Zima, Gordon 1920- 90
Zimelman, Nathan 1921- 65
  Brief entry 37
Zimmer, Dirk 1943- 147
  Earlier sketch in SATA 65
Zimmer, Tracie Vaughn 169
Zimmermann, Andrea 1950- 192
  Earlier sketch in SATA 123
Zimmerman, Andrea Griffing
  See Zimmerman, Andrea
Zimmerman, H. Werner 1951- 101
Zimmerman, Heinz Werner
  See Zimmerman, H. Werner
Zimmerman, Naoma 1914-2004 10
Zimmermann, Arnold E. 1909- 58
Zimmermann, Karl 1943- 211
Zimmermann, Karl R.
  See Zimmermann, Karl
Zimmett, Debbie
  See Becker, Deborah Zimmett
Zimmy
  See Stratemeyer, Edward L.
Zimnik, Reiner 1930- 36
  See also CLR 3
Zindel, Bonnie 1943- 34
Zindel, Lizabeth 187

Zindel, Paul 1936-2003 .... *102*
  Obituary *142*
  Earlier sketches in SATA *16, 58*
  See also CLR *85*
Ziner, Feenie
  See Ziner, Florence
Ziner, Florence 1921- *5*
Zingara, Professor
  See Leeming, Joseph
Zinger, Yitskhok
  See Singer, Isaac Bashevis
Zink, Michelle 1969- *220*
Zion, Eugene 1913-1975 .... *18*
Zion, Gene
  See Zion, Eugene
Zobel, Allia
  See Zobel Nolan, Allia
Zobel Nolan, Allia *218*
Zoehfeld, Kathleen Weidner 1954- *193*
Zohorsky, Janet R. 1958- *148*
Zolkower, Edie Stoltz *171*
Zolkowski, Cathy (A.) 1969- *121*

Zollars, Jaime *191*
Zolotow, Charlotte 1915- *138*
  Earlier sketches in SATA *1, 35, 78*
  See also CLR *77*
Zolotow, Charlotte Gertrude Shapiro
  See Zolotow, Charlotte
Zolotow, Ellen
  See Dragonwagon, Crescent
Zonderman, Jon 1957- *92*
Zonia, Dhimitri 1921- *20*
Zonta, Pat 1951- *143*
Zubrowski, Bernard 1939- *90*
  Earlier sketch in SATA *35*
Zubrowski, Bernie
  See Zubrowski, Bernard
Zucker, Jonny *228*
Zucker, Miriam S.
  See Reichert, Miriam Zucker
Zuckerman, Amy *217*
Zuckerman, Andrew 1977- *224*
Zuckerman, Linda *190*
Zudeck, Darryl 1961- *61*

Zug, Mark *204*
Zulkey, Claire 1979- *225*
Zupa, G. Anthony
  See Zeck, Gerald Anthony
Zupancic, Lilijana Praprotnik
  See Prap, Lila
Zurbo, Matt(hew) 1967- *98*
Zurhorst, Charles (Stewart, Jr.) 1913-1989 .. *12*
Zurlo, Tony 1941- *145*
Zuromskis, Diane
  See Stanley, Diane
Zuromskis, Diane Stanley
  See Stanley, Diane
Zusak, Markus 1975- *149*
Zwahlen, Diana 1947- *88*
Zweifel, Frances W. 1931- *14*
Zwerger, Lisbeth 1954- *194*
  Earlier sketches in SATA *66, 130*
  See also CLR *46*
  See also SAAS *13*
Zwinger, Ann (H.) 1925- *46*
Zymet, Cathy Alter 1965- *121*